www.wadsworth.com

wadsworth.com is the World Wide Web site for Wadsworth and is your direct source to dozens of online resources.

At *wadsworth.com* you can find out about supplements, demonstration software, and student resources. You can also send email to many of our authors and preview new publications and exciting new technologies.

wadsworth.com
Changing the way the world learns®

Wayne Weiten is a graduate of Bradley University and earned his Ph.D. from the University of Illinois at Chicago in 1981. He is the author of *Psychology: Themes and Variations* (Wadsworth, 1998) and teaches psychology at Santa Clara University. He has received distinguished teaching awards from Division 2 of the American Psychological Association and the College of DuPage, where he taught until 1991. He served as President of the Society for the Teaching of Psychology (Division 2 of the American Psychological Association) in 1996–1997. He has conducted research on a wide range of topics, including cerebral specialization, educational measurement, jury behavior, attribution theory, pressure as a form of stress, and the technology of textbooks.

Margaret A. Lloyd is a graduate of the University of Denver and received her Ph.D. in psychology from the University of Arizona in 1973. She is the author of *Adolescence* (Harper & Row, 1985), she is a past President of the Society for the Teaching of Psychology (Division 2 of the American Psychological Association), and currently serves as the Executive Director of the Society's Office of Teaching Resources in Psychology. She is Professor of Psychology at Georgia Southern University and recipient of that institution's Award for Excellence for Contributions to Instruction. She has served as Chair of the psychology departments at Suffolk University (1980–1988) and Georgia Southern University (1988–1993) and is the founding Chair of the Council of Undergraduate Psychology Programs. Her scholarly interests lie in the areas of identity and gender roles.

SIXTH EDITION

Psychology Applied to Modern Life

ADJUSTMENT AT THE TURN OF THE CENTURY

Wayne Weiten
Santa Clara University

Margaret A. Lloyd
Georgia Southern University

Wadsworth
Thomson Learning

Australia • Canada • Mexico • Singapore • Spain • United Kingdom • United States

To two pillars of stability in this era of turmoil—my parents
W.W.

To my father and the memory of my mother—models of integrity and courage
M.A.L.

Psychology Editor: Eileen Murphy
Assistant Editor: Julie Martinez
Marketing Manager: Joanne Terhaar
Marketing Assistant: Jenna Burrill
Project Editor: Tanya Nigh
Print Buyer: Karen Hunt
Permissions Editor: Roberta Broyer
Production Service: Thomas E. Dorsaneo/Publishing Consultants

Text Designer: Gladys Rosa-Mendoza, rosa+wesley
Photo Researcher: Linda Rill
Copy Editor: Jackie Estrada
Illustrator: Jeff Grunewald
Cover Designer: Gladys Rosa-Mendoza, rosa+wesley
Cover Image: Alan Giana
Text and cover Printer: Von Hoffman Press, Inc.
Compositor: Brian Wenberg, rosa+wesley

Printed in the United States of America
1 2 3 4 5 6 7 03 02 01 00 99

For permission to use material from this text,
contact us by **Web:** http://www.thomsonrights.com
Fax: 1-800-730-2215
Phone: 1-800-730-2214

Library of Congress Cataloging-in-Publication Data

Weiten, Wayne,
    Psychology applied to modern life : adjustment at the turn of the century / Wayne Weiten, Margaret A. Lloyd. — 6th ed.
        p.   cm.
    Includes bibliographical references and index.
    ISBN 0-534-35553-6
    1. Adjustment (Psychology). 2. Interpersonal relations. 3. Adulthood—Psychological aspects. 4. Self-help techniques.
    I. Lloyd, Margaret A. (Margaret Ann). II. Title.
BF335.W423   1999
158—dc21   99-24189
                                                    CIP

For more information, contact
Wadsworth/Thomson Learning
10 Davis Drive
Belmont, CA 94002-3098
USA
http://www.wadsworth.com

International Headquarters
Thomson Learning
International Division
290 Harbor Drive, 2nd Floor
Stamford, CT 06902-7477
USA

UK/Europe/Middle East/South Africa
Thomson Learning
Berkshire House
168-173 High Holborn
London WC1V 7AA
United Kingdom

Asia
Thomson Learning
60 Albert Street, #15-01
Albert Complex
Singapore 189969

Canada
Nelson Thomson Learning
1120 Birchmount Road
Toronto, Ontario M1K 5G4
Canada

This book is printed on acid-free recycled paper.

To the Instructor

Many students enter adjustment courses with great expectations. They've ambled through their local bookstores, and in the 'Psychology' section they've seen numerous self-help books that offer highly touted recipes for achieving happiness for a mere $6.^{95}. After paying far more money to enroll in a collegiate course that deals with the same issues as the self-help books, many students expect a revelatory experience. However, the majority of us with professional training in psychology or counseling take a rather dim view of self-help books and the pop psychology they represent. We tend to see this literature as oversimplified, intellectually dishonest, and opportunistic. Often we summarily dismiss the pop psychology that so many of our students have embraced. We then try to supplant it with our more sophisticated academic psychology, which is more complex and less accessible.

In this textbook, we have tried to come to grips with this problem of differing expectations between student and teacher. Our goal has been to produce a comprehensive, serious, research-oriented treatment of the topic of adjustment that also acknowledges the existence of popular psychology and looks critically at its contributions. Our approach involves the following:

● In Chapter 1 we confront the phenomenon of popular self-help books. We try to take the student beneath the seductive surface of such books and analyze some of their typical flaws. Our goal is to make the student a more critical consumer of this type of literature.
● While encouraging a more critical attitude toward self-help books, we do not suggest that they should all be dismissed. Instead, we acknowledge that some of them offer authentic insights. With this in mind, we highlight some of the better books in Recommended Reading boxes sprinkled throughout the text. These recommended readings tie in with the adjacent topical coverage and show the student the interface between academic and popular psychology.
● We try to provide the student with a better appreciation of the merit of the empirical approach. This effort to clarify the role of research, which is rare for an adjustment text, appears in the first chapter.
● Recognizing that adjustment students want to leave the course with concrete, personally useful information, we end each chapter with an application section. The Applications are 'how to' discussions that address everyday problems. While they focus on issues that are relevant to the content of the particular chapter, they contain more explicit advice than the text proper.

In summary, we have tried to make this book both rigorous and applied. We hope that our approach will help students to better appreciate the value of scientific psychology.

Philosophy

A certain philosophy is inherent in any systematic treatment of the topic of adjustment. Our philosophy can be summarized as follows:

● We believe that an adjustment text should be a resource book for students. We have tried to design this book so that it encourages and facilitates the pursuit of additional information on adjustment-related topics. It should serve as a point of departure for more learning.
● We believe in theoretical eclecticism. This book will not indoctrinate your students along the lines of any single theoretical orientation. The psychodynamic, behavioral, and humanistic schools of thought are all treated with respect, as are cognitive, biological, evolutionary, and other perspectives.
● We believe that effective adjustment requires 'taking charge' of one's own life. Throughout the book we try to promote the notion that active coping efforts are generally superior to passivity and complacency.

Changes in the Sixth Edition

One of the exciting things about psychology is that it is not a stagnant discipline. It continues to progress at what seems a faster and faster pace. A good textbook must evolve with the discipline. Although the professors and students who used the first five editions of this book did not clamor for change, there are some significant alterations.

CONTENT CHANGES

To improve the book and keep up with new developments in psychology, we have made a variety of content changes—adding and deleting some topics, condensing and reorganizing others, updating everything (there are 895 new references). The major alterations from the previous edition include the following.

Chapter 1: Adjusting to Modern Life. We focus on new examples of the search for direction, including cults, the Christian men's movement, and "Dr. Laura." Our evaluation of the codependency movement has been updated and we discuss new research on the correlates of happiness

Chapter 2: Theories of Personality. This chapter tends to stay relatively stable, but we expanded the discussion of the five-factor model of personality, including new evidence from twin studies of the Big Five traits. We have also added coverage of the evolutionary perspective on personality.

Chapter 3: Stress and Its Effects. Besides the usual updating, we have a new Recommended Reading box on technostress, a revised discussion of choking under pressure, revised coverage of posttraumatic stress disorder, and a new discussion of conscientiousness and stress tolerance, along with six new figures.

Chapter 4: Coping Processes. This chapter includes new coverage of addiction to the Internet, a revised discussion of whether personal illusions can be healthy, new coverage of procrastination, new evidence on the repercussions of inhibiting emotions, and new coverage of emotional intelligence.

Chapter 5: The Self. This chapter contains a great deal of new material, including a new discussion of confusion about self-concept, a new section on gender, ethnicity and identity, a new section on self-esteem and adjustment, and a new discussion of whether high self-esteem is always good.

Chapter 6: Social Cognition and Social Influence. This chapter should benefit from extensive new coverage of prejudice, the elaboration likelihood model, and subliminal persuasion, as well as additional material on resisting conformity pressures.

Chapter 7: Interpersonal Communication. We have taken a more practical approach to our discussion of verbal communication and streamlined and reorganized our coverage of self-disclosure. The chapter also includes a new discussion of culture and self-disclosure, and a new section on interpersonal conflict in an adversarial culture.

Chapter 8: Friendship and Love. Among the changes to this chapter, you will find revised coverage of close relationships, a new sequential slant on factors influencing interpersonal attraction, a revised discussion of romantic love as attachment, and a new Application on date rape.

Chapter 9: Marriage and Intimate Relationships. The major change in this chapter is the expanded coverage of family violence and child abuse in the Application. You will also find a new discussion of role overload and interrole conflict among wives, new data on correlates of divorce, and a new discussion of why marriage is correlated with greater health and happiness.

Chapter 10: Gender and Behavior. This chapter features new material on gender differences in behavior, additional coverage of the evolutionary perspective on gender, an updated discussion of environmental factors in gender differences, and new material on problems associated with the traditional male role.

Chapter 11: Development in Adolescence and Adulthood. The coverage of adult development has been thoroughly revised and you will find new material on the mid-life crisis, retirement, death anxiety, coping with bereavement, and the effects of parenting styles on outcomes for children.

Chapter 12: Careers and Work. This chapter features a new emphasis on crucial issues in selecting a career, an updated discussion of workplace trends, a new discussion of unemployment, and new research on the effects of using the Internet.

Chapter 13: Development and Expression of Sexuality. Our coverage includes new material on attitudes toward homosexuality, the effects of cyberporn, the positive use of peers in sex education, and emotional versus sexual affairs.

Chapter 14: Psychology and Physical Health. This chapter highlights new data on emotional reactions and heart disease, and includes a new discussion of dietary restraint and overeating. You will also find expanded coverage of communication with health providers, new material on designer drugs, and five new figures.

Chapter 15: Psychological Disorders. The major change in this chapter is the addition of a new Application on eating disorders. You will also find revised coverage of personality factors in anxiety disorders, dissociative identity disorder, and positive versus negative symptoms in schizophrenic disorders.

Chapter 16: Psychotherapy. This chapter contains new research on who seeks therapy, a revised discussion of the relative efficacy of different approaches to therapy, revised coverage of the controversy over the recovery of repressed memories in therapy, and thoroughly updated coverage of drug treatments.

OTHER CHANGES

As you look through this edition, you will see many other changes besides those in content. For example, to conserve on space, we have shifted to a full two-column layout. This change in design made it possible for us to add a major, new pedagogical feature—the Practice Tests found at the end of the chapters. Cognizant of the impact of the Internet on students, we have integrated recommended Web sites throughout the chapters to help your students pursue additional information on many of the topics covered in the book. For those students who are not already sophisticated about cyberspace, we have added a wonderful introductory essay on the Internet by Professor Vincent Hevern.

Writing Style

This book has been written with the student reader in mind. We have tried to integrate the technical jargon of our discipline into a relatively informal and down-to-earth writing style. We use concrete examples extensively to clarify complex concepts and to help maintain student interest.

Features

This text contains a number of features intended to stimulate interest and enhance students' learning. These special features include Applications, Recommended Reading boxes, Internet-related features, Practice Tests, a didactic illustration program, and cartoons.

APPLICATIONS

The Applications should be of special interest to most students. They are tied to chapter content in a way that should show students how practical applications emerge out of theory and research. Although some of the material covered in these sections shows up frequently in adjustment texts, much of it is unique. Some of the Applications include the following:

- Understanding Intimate Violence
- Monitoring Your Stress
- Understanding Eating Disorders
- Getting Ahead in the Job Game
- Building Self-Esteem
- Enhancing Sexual Relationships
- Bridging the Gender Gap in Communication

RECOMMENDED READING BOXES

Recognizing students' interest in self-help books, we have sifted through hundreds of them to identify some that may be especially useful. These are highlighted in boxes that briefly review the book and include a provocative excerpt or two. These Recommended Reading boxes are placed where they are germane to the material being covered in the text. Some of the recommended books are very well known, whereas others are obscure. Although we make it clear that we don't endorse every idea in every book, we think they all have something worthwhile to offer. This feature replaces the conventional suggested readings lists that usually appear at the ends of chapters, where they are almost universally ignored by students.

INTERNET-RELATED FEATURES

The Internet is rapidly altering the landscape of modern life, and students clearly need help dealing with the information explosion in cyberspace. To assist them, we have added two features. First, we recruited web expert Vincent Hevern to write a concise essay that explains the essentials of the Internet to the uninitiated. This essay, which appears in the front of the book, briefly explains URLs, domain names, hyperlinks, search engines, and so forth. It also provides students with realistic warnings about the instability of URLs and the questionable validity of much of the information available on the Web. Second, we also asked Professor Hevern to evaluate hundreds of psychology- and adjustment-related sites on the Web and come up with some recommended sites that appear to provide reasonably accurate, balanced, and empirically sound information. Short descriptions of these recommended Web sites are dispersed throughout the chapters, adjacent to related topical coverage. Because URLs change frequently, we have relegated the URLs for our Web Links to an Appendix in the back of the book. Insofar as students are interested in visiting these sites, we recommend that they do so through the *Psychology Applied to Modern Life* home page at the Wadsworth Psychology Study Center Web site (http://psychology.wadsworth.com). Links to all the recommended Web sites will be maintained there, and the Wadsworth Webmaster will periodically update the URLs.

PRACTICE TESTS

Each chapter ends with a 10-item multiple-choice Practice Test that should give students a pretty realistic assessment of their mastery of that chapter and valuable practice taking the type of test that many of them will face in the classroom (if the instructor uses the Test Bank). This new feature grew out of some research on students' use of textbook pedagogical devices (see Weiten, Guadagno, & Beck, 1996). This research indicated that students pay scant attention to some standard pedagogical devices. When students were grilled to gain a better undertstanding of this perplexing finding, it quickly became apparent that students are very pragmatic about pedagogy. Essentially, their refrain was "We want study aids that will help us pass the next test." With this mandate in mind, we added the Practice Tests. They should be very realistic, as many of the items came from the Test Bank for the previous edition (these items do not appear in the Test Bank for the current edition).

DIDACTIC ILLUSTRATION PROGRAM

The illustration program is once again in full color and we have added many new photographs and figures. Although the illustrations are intended to make the book attractive and to help maintain student interest, they are not merely decorative. They have been carefully selected for their didactic value to enhance the educational goals of the text.

CARTOONS

Because a little comic relief usually helps keep a student interested, numerous cartoons are sprinkled throughout the book. Like the figures, most of these have been chosen to reinforce ideas in the text.

Learning Aids

Because this book is rigorous, substantive, and sizable, a number of learning aids have been incorporated into the text to help the reader digest the wealth of material:

- *The outline* at the beginning of each chapter provides the student with a preview and overview of what will be covered.
- *Headings* are employed very frequently to keep material well organized.
- To help alert your students to key points, *learning objectives* are distributed throughout the chapters, after the level-1 headings.
- *Key terms* are identified with ***italicized boldface*** type to indicate that these are important vocabulary items that are part of psychology's technical language.
- *An integrated running glossary* provides an on-the-spot definition of each key term as it is introduced in the text. These formal definitions are printed in **boldface** type.
- *An alphabetical glossary* is found in the back of the book, since key terms are usually defined in the integrated running glossary only when they are first introduced.
- *Italics* are used liberally throughout to emphasize important points.
- *A chapter review* is found at the end of each chapter. Each review includes a concise but thorough summary of the chapter's key ideas, a list of the key terms that were introduced in the chapter, and a list of important theorists and researchers who were discussed in the chapter.

Supplementary Materials

A complete teaching/learning package has been developed to supplement *Psychology Applied to Modern Life.* These supplementary materials have been carefully coordinated to provide effective support for the text.

INSTRUCTOR'S MANUAL

An instructor's manual is available as a convenient aid for your educational endeavors. Written by William Addison, it provides a thorough overview of each chapter, along with a list of relevant films. It also includes a wealth of suggestions for lecture topics, class demonstrations, exercises, and discussion questions, organized around the content of each chapter in the text.

TEST BANK

Bill Addison has taken on the task of revising the test bank. It contains an extensive collection of multiple-choice questions for objective tests. The questions are closely tied to the learning objectives found in the text chapters. We're confident that you will find this to be a dependable and usable test bank.

STUDY GUIDE

The study guide has been revised by William Addison, who has built on the outstanding work of Michael Sosulski, a dear friend and colleague who passed away. The study guide is designed to help students master the information contained in the text. For each chapter, it contains a brief overview, learning objectives, a programmed review, several other types of review exercises, and a self-test. We're confident that your students will find it very helpful in their study efforts.

CULTURE AND MODERN LIFE

Culture and Modern Life is a small paperback that is intended to help your students appreciate how cultural factors moderate psychological processes and how the viewpoint of one's own culture can distort one's interpretation of the behavior of people from other cultures. Written by David Matsumoto, a leading authority on cross-cultural psychology, this supplementary book should greatly enhance your students' understanding of how culture can influence adjustment. *Culture and Modern Life* can be ordered shrinkwrapped with the text.

PERSONAL EXPLORATIONS WORKBOOK

The Personal Explorations Workbook is a small booklet assembled by Wayne Weiten. It contains experiential exercises for each text chapter, designed to help your students achieve personal insights. The Questionnaires are psychological tests or scales that your students can administer and score for themselves. The Personal Probes consist of questions intended to help students think about themselves in relation to issues raised in the text. Most students find these exercises interesting. They can also be fruitful in stimulating class discussion. The *Personal Explorations Workbook* can be ordered shrinkwrapped with the text.

Acknowledgements

This book has been an enormous undertaking, and we want to express our gratitude to the innumerable people who have influenced its evolution. To begin with, we must cite the contribution of our students who have taken the adjustment course. It is trite to say that they have been a continuing inspiration—but they have.

We also want to express our appreciation for the time and effort invested by the authors of our Internet essay and various ancillary books: Vinny Hevern (LeMoyne College), Bill Addison (Eastern Illinois University), and David Matsumoto (San Francisco State University). In spite of tight schedules, they all did commendable work.

The quality of a textbook depends greatly on the quality of the prepublication reviews by psychology professors around the country. The reviewers listed on page x have contributed to the development of this book by providing constructive reviews of various portions of the manuscript in this or earlier editions. We are very grateful to all of them.

We would also like to thank Eileen Murphy, who has served as editor of this and the previous edition. She has done a wonderful job following in the footsteps of Claire Verduin, a legend in textbook publishing circles, who we remain indebted to. We are also grateful to Jackie Estrada, for an excellent job of copy editing and indexing, Tom Dorsaneo, who performed superbly as our production editor, Gladys Rosa-Mendoza, who created the efficient, new design and the chapter opening art, Brian Wenberg, who did valiant work on the page layouts, Linda Rill, who provided outstanding photo research, and Fiorella Ljunggren, who shepherded previous editions into existence. Others who have made significant contributions to this project include: Joanne Terhaar (marketing), Annie Berterretche (editorial assistant), Tanya Nigh (project editor), Stephen Rapley (creative director), and Leslie Krongold (media editor).

In addition, Wayne Weiten would like to thank his wife, Beth Traylor, who has been a steady source of emotional support in spite of the intense demands of her medical career, and his six-year-old son, T.J., who adds a wealth of laughter to his dad's life. He is also grateful to his former colleagues at the College of DuPage and his current colleagues at Santa Clara University, for their counsel and assistance. Marky Lloyd would like to thank graduate students Penny Mills, Mark Tichon, and Kelli Taylor, and librarian Suzanne Metcalf for their help with library research. She is also grateful to her colleagues Janis Bohan, Virginia Rowden, and Edward W. L. Smith for their assistance. Finally, she wishes to thank Judith A. Holleman for her support and encouragement.

Wayne Weiten
Margaret A. Lloyd

Reviewers

Marsha K. Beauchamp
Mt. San Antonio College

John R. Blakemore
Monterey Peninsula College

Paul Bowers
Grayson County College

George Bryant
East Texas State University

James F. Calhoun
University of Georgia

Robert Cameron
Fairmont State College

M. K. Clampit
Bentley College

Meg Clark
California State Polytechnic University–Pomona

Stephen S. Coccia
Orange County Community College

Dennis Coon
Santa barbara City College

Tori Crews
American River College

Salvatore Cullari
Lebanon Valley College

Kenneth S. Davidson
Wayne State University

Richard Fuhrer
University of Wisconsin–Eau Claire

Lee Gills
Georgia College

Lawrence Grebstein
University of Rhode Island

Robert Helm
Oklahoma State University

Barbara Hermann
Gainesville College

Robert Higgins
Central Missouri State University

Clara E. Hill
University of Maryland

Michael Hirt
Kent State University

Fred J. Hitti
Monroe Community College

Joseph Horvat
Weber State University

Kathy Howard
Harding University

Walter Jones
College of DuPage

Wayne Joose
Clavin College

Margaret Karolyi
University of Akron

Susan Kupisch
Austin Peay State University

Barbara Hansen Lemme
College of DuPage

Harold List
Massachusetts Bay Community College

Louis A. Martone
Miami–Dade Community College

Richard Maslow
San Joaquin Delta College

William T. McReynolds
University of Tampa

Fred Medway
University of South Carolina–Columbia

Frederick Meeker
California State Polytechnic University–Pomona

John Moritsugu
Pacific Lutheran University

Jeanne O'Kon
Tallahassee Community College

Gary Oliver
College of DuPage

Joseph Philbrick
California State Polytechnic University–Pomona

William Penrod
Middle Tennessee State University

Barbara M. Powell
Eastern Illinois University

James Prochaska
University of Rhode Island

Joan Royce
Riverside Community College

Joan Rykiel
Ocean County College

John Sample
Slippery Rock University

Thomas K. Savill
Metropolitan State College of Denver

Carol Schachat
DeAnza Community College

Norman R. Schultz
Clemson University

Dale Simmons
Oregon State University

Karl Swain
Community College of South Nevada

Kenneth L. Thompson
Central Missouri State University

David L. Watson
University of Hawaii

Deborah S. Weber
University of Akron

Clair Wiederholt
Madison Area Tech College

J. Oscar Williams
Diablo Valley College

Raymond Wolfe
Moraine Park Technical College

Raymond Wolfe
State University of New York at Geneseo

Michael Wolff
Southwestern Oklahoma State University

Norbert Yager
Henry Ford Community College

Brief Contents

Contents

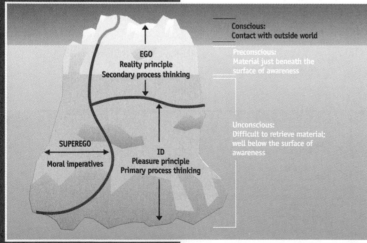

CHAPTER 2
Theories of Personality

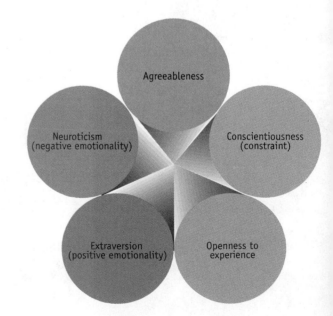

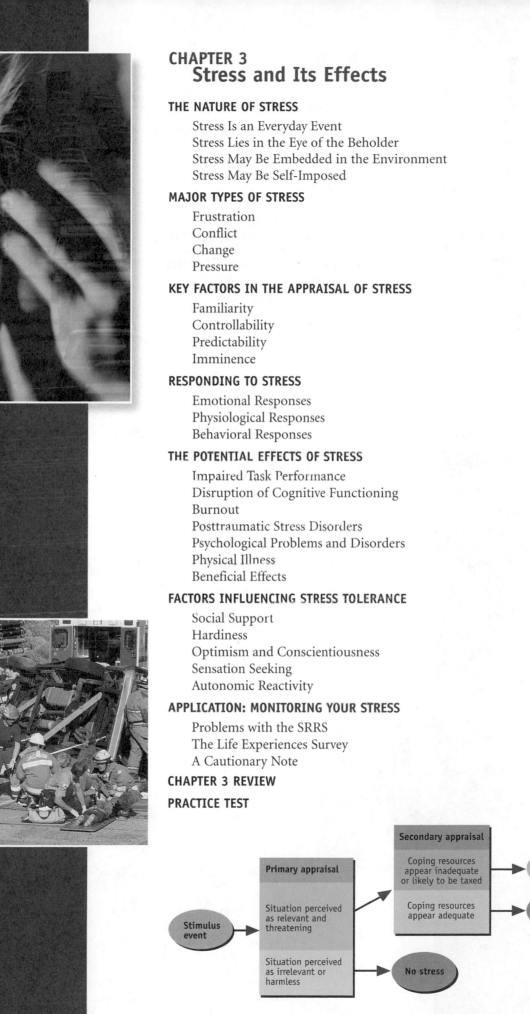

Secondary appraisal

Coping resources appear inadequate or likely to be taxed → Stress

Coping resources appear adequate → No stress

Primary appraisal

Situation perceived as relevant and threatening

Stimulus event →

Situation perceived as irrelevant or harmless → No stress

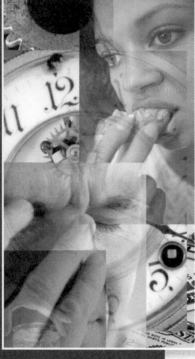

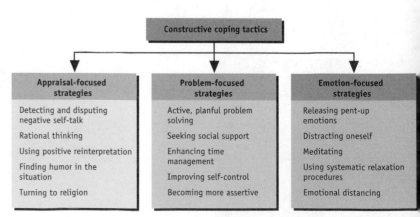

Constructive coping tactics		
Appraisal-focused strategies	**Problem-focused strategies**	**Emotion-focused strategies**
Detecting and disputing negative self-talk	Active, planful problem solving	Releasing pent-up emotions
Rational thinking	Seeking social support	Distracting oneself
Using positive reinterpretation	Enhancing time management	Meditating
Finding humor in the situation	Improving self-control	Using systematic relaxation procedures
Turning to religion	Becoming more assertive	Emotional distancing

PART TWO
The Interpersonal Realm

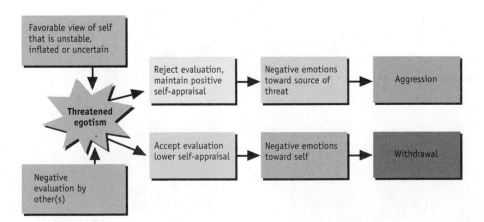

CHAPTER 6
Social Cognition and Social Influence

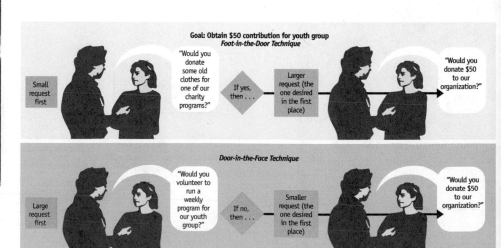

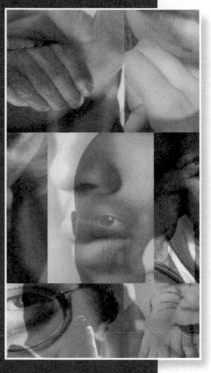

CHAPTER 7
Interpersonal Communication

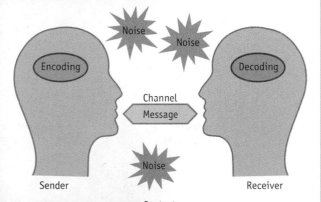

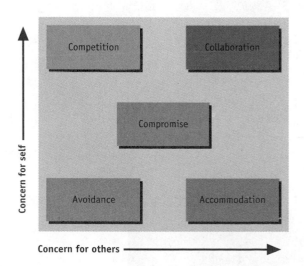

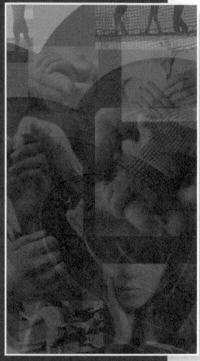

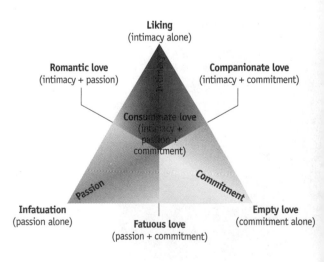

Liking
(intimacy alone)

Romantic love
(intimacy + passion)

Companionate love
(intimacy + commitment)

Consummate love
(intimacy +
passion +
commitment)

Passion

Commitment

Infatuation
(passion alone)

Fatuous love
(passion + commitment)

Empty love
(commitment alone)

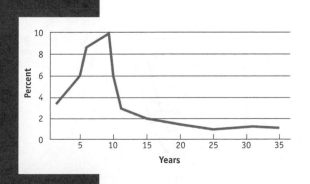

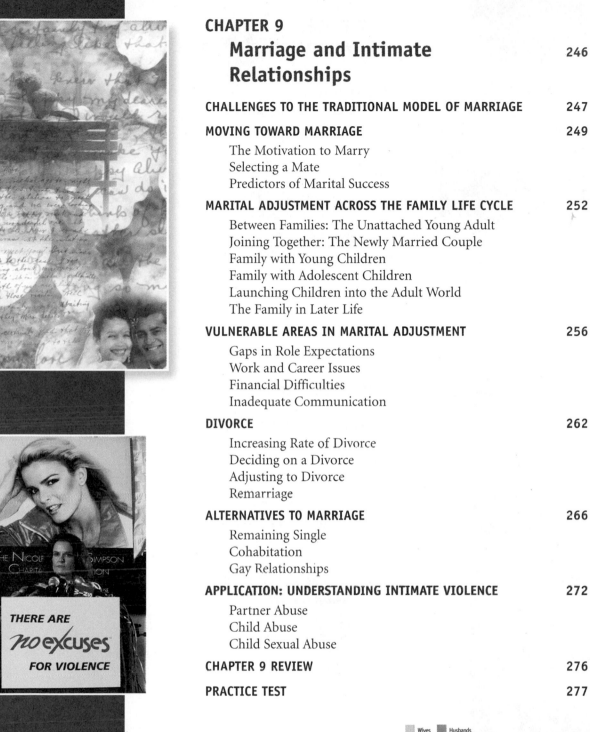

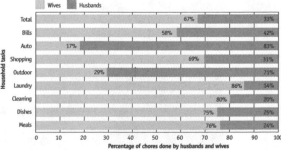

PART THREE
Developmental Transitions

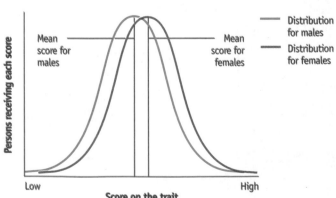

CHAPTER 11
Development in Adolescence and Adulthood

	Parental Acceptance	
	Low	**High**
High	**Authoritarian** (low acceptance, high control)	**Authoritative** (high acceptance, high control)
Low	**Neglectful** (low acceptance, low control)	**Permissive** (high acceptance, low control)

Parental Control

CHAPTER 12
Careers and Work

Relatives 3%   Acquaintances 3%

Work associates 9%

85%
Robberies and crimes

Sources of on-the-job homicides

CHAPTER 13
Development and Expression of Sexuality

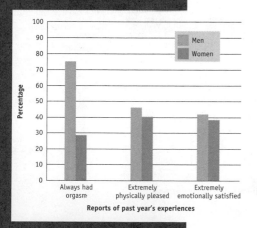

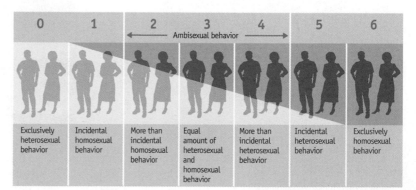

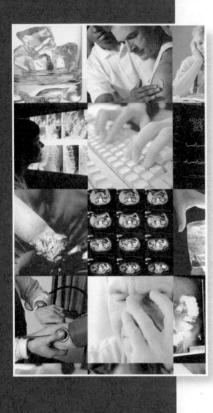

PART FOUR
Mental and Physical Health

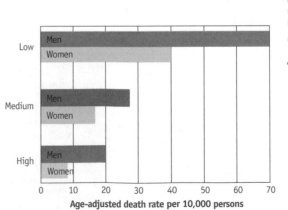

Participants were divided into fiv
categories based on their fitness
ranging from least fit (group 1) 1
most fit (group 5).

Low fitness:
Group 1

Medium fitness:
Groups 2 and 3

High fitness:
Groups 4 and 5

CHAPTER 15
Psychological Disorders

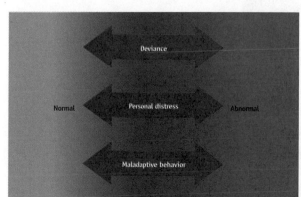

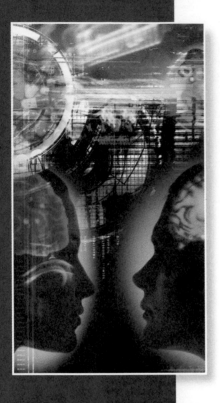

To the Student

In most college courses students spend more time with their textbooks than with their professors. Given this reality, it helps if you like your textbook. Making textbooks likable, however, is a tricky proposition. By its very nature, a textbook must introduce a great many new concepts, ideas, and theories. If it doesn't, it isn't much of a textbook, and instructors won't choose to use it—so you'll never see it anyway. Consequently, we have tried to make this book as likable as possible without compromising the academic content that your instructor demands. Thus, we have tried to make the book lively, informal, engaging, well organized, easy to read, practical, and occasionally humorous. Before you plunge into Chapter 1, let us explain some of the key features that can help you get the most out of the book.

Learning Aids

Mastering the content of this text involves digesting a great deal of information. To facilitate this learning process, we've incorporated a number of instructional aids into the book.

- *Outlines* at the beginning of each chapter provide you with both a preview and an overview of what will be covered.
- *Headings* are employed very frequently to keep material well organized.
- To help alert you to key points, *learning objectives* are found throughout the chapters, immediately after the level-1 headings.
- *Key terms* are identified with ***italicized boldface*** type to indicate that these are important vocabulary items that are part of psychology's technical language.
- *An integrated running glossary* provides an on-the-spot definition of each key term as it's introduced in the text. These formal definitions are printed in **boldface** type. It is often difficult for students to adapt to the jargon used by scientific disciplines. However, learning this terminology is an essential part of your educational experience. The integrated running glossary is meant to make this learning process as painless as possible.
- *An alphabetical glossary* is provided in the back of the book, since key terms are usually defined in the running glossary only when they are first introduced. If you run into a technical term that was introduced in an earlier chapter and you can't remember its meaning, you can look it up in the alphabetical glossary instead of backtracking to find the place where it first appeared.
- *Italics* are used liberally throughout the book to emphasize important points.

- A *chapter review* is found near the end of each chapter. Each review includes a thorough summary of the chapter, a list of key terms, and a list of important theorists and researchers. Reading over these review materials can help you ensure that you've digested the key points in the chapter.
- Each chapter ends with a 10-item *practice test* that should give you a realistic assessment of your mastery of that chapter and valuable practice taking multiple-choice tests that probably will be representative of what you will see in class (if your instructor uses the test bank designed for this book).

Recommended Reading Boxes

This text should function as a resource book. To facilitate this goal, particularly interesting self-help books on various topics are highlighted in boxes within the chapters. Each box provides a brief description of the book and a provocative excerpt. We do not agree with everything in these recommended books, but all of them are potentially useful or intriguing. The main purpose of this feature is to introduce you to some of the better self-help books that are available.

Web Links (by Vincent Hevern)

To help make this book a rich resource guide, we have included Web Links, which are recommended Web sites that can provide you with additional information on adjustment-related topics. The recommended sites were selected by Vincent Hevern, the Web Editor for the Society for the Teaching of Psychology. Professor Hevern sought out sites that are interesting, relevant to adjustment, and that provide accurate, empirically sound information. As with the Recommended Reading Boxes, we cannot say that we agree with everything posted on these Web pages, but we think they have some real value. The Web Links are dispersed throughout the chapters, adjacent to related topical coverage. Because URLs change frequently, we have relegated the URLs for our Web Links to an Appendix in the back of the book. If you are interested in visiting these sites, we recommend that they do so through the *Psychology Applied to Modern Life* home page at the Wadsworth Psychology Study Center Web site (http://psychology.wadsworth.com). Links to all the recommended Web sites will be maintained there and the Wadsworth Webmaster will periodically update the URLs. By the way, if you are not particularly sophisticated about the Internet, we strongly suggest that you read Professor Hevern's essay on the Internet, which follows this preface.

Study Guide

The study guide that accompanies this text is an excellent resource designed to assist you in mastering the information contained in the book. It includes a wealth of review exercises to help you organize information and a self-test for assessing your mastery. You should be able to purchase it at your college bookstore.

A Concluding Note

We sincerely hope that you find this book enjoyable. If you have any comments or advice that might help us improve the next edition, please write to us in care of the publisher, Wadsworth Publishing Company, 10 Davis Drive, Belmont, California 94002. There is a form in the back of the book that you can use to provide us with feedback. Finally, let us wish you good luck. We hope you enjoy your course and learn a great deal.

Wayne Weiten
Margaret A. Lloyd

Applied Psychology and the Internet: What Should a Student Know?

BY VINCENT W. HEVERN, LE MOYNE COLLEGE

Imagine walking into a huge bookstore at a mall to look for a good book in "applied psychology". Your first reaction is confusion. The store is gigantic and you're unsure even where to begin your search. No one seems to be around to tell you where to look. Eventually you discover that some titles of interest are shelved in a "Psychology" section but a lot of others are found in a separate "Self Help" section. What's the difference, you wonder? After a careful look at the books, you begin to notice that many (not all) of the *psychology* books contain research references to support their conclusions. But, many (not all) of the *self-help* books don't have any references. Indeed, many self-help books have catchy titles, flashy covers, bold claims, but very little scientific support for the claims they make.

The World Wide Web (WWW or "the Web") on the Internet ("the Net") is very much like one of those huge bookstores. It's enormous and sometimes difficult to find what you're looking for. For many browsers, the Net can seem intimidating and students may feel they don't know how the Net works. On top of that, much of the Web is filled with weak or poor resources of dubious validity. So what can you do?

Wayne Weiten and Marky Lloyd, the authors of this textbook, asked me to put together some advice and guidelines for students like yourself who may turn to the Net for help. They know that I've been using the Net intensively for about five years in teaching and research with undergraduates. So, I'm going to share with you here what I believe to be the really important stuff about the Internet—information that should make your life as a student easier and, in the end, help you to learn even more about the fascinating world of applied psychology.

General Comments about the Internet

We now know that something of a fundamental change in the way people exchange ideas and information took place around the time many of you were beginning junior high or high school. For over twenty years, the Internet had been the tool of a relatively small group of lab scientists communicating mostly with each other. Suddenly, in the mid-1990s, the Net began to expand rapidly beyond the research laboratory. It first reached tens and, then, hundreds of millions of people as vast numbers of computers, large and small, were interconnected to form what is often called *cyberspace*. Thus, in the 21st century, learning to navigate the Internet will become as crucial as learning to read or to write—most of us will probably employ the Net in some form at work or at home for the rest of our lives.

So, what are some basic notions to understand the Internet and how it works? Let me propose briefly eight crucial ideas.

1. *The goal of the Internet is communication—the rapid exchange of information—between people separated from each other.* Electronic mail (e-mail) and the World Wide Web are currently the two most important ways of communicating in cyberspace even though the Net also uses other formats to do so.

2. *Every piece of information on the Net—every Web page, every graphic, every movie or sound, every e-mail box—has a unique, short, and structured address called a URL (or uniform resource locator).* Take, for example, the URL for the online Psychology Textbook Catalogue of the publisher of this book:

http://psychology.wadsworth.com/psych_dis.html

This example shows all three elements of a URL: (a) to the left of the double forward slashes (//) is the protocol that tells the Net how to transfer the information. Here it is *http:* which means "use hypertext transfer protocol"—the most frequent protocol on the Net; (b) to the right of the double slashes up to the first forward slash (/) is the *domain name* that indicates which computer on the Net from which to get the information. Here the name of the computer is "psychology.wadsworth.com". (c) finally, everything after the first forward slash is called the *pathway* which indicates where the information is located within that particular computer. Here the pathway comprises the location "psych_dis.html".

3. *The foundation of the Web rests upon hypertext links ("hyperlinks") which are contained within documents (or "web pages") displayed online.* A hyperlink is a highlighted word, phrase, or graphic image within an onscreen document which refers to some other document or web page elsewhere. Part of every hyperlink on a computer screen includes the URL of the document which is hidden from view on the screen but stored within the computer displaying the document. Users can easily move from one document to another on screen because of hypertext links and their URLs.

4. *Pay attention to the last element of the domain name (the "domain" itself) which indicates what type of organization sponsors the link.* Four important domains are: *.com* (commercial businesses), *.edu* (colleges and universities), *.gov* (governmental agencies) and *.org* (non-profit organizations).

5. *The Internet is too large for any one individual to know all the important resources which can be found there.* Users, even experienced ones, often need help to find what they're looking for. In the chapters ahead, you will find many recommended web sites, called Web Links, that I have carefully selected based on their quality and their suitability for undergraduates. In making these selections, I emphasized quality over quantity and strived to send you to excellent gateway sites that are rich in links to related sites. I hope these links help you to begin to explore the field of applied psychology on the Internet.

6. *URLs are relatively unstable.* Many web sites are moved or changed each year and new computer systems are installed to replace older ones. Thus, links or URLs which are good one day may be useless the next. That is why we have relegated the URLs for our Web Links to an Appendix found in the back of this book. If you want to check out a recommended web site, we suggest that you do so through the *Psychology: Applied to Modern Life* home page at the Wadsworth Psychology Study Center web site (http://psychology. wadsworth. com). Links to all of the recommended web sites will be maintained there and the Wadsworth Webmaster will periodically update the URLs.

7. *The Web is a world-wide democracy on which anyone can post materials.* Hence, the quality of information found online varies tremendously. Some is first-rate, up-to-date, and backed up by good research and professional judgment. But, a great deal of information online is junk—second-rate, based on poor or invalid research, and filled with many errors. Frankly, some sites are downright wacky and others are run by hucksters and hate-mongers. Thus, users need to learn to tell the difference between reputable and disreputable Web resources.

8. *Knowledge has a monetary value.* Although the Internet started out as a non-commercial enterprise where almost everything was free, things have changed swiftly. Owners of knowledge (the holders of commercial "copyrights") usually expect to be paid for sharing what they own over the Net. Thus, many commercial businesses like the publishers of academic journals or books either do *not* make journal articles available on line for free or expect users to pay some type of fee for accessing their materials. Cognizant of this problem, the publisher of this text has entered into an agreement with a major online resource for magazine and journal articles and other types of information called *InfoTrac*. Your text may have come bundled with a four-month subscription to *InfoTrac*, which provides easy access to full-text versions of thousands of periodicals. If you received an *InfoTrac* subscription with this book, it would be wise to take advantage of this valuable resource.

Some Suggestions for Action

In light of these ideas, how might students approach the Internet? What should you do? Let's review some general suggestions for exploring the Internet.

1. *Learn to navigate the Net before you get an assignment requiring you to do so.* If you've never employed the Net before, start now to get a feel for it. Consider doing what lots of students do: ask a friend who knows the Net to work with you directly so you can quickly get personal experience in cyberspace. What if you "hate" computers or they make you uncomfortable? Recent research has shown that students' fears of using computers tends to diminish once they get some practical experience in the course of a single semester.

2. *Learn how the software browser on your computer works.* The two most popular Web browser programs, *Netscape® Navigator* and *Microsoft® Internet Explorer®*, are filled with many simple tricks and helpful shortcuts. Ask your friends or the computer consultants at school. When you learn the tricks, it makes Net-based research much easier. (Hint: find out what happens when you hold down the right-hand mouse button on a PC or the whole button on a Mac once you have the cursor on top of a hyperlink.)

3. *Get to know the different types of online help to find resources on the Web.* These currently fall into three general categories. (a) *General Guides or Directories* like Yahoo! (www.yahoo.com) are similar to the Yellow Pages for telephones. You ask the online guide to show you what's listed in its directory under a category heading you supply. (b) *Search Engines* such as AltaVista (www.altavista.com) or Hotbot (www.hotbot.com), and *Meta-search Engines* such as Metacrawler (www.metacrawler.com) are huge databases which generally collect the names and URLs of millions of pages on the Net along with many lines of text from these pages. They can be searched by either keywords or phrases and provide ranked listings of Web pages which contain the search target words or phrases. (c) *Expert Subject Guides* such as Russ Dewey's *PsychWeb* (www.gasou.edu/psychweb/psychweb.html) or Jeffrey Browndyke's *Neuropsychology Central* (www.premier .net/~cogito/neuropsy.html) provide links to online resources in more narrow or specific fields. Volunteer specialists who claim to be experts on the topic of the guide select the links.

4. *Check very carefully everything you type online because even the slightest error in spelling a URL or an e-mail address will cause a failure to retrieve the web page or to deliver the e-mail message.* Remember that computers are stupid and will do exactly and only what you tell them to do. They don't read minds.

Using the Internet in Psychology

Are there specific suggestions for students of psychology about using the Net? Here's four that I think are very important.

1. *Think out what you are looking for in research before going online.* Too many psychology students jump right to the Web when they're given a research task before giving careful thought about what they're looking for. They easily get frustrated because the Web doesn't seem to have anything about the topic. It would be better (a) to think about the subject you are researching and what specifically you want to learn about that topic, (b) to recall what you already know that relates to the topic, especially psychological concepts and vocabulary words associated with the topic, and (c) to devise a strategy for getting the information you desire. Consult your school's reference library staff or your teachers for suggestions.

2. *The Internet should not be the principal or only source of data or references in a research project* (especially if you want a good grade). The Net may be easy to use, but your teachers will expect you to cite journal articles, books, and other printed sources more than you cite Internet materials in research. Developing your library skills is essential.

3. As noted before, don't expect to find many full-text journal articles or other copyrighted commercial materials online for free. Consult your school's reference librarians about online access to such materials. You are more likely to uncover government reports, specialized technical materials from non-profit organizations, current news and opinion, and general sorts of information rather than findings of specific research studies (though, if they were recently in the news, you may find some of these too.)

4. *Learn to recognize the characteristics of a good online resource site.* Good sites have webmasters or editors personally identified by name and affiliation. Such persons may be professionals or staff members at a reputable institution such as a hospital or university. These sites seem to provide a broad set of resources, are balanced and reasonably objective in their content and avoid sensational or one-sided viewpoints. More reputable sites tend not to promote specific products or services for money or, if they do, acknowledge there are other resources which browsers may consider. Libraries have taken the lead on guidelines about what to look for. I suggest you read the excellent Widener University Library materials at http://www.science.widener.edu/~withes/webeval.htm.

I hope some of these ideas and suggestions help. The Internet offers an awesome array of learning resources related to psychology. Welcome to an exciting new world of discovery.

Psychology Applied to Modern Life

ADJUSTMENT AT THE TURN OF THE CENTURY

CHAPTER 1

Adjusting to Modern Life

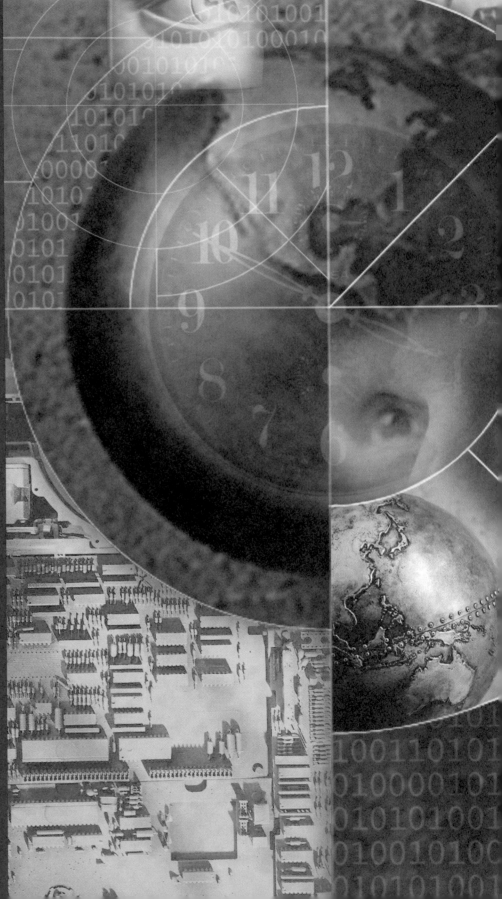

The immense Boeing 747 lumbers into position to accept its human cargo. The eager passengers-to-be scurry on board. In a tower a few hundred yards away, air traffic controllers diligently monitor radar screens, radio transmissions, and digital readouts of weather information. At the reservation desks in the airport terminal, clerks punch up the appropriate ticket information on their computer terminals and quickly process the steady stream of passengers. Mounted on the wall are video terminals displaying up-to-the-minute information on flight arrivals, departures, and delays. Back in the cockpit of the plane, the flight crew calmly scans the complex array of dials, meters, and lights to assess the aircraft's readiness for flight. In a few minutes, the airplane will slice into the cloudy, snow-laden skies above Chicago. In a mere three hours its passengers will be transported from the piercing cold of a Chicago winter to the balmy beaches of the Bahamas. Another everyday triumph for technology will have taken place.

The Paradox of Progress

LEARNING OBJECTIVES

- Describe four examples of the paradox of progress.
- Explain what is meant by the paradox of progress and how theorists have explained it.

We are the children of technology. We take for granted such impressive feats as transporting 300 people over 1500 miles in a matter of hours. After all, we live in the space age—a time of unparalleled progress. Our modern Western society has made extraordinary strides in transportation, energy, communication, agriculture, and medicine. Yet in spite of our technological progress, social problems and personal difficulties seem more prevalent and more prominent than ever before. This paradox is evident in many aspects of contemporary life, as seen in the following examples.

Point. Modern technology has provided us with countless time-saving devices—automobiles, telephones, vacuum cleaners, dishwashers, photocopiers, fax machines. Today, cellular phones allow people to talk to friends or colleagues and battle rush hour at the same time. In a matter of seconds a personal computer can perform calculations that would take months if done by hand.

Counterpoint. Nonetheless, most of us complain about not having enough time. Our schedule books are overflowing with appointments, commitments, and plans. Surveys suggest that most of us spend more and more time working and have less and less time for themselves (Gilbert, 1988; Schor, 1991). Time has become such a precious commodity that a 1995 *U.S. News & World Report* survey found that 51% of the adult respondents would rather have more time than more money (Weil & Rosen, 1997). As social critic Jeremy Rifkin (1989) notes, "It is ironic in a culture so committed to saving time that we feel increasingly deprived of the very thing we value. The modern world of streamlined transportation, instantaneous communication, and time-saving technologies was supposed to free us from the dictates of the clock and provide us with increased leisure. Instead there seems never to be enough time.... Despite our alleged efficiency, as compared to almost every other period in history, we seem to have less time for ourselves and far less time for each other" (p. 19). Where has all our free time gone? Recent research suggests that virtually all the additional leisure time gained over the last 30 years has been absorbed by technology's most seductive invention—television (Robinson & Godbey, 1997).

Point. Thanks in large part to technological advances, we live in extraordinary affluence. Undeniably, there are pockets of genuine poverty, but Paul Wachtel (1989) argues convincingly that the middle and upper classes are larger and wealthier than ever before. Most of us take for granted things that were once considered luxuries, such as color television and air conditioning. People spend vast amounts of money on expensive automobiles, stereo systems, computers, projection TVs, clothing, and travel. Wachtel quotes a New York museum director who asserts that "shopping is the chief cultural activity in the United States" (p. 23).

Counterpoint. In spite of this economic abundance, Wachtel notes that a "sense of economic decline is widespread nowadays.... [We feel] that declining productivity has pinched our pocketbooks, that inflation has eaten up our buying power, that we can't catch up, much less get ahead" (p. 9). According to Wachtel, our economic system's commitment to growth, coupled with the effects of mass media advertising, has created an insatiable thirst for consumption. Although our standard of living has improved, most of us feel like we still need more goods and services. Rich by any

previous standard, we are nevertheless subjectively distressed about our economic plight.

Point. In recent years, our ability to process, store, and communicate information has improved exponentially. Using satellites, TV networks can beam live telecasts around the globe almost instantaneously. Small satellite dishes and digital cable bring hundreds of TV channels into our homes. We can use online computerized databases to access millions of magazine and journal articles. We can use the Internet to track the stock market, view airline schedules, shop for books or cars, communicate with friends or strangers in distant places, or visit a seemingly infinite universe of Web sites. In this "wired" world, computer technology has even seeped into many people's sense of identity. As Weil and Rosen (1997) note, "People at social gatherings and at work compare baud rates and hard drive storage space as though they are in a gym, flexing muscles" (p. 64).

Counterpoint. However, in his book *Data Smog*, David Shenk (1997) asserts that this information glut "no longer adds to our quality of life, but instead begins to cultivate stress, confusion, and even ignorance" (p. 15). Shenk argues that most of us are simply overwhelmed by the deluge of information that we routinely receive. Reasoning along similar lines, Richard Saul Wurman (1990) maintains that nearly everyone suffers from *information anxiety*—concern about the ever-widening gap between what we understand and what we think we

should understand. The crux of the problem is the explosive growth of available information, which now doubles about every five years. Wurman points out that a single weekday edition of the *New York Times* "contains more information than the average person was likely to come across in a lifetime in 17th-century England" (p. 32). According to Wurman, people exhibit symptoms of information anxiety when they complain about stacks of unread periodicals, when they bemoan their inability to keep up with what's going on, when they pretend that they are familiar with a book or artist that they've never heard of, when they feel overwhelmed by the hundreds of TV channels available, and when they feel bewildered by the intricacies of their computers, VCRs, cellular phones, fax machines, and pagers.

Point. In the medical arena, we have made stunning advances. Doctors can reattach severed limbs, use lasers to correct microscopic defects in the eye, and even replace the human heart. Contagious diseases (those caused by infectious agents), such as tuberculosis, typhoid fever, smallpox, and cholera, are largely under control. Since the turn of the century, life expectancy in the United States has increased from 47 to 75 years.

Counterpoint. Nonetheless, as noted in a *Time* magazine article, "Never have doctors been able to do so much for their patients, and rarely have patients seemed so ungrateful" (Gibbs, 1989, p. 49). The cost of medical care has skyrocketed and malpractice lawsuits have increased dramatically, while patients' access to quality care and their trust in the medical profession have declined noticeably (Kassler, 1994). Moreover, as we'll discuss in Chapter 14, the void left by contagious diseases has been filled all too quickly by chronic diseases that develop gradually, such as cancer, heart disease, hypertension, and ulcers. The increase in chronic diseases is partly attributable to stress and certain features of our modern lifestyle, such as the penchant for smoking and overeating and the tendency to get little physical exercise.

The apparent contradictions just discussed all reflect the same theme: *The technological advances of the 20th century, impressive though they may be, have not led to perceptible improvement in our collective health and happiness.* Indeed, many social critics argue that the quality of our lives and our sense of personal fulfillment have declined rather than increased. This is the paradox of progress.

What is the cause of this paradox? There are many potential explanations. Erich Fromm (1963, 1981) has argued that the progress we value so much has scrambled our value systems and undermined our traditional sources of emotional security, such as family, community, and religion. Alvin Toffler (1970, 1980) attributes our collective alienation and distress to our being overwhelmed by rapidly accelerating cultural change. Robert Kegan (1994) maintains that the mental demands of modern life have become so complex, confusing, and contradictory that most of us are "in over our heads." Whatever the explanation, many theorists agree that *the basic challenge of modern life has become the search for meaning or a sense of direction* (Naylor, Willimon, & Naylor, 1994). This search involves struggling with such problems as forming a solid sense of identity, arriving at a coherent philosophy of life, and developing a clear vision of a future that realistically promises fulfillment. Centuries ago, problems of this kind were probably much simpler. As we'll see in the next section, today it appears that many of us are floundering in a sea of confusion.

The Search for Direction

LEARNING OBJECTIVES

● *Explain the key ideas of codependency theory.*
● *Discuss some strengths of codependency theory.*
● *Summarize the text's critique of codependency theory.*
● *Describe three problems that are common in popular self-help books.*
● *Summarize advice about what to look for in quality self-help books.*
● *Summarize the philosophy underlying this textbook.*

We live in a time of unparalleled social and technological mutation. According to a host of social critics, the kaleidoscope of change that we see around us creates feelings of anxiety and uncertainty, which we try to alleviate by searching for a sense of direction. This search, which sometimes goes awry, is manifested in many ways.

● For example, we could discuss how hundreds of thousands of Americans have invested large sums of money to enroll in "self-realization" programs such as est training, Scientology, and Silva Mind Control. These programs typically promise to provide profound enlightenment and quickly turn one's life around. Many participants claim that the programs have revolutionized their lives. However, most experts characterize these programs as intellectually bankrupt, and magazine exposés reveal that they are simply lucrative money-making schemes (Behar, 1991; Pressman, 1993). More than anything else, the success of these programs demonstrates just how desperate some people are for a sense of direction and purpose in their lives.

● We could also discuss how a host of unorthodox religious groups—commonly called *cults*—have attracted hundreds of thousands of converts who voluntarily embrace a life of regimentation, obedience, and zealous ideology. Most of these cults flourish in obscurity, unless bizarre incidents—such as the mass suicide of the Heaven's Gate cult—attract public attention. It is widely believed that cults use brainwashing and mind control to seduce lonely outsiders, but in reality converts are a diverse array of normal people who are swayed by remarkably ordinary social influence strategies (Deikman, 1990; Zimbardo, 1997) According to Philip Zimbardo (1992), people join cults because they appear to provide simple solutions to complex problems, a sense of purpose, and a structured lifestyle that reduces feelings of uncertainty.

● If you would prefer a less exotic and much healthier example of our collective search for a sense of direction, we could talk about the recent emergence of the Christian men's movement, as exemplified by the

There are many manifestations of our search for a sense of direction, including the emergence of religious cults, such as the Heaven's Gate cult that attracted attention with its mass suicide, the remarkable growth of the Christian men's movement, as exemplified by the Promise Keepers, and the astonishing popularity of "Dr. Laura."

Promise Keepers. Founded in 1991 by Bill McCartney, a former Colorado football coach, this grassroots organization has drawn millions of men to a series of huge convocations in stadiums, where they pray for the strength to lead their families as good Christian fathers and husbands. Although some mainstream religious leaders are skeptical about the value of "arena-stretching rallies," the massive turnouts clearly demonstrate that many men have unfulfilled spiritual needs and are searching for inspiration, support, and guidance (Rabey, 1996).

• And, if you would like a mundane, everyday example of our search for direction, you need look no farther than your radio, where you will find that the hottest nationally syndicated personality is "Dr. Laura," who doles out advice to over 15 million listeners a week over a network of nearly 300 stations (Bendis, 1997). Although only seven or eight people get through to her during each show, an astonishing 75,000 people call each day to seek her unique brand of blunt, outspoken, judgmental advice. Dr. Laura is the first to emphasize that—contrary to public perception—she does not do therapy over the air. As she puts it, I "preach, teach, and nag." As you will learn in Chapter 16, therapists generally do *not* tell people how to live their lives, whereas Dr. Laura is not the least bit bashful about doing so. Analyzing callers' problems in more of a moral than psychological framework, she unabashedly preaches to her audience about how they ought to live their lives. The remarkable popularity of her highly prescriptive advice demonstrates once again that many people are eager for guidance and direction.

Although we might choose to examine any of these examples of people's search for a sense of direction, we will reserve our in-depth analysis for two other manifestations of this search that are even more germane to our focus on everyday adjustment: the recent popularity of the codependency movement, and the spectacular success of best-selling "self-help" books.

The Codependency Movement

One highly visible indication of our collective malaise and never-ending search for fulfillment is the codependency movement, which has grown like a firestorm on a dry, windy prairie. The fire was ignited in 1987 with the publication of *Codependent No More* by Melody Beattie. Beattie's description of the codependency syndrome clearly struck a chord, as it has become "the chic neurosis of our time" (Lyon & Greenberg, 1991, p. 435). The movement spawned a host of books, workshops, seminars, support groups, and treatment programs designed to help people overcome their codependency. By 1991, there were over 500 bookstores in the United States devoted entirely to codependency literature (Jones, 1993).

DESCRIPTION

What is codependency? It was an obscure concept in the field of alcoholism counseling before Beattie (1987, 1989, 1993) and others (Bradshaw, 1988; Schaef, 1986, 1992; Whitfield, 1987, 1993) borrowed, broadened, and popularized it. The term originally referred to the tendency of alcoholics' spouses—typically wives of alcoholic men—to get entangled in their partner's addictions in ways that inadvertently supported the addictive behavior (Cocores, 1987). For example, the wife of an alcoholic might protect him from the consequences of his addiction by not confronting him about his problem, by lying to people to cover up his drinking, and by taking on many of his parental, household, and financial responsibilities.

Beattie (1987) greatly expanded the codependency concept. Arguing that people can be addicted to love, sex, work, food, gambling, or shopping as well as to drugs and alcohol, she described the codependent person as anyone who has let another person's addictive behavior affect him or her and is obsessed with controlling that behavior. By equating any kind of self-control problem with addiction, Beattie made the notion of codependency applicable to an enormous range of people. Indeed, she estimated that as many as 80 million Americans suffer from codependency. Other theorists have offered a variety of somewhat different definitions of codependency, and some are even broader than Beattie's conception (Whitfield, 1991).

According to most theorists, codependency is not a matter of happenstance. They maintain that many people—especially women—unwittingly *seek out* relationships with troubled individuals to satisfy an excessive need to be needed (O'Brien & Gaborit, 1992; Wright & Wright, 1991). In these relationships, codependents become obsessed with trying to protect, control, and change their partners. Pouring their energy into these largely unsuccessful efforts, codependent people consistently subordinate their own needs to those of their partner. Hence, they end up leading anguished, unfulfilling lives. The codependency literature provides lengthy recitations of the personal problems that may be attributable to codependency (Loughead, 1991). These symptoms of codependency range from minor, common problems, such as boredom, indecision, and lack of spontaneity, to profound, debilitating problems, such as anorexia, depression, and suicide.

What's the solution to the widespread affliction of codependency? Most codependency experts advocate recovery programs, such as Codependents Anonymous, which follow the Alcoholics Anonymous model developed in 1935 as a treatment for drinking problems.

According to this model, codependency is an addictive disease and recovery can only begin when people admit that they have lost control over their disease. Victims must then commit to the Twelve Step path to recovery. The Twelve Step program requires a spiritual conversion in which addicts turn their lives over to a "higher power." Recovery programs also depend heavily on peer self-help groups in which codependent people meet to discuss their problems, vent their emotions, exchange insights, and provide encouragement for each other.

EVALUATION

Is the codependency movement just another pop psych fad? Or does it contribute genuine insights about human suffering and effective methods for alleviating this suffering? The answer appears to lie somewhere in between these two extremes.

On the one hand, there is much to be said for the family systems perspective adopted by the codependency movement. Clinical work provides evidence that addicts and their family members are often enmeshed in dysfunctional relationships that contribute to the addicts' problems and undermine the morale and mental health of the family members (Cermak, 1986; Mendenhall, 1989). Spouses and family members clearly have complex, reciprocal influences on each other (Robins, 1990), and the codependency movement has increased the public's appreciation of this reality. Furthermore, the popularity of the codependency movement suggests that it has uncovered a genuine malady that meshes with the subjective experience of many people in our society. As Haaken (1990) puts it, "The codependence literature expresses the pain, anguish and helplessness, combined with an overwhelming, wearisome responsibility for others, that dominates the lives of many women" (p. 397).

What about the recovery programs advocated by codependency theorists? Their efficacy hasn't been evaluated adequately (Harper & Capdevila, 1990), but they include elements that appear to have some legitimate value. For example, recovery groups seek to provide participants with social support, which can be valuable in helping people cope with stress (Hobfoll & Vaux, 1993), as you'll see in Chapter 3. Recovery groups also encourage participants to talk about their problems and vent their emotions. Research suggests that these are healthy coping strategies (Pennebaker, Colder, & Sharp, 1990), as you will learn in Chapter 4. Thus, it is plausible that many people benefit from their participation in the recovery programs promoted by the codependency movement.

On the other hand, critics argue that codependency theory is riddled with holes and that the commotion about codependency has far outstripped the substance of what is known (Babcock, 1995; Collins, 1993). Specific concerns include the following:

1. Definitions of codependency vary considerably. Because different theorists are often discussing different problems, the concept of codependency remains vaguely defined, at best (Prest & Protinsky, 1993; Uhle, 1994). People who label themselves as codependent are making highly subjective self-diagnoses of dubious validity based on simplistic stereotypes.

2. Controlled, scientific research on codependency is in its infancy, and little or no evidence exists to support many of the basic tenets of codependency theory (Babcock, 1995; Wright & Wright, 1991). For example, researchers have only just begun to test the idea that codependency occurs because people seek out relationships with troubled individuals (Lyon & Greenberg, 1991) or to study the applicability of the codependency concept to problems such as compulsive eating, gambling, and shopping (O'Brien & Gaborit, 1992).

3. As Kaminer (1995) notes, in codependency theory "every conceivable form of arguably compulsive behavior is classified as an addiction. We are a nation of sexaholics, rageaholics, shopaholics, and rushaholics" (p. 70). Critics assert that this view trivializes the concept of addiction, making it virtually meaningless (Anderson, 1994). Other theorists object to the *medicalization* of interpersonal difficulties in families. Krestan and Bebko (1995), for instance, argue that the success of the codependency movement "speaks to the power of our descriptions of reality to invent reality and to invent disease for economic and political gain

whereby certain segments of society profit from treating others whose experience is controlled by being defined as sick" (p. 108).

4. Codependency theorists tend to blame addiction and codependence for virtually every conceivable type of psychological problem. Beattie's (1987) first book listed 234 symptoms of condependency! This tendency to explain everything in terms of addiction and codependency clearly represents a vast oversimplification of the complex causes of psychological maladies (Haaken, 1990, 1993). As Carol Tavris (1995, p. 193) notes, "This is a curious kind of disease. What physician would write a book on diabetes, for example, that says 'Diabetes is anything, and everyone is diabetic'?"

5. The codependency movement speaks primarily to women, with an apparently sincere intent to help them grapple with certain problems associated with the traditional female role in our society. However, some critics argue that "codependent" has become a derogatory label that is applied to women in a discriminatory fashion (Van Wormer, 1995). Some observers are also concerned that codependency theory implicitly blames women for their own suffering, their dysfunctional relations with men, and their husbands' problems (Kokin & Walker, 1995; Tavris, 1992).

In sum, codependency started out as a specific, researchable, and potentially insightful idea about how family dynamics may sometimes contribute to addictive behavior. Unfortunately, in the rush to popularize the concept, it has become a catchall scapegoat that is blamed for nearly every form of human misery. Nonetheless, the codependency movement provides another demonstration that many people are desperately searching for simple answers to complex questions about adjustment in contemporary society.

Self-Help Books

Another fascinating example of our search for a sense of direction is the popularity of "self-help books" that offer do-it-yourself treatments for common personal problems. A glance at the best-seller lists of recent years reveals that readers have a voracious appetite for self-help books such as *I'm OK-You're OK* (Harris, 1967), *Your Erroneous Zones* (Dyer, 1976), *How to Be Awake and Alive* (Newman & Berkowitz, 1976), *Winning Through Intimidation* (Ringer, 1978), *Living, Loving & Learning* (Buscaglia, 1982), *The Art of Self-Fulfillment* (Litwack & Resnick, 1984), *Willpower's Not Enough* (Watson & Boundy, 1989), *Awakening the Giant Within* (Robbins, 1991), *Men Are from Mars, Women Are from Venus* (Gray, 1992), *Ageless Body, Timeless Mind* (Chopra, 1993), *Ten Stupid Things Women Do to Mess Up Their Lives* (Schlessinger, 1995), *Finding Serenity in the Age of Anxiety* (Gerzon, 1997), and *Don't Sweat the Small Stuff. . . and It's All Small Stuff* (Carlson, 1997). With their simple recipes for achieving happiness, these books have generally not been timid about promising to change the quality of the reader's life. Consider the following excerpt from the back cover of a self-help book titled *Self Creation* (Weinberg, 1979):

More than any book ever written, Self Creation *shows you who you are and reveals the secret to controlling your own life. It contains an action blueprint built around a clear-cut principle as basic and revolutionary as the law of gravity. With it you will discover how to conquer bad habits, solve sexual problems, overcome depression and shyness, deal with infuriating people, be decisive, enhance your career, increase creativity. And it will show you how to love and be loved. You created you. Now you can start to reap the boundless benefits of self-confidence, self-reliance, self-determination with* Self Creation.

If only it were that easy! If only someone could hand you a book that would solve all your problems! Unfortunately, it is not that simple. Merely reading a book is not likely to turn your life around. If the consumption of these literary narcotics were even remotely as helpful as their publishers claim, we would be a nation of serene, happy, well-adjusted people. It is clear, however, that serenity is not the dominant national

A glance at bookstore shelves verifies that the boom in self-help books continues unabated, fueled by people's ongoing need for guidance and direction in their personal lives.

high-energy experience" are typical examples of this language. At best, such terminology is ill-defined; at worst, it is meaningless. Consider the following example, taken from a question/answer booklet promoting *est* training:

The EST training doesn't change the content of anyone's life, nor does it change what anyone knows. It deals with the context or the way we hold the content. . . . Transformation occurs as a recontextualization. . . . "Getting it" means being able to discover when you have been maintaining (or are stuck with) a position which costs you more in aliveness than it is worth, realizing that you are the source of that position, and being able to choose to give up that position or hold it in a way that expands the quality of your life.

What exactly does this paragraph say? Who knows? The statements are so ambiguous and enigmatic that you can read virtually any meaning into them. Therein lies the problem with psychobabble; it is often so obscure as to be unintelligible. Clarity is sacrificed in favor of a hip jargon that prevents, rather than enhances, effective communication.

mood. The multitude of self-help books that crowd bookstore shelves represent just one more symptom of our collective distress and our search for the elusive secret of happiness.

THE VALUE OF SELF-HELP BOOKS

It is somewhat unfair to lump all self-help books together for a critique, because they vary widely in quality (Fried & Schultis, 1995; Santrock, Minnett, & Campbell, 1994). Surveys exploring psychotherapists' opinions of self-help books suggest that there are some excellent books that offer authentic insights and sound advice (Starker, 1990, 1992). Surveys also reveal that many therapists encourage their patients to read selected self-help books (Pardeck, 1991; Warner, 1991). Thus, it would be foolish to dismiss all these books as shallow drivel. In fact, some of the better self-help books are highlighted in the Recommended Reading boxes that appear throughout this text. Unfortunately, however, the gems are easily lost in the mountains of rubbish. A great many self-help books offer little of real value to the reader. Generally, they have three fundamental shortcomings.

First, they are dominated by "psychobabble." The term *psychobabble,* coined by R. D. Rosen (1977), seems appropriate to describe the "hip" but hopelessly vague language used in many of these books. Statements such as "It's beautiful if you're unhappy," "You've got to get in touch with yourself," "You have to be up front," "You gotta be you 'cause you're you," and "You need a real

● Recommended Reading

I'm Dysfunctional, You're Dysfunctional
by Wendy Kaminer (Addison-Wesley, 1992)

This book takes a penetrating look at self-help books, self-realization programs, the codependency movement, New Age spiritualism, and the curious tendency of people to go on TV talk shows to share their innermost secrets and their most embarrassing frailties with millions of strangers. Kaminer, a social critic who writes about politics, culture, and law, maintains that most self-help books are riddled with psychobabble and sloppy thinking, which undermine our intellectual standards. She also argues that the self-help tradition discourages independent thinking by touting the idea that there are universally applicable solutions for everyone's problems. Kaminer explains how people who jump on the self-help bandwagon give up their freedom to think for themselves by passively submitting to "expert" authority figures who provide simplistic prescriptions for attaining happiness and contentment. In her analysis of the codependency movement, Kaminer questions the value of encouraging people to view themselves as helpless victims of their families and the wisdom of characterizing traditional feminine traits as pathological. She also questions the assertion that women remain in relationships with troubled, abusive men because they have a masochistic streak. Kaminer's book is a wide-ranging, easy-to-read, thought-provoking analysis of contemporary pop psychology.

The self-help tradition has always been covertly authoritarian and conformist, relying as it does on a mystique of expertise, encouraging people to look outside themselves for standardized instructions on how to be, teaching us that different people with different problems can easily be saved by the same techniques. It is anathema to independent thought. [p. 6]

A second problem is that self-help books tend to place more emphasis on sales than on scientific soundness. The advice offered in these books is far too rarely based on solid, scientific research (Ellis, 1993; Rosen, 1987). Instead, the ideas are frequently based on the authors' intuitive analyses, which may be highly speculative. Moreover, even when responsible authors provide scientifically valid advice and are careful not to mislead their readers, sales-hungry publishers often slap outrageous, irresponsible promises on the books' covers (much to the dismay of some authors).

The third shortcoming is that self-help books usually don't provide explicit directions about how to change your behavior. These books tend to be smoothly written and "touchingly human" in tone. They often strike responsive chords in the reader by aptly describing a common problem that many of us experience. The reader says "Yes, that's me!" Unfortunately, when the book focuses on how to deal with the problem, it usually provides only a vague distillation of simple common sense, which could be covered in 2 rather than 200 pages. These books often fall back on inspirational cheerleading in the absence of sound, explicit advice.

WHAT TO LOOK FOR IN SELF-HELP BOOKS

Because self-help books vary so widely in quality, it seems a good idea to provide you with some guidelines about what to look for in seeking genuinely helpful books. The following thoughts give you some criteria for judging books of this type.

1. Clarity in communication is essential. Advice won't do you much good if you can't understand it. Try to avoid drowning in the murky depths of psychobabble.

2. This may sound backward, but look for books that do not promise too much in the way of immediate change. The truly useful books tend to be appropriately cautious in their promises and realistic about the challenge of altering one's behavior.

3. Try to select books that mention, at least briefly, the theoretical or research basis for the program they advocate. It is understandable that you may not be interested in a detailed summary of research that supports a particular piece of advice. However, you should be interested in whether the advice is based on published research, widely accepted theory, anecdotal evidence, clinical interactions with patients, or pure speculation by the author. Books that are based on more than personal anecdotes and speculation should have a list of references in the back (or at the end of each chapter).

4. Intellectually honest authors don't just talk about what we know—they also discuss what we do *not* know. There is much to be said for books that are candid about the limits of what the so-called experts really know.

5. Look for books that provide detailed, explicit directions about how to alter your behavior. Generally, these directions represent the crucial core of the book. If they are inadequate in detail, you have been shortchanged.

6. More often than not, books that focus on a particular kind of problem, such as overeating, loneliness, or marital difficulties, deliver more than those that promise to cure all of life's problems with a few simple ideas. Books that cover everything are usually superficial and disappointing. Books that devote a great deal of thought to a particular topic tend to be written by authors with genuine expertise on that topic. Such books are more likely to pay off for you. Figure 1.1 lists 15 self-help books that were among the most highly recommended in a national survey of clinical and counseling psychologists (Santrock et al., 1994). As you can see, they largely focus on specific topics.

The Approach of This Textbook

Clearly, in spite of our impressive technological progress, we are a people beset by a great variety of personal problems. Living in our complex, modern society is a formidable challenge. This book is about that challenge. It is about you. It is about life. Specifically, it summarizes for you the scientific research on human behavior that appears relevant to the challenge of living effectively in contemporary society. It draws primarily, but not exclusively, from the science we call psychology.

This text deals with the same kinds of problems addressed by self-help books, self-realization programs, the codependency movement, and Dr. Laura: anxiety, stress, interpersonal relationships, frustration, loneliness, depression, self-control. However, it makes no

● **Recommended Reading**

What You Can Change & What You Can't
by Martin E. P. Seligman (Knopf, 1994)

Martin Seligman is a prominent psychologist who has conducted influential research on learned helplessness, attributional style, optimism, depression, and phobias. In this book he synthesizes research on a host of issues to help people understand what they can and cannot change about themselves. Seligman points out that self-improvement programs of all types—from meditation to self-help books to professional therapy—are predicated on the assumption that people can permanently change themselves for the better. He notes, however, that recent, highly publicized research in biological psychiatry is at odds with this assumption. This research suggests that individuals' personality, intelligence, physique, and vulnerability to psychological disorders are predominantly determined by their genetic inheritance and hence largely immutable. Seligman asserts that both viewpoints are too extreme—that the architects of self-improvement programs are too optimistic and the authorities on biological psychiatry too pessimistic about people's capacity for change. Thus, he sets out to review the empirical evidence on what can be modified with reliable success, and what can't be. Seligman's coverage is wide ranging. He discusses treatments for sexual difficulties, alcoholism, weight problems, anxiety, depression, obsessions, and posttraumatic stress syndrome, among other things. His discussions are lively, readable, objective, sophisticated, and thoroughly grounded in research.

As the ideologies of biological psychiatry and self-improvement collide, a resolution is apparent. There are some things about ourselves that can be changed, others that cannot, and some that can be changed only with extreme difficulty. [p. 4]

boldly seductive promises about solving your personal problems, turning your life around, or helping you achieve tranquility. Such promises simply aren't realistic. Psychologists have long recognized that changing a person's behavior is a difficult challenge, fraught with frustration and failure (Seligman, 1994). Troubled individuals sometimes spend years in therapy without resolving their problems.

FIGURE 1.1.

Top rated self-help books.
Based on a national survey of over 500 clinical and counseling psychologists, Santrock, Minnet, and Campbell (1994) compiled a list of the 25 most highly recommended self-help books. Ten of the books on their list deal with parenting or children. These books are listed in Chapter 11, where we discuss parent-child relations. The remaining 15 self-help books from their top-rated list are shown here.

Top-Rated Self-Help Books

The Courage to Heal
by Ellen Bass and Laura Davis

Feeling Good
by David Burns

How to Survive the Loss of a Love
by Melba Cosgrove, Harold Bloomfield, & Peter McWilliams

The Dance of Anger
by Harriet Lerner

The Feeling Good Handbook
by David Burns

Your Perfect Right
by Robert Alberti and Michael Emmons

What Color Is Your Parachute?
by Robert Bolles

The Relaxation Response
by Herbert Benson

The New Aerobics
by Kenneth Cooper

Learned Optimism
by Martin Seligman

Man's Search for Meaning
by Victor Frankl

You Just Don't Understand
by Deborah Tannen

The Dance of Intimacy
by Harriet Lerner

Beyond the Relaxation Response
by Herbert Benson

The Battered Woman
by Lenore Walker

This does not mean that you should be pessimistic about your potential for personal growth. You most certainly can change your behavior. Moreover, you can often change it on your own without consulting a professional psychologist. We would not be writing this text if we did not believe that some of our readers could experience some personal benefit from this literary encounter. But it is important that you have realistic expectations. Reading this book will not be a revelatory experience. There are no mysterious secrets about to be unveiled. All this book can do is give you some potentially useful information and point you in some potentially beneficial directions. The rest is up to you.

In view of our criticisms of many self-realization programs and self-help books, it seems essential that we explicitly lay out the philosophy that underlies the writing of this text. The following statements summarize the assumptions and goals of this book.

1. *This text is based on the premise that accurate knowledge about the principles of psychology can be of value to you in everyday life.* It has been said that knowledge is power. Greater awareness of why people behave as they do should help you in interacting with others as well as in trying to understand yourself.

2. *This text attempts to foster a critical attitude about psychological issues and to enhance your critical thinking skills.* Information is important, but people also need to develop effective strategies for evaluating information. Critical thinking involves subjecting ideas to systematic,

Web Link 1.3

The Critical Thinking Community
How can students best develop those skills that go beyond merely acquiring information to actively weighing and judging information? The many resources at The Critical Thinking Community at Sonoma State University are directed primarily toward teachers at every level to help them develop their students' critical thinking abilities.

skeptical scrutiny. Critical thinkers ask tough questions, such as: What exactly is being asserted? What assumptions underlie this assertion? What evidence or reasoning supports this assertion? Are there alternative explanations? Some general guidelines for thinking critically are outlined in Figure 1.2. We have already attempted to illustrate the importance of a critical attitude in our evaluation of the codependency movement and self-help books, and we'll continue to model critical thinking strategies throughout the text.

3. *This text should open doors.* The coverage in this book is very broad; we tackle many topics. Therefore, in some places it may lack the depth or detail that you would like. However, you should think of it as a resource book that can introduce you to other books or techniques or therapies, which you can then pursue on your own.

4. *This text assumes that the key to effective adjustment is to "take charge" of your own life.* If you are dissatisfied with some aspect of your life, it does no good to sit around and mope about it. You have to take an

FIGURE 1.2.
Guidelines for thinking critically. Critical thinking should not be equated with negative thinking; it's not a matter of learning how to tear down others' ideas. Rather, critical thinkers carefully subject others' ideas—and their own—to careful, systematic, objective evaluation. The guidelines shown here, taken from Wade and Tavris (1990), provide a succint overview of what it means to think critically.

Guidelines for Thinking Critically

1 **Ask questions; be willing to wonder.** To think critically you must be willing to think creatively—that is, to be curious about the puzzles of human behavior; to wonder why people act the way they do, and to question received explanations and examine new ones.

2 **Define the problem.** Identify the issues involved in clear and concrete terms, rather than vague generalities such as "happiness," "potential," or "meaningfulness." What does meaningfulness mean, exactly?

3 **Examine the evidence.** Consider the nature of the evidence that supports all aspects of the problem under examination. Is it reliable? Valid? Is it someone's personal assertion or speculation? Does the evidence come from one or two narrow studies, or from repeated research?

4 **Analyze biases and assumptions**—your own and those of others. What prejudices, deeply held values, and other personal biases do you bring to your evaluation of a problem? Are you willing to consider evidence that contradicts your beliefs? Be sure you can identify the bias of others, in order to evaluate their arguments as well.

5 **Avoid emotional reasoning** ("If I feel this way, it must be true"). Remember that everyone holds convictions and ideas about how the world should operate—and that your opponents are as serious about their convictions as you are about yours. Feelings are important, but they should not substitute for careful appraisal of arguments and evidence.

6 **Don't oversimplify.** Look beyond the obvious. Reject simplistic, either-or thinking. Look for logical contradictions in arguments. Be wary of "arguments by anecdote."

7 **Consider other interpretations.** Before you leap to conclusions, think about other explanations. Be especially careful about assertions of cause and effect.

8 **Tolerate uncertainty.** This may be the hardest step in becoming a critical thinker, for it requires the ability to accept some guiding ideas and beliefs—yet the willingness to give them up when evidence and experience contradict them.

active role in attempting to improve the quality of your life. Doing so may involve learning a new skill or pursuing a particular kind of help. In any case, it is generally best to meet problems head on rather than trying to avoid them.

The Psychology of Adjustment

LEARNING OBJECTIVES

- *Describe the two key facets of psychology.*
- *Explain the concept of adjustment.*

Now that we have spelled out our approach in writing this text, it is time to turn to the task of introducing you to some basic concepts. In this section, we'll discuss the nature of psychology and the concept of adjustment.

What Is Psychology?

Psychology **is the science that studies behavior and the physiological and mental processes that underlie it and the profession that applies the accumulated knowledge of this science to practical problems.**

Psychology leads a complex dual existence as both a *science* and a *profession*. Let's examine the science first. Psychology is an area of scientific study, much like biology or physics. Whereas biology focuses on life processes, and physics on matter and energy, psychology focuses on *behavior* and *related processes*.

Psychology looks at behavior. **Behavior is any overt (observable) response or activity by an organism.** Psychology does *not* confine itself to the study of human behavior. Many psychologists believe that the principles of behavior are much the same for animals and humans. As a result, these psychologists often prefer to study animals—mainly because they can exert more control over the factors influencing the animals' behavior.

Psychology is also interested in the mental processes—the thoughts, feelings, and wishes—that accompany behavior. Mental processes are more difficult to study than behavior because they are private and not directly observable. However, they exert critical influence over human behavior, so psychologists have strived to improve their ability to "look inside the mind."

Finally, psychology includes the study of the physiological processes that underlie behavior. Thus, some psychologists try to figure out how bodily processes such as neural impulses, hormonal secretions, and genetic coding regulate behavior.

Practically speaking, all this means that psychologists study a great variety of phenomena. Psychologists are interested in maze running in rats, salivation in dogs, and brain functioning in cats, as well as visual perception in humans, play in children, and social interaction in adults.

As you probably know, psychology is not all pure science. It has a highly practical side, represented by the many psychologists who provide a variety of professional services to the public. Although the profession of psychology is quite prominent today, this aspect of psychology was actually slow to develop. Psychology emerged as an independent science back in the 19th century, but until the 1950s psychologists were found almost exclusively in the halls of academia, teaching and doing research. However, the demands of World War II (1942–1945) stimulated rapid growth in psychology's first professional specialty—clinical psychology. *Clinical psychology* **is the branch of psychology concerned with the diagnosis and treatment of psychological problems and disorders.** During World War II, a multitude of academic psychologists were pressed into service as clinicians to screen military recruits and treat soldiers suffering from trauma. Many found their clinical work interesting and returned from the war to set up training programs to meet the continued high demand for clinical services. Soon, about half of the new Ph.D.'s in psychology were specializing in clinical work. Psychology had come of age as a profession.

What Is Adjustment?

We have used to the term *adjustment* several times without clarifying its exact meaning. The concept of adjustment was originally borrowed from biology. It was modeled after the biological term *adaptation*, which refers to efforts by a species to adjust to changes in its environment. Just as a field mouse has to adapt to an unusually brutal winter, a person has to adjust to changes in circumstances such as a new job, a financial setback, or the loss of a loved one. Thus, *adjustment* **refers to the psychological processes through which people manage or cope with the demands and challenges of everyday life.**

The demands of everyday life are diverse, so in studying the process of adjustment we will encounter a broad variety of topics. In the first section of this book, "The Dynamics of Adjustment," we discuss general issues, such as how personality affects people's patterns of adjustment, how individuals are affected by stress, and how they use coping strategies to deal with stress. In the second section, "The Interpersonal Realm," we examine the adjustments that people make in their social relationships, exploring topics such as how individuals view others, communication, behavior in groups, friendship, and intimate relationships. In the third section, "Developmental Transitions," we look at how individuals adjust to changing demands as they grow older. We discuss such topics as the development of gender roles, the emergence of sexuality, phases of adult development, and transitions in the world of work. Finally, in the fourth section, "Mental and Physical Health," we discuss how the process of adjustment influences a person's psychological and physical wellness.

As you can see, the study of adjustment delves into nearly every corner of people's lives, and we'll be discussing a diverse array of issues and topics. Before we begin considering these topics in earnest, however, we need to take a closer look at psychology's approach to investigating behavior—the scientific method.

The Scientific Approach to Behavior

LEARNING OBJECTIVES

- Explain the nature of empiricism.
- Explain two advantages of the scientific approach to understanding behavior.
- Describe the experimental method, distinguishing between independent and dependent variables and between experimental and control groups.
- Distinguish between positive and negative correlation and explain what the size of a correlation coefficient means.
- Describe three correlational research methods.
- Compare the advantages and disadvantages of experimental versus correlational research.

We all expend a great deal of effort in trying to understand our own behavior as well as the behavior of others. We wonder about any number of behavioral questions: Why am I so anxious when I interact with new people? Why is Sam always trying to be the center of attention at the office? Why does Joanna cheat on her wonderful husband? Are extraverts happier than introverts? Is depression more common during the Christmas holidays? Given that psychologists' principal goal is to explain behavior, how are their efforts different from everyone else's? The key difference is that psychology is a *science*, committed to *empiricism*.

The Commitment to Empiricism

Empiricism is the premise that knowledge should be acquired through observation. When we say that scientific psychology is empirical, we mean that its conclusions are based on systematic observation rather than on reasoning, speculation, traditional beliefs, or common sense. Scientists are not content with having ideas that sound plausible; they must conduct research to *test*

their ideas. Whereas our everyday speculations are informal, unsystematic, and highly subjective, scientists' investigations are formal, systematic, and objective.

In these investigations, scientists formulate testable hypotheses, gather data (make observations) relevant to their hypotheses, use statistics to analyze these data, and report their results to the public and other scientists, typically by publishing their findings in a technical journal. The process of publishing scientific studies allows other experts to evaluate and critique new research findings.

Advantages of the Scientific Approach

Science is certainly not the only method that can be used to draw conclusions about behavior. We can also turn to logic, casual observation, and good old-fashioned common sense. Because the scientific method often requires painstaking effort, it seems reasonable to ask: What exactly are the advantages of the empirical approach?

The scientific approach offers two major advantages. The first is its clarity and precision. Commonsense notions about behavior tend to be vague and ambiguous. Consider the old truism "Spare the rod and spoil the child." What does this generalization about child-rearing amount to? How severely should children be punished if parents are not to "spare the rod"? How do parents assess whether a child qualifies as "spoiled"? Such statements can have different meanings to different people. When people disagree about this assertion, it may be because they are talking about entirely different things. In contrast, the empirical approach requires that scientists specify *exactly* what they are talking about when they formulate hypotheses. This clarity and precision enhance communication about important ideas.

The second advantage offered by the scientific approach is its relative intolerance of error. Scientists subject their ideas to empirical tests. They also scrutinize one another's findings with a critical eye. They demand objective data and thorough documentation before they accept ideas. When the findings of two studies conflict, they try to figure out why the studies reached different conclusions, usually by conducting additional research. In contrast, common sense and casual observation often tolerate contradictory generalizations, such as "Opposites attract" and "Birds of a feather flock together." Furthermore, commonsense analyses involve little effort to verify ideas or detect errors, so that many myths about behavior come to be widely believed.

All this is not to say that science has a copyright on truth. However, the scientific approach does tend to yield more accurate and dependable information than casual analyses and armchair speculation. Knowledge of empirical data can thus provide a useful benchmark against which to judge claims and information from other kinds of sources.

Now that we have an overview of how the scientific enterprise works, we can look at some of the specific research methods that psychologists depend on most. The two main types of research methods in psychology are *experimental research methods* and *correlational research methods*. We discuss them separately because there is an important distinction between them.

Experimental Research: Looking for Causes

Does misery love company? This question intrigued social psychologist Stanley Schachter. How does anxiety affect people's desire to be with others? When they feel anxious, do they want to be left alone, or do they prefer to have others around? Schachter's hypothesis was that increases in anxiety would cause increases in the desire to be with others, which psychologists call the *need for affiliation*. To test this hypothesis, Schachter (1959) designed a clever experiment. **The *experiment* is a research method in which the investigator manipulates one (independent) variable under carefully controlled conditions and observes whether any changes occur in a second (dependent) variable as a result.** Psychologists depend on this method more than any other.

INDEPENDENT AND DEPENDENT VARIABLES

An experiment is designed to find out whether changes in one variable (let's call it x) cause changes in another variable (let's call it y). To put it more concisely, we want to know how x affects y. In this formulation, we refer to x as the independent variable, and we call y the dependent variable. **An *independent variable* is a condition or event that an experimenter varies in order to see its impact on another variable.** The independent variable is the variable that the experimenter controls or manipulates. It is hypothesized to have some effect on the dependent variable. The experiment is conducted to verify this effect. **The *dependent variable* is the variable that is thought to be affected by the manipulations of the independent variable.** In psychology studies, the dependent variable usually is a measurement of some aspect of the subjects' behavior.

In Schachter's experiment, *the independent variable was the participants' anxiety level,* which he manipulated in the following way. Subjects assembled in his laboratory were told by a Dr. Zilstein that they would be participating in a study on the physiological effects of electric shock and that they would receive a series of electric shocks. Half of the participants were warned that the shocks would be very painful. They made up the *high-anxiety* group. The other half of the participants, assigned to the *low-anxiety* group, were told that the shocks would be mild and painless. These procedures were simply intended to evoke different levels of anxiety. In reality, no one was actually shocked at any time. Instead, the experimenter indicated that there would be a delay while he prepared the shock apparatus for use. The participants were asked whether they would prefer to wait alone or in the company of others. *This measure of the subjects' desire to affiliate with others was the dependent variable.*

EXPERIMENTAL AND CONTROL GROUPS

To conduct an experiment, an investigator typically assembles two groups of participants who are treated differently in regard to the independent variable. We call these groups the experimental and control groups. **The *experimental group* consists of the subjects who receive some special treatment in regard to the independent variable. The *control group* consists of similar subjects who do not receive the special treatment given to the experimental group.**

Let's return to the Schachter study to illustrate. In this study, the participants in the high-anxiety condition were the experimental group. They received a special treatment designed to create an unusually high level of anxiety. The participants in the low-anxiety condition were the control group.

It is crucial that the experimental and control groups be very similar except for the different treatment they receive in regard to the independent variable. This stipulation brings us to the logic that underlies the experimental method. If the two groups are alike in all respects *except for the variation created by the manipulation of the independent variable,* then any differences between the two groups on the dependent variable *must be due to this manipulation of the independent variable.* In this way researchers isolate the effect of the independent variable on the dependent variable. In his experiment, Schachter isolated the impact of anxiety on need for affiliation. What did he find? As predicted, he found that increased anxiety led to increased affiliation. The percentage of people who wanted to wait with others was nearly twice as high in the high-anxiety group as in the low-anxiety group.

Web Link 1.4

Research Methods Tutorials
Bill Trochim's classes in research and program design at Cornell University have assembled tutorial guides for undergraduate and graduate students on more than 35 topics. Students new to research design may find some of these tutorials very helpful.

The logic of the experimental method rests heavily on the assumption that the experimental and control groups are alike in all important matters except for their different treatment with regard to the independent variable. Any other differences between the two groups cloud the situation and make it difficult to draw solid conclusions about the relationship between the independent variable and the dependent variable. To summarize our discussion of the experimental method, Figure 1.3 provides an overview of the various elements in an experiment, using Schachter's study as an example.

ADVANTAGES AND DISADVANTAGES

The experiment is a powerful research method. Its principal advantage is that it allows scientists to draw conclusions about cause and effect relationships between variables. Researchers can draw these conclusions about causation because the precise control available in the experiment permits them to isolate the relationship between the independent variable and the dependent variable. No other research method can duplicate this advantage.

For all its power, however, the experimental method has its limitations. One disadvantage is that reserchers are often interested in the effects of variables that cannot be manipulated (as independent variables) because of ethical concerns or practical realities. For example, you might want to know whether being brought up in an urban area as opposed to a rural area affects people's values. A true experiment would require you to assign similar families to live in urban and rural areas, which obviously is impossible to do. To explore this question, you would have to use correlational research methods, which we turn to next.

Correlational Research: Looking for Links

As we just noted, in some situations psychologists cannot exert experimental control over the variables they want to study. In such situations, all a researcher can do is make systematic observations to see whether a link or association exists between the variables of interest. Such an association is called a correlation. **A correlation exists when two variables are related to each other.** The definitive aspect of correlational studies is that the researchers cannot control the variables under study.

MEASURING CORRELATION

The results of correlational research are often summarized with a statistic called the *correlation coefficient*. We'll be refering to this widely used statistic frequently as we discuss studies throughout the remainder of this text. **A *correlation coefficient* is a numerical index of the degree of relationship that exists between two variables.** A correlation coefficient indicates (1) how strongly related two variables are and (2) the direction (positive or negative) of the relationship.

Two *kinds* of relationships can be described by a correlation. A *positive* correlation indicates that two variables covary in the same direction. This means that high scores on variable *x* are associated with high scores on variable *y* and that low scores on variable *x* are associated with low scores on variable *y*. For example, there is a positive correlation between high school grade point average (GPA) and subsequent college GPA. That is, people who do well in high school tend to do well in college, and those who perform poorly in high school tend to perform poorly in college (see Figure 1.4).

In contrast, a *negative* correlation indicates that two variables covary in the opposite direction. This means that people who score high on variable *x* tend to score low on variable *y*, whereas those who score low on *x* tend to score high on *y*. For example, in most college

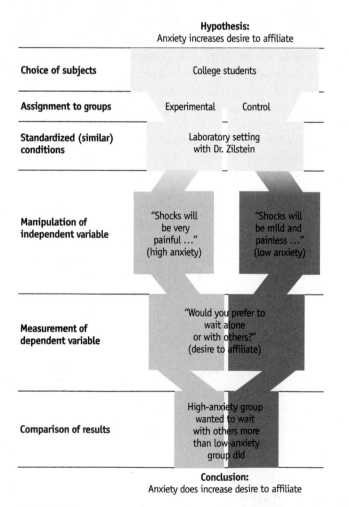

Hypothesis:
Anxiety increases desire to affiliate

Choice of subjects	College students
Assignment to groups	Experimental / Control
Standardized (similar) conditions	Laboratory setting with Dr. Zilstein
Manipulation of independent variable	"Shocks will be very painful ..." (high anxiety) / "Shocks will be mild and painless ..." (low anxiety)
Measurement of dependent variable	"Would you prefer to wait alone or with others?" (desire to affiliate)
Comparison of results	High-anxiety group wanted to wait with others more than low-anxiety group did

Conclusion:
Anxiety does increase desire to affiliate

FIGURE 1.3.
The basic elements of an experiment. This diagram provides an overview of the key features of the experimental method, as illustrated by Schachter's study of anxiety and affiliation. The logic of the experiment rests on treating the experimental and control groups alike except for the manipulation of the independent variable.

FIGURE 1.4.

FIGURE 1.4.
Positive and negative correlations. Variables are positively correlated if they tend to increase and decrease together and negatively correlated if one variable tends to increase when the other decreases. Hence, the terms *positive correlation* and *negative correlation* refer to the *direction* of the relationship between two variables.

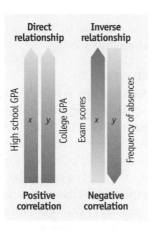

courses, there is a negative correlation between how frequently a student is absent and how well the student performs on exams. Students who have a high number of absences tend to earn low exam scores, while students who have a low number of absences tend to get higher exam scores (see Figure 1.4).

While the positive or negative sign indicates whether an association is direct or inverse, the *size* of the coefficient indicates the *strength* of the association between two variables. A correlation coefficient can vary between 0 and +1.00 (if positive) or between 0 and −1.00 (if negative). A coefficient near zero tells us there is no relationship between the variables. The closer the correlation to either −1.00 or +1.00, the stronger the relationship (see Figure 1.5). Thus, a correlation of +.90 represents a stronger tendency for variables to be associated than a correlation of +.40 does. Likewise, a correlation of −.75 represents a stronger relationship than a correlation of −.45. Keep in mind that the *strength* of

a correlation depends only on the size of the coefficient. The positive or negative sign simply shows whether the correlation is direct or inverse. Therefore, a correlation of −.60 reflects a stronger relationship than a correlation of +.30.

There are a variety of correlational research methods, including naturalistic observation, case studies, and surveys. Let's examine each of these methods to see how researchers use them to detect associations between variables.

NATURALISTIC OBSERVATION

In *naturalistic observation* a researcher engages in careful observation of behavior without intervening directly with the subjects. This type of research is called *naturalistic* because behavior is allowed to unfold naturally (without interference) in its natural environment—that is, the setting in which it would normally occur.

As an example, consider a study by Stoffer, Davis, and Brown (1977), which sought to determine whether it is a good idea for students to reconsider and change answers on multiple-choice tests. The conventional wisdom is that "your first hunch is your best hunch," and it is widely believed that students should not go back and change their answers. To put this idea to an empirical test, Stoffer and his colleagues studied the answer changes made by college students on their regular exams in a psychology course. They simply examined students' answer sheets for evidence of response changes, such as erasures or crossing out of responses. As Figure 1.6 on the next page shows, they found that changes that went from a wrong answer to a right

FIGURE 1.5.
Interpreting correlation coefficients. The magnitude of a correlation coefficient indicates the strength of the relationship between two variables. The closer a correlation is to either +1.00 or −1.00, the stronger the relationship between the variables. The square of a correlation (called the coefficient of determination) is an index of the correlation's predictive power. The coefficient of determination tells us the percentage of variation in one variable that can be predicted based on the other variable. For example, the correlation between SAT scores and college grade point average is roughly .50, which means that the abilities measured by SAT scores can account for about 25% of the variation among students in grade point average.

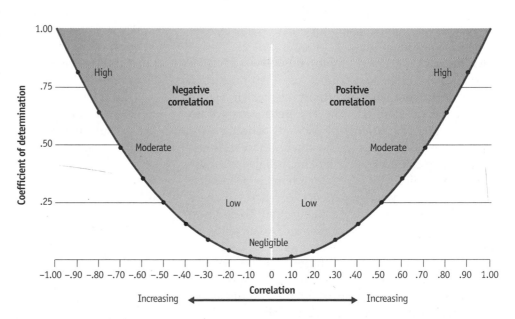

FIGURE 1.6.

The effects of answer changing on multiple-choice exams. In a study of answer changes, Stoffer et al. (1977) found that wrong-to-right changes outnumbered right-to-wrong changes by a sizable margin. These results are similar to those of other studies on this issue.

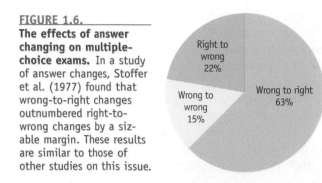

answer outnumbered changes that went from a right answer to a wrong answer by a margin of nearly 3 to 1! The correlation between the number of changes students made and their net gain from answer changing was +.49, indicating that the more answer changing students engaged in, the more they improved their scores. These results, which have been replicated in a number of other studies (Benjamin, Cavell, & Shallenberger, 1984), show that popular beliefs about the harmful effects of answer changing are inaccurate.

CASE STUDIES

A *case study* is an in-depth investigation of an individual participant. Psychologists typically assemble case studies in clinical settings where an effort is being made to diagnose and treat some psychological problem. To achieve an understanding of an individual, a clinician may use a variety of procedures, including interviewing the person, interviewing others who know the individual, direct observation, examination of records, and psychological testing. Usually, a single case study does not provide much basis for deriving general laws of behavior. If researchers have a number of case studies available, however, they can look for threads of consistency among them, and they may be able to draw some general conclusions.

This was the strategy employed by a research team (Farina et al., 1986) that studied psychiatric patients' readjustment to their community after their release from a mental hospital. The researchers wanted to know whether the patients' physical attractiveness was related to their success in readjustment. As we'll discuss in upcoming chapters, good-looking people tend to be treated more nicely by others than homely people are, suggesting that attractive patients may have an easier time adjusting to life outside the hospital. To find out, the research team compiled case history data (and ratings of physical attractiveness) for patients just before their discharge from a mental hospital and six months later. A modest positive correlation (+.38) was found between patients' attractiveness and their postdischarge social adjustment. Thus, the better-looking patients were better off, suggesting that physical attractiveness

plays a role in psychiatric patients' readjustment to community living.

SURVEYS

Surveys **are structured questionnaires designed to solicit information about specific aspects of participants' behavior.** They are sometimes used to measure dependent variables in experiments, but they are mainly used in correlational research. Surveys are commonly used to gather data on people's attitudes and on aspects of behavior that are difficult to observe directly (marital interactions, for instance).

As an example, consider an influential study by Thomas Holmes and his colleagues (Wyler, Masuda, & Holmes, 1971) that explored the possible relationship between life stress and physical illness. They hypothesized that high stress would be associated with a relatively high frequency of physical illness. To test this hypothesis, the researchers gave 232 participants a questionnaire that assessed the amount of stress they had experienced in the past year and another questionnaire that assessed the amount of illness they had recently experienced. As predicted, there was a positive correlation (+.32) between participants' level of stress and their amount of illness. This groundbreaking investigation inspired hundreds of follow-up studies that have enhanced our understanding of how stress is related to physical health (see Chapter 3).

ADVANTAGES AND DISADVANTAGES

Correlational research methods give us a way to explore questions that we could not examine with experimental procedures. Consider the Holmes study on the association between life stress and health. Obviously, Holmes and his colleagues could not manipulate the life stress experienced by the people in their study—divorces, retirements, pregnancies, and mortgages were far beyond the researchers' control. But correlational methods allowed them to gather useful information on whether a link exists between life stress and illness. Thus, *correlational research broadens the scope of phenomena that psychologists can study.*

Unfortunately, correlational methods have one major disadvantage. The investigator does not have the

Web Link 1.5

American Psychological Association (APA)
As the largest professional organization of psychologists, the APA continually publicizes the latest research findings for most topics discussed in this textbook. Students should consider using the excellent search engines at the APA's online site when looking for leads to new scientific research on adjustment issues.

opportunity to control events in a way to isolate cause and effect. *Consequently, correlational research cannot demonstrate conclusively that two variables are causally related.* The crux of the problem is that correlation is no assurance of causation.

When we find that variables *x* and *y* are correlated, we can safely conclude only that *x* and *y* are related. We do not know *how x* and *y* are related. We do not know whether *x* causes *y*, whether *y* causes *x*, or whether both are caused by a third variable. For example, survey studies show that there is a positive correlation between marital satisfaction and sexual satisfaction (Hunt, 1974; Tavris & Sadd, 1977). Although it's clear that good sex and a healthy marriage go hand in hand, it's hard to tell what's causing what. We don't know whether healthy marriages promote good sex or whether good sex promotes healthy marriages. Moreover, we can't rule out the possibility that both are caused by a third variable. Perhaps sexual satisfaction and marital satisfaction are both caused by compatibility in values. The plausible causal relationships in this case are diagrammed for you in Figure 1.7, which illustrates the "third-variable problem" in interpreting correlations. This problem occurs frequently in correlational research. Indeed, it will surface in the next section, where we review the empirical research on the determinants of happiness.

The Roots of Happiness: An Empirical Analysis

LEARNING OBJECTIVES

- Discuss the prevalence of reported happiness in modern society.
- List the various factors that are surprisingly unrelated to happiness.
- Explain how health, social activity, religion, and culture are related to happiness.
- Discuss how love, work, and personality are related to happiness.
- Summarize the conclusions drawn about the determinants of happiness.

What exactly makes a person happy? This question has been the subject of much speculation. Commonsense hypotheses about the roots of happiness abound. For example, you have no doubt heard that money cannot buy happiness. But do you believe it? A television commercial says, "If you've got your health, you've got just about everything." Is health indeed the key? What if you're healthy but poor, unemployed, and lonely? We often hear about the joys of parenthood, the joys of youth, and the joys of the simple, rural life. Are these the factors that promote happiness?

In recent years, social scientists have begun putting these and other hypotheses to empirical test. Quite a number of survey studies have been conducted to explore the determinants of happiness—or *subjective well-being*, as social scientists like to call it. The findings of these studies are quite interesting. We review this research because it illustrates the value of collecting data and putting ideas to an empirical test. As you will see, many commonsense notions about happiness appear to be inaccurate.

The first of these is the apparently widespread assumption that most people are relatively unhappy. Writers, social scientists, and the general public seem to believe that people around the world are predominantly dissatisfied, yet empirical surveys consistently find that the vast majority of respondents—even those who are poor or disabled—characterize themselves as fairly happy (Diener & Diener, 1996; Myers & Diener, 1995). When people are asked to rate their happiness, only a small minority place themselves below the neutral point on the various scales used (see Figure 1.8 on the following page). When the average subjective well-being of entire nations is computed, based on almost 1000 surveys, the means cluster toward the positive end of the scale, as shown in Figure 1.9 on the following page (Veenhoven, 1993). That's not to say that everyone is equally happy. Researchers have found substantial and thought-provoking disparities among people in subjective well-being, which we will analyze momentarily. But the overall picture seems rosier than anticipated.

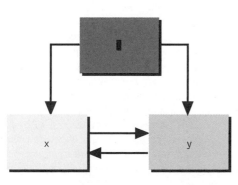

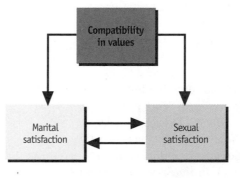

FIGURE 1.7.
Possible causal relations between correlated variables. When two variables are correlated, there are several possible explanations. It could be that *x* causes *y*, that *y* causes *x*, or that a third variable, *z*, causes changes in both *x* and *y*. As the correlation between marital satisfaction and sexual satisfaction illustrates, the correlation itself does not provide the answer.

Community. According to Freedman (1978), when asked where they would most like to live, people show a clear preference for the stereotype of the tranquil, pastoral life believed to exist in rural areas. However, when actual reported happiness is related to community type, people living in urban, suburban, and rural areas are found to be equally happy.

What Is Somewhat Important?

Research has identified four facets of life that appear to have a moderate impact on subjective well-being: health, social activity, religious belief, and culture.

Health. Good physical health would seem to be an essential requirement for happiness, but people adapt to health problems. Research reveals that individuals who develop serious, disabling health conditions aren't as unhappy as one might guess (Myers, 1992). Furthermore, Freedman (1978) argues that good health does not, by itself, produce happiness, because people tend to take good health for granted. Such considerations may help explain why researchers find only a moderate positive correlation (average = .32) between health status and subjective well-being (Diener, 1984).

Social activity. Humans are social animals, and people's interpersonal relations *do* appear to contribute to their happiness. People who are satisfied with their friendship networks and who are socially active report above-average levels of happiness (Cooper, Okamura, & Gurka, 1992; Diener, 1984). At the other end of the spectrum, people troubled by loneliness tend to be very unhappy (Argyle, 1987).

Religion. The link between religiosity and subjective well-being is modest, but a number of large-scale surveys suggest that people with heartfelt religious convictions are more likely to be happy than people who characterize themselves as nonreligious (Argyle, 1987; Poloma & Pendleton, 1990). Researchers aren't sure how religious faith fosters happiness, but Myers (1992) offers some interesting conjectures. Among other things, he discusses how religion can give people a sense of purpose and meaning in their lives, help them to accept their setbacks gracefully, connect them to a caring, supportive community, and comfort them by putting their ultimate mortality in perspective.

Culture. Researchers have found some modest cultural variations in average subjective well-being and in the key sources of happiness (Diener, Diener, & Diener, 1995; Suh et al., 1998). These variations have mostly been related to cultural differences in *individualism versus collectivism* (see Chapter 5). **Individualism** involves putting personal goals ahead of group goals and defining one's identity in terms of personal attributes rather than group memberships. In contrast, **collectivism** involves putting group goals ahead of personal goals and defining one's identity in terms of the groups one belongs to (such as one's family, tribe, work group, social class, caste, and so on). In comparison to individualistic cultures, collectivist cultures place a higher priority on shared values and resources, cooperation, mutual interdependence, and concern for how one's actions will affect other group members. Consistent with these realities, *relationship harmony*

● Recommended Reading

The Pursuit of Happiness: Who Is Happy—and Why by David G. Myers (William Morrow, 1992)

The Pursuit of Happiness provides a thorough, accurate, up-to-date review of the empirical research on the determinants of happiness, seasoned nicely with illustrative personal anecdotes and low-key, practical advice. Myers is a respected social psychologist and hard-nosed scientist who acknowledges that his reflections on happiness are "colored by Christian values and spirituality." Emphasizing the finding that objective circumstances have a limited impact on happiness, Myers discusses how people might alter their subjective assessments of their lives to foster greater happiness. Working from the insight that happiness is relative, he offers suggestions for how to manage your comparisons to others and restraining your expectations to enhance your well-being. Myers's book is a superb example of what self-help books could and should be, but rarely are. It is clearly written and appropriately cautious about the limits of our knowledge. It is carefully documented, and assertions are closely tied to research and theory. The author's conjectures—which are often fascinating—are accurately presented as learned speculation rather than scientific fact, and readers are encouraged to think for themselves. Complicated issues are not reduced to sound bites and bumper sticker slogans. Myers does not encourage a self-centered approach to life (quite the opposite!) and he refrains from offering simple prescriptions for how to live. Given these realities, *The Pursuit of Happiness* probably won't make any best-seller lists, but it is well worth reading.

Happiness is relative not only to our personal past experience, but also to our social experience. We are always comparing ourselves to others. And we feel good or bad depending on whom we compare ourselves to. . . . Today's middle class has double the spending power of three decades ago, yet, because the rising tide lifts all boats, feels relatively deprived compared to their better-off neighbors. Even the rich seldom feel rich. . . . To those earning $10,000 a year, it takes a $50,000 income to be rich. To those making $500,000, rich may be a $1 million income. . . . Advertisers exploit our eagerness to compare upward by bombarding us with images of people whose elegant possessions awaken our envy. Many television programs similarly enlarge our circle of comparisons, whetting our appetites for what some others have. [pp. 56–58]

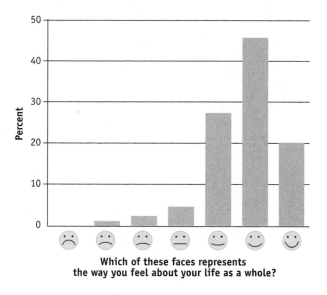

**Which of these faces represents
the way you feel about your life as a whole?**

FIGURE 1.8.

Measuring happiness with a nonverbal scale. Researchers have used a variety of methods to estimate the distribution of happiness. For example, in one study in the United States, respondents were asked to examine the seven facial expressions shown and select the one that "comes closest to expressing how you feel about your life as a whole." As you can see, the vast majority of participants chose happy faces. (Data adapted from Myers, 1992)

What Isn't Very Important?

Let us begin our discussion of individual differences in happiness by highlighting those things that turn out to be relatively unimportant determinants of subjective well-being. Quite a number of factors that one might expect to be influential appear to bear little or no relationship to general happiness.

Money. There *is* a positive correlation between income and subjective feelings of happiness, but the association is surprisingly weak (Myers & Diener, 1995). For example, one study found a correlation of just .12 between income and happiness in the United States (Diener et al., 1993). Admittedly, being very poor can make people unhappy, but once people ascend above the poverty level, there is little relation between income and happiness. On the average, even wealthy people are only marginally happier than those in the middle classes. The problem with money is that in this era of voracious consumption, most people find a way to spend all their money and come out short, no matter how much they make. Complaints about not having enough money are routine even among affluent people who earn six-figure incomes.

Age. Age and happiness are consistently found to be unrelated. Age accounts for less than 1 percent of the variation in people's happiness (Inglehart, 1990; Myers & Diener, 1997). The key factors influencing subjective

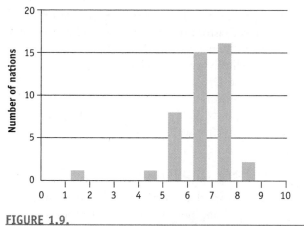

FIGURE 1.9.

The subjective well-being of nations. Veenhoven (1993) combined the results of almost 1000 surveys to calculate the average subjective well-being reported by representative samples from 43 nations. The mean happiness scores clearly pile up at the positive end of the distribution, with only two scores falling below the neutral point of 5. (Data adapted from Diener and Diener, 1996)

well-being may shift some as people grow older—work becomes less important, health moreso—but people's average level of happiness tends to remain remarkably stable over the life span.

Gender. Women are treated for depressive disorders about twice as often as men, so one might expect that women are less happy on the average. However, like age, gender accounts for less than 1 percent of the variation in people's subjective well-being (Myers, 1992).

Parenthood. Children can be a tremendous source of joy and fulfillment, but they can also be a tremendous source of headaches and hassles. Compared to childless couples, parents worry more and experience more marital problems (Argyle, 1987). Apparently, the good and bad aspects of parenthood balance each other out, because the evidence indicates that people who have children are neither more nor less happy than people without children.

Intelligence. Intelligence is a highly valued trait in modern society, but researchers have not found an association between IQ scores and happiness (Diener, 1984). Educational attainment also appears to be unrelated to life satisfaction (Ross & Van Willigen, 1997).

Physical attractiveness. Good-looking people enjoy a variety of advantages in comparison to unattractive people (see Chapters 6 and 8). Given that physical attractiveness is an important resource in Western society, we might expect attractive people to be happier than others, but the available data indicate that the correlation between attractiveness and happiness is negligible (Diener, Wolsic, & Fujita, 1995).

appears to be a more important determinant of happiness in collectivist cultures than in individualistic cultures (Kwan, Bond, & Singelis, 1997). Interestingly, people from individualistic cultures report somewhat higher average levels of happiness than people from collectivist cultures (Diener et al., 1995). Researchers have just begun to analyze the causes of cultural disparities in subjective well-being.

What Is Very Important?

The list of factors that turn out to be very important ingredients of happiness is surprisingly short. Only a few variables are strongly related to overall happiness.

Love and marriage. Romantic relationships can be stressful, but people consistently rate being in love as one of the most critical ingredients of happiness (Diener, 1984). Furthermore, although people complain a lot about their marriages, the evidence indicates that marital status is a key correlate of happiness. Among both men and women, married people are happier than people who are single or divorced (see Figure 1.10; Myers & Diener, 1995). However, the causal relations underlying this correlation are unclear. It may be that happiness causes marital satisfaction more than marital satisfaction promotes happiness. Perhaps people who are happy tend to have better intimate relationships and more stable marriages, while people who are unhappy have more difficulty finding and keeping mates.

Work. Given the way people often complain about their jobs, we might not expect work to be a key source

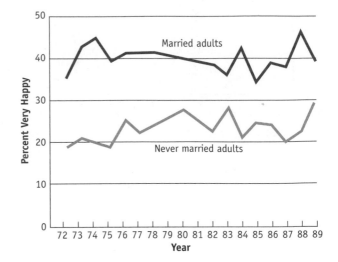

FIGURE 1.10.

Happiness and marital status. This graph shows that the percentage of adults characterizing themselves as "Very happy" has consistently been much higher among married people than among those who never married (Lee, Seccombe, & Shehan, 1991). These data and many others suggest that marital satisfaction is a key ingredient of happiness. (From Myers & Diener, 1995)

of happiness, but it is. Although less critical than love and marriage, job satisfaction is strongly related to general happiness (Argyle, 1987). Studies also show that unemployment has devastating effects on subjective well-being (Diener, 1984). It is difficult to sort out whether job satisfaction causes happiness or vice versa, but evidence suggests that causation flows both ways (Argyle, 1987).

Research on the correlates of happiness suggests that two key ingredients of happiness are satisfaction in intimate relationships and a rewarding work life.

Personality. The best predictor of individuals' future happiness is their past happiness (Myers, 1992). Some people seem destined to be happy and others unhappy, regardless of their triumphs or setbacks. The limited influence of life events was apparent in a study that found only marginal differences between lottery winners and quadriplegics in overall happiness (Argyle, 1987). Several lines of evidence suggest that happiness does not depend on external circumstances—having a nice house, good friends, and an enjoyable job—as much as internal factors, such as one's outlook on life. With this reality in mind, researchers have begun to look for links between personality and subjective well-being, and they have found some relatively strong correlations. For example, self-esteem is one of the best predictors of happiness. Not surprisingly, people who like themselves tend to be happier than those who do not. Other personality correlates of happiness include extraversion, optimism, and a sense of personal control over one's life (Myers & Diener, 1995).

Conclusions

We must be cautious in drawing inferences about the causes of happiness, because most of the available data are correlational data (see Figure 1.11). Nonetheless, the empirical evidence suggests that many popular beliefs about the sources of happiness are unfounded. The data also demonstrate that happiness is shaped by a complex constellation of variables. In spite of this complexity, however, a number of worthwhile insights about human adjustment can be gleaned from research on the correlates of subjective well-being.

First, research on happiness demonstrates that the determinants of subjective well-being are precisely that: subjective. Objective realities are not as important as subjective feelings. In other words, your health, your wealth, your job, and your age are not as influential as how you *feel* about your health, wealth, job, and age (Argyle, 1987).

Second, in making the subjective assessments that shape a person's happiness, everything is relative (Myers, 1992). In other words, you evaluate what you have relative to what the people around you have and relative to what you expected to have. Generally, people compare themselves with others who are similar. Thus,

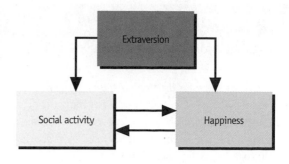

FIGURE 1.11.

Possible causal relations among the correlates of happiness. Although considerable data exist on the correlates of happiness, it is difficult to untangle the possible causal relationships. For example, we know that a moderate positive correlation exists between social activity and happiness, but we can't say for sure whether high social activity causes happiness or whether happiness causes people to be more socially active. Moreover, in light of the finding that a third variable—extraversion—correlates with both variables, we have to consider the possibility that extraversion causes both greater social activity and greater happiness.

wealthy people assess what they have by comparing themselves with their wealthy friends and neighbors. This is one reason why there is little correlation between wealth and happiness. You might have a lovely home, but if it sits next door to a neighbor's palatial mansion, it might be a source of more dissatisfaction than happiness. In addition to comparing themselves with others, people compare what they have with what they expected to have. Those who exceed their expectations are more likely to be happy. Thus, people living in a lovely home next door to a much lovelier mansion could still be quite happy—if they never expected to live in such an affluent neighborhood. To a large degree then, happiness is measured on a relative, rather than an absolute, scale.

Third, although there is no simple recipe for happiness, research shows that the quest for happiness is never hopeless (Freedman, 1978; Myers, 1992). The evidence indicates that some people find happiness in spite of seemingly insurmountable problems. There is nothing, short of terminal illness—no setback, shortcoming, difficulty, or inadequacy—that makes happiness impossible.

Improving Academic Performance

LEARNING OBJECTIVES

● *List three steps for developing sound study habits.*

● *Describe the SQ3R method and what makes it effective.*

● *Summarize advice on how to get more out of lectures.*

● *Summarize how memory is influenced by practice, interference, and organization.*

● *Describe several verbal and visual mnemonic devices.*

Although some students downplay the importance of study efforts, the reality is that effective study habits are crucial to academic success.

Answer the following true or false.

_____ 1. It's a good idea to study in as many different locations (your bedroom or kitchen, the library, lounges around school, and so forth) as possible.

_____ 2. If you have a professor who delivers chaotic, hard-to-follow lectures, there is little point in attending class.

_____ 3. Cramming the night before an exam is an efficient way to study.

_____ 4. In taking lecture notes, you should try to be a "human tape recorder" (that is, take down everything exactly as said by your professor).

_____ 5. Outlining reading assignments is a waste of time.

As you will soon learn, all of the statements above are false. If you answered them all correctly, you may already have acquired the kinds of skills and habits that lead to academic success. If so, however, you are not typical. Today, a huge number of students enter college with remarkably poor study skills and habits—and it's not entirely their fault. Our educational system generally does not provide much in the way of formal instruction on good study techniques. In this first Application, we will try to remedy this deficiency to some extent by sharing some insights that psychology can provide on how to improve your academic performance. We will discuss how to promote better study habits, how to enhance reading efforts, how to get more out of lectures, and how to make your memory more effective.

Developing Sound Study Habits

Effective study is crucial to success in college. You may run into a few classmates who boast about getting good grades without studying. But you can be sure that if they perform well on exams, they study. Students who claim otherwise simply want to be viewed as extremely bright rather than as studious.

Learning can be immensely gratifying, but studying usually involves hard work. The first step toward effective study habits is to face this reality. You don't have to feel guilty if you don't look forward to studying. Most students don't. Once you accept the premise that studying doesn't come naturally, it should be clear that you need to set up an organized program to promote adequate study. Such a program should include the following considerations (Siebert, 1995).

Set up a schedule for studying. If you wait until the urge to study hits you, you may still be waiting when the exam rolls around. Thus, it is important to allocate definite times to studying. Review your time obligations (work, housekeeping, and so on) and figure out in advance when you can study. In allotting certain times to studying, keep in mind that you need to be wide awake and alert. Be realistic, too, about how long you can study at one time before you wear down from fatigue. Allow time for study breaks; they can revive sagging concentration.

It's important to write down your study schedule. Writing it down serves as a reminder and increases your commitment to the schedule. As shown in Figure 1.12, you should begin by setting up a general schedule for the quarter or semester. Then, at the beginning of each week, plan the specific assignments that you intend to work on during each study session. This approach should help you to avoid cramming for exams at the last minute.

In planning your weekly schedule, try to avoid the tendency to put off working on major tasks such as term papers and reports. Time management experts such as Alan Lakein (1973) point out that many of us tend to tackle simple, routine tasks first, while saving larger tasks for later, when we supposedly will have more time. This common tendency leads many of us to delay working on major assignments until it's too late to do a good job. You can avoid this trap by breaking major assignments into smaller component tasks that you schedule individually.

	Mon	Tues	Wed	Thurs	Fri	Sat	Sun
8 A.M.						Work	
9 A.M.	History	Study	History	Study	History	Work	
10 A.M.	Psych		Psych		Psych	Work	
11 A.M.	Study	French	Study	French	Study	Work	
Noon	Math	Study	Math	Study	Math	Work	Study
1 P.M.							Study
2 P.M.	Study		Study		Study		Study
3 P.M.	Study	English	Study	English	Study		Study
4 P.M.							
5 P.M.							
6 P.M.	Work	Study	Work				Study
7 P.M.	Work	Study	Work				Study
8 P.M.	Work	Study	Work				Study
9 P.M.	Work	Study	Work				Study
10 P.M.	Work		Work				

FIGURE 1.12.

Example of an activity schedule. One student's general activity schedule for a semester is shown here. Each week the student fills in the specific assignments to work on during the upcoming study sessions.

Find a place to study where you can concentrate. Where you study is also important. The key is to find a place where distractions are likely to be minimal. Most people cannot study effectively while watching TV, listening to loud music, or overhearing conversations. Don't depend on willpower to carry you through these distractions. It's much easier to plan ahead and avoid the distractions altogether.

There is evidence that it helps to set up one or two specific places for study. If possible, use these places for nothing else. These places may become strongly associated with studying, so that they serve as cues that evoke good study behavior (Hettich, 1998). In contrast, places associated with other activities may serve as cues for these other activities. For example, studying in your kitchen may evoke more eating than reading.

Reward your studying. One of the reasons it is so difficult to motivate oneself to study regularly is that the payoffs for studying often lie in the distant future. The ultimate reward, a degree, may be years away. Even more short-term rewards, such as an A in the course, may be weeks or months away. To combat this problem, it helps to give yourself immediate rewards for studying. It is easier to motivate yourself to study if you reward yourself with a tangible payoff, such as a snack, TV show, or phone call to a friend, when you finish. Thus, you should set realistic study goals for yourself and then reward yourself when you meet them. This systematic manipulation of rewards involves harnessing the principles of *behavior modification,* which are described in some detail in the Chapter 4 Application.

Improving Your Reading

Much of your study time is spent reading and absorbing information. *These efforts must be active.* If you engage in passive reading, the information will pass right through you. Many students deceive themselves into thinking that they are studying by running a marker through a few sentences here and there in their text. If such highlighting isn't done with thoughtful selectivity, the student is simply turning a textbook into a coloring book. Underlining in your text can be useful, but you have to distinguish between important ideas and mere supportive material.

You can choose from a number of ways for actively attacking your reading assignments. One of the more worthwhile strategies is Robinson's (1970) SQ3R method. **SQ3R is a study system designed to promote**

effective reading that includes five steps: survey, question, read, recite, and review. Its name is an abbreviation for the five steps in the procedure:

Step 1: Survey. Before you plunge into the actual reading, glance over the topic headings in the chapter and try to get an overview of the material. Try to understand how the various chapter segments are related. If there is a chapter outline or summary, consult it to get a feel for the chapter. If you know where the chapter is going, you can better appreciate and organize the information you are about to read.

Step 2: Question. Once you have an overview of your reading assignment, proceed through it one section at a time. Take a look at the heading of the first section and convert it into a question. This is usually quite simple. If the heading is "Prenatal Risk Factors," your question should be "What are sources of risk during prenatal development?" If the heading is "Stereotyping," your question should be "What is stereotyping?" Asking these questions gets you actively involved in your reading and helps you to identify the main ideas.

Step 3: Read. Only now, in the third step, are you ready to sink your teeth into the reading. Read only the specific section that you have decided to tackle. Read it with an eye toward answering the question that you just formulated. If necessary, reread the section until you can answer that question. Decide whether the segment addresses any other important questions and answer them as well.

Step 4: Recite. Now that you can answer the key question for the section, recite it out loud to yourself. Use your own words for the answer, because that requires understanding instead of simple memorization. Don't move on to the next section until you understand the main idea(s) of the current section. You may want to write down these ideas for review later. When you have fully digested the first section, go on to the next. Repeat steps 2 through 4 with the next section. Once you have mastered the crucial points there, you can continue. Keep repeating steps 2 through 4, section by section, until you finish the chapter.

Step 5: Review. When you have read the chapter, test and refresh your memory by going back over the key points. Repeat your questions and try to answer them without consulting your book or notes. This review should fortify your retention of the main ideas and alert you to any key ideas that you haven't mastered. It should also help you to see the relationships between the main ideas.

The SQ3R method does not have to be applied rigidly. For example, it is often wise to break your reading assignment into smaller segments than those separated by section headings. In fact, you should probably apply SQ3R to many texts on a paragraph by paragraph basis. Obviously, this will require you to formulate some questions without the benefit of topic headings. However, the headings are not absolutely necessary to use this technique. If you don't have enough headings, you can simply reverse the order of steps 2 and 3. Read the paragraph first and then formulate a question that addresses the basic idea of the paragraph. The point is that you can be flexible in your use of the SQ3R technique. *What makes SQ3R effective is that it breaks a reading assignment down into manageable segments and requires understanding before you move on.* Any method that accomplishes these goals should enhance your reading.

It is easier to use the SQ3R method when your textbook has plenty of topic headings. This brings up another worthwhile point about improving your reading. It pays to take advantage of the various learning aids incorporated into many textbooks. If a book provides a chapter outline or chapter summary, don't

Recommended Reading

Learning Skills for College and Career
by Paul I. Hettich (Brooks/Cole, 1998)

Dozens of books are available on how to survive the trials and tribulations of college life. Most of them are sound in their advice, but this new entry stands out as one of the very best. The book covers the full range of topics relevant to succeeding in college, including time management, organization, study techniques, memory improvement, testwiseness, reading, and note taking in class. It also contains unusual chapters on the covert curriculum, study groups, and interpersonal skills, and Jane Halonen has contributed a wonderful chapter on critical thinking. The book is easy to read and includes an extensive collection of self-analysis exercises.

> *One of the most burdensome beliefs often held by the beginning student is the tendency to see the academic challenge of college as a relatively simple matter of information storage. Students with this belief see their texts as so many pages of material to be memorized and regurgitated at test time. One of my students once referred to this process as the "bulimic" model of education. . . . In fact, most academic disciplines are quite dynamic. Truths in one decade may be cast aside for new truths in the next. Although new students may be tempted to see a discipline as unchanging, most disciplines show relentless growth. [pp. 284–285]*

Web Link 1.6

CalREN Project Study Tips
The staff at the University of California, Berkeley, assembled this excellent set of study resources, with an emphasis on the needs and questions of the "nontraditional age" student.

ignore them. They can help you to recognize the important points in the chapter and understand how the various parts of the chapter are interrelated. If your book furnishes learning objectives, use them. They tell you what you should get out of your reading.

Getting More Out of Lectures

Although lectures are sometimes boring and tedious, it is a simple fact that poor class attendance is associated with poor grades. For example, in one study, Lindgren (1969) found that absences from class were much more common among "unsuccessful" students (grade average: C– or below) than among "successful" students (grade average: B or above), as is shown in Figure 1.13. Even when you have an instructor who delivers hard-to-follow lectures from which you learn virtually nothing, it is still important to go to class. If nothing else, you'll get a feel for how the instructor thinks. This can help you anticipate the content of exams and respond in the manner your professor expects.

Fortunately, most lectures are reasonably coherent. Research indicates that accurate note taking is related to better test performance (Palkovitz & Lore, 1980). Good note taking requires you to actively process lecture information in ways that should enhance both memory and understanding. Books on study skills (Longman & Atkinson, 1996; Sotiriou, 1996) offer a number of suggestions on how to take good lecture notes. Here are a few of them:

• Use *active listening procedures*, which are described in more detail in Chapter 7. With active listening, you focus full attention on the speaker. Try to anticipate what's coming and search for deeper meanings. Pay attention to nonverbal signals that may serve to further clarify the lecturer's intent or meaning.

• When course material is especially complex and difficult, it is a good idea to prepare for the lecture by reading ahead on the scheduled subject in your text. Then you have less information to digest that is brand new.

• Don't try to be a human tape recorder. Instead, try to write down the lecturer's thoughts in your own words. Doing so forces you to organize the ideas in a way that makes sense to you. In taking notes, look for subtle and not-so-subtle clues about what the instructor considers to be important. These clues may range from simply repeating main points to saying things like "You'll run into this again."

• Ask questions during lectures. Doing so keeps you actively involved and allows you to clarify points you may have misunderstood. Many students are more bashful about asking questions than they should be. They don't realize that most professors welcome questions.

Applying Memory Principles

Scientific investigation of memory processes dates back to 1885, when Hermann Ebbinghaus published a series of insightful studies. Since then, psychologists have discovered a number of principles about memory that are relevant to helping you improve your study skills.

ENGAGE IN ADEQUATE PRACTICE

Practice makes perfect, or so you've heard. In reality, practice is not likely to guarantee perfection, but repeatedly reviewing information usually leads to improved retention. Studies show that retention improves with increased rehearsal (Greene, 1992). Continued rehearsal may also pay off by improving your *understanding* of assigned material (Bromage & Mayer, 1986). As you go over information again and again, your increased familiarity with the material may permit you to focus selectively on the most important points, thus enhancing your understanding.

There is evidence that it even pays to overlearn material (Driskell, Wilis, & Copper, 1992). **Overlearning refers to continued rehearsal of material after you first appear to master it.** In one study, after participants mastered a list of nouns (they recited the list without error), Krueger (1929) required them to continue rehearsing for 50% or 100% more trials. Measuring retention at intervals of up to 28 days, Kreuger found that overlearning led to better recall of the list. The

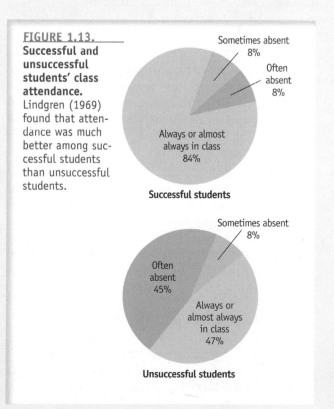

FIGURE 1.13.
Successful and unsuccessful students' class attendance. Lindgren (1969) found that attendance was much better among successful students than unsuccessful students.

Sometimes absent 8%
Often absent 8%
Always or almost always in class 84%

Successful students

Sometimes absent 8%
Often absent 45%
Always or almost always in class 47%

Unsuccessful students

implication of this finding is simple: You should not quit rehearsing material as soon as you appear to have mastered it.

USE DISTRIBUTED PRACTICE

Let's assume that you are going to study 9 hours for an exam. Is it better to "cram" all of your study into one 9-hour period (massed practice) or distribute it among, say, three 3-hour periods on successive days (distributed practice)? The evidence indicates that retention tends to be greater after distributed practice than massed practice (Glenberg, 1992; Payne & Wenger, 1996). This advantage is especially apparent if the intervals between practice periods are fairly long, such as 24 hours (Zechmeister & Nyberg, 1982). The inefficiency of massed practice means that cramming is an ill-advised study strategy for most students. Cramming will strain your memorization capabilities and tax your energy level. It may also stoke the fires of test anxiety.

MINIMIZE INTERFERENCE

Interference **occurs when people forget information because of competition from other learned material.** Research suggests that interference is a major cause of forgetting, so you'll probably want to think about how you can minimize interference. Doing so is especially important for students, because memorizing information for one course can interfere with retaining information in another course. It may help to allocate study for specific courses to specific days. Thorndyke and Hayes-Roth (1979) found that similar material produced less interference when it was learned on different days. Thus, the day before an exam in a course, it is probably best to study for that course only. If demands in other courses make that impossible, study the test material last. Of course, studying for other classes is not the only source of interference in a student's life. Other normal waking activities also produce interference.

Therefore, it is a good idea to conduct one last, thorough review of material as close to exam time as possible (Anderson, 1980). This last-minute review helps you to avoid memory loss due to interference from intervening activities.

ORGANIZE INFORMATION

Retention tends to be greater when information is well organized. Gordon Bower (1970) has shown that hierarchical organization is particularly helpful when it is applicable. Thus, it may be a good idea to *outline* reading assignments for school. Consistent with this reasoning, there is some empirical evidence that outlining material from textbooks can enhance retention of the material (McDaniel, Waddill, & Shakesby, 1996).

USE VERBAL MNEMONICS

People retain information better when they make the information more meaningful (Roediger, 1992). A useful strategy is to make material *personally* meaningful. When you read your textbooks, try to relate information to your own life and experience. For example, if you're reading in your psychology text about the personality trait of assertiveness, you can think of someone you know who is very assertive.

Of course, it's not always easy to make something personally meaningful. When you study chemistry, you may have a hard time relating to polymers at a personal level. This problem has led to the development of many *mnemonic devices,* **or strategies for enhancing memory,** that are designed to make abstract material more meaningful.

Acrostics and acronyms. Acrostics are phrases (or poems) in which the first letter of each word (or line) functions as a cue to help you recall the abstract words that begin with the same letter. For instance, you may remember the order of musical notes with the saying

"Every good boy does fine" (or "deserves favor"). A variation on acrostics is the *acronym*—a word formed out of the first letters of a series of words. Students memorizing the order of colors in the light spectrum often store the name "Roy G. Biv" to remember red, orange, yellow, green, blue, indigo, and violet.

Narrative methods. Another useful way to remember a list of words is to create a story that includes each of the words in the right order. The narrative increases the meaningfulness of the words and links them in a specific order. Examples of this technique can be seen in Figure 1.14. Bower and Clark (1969) found that this procedure enhanced subjects' recall of lists of unrelated words.

Rhymes. Another verbal mnemonic that people often rely on is rhyming. You've probably repeated, "I before E except after C" thousands of times. Perhaps you also remember the number of days in each month with the old standby, "Thirty days hath September . . ." Rhyming something to remember it is an old and useful trick.

USE VISUAL IMAGERY

Memory can be improved through the use of visual imagery. One influential theory (Paivio, 1986) proposes that visual images create a second memory code and that two codes are better than one. Many popular mnemonic devices depend on visual imagery, including the link method and the method of loci.

Link method. The *link* method involves forming a mental image of items to be remembered in a way that links them together. For instance, suppose that you are going to stop at the drugstore on the way home and you need to remember to pick up a news magazine, shaving cream, film, and pens. To remember these items, you might visualize a public figure likely to be in the magazine shaving with a pen while being photographed. Some researchers suggest that bizarre images may be remembered better (Iaccino, 1996; Worthen, 1997).

Method of loci. The *method of loci* involves taking an imaginary walk along a familiar path where you have associated images of items you want to remember with certain locations. The first step is to commit to memory a series of loci, or places along a path. Usually these loci are specific locations in your home or neighborhood. Then envision each thing you want to remember in one of these locations. Try to form distinctive, vivid images. When you need to remember the items, imagine yourself walking along the path. The various loci on your path should serve as retrieval cues for the images that you formed (see Figure 1.15). The method of loci assures that items are remembered in their correct order because the order is determined by the sequence of locations along the pathway. Empirical studies have supported the value of this method for memorizing lists (Crovitz, 1971; De Beni, Mo, & Cornoldi, 1997).

FIGURE 1.14.

The narrative method. Two examples of the narrative method for memorizing lists are shown here (Bower & Clark, 1969). The words to be memorized are listed on the left, and the stories constructed to remember them are shown on the right.

Word Lists to Be Memorized and Stories Constructed from Them		
Word lists		**Stories**
Bird	Nurse	A man dressed in a *Bird Costume* and wearing a *Mailbox* on his *Head* was seen leaping into the *River*. A *Nurse* ran out of a nearby *Theater* and applied *Wax* to his *Eyelids,* but her efforts were in vain. He died and was tossed into the *Furnace*.
Costume	Theater	
Mailbox	Wax	
Head	Eyelid	
River	Furnace	
Rustler	Fuzz	A *Rustler* lived in a *Penthouse* on top of a *Mountain*. His specialty was the three-toed *Sloth*. He would take his captive animals to a *Tavern* where he would remove *Fuzz* from their *Glands*. Unfortunately, all this exposure to sloth fuzz caused him to grow *Antlers*. So he gave up his profession and went to work in a *Pencil* factory. As a precaution he also took a lot of *Vitamin* E.
Penthouse	Gland	
Mountain	Antler	
Sloth	Pencil	
Tavern	Vitamin	

FIGURE 1.15.

The method of loci. In this example from Bower (1970), a person about to go shopping pairs items to be remembered with familiar places (loci) arranged in a natural sequence: (1) hot dogs/driveway; (2) cat food/garage; (3) tomatoes/front door; (4) bananas/coat closet; (5) whiskey/kitchen sink. As the last panel shows, the shopper recalls the items by mentally touring the loci associated with them.

Key Ideas

THE PARADOX OF PROGRESS
● Although our modern era has seen great technological progress, personal problems have not diminished. In spite of many time-saving devices, people tend to have less free time. Although affluence is widespread, most people worry about economic decline.

● The ability to process and communicate information has increased exponentially, yet people are troubled by information anxiety. In spite of stunning medical advances, patients' access to quality care has worsened. Thus, many theorists argue that our progress has brought new, and possibly more difficult, adjustment problems.

THE SEARCH FOR DIRECTION
● According to many theorists, the basic challenge of modern life has become the search for a sense of direction and meaning. This search has many manifestations, including the appeal of self-realization programs, religious cults, the Christian men's movement, and media psychologists, such as Dr. Laura.

● The codependency movement suggests that millions of people are enmeshed in dysfunctional relationships that breed addiction to alcohol, drugs, and a host of unhealthy behaviors. The codependency movement is motivated by good intentions, but it vastly oversimplifies the roots of human distress and has little empirical basis.

● The enormous popularity of self-help books is an interesting manifestation of people's struggle to find a sense of direction. Some self-help books offer worthwhile advice, but most are dominated by psychobabble and are not based on scientific research. Many also lack explicit advice on how to change behavior.

● Although this text deals with many of the same issues as self-realization programs, Dr. Laura, the codependency movement, self-help books, and other types of pop psychology, its philosophy and approach are quite different.

THE PSYCHOLOGY OF ADJUSTMENT
● Psychology is both a science and a profession that focuses on behavior and related mental and physiological processes. Adjustment is a broad area of study in psychology concerned with how people adapt effectively or ineffectively to the demands and pressures of everyday life.

THE SCIENTIFIC APPROACH TO BEHAVIOR
● The scientific approach to understanding behavior is empirical. Psychologists base their conclusions on formal, systematic, objective tests of their hypotheses, rather than reasoning, speculation, or common sense. The scientific approach is advantageous in that it puts a premium on clarity and has little tolerance for error.

● Experimental research involves manipulating an independent variable to discover its effects on a dependent variable. The experimenter usually does this by comparing experimental and control groups, which must be alike except for the variation created by the manipulation of the independent variable. Experiments permit conclusions about cause-effect relationships between variables, but this method isn't usable for the study of many questions.

● Psychologists conduct correlational research when they are unable to exert control over the variables they want to study. The correlation coefficient is a numerical index of the degree of relationship between two variables. Correlational research methods include naturalistic observation, case studies, and surveys. Correlational research facilitates the investigation of many issues that are not open to experimental study, but it cannot demonstrate that two variables are causally related.

THE ROOTS OF HAPPINESS: AN EMPIRICAL ANALYSIS
● A scientific analysis of happiness reveals that many commonsense notions about the roots of happiness appear to be incorrect, including the notion that most people are unhappy. Factors such as money, age, gender, parenthood, intelligence, and attractiveness are not correlated with subjective well-being.

● Physical health, social relationships, religious faith, and culture appear to have a modest impact on feelings of happiness.

● The only factors that are clearly and strongly related to happiness are love and marriage, work satisfaction, and personality.

● There are no simple recipes for achieving happiness, but it helps to understand that happiness is a relative concept mediated by people's highly subjective assessments of their lives.

APPLICATION: IMPROVING ACADEMIC PERFORMANCE
● To foster sound study habits, you should devise a written study schedule and reward yourself for following it. You should also try to find one or two specific places for studying that are relatively free of distractions.

● You should use active reading techniques, such as SQ3R, to select the most important ideas from the material you read. Good note taking can help you get more out of lectures. It's important to use active listening techniques and to record lecturers' ideas in your own words.

● Rehearsal, even when it involves overlearning, facilitates retention. Distributed practice tends to be more efficient than massed practice. It is wise to plan study sessions so as to minimize interference. Evidence also suggests that organization facilitates retention, so outlining reading assignments can be valuable.

● Meaningfulness can be enhanced through the use of verbal mnemonics such as acrostics, acronyms, and narrative methods. The link method and the method of loci are mnemonic devices that depend on the value of visual imagery.

Key Terms

Adjustment
Behavior
Case study
Clinical psychology
Collectivism
Control group
Correlation
Correlation coefficient
Dependent variable
Empiricism
Experiment
Experimental group
Independent variable
Individualism
Interference
Mnemonic devices
Naturalistic observation
Overlearning
Psychology
SQ3R
Surveys

Key People

David Myers   Martin Seligman

Practice Test

1. Technological advances have not led to perceptible improvement in our collective health and happiness. This statement defines
   a. escape from freedom.
   b. the point/counterpoint phenomenon.
   c. modern society.
   d. the paradox of progress.

2. _____ is the tendency to become enmeshed in a dysfunctional relationship marked by excessive preoccupation with another's needs and problems to the virtual exclusion of one's own.
   a. Addiction
   b. Codependency
   c. Neurosis
   d. Psychobabble

3. Which of the following is not offered in the text as a criticism of self-help books?
   a. They are infrequently based on solid research.
   b. Most don't provide explicit directions for changing behavior.
   c. The topics they cover are often quite narrow.
   d. Many are dominated by psychobabble.

4. The adaptation of animals when environments change is similar to _____ in humans.
   a. orientation
   b. adjustment
   c. evolution
   d. assimilation

5. An experiment is a research method in which the investigator manipulates the _____ variable and observes whether there are changes in a _____ variable as a result.
   a. independent; dependent
   b. control; experimental
   c. experimental; control
   d. dependent; independent

6. A researcher wants to determine whether a certain diet causes children to learn better in school. In the study, the independent variable is
   a. the type of diet.
   b. a measure of learning performance.
   c. age or grade level of the children.
   d. intelligence level of the children.

7. A psychologist collected background information about a psychopathic killer, talked to him and people who knew him, and gave him psychological tests. Which research method was she using?
   a. Case study
   b. Naturalistic observation
   c. Survey
   d. Experiment

8. The principal advantage of experimental research is that
   a. it has a scientific basis and is therefore convincing to people.
   b. experiments replicate real-life situations.
   c. an experiment can be designed for any research problem.
   d. it allows the researcher to draw cause-and-effect conclusions.

9. Research has shown that which of the following is very important for one's happiness?
   a. Money
   b. Intelligence
   c. Job satisfaction
   d. Parenthood

10. A good reason for taking notes in your own words, rather than verbatim, is that
    a. most lecturers are quite wordy.
    b. "translating" on the spot is good mental exercise.
    c. doing so reduces the likelihood that you'll later engage in plagiarism.
    d. it forces you to assimilate the information in a way that makes sense to you.

Answers

1. d page 1
2. b page 4
3. c pages 8–9
4. b page 11
5. a page 13
6. a page 13
7. a page 16
8. d page 14
9. c pages 20–21
10. d page 25

INFOTRAC
COLLEGE EDITION

Go to the Wadsworth Psychology Study Center (http://psychology.wadsworth.com/) for quiz questions, research updates, hot topics, interactive exercises, and suggested readings in INFOTRAC related to this chapter.

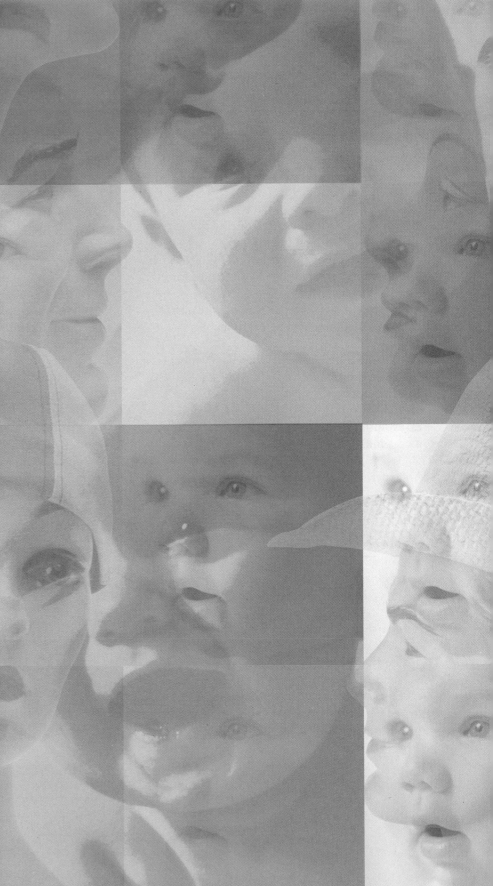

CHAPTER 2

Theories of Personality

Imagine that you are hurtling upward in an elevator with three other persons when suddenly a power blackout brings the elevator to a halt 45 stories above the ground. Your three companions might adjust to this predicament differently. One might crack jokes to relieve tension. Another might make ominous predictions that "we'll never get out of here." The third person might calmly think about how to escape from the elevator. These varied ways of coping with the same stressful situation occur because each person has a different personality. Personality differences significantly influence people's patterns of adjustment. Thus, theories intended to explain personality can contribute to our effort to understand adjustment processes.

In this chapter, we will introduce you to various theories that attempt to explain the structure and development of personality. Our review of personality theory will also serve to acquaint you with four major theoretical perspectives in psychology: the psychodynamic, behavioral, humanistic, and biological perspectives. These theoretical approaches are conceptual models that help us explain behavior. Familiarity with them will help you understand many of the ideas that you will encounter in this book, as well as in other books about psychology.

The Nature of Personality

LEARNING OBJECTIVES

- Explain the concepts of personality and traits.
- Describe the "Big Five" personality traits.

To discuss theories of personality effectively, we need to digress momentarily to come up with a definition of personality and to discuss the concept of personality traits.

What Is Personality?

What does it mean if you say that a friend has an optimistic personality? Your assertion indicates that the person has a fairly *consistent tendency* to behave in a cheerful, hopeful, enthusiastic way, looking at the bright side of things, across a wide variety of situations. In a similar vein, if you note that a friend has an "outgoing" personality, you mean that she or he consistently behaves in a friendly, open, and extraverted manner in

a variety of circumstances. Although no one is entirely consistent in his or her behavior, this quality of *consistency across situations* lies at the core of the concept of personality.

Distinctiveness is also central to the concept of personality. Everyone has traits seen in other people, but each individual has her or his own, distinctive *set* of personality traits. Each person is unique. Thus, as illustrated by our chapter-opening scenario, the concept of personality is used to explain why people don't all act alike in the same situation.

In summary, we use the idea of personality to explain (1) the stability in a person's behavior over time and across situations (consistency) and (2) the behavioral differences among people reacting to the same situation (distinctiveness). We can combine these ideas into the following definition: **personality refers to an individual's unique constellation of consistent behavioral traits.** Let's look more closely at the concept of traits.

What Are Personality Traits?

We all make remarks like "Melanie is very *shrewd*" or "Doug is too *timid* to succeed in that job" or "I wish I could be as *self-assured* as Jamie." When we attempt to describe an individual's personality, we usually do so in terms of specific aspects of personality, called traits. **A *personality trait* is a durable disposition to behave in a particular way in a variety of situations.** Adjectives such as *honest, dependable, moody, impulsive, suspicious, anxious, excitable, domineering,* and *friendly* describe dispositions that represent personality traits.

Most trait theories of personality, such as those of Gordon Allport (1937, 1961) and Raymond Cattell (1950, 1966) assume that some traits are more basic than others. According to this notion, a small number of fundamental traits determine other, more superficial traits. For example, a person's tendency to be impulsive, restless, irritable, boisterous, and impatient might all derive from a more basic tendency to be excitable.

In recent years, Robert McCrae and Paul Costa (1987, 1997) have stimulated a lively debate among psychologists by arguing that the vast majority of personality traits derive from just five higher-order traits that have come to be known as the "Big Five": extraversion, neuroticism, openness to experience, agreeableness, and conscientiousness (see Figure 2.1 on the next page). Let's take a closer look at these traits:

1. *Extraversion.* People who score high in extraversion are characterized as outgoing, sociable, upbeat, friendly, assertive, and gregarious. Referred to as *positive emotionality* in some trait models, extraversion has been studied extensively in research for many decades (Watson & Clark, 1997).

2. *Neuroticism.* People who score high in neuroticism tend to be anxious, hostile, self-conscious, insecure, and vulnerable. Like extraversion, this trait has been the subject of thousands of studies. In some trait models it is called *negative emotionality* (Church, 1994).

3. *Openness to experience.* Openness is associated with curiosity, flexibility, vivid fantasy, imaginativeness, artistic sensitivity, and unconventional attitudes. McCrae (1996) maintains that its importance has been underestimated. Citing evidence that openness fosters liberalism, he argues that this trait is the key determinant of people's political attitudes and ideology.

4. *Agreeableness.* Those who score high in agreeableness tend to be sympathetic, trusting, cooperative, modest, and straightforward. People who score at the opposite end of this personality dimension are characterized as suspicious, antagonistic, and aggressive. Agreeableness may have its roots in childhood temperament and appears to promote altruistic (helping) behavior in social interactions (Graziano & Eisenberg, 1997).

5. *Conscientiousness.* Conscientious people tend to be diligent, disciplined, well-organized, punctual, and dependable. Referred to as *constraint* in some trait models, conscientiousness is associated with higher productivity in a variety of occupational areas (Hogan & Ones, 1997).

McCrae and Costa maintain that personality can be described adequately by measuring the five basic traits that they've identified. Their bold claim has been supported in many studies by other researchers, and the five-factor model has become the dominant conception of personality structure in contemporary psychology (Goldberg, 1993; Ozer & Reise, 1994, Wiggins & Trapnell, 1997). However, some theorists maintain that more than five traits are necessary to account for most of the variation seen in human personality (Benet & Waller, 1995; Cattell, 1990; Wiggins, 1992). Ironically, other theorists have argued for three- or four-factor models of personality (Church & Burke, 1994; Eysenck, 1992).

The debate about how many dimensions are necessary to describe personality is likely to continue for many years to come. As you'll see throughout the chapter, the study of personality is an area in psychology that has a long history of "dueling theories." We'll begin our tour of these theories by examining the influential work of Sigmund Freud and his followers.

Psychodynamic Perspectives

LEARNING OBJECTIVES

- *Describe Freud's three components of personality and how they are distributed across levels of awareness.*
- *Explain the importance of sexual and aggressive conflicts in Freud's theory.*
- *Describe seven defense mechanisms identified by Freud.*
- *Outline Freud's stages of psychosexual development and their theorized relations to adult personality.*
- *Summarize Jung's views on the unconscious.*
- *Summarize Adler's views on key issues relating to personality.*
- *Evaluate the strengths and weaknesses of psychodynamic theories of personality.*

Psychodynamic theories **include all the diverse theories descended from the work of Sigmund Freud, which focus on unconscious mental forces.** Freud inspired many brilliant scholars who followed in his intellectual footsteps. Some of these followers simply refined and updated Freud's theory. Others veered off in new directions and established independent, albeit related, schools of thought. Today, the psychodynamic umbrella covers a large collection of related theories. In this section, we'll examine the ideas of Sigmund Freud in some detail and then take a brief look at the work of two of his most significant followers, Carl Jung and

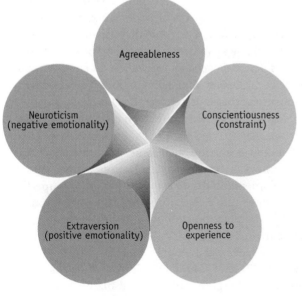

FIGURE 2.1.

The five-factor model of personality. Trait models attempt to analyze personality into its basic dimensions. McCrae and Costa (1987, 1997) maintain that personality can be described adequately with the five higher-order traits identified here.

Freud's psychoanalytic theory was based on decades of clinical work. He treated a great many patients in the consulting room pictured here. The room contains numerous artifacts from other cultures—and the original psychoanalytic couch.

Alfred Adler. Another psychodynamic theorist, Erik Erikson, is covered in a later chapter on adolescent and adult development (see Chapter 11).

Freud's Psychoanalytic Theory

Born in 1856, Sigmund Freud grew up in a middle-class Jewish home in Vienna, Austria. He showed an early interest in intellectual pursuits and became an intense, hard-working young man. He dreamed of achieving fame by making an important discovery. His determination was such that in medical school he dissected 400 male eels to prove for the first time that they had testes. His work with eels did not make him famous. However, his later work with people made him one of the most influential and controversial figures of modern times.

Sigmund Freud

Freud was a physician specializing in neurology when he began his medical practice in Vienna toward the end of the 19th century. Like other neurologists in his era, he often treated people troubled by nervous problems such as irrational fears, obsessions, and anxieties. Eventually he devoted himself to the treatment of mental disorders using an innovative procedure he developed, called *psychoanalysis.*

Psychoanalysis required lengthy verbal interactions in which Freud probed deeply into a patient's life. Decades of experience with his patients provided much of the inspiration for Freud's theory of personality. He also gathered material by looking inward and examining his own anxieties and conflicts. For over 40 years, Freud devoted the last half-hour of each workday to self-analysis.

Freud's theory gradually gained prominence, but most of Freud's contemporaries were uncomfortable with his theory for at least three reasons. First, he argued that unconscious forces govern human behavior. This idea was disturbing because it suggested that people are not masters of their own minds. Second, he claimed that childhood experiences strongly determine adult personality. This notion distressed people because it suggested that people are not masters of their own destinies. Third, he said that individuals' personalities are shaped by how they cope with their sexual urges. This assertion offended the conservative, Victorian values of his time. Thus, Freud endured a great deal of criticism, condemnation, and outright ridicule, even after his work began to attract more favorable attention. Let's examine the ideas that generated so much controversy.

STRUCTURE OF PERSONALITY

Freud (1901, 1920) divided personality structure into three components: the id, the ego, and the superego. He saw a person's behavior as the outcome of interactions among these three components.

The *id* **is the primitive, instinctive component of personality that operates according to the pleasure principle.** Freud referred to the id as the reservoir of psychic energy. By this he meant that the id houses the raw biological urges (to eat, sleep, defecate, copulate, and so on) that energize human behavior. The id operates according to the *pleasure principle,* **which demands immediate gratification of its urges.** The id engages in *primary process thinking,* which is primitive, illogical, irrational, and fantasy-oriented.

The *ego* **is the decision-making component of personality that operates according to the reality principle.** The ego mediates between the id, with its forceful desires for immediate satisfaction, and the external social world, with its expectations and norms regarding suitable behavior. The ego considers social realities—society's norms, etiquette, rules, and customs—in deciding how to behave. The ego is guided by the *reality principle,* **which seeks to delay gratification of the id's urges until appropriate outlets and situations can be found.** In short, to stay out of trouble, the ego often works to tame the unbridled desires of the id. As Freud put it, the ego is "like a man on horseback, who has to hold in check the superior strength of the horse" (Freud, 1923, p. 15).

In the long run, the ego wants to maximize gratification, just like the id. However, the ego engages in *secondary process thinking,* which is relatively rational, realistic, and oriented toward problem solving. Thus, the ego strives to avoid negative consequences from society and its representatives (for example, punishment by parents or teachers) by behaving "properly." It also attempts to achieve long-range goals that sometimes require putting off gratification.

While the ego concerns itself with practical realities, the *superego* **is the moral component of personality that incorporates social standards about what represents right and wrong.** Throughout their lives, but especially during childhood, individuals receive training about what is good and bad behavior. Eventually they internalize many of these social norms. This means that they truly *accept* certain moral principles, and then *they* put pressure on *themselves* to live up to these standards. The superego emerges out of the ego at around 3 to 5 years of age. In some people, the superego can become irrationally demanding in its striving for moral perfection. Such people are plagued by excessive guilt.

According to Freud, the id, ego, and superego are distributed across three levels of awareness. He contrasted the unconscious with the conscious and preconscious (see Figure 2.2). **The *conscious* consists of whatever one is aware of at a particular point in time.** For example, at this moment your conscious may include the current train of thought in this text and a dim awareness in the back of your mind that your eyes are getting tired and you're beginning to get hungry. **The *preconscious* contains material just beneath the surface of awareness that can be easily retrieved.** Examples might include your middle name, what you had for supper last night, or an argument you had with a friend yesterday. **The *unconscious* contains thoughts, memories, and desires that are well below the surface of conscious awareness, but that nonetheless exert great influence on one's behavior.** Examples of material that might be found in your unconscious would include a forgotten trauma from childhood or hidden feelings of hostility toward a parent.

CONFLICT AND DEFENSE MECHANISMS

Freud assumed that behavior is the outcome of an ongoing series of internal conflicts. Internal battles among the id, ego, and superego are routine. Why? Because the id wants to gratify its urges immediately, but the norms of civilized society frequently dictate otherwise. For example, your id might feel an urge to clobber a co-worker who constantly irritates you. However, society frowns on such behavior, so your ego would try to hold this urge in check, and you would find yourself in a conflict. You may be experiencing conflict at this very moment. In Freudian terms, your id may be secretly urging you to abandon reading this chapter so you can watch television. Your ego may be weighing this appealing option against your society-induced need to excel in school.

Freud believed that conflicts dominate people's lives. He asserted that individuals career from one conflict to another. The following scenario provides a fanciful illustration of how the three components of personality interact to create constant conflicts.

Imagine your alarm clock ringing obnoxiously as you lurch across the bed to shut it off. It's 7 A.M. and time to get up for your history class. However, your id (operating according to the pleasure principle) urges you to return to the immediate gratification of additional sleep. Your ego (operating according to the reality principle) points out that you really must go to class since you haven't been able to decipher the stupid textbook on your own. Your id (in its typical unrealistic fashion) smugly assures you that you will get the A that you need. It suggests lying back to dream about how impressed your roommate will be. Just as you're relaxing, your superego jumps into the fray. It tries to make you feel guilty about the tuition your parents paid for the class that you're about to skip. You haven't even gotten out of bed yet—and there is already a pitched battle in your psyche.

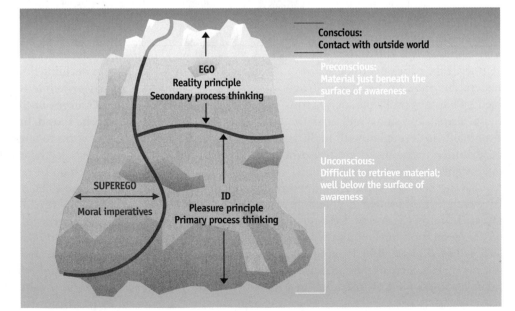

FIGURE 2.2.

Freud's model of personality structure. Freud theorized that awareness occurs at three levels: the conscious, preconscious, and unconscious. To dramatize the size of the unconscious, he compared it to the portion of an iceberg that lies beneath the water's surface. Freud also divided personality structure into three components—id, ego, and superego—which operate according to different principles and exhibit different modes of thinking. In Freud's model, the id is entirely unconscious, but the ego and superego operate at all three levels of awareness.

Conscious:
Contact with outside world

Preconscious:
Material just beneath the surface of awareness

Unconscious:
Difficult to retrieve material; well below the surface of awareness

EGO
Reality principle
Secondary process thinking

SUPEREGO
Moral imperatives

ID
Pleasure principle
Primary process thinking

Let's say your ego wins the battle. You pull yourself out of bed and head for class. On the way, you pass a donut shop and your id clamors for cinnamon rolls. Your ego reminds you that you're getting overweight and that you are supposed to be on a diet. Your id wins this time. After you've attended your history lecture, your ego reminds you that you need to do some library research for a paper in philosophy. However, your id insists on returning to your apartment to watch some sitcom reruns. As you reenter your apartment, you notice how messy it is. It's your roommates' mess and your id suggests that you tell them off. As you're about to lash out, however, your ego convinces you that diplomacy will be more effective. Three sitcoms later, you find yourself in a debate about whether to go to the gym to work out or to the student union to hang out. It's only midafternoon— and already you have been through a series of internal conflicts.

Freud believed that conflicts centering on sexual and aggressive impulses are especially likely to have far-reaching consequences. Why did he emphasize sex and aggression? Two reasons were prominent in his thinking. First, Freud thought that sex and aggression are subject to more complex and ambiguous social controls than other basic motives. The norms governing sexual and aggressive behavior are subtle, and people often get mixed messages about what is appropriate. Thus, he believed that these two drives are the source of much confusion.

Second, Freud noted that the sexual and aggressive drives are thwarted more regularly than other basic biological urges. Think about it: If you get hungry or thirsty, you can simply head for a nearby vending machine or a drinking fountain. But if a department store clerk infuriates you, you aren't likely to slug the clerk, because that isn't socially acceptable. Likewise, when you see an attractive person who inspires lustful urges, you don't normally walk up and propose a tryst in a nearby broom closet. There is nothing comparable to vending machines or drinking fountains for the satisfaction of sexual and aggressive urges. Thus, Freud ascribed great importance to these needs because social norms dictate that they are routinely frustrated.

Most psychic conflicts are trivial and quickly resolved one way or the other. Occasionally, however, a conflict will linger on for days, months, and even years, creating internal tension. Indeed, Freud believed that lingering conflicts rooted in childhood experiences cause most personality disturbances. More often than

"ALL I WANT FROM THEM IS A SIMPLE MAJORITY ON THINGS."

© 1999 by Sidney Harris.

not, these prolonged and troublesome conflicts involve sexual and aggressive impulses that society wants to tame. These conflicts are often played out entirely in the unconscious. Although you may not be aware of these unconscious battles, they can produce *anxiety* that slips to the surface of conscious awareness. This anxiety is attributable to your ego worrying about the id getting out of control and doing something terrible.

The arousal of anxiety is a crucial event in Freud's theory of personality functioning (see Figure 2.3). Anxiety is distressing, so people try to rid themselves of this unpleasant emotion any way they can. This effort to ward off anxiety often involves the use of defense mechanisms. **Defense mechanisms are largely unconscious reactions that protect a person from painful emotions such as anxiety and guilt.** Typically, they are mental maneuvers that work through self-deception. A common example is *rationalization,* **which involves creating false but plausible excuses to justify unacceptable behavior.** You would be rationalizing if, after cheating someone in a business transaction, you tried to reduce your guilt by explaining that "everyone does it."

Characterized as "the flagship in the psychoanalytic fleet of defense mechanisms" (Paulhus, Fridhandler, & Hayes, 1997, p. 545), repression is the most basic and

FIGURE 2.3.

Freud's model of personality dynamics. According to Freud, unconscious conflicts among the id, ego, and superego sometimes lead to anxiety. This discomfort may lead to the use of defense mechanisms, which may temporarily relieve the anxiety.

Intrapsychic conflict (among id, ego, and superego) → Anxiety → Reliance on defense mechanisms

widely used defense mechanism. *Repression* involves **keeping distressing thoughts and feelings buried in the unconscious.** People tend to repress desires that make them feel guilty, conflicts that make them anxious, and memories that are painful. Repression is "motivated forgetting." If you forget a dental appointment or the name of someone you don't like, repression may be at work.

Self-deception can also be seen in the mechanisims of projection and displacement. *Projection* involves **attributing one's own thoughts, feelings, or motives to another.** For example, if your lust for a co-worker makes you feel guilty, you might attribute any latent sexual tension between the two of you to the *other person's* desire to seduce you. *Displacement* involves **diverting emotional feelings (usually anger) from their original source to a substitute target.** If your boss gives you a hard time at work and you come home and slam the door, kick the dog, and scream at your spouse, you are displacing your anger onto irrelevant targets. Unfortunately, social constraints often force people to hold back their anger until they end up lashing out at the people they love the most.

Other prominent defense mechanisms include reaction formation, regression, and identification. *Reaction formation* involves **behaving in a way that is exactly the opposite of one's true feelings.** Guilt about sexual desires often leads to reaction formation. Freud theorized that many males who ridicule homosexuals are defending against their own latent homosexual impulses. As far-fetched as this idea may sound, it was supported in a recent study of homophobic men (Adams, Wright, & Lohr, 1996). The telltale sign of

Web Link 2.1

Sigmund Freud Museum, Vienna, Austria
This online museum, in English and German versions, offers a detailed chronology of Freud's life and an explanation of the most important concepts of psychoanalysis. The highlights here, though, are the rich audiovisual resources, including online photos, amateur movie clips, and voice recordings of Freud.

reaction formation is the exaggerated quality of the opposite behavior.

Regression involves **a reversion to immature patterns of behavior.** When anxious about their self-worth, some adults respond with childish boasting and bragging (as opposed to subtle efforts to impress others). For example, a fired executive having difficulty finding a new job might start making ridiculous statements about his incomparable talents and achievements. Such bragging is regressive when it is marked by massive exaggerations that anyone can see through.

Identification involves **bolstering self-esteem by forming an imaginary or real alliance with some person or group.** For example, youngsters often shore up precarious feelings of self-worth by identifying with rock-star heroes, movie stars, or famous athletes. Adults may join exclusive country clubs or civic organizations with which they identify.

Additional examples of the defense mechanisms we've described can be found in Figure 2.4. If you see defensive maneuvers that you have used, you shouldn't be surprised. According to Freud, everyone uses defense mechanisms to some extent. They become problematic only when a person depends on them excessively. The

FIGURE 2.4.

Defense mechanisms.
According to Freud, people use a variety of defense mechanisms to protect themselves from painful emotions. Definitions of seven commonly used defense mechanisms are shown on the left, along with examples of each on the right. This list is not exhaustive; additional defense mechanisms are discussed in Chapter 4.

Defense Mechanisms, with Examples

Definition	Example
Repression involves keeping distressing thoughts and feelings buried in the unconscious.	A traumatized soldier has no recollection of the details of a close brush with death.
Projection involves attributing one's own thoughts, feelings, or motives to another person.	A woman who dislikes her boss thinks she likes her boss but feels that the boss doesn't like her.
Displacement involves diverting emotional feelings (usually anger) from their original source to a substitute target.	After a parental scolding, a young girl takes her anger out on her little brother.
Reaction formation involves behaving in a way that is exactly the opposite of one's true feelings.	A parent who unconsciously resents a child spoils the child with outlandish gifts.
Regression involves a reversion to immature patterns of behavior.	An adult has a temper tantrum when he doesn't get his way.
Rationalization involves the creation of false but plausible excuses to justify unacceptable behavior.	A student watches TV instead of studying, saying that "additional study wouldn't do any good anyway."
Identification involves bolstering self-esteem by forming an imaginary or real alliance with some person or group.	An insecure young man joins a fraternity to boost his self-esteem.

seeds for psychological disorders are sown when defenses lead to wholesale distortion of reality.

Various theorists have added to Freud's original list of defenses (Vaillant, 1994). We'll examine some of these additional defense mechanisms in Chapter 4 when we discuss the role of defenses in coping with stress. For now, however, let's turn our attention to Freud's ideas about the development of personality.

DEVELOPMENT: PSYCHOSEXUAL STAGES

Freud made the startling assertion that the foundation of an individual's personality is laid down by the tender age of 5! To shed light on these crucial early years, Freud formulated a stage theory of development. He emphasized how young children deal with their immature, but powerful, sexual urges (he used the term "sexual" in a general way to refer to many urges for physical pleasure, not just the urge to copulate). According to Freud, these sexual urges shift in focus as children progress from one stage to another. Indeed, the names for the stages (oral, anal, genital, and so on) are based on where children are focusing their erotic energy at the time. Thus, **_psychosexual stages_ are developmental periods with a characteristic sexual focus that leave their mark on adult personality.**

Freud theorized that each psychosexual stage has its own unique developmental challenges or tasks, as outlined in Figure 2.5. The way these challenges are handled supposedly shapes personality. The notion of *fixation* plays an important role in this process. **_Fixation_ is a failure to move forward from one stage to another as expected.** Essentially, the child's development stalls for awhile. Fixation is caused by *excessive gratification* of needs at a particular stage or by *excessive frustration* of those needs. Either way, fixations left over from childhood affect adult personality. Generally, fixation leads to an overemphasis on the psychosexual needs that were prominent during the fixated stage. Freud described a series of five psychosexual stages. Let's examine some of the major features of each stage.

According to Freudian theory, a child's feeding experiences are crucial to later development. Fixation at the oral stage could lead to an overemphasis on, for example, smoking or eating in adulthood.

Oral stage. This stage usually encompasses the first year of life. During this stage the main source of erotic stimulation is the mouth (in biting, sucking, chewing, and so on). How caretakers handle the child's feeding experiences is supposed to be crucial to subsequent development. Freud attributed considerable importance to the manner in which the child is weaned from the breast or the bottle. According to Freud, fixation at the oral stage could form the basis for obsessive eating or smoking later in life (among many other things).

Anal stage. In their second year, children supposedly get their erotic pleasure from their bowel movements, through either the expulsion or retention of the feces.

FIGURE 2.5.
Freud's stages of psychosexual development. Freud theorized that people evolve through the series of psychosexual stages summarized here. The manner in which certain key tasks and experiences are handled during each stage is thought to leave a lasting imprint on adult personality.

Freud's Stages of Psychosexual Development			
Stage	**Approximate ages**	**Erotic focus**	**Key tasks and experiences**
Oral	0–1	Mouth (sucking, biting)	Weaning (from breast or bottle)
Anal	2–3	Anus (expelling or retaining feces)	Toilet training
Phallic	4–5	Genitals (masturbating)	Identifying with adult role models; coping with Oedipal crisis
Latency	6–12	None (sexually repressed)	Expanding social contacts
Genital	Puberty onward	Genitals (being sexually intimate)	Establishing intimate relationships; contributing to society through working

The crucial event at this time involves toilet training, which represents society's first systematic effort to regulate the child's biological urges. Severely punitive toilet training is thought to lead to a variety of possible outcomes. For example, excessive punishment might produce a latent feeling of hostility toward the "trainer," who usually is the mother. This hostility might generalize to women in general. Another possibility is that heavy reliance on punitive measures might lead to an association between genital concerns and the anxiety that the punishment arouses. This genital anxiety derived from severe toilet training could evolve into anxiety about sexual activities later in life.

Phallic stage. Around age 4, the genitals become the focus for the child's erotic energy, largely through self-stimulation. During this pivotal stage, the *Oedipal complex* emerges. Little boys develop an erotically tinged preference for their mother. They also feel hostility toward their father, whom they view as a competitor for mom's affection. Little girls develop a special attachment to their father. At about the same time, they learn that their genitals are very different from those of little boys, and they supposedly develop *penis envy*. According to Freud, girls feel hostile toward their mother because they blame her for their anatomical "deficiency."

To summarize, **in the *Oedipal complex* children manifest erotically tinged desires for their other-gender parent, accompanied by feelings of hostility toward their same-gender parent.** The name for this syndrome was taken from the Greek myth in which Oedipus is separated from his parents at birth. Not knowing the identity of his real parents, he inadvertently kills his father and marries his mother.

According to Freud, the way parents and children deal with the sexual and aggressive conflicts inherent in the Oedipal complex is of paramount importance. The child has to resolve the Oedipal dilemma by giving up the sexual longings for the other-gender parent and the hostility toward the same-gender parent. Healthy psychosexual development is supposed to hinge on the resolution of the Oedipal conflict. Why? Because continued hostile relations with the same-sex parent may prevent the child from identifying adequately with that parent. Without such identification, Freudian theory predicts that many aspects of the child's development won't progress as they should.

Latency and genital stages. Freud believed that from age 6 through puberty, the child's sexuality is suppressed—it becomes "latent." Important events during this *latency stage* center on expanding social contacts beyond the family. With the advent of puberty, the child evolves into the *genital stage*. Sexual urges reappear and

focus on the genitals once again. At this point the sexual energy is normally channeled toward peers of the other sex, rather than toward oneself, as in the phallic stage.

In arguing that the early years shape personality, Freud did not mean that personality development comes to an abrupt halt in middle childhood. However, he did believe that the foundation for one's adult personality is solidly entrenched by this time. He maintained that future developments are rooted in early, formative experiences and that significant conflicts in later years are replays of crises from childhood.

In fact, Freud believed that unconscious sexual conflicts rooted in childhood experiences cause most personality disturbances. His steadfast belief in the psychosexual origins of psychological disorders eventually led to bitter theoretical disputes with two of his most brilliant colleagues: Carl Jung and Alfred Adler. Jung and Adler both argued that Freud overemphasized sexuality. Freud summarily rejected their ideas, and the other two theorists felt compelled to go their own way, developing their own psychodynamic theories of personality.

Jung's Analytical Psychology

Swiss psychiatrist Carl Jung called his new approach *analytical psychology* to differentiate it from Freud's psychoanalytic theory. Like Freud, Jung (1921, 1933) emphasized the unconscious determinants of personality. However, he proposed that the unconscious consists of two layers. The first layer, called the *personal unconscious,* is essentially the same as Freud's version of the unconscious. The personal unconscious houses material that is not within one's conscious awareness because it has been repressed or forgotten. In addition, Jung theorized the existence of a deeper layer he called the collective unconscious. **The *collective unconscious* is a storehouse of latent memory traces inherited from people's ancestral past that is shared with the entire human race.** Jung called these ancestral memories *archetypes*. They are not memories of actual,

Carl Jung

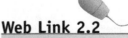

Web Link 2.2

C. G. Jung, Analytical Psychology, and Culture
Synchronicity, archetypes, collective unconscious, introversion, extraversion—these and many other important concepts arising from analytical psychology and Jung's tremendously influential theories are examined at this comprehensive site.

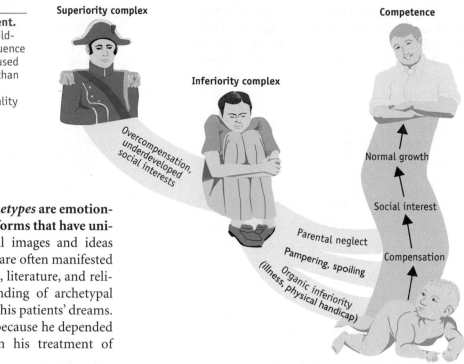

FIGURE 2.6.

Adler's view of personality development.
Like Freud, Adler believed that early child-hood experiences exert momentous influence over adult personality. However, he focused on children's social interactions rather than on their grappling with their sexuality. According to Adler, the roots of personality disturbances typically lie in excessive parental neglect or pampering.

personal experiences. Instead, ***archetypes* are emotionally charged images and thought forms that have universal meaning.** These archetypal images and ideas show up frequently in dreams and are often manifested in a culture's use of symbols in art, literature, and religion. Jung felt that an understanding of archetypal symbols helped him make sense of his patients' dreams. This was of great concern to him because he depended extensively on dream analysis in his treatment of patients.

Jung's unusual ideas about the collective unconscious had little impact on the mainstream of thinking in psychology. Their influence was felt more in other fields, such as anthropology, philosophy, art, and religious studies. However, many of Jung's other ideas *have* been incorporated into the mainstream of psychology. For instance, Jung was the first to describe the introverted (inner-directed) and extraverted (outer-directed) personality types. ***Introverts* tend to be preoccupied with the internal world of their own thoughts, feelings, and experiences.** They generally are contemplative and aloof. In contrast, ***extraverts* tend to be interested in the external world of people and things.** They're more likely to be outgoing, talkative, and friendly, instead of reclusive.

Adler's Individual Psychology

Alfred Adler was a charter member of Freud's inner circle—the Vienna Psychoanalytic Society. However, he soon began to develop his own theory of personality, which he christened *individual psychology*. Adler's (1917, 1927) theory stressed the social context of personality development (Hoffman, 1994). For instance, it was Adler who first focused attention on the possible importance of *birth order* as a factor shaping personality. Adler's view of human nature was much more optimistic than Freud's. For example, he asserted that human nature includes a unique *social interest*—an innate sense of kinship and belongingness with the human race. He saw this social interest as the source of people's willingness to work together, in a spirit of cooperation, for the common good of the society.

Adler argued that the foremost human drive is not sexuality, but a *striving for superiority*. Adler viewed striving for superiority as a universal drive to adapt, improve oneself, and master life's challenges. He noted that young children understandably feel weak and helpless in comparison to more competent older children and adults. These early inferiority feelings supposedly motivate individuals to acquire new skills and develop new talents.

Adler asserted that everyone has to work to overcome some feelings of inferiority. ***Compensation* involves efforts to overcome imagined or real inferiorities by developing one's abilities.** Adler believed that compensation is entirely normal. However, in some people inferiority feelings can become excessive, resulting in what is widely known today as an *inferiority complex*—exaggerated feelings of weakness and inadequacy. Adler thought that either parental pampering or parental neglect (or actual physical handicaps) could cause an inferiority problem. Thus, he agreed with Freud on the importance of early childhood, although he focused on different aspects of parent-child relations.

Alfred Adler

Adler explained personality disturbances by noting that an inferiority complex can distort the normal process of striving for superiority (see Figure 2.6). He maintained that some people engage in *overcompensation* in order to conceal, even from themselves, their feelings of inferiority. Instead of working to master life's challenges, people with an inferiority complex work to achieve status, gain power over others, and acquire the trappings of success (fancy clothes, impressive cars, or whatever looks important to them). They tend to flaunt their success in an effort to cover up their underlying inferiority complex. The problem is that such people engage in unconscious self-deception, worrying more about *appearances* than *reality*.

Evaluating Psychodynamic Perspectives

The psychodynamic approach has given us a number of far-reaching theories of personality. These theories yielded some bold new insights for their time (Kihlstrom, 1990; Westen, 1990). Psychodynamic theory and research have demonstrated (1) that unconscious forces can influence behavior, (2) that internal conflict often plays a key role in generating psychological distress, and (3) that early childhood experiences can exert considerable influence over adult personality. Psychodynamic models have also been praised because they probe beneath the surface of personality and because they focus attention on how personality develops over time. Many widely used concepts in psychology emerged out of psychodynamic theories, including the unconscious, defense mechanisms, introversion-extraversion, and the inferiority complex.

In a more negative vein, psychodynamic formulations have been criticized on several grounds, including the following (Fine, 1990; Macmillan, 1991; Torrey, 1992):

1. *Poor testability.* Scientific investigations require testable hypotheses. Psychodynamic ideas have often been too vague to permit a clear scientific test. Concepts such as the superego, the preconscious, and collective unconscious are difficult to measure.

2. *Inadequate evidence.* The empirical evidence on psychodynamic theories has often been characterized as inadequate. The approach depends too much on case studies, in which it is easy for clinicians to see what they expect to see based on their theory. Recent re-examinations of Freud's own clinical work suggest that he sometimes distorted his patients' case histories to mesh with his theory (Esterson, 1993; Sulloway, 1991) and that there was a substantial disparity between Freud's writings and his actual therapeutic methods (Lynn & Vaillant, 1998). Insofar as researchers have accumulated evidence on psychodynamic theories, it has provided only modest support for the central hypotheses (Fisher & Greenberg, 1985, 1996).

3. *Sexism.* Many critics have argued that psychodynamic theories harbor a bias against women. Freud believed that females' penis envy made them feel inferior to men. He also thought that females tended to develop weaker superegos and to be more prone to neurosis than men. He dismissed female patients' reports of sexual molestation during childhood as mere fantasies. Admittedly, sexism isn't unique to Freudian theories, and the sex bias in modern psychodynamic theories has been reduced to some degree. But the psychodynamic approach has generally provided a rather male-centered viewpoint (Chehrazi, 1986; Chodorow, 1978).

It's easy to ridicule Freud for concepts such as penis envy and to point to ideas that have turned out to be wrong. Remember, though, that Freud, Jung, and Adler began to fashion their theories over a century ago. It is not entirely fair to compare these theories to other models that are only a decade old. That's like asking the Wright brothers to race the Concorde. Freud and his psychodynamic colleagues deserve great credit for breaking new ground. Standing at a distance a century later, one has to be impressed by the extraordinary impact that psychodynamic theory has had on modern thought. No other theoretical perspective in psychology has been as influential, except for the one we turn to next—behaviorism.

Behavioral Perspectives

LEARNING OBJECTIVES

● *Describe Pavlov's classical conditioning and its contribution to understanding personality.*

● *Discuss how Skinner's principles of operant conditioning can be applied to personality development.*

● *Describe Bandura's social learning theory and his concept of self-efficacy.*

● *Evaluate the strengths and weaknesses of behavioral theories of personality.*

Behaviorism **is a theoretical orientation based on the premise that scientific psychology should study observable behavior.** Behaviorism has been a major school of thought in psychology since 1913, when John B. Watson published an influential article. Watson argued that psychology should abandon its earlier focus on the mind and mental processes and focus exclusively on overt behavior. He contended that psychology could not study mental processes in a scientific manner because they are private and not accessible to public observation.

In completely rejecting mental processes as a suitable subject for scientific study, Watson took an extreme position that is no longer dominant among

FIGURE 2.7.

A behavioral view of personality. Behaviorists devote little attention to the structure of personality because it is unobservable, but they implicitly view personality as an individual's collection of response tendencies. A possible hierarchy of response tendencies for a specific stimulus situation is shown here.

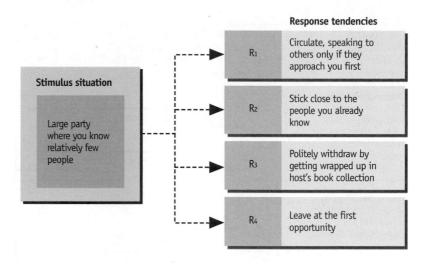

Response tendencies

Stimulus situation

Large party where you know relatively few people

R₁	Circulate, speaking to others only if they approach you first
R₂	Stick close to the people you already know
R₃	Politely withdraw by getting wrapped up in host's book collection
R₄	Leave at the first opportunity

modern behaviorists. Nonetheless, his influence was enormous, as psychology did shift its primary focus from the study of the mind to the study of behavior.

The behaviorists have shown little interest in internal personality structures similar to Freud's id, ego, and superego, because such structures can't be observed. They prefer to think in terms of response tendencies, which can be observed. Thus, most behaviorists view an individual's personality as a *collection of response tendencies that are tied to various stimulus situations.* A specific situation may be associated with a number of response tendencies that vary in strength, depending on an individual's past experience (see Figure 2.7).

Although behaviorists have shown relatively little interest in personality structure, they have focused extensively on personality *development.* They explain development the same way they explain everything else—through learning. Specifically, they focus on how children's response tendencies are shaped through classical conditioning, operant conditioning, and observational learning. Let's look at these processes.

Pavlov's Classical Conditioning

Do you go weak in the knees when you get a note at work that tells you to go see your boss? Do you get anxious when you're around important people? When you're driving, does your heart skip a beat at the sight of a police car—even when you're driving under the speed limit? If so, you probably acquired these common responses through classical conditioning. *Classical conditioning is a type of learning in which a neutral stimulus acquires the capacity to evoke a response that was originally evoked by another stimulus.* This process, which is also

Ivan Pavlov

called *respondent conditioning,* was first described back in 1903 by Ivan Pavlov.

Pavlov was a prominent Russian physiologist who did Nobel Prize–winning research on digestion. He was a dedicated scientist who was obsessed with his research. Legend has it that Pavlov severely reprimanded an assistant who was late for an experiment because he was trying to avoid street fighting in the midst of the Russian Revolution. The assistant defended his tardiness, saying, "But Professor, there's a revolution going on, with shooting in the streets!" Pavlov supposedly replied, "Next time there's a revolution, get up earlier!" (Fancher, 1979; Gantt, 1975).

THE CONDITIONED REFLEX

Pavlov (1906) was studying digestive processes in dogs when he discovered that the dogs could be trained to salivate in response to the sound of a tone. What was so significant about a dog salivating when a tone was rung? The key was that the tone started out as a *neutral* stimulus; that is, originally it did not produce the response of salivation (after all, why should it?). However, Pavlov managed to change that by pairing the tone with a stimulus (meat powder) that did produce the salivation response. Through this process, the tone acquired the capacity to trigger the response of salivation. What Pavlov had demonstrated was *how learned reflexes are acquired.*

At this point we need to introduce the special vocabulary of classical conditioning. In Pavlov's experiment the bond between the meat powder and salivation was a natural association that was not created through conditioning. In unconditioned bonds, **the unconditioned stimulus (UCS) is a stimulus that evokes an unconditioned response without previous conditioning. The *unconditioned response (UCR)* is an unlearned reaction to an unconditioned stimulus that occurs without previous conditioning.**

In contrast, the link between the tone and salivation

FIGURE 2.8.

The process of classical conditioning. The sequence of events in classical conditioning is outlined here. As you encounter new examples of classical conditioning throughout the book, we will see diagrams like that shown in the fourth panel, which summarizes the process.

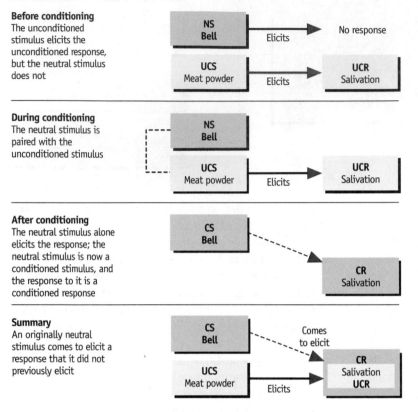

Before conditioning
The unconditioned stimulus elicits the unconditioned response, but the neutral stimulus does not

During conditioning
The neutral stimulus is paired with the unconditioned stimulus

After conditioning
The neutral stimulus alone elicits the response; the neutral stimulus is now a conditioned stimulus, and the response to it is a conditioned response

Summary
An originally neutral stimulus comes to elicit a response that it did not previously elicit

was established through conditioning. In conditioned bonds, **the *conditioned stimulus (CS)* is a previously neutral stimulus that has acquired the capacity to evoke a conditioned response through conditioning. The *conditioned response (CR)* is a learned reaction to a conditioned stimulus that occurs because of previous conditioning.** Note that the unconditioned response and conditioned response often involve the same behavior (although there may be subtle differences). In Pavlov's initial demonstration, salivation was an unconditioned response when evoked by the UCS (meat powder) and a conditioned response when evoked by the CS (the tone). The procedures involved in classical conditioning are outlined in Figure 2.8.

Pavlov's discovery came to be called the *conditioned reflex.* Classically conditioned responses are viewed as reflexes because most of them are relatively involuntary. Responses that are a product of classical conditioning are said to be *elicited.* This word is meant to convey the idea that these responses are triggered automatically.

CLASSICAL CONDITIONING IN EVERYDAY LIFE

What is the role of classical conditioning in shaping personality in everyday life? Previously, it contributes to the acquisition of emotional responses, such as

anxieties, fears, and phobias (Merckelbach et al., 1989). This is a relatively small but important class of responses, as maladaptive emotional reactions underlie many adjustment problems. For example, one middle-aged woman reported being troubled by a bridge phobia so severe that she couldn't drive on interstate highways because of all the viaducts she would have to cross. She was able to pinpoint the source of her phobia. Many years before, when her family would drive to visit her grandmother, they had to cross a little-used, rickety, dilapidated bridge out in the countryside. Her father, in a misguided attempt at humor, made a major production out of these crossings. He would stop short of the bridge and carry on about the enormous danger of the crossing. Obviously, he thought the bridge was safe or he wouldn't have driven across it. However, the naive young girl was terrified by her father's scare tactics, and the bridge became a conditioned stimulus eliciting great fear (see Figure 2.9). Unfortunately, the fear spilled over to all bridges, and 40 years later she was still carrying the burden of this phobia. Although a number of processes can cause phobias (Marks, 1987), it is clear that classical conditioning is responsible for many of our irrational fears.

Classical conditioning also appears to account for more realistic and moderate anxiety. For example, imagine a news reporter in a high-pressure job where he consistently gets negative feedback about his work from his bosses. The negative comments from his supervisors function as a UCS eliciting anxiety. These reprimands are paired with the noise and sight of the newsroom, so that the newsroom becomes a CS triggering anxiety, even when his supervisors are absent (see Figure 2.10). Our poor reporter might even reach a

FIGURE 2.9.

Classical conditioning of a phobia. Many emotional responses that would otherwise be puzzling can be explained as a result of classical conditioning. In the case of the woman's bridge phobia, the fear originally elicited by her father's scare tactics became a conditioned response to the stimulus of bridges.

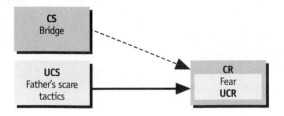

FIGURE 2.10.

Classical conditioning of anxiety. A stimulus (in this case, a newsroom) that is frequently paired with anxiety-arousing events (reprimands and criticism) may come to elicit anxiety by itself, through classical conditioning.

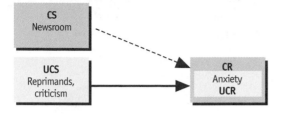

point at which the mere *thought* of the newsroom elicits anxiety when he is elsewhere.

Fortunately, not every frightening experience leaves a conditioned fear in its wake. A variety of factors influence whether a conditioned response is acquired in a particular situation. Furthermore, a newly formed stimulus-response bond does not necessarily last indefinitely. The right circumstances can lead to **extinction—the gradual weakening and disappearance of a conditioned response tendency.** What leads to extinction in classical conditioning? The consistent presentation of the CS *alone*, without the UCS. For example, when Pavlov consistently presented *only* the tone to a previously conditioned dog, the tone gradually stopped eliciting the response of salivation. How long it takes to extinguish a conditioned response depends on many factors. Foremost among them is the strength of the conditioned bond when extinction begins. Some conditioned responses extinguish very quickly, while others are very difficult to weaken.

Skinner's Operant Conditioning

Even Pavlov recognized that classical conditioning is not the only form of conditioning. Classical conditioning best explains reflexive responding controlled by stimuli that *precede* the response. However, both animals and humans make many responses that don't fit this description. Consider the response you are engaging in right now—studying. It is definitely not a reflex (life might be easier if it were). The stimuli that govern it (exams and grades) do not precede it. Instead, your studying response is mainly influenced by events that follow it—specifically, its *consequences*.

This kind of learning is called *operant conditioning*. **Operant conditioning is a form of learning in which voluntary responses come to be controlled by their consequences.** Operant conditioning probably governs a larger share of human behavior than classical conditioning, since most human responses are voluntary rather than reflexive. Because they are voluntary, operant responses are said to be *emitted* rather than *elicited*.

The study of operant conditioning was led by B. F. Skinner (1953, 1974, 1990), a Harvard University psychologist who spent most of his career studying simple responses made by laboratory rats and pigeons. The fundamental principle of operant conditioning is uncommonly simple. Skinner demonstrated that *organisms tend to repeat those responses that are followed by favorable consequences, and that they tend not to repeat those responses that are followed by neutral or unfavorable consequences.* In Skinner's scheme, favorable, neutral, and unfavorable consequences involve reinforcement, extinction, and punishment, respectively. We'll look at each of these concepts in turn.

B. F. Skinner

THE POWER OF REINFORCEMENT

According to Skinner, reinforcement can occur in two ways, which he called *positive reinforcement* and *negative reinforcement*. **Positive reinforcement occurs when a response is strengthened (increases in frequency) because it is followed by the arrival of a (presumably) pleasant stimulus.** Positive reinforcement is roughly synonymous with the concept of reward. Notice, however, that reinforcement is defined *after the fact*, in

Skinner placed rats and other animal subjects in controlled environments where reinforcement could be regulated and responses accurately measured.

terms of its effect on behavior. Why? Because reinforcement is subjective. Something that serves as a reinforcer for one person may not function as a reinforcer for another. For example, peer approval is a potent reinforcer for most people, but not all.

Positive reinforcement motivates much of everyday behavior. You study hard because good grades are likely to follow as a result. You go to work because this behavior produces paychecks. Perhaps you work extra hard in the hopes of winning a promotion or a pay raise. In each of these examples, certain responses occur because they have led to positive outcomes in the past.

Positive reinforcement influences personality development in a straightforward way. Responses followed by pleasant outcomes are strengthened and tend to become habitual patterns of behavior. For example, a youngster might clown around in class and gain appreciative comments and smiles from schoolmates. This social approval will probably reinforce clowning-around behavior (see Figure 2.11). If such behavior is reinforced with some regularity, it will gradually become an integral element of the youth's personality. Similarly, whether or not a youngster develops traits such as independence, assertiveness, or selfishness depends on whether the child is reinforced for such behaviors by parents and by other influential persons.

Negative reinforcement **occurs when a response is strengthened (increases in frequency) because it is followed by the removal of a (presumably) unpleasant stimulus.** Don't let the word *negative* here confuse you. Negative reinforcement is reinforcement. Like positive reinforcement, it strengthens a response. However, this strengthening occurs because the response gets rid of an aversive stimulus. Consider a few examples: You rush home in the winter to get out of the cold. You clean your house to get rid of a mess. Parents give in to their child's begging to halt his whining.

Negative reinforcement plays a major role in the development of avoidance tendencies. As you may have noticed, many people tend to avoid facing up to awkward situations and sticky personal problems. This personality trait typically develops because avoidance behavior gets rid of anxiety and is therefore negatively reinforced. Recall our imaginary newspaper reporter, whose work environment (the newsroom) elicits anxi-

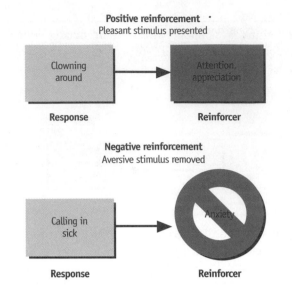

FIGURE 2.11.

Positive and negative reinforcement in operant conditioning. Positive reinforcement occurs when a response is followed by a favorable outcome, resulting in the response being strengthened. In negative reinforcement, the removal (symbolized here by the "No" sign) of an aversive stimulus serves as a reinforcer. Negative reinforcement produces the same result as positive reinforcement: The person's tendency to emit the reinforced response is strengthened (the response becomes more frequent).

ety (due to classical conditioning). He might notice that on days when he calls in sick, his anxiety evaporates, so that this response is gradually strengthened—through negative reinforcement (shown in Figure 2.11). If his avoidance behavior continues to be successful in reducing his anxiety, it might carry over into other areas of his life and become a central aspect of his personality.

EXTINCTION AND PUNISHMENT

Like the effects of classical conditioning, the effects of operant conditioning may not last forever. In both types of conditioning, *extinction* refers to the gradual weakening and disappearance of a response. In operant conditioning, extinction begins when a previously reinforced response stops producing positive consequences. As extinction progresses, the response typically becomes less and less frequent and eventually disappears.

Thus, the response tendencies that make up one's personality are not necessarily permanent. For example, the youngster who found that his classmates reinforced clowning around in grade school might find that his attempts at comedy earn nothing but indifferent stares in high school. This termination of reinforcement would probably lead to the gradual extinction of the clowning-around behavior. How quickly an operant response extinguishes depends on many factors in the person's earlier reinforcement history.

Some responses may be weakened by punishment. In Skinner's scheme, *punishment* **occurs when a response is weakened (decreases in frequency) because it is followed by the arrival of a (presumably) unpleasant stimulus.** The concept of punishment in operant conditioning confuses many students on two counts. First, it is often mixed up with negative reinforcement because both involve aversive stimuli. Please note, however, that they are altogether different events with opposite outcomes! In negative reinforcement, a response leads to the removal of something aversive, and this response is strengthened. In punishment, a response leads to the arrival of something aversive, and this response tends to be weakened.

The second source of confusion involves viewing punishment as only a disciplinary procedure used by parents, teachers, and other authority figures. In the operant model, punishment occurs whenever a response leads to negative consequences. Defined in this way, the concept goes far beyond actions such as parents spanking children or teachers handing out detentions. For example, if you wear a new outfit and your friends make fun of it and hurt your feelings, your behavior has been punished, and your tendency to wear this clothing will decline. Similarly, if you go to a restaurant and have a horrible meal, in Skinner's terminology your response has led to punishment.

The impact of punishment on personality development is just the opposite of reinforcement. Generally speaking, those patterns of behavior that lead to punishing (that is, negative) consequences tend to be weakened. For instance, if your impulsive decisions always backfire, your tendency to be impulsive should decline.

According to Skinner (1987), conditioning in humans operates much as it does in the rats and pigeons that he has studied in his laboratory. Hence, he assumes that conditioning strengthens and weakens people's response tendencies "mechanically"—that is, without their conscious participation. Like John Watson (1913) before him, Skinner asserts that we can explain behavior without being concerned about individuals' mental processes.

Skinner's ideas continue to be very influential, but his mechanical view of conditioning has not gone unchallenged by other behaviorists. Theorists such as Albert Bandura have developed somewhat different behavioral models in which cognition plays a role. *Cognition* **refers to the thought processes involved in acquiring knowledge.** In other words, cognition is another name for the mental processes that behaviorists have traditionally shown little interest in.

Bandura and Social Learning Theory

Albert Bandura is one of several behaviorists who have added a cognitive flavor to behaviorism since the 1960s. Bandura (1977), Walter Mischel (1973), and Julian Rotter (1982) take issue with Skinner's view. They point out that humans obviously are conscious, thinking, feeling beings. Moreover, these theorists argue that in neglecting cognitive processes, Skinner ignores the most distinctive and important feature of human behavior. Bandura and like-minded theorists call their modified brand of behaviorism *social learning theory.*

Albert Bandura

Bandura (1977, 1986) agrees with the basic thrust of behaviorism in that he believes that personality is largely shaped through learning. However, he contends that conditioning is not a mechanical process in which people are passive participants. Instead, he maintains that individuals actively seek out and process information about their environment in order to maximize their favorable outcomes.

OBSERVATIONAL LEARNING

Bandura's foremost theoretical contribution has been his description of observational learning. *Observational learning* **occurs when an organism's responding is influenced by the observation of others, who are called models.** Bandura does not view observational learning as entirely separate from classical and operant conditioning. Instead, he asserts that both classical and operant conditioning can take place indirectly when one person observes another's conditioning (see Figure 2.12).

To illustrate, suppose you observe a friend behaving assertively with a car salesman. Let's say that her assertiveness is reinforced by the exceptionally good

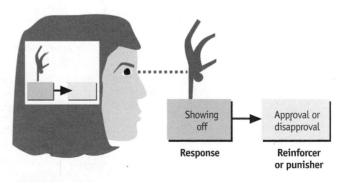

FIGURE 2.12.

Observational learning. In observational learning, an observer attends to and stores a mental representation of a model's behavior (for example, showing off by doing handstands) and its consequences (such as approval or disapproval from others). According to social learning theory, many of one's characteristic responses are acquired through observation of others' behavior.

buy she obtains on the car. Your own tendency to behave assertively with salespeople might well be strengthened as a result. Notice that the favorable consequence is experienced by your friend, not you. Your friend's tendency to bargain assertively should be reinforced directly. But your tendency to bargain assertively may also be reinforced indirectly.

The theories of Skinner and Pavlov make no allowance for this type of indirect learning. After all, this observational learning requires that you pay *attention* to your friend's behavior, that you *understand* its consequences, and that you store this *information* in *memory*. Obviously, attention, understanding, information, and memory involve cognition, which behaviorists used to ignore.

As social learning theory has been refined, it has become apparent that some models are more influential than others (Bandura, 1986). Both children and adults tend to imitate people they like or respect moreso than people they don't. People are also especially prone to imitate the behavior of those they consider attractive or powerful (such as rock stars). In addition, imitation is more likely when individuals see similarity between the model and themselves. Thus, children imitate same-gender role models somewhat more than other-gender models. Finally, as noted before, people are more likely to copy a model if they see the model's behavior leading to positive outcomes.

According to social learning theory, models have a great impact on personality development. Children learn to be assertive, conscientious, self-sufficient, dependable, easygoing, and so forth by observing others behaving in these ways. Parents, teachers, relatives, siblings, and peers serve as models for young children.

Bandura and his colleagues have done extensive research showing how models influence the development of aggressiveness, gender roles, and moral standards in children (Bandura, 1973; Bussey & Bandura, 1984; Mischel & Mischel, 1976). Their research on modeling and aggression has been particularly influential.

SELF-EFFICACY

Bandura (1990a, 1993) believes that *self-efficacy* is a crucial element of personality. **Self-efficacy is one's belief about one's ability to perform behaviors that should lead to expected outcomes.** When a person's self-efficacy is high, he or she feels confident in executing the responses necessary to earn reinforcers. When self-efficacy is low, the individual worries that the necessary responses may be beyond her or his abilities. Perceptions of self-efficacy are subjective and specific to different kinds of tasks. For instance, you might feel extremely confident about your ability to handle difficult social situations but doubtful about your ability to handle academic challenges. Although specific perceptions of self-efficacy predict behavior best, these perceptions are influenced by general feelings of self-efficacy, which can be measured with the scale shown in Figure 2.13 (Sherer et al., 1982).

Perceptions of self-efficacy can influence which challenges one tackles and how well one performs. Studies have found that feelings of greater self-efficacy are associated with greater success in giving up smoking and following an exercise regimen (Schwarzer & Fuchs, 1995), greater persistence and effort in academic pursuits and higher levels of academic performance (Zimmerman, 1995), enhanced performance in athletic competition (Bandura, 1990a), and consideration of a

FIGURE 2.13.

Sample items from the Self-Efficacy Scale. The eight items shown here are taken from the Self-Efficacy Scale, developed by Sherer et al. (1982), which is a 23-item measure of general expectations of self-efficacy that are not tied to specific situations. The more items you agree with, the stronger your self-efficacy is. High scores on the complete scale are predictive of vocational and educational success.

The Self-Efficacy Scale

Instructions: This questionnaire is a series of statements about your personal attitudes and traits. Each statement represents a commonly held belief. Read each statement and decide to what extent it describes you. There are no right or wrong answers. You will probably agree with some statements and disagree with others. Please indicate your own personal feelings about each statement below by marking the letter that describes your attitude or feeling. Please be very truthful and describe yourself as you really are, not as you would like to be.

A = Disagree strongly   D = Agree moderately
B = Disagree moderately   E = Agree strongly
C = Neither agree nor disagree

1. _____ When I make plans I am certain I can make them work.
2. _____ If I can't do a job the first time, I keep trying until I can.
3. _____ If I see someone I would like to meet, I go to that person instead of waiting for him or her to come to me.
4. _____ When I have something unpleasant to do, I stick to it until I finish it.
5. _____ When I decide to do something, I go right to work on it.
6. _____ When I'm trying to become friends with someone who seems uninterested at first, I don't give up very easily.
7. _____ Failure just makes me try harder.
8. _____ I am a self-reliant person.

broader range of occupations in making career choices (Bores-Rangel et al., 1990), among many other things.

Evaluating Behavioral Perpectives

Behavioral theories are firmly rooted in empirical research rather than clinical intuition. Pavlov's model has shed light on how conditioning can account for people's sometimes troublesome emotional responses. Skinner's work has demonstrated how personality is shaped by the consequences of behavior. Bandura's social learning theory has shown how people's observations mold their characteristic behavior.

Behaviorists, in particular Walter Mischel (1973, 1990), have also provided the most thorough account of why people are only moderately consistent in their behavior. For example, a person who is shy in one context might be quite outgoing in another. Other models of personality largely ignore this inconsistency. The behaviorists have shown that this inconsistency occurs because people behave in ways they think will lead to reinforcement in the situation at hand. In other words, situational factors play a significant role in controlling behavior.

Of course, each theoretical approach has its shortcomings, and the behavioral approach is no exception. Major lines of criticism include the following (Liebert & Spiegler, 1994; Maddi, 1989):

1. *Dilution of the behavioral approach.* The behaviorists used to be criticized because they neglected cognitive processes, which clearly are important factors in human behavior. The rise of social learning theory, which focuses heavily on cognitive factors, blunted this criticism. However, social learning theory undermines the foundation on which behaviorism was built—the idea that psychologists should study only observable behavior. Thus, some critics complain that behavioral theories aren't very behavioral anymore.

2. *Overdependence on animal research.* Many principles in behavioral theories were discovered through research on animals. Some critics, especially humanistic theorists, argue that behaviorists depend too much on animal research and that they indiscriminately generalize from the behavior of animals to the behavior of humans.

Humanistic Perspectives

LEARNING OBJECTIVES
● Discuss humanism as a school of thought in psychology.
● Explain Rogers's views on self-concept, development, and defensive behavior.
● Describe Maslow's hierarchy of needs and summarize his findings on self-actualizing persons.
● Evaluate the strengths and weaknesses of humanistic theories of personality.

Humanistic theory emerged in the 1950s as something of a backlash against the behavioral and psychodynamic theories. The principal charge hurled at these two models was that they were dehumanizing. Freudian theory was criticized for its belief that primitive, animalistic drives dominate behavior. Behaviorism was criticized for its preoccupation with animal research. Critics argued that both schools view people as helpless pawns controlled by their environment and their past, with little capacity for self-direction. Many of these critics blended into a loose alliance that was christened the "third force" in psychology because it surfaced as an alternative to the two dominant "forces" at the time (the psychodynamic and behavioral orientations).

This third force came to be known as humanism because of its exclusive interest in human behavior. *Humanism* **is a theoretical orientation that emphasizes the unique qualities of humans, especially their free will and their potential for personal growth.** Humanistic psychologists are interested only in issues important to human existence, such as love, creativity, loneliness, and personal growth. They do not believe that we can learn anything of any significance about the human condition from animal research.

Humanistic theorists take an optimistic view of human nature. In contrast to most psychodynamic and behavioral theorists, humanistic theorists believe (1) that human nature includes an innate drive toward personal growth, (2) that individuals have the freedom to chart their courses of action and are not pawns of their environment, and (3) that humans are largely conscious and rational beings who are not dominated by unconscious, irrational needs and conflicts. Humanistic theorists also maintain that one's subjective view of the world is more important than objective reality. According to this notion, if you *think* you are homely, or bright, or sociable, these beliefs will influence your behavior more than the actual realities of how homely, bright, or sociable you are.

The humanistic approach clearly provides a different perspective on personality than either the psychodynamic or behavioral approach. In this section we'll review the ideas of the two most influential humanistic theorists, Carl Rogers and Abraham Maslow.

Rogers's Person-Centered Theory

Carl Rogers (1951, 1961, 1980) was one of the founders of the human potential movement, which emphasizes personal growth through sensitivity training, encounter groups, and other exercises intended to help people get in touch with their true selves. Working at the University of Chicago in the 1940s, Rogers devised a major new approach to psychotherapy. Like Freud, Rogers based his personality theory on his extensive therapeutic interactions with many clients. Because of his emphasis on a person's subjective point of view, Rogers called his approach a *person-centered theory.*

Carl Rogers

THE SELF AND ITS DEVELOPMENT

Rogers viewed personality structure in terms of just one construct. He called this construct the self, although it is more widely known today as the *self-concept.* **A self-concept is a collection of beliefs about one's own nature, unique qualities, and typical behavior.** Your self-concept is your mental picture of yourself. It is a collection of self-perceptions. For example, a self-concept might include such beliefs as "I am easygoing" or "I am pretty" or "I am hard-working."

Rogers stressed the subjective nature of the self-concept. Your self-concept may not be entirely consistent with your actual experiences. To put it more bluntly, your self-concept may be inaccurate. Most people are prone to distort their experiences to some extent to promote a relatively favorable self-concept. For example, you may believe that you are quite bright academically, but your grade transcript might suggest otherwise. Rogers used the term ***incongruence* to refer to the disparity between one's self-concept and one's actual experience.** In contrast, if a person's self-concept is reasonably accurate, it is said to be *congruent* with reality. Everyone experiences *some* incongruence; the crucial issue is how much (see Figure 2.14). Rogers maintained that a great deal of incongruence undermines a person's psychological well-being.

In terms of personality development, Rogers was concerned with how childhood experiences promote congruence or incongruence. According to Rogers, everyone has a strong need for affection, love, and acceptance from others. Early in life, parents provide most of this affection. Rogers maintained that some parents make their affection *conditional.* That is, they make it depend on the child's behaving well and living up to expectations. When parental love seems conditional, children often distort and block out of their self-concept those experiences that make them feel unworthy of love. At the other end of the spectrum, Rogers asserted that some parents make their affection *unconditional.* Their children have less need to block out unworthy experiences because they have been assured that they are worthy of affection no matter what they do.

Rogers believed that unconditional love from parents fosters congruence and that conditional love fosters incongruence. He further theorized that individuals who grow up believing that affection from others (besides their parents) is conditional, go on to distort more and more of their experiences in order to feel worthy of acceptance from a wider and wider array of people, making the incongruence grow.

ANXIETY AND DEFENSE

According to Rogers, experiences that threaten people's personal views of themselves are the principal cause of troublesome anxiety. The more inaccurate your self-concept, the more likely you are to have experiences that clash with your self-perceptions. Thus, people with highly incongruent self-concepts are especially likely to be plagued by recurrent anxiety (see Figure 2.15).

To ward off this anxiety, such people often behave defensively. Thus, they ignore, deny, and twist reality to protect their self-concept. Consider a young woman who, like most of us, considers herself a "nice person." Let us suppose that in reality she is rather conceited and selfish, and she gets feedback from both boyfriends and girlfriends that she is a "self-centered, snotty brat." How might she react in order to protect her self-concept? She might ignore or block out those occasions when she behaves selfishly and then deny the accusations by her friends that she is self-centered. She might also attribute her girlfriends' negative comments to their jealousy of her good looks and blame the boyfriends'

<u>FIGURE 2.14.</u>
Rogers's view of personality structure. In Rogers's model, the self-concept is the only important structural construct. However, Rogers acknowledged that one's self-concept may not jibe with the realities of one's actual experience—a condition called incongruence. Different people have varied amounts of incongruence between their self-concept and reality.

Self-concept   Actual experience

Congruence
Self-concept meshes well with actual experience (some incongruence is probably unavoidable)

Self-concept   Actual experience

Incongruence
Self-concept does not mesh well with actual experience

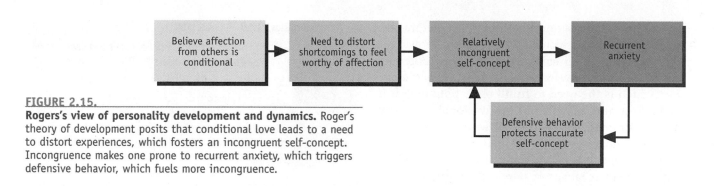

FIGURE 2.15.

Rogers's view of personality development and dynamics. Roger's theory of development posits that conditional love leads to a need to distort experiences, which fosters an incongruent self-concept. Incongruence makes one prone to recurrent anxiety, which triggers defensive behavior, which fuels more incongruence.

negative remarks on their disappointment because she won't get more serious with them. Meanwhile, she might start doing some kind of charity work to show everyone (including herself) that she really is a nice person. As you can see, people often go to great lengths to defend their self-concept.

Rogers's theory can explain defensive behavior and personality disturbances, but he also emphasized the importance of psychological health. Rogers held that psychological health is rooted in a congruent self-concept. In turn, congruence is rooted in a sense of personal worth, which stems from a childhood saturated with unconditional affection from parents and others. These themes are similar to those emphasized by the other major humanistic theorist, Abraham Maslow.

Maslow's Theory of Self-Actualization

Abraham Maslow grew up in Brooklyn and spent much of his career at Brandeis University, where he provided crucial leadership for the fledgling humanistic movement. Like Rogers, Maslow (1968, 1970) argued that psychology should take a greater interest in the nature of the healthy personality, instead of dwelling on the causes of disorders. "To oversimplify the matter somewhat," he said, "it is as if Freud supplied to us the sick half of

psychology and we must now fill it out with the healthy half" (Maslow, 1968, p. 5). Maslow's key contributions were his analysis of how motives are organized hierarchically and his description of the healthy personality.

HIERARCHY OF NEEDS

Maslow proposed that human motives are organized into a *hierarchy of needs*—a systematic arrangement of needs, according to priority, in which basic needs must be met before less basic needs are aroused. This hierarchical arrangement is usually portrayed as a pyramid (see Figure 2.16). The needs toward the bottom of the pyramid, such as physiological or security needs, are the most basic. Higher levels in the pyramid consist of progressively less basic needs. When a person manages to satisfy a level of needs reasonably well (complete satisfaction is not necessary), *this satisfaction activates needs at the next level.*

Like Rogers, Maslow argued that humans have an innate drive toward personal growth—that is, evolution toward a higher state of being. Thus, he described

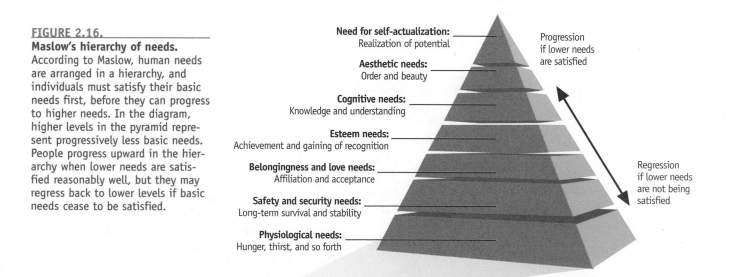

FIGURE 2.16.

Maslow's hierarchy of needs. According to Maslow, human needs are arranged in a hierarchy, and individuals must satisfy their basic needs first, before they can progress to higher needs. In the diagram, higher levels in the pyramid represent progressively less basic needs. People progress upward in the hierarchy when lower needs are satisfied reasonably well, but they may regress back to lower levels if basic needs cease to be satisfied.

Need for self-actualization: Realization of potential

Aesthetic needs: Order and beauty

Cognitive needs: Knowledge and understanding

Esteem needs: Achievement and gaining of recognition

Belongingness and love needs: Affiliation and acceptance

Safety and security needs: Long-term survival and stability

Physiological needs: Hunger, thirst, and so forth

Progression if lower needs are satisfied

Regression if lower needs are not being satisfied

the needs in the uppermost reaches of his hierarchy as *growth needs*. These include the needs for knowledge, understanding, order, and aesthetic beauty. Foremost among the growth needs is the ***need for self-actualization,*** **which is the need to fulfill one's potential; it is the highest need in Maslow's motivational hierarchy.** Maslow summarized this concept with a simple statement: "What a man *can* be, he *must* be." According to Maslow, people will be frustrated if they are unable to fully utilize their talents or pursue their true interests. For example, if you have great musical talent but must work as an accountant, or if you have scholarly interests but must work as a sales clerk, your need for self-actualization will be thwarted.

THE HEALTHY PERSONALITY

Because of his interest in self-actualization, Maslow set out to discover the nature of the healthy personality. He tried to identify people of exceptional mental health so that he could investigate their characteristics. In one case, he used psychological tests and interviews to sort out the healthiest 1% of a sizable population of college students. He also studied admired historical figures (such as Thomas Jefferson and psychologist-philosopher William James) and personal acquaintances characterized by superior adjustment. Over a period of years, he accumulated his case histories and gradually sketched, in broad strokes, a picture of ideal psychological health.

Maslow called people with exceptionally healthy personalities *self-actualizing persons* because of their commitment to continued personal growth. He identified various traits characteristic of self-actualizing people, which are listed in Figure 2.17. In brief, Maslow found that self-actualizers are accurately tuned in to reality and that they are at peace with themselves. He found that they are open and spontaneous and that they retain a fresh appreciation of the world around them. Socially, they are sensitive to others' needs and enjoy rewarding interpersonal relations. However, they are not dependent on others for approval, nor are they uncomfortable with solitude. They thrive on their work, and

they enjoy their sense of humor. Maslow also noted that they enjoy "peak experiences" (profound emotional highs) more often than others. Finally, he found that they strike a nice balance between many polarities in personality, so that they can be both childlike and mature, rational and intuitive, conforming and rebellious.

FIGURE 2.17.
Characteristics of self-actualizing people.
Humanistic theorists emphasize psychological health instead of maladjustment. Maslow's sketch of the self-actualizing person provides a provocative picture of the healthy personality.

Characteristics of Self-Actualizing People	
• Clear, efficient perception of reality and comfortable relations with it	• Mystical and peak experiences
• Spontaneity, simplicity, and naturalness	• Feelings of kinship and identification with the human race
• Problem centering (having something outside themselves they "must" do as a mission)	• Strong friendships, but limited in number
• Detachment and need for privacy	• Democratic character structure
• Autonomy, independence of culture and environment	• Ethical discrimination between means and ends, between good and evil
• Continued freshness of appreciation	• Philosophical, unhostile sense of humor
	• Balance between polarities in personality

PEANUTS reprinted by permission of United Feature Syndicate, Inc.

Evaluating Humanistic Perspectives

The humanists added a refreshing perspective to the study of personality. Their argument that a person's subjective views may be more important than objective reality has proven compelling. Today, even behavioral theorists have begun to consider subjective personal factors such as beliefs and expectations. The humanistic approach also deserves credit for making the self-concept an important construct in psychology. Finally, the humanists have often been applauded for focusing attention on the issue of what constitutes a healthy personality.

Of course, there is a negative side to the balance sheet as well. Critics have identified some weaknesses in the humanistic approach to personality, including the following (Burger, 1993):

1. *Poor testability.* Like psychodynamic theorists, the humanists have been criticized for proposing hypotheses that are difficult to put to a scientific test. Humanistic concepts like personal growth and self-actualization are difficult to define and measure.

2. *Unrealistic view of human nature.* Critics also charge that the humanists have been overly optimistic in their assumptions about human nature and unrealistic in their descriptions of the healthy personality. For instance, Maslow's self-actualizing people sound *perfect*. In reality, Maslow had a hard time finding self-actualizing persons. When he searched among the living, the results were so disappointing that he turned to the study of historical figures. Thus, humanistic portraits of psychological health are perhaps a bit unrealistic.

3. *Inadequate evidence.* Humanistic theories are based primarily on discerning but uncontrolled observations in clinical settings. Case studies can be valuable in generating ideas, but they are ill-suited for building a solid database. More experimental research is needed to catch up with the theorizing in the humanistic camp. This is precisely the opposite of the situation that you'll encounter in the next section, on biological perspectives, where more theorizing is needed to catch up with the research.

Biological Perspectives

LEARNING OBJECTIVES

- *Describe Eysenck's views on personality structure and development.*
- *Summarize recent twin studies that support the idea that personality is largely inherited.*
- *Summarize evolutionary analyses of why certain personality traits appear to be important.*
- *Evaluate the strengths and weaknesses of biological theories of personality.*

Like many identical twins reared apart, Jim Lewis and Jim Springer found they had been leading eerily similar lives. Separated four weeks after birth in 1940, the Jim twins grew up 45 miles apart in Ohio and were reunited in 1979. Eventually, they discovered that both drove the same model blue Chevrolet, chain-smoked Salems, chewed their fingernails, and owned dogs named Toy. Each had spent a good deal of time vacationing at the same three-block strip of beach in Florida. More important, when tested for such personality traits as flexibility, self-control, and sociability, the twins responded almost exactly alike. [Leo, 1987, p. 63]

So began a *Time* magazine summary of a major twin study conducted at the University of Minnesota, where investigators have been exploring the hereditary roots of personality. The research team has managed to locate and complete testing on 44 rare pairs of identical twins separated early in life. Not all the twin pairs have been as similar as Jim Lewis and Jim Springer, but many of the parallels have been uncanny. Identical twins Oskar Stohr and Jack Yufe were separated soon after birth. Oskar was sent to a Nazi-run school in Czechoslovakia, while Jack was raised in a Jewish home on a Caribbean

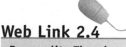

Web Link 2.4

Personality Theories
C. George Boeree, who teaches personality theory at Shippensburg University, has assembled an online textbook that discusses more than 20 important personality theorists in depth. All of the important figures cited in this chapter (except for the behaviorists like Skinner and Pavlov) receive attention at this valuable site.

The striking parallels in the lives of Jim Lewis and Jim Springer, identical twins separated soon after birth and reunited as adults, suggest that heredity may have a powerful impact on personality.

island. When they were reunited for the first time during middle age, they both showed up wearing similar mustaches, haircuts, shirts, and wire-rimmed glasses. A pair of previously separated female twins both arrived at the Minneapolis airport wearing seven rings on their fingers. One had a son named Richard Andrew, and the other had a son named Andrew Richard! Still another pair of separated twin sisters shared the same phobia of water. They even dealt with it in the same peculiar way—by backing into the ocean.

Could personality be largely inherited? These anecdotal reports of striking resemblances between identical twins reared apart certainly raise this possibility. In this section we'll discuss Hans Eysenck's theory, which emphasizes the influence of heredity, and look at behavioral genetics and evolutionary perspectives on personality.

Eysenck's Theory

Hans Eysenck was born in Germany but fled to London during the era of Nazi rule. He went on to become one of Britain's most prominent psychologists. According to Eysenck (1967), "Personality is determined to a large extent by a person's genes" (p. 20). How is heredity linked to personality in Eysenck's model? In part, through conditioning concepts borrowed from behavioral theory. Eysenck (1967, 1982, 1991) theorizes that some people can be conditioned more readily than others because of inherited differences in their physiological functioning (specifically, their level of arousal). These variations in "conditionability" are assumed to influence the personality traits that people acquire through conditioning.

Eysenck views personality structure as a hierarchy of traits. Numerous superficial traits are derived from a smaller number of more basic traits, which are derived from a handful of fundamental higher-order traits, as shown in Figure 2.18. Eysenck has shown a special interest in explaining variations in *extraversion-introversion*, the trait dimension first described years earlier by Carl Jung. He has proposed that introverts tend to have higher levels of physiological arousal than extraverts. This higher arousal purportedly motivates them to avoid social situations that will further elevate their arousal and makes them more easily conditioned than extraverts. According to Eysenck, people who condition easily acquire more conditioned inhibitions than others. These inhibitions, coupled with their relatively high arousal, make them more bashful, tentative, and uneasy in social situations. This social discomfort leads them to turn inward. Hence, they become introverted.

Is there any research to support Eysenck's explanation of the origins of introversion? Yes, but the evidence is rather inconsistent. Many studies *have* found that introverts tend to exhibit higher levels of arousal than extraverts (Bullock & Gilliland, 1993; Wilson, 1990),

Hans Eysenck

FIGURE 2.18.

Eysenck's model of personality structure. Eysenck describes personality structure as a hierarchy of traits. In this scheme, a few higher-order traits (such as extraversion) determine a host of lower-order traits (such as sociability), which determine habitual responses (such as going to lots of parties). In turn, these habitual responses determine specific responses to situations.

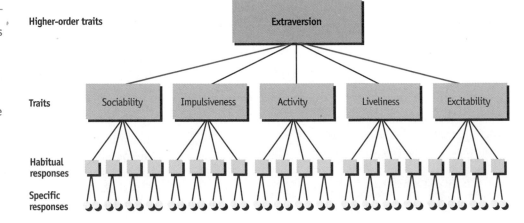

but many studies have also failed to find the predicted differences (Gale, 1983). Even Eysenck (1990) acknowledges that the evidence on his theory is mixed and that the concept of physiological arousal has turned out to be much more multifaceted and difficult to measure than he originally anticipated. It will be interesting to see whether more consistent results are obtained in the future, as investigators improve and refine their methods for measuring physiological arousal.

Recent Research in Behavioral Genetics

Recent twin studies have provided impressive support for Eysenck's hypothesis that personality is largely inherited. In *twin studies* researchers assess hereditary influence by comparing the resemblance of identical twins and fraternal twins on a trait. The logic underlying this comparison is as follows. *Identical twins* emerge from one egg that splits, so that their genetic makeup is exactly the same (100% overlap). *Fraternal twins* result when two eggs are fertilized simultaneously; their genetic overlap is only 50%. Both types of twins *usually* grow up in the same home, at the same time, exposed to the same relatives, neighbors, peers, teachers, events, and so forth. Thus, both kinds of twins normally develop under similar environmental conditions, but identical twins share more genetic kinship. Hence, if sets of identical twins exhibit more personality resemblance than sets of fraternal twins, this greater similarity is probably attributable to heredity rather than environment.

The accumulating evidence from twin studies suggests that heredity is a key factor shaping personality (Rowe, 1997). For instance, Figure 2.19 shows the mean correlations observed for identical and fraternal twins in studies of the Big Five personality traits summarized by Loehlin (1992). Higher correlations are indicative of greater similarity on a trait. On all five traits, identical twins have been found to be much more similar than fraternal twins. Based on these and many other data, Loehlin (1992) concludes that genetic factors exert considerable influence over personality.

Some skeptics still wonder whether identical twins might exhibit more personality resemblance than fraternal twins because they are raised more similarly. In other words, they wonder whether environmental factors (rather than heredity) could be responsible for identical twins' greater similarity. This nagging question can be answered only by studying identical twins who have been reared apart. Which is where the twin study at the University of Minnesota comes in.

The Minnesota study (Tellegen et al., 1988) is the first to administer the same personality test to identical and fraternal twins reared together as well as apart. Most of the twins reared apart were separated quite

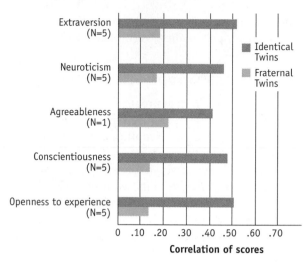

FIGURE 2.19.

Twin studies of personality. Loehlin (1992) has summarized the results of twin studies that have examined the Big Five personality traits. The N under each trait indicates the number of twin studies that have examined that trait. The chart plots the average correlations obtained for identical and fraternal twins in these studies. As you can see, identical twins have shown greater resemblance in personality than fraternal twins have, suggesting that personality is partly inherited.

early in life (median age of 2.5 months) and remained separated for a long time (median period of almost 34 years). Nonetheless, on all three of the higher-order traits examined, the identical twins reared apart displayed more personality resemblance than fraternal twins reared together. Based on the pattern of correlations observed, the researchers estimate that genetic inheritance accounts for at least 50% of the variation among people in personality.

Research on the genetic bases of personality has inadvertently turned up another interesting finding. A number of recent studies have found that shared family environment has surprisingly little impact on personality (Beer, Arnold, & Loehlin, 1998; Halverson & Wampler, 1997). For many years, social scientists have assumed that the environment shared by children growing up together leads to some personality resemblance among them. However, recent findings seriously undermine this widespread belief.

These findings have led Robert Plomin (1990) to ask, "Why are children in the same family so different from one another?" Researchers have only just begun to explore this perplexing question. Plomin speculates that children in the same family experience home environments that are not nearly as homogeneous as previously assumed. He notes that children in the same home may be treated quite differently, because gender and birth order can influence parents' approaches to child-rearing. Temperamental differences between children may also evoke differences in styles of parenting. Focusing on how environmental factors vary *within* families represents a promising new way to explore the determinants of personality (Vernon et al., 1997).

The Evolutionary Approach to Personality

In the realm of biological approaches to personality, the most recent development has been the emergence of an evolutionary perspective. Evolutionary psychologists assert that personality has a biological basis because natural selection has favored certain traits over the course of human history. Thus, evolutionary analyses focus on how various personality traits—and the ability to recognize these traits in others—may have contributed to reproductive fitness in ancestral human populations.

For example, David Buss (1991, 1995, 1997) has argued that the Big Five personality traits stand out as important dimensions of personality across a variety of cultures because those traits have had significant adaptive implications. Buss points out that humans historically have depended heavily on groups, which afford protection from predators or enemies, opportunities for sharing food, and a diverse array of other benefits. In the context of these group interactions, people have had to make difficult but crucial judgments about the characteristics of others, asking such questions as: Who will make a good member of my coalition? Who can I depend on when in need? Who will share their resources? Thus, Buss (1995) argues, "those individuals able to accurately discern and act upon these individual differences likely enjoyed a considerable reproductive advantage" (p. 22). According to Buss, the Big Five emerge as fundamental dimensions of personality because humans have evolved special sensitivity to variations in the ability to bond with others (extraversion), the willingness to cooperate and collaborate (agreeableness), the tendency to be reliable and ethical (conscientiousness), the capacity to be an innovative problem solver (openness to experience), and the ability to handle stress (low neuroticism). In a nutshell, the Big Five supposedly reflect the most salient features of ancestral humans' adaptive landscape.

Evaluating Biological Perspectives

Although evolutionary analyses of personality are pretty speculative, recent research in behavioral genetics has provided convincing evidence that biological factors help shape personality. Nonetheless, we must take note of some weaknesses in biological approaches to personality:

1. *Problems with estimates of hereditary influence.* Efforts to carve personality into genetic and environmental components with statistics are ultimately artificial. The effects of heredity and environment are twisted together in complicated interactions that can't be separated cleanly (Brody & Crowley, 1995; Scarr, 1992). Although estimates of the genetic component in personality sound precise, they are estimates based on a complicated chain of inferences that are subject to debate.

2. *Lack of adequate theory.* At present there is no comprehensive biological theory of personality. Eysenck's model does not provide a systematic overview of how biological factors govern personality development (and it was never intended to). Evolutionary analyses of personality are even more limited in scope. Additional theoretical work is needed to catch up with recent empirical findings on the biological basis for personality.

An Epilogue on Theoretical Diversity

LEARNING OBJECTIVES

● Discuss why the subject of personality has generated so much theoretical diversity.
● Compare and contrast the personality theories of Freud, Skinner, Rogers, and Eysenck.

Figure 2.20 provides a comparative overview of the ideas of Freud, Skinner, Rogers, and Eysenck, as representatives of the psychodynamic, behavioral, humanistic, and biological approaches to personality. Most of this information was covered in the chapter, but the figure organizes it so that the similarities and differences between the theories become more apparent. As you can see, there are many fundamental points of disagreement. Our review of perspectives on personality should have made one thing abundantly clear: Psychology is marked by theoretical diversity.

Why do we have so many competing points of view? One reason is that no single theory can adequately explain everything that we know about personality. Sometimes different theories focus on different aspects of behavior. Sometimes there is simply more than one way to look at something. Is the glass half empty or half full? Obviously, it is both. To take an example from another science, physicists wrestled for years with the nature of light. Is it a wave, or is it a particle? In the end, it proved useful to think of light sometimes as a wave, and sometimes as a particle. Similarly, if a business executive lashes out at her employees with stinging criticism, is she releasing pent-up aggressive urges (a psychoanalytic view)? Is she making a habitual response to the stimulus of incompetent work (a behavioral view)? Is she trying to act like a tough boss because that's a key

FIGURE 2.20.

Comparison of four theoretical perspectives on personality. This chart compares the theories of Freud, Skinner, Rogers, and Eysenck to highlight the similarities and differences among the psychodynamic, behavioral, humanistic, and biological approaches to personality.

Overview of Four Approaches to Personality			
	Sigmund Freud: A psychodynamic view	**B. F. Skinner: A behavioral view**	**Carl Rogers: A humanistic view**	**Hans Eysenck: A biological view**
Source of data and observations	Case studies from clinical practice of psychoanalysis	Laboratory experiments primarily with animals	Case studies from clinical practice of client-centered therapy	Twin, family, and adoption studies of hereditary influence; factor analysis studies of personality structure
Key motivational forces	Sex and aggression; need to reduce tension produced by internal conflicts	Pursuit of primary (unlearned) and secondary (learned) reinforcers; priorities depend on personal history	Actualizing tendency (need for personal growth) and self-actualizing tendency (need to maintain self-concept)	No specific motivational forces singled out
Model of personality structure	Three interacting components (id, ego, superego) operating at three levels of consciousness	Collection of response tendencies tied to specific stimulus situations	Self-concept, which may or may not be congruent with actual experience	Hierarchy of traits, with specific traits derived from more fundamental, general traits
View of personality development	Emphasis on fixation or progress through psychosexual stages; experiences in early childhood leave lasting mark on adult personality	Personality evolves gradually over the life span (not in stages); responses followed by reinforcement become more frequent	Children who receive unconditional love have less need to be defensive; they develop more accurate, congruent self-concepts; conditional love fosters incongruence	Emphasis on unfolding of genetic blueprint with maturation; inherited predispositions interact with learning experiences
Roots of disorders	Unconscious fixations and unresolved conflicts from childhood, usually centered around sex and aggression	Maladaptive behavior due to faulty learning; the "symptom" is the problem, not a sign of underlying disease	Incongruence between self-concept and actual experience; overdependence on others for approval and sense of worth	Genetic vulnerability activated in part by environmental factors
Importance of nature (biology, heredity) vs. nurture (environment, experience)	Nature: emphasis on biological basis of instinctual drives	Nurture: strong emphasis on learning, conditioning, role of experience	Nurture: interested in innate potentials, but humanists believe we can rise above our biological heritage	Nature: strong emphasis on how hereditary predispositions shape our personalities
Importance of person factors vs. situation factors	Person: main interest is in internal factors (id, ego, conflicts, defenses, etc.)	Situation: strong emphasis on how we respond to specific stimulus situations	Person: focus on self-concept, which is stable	Person: interested in stable traits molded by heredity

aspect of her self-concept (a humanistic view)? Or is she exhibiting an inherited tendency to be aggressive (a biological view)? In some cases, all four of these explanations might have some validity.

In short, it is an oversimplification to expect that one view has to be right while all others are wrong. Life is rarely that simple. In view of the complexity of personality, it would be surprising if there were *not* a number of different theories. It's probably best to think of the various theoretical orientations in psychology as complementary viewpoints, each with its own advantages and limitations. Indeed, modern psychologists increasingly recognize that theoretical diversity is a strength rather than a weakness (Hilgard, 1987; Kleinginna & Kleinginna, 1988). As we proceed through this text, you will see how differing theoretical perspectives often inspire fruitful research and how they sometimes converge on a more complete understanding of behavior than could be achieved by any one perspective alone.

Assessing Your Personality

- *Explain the concepts of standardization, test norms, reliability, and validity.*
- *Discuss the value and the limitations of self-report inventories.*
- *Discuss the value and limitations of projective tests.*

Answer the following true or false.

____ 1. Responses to personality tests are subject to unconscious distortion.

____ 2. The results of personality tests are often misunderstood.

____ 3. Personality test scores should be interpreted with caution.

____ 4. Personality tests may be quite useful in helping people to learn more about themselves.

If you answered "true" to all four questions, you earned a perfect score. Yes, personality tests are subject to distortion. Admittedly, test results are often misunderstood, and they should be interpreted cautiously. In spite of these problems, however, psychological tests can be very useful.

We all engage in efforts to size up our own personality as well as that of others. When you think to yourself that "this salesman is untrustworthy," or when you remark to a friend that "Howard is too timid and submissive," you are making personality assessments. In a sense, then, personality assessment is part of daily life. However, psychological tests provide much more systematic assessments than casual observations do.

The value of psychological tests lies in their ability to help people form a realistic picture of their personal qualities. In light of this value, we have included a variety of personality tests in the *Personal Explorations Workbook* that is available to accompany this text, and we have sprinkled a number of short tests throughout the text itself. Most of these questionnaires are widely used personality tests. We hope that you may gain some insights by responding to these scales. But it's important to understand the logic and limitations of such tests. To facilitate your use of these and other tests, this Application discusses some of the basics of psychological testing.

Key Concepts in Psychological Testing

A *psychological test* is a standardized measure of a sample of a person's behavior. Psychological tests are measurement instruments. They are used to measure abilities, aptitudes, and personality traits.

Note that your responses to a psychological test represent a *sample* of your behavior. This reality should alert you to one of the key limitations of psychological tests: It's always possible that a particular behavior sample is not representative of your characteristic behavior. We all have our bad days. A stomachache, a fight with a friend, a problem with your car—all might affect your responses to a particular test on a particular day. Because of the limitations of the sampling process, test scores should always be interpreted *cautiously*. Most psychological tests are sound measurement devices, but test results should not be viewed as the "final word" on one's personality and abilities because of the ever-present sampling problem.

Most psychological tests can be placed in one of two broad categories: (1) mental ability tests, and (2) personality tests. *Mental ability tests*, such as intelligence tests, aptitude tests, and achievement tests, often serve as gateways to schooling, training programs, and jobs. *Personality* tests measure various aspects of personality, including motives, interests, values, and attitudes. Many psychologists prefer to call these tests personality *scales*, since the questions do not have right and wrong answers as do those on tests of mental abilities.

STANDARDIZATION AND NORMS

Both personality scales and tests of mental abilities are *standardized* measures of behavior. **Standardization refers to the uniform procedures used to administer and score a test.** All subjects get the same instructions, the same questions, the same time limits, and so on, so that their scores can be compared meaningfully.

The standardization of a test's scoring system includes the development of test norms. **Test norms provide information about where a score on a psychological test ranks in relation to other scores on that test.** Why do we need test norms? Because in psychological testing, everything is relative. Psychological tests tell you how you score *relative to other people*. They tell you, for instance, that you are average in impulsiveness, or slightly above average in assertiveness, or far below average in anxiety. These interpretations are derived from the test norms.

RELIABILITY AND VALIDITY

Any kind of measuring device, whether it's a tire gauge, a stopwatch, or a psychological test, should be reasonably consistent. That is, repeated measurements should yield reasonably similar results. To appreciate the importance of reliability, think about how you would react if a tire pressure gauge gave you several different readings for the same tire. You would probably conclude that the gauge was broken and toss it into the garbage, because you know that consistency in measurement is essential to accuracy.

Reliability refers to the measurement consistency of a test. A reliable test is one that yields similar results

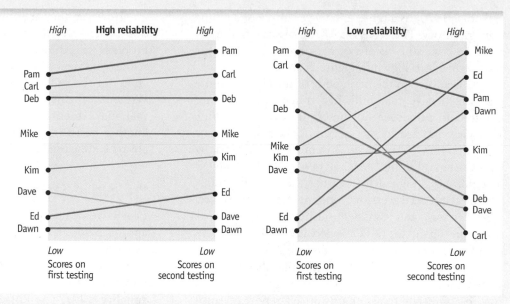

FIGURE 2.21.

Test reliability. Subjects' scores on the first administration of an assertiveness test are represented on the left, and their scores on a second administration (a few weeks later) are represented on the right. If subjects obtain similar scores on both administrations, the test measures assertiveness consistently and is said to have high reliability. If subjects get very different scores when they take the assertiveness test a second time, the test is said to have low reliability.

High reliability

High — Pam, Carl, Deb, Mike, Kim, Dave, Ed, Dawn — Low
Scores on first testing

High — Pam, Carl, Deb, Mike, Kim, Ed, Dave, Dawn — Low
Scores on second testing

Low reliability

High — Pam, Carl, Deb, Mike, Kim, Dave, Ed, Dawn — Low
Scores on first testing

High — Mike, Ed, Pam, Dawn, Kim, Deb, Dave, Carl — Low
Scores on second testing

upon repetition of the test (see Figure 2.21). Like most other types of measuring devices, psychological tests are not perfectly reliable. They usually do not yield the exact same score when repeated. A certain amount of inconsistency is unavoidable because human behavior is variable. Personality tests tend to have lower reliability than mental ability tests because daily fluctuations in mood influence how people respond to such tests.

Even if a test is quite reliable, we still need to be concerned about its validity. **Validity refers to the ability of a test to measure what it was designed to measure.** If we develop a new test of assertiveness, we have to provide some evidence that it really measures assertiveness. Validity can be demonstrated in a variety of ways. Most of them involve correlating scores on a test with other measures of the same trait, or with related traits.

Self-Report Inventories

The vast majority of personality tests are self-report inventories. **Self-report inventories are personality scales that ask individuals to answer a series of questions about their characteristic behavior.** When you take a self-report personality scale, you endorse statements as true or false as applied to you, you indicate how often you behave in a particular way, or you rate yourself with respect to certain qualities. For example, on the Minnesota Multiphasic Personality Inventory, people respond "true," "false," or "cannot say" to 550 statements such as the following:

I get a fair deal from most people.
I have the time of my life at parties.
I am glad that I am alive.
Several people are following me everywhere.

The logic underlying this approach is simple: Who knows you better than you do? Who has known you

longer? Who has more access to your private feelings?

The entire range of personality traits can be measured with self-report inventories. Some scales measure just one trait dimension, such as the Self-Efficacy Scale (see Figure 2.13) or the brief measure of introversion-extraversion shown in Figure 2.22. Others simultaneously assess a multitude of traits. The Sixteen Personality Factor Questionnaire (16PF), developed by Raymond Cattell and his colleagues (Cattell, Eber, &

The Maudsley Personality Inventory, Short Form

Instructions: The following questions pertain to the way people behave, feel, and act. Decide whether the items represent your usual way of acting or feeling, and circle either a "yes" or "no" for each. If you find it absolutely impossible to decide, circle the "?" answer; but use this answer sparingly.

1. Do you prefer action to planning for action?
   YES   ?   NO

2. Are you happiest when you get involved in some project that calls for rapid action?
   YES   ?   NO

3. Do you usually take the initiative in making new friends?
   YES   ?   NO

4. Are you inclined to be quick and sure in your actions?
   YES   ?   NO

5. Would you rate yourself as a lively individual?
   YES   ?   NO

6. Would you be very unhappy if you were prevented from making numerous social contacts?
   YES   ?   NO

FIGURE 2.22.

Measuring extraversion-introversion. The items shown here, taken from the Maudsley Personality Inventory, Short Form, provide a brief measure of one's extraversion-introversion. The items are worded so that a "yes" response is indicative of extraverted tendencies. If you answered "yes" to all six questions, you are probably more extraverted than introverted, although you should be cautious about drawing conclusions based on such a short scale.

Tatsuoka, 1970), is a representative example of a multi-trait inventory. The 16PF is a 187-item scale that measures 16 basic dimensions of personality, called *source traits*, which are shown in Figure 2.23.

As we noted in the main body of the chapter, some theorists believe that only five trait dimensions are required to provide a full description of personality. This view has led to the creation of a relatively new test—the NEO Personality Inventory. Developed by Paul Costa and Robert McCrae (1985, 1992), the NEO Inventory is designed to measure the Big Five traits: neuroticism, extraversion, openness to experience, agreeableness, and conscientiousness. In spite of its short life span, the NEO is already widely used in research and clinical work. Some testing experts, such as Joseph Mattarazzo (1992), believe that the NEO represents the wave of the future in personality assessment.

To appreciate the strengths of self-report inventories, consider how else you might assess your personality. For instance, how assertive are you? You probably have some vague idea, but can you accurately estimate how your assertiveness compares to others'? To do that, you need a great deal of comparative information about others' usual behavior—information that all of us lack. In contrast, a self-report inventory inquires about your typical behavior in a wide variety of circumstances requiring assertiveness and generates an exact comparison with the typical behavior reported by many other respondents for the same circumstances. Thus, self-report inventories are much more thorough and precise than casual observations are.

However, they are only as accurate as the information people give them. Deliberate deception can be a problem with these tests, and some people are unconsciously influenced by the social desirability or acceptability of the statements (Kline, 1995; Paulhus, 1991). Without realizing it, they endorse only those statements that make them look good. This problem provides another reason why personality test results should always be regarded as suggestive rather than definitive.

Projective Tests

Projective tests, which all take a rather indirect approach to the assessment of personality, are used extensively in clinical work. *Projective tests* **ask people to respond to vague, ambiguous stimuli in ways that may reveal the respondents' needs, feelings, and personality traits.** The Rorschach test, for instance, consists of a series of ten inkblots. Respondents are asked to describe what they see in the blots (see the adjacent photo). In the Thematic Apperception Test (TAT), a series of pictures of simple scenes is presented to subjects who are asked to tell stories about what is happening in the scenes and what the characters are feeling. For instance, one TAT card shows a young boy contemplating a violin resting on a table in front of him.

The assumption underlying projective testing is that ambiguous materials can serve as a blank screen onto which people project their characteristic concerns, conflicts, and desires. Thus, a competitive person who is shown the TAT card of the boy at the table with the

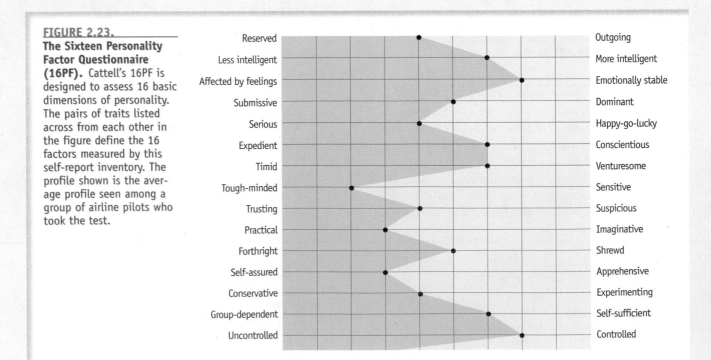

FIGURE 2.23.

The Sixteen Personality Factor Questionnaire (16PF). Cattell's 16PF is designed to assess 16 basic dimensions of personality. The pairs of traits listed across from each other in the figure define the 16 factors measured by this self-report inventory. The profile shown is the average profile seen among a group of airline pilots who took the test.

Reserved	Outgoing
Less intelligent	More intelligent
Affected by feelings	Emotionally stable
Submissive	Dominant
Serious	Happy-go-lucky
Expedient	Conscientious
Timid	Venturesome
Tough-minded	Sensitive
Trusting	Suspicious
Practical	Imaginative
Forthright	Shrewd
Self-assured	Apprehensive
Conservative	Experimenting
Group-dependent	Self-sufficient
Uncontrolled	Controlled

In projective tests, such as the Rorschach, stimuli are deliberately vague and ambiguous to serve as a blank screen onto which subjects can project their concerns, conflicts, and desires.

In taking the Thematic Apperception Test (TAT), a respondent is asked to tell stories about scenes such as this one. The themes apparent in each story can be scored to provide insight about the respondent's personality.

violin might concoct a story about how the boy is contemplating an upcoming musical competition at which he hopes to excel. The same card shown to a person high in impulsiveness might elicit a story about how the boy is planning to sneak out the door to go dirt-bike riding with friends.

Proponents of projective tests assert that the tests have two unique strengths. First, they are not transparent to subjects. That is, the subject doesn't know how the test provides information to the tester. Hence, it's difficult for people to engage in intentional deception. Second, the indirect approach used in these tests may

make them especially sensitive to unconscious features of personality.

Unfortunately, there is inadequate evidence for the reliability (consistency) and validity of projective measures (Lanyon & Goodstein, 1997). In particular, doubts have been raised about the research evidence on the Rorschach test (Wood, Nezworski, & Stejskal, 1996). The principal criticism of projective tests is that they are poorly standardized and highly subjective; different clinicians administer and score them differently, making the reliability of the tests distressingly low.

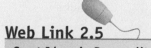

Web Link 2.5

Great Ideas in Personality
At this great site, Northwestern University personality psychologist G. Scott Acton demonstrates that scientific research programs in personality generate broad and compelling ideas about what it is to be a human being. He charts the contours of 12 research perspectives, including behaviorism, behavioral genetics, and sociobiology, and backs them up with extensive links to published and online resources associated with each perspective.

Key Ideas

THE NATURE OF PERSONALITY
● The concept of personality explains the consistency in individuals' behavior over time and situations while also explaining their distinctiveness. Personality traits are dispositions to behave in certain ways. Recent research suggests that the complexity of personality can be reduced to just five basic traits: extraversion, neuroticism, openness to experience, agreeableness, and conscientiousness.

PSYCHODYNAMIC PERSPECTIVES
● Freud's psychoanalytic theory emphasizes the importance of the unconscious. Freud described personality structure in terms of three components (id, ego, and superego) that are involved in internal conflicts, which generate anxiety.
● According to Freud, people often ward off anxiety and other unpleasant emotions with defense mechanisms, which work through self-deception. Freud believed that the first five years of life are extremely influential in shaping adult personality. He describes five psychosexual stages that children undergo in their personality development.
● Jung's analytical psychology stresses the importance of the collective unconscious. Adler's individual psychology emphasizes how people strive for superiority in order to compensate for feelings of inferiority.

BEHAVIORAL PERSPECTIVES
● Behavioral theories view personality as a collection of response tendencies shaped through learning. Pavlov's classical conditioning can explain how people acquire emotional responses.
● Skinner's model of operant conditioning shows how consequences such as reinforcement, extinction, and punishment shape behavior. Bandura's social learning theory adds a cognitive flavor to behaviorism. It shows how people can be conditioned indirectly through observation.

HUMANISTIC PERSPECTIVES
● Humanistic theories take an optimistic view of people's conscious, rational ability to chart their own courses of action. Rogers focused on the self-concept as the critical aspect of personality. He maintained that incongruence between one's self-concept and reality creates anxiety and leads to defensive behavior.
● Maslow theorized that needs are arranged hierarchically. He asserted that psychological health depends on fulfilling the need for self-actualization.

BIOLOGICAL PERSPECTIVES
● Eysenck believes that inherited individual differences in physiological functioning affect conditioning and thus influence personality. Recent twin studies have provided impressive evidence that genetic factors shape personality. Behavioral genetics research also suggests that the family has surprisingly little influence over personality. Evolutionary psychologists maintain that natural selection has favored the emergence of the Big Five traits as crucial dimensions of personality.

AN EPILOGUE ON THEORETICAL DIVERSITY
● The study of personality illustrates how great the theoretical diversity in psychology is. This diversity is a strength in that it fuels research that helps psychology move toward a more complete understanding of behavior.

APPLICATION: ASSESSING YOUR PERSONALITY
● Psychological tests are standardized measures of behavior—usually mental abilities or aspects of personality. Test norms indicate what represents a high or low score. Psychological tests should produce consistent results upon retesting, a quality called reliability. Validity refers to the degree to which a test measures what it was designed to measure.
● Self-report inventories, such as the 16PF and NEO Personality Inventory, ask respondents to describe themselves. Self-report inventories can provide a better snapshot of personality than can casual observations, but they are vulnerable to deception and social desirability bias.
● Projective tests, such as the Rorschach and TAT, assume that people's responses to ambiguous stimuli reveal something about their personality. Although the projective hyothesis is plausible, projective tests' reliability and validity appear to be disturbingly low.

Key Terms

Archetypes
Behaviorism
Classical conditioning
Cognition
Collective unconscious
Compensation
Conditioned response (CR)
Conditioned stimulus (CS)
Conscious
Defense mechanisms
Displacement
Ego
Extinction
Extraverts
Fixation
Hierarchy of needs
Humanism
Id
Identification
Incongruence
Introverts
Need for self-actualization
Negative reinforcement
Observational learning
Oedipal complex
Operant conditioning
Personality
Personality trait
Pleasure principle
Positive reinforcement
Preconscious
Projection
Projective test
Psychodynamic theories
Psychological test
Psychosexual stages
Punishment
Rationalization
Reaction formation
Reality principle
Regression
Reliability
Repression
Self-concept
Self-efficacy
Self-report inventories
Standardization
Superego
Test norms
Twin studies
Unconditioned response (UCR)
Unconditioned stimulus (UCS)
Unconscious
Validity

Key People

Alfred Adler
Albert Bandura
Hans Eysenck
Sigmund Freud
Carl Jung
Abraham Maslow
Ivan Pavlov
Carl Rogers
B. F. Skinner

Practice Test

1. Which of the following is not included in McCrae and Costa's five-factor model of personality?
   a. Neuroticism
   b. Extraversion
   c. Conscientiousness
   d. Intelligence

2. You're feeling guilty after your third bowl of ice cream. You tell yourself it's all right because yesterday you skipped lunch. Which defense mechanism is at work?
   a. Conceptualization
   b. Displacement
   c. Rationalization
   d. Identification

3. According to Adler, _____ is a universal drive to adapt, improve oneself, and master life's challenges.
   a. compensation
   b. striving for superiority
   c. avoiding inferiority
   d. social interest

4. The strengthening of a response tendency by virtue of the fact that the response leads to the removal of an unpleasant stimulus is
   a. negative reinforcement.
   b. positive reinforcement.
   c. primary reinforcement.
   d. secondary reinforcement.

5. Self-efficacy is
   a. the ability to fulfill one's potential.
   b. the belief about one's ability to perform behaviors that should lead to expected outcomes.
   c. a durable disposition to behave in a particular way in a variety of situations.
   d. a collection of beliefs about one's nature, unique qualities, and typical behavior.

6. According to Rogers, disparity between one's self-concept and actual experience is referred to as
   a. a delusional system.
   b. dissonance.
   c. conflict.
   d. incongruence.

7. The humanistic theorist who emphasized the need for self-actualization and the hierarchical organization of needs was
   a. Abraham Maslow.
   b. Carl Rogers.
   c. B.F. Skinner.
   d. Alfred Adler.

8. According to Eysenck, the way that heredity is linked to extraversion-introversion is that
   a. genes for this trait are passed from parent to offspring.
   b. some people can be conditioned more easily than others.
   c. people who inherit certain types of body builds are more extraverted.
   d. people who inherit more "socially admired" traits are more extraverted.

9. If identical twins exhibit more personality resemblance than fraternal twins, it's probably due mostly to
   a. similar treatment from parents.
   b. their strong identification with each other.
   c. their greater genetic overlap.
   d. others' expectations that they should be similar.

10. In psychological testing, consistency of results over repeated measurements refers to
    a. standardization.
    b. validity.
    c. statistical significance.
    d. reliability.

Answers

1. d pages 31–32
2. c page 35
3. b page 39
4. a page 44
5. b page 46
6. d page 48
7. a pages 49–50
8. b page 52
9. c page 53
10. d pages 56–57

INFOTRAC COLLEGE EDITION

Go to the Wadsworth Psychology Study Center (http://psychology.wadsworth.com/) for quiz questions, research updates, hot topics, interactive exercises, and suggested readings in INFOTRAC related to this chapter.

CHAPTER 3

Stress and Its Effects

You're in your car headed home from school with a classmate. Traffic is barely moving. A radio report indicates that the traffic jam is only going to get worse. You groan audibly as you fiddle impatiently with the radio dial. Another motorist nearly takes your fender off trying to cut into your lane. Your pulse quickens as you shout insults at the unknown driver, who cannot even hear you. You think about the term paper that you have to work on tonight. Your stomach knots up as you recall all the crumpled drafts you tossed into the wastebasket last night. If you don't finish the paper soon, you won't be able to find any time to study for your math test, not to mention your biology quiz. Suddenly you remember that you promised the person you're dating that the two of you would get together tonight. There's no way. Another fight looms on the horizon. Your classmate asks how you feel about the tuition increase the college announced yesterday. You've been trying not to think about it. You're already in debt up to your ears. Your parents are bugging you about changing schools, but you don't want to leave your friends. Your heartbeat quickens as you contemplate the debate you'll have to wage with your parents. You feel wired with tension as you realize that the stress in your life never seems to let up.

Many circumstances can create stress in our lives. Stress comes in all sorts of packages: large and small, pretty and ugly, simple and complex. All too often, the package is a surprise. In this chapter, we'll try to sort out these packages. We'll analyze the nature of stress, outline the major types of stress, and discuss how people respond to stressful events at several levels.

In a sense, stress is what a course on adjustment is all about. Recall from Chapter 1 that adjustment essentially deals with how people manage to cope with various demands and pressures. These demands or pressures that require adjustment represent the core of stressful experience. Thus, the central theme in a course such as this is: How do people adjust to stress, and how might they adjust more effectively?

The Nature of Stress

LEARNING OBJECTIVES

● Explain the nature of stress and discuss how common it is.
● Distinguish between primary and secondary appraisal of stress.
● Summarize the evidence on ambient stress.

Over the years, the term *stress* has been used in different ways by different theorists. Some have viewed stress as a *stimulus* event that presents difficult demands (a divorce, for instance), while others have viewed stress as the *response* of physiological arousal elicited by a troublesome event (Whitehead, 1994). However, the emerging consensus among contemporary researchers is that stress is neither a stimulus nor a response but a special stimulus-response transaction in which one feels threatened. Hence, we will define **stress as any circumstances that threaten or are perceived to threaten one's well-being and thereby tax one's coping abilities.** The threat may be to one's immediate physical safety, long-range security, self-esteem, reputation, or peace of mind. This is a complex concept—so let's dig a little deeper.

Stress Is an Everyday Event

The term *stress* tends to spark images of overwhelming, traumatic crises. People think of hijackings, hurricanes, military combat, and nuclear accidents. Undeniably, these are extremely stressful events. Studies conducted in the aftermath of tornadoes, floods, earthquakes, and the like typically find elevated rates of anxiety, depression, and drug abuse in the communities affected by these disasters (Rubonis & Bickman, 1991; Weisaeth, 1993). However, these unusual and infrequent events represent the tip of the iceberg. Many everyday events such as waiting in line, having car trouble, shopping for Christmas presents, misplacing your checkbook, and staring at bills you can't pay are also stressful. Of course, major and minor stressors are not entirely independent. A major stressful event, such as going through a divorce, can trigger a cascade of minor stressors, such as looking for an attorney, taking on new household responsibilities, and so forth (Pillow, Zautra, & Sandler, 1996).

You might guess that minor stresses would produce minor effects, but that isn't necessarily true. Research shows that routine hassles may have significant negative effects on a person's mental and physical health (Delongis, Folkman, & Lazarus, 1988). Richard Lazarus and his colleagues have devised a scale to measure stress in the form of daily hassles. Their scale lists 117 everyday problems, such as misplacing things, struggling with rising prices, dealing with delays, and so forth. When they compared their hassles scale against another scale that assessed stress in the form of major life events (Kanner et al., 1981), they found that scores on their hassles scale were more strongly related to subjects' mental health than the scores on the other scale were. Other investigators, working with different types of samples and different measures of hassles, have also found that everyday hassles are predictive of mental and physical health (Johnson & Sherman, 1997; Kohn, Lafreniere, & Gurevich, 1991).

Why would minor hassles be more strongly related to mental health than major stressful events? The answer isn't entirely clear yet, but most theories of stress assume that stressful events have a *cumulative* impact (Seta, Seta, & Wang, 1991). In other words, stress adds up. Routine stresses at home, at school, and at work might be fairly benign individually, but collectively they could create great strain.

Richard Lazarus

Stress Lies in the Eye of the Beholder

The experience of feeling threatened depends on what events you notice and how you choose to appraise or interpret them (Monroe & Kelley, 1995). Events that are stressful for one person may be "ho-hum" routine for another. For example, many people find flying in an airplane somewhat stressful, but frequent fliers may not even raise an eyebrow. Some people enjoy the excitement of going out on a date with someone new; others find the uncertainty terrifying.

In discussing appraisals of stress, Lazarus and Folkman (1984) distinguish between primary and secondary appraisal (see Figure 3.1). **Primary appraisal is an initial evaluation of whether an event is (1) irrelevant to you, (2) relevant, but not threatening, or (3) stressful.** When you view an event as stressful, you are likely to make a **secondary appraisal, which is an evaluation of your coping resources and options for dealing with the stress.** Thus, your primary appraisal would determine whether you saw an upcoming job

interview as stressful. Your secondary appraisal would determine how stressful the interview appeared, in light of your assessment of your ability to deal with the event.

Often, people are not very objective in their appraisals of potentially stressful events. A study of hospitalized patients awaiting surgery showed only a slight correlation between the objective seriousness of a person's upcoming surgery and the amount of fear the person experienced (Janis, 1958). Clearly, some people are more prone to feel threatened by life's difficulties than

FIGURE 3.1.
Primary and secondary appraisal of stress. According to Lazarus and Folkman (1984), the appraisal of potentially stressful events is a two-step process. First people make a *primary appraisal* of whether an event appears threatening. If the answer is yes, they make a *secondary appraisal* of whether they have the resources to cope with the challenge. Stress occurs when people feel that they may have difficulty coping with the event.

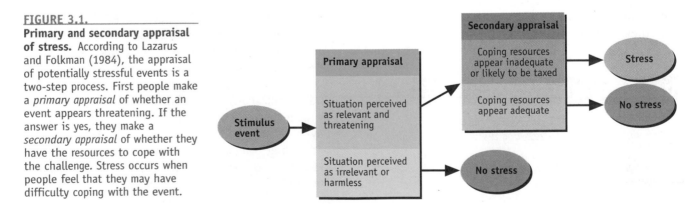

others. A number of studies have shown that anxious, neurotic people report more stress than others (Brett et al. 1990), as do people who are relatively unhappy (Seidlitz & Diener, 1993). Thus, stress lies in the eye (actually, the mind) of the beholder, and people's appraisals of stressful events are highly subjective.

Stress May Be Embedded in the Environment

Although the perception of stress is a highly personal matter, many kinds of stress emanate from the environmental circumstances that individuals share with others. *Ambient stress* **consists of chronic environmental conditions that, although not urgent, are negatively valued and that place adaptive demands on people** (Holahan, 1986). Features of the environment such as excessive noise, heat, and pollution can threaten well-being and leave their mark on mental and physical health.

For example, investigators have found an association between chronic exposure to high levels of noise and elevated blood pressure among children attending school near Los Angeles International Airport (Cohen et al., 1980). A more recent study of the effects of airport noise (Evans, Hygge, & Bullinger, 1995) also found elevated stress hormones, reading deficits, and poor task persistence in a sample of children who lived near Munich International Airport (see Figure 3.2). Although the relationships are complex, evidence suggests that excessive heat may impair task performance and increase the likelihood of aggressive behavior (Bell et al., 1996). In a study conducted in Dayton, Ohio, Rotton and Frey (1984) found that psychiatric emergencies increased when air pollution was high.

Crowding is another source of environmental stress. Temporary experiences of crowding, such as being packed into a rock concert with thousands of

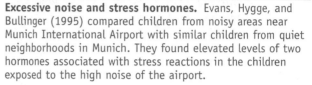

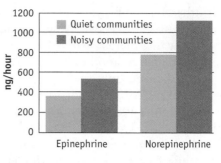

FIGURE 3.2.

Excessive noise and stress hormones. Evans, Hygge, and Bullinger (1995) compared children from noisy areas near Munich International Airport with similar children from quiet neighborhoods in Munich. They found elevated levels of two hormones associated with stress reactions in the children exposed to the high noise of the airport.

other fans, can be stressful, but most of the research on crowding has focused on the effects of residential density. Generally, studies find an association between high density and increased physiological arousal, psychological distress, and social withdrawal (Baum & Paulus, 1987; Evans, LePore, & Schroeder, 1996). One does not have to live in an urban skyscraper or tenement to experience crowding. Even an overcrowded dormitory, with three students in rooms built for two, can be stressful (Mullen & Felleman, 1990). Psychologists have also explored the repercussions of living in areas that are at risk for disaster. For instance, studies suggest that people who live near a nuclear power plant or in an area prone to earthquakes may experience increased stress (Baum; 1990, Nolen-Hocksema & Morrow, 1991).

Stress can be caused by environmental circumstances such as excessive noise, crowding, and traffic.

As with other types of stress, the experience of environmental stress is subjective. A specific level of noise, heat, or crowding that is aversive for one person may not be bothersome to another. Even in the aftermath of a major disaster, only some people will feel stressed out. For example, in a study of Stanford students' adjustment to the 1989 Loma Prieta earthquake that crippled the San Francisco bay area, Nolen-Hoeksema and Morrow (1991) found negative emotional effects primarily among students who tended to ruminate about their problems and those who were depressed before the earthquake.

Stress May Be Self-Imposed

We tend to think of stress as something imposed on us from without by others and their demands. However, a recent study of college students' stress found that stress is self-imposed surprisingly often (Epstein & Katz, 1992). For example, you might sign up for extra classes to get through school quickly. Or you might actively seek additional responsibilities at work to impress your boss. People frequently put pressure on themselves to get good grades or to climb the corporate ladder rapidly. Many people create stress by embracing unrealistic expectations for themselves. Because stress is often self-imposed, people have more control over their stress than they realize. However, to exert this control, individuals need to be able to recognize the sources of stress in our lives. Hence, in the next section we'll discuss the major types of stress.

Major Types of Stress

LEARNING OBJECTIVES
- List and describe four principal types of stress.
- Describe frustration as a form of stress.
- Describe three types of conflict and discuss typical reactions to conflicts.
- Summarize evidence on life change as a form of stress.
- Summarize evidence on pressure as a form of stress.

An enormous variety of events can be stressful for one person or another. To achieve a better understanding of stress, theorists have tried to classify the principal types of stress. None of their schemes has turned out to be altogether satisfactory. It's virtually impossible to classify stressful events into nonintersecting categories. Although this problem presents conceptual headaches for researchers, it need not prevent us from describing four major types of stress: frustration, conflict, change, and pressure. As you read about each of them, you'll surely recognize four very familiar adversaries.

Frustration

"It has been very frustrating to watch the rapid deterioration of my parents' relationship. Over the last year or two they have argued constantly and have refused to seek any professional help. I have tried to talk to them, but they kind of shut me and my brother out of their problem. I feel very helpless and sometimes even very angry, not at them, but at the whole situation."

This scenario illustrates frustration. As psychologists use the term, **frustration occurs in any situation in which the pursuit of some goal is thwarted.** In essence, you experience frustration when you want something and you can't have it. Everyone has to deal with frustration virtually every day. Traffic jams and difficult daily commutes, for instance, are a routine source of frustration that can affect mood, blood pressure, and health (Novaco, Stokols, & Milanesi, 1990; Schaeffer, Street, & Singer, 1988). Fortunately, most frustrations are brief and insignificant. You may be quite upset when you go to a repair shop to pick up your ailing stereo and find that it hasn't been fixed as promised. However, a week later you'll probably have your precious stereo, and all will be forgotten.

Of course, some frustrations can be sources of significant stress. *Failures* and *losses* are two common kinds of frustration that are often very stressful. All people fail in at least some of their endeavors. Some make failure almost inevitable by setting unrealistic goals for themselves. People tend to forget that for every newly appointed vice-president in the business world, there are dozens of middle-level executives who don't get promoted. Losses may be especially frustrating because you are deprived of something you are accustomed to having. For example, there are few things that are more frustrating than losing a dearly loved boyfriend, girlfriend, or spouse.

More often than not, frustration appears to be the culprit at work when people feel troubled by environmental stress (Graig, 1993). Insofar as excessive noise, heat, pollution, and crowding are stressful, it's probably because they frustrate the desire for quiet, a comfortable body temperature, clean air, and adequate privacy.

Conflict

"Should I or shouldn't I? I became engaged at Christmas. My fiancé surprised me with a ring. I knew if I refused the ring he would be terribly hurt and our relationship would suffer. However, I don't really know whether or not I want to marry him. On the other hand, I don't want to lose him either."

Like frustration, conflict is an unavoidable feature of everyday life. That perplexing question "Should I or shouldn't I?" comes up countless times on a daily basis. **Conflict occurs when two or more incompatible**

motivations or behavioral impulses compete for expression. As we discussed in Chapter 2, Sigmund Freud proposed nearly a century ago that internal conflicts generate considerable psychological distress. This link between conflict and distress was measured with new precision in recent studies by Laura King and Robert Emmons (1990, 1991). They used an elaborate questionnaire to assess the overall amount of internal conflict experienced by subjects in several studies. They found higher levels of conflict to be associated with higher levels of psychological distress.

Neal Miller

Conflicts come in three types, which were originally described by Kurt Lewin (1935) and investigated extensively by Neal Miller (1944, 1959). These types—approach-approach, avoidance-avoidance, and approach-avoidance—are diagrammed in Figure 3.3.

In an ***approach-approach conflict*** **a choice must be made between two attractive goals.** The problem, of course, is that you can choose just one of the two goals. For example, you have a free afternoon; should you play tennis or racquetball? You're out for a meal; do you want to order the pizza or the spaghetti? You can't afford both; should you buy the blue sweater or the gray jacket?

Among the three kinds of conflict, the approach-approach type tends to be the least stressful. People usually don't stagger out of restaurants, exhausted by the stress of choosing which of several appealing entrees to eat. In approach-approach conflicts you typically have a reasonably happy ending, whichever way you decide to go. Nonetheless, approach-approach conflicts centering on important issues may sometimes be troublesome. If you are torn between two appealing college majors or two attractive boyfriends, you may find the decision-making process quite stressful.

In an ***avoidance-avoidance conflict*** **a choice must be made between two unattractive goals.** Forced to choose between two repelling alternatives, you are, as they say, "caught between a rock and a hard place." For example, let's say you have painful backaches. Should you submit to surgery that you dread, or should you continue to live with the pain?

Obviously, avoidance-avoidance conflicts are most unpleasant and highly stressful. Typically, people keep delaying their decision as long as possible, hoping that they will somehow be able to escape the conflict situation. For example, you might delay surgery in the hope that your backaches will disappear on their own.

In an ***approach-avoidance conflict*** **a choice must be made about whether or not to pursue a single goal that has both attractive and unattractive aspects.** For instance, imagine that you're offered a career promotion that will mean a large increase in pay. The catch is that you will have to move to a city that you hate. Approach-avoidance conflicts are common, and they can be very stressful. Any time you have to take a risk to pursue some desirable outcome, you are likely to find yourself in an approach-avoidance conflict. Should you risk rejection by asking out that attractive person in class? Should you risk your savings by investing in a new business that could fail?

Approach-avoidance conflicts often produce *vacillation*. That is, people go back and forth, beset by indecision. They decide to go ahead, then not to, then to go ahead again. Humans are not unique in this respect. Many years ago, Neal Miller (1944) observed the same vacillation in his groundbreaking research with rats. He created approach-avoidance conflicts in hungry rats by alternately feeding and shocking them at one end of a

FIGURE 3.3.

Types of conflict. Psychologists have identified three basic types of conflict. In approach-approach or avoidance-avoidance conflicts, the person is torn between two goals. In an approach-avoidance conflict, only one goal is under consideration, but it has both positive and negative aspects.

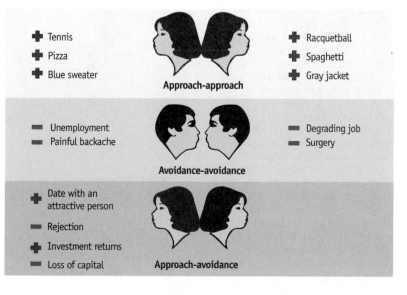

+ Tennis
+ Pizza
+ Blue sweater

Approach-approach

+ Racquetball
+ Spaghetti
+ Gray jacket

− Unemployment
− Painful backache

Avoidance-avoidance

− Degrading job
− Surgery

+ Date with an attractive person
− Rejection
+ Investment returns
− Loss of capital

Approach-avoidance

runway apparatus. Eventually, these rats tended to hover near the center of the runway. They would alternately approach and retreat from the goal box at the end of the alley.

In a series of studies, Miller (1959) plotted out how an organism's tendency to approach a goal (the approach gradient in Figure 3.4a) and to retreat from a goal (the avoidance gradient in Figure 3.4a) increase as the organism nears the goal. He found that avoidance motivation increases more rapidly than approach motivation (as reflected by the avoidance gradient's steeper slope in Figure 3.4a). Based on this principle, Miller concluded that *in trying to resolve an approach-avoidance conflict, we should focus more on decreasing avoidance motivation than on increasing approach motivation.*

How would this insight apply to complex human dilemmas? Imagine that you are counseling a friend who is vacillating over whether to ask someone out on a date. Miller would assert that you should attempt to downplay the negative aspects of possible rejection (thus lowering the avoidance gradient) rather than dwelling on how much fun the date could be (thus raising the approach gradient). Figure 3.4b shows the effects of lowering the avoidance gradient. If it is lowered far enough, the person should reach the goal (make a decision and take action).

Change

"After my divorce, I lived alone for four years. Six months ago, I married a wonderful woman who has two children from her previous marriage. My biggest stress is suddenly having to adapt

Web Link 3.1

Stress and Workstress Directory
Dutch physician and stress researcher Theo Compernolle offers a generous set of resource links relating to the impact of stress in general and in the workplace.

to living with three people instead of by myself. I was pretty set in my ways. I had certain routines. Now everything is chaos. I love my wife and I'm fond of the kids, and they're not really doing anything wrong, but my house and my life just aren't the same and I am having trouble dealing with it all."

Life changes may represent a key type of stress. **Life changes are any noticeable alterations in one's living circumstances that require readjustment.** Research on life change began when Thomas Holmes, Richard Rahe, and their colleagues set out to explore the relation between stressful life events and physical illness (Holmes & Rahe, 1967; Rahe & Arthur, 1978). They interviewed thousands of tuberculosis patients to find out what kinds of events preceded the onset of their disease. Surprisingly, the frequently cited events were not uniformly negative. There were plenty of aversive events, as expected, but there were also many seemingly positive events, such as getting married, having a baby, or getting promoted.

Why would positive events, such as moving to a nicer home, produce stress? According to Holmes and Rahe, it is because they produce *change.* Their thesis is that disruptions of daily routines are stressful.

FIGURE 3.4.

Approach-avoidance conflict.
(a) According to Neal Miller (1959), as you near a goal that has positive and negative features, avoidance motivation tends to rise faster than approach motivation (that's why the avoidance gradient has a steeper slope than the approach gradient), sending you into retreat. However, if you retreat far enough, you'll eventually reach a point where approach motivation is stronger than avoidance motivation, and you may decide to go ahead once again. The ebb and flow of this process leads to vacillation around the point where the two gradients intersect. (b) As the avoidance gradient is lowered, the person comes closer and closer to the goal. If the avoidance gradient can be lowered far enough, the person should be able to resolve the conflict and reach the goal.

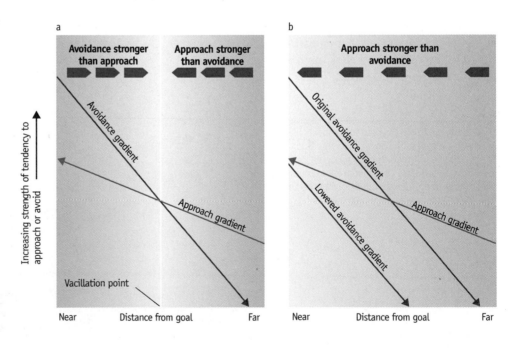

According to their theory, changes in personal relationships, changes at work, changes in finances, and so forth can be stressful even when the changes are welcomed.

Based on this analysis, Holmes and Rahe (1967) developed the Social Readjustment Rating Scale (SRRS) to measure life change as a form of stress. The scale assigns numerical values to 43 major life events that are supposed to reflect the magnitude of the readjustment required by each change (see Figure 3.5). In responding to the scale, respondents are asked to indicate how often they experienced any of these 43 events during a certain time period (typically, the past year). The person then adds up the numbers associated with each event checked. This sum is an index of the amount of change-related stress the person has recently experienced.

The SRRS and similar scales have been used in thousands of studies by researchers all over the world. Overall, these studies have shown that people with higher scores on the SRRS tend to be more vulnerable to many kinds of physical illness—and many types of psychological problems as well (Creed, 1993; Derogatis & Coons, 1993; Gruen, 1993). These results have attracted a great deal of attention, and the SRRS has been reprinted in many newspapers and popular magazines. The attendant publicity has led to the widespread conclusion that life change is inherently stressful.

More recently, however, experts have criticized this research, citing problems with the methods used (Johnson & Bornstein, 1991; Monroe & McQuaid, 1994; Raphael, Cloitre, & Dohrenwend, 1991) and in interpreting the findings (Brett et al., 1990; Critelli & Ee, 1996; Watson & Pennebaker, 1989). At this point, it is a key interpretive issue that concerns us. Many critics have argued that the SRRS does not measure *change* exclusively. The list of life changes on the SRRS is dominated by events that are clearly negative or undesirable (death of a spouse, fired at work, and so on). These negative events probably generate great frustration. So even though the scale contains some positive events, it could be that frustration (generated by negative events), rather than change, creates most of the stress assessed by the scale.

To investigate this possibility, researchers have begun to take into account the desirability and undesirability of subjects' life changes. Subjects are asked to indicate the desirability of the events that they check off on the SRRS and similar scales. The findings in these studies clearly indicate that life change is *not* the crucial dimension measured by the SRRS. Undesirable or negative life events cause most of the stress tapped by the SRRS (McLean & Link, 1994; Turner & Wheaton, 1995).

Should we discard the notion that change is stressful? Not entirely. Other lines of research, independent of work with the SRRS, support the hypothesis that change is an important form of stress. For instance, researchers have found associations between geographic mobility and impaired mental and physical health that presumably reflect the impact of change (Brett, 1980; Shuval, 1993). And research on becoming a parent, which is a highly positive life change for the

FIGURE 3.5.
Social Readjustment Rating Scale (SRRS). Devised by Holmes and Rahe (1967), this scale measures the change-related stress in one's life. The numbers on the right are supposed to reflect the average amount of stress (readjustment) produced by each event. Respondents check off the events that have occurred to them recently and add up the associated numbers to arrive at their stress scores. See this chapter Application for a detailed critique of the SRRS.

Social Readjustment Rating Scale

Life event	Mean value	Life event	Mean value
Death of a spouse	100	Son or daughter leaving home	29
Divorce	73	Trouble with in-laws	29
Marital separation	65	Outstanding personal achievement	28
Jail term	63	Spouse begins or stops work	26
Death of close family member	63	Begin or end school	26
Personal injury or illness	53	Change in living conditions	25
Marriage	50	Revision of personal habits	24
Fired at work	47	Trouble with boss	23
Marital reconciliation	45	Change in work hours or conditions	20
Retirement	45	Change in residence	20
Change in health of family member	44	Change in school	20
Pregnancy	40	Change in recreation	19
Sex difficulties	39	Change in church activities	19
Gain of a new family member	39	Change in social activities	18
Business readjustment	39	Mortgage or loan for lesser purchase (car, TV, etc.)	17
Change in financial state	38	Change in sleeping habits	16
Death of a close friend	37	Change in number of family get-togethers	15
Change to a different line of work	36	Change in eating habits	15
Change in number of arguments with spouse	35	Vacation	13
Mortgage or loan for major purchase (home, etc.)	31	Christmas	12
Foreclosure of mortgage or loan	30	Minor violations of the law	11
Change in responsibilities at work	29		

Pressure comes in two varieties: the pressure to perform *and to* conform. *For example, suburban homeowners are expected to keep their yards in attractive shape (conformity pressure) and public speakers are expected to be articulate and persuasive (performance pressure).*

vast majority of people, shows that this transition can be extremely stressful (Miller & Sollie, 1986). A study by Brown and McGill (1989) suggests that desirable life changes may be stressful for some people, but not for others. They found a link between positive life changes and increased illness only among subjects low in self-esteem. In contrast, positive events were correlated with improved health among their high self-esteem subjects. Based on these results, Brown and McGill suggest that positive events are stressful to the extent that they disrupt one's sense of identity.

More research is needed, but it is quite plausible that change constitutes a major type of stress in people's lives. However, there is little reason to believe that change is *inherently* or *inevitably stressful.* Some life changes may be quite challenging, while others may be quite benign.

Pressure

"My father questioned me at dinner about some things I did not want to talk about. I know he doesn't want to hear my answers, at least not the truth. My father told me when I was little that I was his favorite because I was 'pretty near perfect' and I've spent my life trying to keep that up, even though it's obviously not true. Recently, he has begun to realize this and it's made our relationship very strained and painful."

At one time or another, most of us have probably remarked that we were "under pressure." What does this mean? **Pressure involves expectations or demands that one behave in a certain way.** Pressure can be divided into two subtypes: the pressure to *perform* and the pressure to *conform.* You are under pressure to perform when you are expected to execute tasks and responsibilities quickly, efficiently, and successfully. For

example, salespeople are usually under pressure to move lots of merchandise. Professors at research institutions are often under pressure to publish in prestigious journals. Comedians are under pressure to be amusing. Secretaries are often under pressure to complete lots of clerical work in very little time. Pressures to conform to others' expectations are also common. Businessmen are expected to wear suits and ties. Suburban homeowners are expected to keep their lawns manicured. Teenagers are expected to adhere to their parents' values and rules. Young adults are expected to get themselves married by the time they're 30.

Although widely discussed by the general public, the concept of pressure has received scant attention

FIGURE 3.6.

Pressure and psychological symptoms. A comparison of pressure and life change as sources of stress suggests that pressure may be more strongly related to mental health than change. In one study, Weiten (1988) found a correlation of .59 between scores on the Pressure Inventory (PI) and symptoms of psychological distress. In the same sample, the correlation between SRRS scores and psychological symptoms was only .28.

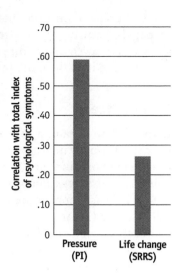

from researchers. However, recent years have seen the development of a scale to measure pressure as a form of life stress (Weiten, 1988). In studies with this scale, a strong relationship has been found between pressure and a variety of psychological symptoms and problems (Weiten, 1988, 1998). In fact, pressure has turned out to be more strongly related to measures of mental health than the SRRS and other established measures of stress (see Figure 3.6). These findings suggest that pressure may be an important form of stress that merits more attention from researchers.

Key Factors in the Appraisal of Stress

LEARNING OBJECTIVES

● *Explain how familiarity and controllability influence the appraisal of stress.*

● *Explain how predictability and imminence influence the appraisal of stress.*

We noted earlier that stress lies in the eye of the beholder. Quite a variety of factors influence people's subjective appraisals of potentially stressful events. Four that stand out are (1) the individual's familiarity with the challenge, (2) the controllability of the events, (3) the predictability of the events, and (4) the imminence of the threat.

Familiarity

An important consideration in your appraisal of stress is your familiarity with the stressful demands. Generally, the more unfamiliar you are with a potentially stressful event, the more threatened you are likely to feel (McGrath, 1977). The importance of familiarity

was apparent in a study that compared the arousal of novice and experienced parachute jumpers as they prepared for a jump (Fenz & Epstein, 1967). As one might expect, and as Figure 3.7 shows, the novices experienced considerably more arousal during the jump than the experienced parachutists. Given the influence of familiarity, a person's first major job interview, first appearance in a courtroom, or first purchase of a home tends to be more stressful than subsequent similar events. Familiarity with a challenge can make yesterday's crisis today's routine.

Controllability

Another factor that influences your appraisal of stress is your perception of how much control you can exert over the event in question. For example, if you are facing surgery and a lengthy rehabilitation period, your feelings might range from a sense of powerlessness to a firm belief that you will be able to speed up the recovery process. Stern, McCants, and Pettine (1982) found that when events are viewed as controllable, they tend to be less stressful.

The finding that controllability reduces stress is fairly typical for this line of research, although it is not universal (Thompson & Spacapan, 1991). Jerry Burger (1989) has identified some situations in which greater

FIGURE 3.7.

Familiarity and physiological arousal. Using heart rate as an index of stress-induced physiological arousal, Fenz and Epstein (1967) compared a group of experienced parachute jumpers with a group of novices as both groups went through a jump. As the graph shows, the two groups started out with similar levels of arousal, but as the time for the jump approached, the novices experienced greater arousal. The lower arousal seen in the experienced jumpers shows how familiarity with a stressful event can sometimes make it less stressful.

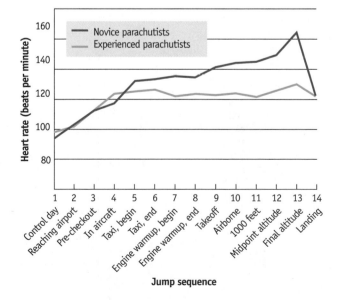

control is associated with *increased* stress. Burger points out that control has negative as well as positive aspects. On the negative side, when events are controllable, people have to accept greater responsibility for their outcomes. *Hence, people who are very concerned about how others will evaluate them often find being in control quite stressful.* Nonetheless, the general trend is for people to view events over which they have more control as less stressful.

Predictability

If you experience a stressful event—for instance, being fired at work—is it more traumatic when the event comes out of nowhere (unpredictable stress) or when you can see the event coming for some time (predictable stress)? In general, it appears that people prefer predictable stress over surprise packages. When researchers expose subjects to the stress of predictable and unpredictable noise, they usually find that subjects are bothered more by the unpredictable noise (Matthews et al., 1989). Major stressors, such as the progression of an illness or job loss, seem to be less devastating when they can be anticipated over a period of time. People may prefer predictability because it allows them to engage in anticipatory coping to prepare for the stress.

However, the effects of predictability are complex. There are some situations in which people prefer *not* to know about stress in advance (Burger, 1989). For instance, when understudy actors or rookie athletes are pressed into service as last-minute substitutes for more experienced performers, many comment, "It was better that way. I didn't have time to dwell on it and get nervous." The value of predictability probably depends on whether there's much that you can do to prepare for the stress. If preparation won't help (or if you already feel prepared), knowing about stress in advance may only allow you to dwell on the threatening event, which will usually make it all the more threatening.

Imminence

If you *do* know about a threatening event in advance, your stress usually increases as the event becomes more imminent (closer in time). When a threat lies in the distant future, its stressfulness may be minimal. However, as the challenge looms near, concern and distress typically escalate (Lazarus & Folkman, 1984). Thus, as you approach the day on which you have to take a critical exam, submit to serious surgery, or speak at a convention, you generally will find the stress increasing (Bolger, 1990). In fact, your stress may peak during the period of anticipation, rather than with the event itself (see Figure 3.8). For example, after a big exam, students often remark, "Taking it wasn't nearly as bad as anticipating it and worrying about it."

In summary, the appraisal of stress is a complicated process. Factors such as controllability and predictability have varied effects on the appraisal of stress, depending on the exact circumstances. However, research on this process is important because people's stress appraisals make all the difference in the world to how they respond to stress, which is our next topic.

Responding to Stress

LEARNING OBJECTIVES

● *List three dimensions of emotion commonly elicited by stress.*

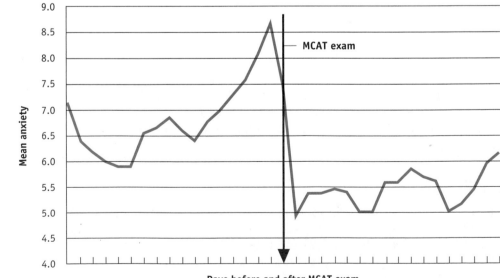

FIGURE 3.8.

Imminence as a factor in appraisals of stress. In a study of personality and coping styles, Bolger (1990) tracked daily levels of anxiety in 50 premedical students for 35 days surrounding the administration of the highly stressful Medical College Admissions Test (MCAT). As you can see, anxiety increased steadily as the stressful event became more imminent and peaked just prior to the event rather than during the event itself.

- Discuss the effects of emotional arousal on coping efforts and the inverted-U hypothesis.
- Describe the fight-or-flight response.
- Describe the three stages of the general adaptation syndrome.
- Describe the two major pathways along which the brain sends signals to the endocrine system in response to stress.
- Describe the nature of behavioral responses to stress.

Web Link 3.2

Stress, Anxiety, Fears, and Psychosomatic Disorders
This resource, which constitutes Chapter 5 of Clayton E. Tucker-Ladd's online text, *Psychological Self-Help*, provides a particularly fine discussion of the nature of stress and its relationship to psychological and physical disorders.

The human response to stress is complex and multidimensional. Stress affects people at several levels. Consider again the chapter's opening scenario, in which you're driving home in heavy traffic, thinking about overdue papers, tuition increases, and parental pressures. Let's look at some of the reactions we mentioned. When you groan audibly in reaction to the traffic report, you're experiencing an *emotional response* to stress, in this case, annoyance and anger. When your pulse quickens and your stomach knots up, you're exhibiting *physiological responses* to stress. When you shout insults at another driver, your verbal aggression is a *behavioral response* to the stress at hand. Thus, we can analyze people's reactions to stress at three levels: (1) their emotional responses, (2) their physiological responses, and (3) their behavioral responses. Figure 3.9 depicts these three levels of response.

Emotional Responses

Emotion is an elusive concept. Psychologists debate about how to define emotion, and many conflicting theories purport to explain emotion. However, everyone has had extensive personal experience with emotions. Everyone has a good idea of what it means to be anxious, elated, gloomy, jealous, disgusted, excited, guilty, or nervous. So rather than pursue the technical debates about emotion, we'll rely on your familiarity with the concept and simply note that **emotions are powerful, largely uncontrollable feelings, accompanied by physiological changes.** When people are under stress, they often react emotionally. More often than not, stress tends to elicit unpleasant emotions rather than pleasurable feelings (Lazarus, 1993).

The link between stress and emotion was apparent in a study of 96 women who filled out diaries about stresses and moods they experienced over 28 days (Caspi, Bolger, & Eckenrode, 1987). The investigators found that daily fluctuations in stress correlated with daily fluctuations in mood. As stress increased, mood tended to become more negative. As the researchers put it, "Some days everything seems to go wrong, and by day's end, minor difficulties find their outlet in rotten moods" (p. 184). Other studies that have tracked daily stress and mood fluctuations have also found strong relations between the two (Affleck et al., 1994; Repetti, 1993).

EMOTIONS COMMONLY ELICITED

There are no simple one-to-one connections between certain types of stressful events and particular emotions, but researchers *have* begun to uncover some strong links between specific *cognitive reactions to stress (appraisals)* and specific emotions (Smith & Lazarus, 1993). For example, self-blame tends to lead to guilt, helplessness to sadness, and so forth. Although many emotions can be evoked by stressful events, some are

FIGURE 3.9.

The multidimensional response to stress. A potentially stressful event, such as a major exam, will elicit a subjective, cognitive appraisal of how threatening the event is. If the event is viewed with alarm, the stress may trigger emotional, physiological, and behavioral reactions.

Potentially stressful objective events
A major exam, a big date, trouble with the boss, or a financial setback, which may lead to frustration, conflict, change, or pressure

Subjective cognitive appraisal
Personalized perceptions of threat, which are influenced by familiarity with the event, its controllability, its predictability, and so on

Emotional response
Annoyance, anger, anxiety, fear, dejection, grief, guilt, shame, envy, disgust

Physiological response
Autonomic arousal, hormonal fluctuations, neurochemical changes, and so on

Behavioral response
Coping efforts, such as lashing out at others, blaming oneself, seeking help, solving problems, and releasing emotions

certainly more likely than others. Common emotional responses to stress include (Lazarus, 1993; Woolfolk & Richardson, 1978):

- *Annoyance, anger, and rage.* Stress commonly produces feelings of anger ranging in intensity from mild annoyance to uncontrollable rage. Frustration is particularly likely to generate anger.
- *Apprehension, anxiety, and fear.* Stress probably evokes anxiety and fear more frequently than any other emotions. As we saw in Chapter 2, Freudian theory has long recognized the link between conflict and anxiety. However, anxiety can also be elicited by the pressure to perform, the threat of impending frustration, or the uncertainty associated with change.
- *Dejection, sadness, and grief.* Sometimes stress—especially frustration—simply brings one down. Routine setbacks, such as traffic tickets and poor grades, often produce feelings of dejection. More profound setbacks, such as deaths and divorces, typically leave one grief-stricken.

Of course, the above list is not exhaustive. In his insightful analyses of stress-emotion relations, Richard Lazarus (1991, 1993) mentions five other emotions that often figure prominently in reactions to stress: guilt, shame, envy, jealousy, and disgust.

EFFECTS OF EMOTIONAL AROUSAL

Emotional reponses are a natural and normal part of life. Even unpleasant emotions serve important purposes. Like physical pain, painful emotions can serve as warnings that one needs to take action. However, it's important to note that strong emotional arousal may sometimes interfere with efforts to cope with stress. For example, research has found that high emotional arousal can interfere with attention and memory retrieval and impair judgment and decision making (Janis, 1993; Mandler, 1993).

The well-known problem of *test anxiety* illustrates how emotional arousal can hurt performance. Often students who score poorly on an exam will nonetheless insist that they know the material. Many of them are probably telling the truth. Many researchers have found a negative correlation between test-related anxiety and exam performance. That is, students who display high test anxiety tend to score low on exams (Hembre, 1988; Naveh-Benjamin et al., 1997). Test anxiety can interfere with test taking in several ways, but one critical consideration appears to be the disruption of attention to the test (Jones & Petruzzi, 1995; Sarason, 1984). Many test-anxious students waste too much time worrying about how they're doing and wondering whether others are having similar problems. In other words, their minds wander too much from the task of taking the test.

Although emotional arousal may hurt coping efforts, this isn't *necessarily* the case. The *inverted-U hypothesis* predicts that task performance should improve with increased emotional arousal—up to a point, after which further increases in arousal become disruptive and performance deteriorates (Anderson, 1990; Mandler, 1993). This idea is referred to as the inverted-U hypothesis because when performance is plotted as a function of arousal, the resulting graphs approximate an upside-down U (see Figure 3.10). In these graphs, the level of arousal at which performance peaks is characterized as the *optimal level of arousal* for a task.

This optimal level of arousal appears to depend in part on the complexity of the task at hand. The conventional wisdom is that *as a task becomes more complex, the optimal level of arousal (for peak performance) tends to decrease.* This relationship is depicted in Figure 3.10. As you can see, a fairly high level of arousal should be optimal on simple tasks (such as driving eight hours to help a friend in a crisis). However, performance should peak at a lower level of arousal on complex tasks (such as making a major decision in which you have to weigh many factors).

The research evidence on the inverted-U hypothesis is inconsistent and subject to varied interpretations (Neiss, 1988, 1990). Hence, it may be risky to generalize this principle to the complexities of everyday coping efforts. Nonetheless, the inverted-U hypothesis provides a plausible model of how emotional arousal could have either beneficial or disruptive effects on coping, depending on the nature of the stressful demands.

Physiological Responses

As we have seen, stress frequently elicits strong emotional responses. These responses bring about important physiological changes. Even in cases of moderate stress, you may notice that your heart has started beating faster, you have begun to breathe harder, and you are perspiring more than usual. How does all this (and much more) happen? Let's see.

THE "FIGHT OR FLIGHT" RESPONSE
The *fight-or-flight response* is a physiological reaction to threat that mobilizes an organism for attacking

Web Link 3.3

Stress Management and Peak Performance
From the University of Nebraska's (Lincoln) Department of Health and Human Performance, Wesley Sime provides both a general overview and an educational tutorial for issues involved in human stress management.

FIGURE 3.10.

Arousal and performance. Graphs of the relationship between emotional arousal and task performance tend to resemble an inverted U, as increased arousal is associated with improved performance up to a point, after which higher arousal leads to poorer performance. The optimal level of arousal for a task depends on the complexity of the task. On complex tasks, a relatively low level of arousal tends to be optimal. On simple tasks, however, performance may peak at a much higher level of arousal.

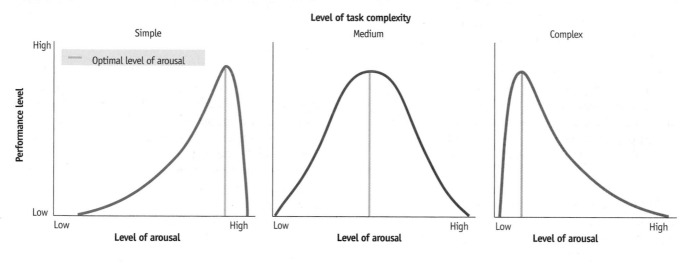

Level of task complexity

(fight) or fleeing (flight) an enemy. First described by Walter Cannon (1932), the fight-or-flight response occurs in the body's autonomic nervous system. **The autonomic nervous system (ANS) is made up of the nerves that connect to the heart, blood vessels, smooth muscles, and glands.** As its name hints, the autonomic nervous system is somewhat *autonomous.* That is, it controls involuntary, visceral functions that people don't normally think about, such as heart rate, digestion, and perspiration.

The autonomic nervous system can be broken into two divisions (see Figure 3.11). The *parasympathetic division* of the ANS generally conserves bodily resources. For instance, it slows heart rate and promotes digestion to help the body save and store energy.

The fight-or-flight response is mediated by the *sympathetic division* of the autonomic nervous system, which mobilizes bodily resources for emergencies. In one experiment, Cannon studied the fight-or-flight response in cats by confronting them with dogs. Among other things, he noticed an immediate acceleration in breathing and heart rate and a reduction in digestive processes.

Elements of the fight-or-flight response are also seen in humans. Imagine your reaction if your car nearly spun out of control on the highway. Your heart would race, and your blood pressure would surge. You might get "goosebumps" and experience a "knot in your stomach." These reflex responses are part of the fight-or-flight response.

FIGURE 3.11.

The autonomic nervous system (ANS). The ANS is composed of the nerves that connect to the heart, blood vessels, smooth muscles, and glands. The ANS is subdivided into the *sympathetic division*, which mobilizes bodily resources in times of need, and the *parasympathetic division*, which conserves bodily resources. Some of the key functions controlled by each division of the ANS are summarized in the center of the diagram.

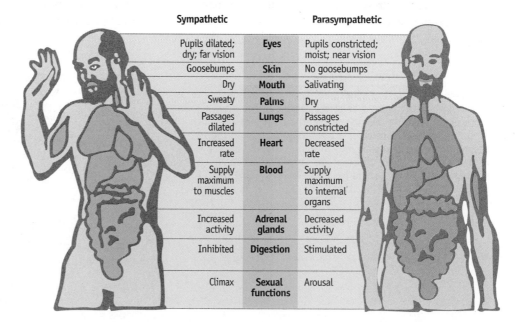

Sympathetic		Parasympathetic
Pupils dilated; dry; far vision	**Eyes**	Pupils constricted; moist; near vision
Goosebumps	**Skin**	No goosebumps
Dry	**Mouth**	Salivating
Sweaty	**Palms**	Dry
Passages dilated	**Lungs**	Passages constricted
Increased rate	**Heart**	Decreased rate
Supply maximum to muscles	**Blood**	Supply maximum to internal organs
Increased activity	**Adrenal glands**	Decreased activity
Inhibited	**Digestion**	Stimulated
Climax	**Sexual functions**	Arousal

In a sense, this automatic reaction is a leftover from our evolutionary past. It is clearly an adaptive response in the animal kingdom, where the threat of predators often requires a swift response of fighting or fleeing. But among humans, the fight-or-flight response appears less adaptive. Most modern stresses cannot be handled simply through fight or flight. Work pressures, marital problems, and financial difficulties require far more complex responses. Moreover, these stresses often continue for lengthy periods of time, so that the fight-or-flight response leaves one in a state of enduring physiological arousal. Concern about the effects of prolonged physical arousal was first voiced by Hans Selye, a Canadian scientist who conducted extensive research on stress.

THE GENERAL ADAPTATION SYNDROME

The concept of stress was added to our language by Hans Selye (1936, 1956, 1982). Selye was born in Vienna but spent his entire professional career at McGill University in Montreal. Beginning in the 1930s, Selye exposed laboratory animals to a diverse array of both physical and psychological stressors (heat, cold, pain, mild shock, restraint, and so on). The patterns of physiological arousal he observed in the animals were largely the same, regardless of the type of stress. Thus, Selye concluded that stress reactions are *nonspecific*. In other words, he maintained that they do not vary according to the specific type of stress encountered. Initially, Selye wasn't sure what to call this nonspecific response to a variety of noxious agents. In the 1940s, he decided to call it *stress,* and the word has been part of our vocabulary ever since.

Hans Selye

Web Link 3.4

Stress and You: History of Chronic Fatigue
The highlight of this particular subpage is an excellent chart that illustrates the stages of the general adaptation syndrome, Hans Selye's seminal theory of how stress affects the entire organism.

Selye (1956, 1974) formulated an influential theory of stress reactions called the general adaptation syndrome (see Figure 3.12). **The *general adaptation syndrome* is a model of the body's stress response, consisting of three stages: alarm, resistance, and exhaustion.** In the first stage of the general adaptation syndrome, an *alarm reaction* occurs when an organism recognizes the existence of a threat. Physiological arousal increases as the body musters its resources to combat the challenge. Selye's alarm reaction is essentially the fight-or-flight response originally described by Cannon.

However, Selye took his investigation of stress a couple of steps further by exposing laboratory animals to *prolonged stress,* similar to the chronic stress often endured by humans. If stress continues, the organism may progress to the second phase of the general adaptation syndrome, called the *stage of resistance.* During this phase, physiological changes stabilize as coping efforts get under way. Typically, physiological arousal continues to be higher than normal, although it may level off somewhat as the organism becomes accustomed to the threat.

If the stress continues over a substantial period of time, the organism may enter the third stage, called the *stage of exhaustion.* According to Selye, the body's resources for fighting stress are limited. If the stress cannot be overcome, the body's resources may be depleted, and physiological arousal will decrease. Eventually, there may be a collapse from exhaustion. During this phase,

FIGURE 3.12.

The general adaptation syndrome. According to Selye, the physiological response to stress can be broken into three phases. During the first phase, the body mobilizes its resources for resistance after a brief initial shock. In the second phase, resistance levels off and eventually begins to decline. If the third phase of the general adaptation syndrome is reached, resistance is depleted, leading to health problems and exhaustion.

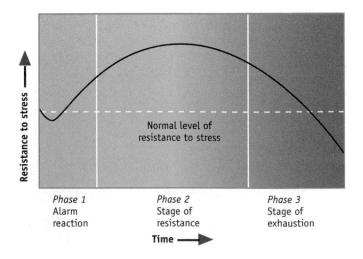

the organism's resistance declines. This reduced resistance may lead to what Selye called "diseases of adaptation," such as ulcers or high blood pressure.

Selye's theory and research forged a link between stress and physical illness. He showed how prolonged physiological arousal that is meant to be adaptive could lead to diseases. His theory has been criticized because it ignores individual differences in the appraisal of stress (Lazarus & Folkman, 1984), and his belief that stress reactions are nonspecific remains controversial (Baum, 1990; Weiner, 1992). However, his model provided guidance for a generation of researchers who worked out the details of how stress reverberates throughout the body. Let's look at some of those details.

BRAIN-BODY PATHWAYS

When you experience stress, your brain sends signals to the endocrine system along two major pathways (Felker & Hubbard, 1998; Koranyi, 1989). **The *endocrine system* consists of glands that secrete chemicals called hormones into the bloodstream.** The major endocrine glands, such as the pituitary, pineal, thyroid, and adrenal glands, are shown in Figure 3.13.

The hypothalamus, a small structure near the base of the brain, appears to initiate action along both of the pathways. The first pathway (shown on the right in Figure 3.14 on the next page) is routed through the autonomic nervous system. The hypothalamus activates the sympathetic division of the ANS. A key part of this activation involves stimulating the central part of the adrenal glands (the adrenal medulla) to release large amounts of *catecholamines* into the bloodstream. These hormones radiate throughout your body, producing many important physiological changes. The net result of catecholamine elevation is that your body is mobilized for action. Heart rate and blood flow increase, pumping more blood to your brain and muscles. Respiration and oxygen consumption speed up, facilitating alertness. Digestive processes are inhibited to conserve your energy. The pupils of your eyes dilate, increasing visual sensitivity.

The second pathway (shown on the left in Figure 3.14) involves more direct communication between the brain and the endocrine system. The hypothalamus sends signals to the so-called master gland of the endocrine system, the pituitary gland. The pituitary secretes a hormone (ACTH) that stimulates the outer part of the adrenal glands (the adrenal cortex) to release another important set of hormones—*corticosteroids*. These hormones stimulate the release of more fats and proteins into your circulation, thus helping increase your energy. They also mobilize chemicals that help inhibit tissue inflammation in case of injury.

Stress can also produce other physiological changes that we are just beginning to understand. The most

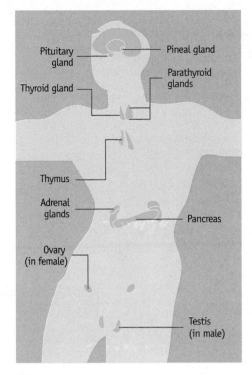

FIGURE 3.13.

The endocrine system. The endocrine glands secrete hormones into the bloodstream. The locations of the principal endocrine glands are shown here. The hormones released by these glands regulate a variety of physical functions and play a key role in our response to stress.

critical changes occur in the immune system. Your immune system provides you with resistance to infections. However, mounting evidence indicates that stress can suppress the functioning of the immune system, making it less effective in repelling invasions by infectious agents (Kiecolt-Glaser & Glaser, 1995; La Via & Workman, 1998). The exact mechanisms underlying immunal suppression remain a mystery for the moment, but it appears likely that both sets of stress hormones (catecholamines and corticosteroids) contribute (Dantzer & Mormede, 1995). In any case, it is becoming clear that physiological responses to stress extend into every corner of the body. Moreover, some of these responses may persist long after a stressful event has ended (Esterling et al., 1994). As you will see, these physiological reactions can have an impact on both mental and physical health.

Behavioral Responses

Although people respond to stress at several levels, their behavior is the crucial dimension of these reactions. Emotional and physiological responses to stress—which are often undesirable—tend to be largely automatic. However, dealing effectively with stress at the behavioral level may shut down these potentially harmful emotional and physiological responses.

FIGURE 3.14.

Brain-body pathways in stress. In times of stress, the brain sends signals along two pathways. The pathway through the autonomic nervous system (shown in blue on the right) controls the release of catecholamine hormones that help mobilize the body for action. The pathway through the pituitary gland and the endocrine system (shown in brown on the left) controls the release of corticosteroid hormones that increase energy and ward off tissue inflammation.

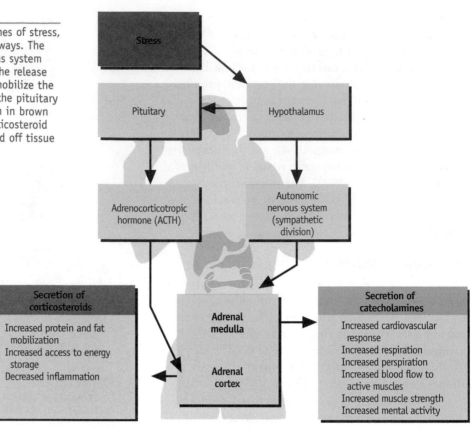

Most behavioral responses to stress involve coping. *Coping* **refers to active efforts to master, reduce, or tolerate the demands created by stress.** Notice that this definition is neutral as to whether coping efforts are healthy or maladaptive. The popular use of the term often implies that coping is inherently healthy. When we say that someone "coped with her problems," we imply that she handled them effectively.

In reality, coping responses may be either healthy or unhealthy (Moos & Schaefer, 1993). For example, if you were flunking a history course at midterm, you might cope with this stress by (1) increasing your study efforts, (2) seeking help from a tutor, (3) blaming your professor for your poor grade, or (4) giving up on the class. Clearly, the first two coping responses would be healthier than the second two. Thus, coping efforts may range from healthy to unhealthy.

People cope with stress in an endless variety of ways. Because of the complexity and importance of coping processes, we'll devote all of the next chapter to ways of coping. At this point, it is sufficient to note that coping strategies help to determine whether stress has any positive or negative effects on an individual. In the next section, we'll see what some of those effects can be as we discuss the possible outcomes of people's struggles with stress.

The Potential Effects of Stress

LEARNING OBJECTIVES

- Discuss the effects of stress on task performance and the phenomenon of choking under pressure.
- Discuss the likely effect of stress on cognitive functioning.
- Describe the symptoms and causes of burnout.
- Discuss the prevalence, symptoms, and causes of posttraumatic stress disorder.
- Discuss the potential impact of stress on mental and physical health.
- Discuss three ways in which stress might lead to beneficial effects.

People struggle with many stresses every day, most of which come and go without leaving any enduring imprint. However, when stress is severe or when demands pile up, stress may have long-lasting effects. These effects are often called "adaptational outcomes." They are relatively durable (though not necessarily permanent) consequences of exposure to stress. Although stress can have beneficial effects, research has focused mainly on possible negative outcomes (Cohen, 1988), so you'll find our coverage slanted in that direction.

Impaired Task Performance

Frequently, stress takes its toll on our ability to perform effectively on the task at hand. For instance, Roy Baumeister's work shows how pressure can interfere with performance. Baumeister's (1984) theory assumes that pressure to perform often makes people self-conscious and that this elevated self-consciousness disrupts their attention. He theorizes that attention may be distorted in two ways. First, elevated self-consciousness may divert attention from the demands of the task, creating distractions. Second, on well-learned tasks that should be executed almost automatically, the self-conscious person may focus *too* much attention on the task. Thus, the person thinks too much about what he or she is doing.

Baumeister (1984) found support for his theory in a series of laboratory experiments in which he manipulated the pressure to perform well on a simple perceptual-motor task. Even more impressive, his theory was supported in a study of the past performance of professional sports teams in championship contests (Baumeister & Steinhilber, 1984). According to Baumeister, when a championship series such as baseball's World Series goes to the final, decisive game, the home team is under greater pressure than the visiting team. Why? Because players desperately want to succeed in front of their hometown fans. Conventional wisdom suggests that home teams have the advantage in sports. But Baumeister and Steinhilber (1984) analyzed past championships in professional baseball (from 1924 to 1982) and basketball (from 1967 to 1982) and found that the winning percentage for home teams was significantly lower in final games than in early games in both sports (see Figure 3.15). In other words the home team "choked."

More recently, Schlenker and colleagues (1995) have pointed out that home team championship choking has been infrequent in professional baseball and basketball since the Baumeister and Steinhilber (1984) study, and they question the reliability of the phenomenon. In reply, Baumeister (1995) argues that a modest home choking effect is still apparent even when the data from 1983–1993 are included (see Figure 3.15). He also speculates that changes in the nature of American professional sports may have made modern athletes less susceptible to choking under pressure. The bottom line is that looking for a choking effect in professional sports represents an inordinately difficult test of the hypothesis that pressure impairs performance. In professional sports championships, both teams are under incredible pressure, and the disparity between the home and visiting teams may not amount to much. Moreover, gifted professional athletes are probably less likely to choke under pressure than virtually any other sample one might assemble. Laboratory research on "normal" subjects is much more pertinent to the issue, and it suggests that choking under pressure is fairly common (Baumeister, 1995; Lewis & Linder, 1997).

Disruption of Cognitive Functioning

An interesting experimental study suggests that Baumeister is on the right track in looking to *attention* to explain how stress impairs task performance. In a study of stress and decision making, Keinan (1987) was able to measure three specific aspects of subjects' attention under stressful and nonstressful conditions. Keinan placed subjects under stress by telling them that they might receive painful but harmless electric shocks while working on a decision-making task at a computer. No one was actually shocked, and subjects were given the option of quitting the study when they were told about the shock. Keinan found that stress disrupted two out of the three aspects of attention

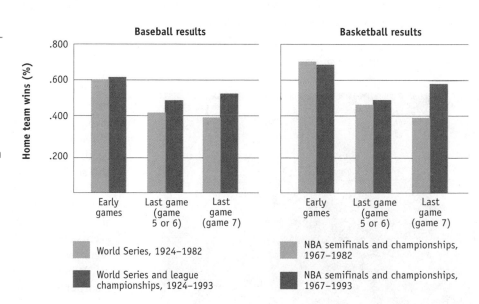

FIGURE 3.15.

Choking under pressure? The results graphed in orange were reported in Baumeister and Steinhilber's (1984) study, which summarized World Series and NBA championship contests in each sport's modern era up through 1982. The results graphed in red include more recent years in both sports and the league championships in baseball, as compiled by Schlenker and colleagues (1995). The earlier study suggested that when it comes to the last game, the home team frequently chokes under pressure. With more recent results added in, the choking effect is much less pronounced, although home teams still fare more poorly in final games than in earlier games.

measured in the study. Stress increased subjects' tendency (1) to jump to a conclusion too quickly without considering all their options and (2) to do an unsystematic, poorly organized review of their available options.

Severe stress may leave people dazed and confused, in a state of shock (Weisaeth, 1993). In these states, people report feeling emotionally numb, and they respond in a flat, apathetic fashion to events around them. They often stare off into space and have difficulty maintaining a coherent train of thought. Their behavior frequently has an automatic, rigid, stereotyped quality. Fortunately, this disorientation usually occurs only in extreme situations involving overwhelming stress, such as surviving a fire, a flood, or a tornado.

Burnout

Burnout is an overused buzzword that means different things to different people. Nonetheless, a few researchers have described burnout in a systematic way that has facilitated scientific study of the syndrome (Leiter & Maslach, 1988; Maslach, 1982; Pines, 1993). **Burnout involves physical, mental, and emotional exhaustion that is attributable to work-related stress.** The physical exhaustion includes chronic fatigue, weakness, and low energy. The mental exhaustion is manifested in highly negative attitudes toward oneself, one's work, and life in general. The emotional exhaustion includes feeling hopeless, helpless, and trapped.

What causes burnout? According to Ayala Pines and her colleagues (1981), "it usually does not occur as the result of one or two traumatic events but sneaks up through a general erosion of the spirit" (p. 3). They view burnout as an emotional disturbance brought on gradually by heavy, chronic, job-related stress.

Initially, theorists thought that burnout was unique to the helping professions, such as social work, clinical psychology, and counseling. The high burnout rate in

Severe accidents are just one of about a half-dozen types of calamitous events that can lead to posttraumatic stress disorder.

Web Link 3.5

The Road to Burnout
This resource, maintained by the American Psychological Association, describes various stages and warning signs of burnout—that "state of physical, emotional, and mental exhaustion caused by unrealistically high aspirations and illusory and impossible goals," as this page describes it.

the helping professions was blamed on helpers' emotionally draining relations with their clients. However, it has gradually become clear that burnout is a potential problem in a wide variety of occupations (Lee & Ashforth, 1996). Indeed, work stress may not be the only cause of burnout. It's possible that chronic stress from other roles, such as parenting or being a student, may lead to burnout.

Posttraumatic Stress Disorders

Extremely stressful, traumatic incidents can leave a lasting imprint on victims' psychological functioning. **The** *posttraumatic stress disorder (PTSD)* **involves enduring psychological disturbance attributed to the experience of a major traumatic event.** Researchers began to appreciate the frequency and severity of posttraumatic stress disorders after the Vietnam war ended in 1975 and a great many psychologically scarred veterans returned home. These veterans displayed a diverse array of psychological problems and symptoms that in many cases lingered much longer than expected. Studies suggest that nearly a half million Vietnam veterans were still suffering from PTSD over a decade after the end of the war (Schlenger et al., 1992).

Although posttraumatic stress disorders are widely associated with the experiences of Vietnam veterans, they are seen in response to other cases of traumatic stress as well, and they appear to be much more common than originally believed. Recent research suggests that about 8% of people have suffered from PTSD at some point in their lives (Solomon & Canino, 1990). About 60% of these cases turn out to be long-lasting (Kessler et al., 1995).

What types of stress besides combat are severe enough to produce PTSD? The syndrome is frequently seen after a rape, a serious automobile accident, a robbery or assault, or the witnessing of someone's death (Stein et al., 1997). Studies indicate that PTSD is also somewhat common in the wake of major disasters, such as floods, hurricanes, earthquakes, fires, and so forth (Koopman, Classen, & Spiegel, 1994; Vernberg et al., 1996). Unfortunately, these types of traumatic events are more common than most people realize (see Figure 3.16).

What are the symptoms of posttraumatic stress disorders? Common symptoms include reexperiencing the traumatic event in the form of nightmares and flashbacks, emotional numbing, alienation, problems in social relations, and elevated arousal, anxiety, and guilt (Foa & Riggs, 1995). PTSD is also associated with an elevated risk for substance abuse, depression, and suicide attempts (Warshaw et al., 1993). The frequency and severity of posttraumatic symptoms usually decline gradually over time, but in many cases the symptoms never completely disappear.

Although PTSD is common in the wake of traumatic events, the majority of people who experience such events do not develop PTSD. Hence, a current focus of research is to determine what factors make certain people more resilient than others to the ravages of severe stress. One recent study identified *social support* and the personality syndrome of *hardiness* as key factors promoting resistance to PTSD (King et al., 1998). We will discuss the importance of social support and hardiness in our upcoming section on factors influencing stress tolerance.

Psychological Problems and Disorders

Posttraumatic stress disorders are caused by a single episode of extreme stress. Of greater relevance to most of us are the effects of chronic, prolonged, everyday stress. On the basis of clinical impressions, psychologists have long suspected that chronic stress might contribute to many types of psychological problems and mental disorders. Since the late 1960s, advances in the measurement of stress have allowed researchers to verify these suspicions in empirical studies. In the domain of common psychological problems, studies indicate that stress may contribute to poor academic performance (Dawod, 1995), insomnia (Roehrs, Zorick, & Roth, 1994) nightmares (Hartmann, 1993), sexual difficulties (Lemack, Uzzo, & Poppas, 1998), alcohol abuse

Web Link 3.6

David Baldwin's Trauma Information Pages
This site has long been recognized as the premier repository for Web-based and other resources relating to emotional trauma, traumatic stress, and posttraumatic stress disorder. David Baldwin has assembled more than 1,000 links to information about these issues.

(Jennison, 1992), drug abuse (Franco, Hubbard, & Martin, 1998), and unhappiness (Heady & Wearing, 1989).

Above and beyond these everyday problems, research reveals that stress often contributes to the onset of full-fledged psychological disorders, including depression (Gruen, 1993), schizophrenia (Fowles, 1992), anxiety disorders (Falsetti & Ballenger, 1998), and eating disorders (Cooper, 1995). We'll discuss these relations between stress and mental disorders in detail in Chapter 15. Of course, stress is only one of many factors that may contribute to psychological disorders. Nonetheless, it is sobering to realize that stress can have such a dramatic impact on one's mental health.

Physical Illness

It is just as sobering to realize that stress can also have a dramatic impact on one's physical health. The idea that stress can contribute to physical diseases is not entirely new. Evidence that stress can cause physical illness began to accumulate back in the 1930s. By the 1950s, the concept of psychosomatic disease was widely accepted. **Psychosomatic diseases (or psychophysiological disorders) are genuine physical ailments caused in part by psychological factors.** The underlying assumption is that stress-induced autonomic arousal contributes to most psychosomatic diseases. Please note, these diseases are not *imagined* physical ailments.

FIGURE 3.16.

The prevalence of traumatic events. We tend to think that traumatic events are relatively unusual and infrequent, but research by Stein et al. (1997) suggests otherwise. They interviewed over 1000 people in Winnipeg and found that 74.2% of the women and 81.3% of the men reported having experienced at least one highly traumatic event. The graph summarizes the percentage of respondents reporting specific types of traumatic events.

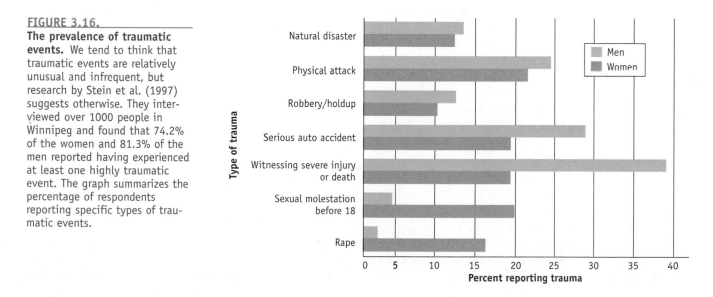

The term *psychosomatic* is often misused to refer to ailments that are "all in the head." This is an entirely different syndrome (see Chapter 15).

Common psychosomatic diseases include high blood pressure, ulcers, asthma, skin disorders such as eczema and hives, and migraine and tension headaches (Kaplan, 1989). These diseases do not *necessarily* have a strong psychological component in every affected individual. There is a genetic predisposition to most psychosomatic diseases, and in some people these diseases are largely physiological in origin (Weiner & Fawzy, 1989). More often than not, however, psychological factors contribute to psychosomatic diseases. When they do, stress is one of the chief culprits at work (Creed, 1993).

Prior to the 1970s, it was thought that stress contributed to the development of only a few physical diseases (the psychosomatic diseases). In the 1970s, however, researchers began to uncover new links between stress and a great variety of diseases previously believed to be purely physiological in origin. Although there is room for debate on some specific diseases, stress may influence the onset and course of heart disease, stroke, tuberculosis, multiple sclerosis, arthritis, diabetes, leukemia, cancer, various types of infectious disease, and the common cold (Critelli & Ee, 1996; Elliott, 1989; Hubbard & Workman, 1998). We'll take a more detailed look at the evidence linking stress to some of these diseases in Chapter 14.

Beneficial Effects

The beneficial effects of stress are more difficult to pinpoint than the harmful effects because they tend to be more subtle. Although research data are sparse, there are at least three ways in which stress can have positive effects.

First, stressful events help satisfy the need for stimulation and challenge. Studies suggest that most people prefer an intermediate level of stimulation and challenge in their lives (Suedfeld, 1979). Although we think of stress in terms of stimulus overload, underload can be extremely unpleasant as well (Goldberger, 1993). Thus, most people would experience a suffocating level of boredom if they lived a stress-free existence. In a sense, then, stress fulfills a basic need of the human organism.

Second, stress can promote personal growth or self-improvement (Holahan & Moos, 1990). Stressful events sometimes force people to develop new skills, learn new insights, and acquire new strengths. In other words, the adaptation process initiated by stress may lead to personal changes that are changes for the better. Confronting and conquering a stressful challenge may lead to improvements in specific coping abilities and to an enhanced self-concept (Schaefer & Moos, 1992). For example, a breakup with a boyfriend or a girlfriend may lead individuals to change aspects of their behavior that they find unsatisfactory. Moreover, even if people do not conquer stressors, they may be able to learn from their mistakes. Thus, researchers have begun to explore the growth potential of stressful events (Park, Cohen, & Murch, 1996; Tedeschi & Calhoun, 1996).

Third, today's stress can inoculate individuals so that they are less affected by tomorrow's stress. Some studies suggest that exposure to stress can increase stress tolerance—as long as the stress isn't overwhelming (Meichenbaum, 1993). Thus, a woman who has previously endured business setbacks may be much better prepared than most people to deal with a bank foreclosure on her home. In light of the negative effects that stress can have, improved stress tolerance is a desirable goal. We'll look next at the factors that influence the ability to tolerate stress.

Factors Influencing Stress Tolerance

LEARNING OBJECTIVES

- Discuss how social support moderates the impact of stress.
- Describe the hardiness syndrome and how it influences stress tolerance.
- Discuss how optimism and conscientiousness are related to stress tolerance.
- Discuss how sensation seeking can be both adaptive and maladaptive.
- Describe the relationship between autonomic reactivity and stress tolerance.

Some people seem to be able to withstand the ravages of stress better than others (Holahan & Moos, 1990, 1994). Why? Because a number of *moderator variables* can soften the impact of stress on physical and mental health. To shed light on differences in how well people tolerate stress, we'll look at a number of key moderator variables, including social support, hardiness, optimism, conscientiousness, sensation seeking, and autonomic reactivity. As you'll see, these factors influence people's appraisals of potentially stressful events and their emotional, physical, and behavioral responses to stress. These complexities are diagrammed in Figure 3.17, which builds on Figure 3.9 to provide a more complete overview of all the factors involved in individual reactions to stress.

Social Support

Friends may be good for your health! This startling

FIGURE 3.17.

Overview of the stress process. This diagram builds on Figure 3.9 to provide a more complete overview of the factors involved in stress. This diagram adds the potential effects of stress (seen on the far right) by listing some of the positive and negative adaptational outcomes that may result from stress. It also completes the picture by showing that moderating variables (seen at the top) can intervene to influence the effects of stress.

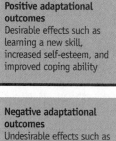

Moderating variables influencing stress tolerance
Such as social support, hardiness, optimism, sensation seeking, and autonomic reactivity

Potentially stressful objective events
A major exam, a big date, trouble with boss, or a financial setback, which may lead to frustration, conflict, change, or pressure

Subjective cognitive appraisal
Personalized perceptions of threat, which are influenced by familiarity with the event, its controllability, its predictability, and so on

Emotional response
Annoyance, anger, anxiety, fear, dejection, grief, guilt, shame, envy, disgust

Physiological response
Autonomic arousal, hormonal fluctuations, neurochemical changes, and so on

Behavioral response
Coping efforts, such as lashing out at others, blaming oneself, seeking help, solving problems, and releasing emotions

Positive adaptational outcomes
Desirable effects such as learning a new skill, increased self-esteem, and improved coping ability

Negative adaptational outcomes
Undesirable effects such as physical illness, psychological problems, burnout, and impaired task performance

conclusion emerges from studies on social support as a moderator of stress. *Social support* refers to various types of aid and succor provided by members of one's social networks. For example, Jemmott and Magloire (1988) examined the effect of social support on immunal functioning in a group of students going through the stress of final exams. They found that students who reported stronger social support had higher levels of an antibody that plays a key role in warding off respiratory infections. Positive correlations between high social support and greater immunal functioning were also seen in another study, which focused on spouses of cancer patients (Baron et al., 1990)

Many studies have found evidence that social support is favorably related to physical health (Uchino, Cacioppo, & Kiecolt-Glaser, 1996; Vogt et al., 1992). Indeed, in a major review of the relevant research, House, Landis, and Umberson (1988) argue that the evidence linking social support to health is roughly as strong as the evidence linking smoking to cancer. Social support seems to be good medicine for the mind as well as the body, as most studies find an association between social support and mental health and emotional well-being (Davis, Morris, & Kraus, 1998; Sarason, Pierce, & Sarason, 1994). The mechanisms underlying the connection between social support and wellness are the subject of considerable debate (Hobfoll & Vaux, 1993). It appears that social support serves as a protective buffer during times of high stress, reducing the negative

impact of stressful events—and that social support has its own positive effects on health, which may be apparent even when people aren't under great stress (Cohen & Syme, 1985; Peirce et al., 1996). The stress-buffering effects of social support were apparent in a recent study which found that strong social support was a key factor reducing the likelihood of posttraumatic stress disorders among Vietnam veterans (King et al., 1998).

The power of social support is such that even pets may provide social bonds that buffer the effects of stress! For instance, Siegel (1990) found that elderly pet owners required less medical care than comparable subjects who did not own pets. In another study, women exposed to brief stress showed less physiological reaction when in the company of their pets (Allen et al., 1991).

Of course, social *bonds* are not equivalent to social *support* (Rook, 1990). Indeed, some people in one's social circles may be a source of more *stress* than *support* (Lepore, 1992; Vinokur & van Ryn, 1993). Friends and family can put one under pressure, make one feel guilty, break promises, and so forth. Pagel, Erdly, and Becker (1987) looked at both the good and the bad sides of social relations in measuring subjects' satisfaction with their social networks. They found that the helpfulness of friends and family wasn't as important as whether friends and family caused emotional distress. Adapting a line from an old Beatles song, the investigators concluded that "We get by with [*and in spite of*] a little help from our friends." To some extent, then, people who report good social support may really mean that their friends and family aren't driving them crazy.

Hardiness

Another line of research indicates that a syndrome called *hardiness* may moderate the impact of stressful events. Suzanne Ouellette (Kobasa) reasoned that if stress affects some people less than others, then some people must be *hardier* than others. Hence, she set out to ascertain what factors might be the key to these differences in hardiness.

Suzanne Ouellette

Kobasa (1979) used a modified version of the Holmes and Rahe (1967) stress scale (SRRS) to measure the amount of stress experienced by a group of executives. As in most other studies, she found a modest correlation between stress and the incidence of physical illness. However, she carried her investigation one step further than previous studies. She compared the high-stress executives who exhibited the expected high incidence of illness against the high-stress executives who stayed healthy. She administered a battery of psychological tests and found that the hardier executives "were more committed, felt more in control, and had bigger appetites for challenge" (Kobasa, 1984, p. 70). These traits have also shown up in many other studies of hardiness (Ouellette, 1993).

Thus, **hardiness is a syndrome marked by commitment, challenge, and control that is purportedly associated with strong stress resistance.** Hardiness may reduce the effects of stress by altering stress appraisals (Florian, Mikulincer, & Taubman, 1995). The benefits of hardiness showed up in a recent study of Vietnam veterans, which found that higher hardiness was related to a lower likelihood of developing post-traumatic stress disorders (King et al., 1998).

Although the research on hardiness is promising, doubts exist about the relevance of the hardiness syndrome to women, and debate continues about the key elements of hardiness (Funk, 1992; Wiebe, 1991; Younkin & Betz, 1996).

Optimism and Conscientiousness

Defining **optimism as a general tendency to expect good outcomes,** Michael Scheier and Charles Carver (1985) found a correlation between a measure of optimism (see Figure 3.18) and relatively good physical health in a sample of college students. In another study that focused on surgical patients, optimism was found

to be associated with a faster recovery and a quicker return to normal activities after coronary artery bypass surgery (Scheier et al., 1989). Yet another study found that optimism was associated with more effective immunal functioning (Segerstrom et al., 1998).

Research suggests that optimists cope with stress in more adaptive ways than pessimists (Aspinwall & Taylor, 1992; Chang, 1996; Scheier & Carver, 1992). Optimists are more likely to engage in action-oriented, problem-focused coping and are more willing than pessimists to seek social support. In comparison, pessimists are more likely to deal with stress by giving up or engaging in denial. A recent study also found that optimists are more likely to emphasize the positive in their secondary appraisals of stressful events (Chang, 1998).

In a related line of research, Christopher Peterson and Martin Seligman have studied how people explain

FIGURE 3.18.

The Life Orientation Test (LOT). The personality trait of optimism, which appears to foster resilience in the face of stress, can be measured by the Life Orientation Test (LOT) developed by Scheier and Carver (1985). Follow the instructions for this scale to obtain an estimate of your own optimism. High and low scores are based on scoring three-fifths of a standard deviation above or below the mean.

Measuring Optimism

In the following spaces, mark how much you agree with each of the items, using the following scale:

4 = strongly agree
3 = agree
1 = disagree
2 = neutral
0 = strongly disagree

_____ 1. In uncertain times, I usually expect the best.
_____ 2. It's easy for me to relax.
_____ 3. If something can go wrong for me, it will.
_____ 4. I always look on the bright side of things.
_____ 5. I'm always optimistic about my future.
_____ 6. I enjoy my friends a lot.
_____ 7. It's important for me to keep busy.
_____ 8. I hardly ever expect things to go my way.
_____ 9. Things never work out the way I want them to.
_____ 10. I don't get upset too easily.
_____ 11. I'm a believer in the idea that "every cloud has a silver lining."
_____ 12. I rarely count on good things happening to me.

Scoring

Cross out and ignore the responses you entered for items 2, 6, 7, and 10, which are "filler" items. For items 3, 8, 9, and 12, you need to reverse the numbers you entered. If you entered a 4, change it to 0. If you entered a 3, change it to 1. If you entered a 2, leave it unchanged. If you entered a 1, change it to 3. If you entered a 0, change it to 4. Now add up the numbers for items 1, 3, 4, 5, 8, 9, 11, 12, using the new numbers for the reversed items. This sum is your score on the Life Orientation Test. For college students, approximate norms are as follows: High score (25–32), Intermediate score (18–24), Low score (0–17).

bad events (personal setbacks, mishaps, disappointments, and such). They identified a *pessimistic explanatory style* in which people tend to blame setbacks on their own personal shortcomings. In two retrospective studies of people born many decades ago, they found an association between this pessimistic explanatory style and relatively poor health (Peterson, Seligman, & Vaillant, 1988) and elevated mortality (earlier death) (Peterson et al., 1998). In their attempt to explain these

associations, they speculate that pessimism may lead to passive coping efforts, poor health care practices, and risky lifestyles.

Recent research by Howard Friedman and his colleagues (1993, 1995) suggests that *conscientiousness,* one of the Big Five personality traits discussed in Chapter 2, may also have an impact on stress reactions and physical health. **Conscientiousness consists of the tendency to be diligent, punctual, and dependable.** Friedman

●Recommended Reading

Learned Optimism: How to Change Your Mind and Your Life by Martin E. P. Seligman (Pocket Books, 1990)

Martin Seligman is an outstanding researcher who has done pioneering work on optimism. *Learned Optimism* is a highly personal book in which Seligman describes how his research on optimism grew out of his earlier work on learned helplessness and depression. It offers some interesting insights into how a scientist's thinking evolves as research progresses and new evidence emerges. According to Seligman, people have characteristic ways of explaining and thinking about their successes, their failures, and their challenges in life. Pessimists expect the worst possible scenario from every setback and blame themselves for their failures. Optimists are much the opposite. They see life's difficulties in the least threatening light and tend to attribute setbacks to circumstances rather than their personal flaws and inadequacies. Seligman reviews research on how these differences in explanatory style affect mental and physical health, as well as performance in school, sports, and work. Seligman also offers extensive advice about how people can change their characteristic way of thinking, borrowing liberally from the ideas of other influential theorists, such as Albert Ellis and Aaron Beck. *Learned Optimism* is a well-written, readable, practical book, loaded with fascinating anecdotes, that is firmly grounded in empirical research.

There was a lot of hype in the press about Berkeley swimming star Matt Biondi's chances in the 1988 Seoul Olympics. . . .
The first event Biondi swam was the two-hundred-meter freestyle. He finished a disappointing third. The second event

was the one-hundred-meter butterfly, not his premier event. Overpowering the field, he led all the way. But in the last two meters, rather than taking one extra stroke and crashing into the finish wall, he appeared to relax and coast the final meter. You could hear the groan in Seoul, and imagine it across America, as he was inched (centimetered?) out by Anthony Nesty of Surinam, who took the extra stroke to win Surinam's first medal ever. The "agony of defeat" interviewers hammered Biondi on the disappointment of a bronze and a silver medal and speculated that he might not be able to rebound. Would Biondi carry home gold in his five remaining events after this embarrassing start?

I sat in my living room confident that he would. I had reason to believe this, because we had tested Matt Biondi in Berkeley four months before to determine his capacity to do just what he had to do now—come back from defeat.

Along with his teammates, he had taken the Attributional Style Questionnaire, and he had come out in the top quarter of optimism of an optimistic bunch. We had then simulated defeat under controlled conditions in the pool. Nort Thornton, Biondi's coach, had him swim the one-hundred-yard butterfly all out. Biondi swam it in 50.2 seconds, a very respectable time. But Thornton told him he had swum 51.7, a very slow time for Biondi. Biondi looked disappointed and surprised. Thornton told him to rest up for a few minutes and then swim it again—all out. Biondi did. His actual time got even faster, 50.0. Because his explanatory style was highly optimistic and he had shown us that he got faster—not slower—after defeat, I felt he would bring back gold from Seoul.

In his last five events in Seoul, Biondi won five gold medals. [pp. 163–164]

and colleagues related personality measures to longevity in a large sample of gifted children that has been followed closely by researchers since 1921. Data were available on six personality traits, which were measured when the subjects were children. The one trait that predicted greater longevity was conscientiousness. At first the researchers reasoned, logically enough, that conscientiousness may simply have fostered better health habits, but a follow-up study found little evidence that this was the case. Hence, the investigators have now turned their attention to how conscientiousness may have affected subjects' coping or stress tolerance.

Sensation Seeking

Sensation seeking is yet another personality trait that affects how individuals respond to stress. First described by Marvin Zuckerman (1979, 1990, 1995), *sensation seeking is a generalized preference for high or low levels of sensory stimulation* (see Figure 3.19).

People who are high in sensation seeking prefer, and perhaps even need, a high level of stimulation. They are easily bored, and they enjoy challenges. They like activities that may involve some physical risk, such as mountain climbing, whitewater rafting, and surfing. They may satisfy their appetite for stimulation by experimenting with drugs, numerous sexual partners, and novel experiences (such as travel to unusual places). They tend to relish gambling, spicy foods, provocative art, wild parties, and unusual friends.

Obviously, high sensation seekers actively pursue experiences that many people would find highly stressful. However, now that you know how subjective stress is, it should come as no surprise that sensation seekers see these experiences as less threatening, risky, and anxiety provoking than other people would (De Brabander et al., 1996; Franken, Gibson, & Rowland, 1992). According to Zuckerman (1991, 1996), some people have a biological predisposition toward high sensation seeking.

FIGURE 3.19.

A brief scale to assess sensation seeking as a trait. As the text explains, people high in sensation seeking tend to appraise potentially stressful events as less threatening than others. Follow the instructions for this scale to obtain a rough estimate of your own sensation seeking tendencies.

Measuring Sensation Seeking

Answer "true" or "false" to each of the items listed below by circling "T" or "F." A "true" means that the item expresses your preference most of the time. A "false" means that you do not agree that the item is generally true for you. After completing the test, score your responses according to the instructions that follow the test items.

T F **1.** I would really enjoy skydiving.

T F **2.** I can imagine myself driving a sports car in a race and loving it.

T F **3.** My life is very secure and comfortable—the way I like it.

T F **4.** I usually like emotionally expressive or artistic people, even if they are sort of wild.

T F **5.** I like the idea of seeing many of the same warm, supportive faces in my everyday life.

T F **6.** I like doing adventurous things and would have enjoyed being a pioneer in the early days of this country.

T F **7.** A good photograph should express peacefulness creatively.

T F **8.** The most important thing in living is fully experiencing all emotions.

T F **9.** I like creature comforts when I go on a trip or vacation.

T F **10.** Doing the same things each day really gets to me.

T F **11.** I love snuggling in front of a fire on a wintry day.

T F **12.** I would like to try several types of drugs as long as they didn't harm me permanently.

T F **13.** Drinking and being rowdy really appeals to me on the weekend.

T F **14.** Rational people try to avoid dangerous situations.

T F **15.** I prefer Figure A to Figure B.

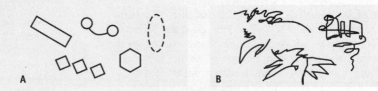

A   B

Give yourself 1 point for answering "true" to the following items: 1, 2, 4, 8, 10, 12, and 13. Also give yourself 1 point for answering "false" to the following items: 3, 5, 7, 9, 11, 14, and 15. Add up your points, and compare your total to the following norms: 11–15, high sensation seeker; 6–10, moderate sensation seeker; 0–5, low sensation seeker. Bear in mind that this is a shortened version of the Sensation Seeking Scale and that it provides only a rough approximation of your status on this personality trait.

High sensation seekers actively pursue stimulation and risk. They enjoy experiences, such as bungee jumping, that most would find stressful and unpleasant.

Although sensation seeking may be associated with stress resistance, we hasten to point out that high sensation seeking may often be more maladaptive than adaptive. In comparison to others, high sensation seekers are more likely to indulge in drug abuse, have difficulty in school, exhibit unhealthy habits, engage in risky sexual behavior, drive in a reckless mannner, and display impulsive behavior, including fighting with others (Arnett, 1996; Jonah, 1997; Zuckerman, 1979, 1990). Some studies have even found associations between high sensation seeking and antisocial behavior, sexual coercion, and criminal activity (Lalumiere & Quinsey, 1996; Stacy, Newcomb, & Bentler, 1993; Thornquist & Zuckerman, 1995). Thus, the disadvantages of high sensation seeking may well outweigh the advantages.

Autonomic Reactivity

In light of the physiological response that people often make to stress, it makes sense that physical makeup might influence stress tolerance. According to this line of thinking, those individuals who have a relatively placid autonomic nervous system should be less affected by stress than those who are equipped with a highly reactive ANS. Thus far, most of the research on autonomic reactivity has focused on autonomically regulated cardiovascular (heart rate and blood pressure) reactivity in response to stress.

Subjects who are exposed to stressful tasks in laboratory settings show fairly consistent personal differences in cardiovascular reactivity over time and across a variety of tasks (Manuck et al., 1993; Sherwood, 1993). There may be a genetic basis for these differences in cardiovascular reactivity (Smith et al., 1987), which can be seen even in children (Matthews, Woodall, & Stoney, 1990). However, the research thus far has largely focused on reactions to simple, short-term stressors in the laboratory (challenging mental tasks) that are relatively pale imitations of real-life stress. Hence, more research is needed on reactions to chronic, ongoing stress and stress emanating from social interactions (Kelsey, 1993; Lassner, Matthews, & Stoney, 1994). Nonetheless, the preponderance of evidence suggests that certain patterns of cardiovascular reactivity *probably* make some people more vulnerable than others to stress-related heart disease (Blascovich & Katkin, 1993).

Monitoring Your Stress

● List five problems with the SRRS that are described in the application section.

● Summarize how the LES corrects some of the problems that are characteristic of the SRRS.

● Explain why one should be cautious in interpreting scores on stress scales.

Rank the following five events in terms of how stressful they would be for you (1 = most stressful, 5 = least stressful).

_____ 1. Change in residence

_____ 2. Fired at work

_____ 3. Death of a close family member

_____ 4. Pregnancy

_____ 5. Personal injury or illness

All five events appear on the Social Readjustment Rating Scale (SRRS), developed by Holmes and Rahe (1967), which we described earlier (see Figure 3.5). If you ranked them in the same order as Holmes and Rahe's subjects, the rankings would be 5, 3, 1, 4, and 2. If you didn't rank them in that order, don't worry about it. That merely shows that the perception of stress is personal and subjective. Unfortunately, the SRRS fails to take this subjectivity into account. That is just one of a number of basic problems with the SRRS.

The SRRS and the research associated with it have received a great deal of publicity. The scale has been reprinted in many popular newspapers and magazines. In these articles, readers have been encouraged to attribute great significance to their scores. They have sometimes been told that they should reduce or minimize change in their lives if their scores are high (Cohen, 1979). Such bold advice could be counterproductive and needs to be qualified carefully. Therefore, in this application section we'll elaborate on some of the problems with the SRRS as a measurement scale, introduce you to an improved scale for measuring stress, and explain why your scores on any stress scale should be interpreted with caution.

Problems with the SRRS

As you learned earlier in this chapter, the SRRS was developed in the early 1960s by Thomas Holmes and Richard Rahe (1967). They designed the scale to measure the amount of change-related stress that people experience. The scale assigns normative values to 43 life events that supposedly indicate the stressfulness of those events. You respond to the scale by checking off those events that have happened to you in a recent time period. Then you add up the values of the checked

events to arrive at your score. In a host of studies, these scores have been found to be related to the likelihood of developing an intimidating array of physical illnesses and psychological problems (Creed, 1993; Derogatis & Coons, 1993; Elliott, 1989; T. Miller, 1989; Turner & Wheaton, 1995).

Thomas Holmes

Before we discuss the shortcomings of the SRRS, we should emphasize that Holmes and Rahe deserve enormous credit for having had the imagination to tackle the difficult task of measuring life stress over three decades ago. They had the insight to recognize the potential importance of stress and the ingenuity to develop a scale that would permit its measurement. They pioneered a new area of research that has turned out to be extremely productive. However, their groundbreaking foray into the assessment of stress was not without its flaws, and their scale has been improved on. So, borrowing from the analyses of a number of critics (notably, Cleary, 1980; Derogatis, 1982; Monroe & McQuaid, 1994; Rabkin, 1993; Schroeder & Costa, 1984), let's look at some of the major problems with the SRRS. Although our list is not exhaustive, we have highlighted the key problems.

First, as already discussed, the assumption that the SRRS measures change exclusively has been shown to be inaccurate. We now have ample evidence that the desirability of events affects adaptational outcomes more than the amount of change that they require (Brown & McGill, 1989; Turner & Wheaton, 1995). Thus, it seems prudent to view the SRRS as a measure of diverse forms of stress, rather than as a measure of change-related stress (McLean & Link, 1994).

Second, the SRRS fails to take into account differences among people in their subjective perception of how stressful an event is. For instance, while divorce may deserve a stress value of 73 for *most* people, a particular person's divorce might generate much less stress and merit a value of only 25. Cohen, Karmack, and Mermelstein (1983) have suggested that it might be better to have respondents rate how personally stressful events are, rather than use the standardized, average weights, which may not capture the true impact of an event on a particular person.

Third, many of the events listed on the SRRS and similar scales are highly ambiguous, leading people to be inconsistent as to which events they report experiencing (Monroe & McQuaid, 1994; Raphael, Cloitre, & Dohrenwend, 1991). For instance, what qualifies as "trouble with boss"? Should you check that because you're sick and tired of your supervisor? What constitutes a "change in living conditions"? Does your purchase of a great new stereo qualify? How should the "pregnancy" item be interpreted? Should a man who has a pregnant wife check that item? As you can see, the SRRS includes many "events" that are described inadequately, producing considerable ambiguity about the meaning of one's response. Problems in recalling events over a period of a year also lead to inconsistent responding on stress scales, thus lowering their reliability (Klein & Rubovits, 1987).

Fourth, the SRRS does not sample from the domain of stressful events very thoroughly. Do the 43 events listed on the SRRS exhaust all the major stresses that people typically experience? Studies designed to explore that question have found many significant omissions (Dohrenwend et al., 1993; McLean & Link, 1994; Wheaton, 1994).

Fifth, the correlation between SRRS scores and health outcomes may be inflated because subjects' neuroticism affects both their responses to stress scales and their self-reports of health problems. Neurotic individuals have a tendency to recall more stress than others and to recall more symptoms of illness than others (Brett et al., 1990; Watson & Pennebaker, 1989). These tendencies mean that some of the correlation between high stress and high illness may simply reflect the effects of subjects' neuroticism (Critelli & Ee, 1996). This is another case of the third variable problem in correlation that we introduced in Chapter 1 (see Figure 3.20). The possible contaminating effects of neuroticism obscure the meaning of scores on the SRRS and similar measures of stress.

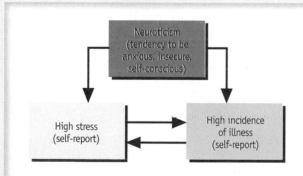

FIGURE 3.20.

Neuroticism as a possible factor underlying the stress-illness correlation. Many studies have found a correlation between subjects' scores on self-report stress scales, such as the SRRS, and their reports of how much illness they have experienced. However, neurotic subjects, who are anxious, insecure, and self-conscious, tend to recall more stress *and* more illness than others. Although there is a great deal of evidence that stress contributes to the causation of illness, some of the stress-illness correlation may be due to neuroticism causing high recall of both stress and illness.

The Life Experiences Survey

In light of the problems outlined above, a number of researchers have attempted to develop improved versions of the SRRS. One scale that seems to be gaining use is the Life Experiences Survey (LES), assembled by Irwin Sarason and colleagues (1978). The LES has become a widely used measure of stress in contemporary research (for examples see Gillis, 1993; Lightsey, 1994; Mullis et al., 1993). The LES revises and builds on the SRRS in a variety of ways that correct, at least in part, most of the problems just discussed.

Specifically, the LES recognizes that stress involves more than mere change and asks respondents to indicate whether events had a positive or negative impact on them. This strategy permits the computation of positive change, negative change, and total change scores, which helps researchers to gain much more insight into which facets of stress are most crucial.

The LES also takes into consideration differences among people in their appraisal of stress, by dropping the normative weights and replacing them with personally assigned weightings of the impact of relevant events. Ambiguity in items is decreased by providing more elaborate descriptions of many items to clarify their meaning. There is still some ambiguity in the scale, but there is no complete solution for this problem.

The LES deals with the failure of the SRRS to sample the full domain of stressful events in several ways. First, some significant omissions from the SRRS have been added to the LES. Second, the LES allows the respondent to write in personally important events that are not included on the scale. Third, the LES reprinted here (in Figure 3.21 on pages 90–92) has an extra section just for students. Sarason et al. (1978) suggest that special, tailored sections of this sort be added for specific populations whenever it is useful.

Arriving at your scores on the LES is very simple. Respond to the items in Figure 3.21, and add up all the positive impact ratings on the right side. That sum is your positive change score. Your negative change score is the sum of all of the negative impact ratings that you made on the left. Adding these two values yields your total change score. Approximate norms for all three of these scores are listed in Figure 3.22 on page 93, so that you can get some idea of what your score means.

Research to date suggests that the negative change score is the crucial one; positive change has not been found to be a good predictor of adaptational outcomes. Thus far, research has shown that negative change scores are related to a variety of negative adaptational outcomes. For instance, the negative change score has turned out to be a better predictor of mental and physical health than SRRS scores (Sarason et al., 1978).

FIGURE 3.21.

The Life Experiences Survey (LES). Like the SRRS, the LES is designed to measure change-related stress. However, Sarason, Johnson, and Siegel (1978) corrected many of the problems apparent in the SRRS. Follow the instructions in the text to determine your positive, negative, and total change scores.

Instructions. Listed below are a number of events that sometimes bring about change in the lives of those who experience them and that necessitate social readjustment. Please check those events you have experienced in the recent past and indicate the time period during which you have experienced each event. Be sure that all checkmarks are directly across from the times that they correspond to. Also, for each item checked below, please indicate the extent to which you viewed the event as having either a positive or negative impact on your life at the time the event occurred. That is, indicate the type and extent of impact that the event had. A rating of −3 would indicate an extremely negative impact. A rating of 0 suggests no impact, either positive or negative. A rating of +3 would indicate an extremely positive impact.

The Life Experiences Survey (LES)	0 to 6 mo	7 mo to 1 yr	Extremely negative	Moderately negative	Somewhat negative	No impact	Slightly positive	Moderately positive	Extremely positive
Section 1									
1. Marriage			−3	−2	−1	0	+1	+2	+3
2. Detention in jail or comparable institution			−3	−2	−1	0	+1	+2	+3
3. Death of spouse			−3	−2	−1	0	+1	+2	+3
4. Major change in sleeping habits			−3	−2	−1	0	+1	+2	+3
5. Death of a close family member			−3	−2	−1	0	+1	+2	+3
a. Mother			−3	−2	−1	0	+1	+2	+3
b. Father			−3	−2	−1	0	+1	+2	+3
c. Brother			−3	−2	−1	0	+1	+2	+3
d. Sister			−3	−2	−1	0	+1	+2	+3
e. Grandmother			−3	−2	−1	0	+1	+2	+3
f. Grandfather			−3	−2	−1	0	+1	+2	+3
g. Other (specify)			−3	−2	−1	0	+1	+2	+3
6. Major change in eating habits (much more or much less food intake)			−3	−2	−1	0	+1	+2	+3
7. Foreclosure on mortgage or loan			−3	−2	−1	0	+1	+2	+3
8. Death of a close friend			−3	−2	−1	0	+1	+2	+3
9. Outstanding personal achievement			−3	−2	−1	0	+1	+2	+3
10. Minor law violations			−3	−2	−1	0	+1	+2	+3
11. Male: Wife/girlfriend's pregnancy			−3	−2	−1	0	+1	+2	+3
12. Female: Pregnancy			−3	−2	−1	0	+1	+2	+3
13. Changed work situation (different work responsibility, major change in working conditions, working hours, etc.)			−3	−2	−1	0	+1	+2	+3
14. New job			−3	−2	−1	0	+1	+2	+3
15. Serious illness or injury of close family member:									
a. Mother			−3	−2	−1	0	+1	+2	+3
b. Father			−3	−2	−1	0	+1	+2	+3
c. Brother			−3	−2	−1	0	+1	+2	+3
d. Sister			−3	−2	−1	0	+1	+2	+3
e. Grandmother			−3	−2	−1	0	+1	+2	+3
f. Grandfather			−3	−2	−1	0	+1	+2	+3
g. Spouse			−3	−2	−1	0	+1	+2	+3
h. Other (specify)			−3	−2	−1	0	+1	+2	+3

	0 to 6 mo	7 mo to 1 yr	Extremely negative	Moderately negative	Somewhat negative	No impact	Slightly positive	Moderately positive	Extremely positive
16. Sexual difficulties			−3	−2	−1	0	+1	+2	+3
17. Trouble with employer (in danger of losing job, being suspended, being demoted, etc.)			−3	−2	−1	0	+1	+2	+3
18. Trouble with in-laws			−3	−2	−1	0	+1	+2	+3
19. Major change in financial status (a lot better off or a lot worse off)			−3	−2	−1	0	+1	+2	+3
20. Major change in closeness of family members (increased or decreased closeness)			−3	−2	−1	0	+1	+2	+3
21. Gaining a new family member (through birth, adoption, family member moving in, etc.)			−3	−2	−1	0	+1	+2	+3
22. Change in residence			−3	−2	−1	0	+1	+2	+3
23. Marital separation from mate (due to conflict)			−3	−2	−1	0	+1	+2	+3
24. Major change in church activities (increased or decreased attendance)			−3	−2	−1	0	+1	+2	+3
25. Marital reconciliation with mate									
26. Major change in number of arguments with spouse (a lot more or a lot fewer)			−3	−2	−1	0	+1	+2	+3
27. Married male: Change in wife's work outside the home (beginning work, ceasing work, changing to a new job, etc.)			−3	−2	−1	0	+1	⏐2	+3
28. Married female: Change in husband's work (loss of job, beginning new job, retirement, etc.)			−3	−2	−1	0	+1	+2	+3
29. Major change in usual type and/or amount of recreation			−3	−2	−1	0	+1	+2	+3
30. Borrowing for a major purchase (buying a home, business, etc.)			−3	−2	−1	0	+1	+2	+3
31. Borrowing for a smaller purchase (buying a car or TV, getting school loan, etc.)			−3	−2	−1	0	+1	+2	+3
32. Being fired from job			−3	−2	−1	0	+1	+2	+3
33. Male: Wife/girlfriend having abortion									
34. Female: Having abortion			−3	−2	−1	0	+1	+2	+3
35. Major personal illness or injury			−3	−2	−1	0	+1	+2	+3
36. Major change in social activities, e.g., parties, movies, visiting (increased or decreased participation)			−3	−2	−1	0	+1	+2	+3

	0 to 6 mo	7 mo to 1 yr	Extremely negative	Moderately negative	Somewhat negative	No impact	Slightly positive	Moderately positive	Extremely positive
37. Major change in living conditions of family (building new home, remodeling, deterioration of home or neighborhood, etc.)			−3	−2	−1	0	+1	+2	+3
38. Divorce			−3	−2	−1	0	+1	+2	+3
39. Serious injury or illness of close friend			−3	−2	−1	0	+1	+2	+3
40. Retirement from work			−3	−2	−1	0	+1	+2	+3
41. Son or daughter leaving home (due to marriage, college, etc.)			−3	−2	−1	0	+1	+2	+3
42. End of formal schooling			−3	−2	−1	0	+1	+2	+3
43. Separation from spouse (due to work, travel, etc.)			−3	−2	−1	0	+1	+2	+3
44. Engagement			−3	−2	−1	0	+1	+2	+3
45. Breaking up with boyfriend/girlfriend			−3	−2	−1	0	+1	+2	+3
46. Leaving home for the first time			−3	−2	−1	0	+1	+2	+3
47. Reconciliation with boyfriend/girlfriend			−3	−2	−1	0	+1	+2	+3
Other recent experiences that have had an impact on your life. List and rate.									
48. _____			−3	−2	−1	0	+1	+2	+3
49. _____			−3	−2	−1	0	+1	+2	+3
50. _____			−3	−2	−1	0	+1	+2	+3

Section 2. Students only

	0 to 6 mo	7 mo to 1 yr	Extremely negative	Moderately negative	Somewhat negative	No impact	Slightly positive	Moderately positive	Extremely positive
51. Beginning a new school experience at a higher academic level (college, graduate school, professional school)			−3	−2	−1	0	+1	+2	+3
52. Changing to a new school at the same academic level (undergraduate, graduate, etc.)			−3	−2	−1	0	+1	+2	+3
53. Academic probation			−3	−2	−1	0	+1	+2	+3
54. Being dismissed from dormitory or other residence			−3	−2	−1	0	+1	+2	+3
55. Failing an important exam			−3	−2	−1	0	+1	+2	+3
56. Changing a major			−3	−2	−1	0	+1	+2	+3
57. Failing a course			−3	−2	−1	0	+1	+2	+3
58. Dropping a course			−3	−2	−1	0	+1	+2	+3
59. Joining a fraternity/ sorority			−3	−2	−1	0	+1	+2	+3
60. Financial problems concerning school (in danger of not having sufficient money to continue)			−3	−2	−1	0	+1	+2	+3

FIGURE 3.22.
Norms for the Life Experiences Survey (LES). Approximate norms for college students taking the LES are shown for negative, positive, and total change scores. These norms are based on 345 undergraduates studied by Sarason et al. (1978). Data for males and females were combined, as gender differences were negligible. Negative change scores are the best predictor of adaptational outcomes.

Norms for LES			
Score category	Negative change	Positive change	Total change
High	14 and above	16 and above	28 and above
Medium	4–13	7–15	12–27
Low	0–3	0–6	0–11

A Cautionary Note

There is merit in getting an estimate of how much stress you have experienced lately, but scores on the LES or any measure of stress should be interpreted with caution. You need not panic if you add up your negative change score and find that it falls in the "high" category. Although it is clear that there is a connection between stress and a variety of undesirable adaptational outcomes, there are a couple of reasons why a high score shouldn't cause undue concern.

First, the strength of the association between stress and adaptational problems is modest. Most of the correlations observed between stress scores and illness have been relatively low, often less than .30 (Dohrenwend & Dohrenwend, 1981; Kobasa, 1979; Monroe & McQuaid, 1994). For researchers and theorists, it is interesting to find any relationship at all. However, the link between stress and adaptational problems is too weak to permit us to make confident predictions about individuals. Many people endure high levels of stress without developing significant problems.

Second, stress is only one of a multitude of variables that affect your susceptibility to various maladies. Stress interacts with many other factors, such as your lifestyle, coping skills, social support, hardiness, and genetic inheritance, in influencing your mental and physical health. It's important to remember that stress is only one actor on a crowded stage. In light of these considerations, you should evaluate the potential meaning of SRRS or LES scores with caution. A high score should be food for thought, but not reason for alarm.

Key Ideas

THE NATURE OF STRESS

⬤ Stress involves transactions with the environment that are perceived to be threatening. Stress is a common, everyday event, and even routine hassles can be problematic. To a large degree, stress lies in the eye of the beholder. According to Lazarus and Folkman, primary appraisals determine whether events appear threatening, and secondary appraisals assess whether one has the resources to cope with challenges.

⬤ Some of the stress that people experience emanates from their environment. Examples of environmental stimuli that can be stressful include excessive noise, heat, pollution, and crowding. Much everyday stress is self-imposed.

MAJOR TYPES OF STRESS

⬤ Major types of stress include frustration, conflict, change, and pressure. Frustration occurs when an obstacle prevents one from attaining some goal. There are three principal types of conflict: approach-approach, avoidance-avoidance, and approach-avoidance. The latter is especially stressful. Vacillation is a common response to approach-avoidance conflict.

⬤ A large number of studies with the SRRS suggest that change is stressful. Although this may be true, it is now clear that the SRRS is a measure of general stress rather than just change-related stress. Two kinds of pressure (to perform and to conform) also appear to be stressful.

KEY FACTORS IN THE APPRAISAL OF STRESS

⬤ Appraisals of potentially threatening events are highly subjective. Stressful events are usually viewed as less threatening when they are familiar, controllable, and predictable, and when they lie in the distant future. However, controllability and predictability have varied effects on the appraisal of stress.

RESPONDING TO STRESS

⬤ Emotional reactions to stress typically involve anger, fear, or sadness. Emotional arousal may interfere with coping. As tasks get more complex, the optimal level of arousal declines. Physiological arousal in response to stress was originally called the fight-or-flight response by Cannon. Selye's general adaptation syndrome describes three stages in the physiological reaction to stress: alarm, resistance, and exhaustion. Diseases of adaptation may appear during the stage of exhaustion.

⬤ In response to stress, the brain sends signals along two major pathways to the endocrine system. Actions along these paths release two sets of hormones into the bloodstream, catecholamines and corticosteroids. Stress can also lead to suppression of the immune response. Behavioral responses to stress involve coping, which may be healthy or maladaptive. If people cope effectively with stress, they can short-circuit potentially harmful emotional and physical responses.

THE POTENTIAL EFFECTS OF STRESS

⬤ Although stress can have positive effects, research on the effects of stress has concentrated on negative outcomes. Common negative effects include impaired task performance including choking under pressure, disruption of attention

and other cognitive processes, pervasive emotional exhaustion known as burnout, posttraumatic stress disorders, a host of everyday psychological problems, full-fledged psychological disorders, and varied types of damage to physical health. However, stress fulfills a basic human need for challenge and can lead to personal growth and self-improvement.

FACTORS INFLUENCING STRESS TOLERANCE

⬤ People differ in how much stress they can tolerate without experiencing ill effects. A person's social support can be a key consideration in buffering the effects of stress. The personality factors associated with hardiness—commitment, challenge, and control—may increase stress tolerance. People high in optimism and conscientiousness also have advantages in coping with stress. Although there is a dark side to high sensation seeking, this personality trait is associated with high tolerance for many forms of stress. A relatively placid autonomic nervous system may also shield people from some of the detrimental health effects associated with stress.

APPLICATION: MONITORING YOUR STRESS

⬤ It can be useful to attempt to measure the amount of stress in one's life, but the much-used SRRS is marred by a variety of shortcomings. It does not really measure change exclusively and it fails to account for the subjective nature of stress. Some of the items on the SRRS are ambiguous, and the scale does not sample the domain of stress thoroughly.

⬤ In contrast, the LES is an improved measure of stress that recognizes the subjectivity of stress and the importance of the desirability of many life events. The LES also samples the domain of stressful events a little more thoroughly and has less ambiguity than the SRRS. Negative change scores on the LES have been found to be predictive of a variety of adaptational outcomes.

Key Terms

Ambient stress
Approach-approach conflict
Approach-avoidance conflict
Autonomic nervous system (ANS)
Avoidance-avoidance conflict
Burnout

Conflict
Conscientiousness
Coping
Emotions
Endocrine system
Fight-or-flight response
Frustration
General adaptation syndrome
Hardiness
Life changes
Optimism

Posttraumatic stress disorder (PTSD)
Pressure
Primary appraisal
Psychophysiological disorders
Psychosomatic diseases
Secondary appraisal
Sensation seeking
Social support
Stress

Key People

Thomas Holmes and Richard Rahe
Suzanne Ouellette (Kobasa)
Richard Lazarus

Neal Miller
Hans Selye
Marvin Zuckerman

Practice Test

1. Concerning the nature of stress, which statement is not accurate?
   a. Stress is an everyday event.
   b. Stress lies in the eye of the beholder.
   c. Stress may be embedded in the environment.
   d. Stress is always imposed on us by others.

2. Secondary appraisal refers to:
   a. second thoughts about what to do in a stressful situation.
   b. second thoughts about whether an event is genuinely threatening.
   c. initial evaluation of an event's relevance, threat, and stressfulness.
   d. evaluation of coping resources and options for dealing with a stressful event.

3. An approach-avoidance conflict may best be resolved by _____ the avoidance motivation rather than _____ the approach motivation.
   a. decreasing, decreasing
   b. decreasing, increasing
   c. increasing, decreasing
   d. increasing, increasing

4. Generally, familiarity with a stressful event:
   a. tends to make it less stressful.
   b. tends to make it more stressful.
   c. has little effect on stressfulness.
   d. tends to affect stressfulness according to temperament.

5. The optimal level of arousal for a task appears to depend in part on:
   a. one's position on the optimism/pessimism scale.
   b. how much physiological change an event stimulates.
   c. the complexity of the task at hand.
   d. how imminent a stressful event is.

6. The fight-or-flight response is mediated by the:
   a. sympathetic division of the autonomic nervous system.
   b. endocrine system.
   c. visceral division of the peripheral nervous system.
   d. parasympathetic division of the autonomic nervous system.

7. When Selye exposed lab animals to various stressors, he found that:
   a. each type of stress causes a particular physiological response.
   b. each type of animal responds to stress differently.
   c. patterns of physiological arousal were similar, regardless of the type of stress.
   d. patterns of physiological arousal were different, even when stressors were similar.

8. Stress can _____ the functioning of the immune system.
   a. stimulate
   b. destroy
   c. suppress
   d. enhance

9. Psychosomatic diseases are:
   a. imaginary physical ailments caused partly by psychological factors.
   b. genuine physical ailments caused partly by psychological factors.
   c. diseases that exist only "in the head."
   d. imagined diseases with no physical symptoms.

10. A personality syndrome marked by commitment, challenge, and control and that appears to be related to stress resistance is called:
    a. hardiness.
    b. optimism.
    c. courage.
    d. sensation seeking.

Answers

1. d pages 63–66
2. d page 64
3. b page 68
4. a page 71
5. c page 74

6. a pages 74–75
7. c page 76
8. c page 77
9. b page 81
10. a page 84

INFOTRAC
COLLEGE EDITION

Go to the Wadsworth Psychology Study Center (http://psychology.wadsworth.com/) for quiz questions, research updates, hot topics, interactive exercises, and suggested readings in INFOTRAC related to this chapter.

CHAPTER 4

Coping Processes

"*I have begun to believe that I have intellectually and emotionally outgrown my husband. However, I'm not really sure what this means or what I should do. Maybe this feeling is normal and I should ignore it and continue my present relationship. This seems to be the safest route. Maybe I should seek a lover while continuing with my husband. Then again, maybe I should start anew and hope for a beautiful ending with or without a better mate.*"

The woman quoted above is in the throes of a thorny conflict. Although it is hard to tell just how much emotional turmoil she is experiencing, it's clear that she is under substantial stress. What should she do? Is it psychologically healthy to remain in an emotionally hollow marriage? Is seeking a secret lover a reasonable way to cope with this unfortunate situation? Should she just strike out on her own and let the chips fall where they may? There are no simple answers to these questions. As you'll soon see, decisions about how to cope with life's difficulties can be terribly complex.

This chapter focuses on how people cope with stress. In the previous chapter we discussed the nature of stress and its effects. We learned that stress can be a challenging, exciting stimulus to personal growth. However, we also saw that stress can prove damaging to people's psychological and physical health because it often triggers physiological responses that may be harmful. These responses to stress tend to be largely automatic. Controlling them depends on the coping responses people make to stressful situations. Thus, a person's mental and physical health depends, in part, on his or her ability to cope effectively with stress.

Here's our plan of attack for this chapter: We'll begin with a general discussion of the concept of coping. Then we'll review some common coping patterns that tend to have relatively little value. After discussing these ill-advised coping techniques, we'll sketch an overview of what it means to engage in healthier, "constructive" coping. In the remainder of the chapter we'll expand on the specifics of constructive coping. We hope our discussion will provide you with some new ideas about how to deal with the stresses of modern life.

The Concept of Coping

LEARNING OBJECTIVES

● *Discuss the variety of coping strategies that people employ.*

● *Discuss whether individuals display distinctive styles of coping.*

In Chapter 3, you learned that **coping refers to efforts to master, reduce, or tolerate the demands created by stress.** Let's take a closer look at this concept and discuss some general points about coping.

People cope with stress in many different ways. A number of researchers have attempted to identify and classify the various coping techniques that people use in dealing with stress. Their work reveals quite a variety of coping strategies. For instance, in a study of how 255 adult subjects dealt with stress, McCrae (1984) identified 28 different coping techniques. In another study, Carver, Scheier, and Weintraub (1989) found that they could sort their subjects' coping tactics into 14 categories, which are listed in Figure 4.1 on the next page. Thus, in grappling with stress, people select their coping tactics from a large and varied menu of options.

Individuals have their own styles of coping. Even with a large menu of coping tactics to choose from, most people come to rely on some strategies more than others (Folkman et al., 1986; Heszen-Niejodek, 1997). Of course, an individual's coping strategies are also influenced by situational demands. For instance, in situations involving uncontrollable stress, emotion-focused coping is especially likely, whereas when stress is more controllable, problem-focused coping comes to the fore (Terry, 1994). Nonetheless, people's coping strategies show moderate stability across a wide variety of situations (Carver & Scheier, 1994). To some extent, each person has an individual style of coping with life's difficulties. As we progress through this chapter, it may be fruitful for you to analyze your own style of coping.

Coping strategies vary in their adaptive value. In everyday terms, when we say that someone "coped with her problems," we imply that she handled them effectively. In reality, however, coping processes range from the helpful to the destructive (Carver et al., 1989). For example, coping with the disappointment of not getting a promotion by plotting to sabotage your company's computer system, would be a negative way of coping. Hence, we will distinguish between coping patterns that tend to be helpful and those that tend to be maladaptive. Bear in mind, however, that our generalizations about the adaptive value of various coping strategies are based on trends or tendencies. No coping strategy can ensure a successful outcome. Furthermore, the adaptive value of a coping technique depends on the exact nature of the situation. As you'll see in the next section, even ill-advised coping strategies may have adaptive value in some instances.

FIGURE 4.1.

Classifying coping strategies.
Carver, Scheier, and Weintraub (1989) sorted their subjects' coping responses into 14 categories. The categories are listed here (column 1) with a representative example from each category (column 2). As you can see, people use quite a variety of coping strategies.

Types of Coping Strategies

Coping strategy	Example
Active coping	I take additional action to try to get rid of the problem.
Planning	I come up with a strategy about what to do.
Suppression of competing activities	I put aside other activities in order to concentrate on this.
Restraint coping	I force myself to wait for the right time to do something.
Seeking social support for instrumental reasons	I ask people who have had similar experiences what they did.
Seeking social support for emotional reasons	I talk to someone about how I feel.
Positive reinterpretation and growth	I look for the good in what is happening.
Acceptance	I learn to live with it.
Turning to religion	I seek God's help.
Focus on and venting of emotions	I get upset and let my emotions out.
Denial	I refuse to believe that it has happened.
Behavioral disengagement	I give up the attempt to get what I want.
Mental disengagement	I turn to work or other substitute activities to take my mind off things.
Alcohol-drug disengagement	I drink alcohol or take drugs in order to think about it less.

Common Coping Patterns of Limited Value

LEARNING OBJECTIVES

- Discuss the adaptive value of giving up as a response to stress.
- Discuss the adaptive value of aggression as a response to stress.
- Discuss the adaptive value of indulging yourself as a response to stress.
- Discuss the adaptive value of negative self-talk as a response to stress.
- Explain how defense mechanisms work.
- Discuss the adaptive value of defense mechanisms, including recent work on healthy illusions.

"Recently, after an engagement of 22 months, my fiancée told me that she was in love with someone else, and that we were through. I've been a wreck ever since. I can't study because I keep thinking about her. I think constantly about what I did wrong in the relationship and why I wasn't good enough for her. Getting drunk is the only way I can get her off my mind. Lately, I've been getting plastered about five or six nights a week. My grades are really hurting, but I'm not sure that I care."

This young man is going through a difficult time and does not appear to be handling it very well. He's blaming himself for the breakup with his fiancée. He's turning to alcohol to dull the pain that he feels, and it sounds like he may be giving up on school. Given his situation, these coping responses aren't particularly unusual, but they're only going to make his problems worse.

In this section, we'll examine some relatively common coping patterns that tend to be less than optimal. Specifically, we'll discuss giving up, aggression, blaming yourself, indulging yourself, and defense mechanisms. Some of these coping tactics may be helpful in certain circumstances, but more often than not, they are counterproductive.

Giving Up

When confronted with stress, people sometimes simply give up and withdraw from the battle. This response of apathy and inaction tends to be associated with the emotional reactions of sadness and dejection. Bruno Bettelheim (1943) observed this reaction among prisoners in the Nazi concentration camps of World War II. Some prisoners aggressed against their captors through acts of sabotage and worked valiantly to maintain their will to live. However, many others sank into apathy and made no effort to adapt and survive.

Martin Seligman (1974, 1992) has developed a model of this giving-up syndrome that appears to shed light on its causes. In Seligman's original research, animals were subjected to electric shocks they could not escape. The animals were then given an opportunity to learn a response that

Martin Seligman

would allow them to escape the shock. However, many of the animals became so apathetic and listless they didn't even try to learn the escape response. When researchers made similar manipulations with *human* subjects using inescapable noise (rather than shock) as the stressor, they observed parallel results (Hiroto & Seligman, 1975). This syndrome is referred to as learned helplessness. **Learned helplessness is passive behavior produced by exposure to unavoidable aversive events.** Unfortunately, this tendency to give up may be transferred to situations in which one is not really helpless. Hence, some people routinely respond to stress with fatalism and resignation, passively accepting setbacks that might be dealt with effectively.

Seligman originally viewed learned helplessness as a product of conditioning. However, research with human subjects has led Seligman and his colleagues to revise their theory. Their current model proposes that people's *cognitive interpretation* of aversive events determines whether they develop learned helplessness. Specifically, helplessness seems to occur when individuals come to believe that events are beyond their control. This belief is particularly likely to emerge in people who exhibit a pessimistic explanatory style. Among other things, such people tend to attribute setbacks to personal inadequacies instead of situational factors (Abramson, Seligman, & Teasdale, 1978; Seligman, 1990).

As you might guess, giving up is not a highly regarded method of coping. Carver and his colleagues (1989, 1993) have studied this coping strategy, which they refer to as *behavioral disengagement*, and found that it is associated with increased rather than decreased distress. Furthermore, many studies suggest that learned helplessness can contribute to depression (Nolen-Hoeksema, Girgus, & Seligman, 1992; Peterson & Seligman, 1984).

A related coping tactic that may have more adaptive value is *social withdrawal*. In response to stress, many people pull back from their interactions with others, becoming socially distant and preoccupied. This coping strategy has not been the focus of much research yet. Repetti (1992) speculates that social withdrawal may be adaptive in the short run, perhaps allowing people to reduce stress-induced arousal and replenish their energy, but that it is probably maladaptive as a long-term coping response.

However, giving up could be adaptive in some instances. For example, if you were thrown into a job that you were not equipped to handle, it might be better to quit rather than face constant pressure and diminishing self-esteem. There is something to be said for recognizing one's limitations. There may also be occasions when people need to recognize that their goals are unrealistic. The highly competitive nature of

American society leads many people to push themselves toward heights that are very difficult to achieve. Goals such as gaining admission to medical school, becoming a professional actress, or buying an expensive home may be better discarded if they are not realistic. The value of any coping response depends on the situation. Even a coping strategy such as giving up, which sounds uninspiring, may sometimes be adaptive. As you will see again and again, there are no simple rules regarding the best ways to cope with life's challenges.

Striking Out at Others

A young man, aged 17, cautiously edged his car into traffic on the Corona Expressway in Los Angeles. His slow speed apparently irritated the men in a pickup truck behind him. Unfortunately, he angered the wrong men—they shot him to death. During that same weekend there were six other roadside shootings in the Los Angeles area. All of them were triggered by minor incidents or "fender benders." Frustated motorists are attacking each other more and more frequently, especially on the overburdened highways of Los Angeles.

These tragic incidents of highway violence—so called "road rage"—vividly illustrate that people often respond to stressful events by striking out at others with aggressive behavior. **Aggression is any behavior intended to hurt someone, either physically or verbally.** Snarls, curses, and insults are much more common than shootings or fistfights, but aggression of any kind can be problematic. Many years ago, a team of psychologists (Dollard et al., 1939) proposed the frustration-aggression hypothesis, which held that aggression is always due to frustration. Decades of research have verified their idea of a causal link between frustration and aggression. However, this research has been unable to show an inevitable, one-to-one correspondence between frustration and aggression.

In discussing qualifications to the frustration-aggression hypothesis, Leonard Berkowitz (1969, 1989) concludes (1) that frustration does not *necessarily* lead to aggression, (2) that many factors in addition to frustration (such as one's personality) influence the likelihood of aggression, and (3) that frustration may produce responses other than aggression (for example, apathy). Although these are important qualifications, it is clear that frustration often leads to aggression.

People often lash out aggressively at others who had nothing to do with their frustration, especially when they can't vent their anger at the real source of their frustration. Thus, you'll probably suppress your anger rather than lash out verbally at a police officer who gives you a speeding ticket. Twenty minutes later, however, you might be downright brutal in rebuking a waiter who is slow in servicing your table. As we discussed in Chapter 2, this diversion of anger to a substitute target was noticed long ago by Sigmund Freud, who called it *displacement*.

Freud theorized that behaving aggressively could get pent-up emotion out of one's system and thus be adaptive. He coined the term ***catharsis* to refer to this release of emotional tension.** There is some experimental evidence to support Freud's theory of catharsis. In a widely cited study, Hokanson and Burgess (1962) found that the opportunity to aggress physically or verbally after frustration led to a smaller increase in subjects' blood pressure (see Figure 4.2). Given the potential negative effects of emotional arousal, this study suggests that expressing aggression may have some adaptive value.

However, after reviewing additional research by Hokanson and others, Carol Tavris (1982, 1989) concludes that aggressive behavior does not reliably lead to catharsis. She asserts, "Aggressive catharses are almost impossible to find in continuing relationships because parents, children, spouses and bosses usually feel obliged to aggress back at you; and indirect, 'displaced' aggression does nothing but make you angrier and more upset" (1982, p. 131). Thus, the adaptive value of aggressive behavior tends to be minimal. Hurting

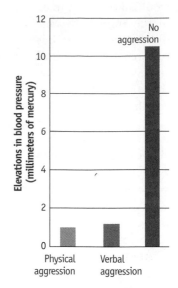

FIGURE 4.2.

Aggression and blood pressure. After frustrating subjects, Hokanson and Burgess (1962) found that those who were allowed to engage in either physical or verbal aggression showed smaller increases in blood pressure than subjects who had no opportunity for aggression. These findings support the idea that aggressive behavior permits people to cathart (drain off) emotional tension. As the text notes, however, many other studies have failed to support the catharsis value of aggression.

someone, especially an irrelevant someone, is not likely to alleviate frustration. Moreover, the interpersonal conflicts that often emerge from aggressive behavior may produce additional stress. If you pick a fight with your spouse after a terrible day at work, you may create new stress and lose valuable empathy and social support as well.

Indulging Yourself

Stress sometimes leads to self-indulgence. For instance, after an exceptionally stressful day, some people head for their kitchen, a grocery store, or a restaurant in pursuit of something chocolate. In a similar vein, others cope with stress by making a beeline for the nearest shopping mall for a spending spree. Still others respond to stress by indulging in injudicious patterns of drinking, smoking, gambling, and drug use.

In their classification of coping responses, Moos and Billings (1982) list *developing alternative rewards* as a common response to stress. It makes sense that when things are going poorly in one area of your life, you may try to compensate by pursuing substitute forms of satisfaction. Thus, it is not surprising that there is evidence relating stress to increases in eating (Grunberg & Straub, 1992), smoking (Cohen & Lichtenstein, 1990), and the consumption of alcohol and drugs (Peyser, 1993).

A new manifestation of this coping strategy is the tendency to immerse oneself in the online world of the Internet. Kimberly Young (1996, 1998) has described a syndrome called ***Internet addiction*, which consists of spending an inordinate amount of time on the Internet and inability to control online use** (see Figure 4.3). People who exhibit this syndrome often use the

Recommended Reading

Anger: The Misunderstood Emotion
by Carol Tavris (Simon & Schuster, 1989)

With the possible exception of anxiety, anger is the emotion elicited by stress more than any other. It's a powerful emotion that can be harnessed to achieve admirable goals. The work of some of the world's great reformers and leaders has been fueled by moral outrage. However, anger also lies at the center of many human woes—wrecked friendships, destroyed marriages, murders, and wars. Hence, anger is a profoundly important emotion. Carol Tavris analyzes virtually every facet of anger in her book. She carefully scrutinizes common beliefs about anger and concludes that many of them are inaccurate. For instance, she argues convincingly against the idea that aggression can drain off anger through catharsis and the idea that anger and aggression are overpowering, instinctual responses. Tavris's book is a delight to read. It's witty, lively, practical, thought-provoking, and frequently eloquent.

Our contemporary ideas about anger have been fed by the anger industry, psychotherapy, which too often is based on the belief that inside every tranquil soul a furious one is screaming to get out. Psychiatric theory refers to anger as if it were a fixed amount of energy that bounces through the system: if you pinch it in here, it is bound to pop out there—in bad dreams, neurosis, hysterical paralysis, hostile jokes, or stomachaches. Therapists are continually "uprooting" anger or "unearthing" it, as if it were a turnip. [p. 23]

FIGURE 4.3.

Measuring addiction to the Internet. The questions on Young's (1998) Internet Addiction Test highlight the traits that make up this syndrome. You can see whether you exhibit any signs of Internet addiction by responding to the items and computing your score.

Internet Addiction Test

To assess your level of addiction, answer the following questions using this scale:

1 = Not at all	2 = Rarely	3 = Occasionally	4 = Often	5 = Always

Question	1	2	3	4	5
1. How often do you find that you stay on-line longer than you intended?	1	2	3	4	5
2. How often do you neglect household chores to spend more time on-line?	1	2	3	4	5
3. How often do you prefer the excitement of the Internet to intimacy with your partner?	1	2	3	4	5
4. How often do you form new relationships with fellow on-line users?	1	2	3	4	5
5. How often do others in your life complain to you about the amount of time you spend on-line?	1	2	3	4	5
6. How often do your grades or school work suffer because of the amount of time you spend on-line?	1	2	3	4	5
7. How often do you check your e-mail before something else that you need to do?	1	2	3	4	5
8. How often does your job performance or productivity suffer because of the Internet?	1	2	3	4	5
9. How often do you become defensive or secretive when anyone asks you what you do on-line?	1	2	3	4	5
10. How often do you block out disturbing thoughts about your life with soothing thoughts of the Internet?	1	2	3	4	5
11. How often do you find yourself anticipating when you will go on-line again?	1	2	3	4	5
12. How often do you fear that life without the Internet would be boring, empty, and joyless?	1	2	3	4	5
13. How often do you snap, yell, or act annoyed if someone bothers you while you are on-line?	1	2	3	4	5
14. How often do you lose sleep due to late-night log-ins?	1	2	3	4	5
15. How often do you feel preoccupied with the Internet when off-line, or fantasize about being on-line?	1	2	3	4	5
16. How often do you find yourself saying "just a few more minutes" when on-line?	1	2	3	4	5
17. How often do you try to cut down the amount of time you spend on-line and fail?	1	2	3	4	5
18. How often do you try to hide how long you've been on-line?	1	2	3	4	5
19. How often do you choose to spend more time on-line over going out with others?	1	2	3	4	5
20. How often do you feel depressed, moody, or nervous when you are off-line, which goes away once you are back on-line?	1	2	3	4	5

After you've answered all the questions, add the numbers you selected for each response to obtain a final score. The higher your score, the greater your level of addiction and the problems your Internet usage causes. Here's a general scale to help measure your score.

20–39 points: You are an average on-line user. You may surf the Web a bit too long at times, but you have control over your usage.

40–69 points: You are experiencing frequent problems because of the Internet. You should consider their full impact on your life.

70–100 points: Your Internet usage is causing significant problems in your life. You need to address them now.

online world as an escape from their problems in the real world. Their Internet use is so excessive, it begins to interfere with their functioning at work, at school, or at home, leading victims to start concealing the extent of their dependence on the Internet. There are no data yet on the prevalence of this new form of self-indulgence, but Young (1996) had little difficulty recruiting a sample of 396 Internet addicts, so the syndrome does *not* appear to be rare. The findings from her sample suggest that Internet addiction is not limited to shy, male computer whizzes, as one might expect. Although there is active debate about the wisdom of characterizing excessive Internet surfing as an *addiction*, it is clear that this new coping strategy is likely to become increasingly common.

There is nothing inherently maladaptive about indulging oneself as a way of coping with life's stresses. The pursuit of alternative rewards is a readily available

Experts disagree about whether excessive Internet use should be characterized as an addiction, *but inability to control online use appears to be an increasingly common syndrome.*

coping strategy that may have merit if kept under control. If a hot fudge sundae or some new clothes can calm your nerves after a major setback, who can argue? However, if a person consistently responds to stress with chronic and excessive self-indulgence, obvious problems are likely to develop. Excesses in eating may produce obesity. Excesses in drinking can lead to alcoholism, drunk driving, and a host of other problems. Excesses in drug use may endanger one's health and result in drug dependence. Excesses in spending may create havoc in one's personal finances. Given the risks associated with self-indulgence, it has rather marginal adaptive value.

Blaming Yourself

In a postgame interview after a tough defeat, a prominent football coach was brutally critical of himself. He said that he had been outcoached, that he had made poor decisions, and that his game plan was faulty. He almost eagerly assumed all the blame for the loss himself. In reality, he had taken some reasonable chances that didn't go his way and had suffered the effects of poor execution by his players. Looking at it objectively, the loss was attributable to the collective failures of 50 or so players and coaches. However, the coach's unrealistically negative self-evaluation was a fairly typical response to frustration. When confronted by stress (especially frustration and pressure), people often become highly self-critical.

The tendency to engage in negative self-talk in response to stress has been noted by a number of influential theorists. Albert Ellis (1973, 1987) calls this phenomenon "catastrophic thinking" and focuses on how it is rooted in irrational assumptions. Aaron Beck (1976, 1987) analyzes negative self-talk into specific tendencies. Among other things, he asserts that people often (1) unreasonably attribute their failures to personal shortcomings, (2) focus on negative feedback from others while ignoring favorable feedback, and (3) make unduly pessimistic projections about the future. Thus, if you performed poorly on an exam, you might blame it on your woeful stupidity, dismiss a classmate's comment that the test was unfair, and hysterically predict that you will flunk out of school.

Although there is some value in recognizing one's weaknesses, Ellis and Beck agree that negative self-talk tends to be counterproductive. According to Ellis, catastrophic thinking causes, aggravates, and perpetuates emotional reactions to stress that are often problematic. Along even more serious lines, Beck marshals evidence that negative self-talk can contribute to the development of depressive disorders. The bottom line is that people who blame themselves for their difficulties tend to be less happy and less well adjusted than those who

do not use this coping style (Healy, Stewart, & Copeland, 1993; Revenson & Felton, 1989; Vitaliano et al., 1989). In general, then, it appears that self-blame and self-criticism are not very healthy ways to cope with stress.

Using Defensive Coping

Defensive coping is a common response to stress. We noted in Chapter 2 that the concept of defense mechanisms was originally developed by Sigmund Freud. Though rooted in the psychoanalytic tradition, this concept has gained acceptance from psychologists of most persuasions. Building on Freud's initial insights, modern psychologists have broadened the scope of the concept and added to Freud's list of defense mechanisms.

THE NATURE OF DEFENSE MECHANISMS

Defense mechanisms are largely unconscious reactions that protect a person from unpleasant emotions such as anxiety and guilt. A number of strategies fit this definition. For example, Laughlin (1979) lists 49 different defenses. In our discussion of Freud's theory in Chapter 2, we described seven common defenses. Figure 4.4 introduces another five defenses that people use with some regularity. Although widely discussed in the popular press, defense mechanisms are often misunderstood. We will use a question-answer format to elaborate on the nature of defense mechanisms in the hopes of clearing up any misconceptions.

What do defense mechanisms defend against? Above all else, defense mechanisms shield the individual from the *emotional discomfort* elicited by stress. Their main purpose is to ward off unwelcome emotions or to reduce their intensity. Foremost among the emotions guarded against is anxiety. People are especially defensive when the anxiety is due to some threat to their self-esteem. They also use defenses to suppress dangerous feelings of anger to avoid exploding into acts of aggression. Guilt and dejection are two other emotions that people often try to evade through defensive maneuvers.

How do they work? Defense mechanisms work through *self-deception*. They accomplish their goals by distorting reality so it does not appear so threatening. Let's say you're doing poorly in school and are in danger of flunking out. Initially, you might use *denial* to block awareness of the possibility that you could flunk out. This tactic might temporarily fend off feelings of anxiety. If it becomes difficult to deny the obvious, you might resort to *fantasy*, daydreaming about how you will salvage adequate grades by getting spectacular

FIGURE 4.4.

Additional defense mechanisms. Like the seven defense mechanisms described in our discussion of Freudian theory in Chapter 2 (see Figure 2.4), these five defenses are frequently used in people's efforts to cope with stress.

Common Defense Mechanisims

Mechanism	Example
Denial of reality. Protecting oneself from unpleasant reality by refusing to perceive or face it.	A smoker concludes that the evidence linking cigarette use to health problems is scientifically worthless.
Fantasy. Gratifying frustrated desires by imaginary achievements.	A socially inept and inhibited young man imagines himself chosen by a group of women to provide them with sexual satisfaction.
Intellectualization (isolation). Cutting off emotion from hurtful situations or separating incompatible attitudes in logic-tight compartments.	A prisoner on death row awaiting execution resists appeal on his behalf and coldly insists that the letter of the law be followed.
Undoing. Atoning for or trying to magically dispel unacceptable desires or acts.	A teenager who feels guilty about masturbation ritually touches door knobs a prescribed number of times after each occurrence of the act.
Overcompensation. Covering up felt weaknesses by emphasizing some desirable characteristic, or making up for frustration in one area by overgratification in another.	A dangerously overweight woman goes on eating binges when she feels neglected by her husband.

scores on the upcoming final exams, when the objective fact is that you are hopelessly behind in your studies. Thus, defense mechanisms work their magic by bending reality in self-serving ways.

Are they conscious or unconscious? Freud originally assumed that defenses operate entirely at an unconscious level. However, the concept of defense mechanisms has been broadened by other theorists to include maneuvers that people may be aware of. Thus, defense mechanisms operate at varying levels of awareness, although they are largely unconscious.

Are they normal? Definitely. Everyone uses defense mechanisms on a fairly regular basis. They are entirely normal patterns of coping. The notion that only neurotic people use defense mechanisms is inaccurate.

CAN ILLUSIONS BE HEALTHY?

The most critical question concerning defense mechanisms is: *Are they healthy?* This is a complicated question. More often than not, the answer is no. Generally, defense mechanisms are poor ways of coping, for a number of reasons. First, defensive coping is an avoidance strategy, and avoidance rarely provides a genuine solution to our problems. Holahan and Moos (1985, 1990) have found that people who exhibit relatively high resistance to stress use avoidance strategies less than people who are frequently troubled by stress. Second, defenses such as denial, fantasy, and projection represent "wishful thinking," which is likely to accomplish little. In fact, in a study of how students coped with the stress of taking the Medical College Admissions Test (MCAT), Bolger (1990) found that students who engaged in a lot of wishful thinking experienced greater increases in anxiety than other students as the exam approached. Third, a repressive coping style has been related to poor health, in part because repression often leads people to delay facing up to their problems (Weinberger, 1990). For example, if you were to block out obvious warning signs of cancer or diabetes and fail to obtain needed medical care, your defensive behavior could be fatal. Fourth, defensive tactics use up energy that could be spent more wisely by

tackling the problem. In other words, defensive pseudosolutions may keep people from using more constructive coping strategies.

Although defensive behavior tends to be relatively unhealthy, some defenses are healthier than others, and defense mechanisms can sometimes be adaptive (Erickson, Feldman, & Steiner, 1996; Vaillant, 1994). For example, *overcompensation* for athletic failures could lead you to work extra hard in the classroom. And creative use of *fantasy* is sometimes the key to helping people deal effectively with a temporary period of frustration, such as a stint in the military service or a period of recovery in the hospital.

Most theorists used to regard accurate contact with reality as the hallmark of sound mental health (Jahoda, 1958; Jourard & Landsman, 1980). However, after studying denial and other defenses, Richard Lazarus acknowledges that sometimes "illusion and self-deception can have positive value in a person's psychological economy" (Goleman, 1979, p. 47). Consistent with this notion, Ward, Leventhal, and Love (1988) found that cancer patients who relied on repression experienced fewer treatment side effects than patients who carefully monitored the course of their disease.

Shelley Taylor and Jonathon Brown (1988, 1994) have reviewed several lines of evidence suggesting that "illusions" may be adaptive for mental health and well-being. First, they note that "normal" people tend to have overly favorable self-images. In contrast, depressed subjects exhibit less favorable—but more realistic—self-concepts. Second, normal subjects overestimate the degree to which they control chance events. In comparison, depressed subjects are less prone to this illusion of control. Third, normal individuals are more likely than depressed subjects to display unrealistic optimism in making projections about the future.

Shelly Taylor

Colvin and Block (1994) have expressed considerable skepticism about the idea that illusions are adaptive. They make a pretty eloquent case for the traditional view that accuracy and realism are healthy. Moreover, they report data showing that overly favorable self-ratings are correlated with maladaptive personality traits (Colvin, Block, & Funder, 1995). Part of the problem in sorting out the evidence on this complex issue is that both ends of the correlational equation are difficult to measure (Asendorpf & Ostendorf, 1998). What exactly is an illusion? It is not easy to precisely determine whether a subject's self-concept is overly favorable. In a similar vein, mental health and well-being are difficult to quantify. Thus, the contradic-

tory findings on this issue are partly attributable to researchers defining illusions and mental health in different ways.

To summarize, it is hard to make sweeping generalizations about the adaptive value of self-deception. Some personal illusions may help some people deal with some of life's difficulties. But Taylor and Brown would be the first to stress that they are talking about modest illusions, not wholesale distortions of reality. Roy Baumeister (1989) theorizes that it's all a matter of degree and that there is an "optimal margin of illusion." According to Baumeister, extreme distortions of reality are maladaptive, but small illusions are often beneficial.

The Nature of Constructive Coping

LEARNING OBJECTIVES

- Describe the nature of constructive coping.
- List the three categories of constructive coping tactics.

Our discussion thus far has focused on coping strategies that tend to be less than ideal. Of course, people also exhibit many healthful strategies for dealing with stress. We will use the term **constructive coping to refer to efforts to deal with stressful events that are judged to be relatively healthful.** No strategy of coping can guarantee a successful outcome. Even the healthiest coping responses may turn out to be ineffective in some cases. Thus, the concept of constructive coping is simply meant to convey a healthy, positive connotation, without promising success.

Constructive coping does not appear to depend particularly on one's intelligence—at least not the abstract, "academic" intelligence measured by conventional IQ tests. Seymour Epstein (1990), a professor at the University of Massachusetts, has shown an interest in "why smart people think dumb." His interest was stimulated in part by a course that he teaches in which students keep daily records of their most positive and negative emotional experiences, for class discussion. Commenting on these discussions, Epstein says, "One cannot help but be impressed, when observing students in such a situation, with the degree to which some otherwise bright people lead their lives in a manifestly unintelligent and self-defeating manner" (Epstein & Meier, 1989, p. 333).

To investigate this matter more systematically, Epstein and Petra Meier (1989) devised an elaborate scale to assess the degree to which people engage in constructive coping and thinking. They found constructive thinking to be favorably related to mental and physical health and to measures of "success" in work,

Reprinted with special permission of North America Syndicate.

love, and social relationships. However, subjects' IQ scores were only weakly related to their constructive coping scores and were largely unrelated to the measures of success in work, love, and social relationships.

In subsequent studies, Epstein and his colleagues have compared good versus poor constructive thinkers as they worked on laboratory tasks that subjected them to modest stress (Katz & Epstein, 1991; Scheuer & Epstein, 1997). Under stress, the good constructive thinkers reported fewer negative thoughts and less negative emotion. They also exhibited lower physiological arousal. In another study, Epstein and Katz (1992) uncovered a negative correlation between constructive thinking and a measure of self-produced stress, thus supporting the notion that "some people, because of their disorganized, provocative, or otherwise maladaptive behavior, instigate more stressors in their lives than do others" (p. 814). In other words, they found that good constructive thinkers not only cope more effectively with stress, they also create less stress for themselves than poor constructive thinkers do.

What makes a coping strategy constructive? Frankly, in labeling certain coping responses constructive or healthy, psychologists are making value judgments. It's a gray area in which opinions will vary to some extent. Nonetheless, some consensus emerges from the burgeoning research on coping and stress management. Key themes in this literature include the following:

1. Constructive coping involves confronting problems directly. It is task-relevant and action-oriented. It involves a conscious effort to rationally evaluate your options in an effort to solve your problems.

2. Constructive coping is based on reasonably realistic appraisals of your stress and coping resources. A little self-deception may sometimes be adaptive, but excessive self-deception and highly unrealistic negative thinking are not.

3. Constructive coping involves learning to recognize and manage potentially disruptive emotional reactions to stress.

4. Constructive coping involves learning to exert some control over potentially harmful or destructive habitual behaviors. It requires the acquisition of some behavioral self-control.

● Recommended Reading

You're Smarter Than You Think
by Seymour Epstein, with Archie Brodsky
(Simon & Schuster, 1993)

In an ongoing effort to understand "why smart people think dumb," Seymour Epstein has conducted pioneering research on what he calls *constructive thinking*. In this book, he summarizes his research for the layperson and offers sage advice on how people can make their thinking more constructive. He begins with a self-administered scale intended to measure the reader's tendency to engage in constructive thinking. This brief (30 items) version of the scale he has used extensively in his research assesses the reader's emotional coping, behavioral coping, categorical thinking, superstitious thinking, esoteric thinking, and naive optimism. He provides test norms so readers can understand how they stack up on each dimension.

After this intriguing venture in self-assessment, Epstein tackles the paradox of how bright people can be remarkably foolhardy. He argues that people operate with two minds—a rational mind and an experiential mind. Although a person's rational mind may rack up high scores on IQ and academic tests, the experiential mind has more influence over everyday coping behavior. The metaphor of two minds may be more confusing than helpful to many readers, but Epstein goes on to provide a great deal of worthwhile advice on how to cope more effectively with emotional distress, relationship problems, work stress, and the challenge of parenting, among other things.

Why do "smart" people think "dumb" and vice versa? The answer, I have found, is that there is a second kind of intelligence that is unrelated to IQ tests, but is related, instead, to common sense, social skills, and coping with emotions....Your experiential mind is much more closely connected with your emotions than is your rational mind. Operating outside of rational awareness, it comes up with automatic, gut-level, reactions based on memories of past experiences. Your experiential mind is vital to your well-being because it automatically interprets what is going on around you, how you feel about it, and what you should do about it. [pp. 11–12]

These points should give you a general idea of what we mean by constructive coping. They will guide our discourse in the remainder of this chapter as we discuss how to cope more effectively with stress. To organize our discussion, we will use a classification scheme proposed by Rudolph Moos and Andrew Billings (1982) to divide constructive coping techniques into three broad groups, which are classified according to their focus or goal (see Figure 4.5):

• *Appraisal-focused coping* involves efforts to reevaluate the apparent demands or redefine the apparent meaning of stressful events. Its goal is to alter your appraisal of the threat in the situation.

• *Problem-focused coping* involves efforts to circumvent, modify, remedy, or conquer the problem and its consequences. Its goal is to directly master the threat or problem itself.

• *Emotion-focused coping* involves efforts to control and usually reduce the emotional reactions aroused by stress. Its goal is to reestablish a healthy emotional equilibrium.

Of course, like most efforts to classify complex behavior, this scheme is not entirely satisfactory. Some coping tactics are difficult to categorize because they have more than one goal. Nonetheless, this scheme gives us a framework for analyzing healthy approaches to coping.

Appraisal-Focused Constructive Coping

- Explain Ellis's analysis of the causes of maladaptive emotions.
- Describe some assumptions that contribute to catastrophic thinking.

- Discuss the merits of positive reinterpretation and humor as coping strategies.

People often underestimate the importance of the appraisal phase in the stress process. They fail to appreciate the highly subjective feelings that color the perception of threat to one's well-being. A useful way to deal with stress is to alter your appraisal of threatening events. In this section, we'll examine Albert Ellis's ideas about reappraisal and discuss the value of using humor and positive reinterpretation to cope with stress.

Ellis's Rational Thinking

Albert Ellis (1977, 1985, 1996) is a prominent theorist who believes that people can short-circuit their emotional reactions to stress by altering their appraisals of stressful events. Ellis's insights about stress appraisal are the foundation for a widely used system of therapy that he devised. **Rational-emotive therapy is an approach to therapy that focuses on altering clients' patterns of irrational thinking to reduce maladaptive emotions and behavior.**

Ellis maintains that *you feel the way you think*. He argues that problematic emotional reactions are caused by negative self-talk, which he calls catastrophic thinking. **Catastrophic thinking involves unrealistic appraisals of stress that exaggerate the magnitude of one's problems.** Ellis uses a simple A-B-C sequence to explain his ideas (see Figure 4.6).

Albert Ellis

A. *Activating event.* The A in Ellis's system stands for the activating event that produces the stress. The activating event may be any potentially stressful transaction. Examples might include an automobile accident, the cancellation of a date, a delay while waiting in

FIGURE 4.5.

Overview of constructive coping tactics. Coping tactics can be organized in several ways, but we will use the classification scheme shown here, which consists of three categories: appraisal-focused, problem-focused, and emotion-focused. The list of coping tactics in each category is not exhaustive. We will discuss most, but not all, of the listed strategies in our coverage of constructive coping.

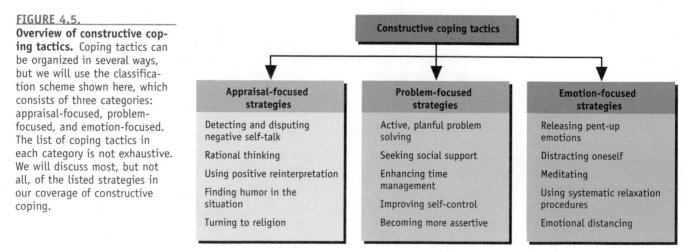

Constructive coping tactics		
Appraisal-focused strategies	**Problem-focused strategies**	**Emotion-focused strategies**
Detecting and disputing negative self-talk	Active, planful problem solving	Releasing pent-up emotions
Rational thinking	Seeking social support	Distracting oneself
Using positive reinterpretation	Enhancing time management	Meditating
Finding humor in the situation	Improving self-control	Using systematic relaxation procedures
Turning to religion	Becoming more assertive	Emotional distancing

line at the bank, or a failure to get a promotion you were expecting.

B. *Belief system.* B stands for your belief about the event. This represents your appraisal of the stress. According to Ellis, people often view minor setbacks as disasters, engaging in catastrophic thinking: "How awful this is. I can't stand it! Things never turn out fairly for me. I'll be in this line forever. I'll never get promoted."

C. *Consequence.* C stands for the consequence of your negative thinking. When your appraisals of stressful events are highly negative, the consequence tends to be emotional distress. Thus, you feel angry, outraged, anxious, panic-stricken, disgusted, or dejected.

Ellis asserts that most people do not understand the importance of phase B in this three-stage sequence. They unwittingly believe that the activating event (A) *causes* the consequent emotional turmoil (C). However, Ellis maintains that A does not cause C. It only appears to do so. Instead, Ellis asserts that B causes C. Emotional distress is actually caused by one's catastrophic thinking in appraising stressful events.

According to Ellis, it is common for people to turn inconvenience into disaster and make "mountains out of molehills." For instance, imagine that someone stands you up on a date that you were eagerly looking forward to. You might think, "Oh, this is terrible. I'm going to have another rotten, boring weekend. People always mistreat me. I'll never find anyone to fall in love with. I must be a crummy, worthless person." Ellis would argue that such thoughts are irrational. He would point out that it does not follow logically from being stood up that you (1) must have a lousy weekend, (2) will never fall in love, or (3) are a worthless person.

THE ROOTS OF CATASTROPHIC THINKING

Ellis (1994, 1995) theorizes that unrealistic appraisals of stress are derived from the irrational assumptions that people hold. He maintains that if you scrutinize your catastrophic thinking, you will find that your reasoning is based on an indefensibly unreasonable premise, such as "I must have approval from everyone" or "I must perform well in all endeavors." These faulty assumptions, which most people hold unconsciously, generate catastrophic thinking and emotional turmoil. To facilitate emotional self-control, it is important to learn to spot irrational assumptions and the unhealthy patterns of thought that they generate. Let's look at four particularly common irrational assumptions.

FIGURE 4.6.

Albert Ellis's A-B-C model of emotional reactions. Most people are prone to attribute their negative emotional reactions (C) directly to stressful events (A). However, Ellis argues that emotional reactions are really caused by the way people think about these events (B).

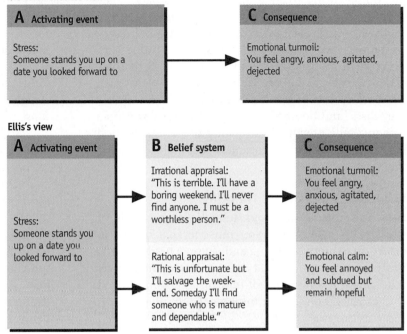

1. *I must have love and affection from certain people.* Everyone wants to be liked and loved. There is nothing wrong with that. However, many people foolishly believe that they should be liked by everyone they come into contact with. If you stop to think about it, that's clearly unrealistic. Once individuals fall in love, they tend to believe that their future happiness depends absolutely on the continuation of that one, special relationship. They believe that if their current love relationship were to end, they would never again be able to achieve a comparable one. This is an unrealistic view of the future. Such views make the person anxious during a relationship and severely depressed if it comes to an end.

2. *I must perform well in all endeavors.* We live in a highly competitive society. We are taught that victory brings happiness. Consequently, we feel that we must always win. For example, many sports enthusiasts are never satisfied unless they perform at their best level. However, by definition, their best level is not their typical level, and they set themselves up for inevitable frustration.

3. *Other people should always behave competently and be considerate of me.* People are often angered by others' stupidity and selfishness. For example, you may become outraged when a mechanic fails to fix your car properly or when a salesperson treats you rudely. It would be nice if others were always competent and considerate, but you know better—they are not! Yet many people go through life unrealistically expecting others' efficiency and kindness.

4. Events should always go the way I like. Some people simply won't tolerate any kind of setback. They assume that things should always go their way. For example, some commuters become tense and angry each time they get stuck in a rush-hour traffic jam. They seem to believe that they are entitled to coast home easily every day, even though they know that rush hour rarely is a breeze. Such expectations are clearly unrealistic and doomed to be violated. Yet few people recognize the obvious irrationality of the assumption that underlies their anger unless it is pointed out to them.

REDUCING CATASTROPHIC THINKING

How can you reduce your unrealistic appraisals of stress? Ellis asserts that you must learn (1) how to detect catastrophic thinking and (2) how to dispute the irrational assumptions that cause it. Detection involves acquiring the ability to spot unrealistic pessimism and wild exaggeration in your thinking. Examine your self-

● Recommended Reading

How to Stubbornly Refuse to Make Yourself Miserable about Anything—Yes, Anything!
by Albert Ellis (Carol Communications, 1988)

This is one of the better "popular" books by Albert Ellis, the world-renowned architect of rational-emotive therapy. At last count, Ellis had written around 50 books, about evenly divided between popular books intended for a general audience and technical books intended for mental health professionals. This book doesn't break any new ground for Ellis, but it does bring his ideas together in one succinct, readable summary, complete with exercises. Ellis is a bit prone to overstatement, asserting that his book "will help you achieve a profound philosophic change and a radically new outlook on life." Whether it does so or not, his ideas clearly can be helpful in coping with stress more effectively. If you're a chronic victim of catastrophic thinking, this book is worth reading. The writing is casual and down-to-earth. For instance, the following passage comes from a chapter titled *"Forget Your 'Godawful' Past."*

For several years I was a highly successful psychoanalyst and thought that I was greatly helping my clients by exploring the gory details of their early life and showing them how these experiences made them disturbed—and how they could now understand and remove these early influences.

How wrong I was!

After I honestly admitted that my psychoanalytic "cures" were hardly as good as I would have liked them to be, I began to see that helping people to understand their past was not only doing them little good but was actually blocking their dealing with their present problems. [p. 69]

talk closely. Ask yourself why you're getting upset. Force yourself to verbalize your concerns, covertly or out loud. Look for key words that often show up in catastrophic thinking, such as *should, ought, never,* and *must.*

Disputing your irrational assumptions requires subjecting your entire reasoning process to scrutiny. Try to root out the assumptions from which your conclusions are derived. Most of us are unaware of these assumptions. Once they are unearthed, their irrationality may be quite obvious. If your assumptions seem reasonable, ask yourself whether your conclusions follow logically. Try to replace your catastrophic thinking with more low-key, rational analyses. These strategies should help you to redefine stressful situations in ways that are less threatening. Strangely enough, another way to defuse such situations is to turn to humor.

Humor as a Stress Reducer

A number of years ago, the Chicago area experienced its worst flooding in about a century. Thousands of people saw their homes wrecked when two rivers spilled over their banks. As the waters receded, the flood victims returning to their homes were subjected to the inevitable TV interviews. A remarkable number of victims, surrounded by the ruins of their homes, *joked* about their misfortune. When the going gets tough, it may pay to laugh about it. In a study of coping styles, McCrae (1984) found that 40% of his subjects reported using humor to deal with stress.

In analyzing the stress-reducing effects of humor, Dixon (1980) emphasizes its impact on the appraisal of stress. Finding a humorous aspect in a stressful situation redefines the situation in a less threatening way. Dixon notes that laughter can also discharge pent-up emotions. These dual functions of humor may make joking about life's difficulties a particularly useful coping strategy.

Empirical evidence showing that humor moderates the impact of stress has been accumulating over the last 25 years. For instance, in one influential study, Martin and Lefcourt (1983) found that a good sense of humor functioned as a buffer to lessen the negative impact of stress on mood. Some of their results are shown in Figure 4.7, which plots how mood disturbance increased as stress went up in two groups of subjects—

those who were high or low in their use of humor. Notice how higher stress leads to a smaller increase in mood disturbance in the high-humor group. Similar findings have been observed in many other studies (Abel, 1998; Martin, 1996). Lefcourt and colleagues (1995) argue that high-humor people may benefit from not taking themselves as seriously as low-humor people. As they put it, "If persons do not regard themselves too seriously and do not have an inflated sense of self-importance, then defeats, embarrassments, and even tragedies should have less pervasive emotional consequences for them" (p. 375).

Positive Reinterpretation

When you are feeling overwhelmed by life's difficulties, you might try the commonsense strategy of recognizing that "things could be worse." No matter how terrible your problems seem, you probably know someone who has even bigger troubles. That is not to say that you should derive satisfaction from others' misfortune. However, comparing your own plight with others' even tougher struggles can help you put your problems in perspective. Research by McCrae (1984) suggests that this strategy of making positive comparisons with others is a widely used coping mechanism. It seems to be a relatively healthy one, in that it can facilitate calming reappraisals of stress without the necessity of distorting reality.

Another way to engage in positive reinterpretation is to search for something good in a bad experience. Distressing though they may be, many setbacks have positive elements. After experiencing divorces, illnesses, firings, financial losses, and such, many people remark that "I came out of the experience better than I went in," or "I grew as a person." The positive aspects of a personal setback may be easy to see after the stressful event is behind you. The challenge is to recognize these positive aspects while you are still struggling with the setback, so that it becomes less stressful. Research suggests that positive reinterpretation is in fact an effective coping method (Folkman et al., 1986; Park, Cohen, & Murch, 1996).

Problem-Focused Constructive Coping

LEARNING OBJECTIVES

- List and describe four steps in systematic problem solving.
- Discuss the adaptive value of seeking help as a coping strategy.
- Explain five common causes of wasted time.
- Summarize evidence on the causes and consequences of procrastination.
- Summarize advice on managing time effectively.

Problem-focused coping includes efforts to remedy or conquer the stress-producing problem itself. In this category, we'll discuss systematic problem solving, the importance of seeking help, effective time management, and improvement of self-control.

Using Systematic Problem Solving

In dealing with life's problems, the most obvious course of action is to tackle the problems head-on. In the study of coping by Carver, Scheier, and Weintraub (1989), the two coping tactics that reflect this approach (active coping and planning) were favorably related to higher self-esteem and lower anxiety. In another study, D'Zurilla and Sheedy (1991) took a more focused look at the link between problem solving and stress. They used two scales to evaluate key aspects of subjects' social problem-solving ability. One scale gauged subjects' *problem orientation*—that is, whether they approached problems with a positive attitude, viewing them as challenges and opportunities. The other scale assessed a set of four *problem-solving skills:* (1) defining and formulating the problem, (2) generating alternative solutions, (3) making decisions, and (4) implementing and verifying solutions. Three months after the assessment of their problem-solving ability, subjects completed the Derogatis Stress Profile (Derogatis, 1987), which measures various symptoms of stress. D'Zurilla and Sheedy found that subjects' level of stress symptoms correlated −.53 with their problem orientation and −.23 with their problem-solving skills. In other

FIGURE 4.7.

Humor and coping. Martin and Lefcourt (1983) related stress to mood disturbance in subjects who were either high or low in their use of humor. Increased stress led to smaller increases in mood disturbance in the high-humor group, suggesting that humor has some value in efforts to cope with stress.

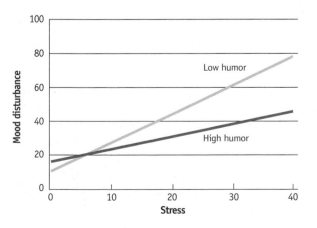

words, the better subjects' problem-solving abilities were, the fewer stress-related difficulties they experienced. Consistent with this finding, research reveals that the acquisition of systematic problem-solving skills can help depressed patients reduce their feelings of depression (Nezu, 1986).

Because an infinite number of personal problems can arise, we can only sketch a general outline of how to engage in systematic problem solving. The problem-solving plan described here is a synthesis of observations by various experts, especially Mahoney (1979), Miller (1978), and Chang and Kelly (1993). The four steps, which closely parallel the four problem-solving skills measured by D'Zurilla and Sheedy (1991), include (1) clarifying the problem, (2) generating alternative courses of actions, (3) evaluating alternatives and selecting a course of action, and (4) taking action while maintaining flexibility.

CLARIFY THE PROBLEM

You can't tackle a problem if you're not sure what the problem is. Therefore, the first step in any systematic problem-solving effort is to clarify the nature of the problem. Sometimes the problem will be all too obvious. At other times the source of trouble may be quite difficult to pin down. In any case, you need to arrive at a specific concrete definition of your problem .

Two common tendencies typically hinder people's efforts to get a clear picture of their problems. First, they often describe their problems in vague generalities ("My life isn't going anywhere" or "I never have enough time"). Second, they tend to focus too much on negative feelings, thereby confusing the consequences of problems ("I'm so depressed all the time" or "I'm so nervous I can't concentrate") with the problems themselves.

GENERATE ALTERNATIVE COURSES OF ACTION

The second step in systematic problem solving is to generate alternative courses of action. Notice that we did not call these alternative *solutions*. Many problems do not have a readily available solution that will completely resolve the problem. If you think in terms of searching for complete solutions, you may prevent yourself from considering many worthwhile courses of action. Instead, it is more realistic to search for alternatives that may produce some kind of improvement in your situation.

Besides avoiding the tendency to insist on solutions, you need to avoid the temptation to go with the first alternative that comes to mind. Many people are a little trigger-happy. They thoughtlessly try to follow through on the first response that occurs to them. Various lines of evidence suggest that it is wiser to engage in brainstorming about a problem. *Brainstorming* **is generating as many ideas as possible**

Web Link 4.2

Mind Tools
James Manktelow's British site details practical techniques to help cope more efficiently and effectively. Particularly useful are a set of problem-solving and stress-reduction techniques grouped as the "strategies for high-performance living."

while withholding criticism and evaluation. In other words, you generate alternatives without paying any attention to their apparent practicality. This approach facilitates creative expression of ideas.

EVALUATE YOUR ALTERNATIVES AND SELECT A COURSE OF ACTION

Once you generate as many alternatives as you can, you need to start evaluating the possibilities. There are no simple criteria for judging the relative merits of your alternatives. However, you will probably want to address three general issues. First, ask yourself whether each alternative is a realistic plan. In other words, what is the probability that you can successfully execute the intended course of action? Try to think of any obstacles you may have failed to anticipate. In making this assessment, it is important to try to avoid both foolish optimism and unnecessary pessimism.

Second, consider any costs or risks associated with each alternative. The "solution" to a problem is sometimes worse than the problem itself. Assuming you can successfully implement your intended course of action, what are the possible negative consequences? Finally, compare the desirability of the probable outcomes of each alternative. After eliminating the unrealistic possibilities, list the probable consequences (both good and bad) associated with each alternative. Then review and compare the desirability of these potential outcomes. In making your decision, you have to ask yourself "What is important to me? Which outcomes do I value the most?"

TAKE ACTION WHILE MAINTAINING FLEXIBILITY

After you have chosen your course of action, you should follow through in implementing your plan. In so doing, try to maintain flexibility. Do not get locked into a particular course of action. Few choices are truly irreversible. You need to monitor results closely and be willing to revise your strategy.

In evaluating your course of action, try to avoid the simplistic success/failure dichotomy. You should simply look for any improvement of any kind. If your plan doesn't work out too well, consider whether it was undermined by any circumstances that you could not have anticipated. Finally, remember that you can learn from your failures. Even if things did not work out, you may now have new information that will facilitate a new attack on the problem.

Seeking Help

In Chapter 3, we learned that social support can be a powerful force that helps buffer the deleterious effects of stress. We discussed social support as if it were a stable, external resource available to different people in varying degrees. In reality, social supports fluctuate over time and evolve out of an individual's interactions with others (Newcomb, 1990). Some people have more support than others, because they have personal characteristics that attract more support or because they make more effort to seek support.

In trying to tackle problems directly, it pays to keep in mind the value of seeking aid from friends, family, co-workers, and neighbors. Because of potential embarrassment, many people are reluctant to acknowledge their problems and seek help from others. What makes this reality so lamentable is that others can provide a great deal of help in many ways.

Using Time More Effectively

Do you constantly feel that you have too much to do, and too little time to do it in? Do you feel overwhelmed by your responsibilities at work, at school, and at home? Do you feel like you're always rushing around, trying to meet an impossible schedule? If you answered yes to some of these questions, you're struggling with time pressure. You can estimate how well you manage time by responding to the brief questionnaire in Figure 4.8. If the results suggest that your time is out of your control, you may be able to make your life less stressful by learning sound time-management strategies.

R. Alec Mackenzie (1997), a prominent time-management researcher, points out that time is a nonrenewable resource. It can't be stockpiled like money, food, or other precious resources. You can't turn back the clock. Furthermore, everyone, whether rich or poor, gets an equal share of time—24 hours per day, 7 days a week. Although time is our most equitably distributed resource, some people spend it much more wisely than others. Let's look at some of the ways in which people let time slip through their fingers without accomplishing much.

THE CAUSES OF WASTED TIME

When people complain about "wasted time," they're usually upset because they haven't accomplished what they really wanted to do with their time. Wasted time is time devoted to unnecessary, unimportant, or unenjoyable activities. Why waste time on such activities? There are many reasons.

Inability to set or stick to priorities. Time consultant Alan Lakein (1996) emphasizes that it's often tempting to deal with routine, trivial tasks ahead of

FIGURE 4.8.

Assessing your time management. The brief questionnaire shown here is designed to evaluate the quality of one's time management. Although it is geared more for working adults than for college students, it should allow you to get a rough handle on how well you manage your time. (From LeBoeuf, 1980)

How Well Do You Manage Your Time?

Listed below are ten statements that reflect generally accepted principles of good time management. Answer these items by circling the response most characteristic of how you perform your job. Please be honest. No one will know your answers except you.

1. Each day I set aside a small amount of time for planning and thinking about my job.
   0. Almost never 1. Sometimes 2. Often 3. Almost always

2. I set specific, written goals and put deadlines on them.
   0. Almost never 1. Sometimes 2. Often 3. Almost always

3. I make a daily "to do list," arrange items in order of importance, and try to get the important items done as soon as possible.
   0. Almost never 1. Sometimes 2. Often 3. Almost always

4. I am aware of the 80/20 rule and use it in doing my job. (The 80/20 rule states that 80 percent of your effectiveness will generally come from achieving only 20 percent of your goals.)
   0. Almost never 1. Sometimes 2. Often 3. Almost always

5. I keep a loose schedule to allow for crises and the unexpected.
   0. Almost never 1. Sometimes 2. Often 3. Almost always

6. I delegate everything I can to others.
   0. Almost never 1. Sometimes 2. Often 3. Almost always

7. I try to handle each piece of paper only once.
   0. Almost never 1. Sometimes 2. Often 3. Almost always

8. I eat a light lunch so I don't get sleepy in the afternoon.
   0. Almost never 1. Sometimes 2. Often 3. Almost always

9. I make an active effort to keep common interruptions (visitors, meetings, telephone calls) from continually disrupting my work day.
   0. Almost never 1. Sometimes 2. Often 3. Almost always

10. I am able to say no to others' requests for my time that would prevent my completing important tasks.
    0. Almost never 1. Sometimes 2. Often 3. Almost always

To get your score, give yourself
3 points for each "almost always"
2 points for each "often"
1 point for each "sometimes"
0 points for each "almost never"
Add up your points to get your total score.

If you scored
0–15 Better give some thought to managing your time.
15–20 You're doing OK, but there's room for improvement.
20–25 Very good.
28–30 You cheated!

larger and more difficult tasks. Thus, students working on a major term paper often read their mail, do the dishes, fold the laundry, reorganize their desk, or dust the furniture instead of concentrating on the paper. Routine tasks are easy, and working on them allows people to rationalize their avoidance of more important tasks. Unfortunately, they often use up too much time on trivial pursuits, leaving their more important tasks undone.

Inability to say no. Other people are constantly making demands on our time. They want us to exchange gossip in the hallway, go out to dinner on Friday night, cover their hours at work, help with a project, listen to their sales pitch on the phone, join a committee, or coach Little League. Clearly, we can't do everything that everyone wants us to. However, some people just can't say no to others' requests for their time. Such people end up fulfilling others' priorities instead of their own. Thus, McDougle (1987) concludes, "Perhaps the most successful way to prevent yourself from wasting time is by saying *no*" (p. 112).

Inability to delegate responsibility. Some tasks should be delegated to others—secretaries, subordinates, fellow committee members, assistant coaches, spouses, children, and so on. However, many people have difficulty delegating work to others. Barriers to delegation include unwillingness to give up any control, lack of confidence in subordinates, fear of being disliked, the need to feel needed, and the attitude that "I can do it better myself" (Mitchell, 1987). The problem, of course, is that people who can't delegate waste a lot of time on trivial work or others' work.

Inability to throw things away. Some people are "pack rats" who can't throw anything into the wastebasket. Their desks are cluttered with piles of mail, newspapers, magazines, reports, and books. Their filing cabinets overflow with old class notes or ancient memos. At home, their kitchen drawers bulge with rarely used utensils, their closets bulge with old clothes that are never worn, and their attics bulge with discarded junk. Pack rats waste time in at least two ways. First, they lose time looking for things that are lost amongst all the chaos. Second, they end up reshuffling the same paper, rereading the same mail, resorting the same reports, and so on. According to Mackenzie (1997), they would be better off if they made more use of their wastebaskets.

Inability to accept anything less than perfection. High standards are admirable, but some people have difficulty finishing projects because they expect them to be flawless. They can't let go. They dwell on minor problems and keep making microscopic changes in their papers, projects, and proposals. They are caught in what Emanuel (1987) calls the "paralysis of perfection." They end up spinning their wheels, redoing the same work over and over.

THE PROBLEM OF PROCRASTINATION

Another time-related problem is *procrastination*—**the tendency to delay tackling tasks until the last minute.** Almost everyone procrastinates on occasion, but research suggests that about 20% of adults are chronic procrastinators (Harriott & Ferrari, 1996). Procrastination is more likely when people have to work on aversive tasks and when they anticipate that their performance will be evaluated (Milgram, Marshevsky, & Sadeh, 1995; Senecal, Lavoie, & Koestner, 1997).

Although many people rationalize their delaying tactics by claiming that "I work best under pressure," (Ferrari, 1992; Lay, 1995), the empirical evidence suggests otherwise. Studies show that procrastination tends to have a negative impact on the quality of task performance (Ferrari, Johnson, & McCown, 1995; Tice & Baumeister, 1997). Why? Late starters may often underestimate how much time will be required to complete a task effectively or experience unforeseen delays and then run out of time because they didn't allow any "cushion." Another consideration is that waiting until the last minute may make a task more stressful—and as we saw in Chapter 3, performance often suffers under conditions of high stress. Moreover, performance may not be the only thing that suffers when people procrastinate. Studies indicate that as a deadline looms, procrastinators tend to experience elevated anxiety and increased health problems (Lay et al., 1989; Tice & Baumeister, 1997).

Why do people procrastinate? Personality factors that contribute to procrastination include low conscientiousness (Lay, Kovacs, & Danto, 1998), low self-efficacy (Haycock, McCarthy, & Skay, 1998), and excessive perfectionism (Flett, Hewitt, & Martin, 1995). The type of irrational thinking described by Albert Ellis also seems to foster procrastination (Bridges & Roig, 1997), as does a strong fear of failure (Lay, 1992). Roy Baumeister (1997) argues that procrastination is one of many types of self-defeating behavior in which people choose courses of action that yield short-term gains in spite of their long-term costs. In the case of procrastination, the short-term payoff is the avoidance of an unpleasant task, whereas the long-term costs consist of impaired performance and increased stress.

TIME-MANAGEMENT TECHNIQUES

What's the key to better time management? Most people assume that it's increased *efficiency*—that is, learning to perform tasks more quickly. Improved efficiency may help a little, but time-management experts maintain that efficiency is overrated. They emphasize that the key to better time management is increased *effectiveness*—that is, learning to allocate time to your most important tasks. This distinction is captured by a widely quoted slogan in the time-management literature: "Efficiency is doing the job right, while effectiveness is doing the right job." Let's look at the experts' suggestions about how to use time more effectively (based on Lakein, 1996; Lebov, 1980; Mackenzie, 1997):

1. *Monitor your use of time.* The first step toward better time management is to monitor your use of time to see where it all goes (Douglass & Douglass, 1993). This requires keeping a written record of your activities, similar to that shown in Figure 4.9. At the end of each week, you should analyze how your time was allocated. Based on your personal roles and responsibilities, create categories of time use such as studying, child care, housework, commuting, work at the office, work at home, eating, and sleeping. For each day, add up the hours allocated to each category. Record this information on a summary sheet like that in Figure 4.10. Two weeks of record keeping should allow you to draw some conclusions about where your time goes. Your records

	Monday	Tuesday	Wednesday	Thursday	Friday	Saturday	Sunday
7 am	Wake-up, jogging, shower, breakfast with family					Sleep in	Sleep in
8							
9	Bus to campus	Molly to day care	Bus to campus	Molly to day care	Bus to campus	Walk at beach with Vic	Waffles for family, Read Sunday paper
10	Medical Anthropology	prepare lecture	Medical Anthropology	prepare lecture	Medical Anthropology	Breakfast	
11		Teach class		Teach class		Clean house	
12 noon	lunch	lunch	lunch	lunch and shopping with Barbara	lunch		Hiking and picnic with family and Tom
1	Biology seminar	pick up Molly at day care	writing at home		pick up Molly at day care	Work in garden	
2		writing at home		Lab work	writing at home		
3							
4		Drive Florrie to piano lesson			Molly to dentist		
5			Grocery shopping			Practice guitar	
6	Dinner at home	Dinner at home	Dinner at home	Dinner at home	Dinner out with Vic	Pick up babysitter	
7	Spend time with Vic and kids			Spend time with Vic and kids		Party at Reid's	Call Mother
8	Guitar lesson		Women's meeting	Band rehearsal			
9		Practice guitar	Practice guitar				Watch Masterpiece Theater
10	Reading and journal						
11	sleep						
12							
1 am							

FIGURE 4.9.
Example of a time log. Experts recommend keeping a detailed record of how you use your time if you are to improve your time management. The example depicted here shows the kind of record keeping that should be done.

will help you make informed decisions about reallocating your time. When you begin your time-management program, these records will also give you a baseline for comparison, so that you can see whether your program is working.

2. *Clarify your goals.* You can't wisely allocate your time unless you decide what you want to accomplish with your time. Lakein (1996) suggests that you ask yourself, "What are my lifetime goals?" Write down all the goals that you can think of, even relatively frivolous things like going deep-sea fishing or becoming a wine expert. Some of your goals will be in conflict. For instance, you can't become a vice-president at your company in Wichita and move to the West Coast. Thus, the tough part comes next. You have to wrestle with your goal conflicts. Figure out which goals are most important to you, and order them in terms of priority. These priorities should guide you as you plan your activities on a daily, weekly, and monthly basis.

3. *Plan your activities using a schedule.* People resist planning because it takes time, but in the long run it saves time. Thorough planning is essential to effective time management (McGee-Cooper & Trammell, 1994). At the beginning of each week, you should make up a list of short-term goals. This list should be translated into daily "to do" lists of planned activities. To avoid the tendency to put off larger projects, break them into smaller, manageable components, and set deadlines for completing the components. Your planned activities should be allocated to various time slots on a written schedule. Schedule your most important activities into the time periods when you tend to be most energetic and productive.

4. *Protect your prime time.* The best-laid plans can quickly go awry because of interruptions. There isn't any foolproof way to eliminate interruptions, but you may be able to shift most of them into certain time slots while protecting your most productive time. The trick is to announce to your family, friends, and co-workers that you're blocking off certain periods of "quiet time" when visitors and phone calls will be turned away. Of course, you also have to block off periods of "available time" when you're ready to deal with everyone's problems.

5. *Increase your efficiency.* Although efficiency is not the key to better time management, it's not irrelevant. Time-management experts do offer some suggestions for improving efficiency, including the following (Klassen, 1987; Schilit, 1987):

• *Handle paper once.* When memos, letters, reports, and such arrive on your desk, they should not be stashed away to be read again and again before you deal with them. Most paperwork can and should be dealt with immediately.

• *Tackle one task at a time.* Jumping from one problem to another is inefficient. Insofar as possible, stick with a task until it's done. In scheduling your activities, try to allow enough time to complete tasks.

• *Group similar tasks together.* It's a good idea to bunch up small tasks that are similar. This strategy is useful when you're paying bills, replying to letters, returning phone calls, and so forth.

• *Make use of your downtime.* Most of us endure a lot of "downtime," waiting in doctors' offices, sitting in needless meetings, riding on buses and trains. In many of these situations, you may be able to get some of your easier work done—if you think ahead and bring it along.

Improving Self-Control

Self-discipline and self-control are the key to handling many of life's problems effectively. All four forms of stress described in Chapter 3 can create challenges to

Time Use Summary Form									
Activity	Mon.	Tues.	Wed.	Thurs.	Fri.	Sat.	Sun.	Total	%
1. Sleeping	8	6	8	6	8	7	9	52	31
2. Eating	2	2	3	2	3	2	3	17	10
3. Commuting	2	2	2	2	2	0	0	10	6
4. Housework	0	1	0	3	0	0	2	6	4
5. In class	4	2	4	2	4	0	0	16	9
6. Part-time job	0	5	0	5	0	3	0	13	8
7. Studying	3	2	4	2	0	4	5	20	12
8. Relaxing	5	4	3	2	7	8	5	34	20
9.									
10.									

FIGURE 4.10.

Time use summary. To analyze where your time goes, you need to review your time log and create a weekly time use summary, like the one shown here. The exact categories to be listed on the left depend on your circumstances and responsibilities.

your self-control. Whether you're struggling with the *frustration* of poor grades in school, constant *conflicts* about your overeating, *pressure* to do well in sports, or downhill *changes* in finances that require readjustment, you will need reasonable self-control if you expect to make much progress.

For many people, however, satisfactory self-control is difficult to achieve. Fortunately, the last several decades have produced major advances in the technology of self-control. These advances have emerged from research on *behavior modification,* an approach to controlling behavior that utilizes the principles of learning and conditioning. Because of its importance, we'll devote the entire Application at the end of this chapter to improving self-control through behavior modification.

Emotion-Focused Constructive Coping

LEARNING OBJECTIVES

- Discuss the adaptive value of releasing pent-up emotions and distracting yourself.
- Summarize the evidence on the effects of meditation.
- Describe the requirements and procedure for Benson's relaxation response.

Let's be realistic: There are going to be occasions when appraisal-focused coping and problem-focused coping are not successful in warding off emotional turmoil. Some problems are too serious to be whittled down much by reappraisal, and others simply can't be "solved." Moreover, even well-executed coping strategies may take time to work before emotional tensions begin to subside. Hence, it is helpful to have some coping mechanisms that are useful in reducing emotional arousal. We'll discuss the merits of four such coping

strategies in this section: releasing pent-up emotions, distracting yourself, meditating, and doing relaxation exercises.

Releasing Pent-Up Emotions

Try as you might to redefine situations as less stressful, you no doubt still go through times when you feel wired with stress-induced tension. When this happens, there's merit in the commonsense notion that you should try to release the emotions welling up inside. Why? Because the physiological arousal that accompanies emotions can become problematic. For example, research suggests that people who inhibit the expression of anger and other emotions are somewhat more likely than other people to have elevated blood pressure (Jorgensen et al., 1996). Moreover, research suggests that efforts to actively suppress emotions result in increased autonomic arousal (Gross, 1998; Gross & Levenson, 1997).

A recent study looked at the repercussions of "psychological inhibition" in gay men who conceal their homosexual identity (Cole et al., 1996). Many gay individuals inhibit the public expression of their homosexuality to avoid stigmatization, discrimination, and even physical assault. Although hiding one's gay identity may be a sensible strategy, it entails vigilant inhibition of one's true feelings. To investigate the possible effects of this inhibition, Cole et al. (1996) tracked the incidence of cancer, pneumonia, bronchitis, sinusitis, and tuberculosis in a sample of 222 HIV-negative gay and bisexual men over a period of five years. As you can see in Figure 4.11 on the next page, they found that the overall incidence of these diseases was noticeably higher among the men who concealed their homosexual identity. The investigators speculate that psychological inhibition may be detrimental to people's health.

If inhibition is bad, perhaps expression is good. Although there's no guarantee of it, you can sometimes

reduce your physiological arousal by *expressing* your emotions. The key, of course, is to express your emotions in a mature and socially acceptable manner. This is particularly important when the emotion is anger.

Evidence is accumulating that verbalization or "talking it out" can be valuable in dealing with stress (Clark, 1993). James Pennebaker and his colleagues have shown that talking or writing about traumatic events can have beneficial effects. For example, in one study of college students, half the subjects were asked to write three essays about their difficulties in adjusting to college. The other half wrote three essays about superficial topics. The subjects who wrote about their personal problems and traumas enjoyed better health in the following months than the other subjects did (Pennebaker, Colder, & Sharp, 1990). Subsequent, similar studies have replicated this finding (Francis &

Pennebaker, 1992; Greenberg, Wortman, & Stone, 1996) and shown that emotional disclosure is associated with better immunal functioning (Esterling et al., 1994).

Thus, if you can find a good listener, it may be wise to try to discharge problematic emotions by letting your secret fears, misgivings, and suspicions spill out in a candid conversation. Admittedly, talking about one's problems can be awkward and difficult. Pennebaker's research suggests that confiding in others does have short-term costs in that it may elicit anxiety and other negative emotions. However, in the long run, those who open up to others enjoy better mental and physical health than those who hold back.

Distracting Yourself

Distraction involves diverting your attention from a problem by thinking about other things or engaging in other activities. Substantial reliance on this strategy was observed in a study of the coping efforts of 60 married couples (Stone & Neale, 1984). If your stomach is churning over a snafu at work, it may be a good idea to go out to a movie, take up your knitting, or head for the bowling alley. Activities that require focused attention are probably best when using this strategy.

The adaptive merits of distraction are open to debate. On the one hand, distracting yourself is probably inferior to problem-focused coping that might yield a longer-lasting solution. On the other hand, distracting yourself is clearly a better idea than self-indulgence, lashing out at others, or getting bogged down in negative self-talk. Thus, it appears to be a strategy that has modest, short-term value when more direct tactics have failed to produce progress.

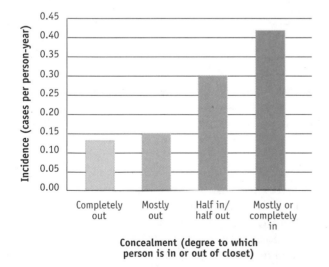

FIGURE 4.11.
Elevated health risk among gay men who conceal their homosexual identity. In a sample of gay and bisexual men, Cole et al. (1996) found that the more the men concealed their homosexual identity, the more likely they were to experience various diseases. The investigators speculate that the elevated incidence of disease may reflect the costs of inhibiting one's true feelings.

Meditating

Recent years have seen an explosion of interest in meditation as a method for relieving stress. **Meditation refers to a family of mental exercises in which a con-**

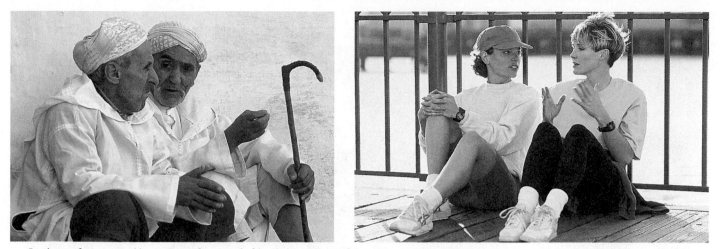

In times of stress, seeking support from one's friends is a very useful coping strategy. Releasing pent-up emotions by talking about one's difficulties appears to be a particularly beneficial coping mechanism.

scious attempt is made to focus attention in a nonanalytical way. There are many approaches to meditation. In the United States, the most widely practiced approaches are those associated with yoga, Zen, and transcendental meditation (TM). Although all three of these approaches are rooted in Eastern religions (Hinduism, Buddhism, and Taoism), most Americans who practice meditation have only vague ideas regarding its religious significance. Of interest to us is the idea that meditation can calm inner emotional turmoil.

Most meditative techniques look deceptively simple. For example, in TM a person is supposed to sit in a comfortable position with eyes closed and silently focus attention on a *mantra,* a specially assigned Sanskrit word that creates a resonant sound. This exercise in mental self-discipline is to be practiced twice daily for 20 minutes. The technique has been described as "diving from the active surface of the mind to its quiet depths" (Bloomfield & Kory, 1976, p. 49).

Advocates of TM claim that it can improve learning, energy level, work productivity, physical health, mental health, and general happiness while reducing tension and anxiety caused by stress (Alexander et al., 1990; Bloomfield & Kory, 1976). These are not exactly humble claims. Moreover, TM advocates assert that they can back up their claims with scientific evidence. Let's examine that evidence.

What are the *physical effects* of going into the meditative state? Some studies suggest that changes occur in the electrochemical activity of the brain. Most studies also find decreases in subjects' heart rate, respiration rate, oxygen consumption, and carbon dioxide elimination (see Figure 4.12). Many researchers have also observed increases in skin resistance and decreases in blood lactate—physiological indicators associated with relaxation. Taken together, these bodily changes suggest that meditation can lead to a potentially beneficial physiological state characterized by relaxation and suppression of arousal (Carrington, 1993; Fenwick, 1987).

● Recommended Reading

Emotional Intelligence: Why It Can Matter More Than IQ by Daniel Goleman (Bantam Books, 1995)

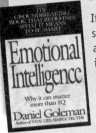

It's great to see a book like this make the bestseller lists. It is a serious, scholarly, yet readable analysis of how emotional functioning is so important in everyday life. Daniel Goleman is both a psychologist and a journalist who writes about the behavioral sciences for the *New York Times.* In this book, he synthesizes the research of many investigators as he argues that emotional intelligence may be more important to success than high IQ.

The concept of emotional intelligence was originally formulated by Peter Salovey and John Mayer (1990). They define emotional intelligence as the ability to monitor, access, express, and regulate one's own emotions and to identify, interpret, and understand others' emotions (Mayer & Salovey, 1997). Their concept, which focused squarely on being savvy about emotions, languished in relative obscurity until Goleman's book attracted attention. Goleman views emotional intelligence more broadly than Salovey and Mayer. He includes all of their ingredients but adds social poise and skill, strong motivation and persistence, and some desirable personality traits, such as optimism and conscientiousness.

One can argue that Goleman's concept of emotional intelligence is too much of a hodgepodge of traits to be measureable or meaningful, but his broad view yields a wide-ranging book that discusses innumerable examples of how social finesse and emotional sensitivity can foster career success, marital bliss, and physical and mental health. In the course of this analysis, Goleman discusses state-of-the-art research on a diverse array of topics in an exceptionally lucid manner.

And that is the problem: academic intelligence offers virtually no preparation for the turmoil—or opportunity—life's vicissitudes bring. Yet even though a high IQ is no guarantee of prosperity, prestige, or happiness in life, our schools and our culture fixate on academic abilities, ignoring emotional intelligence, a set of traits—some might call it character—that also matters immensely for our personal destiny. Emotional life is a domain that, as surely as math or reading, can be handled with greater or lesser skill, and requires its unique set of competencies.

One constructive means of coping with daily stress is meditating.

These findings generated quite a bit of excitement in the 1970s. However, additional research using better experimental controls soon dampened some of this enthusiasm. It turns out that these physical changes may not be unique to meditation. A variety of systematic relaxation training procedures may be able to produce similar results (Holmes, 1987; Shapiro, 1984).

The findings on the psychological effects of meditation are also promising but controversial. Some studies have found that meditation can improve mood, lessen fatigue, and reduce anxiety and drug abuse (Carrington, 1987; Eppley, Abrams, & Shear, 1989; Gelderloos et al., 1991). Studies also suggest that meditation is associated with improved physical health (Orme-Johnson, 1987), superior mental health (Alexander, Rainforth, & Gelderloos, 1991), and even increased longevity among the elderly (Alexander et al., 1989). However, some psychologists argue that at least some of these effects may be just as attainable through systematic relaxation or other mental focusing procedures (Holmes, 1984; Shapiro, 1987). At present, the evidence on this issue is too inconsistent and fragmentary to permit any solid conclusions (Lehrer & Woolfolk, 1993).

What's the bottom line? If you are troubled by chronic emotional tension, learning to meditate may be an effective way to reduce your troublesome arousal.

FIGURE 4.12.

Transcendental meditation (TM) and physiological arousal. The physiological changes shown on this graph (based on Wallace & Benson, 1972) indicate that meditation suppresses arousal, thus leading to a physical state that may have beneficial effects.

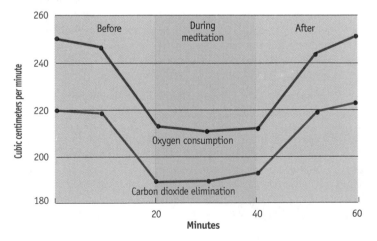

Web Link 4.4

The Anxiety-Panic Internet Resource: Relaxation
This veteran Web site dealing with anxiety, panic, and stress gathers together a broad set of coping hints, tips, and strategies, all designed to help enhance one's experience of relaxation.

Bear in mind, however, that the benefits of meditation may not be as spectacular as some proponents have claimed. Furthermore, you may be able to attain some of the same benefits through less exotic techniques, such as the relaxation procedures that we discuss next.

Using Relaxation Procedures

Ample evidence suggests that systematic relaxation procedures can soothe emotional turmoil and reduce problematic physiological arousal (Lehrer & Woolfolk, 1984, 1993). One study even proposes that relaxation training may improve the effectiveness of one's immune response (Kiecolt-Glaser et al., 1985). There are a number of worthwhile approaches to achieving beneficial relaxation. The most prominent systems are Jacobson's (1938) *progressive relaxation* (see McGuigan, 1993), Schultz and Luthe's (1969) *autogenic training* (see Linden, 1993), and Benson's (1975; Benson & Klipper, 1988) *relaxation response.* We'll discuss Benson's approach because it is a simple one that virtually anyone can learn to use.

After studying various approaches to meditation, Herbert Benson, a Harvard Medical School cardiologist, concluded that elaborate religious rituals and beliefs are not necessary to profit from meditation. He also concluded that what makes meditation beneficial is the relaxation it induces. After "demystifying" meditation, Benson (1975) set out to devise a simple, nonreligious procedure that could provide similar benefits. He calls his procedure the "relaxation response." According to Benson, four factors are critical to effective practice of the relaxation response:

1. *A quiet environment.* It is easiest to induce the relaxation response in a distraction-free environment. After you become skilled at the relaxation response, you may be able to accomplish it in a crowded subway. Initially, however, you should practice it in a quiet, calm place.

2. *A mental device.* To shift attention inward and keep it there, you need to focus it on a constant stimulus, such as a sound or word that you recite over and over. You may also choose to gaze fixedly at a bland object, such as a vase. Whatever the case, you need to focus your attention on something.

3. *A passive attitude.* It is important not to get upset when your attention strays to distracting thoughts. You must realize that such distractions are inevitable. Whenever your mind wanders from your attentional focus, calmly redirect attention to your mental device.

4. *A comfortable position.* Reasonable body comfort is essential to avoid a major source of potential distraction. Simply sitting up straight works well for most people. Some people can practice the relaxation response lying down, but for most people such a position is too conducive to sleep.

Benson's (1975, pp. 114–115) actual procedure for inducing the relaxation response is deceptively simple. The procedure is described in Figure 4.13. For full benefit, it should be practiced daily.

FIGURE 4.13.

Benson's relaxation response. The relaxation procedure advocated by Herbert Benson (1975) is a simple one that should be practiced daily.

1 Sit quietly in a comfortable position.

2 Close your eyes.

3 Deeply relax all your muscles, beginning at your feet and progressing up to your face. Keep them relaxed.

4 Breathe through your nose. Become aware of your breathing. As you breathe out, say the word "one" silently to yourself. For example, breathe in . . . out, "one"; in . . . out, "one"; and so forth. Breathe easily and naturally.

5 Continue for 10 to 20 minutes. You may open your eyes to check the time, but do not use an alarm. When you finish, sit quietly for several minutes, at first with your eyes closed and later with your eyes opened. Do not stand up for a few minutes.

6 Do not worry about whether you are successful in achieving a deep level of relaxation. Maintain a passive attitude and permit relaxation to occur at its own pace. When distracting thoughts occur, try to ignore them by not dwelling on them, and return to repeating "one." With practice, the response should come with little effort. Practice the technique once or twice daily but not within two hours after any meal, since digestive processes seem to interfere with the elicitation of the relaxation response.

Achieving Self-Control

LEARNING OBJECTIVES

- *Explain why traits cannot be target behaviors in self-modification programs.*
- *Discuss the three kinds of information you should pursue in gathering your baseline data.*
- *Discuss how to use reinforcement to increase the strength of a response.*
- *Discuss how to use reinforcement, control of antecedents, and punishment to decrease the strength of a response.*
- *Discuss issues related to fine-tuning and ending a self-modification program.*

Answer the following "yes" or "no."

____ **1.** Do you have a hard time passing up food, even when you're not hungry?

____ **2.** Do you wish you studied more often?

____ **3.** Would you like to cut down on your smoking or drinking?

____ **4.** Do you experience difficulty in getting yourself to exercise regularly?

____ **5.** Do you wish you had more willpower?

If you answered "yes" to any of these questions, you have struggled with the challenge of self-control. This Application discusses how you can use the techniques of behavior modification to improve your self-control. If you stop to think about it, self-control—or rather a lack of it—underlies many of the personal problems that people struggle with in everyday life.

***Behavior modification* is a systematic approach to changing behavior through the application of the principles of conditioning.** Advocates of behavior modification assume that behavior is a product of learning, conditioning, and environmental control. They further assume that *what is learned can be unlearned.* Thus, they set out to "recondition" people to produce more desirable patterns of behavior.

The technology of behavior modification has been applied with great success in schools, businesses, hospitals, factories, child-care facilities, prisons, and mental health centers (Goodall, 1972; Kazdin, 1982; Rachman, 1992). Moreover, behavior modification techniques have proven particularly valuable in efforts to improve self-control. Our discussion will borrow liberally from an excellent book on self-modification by David Watson and Roland Tharp (1997). We will discuss five steps in the process of self-modification, which are outlined in Figure 4.14.

Specifying Your Target Behavior

The first step in a self-modification program is to specify the target behavior(s) that you want to change. Behavior

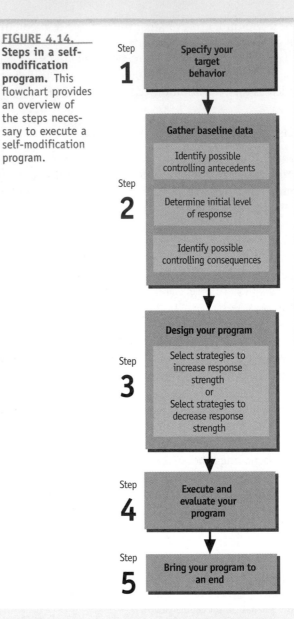

FIGURE 4.14.
Steps in a self-modification program. This flowchart provides an overview of the steps necessary to execute a self-modification program.

Step **1** Specify your target behavior

Step **2** Gather baseline data
- Identify possible controlling antecedents
- Determine initial level of response
- Identify possible controlling consequences

Step **3** Design your program
- Select strategies to increase response strength
- or
- Select strategies to decrease response strength

Step **4** Execute and evaluate your program

Step **5** Bring your program to an end

modification can only be applied to a clearly defined, overt response, yet many people have difficulty pinpointing the behavior they hope to alter. They tend to describe their problems in terms of unobservable personality *traits* rather than overt behaviors. For example, asked what behavior he would like to change, a man might say, "I'm too irritable." That may be true, but it is of little help in designing a self-modification program. To use a behavioral approach, you need to translate vague statements about traits into precise descriptions of specific target behaviors.

To identify target responses, you need to ponder past behavior or closely observe future behavior and list specific *examples* of responses that lead to the trait description. For instance, the man who regards himself as "too irritable" might identify two overly frequent responses, such as arguing with his wife and snapping at his children. These are specific behaviors for which he could design a self-modification program.

Gathering Baseline Data

The second step in behavior modification is to gather baseline data. You need to systematically observe your target behavior for a period of time (usually a week or two) before you work out the details of your program. In gathering your baseline data, you need to monitor three things.

First, you need to determine the initial response level of your target behavior. After all, you can't tell whether your program is working effectively unless you have a baseline for comparison. In most cases, you would simply keep track of how often the target response occurs in a certain time interval. Thus, you might count the daily frequency of snapping at your children, smoking cigarettes, or biting your fingernails. If studying is your target behavior, you will probably monitor hours of study. If you want to modify your eating, you will probably keep track of how many calories you consume. Whatever the unit of measurement, *it is crucial to gather accurate data*. You should keep permanent written records, preferable in the form of some type of chart or graph (see Figure 4.15).

Second, you need to monitor the antecedents of your target behavior. ***Antecedents* are events that typically precede the target response.** Often these events play a major role in evoking your target behavior. For example, if your target is overeating, you might discover that the bulk of your overeating occurs late in the evening while you watch TV. If you can pinpoint this kind of antecedent-response connection, you may be able to design your program to circumvent or break the link.

Third, you need to monitor the typical consequences of your target behavior. Try to identify the reinforcers that are maintaining an undesirable target behavior or the unfavorable outcomes that are suppressing a desirable target behavior. In trying to identify reinforcers, remember that avoidance behavior is usually maintained by negative reinforcement (see Chapter 2). That is, the payoff for avoidance is usually the removal of something aversive, such as anxiety or a threat to self-esteem. You should also take into account the fact that a response may not be reinforced every time, as most behavior is maintained by intermittent reinforcement.

Designing Your Program

Once you have selected a target behavior and gathered adequate baseline data, it is time to plan your intervention program. Generally speaking, your program will be designed either to increase or to decrease the frequency of a target response.

INCREASING RESPONSE STRENGTH

Efforts to increase the frequency of a target response depend largely on the use of positive reinforcement. In other words, you reward yourself for behaving properly. Although the basic strategy is quite simple, doing it skillfully involves a number of considerations.

Selecting a Reinforcer. To use positive reinforcement, you need to find a reward that will be effective for you. Reinforcement is subjective—what is reinforcing for

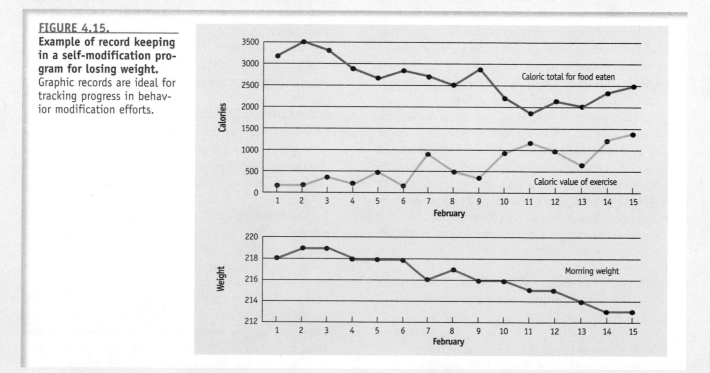

FIGURE 4.15.

Example of record keeping in a self-modification program for losing weight. Graphic records are ideal for tracking progress in behavior modification efforts.

one person may not be reinforcing for another. Figure 4.16 lists questions you can ask yourself to help you determine your personal reinforcers. Be sure to be realistic and choose a reinforcer that is really available to you.

You don't have to come up with spectacular new reinforcers that you've never experienced before. *You can use reinforcers that you are already getting.* However, you have to restructure the contingencies so that you get them only if you behave appropriately. For example, if you normally buy two compact discs per week, you might make these purchases contingent on studying a certain number of hours during the week. Making yourself earn rewards that you used to take for granted is often a useful strategy in a self-modification program.

Arranging the Contingencies. Once you have chosen your reinforcer, you have to set up reinforcement contingencies. These contingencies will describe the exact behavioral goals that must be met and the reinforcement that may then be awarded. For example, in a program to increase exercise, you might make spending $40 on clothes (the reinforcer) contingent on having jogged 15 miles during the week (the target behavior).

Try to set behavioral goals that are both challenging and realistic. You want your goals to be challenging so that they lead to improvement in your behavior. However, setting unrealistically high goals—a common mistake in self-modification—often leads to unnecessary discouragement.

You also need to be concerned about doling out too much reinforcement. If reinforcement is too easy to get, you may become *satiated,* and the reinforcer may lose its motivational power. For example, if you were to reward yourself with virtually all the compact discs you wanted, this reinforcer would lose its incentive value.

One way to avoid the satiation problem is to put yourself on a token economy. **A *token economy* is a system for doling out symbolic reinforcers that are exchanged later for a variety of genuine reinforcers.** Thus, you might develop a point system for exercise behavior, accumulating points that can be spent on compact discs, movies, restaurant meals, and so forth. You can also use a token economy to reinforce a variety of related target behaviors, as opposed to a single, specific response. The token economy in Figure 4.17, for instance, is set up to strengthen three different, though related, responses (jogging, tennis, and sit-ups).

Shaping. In some cases, you may want to reinforce a target response that you are not currently capable of making, such as speaking in front of a large group or jogging ten miles a day. This situation calls for *shaping,* **which is accomplished by reinforcing closer and closer approximations of the desired response.** Thus,

FIGURE 4.16.

Selecting a reinforcer. The questions listed here may help you to identify your personal reinforcers. (From Watson & Tharp, 1993, pp. 213–214)

What Are Your Reinforcers?

1. What will be the rewards of achieving your goal?
2. What kind of praise do you like to receive, from yourself and others?
3. What kinds of things do you like to have?
4. What are your major interests?
5. What are your hobbies?
6. What people do you like to be with?
7. What do you like to do with those people?
8. What do you do for fun?
9. What do you do to relax?
10. What do you do to get away from it all?
11. What makes you feel good?
12. What would be a nice present to receive?
13. What kinds of things are important to you?
14. What would you buy if you had an extra $20? $50? $100?
15. On what do you spend your money each week?
16. What behaviors do you perform every day? (Don't overlook the obvious or commonplace.)
17. Are there any behaviors you usually perform instead of the target behavior?
18. What would you hate to lose?
19. Of the things you do every day, which would you hate to give up?
20. What are your favorite daydreams and fantasies?
21. What are the most relaxing scenes you can imagine?

you might start jogging two miles a day and add a half-mile each week until you reach your goal. In shaping your behavior, you should set up a schedule spelling out how and when your target behaviors and reinforcement contingencies should change. Generally, it is a good idea to move forward gradually.

DECREASING RESPONSE STRENGTH

Let's turn now to the challenge of reducing the frequency of an undesirable response. You can go about this task in a number of ways. Your principal options are reinforcement, control of antecedents, and punishment.

Reinforcement. Reinforcers can be used in an indirect way to decrease the frequency of a response. This may sound paradoxical, since you have learned that reinforcement strengthens a response. The trick lies in how you define the target behavior. For example, in the case of overeating you might define your target behavior as eating more than 1600 calories a day (an excess response that you want to decrease) or eating less than 1600 calories a day (a deficit response that you want to increase). You can choose the latter definition and

Self-control issues, such as working out frequently enough and giving up smoking, can often be dealt with through the use of self-modification techniques.

reinforce yourself whenever you eat less than 1600 calories in a day. Thus, you can reinforce yourself for not emitting a response, or for emitting it less, and thereby decrease a response through reinforcement.

Control of Antecedents. A worthwhile strategy for decreasing the occurrence of an undesirable response

FIGURE 4.17.
Example of a token economy to reinforce exercise. This token economy was set up to strengthen three types of exercise behavior. The person can exchange tokens for four types of reinforcers.

Responses Earning Tokens		
Response	**Amount**	**Number of Tokens**
Jogging	1/2 mile	4
Jogging	1 mile	8
Jogging	2 miles	16
Tennis	1 hour	4
Tennis	2 hours	8
Sit-ups	25	1
Sit-ups	50	2

Redemption Value of Tokens	
Reinforcer	**Tokens required**
Purchase one compact disc of your choice	30
Go to movie	50
Go to nice restaurant	100
Take special weekend trip	500

may be to identify its antecedents and avoid exposure to them. This strategy is especially useful when you are trying to decrease the frequency of a consummatory response, such as smoking or eating. In the case of overeating, for instance, the easiest way to resist temptation is to avoid having to face it. Thus, you might stay away from enticing restaurants, minimize time spent in your kitchen, shop for groceries just after eating (when willpower is higher), and avoid purchasing favorite foods. Figure 4.18 on the next page lists a variety of suggestions for controlling antecedents to reduce overeating. Control of antecedents can also be helpful in a program to increase studying. The key often lies in *where* you study. You can reduce excessive socializing by studying somewhere devoid of people. Similarly, you can reduce loafing by studying someplace where there is no TV, stereo, or phone to distract you.

Punishment. The strategy of decreasing unwanted behavior by punishing yourself for that behavior is an obvious option that people tend to overuse. The biggest problem with punishment in a self-modification effort is that it is difficult to follow through and punish yourself. Nonetheless, there may be situations in which your manipulations of reinforcers need to be bolstered by the threat of punishment. If you're going to use punishment, keep two guidelines in mind. First, do not use punishment alone. Use it in conjunction with positive reinforcement. If you set up a program in which you can earn only negative consequences, you probably

FIGURE 4.18.

Control of antecedents. Controlling antecedents that trigger overeating is often a crucial part of behavioral programs for weight loss. The tips listed here have proven useful to many people.

Controlling the Antecedents of Overeating

A. Shopping for food

1. Do not purchase problematic foods. These include
   a. very fattening, high-calorie foods
   b. your favorite foods, unless they have very low caloric values (you will be tempted to overconsume favorite foods)
   c. foods requiring little preparation (they make it too easy to eat)

2. To facilitate the above, you should
   a. use a shopping list from which you do not deviate
   b. shop just after eating (your willpower is reduced to jelly when you're hungry)
   c. carry only enough money to pay for items on your list

B. In your kitchen

1. Don't use your kitchen for anything other than food preparation and consumption.
2. Keep food stock stored out of sight.
3. If you have problematic foods in your kitchen (for other household members, of course), arrange cupboards and the refrigerator so that these foods are out of reach or in the rear.
4. Don't hover over cooking food. It will cook itself.
5. Prepare only enough food for immediate consumption.

C. While eating

1. Don't do anything besides eating. Watching TV or reading promotes mindless consumption.
2. Leave serving dishes on the kitchen counter or stove. Don't set them right in front of you.
3. Eat from a smaller dish. It will make a quantity of food appear greater.
4. Slow the pace of eating. Relax and enjoy your food.

D. After eating

1. Quickly put away or dispose of leftover foods.
2. Leave the kitchen as soon as you are through.

E. In regard to restaurants

1. Insofar as possible, do not patronize restaurants. Menus are written in a much too seductive style.
2. If social obligations require that you eat out, go to a restaurant that you don't particularly like.
3. When in restaurants, don't linger over the menu, and don't gawk at the food on other tables.
4. Avoid driving down streets and going to shopping centers that are loaded with alluring fast-food enterprises.

F. In general

1. Try to avoid boredom. Keep yourself busy.
2. Try to avoid excessive sleep loss and fatigue. Your self-control diminishes when you are tired.
3. Avoid excessive fasting. Skipping meals often leads to overeating later.

won't stick to it. Second, use a relatively mild punishment so that you will actually be able to administer it to yourself. Nurnberger and Zimmerman (1970) developed a creative method of self-punishment. They had subjects write out a check to an organization they hated (for instance, the campaign of a political candidate whom they despised). The check was held by a third party who mailed it if subjects failed to meet their behavioral goals. Such a punishment is relatively harmless, but it can serve as a strong source of motivation.

Executing and Evaluating Your Program

Once you have designed your program, the next step is to put it to work by enforcing the contingencies that you have carefully planned. During this period, you need to continue to accurately record the frequency of your target behavior so you can evaluate your progress. The success of your program depends on your not "cheating." The most common form of cheating is to reward yourself when you have not actually earned it.

You can do two things to increase the likelihood that you will comply with your program. One is to make up a *behavioral contract*—a written agreement outlining a promise to adhere to the contingencies of a behavior modification program (see Figure 4.19). The formality of signing such a contract in front of friends or family seems to make many people take their program more seriously. You can further reduce the likelihood of cheating by having someone other than yourself dole out the reinforcers and punishments.

Behavior modification programs often require some fine-tuning. So don't be surprised if you need to make a few adjustments. Several flaws are especially common in designing self-modification programs. Among those that you should look out for are (1) depending on a weak reinforcer, (2) permitting lengthy delays between appropriate behavior and delivery of reinforcers, and (3) trying to do too much too quickly by setting unrealistic goals. Often, a small revision or two can turn a failing program around and make it a success.

Ending Your Program

Generally, when you design your program you should spell out the conditions under which you will bring it to an end. This involves setting terminal goals such as reaching a certain weight, studying with a certain regularity, or going without cigarettes for a certain length of time. Often, it is a good idea to phase out your program by planning a gradual reduction in the frequency or potency of your reinforcement for appropriate behavior.

FIGURE 4.19.
A behavioral contract.
Behavior modification experts
recommend the use of a formal,
written contract similar to that
shown here.

I, _____, do hereby agree to initiate my self-change strategy as of

(date) _____ and to continue it for a minimum period of _____

weeks—that is, until (date) _____ .

My specific self-change strategy is to _____

_____

_____

I will do my best to execute this strategy to my utmost ability and to evaluate its effectiveness only after
it has been honestly tried for the specified period of time.

Optional Self-Reward Clause: For every _____ day(s) that I successfully comply with my

self-change contract, I will reward myself with _____

_____

In addition, at the end of my minimum period of personal experimentation, I will reward myself for having

persisted in my self-change efforts. My reward at that time will be_____

_____

I hereby request that the witnesses who have signed below support me in my self-change efforts and
encourage my compliance with the specifics of this contract. Their cooperation and encouragement
throughout the project will be appreciated.

Signed _____

Date _____

Witness:

Witness:

If your program is successful, it may fade away
without a conscious decision on your part. Often, new,
improved patterns of behavior become self-maintaining.
Responses such as eating right, exercising regularly,
and studying diligently may become habitual. Whether
you end your program intentionally or not, you should
always be prepared to reinstitute the program if you
find yourself slipping back to your old patterns of
behavior.

Key Ideas

THE CONCEPT OF COPING
● Coping involves behavioral efforts to master, reduce, or tolerate the demands created by stress. People cope with stress in many ways, but most have certain styles of coping. Coping strategies vary in their adaptive value.

COMMON COPING PATTERNS OF LIMITED VALUE
● Giving up, possibly best understood in terms of learned helplessness, is a common coping pattern that tends to be of limited value. Another is striking out at others with acts of aggression. Frequently caused by frustration, aggression tends to be counterproductive because it often creates new sources of stress.

● Indulging oneself is a common coping strategy that is not inherently unhealthy, but it is frequently taken to excess and thus becomes maladaptive. Internet addiction is a new form of self-indulgence. Blaming yourself with negative self-talk is associated with depression.

● Defensive coping is particularly common and may involve any of a number of defense mechanisms. Although the adaptive value of defensive coping tends to be less than optimal, it depends on the situation. Taylor and Brown have argued that some illusions may be healthful, but their thesis has been controversial.

THE NATURE OF CONSTRUCTIVE COPING
● Constructive coping, which includes efforts to deal with stress that are judged as relatively healthful, does not appear to depend on one's intelligence. Constructive coping is rational, realistic, and action oriented. It also involves managing emotions and learning self-control.

APPRAISAL-FOCUSED CONSTRUCTIVE COPING
● Appraisal-focused constructive coping is facilitated by Ellis's suggestions on how to reduce catastrophic thinking by digging out the irrational assumptions that cause it. Other valuable strategies include using humor to deal with stress and looking for the positive aspects of setbacks and problems.

PROBLEM-FOCUSED CONSTRUCTIVE COPING
● Systematic problem solving can be facilitated by following a four-step process: (1) clarify the problem, (2) generate alternative courses of action, (3) evaluate your alternatives and select a course of action, and (4) take action while maintaining flexibility.

● Other problem-focused coping tactics with potential value include seeking social support and acquiring strategies to improve self-control. Better time management can also aid problem-focused coping. Effective time management doesn't depend on increased efficiency as much as on setting priorities and allocating time wisely. It is also helpful to avoid the common tendency to procrastinate on aversive tasks.

EMOTION-FOCUSED CONSTRUCTIVE COPING
● Our discussion of emotion-focused coping noted the possible value of releasing pent-up emotions. The inhibition of emotions appears to be associated with increased health problems. Distracting yourself in times of stress is a coping strategy that has some short-term value.

● Research suggests that meditation can be helpful in reducing emotional turmoil. Although less exotic, systematic relaxation procedures, such as Benson's relaxation response, can also be effective in coping with troublesome emotional arousal.

APPLICATION: ACHIEVING SELF-CONTROL
● In behavior modification, the principles of learning are used to change behavior directly. Behavior modification techniques can be used to increase one's self-control. The first step in self-modification is to specify the overt target behavior to be increased or decreased.

● The second step is to gather baseline data about the initial rate of the target response and identify any typical antecedents and consequences associated with the behavior. The third step is to design a program. If you are trying to increase the strength of a response, you'll depend on positive reinforcement. The reinforcement contingencies should spell out exactly what you have to do to earn your reinforcer.

● A number of strategies can be used to decrease the strength of a response, including reinforcement, control of antecedents, and punishment. The fourth step is to execute and evaluate the program. Self-modification programs often require some fine-tuning. The final step is to determine how and when you will phase out your program.

Key Terms

Aggression
Antecedents
Behavioral contract
Behavior modification
Brainstorming
Catastrophic thinking
Catharsis
Constructive coping
Coping
Defense mechanisms
Internet addiction
Learned helplessness
Meditation
Procrastination
Rational-emotive therapy
Shaping
Token economy

Key People

Herbert Benson
Albert Ellis
Seymour Epstein
Sigmund Freud
Martin Seligman
Shelley Taylor

Practice Test

1. The release of emotional tension as termed by Freud is called:
   a. overreaction.
   b. catharsis.
   c. discharge.
   d. diversion.

2. Defense mechanisms involve the use of _____ to guard against negative _____.
   a. self-deception, behaviors
   b. self-deception, emotions
   c. self-denial, behaviors
   d. self-denial, emotions

3. Taylor and Brown found that normal people's self-images tend to be _____; depressed people's tend to be _____.
   a. accurate, inaccurate
   b. less favorable, more favorable
   c. overly favorable, more realistic
   d. more realistic, overly favorable

4. According to Albert Ellis, people's emotional reactions to life events result mainly from:
   a. their arousal level at the time.
   b. the consequences following events.
   c. congruence between events and expectations.
   d. their beliefs about events.

5. According to D'Zurilla and Sheedy, the first step in systematic problem solving is:
   a. clarifying the problem.
   b. generating alternative courses of action.
   c. selecting a course of action.
   d. taking action.

6. Which of the following is not listed in your text as a cause of wasted time?
   a. Inability to set priorities
   b. Inability to delegate responsibility
   c. Inability to work diligently
   d. Inability to throw things away

7. Time-management experts agree that the key to better time management is increased:
   a. willpower
   b. efficiency
   c. self-discipline
   d. effectiveness

8. Which of the following is *not* a type of emotion-focused constructive coping described in the text?
   a. Using time more effectively
   b. Distracting oneself
   c. Learning to relax
   d. Releasing pent-up emotions

9. The first step in a self-modification program is:
   a. designing your program.
   b. gathering baseline data.
   c. specifying your target behavior.
   d. any of the above; it doesn't matter.

10. A system providing for symbolic reinforcers is called a(n)
    a. extinction system
    b. token economy
    c. endocrine system
    d. symbolic reinforcement system

Answers

1. b page 100
2. b page 102
3. c page 104
4. d page 107
5. a page 110

6. c pages 111–112
7. d page 113
8. a pages 115–118
9. c page 120
10. b page 122

INFOTRAC COLLEGE EDITION

Go to the Wadsworth Psychology Study Center (http://psychology.wadsworth.com/) for quiz questions, research updates, hot topics, interactive exercises, and suggested readings in INFOTRAC related to this chapter.

CHAPTER 5 The Self

You've just taken your first exam in your first psychology course. Expecting a B, you're looking forward to getting your test back. Your instructor hands you your exam and you look at your grade: a C–. You're stunned! How could this be? You thought that you knew the material really well. As you sit there taking in this disappointing and disturbing turn of events, you anxiously search for possible explanations for your performance. "Did I study long enough? Do I need to revamp my study methods? Is this course a lot harder than I had thought? Am I really 'college material'?" As you leave the class, your mood has shifted from up to down. You're feeling dejected and already worrying about how you'll do on the next exam.

This scenario illustrates the process of self-perception and the effect self-perception can have on emotions, self-esteem, and goal setting. People engage in this process constantly to understand the causes of their own behavior.

In this chapter, we focus on the self and its role in adjustment. We'll start off by looking at three major components of the self: self-concept, identity, and self-esteem. Then we'll review some key principles of the self-perception process. Next, we'll turn to the important topic of self-regulation. Finally, we'll focus on how people present themselves to others. In the Application, we offer some suggestions for building self-esteem.

Self-Concept

LEARNING OBJECTIVES

- Describe some key aspects of the self-concept.
- Explain how self-complexity protects against stress.
- Cite two types of self-discrepancies and describe their effects.
- Describe two ways of coping with self-discrepancies.
- Discuss important factors that help form the self-concept.
- Discuss how individualism and collectivism influence self-concept.

If you were asked to describe yourself, what would you say? You'd probably start off with some physical attributes such as "I'm tall," "I'm of average weight," or "I'm blonde." Soon you'd move on to psychological characteristics: "I'm friendly," "I'm honest," "I'm reasonably intelligent," and so forth. How did you develop these beliefs about yourself? Have your self-views changed over time? Read on.

The Nature of the Self-Concept

The *self-concept* is a set of beliefs about one's personal qualities and typical behavior. Although we usually talk about the self-concept as a single entity, it is probably more accurate to say that people have a number of specific self-concepts that operate in different situations (Harter, 1990). Don Hamachek (1992) has suggested that people have separate concepts of their physical, social, emotional, and intellectual selves.

Each of these various self-concepts is characterized by relatively distinct thoughts and feelings. For instance, you might have considerable information about your social skills and feel quite capable about them but have limited information and less confidence about your physical skills. Current thinking is that only a portion of the total self-concept operates at any one time. The self-concept that is currently accessible has been termed the *working self-concept* by Hazel Markus, a leading researcher in this area (Markus & Wurf, 1987). When a particular self-concept is operating, its attendant thoughts and feelings strongly influence the way one processes information about that aspect of the self (Fiske & Taylor, 1991). When you're in class, for example, the beliefs and emotions associated with your intellectual self-concept usually dominate how you process information you receive in that setting. Similarly, when you're at a party (or thinking about a party when you're in class!), you tap into your social self-concept and the thoughts and feelings related to it.

Hazel Markus

Not only do self-concepts affect current behavior, they also influence future behavior. Markus uses the term ***possible selves* to refer to one's conceptions about the kind of person one might become in the future** (Markus & Nurius, 1986). If you have narrowed your career choices to personnel manager and psychologist, these represent two possible selves in the career realm. Possible selves are developed from past experiences, current behavior, and future expectations. They make people more attentive to goal-related information and role models and more mindful of the need to practice goal-related skills. As such, they help individuals not only to envision desired future goals but also to achieve them (Markus & Ruvulo, 1989). Interestingly, it has been found that, for individuals who have experienced traumatic events, psychological adjustment is best among those who are able to envision a variety of positive selves (Morgan & Janoff-Bulman, 1994). Sometimes, possible selves are negative and represent what one fears one might become—an alcoholic like our Uncle George or an adult without an intimate relationship. In this case, possible selves function as images to be avoided.

Self-concepts are not set in concrete—but they are not easily changed, either. As you will see, people are strongly motivated to maintain a consistent view of the self. Thus, once the self-concept is established, the individual has a tendency to preserve and defend it. In the context of this stability, however, self-concepts do have a certain dynamic quality (Markus & Wurf, 1987). The self-concept seems to be most susceptible to change when there are major modifications in one's social environment—for example, when moving from elementary to junior high school or from high school to college (Harter, 1993). In any case, the key factor seems to be the shift from a familiar social setting to an unfamiliar one. These findings clearly underscore the social foundations of the self-concept.

Self-concepts are not merely an abstract idea of interest to psychologists. Because they guide the processing of self-relevant information, self-concepts obviously play a powerful role in how people see themselves and others, how they feel, and how they behave. For instance, if you have been eyeing an attractive classmate

Web Link 5.1

Research Sources: Concepts of Person, Self, and Personal Identity
Over the past century psychologists, philosophers, and many others contemplated the meaning of terms like person and self. Professor Shaun Gallagher of Canisius College's Philosophy Department provides a variety of resources for exploring these concepts.

recently, your social self-concept may be the critical factor that determines whether you actually approach that person.

Self-Complexity

Individuals' self-concepts vary in complexity. *Self-complexity refers to how simple or elaborate the self-concept is.* People with greater self-complexity have a number of different aspects to their self-concept so each single component makes up a small part of the whole (see Figure 5.1a). In contrast, those who are low in self-complexity have relatively few different self-components so each one makes up a large part of the whole (see Figure 5.1b). According to Patricia Linville (1985, 1987), a positive or negative event (winning a tennis match or having a fight with your partner) directly affects only that self-component that is related to the event. When one of only a few components is affected, the impact will be greater than when one of many components is involved. Thus, if you have many different selves and have a fight with your partner, you may feel bad, but not as bad as a person who has only a few self-components. Conversely, if you have many

FIGURE 5.1.

Self-complexity. (a) This woman perceives herself to have many different self-components, so she rates high in self-complexity. (b) This woman sees herself as having relatively few self-components and thus has low self-complexity.

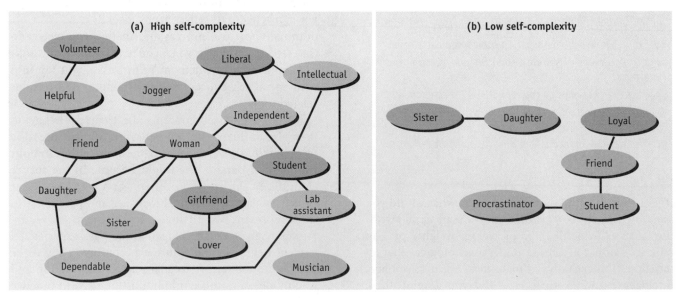

different selves and win a tennis match, your elation will be less intense than that experienced by a person with fewer selves. In other words, Linville asserts that people who are low in self-complexity should experience greater swings in emotion and self-esteem than those who are high in self-complexity.

Are there any data to support this idea? In one study, college students who differed in self-complexity were told that they had either done well or failed on an aptitude test (Linville, 1985). Those who were low in self-complexity reported more positive moods if they experienced success and more negative moods if they experienced failure compared to those who were high in self-complexity. That is, those with low self-complexity experienced greater mood fluctuations than did those with high self-complexity (see Figure 5.2). Linville also found that college students who were low in self-complexity had more emotional ups and downs over a two-week period than those who were high in self-complexity.

Because self-complexity contributes to stable emotions and self-esteem, it seems to be a desirable quality. Is it something people can develop? According to Linville (1987), it helps to be involved in a variety of roles, relationships, and situations (student, worker, friend, sibling, son or daughter, musician, tennis player, community volunteer, and romantic partner). She also believes that having a broad range of experiences in these different roles and relationships can foster self-complexity. Once people have developed self-complexity, there is more good news. Research has shown that people with high self-complexity can offset the impact of negative events by setting up positive events that affect different self-components (Linville & Fischer, 1991). For instance, if you have a disagreement with a co-worker (negative experience for the "work-self"), you can arrange to socialize with a friend (positive experience for the "friend-self"), thereby diminishing to a degree the negative experience affecting the "work self."

Self-Discrepancies

Some people perceive themselves pretty much the way they'd like to see themselves. Others experience a gap between what they actually see and what they'd like to see. For example, Jack describes his actual self as "shy"

◉ Recommended Reading

Encounters with the Self by Don Hamachek (Harcourt Brace Jovanovich, 1992)

This book is about the many aspects of the self-concept. It describes how the contours of the self-concept are molded by one's interactions with others, how the self-concept continues to undergo metamorphosis throughout life, and how the self-concept is expressed in everyday behavior. Though reasonably compact in size, the book is quite broad in scope, and Hamachek manages to cover a number of intriguing topics, including defense mechanisms, perception of others, the role of physical appearance in shaping self-concept, the influences of child-rearing styles on self-concept, the effect of self-perceptions on academic adjustment, feelings of inferiority, and ways to pursue a more positive self-image.

This is one of those rare books that can provide satisfactory reading for both the layperson and the sophisticated professional. Academicians will appreciate the well-documented and thorough review of relevant research. Nonprofessional readers will find the book highly readable and brimming with practical insights and advice. Although the author disavows any intention of writing a "self-help" book, this volume is likely to be about as helpful to readers as any mere book can be.

Some individuals avoid finding out more about themselves for fear of having to give up a self with which they have grown comfortable or "satisfied." Most people have an initial inclination to resist personal change anyway, but this resistance is even stronger for those who refuse to insert new or changed behavior into their current concept of self. For example, a shy, timid, submissive person may not want to know his strengths and assets for fear that he might have to be more assertive and socially aggressive. If shyness has become a way of life designed to protect him from the risks of social disapproval (in this case, nothing ventured, nothing lost—in terms of self-esteem), then it may be difficult indeed for him to give up being timid. Other individuals are reluctant to find out more about themselves because of the threat of having to become more personally mature. Maturity implies many things, among which are a certain degree of independence and autonomy, capacity for self-discipline, certainty about goals and values, and motivation toward some level of personal achievement. Most of all, greater maturity means greater responsibility, and for some this may be a frightening possibility. [p. 53]

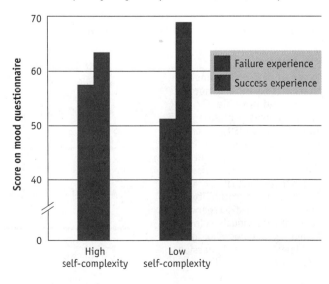

FIGURE 5.2.

Self-complexity as a buffer against depression. The moods of subjects high in self-complexity fluctuated less in response to failure and success experiences than did the moods of low-self-complexity subjects. (Based on Linville, 1985)

but his ideal self as "outgoing." **This mismatching of self-perceptions is termed** *self-discrepancy.* According to E. Tory Higgins (1989), individuals have several different self-perceptions: the *actual self* (qualities that you or others believe you *actually* possess), the *ideal self* (characteristics that you or others would *like* you to have), and the *ought self* (traits that you or others believe that you *should* possess). Although self-discrepancy theory is concerned with both self-perceptions and how significant others see one, we'll limit our discussion to the self-discrepancies associated with one's own self-perceptions.

SELF-DISCREPANCIES AND THEIR EFFECTS

According to Higgins, when people live up to their personal standards (ideal or ought selves), they experience high self-esteem; when they don't meet their own expectations, their self-esteem suffers (Moretti & Higgins, 1990). In addition, he says, certain types of self-discrepancies are associated with specific emotions (see Figure 5.3). One type of self-discrepancy occurs when the *actual* self is at odds with the *ideal* self. These instances trigger *dejection-related* emotions (sadness, disappointment). Consider Mary's situation: She knows that she's attractive, but she is also overweight and would like to be thinner. Self-discrepancy theory would predict that she would feel dissatisfied and dejected. Interestingly, research has shown an association between discrepant actual/ideal views of body shape and eating disorders (Strauman, et al., 1991).

A second type of discrepancy involves a mismatch between *actual* and *ought* selves. Perhaps you don't stay in touch with your grandparents as often as you feel you should. As a result of this actual/ought self-discrepancy, Higgins predicts that you would experience *agitation-related* emotions (irritability, anxiety, and guilt). Extreme discrepancies of this type can result in anxiety-related psychological disorders.

Everyone experiences self-discrepancies, yet most people manage to feel reasonably good about themselves. How is this possible? Two factors seem to be important: (1) the amount of discrepancy experienced and (2) awareness of the discrepancy. Thus, those with self-discrepancies feel more emotional discomfort than those who are self-congruent. Similarly, those who are more aware of self-discrepancies are more vulnerable to negative feelings than those who are less aware of them (Higgins, et al., 1986).

COPING WITH SELF-DISCREPANCIES

Can individuals do anything to blunt the negative emotions and blows to self-esteem associated with self-discrepancies? Well, for one thing, people can *change their behavior* to bring it more in line with their personal standards (ideal or ought selves). For instance, if your ideal self is a person who gets above-average grades and your actual self just got a D on a test, you can study more effectively for the next test to improve your grade. But what about the times you can't match your ideal standards? Perhaps you had your heart set on making the varsity tennis team but didn't make the cut. Maybe you had planned to go to medical school, but barely eked out C's in your science courses. One way to ease the discomfort associated with such discrepancies is to bring your actual self a bit more in line with your actual abilities. Another option is to *blunt your self-awareness.* Sometimes you do so by avoiding situations that increase your self-awareness—you don't go to a party if you expect to spend a miserable evening talking to yourself.

Some people use alcohol to blunt self-awareness. In one study, college students were first put into either a high or a low self-awareness group based on test scores (Hull & Young, 1983). Then, both groups were given a brief version of an intelligence test as well as false feedback on their test performance. Half of the high self-aware group were told that they had done quite well on the test, and the other half were told that they had done quite poorly. Next, supposedly as part of a separate study, these participants were asked to taste and evaluate different wines for 15 minutes. The experimenters predicted that the high self-awareness participants who

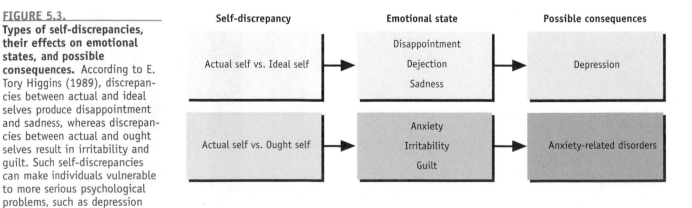

FIGURE 5.3.
Types of self-discrepancies, their effects on emotional states, and possible consequences. According to E. Tory Higgins (1989), discrepancies between actual and ideal selves produce disappointment and sadness, whereas discrepancies between actual and ought selves result in irritability and guilt. Such self-discrepancies can make individuals vulnerable to more serious psychological problems, such as depression and anxiety-related disorders.

had been told that they had done poorly on the IQ test would drink more than the other groups, and this is what the study found (see Figure 5.4). In other words, those who couldn't escape negative information about themselves drank more alcohol to reduce their self-awareness. Similarly, in the real world it has been found that alcoholics who have high self-awareness and who experience negative or painful life events relapse more quickly and completely (Hull, Young, & Jouriles, 1986).

Heightened self-awareness doesn't always make people focus on self-discrepancies and negative aspects of the self. If that were true, most people would feel a lot worse about themselves than they actually do! As you recall, self-concepts are made up of numerous self-beliefs—many of them positive, some negative. Because individuals have a need to feel good about themselves, they tend to focus on their positive features rather than their "warts" (Showers, 1992).

Factors Shaping the Self-Concept

A variety of sources influence one's self-concept. Chief among them are one's own observations, feedback from others, and cultural values.

PERSONAL OBSERVATIONS

Your observations of your own behavior are obviously a major source of information about what you are like. Individuals begin observing their own behavior and drawing conclusions about themselves early in life.

When people don't live up to their personal standards, self-esteem suffers, and some turn to alcohol to blunt their awareness of the discrepancy.

Young children will make statements about who is the tallest, who can run fastest, or who can swing the highest. Leon Festinger's (1954) *social comparison theory* **proposes that individuals compare themselves with others in order to assess their abilities and opinions.** People compare themselves to others to determine how attractive they are, how they did on the history exam, how their social skills stack up, and so forth.

Although Festinger's original theory claimed that people engage in social comparison for the purpose of accurately assessing their abilities, recent research suggests that they also engage in social comparison to maintain their self-image and to improve their skills (Buunk et al., 1990). Furthermore, the reasons people engage in social comparison determine whom they choose for a point of comparison. **A *reference group* is a set of people against whom individuals compare themselves.** For example, if you want to know how you did on your first test in social psychology (ability appraisal), your reference group will be the entire class. On the other hand, if you want to improve your tennis game (skill development), your reference group will probably be limited to those of superior ability because their skills give you something to strive for. And, if your self-esteem needs bolstering, you will probably compare yourself to those whom you perceive to be worse off than you are so you can feel better about yourself.

The potential impact of such social comparisons was dramatically demonstrated in the classic "Mr. Clean/Mr. Dirty" study (Morse & Gergen, 1970). Subjects thought they were being interviewed for a job.

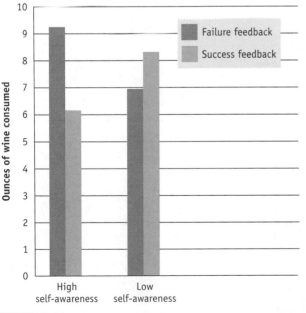

FIGURE 5.4.

Self-awareness and alcohol consumption. Individuals who were high in self-awareness drank significantly more wine in a 15-minute period if they believed that they had performed poorly on an IQ test than did any other group. (Based on Hull & Young, 1983)

Half the subjects met another applicant who was neatly dressed and who appeared to be very competent. The other half were exposed to a competitor who was unkempt and disorganized. All subjects filled out measures of self-esteem both before and after the bogus job interviews. The results indicated that subjects who encountered the impressive competitor showed a decrease in self-esteem after the interview while those who met the unimpressive competitor showed increases in self-esteem. Thus, comparisons with others can have immediate effects on one's self-concept.

People's observations of their own behavior are not entirely objective. The general tendency is to distort reality in a positive direction (see Figure 5.5). Research findings support the idea that most people tend to evaluate themselves in a more positive light than they really merit (Taylor & Brown, 1988, 1994). The strength of this tendency was highlighted in a large survey—conducted as part of the Scholastic Aptitude Test (SAT)—of some 829,000 high school seniors (Myers, 1980). In this survey, 70% of the students rated themselves above average in "leadership ability." Only 2% rated themselves below average. Obviously, by definition, 50% must be "above average" and 50% below. Nonetheless, in regard to "ability to get along with others," 100% of the subjects saw themselves as above average!

Furthermore, 25% of the respondents thought that they belonged in the top 1%. These findings call to mind Garrison Keillor's description of the inhabitants of Lake Woebegone, the mythical town where "... all the women are strong, all the men are good-looking, and all the children are above average."

Although the general tendency is to distort reality in a positive direction, most people tend to make both negative and positive distortions. For example, you might overrate your social skill, emotional stability, and intellectual ability while underrating your physical attractiveness. Also, a minority of people constantly evaluate themselves in an unrealistically negative way. Thus, the tendency to see oneself in an overly favorable light is strong but not universal.

FEEDBACK FROM OTHERS

Your self-concept is shaped significantly by the feedback you get from other people about your behavior. Of course, it's obvious that not everyone has equal influence in your life. Early on, your parents and other family members played a dominant role in providing you with feedback. As you grew older, the number of significant others who gave you feedback increased (Harter, 1990).

FIGURE 5.5.

Distortions in self-images.
How people see themselves may be very different from how others see them. These pictures and text illustrate the subjective quality of self-concept and people's perception of others. Generally, self-images tend to be distorted in a positive direction.

As she sees herself: Unchanged since age 22. Sociable, scintillating, sexy.

As the husband sees her: Older than her years. Someone more suited to suburban domesticity and PTA.

As he sees himself: Stylish haircut, rakish moustache, benevolent, generous, powerful. A smooth operator.

As the wife sees him: Somewhat of a slob, moody, not very decisive or strong.

Parents give their children a great deal of direct feedback. They constantly express approval or disapproval, making statements such as "I'm so proud of you" or "You're a lazy bum just like your Uncle John." Most people, especially when young, take this sort of feedback to heart. Thus, it comes as no surprise that studies find an association between parents' views of a child and the child's self-concept (Berne & Savary, 1993; Burhans & Dweck, 1995). There is even stronger evidence for a relationship between children's perceptions of their parents' attitudes toward them and their own self-perceptions (Felson, 1989).

Interestingly, people are not particularly accurate perceivers of how specific individuals evaluate them; they are better at judging how other people, in general, view them (DePaulo et al., 1987; Kenny & DePaulo, 1993). Also, when individuals have access to "objective" information (such as course grades), their perceptions of others' judgments don't seem to carry as much weight as when they are evaluating themselves in areas for which they must rely solely on socially defined standards, such as physical attractiveness (Felson, 1989).

Parents and family are not the only source of feedback during childhood. Teachers, coaches, Scout leaders, and others also provide significant feedback. In adolescence, as one's peer group becomes more influential, friends play an important role in the development of self-concept (Harter, 1990; Smollar & Youniss, 1985). Of course, the feedback from others is filtered through one's social perception systems. As a consequence, it may be as distorted as one's own self-observations.

CULTURAL GUIDELINES

Your self-concept is also shaped by cultural values. The society in which you are brought up defines what is desirable and undesirable in personality and behavior. For example, American culture tends to put a premium on individuality, competitive success, strength, and skill. When individuals meet cultural expectations, they feel good about themselves and experience increases in self-esteem and vice versa (Matsumoto, 1994).

Recent cross-cultural studies by Hazel Markus and others suggest that different cultures shape different conceptions of the self (Markus & Kitayama, 1991; Matsumoto, 1994). One important way cultures differ is on the dimension of individualism versus collectivism (Hofstede, 1983; Triandis, 1989, 1994). *Individualism* **involves putting personal goals ahead of group goals and defining one's identity in terms of personal attributes rather than group memberships.** In contrast, *collectivism* **involves putting group goals ahead of personal goals and defining one's identity in terms of the groups to which one belongs** (such as one's family, tribe, work group, social class, caste, and so on). In comparison to individualistic cultures, collec-

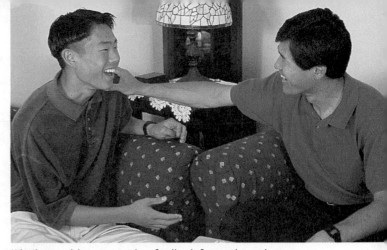

Whether positive or negative, feedback from others plays an important role in shaping a youngster's self-concept.

tivist cultures place a higher priority on shared values and resources, cooperation, mutual interdependence, and concern for how one's actions will affect other group members. Child-rearing patterns in collectivist cultures emphasize the importance of obedience, reliability, and proper behavior, whereas individualistic cultures emphasize the development of independence, self-esteem, and self-reliance.

A variety of factors influence whether societies cherish individualism as opposed to collectivism. Among other things, increases in a culture's affluence, education, urbanization, and social mobility tend to foster more individualism (Triandis, 1994). Many contemporary societies are in transition, but generally speaking North American and Western European cultures tend to be individualistic, whereas Asian, African, and Latin American cultures tend to be collectivistic (Hofstede, 1980, 1983).

Individuals reared in individualistic cultures usually have an *independent* view of the self, perceiving themselves as unique, self-contained, and distinct from others. In contrast, individuals reared in collectivist cultures typically have an *interdependent* view of the self. They see themselves as connected to others and believe that harmonious relationships with others are of utmost importance. Figure 5.6 (on the next page) depicts the self-conceptions of individuals from these contrasting cultures.

Individuals with an independent view of the self are socialized to maintain their sense of self as a separate person—to "look out for number one," claim more than their share of credit for group successes, and disavow responsibility for group failure. Those with an interdependent view of the self are socialized to adjust themselves to the needs of the groups to which they belong and to maintain the interdependence among individuals. Thus, social duties and obligations assume great importance and people are likely to see themselves as responsible for group failures (Matsumoto, 1994).

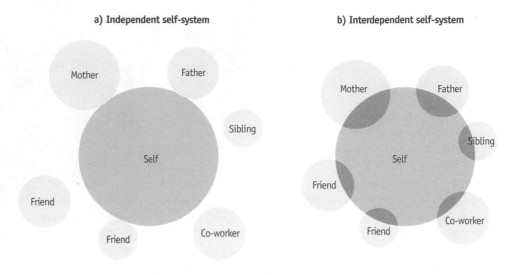

FIGURE 5.6.

Independent and interdependent views of the self. (a) Individuals in cultures that support an independent view of the self perceive the self as clearly separated from significant others. (b) Individuals in cultures that support an interdependent view of the self perceive the self as inextricably connected to others. (Adapted from Markus & Kitayama, 1991)

A number of researchers have noted parallels between the views of self promoted by individualistic and collectivist cultures and the self-views of many Northern American men and women, respectively (Dion & Dion, 1993; Lykes, 1985). That is, many American women seem to have an interdependent view of the self and many American men tend to have an independent view of the self. These hypothesized gender differences in self-conceptions are provocative and warrant further investigation. For instance, this research might be able to shed light on gender differences related to the experience of romantic love and the capacity for intimacy (see Chapter 8).

Cultural values are also responsible for various *stereotypes* that may mold people's self-perceptions. For instance, gender stereotypes influence males' and females' self-perceptions and behavior. One study found that college students' gender stereotypes predicted which activities they tried and how much they enjoyed them (Carter & Myerowitz, 1984). In a similar manner, stereotypes about ethnicity, class, sexual orientation, and religion can influence self-conceptions.

Identity

LEARNING OBJECTIVES

● *Define identity and explain when it develops.*
● *Identify the key differences among Marcia's four identity statuses.*
● *Describe how gender and ethnicity affect identity.*

In childhood, a key task is identifying the attributes that are perceived as "me" and integrating them into a self-concept. In adolescence, the work of developing a sense of self continues but shifts to a broader arena. As adulthood looms closer, individuals turn their attention to finding a meaningful place in the larger society. Thus, adolescents are preoccupied with clarifying their career goals and the moral, religious, and political values that will guide their decisions as members of the larger social order. Erik Erikson (1968), an influential psychoanalytic theorist (see Chapter 11), contributed the term "identity" to express this important psychological connection between self and society. **Identity refers to having a relatively clear and stable sense of who one is in the larger society.** Although much of the process of identity formation is unconscious, a key point is that individuals create their identity; they do not just unquestioningly assume the roles and beliefs designated for them by parents and society.

Development of Identity

Identity has its roots in childhood, and, ideally, it continues to develop throughout adulthood (Marcia, 1991). However, Erikson saw adolescence as the most significant period for identity development, and research has supported his view. Studies show that identity concerns are particularly prominent among those in late adolescence (college-age individuals) (Archer, 1982; Marcia, 1980; Meilman, 1979). The fact that identity achievement is a concern during late adolescence probably reflects the conjunction of several developmental milestones during this time (Lloyd, 1985). That is, the achievement of a stable and familiar sense of self depends on physical and sexual maturity, competence in abstract thought, and a degree of emotional stability. In addition, identity achievement requires a certain amount of freedom from the constraining influences of parents and peers (Harter, 1990). As it happens, late adolescence is the period during which such conditions are first likely to exist.

Identity Statuses

According to Erikson, identity emerges out of crisis. For Erikson, the term identity crisis refers to a period of personal questioning during which individuals reflect on and experiment with various occupational possibilities and value choices (political, religious, and so forth). For most people, an identity crisis is not a sudden or personally agonizing experience, but rather the gradual evolution of a sense of who one is. This search for identity is part of the normal developmental process.

The experience of an identity crisis usually results in a commitment to a specific career and personal value system. According to Marcia, these two factors of crisis and commitment combine in various ways to produce four identity statuses (see Figure 5.7). These are not stages that people pass through, but rather statuses that characterize a person's identity orientation at any particular time. In other words, it is possible that a person may never experience some of the statuses, including that of identity achievement. Let's examine the four identity statuses described by Marcia.

Identity Foreclosure. Not everyone develops a unique, personal identity. Rather than going through the process of developing their own beliefs and career choices (identity crisis), individuals in the foreclosure status unquestioningly adopt the values and expectations of their parents. For example, adolescents or adults who select careers their parents have chosen for them would be classified as "foreclosures." These individuals have made commitments—or, rather, adopted the commitments of others—but because they haven't gone through an identity crisis, they don't qualify as having achieved an independent identity.

Moratorium. Individuals in the midst of struggling with a sense of identity are classified as being in the moratorium status. As part of the process of evolving a personally satisfying identity, adolescents are likely to engage in a variety of identity experiments, trying on different roles, beliefs, and behaviors. Most move on to the identity achievement status, but some drift into the status of identity diffusion.

Web Link 5.2

Identity and Self

Professor Andy Lock at Massey University in New Zealand has posted the outline of a possible upper-level course that would explore contemporary psychological conceptions of the self and identity development, particularly from the social constructivist and cultural viewpoints. A full set of bibliographical and topical guides are included.

Identity Diffusion. Identity diffusion is characterized by a failure to achieve a stable and integrated sense of self. Individuals in this category experience considerable self-doubt, but they don't appear able to change the situation. Hence, they are different from those in the moratorium status, who are still struggling to resolve identity conflicts. People in the diffusion status are not currently experiencing an identity crisis, nor are they able to make career or value commitments. Identity diffusion is a serious problem for only a small number of adolescents, usually in cases where it is prolonged.

Identity Achievement. The preferred identity status is that of identity achievement. In this case, the individual has successfully passed through an identity crisis and is now able to make a commitment to a career objective and a set of personally meaningful beliefs. Once this status is attained, the active search for identity ends. Over the course of a lifetime, however, significant personal crises such as divorce may trigger the reworking of an established identity (Marcia, 1991).

Both identity achievement and identity foreclosure can be seen as resolutions of the identity crisis because a sense of commitment characterizes both statuses. Of course, in foreclosure, the commitment is not an independently developed one, as is desirable. Individuals in both the moratorium and diffusion statuses have only vague, or sometimes no, commitments. While those in identity diffusion have given up the search for identity, those in moratorium are still pursuing it.

Considerable research has been done on identity statuses and their characteristics (Marcia, 1980; 1991). Compared to those in other statuses, *identity achievers* are more cognitively flexible, function at higher levels

---

FIGURE 5.7.

Marcia's four identity statuses. According to Marcia, the occurrence of an identity crisis and the development of personal commitments can combine into four possible identity statuses, as shown in this diagram.

Marcia's Four Identity Statuses		
	Crisis present	**Crisis absent**
Commitment present	*Identity achievement* (succesful achievement of a sense of identity)	*Identity foreclosure* (unquestioning adoption of parental or societal values)
Commitment absent	*Identity moratorium* (active struggling for a sense of identity)	*Identity diffusion* (absence of struggle for identity, with no obvious concern about this)

of moral reasoning, and have the capacity for more emotionally intimate relationships (Marcia, 1991). Those in the *moratorium* status are conflicted between conforming and rebelling, have ambivalent feelings toward their parents, and are perceived by others as intense. *Foreclosures* are strongly connected to their families, cognitively rigid, and conventional, and they hold conservative values. Those in the *identity diffusion* status feel alienated from their parents, are at the lower levels of moral reasoning, and are less capable of emotional intimacy than the other statuses.

Gender, Ethnicity, and Identity

Although they are changing, adult roles for American men are still primarily focused on work, whereas adult roles for American women typically include marriage, child-rearing, and, increasingly, work. Because identity is based on social roles, one would predict that there are gender differences in identity, and research supports this idea (Harter, 1993). Males are encouraged to be autonomous and to focus on individual achievement; thus, their identity is largely defined in terms of occupational choice. Females are encouraged, above all, to form close connections with others; thus, their identity is rooted most strongly in their relationships (friends, husband, children). Yet, because work is becoming increasingly important in women's lives, contemporary women are challenged to integrate both work and family roles. This makes identity development a more complex and conflicted process for females than for males, who typically deal with only a single component of identity. (We'll explore these and other gender issues in greater detail in Chapter 10.)

The United States contains many ethnic minority groups (African Americans, Hispanic Americans, Asian Americans, Native Americans, and so forth). How does ethnic group membership influence identity? According to Jean Phinney (1989), ethnic identity usually develops during adolescence and seems to proceed in three stages. In the first stage, individuals don't see ethnic identity as a personal concern; thus, they have minimal interest in ethnic issues. In the second stage, adolescents become curious about their ethnic heritage and are eager to learn about their group's history and

Gender and ethnicity are key components of identity.

unique customs. In the third stage, individuals come to feel a part of their ethnic group and develop a distinct ethnic self-concept. Here's how a Filipino youth described his ethnic identity: "I have been born Filipino and am born to be Filipino . . . I'm here in America, and people of many different cultures are here, too. So I don't consider myself only Filipino, but also American" (Phinney, 1989, p. 44). Members of minority groups differ in how strongly they identify with the mainstream culture and their special ethnic culture. While some identify strongly with both cultures, others identify more strongly with one culture than the other (Phinney, 1990).

Self-Esteem

LEARNING OBJECTIVES

● *Discuss how low and high self-esteem are related to adjustment.*

● *Cite two important determinants of self-esteem.*

● *Explain why minority group members don't have lower self-esteem than those in the dominant group.*

Self-esteem refers to one's overall assessment of one's worth as a person; it is the evaluative component of the self-concept. Self-esteem is a global evaluation that blends many specific evaluations about your adequacy as a student, an athlete, a worker, a spouse, a parent, or whatever is relevant to you. Figure 5.8 shows how specific elements of self-concept may contribute to self-esteem. If you feel basically good about yourself, you probably have high self-esteem. Sometimes the term "positive self-concept" is used as a synonym for self-esteem.

Although people are typically described as having either high or low self-esteem, those characterized as

Web Link 5.3

Classic Theories of Child Development
Erik Erikson, who fashioned the crucial notion of identity development in adolescent personality formation, is one of several theorists discussed at psychotherapist Linda Chapman's popular site.

having low self-esteem in fact have moderate or average self-esteem. It is only because they score lower on self-esteem tests than individuals who rate themselves very positively that they are classified as having low self-esteem. Very few individuals actually score low on such tests.

Studies generally show self-esteem to be quite stable over time (Baumeister, 1991). Thus, those who have high self-esteem today are likely to have high self-esteem six months or two years from now. While it's true that baseline self-esteem is stable, it's also true that the ups and downs of daily life can produce short-term fluctuations from baseline self-esteem. Recall the temporary boost in your self-esteem when that good-looking person at work asked you out, and the short-term dip when you saw that C– staring back at you on your last calculus exam.

Investigating self-esteem is difficult for several reasons. For one thing, there is some doubt about the validity of many measures of self-esteem. The problem is that researchers tend to rely on self-reports from subjects, which obviously may be biased. As we noted in Chapter 4, most individuals typically hold unrealistically positive views about themselves; moreover, some people may choose not to disclose their actual self-esteem on a questionnaire. Second, in probing self-esteem it is often quite difficult to separate cause from effect. A large volume of correlational data tells us that certain behavioral characteristics are associated with positive or negative self-esteem. For instance, we saw in Chapter 1 that self-esteem is a good predictor of happiness. However, it is hard to tell whether these behavioral tendencies are the cause or the effect of a particular level of self-esteem. This problem in pinpointing causation should be kept in mind as we take a closer look at this fascinating topic.

The Importance of Self-Esteem

Among researchers, self-esteem has always been a popular concept. In recent years, the topic has captured the public's attention as well. Of particular interest to our discussion are the connections between self-esteem and adjustment.

SELF-ESTEEM AND ADJUSTMENT

It has long been thought that individuals with low self-esteem hold strong negative views about themselves. Recent research has called this assumption into question. For instance, it seems the self-views of these individuals are not more negative but rather less clear, less complete, more self-contradictory, and more susceptible to short-term fluctuations than the self-views of people with high self-esteem. Roy Baumeister (1998), a leading researcher on the self, spells out the likely connection between "self-concept confusion" (Campbell & Lavallee, 1993) and lower scores on self-esteem tests: Individuals with low self-esteem simply don't know themselves well enough to strongly endorse many personal attributes on self-esteem tests (which results in lower scores). Lack of self-concept clarity also figures in

Roy Baumeister

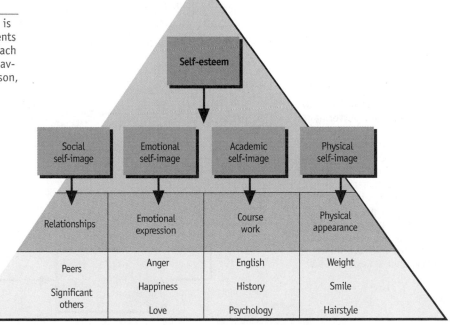

FIGURE 5.8.

The structure of self-esteem. Self-esteem is a global evaluation that combines assessments of different aspects of one's self-concept, each of which is built up from many specific behaviors and experiences. (Adapted from Shavelson, Hubner, & Stanton, 1976)

the differences in goal setting found between those with high and low self-esteem. Because those with low self-esteem are less sure of their capabilities, they are less confident of their success. Therefore, they tend to underestimate their abilities and set lower goals for themselves. Relatedly, individuals with high self-esteem persist longer in the face of failure, although sometimes they fail to recognize when it is pointless to persevere (McFarlin, Baumeister, & Blascovich, 1984).

In the emotional sphere, low self-esteem is more often associated with less pleasant moods and greater emotional ups and downs than high self-esteem (Campbell, Chew, & Scratchley, 1991). Also, people with low self-esteem tend to develop more emotional problems than those with high self-esteem (Leary & Kowalski, 1995; Pillow, West, & Reich 1991). Among other things, they are more likely to report that they are troubled by anxiety, depression, irritability, aggressiveness, feelings of resentment and alienation, unhappiness, insomnia, and psychosomatic symptoms.

Low self-esteem is also associated with less effective social skills. Compared to those with high self-esteem, people low in self-esteem often feel socially awkward, self-conscious, and especially vulnerable to rejection (Rosenberg, 1985). Unlike those with high self-esteem, they are reluctant to "toot their own horn," perhaps out of fear of the humiliation that would result if others discovered that their claims were exaggerated. Instead, they fall back on indirect strategies, such as putting others down, to maintain or boost their self-esteem (Tice, 1993). This fear of standing out in a negative way also makes them tentative and cautious in their interactions with others (Baumeister, Tice, & Hutton, 1989; Heatherton & Ambady, 1993). By contrast, those with high self-esteem expect and want to stand out in a positive way, so they are usually more assertive in their social interactions. Because low self-esteem people have difficulties in social encounters, they are also often lonely (Olmstead et al., 1991). Finally, individuals with

low self-esteem are more easily persuaded to change their views and more likely to conform to peer pressure (Brockner, 1983).

Because self-esteem affects expectations, it operates in a self-perpetuating fashion. As can be seen in Figure 5.9, individuals with low self-esteem may have negative expectations about their performance (in a social situation, at a job interview, on a test). As a result, they feel anxious and may not prepare for the challenge. Then, when they fail, they often blame themselves—delivering one more blow to their already battered self-esteem (Brockner, 1983). Of course, this repeating loop also works for those with high self-esteem: Positive expectations usually produce high effort and low anxiety, successful outcomes, and self-praise. Thus, positive feelings about the self are perpetuated. In either case, the important point is that self-esteem affects not only the present, but also the future.

IS HIGH SELF-ESTEEM ALWAYS GOOD?

From the discussion thus far, it might seem that high self-esteem is a very desirable quality. Intriguingly, there is mounting evidence that certain forms of high self-esteem play a significant role in the hostility and aggression seen in partner abuse, rape, gang aggression, individual and group hate crimes, and political terrorism (Baumeister, Smart, & Boden, 1996). How can this be? The darker side of high self-esteem seems to emerge when a person's self-appraisal is unrealistically high, heavily dependent on confirmation by others, or subject to short-term fluctuations. When such individuals experience threats to their self-views (ego threats), violence can flare. By contrast, individuals whose self-appraisals are realistically positive, less dependent on external validation, or more stable are not so susceptible to ego threats. Moreover, when they experience ego threats, they do not resort to violence.

Let's take a closer look at this phenomenon. As we noted earlier, when people are confronted with

FIGURE 5.9.

The vicious circle of low-self-esteem and poor performance. Low self-esteem is associated with low or negative expectations about performance. These low expectations often result in inadequate preparation and high anxiety, which heighten the likelihood of poor performance. Unsuccessful performance triggers self-blame, which feeds back to low self-esteem. (From Brehm & Kassin, 1993)

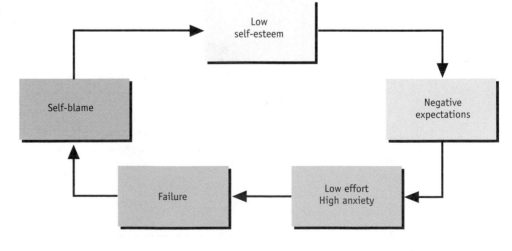

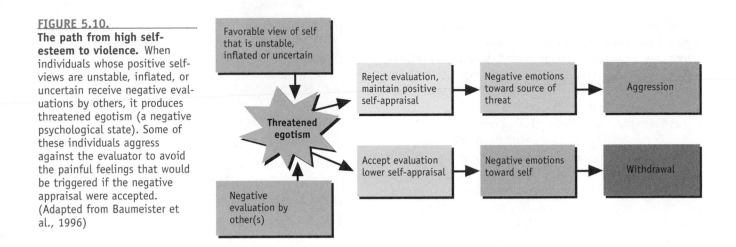

FIGURE 5.10.

The path from high self-esteem to violence. When individuals whose positive self-views are unstable, inflated, or uncertain receive negative evaluations by others, it produces threatened egotism (a negative psychological state). Some of these individuals aggress against the evaluator to avoid the painful feelings that would be triggered if the negative appraisal were accepted. (Adapted from Baumeister et al., 1996)

self-discrepancies, one option is to accept the negative external evaluation and revise self-perception downward. However, since this path results in unpleasant feelings (anxiety, dejection), it is not the preferred response (Swann, 1987; Taylor & Brown, 1988). Instead, individuals usually reject unfavorable feedback and cling to their favorable self-views. A small subset of people who refuse to accept unflattering evaluations also feel extreme hostility toward the source of the negative feedback and lash out—particularly if the target is perceived as weak. Baumeister speculates that when individuals are confronted with unflattering feedback, they face a choice point, and the path they choose will determine their emotional reaction to the negative information (Baumeister et al., 1996). These two pathways and their outcomes are illustrated in Figure 5.10.

These findings have important practical implications (Baumeister et al., 1996). Most rehabilitation programs for spousal abusers, delinquents, and criminals are based on the inaccurate belief that these individuals suffer from low self-esteem. In opposition to this view, current research suggests that efforts to boost (already high) self-esteem are misguided; a better approach would be to help such individuals develop more self-control and more realistic views of themselves.

Determinants of Self-Esteem

The foundations for high or low self-esteem appear to be laid early in life. For this reason, psychologists have focused much of their attention on the role of parenting in self-esteem development. Indeed, there is ample evidence that parental involvement, acceptance, support, and exposure to clearly defined limits have marked influence on children's self-esteem (Baumrind, 1978; Felson, 1989; Harter, 1993). Let's review the findings of a classic study of self-esteem in young boys conducted by Stanley Coopersmith (1967, 1975). He compared the child-rearing styles of parents of boys

with high self-esteem and low self-esteem. Compared to parents of boys with low self-esteem, parents whose boys had high self-esteem (1) expressed more affection to their children, (2) were more interested in their children's activities, (3) were more accepting of their children, (4) used sound, consistent disciplinary procedures, and (5) had relatively high self-esteem themselves (see Figure 5.11). In particular, it was parents' sincere interest in their children that seemed most strongly related to the development of a positive self-concept. As children grow into adolescents, peers begin to rival parents as a source of self-esteem; by college age, peers have much more impact on self-esteem than parents (Harter, 1993).

While parental feedback may be the crucial determinant of self-esteem, it is clear that children (and

FIGURE 5.11.

Self-esteem and parents' child-rearing techniques. Parents strongly influence youngsters' self-esteem. Coopersmith (1975) found interesting differences in child-rearing practices among the mothers of boys with high, medium, and low self-esteem.

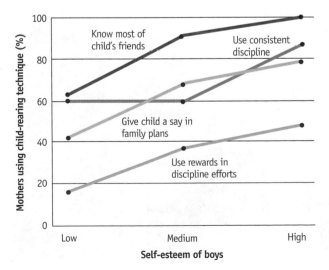

adults) make their own judgments about themselves as well. Of particular significance in these self-evaluations is perceiving oneself as being successful in domains that one values highly (Harter, 1993). For instance, if Andrea values success in the scholastic and social areas and sees herself as competent in these arenas, she will have higher self-esteem than Beth, who also values these domains but rates herself low on one or both of them. An important basis for self-judgments is how well one "stacks up" against others one chooses as a reference group. For example, one study found that preadolescents' self-esteem was affected by the quality of competition they faced in school (Marsh & Parker, 1984). In this study, children from schools in higher-socioeconomic-class areas with "high-quality" competition (high-ability reference group) were compared with children of similar ability from schools in lower-class areas with "low-quality" competition (low-ability reference group). Surprisingly, the children in the low-quality schools tended to display greater self-esteem than children of similar academic ability who were enrolled in the high-quality schools. This finding that one's self-esteem is boosted by being a "big fish in a little small pond" has found widespread support (McFarland & Buehler, 1995). Thus, it seems that individuals compare themselves to others in their specific reference group (other students in their school), not to a general reference group (other students in the country). The fact that individuals with similar talents may vary in self-esteem, depending on their reference group, demonstrates the immense importance of social comparison in the development of self-esteem.

Role models from a person's own in-group are critical to the development of self-esteem.

Web Link 5.4

Distinctions between Self-Esteem and Narcissism: Implications for Practice

The importance of self-esteem in early childhood education may be undermined by uncritical approaches to how it should be developed. Lilian G. Katz explores durable foundations for a child's self-worth in this online book from ERIC, the Educational Resources Information Center.

Minority Group Membership and Self-Esteem

Because prejudice and discrimination are still present in the United States, it has generally been assumed (and sometimes found) that members of minority groups have lower self-esteem than members of the dominant majority group. In fact, there is a good deal of evidence to the contrary (Crocker & Major, 1989; Garnets & Kimmel, 1991; Harter, 1993).

How does it happen that minority group members often have high self-esteem when it seems they shouldn't? A review of studies in this area suggested a number of strategies minority group members use to protect their self-esteem from the effects of being stigmatized (Crocker & Major, 1989). These include attributing negative appraisals to prejudice against their group instead of to themselves, and devaluing those qualities on which their group fares poorly and valuing those attributes on which their group excels. In addition, minority group members use their own group as their dominant reference group, not the relatively advantaged majority group. This in-group comparison ensures that minority group individuals are similar to others and, therefore, that they compare positively to them. This experience leads them to feel good about themselves.

An important implication here is that minority group role models play a critical part in the development of self-esteem. Because of recognizable markers (skin color, gender, body weight, physical handicaps), many minority groups are visible, enabling group members to easily identify in-group role models. Of course, this situation isn't the case for homosexuals, because sexual orientation isn't obvious unless individuals choose to make it so. Because of the social stigma still attached to homosexuality, many homosexual individuals prefer not to declare their sexual orientation openly. Although this is understandable, it means that gay male and lesbian role models are more difficult to identify. Obviously, role models are important for self-esteem development for anyone. However, members of the dominant majority typically have lots of role models to choose from, whereas minority group members do not. Hence, it's the relative availability of role models that distinguishes minority and majority group members, not the need for them.

Basic Principles of Self-Perception

LEARNING OBJECTIVES

- *Define self-attributions and identify the key dimensions of attributions.*
- *Explain how optimistic and pessimistic attributional styles are related to adjustment.*
- *Discuss some important methods individuals use to maintain self-consistency.*
- *Describe three strategies individuals use to maintain positive feelings about the self.*

Now that you're familiar with some of the major aspects of the self, let's explore some of the processes people use to construct and maintain a coherent view of the self. We'll look at self-attributions, attributional style, two important motives that influence self-perception, and some interesting strategies people use to maintain positive feelings about the self.

Self-Attributions

Let's say that you win a critical match for your school's tennis team. To what do you attribute your success? Has your new practice routine started to pay off? Did you have the home court advantage? Perhaps your opponent was playing with a minor injury? This example from everyday life illustrates the nature of the self-attribution process. **Self-attributions are inferences that people draw about the causes of their own behavior.** People routinely make attributions to make sense out of their experiences. These attributions involve inferences that ultimately represent guesswork on the individual's part.

KEY DIMENSIONS OF SELF-ATTRIBUTIONS

Fritz Heider (1958) was the first to assert that people tend to locate the cause of a behavior either within a person, attributing it to personal factors, or outside of a person, attributing it to environmental factors. He thus established one of the crucial dimensions along which attributions are made.

Internal or external. Elaborating on Heider's insight, various theorists have agreed that explanations of behavior and events can be categorized as internal or external attributions (Jones & Davis, 1965; Kelley, 1967; Weiner, 1974). *Internal attributions* **ascribe the causes of behavior to personal dispositions, traits, abilities, and feelings.** *External attributions* **ascribe the causes of behavior to situational demands and environmental constraints.** For example, if you explain your poor statistics grade to your failure to prepare adequately for the test or to getting overly anxious during the test, you are making an internal attribution.

Whether one's self-attributions are internal or external can have a tremendous impact on one's personal adjustment. As you'll see in Chapter 8, lonely people tend to attribute the cause of their loneliness to stable, internal causes ("I'm unlovable"). Similarly, studies suggest that people who attribute their setbacks to internal, personal causes while discounting external, situational explanations may be more prone to depression than people who display opposite tendencies (Alloy, Clements, & Kolden, 1985; Huesmann & Morikawa, 1985).

Stable or unstable. A second dimension people use in making causal attributions is the stability of the causes underlying behavior (Weiner, 1974; Weiner et al., 1972). A stable cause is one that is more or less permanent and unlikely to change over time. For example, a sense of humor and intelligence are *stable internal* causes of behavior. *Stable external* causes of behavior include such things as laws and rules (speed limits, no smoking areas). An unstable cause of behavior is one that is variable or subject to change. *Unstable internal* causes of behavior include such things as mood (good or bad) and motivation (strong or weak). *Unstable external* causes could be the weather and the presence or absence of other people. According to Weiner, the stable-unstable dimension in attribution cuts across the internal-external dimension, creating four types of attributions for success and failure, as shown in Figure 5.12.

Let's apply Weiner's model to a concrete event. Imagine that you are contemplating why you just landed the job you wanted. You might attribute your good

FIGURE 5.12.

Key dimensions of attributional thinking. Weiner's model assumes that people's explanations for success and failure emphasize internal versus external causes and stable versus unstable causes. For example, if you attribute an outcome to great effort or to lack of effort, you are citing causes within the person. Since effort can vary over time, the causal factors at work are unstable. Other examples of causal factors that fit into each of the four cells in Weiner's model are shown in the diagram. (From Weiner et al., 1972)

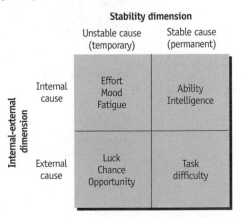

fortune to internal factors that are stable (excellent ability) or unstable (hard work on your eye-catching résumé). Or you might attribute the outcome to external factors that are stable (lack of top-flight competition) or unstable (good luck). If you failed to get the job, the explanations you might offer for the outcome would fall in the same four categories: internal-stable (lack of ability), internal-unstable (inadequate effort on your résumé), external-stable (too much competition in your field), and external-unstable (bad luck).

Controllable-uncontrollable. A third dimension in the attribution process concerns the controllability of the causes underlying one's actions (Weiner, 1986). For example, the amount of effort you expend on a task is typically perceived as something under your control, whereas an aptitude for music is viewed as something you are born with (beyond your control). This dimension acknowledges the fact that sometimes behavior is under one's control and sometimes it isn't. Controllability can vary with each of the other two factors.

These three dimensions appear to be the central ones in the attribution process. Research has documented that self-attributions can influence future expectations (success or failure) and emotions (pride, hopelessness, guilt) and that these combine to influence subsequent performance (Weiner, 1986; Fiske & Taylor, 1991). Thus, self-attributions play a key role in one's feelings, motivational state, and behavior.

Attributional Style

Carlos and Scott are college freshmen who have just tried to get their first college date. Unfortunately, they both struck out. Afterward, they reflect on the possible reasons for this disappointing turn of events. Carlos suspects that his approach was too subtle. Looking back, he recalls that he was nervous about asking the woman out, so he wasn't very direct. When she didn't reply, he didn't pursue the issue for fear that she really didn't want to go out with him. On further reflection, he reasons that she probably didn't respond because she wasn't really sure of his intentions. He vows to be more direct the next time. Scott, on the other hand, mopes, "I guess I just can't compete in the college dating scene. I wonder what's wrong with me?" On the basis of these comments, who do you think is likely to get a date in the future? If you guessed Carlos, you are probably correct. Let's see why.

Attributional style **is the tendency to use similar causal explanations for a wide variety of events in one's life.** According to Martin Seligman (1990), people tend to exhibit, to varying degrees, one of two attributional styles—either an *optimistic explanatory style* or a *pessimistic explanatory style* (see Figure 5.13). The person with an optimistic explanatory style has a tendency to attribute setbacks to external, unstable, and specific factors. A person who fails to get a desired job, for example, might attribute this outcome to bad luck in the interview rather than to personal shortcomings. This style can help people discount their setbacks and

FIGURE 5.13.

The effects of attributional style on expectations, emotions, and behavior. The pessimistic explanatory style is seen in the top set of boxes. This attributional style, which attributes setbacks to internal, stable, and global causes, tends to result in an expectation of lack of control over future events, depressed feelings, and passive behavior. A more adaptive, optimistic attributional style is shown in the bottom set of boxes.

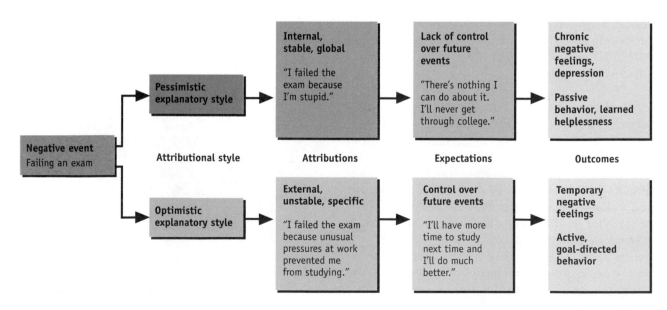

thus maintain positive expectations for the future and a favorable self-image. Not surprisingly, an optimistic attributional style is associated with students' academic success and salespersons' job success (Fiske & Taylor, 1991).

In contrast, people with a pessimistic explanatory style tend to attribute their setbacks to internal, stable, and global (or pervasive) factors. These attributions make them feel bad about themselves and pessimistic about their ability to handle challenges in the future. Research shows that such a style can foster passive behavior and make one more vulnerable to learned helplessness and depression (Peterson, Maier, & Seligman, 1993). Thankfully, several new forms of therapy appear to be successful in helping depressed individuals change a self-defeating attributional style (Robinson, Berman, & Neimeyer, 1990). With these approaches, individuals learn to stop always blaming themselves for negative outcomes (especially when they can't be avoided) and to take personal credit for positive outcomes.

The Premium on Consistency

The desire to maintain a consistent self-image is a powerful motive. This tendency to strive for a consistent self-image is the major reason that individual's self-concepts are relatively stable, as we noted earlier. People maintain consistent self-perceptions in a number of subtle ways and are often unaware of doing so. For example, individuals tend to reconstruct their personal history to match new information about themselves. Thus, they are able to maintain consistency between past and present behavior by erasing past memories that conflict with current ones. To illustrate, people who were once shy and who later became outgoing have been shown to recall memories about themselves indicating that they now perceive themselves as always having been outgoing (Ross & Conway, 1986). This inclination to revise the past in favor of the present may lie behind the oft-heard parental reproof, "When I was your age . . ." What is probably going on here is that parents have conveniently erased memories of their childhood behavior—which was probably similar to that of their children—and, instead, compare their children's behavior to their own *current* behavior (Ross, McFarland, & Fletcher, 1981).

Another way people maintain self-consistency is by seeking out feedback and situations that will confirm their existing self-perceptions and avoiding situations or feedback that might disconfirm their self-image. According to William Swann's *self-verification theory,* **people prefer to receive feedback from others that is consistent with their own self-views.** Thus, those with positive self-concepts should prefer positive feedback from others and those with negative self-concepts should prefer negative feedback. And research has found this is usually the case (Swann et al., 1990; Swann, Stein-Serioussi, & Geisler, 1992). In one study, college men were divided into either a positive self-concept group or a negative self-concept group based on test scores. They were then asked to choose a partner for a subsequent 2 to 3-hour interaction. Participants were led to believe that one of the prospective partners held views of him that were consistent with his self-views and that the other held views of him that were inconsistent with his self-views. As predicted, subjects with positive self-views preferred partners who viewed them positively, whereas those with negative self-views chose partners who viewed them negatively (Swann et al., 1992).

The Need for Self-Enhancement

Typically, self-perceptions are biased in a positive direction. **This tendency to maintain positive feelings about the self is termed** *self-enhancement.* Evidence of self-enhancement is widespread. For example, individuals exaggerate their control over life events (Taylor, 1989), predict they will have a brighter future than others (Weinstein, 1980), view themselves as better than others (Allison, Messick, & Goethals, 1989), seek more information about their strengths than their weaknesses (J. Brown, 1990), and perceive that their own personality traits are more desirable than those they believe are not self-descriptive (Dunning, Perie, & Story, 1991). While self-enhancement is quite common, it is not universal. As we noted in Chapter 4, high self-esteem or nondepressed individuals have more positive self-views than do those individuals who have low self-esteem or are moderately depressed (Taylor & Brown, 1988, 1994). Thus, self-enhancement seems to operate less in the latter group. Let's explore four cognitive strategies individuals frequently employ to maintain positive feelings about the self.

DOWNWARD COMPARISONS
Earlier in the chapter, we mentioned that people compare themselves to others as a means of learning more about themselves (social comparison). Individuals engage in social comparison whether or not they expect to feel threatened by the information they'll receive. Once threat enters the picture, however, it seems to change the type of person one chooses to compare oneself with. That is, when people feel threatened, they frequently choose to compare themselves with someone who is worse off than they are (Wood, 1989). **This defensive tendency to compare oneself with someone whose troubles are more serious than one's own is termed** *downward social comparison.* Studies show

positive increases in both mood and self-esteem when downward social comparisons are made (Reis, Gerrard, & Gibbons, 1993).

Let's look at some examples of downward comparisons. If you have ever been in a serious car accident in which your car was "totaled," you probably reassured yourself by reflecting on the fact that at least no one was seriously injured. Similarly, people with chronic illnesses may compare themselves with those who have life-threatening diseases. Talk shows that feature people with assorted life tragedies provide numerous opportunities for downward social comparison. No doubt, this factor contributes to their popularity.

THE SELF-SERVING BIAS

Suppose that you and three other individuals apply for a part-time job in the parks and recreation department and you are selected for the position. How do you explain your good fortune? Chances are you tell yourself that you were hired because you had the most outstanding qualifications for the job. But, how do the other three people who weren't hired interpret their negative outcome? Do they tell themselves that you got the job because you were the most able? Unlikely! Instead, they probably attribute their loss to "bad luck" or to not having had time to prepare for the interview. These different explanations for success and failure reflect the *self-serving bias* or the tendency to attribute one's successes to personal factors and one's failures to situational factors (Miller and Ross, 1975).

Research indicates that the self-serving bias is quite a potent one, although it seems that people are more likely to take credit for their successes than they are to disavow their failures (Brown & Rogers, 1991). And, there are some occasions when people don't rush to take credit for their successes. For instance, if your role in a success is quite obvious, you may opt for modesty—at least to others (Schlenker, Weigold, & Hallum, 1990). Ironically, this strategy also turns out to be self-serving because you may fear that "blowing your horn" too loudly could cause others to dislike you.

BASKING IN REFLECTED GLORY

Robert Cialdini

When your favorite sports team won the national championship last year, did you make a point of wearing the team cap? And, when your best friend won that special award, remember how you looked for opportunities to tell others the good news about *your* friend? Of course, if you played a role in someone's success, it's understandable that you would want to share in the recognition; however, people often bask in reflected glory even when they have had nothing at all to do with an outstanding achievement. Robert Cialdini and his colleagues (1976) describe the tendency to enhance one's image by publicly announcing one's association with those who are successful as *basking in reflected glory.*

Cialdini and his colleagues (1976) studied this phenomenon on college campuses with nationally ranked football teams. They predicted that, when asked how their team had fared in a recent football game, students would be more likely to say "we won" (in other words, to bask in reflected glory or to "BIRG"—pronounced with a soft "g") when the home team had been successful than when it had been defeated (in which case they would identify less with the home team and say, "They won"). In addition, they reasoned that students who had just experienced a personal failure would be more likely to BIRG than students who had just experienced a personal success. They tested their hypotheses by having college students take a test on their knowledge of various campus issues. Afterward, half of the students were told that they had done very well on the test and the other half were told that they had done rather poorly. Then, participants were asked to describe the outcome of a recent school football game. As predicted, students were more likely to BIRG when their team won than when it lost. Also, subjects who believed that they had just failed the test were more likely to use the

PEANUTS reprinted by permission of United Feature Syndicate, Inc.

words "*We* won" than those who believed they had performed well.

There is evidence not only for basking in reflected glory but also for the opposite tendency: to "CORF," or cut off reflected failure. Because self-esteem is partly tied to an individual's associations with others, people often protect their self-esteem by distancing themselves from those who are *un*successful (Cialdini et al., 1976; Snyder, Lassegard, & Ford, 1986). Thus, if your cousin is arrested for drunk driving, you may tell others that you and he don't really know each other that well.

SELF-HANDICAPPING

Another self-enhancement strategy comes into play when people need to "save face" because they have failed at an important task. Maybe they were cut from the soccer team, failed to get a job they wanted, or did poorly on a big exam. When this happens, individuals can usually come up with a face-saving excuse, and such excuses are even more convincing if used *before* an outcome is known: "I'm having a hard time studying for my biology exam because I'm not feeling very well." However, some people use a different, but related, strategy to avoid the disapproval that follows poor performance. They actually behave in a way that sets them up to fail so they have a ready-made excuse for failure, should it occur. For example, when a big test is coming up, these individuals might put off studying until the last minute or go out drinking the night before the test. When exam day arrives, chances are they don't do very well. How do these individuals explain their poor performance to others? Isn't it obvious: They didn't do well because they didn't prepare for the test. (After all, wouldn't you rather have others believe that your poor performance is due to inadequate preparation rather than lack of ability?) **This tendency to sabotage one's performance to provide an excuse for possible failure is termed *self-handicapping*** (Berglas & Jones, 1978). A number of studies reveal that people use a variety of tactics by which to handicap their performance, including alcohol, drugs, procrastination, a bad mood, a distracting stimulus, anxiety, depression, and being overcommitted (Fiske & Taylor, 1991).

Some people engage in self-handicapping more than others. Men use this strategy more often than women, as do those who are more conscious of how others view them (Shepperd & Arkin, 1989). Moreover, individuals vary in the *means* they use for self-handicapping. For example, men are more likely to use the strategies of not practicing or of taking drugs, whereas women more often report physical symptoms or stress (Hirt, Deppe, & Gordon, 1991). Finally, there are individual differences in the *reasons* for self-handicapping. People with low self-esteem more often engage in self-handicapping to maintain a positive impression (or to avoid failing), while those with high self-esteem are more likely to handicap themselves to enhance their image (Rhodewalt et al., 1991; Tice, 1991). That is, if they happen to do well, they can claim that they are especially capable, given their excellent performance with minimal preparation. In one study, college students were categorized as high or low in self-esteem based on test scores (Tice, 1991). They were then told that they would be completing either a test of nonverbal intelligence (a task important to their self-esteem) or a test of eye-hand coordination (a task unimportant to their self-esteem). Finally, half of the subjects taking each test were told that it identified only individuals who were intellectually deficient (motivating them to want to protect their self-esteem by avoiding failure) and half were told that the test identified only those who were highly gifted (motivating them to want to enhance their image). After hearing this information, all subjects were allowed to practice as long as they wished. As predicted, when the task was important to their self-esteem, those who practiced less (self-handicapped) were the low-self-esteem subjects in the self-protection condition and the high self-esteem subjects in the self-enhancement condition (see Figure 5.14).

Thus, self-handicapping seems like a win-win strategy: If you fail, you have a face-saving excuse at the ready, and if you happen to succeed, you can claim that you are unusually gifted! However, it probably has not

FIGURE 5.14.

Motives for self-handicapping vary depending on self-esteem. When subjects were told that they would be taking a test that identified only people who were intellectually deficient (self-esteem protection condition), low-self-esteem subjects practiced less (self-handicapped) than high-self-esteem subjects. In contrast, when subjects were told that the test identified only people who were highly gifted (self-esteem enhancement condition), high-self-esteem subjects practiced less (self-handicapped) than low-self-esteem subjects. Thus, both high- and low-self-esteem individuals self-handicap, but they have different motives for doing so. (Based on Tice, 1991)

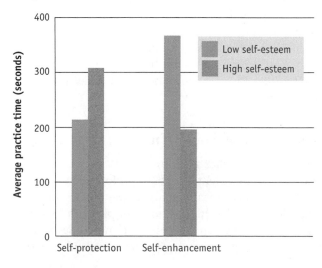

escaped your attention that there is a big risk associated with self-handicapping. That is, in the process of giving yourself an attributional "out" to use in case of failure, your self-defeating behavior is likely to result in poor performance (Baumgardner & Brownlee, 1987). Moreover, while self-handicapping may keep others from attributing your poor performance to low ability, it does not prevent them from making negative attributions about you. For example, there is evidence that people believe that individuals are less competent when they self-handicap than when they don't (Rhodewalt et al., 1995). Also, if you self-handicap, others may perceive you as lazy, inclined to drink too much, or highly anxious, depending on the means you use to self-handicap. Consequently, this self-enhancement tactic has serious drawbacks.

Self-Regulation

LEARNING OBJECTIVES

- *Explain why self-efficacy is important to psychological adjustment.*
- *Describe how individuals develop self-efficacy.*

People are constantly making decisions about the goals they want to pursue and developing strategies by which to reach those goals. If they fall short of a goal, they take stock and often devise a different way to get where they want to go. **This work of directing and controlling one's behavior is termed *self-regulation.*** We'll review self-regulation from the perspective of Albert Bandura's theory of self-efficacy. As you recall from our brief discussion of this topic in Chapter 2, *self-efficacy* **refers to people's conviction that they can achieve specific goals.** Obviously, efficacy beliefs vary according to one's skills. A person may have high self-efficacy when it comes to making friends but low self-efficacy when it comes time to speak in front of a group. However, simply having a skill doesn't guarantee that one will be able to put it into practice; one must also *believe* that one is capable of doing so. As Bandura (1986) puts it, self-efficacy "is concerned not with the skills one has, but with judgments of what one can do with whatever skills one possesses" (p. 391).

Correlates of Self-Efficacy

A number of studies show that self-efficacy affects individuals' commitments to goals, performance on tasks, and persistence toward goals in the face of obstacles (Bandura, 1990b). In addition, people with high self-efficacy anticipate success in future outcomes and can "tune out" negative thoughts that can lead to failure

(Bandura, 1989). Research has also demonstrated that self-efficacy is related to career choice (Betz & Hackett, 1986), health habits, and responses to stress (Bandura, 1997).

Albert Bandura

Because of its importance in psychological adjustment, it is worth noting that self-efficacy is learned and can be changed. Studies have demonstrated that increasing a person's self-efficacy is an effective way to treat psychological problems such as test anxiety (Smith, 1989), fear of sexual assault (Ozer & Bandura, 1990), post-traumatic stress disorder (Solomon et al., 1988), and drug addiction (DiClemente, 1986).

Developing Self-Efficacy

Self-efficacy plays a key role in the ability to make commitments to goals and to meet the goals one sets. How do people acquire this valuable characteristic? Bandura (1986) suggests there are four sources of self-efficacy: mastery experiences, vicarious experiences, persuasion/encouragement, and interpretation of emotional arousal.

Mastery experiences. The most important path to self-efficacy is through a history of mastering new skills. Sometimes new skills come easily—learning how to use the copy machine in the library, for instance. Some skills are harder to master—learning how to use a new word-processing program or how to play the piano. In acquiring more difficult skills, people usually make mistakes. How they handle these failure experiences is the key to learning self-efficacy. If you give up when you make mistakes, your failure instills self-doubts or low self-efficacy. On the other hand, if you persist through failure experiences to eventual success, you learn the lesson of self-efficacy: I *can* do it! A practical implication for parents, teachers, and coaches is that they should set high, but attainable, goals for children and encourage them to learn from their mistakes and to persevere until they succeed. This approach provides the mastery experiences children need to build self-efficacy and will enable them to approach future challenges with confidence. Well-intentioned parents, teachers, and supervisors who sometimes do their children's or employees' work or who regularly allow others to opt out of obligations with no consequences are unwittingly depriving individuals of opportunities to develop self-efficacy.

Vicarious Experiences. Another way to improve self-efficacy is by watching others perform a skill you want to learn. It's important that you choose a model who is competent at the task, and it helps if the model is similar to you (in age, gender, and ethnicity). For example, if you're afraid of speaking up for yourself, observing someone who is skilled at doing so can help you develop the confidence to do it. In addition, it's important that the person you use as a model not experience negative consequences; watching someone engage in behavior that results in adverse effects can undermine self-efficacy.

Persuasion and Encouragement. Although it is less effective than the first two approaches, a third way to develop self-efficacy is through others' telling you that you are up to a particular task. For example, if you're having a hard time asking someone for a date, a friend's encouragement might give you just the push you need. Of course, persuasion doesn't always work. And, unless encouragement is accompanied by specific and concrete suggestions, this tactic is unlikely to be successful. Too, if people attempt a skill they're doubtful about and do it poorly, it can have a negative effect on self-efficacy.

Interpretation of Emotional Arousal. The physiological responses that accompany feelings and one's interpretations of these responses are another source of self-efficacy. Let's say you're sitting in class waiting for the instructor to distribute an exam. You notice that your palms are moist and your heart is pounding. If you attribute these behaviors to fear, you can temporarily lower your self-efficacy, thus increasing the chances that you will do poorly on the test. Alternatively, if you interpret your sweaty palms and racing heart to the arousal everyone needs in order to perform well, you may be able to boost your self-efficacy and increase your chances of doing well.

To summarize, the ability to set goals, to design strategies by which to actually accomplish these goals, and to persist through failure to eventual success plays a key role in psychological adjustment.

Self-Presentation

LEARNING OBJECTIVES

- Explain why and when individuals engage in impression management.
- Cite some strategies people use to make positive impressions on others.
- Describe how high self-monitors differ from low self-monitors.
- Explain how excessive impression management can negatively affect adjustment.

Whereas your self-concept involves how you see yourself, your public self involves how you want others to see you. **A *public self* is an image or facade presented to others in social interactions.** People rarely behave totally spontaneously. Let's face it: Most people see only an edited version of your behavior, which is usually calculated to present a certain image. This presentation of a public self may sound deceitful, but it is perfectly normal, and everyone does it (Schlenker & Weigold, 1992). Actually, most people are not limited to a single public self. Typically, individuals have a number of public selves that are tied to certain situations and certain people with whom they interact. For instance, you may have one public self for your parents and another for your siblings. You may have still others for your teachers, your same-gender friends, your other-gender friends, your spouse, your boss, your colleagues, your customers, and your neighbors.

Impression Management

In presenting themselves to others, people normally strive to make a positive impression (Baumeister, Tice, & Hutton, 1989). This is obviously important if they want to be liked, respected, hired, and so forth. *Impression management* refers to usually conscious efforts by people to influence how others think of them. To see impression management in operation, let's look at a study of behavior in simulated job interviews (von Baeyer, Sherk, & Zanna, 1981). In this study, female job applicants were led to believe that the man who would interview them held either very traditional, "chauvinistic" views of women or just the opposite. The result? Applicants who expected a chauvinist presented themselves in a more "traditionally feminine" manner than subjects in the other condition. Their self-presentation efforts affected both their appearance (they wore more makeup) and their communication style (they talked less and gave more traditional answers to a question about marriage and children). The bottom line is this: Impression management is a normal feature of everyday social interactions. Although people certainly don't engage in it all the time, they probably do it a lot more than many realize. In the next section, we'll explore some typical strategies individuals use to make favorable impressions on others.

SELF-PRESENTATION STRATEGIES

Politicians, rapsters, and judges present themselves quite differently to others. You, too, select your type of dress, hairstyle, and manner of speech to present a certain image of yourself. Thus, one reason people engage in self-presentation is to claim a particular identity (Baumeister, 1998). A second motive for impression management is to gain liking and approval from

Basketball star Dennis Rodman attracts press attention for his unusual self-presentation behavior.

others—by editing what one says about oneself and by using various nonverbal cues such as smiles, gestures, and eye contact. Because self-presentation is practiced so often, people usually do it automatically. At other times, however, impression management may be used intentionally—to get a job, a date, a promotion, and so forth. Some common self-presentation strategies include the following (Jones, 1990).

Ingratiation. Of all the self-presentation strategies, this is the most fundamental and frequently used. ***Ingratiation is behaving in ways to make oneself likable to others.*** People behave in ways they hope will produce favorable evaluations. *Giving compliments* is a common ingratiation strategy; however, it's best to be sincere, as people dislike insincerity and can often detect it. *Doing favors for others* is also an effective tactic (Morrison & Bies, 1991). Generally, people like these little attentions; however, the favors shouldn't be too spectacular, or they may leave the target person with the uncomfortable feeling of social indebtedness. Other useful ingratiation tactics include *expressing liking for others* (Wayne & Ferris, 1990) and *going along with others* (to get others to like you, it helps to do the things that they want to do).

Self-promotion. While people use the strategy of ingratiation to get others to like them, they use self-promotion to get others to *respect* them. Self-promotion involves playing up your strong points to present yourself as competent. For instance, in a job interview, you might find ways of mentioning the fact that you earned good grades at a school with a fine academic reputation and that you were president of the student body and a member of the soccer team. You want to avoid going overboard with self-promotion—it's important not to come across as a braggart. For this reason, false modesty often works well.

Exemplification. Most people try to project an honest image; thus, individuals who want to claim special credit for integrity or strength of character have to seek out situations that will allow them to demonstrate exemplary behavior. For example, danger-fraught occupations such as the military or the police provide obvious opportunities to exemplify moral virtue. A less dramatic, but still effective, strategy is to demonstrate consistent behavior of a high moral tone in many different situations. Obviously, this strategy has its risks. Exemplifiers can come across as self-righteous; when they are discovered to have "feet of clay," they are labeled hypocrites.

Intimidation. This strategy sends the message, "Don't mess with me" and usually only works in nonvoluntary relationships—for instance, when it's hard for an employee to find another employer or for an economically dependent spouse to leave her or his partner. Obvious intimidation tactics include threats and the withholding of valuable resources (salary increases, promotions, sex). A more subtle tactic is emotional intimidation—holding over a person's head the threat of an aggressive outburst if you don't get your way. Whereas the other self-presentation strategies work by creating a favorable impression, intimidation usually generates dislike. Nonetheless, it can work.

Supplication. This is usually the tactic of last resort (recall the song, "Ain't Too Proud to Beg"). Here, individuals try to present themselves as weak and dependent to get favors from others. For example, it is not unheard of for students to plead or break into tears in an instructor's office in an attempt to get a grade changed. Because of the social norm to help those who are needy, supplication may work; however, unless the supplicator has something to offer the potential benefactor in return, it's not a very effective strategy.

Individuals tailor their use of self-presentation strategies to match the situation. For instance, it's unlikely that you'd try intimidating your boss; you'd be more likely to ingratiate or promote yourself with her. As you can see in Figure 5.15, each of these strategies carries a risk. Thus, to make a good impression, you must use these strategies skillfully. In the next section,

FIGURE 5.15.

Strategic Self-Presentation Strategies. Individuals rely on a variety of self-presentation strategies to present a certain image of themselves to others. To avoid the risks associated with the strategies, it's important to use the tactics skillfully. (Based on Jones, 1990)

Strategic Self-Presentation Strategies			
Presentation Strategy	Impression Sought	Emotion to Be Aroused in Target	Negative Impressions Risked
Ingratiation	Likable	Affection	Boot-licker, conformist
Self-promotion	Competent	Respect	Conceited, defensive
Exemplification	Morally superior	Guilt	Hypocrite, sanctimonious
Intimidation	Dangerous	Fear	Blusterer, ineffectual
Supplication	Helpless	Obligation	Undeserving, lazy

we'll dig deeper into the fascinating topic of self-presentation.

PERSPECTIVES ON SELF-PRESENTATION

Interestingly, almost all research on self-presentation has been conducted on first meetings between strangers, yet the vast majority of actual social interactions take place between people who already know each other. Noting the gap between reality and research, Dianne Tice and her colleagues (1995) investigated whether self-presentation varied in these different situations. Their findings confirmed the tendency for people to make positive impressions on others when interacting with strangers but revealed a shift toward modesty and neutral self-presentations when interacting with friends. Why the difference? Since strangers don't know you, you want to give them positive information so they'll form a good impression of you. Besides, strangers have no way of knowing whether you are bending the truth or not. On the other hand, your friends already know your positive qualities. Thus, belaboring them is unnecessary and may be off-putting if you come across as immodest. Likewise, your friends know you well enough to know whether you are exaggerating, so there's no point in doing so.

Can self-presentation be hazardous to your health? It seems that the need to project a positive public image can lead individuals into a number of dangerous practices (Leary, Tchividjian, & Kraxberger, 1994). Consider the following familiar scenarios. To avoid the embarrassment of buying condoms or talking with their sex partners, people practice unprotected sex and heighten their risk of contracting AIDS. In pursuit of an attractive tan, people spend hours in the sun, thereby increasing their chances of getting skin cancer. Interestingly, research indicates that concerns about appearance influence sunbathing behavior much more strongly than concerns about skin cancer (Leary & Jones, 1993). To keep thin, many, especially women, use strong diet medications and develop full-blown eating disorders (see the Chapter 15 Application). To impress their peers some adolescents take up drinking and smoking and even drug abuse. Finally, out of the desire to appear brave and daring, some people engage in reckless behavior that ends in accidents and death.

To conclude, the need to present a favorable image results in wide-ranging outcomes. Most of these outcomes are positive, but self-presentation can operate to one's detriment.

Self-Monitoring

According to Mark Snyder (1979, 1986), people vary in their awareness of how they are perceived by others. **Self-monitoring refers to the degree to which people attend to and control the impressions they make on others.** People who are high self-monitors are sensitive to their impact on others. Low self-monitors are less concerned about impression management and behave more spontaneously.

Compared to low self-monitors, high self-monitors actively seek information about how they are expected to behave and try to tailor their actions accordingly (Snyder & Campbell, 1982); they are sensitive to situational cues and relatively skilled at deciphering what others want to see, and they tend to act more in accordance with situational expectations than with their true feelings or attitudes (Zanna & Olson, 1982). Because high self-monitors control

Mark Snyder

Web Link 5.5

Impression Management and Dramaturgy
This site contains PowerPoint slides used by Professor Douglas Martin at Northwest Missouri State University when he lectures on impression management to his social psychology classes.

their emotions well and deliberately regulate nonverbal signals that are more spontaneous in others, they are relatively talented at self-presentation (Friedman & Miller-Herringer, 1991). In addition, they have been shown to be more accurate in judging other people's feelings (Geiser, Rarick, & Soldow, 1977). In contrast, low self-monitors are more likely to express their true beliefs, since they are more motivated to behave consistently with their internal feelings (McCann & Hancock, 1983).

As you might infer, these two personality types view themselves rather differently (Baumeister, 1998). Low self-monitors see themselves as having strong principles and behaving in line with them. In contrast, high self-monitors perceive themselves as flexible and pragmatic. Because high self-monitors don't see a necessary connection between their private beliefs and their public actions, they aren't troubled by discrepancies between beliefs and behavior. Perhaps you're wondering whether these groups differ on psychological adjustment? Interestingly, researchers who have looked at this question have found that greater adjustment problems are found among individuals who score either very high or very low on self-monitoring compared to those whose scores are closer to the middle (Miller & Thayer, 1989).

Self-Presentation and Authenticity

Although people may be aware of the dubious accuracy of their self-presentations, research indicates that individuals sometimes come to believe their fabrications (Jones et al., 1981; Rhodewalt & Agustsdottir, 1986). In other words, if you present yourself in a certain way often enough, you may begin to actually see yourself in that way. For example, if you are really quite conceited but you incorporate false humility into many of your public selves, you might begin to view yourself as a humble person.

Although everyone engages in some impression management, people vary greatly in how much they edit their behavior. As you have seen, some people are more concerned than others about portraying themselves appropriately for various audiences. Moreover, people differ in the degree of congruence or overlap among their various public selves (see Figure 5.16). Recall Erikson's emphasis on the congruence between one's own sense of self and others' perceptions of one. Similarly, Sidney Jourard (1971), a well-respected humanistic psychologist, maintained that constant misrepresentation for purposes of impression management may lead people to lose touch with their "authentic" selves. Jourard argued that this kind of confusion is dangerous and may cause much psychological distress.

It is this identity-related confusion that leads many people to be concerned about "finding" themselves. This search for the real self became something of a fad in the 1970s, and many people used the concept to rationalize their "rudderless" lives. It has since become common to ridicule people who say they are "looking for the real me." However, this search for the authentic self may often be a genuine effort to come to grips with a self-concept and an identity that are in disarray.

To conclude, it is probably a good idea to avoid going overboard on self-presentation efforts. Taken to an excess, impression management may be harmful to accurate self-perception. Also, most people are sensitive to sincerity in others; when they doubt the sincerity of flattering statements, they may like the flatterer less (Jones, 1990).

In the upcoming Application, we'll redirect our attention to the critical issue of self-esteem and outline seven steps for building self-esteem.

FIGURE 5.16.

Public selves and identity confusion. Person 1 has divergent public selves with relatively little overlap among them. Person 1 is more likely to develop identity confusion than Person 2, whose public selves are more congruent with each other.

Public selves for
(a) spouse
(b) parents
(c) neighbors
(d) boss
(e) colleagues at work

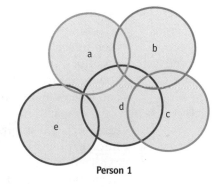

Person 1

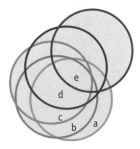

Person 2

Building Self-esteem

- Describe seven ways to build self-esteem.
- Describe the vicious circle of low self-esteem and rejection.

Answer the following "yes" or "no."

___ **1.** I am very sensitive to criticism.

___ **2.** I tend to have a hard time accepting praise or flattery.

___ **3.** I have very little confidence in my abilities.

___ **4.** I often feel awkward in social situations and just don't know how to take charge.

___ **5.** I tend to be highly critical of other people.

If you answered "yes" to most of these questions, you may be suffering from what Alfred Adler called an inferiority complex (see Chapter 2). This syndrome, which is dominated by low self-esteem, is fairly common. It is also quite unfortunate. People with very low self-esteem tend to develop more emotional problems than others, set low goals for themselves, become socially invisible, conform against their better judgment, and court rejection by putting down others.

Self-esteem is obviously an important component of your self-concept. It appears that an overly negative self-image can contribute to many kinds of behavioral problems. An overly positive image can also cause problems, but people characterized by excessive conceit do not suffer in the same way that self-critical people do.

In this Application, we will describe seven guidelines for building higher self-esteem. These guidelines are based on our own distillation of the advice of many theorists, including Bednar & Peterson (1995), Rogers (1977), Ellis (1984), Jourard (Jourard & Landsman, 1980), Hamachek (1992), and Zimbardo (1977).

1. Recognize That You Control Your Self-Image

The first thing you must do is recognize that you ultimately control how you see yourself. You do have the power to change your self-image. True, we have discussed at length how feedback from others influences your self-concept. Yes, social comparison theory suggests that people need such feedback and that it would be unwise to ignore it completely. However, the final choice about whether to accept or reject such feedback rests with you. Your self-image resides in your mind and is a product of your thinking. Although others may influence your self-concept, you are the final authority.

2. Don't Let Others Set Your Goals

A common trap that many people fall into is letting others set the standards by which they evaluate themselves. Other people are constantly telling you that you should do this or you ought to do that. Thus, you hear that you "should study computer science" or "ought to lose weight" or "must move to a better neighborhood." Most of these people are well-intentioned, and many of them may have good ideas. Still, as you will recall from our discussion of identity, it is important that you make your *own* decisions about what you will do and what you will believe in. For example, consider a business executive in his early forties who sees himself in a negative light because he has not climbed very high in the corporate hierarchy. The crucial question is: Did he ever really want to make that arduous climb? It could be that he has misgivings about the value of such an effort. Perhaps he has gone through life thinking he should pursue that kind of success only because that standard was imposed on him by his parents or by society. You should think about the source of and basis for your personal goals and standards. Do they really represent ideals that *you* value? Or are they beliefs that you have passively accepted from others without thinking?

3. Recognize Unrealistic Goals

Even if you truly value certain ideals and sincerely want to achieve certain goals, another question remains: Are your goals realistic? Many people get in the habit of demanding too much of themselves. They always want to perform at their best, which is obviously impossible. For instance, you may have a burning desire to achieve national acclaim as an actress. However, the odds against such an achievement are enormous. It is

© Punch/Rothco

"I don't suppose it's much compared with other inferiority complexes"

important to recognize this reality so that you do not condemn yourself for failure. Some overly demanding people pervert the social comparison process by always comparing themselves against the best rather than against similar others. They assess their looks by comparing themselves with famous models, and they judge their finances by comparing themselves with the wealthiest people they know. Such comparisons are unrealistic and almost inevitably undermine self-esteem.

4. Modify Negative Self-Talk

The way you analyze your life influences how you see yourself (and vice versa). People who are low in self-esteem tend to engage in various counterproductive modes of thinking. For example, when they succeed, they may attribute their success to good luck, and when they fail, they may blame themselves. Quite to the contrary, you should take credit for your successes and consider the possibility that your failures may not be your fault. As discussed in Chapter 4, Albert Ellis has pointed out that people often think irrationally and draw unwarranted negative conclusions about themselves. For example, if you apply for a job and are rejected, you might think, "They didn't hire me. I must be a worthless, inept person." The conclusion that you are a "worthless person" does not follow logically from the

fact that you were not hired. Such irrational thinking and negative self-talk breed poor self-esteem. It is important to recognize the destructive potential of negative self-talk and bring it to a halt.

5. Emphasize Your Strengths

This advice may seem trite, but it has some merit. People with low self-esteem often derive little satisfaction from their accomplishments and virtues. They dismiss compliments as foolish, unwarranted, or insincere. They pay little heed to their good qualities while talking constantly about their defeats and frailties. The fact is that everyone has strengths and weaknesses. You should accept those personal shortcomings that you are powerless to change and work on those that are changeable, without becoming obsessed about it. At the same time, you should take stock of your strengths and learn to appreciate them.

6. Work to Improve Yourself

As just mentioned, some personal shortcomings can be overcome. Although it is important to reassess your goals and discard those that are unrealistic, this advice is not intended to provide a convenient rationalization for complacency. There is much to be said for setting out to conquer personal problems. In a sense, this

If you like rock star Ricky Martin, or actress Elizabeth Hurley, that's fine, but they are not sensible benchmarks for evaluating your attractiveness or your success. Some people distort the social comparison process and undermine their self-esteem by always comparing themselves to the most attractive and successful people they see in the media.

FRANK & ERNEST reprinted by permission of Newspaper Enterprise Association, Inc.

entire text is based on a firm belief in the value of self-control and self-improvement. As we saw in our discussion of self-efficacy, there is ample evidence that efforts at self-improvement can pay off by boosting self-esteem.

7. Approach Others with a Positive Outlook

People who are low in self-esteem often try to cut others down to their (subjective) size through constant criticism. As you can readily imagine, this faultfinding and generally negative approach to interpersonal transactions does not go over well with other people. Instead, it leads to tension, antagonism, and rejection. This rejection lowers self-esteem still further (see Figure 5.17). Efforts to build self-esteem can be facilitated by recognizing and reversing this self-defeating tendency. Approaching people with a positive, supportive outlook will promote rewarding interactions and help you earn their acceptance. There is probably nothing that enhances self-esteem more than acceptance and genuine affection from others.

●Recommended Reading

Self-Esteem by Matthew McKay and Patrick Fanning (New Harbinger Publications, 1994)

If you want to assess, raise, and maintain your self-esteem, this book can help you. The authors work from the premise that everyone has a "pathological critic," an inner voice that is judgmental and fault finding. Some people have an overly active and harsh pathological critic that, over time, erodes self-esteem. Through the use of cognitive restructuring, the reader is shown how to deal with these destructive self-statements.

This book is easily understood, is written in an interesting style, and packs a lot of information in a few pages. It is most useful for those whose self-esteem problems are limited to a specific area (work, parenting, sex, etc.). While also helpful to those whose esteem problems are more serious, the authors suggest that the book will be most effective for this group when used along with psychotherapy.

In the following excerpt, the authors discuss how parents' reactions to children can contribute to low self-esteem.

Many parents label poor judgment as moral error. For example, a child who puts off a school project until the very end and is then forced to stay up late doing a rather slipshod job is guilty of poor judgment or poor impulse control (or both). But a parent who labels this behavior as lazy or stupid or "screwed up" is communicating to the child that he is morally bad. . . . The more your parents confused matters of taste, preference, judgment, and convenience with moral issues, the more likely you are to have fragile self-esteem. [1992, p. 112]

FIGURE 5.17.
The vicious circle of low self-esteem and rejection.
A negative self-image can make expectations of rejection a self-fulfilling prophecy, because people with low self-esteem tend to approach others in negative, hurtful ways. Real or imagined rejections lower self-esteem still further, creating a vicious circle.

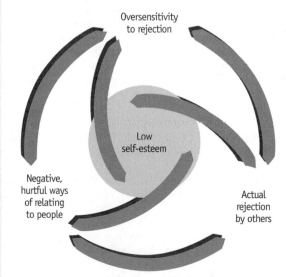

Key Ideas

SELF-CONCEPT

● The self-concept is composed of a number of beliefs about what one is like, and it is not easily changed. It governs both current and future behavior. People with complex self-concepts are likely to have stable emotions and high self-esteem. Discrepancies between the ideal self and the actual or ought self can produce negative emotions and lowered self-esteem. To cope with these negative states, individuals may bring their behavior in line with their ideal selves or blunt their awareness of self-discrepancies.

● The self-concept is shaped by several factors, including individuals' observations of their own behavior, which often involve social comparisons with others. Self-observations tend to be biased in a positive direction. In addition, feedback from others shapes the self-concept; this information is also filtered to some extent. Cultural guidelines also affect the way people see themselves. Members of individualistic cultures usually have an independent view of the self, whereas those in collectivist cultures often have an interdependent view of the self.

IDENTITY

● Identity refers to having a sense of who one is in the larger society. According to Erik Erikson, developing a sense of identity is a key challenge of adolescence. James Marcia has proposed that identity outcomes include foreclosure, moratorium, diffusion, and achievement.

● Male identity is typically defined in terms of occupational choice, whereas female identity is rooted in relationships. For members of ethnic minority groups, adolescence is also a time when ethnic identity is developed.

SELF-ESTEEM

● Self-esteem is a person's global evaluation of his or her worth. Like the self-concept, it tends to be stable, but it can fluctuate in response to daily ups and downs. Compared to those with high self-esteem, individuals with low self-esteem have unclear and contradictory self-views, more emotional problems, and more difficulties in social interactions. A subset of individuals with unstable high self-esteem are prone to violence when self-esteem is threatened.

● Because self-esteem affects expectations, it operates in a self-perpetuating fashion. Parents are especially important in determining self-esteem. Members of minority groups use a number of strategies to protect their self-image from the effects of being stigmatized.

BASIC PRINCIPLES OF SELF-PERCEPTION

● Individuals make use of a number of processes to construct and maintain a coherent view of the self. To explain the causes of their behavior, individuals make self-attributions. Generally, people attribute their behavior to internal or external factors and to stable or unstable factors. Controllability-uncontrollability is another key dimension of self-attributions. People tend to use either an optimistic explanatory style or a pessimistic explanatory style to explain various events that occur in their lives, and these attributional styles are related to psychological adjustment.

● Individuals strive to maintain a consistent self-view, even though this means that self-perceptions are not necessarily accurate. Individuals also actively strive to maintain a positive view of themselves. Common self-enhancement strategies include downward comparisons, the self-serving bias, basking in reflected glory, and self-handicapping.

SELF-REGULATION

● Self-regulation involves setting goals and directing behavior to meet those goals. A key aspect of self-regulation is self-efficacy—an individual's belief that he or she can achieve specific goals. Self-efficacy plays a key role in adjustment and can be learned through mastery experiences, vicarious experiences, persuasion, and positive interpretations of emotional arousal.

SELF-PRESENTATION

● Public selves are the various images that individuals project to others. Generally, people try to create positive impressions for others by using a variety of self-presentation strategies. People who are high in self-monitoring are especially sensitive to the impressions they make on others.

● In striving to make positive impressions on others, it is unwise to stray too far from the truth. This misguided tactic may interfere with accurate self-perception and cause others to distrust and dislike you.

APPLICATION: BUILDING SELF-ESTEEM

● Suggested ways to improve self-esteem include (1) recognize that you control your self-image, (2) don't let others set your goals, (3) recognize unrealistic goals, (4) modify negative self-talk, (5) emphasize your strengths, (6) work to improve yourself, and (7) approach others with a positive outlook.

Key Terms

Attributional style
Basking in reflected glory
Collectivism
Downward social comparison
External attributions
Identity
Impression management
Individualism
Ingratiation
Internal attributions
Possible selves
Public self
Reference group
Self-attributions
Self-complexity
Self-concept
Self-discrepancy
Self-efficacy
Self-enhancement
Self-esteem
Self-handicapping
Self-monitoring
Self-regulation
Self-serving bias
Self-verification theory
Social comparison theory

Key People

Albert Bandura
Roy Baumeister
Robert Cialdini
Erik Erikson
Hazel Markus
Mark Snyder

Practice Test

1. People who are low in self-complexity:
   a. experience more stable emotions and self-esteem than those high in self-complexity.
   b. experience less stable emotions and self-esteem than those high in self-complexity.
   c. cannot develop greater self-complexity.
   d. have many different self-components.

2. In the study (Hull & Young, 1983) that looked at self-awareness and alcohol consumption, it was found that those who drank the most were:
   a. self-aware and believed that they had done poorly on an IQ test.
   b. self-aware and believed that they had done well on an IQ test.
   c. not self-aware and believed that they had done poorly on an IQ test.
   d. not self-aware and believed that they had done well on an IQ test.

3. Which identity status describes those who are searching for a sense of identity?
   a. Foreclosure
   b. Achievement
   c. Moratorium
   d. Diffusion

4. Low self-esteem is associated with:
   a. few emotional problems.
   b. effective social skills.
   c. setting high personal goals.
   d. self-concept confusion.

5. Hostility and aggression are more likely in a small subset of individuals with:
   a. high self-esteem.
   b. moderate self-esteem.
   c. low self-esteem.
   d. no self-esteem.

6. Which of the following is *not* a basic principle of self-perception?
   a. People make inferences about the causes of their behavior.
   b. People's explanatory style is unrelated to adjustment.
   c. People prefer to receive information that is consistent with their self-views.
   d. People want to maintain positive feelings about the self.

7. Keisha is upset when a textbook is stolen, but she feels better after she hears that a classmate's book bag, including her cell phone, was stolen. This is an example of:
   a. the self-serving bias.
   b. basking in reflected glory.
   c. downward comparison.
   d. self-handicapping.

8. Which of the following statements about self-efficacy is TRUE?
   a. It can be developed by persevering through failure to success.
   b. It is something that one is born with.
   c. It refers to a person's general self-confidence.
   d. It refers to conscious efforts to make a certain impression on others.

9. The self-presentation strategy of ingratiation involves trying to make others:
   a. respect you.
   b. fear you.
   c. feel sorry for you.
   d. like you.

10. Which of the following will *not* help you build higher self-esteem?
    a. Minimizing negative self-talk
    b. Comparing yourself with those who are the best in a given area
    c. Working to improve yourself
    d. Approaching others with positive expectations

Answers

1. b pages 130–131
2. a pages 132–133
3. c page 137
4. d pages 139–140
5. a pages 140–141
6. b pages 144–145
7. c pages 145–146
8. a pages 148–149
9. d page 150
10. b pages 153–154

INFOTRAC
COLLEGE EDITION

Go to the Wadsworth Psychology Study Center (http://psychology.wadsworth.com/) for quiz questions, research updates, hot topics, interactive exercises, and suggested readings in INFOTRAC related to this chapter.

CHAPTER 6

Social Cognition and Social Influence

You've had your eye on that attractive brunette in the first row of your algebra class since the term began. Should you ask her out? As you ponder the wisdom of this action, you watch her, hoping to pick up some clues to help you make your decision. You notice that there is a sorority decal on her notebook. But you don't belong to a fraternity and you've never dated a sorority woman. You've heard that some of them can be snobbish, although she seems to be friendly and approachable. Still, you're only a sophomore; what if she's a senior? That could be awkward. As you continue to contemplate what to do, similar thoughts flit through your mind.

In this scenario, you can see the process of person perception at work. People are constantly constructing impressions of others to understand them and predict their behavior. In this chapter, we'll explore what's involved in forming these impressions and how and why they are often inaccurate. Expanding our discussion of social cognition, we'll turn to the problem of prejudice. Next, we'll look at how others try to influence your beliefs and behavior. Specifically, we'll focus on the power of persuasive messages and the pressures to conform and obey. As you'll see, social thinking and social influence play significant roles in personal adjustment.

Forming Impressions of Others

LEARNING OBJECTIVES

● Cite the five sources of information people use to form impressions of others.

● Describe the key differences between snap judgments and systematic judgments.

● Define attributions and explain when people are likely to make them.

● Describe how expectancies distort people's perceptions and influence others' behavior.

● Explain how four important cognitive distortions operate.

● Describe some ways in which perceptions of others are efficient, selective, and stable.

Can you remember the first time you met your freshman roommate? She seemed pleasant enough but came across as a little reserved. In fact, you were worried whether you would become friends. To your relief,

within a week it seemed as though you had known each other for years. As people interact with others, they constantly engage in *person perception*, **the process of forming impressions of others**. Because impression formation is usually such an easy and automatic process, people are unaware that it is taking place. Nonetheless, the process is a complex one. Let's review some of its essential aspects.

Key Sources of Information

Because you can't read other people's minds, you are dependent on *observations* of others to determine what they are like. In forming impressions of others, people rely on five key sources of observational information: appearance, verbal statements, actions, nonverbal messages, and situational cues.

● *Appearance.* Despite the admonition, "You can't judge a book by its cover," people frequently do exactly that. Physical features such as height, weight, skin color, and hair color are some of the cues used to "read" other people. Regardless of their accuracy, beliefs about physical features are used to form impressions of others (Bull & Rumsey, 1988). For example, Americans learn to associate red hair with "hot" tempers and the wearing of eyeglasses with studiousness.

● *Verbal statements.* Another obvious source of information about others is what they say. If Mark tells

In forming impressions of others, people rely on cues such as appearance, actions, verbal and nonverbal messages, as well as the nature of the situation.

you that he goes out drinking every weekend and Jeremy says that he never drinks, you form quite different impressions of these two individuals. If Mary speaks negatively about most people she knows, you will probably conclude that she is a critical person.

• *Actions.* Because people don't always tell the truth, you must rely on people's behavior to provide insights about them. In impression formation, people follow the adage, "Actions speak louder than words." If you know that Linda volunteers five hours a week at the local homeless shelter, you are likely to infer that she is a caring person.

• *Nonverbal messages.* Another key source of information about others is nonverbal communication: facial expressions, eye contact, body language, and gestures (Ambady & Rosenthal, 1992; Ekman, 1992). These nonverbal cues provide information about people's emotional states and dispositions. For example, a bright smile and good eye contact signal friendliness and openness. Also, because people know that verbal behavior is more easily manipulated than nonverbal behavior, they often rely on nonverbal cues to determine the truth of what others say (DePaulo, LeMay, & Epstein, 1991).

• *Situations.* The setting in which behavior occurs provides crucial information about how to interpret a person's behavior. For example, if Doug guffaws at a joke at a local student hangout, no one bats an eye. But if he bursts out laughing in the middle of a serious lecture, it will raise eyebrows and generate speculations about why he behaved this way. As this example illustrates, people pay particular attention to behavior that is negative or unexpected (Weiner, 1985).

Snap Judgments Versus Systematic Judgments

Snap judgments about others are those made quickly and on the basis of only a few bits of information and preconceived notions. Thus, they may not be particularly accurate. Nevertheless, people get by with superficial assessments of others quite often. As Susan Fiske

Susan Fiske

(1993) puts it: "People are good enough perceivers" (p. 156). Often, interactions with others are so fleeting or inconsequential that it makes little difference that such judgments are imprecise. Does it really matter that you mistakenly infer that the blonde postal clerk is a fun-loving person, or that your bespectacled restaurant server is an intellectual? You may never interact with them again and even if you do, your interactions are not likely to be significant to either of you.

On the other hand, when it comes to selecting a friend, a mate, a boss, or an employee, it's essential that your impressions be as accurate as possible. Hence, it's not surprising that people are motivated to take more care in these assessments. In forming impressions of those who can affect their welfare and happiness, people make *systematic judgments* rather than snap decisions (see Figure 6.1). That is, they take the time to observe the person in a variety of situations and to compare that person's behavior with that of others in similar situations.

Two different cognitive processes underlie these two types of judgments. To conserve their limited cognitive resources (attention, memory, and so forth), people quite often operate on "cognitive automatic pilot." More effortful, thoughtful processing only kicks in when people expect a person or situation to be personally relevant. Ellen Langer (1989) describes these two states as *mindlessness* and *mindfulness*, respectively. As you'll see, these two different modes of processing operate in a variety of social situations.

In assessing what a significant individual is like, people are particularly interested in learning *why* the person behaves in a certain way. This deeper level of understanding is vital if one is to make accurate predictions about their future behavior. After all, when you're looking for a roommate, you don't want to end up with an inconsiderate slob. To determine the causes of others' behavior, people engage in the process of causal attribution.

FIGURE 6.1.

The process of person perception. In forming impressions of others, perceivers rely on five sources of observational information. When it's important to form accurate impressions of others, people are motivated to make systematic judgments, including attributions. When accuracy isn't a priority, people make snap judgments about others. (Adapted from Brehm & Kassin, 1993)

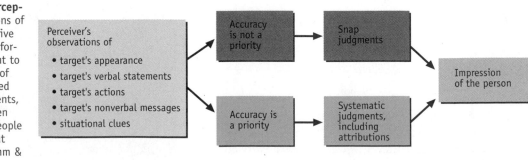

Attributions

As you have seen in earlier chapters, *attributions* **are inferences that people draw about the causes of their own behavior, others' behavior, and events.** In the previous chapter, we focused on *self*-attributions. Here, we'll apply attributions to the behavior of *other people*. For example, suppose that your boss bawls you out for doing a sloppy job on an insignificant project. To what do you attribute this tongue-lashing? Was your work really that bad? Was your boss just in a grouchy mood? Is your boss under too much pressure? Or, let's say that you overhear Amy compliment Tracy on her clothing. To what do you attribute the compliment? Does Amy really like Tracy's outfit? Or was the compliment merely part of everyday social routine? Is it possible that the compliment was an attempt to butter Tracy up?

In Chapter 5, we noted that there are three key dimensions of attributions: internal or external, stable or unstable, and controllable and uncontrollable (Jones & Davis, 1965; Kelley, 1967; Weiner, 1974). For the purposes of our current discussion, we'll focus only on the internal/external dimension. When people ascribe the causes of someone's behavior to personal dispositions, traits, abilities, or feelings, they are making *internal* attributions. When they impute the causes of behavior to situational demands and environmental constraints, they are making *external* attributions. For example, if a friend's business fails, you might attribute the failure to your friend's lack of business acumen (an internal factor) or to negative trends in the economy (an external explanation). Parents who discover that their teenage son just banged up the family car may blame it on his carelessness (an internal attribution) or on slippery road conditions (an external attribution).

The types of attributions people make about others can have a tremendous impact on everyday social interactions. For example, blaming a friend's business failure on poor business "smarts" rather than a poor economy will obviously affect how you view your friend—not to mention whether you'll lend her money! Likewise, if parents attribute their son's automobile accident to slippery road conditions, they are likely to deal with him differently than if they attribute it to his carelessness. In addition, there is evidence that the attributions spouses make to explain each other's behavior can affect their marital satisfaction (Bradbury & Fincham, 1988).

Obviously, people don't make attributions about everyone they meet. Research suggests that people are relatively selective about this (Hilton, Fein, & Miller, 1993; E. Jones, 1990). It seems that people are most likely to make attributions (1) when unusual events grab their attention, (2) when events have personal consequences, (3) when others behave in unexpected ways, and (4) when they are suspicious about the motives underlying someone's behavior.

Some aspects of the attribution process are logical (Brewer, 1988). Nonetheless, research also shows that the process of person perception is sometimes illogical and unsystematic, as in the case of snap judgments. Biases also creep into the person perception process, a topic we'll take up next.

Perceiver Expectancies

Remember Evan, that bully from your elementary school? He made your nine-year-old life a total misery—constantly looking for opportunities to poke fun at you and beat you up. Now, when you meet someone named Evan, you notice that your initial reaction is negative and that it takes a while before you warm up to him. Why? Your negative past experiences with males named Evan lead you expect the worst, whether or not it's warranted. Let's see how people's expectations can influence their perceptions of others.

CONFIRMATION BIAS

Shortly after you begin interacting with someone, you start forming hypotheses about what the person is like. In turn, these hypotheses can influence your behavior toward that person in such a way as to confirm your expectations. Thus, if when you first meet Dana she has a camera slung around her neck, you will probably hypothesize that she has an interest in photography and question her selectively about her interests in this area. You might also neglect to ask more wide-ranging questions that would give you a more accurate picture of her. **This tendency to behave toward others in ways that confirm your expectations about them is termed** *confirmation bias.*

In a study that shows confirmation bias in operation, male students were asked to have a brief telephone conversation with a female student (Snyder, Tanke, & Berscheid, 1977). Before their conversations, the men were given a folder with a photo of and background information on their telephone partners. Half of the men saw a photo of an attractive woman and half saw a photo of an unattractive woman. (In reality, the women in the photos did not participate in the study and there was no difference in the attractiveness of the actual female telephone partners. The background information was provided by the real partners.) Prior to the actual telephone conversations, the men rated their partners-to-be. Those who believed their partners were attractive judged that the women would be poised, humorous, outgoing, and socially adept, whereas those who believed their partners were unattractive judged them to be awkward, serious, unsociable, and socially inept. Generalizing from this example, we can surmise that confirmation bias occurs not only in casual social interactions but also in job interviews and in courtrooms, in which the interviewer or attorney may ask leading questions (Fiske, & Talyor, 1991).

Confirmation bias also occurs because individuals selectively recall facts that fit with the schemas they apply to others. Evidence for such a tendency was found in a study by Cohen (1981). In this experiment, participants watched a videotape of a woman who engaged in a variety of activities, including listening to classical music, drinking beer, and watching TV. Half of the participants were told that the woman was a waitress and the other half were led to believe that the woman was a librarian. When asked to recall what the woman did during the filmed sequence, participants tended to remember activities consistent with their stereotypes of waitresses and librarians. For instance, participants who thought that the woman was a waitress recalled her beer drinking, while participants who thought she was a librarian recalled her listening to classical music.

Although confirmation bias does occur, there is some question about how pervasive it is. For example, Susan Fiske (1993) notes that when people have a high need for accuracy in their impression of someone, they are less likely to engage in selective questioning. Instead, they ask *diagnostic* questions such as, "Would you rather have a few, close relationships or a lot of less intimate ones?" Diagnostic questions provide people with information about the accuracy of their expectations, in contrast to biased questions that seek mainly to confirm their initial hypotheses.

Normally, people remain unaware of the biases in their perceptions. They go blithely along, assuming that their version of reality is accurate. And most of the time this works (Fiske, 1993). It's only when someone disagrees with a perception that a person is brought up short. When this happens, the individual may alter his or her views, conclude that the other person's perception is "off," or look for another satisfactory explanation for the difference in perceptions.

SELF-FULFILLING PROPHECIES

Sometimes a perceiver's expectations can actually change another person's behavior. For instance, in the study by Snyder and colleagues (1977), after the men had completed their ratings of their partners, they spoke with their partners for ten minutes on the telephone. Later, audiotapes of these conversations were analyzed by judges who were "blind" to the nature of the study. The judges rated the comments of the men with "attractive" partners as more sociable and outgoing than those of the men with "unattractive" partners. How did independent judges rate the women's comments? The "attractive" women were rated as more confident and animated than the "unattractive" women; they were also judged to have enjoyed their conversations and liked the men they spoke with more than the "unattractive" women.

This process whereby expectations about a person cause the person to behave in ways that confirm the expectations is termed the *self-fulfilling prophecy*. This term was coined by sociologist Robert Merton (1948) to explain such phenomena as "runs" on banks that occurred during the Depression. That is, when unfounded rumors would circulate that a bank couldn't cover its deposits, people would rush to the bank and withdraw their funds, thereby draining the deposits from the bank and making real what was initially untrue.

Figure 6.2 depicts the three steps in a self-fulfilling prophecy. First, the perceiver has an initial impression of someone (the target person). Then the perceiver behaves toward the target person in line with his or her expectations. The third step in the process occurs when the target person adjusts his or her behavior to the perceiver's actions, which confirms the perceiver's hypothesis about the target person. Note that both individuals are unaware that this process is operating. Also note that because perceivers are unaware of their expectations and of the effect they can have on others, they

FIGURE 6.2.

The three steps of the self-fulfilling prophecy. Through a three-step process, your expectations about a person can cause that person to behave in ways that confirm those expectations. First, you form an impression of someone. Second, you behave toward that person in a way that is consistent with your impression. Third, the person exhibits the behavior you encourage, thereby confirming your initial impression. (Adapted from Smith & Mackie, 1995)

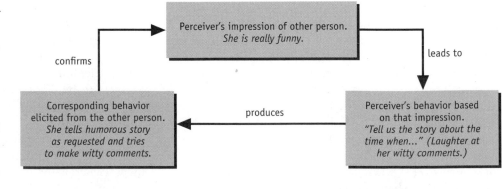

mistakenly attribute the target person's behavior to an internal cause (personal disposition), rather than an external one (the perceiver's behavior/expectations).

The best-known experiments on the self-fulfilling prophecy have been conducted in the classroom setting, looking at the effect of teachers' expectations on students' academic performance (Rosenthal, 1985). In a review of the 400 studies on this question over a period of 30 years, it was reported that teacher expectations significantly influenced student performance in 36% of the 400 experiments. Of course, the self-fulfilling prophecy can also work in other settings.

Thankfully, research also indicates that there are limits on the self-fulfilling prophecy. Two conditions minimize the effects of the perceiver's expectations on a target person's behavior. First, if target persons are aware of another's beliefs and these beliefs contradict their self-views, target persons work hard to change the perceiver's perceptions and are usually successful in doing so (Hilton & Darley, 1985). Second, when target persons are confident about their self-views, they are less likely to be influenced by a perceiver with different perceptions (Swann & Ely, 1984). But when perceivers are confident about their beliefs and target persons are uncertain about their self-views, the self-fulfilling prophecy comes into play.

Cognitive Distortions

Another source of error in person perception comes from distortions in the minds of perceivers. These errors in judgment are most likely to occur when the perceiver is in a hurry, is distracted, or is not motivated to pay careful attention to another person.

CATEGORIZING

People commonly categorize others on the basis of race, gender, age, sexual orientation, and so forth. Individuals perceive those like themselves as being members of their *ingroup* ("us") and those who are dissimilar to be in the *outgroup* ("them"). Such categoriz-

Web Link 6.1

Social Psychology Network
Wesleyan University social psychologist Scott Plous offers a broad collection of more than 4,000 Web links related to all aspects of social and general psychology, including how people understand and influence each other interpersonally.

ing has three important results. First, people usually have less favorable attitudes toward outgroup members than ingroup members (Meindl & Lerner, 1984). Second, individuals usually see outgroup members as being much more similar to each other than they really are, whereas they see members of the ingroup as unique individuals. In other words, people frequently explain the behavior of outgroup members on the basis of the characteristic that sets them apart ("Those Nerdians are all drunks"). By contrast, people attribute the same behavior by an ingroup member to unique personality traits ("Jack's a heavy drinker"). This phenomenon is termed the *outgroup homogeneity effect*.

A third result of categorizing is that it heightens the visibility of outgroup members when there are only a few of them within a larger group. In other words, minority group status in a group makes more salient the quality that distinguishes the person—race, gender, whatever. When people are perceived as being unique or distinctive, they are also seen as having more influence in a group, and their good and bad qualities are given extra weight (Crocker & McGraw, 1984). Such distinctiveness also makes it more likely that stereotypes will be invoked. This explains why many people notice nagging women (but not men), noisy blacks (but not whites), and Jewish names (but not white, Anglo-Saxon Protestant names) among cheating stockbrokers.

STEREOTYPES

Stereotypes **are widely held beliefs that people have certain characteristics because of their membership in a particular group.** For example, many people assume that Jews are shrewd and ambitious and that African

Americans have special athletic and musical abilities. Although a kernel of truth may underlie some stereotypes, it should be readily apparent that not all Jews, African Americans, and so forth behave alike. If you take the time to think about it, you recognize that there is enormous diversity in behavior within any group.

The most prevalent stereotypes in America are those based on gender, age, and ethnicity (Fiske, 1993). Gender stereotypes, although in transition, remain pervasive. For example, in a study of gender stereotypes in 30 countries, males were typically characterized as adventurous, powerful, and independent, while females were characterized as sentimental, submissive, and superstitious (Williams & Best, 1982). Because of their wide-ranging significance, we will focus on gender stereotypes in detail in our chapter on gender roles (Chapter 10).

Stereotypes are also based on physical appearance. In particular, there is plenty of evidence that physically attractive people are believed to possess desirable personality traits. In fact, this perception is so widespread that social psychologists have developed a term for it: the *"what-is-beautiful-is-good"* stereotype (Dion, Berscheid, & Walster, 1972). Specifically, beautiful people are usually viewed as more socially competent, more assertive, better adjusted, and more intellectually competent than those who are less attractive (Eagly et al., 1991). Yet there is little basis in fact for most of these perceptions.

Attractive people do have an advantage in the social arena. For example, they have better social skills, are more popular, are less socially anxious (especially about interactions with the other gender), are less lonely, and are more sexually experienced (Feingold, 1992). However, they are not any different from others on intelligence, personality traits, mental health, or self-esteem (Feingold, 1992b). Thus, attractive people are perceived in a more favorable light than is actually justified (Dion, 1986; Eagly et al., 1991; Feingold, 1992b). Unfortunately, the positive biases toward attractive people also operate in reverse. Thus, unattractive people are unjustifiably seen as less well adjusted and less intellectually competent than others.

Why do stereotypes persist? For one thing, they are functional. Because people are deluged with much more information than they can process, their tendency is to reduce complexity to simplicity. But, as we noted earlier, the tradeoff for simplification is inaccuracy. Stereotypes also endure because of confirmatory biases. Thus, when individuals encounter members of groups that they view with prejudice, they are likely to see what they expect to see (Stephan, 1989). Self-fulfilling prophecy is a third reason stereotypes persist: Beliefs about another person may actually elicit the anticipated behavior and confirm biased expectations.

THE FUNDAMENTAL ATTRIBUTION ERROR

To explain the causes of others' behavior, people invoke personality-based attributions and discount the importance of extenuating circumstances and situational factors. Although this tendency is not universal (Harvey, Town, & Yarkin, 1981), it is strong enough that Lee Ross (1977) called it the *fundamental* attribution error. **The *fundamental attribution error* refers to the tendency to explain other people's behavior as the result of personal, rather than situational, factors.** This bias leads people to leap to conclusions about others' personal qualities.

The fundamental attribution error is different from stereotyping in that inferences are based on actual behavior. Nonetheless, those inferences may still be inaccurate. Because the importance of situational factors is underestimated, individuals may attribute to others motives and traits that they don't actually have. For instance, imagine that you're at your bank and the person in line ahead of you flies into a rage over an error made in his account. You will probably infer that this person is temperamental or quarrelsome—and you may be right. However, this person may be a normally easygoing individual who is late for an appointment, has waited in line for 30 minutes, and already straightened out a similar error by the same bank just last week. Thus, a person's behavior at a given time may or may not be reflective of his or her personality—but observers tend to assume that it is.

Lee Ross

Cultural values seem to promote different attributional errors. You'll recall from our discussion in Chapter 5 that Western societies tend to be *individualistic,* viewing people as autonomous individuals who are responsible for their actions (Matsumoto, 1994). Endorsing beliefs such as "You can do anything you put your mind to" or "You have no one to blame but yourself," Westerners typically explain behavior in terms of people's personality traits and unique abilities. In contrast, members of *collectivist* societies value interdependence and obedience; hence, they tend to assume that one's behavior reflects adherence to group norms. Consistent with this analysis, researchers have found that American subjects explain others' behavior in terms of internal attributions more than Hindu (Miller, 1984) or Japanese subjects do (Weisz, Rothbaum, & Blackburn, 1984). A recent study found that English-language newspapers used more dispositional explanations and Chinese-language newspapers used more situational explanations for the same crimes (Morris & Peng, 1994).

A common example of defensive attribution is the tendency to blame the homeless for their plight.

DEFENSIVE ATTRIBUTION

Observers are especially likely to make internal attributions in trying to explain the calamities and setbacks that befall other people. Examples easily come to mind. When a woman is abused by a boyfriend or husband, people frequently blame the victim by remarking how stupid she is to stay with the man rather than condemning the aggressor for his behavior (Kristiansen & Giulietti, 1990). Similarly, rape victims are often judged to have "asked for it."

Defensive attribution **is a tendency to blame victims for their misfortune, so that one feels less likely to be victimized in a similar way.** Blaming victims for their calamities also helps people maintain their belief that they live in a "just world" where people get what they deserve and deserve what they get (Lerner & Miller, 1978). Acknowledging to oneself that the world is not just—that unfortunate events can happen as a result of chance factors—would mean having to admit the frightening possibility that the catastrophes that happen to others could also happen to oneself. Making defensive attributions allows people to avoid such unnerving thoughts (Salminen, 1992; Thornton, 1984, 1992). Unfortunately, when victims are blamed for their setbacks, people unfairly attribute undesirable traits to them, such as incompetence, foolishness, and laziness.

Key Themes in Person Perception

As you have seen, the process of person perception is a complex one. Nonetheless, we can detect three recurrent themes in this process: efficiency, selectivity, and stability.

EFFICIENCY

In forming impressions of others, people prefer to exert no more effort or time than is necessary. According to Susan Fiske (1993), people are like government bureaucrats, who "only bother to gather information on a 'need to know' basis" (p. 175). After all, you're a busy person with lots of important things to attend to. It boggles the mind to consider what life would be like if you had to take the time to make careful observations and judgments of everyone you meet. Obviously, the human penchant for efficiency has important advantages: People can make judgments quickly and keep things simple. Of course, there is a big disadvantage: Errors can occur in these judgments. Still, on balance, efficiency works pretty well as an operating principle.

SELECTIVITY

There is an old saying that "people see what they expect to see." This commonsense notion that expectations influence perceptions has been confirmed repeatedly by social scientists. In a classic study, Harold Kelley (1950) showed how a person is preceded by his or her reputation. Students in a class at the Massachusetts Institute of Technology (MIT) were told that a new lecturer would be speaking to them that day. Before the instructor arrived, the students were given a short description of him, with one important variation: Half the students were led to expect a "warm" person, while the other half were led to expect a "cold" one (see Figure 6.3). All the participants were exposed to the same 20 minutes of

FIGURE 6.3.
Descriptions of the guest lecturer in Kelley's (1950) study. These two descriptions, provided to two groups of students before the lecturer spoke, differ by only a single word, but that one small difference caused the two groups to form altogether different perceptions of the lecturer.

Mr. Blank is a graduate student in the Department of Economics and Social Science here at M.I.T. He has had three semesters of teaching experience in psychology at another college. This is his first semester teaching Ec. 70. He is 26 years old, a veteran, and married. People who know him consider him to be a rather cold person, industrious, critical, practical, and determined.

Mr. Blank is a graduate student in the Department of Economics and Social Science here at M.I.T. He has had three semesters of teaching experience in psychology at another college. This is his first semester teaching Ec. 70. He is 26 years old, a veteran, and married. People who know him consider him to be a very warm person, industrious, critical, practical, and determined.

Web Link 6.2

Social Cognition Paper Archive and Information Center
Eliot R. Smith at Purdue University maintains a popular site that includes information about papers (abstracts, mostly) and people and provides links to the wider social psychological research community.

lecture and interaction with the new instructor. However, those who were led to expect a warm person rated the instructor as significantly more considerate, sociable, humorous, good-natured, informal, and humane than those who were led to expect a cold person.

Especially if there's any ambiguity in someone's behavior, people are likely to interpret what they see in a way that fits their expectations (E. Jones, 1990). Thus, after dealing with an assertive female customer, a salesman who holds traditional gender stereotypes might characterize the woman as "pushy." By contrast, he might fail to notice the same behavior in a man because he would have mindlessly interpreted it as appropriate male behavior.

STABILITY

Although the evidence is not overwhelming, some studies suggest that first impressions have a powerful influence on perceptions of others (Friedman, 1983; Hodges, 1974). **A *primacy effect* occurs when initial information carries more weight than subsequent information.** First impressions tend to be particularly potent for a couple of reasons. In part, this tendency is caused by the fact that people see what they expect to see. Moreover, as we have already noted, confirmatory biases may lead people to discount later information that contradicts their initial impression. Interestingly, when the initial impression is negative, it may be especially difficult to change (Mellers, Richards, & Birnbaum, 1992). Thus, "getting off on the wrong foot" may be particularly damaging.

Of course, it is possible to override a primacy effect. If you're *actively* looking for change in a person or have compelling evidence that contradicts your initial impression, you can change your opinion. Still, since people usually expect others to stay the same, their initial impressions don't change very often.

In summary, the process of person perception is highly subjective. In forming impressions of others, people are efficient and selective perceivers, and they tend to hold on to their initial views. Although perceptions of others can be erroneous, these errors are quite often harmless. However, there clearly are occasions when these inaccuracies interfere with rewarding social interactions. This is certainly true in the case of prejudice, which we consider next.

The Problem of Prejudice

LEARNING OBJECTIVES

- *Explain how "old-fashioned" and modern discrimination differ.*
- *Describe some of the key determinants of prejudice and explain how they work.*
- *Explain how prejudice can be reduced.*

"Can't we all just get along?" implored Rodney King, a victim of police brutality because of his race. These words echo the sentiments of most Americans. Yet antagonism between groups continues to be a problem, both in this country and internationally—in the Middle East and the former Yugoslavia, for instance. Why is it so hard for members of different groups to get along? In this section, we'll address the problem of prejudice—and the equally important question of how to deal with this enduring social problem.

Let's begin by clarifying a couple of terms that are often confused. ***Prejudice* is a negative attitude toward members of a group; *discrimination* involves behaving differently, usually unfairly, toward the members of a group.** Prejudice and discrimination do tend to go together, but there is no necessary correspondence between the two (see Figure 6.4). For example, a restaurant owner might be prejudiced against Chicanos and yet treat them like anyone else because he needs their business. This is an example of prejudice without discrimination. Although it is probably less common, discrimination without prejudice may also occur. For example, an executive who has favorable attitudes toward blacks may not hire them because his boss would be upset.

FIGURE 6.4.

Prejudice and discrimination. Prejudice and discrimination are highly correlated but they don't necessarily go hand in hand. As the examples in the yellow cells show, there can be prejudice without discrimination and discrimination without prejudice.

Discrimination	Prejudice: Absent	Prejudice: Present
Absent	No relevant behaviors	A restaurant owner who is bigoted against Hispanics treats them fairly because she needs their business
Present	An executive with favorable attitudes toward blacks doesn't hire them because he would get in trouble with his boss	A professor who is hostile toward women grades his female students unfairly

"Old-Fashioned" Versus Modern Discrimination

James Byrd, Jr., a 49-year-old black man, was walking home from a family gathering in the summer of 1998 when he was offered a ride by three white men, one of whom he knew. Shortly thereafter, pieces of Byrd's savagely beaten body were found strewn along a rural road in Texas. He had been beaten, then shackled by his ankles to the back of the truck and dragged to death over 2¹/₂ miles of road. Police say that Byrd was targeted simply because he was black. Thankfully, such incidents are rare these days. Nonetheless, this racially motivated and gruesome murder reminds us that racism still exists in the United States.

Over the past 40 years, prejudice and discrimination against minority groups have diminished. Racial segregation is illegal, and discrimination based on race, ethnicity, gender, and religion is much less common now than it was in the 1950s and 1960s. Thus, the good news is that blatant or "old-fashioned" discrimination against minority groups has declined (but not disappeared, as noted above). The bad news is that a more subtle form of prejudice and discrimination has emerged (Gaertner & Dovidio, 1986; McConahay, 1986). That is, people may privately harbor negative attitudes toward minority groups (including women) but express them only when they feel that such views are justified or that it's safe to do so. This new form of prejudice is termed *modern discrimination* (also called "symbolic racism"). Modern discrimination is also operating when people endorse equality as an abstract principle but oppose concrete programs intended to promote equality on the grounds that discrimination against minority groups no longer exists (Sears, 1987; Swim, et al., 1995). Similar distinctions between blatant and subtle discrimination have been found in European countries as well—for example, in British attitudes toward West Indians and Asians, in French attitudes toward North Africans and Asians, and in German attitudes toward Turks (Pettigrew & Meertens, 1995). While symbolic racists do not wish to return to the days of segregation, they also feel that minority groups should not push too fast for advancement or receive special treatment by the government.

Researchers have found that individuals who endorse modern discrimination ("Blacks are getting too demanding in their push for equal rights") are much more likely to vote against a black political candidate, to oppose school busing, and to favor tax laws that benefit whites at the expense of blacks, when compared to those who do not endorse such views (Kinder & Sears, 1981; Sears & Citrin, 1985). Interestingly, the endorsement of statements such as "I do not like black people" (old-fashioned racism) does *not* reliably predict an individual's political actions (because many people who might personally agree with such a statement are reluctant to publicly endorse it).

Causes of Prejudice

Prejudice is obviously a complex issue and has multiple causes. While we can't thoroughly examine all of the causes of prejudice, we'll review some of the major psychological and social factors that contribute to this vexing problem.

COGNITIVE DISTORTIONS

Much of prejudice is rooted in cognitive processes that kick in automatically. As you have seen, *categorizing* predisposes people to divide the social world into ingroups and outgroups. Perhaps no factor plays a larger role in prejudice than *stereotyping*. Many people fall prey to derogatory stereotypes of various ethnic groups. Although racial stereotypes have declined over the last 50 years, they're not entirely a thing of the past (Dovidio & Gaertner, 1986).

It seems that people are particularly likely to make the *fundamental attribution error* when evaluating targets of prejudice (Hewstone, 1990; Pettigrew, 1979). Thus, when people take note of ethnic neighborhoods dominated by crime and poverty, they blame the personal qualities of the residents for these problems and downplay or ignore situationally based explanations (job discrimination, poor police service, and so on). The old saying, "They should pull themselves up by their own bootstraps" is a blanket dismissal of how situational factors may make it especially difficult for minorities to achieve upward mobility.

Defensive attributions, in which people unfairly blame victims of adversity to reassure themselves that they are unlikely to experience a similar fate, can also contribute to prejudice. For example, individuals who claim that people who contract AIDS deserve it or that rape victims "asked for it" may be trying to reassure themselves that they won't suffer a similar fate.

Unfortunately, the automatic and selective nature of social thinking means that people usually see what they expect to see when they encounter minorities they view with prejudice.

THE AUTHORITARIAN PERSONALITY

In some of the earliest research on prejudice, Adorno and his colleagues (1950) identified a personality type characterized by prejudice toward any group perceived to be different from oneself. Individuals of this type are found to hold conventional views, to be submissive to those in authority, and to have punitive attitudes toward minorities and toward those who violate conventional standards of behavior. Adorno termed this cluster of characteristics the *authoritarian personality*. Recent research has found that prejudice toward a variety of groups—African Americans, ethnic minorities, women, homosexuals—is often found in the same person (Bierly, 1985; Snyder & Ickes, 1985). According to Bob Altemeyer (1988a, 1988b), a contemporary researcher on the authoritarian personality, such individuals are unduly threatened by social change—a fear picked up from their parents, who believe that "the world is a dangerous and hostile place" (1988b, p. 38). He also notes that such attitudes are reinforced by the mass media's emphasis on crime and violence.

COMPETITION BETWEEN GROUPS

Back in 1954, Muzafer Sherif and his colleagues conducted a now-classic study at Robbers' Cave State Park in Oklahoma to look at competition and prejudice (Sherif et al., 1961). In this study, 11-year-old white boys were invited, with parental permission, to attend a three-week summer camp. What the boys didn't know was that they were participants in an experiment. The boys were randomly assigned to one of two groups; at camp, they went directly to their assigned campsites and had no knowledge of the other group's existence. During the first week, the boys got to know the other members of their own group through typical camp activities (hiking, swimming, camping out); each group also chose a name (the Rattlers and the Eagles).

In the second week, the Rattlers and Eagles were introduced to each other through intergroup competitions. Events included a football game, a treasure hunt, and a tug of war, with medals, trophies, and other impressive prizes for the winning team. Almost immediately after competitive games were introduced, hostile feelings (prejudice) erupted between the two groups and then quickly escalated to highly aggressive behavior: Cabins were ransacked, group flags were burned, and food fights broke out in the mess hall.

This experimental demonstration of the effects of competition on prejudice is often mirrored in the real world. The lack of jobs or other important resources fosters competition between social groups and breeds fear of losing status. Interestingly, people seem more concerned about threats to the status of their ingroup than to themselves, personally (Bobo, 1988). If individuals perceive their ingroup to be threatened, they often look for scapegoats in outgroups. For example, it has been consistently documented that the strongest prejudice against blacks is held by whites of modest economic means (Pettigrew, 1978). Similarly, disputes over territory are a key factor in the Israeli-Palestinian conflict. Thus, there is ample evidence that conflict over scarce resources can prejudice individuals toward outgroup members.

THREATS TO SOCIAL IDENTITY

Although group membership provides individuals with a sense of identity and pride, it can also foster prejudice and discrimination. To get a better understanding of this idea, we turn to *social identity theory*, developed by Henri Tajfel (1982) and John Turner (1987). According to this theory, self-esteem is partly determined by one's *social identity* or collective self, which is tied to one's group memberships (nationality, gender, major, occupation, and so forth) (Luhtanen & Crocker, 1992). Whereas your personal self-esteem is elevated by individual accomplishments (you got an A on a government exam), your collective self-esteem is boosted when an ingroup is successful (your team wins the intramural softball award, your country wins a war). Likewise, your self-esteem can be threatened on both the personal level (you didn't get called for that job interview) and the collective level (your football team loses the championship game, your country is defeated in a war).

Threats to both personal and social identity motivate individuals to restore self-esteem, but threats to social identity are more likely to provoke responses that foster prejudice and discrimination (Crocker & Luhtanen, 1990). When collective self-esteem is threatened, individuals react in two key ways to bolster it. The most common response is to show *ingroup favoritism*—for example, tapping an ingroup member for a job opening or rating the performance of an ingroup member higher than that of an outgroup member (Branscombe et al., 1993). Another way to deal with threats to social identity is to engage in *outgroup derogation*—to "trash" outgroups that are perceived as threatening. As you might suspect, this latter tactic is more often used by individuals who identify especially strongly with an ingroup (Branscome & Wann, 1994). Figure 6.5 depicts the various elements of social identity theory.

Reducing Prejudice

For decades psychologists have been looking for ways to reduce prejudice. Such a complicated problem requires solutions on a number of levels. Let's look at a few interventions that have been shown to work.

COGNITIVE STRATEGIES

Because stereotypes are part of the social air that Americans breathe, practically everyone learns stereotypes about various groups. This means that stereotyped thinking about others becomes a mindless habit—even for individuals who have been taught to be tolerant of those who are different (Devine, 1989).

While it's true that stereotypes kick in automatically and unintentionally, individuals *can* override

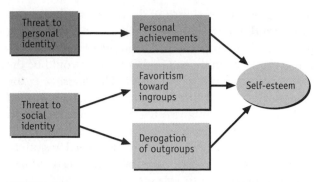

FIGURE 6.5.

Social identity theory. According to Tajfel and Turner, individuals have both a personal identity (based on a unique sense of self) and a social identity (based on group memberships). When social identity is threatened, people are motivated to restore self-esteem either by showing favoritism to ingroup members or by derogating members of outgroups. These tactics contribute to prejudice and discrimination. (Adapted from Brehm & Kassin, 1993)

them—with some cognitive effort. Thus, if you meet someone who speaks with an accent, your initial, automatic reaction might be negative. However, if you believe that prejudice is wrong and if you are aware that you are stereotyping, you can intentionally inhibit such thoughts. According to Patricia Devine's (1989) model of prejudice reduction, this process requires an intentional shift from *automatic processing* to *controlled processing* (or from mindlessness to mindfulness, in Langer's terms).

Research supports the idea that controlled, mindful thinking can actually reduce stereotyping and prejudice. In one study, children who were shown slides of handicapped individuals and were asked questions that required them to think carefully about the disabled individuals showed less prejudice and more willingness to play with a handicapped peer than did children who saw the same slides but who were asked to make only mindless responses to the slides (Langer, Bashner, & Chanowitz, 1985). Thus, you can reduce prejudice by paying careful attention to what and how you think.

INTERGROUP CONTACT

Recall now the Robbers' Cave study. When we left them, the Rattlers and Eagles were busy with food fights and flag burning. Understandably, the experimenters were eager to restore peace. First, they tried speaking with each group, talking up the other group's good points and minimizing their differences. They also made the Eagles and the Rattlers sit together at meals and "fun" events (movies). Unfortunately, these tactics fell flat.

Next, the experimenters designed intergroup activities based on the principle of **superordinate goals** (also termed **cooperative interdependence**), or requiring **two groups to work together to achieve a mutual goal.** For example, each boy had to contribute in some

way (building a fire, preparing the food) on a cookout so that all could eat. After the boys had participated in a variety of such activities, the hostility between the two groups was much reduced. In fact, at the end of the three-week camping period, the Eagles and the Rattlers voted to ride on the same bus back home.

Researchers have identified four necessary ingredients in the recipe for reducing intergroup hostility (Brewer & Brown, 1997). First, groups must work together for a common goal (merely bringing hostile groups into contact is not an effective way to reduce intergroup antagonism and may actually exacerbate it). Second, there must be *successful outcomes* to cooperative efforts (if groups fail at a cooperative task, they are likely to blame each other for the failure). Third, group members must have the opportunity to establish *meaningful connections* with one another and not merely go through the motions of interacting. The fourth factor of *equal status contact* requires bringing together members of different groups in ways that ensure that everyone has equal status.

The "jigsaw classroom" is an excellent example of how these principles can reduce prejudice in schoolchildren (Aronson et al., 1978). In this intervention, six children are first assigned to an "expert group" in which they help each other learn specialized information prepared by the teacher about the topic under study. Thus, each child becomes an "expert" on a subtopic. Then the children are assigned to ethnically mixed groups of six where they teach each other their school lessons (cooperative interdependence). This arrangement puts all children on an equal footing (equal status contact) and reduces competition for the teacher's attention and grades (scarce resources).

Children taught in a jigsaw classroom learn as much as peers taught in a traditional classroom setting. In addition, "jigsaw" children get an important bonus: Prejudice is replaced with positive feelings for ethnically different children, and the self-esteem of minority kids gets a big boost.

To conclude, although prejudice remains a complex and distressing social problem, there are some effective strategies to combat it.

The Power of Persuasion

LEARNING OBJECTIVES

● Cite the key elements in the persuasion process.

● Describe several source factors that influence persuasion.

● Discuss the evidence on one-sided versus two-sided messages, and the value of arousing fear or positive feelings in persuasion.

- Describe several receiver factors that influence persuasion.
- Explain how the two cognitive routes to persuasion operate.
- Discuss the effectiveness of subliminal persuasion.

Every day you are bombarded by efforts to alter your attitudes through persuasion. You may not even be out of bed before you start hearing radio advertisements that are meant to persuade you to buy specific mouthwashes, computers, and tennis shoes. When you open your newspaper, you find statements from numerous government officials, all of which have been carefully crafted to shape your opinions. On your way to school, you see billboards showing attractive models draped over automobiles and bottles of scotch in the hopes that they'll affect your feelings about these products. Arriving on campus, you encounter a group passing out leaflets that urge you to vote for their political candidate. In class, your economics professor champions the wisdom of the free market in international trade. "Does it ever let up?" you wonder.

When it comes to persuasion, the answer is "no." As Anthony Pratkanis and Elliot Aronson (1998) put it, we live in "the age of propaganda" (see Recommended Reading on this page). In light of this reality, let's examine some of the factors that determine whether persuasion works.

Persuasion involves the communication of arguments and information intended to change another person's attitudes. What are attitudes? For the purposes of our discussion, we'll define **attitudes as beliefs and feelings about people, objects, and ideas.** Let's look more closely at two of the terms in this definition. We use the term *beliefs* to mean thoughts and judgments about people, objects, and ideas. For example, someone may *believe* that equal pay for equal work is a fair policy or that capital punishment is not an effective deterrent to crime. The "feeling" component of attitudes refers to the positivity and negativity of one's feelings about an issue as well as how strongly one feels about it. For example, you may *strongly favor* equal pay for equal work, but only *mildly disagree* with the idea that capital punishment reduces the crime rate.

The Elements of the Persuasion Process

Have you ever noticed how many commercials feature physically attractive actors and upbeat music? In this section, we'll tell you why that is, as well as answer the more general question of what's involved in a successful persuasion attempt.

The process of persuasion includes four basic elements (see Figure 6.6). The **source is the person who** sends a communication, and the *receiver* is the person to whom the message is sent. Thus, if you watched a presidential address on TV, the president would be the source. You and millions of other viewers would be the receivers in this persuasive effort. **The *message* is the information transmitted by the source. The *channel* is the medium through which the message is sent.** In the case of the president's address, the message is the content of the speech, and the medium is television. In examining communication channels, investigators have often compared face-to-face interaction against appeals sent via mass media such as television and radio. Although the research on communication channels is interesting, we'll confine our discussion to source, message, and receiver variables.

Recommended Reading

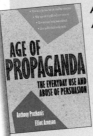

Age of Propaganda: The Everyday Use and Abuse of Persuasion by Anthony R. Pratkanis and Elliot Aronson (W. H. Freeman, 1998)

The two social psychologists who wrote this book did so out of their concern that the increased use of propaganda in contemporary American society is having harmful consequences. Propaganda discourages careful reasoning and scrutiny, and its use by contemporary political leaders and the advertising industry is seen as particularly problematic in a democracy. For a democratic form of government to survive in an age of propaganda, according to Pratkanis and Aronson, it must have "communicators who know how to present their message clearly and fairly, coupled with an informed electorate who knows the difference between a fair presentation and a con job" (p. xiii). The authors have written the book to help Americans understand how their attitudes are being manipulated. Using an engaging writing style, they do an excellent job of applying research evidence to historical events (Nazi Germany, the Vietnam War, Iran-Contra, and Watergate) and contemporary situations (televangelism, political campaigns, and commercials).

We define factoids as an assertion of fact that is not backed up by evidence, usually because the fact is false or because evidence in support of the assertion cannot be obtained. . . . In our work places and neighborhoods, they are known as rumors or gossip. In courts of law, factoids are called hearsay and inadmissible evidence. In the mass media, they are called libel, slander, innuendo, and the reporting of currently circulating rumors, gossip, and hearsay as news. . . .

But do factoids really influence our judgments and beliefs? After all, some of them are often just plain unbelievable. . . . It appears that simply questioning a [political] candidate's connection with unseemly activities can be enough to damage that candidate's public image. What's more, the source of the innuendo made little difference: The candidates were still rated negatively even if the source of headline was a newspaper lacking in credibility (the National Enquirer *or the* Midnight Globe *as opposed to the* New York Times *or the* Washington Post*). Negative political advertising and slur campaigns often do indeed pay off. [pp. 71–73]*

FIGURE 6.6.

Overview of the persuasion process. The process of persuasion essentially boils down to *who* (the source) communicates *what* (the message) *by what means* (the channel) *to whom* (the receiver). Thus, there are four sets of variables that influence the process of persuasion: source, message, channel, and receiver factors. The diagram lists some of the more important factors in each category (including some that are not discussed in the text due to space limitations). (Based on Lippa, 1994)

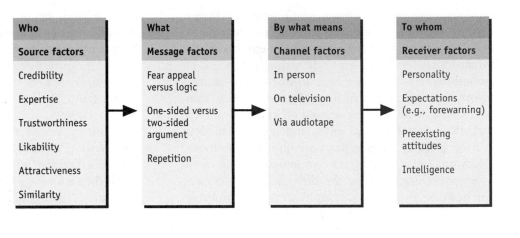

Who	What	By what means	To whom
Source factors	**Message factors**	**Channel factors**	**Receiver factors**
Credibility	Fear appeal versus logic	In person	Personality
Expertise	One-sided versus two-sided argument	On television	Expectations (e.g., forewarning)
Trustworthiness		Via audiotape	Preexisting attitudes
Likability	Repetition		Intelligence
Attractiveness			
Similarity			

SOURCE FACTORS

Persuasion tends to be more successful when the source has high *credibility* (O'Keefe, 1990). What makes a person credible? Either *expertise* or trustworthiness. People try to convey their expertise by mentioning their degrees, their training, and their experience or by showing an impressive grasp of the issue at hand (Wood & Kallgren, 1988).

Expertise is a plus, but *trustworthiness* is even more important (McGinnies & Ward, 1980). Whom would you believe if you were told that your state needs to reduce corporate taxes to stimulate its economy—the president of a huge corporation in your state or an economics professor from out of state? Probably the latter. Trustworthiness is undermined when a source, such as the corporation president, appears to have something to gain. In contrast, trustworthiness is enhanced when people appear to argue against their own interests (Hunt, Smith, & Kernan, 1985). This effect explains why salespeople often make remarks like "Frankly, my snowblower isn't the best, and they have a better brand down the street if you're willing to spend a bit more . . ."

Likability also increases the effectiveness of a persuasive source (Roskos-Ewoldson & Fazio, 1992). Likability depends on a host of factors (see Chapter 8). A key consideration is a person's physical attractiveness. The favorable effect of physical attractiveness on persuasion was apparent in a study by Chaiken (1979), in which students were asked to obtain signatures for a petition. Chaiken found that the more attractive students were more successful. Other studies have also shown the effect of physical attractiveness on persuasion (Kahle & Homer, 1985; Pallak, 1983). People also respond better to sources who are *similar* to them in ways that are relevant to the issue at hand (Mackie, Worth, & Asuncion, 1990).

The importance of source variables can be seen in advertising. Many companies spend a fortune to obtain an ideal spokesperson, like Bill Cosby, who combines trustworthiness, expertise (a doctorate in education), likability, and a knack for connecting with the average person. Companies quickly abandon spokespersons whose likability declines. For example, Hertz dropped O. J. Simpson as their spokesperson when he became a controversial figure. And the *Ellen* TV show had difficulty getting sponsors after the "coming out" episode. Thus, source variables are extremely important factors in persuasion.

MESSAGE FACTORS

Imagine that you are going to give a speech to a local community group advocating a reduction in state taxes on corporations. In preparing your speech, you will probably wrestle with questions about how to structure your message. Should you look at both sides of the issue or just present your own side? Should you deliver a low-key, logical speech, or should you try to strike fear in the hearts of your listeners? Let's look at these message factors.

To begin with, you're aware that there are two sides to the taxation issue. On the one hand, you are convinced that lower corporate taxes will bring new companies and factories to your state, stimulate economic growth, and create jobs. On the other hand, you realize the reduced tax revenues may gradually hurt the quality of education and roads in your state. Nevertheless, you believe that the benefits of a lower tax rate will outweigh the costs. Should you present a *one-sided argument* that ignores the possible problems of education and road quality? Or should you present a *two-sided argument* that acknowledges concern about education and road quality and then downplays the magnitude of these problems?

In general, two-sided arguments seem to be more effective (O'Keefe, 1990). Just mentioning that there are two sides to an issue can increase your credibility with an audience (Jones & Brehm, 1970). One-sided messages work only when your audience is uneducated about the issue or when they are already very favorably disposed to your point of view.

Persuasive messages frequently attempt to arouse fear. Opponents of nuclear power scare us with visions of meltdowns. Antismoking campaigns emphasize the threat of cancer. Deodorant ads highlight the risk of embarrassment. Does *fear arousal* work? Yes—studies involving a wide range of issues (nuclear policy, auto safety, and dental hygiene among others) have shown that the arousal of fear often increases persuasion (Perloff, 1993). However, there are limiting conditions (Johnson, 1991). Fear appeals are most likely to work when your listeners view the dire consequences that you describe as exceedingly unpleasant, fairly probable if they don't take your advice, and avoidable if they do. If you induce a high level of fear in your audience without providing a manageable solution to the problem (such as a sure-fire stop-smoking or weight-loss program), you may make your audience defensive, causing them to tune you out.

Generating *positive feelings* is also an effective way to persuade people. Familiar examples of such tactics include the use of music in TV commercials, the practice of wining and dining prospective customers, and the ploy of offering small gifts (key chains, pencils, etc.). Recent research has shown that producing positive feelings in order to win people over can be effective—provided they don't care too much about the issue. If people do care about the topic, it takes more than good feelings to move them. For example, one study showed that the use of music in TV commercials was effective in persuading viewers, but only when the message concerned a trivial topic (Park & Young, 1986).

RECEIVER FACTORS

What about the receiver of the persuasive message—are some people easier to persuade than others? Undoubtedly, but the personality traits that account for these differences interact with other considerations in complicated ways. Transient factors, such as forewarning the receiver about a persuasive effort and a receiver's initial position on an issue, seem to be more influential than a receiver's personality. When you shop for a new TV, you expect salespeople to work at persuading you. To some extent this *forewarning* reduces the impact of their arguments (Petty & Cacioppo, 1979; Pfau et al., 1990). Thus, there is some truth to the old saying, "To be forewarned is to be forearmed."

Receivers are also harder to persuade when they encounter a position that is incompatible with their existing beliefs. In general, people display a *disconfirmation* bias in evaluating such arguments (Edwards & Smith, 1996). Attitudes that are personally important to a receiver are also very hard to change (Zuwerink & Devine, 1996).

The effect of a persuasion attempt also depends on the discrepancy between a *receiver's initial position* on

an issue and the position advocated by the source. Persuasion tends to work best when there is a moderate discrepancy between the two. Why? According to *social judgment theory*, people are usually willing to consider alternative views on an issue if the views aren't too different from their own (Sherif & Hovland, 1961; Upshaw, 1969). This range of potentially acceptable positions on an issue is referred to as the *latitude of acceptance*. Persuasive messages that fall outside a receiver's latitude of acceptance usually fall on deaf ears. When a message falls within a receiver's latitude of acceptance, successful persuasion is much more likely (Rajecki, 1990).

Within the latitude of acceptance, however, a *larger* discrepancy between the receiver's initial position and the position advocated should produce greater attitude change than a smaller discrepancy. The reason is that people often "meet partway" to resolve disagreement. Figure 6.7 shows how this theory could apply to an audience member who heard your presentation advocating reduced corporate taxation.

The Whys of Persuasion

In the previous section, we looked at a number of effective techniques that are used to change attitudes. But *why* do people change their attitudes? What underlying cognitive processes actually cause a juror to believe that a defendant is guilty or a voter to believe that one candidate is better than another? Thanks to the work of Richard Petty and John Cacioppo (1986), psychologists have a much better understanding of this issue.

According to the **elaboration likelihood model, an individual's thoughts about a persuasive message (rather than the message itself) determine whether attitude change will occur** (Petty & Cacioppo, 1986).

FIGURE 6.7

Latitude of acceptance and attitude change. A, B, and C are positions on the tax rate that one might advocate. A and B both fall within the receiver's latitude of acceptance, but position B should produce a larger attitude shift. Position C is outside the receiver's latitude of acceptance and should fall on deaf ears.

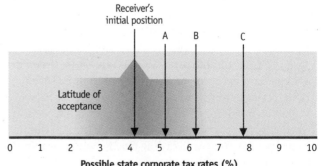

As we have noted before, people often make quick, sloppy decisions (automatic processing, mindlessness, snap judgments), whereas at other times they process information carefully (controlled processing, mindfulness, systematic judgments). These processes also operate in persuasion.

When people are distracted, tired, or uninterested in a persuasive message, they fail to key in on the main points of a message. They process information, but not carefully. Surprisingly, even when people do not carefully evaluate a message, attitude change can occur (Petty & Cacioppo, 1990). What happens is that the receiver is persuaded by cues that are peripheral to the message—hence the term the *peripheral route* (see Figure 6.8). Just because you're not mindfully analyzing a TV commercial for a new fruit drink doesn't mean that you're totally tuned out. You may not be paying attention to the substance of the commercial, but you are aware of superficial aspects of the ad—you like the music, the source is attractive, your favorite basketball player is pitching the product, and so forth.

Although persuasion usually occurs via the peripheral route, there is another route to attitude change—the *central route* (Figure 6.8). In this case, receivers process persuasive messages carefully, by thinking about the logic and merits of the pertinent (or central) arguments. In other words, the receiver cognitively *elaborates* on the persuasive message—hence, the name of the model. If people have a favorable reaction to their thoughtful evaluation of a message, positive attitude change occurs; an unfavorable evaluation results in negative attitude change.

For the central route to override the peripheral route, there are two requirements. First, receivers must be *motivated* to process the persuasive message carefully. They must be interested in the issue, find it personally relevant, and have time and energy to think carefully about it. Second, receivers must also be *able to understand* the message—that is, the message must be comprehensible, and individuals must be capable of understanding it. If people are distracted, are tired, or find a message uninteresting or irrelevant, they are obviously not going to pay careful attention to it, and superficial cues will become salient.

The two routes to persuasion are not equally effective. Attitudes formed via the central route are longer

Political candidates use music, flags, and slogans to persuade via the peripheral route; when they present their views on an issue, they are going for the central route.

lasting and more resistant to challenge than those formed via the peripheral route. They are also better predictors of a person's behavior (Petty, Priester, & Wegener, 1994).

Subliminal Persuasion

People spend millions of dollars annually on the purchase of tapes that purport to help them relax, lose weight, and improve their sex life and self-esteem by listening to subliminal messages embedded in soft music, nature sounds, and the like. **Subliminal persuasion refers to persuasion through messages that are presented below the level of conscious awareness.** Does subliminal persuasion really work? Let's look at the evidence.

Stimuli (a word, an object, a face) that are presented below conscious awareness (for mere milliseconds) *are* rated more favorably than those to which subjects have not been exposed (Bornstein & D'Agostino, 1992). On the other hand, the effect of subliminal messages seems to be limited. Several researchers in this area state quite strongly that subliminal advertising is simply ineffective (Merikle & Skanes, 1992; Moore, 1982).

Subliminal self-help tapes have also been shown to be ineffective. In one study, subjects listened for five weeks to a music tape that contained a subliminal message designed either to improve memory or to raise

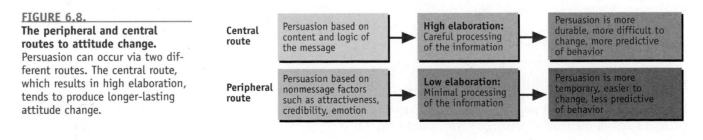

<u>FIGURE 6.8.</u>
The peripheral and central routes to attitude change. Persuasion can occur via two different routes. The central route, which results in high elaboration, tends to produce longer-lasting attitude change.

| Central route | Persuasion based on content and logic of the message | High elaboration: Careful processing of the information | Persuasion is more durable, more difficult to change, more predictive of behavior |
| Peripheral route | Persuasion based on nonmessage factors such as attractiveness, credibility, emotion | Low elaboration: Minimal processing of the information | Persuasion is more temporary, easier to change, less predictive of behavior |

self-esteem (Greenwald et al., 1991). But, there was a twist: Half of the subjects in each condition received a correctly labeled tape (memory tape with memory label, self-esteem tape with self-esteem label), but half received an incorrectly labeled tape (self-esteem tape/memory label, memory tape/self-esteem label).

According to the results, subjects showed no actual improvement (objective scores) in memory or self-esteem, although all subjects *believed* that they had improved. More specifically and importantly, subjects' perceptions of their improvement were based on the tape label, not the message! In other words, subjects' perceptions of reality were determined by their expectations (a case of confirmation bias). Thus, this study, like others, found that subliminal persuasion is basically ineffective.

Although we can't do anything to stem the tide of persuasive messages bombarding you every day, we hope we've helped you to be a more vigilant and informed recipient of persuasion attempts. Of course, persuasion is not the *only* method through which people try to influence you, as you'll see in the next section.

The Power of Social Pressure

LEARNING OBJECTIVES

- *Summarize what Asch discovered about conformity.*
- *Discuss how individuals can cope with conformity pressures.*
- *Describe the determinants of obedience to authority.*
- *Cite some points to keep in mind for resisting inappropriate demands of authority figures.*
- *Explain the roles of persuasion and social influence in the tragedies of Jonestown, Waco, and Heaven's Gate.*
- *Describe the ways in which culture influences responses to social pressure.*

In the previous section, we showed you how others attempt to change your *attitudes.* Now, you'll see how others attempt to change your *behavior*—by trying to get you to agree to their requests and demands.

Conformity and Compliance Pressures

If you extol the talents of popular singer Ricky Martin or keep a well-manicured lawn, are you exhibiting conformity? According to social psychologists, it depends on whether your behavior is freely chosen or the result of group pressure. **Conformity occurs when people yield to real or imagined social pressure.** For example, if you like Ricky Martin because you genuinely enjoy his music, that's not conformity. However, if you like his because it's "hip" and your friends would question your taste if you didn't, then you're conforming. Similarly, if you maintain a well-groomed lawn only to avoid complaints from your neighbors, you're yielding to social pressure.

THE DYNAMICS OF CONFORMITY

To see how psychologists study conformity and what they know about the topic, let's re-create one of the classic experiments on conformity devised by Solomon Asch (1955). The participants are male undergraduates recruited for a study of visual perception. A group of seven participants are shown a large card with a vertical line on it and asked to indicate which of three lines on a second card matches the original "standard line" in length (see Figure 6.9). All seven participants are given a turn at the task, and each announces his choice to the group. The subject in the sixth chair doesn't know it, but everyone else in the group is an accomplice of the experimenter.

The accomplices give accurate responses on the first two trials. On the third trial, line 2 clearly is the correct response, but the first five participants all say that line 3 matches the standard line. The genuine subject can't believe his ears. Over the course of the experiment, the accomplices all give the same incorrect response on 12 out of 18 trials. Asch wanted to see how the subject would respond in these situations. The line judgments are easy and unambiguous. Working alone, people achieve better than 95% accuracy in matching the lines. So, if the subject consistently agrees with the accomplices, he isn't making honest mistakes—he is conforming. Will the subject stick to his guns or will he go along with the group? Averaging across 50 participants, Asch (1955) found that the young men

FIGURE 6.9.

Stimuli used in Asch's conformity studies.
Subjects were asked to match a standard line (top) with one of three other lines displayed on another card (bottom). The task was easy—until experimental accomplices started responding with obviously incorrect answers, creating a situation in which Asch evaluated subjects' conformity. (Adapted from Asch, 1955)

conformed on 37% of the trials. The participants varied considerably in their tendency to conform, however. Out of the 50 participants, 26% never caved in to the group, while 28% conformed on more than half the trials. Similar levels of conformity were obtained in a replication of Asch's work some 30 years later (Larsen, 1990).

In subsequent studies, Asch (1956) determined that group size and group unanimity are key determinants of conformity. To examine group size, Asch repeated his procedure with groups that included 1 to 15 accomplices. Little conformity was seen when a subject was pitted against just one accomplice. Conformity increased rapidly as group size went from 2 to 4, peaked at a group size of 7, and then leveled off (see Figure 6.10). Thus, Asch concluded that as opposition increases, conformity increases—up to a point. Subsequent research has confirmed the importance of unanimity in fostering conformity (Nemeth & Chiles, 1988).

Asch found that group size made little difference if just one accomplice "broke" with the others, wrecking their unanimous agreement. The presence of another dissenter lowered conformity to about one-quarter of its peak, even when the dissenter made inaccurate judgments that happened to conflict with the majority view. Apparently, the participants just needed to hear someone else question the accuracy of the group's perplexing responses.

CONFORMITY VERSUS COMPLIANCE

At first, Asch wasn't sure whether conforming participants were really changing their beliefs in response to social pressure or just pretending to change them. A study that included a condition in which participants made their responses anonymously, instead of publicly, settled the question. Conformity declined dramatically when participants recorded their responses privately. Thus, it seems that participants were not really changing their beliefs (Deutsch & Gerard, 1955). Based on this evidence, theorists concluded that Asch's experiments evoked a particular type of conformity, called compliance. **Compliance occurs when people yield to social pressure in their public behavior, even though their private beliefs have not changed.**

Compliance often occurs because people are afraid of being criticized or rejected. For example, around the time of the Supreme Court decision in 1954 that outlawed segregated schools, many ministers in Little Rock, Arkansas, favored integration. However, while they would voice their opinions privately, they did not make public proclamations to this effect because they feared that they would lose members and contributions (Campbell & Pettigrew, 1959).

In the Asch studies, compliance resulted from subtle, implied pressure. However, compliance frequently occurs in response to explicit rules, requests, and com-

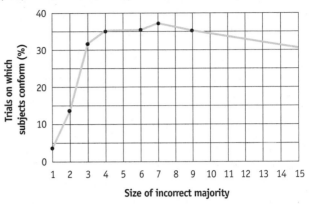

FIGURE 6.10.

Conformity and group size. This graph shows the percentage of trials on which subjects conformed as a function of the number of individuals with an opposing view. Asch found that conformity became more frequent as the number in opposition increased, up to about seven persons, and then leveled off. (Adapted from Asch, 1955)

mands. For example, if you agree to wear formal clothes to a fancy restaurant that requires formal attire, even though you scorn such rules, you're displaying compliance. Similarly, if you reluctantly follow a supervisor's suggestions at work even when you think that the ideas are lousy, you're complying with a superior's wishes.

RESISTING CONFORMITY PRESSURES

Research confirms what every teenager knows—namely, that conformity to peer group norms is an important key to popularity (Brown, Lohr, & McClenahan, 1986). When people yield to conformity pressures, it is often on relatively trivial matters, such as dressing up to go to a nice restaurant. In these cases, conformity and compliance to social norms help minimize the confusion and anxiety people experience when they find themselves in unfamiliar situations. However, when individuals feel pressured to conform to antisocial norms, tragic consequences can sometimes result. Familiar examples of the negative effects of "going along with the crowd" include drinking more than one knows one should because others say, "C'mon, have just one more" and driving at someone's urging when one is under the influence of alcohol or drugs. Other instances include refusing to socialize with someone simply because the person isn't liked by one's social group and failing to come to another's defense when it might make one unpopular. As you might expect, individuals who feel insecure about their status in a social group are more likely to comply when peers put down members of outgroups, when compared to those who feel secure about their status (Noel, Wann, & Branscombe, 1995).

Here are some things to keep in mind to help you resist conformity pressures. First, make an effort to pay more attention to the social forces operating on you. In other words, try to become *mindful* (as opposed to mindless) about the social pressures in your life and their possible implications for you and others. Second, if you find yourself in a situation where others are pressuring you to do something you would rather not do, try to identify someone in the group whose views match yours. (Recall that just one dissenter in Asch's groups significantly reduced conformity pressures.) And, if you know in advance that you're heading into this kind of situation, consider inviting a friend with similar views to go along.

Pressure from Authority Figures

Obedience **is a form of compliance that occurs when people follow direct commands, usually from someone in a position of authority.** In itself, obedience isn't good or bad. To get at that important issue, we need to consider what one is being asked to do. For example, if the fire alarm goes off in your classroom and your instructor "orders" you to leave, obedience is a good idea. On the other hand, if your boss asks you to engage in an illegal act or to do something that goes against your conscience, *disobedience* is probably in order. The consequences of obedience can be serious, so it's important to know how it operates.

THE DYNAMICS OF OBEDIENCE

Like many other people after World War II, social psychologist Stanley Milgram was troubled by how readily the citizens of Germany had followed the orders of dictator Adolf Hitler, even when the orders required morally repugnant actions, such as the slaughter of millions of Jews. Thus, Milgram, who had worked with Solomon Asch, set out to design a standard laboratory procedure for the study of obedience, much like Asch's procedure for studying conformity.

Stanley Milgram

Milgram's (1963) participants were a diverse collection of 40 men from the local community who volunteered for a study on the effects of punishment on learning. When they arrived at the lab, they drew slips of paper from a hat to get their assignments. The drawing was rigged so that the subject always became the "teacher" and an experimental accomplice (a likable 47-year-old accountant) became the "learner."

The teacher watched while the learner was strapped into a chair and as electrodes were attached to his arms (to be used to deliver shocks whenever he made a mistake on the task). The subject was then taken to an adjoining room that housed the shock gen-

erator that he would control in his role as the teacher. Although the apparatus looked and sounded realistic, it was a fake, and the learner was never shocked. The experimenter played the role of the authority figure who told the teacher what to do and who answered any questions that arose.

The experiment was designed such that the learner would make many mistakes, and the teacher was instructed to increase the shock level after each wrong answer. At 300 volts, the learner began to pound on the wall between the two rooms in protest and soon stopped responding to the teacher's questions. From this point forward, participants frequently turned to the experimenter for guidance. Whenever they did so, the experimenter (authority figure) firmly stated that the teacher should continue to give stronger and stronger shocks to the now-silent learner. The dependent variable was the maximum shock the subject was willing to administer before refusing to cooperate.

As Figure 6.11 shows, an astounding 65% of the subjects administered all 30 levels of shock. Although they tended to obey the experimenter, many participants voiced and displayed considerable distress about harming the learner. They groaned, bit their lips, stuttered, trembled, and broke into a sweat—but they continued administering the shocks. Based on these findings, Milgram concluded that obedience to authority was even more common than he or others had anticipated.

According to Milgram, a number of factors produced the obedient behavior. First, the demands on the participants (shocking the learner) *escalated gradually* so that very strong shocks were demanded only after the participant was well into the experiment. Second, when participants asked the authority figure who was responsible if anything happened to the learner, the authority figure always stated that he was ultimately responsible. (One would expect less obedience if the participants believed themselves to be responsible.) Third, subjects experienced a shift in perspective, not evaluating their actions according to their harmful effects on the victim but on how well they were living up to the expectations of the authority figure. Taken together, these findings suggest that actions are determined not so much by the *kind of person* one is as by the *kind of situation* one is in. Applying this insight to Nazi war crimes and other atrocities, Milgram made a chilling assertion: Inhuman and evil visions may originate in the disturbed mind of an authority figure like Hitler, but it is only through the obedient actions of normal people that such ideas can be turned into frightening reality.

After his initial demonstration, Milgram (1974) tried about 20 variations on his experimental procedure, looking for factors that influenced participants'

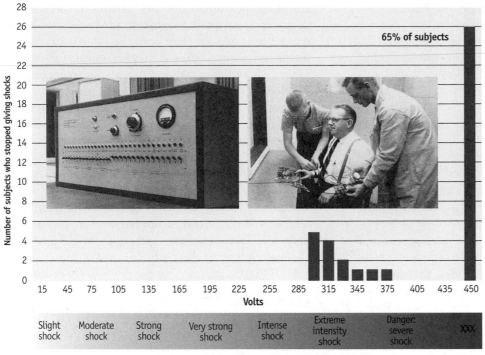

The graph shows:
- Y-axis: Number of subjects who stopped giving shocks (0 to 28)
- X-axis: Volts (15, 45, 75, 105, 135, 165, 195, 225, 255, 285, 315, 345, 375, 405, 435, 450)
- Level of shock (as labeled on Milgram's shock machine): Slight shock, Moderate shock, Strong shock, Very strong shock, Intense shock, Extreme intensity shock, Danger: severe shock, XXX

65% of subjects

FIGURE 6.11.

Milgram's (1963) experiment on obedience. The photos show the fake shock generator and the "learner" being connected to the shock generator during an experimental session. The results of the study are summarized in the bar graph. The vast majority of subjects (65%) delivered the entire series of shocks to the learner.

obedience. For instance, he studied female participants to look at gender differences in obedience (he found no evidence of this).

Milgram's study has been consistently replicated for many years, in diverse settings, with a variety of participants and procedural variations (Miller, 1986). Overall, the weight of evidence supports the generalizability of Milgram's results. Nonetheless, critics have questioned the ethics of Milgram's procedure (Baumrind, 1964). Today, at most universities it would be difficult to obtain permission to replicate Milgram's study—a bizarre epitaph for what may be psychology's best-known experiment.

TO OBEY OR NOT TO OBEY?

After many replications, the data are clear, and their implications are frightening and deplorable. Most people can be coerced into engaging in actions that violate their morals and values. Consider the fact of Chinese troops firing on unarmed civilians during the 1989 Tiananmen Square demonstrations. Nonetheless, some individuals are able to resist pressure from authority figures. Let's look at *dis*obedience in the workplace to see what can be learned.

When they realized that the space shuttle *Challenger* was not safe, three employees of Rockwell International notified NASA officials of the dangerous situation. Unfortunately, NASA officials decided to go ahead with the launch in spite of these warnings because decision-making authority for the launch was transferred from engineers to administrators and because administrators were unwilling to assume responsibility for the costly decision to postpone the launch (Romzek & Dubnick, 1987). The tragic result: on January 20, 1986, seven lives and a multimillion-dollar spacecraft were lost. The courageous actions of the Rockwell "whistleblowers" illustrate resisting obedience pressures.

The term *whistleblowing* applies to a wide variety of actions taken by employees to protest or change ethically questionable organizational practices (Glazer & Glazer, 1990; Graham, 1986). On occasion, whistleblowers take their charges outside the organization, although these cases are relatively rare because of the high risk involved: Karen Silkwood probably died for trying to report unsafe practices at the nuclear power plant where she worked. More often, disobedience to authority is less dramatic and less dangerous, but these "ethical resisters" also risk the loss of credibility, friends, and jobs for the sake of important principles (Glazer & Glazer, 1990).

Is it common for employees to report wrongdoings they observe on the job to their superiors? In a large-scale survey, 8500 civilian employees of the federal government were asked if they had observed any wrongdoing at work during a 12-month period (Graham, 1986). Nearly half of the participants reported that they had personally observed a serious case of wrongdoing, such as tolerating a situation that was dangerous to public safety, accepting bribes, or stealing federal funds. Of those who had witnessed such transgressions, almost 30% said that they had told their bosses about the problem (72% reported that they had done nothing about the situation).

What prompts individuals to blow the whistle? Generalizing from research on social influence and helping behavior, the following factors stand out (Graham, 1986; Latané & Darley, 1970):

1. *Individuals must be aware of a problem.* Obviously, those who don't know that a wrongdoing has taken place or who don't view an activity as unethical have no reason to report a problem. Merely noticing that wrongdoing has occurred, however, does not ensure that a person will act. For that to happen, additional factors must come into play.

2. *People must perceive the problem as serious and believe that they are capable of taking effective action.* Ethical dissenters typically take the view that they are demonstrating company loyalty by helping the organization correct its mistakes rather than ignoring them. Moreover, they place loyalty to the public or principle over loyalty to the company. Nonetheless, even if people see a serious situation, they must believe that something can be done and that they have the necessary skills to do so before they will act. Self-esteem is an issue here, as is the person's position in the organization. People also weigh the perceived costs of acting (and not acting). In some organizations, being demoted or fired is a realistic possibility.

3. *Social support is important.* The presence of co-dissenters increases the likelihood that individuals will take action. Also, when whistleblowing involves risk, aligning oneself with others can decrease anxiety and increase safety. Discussing the problem with others who are sympathetic can provide helpful perspectives on the issue. Some organizations have specially designated individuals to handle such problems.

4. *People must take responsibility for acting and follow through.* In a large organization, individuals who are aware of a problem may persuade themselves that someone else will take responsibility for reporting the issue. This phenomenon is termed **diffusion of responsibility, or the expectation that others who are present**

Web Link 6.4

The Stanford Prison Experiment: Still Powerful After All These Years

A long press release from the Stanford University News office revisits the 1971 Prison Experiment through the eyes of Professors Phil Zimbardo (Stanford) and Christina Maslach (University of California, Berkeley). As director of the experiment (Zimbardo) and a participant (Maslach), these social psychologists offer a penetrating reevaluation of this harrowing experiment in social conformity and pressure a quarter of a century later.

will take responsibility for action. If individuals decide to act, then they must decide precisely what to do and how. Should they keep the information inside the organization or should they go outside the organization? Should they take indirect action (reporting the problem to someone else or reporting it anonymously) or should they act directly (quitting, for example)? In deciding how to respond, individuals obviously consider how the organization is likely to react to their possible actions.

In dealing with pressure from authority figures, keep in mind that social influence is a two-way street: You are not merely a helpless victim. Being mindful of how obedience pressures operate and of factors that make it easier to resist these pressures should make you a stronger player in these situations.

Fatal Social Influence

The Jonestown massacre. Waco. Heaven's Gate. Most people are at a loss to understand how such mass deaths of cult members could happen. Seeking simple answers, many fall back on stereotype-based explanations: "What else would you expect? People who join groups like that are crazy." In fact, experts report that only 5–6% of people who join cults have major psychological disorders prior to joining. About a third have depressive symptoms resulting from loss—usually of a job or an important relationship—but two-thirds are perfectly normal (Singer & Lalich, 1995). Thus, we need to look elsewhere for explanations. The powerful forces of persuasion and social influence are a good place to start.

CONTEMPORARY EXAMPLES

The infamous Jonestown massacre took place in Guyana, South America, in 1978. As you may know, Jim Jones was the charismatic leader of an American religious cult called the People's Temple, which had set up a large encampment in the isolated wilderness of Guyana. Feeling pressured by a U.S. congressional investigation, Jones persuaded all his followers to commit mass suicide by drinking cyanide-laced Kool-Aid. Although a small minority of Jones's followers refused to cooperate (a few escaped, a few were shot), most went along with him and took their own lives. In all, 913 Americans died at Jonestown, including more than 200 children who were poisoned by their parents.

Another case of fatal social influence occurred in 1993 at the Branch Davidian Compound in Waco, Texas. After 51 days of an armed standoff, a catastrophic fire of unknown origin swept through the compound on April 20, killing over 80 adults and children (Gibbs, 1993). David Koresh, the leader of the Branch Davidians, and several others died of gunshot wounds to the head and not from the fire or smoke inhalation.

As a third example, in March, 1997, 39 male and female members of the Heaven's Gate "cult" committed mass suicide in their community home in San Diego. Based on videotapes left behind, it seems that the members of the religious group believed that they had to leave their physical bodies behind in order to rendezvous with aliens on a spaceship that was trailing the Hale-Bopp comet.

How can we explain the extraordinary behavior in these three events?

PERSUASION AND SOCIAL INFLUENCE AT WORK

Social psychologists who have studied the Jonestown massacre tell us that this unusual behavior was due to Jim Jones's highly skilled use of persuasion and social influence tactics (Galanter, 1989; Zimbardo & Leippe, 1991). To begin with, Jonestown members were already heavily dependent on and trusting of Jones as evidenced by their joining his movement and leaving the United States. These individuals were persuaded to join Jonestown in the first place because they felt alienated from American society and, therefore, were particularly vulnerable to Jones's promise of a better life in a better place (*receiver* factors). But the fact that Jones could persuade individuals to move to an isolated location in a foreign country gives us an idea of his impressive rhetorical skills. As a *source,* Jones was perceived by his followers as an expert who was credible and trustworthy (Zimbardo & Leippe, 1991).

Jones also had an unusual amount of control over the content of the information his followers received and how it was presented to them (*message* factors). Specifically, he could prevent his people from coming into contact with ideas or values that differed from those he espoused and permit them to receive only the information he wanted them to have. Of course to have this degree of control over people is quite unusual, and it is one of the key factors that explains how Jones was able to persuade hundreds of individuals to kill themselves.

Social influence tactics were also at work here: the power of social pressure (violating personal standards in order to be liked by other members of a cohesive group), the power of authority (doing what you are told), modeling, and playing on guilt. The persuasion and social influence tactics used by Jim Jones are normal and familiar to everyone. What was unusual was the degree of control he had over his members' psychological environment, which allowed him to use a large number of techniques that combined to produce uncommonly powerful—and tragic—results.

If we were to analyze the Branch Davidian and Heaven's Gate cults, we would see a similar pattern of charismatic leadership and group cohesion.

Although each of the three cases of fatal social influence was unique, there were remarkable similarities among the tactics of persuasion and social influence that the leaders so skillfully used to such tragic ends.

Culture and Social Influence

As we noted in Chapter 5, Western cultures tend to have an individualistic orientation and other cultures, a collectivist orientation. This observed difference in orientations appears to influence people's *attitudes* about the desirability or undesirability of conformity, compliance, and obedience. Thus, individuals in Asian countries view conformity and obedience more positively than do either Americans or citizens of some other Western countries (Matsumoto, 1994). For example, on a values survey, Asian participants endorsed items related to conformity and obedience, whereas British participants endorsed items related to individualism (independence and freedom) (Punetha, Giles, & Young, 1987). It appears that Japanese and Hong Kong Chinese also value obedience more than the British and Italians do (Argyle et al., 1986).

Is conformity *behavior* more prevalent in countries where conformity is viewed more favorably? As you might expect, conformity rates were lower in subjects from individualistic cultures vs. those from collectivist cultures in experiments conducted across 14 countries (Bond & Smith, 1994). Studies have found that Japanese are more conforming than Americans (Buck, Newton, & Muramatsu, 1984) and that Italians are more conforming than Anglo-Australians (Cashmore & Goodnow, 1986). Thus, both beliefs about the desirability of yielding to social influence and conformity behavior are consistent with cultural orientations.

In the upcoming Application, we'll alert you to some fascinating social influence strategies at work in everyday situations.

Seeing Through Compliance Tactics

- Describe the foot-in-the-door compliance strategy.
- Describe the door-in-the-face compliance strategy and how it works.
- Explain how the reciprocity norm is used in social influence efforts.
- Explain how lowballing is used in social influence efforts.
- Discuss how reactance and feigned scarcity can increase someone's attraction to something.
- Explain how modeling effects can be used in social influence attempts.

Which of the following statements is true?

_____ **1.** It's a good idea to ask for a small favor before soliciting the larger favor that you really want.

_____ **2.** It's a good idea to ask for a large favor before soliciting the smaller favor that you really want.

Would you believe that both of these statements are true? Although the two approaches involve opposite strategies, both can be effective ways to get people to do what you want. This paradox illustrates the complexity of social influence processes, which we'll examine from a practical standpoint in this Application. It pays to understand these strategies because advertisers, sales-people, and fundraisers (not to mention friends and neighbors) use them frequently to influence people's behavior. We'll begin by looking at the contradictory strategies described in our opening questions.

The Foot-in-the-Door Technique

Door-to-door salespeople have long recognized the importance of gaining a *little* cooperation from sales targets (getting a "foot in the door") before hitting them with the real sales pitch. **The *foot-in-the-door technique* involves getting people to agree to a small request to increase the chances that they will agree to a larger request later** (see Figure 6.12). This technique is widely used in all walks of life. For example, groups seeking donations often ask people to simply sign a petition first. Salespeople routinely ask individuals to try a product with "no obligations" before they launch their hard sell. In a similar vein, a wife might ask her husband to get her a cup of coffee, and when he gets up to fetch it say, "While you're up, would you make me a grilled cheese sandwich?"

The foot-in-the-door technique was first investigated by Jonathon Freedman and his colleagues. In one study (Freedman & Fraser, 1966), the large request involved telephoning homemakers to ask whether a team of six men doing consumer research could come into their home to classify all their household products. Imagine six strangers tramping through your home, pulling everything out of your closets, cupboards, and

FIGURE 6.12.

The foot-in-the-door and the door-in-the-face techniques. These two influence techniques are essentially the reverse of each other, but both can work. In the foot-in-the-door technique, you begin with a small request and work up to a larger one. In the door-in-the-face technique, you begin with a large request and work down to a smaller one.

Goal: Obtain $50 contribution for youth group
Foot-in-the-Door Technique

Small request first — "Would you donate some old clothes for one of our charity programs?" — If yes, then . . . — Larger request (the one desired in the first place) — "Would you donate $50 to our organization?"

Door-in-the-Face Technique

Large request first — "Would you volunteer to run a weekly program for our youth group?" — If no, then . . . — Smaller request (the one desired in the first place) — "Would you donate $50 to our organization?"

drawers, and you can understand why only 22% of the subjects in the control group agreed to this outlandish request. Subjects in the experimental group were contacted three days before the unreasonable request was made and asked to answer a few questions about the soaps used in their home. When the large request was made three days later, 53% of the experimental group complied with that request.

Many other studies have shown the foot-in-the-door technique to be an effective strategy. Why does it work? Researchers think that the technique's effectiveness rests on people's tendency to behave consistently (with their initial response) (DeJong & Musilli, 1982). Of course, no strategy works all the time. The foot-in-the-door technique may be ineffective if the initial request is too small to create a sense of commitment or if the second request is so large it's unreasonable (Foss & Dempsey, 1979; Zuckerman, Lazzaro, & Waldgeir, 1979).

Web Link 6.5

Influence at Work

This new Web site, by researchers Robert Cialdini and Kelton Rhodes, offers an intriguing set of pages describing a wide variety of social influence phenomena: persuasion, propaganda, brainwashing, and the tactics of various types of cults. These resources supplement readings in an upper-division course on Interpersonal Influence offered by Professor Rhodes at Arizona State University.

The Door-in-the-Face Technique

The door-in-the-face technique reverses the sequence of requests used with the foot-in-the-door technique. **The *door-in-the-face* technique involves making a very large request that is likely to be turned down in order to increase the chances that people will agree to a smaller request later** (see Figure 6.12). The name for this strategy is derived from the expectation that the initial request will be quickly rejected. For example, a husband who wants to coax his frugal wife into agreeing to buy a $25,000 sports car might begin by proposing that they purchase a $35,000 sports car. By the time she has talked her husband out of the $35,000 car, the $25,000 price tag may look quite reasonable to her.

The door-in-the-face technique works for two reasons (Cialdini, 1993). First, everything is relative, and we are easily swayed by *contrast effects*. A 6'3" basketball player, who is really quite tall, can look downright small when surrounded by teammates who all are over 6'8". Similarly, a $25,000 car may seem cheap relative to a $35,000 car. Second, when people make concessions by reducing the size of their requests, most feel obliged to reciprocate by making concessions of their own. Hence, they agree to the smaller request. The belief that people should reciprocate others' kindness is a powerful norm. Let's examine some of the other ways in which it is used in compliance efforts.

Using the Reciprocity Norm

Most people have been socialized to believe in the ***reciprocity norm*—the rule that one should pay back in kind what one receives from others.** Robert Cialdini (1993) has written extensively about how the reciprocity norm is used in social influence efforts. Charities frequently make use of the reciprocity principle. Groups seeking donations for the disabled, the homeless, and so forth routinely send address labels, key rings, and other small gifts with their pleas for donations.

Salespeople using the reciprocity principle distribute free samples to prospective customers. Cialdini (1993) describes the procedures used by the Amway Corporation, which sells such household products as detergent, floor wax, and insect spray. Amway's door-to-door salespeople give homemakers many bottles of their products for a "free trial." When they return a few

days later, most of the homemakers feel obligated to buy some of the products.

The reciprocity rule is meant to promote fair exchanges in social interactions. However, when people manipulate the reciprocity rule, they usually give something of minimal value in the hopes of getting far more in return. For example, a person selling large computer systems may treat a potential customer to dinner at a nice restaurant in an effort to close a deal worth hundreds of thousands of dollars. According to Cialdini, the reciprocity norm is so powerful that it often works even when (1) the gift is uninvited, (2) the gift comes from someone you dislike, or (3) the gift results in an uneven exchange.

The Lowball Technique

Manipulations of the reciprocity rule can involve some trickery, but the lowball technique is even more deceptive. The name for this technique derives from a common practice in automobile sales, in which a customer is offered a terrific bargain on a car. The bargain price gets the customer to commit to buying the car. Soon after this commitment is made, the dealer starts revealing that there are some hidden costs. Typically, the customer learns that options apparently included in the original price are actually going to cost extra. Once they have committed to buying a car, most customers are unlikely to cancel the deal. Thus, **the *lowball technique* involves getting someone to commit to an attractive proposition before its hidden costs are revealed.**

Car dealers aren't the only ones who use this technique. For instance, a friend might ask if you want to spend a week with him at his charming backwoods cabin. After you accept this seemingly generous proposition, he may add, "Of course, there's some work for us to do. We need to repair the pier, paint the exterior, and . . ." You might guess that people would become angry and back out of a deal once its hidden costs are revealed. Although this certainly happens on occasion, lowballing is a surprisingly effective strategy (Burger & Petty, 1981).

Reactance and Feigned Scarcity

A number of years ago, Jack Brehm demonstrated that telling people they can't have something only makes them want it more. This finding emerged in his research on reactance. *Reactance* **occurs when a person's freedom to behave in a certain way is impeded, thus leading to efforts to restore the threatened freedom.**

In one study of reactance (Brehm, 1966), subjects listened to four records and were then asked to rate how much they liked each one. As a reward for participating in the study, some subjects were told that they could have the record of their choice when they returned to make additional ratings on a second occasion. When subjects returned for the second session, they were told that one of the four records would not be available as their reward. The excluded record varied from subject to subject. It was always the record ranked third best by that individual in the first set of ratings. The subjects listened to the four records again and made their second set of ratings. Brehm found that the ratings of the excluded records increased significantly. In other words, the record that a subject could not have became all the more desirable!

This reactance effect helps explain why companies often try to create the impression that their products are in scarce supply. Scarcity threatens your freedom to choose a product, thus creating reactance and an increased desire for the scarce product. Advertisers frequently feign scarcity to drive up the demand for products. Thus, we constantly see ads that scream "limited supply available," "for a limited time only," "while they last," and "time is running out."

The Power of Modeling

As we noted in Chapter 2, *observational learning* occurs when behavior is swayed by observations of others, who, in this context, are called *models*. According to Albert Bandura (1986), much of human behavior is the product of imitation or modeling effects. These modeling effects are sometimes used in social influence efforts.

The power of modeling was demonstrated in an experiment designed to increase the contributions tossed into a Salvation Army kettle during the Christmas holiday (Bryan & Test, 1967). In this study, experimental accomplices posing as shoppers tossed money into a Salvation Army kettle as they walked by it. Thus, they modeled generous behavior for real shoppers who witnessed their contributions. As predicted, the shoppers exposed to these generous models made more contributions than the shoppers in a control condition, where the models were absent.

Advertisers are well aware of people's tendency to be influenced by what others do. That's why they run television ads in which both celebrities and "ordinary people" testify about how they use a particular detergent, deodorant, or gasoline. Modeling effects also explain why television producers use laugh tracks in their comedy shows. Research reveals that canned laughter leads audiences to laugh at jokes more frequently and longer (Fuller & Sheehy-Skeffington, 1974). People try to take advantage of modeling effects in many different situations. For instance, bartenders often slip a few dollar bills into their tip jars to "model" healthy tipping from previous customers.

In summary, people use a host of methods to coax compliance from one another. Despite the fact that many of these influence techniques are more or less dishonest, they're still widely used. There is no way to completely avoid being hoodwinked by influence strategies. However, understanding these various tactics can reduce the likelihood that you'll be a victim of influence artists. As we noted in our discussion of persuasion, "to be forewarned is to be forearmed."

Key Ideas

FORMING IMPRESSIONS OF OTHERS

● In forming impressions of other people, individuals rely on appearance, verbal statements, actions, nonverbal messages, and situational cues. Individuals usually make snap judgments about others unless accurate impressions are important. To explain the causes of other people's behavior, individuals make attributions (either internal or external).

● People often try to confirm their expectations about what others are like, which can result in biased impressions. Self-fulfilling prophecies can actually change a target person's behavior in the direction of a perceiver's expectations. Cognitive distortions also occur and are caused by categorizing, stereotypes, the fundamental attribution error, and defensive attributions. The process of person perception is characterized by the themes of efficiency, selectivity, and stability.

THE PROBLEM OF PREJUDICE

● Prejudice is a particularly unfortunate outcome of the tendency to view others inaccurately. Blatant ("old-fashioned") discrimination occurs relatively infrequently today, but more subtle expressions of prejudice and discrimination ("modern discrimination") have become more common. Common causes of prejudice include cognitive distortions, the authoritarian personality, competition between groups, and threats to social identity. Strategies for reducing prejudice are rooted in social thinking and intergroup contact.

THE POWER OF PERSUASION

● The success of persuasive efforts depends on several factors. A source of persuasion who is expert, trustworthy, likable, physically attractive, and similar to the receiver tends to be relatively effective. Although there are some limitations, two-sided arguments, arousal of fear, and generation of positive feelings are effective elements in persuasive messages. Persuasion is undermined when receivers are forewarned or have beliefs that are extremely discrepant from the position being advocated.

● Persuasion takes place via two different processes. The central route to persuasion requires a receiver to be motivated to process persuasive messages carefully (elaboration). A favorable reaction to such an evaluation will result in positive attitude change. When a receiver is unmotivated or unable to process persuasive messages carefully, persuasion may take place via the peripheral route (on the basis of simple cues such as a catchy tune). Subliminal persuasion is an ineffective tactic.

THE POWER OF SOCIAL PRESSURE

● Asch found that subjects often conform to the group, even when the group reports inaccurate judgments. Asch's experiments may have produced public compliance while subjects'

private beliefs remained unchanged. Being mindful of social pressures and getting support from others with similar views are ways to resist conformity pressures.

● In Milgram's landmark study of obedience to authority, subjects showed a remarkable tendency to follow orders to shock an innocent stranger. Milgram concluded that situational pressure can make decent people do indecent things. Although people often obey authority figures, they are sometimes disobedient, as exemplified by whistleblowing.

● Extremely effective communicators who have almost complete control over groups are able to produce powerful, sometimes tragic, outcomes, as was seen in the Jonestown, Waco, and Heaven's Gate incidents. Although these tragic events seemed inexplicable, normal persuasive principles were at work in each case. The value cultures place on conformity influences the extent to which individuals are likely to conform. Conformity tends to be greater in collectivistic cultures.

APPLICATION: SEEING THROUGH COMPLIANCE TACTICS

● A variety of tactics have been shown to be effective in influencing the behavior of others. These include the foot-in-the-door technique, the door-in-the-face technique, the reciprocity norm, the lowball technique, reactance, feigned scarcity, and modeling. Understanding these strategies can make you less vulnerable to manipulation.

Key Terms

Attitudes	Door-in-the-face	Persuasion
Attributions	technique	Prejudice
Channel	Elaboration like-	Primacy effect
Compliance	lihood model	Reactance
Confirmation	Foot-in-the-door	Receiver
bias	technique	Reciprocity norm
Conformity	Fundamental	Self-fulfilling
Cooperative	attribution	prophecy
interdepen-	error	Source
dence	Lowball	Stereotypes
Defensive	technique	Subliminal
attribution	Message	persuasion
Diffusion of	Obedience	Superordinate
responsibility	Person	goals
Discrimination	perception	

Key People

Solomon Asch	Stanley Milgram	Muzafer Sherif
Robert Cialdini	Richard Petty and	
Susan Fiske	John Cacioppo	

Practice Test

1. Mindfulness operates when people:
   a. make snap judgments.
   b. are on "cognitive automatic pilot."
   c. make systematic judgments.
   d. are not concerned about forming accurate impressions.

2. Which of the following is not a type of cognitive distortion in perception?
   a. Categorizing
   b. "Old-fashioned" discrimination
   c. Stereotypes
   d. Defensive attribution

3. Which of the following is not a theme in person perception?
   a. Efficiency
   b. Selectivity
   c. Stability
   d. Mindfulness

4. "Old-fashioned" discrimination is _____;
   modern discrimination is _____.
   a. blatant; subtle
   b. legal; illegal
   c. common; rare
   d. race-based; gender-based

5. Which of the following is a cause of prejudice?
   a. Mindfulness
   b. The authoritarian personality
   c. Jigsaw classrooms
   d. Activities based on superordinate goals

6. Receivers who are forewarned that someone will try to persuade them will most likely:
   a. be very open to persuasion.
   b. get up and stomp out of the room.
   c. not be very open to persuasion.
   d. heckle the persuader.

7. Compared to attitudes formed via the peripheral route, those formed via the central route:
   a. operate subliminally.
   b. are harder to change.
   c. last only a short time.
   d. are poor predictors of behavior.

8. When people change their outward behavior but not their private beliefs, _____ is operating.
   a. conformity
   b. persuasion
   c. obedience
   d. compliance

9. Conformity behavior is:
   a. more common in collectivist countries.
   b. more common in individualistic countries.
   c. not affected by culture.
   d. viewed very positively in all cultures.

10. When charities send prospective donors free address labels and the like, which of the following compliance tactics are they using?
    a. The lowball technique
    b. The foot-in-the-door technique
    c. The reciprocity norm
    d. The door-in-the-face technique

Answers

1. c page 160
2. b pages 163–165
3. d pages 165–166
4. a page 167
5. b pages 167–168
6. c page 172
7. b page 173
8. d page 175
9. a page 179
10. c pages 181–182

**INFOTRAC
COLLEGE EDITION**

Go to the Wadsworth Psychology Study Center (http://psychology.
wadsworth.com/) for quiz questions, research updates, hot topics, interactive
exercises, and suggested readings in INFOTRAC related to this chapter.

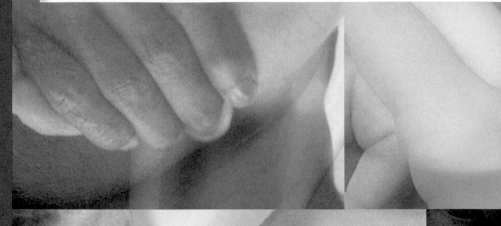

CHAPTER 7 Interpersonal Communication

Have you ever rushed home, eager to relate an interesting incident, only to find no one there to listen to your story? It may not have been a spectacular or earthshaking tale; maybe you simply picked up an intriguing bit of gossip or met someone who was a little unusual. Still, it was something you wanted to share. Chances are you rehearsed your fascinating account all the way home. When you found no receptive ears for your story, do you remember how frustrated you felt? As this common experience illustrates, people have a powerful need to share information with others and to get their reactions.

Interpersonal communication is an integral part of human experience. Moreover, interpersonal skills are highly relevant to adjustment because they can be critical to happiness and success in life. In this chapter, we'll start off with an overview of the communication process and then turn our attention to the important topic of nonverbal communication. Next, we'll discuss ways to communicate more effectively and examine several communication problems. Finally, we'll look at interpersonal conflict, including constructive ways to deal with it. In the Application, we'll consider ways to develop an assertive communication style.

The Process of Interpersonal Communication

LEARNING OBJECTIVES

- List and explain the six components of the communication process.
- Discuss how interpersonal communication is important to adjustment.

Communication can be defined as the process of sending and receiving messages that have meaning. Your personal thoughts have meaning, of course, but when you "talk to yourself," you are engaging in *intra*personal communication. In this chapter, we will focus on *inter*personal communication—the face-to-face transmission of meaning between two or more people. For the most part, we'll concentrate on two-person *interactions*. We will define **interpersonal communication** as an **interactional process whereby one person sends a message to another.**

Note several points about this definition. First, for communication to qualify as *interpersonal*, at least two

people must be involved. Second, interpersonal communication is a *process*. By this, we simply mean that it is usually composed of a series of actions: Kelli talks/Jason listens, Jason responds/Kelli listens, and so on. Third, this process is *interactional*. Communication is generally not a one-way street: Both participants send as well as receive information when they're interacting. A key implication of this fact is that you need to pay attention to both *speaking* and *listening* if you want to improve your communication skills.

Components of the Communication Process

Let's take a look at the essential components of the interpersonal communication process. The key elements are (1) the sender, (2) the receiver, (3) the message, (4) the channel through which the message is sent, (5) noise or interference, and (6) the context in which the message is communicated. As we describe these components, refer to Figure 7.1 to see how they work together.

The sender is the person who initiates the message. In a typical two-way conversation, both people serve as senders (as well as receivers). Keep in mind that each person brings a unique set of expectations and understandings to each communication situation. The receiver is the person to whom the message is targeted.

FIGURE 7.1.

A model of interpersonal communication. Interpersonal communication involves six elements: the sender, the receiver, the message, the channel through which the message is transmitted, distorting noise, and the context in which the message is sent. In conversations, both participants function as sender and receiver.

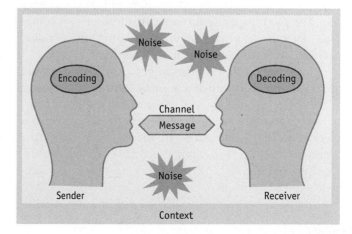

As we have noted, each conversational participant serves as both sender and receiver.

The *message* refers to the information or meaning that is transmitted from the sender to the receiver. The message is the content of the communication—that is, the ideas and feelings conveyed to another person. Two important cognitive processes underlie the transmission of messages. Speakers *encode* or transform their ideas and feelings into symbols and organize them into a message; receivers *decode* or translate a speaker's message into their own ideas and feelings (see Figure 7.1). Generally, fluent speakers of a language are unaware of these processes.The primary means of sending messages is language, but people also communicate to others nonverbally. Nonverbal communication includes the facial expressions, gestures, and vocal inflections used to supplement (and sometimes entirely change) the meaning of verbal messages. For example, when you say, "Thanks a lot," your nonverbal communication can convey either sincere gratitude or heavy sarcasm.

The *channel* refers to the sensory channel through which the message reaches the receiver. Typically, people receive information from multiple channels simultaneously. They not only hear what the other person says, they also see the person's facial expressions, observe his or her gestures, experience eye contact, and sometimes feel the physical touch of the speaker. Note that the messages in the various channels may be consistent or inconsistent with each other, making their interpretation more or less difficult. Sometimes sound is the only channel available for receiving information—when you talk on the telephone, for instance. Through sound, people hear both the literal content of messages and vocal inflections.

Whenever two people talk, miscommunication can occur. **Any stimulus that interferes with accurately expressing or understanding a message is termed *noise*.** Sources of noise include environmental factors (street traffic, loud music) and physical factors (poor hearing, poor vision). Noise can also have semantic origins (Verderber & Verderber, 1998). For instance, profanity, ethnic slurs, or sexist language can cause a listener to disregard the larger message. In addition, psychological factors (defensiveness, anxiety) contribute to noise, a topic we'll consider later in the chapter.

All social communication occurs in a ***context*, the environment in which communication takes place.** These background factors significantly influence communication and include the *physical place* in which a conversation takes place (in private or public), the nature of the participants' *relationship* (employer/employee, friends), their history (previous interactions), their current *mood* (happy, stressed), and their *cultural backgrounds* (Verderber & Verderber, 1998). The cultural context is especially important in the U.S.

because of the varieties of subcultures, many with different rules of communication. The cultural context is also important in the global marketplace, as the marketers of *Coca-Cola* in China discovered too late (Petras & Petras, 1994). It seems that *Coca-Cola* translates to something like "Bite the wax tadpole" in Chinese!

The Importance of Communication

Before we plunge further into the topic of interpersonal communication, let's take a moment to emphasize its significance. Communication with others—friends, lovers, parents, spouses, children, employers, employees—is such an essential and commonplace aspect of everyday life that it's hard to overstate the importance of communicating effectively. Many of life's satisfactions (and frustrations and heartaches, as well) hinge on one's ability to communicate effectively with others. Numerous studies have shown that good communication can enhance satisfaction in marriage and that poor communication can be a factor in marital dissatisfaction (Noller & Guthrie, 1991).

Nonverbal Communication

LEARNING OBJECTIVES

- List five general principles of nonverbal communication.
- Define proxemics and discuss personal space.
- Discuss display rules and what can be discerned from facial cues.
- Summarize the characteristics associated with high levels of eye contact.
- Describe the roles of body movement, posture, and gestures in communication.
- Summarize the research findings on touching and paralanguage.
- Summarize the research evidence on detecting deception from nonverbal cues.
- Explain what polygraphs do and cite some problems with their use.
- Discuss the significance of nonverbal messages in interpersonal relationships.

You're standing at the bar in your favorite lounge, gazing across a dark, smoky room filled with people drinking, dancing, and talking. You motion to the bartender that you'd like another drink. Your companion comments on the loudness of the music, and you nod your head in agreement. You spot an attractive stranger across the bar; your eyes meet for a moment and you smile. In a matter of seconds, you have sent three messages without uttering a syllable. To put it another way, you have just sent three nonverbal messages. ***Nonverbal communica-***

tion **is the transmission of meaning from one person to another through means or symbols other than words.** Communication at the nonverbal level takes place through a variety of behaviors: interpersonal distance, facial expression, eye contact, body posture and movement, gestures, physical touch, and tone of voice. We will discuss each of these in this section.

Some experts maintain that as much as 65% of the message transmissions in face-to-face interactions actually occur at the nonverbal level (Burgoon, Buller, & Woodall, 1989). Clearly, a great deal of information is exchanged through nonverbal channels—probably more than most people realize. You can enhance your communication skills by increasing your knowledge about this important aspect of communication.

General Principles

Let's begin by examining some general principles of nonverbal communication.

1. *Nonverbal communication is multichanneled.* Nonverbal communication typically involves simultaneous messages sent through a number of channels. For instance, information may be transmitted through gestures, facial expressions, eye contact, and vocal tone at the same time. In contrast, verbal communication is limited to a single channel: speech. If you have ever tried to follow two people speaking at once, you are aware of how difficult it is to process multiple inputs of information. The multichanneled nature of nonverbal communication is one of the reasons that many nonverbal transmissions sail by the receiver unnoticed.

2. *Nonverbal communication conveys emotions.* People often communicate their feelings without saying a word—for example, "a look that 'kills.'" Nonverbal demonstrations of positive feelings include sitting or standing close to those you care for, touching them often, and looking at them frequently (Fletcher & Fitness, 1990).

3. *Nonverbal communication is ambiguous.* Nonverbal messages tend to be less clear than spoken words. A shrug or a raised eyebrow can mean different things to different people. Moreover, it is always difficult to know whether nonverbal messages are being sent intentionally. Although some popular books on body language imply otherwise, few nonverbal signals carry universally accepted meanings even within the same culture (DePaolo & Friedman, 1998). Hence, they should be interpreted with caution.

4. *Nonverbal communication may contradict verbal messages.* How often have you seen people proclaim "I'm not angry" even though their bodies shout that they are positively furious? When confronted with such inconsistency, which message should you believe? Because of their greater spontaneity, you're probably better off heeding the nonverbal signs. Research shows that when someone is instructed to tell a lie, deception is most readily detected through nonverbal behavior (DePaulo, LeMay, & Epstein, 1991; DePaulo, Lanier, & Davis, 1983).

5. *Nonverbal communication is culture-bound.* Like language, nonverbal signals are different in different cultures (Matsumoto, 1996). For instance, people of Northern European heritage tend to engage in less physical contact and keep a greater distance between themselves than people of Latin or Middle Eastern heritage. Thus, an Englishman might be quite upset when a well-meaning Brazilian "trespasses" on his personal space. Sometimes cultural differences can be quite dramatic. For example, in Tibet people greet their friends by sticking out their tongues (Ekman, 1975).

Elements of Nonverbal Communication

Nonverbal signals can provide information about many things in interpersonal interactions. As we discuss specific nonverbal behaviors, we will focus on what they communicate about interpersonal attraction and social status.

PERSONAL SPACE

Proxemics **is the study of people's use of interpersonal space.** *Personal space* **is a zone of space surrounding a person that is felt to "belong" to that person.** This personal space that you consider "yours" is like an invisible bubble you carry around with you in your social interactions. The size of this mobile zone is related to your cultural background, social status, personality, age, and gender. Interestingly, animals show a similar tendency, called *territoriality*—the marking off and defending of certain areas as their own.

As you might guess, the amount of distance people feel comfortable with between themselves and others depends on the nature of the relationship and the situation (Darley & Gilbert, 1985; J. A. Hall, 1990). The appropriate distance between people is also regulated by social norms and varies by culture (Hall, 1990). Anthropologist Edward T. Hall has described four interpersonal distance zones that are appropriate for

Web Link 7.1

Nonverbal Communication Research Page
Marvin A. Hecht of Louisiana College, this site's editor, emphasizes that the Internet is not an adequate realm for researching a paper on nonverbal communication. Nevertheless, the links provided here can serve to introduce students and others to major issues, researchers, current news, and examples drawn from this fascinating field.

middle-class encounters in American culture (see Figure 7.2). The general rule is that the more you like someone, the more comfortable you feel being physically close to that person. Of course, there are obvious exceptions, such as in crowded subways and elevators, but these situations are often experienced as stressful. Women seem to have smaller personal-space zones than men do. When talking, women sit or stand closer together than men do (Sussman & Rosenfeld, 1982). There seem to be two reasons for this: Women approach others more closely than men do and others approach women more closely than they do men (Hall, 1984).

Like other aspects of nonverbal communication, personal distance can convey information about status. People of similar status tend to stand closer together than people whose status is unequal (J. A. Hall, 1990). Moreover, it is the prerogative of the more powerful person in an interaction to set the "proper" interpersonal distance (Henley, 1977).

What happens when someone approaches you more closely than you feel is appropriate? Invasions of personal space invariably produce discomfort and attempts to shift the interpersonal distance more in line with your expectations. To illustrate, let's say that you have staked out some territory for yourself at a table in the library. When a stranger sits down at "your" table and forces you to share it, how might you react? One option is to move to another table to reestablish a distance that feels comfortable to you. If moving away is not practical, you will probably reorient your body away from the intruder or place some barrier (for example, a stack of books) between you and the invader. Whatever response you choose, the point is that invasions of personal space rarely go unnoticed, and they usually elicit a variety of reactions.

FACIAL EXPRESSION

More than anything else, facial expressions convey emotions. In an extensive research program, Paul Ekman and his colleagues have identified six primary emotions that have distinctive facial expressions: anger, disgust, fear, happiness, sadness, and surprise (Ekman, 1994; Ekman & Friesen, 1984). The facial expressions conveying these six emotions appear to be universal (Rosenberg & Ekman, 1994). That is, individuals from a variety of cultures are able to identify them correctly. Typically, in such studies, subjects from a variety of Western and non-Western cultures are shown photographs depicting different emotions and are asked to match the photographs with the appropriate emotions.

FIGURE 7.2.

Interpersonal distance zones. According to Edward T. Hall (1966), people like to keep a certain amount of distance between themselves and others. The distance that makes one feel comfortable depends on whom one is interacting with and the nature of the situation. Generally, the zones depicted on the left are appropriate for the people and situations listed on the right.

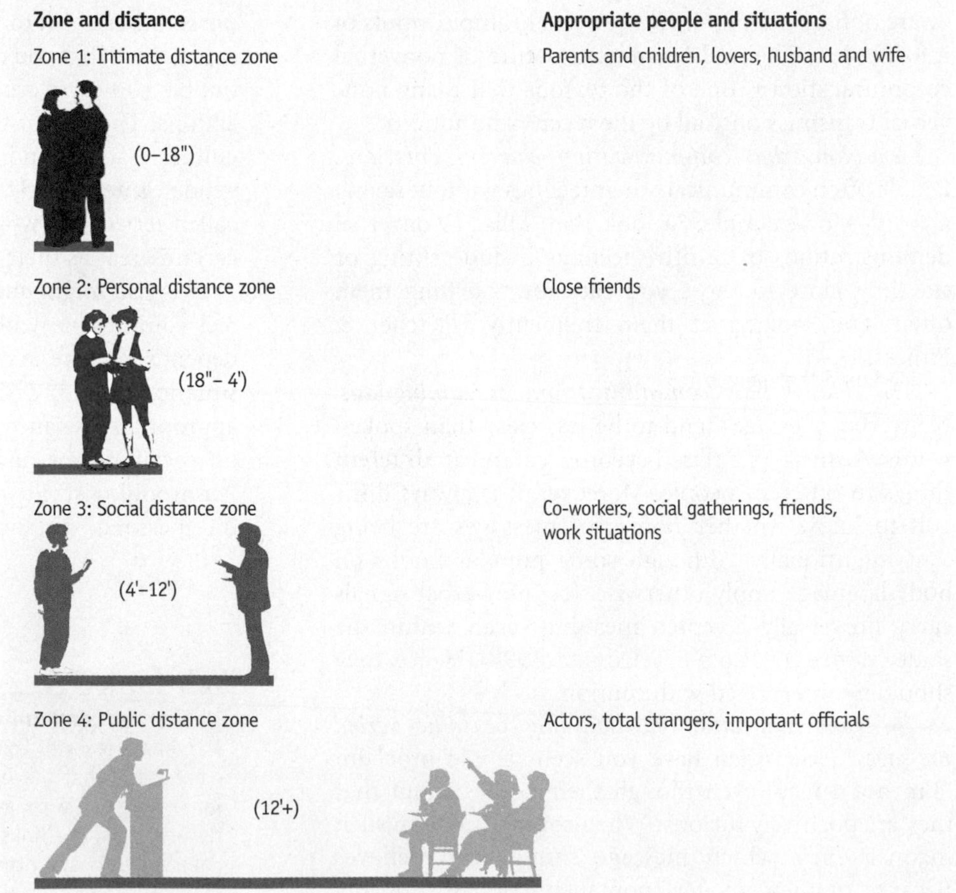

Zone and distance

Zone 1: Intimate distance zone (0–18")

Zone 2: Personal distance zone (18"– 4')

Zone 3: Social distance zone (4'–12')

Zone 4: Public distance zone (12'+)

Appropriate people and situations

Parents and children, lovers, husband and wife

Close friends

Co-workers, social gatherings, friends, work situations

Actors, total strangers, important officials

Display rules require unsuccessful contestants in beauty pageants to suppress the display of resentful, envious, or angry feelings.

Some representative results from this research are depicted in Figure 7.3. Although a small number of basic facial expressions are universally recognizable, other expressions of emotion can vary from culture to culture—as we noted in the earlier example of Tibetans sticking out their tongues to greet their friends.

Each society has social rules that govern whether (and when) it is appropriate to express one's feelings. **These norms that govern the appropriate display of emotions are termed *display rules.*** In the United States, for instance, it is considered bad form to gloat over one's victories or to show envy or anger in defeat. This regulation of facial expression is an aspect of impression management that we discussed in Chapter 5. Is it possible to deliberately deceive others through facial expression? Yes, indeed. In fact, it appears that people are better at sending deceptive messages with their faces than with other areas of their bodies (Ekman, Friesen, & Ellsworth, 1982). Recall the term "poker face," an allusion to poker players who are skilled at controlling their excitement about a good hand of cards (or their dismay about a bad one). As you might predict, high self-monitors are better than low self-monitors at managing their facial expressions when it is inappropriate to show them (Friedman & Miller-Herringer, 1991). At this point, it isn't known whether high self-monitors are really more skilled at regulating their behavior or whether they are just more motivated to do so.

EYE CONTACT
Eye contact (also called mutual gaze) is another major channel of nonverbal communication. Above all, it is the duration of eye contact between people that is most meaningful. A great deal of research has been done on communication through the eyes; we will briefly summarize some of the more interesting findings (Kleinke, 1986).

FIGURE 7.3

Facial expressions and emotions. Ekman and Friesen (1984) found that people in highly disparate cultures showed fair agreement on the emotions portrayed in these photos. This consensus across cultures suggests that the facial expressions associated with certain basic emotions may have a biological basis.

Facial Expressions and Emotions

Emotion Displayed

	Fear	Disgust	Happiness	Anger

Country	Agreement in judging photos (%)			
United States	85	92	97	67
Brazil	67	97	95	90
Chile	68	92	95	94
Argentina	54	92	98	90
Japan	66	90	100	90
New Guinea	54	44	82	50

Chapter 7 *Interpersonal Communication*   **191**

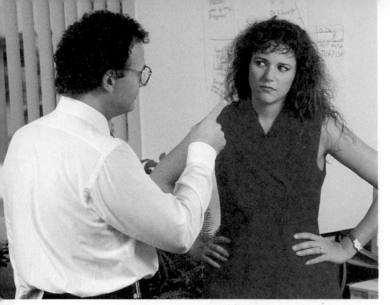

Strong eye contact can convey either very negative or very positive feelings.

People who engage in high levels of eye contact are usually judged as more attentive than those who maintain less eye contact. Speakers, interviewers, and experimenters receive higher ratings of competence when they maintain high rather than low eye contact with their audience. Similarly, those who engage in high levels of mutual gaze are likely to be perceived as having effective social skills and credibility.

Gaze is also a means of communicating the *intensity* (but not the positivity or negativity) of feelings. Thus, eye contact is strongly related to feelings of attraction (Kleinke, 1986). For example, couples who say they are in love spend more time gazing at each other than other couples do (Patterson, 1988). Also, people who engage in high mutual gaze are judged by observers as liking each other more than those who engage in relatively little eye contact. Finally, maintaining moderate (versus constant or no) eye contact with others typically generates positive feelings in them. These positive feelings have even been found to translate into higher tips! One study found that food servers who squatted down next to their customers to take drink orders got higher tips than servers who stood next to their customers (Lynn & Mynier, 1993). Supposedly, the increased eye contact and closeness generated more positive feelings.

In a negative interpersonal context, a steady gaze becomes a stare. A stare causes most people to feel uncomfortable and to flee the situation (Kleinke, 1986). Moreover, like threat displays among nonhuman primates such as baboons and rhesus monkeys, a stare can convey aggressive intent (Henley, 1986). People can also communicate by *reducing* eye contact with others. For example, mutual gaze is usually reduced when an interaction is unpleasant or embarrassing or when people feel that their personal space is being invaded (Kleinke, 1986).

Culture affects patterns of eye contact. For example, Americans get annoyed with people from Asian cultures because they look less directly at the others during social interactions. On the other hand, people from Arab countries get frustrated with Americans because we gaze at them less than they are used to (Matsumoto, 1996).

In the United States, gender and racial differences have been found in eye contact. In interactions, women tend to gaze more at others than men do (Cegala & Sillars, 1989). However, the patterning of eye contact also reflects status, and gender and status are often confounded, as we have noted. Higher-status individuals look at the other person more when speaking than when listening, while lower-status people behave just the opposite. Women usually show the lower-status visual pattern because they are typically accorded lower status than men. As you can see in Figure 7.4, when women are in high-power positions, they show the high-status visual pattern to the same extent that men do (Dovidio et al., 1988). African Americans use more continuous eye contact than European Americans when speaking, but less when listening (Samovar & Potter, 1995). Obviously, such differences can lead to misunderstandings if eye-gaze behaviors intended to convey interest and respect are interpreted as being disrespectful or dishonest.

BODY LANGUAGE

Body movements—those of the head, trunk, hands, legs, and feet—also provide nonverbal avenues of communication. **Kinesics is the study of communication through body movements.** What information does *body movement* convey? For one thing, it provides information about the level of tension or relaxation

FIGURE 7.4.

Visual dominance, status, and gender. Women typically show low visual dominance (see control condition) because they are usually accorded lower status than men (Dovidio et al. 1988). However, when researchers placed women in a high-power position and measured their visual behavior, women showed the high visual dominance pattern and men, the low visual dominance pattern. When men were placed in the high-power position, the visual dominance patterns reversed. Thus, visual dominance seems to be more a function of status than gender.

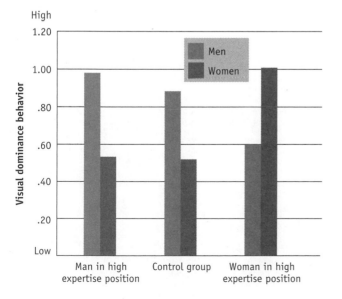

People in higher-status positions tend to adopt an "open" body posture, and those in lower-status roles usually adopt a "closed" position.

that a person is experiencing. For example, frequent touching or scratching suggests nervousness (Harrigan et al., 1991). A person's *gait* (way of walking) can provide cues about age: Younger people walk with more bounce, hip sway, and loose-jointedness than older individuals (Montepare & Zebrowitz-McArthur, 1987).

Body posture also conveys information. Leaning back with arms or legs arranged in an asymmetrical position (an "open" position) conveys a feeling of relaxation. Posture can also indicate a person's attitude toward you (McKay, Davis, & Fanning, 1995). When people lean toward you, it typically indicates interest and a positive attitude. When people angle their bodies away from you or cross their arms, their posture may indicate a negative attitude or defensiveness.

Body posture can also convey status differences. Generally, a higher-status person will look more relaxed. By contrast, a lower-status person will tend to exhibit a more rigid body posture, often sitting up straight with feet together, flat on the floor, and arms close to the body (a "closed" position) (Hall, 1984). Again, as we noted with eye contact, status and gender differences are frequently parallel. That is, men are more likely to exhibit the high-status "open" posture and women the lower-status "closed" posture (J. A. Hall, 1990).

Hand gestures are used primarily to regulate conversations and to supplement speech (McKay et al., 1995). The *referencing gesture* is used to refer to an object or person who is the subject of conversation. For example, you might point at a car that you're commenting on. The *gesture of emphasis* is used to stress a point that is being made verbally. Thus, you might slam your fist onto a desk to emphasize the importance of your statement. *Demonstrative gestures* mimic what is being said. For example, in discussing a cutoff of someone's financial support, you might make chopping motions with your hand.

Finally, as travelers are often surprised to discover, the meaning of gestures is not universal (Cohen & Borsoi, 1996). For instance, a circle made with the thumb and forefinger means that everything is "OK" to an American, but is considered an obscene gesture in some countries.

TOUCH

Touch takes many forms and can express a variety of meanings: support, consolation, and sexual intimacy (DeVito, 1992). Touch can also convey messages of status and power. For example, those who initiate a touch are generally assumed to have higher status than those who receive a touch. It's more common, for example, to see teachers touch students than vice versa. How people interpret the possible messages communicated by touch depends on the age and gender of the two individuals involved, the setting in which the touching takes place, and the relationship between the toucher and recipient, among other things (Major, Schmidlin, & Williams, 1990). Also, there are strong norms about *where* people are allowed to touch friends. These norms are quite different for same-gender as opposed to cross-gender interactions, as can be seen in Figure 7.5.

The results of a large-scale observational study conducted in the Boston area provide several generalizations about touching behavior (Hall & Veccia, 1990, 1991). In this study, researchers observed 4,500 pairs of people interacting in a variety of public places (shopping malls, hotel lobbies, subway stations). Observers recorded instances of touching with the hand as well as other parts of the body and estimated (based on training) the age of the pairs. First, it was found that female-female pairs touch each other significantly more than male-male pairs. Second, although there were no overall differences between the number of men who touched women and vice versa, if we look at these pairs by age, a different pattern emerges. That is, as they age, men tend to touch women less, and women tend to touch men more. Comparable age changes were not found for same-gender pairs.

Regarding people's *responses* to touching, it has been found that women generally respond more favorably to touching than men do (Henley & Freeman, 1981). This gender difference may depend on status differences. Support for this interpretation comes from the finding that both women and men react favorably to touching when the person initiating the touch is higher in status than the recipient (Major, 1981). Of course, in cases where touching is unwelcome (for example, sexual harassment), these findings do not hold.

PARALANGUAGE

The term *paralanguage* refers to *how* something is spoken rather than to *what* is said. Thus, **paralanguage includes all vocal cues other than the content of the verbal message itself.** These cues may include how loudly or softly people speak, how fast they talk, and the rhythm and quality of their speech (McKay et al., 1995). Each of these aspects of vocalization can affect the message being transmitted.

Variations in vocal emphasis can give the same set of words very different meanings. Consider the sentence "I really enjoyed myself!" If you vary the word that is accented, you can speak this sentence in three different ways, each resulting in a different meaning.

FIGURE 7.5.

Where friends touch each other. Social norms govern where friends tend to touch each other. As these diagrams show, the patterns of touching are different in same-gender as opposed to cross-gender interactions. (Adapted from Marsh, 1988)

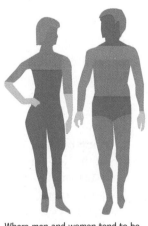

Where men and women tend to be touched by friends of the same gender

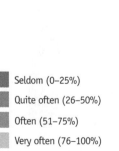

- Seldom (0–25%)
- Quite often (26–50%)
- Often (51–75%)
- Very often (76–100%)

Where men and women tend to be touched by friends of the other gender

- *I* really enjoyed myself!
  (Even though others may not have had a good time, I did.)
- I *really* enjoyed myself!
  (My enjoyment was exceptional or greater than expected.)
- I really *enjoyed* myself!
  (Much to my surprise, I had a great time.)

As you can see from these examples, the way you say something can make a considerable difference in the meaning you convey. In fact, you can actually reverse the literal meaning of a verbal message by how you say it (such as with sarcasm).

Aspects of vocalization can also communicate emotions. For example, rapid speech may mean that a person is happy, frightened, or nervous. Slower speech might be used when a person is uncertain or when he or she wants to emphasize a point. Loud vocalization often indicates anger. A relatively high pitch may indicate anxiety (Verderber & Verderber, 1998). Slow speech, low volume, and low pitch are often associated with sadness. Thus, vocal quality is another clue that you can use to discern someone's true feelings. Keep in mind, however, that it is easy to assign meanings to voice quality that aren't valid, like associating a deep voice with masculinity and maturity and a high, breathy voice with femininity and youth.

In cyberspace communication, e-mail users have adopted various substitutes for the paralanguage cues used in spoken communication. For instance, capital letters are used for emphasis ("I had a GREAT vacation"); however, note that using capital letters throughout is viewed as shouting and considered rude behavior. Other adaptations include arranging punctuation marks to indicate the writer's emotions; thus a positive tone is indicated with :-) and a sad tone with :-(.

Detecting Deception

The spontaneous nature of nonverbal communication often makes it a better index of a person's true feelings than what the person actually says. This reality raises an obvious question. Is it possible to detect deceit by monitoring nonverbal signals? Yes, but it isn't easy. Interestingly, the clues that suggest dishonesty don't necessarily correspond to popular stereotypes about how liars give themselves away.

Evidence on the nonverbal behaviors associated with deception is summarized in Figure 7.6 (based on DePaulo, Stone, & Lassiter, 1985). The vocal and visual cues that have been studied are listed in the first column. The second column indicates whether these cues are really associated with deception. The third column indicates whether the same cues are widely believed to be associated with deception. As you can see, research does not support many stereotypical notions about lying. Contrary to popular belief, lying is *not* associated with slow talking, long pauses before speaking, excessive shifting of posture, reduced smiling, or lack of eye contact.

Nonetheless, some cues are associated with dishonesty (DePaolo & Friedman, 1998). Vocal cues include

Nonverbal Cues and Deceptions		
Kind of Cue	Are cues associated with actual deception?	Are cues believed to be a sign of deception?
Vocal Cues		
Speech hesitations	YES: Liars hesitate more	YES
Voice pitch	YES: Liars speak with higher pitch	YES
Speech errors (stutters, stammers)	YES: Liars make more errors	YES
Speech latency (pause before starting to speak or answer)	NO	YES: People think liars pause more
Speech rate	NO	YES: People think liars talk slower
Response length	YES: Liars give shorter answers	NO
Visual Cues		
Pupil dilation	YES: Liars show more dilation	(No research data)
Adapters (self-directed gestures)	YES: Liars touch themselves more	NO
Blinking	YES: Liars blink more	(No research data)
Postural shifts	NO	YES: People think liars shift more
Smile	NO	YES: People think liars smile less
Gaze (eye contact)	NO	YES: People think liars engage in less eye contact

FIGURE 7.6.

Detecting deception from nonverbal behaviors. This chart summarizes evidence on which nonverbal cues are actually associated with deception and which are believed to be a sign of deception, based on a research review by DePaulo, Stone, and Lassiter (1985).

excessive hesitations and stammering, speaking with a higher pitch, and giving relatively short answers. Visual cues include excessive blinking and dilation of the pupils. Also, liars nervously touch themselves more than normal. Too, it's helpful to look for inconsistencies between messages expressed through the face and those from the lower part of the body. For example, a friendly smile accompanied by a nervous shuffling of feet may be cause for concern. Another clue is whether the facial message lacks spontaneity compared to the verbal message. People take more time to encode and send deceptive nonverbal signals than authentic ones. Because of this tendency, liars' verbal and facial expressions may be out of sync.

If people have trouble detecting deception, might a *machine* be more accurate? **The *polygraph* is a device that records fluctuations in physiological arousal as a person answers questions.** Although called a "lie detector," it's really an emotion detector. The polygraph monitors key indicators of autonomic arousal such as heart rate, blood pressure, respiration rate, and perspiration (or GSR). The assumption is that when subjects lie, they experience emotion that produces noticeable changes in these physiological indicators (see Figure 7.7). Research indicates that polygraphs are inaccurate about one-fourth to one-third of the time (Kleinmuntz & Szucko, 1984). One problem is that people who are telling the truth may experience emotional arousal when they respond to incriminating questions. Thus, polygraph tests often lead to accusations against people who are actually innocent. Another problem is that some people can lie without experiencing physiological arousal. Because of high error rates, polygraph results

cannot be submitted as evidence in most types of courtrooms. In spite of the courts' conservatism, many companies have required prospective and current employees to take lie detector tests to weed out thieves. In 1988, the U.S. Congress passed a law curtailing this practice.

In conclusion, deception is potentially detectable, but detecting it is not a simple matter. The nonverbal behaviors that tend to accompany lying are subtle and can be difficult to spot.

The Significance of Nonverbal Communication

Although people often are unaware of nonverbal communication, it clearly plays an important role in everyone's life. You constantly use nonverbal cues to convey your own feelings to others and to "read" theirs (DePaolo, 1992). Let's consider some ways that nonverbal communication can affect adjustment.

In our society, if you dislike someone, you don't usually say so. Instead, your negative feelings will "leak" through nonverbal channels. Individuals with negative self-concepts seem to have difficulty detecting these nonverbal messages of aversion, which puts them at a social disadvantage (Rosenthal, et al., 1979). To study this issue, researchers tape-recorded 10-minute interactions between two-person, same-gender pairs (Swann, Stein-Seroussi, & McNulty, 1992). Replicating the findings of previous studies, the study found that participants with negative self-views were perceived less favorably than those with positive self-concepts. However, those with negative self-concepts failed to

FIGURE 7.7.

The polygraph measures emotional reactions. A lie detector measures the physiological arousal that most people experience when they tell a lie. After using nonthreatening questions to establish a baseline, a polygraph examiner looks for signs of arousal (such as the sharp change in GSR shown here) on incriminating questions.

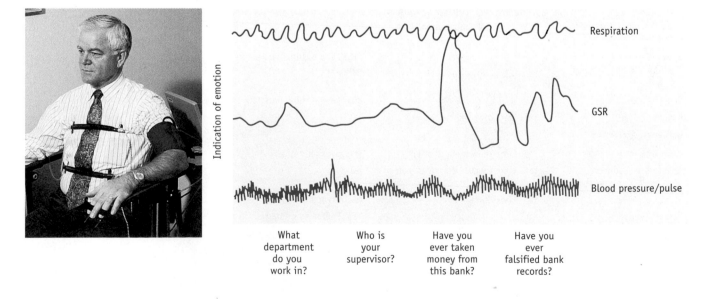

perceive this fact. In another phase of the study, judges evaluated the verbal and nonverbal (voice quality) messages received by the positive- and negative-self-concept individuals. While there were no significant differences in the nature of the verbal messages received by these two groups, there were significant differences in the nonverbal messages. Apparently, those with negative self-views attended to the positive verbal cues and disregarded the negative nonverbal ones. Deprived of this important information, these individuals may fail to learn that or why they alienate others, making it difficult for them to correct their behavior.

Researchers have found that accuracy in reading the emotions of others is related to social competence and status even in children (Feldman, Philipot, & Custrini, 1991; Hubbard & Coie, 1994). Nonverbal communication also plays an important role in marital relationships. For example, it has been shown that husbands and wives in unhappy marriages send more negative nonverbal messages and fewer positive nonverbal messages than do couples who are happily married (Noller & Guthrie, 1991). Of course, relationships depend heavily on other aspects of communication, as well. Thus, we need to do some further exploration.

Toward More Effective Communication

LEARNING OBJECTIVES

- List five suggestions for creating a positive interpersonal climate.
- Cite some suggestions for initiating a conversation.
- Describe the role of self-disclosure in relationships.
- Cite some ways to reduce the risks of self-disclosure.
- Discuss cultural and gender differences in self-disclosure.
- Cite three points good listeners need to keep in mind.

As we've noted, the importance of communication in everyday life can hardly be exaggerated. In this section, we'll turn to some practical issues that will help you become a more effective communicator. We'll review conversational skills, self-disclosure, and effective listening. Because effective communication rests on the foundation of a positive interpersonal climate, we'll begin with that topic.

Creating a Positive Interpersonal Climate

A positive interpersonal climate exists when people feel they can be open rather than guarded or defensive in their communication. You can do your part to create such a climate by putting the following suggestions into practice.

- *Learn to feel and communicate empathy.* **Empathy is adopting another's frame of reference so you can understand his or her point of view.** Being sensitive to others' needs and accepting of their feelings are hallmarks of empathy. Note that being accepting and understanding toward people doesn't require you to condone or endorse their behavior. For example, if your roommate confides that he is worried about his drinking, you can communicate your support for him, as a person, by continuing to be his friend—without encouraging him to continue drinking.

- *Practice withholding judgment.* You can promote an open climate by trying to be nonjudgmental. This doesn't mean that you are giving up your right to have opinions and make judgments. It merely means striving to interact with people in ways that don't put them on the spot (forced to offer an opinion when they would rather not) or make them feel "put down" or inadequate.

- *Strive for honesty.* Mutual trust and respect thrive on authenticity and honesty. So-called hidden agendas don't stay hidden very long. Even if others don't know exactly what your underlying motives are, they often can sense that you're not being entirely honest. Of course, striving for honesty does not require communicating everything that you feel at any time to any person. While it is true that some interactions necessarily involve pain—for example, breaking up with a girlfriend or boyfriend—you can avoid many unpleasant interactions by being truthful without being needlessly hurtful.

- *Approach others as equals.* Most people don't like to be reminded of another's higher status or greater ability. You can go a long way toward effective communication by disregarding status differences in your conversations. Especially when you have the higher status, it is better to approach people on equal terms.

- *Express your opinions tentatively.* Instead of coming across as a "know-it-all," let others know that your beliefs and attitudes are flexible and subject to revision. You can do this by using qualifying words or phrases. For instance, instead of saying, "This is how we should do it," you might say, "There seem to be several ways to go; I lean toward . . . What do you think?"

Keep these points in mind as we delve further into the topic of interpersonal communication.

Conversational Skills

Some people launch right into a conversation with a stranger; others break into a cold sweat as their minds go totally blank. If you fall into the latter category, don't despair! The "art of conversation" is actually based on conversational *skills*. And the good news is that these

Recommended Reading

Messages: The Communication Skills Book by Matthew McKay, Martha Davis, and Patrick Fanning (New Harbinger Publications, 1995)

In this short book, readers will find a wealth of information for improving their communication skills in a wide variety of situations. *Messages* is organized according to six types of communication skills: basic, advanced, conflict, social, family, and public. Within each of these sections, chapters address important issues. For example, the section on family skills includes chapters on sexual communication, parent effectiveness, and family communications; the section on public skills addresses communication in small groups and public speaking; and "advanced skills" deals with hidden agendas, transactional analysis, and the role of culture and gender in communication. The authors have a breezy writing style and use lots of examples to illustrate their points. They have also included numerous exercises to help readers assess their communication skills and practice more effective ways of interacting with others. The following excerpt addresses one of several common "hidden agendas" individuals use in talking with others.

I'm Helpless, I Suffer

This is the agenda of the victim. The stories focus on misfortune, injustice, abuse. The stories are about someone who's stuck, who tries but can't escape, who endures without hope of remedy. The person is implicitly saying, "Don't ask me to do anything about all this pain, I'm not responsible."

A classic I'm Helpless, I Suffer game is Why Does This Always Happen To Me? One man, who'd gotten a little break from his ulcer symptoms, complained of a reoccurrence after he got stuck in traffic without his antacids. "This always happens. I feel a little better and then some crazy thing comes up to set me back. Somebody puts pepper on my salad or sales take a plunge at work. It never fails." The I'm Helpless, I Suffer agenda is ideal for avoiding scary new solutions, or for accepting pain that otherwise suggests the need for a major life decision. "I'm ugly, ill, too nervous" will often help put off the change indefinitely. [pp. 75–76]

skills can be learned. To start you on your way, we'll review a few conversational tips. Our discussion is largely based on *Messages: The Communication Skills Book* by McKay and associates (1995). If you want to explore this topic in greater depth, this book is an excellent source of practical advice (see Recommended Reading box).

In making conversation, here are a few principles to consider. First, follow the Golden Rule: Give to others what you would like to receive from them. In other words, give others your attention and respect and let them know that you like them. Second, focus on the other person instead of yourself. Keep your attention on them and what they are saying, rather than worrying about how you look, what you're going to say next, or winning the argument. Third, as we have noted, use nonverbal cues to communicate your interest in the other person. Like you, others also find it easier to interact with

a person who signals friendliness. A welcoming smile can make a big difference in initial contacts.

Now, how do you actually get the conversational ball rolling? A general strategy, according to McKay and his colleagues, is to keep an eye out for similarities and differences. Look for things you have in common—an earring, a class, a home town—and build a conversation around that. Alternatively, work off of the differences between the two of you. "How did you get interested in science fiction? I'm a mystery fan myself."

Here are a few specific suggestions for breaking the ice (McKay et al., 1995).

- *Use ritual questions.* "What's your name?" "Are you from around here?" "Do you work on campus?" These are easy questions to ask; however, the answers are usually short, so the conversational ball is quickly back in your court. To sustain a conversation, you need to have some specific follow-up questions ready.

- *Ask for information.* "Where's the psychology building?" "Is there a good Mexican restaurant in town?" "I need a good auto mechanic. Can you recommend one?"

- *Give a compliment.* "I like your tattoo!" "That's a cool tie!" "You've got a great tan!"

- *Use humor.* "This (food) line is so long—I hope we don't starve to death before we get our food!"

- *Use current events.* "Are you going to vote in the upcoming election?" "What did you think of *Saving Private Ryan*?"

- *Try being direct.* Another option is to come right to the point. "It's a little scary starting a conversation

THE FAR SIDE © 1991 FARWORKS, INC. Used by permission. All rights reserved.

with a total stranger, but you look like an interesting person so I thought I'd give it try."

Of course, creating a good impression is uppermost in your mind, so you need to be careful about your opening line. Researchers have found that some openers are preferred over others. In one study, participants viewed videotapes of a man or a woman approaching an other-gender stranger and initiating a conversation using a cute/flippant, an innocuous, or a direct opening line (Kleinke, Meeker, & Staneski, 1986). The least preferred openers were of the cute/flippant variety ("Hi, I'm easy—are you?"). In contrast, the preferred openers were either innocuous ("Where are you from?") or direct ("Hi, I'm a little embarrassed about this, but I'd like to get to know you"). Since "cute" lines often backfire, your best bet is probably the conventional approach.

After you've broken the ice and gotten to know a little about another person, you may want to move a relationship to a deeper level. This is where self-disclosure comes into play, a topic we'll address next.

Self-Disclosure

Self-disclosure is the voluntary act of verbally communicating information about yourself to another person. The information doesn't have to be a deeply hidden secret, but it may be. In general terms, self-disclosure involves opening up about yourself to others. Of course, some self-disclosure is superficial—what movie you saw last week or your views on who will win the World Series. Most conversations start here. People typically only share private information—jealousy toward a sister or self-consciousness about their weight—with those they like and feel they can trust (Collins & Miller, 1994). Figure 7.8 illustrates how self-disclosure varies according to type of relationship.

Disclosing personal information to another is critically important to adjustment for several reasons. For one thing, sharing fears and problems with others who are trustworthy and supportive plays a key role in mental health. Expressing your feelings to someone else can reduce stress, as we noted in Chapter 4. Second, emotional (but not factual) self-disclosures lead to feelings of closeness, as long as disclosers feel that listeners are understanding and accepting (Reis & Patrick, 1996; Reis & Shaver, 1988). And, as you saw in Chapter 1, close relationships are an important ingredient of happiness.

Third, self-disclosure in romantic relationships correlates positively with relationship satisfaction (Hansen & Schuldt, 1984). More specifically, it may be *equity* in self-disclosure, rather than high self-disclosure, that is the critical factor that helps couples avoid stress (Bowers, Metts, & Duncanson, 1985).

FIGURE 7.8.
Breadth and depth of self-disclosure. Breadth of self-disclosure refers to how many topics one opens up about; depth refers to how far one goes in revealing private information. Both the breadth and depth of disclosures are greater with best friends as opposed to casual acquaintances or strangers. (Adapted from Altman & Taylor, 1973)

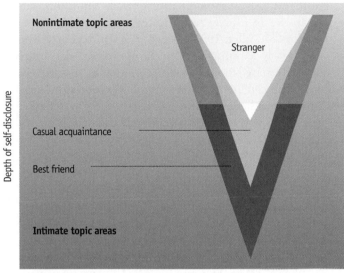

REDUCING THE RISKS OF SELF-DISCLOSURE

Let's face it: Disclosing private information to others is risky business. When you reveal private things about yourself to others, you become more vulnerable to them. Others might reject you or divulge your confidences to someone else. On the other hand, simply discussing a variety of superficial topics won't move a relationship to a deeper level.

How do you steer the conversation toward more intimate topics? We advise using the strategy of *gradual* self-disclosure. In other words, wade into the deep water, don't plunge right in. Moving gradually gives you the chance to observe how the other person reacts to you and what they say in response to your self-disclosures. This is how most relationships develop (Taylor & Altman, 1987). Of course, not all relationships follow the principle of gradual self-disclosure. Many people are capable, early on, of distinguishing between those relationships they wish to remain relatively superficial and those they would like to become more intimate. Still, when you say too much, too soon, it can nip a relationship in the bud. Also, people who frequently talk about their personal problems are often viewed as maladjusted and less likable (Collins & Miller, 1994). Because it entails less risk and stress, we suggest gradual self-disclosure as the optimal route to close relationships.

How can you gauge whether it's safe to share personal information with someone? First off, it pays to be discriminating about sharing private business. If Andrea has a reputation for "loose lips," it's a safe bet that your secrets won't be safe with her. But, let's assume that your conversational partner is discreet. You can get a good idea about her receptivity to your personal disclosures by monitoring her interest in what you have to say. Pay close attention to both verbal and nonverbal cues. If you make a personal disclosure and she reciprocates with a parallel disclosure, this ordinarily signals comfort with more intimacy. It should reassure you to know that self-disclosure is *usually* reciprocated in depth and topic (Collins & Miller, 1994). Of course, some people who aren't very comfortable engaging in self-disclosure themselves are sincerely willing to listen to you anyway. Thus, you can't depend on reciprocity alone as an indicator of another's interest.

This is why tuning in to nonverbal signals is of crucial importance. Usually, when people are uncomfortable, they will send you a nonverbal message to that effect to avoid embarrassing you with a more obvious verbal warning. "Stop" cues include reducing eye contact and displaying a puzzled, apprehensive, or pained facial expression. If seated, the other person may angle his or her body away from you; if the person is standing, he or she may increase the distance between you or shuffle his or her feet impatiently. In contrast, if your listener is leaning forward, appearing relaxed, and maintaining good eye contact, you can be fairly certain that he or she is willing to listen to your self-disclosure.

SELF-DISCLOSURE AND RELATIONSHIP DEVELOPMENT

Earlier, we noted that self-disclosure leads to feelings of intimacy. Actually, it's a little more complicated than that. Research suggests that only certain types of disclosures lead to feelings of closeness (Reis & Shaver, 1988). For instance, factual self-disclosures do not, but emotional self-disclosures do. Moreover, for intimacy to develop in a relationship, a discloser must feel understood, cared for, and validated (Reis & Patrick, 1996). To put it another way, self-disclosure alone doesn't lead to intimacy.

Self-disclosure varies over the course of relationships. As you would expect, high levels of mutual disclosure occur at the beginning of a relationship (Cunningham, Strassberg, & Haan, 1986; Taylor & Altman, 1987). Once relationships are well established, the level of disclosure tapers off. Also, once relationships have become established, people are less likely to reciprocate disclosures. Thus, when a lover or a good friend reveals private information, you frequently respond with words of sympathy and understanding rather than a like disclosure. This movement away from equal exchanges of self-disclosure appears to be based on needs that emerge as intimate relationships develop: (1) the need for support and (2) the need to maintain privacy (Altman, Vinsel, & Brown, 1981). By reciprocating support (versus information), individuals can strengthen relationships while maintaining a sense of privacy. In fact, successfully balancing these twin needs seems to be an important factor in maintaining satisfying close relationships (Baxter, 1988).

When relationships are in distress, self-disclosure seems to change. For example, one or both individuals may decrease the breadth and depth of their self-disclosures, indicating that they are emotionally withdrawing (Baxter, 1988). Also, one study of troubled relationships found that the breadth of self-disclosure decreased but the depth increased, due to the rise in the number of *negative* personal statements expressed (Tolstedt & Stokes, 1984).

CULTURE, GENDER, AND SELF-DISCLOSURE

Americans generally assume that personal sharing is essential to close friendships and happy marriages. This view is consistent with an individualistic culture that emphasizes the individual and the expression of each person's unique feelings and experiences. But collectivist cultures may have a different view of self-disclosure. At least this appears to be true in Japan, a relatively formal and reserved country. One study of cross-

cultural differences in self-disclosure involved several hundred American and Japanese college students (Barnlund, 1989). Although it was found that both Japanese and American students disclosed more to close friends than to distant companions, the Japanese disclosed more than the Americans.

In the United States, it has been found that females tend to be more openly self-disclosing than males, although the disparity seems less large than once believed (Dindia & Allen, 1992). This gender difference is strongest in *same-gender* friendships (Reis, 1998), with female friends sharing more personal information than male friends. (As we'll discuss in Chapter 8, male friends tend to share activities versus personal talk.) In *other-gender* relationships, self-disclosure is more equal, although men who hold traditional gender-role attitudes are less likely to self-disclose because they interpret sharing personal information as a sign of weakness. In other-gender relationships where disclosure is equal, the content of disclosures often varies by gender. Thus, women disclose more personal information and feelings, whereas men disclose more nonpersonal information (Wood, 1993). Also, females talk more often about negative emotions, while males typically disclose positive or neutral feelings.

Gender disparities in self-disclosure are attributed to socialization. In our culture, most men are taught to conceal tender emotions and feelings of vulnerability, especially from other men. But different patterns of self-disclosure are found in other countries. For example, in Jordan and Japan, where early intimacy between males and females is discouraged, close contacts between same-gender friends is encouraged. In one study of American, Jordanian, and Hong Kong Chinese college students, it was found that males from Hong Kong and Jordan disclosed significantly more personal information to same-gender friends than did American males (Reis & Wheeler, 1991).

In *some* situations, however, men may be more prone to self-disclosure than women. In dealing with strangers (as opposed to friends), males tend to be more self-disclosing than females (Rosenfeld, Civikly, & Herron, 1979). And, in the beginning stages of an other-gender relationship, men often disclose more

than women (Derlega et al., 1985). This finding is consistent with the traditional expectations that males should initiate relationships and females should encourage males to talk. Thus, it is an oversimplification to say that women are always more open than men. (We will discuss other aspects of gender and communication in the Chapter 10 Application.)

Effective Listening

Effective listening is a vastly underappreciated skill. As the old saying goes, "We have two ears and only one mouth, so we should listen twice as much as we speak." Because listeners process speech much more rapidly than people speak (600 words per minute versus 100–140 words per minute), it's easy for them to become bored, distracted, and inattentive (Adler & Towne, 1987). This is especially so when the listener knows the speaker well (and, therefore, expects that he or she knows what the speaker will say). Fatigue and preoccupation with one's own thoughts are other factors that interfere with effective listening.

To be a good listener, you need to keep three points in mind. First, *communicate your interest in the speaker by using nonverbal cues.* Face the speaker squarely and lean toward him or her (rather than slouching or leaning back in a chair). This posture sends a clear nonverbal message that you are interested in what the other person has to say. Try not to cross your arms and legs, as this posture can signal defensiveness. Maintaining eye contact with the speaker also indicates your attentiveness. You know how annoying it is to talk with someone whose eyes are roaming around the room. Communicate your feelings about what the speaker is saying by nodding your head or raising your eyebrows.

Second, *engage in active listening* (McKay et al., 1995). Pay careful attention to what the speaker is saying and mindfully process the information. Active listening also involves clarifying and paraphrasing. Inevitably in a conversation, the speaker will skip over an essential point or say something that is confusing. When this happens, you need to ask for clarification. "Was Bill her boyfriend or her brother?" Clarifying ensures that you have an accurate picture of the message and tells the speaker that you are interested.

Paraphrasing takes clarifying another step. To paraphrase means to state concisely what you believe the speaker said. Use words like "Let me see if I've got this straight..." or "What I hear you saying is..." or "Do you mean...?" It's obviously ludicrous to paraphrase every single thing the speaker says; you only need to do that when the speaker says something important. Paraphrasing has a number of benefits. It reassures the speaker that you are "with" him or her, derails misinterpretations, and keeps your attention from wandering.

Web Link 7.4

The Web of Culture
It is hardly a cliché that citizens of the 21st century will be challenged to communicate across cultures with sensitivity and knowledge on a worldwide basis. This business-oriented site suggests a wide range of issues and approaches to increasing cross-cultural understanding.

To develop your skill at paraphrasing, try practicing it with a friend. Have the friend tell you about something; your job is to paraphrase from time to time to be sure that you really understand what your friend is trying to communicate. After each paraphrase, your friend can tell you whether he or she agrees with your interpretation. Don't be surprised if you have to re-paraphrase several times. Keep trying until you get it right. You'll no doubt find that paraphrasing is harder than you think!

Third, *pay attention to the other person's nonverbal signals*. Listeners use the speaker's words to get the "objective" meaning of a message, but depend on nonverbal cues to get the emotional and interpersonal meanings of a message. Your knowledge of body language, tone of voice, and other nonverbal cues can give you deeper understanding of what others are communicating. Remember that these cues are available not only when the other person is speaking, but also when you are talking. If you often get signals that your listener is drifting away, you might have a tendency to be overbearing or, perhaps, to hog the conversation. The antidote is active listening.

The key to effective listening is to devote active effort to the task. Although you probably won't experience a dramatic change in your speaking skills overnight, you *may* be able to substantially improve your listening fairly quickly. For one thing, most people probably are ineffective listeners because they are unaware of the elements of effective listening. Also, effective listening hinges largely on your attitude. If you're willing to work at it, you can become a good listener.

Communication Problems

LEARNING OBJECTIVES

- *Discuss four responses to communication apprehension.*
- *Describe five barriers to effective communication.*

In this section, we'll turn our attention to two problems that can interfere with effective communication: apprehension and barriers.

Web Link 7.5

Effective Presentations
Students often tell teachers that they are terrified of making a presentation in class. Professor Jeff Radel (University of Kansas Medical Center) has crafted an excellent set of guidelines for communicating via oral presentations, visual materials, and posters.

Communication Apprehension

It's the first day of child psychology class and you have just learned that 30-minute oral reports are a course requirement. Do you welcome this as an opportunity to polish your public speaking skills or, panic-stricken, do you race to the registrar's office to drop the class? If you opted for the latter, you may suffer from *communication apprehension,* **or anxiety caused by having to talk with others**. Some people experience communication apprehension in all speaking situations (including one-on-one encounters), but most people who have the problem notice it only when they have to speak before groups.

Bodily experiences associated with communication apprehension can range from small increases in heart rate to "butterflies" in the stomach, cold hands, dry mouth, and a racing heart rate. These physiological effects are stress-induced "fight or flight" responses of the autonomic nervous system (see Chapter 3). Interestingly, it isn't the physiological responses themselves that are the root of communication apprehension, but rather the *interpretation* of these bodily responses. That is, individuals who score high on measures of communication apprehension frequently interpret the bodily changes they experience in public speaking situations as indications of fear. In contrast, those who score low on these measures often chalk up these reactions to the normal excitement in such a situation (McCroskey & Beatty, 1986).

Four responses to communication apprehension have been identified. The most common is *communication avoidance,* a reaction that occurs when people confronted with a communication situation can choose whether they want to participate in it. If they believe that speaking will make them uncomfortable, these individuals will typically avoid participating. *Communication withdrawal* occurs when people unexpectedly find themselves in a communication situation that they can't escape. In this case they may clam up entirely or say as little as possible. *Communication disruption* refers to the inability to make fluent oral presentations or to engage in inappropriate verbal or nonverbal behavior. Of course, inadequate communication skills can produce this same behavioral effect, and it isn't always possible for the average person to identify the actual cause of the problem. *Excessive communication* is a relatively unusual response to high communication apprehension, but it does occur. An example would be the person who attempts to dominate social situations. Although individuals who exhibit this response are perceived as poor communicators, they are not usually identified by the average person as having communication apprehension. This is because people expect to see it only in those who talk very little. Of course, excessive communication may be caused by factors other than communication apprehension.

Being able to speak effectively before a group is a highly useful skill, so it is important to overcome communication apprehension.

James McCroskey, an expert on this topic, suggests that avoidance and withdrawal tactics are only effective *short*-term strategies for coping with communication apprehension (McCroskey & Beatty, 1986). Because it is unlikely that you can go though life without having to speak in front of a group, it is important to learn to cope with this stressful event rather than avoiding it time and again. Allowing the problem to get out of hand can result in self-limiting behavior, such as refusing a job promotion that would entail public speaking. (The Recommended Reading, *Messages,* offers some helpful suggestions for dealing with "stage fright.") Not unexpectedly, research indicates that people with high levels of communication apprehension are likely to have difficulties in interpersonal relationships and in work and educational settings (McCroskey & Beatty, 1986). Both cognitive restructuring (Chapter 4) and systematic desensitization (Chapter 16) have proved to be very effective methods for dealing with this problem.

Barriers to Effective Communication

Earlier in the chapter, we discussed noise and its disruptive effects on interpersonal communication. In this section, we want to take a closer look at some psychological factors that contribute to noise. These psychological barriers to effective communication can reside in the sender, the receiver, or sometimes in both. Common barriers include defensiveness, motivational distortion, self-preoccupation, game playing, and collusion.

DEFENSIVENESS

Perhaps the most basic barrier to effective communication is *defensiveness*—an excessive concern with protecting oneself from being hurt. People are prone to react defensively when they feel threatened, such as when they feel that others are going to evaluate them or when they believe that others are trying to control or manipulate them. Defensiveness is also easily elicited when others act in a superior manner. Thus, those who overemphasize their status, wealth, brilliance, or power often put receivers on the defensive. Dogmatic people who convey "I'm always right" also tend to breed defensiveness. Although you should try to cultivate a communication style that reduces the likelihood of arousing defensiveness in others, you need to remember that you don't have complete control over others' perceptions and reactions.

A threat need not be real to elicit defensive behavior. If you expect that another person won't like you, for example, your interactions with that person will probably not be very positive. And, if the self-fulfilling prophecy kicks in, you may produce the negative reaction you fear.

MOTIVATIONAL DISTORTION

In Chapter 6, we discussed distortions and expectancies in person perception. The same processes operate in communication. That is, people can hear what they want to hear instead of what is actually being said.

Each person has a unique frame of reference—certain attitudes, values, and expectations—that can influence what he or she hears. Information that contradicts an individual's own views often produces emotional discomfort. One way to avoid these unpleasant feelings is to engage in *selective attention*, or actively choosing to attend to information that supports one's beliefs and to ignore information that contradicts them. Similarly, an individual may read meanings that are not intended into statements or jump to erroneous conclusions. This tendency to distort information occurs most often in discussions of issues that people feel strongly about. Certain topics (politics, racism, sexism, abortion) are often highly charged for both the sender and receiver. Misperceptions are especially likely to occur in these situations and to interfere with effective communication.

SELF-PREOCCUPATION

Everyone has had the experience of trying to communicate with someone who is so self-focused as to make enjoyable two-way conversation impossible. These people seem to talk to hear themselves talk. If you try to slip in a word about your problems, they cut you off by saying, "That's nothing. Listen what happened to me!" Further, self-preoccupied people rarely listen attentively. When another person is talking, they're wrapped up in rehearsing what they're going to say next. Because they are self-focused, these individuals are usually unaware of their negative impact on others.

Self-preoccupied people arouse negative reactions in others for several reasons. First, their remarks are usually so self-serving (seeking to impress, to gain unwarranted sympathy, and so on) that others find it offensive. Another problem is that they consistently take up more than their fair share of conversation time. Some individuals do both—talking only about themselves *and* doing so at great length. After a "conversation" with someone like this, listeners feel that their need to communicate has been ignored. Usually they try to avoid such individuals if they can. If they can't, they usually respond only minimally to try to end the conversation as quickly as possible. Needless to say, people who fail to respect the norm that conversations should involve a mutual sharing of information risk alienating others.

GAME PLAYING

"Game playing" is another barrier to effective communication. Game playing was first described by Eric Berne (1964), who originated transactional analysis, a theory of personality and interpersonal relations that emphasizes patterns of communication. In Berne's scheme, **games are manipulative interactions with predictable outcomes, in which people conceal their real motives.** For instance, Yvonne knows that Carlos gets upset when her former boyfriend is mentioned. So when they're out with others, she innocently asks, "Say, has anyone seen Rodrigo lately?" Here, the hidden agenda is to make Carlos feel bad. If Yvonne's behavior produces the desired response, she "wins." In the broadest sense, game playing can include the deliberate (or sometimes unintentional) use of ambiguous, indirect, or deceptive statements. Some game playing involves "verbal fencing" to avoid having to make clear one's meaning or intent. Particularly problematic are repetitive games that result in bad feelings and erode the trust and respect that are essential to good relationships. Games interfere with effective communication and are a destructive element in relationships.

COLLUSION

In contrast to the other barriers to effective communication, collusion requires at least two willing partners. These partners are usually involved in an intimate relationship. **In collusion, two people have an unspoken agreement to deny some problematic aspect of reality in order to sustain their relationship.** To achieve this mutual denial, both suppress all discussion of the problem area. The classic example of collusion is the alcoholic partnership. In this case, the alcoholic requires the partner to join him or her in denying the existence of a drinking problem. To maintain the relationship, the partner goes along with the tacit agreement. The two people go to great lengths to avoid any comment about alcohol-related difficulties. Over time, the drinking usually gets worse and the relationship often deteriorates, thereby making it more difficult for the partner to continue the collusion. Because it is based on a mutual agreement to deny a specific aspect of reality, collusion obviously prevents effective communication.

Communication barriers often provoke interpersonal conflict, the last topic on the agenda.

Interpersonal Conflict

LEARNING OBJECTIVES

- Cite some positive outcomes associated with constructive interpersonal conflict.
- Describe five personal styles of dealing with interpersonal conflict.
- List six guidelines for coping effectively with interpersonal conflict.
- Explain why Deborah Tannen characterizes America as "the argument culture."
- Describe some reasons for increased social contentiousness today.
- Describe what individuals and social institutions can do to reduce the level of public conflict.

People do not have to be enemies to be in conflict, and being in conflict does not make people enemies. **Interpersonal conflict exists whenever two or more people disagree.** By this definition, conflict occurs between friends and lovers as well as between competitors and enemies. The discord may be caused by a simple misunderstanding or be a product of incompatible goals, values, attitudes, or beliefs. Since conflict is an unavoidable aspect of interactions, it's essential to know how to deal constructively with it.

Beliefs About Conflict

Many people assume that any kind of conflict is inherently bad and that it should be suppressed if at all possible. In reality, conflict is neither inherently bad nor inherently good. It is a natural phenomenon that may lead to either good or bad outcomes, depending on how people deal with it. Because people see conflict as negative, they tend to avoid coping with it. Of course, sometimes avoiding conflict can be good. If a relationship or an issue is of little importance to you, or if you believe that the costs of confrontation are too high (your boss might fire you), avoidance might be the best way to handle a conflict. In these situations, there's really no reason to expend a lot of time and energy dealing with conflict. Also, cultures differ in how conflict should be handled. Collectivist cultures (like Japan) often avoid conflict, whereas individualistic cultures tend to encourage direct confrontations (Barnlund, 1989). In individualistic cultures, the type of relationship determines the effects of avoiding conflict.

When relationships and issues are important to you, avoiding conflict is generally counterproductive. For one thing, it can lead to a self-perpetuating cycle (see Figure 7.9).

Also, interpersonal discord that is suppressed usually affects a relationship in spite of efforts to conceal it, and the effects of suppressing it tend to be negative. For example, people in distressed marriages use more avoidance than people in nondistressed or satisfied marriages (Noller et al., 1994).

When dealt with openly and constructively, interpersonal conflict can lead to a variety of valuable outcomes (Johnson & Johnson, 1994). Among other things, constructive confrontation may (1) bring problems out into the open where they can be solved, (2) put an end to chronic sources of discontent in a relationship, and (3) lead to new insights through the airing of divergent views.

Types of Conflict

To manage conflict effectively, you need to know what you're dealing with. According to Verderber and Verderber (1998), conflicts are usually one of four types: pseudoconflicts, content conflicts, value conflicts, or ego conflicts.

A *pseudoconflict* is just what it says, a false conflict. The game playing we mentioned earlier is one type of pseudoconflict. The goal of the game is to get the other person "hooked" so that an unresolved issue comes out. For instance, as Brian and Tina are getting ready to go out, Tina says, "Why don't you wear your new tie?" Mark then retorts, "There you go, telling me what to wear again," a remark intended to draw Tina into a fight about power issues in their relationship. If Tina comes back with something like, "Well, if I don't, you usually look like something the cat dragged in!" she has accepted Mark's invitation to fight. On the other hand, if she identifies the interchange as a pseudoconflict, she can decline the invitation with a response like, "I was just making a suggestion. It's up to you to decide what to wear." The key to managing such encounters is being able to recognize the game and not allowing yourself to be drawn in.

A second type of conflict occurs when people disagree about issues of a factual nature. For instance, Keisha and DeWayne disagree about whether they are

FIGURE 7.9.

The conflict avoidance cycle. Avoiding conflict can lead to a self-perpetuating cycle: (1) people think of conflict as bad, (2) they get nervous about a conflict they are experiencing, (3) they avoid the conflict as long as possible, (4) the conflict gets out of control and must be confronted, and (5) they handle the confrontation badly. In turn, this negative experience sets the stage for avoiding conflict the next time—usually with the same negative outcome. (Adapted from Lulofs, 1994)

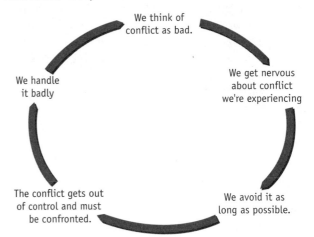

supposed to meet another couple at the restaurant or be picked up so they can all drive in one car. The way to deal with such *content-based conflicts* is to check the facts and then not dwell on who was right and who was wrong. But, note that either party can escalate the disagreement into an argument with insulting comments like, "Can't you ever get anything straight?"

Differing personal values can also lead to conflicts. *Values* are beliefs people use to evaluate the worth of various aspects of life—religion, politics, and various social and aesthetic issues. Some values are obviously more important to people than others, and higher-ranked values usually have more influence on behavior. Thus, if you believe that your family's happiness is more important than your work, you may opt for a career with minimal stress and time demands. *Value-based conflicts* are a particular problem in intimate relationships. If couples can recognize such conflicts as a valued based, they can understand that the issue is important to the other person and that he or she is not just being stubborn. When conflicts can't be resolved, two people may be willing to take turns obliging each other to maintain the relationship. For example, when they go out to eat, they might alternate sitting in the smoking and nonsmoking sections. Also, friends and lovers are sometimes able to agree to disagree. When conflicts are unresolvable and become an ongoing source of distress in marriages, they can lead to divorce. To minimize value-based conflicts, it's best to match up with a person who has similar values.

The most difficult conflicts to manage are those in which one or both parties view the outcome as a measure of self-worth—how competent one is, how much one knows, how much power one has, and so forth. In these *ego-based conflicts*, "winning" becomes more important than finding a fair solution to the problem. Ego-based conflicts often arise when one or both parties lapse into negative personal judgments about a content- or value-based issue under discussion. People most often slip into judgmental statements when they have expertise or a special stake in the discussion. Before you realize it your emotions can become involved, you can lose the ability for rational thought, and you can find yourself saying things you can't take back. Because individuals perceive so much to be at stake, ego-based conflicts are difficult to manage. For this reason, the best way to handle them is to recognize them early on and to move the conflict back to a content level.

Styles of Managing Conflict

How do you react to conflict? Most people have a habitual way or personal style of dealing with dissension. Studies have consistently revealed five distinct patterns of dealing with conflict: avoidance, accommodation, competition, compromise, and collaboration (Putnam, 1990; Thomas, 1988). Two dimensions underlie these different styles: interest in satisfying one's own concerns and interest in satisfying others' concerns (Rahim & Magner, 1995). You can see the location of these five styles on these two dimensions in Figure 7.10. As you read about these five styles, try to determine where you fit.

1. Avoidance (low concern for self and others). Some people simply don't like to face up to the existence of conflict. When a conflict emerges, the avoider will change the subject, deflect discussion with humor, make a hasty exit, or pretend to be preoccupied with something else. This person usually finds conflict extremely unpleasant and distasteful and will go to great lengths to avoid being drawn into a confrontation. People who prefer this style believe that ignoring a problem will make it go away.

For minor problems, this tactic is often a good one—you don't have to react to every little annoyance. However, for bigger conflicts, avoidance is not a good strategy; it generally just delays the inevitable clash. When one person consistently wants to talk and the other consistently does not, relationship difficulties can arise. A particular problem occurs when an avoider has greater power in a relationship (parent, supervisor, romantic partner). This situation prevents the less powerful person from airing his or her concerns and breeds frustration and resentment. We should note here that sometimes it's best to postpone a discussion—especially if one or both individuals is tired or rushed.

FIGURE 7.10.

Five styles of handling interpersonal conflict. In dealing with discord, individuals typically prefer one of five styles. The two dimensions of "concern for self" and "concern for others" underlie each of the five styles.

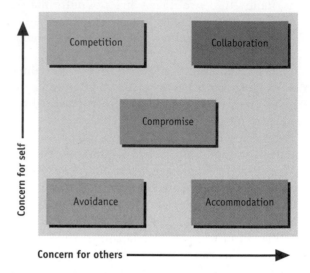

Postponing qualifies as avoiding only if the promised discussion never takes place.

2. Accommodation (low concern for self, high concern for others). Like the avoider, the accommodator feels uncomfortable with conflict. However, instead of ignoring the disagreement, this person brings the conflict to a quick end by giving in easily. People who are overly worried about acceptance and approval from others commonly use this strategy of surrender. Habitual accommodating is a poor way of dealing with conflict because it does not generate creative thinking and genuine solutions. Moreover, feelings of resentment (on both sides) may develop because the accommodator often likes to play the role of a martyr. Of course, when you don't have strong preferences (for instance, where to eat out), occasional accommodating is perfectly appropriate. Also, in some cultures (Japan), it is the preferred style of dealing with conflict (Argyle, 1991).

3. Competition (high concern for self, low concern for others). The competitor turns every conflict into a black-and-white, win-or-lose situation. Competitors will do virtually anything to emerge victorious from confrontations; thus, they can be deceitful and aggressive—including using verbal attacks and physical threats. They rigidly adhere to one position and will use threats and coercion to force the other party to submit. Giving no quarter, competitors often get personal and "hit below the belt." This style is undesirable because, like accommodation, it fails to generate creative solutions to problems. Moreover, this approach is particularly likely to lead to postconflict tension, resentment, and hostility.

4. Compromise (moderate concern for self and others). Compromising is a pragmatic approach to conflict that acknowledges the divergent needs of both parties. Compromisers are willing to negotiate and to meet the other person halfway. With a compromise approach, each person gives up something so both can have partial satisfaction. Because both parties gain some satisfaction, compromise is a fairly constructive approach to conflict, especially when the issue is moderately important.

5. Collaboration (high concern for self and others). While compromise simply entails "splitting the difference" between positions, collaboration involves a sincere effort to find a solution that will maximize the satisfaction of both parties. In this approach, conflict is viewed as a mutual problem to be solved as effectively as possible. Collaboration thus encourages openness and honesty. It also stresses the importance of criticizing the other person's *ideas* in a disagreement rather than the other *person*. Collaboration requires putting a lot of effort into clarifying differences and similarities in positions, so that you can build on the similarities. Generally, this is the most productive approach for dealing with conflict. Instead of resulting in a postconflict residue of tension and resentment, collaboration tends to produce a climate of trust.

Dealing Constructively with Conflict

As you have seen, the most effective approach to conflict management is collaboration. To help you implement such an approach, we will offer some specific suggestions. But, before we get down to specifics, there are a few principles you should keep in mind (Alberti & Emmons, 1990; Verderber & Verderber, 1998). First, in a conflict situation, approach the other person as an equal. If you have a higher status or more power (parent, supervisor), try to set this difference aside. Second, define the conflict as a mutual problem to be solved cooperatively, rather than as a win-lose proposition. Third, choose a mutually acceptable time to sit down and work on resolving the conflict. It is not always best to tackle the conflict when and where it first arises. Fourth, remember to show respect for the other person's position. Do your best to empathize with, and fully understand, their frame of reference. Finally, communicate your flexibility and willingness to modify your position.

Here now are some explicit guidelines to help you deal more effectively with interpersonal conflict (Alberti & Emmons, 1990; Johnson & Johnson, 1994).

- *Make communication honest and open.* Don't withhold information or misrepresent your position. Avoid deceit and manipulation.
- *Use specific behaviors to describe another person's* annoying habits rather than general statements about their personality. Thus, you'll probably get further with your roommate if you say something like, "Please throw your clothes in the hamper" rather than "You're such an inconsiderate slob." Remarks about specific actions are less threatening, and less likely to be taken personally. They also clarify what you hope will change.
- *Avoid "loaded" words.* Certain words are "loaded" in the sense that they tend to trigger negative emotional reactions in listeners. For example, you can discuss politics without using terms such as "right-winger" and "knee-jerk liberal."
- *Use a positive approach.* When giving feedback, try to preface a negative statement with a positive one. But don't use empty praise—most people recognize it and interpret it as patronizing. Also, try to phrase criticism positively rather than negatively. Thus, "I love it when we cook dinner together" will be better received than "You never help with dinner, and I resent it."
- *Limit complaints to recent behavior and to the present situation.* Bringing up past grievances only rekindles old resentments and distracts you from the current problem. Similarly, avoid saying things like "You *always* say you're too busy" or "You *never* do your fair share of the housework." Such categorical statements are bound to put the other person on the defensive.
- *Assume responsibility for your own feelings and preferences.* Instead of "*You* make me mad," say "I am angry." Or, try "I'd appreciate it if you'd water the garden" rather than "Do you think the garden needs watering?"

To this point, we've been focusing on communication in the private sphere—interactions between people in personal relationships. To complete our discussion of interpersonal conflict, we want to examine communication in the public sphere—interactions among members of the same society or community who do not personally know one another.

Public Communication in an Adversarial Culture

Road rage, "flaming," negative campaign ads, the *Jerry Springer Show*—hostile incidents assault Americans on a daily basis. Hoping to attract more listeners and viewers, the news media set up debates between individuals who represent the most extreme views. In some classrooms, students are encouraged to "pick to death" readings and ideas with no larger intellectual purpose in mind. If you've ever been "flamed" in your e-mail or witnessed it, you know that hostility is present on the Internet. Senseless traffic disputes and altercations result in serious injury or death for at least 1500 Americans every year ("Road rage plagues drivers," 1997). Many Americans are worried that public interactions are becoming increasingly conflictual. What is going on?

Sociolinguist Deborah Tannen (1998) characterizes contemporary America as "the argument culture" in her book of the same title (see Recommended Reading). According to Tannen, an atmosphere of "unrelenting contention" (p. 3) pervades American culture and is fueled by a growing tendency for Americans to automatically take an adversarial approach in almost any public situation. She worries that this constant exposure to public arguments is having a "corrosive" effect on Americans' spirits and is creating serious social problems. Hostile public debates usually muddy important public issues rather than clarifying them, inflame emotions, and alienate Americans from each other and their leaders.

Deborah Tannen

CONTRIBUTING FACTORS

Obviously, numerous factors contribute to social contentiousness, and we can touch on only a few of them. We'll start with the fact that the United States is an individualistic culture, which predisposes Americans to be adversarial because the self is perceived to be isolated and in opposition to society. Second, Americans (and those in other Western cultures) have a dualistic view of nature or a tendency to see things in terms of opposites—good *versus* bad, strong *versus* weak, and so on (Tannen, 1998). On the other hand, most Eastern cultures have a nondualistic perspective, in which opposites are seen as complementary partners, both essential to a larger whole (good *and* bad, strong *and* weak).

A third factor is that face-to-face communication is on the decline, fed by advances in technology (Tannen, 1998). Whereas families used to gather around a single radio or television, now many family members have their own radios and TVs. Similarly, many families have more than one telephone and computer. Many families gather only rarely for meals. Instead, to accommodate busy schedules, family members each pop frozen food into the microwave. In the same vein, distance learning classes permit many to take classes they would not otherwise be able to attend, but limit social interactions with peers and instructors. Taken together, such changes mean that individuals spend more time on their own, rather than learning to interact effectively with others.

Excessive exposure to the high levels of physical and verbal aggression, especially on television, is a fourth factor in the equation (Huston & Wright, 1982). Children spend an average of about 2 to 4 hours per day watching television, with viewing time increasing up

through early adolescence. The National Television Violence Study, a large-scale study of the content of network and cable television shows conducted in 1994–1995, revealed that 57% of programs contain violence. By the time a child finishes grade school, he or she will have vicariously witnessed approximately 8,000 murders and 100,000 other acts of violence on TV (Huston et al., 1992).

Over time, excessive exposure to media violence can take its toll in a variety of ways. Numerous studies suggest that extensive exposure to media violence contributes to the development of aggressiveness in some children (Friedrich-Cofer & Huston, 1986). And aggressive children grow up to be aggressive adults (Huesmann & Eron, 1986). In addition, repeated exposure to aggression causes viewers to become numb or

● Recommended Reading

The Argument Culture: Moving from Debate to Dialogue by Deborah Tannen (Random House, 1998)

In this thought-provoking work, Tannen claims that public interchanges in America are increasingly framed as battles or games. Hence, the focus has become trying to win arguments rather than trying to understand what is being said.

While acknowledging that opposition can be useful and necessary, Tannen is concerned with what she sees as a trend for Americans to use an adversarial approach, to the exclusion of other ways of communicating in public. And living in "the argument culture" is having negative effects on Americans and the larger society. Written in an easygoing style, the book brings in research and wide-ranging examples from politics, the media, the legal profession, the classroom, and the Internet to bolster this thesis.

To halt the growth of the argument culture, Tannen advocates using nonadversarial ways to negotiate disagreements and mediate conflicts. For instance, she urges people to start looking for ways that both sides can win in disagreements (as opposed to thinking in terms of one side "winning" and the other "losing"). In addition, she urges people to get out of the "dualism trap." Instead of asking, "What is the other side?" individuals can ask, "What are the other sides?" Tannen recommends setting up discussions with three or more people rather than using the debate-prone two-person format. She also suggests reducing the use of war metaphors (the battle of the sexes, the war on drugs, "annihilating" the other team, and so forth) and replacing them with less combative figures of speech.

Our public interactions have become more and more like having an argument with a spouse. Conflict can't be avoided in our public lives any more than we can avoid conflict with people we love. One of the great strengths of our society is that we can express these conflicts openly. But just as spouses have to learn ways of settling their differences without inflicting real damage on each other, so we, as a society, have to find constructive ways of resolving disputes and differences. Public discourse requires making an argument for a point of view, not having an argument—as in having a fight. [p. 4]

desensitized to violence and its effects on victims (Thomas, 1982), causing them to be more accepting of it. Furthermore, there is evidence that people come to believe that "television reality" depicts actual reality. Thus, people who are exposed to considerable TV violence come to believe that society is more hostile and dangerous than it actually is. In turn, they become more distrustful, so they are more likely to behave aggressively when they perceive that they are in a threatening situation (Gerbner et al., 1980).

RESTORING PRODUCTIVE PUBLIC COMMUNICATION

Must Americans resign themselves to living in an increasingly contentious society, or are there ways to reduce public hostility? Social institutions—the government, media, and schools, for instance—could institute broad-ranging changes that could significantly affect this problem. Politicians could agree to desist from negative campaign rhetoric and enact legislation to reduce access to weapons. Newspapers could encourage reporters to emphasize substance in their reporting and minimize sensationalism; producers could voluntarily reduce the amount of gratuitous violence portrayed on television and in films and increase the number of programs and movies with nonviolent and prosocial messages. And schools could institute programs that teach children social skills and nonviolent ways of resolving conflicts.

But what can *individuals* do? By applying the principles of effective interpersonal communication discussed in this chapter, you can do a lot. Tune in to nonverbal signals, create a positive interpersonal climate, be a good listener, overcome the barriers to effective communication, and practice your conflict management skills. Practice these principles when you're on the Internet, as well. When you're on the road, avoid antagonizing other drivers (see Figure 7.11). And, minimize the amount of media violence you expose yourself to—be selective about the TV programs and movies you watch.

Road rage is one example of increased public conflict in American society.

Parents have a special role to play. They can limit their children's exposure to physical and verbal aggression—on television, in movies, in video games, and in books. And they can ensure that their kids are exposed to TV programs and movies that model positive ways of interacting with others to increase helpfulness and cooperation in children (Hearold, 1986; Liebert & Sprafkin, 1988). Parents can also help by encouraging and rewarding nonaggressive rather than aggressive ways of resolving childhood conflicts (especially in boys). Finally, they can use disciplinary methods that don't model aggressive behavior (for more information, see the Application for Chapter 11, on effective parenting).

In summary, individuals and social institutions can do a number of things to reduce the level of conflictual communication in the public arena. In our upcoming Application, we will discuss assertive communication, a communication style that has proved extremely effective across a wide variety of interpersonal communication situations—for example, making acquaintances, developing relationships, and resolving interpersonal conflicts.

Tips for Avoiding Road Rage
Don't tailgate.
Don't use obscene gestures.
Don't lean on your horn; tap it lightly.
Signal before switching lanes and don't cut someone off when you change lanes.
Don't display bumper stickers or slogans that might antagonize others.
Avoid making eye contact with a hostile motorist.
Be polite and courteous even if the other driver is not.
Don't drive when you are angry, upset, or fatigued.

FIGURE 7.11.

Steering clear of road rage. Studies have shown that these strategies can reduce your chances of being a victim of road rage. ("Road rage plagues drivers," 1997)

Developing an Assertive Communication Style

- Differentiate assertive communication from submissive and aggressive communication.
- Describe five steps that lead to more assertive communication.

Answer the following questions "yes" or "no."

_____ 1. When someone asks you for an unreasonable favor, do you have difficulty saying no?

_____ 2. Do you feel timid about returning flawed merchandise?

_____ 3. Do you have a hard time requesting even small favors from others?

_____ 4. When you're in a group that is hotly debating an issue, are you shy about speaking up?

_____ 5. When a salesperson pressures you to buy something you don't want, do you have a hard time expressing your lack of interest?

If you answered "yes" to several of the questions above, you may have difficulty being assertive. Many people have this problem, but it is more common among females because they are socialized to be more submissive than males—for example, to "be nice" and not to "make waves." Consequently, assertiveness training has become especially popular among women. Men, too, find assertiveness training helpful, both because some males have been socialized to be passive and because some men want to learn to be less aggressive and more assertive. In this Application, we'll elaborate on the differences between assertive, submissive, and aggressive behavior and discuss some procedures for increasing assertiveness.

The Nature of Assertiveness

Assertiveness is acting in your own best interests by expressing your thoughts and feelings directly and honestly (Alberti & Emmons, 1995; Bower & Bower, 1991). Essentially, assertiveness involves standing up for your rights when someone else is about to infringe on them. To be assertive is to speak out openly rather than pull your punches. The nature of assertive communication can best be clarified by contrasting it with submissive communication and aggressive communication.

Submissive communication involves consistently giving in to others on points of possible contention. Submissive people tend to let others take advantage of them. Typically, their biggest problem is that they cannot say "no" to unreasonable requests. A common example is the college student who can't tell her roommate not to borrow her clothes. Submissive people also have difficulty voicing disagreement with others and making requests themselves. In traditional trait terminology, they are timid.

Although the roots of submissiveness have not been investigated fully, they appear to lie in excessive concern about gaining the social approval of others. However, the strategy of not making waves is more likely to garner others' contempt than their approval. Moreover, individuals who use this style often feel bad about themselves (for being "pushovers") and resentful of those whom they allow to take advantage of them. These feelings often lead the submissive individual to try to punish the other person by withdrawing, sulking, or crying (Bower & Bower, 1991). These manipulative attempts to get one's own way are sometimes referred to as "passive aggression" or "indirect aggression."

At the other end of the spectrum, _aggressive communication_ involves an intention to hurt or harm another. Assertive behavior entails no such intention to inflict harm, but it does involve defending your rights. The problem in real life is that assertive and aggressive behaviors _may_ overlap. When someone is about to infringe on their rights, people often lash out at the other party (aggression) while defending their rights (assertion). The challenge, then, is to learn to be firm and assertive without becoming aggressive.

Advocates of assertive communication argue that it is much more adaptive than either submissive or aggressive communication (Alberti & Emmons, 1995; Bower & Bower, 1991). They maintain that submissive behavior leads to poor self-esteem, self-denial, emotional suppression, and strained interpersonal relationships. Conversely, aggressive communication tends to promote guilt, alienation, and disharmony. In contrast, assertive behavior is said to foster high self-esteem and satisfactory interpersonal relationships.

Of course, behaving assertively does not ensure that you will always get what you want. The essential point with assertiveness is that you are able to state what you want clearly and directly. Being able to do so makes you feel good about yourself and will usually make others feel good about you too. And, although being assertive doesn't guarantee your chances for getting what you want, it certainly enhances them.

Steps in Assertiveness Training

Numerous assertiveness training programs are available in book form or through seminars. Some recommendations about books appear in the Recommended Readings box in this section. Most of the programs emphasize gradual improvement and reinforcement of appropriate behavior. Here we will summarize the key steps in assertiveness training.

● Recommended Reading

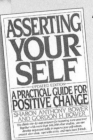

Asserting Yourself: A Practical Guide for Positive Change by Sharon Anthony Bower and Gordon H. Bower (Addison-Wesley, 1991)

Bower and Bower put the problem of non-assertiveness into perspective, relating it to self-esteem and anxiety. They then lay out a systematic program for increasing assertive behavior. They make extensive use of probing questions to help you work out a plan of action that is personally relevant. They also provide sample verbal scripts for numerous common situations that typically call for assertive behavior. Among situations they cover are requesting a raise, saying "no" to unreasonable demands, protesting unjust criticism, dealing with a substance abuser, pointing out annoying habits, and dealing with the silent treatment. They devote a full chapter to the role of assertive behavior in developing friendships—initiating and ending conversations, keeping conversations going, making dates, self-disclosure, listening, and coping with social anxieties. The book is smoothly written in a nonpatronizing tone, as you can tell from the excerpt quoted in this Application.

Other books on assertiveness can also be recommended highly. One of the best is, *Your Perfect Right*, by Robert E. Alberti and Michael L. Emmons (1995), which is now in its seventh edition. Many assertiveness books target women, focusing on the communication problems women tend to encounter. *The Assertive Woman* by Stanlee Phelps and Nancy Austin (1997) is particularly useful.

1. UNDERSTAND WHAT ASSERTIVE COMMUNICATION IS

Most programs begin by clarifying the nature of assertive communication. In order to produce assertive behavior, you need to understand what it looks and sounds like. One way to accomplish this is to imagine situations calling for assertiveness and compare hypothetical submissive (or passive), assertive, and aggressive responses. Let's consider one such comparison. In this example, a woman in assertiveness training is asking her roommate to cooperate in cleaning the apartment once a week. The roommate, who is uninterested in the problem, is listening to music when the conversation begins. In this example, the roommate is playing the role of the antagonist—called the "downer" in the following scripts (excerpted from Bower & Bower, 1991, pp. 8, 9, 11).

The Passive Scene

SHE: *Uh, I was wondering if you would be willing to take time to decide about the housecleaning.*

DOWNER: *(listening to the music) Not now, I'm busy.*

SHE: *Oh, okay.*

The Aggressive Scene

SHE: *Listen, I've had it with you not even talking about cleaning this damn apartment. Are you going to help me?*

DOWNER: *(listening to the music) Not now, I'm busy.*

SHE: *Why can't you look at me when you turn me down? You don't give a damn about the housework or me! You only care about yourself!*

DOWNER: *That's not true.*

SHE: *You never pay any attention to the apartment or to me. I have to do everything around here!*

DOWNER: *Oh, shut up! You're just neurotic about cleaning all the time. Who are you, my mother? Can't I relax with my stereo for a few minutes without you pestering me? This was my apartment first, you know!*

The Assertive Scene

SHE: *I know housework isn't the most fascinating subject, but it needs to be done. Let's plan when we'll do it.*

DOWNER: *(listening to music) Oh, c'mon—not now! I'm busy.*

SHE: *This won't take long. I feel that if we have a schedule, it will be easier to keep up with the chores.*

DOWNER: *I'm not sure I'll have time for all of them.*

SHE: *I've already drawn up a couple of rotating schedules for housework, so that each week we have an equal division of tasks. Will you look at them? I'd like to hear your decisions about them, say, tonight after supper?*

DOWNER: *[indignantly] I have to look at these now?*

SHE: *Is there some other time that's better for you?*

DOWNER: *Oh, I don't know.*

SHE: *Well, then let's discuss plans after supper for fifteen minutes. Is that agreed?*

DOWNER: *I guess so.*

SHE: *Good! It won't take long, and I'll feel relieved when we have a schedule in place.*

If you're unfamiliar with assertive communication, it is critical that you get a handle on what it entails. Reading two or three books on assertiveness is a way to get a good picture of assertive behavior. A helpful way to distinguish among the three types of communication is in terms of how people deal with their own rights and the rights of others. Submissive people sacrifice their own rights. Aggressive people tend to ignore the rights of others. Assertive people consider both their own rights *and* the rights of others.

As we have noted, the nonverbal aspect of communication is extremely important. To ensure that your assertive words have impact, it is important to back them up with congruent nonverbal messages. That is, you'll come across as more assertive if you face the person you're talking with, look directly at him or her, and maintain eye contact, rather than looking away, fidgeting, slouching, and shuffling your feet (Bower & Bower, 1991). Some additional guidelines for behaving assertively are summarized in Figure 7.12 on the next page.

FIGURE 7.12.

Guidelines for assertive behavior. In their book on assertiveness, Bower and Bower (1991) outline a four-step program intended to help readers create successful assertive scripts for themselves. The four steps are (1) *describe* the unwanted behavior from another person (called your "Downer") that is troubling you, (2) *express* your feelings about the behavior to the other person, (3) *specify* the changes needed, and (4) try to provide rewarding *consequences* for the change. Using this framework, the table shown here provides some useful do's and don'ts for achieving effective assertive behavior.

Rules for Assertive Scripts

Number	Do	Don't
Describe		
D1	Describe the other person's behavior objectively.	Describe your emotional reaction to it.
D2	Use concrete terms.	Use abstract, vague terms.
D3	Describe a specified time, place, and frequency of the action.	Generalize for "all time."
D4	Describe the action, not the "motive."	Guess at your Downer's motives or goals.
Express		
E1	Express your feelings.	Deny your feelings.
E2	Express them calmly.	Unleash emotional outbursts.
E3	State feelings in a positive manner, as relating to a goal to be achieved.	State feelings negatively, making put-down attack.
E4	Direct yourself to the specific offending behavior, not to the whole person.	Attack the entire character of the person.
Specify		
S1	Ask explicitly for change in your Downer's behavior.	Merely imply that you'd like a change.
S2	Request a small change.	Ask for too large a change.
S3	Request only one or two changes at one time.	Ask for too many changes.
S4	Specify the concrete actions you want to see stopped, and those you want to see performed.	Ask for changes in nebulous traits or qualities.
S5	Take account of whether your Downer can meet your request without suffering large losses.	Ignore your Downer's needs or ask only for your satisfaction.
S6	Specify (if appropriate) what behavior you are willing to change to make the agreement.	Consider that only your Downer has to change.
Consequences		
C1	Make the consequences explicit.	Be ashamed to talk about rewards and penalties.
C2	Give a positive reward for change in the desired direction.	Give only punishments for lack of change.
C3	Select something that is desirable and reinforcing to your Downer.	Select something that only you might find rewarding.
C4	Select a reward that is big enough to maintain the behavior change.	Offer a reward you can't or won't deliver.
C5	Select a punishment of a magnitude that "fits the crime" of refusing to change behavior.	Make exaggerated threats.
C6	Select a punishment that you are actually willing to carry out.	Use unrealistic threats or self-defeating punishment.

2. MONITOR YOUR ASSERTIVE COMMUNICATION

Most people's assertiveness varies from one situation to another. In other words, they may be assertive in some social contexts and timid in others. Consequently, once you understand the nature of assertive communication, you should monitor yourself and identify when you are nonassertive. In particular, you should figure out who intimidates you, on *what topics*, and in *which situations*.

3. OBSERVE A MODEL'S ASSERTIVE COMMUNICATION

Once you have identified the situations in which you are nonassertive, think of someone who communicates assertively in those situations and observe that person's behavior closely. In other words, find someone to model yourself after. Doing so should help you learn how to behave assertively in situations crucial to you. Your observations should also allow you to see how rewarding assertive communication can be, which should strengthen your assertive tendencies. If an assertive model isn't available, another option is to adapt the relevant scenarios that are depicted in most self-help books.

4. PRACTICE ASSERTIVE COMMUNICATION

Ultimately, the key to achieving assertive communication is to practice it and work toward gradual improvement. Your practice can take several forms. In *covert rehearsal*, you can imagine a situation requiring assertion and the dialogue that you would engage in. In *role playing*, you might get a therapist or friend to play the

KUDZU by Doug Marlette. By permission of Doug Marlette and Creators Syndicate.

role of an antagonist. Then practice communicating assertively in this artificial situation.

Eventually, of course, you want to transfer your assertiveness skills to real-life situations. Most experts recommend that you use *shaping* to increase your assertive communication gradually. As we discussed in the Chapter 4 Application, shaping involves rewarding yourself for making closer and closer approximations of a desired behavior. For example, in the early stages of your behavior-change program, your goal might be to make at least one assertive comment every day, while toward the end you might be striving to make at least eight such comments every day. Obviously, in designing a shaping program it is important to set realistic goals for yourself.

5. ADOPT AN ASSERTIVE ATTITUDE

Most assertiveness training programs have a behavioral orientation and focus on specific responses for specific situations (see Figure 7.13). However, it's obvious that real-life situations are only rarely just like those portrayed in books. Hence, some experts maintain that acquiring a repertoire of verbal responses for certain situations is not as important as developing a new attitude that you're not going to let people push you around (or let yourself push others around, if you're the aggressive type) (Alberti & Emmons, 1995). Although most programs don't talk explicitly about attitudes, they do appear to instill a new attitude indirectly. And a change in attitude is probably crucial to achieving flexible, assertive behavior.

Assertive Responses to Some Common Put-Downs

Nature of Remark	Put-down sentence	Suggested assertive reply
Nagging about details	"Haven't you done this yet?"	"No, when did you want it done?" (Answer without hedging, and follow-up with a question.)
Prying	"I know I maybe shouldn't ask, but. . ."	"If I don't want to answer, I'll let you know," (Indicate that you won't make yourself uncomfortable just to please this person.)
Putting you on the spot socially	"Are you busy Tuesday?"	"What do you have in mind?" (Answer the question with a question.)
Pigeonholing you	"That's a woman for you!"	"That's one woman, not *all* women." (Disagree—assert your individuality.)
Using insulting labels for your behavior	"That's a dumb way to..."	"I'll decide what to call my behavior." (Refuse to accept the label.)
Basing predictions on an amateur personality analysis	"You'll have a hard time. You're too shy."	"In what ways do you think I'm too shy?" (Ask for clarification of the analysis.)

FIGURE 7.13.
Assertive responses to common put-downs.
Having some assertive replies at the ready can increase your confidence in difficult social interactions. (Adapted from Bower & Bower, 1991)

Key Ideas

THE PROCESS OF INTERPERSONAL COMMUNICATION
◐ Interpersonal communication is the interactional process that occurs when one person sends a message to another. Communication takes place when a sender transmits a message to a receiver either verbally or nonverbally. Although people often take it for granted, effective communication contributes to their satisfaction and success in relationships and on the job.

NONVERBAL COMMUNICATION
◐ Nonverbal communication tends to be more spontaneous than verbal communication, and it is more ambiguous. Sometimes it contradicts what is communicated verbally. It is often multichanneled, and like language, it is culturally bound. Nonverbal communication usually conveys emotions. Elements of nonverbal communication include personal space, facial expression, eye contact, body language, touch, and paralanguage.

◐ Certain nonverbal cues are associated with deception, but many of these cues do not correspond to popular beliefs about how liars give themselves away. Discrepancies between facial expressions and other nonverbal signals may suggest dishonesty. The vocal and visual cues associated with lying are so subtle, however, that detecting deception is difficult. Machines used to detect deception (polygraphs) are not particularly accurate. Nonverbal communication plays an important role in adjustment, especially in the quality of interpersonal relationships.

TOWARD MORE EFFECTIVE COMMUNICATION
◐ Effective communication rests on the foundation of a positive interpersonal climate. To promote such a climate, it helps to show empathy, treat people as equals, withhold judgment, strive for honesty, and express opinions tentatively. To be an effective communicator, it's important to know how to initiate a conversation. The most preferred opening lines are innocuous or direct; the least preferred are attempts at cuteness that backfire.

◐ Self-disclosure—opening up to others—can lead to emotional intimacy in relationships. Emotional (but not factual) self-disclosures lead to feelings of closeness. To reduce the risks associated with self-disclosure, it's best to self-disclose gradually. The receiver's nonverbal signals help the speaker know whether to continue or to stop disclosing. The level of self-disclosure varies over the course of relationships. Cultures vary in the preferred level of self-disclosure. American women tend to self-disclose more than men, but this disparity is not so large as it was once was. Effective listening is an essential aspect of interpersonal communication.

COMMUNICATION PROBLEMS
◐ A number of problems can arise that interfere with effective communication. Individuals who become overly anxious when they talk with others suffer from communication apprehension. This difficulty can cause problems in relationships and in work and educational settings. Sometimes communication can produce negative interpersonal outcomes. Barriers to effective communication include defensiveness, motivational distortion, self-preoccupation, game playing, and collusion.

INTERPERSONAL CONFLICT
◐ Dealing constructively with interpersonal conflict is an important aspect of effective communication. Individualistic cultures tend to encourage direct confrontations, whereas collectivist cultures often avoid them. Nonetheless, many Americans have negative attitudes about conflict. Conflicts can be classified as one of four types: pseudoconflicts, content conflicts, value conflicts, or ego conflicts. In dealing with conflict, most people have a preferred style: avoidance, accommodation, competition, compromise, or collaboration. This last style is the most effective in managing conflict.

◐ Public communication in America is becoming increasingly contentious. Contributing factors include living in an individualistic culture, having a dualistic perspective, reduced face-to-face interactions, and excessive exposure to high levels of physical and verbal aggression, especially on television. Individuals and social institutions can institute a number of changes to restore productive communication in the public sphere.

APPLICATION: DEVELOPING AN ASSERTIVE COMMUNICATION STYLE
◐ An assertive style is one that enables individuals to stand up for themselves and to respect the rights of others. To become more assertive, individuals need to understand what assertive communication is, monitor assertive communication, observe a model's assertive communication, practice being assertive, and adopt an assertive attitude.

Key Terms

Assertiveness	Games	Nonverbal
Collusion	Interpersonal	communication
Communication	communication	Paralanguage
apprehension	Interpersonal	Personal space
Context	conflict	Polygraph
Display rules	Kinesics	Proxemics
Empathy	Noise	Self-disclosure

Key People

Sharon Anthony Bower and Gordon Bower	Edward T. Hall
Paul Ekman and Wallace Friesen	James McCroskey
	Deborah Tannen

Practice Test

1. Which of the following is not a component of the interpersonal communication process?
   a. The sender
   b. The receiver
   c. The channel
   d. The meaning

2. Research shows that individuals from a variety of cultures:
   a. agree on the facial expressions that correspond with all emotions.
   b. agree on the facial expressions that correspond with 15 basic emotions.
   c. agree on the facial expressions that correspond with 6 basic emotions.
   d. do not agree on the facial expressions that correspond with any emotions.

3. Which of the following is not an aspect of body language?
   a. Gait
   b. Personal space
   c. Posture
   d. Gestures

4. According to research, which of the following cues is associated with dishonesty?
   a. Speaking with a higher than normal pitch
   b. Speaking slowly
   c. Giving relatively long answers to questions
   d. Lack of eye contact

5. With regard to self-disclosure, it is best to:
   a. share a lot about yourself when you first meet someone.
   b. share very little about yourself for a long time.
   c. gradually share information about yourself.
   d. give no personal information on a first encounter, but share a lot the next time.

6. In same-gender friendships:
   a. most men disclose more to their friends than women.
   b. most women disclose more to their friends than men.
   c. men and women disclose about the same amount to their friends.
   d. men and women disclose about the same amount, but women start disclosing sooner.

7. When people hear what they want to hear instead of what is actually said, _____ is operating.
   a. defensiveness
   b. self-preoccupation
   c. motivational distortion
   d. game playing

8. The most difficult conflicts to manage are:
   a. pseudoconflicts.
   b. content-based conflicts.
   c. value-based conflicts.
   d. ego-based conflicts.

9. Generally, the most productive style for managing conflict is:
   a. collaboration.
   b. compromise.
   c. accommodation.
   d. avoidance.

10. Expressing your thoughts directly and honestly without trampling on other people is a description of which communication style?
    a. Aggressive
    b. Empathic
    c. Submissive
    d. Assertive

Answers

1. d pages 187–188
2. c pages 190–191
3. b page 193
4. a pages 195–196
5. c page 199
6. b page 201
7. c page 203
8. d pages 205–206
9. a page 207
10. d page 210

INFOTRAC COLLEGE EDITION

Go to the Wadsworth Psychology Study Center (http://psychology. wadsworth.com/) for quiz questions, research updates, hot topics, interactive exercises, and suggested readings in INFOTRAC related to this chapter.

CHAPTER 8

Friendship and Love

Jason was so keyed up, he tossed and turned all night. When morning finally arrived, he was elated. In less than two hours, he would meet Sarah for coffee! In his first class, thoughts and images of Sarah constantly distracted him from the lecture. When class was finally over, he had to force himself not to walk too fast to the Student Union, where they had agreed to meet. Sound familiar? Chances are that you recognize Jason's behavior as that of someone falling in love.

Love and friendship play vital roles in people's lives. They also play a large role in psychological adjustment. Given their importance, it's ironic that psychologists didn't start studying these phenomena scientifically until the 1970s. Despite their late start, however, researchers have made up for lost time. Thus, we have a wealth of interesting findings to explore. We'll start off by surveying the array of close relationships and how culture influences ideas about relationships. Then we'll consider why people are attracted to each other and why they stay in or leave relationships. Following that, we'll probe more deeply into friendship and romantic love and examine the problem of loneliness. In the Application section, we'll focus on the distressing problem of date rape.

Perspectives on Close Relationships

LEARNING OBJECTIVES

● Define close relationships and give some examples.
● Describe how members from individualistic cultures and collectivist cultures view love and marriage.

Although you're eager to dive right into the fascinating topic of romantic love, it's important to know something first about the variety of close relationships and how culture influences people's views of relationships. Thus, we'll take a quick look at these foundational issues.

The Ingredients of Close Relationships

Typically, *close relationships* are those that are important, interdependent, and long lasting. In other words, people spend a lot of time and energy maintaining the relationship, and what one person says and does affects the other. As you are aware, close relationships have the capacity to arouse intense feelings—both positive (passion, concern, caring) and negative (rage, jealousy, despair).

Close relationships come in many forms: those with co-workers and family members, friendships, romantic relationships, marriage. Although many close relationships are based on mutual, intimate self-disclosure, many are not. When college students were asked to identify that person to whom they felt closest, 47% named a romantic partner, 36% listed a friend, 14% mentioned a family member, and 3% listed another individual such as a co-worker (Berscheid, Snyder, & Omoto, 1989). Hence, not all close relationships are characterized by emotional intimacy.

Culture and Relationships

Cross-cultural research on close relationships is largely limited to romantic relationships, so we'll focus on this topic. Cultures vary in their emphasis on love—especially romantic love—as a prerequisite for marriage. Interestingly, love as the basis for marriage goes back only to the 18th century of Western culture (Stone, 1977). According to Elaine Hatfield and Richard Rapson (1993), "Marriage-for-love represents an ultimate expression of individualism" (p. 2). By contrast, marriages arranged by families and other go-betweens remain common in cultures high in collectivism, including India (Gupta, 1992), Japan (Iwao, 1993), and China (Xiaohe & Whyte, 1990). This practice is declining in some societies as a result of Westernization, but

Marriages based on romantic love are the norm in Western cultures, whereas arranged marriages prevail in collectivist cultures.

in collectivist societies people contemplating marriage still tend to think in terms of "What will my parents and other people say?" rather than "What does my heart say?" (Triandis, 1994). Studies show that attitudes about love in collectivist societies reflect these cultural priorities (Moghaddam, Taylor, & Wright, 1993). For example, in comparison to Westerners, Japanese respondents report that they value romantic love less (Simmons, von Kolke, & Shimizu, 1986) and rate their relationships as being lower in love commitment (Ting-Toomey, 1991). When compared to Europeans, respondents from India and South Africa also indicated that they valued romantic love less (Furnham, 1984). And a cross-cultural investigation of the meaning of various emotions found that Italians and Americans equated love with happiness, whereas Chinese respondents associated it with sadness and tended to envision unrequited love (Shaver, Wu, & Schwartz, 1991).

People from Western societies are often dumbfounded by collectivist cultures' deemphasis of love and their penchant for arranged marriages. Most people assume that the modern conception of love as the basis for marriage must result in better marital relationships than collectivist cultures' "antiquated" beliefs and practices. However, a variety of researchers have found little empirical support for this ethnocentric view (Dion & Dion, 1993; Triandis, 1994). They cite, for example, a study of couples in India, which found that love tended to grow over the years in arranged marriages, whereas it tended to decline among couples who married for love (Gupta & Singh, 1982). Also, the expectation that marriage will fill diverse psychological needs places greater pressure on marital relationships in individualistic societies than on those in collectivist cultures (Dion & Dion, 1993). These high expectations for personal fulfillment in marriage might be linked to the rapidly escalating divorce rates in these societies (Dion & Dion, 1993). The dearth of cross-cultural research on love means that we can only speculate on these matters. But smug assumptions about the superiority of Western ways look very shaky, given our extremely high divorce rates. The Recommended Reading on this page provides a fascinating look at cultural variability in love and sex.

Recommended Reading

Love and Sex: Cross-Cultural Perspectives
by Elaine Hatfield & Richard L. Rapson
(Allyn & Bacon, 1996)

This book takes a look at romantic relationships and sex from a cross-cultural perspective. Hatfield, a social psychologist, is a distinguished pioneer in research on passionate and companionate love. Rapson, a historian, has had a long interest in the psychological side of American life, past and present.

Hatfield and Rapson, who are husband and wife, have done a fine job melding research and thinking from not only psychology and history but also anthropology, sociology, biology, literature, and art. Moreover, they have pulled together all this fascinating information with an interesting writing style that draws in the reader. They make ample use of first-person accounts and easily readable graphs to illustrate their points. They have also included a number of exercises and tests so readers can assess their own feelings and attitudes.

The book is organized into seven chapters that address key aspects of relationships—or, in their words, "how people meet, mate, fall in love, make love, and fall out of love, usually only to risk it all over again" (p. viii). As they explore these topics, the authors attempt to sort out what is biological and universal and what is culturally specific. The reader will come away with much broader perspectives on love and sex and a greater appreciation for the role culture plays in shaping people's lives.

Today in many parts of the world, parents and matchmakers still arrange their children's marriages. Arranged marriages are common in India, in the Muslim countries, in sub-Saharan Africa, and in cultural enclaves throughout the remainder of the world . . . .

Some problems are serious enough to rule out any thought of marriage. Sometimes, religious advisors would chart the couples' horoscope. Couples born under the wrong sign may be forbidden to marry. . . . Generally, young people are forbidden to marry anyone who is too closely related (say, a brother or a sister or a certain kind of cousin). Sometimes, they are forbidden to marry foreigners . . . . If things look promising, parents and go-betweens begin to talk about the exchange of property, dowries, and the young couple's future obligations and their living arrangements. [p. 46]

Initial Attraction and Relationship Development

LEARNING OBJECTIVES

- Discuss the roles of proximity and familiarity in initial attraction.
- Summarize the findings on physical attractiveness in initial attraction.
- Discuss the role of reciprocal liking in getting acquainted.
- Describe the personality traits that people like in others.
- Explain how similarity affects liking.
- Define the elements of social exchange theory and explain how they influence relationship satisfaction and commitment.

Clearly, a multitude of factors influence the assessment of another person's appeal as a mate or friend. Furthermore, attraction is a two-way street, so there are intricate interactions between factors. To simplify this complex issue, we'll divide our coverage into three segments. First, we'll review the factors that operate in

initial encounters. Then we'll consider factors that come into play as relationships begin to develop. Finally, we'll look at what influences people to stay in or get out of relationships.

Our review of research in this section pertains to both friendships and romantic relationships. In some cases, a particular factor, such as physical attractiveness, may play a more influential role in love than in friendship, or vice versa. However, all the factors discussed in this section enter into both types of relationships.

Initial Encounters

Sometimes initial encounters begin dramatically with two strangers' eyes locking across a room. More often, two people become aware of their mutual interest, usually triggered by each other's looks. What draws two strangers together? Three factors stand out: proximity, familiarity, and physical attractiveness.

PROXIMITY

Obviously, it would be difficult for you to develop a relationship with someone you never met. Although this happens occasionally (between pen pals or over the Internet, for instance), attraction usually depends on proximity: People have to be in the same place at the same time. *Proximity refers to geographic, residential, and other forms of spatial closeness.* Generally, people become acquainted with, and attracted to, someone who lives, works, shops, and plays nearby.

The importance of proximity was apparent in a classic study of friendship patterns among married graduate students living in a university housing project (Festinger, Schachter, & Back, 1950). People whose doors were close together were most likely to become friends. Moreover, those whose homes faced the central court area had more than twice as many friends in the complex as those whose homes faced outward. Using the centralized court area apparently increased the likelihood that people would meet and befriend others.

Proximity effects were also found in a study of Maryland state police trainees (Segal, 1974). At the training academy, both dormitory rooms and classroom seats were assigned on the basis of alphabetical order. Six months after their arrival, participants were asked to name their closest three friends among the group of trainees. The trainees whose last names were closer together in the alphabet were much more likely to be friends than trainees whose names were widely separated in the alphabet.

Proximity effects may seem self-evident, but it is sobering to realize that your friendships and love interests are shaped by seating charts, desk arrangements in offices, and floor assignments in residence halls (Berscheid & Reis, 1998).

FAMILIARITY

You probably walk the same route to your classes several times a week. As the semester progresses, you begin to recognize some familiar faces on your route. Have you also found yourself nodding or smiling at these people? If so, you've experienced the *mere exposure effect*, or an increase in positive feelings toward a novel stimulus (person) based on frequent exposure to it (Zajonc, 1968). Note that the positive feelings arise just on the basis of seeing someone frequently—not because of any interaction. The implications of the mere exposure effect on initial attraction should be obvious. Generally, the more familiar someone is, the more you will like him or her. And greater liking increases the probability that you will strike up a conversation and, possibly, develop a relationship with the person. There is, however, is an important exception to mere exposure effect. If your initial reaction to someone is negative, increased exposure will intensify your dislike (Perlman & Oskamp, 1971).

PHYSICAL ATTRACTIVENESS

Statements such as "Beauty is only skin deep" and "You can't judge a book by its cover" imply that people should be cautious about being seduced by physical beauty. However, research suggests that most people disregard this advice!

Emphasis on Physical Attractiveness. Studies of physical beauty have been conducted in a variety of settings, from college dances to commercial dating services (Walster et al., 1966; Woll, 1986). All show that attractiveness is an important factor in dating. Good looks play a role in friendships as well. People, especially males, prefer attractiveness in their same- and other-gender friends (Berscheid et al., 1971; Buss & Barnes, 1986).

Although women are more likely to report that physical attractiveness is less important to them than males do, research suggests that these differences have been exaggerated (Feingold, 1990; Stevens, Owens, & Schaefer, 1990). When it comes to their behavior, women are as influenced by physical attractiveness as men; however, they downplay this fact in their self-reports. And because most of this research is based on self-reports, the gender difference is artificially heightened.

Do heterosexuals and homosexuals differ in the importance they place on the physical attractiveness of prospective dating partners? Probably not, although the evidence is mixed and plagued by the same problems with self-reports just noted. Researchers who compared the wording of gay and straight personal advertisements in newspapers reported that gender was a more important factor than sexual orientation (Deaux & Hanna, 1984). That is, both heterosexual and homosexual men placed more emphasis on physical attractiveness when describing themselves and their preferences in partners than did either heterosexual or homosexual women. And, regardless of sexual orientation, women placed more importance on psychological characteris-

tics when describing themselves and their preferences in partners. On the other hand, another study found no differences in emphasis on physical attractiveness among heterosexual, homosexual, and bisexual respondents (Engel & Saracino, 1986).

The emphasis on beauty may not be quite as great as the evidence reviewed thus far suggests. Figure 8.1 summarizes the results of a cross-cultural study conducted in 37 countries on the characteristics commonly sought in a mate (Buss, 1985). As you can see, personal qualities, such as kindness-warmth and intelligence, were ranked higher than physical attractiveness by both genders. These results are somewhat reassuring. Still, verbal reports are not necessarily an accurate reflection of how people actually behave.

What Makes Someone Attractive? When you first meet someone, which one or two things about physical appearance do you tend to notice first? This was a question asked by a Roper Poll, and as you can see in Figure 8.2, responses varied widely. Also, what people notice about others often depends on whether they are of the same or other gender.

Researchers who study what constitutes attractiveness focus almost exclusively on physique (body shape) and facial features. Both are important in perceived attractiveness, but an unattractive body is perceived as being a greater liability than an unattractive face (Alicke, Smith, & Klotz, 1986). Males, especially, place more emphasis on body build.

When it comes to *physique*, males who have broad shoulders, slim waists and legs, and small buttocks receive high attractiveness ratings (Singh, 1995). Tall men are also considered attractive (Lynn & Shurgot, 1984), as are men who are not obese (Harris, Harris, & Bochner, 1982). Women of average weight with an "hourglass" figure and medium-sized breasts are rated

FIGURE 8.1.

Characteristics sought in a mate. Buss (1989) surveyed individuals in 37 countries on the characteristics they sought in a mate. Both kindness-understanding and intelligence were ranked higher than physical attractiveness by both genders. Statistically significant gender differences in rankings were found for a variety of characteristics, which are shown in italics. For example, males ranked physical attractiveness higher than females did.

Characteristics Commonly Sought in a Mate		
Rank	Characteristics preferred by men	Characteristics preferred by women
1	Kindness and understanding	Kindness and understanding
2	Intelligence	Intelligence
3	*Physical attractiveness*	Exciting personality
4	Exciting personality	Good health
5	Good health	Adaptability
6	Adaptability	*Physical attractiveness*
7	Creativity	Creativity
8	Desire for children	*Good earning capacity*
9	College graduate	College graduate
10	Good heredity	Desire for children
11	*Good earning capacity*	Good heredity
12	Good housekeeper	Good housekeeper
13	Religious orientation	Religious orientation

FIGURE 8.2.

What men and women first notice about physical appearance. In a Roper Poll, people were asked, "When you first meet someone, which one or two things about physical appearance do you tend to notice first?" The subjects' responses depended to some extent on their gender and on whether they were meeting someone of the same or the other gender. Overall, the subjects' responses were highly varied.

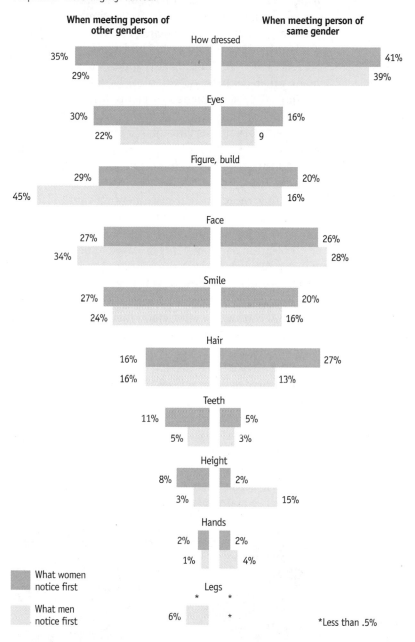

disorders found among adolescent Caucasian girls (Boskind-White, 1985). We explore this important issue in the Chapter 15 Application.

Researchers have also identified a number of *facial features* that are associated with attractiveness. Women who have large eyes, prominent cheekbones, a small nose, and a wide smile get high ratings (Cunningham, 1986). In men, a broad jaw is perceived as attractive (Cunningham, Barbee, & Pike, 1990). Surprisingly, there seems to be widespread agreement across cultures on what constitutes an attractive face (Cunningham et al., 1995). Researchers asked individuals from a number of different countries and ethnic groups to rate the attractiveness of photographs of individuals from a wide array of countries and ethnic groups. Despite the variability in facial features in the photographs, participants strongly agreed on what constitutes attractiveness.

Because our culture particularly values attractiveness in females, being physically attractive appears to be more important for females than for males (Feingold, 1990). This gender gap was apparent in a recent study of the tactics heterosexual individuals used in pursuing romantic relationships. David Buss (1988) asked 208 newlywed individuals to describe the things they did when they first met their spouse, and during the remainder of their courtship, to make themselves more appealing to their partner. Buss found that men were more likely than women to emphasize their material resources by doing such things as flashing lots of money, buying nice gifts, showing off expensive possessions, and bragging about their importance at work (see Figure 8.3 on the next page). In contrast, women were more likely than men to work at enhancing their appearance by dieting, wearing stylish clothes, trying new hairstyles, and getting a tan. Although there were relative differences between the genders in emphasis on physical attractiveness, the data in Figure 8.3 show that both genders relied on tactics intended to enhance or maintain good looks.

Matching Up on Looks. Thankfully, a person does not have to be spectacularly good-looking in order to enjoy a rewarding social life. People apparently take into consideration their own level of attractiveness in the process of dating and mating. **The *matching hypothesis* proposes that people of similar levels of physical**

high in attractiveness (Franzoi & Herzog, 1987; Kleinke & Staneski, 1980; Singh, 1993). A study of white college students found that men exaggerated the extent to which same- and other-gender peers perceived large physiques as most desirable for males. Similarly, women believed that their male and female peers preferred a much thinner female silhouette than was actually the case (Cohn & Adler, 1992). Incidentally, the current emphasis on thinness as the ideal female body shape may underlie the high incidence of eating

FIGURE 8.3.

Similarities and differences between the genders in the tactics of attraction. Buss (1988) asked newlywed subjects to rate how often they had used 23 tactics of attraction to make themselves more appealing to their partner. The tactics used by one gender significantly more often than the other are listed in the first two sections of the figure. Although there were significant differences between the genders, there were also many similarities. The 11 tactics used most frequently by each gender (those above the median) are bold-faced, showing considerable overlap between males and females in the tactics used most. (Note: Higher means in the data reflect higher frequency of use, but the numbers do not indicate frequency per day or week.)

Tactics of Attraction		
	Mean frequency	
Tactics used significantly more by males	Men (N = 102)	Women (N = 106)
Display resources	0.67	0.44
Brag about resources	0.73	0.60
Display sophistication	**1.18**	0.88
Display strength	0.96	0.44
Display athleticism	**1.18**	0.94
Show off	0.70	0.47
Tactics used significantly more by females		
Wear makeup	0.02	**1.63**
Keep clean and groomed	**2.27**	**2.44**
Alter appearance—general	0.39	**1.27**
Wear stylish clothes	**1.22**	**2.00**
Act coy	0.54	0.73
Wear jewelry	0.25	**2.21**
Wear sexy clothes	0.68	0.91
Tactics for which no significant gender differences were found		
Act provocative	0.77	0.90
Flirt	**2.13**	**2.09**
Keep hair groomed	**2.20**	**2.31**
Increase social pressure	0.89	0.90
Act nice	**1.77**	**1.86**
Display humor	**2.24**	**2.28**
Act promiscuous	0.30	0.21
Act submissive	**1.24**	**1.11**
Dissemble (feign agreement)	**1.26**	1.09
Touch	**2.26**	**2.16**

attractiveness gravitate toward each other. This hypothesis is supported by findings that both dating and married heterosexual couples tend to be similar in physical attractiveness (Feingold, 1988). (We are unaware of research on this question regarding homosexual couples.) There is some debate, however, about whether people match up by their own choice (Aron, 1988; Kalick & Hamilton, 1986). Some theorists believe that individuals mostly pursue highly attractive partners and that their matching is the result of social forces beyond their control, such as rejection by more attractive others. Researchers have also found evidence for

matching effects in the same-gender friendships of men, but not women (Duck, 1994). The reasons for this gender difference are not readily apparent.

Resource Exchange. Contradicting the matching hypothesis, several studies have shown that, in heterosexual dating, males "trade" occupational status for physical attractiveness in females, and vice versa (Deaux & Hanna, 1984; Feingold, 1992a; Green, Buchanan, & Heuer, 1984). This finding also appears to hold true in many other cultures. As you already saw in the cross-cultural study summarized in Figure 8.1, men in most countries rate physical attractiveness in a prospective mate as more important than women do, whereas women rate "good financial prospects" and "ambitious and industrious" as more important characteristics than men do (Buss, 1989). Moreover, several studies have shown that more attractive women are more likely to demand high status in their prospective dates than less attractive women (Harrison & Saeed, 1977).

Evolutionary social psychologists such as David Buss (1988) believe that these findings on age, status, and physical attractiveness reflect gender differences in inherited reproductive strategies (Kenrick & Keefe, 1992). According to this view, men are attracted to women of childbearing age because women are limited in the number of years they can reproduce (and men are not). Hence, men display more interest in characteristics that denote a woman's *reproductive capacity* (youth, attractiveness, health). Women, on the other hand, invest more resources in their offspring than men do and are especially desirous of mates who can help feed and protect them and their children. So women focus on a man's capacity for *resource acquisition* (maturity, earning capacity, status). Of course, there are other equally plausible explanations for gender

According to the matching hypothesis, we tend to wind up with someone similar to ourselves in attractiveness. However, other factors such as personality, intelligence, and social status also influence attraction.

Although most couples are similar in age and attractiveness, sometimes men exchange occupational status for physical attractiveness in women, and vice versa.

differences in attraction and mate selection, including traditional gender-role socialization and men's greater economic power (Sprecher, Sullivan, & Hatfield, 1994). For instance, one study found that women's preferences for a physically attractive man increased along with their economic power (Gangestad, 1993).

Getting Acquainted

After several initial encounters, people typically begin the fascinating process of getting to know each other. Is there any way to predict which budding relationships will flower and which will die on the vine? We'll examine three factors that can shed some light on this important question: reciprocal liking, desirable personality characteristics, and perceived similarity.

RECIPROCAL LIKING

An old adage advises, "If you want to *have* a friend, *be* a friend." This suggestion captures the idea of the reciprocity principle in relationships. *Reciprocal liking* **refers to liking those who show that they like you.** Many studies have demonstrated that if you believe another person likes you, you will like him or her (Berscheid & Walster, 1978; Kenny, 1994). Think about it. Assuming that others are sincere, you like it when they flatter you, do favors for you, and use nonverbal behavior to signal their interest in you (eye contact, leaning forward). Moreover, you usually reciprocate such behavior.

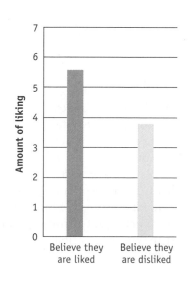

Web Link 8.1

The Student Counseling Virtual Pamphlet Collection
The Student Counseling Office at the University of Chicago had a great idea: gather together links to the very best online information from other counseling centers concerning the problems and issues faced by students. This "best of the best" resource collection includes helpful guides to love, friendship, relationships, and almost any issue an adult in school would face.

You can see the self-fulfilling prophecy at work here. If you believe that someone likes you, you behave in a friendly manner toward them. Your behavior encourages them to respond positively, which confirms your initial expectation. A study by Rebecca Curtis and Kim Miller (1986) shows the self-fulfilling prophecy in action. College students who were strangers were divided into pairs for a 5-minute "get acquainted" conversation. Afterwards, one member of each pair was led to believe that the other student either liked them or did not. Then, the pairs met again and talked about current events for 10 minutes. Raters, blind to the experimental condition of the participants, listened to tape recordings of the 10-minute interactions and rated the participants on a number of behaviors. As predicted, the individuals who believed that they were liked were rated as disclosing more about themselves, behaving more warmly, disagreeing less, and having a more positive tone of voice and general attitude than those who believed that they were disliked (see Figure 8.4).

The strategy of "playing hard to get" (nonreciprocity) seems at odds with the reciprocity principle. Is there any evidence that it works? By and large, this tactic is not advisable. People are usually turned off by others who reject them (Wright & Contrada, 1986). It also seems that individuals prefer those who are *moderately* selective in their liking for others. By contrast, people who like everyone are seen as having no

FIGURE 8.4.

Reciprocal liking.
Research participants were led to believe that their research partner either did or did not like them. The participants who believed that their partners liked them liked their partners more than the participants who believed that their partners did not like them. These results illustrate how reciprocity and the self-fulfilling prophecy can influence attraction to others. (Adapted from Curtis & Miller, 1986)

standards, while those who like very few are perceived as arrogant.

DESIRABLE PERSONALITY CHARACTERISTICS

Personality characteristics are another obvious factor influencing interpersonal attraction. A British study asked college students and dating agency members what personality characteristics they preferred in romantic partners (Goodwin, 1990). The most preferred qualities were kindness-consideration, honesty, and humor. In an American study on dating criteria, college students gave the highest ratings to qualities such as emotionally stable, easygoing, friendly, exciting, and good sense of humor (Kenrick, et al., 1993).

Using a slightly different approach, researchers asked heterosexual college students to rate the physical and psychological characteristics they deemed desirable for both sexual relationships and meaningful, long-term relationships (Nevid, 1984). As you might expect, personal qualities were rated as more important than physical characteristics for meaningful romantic relationships. Also, men placed greater emphasis than women on the physical characteristics of prospective romantic partners, whereas women stressed personal qualities. However, since this research was based on self-reports, these gender differences are probably exaggerated.

SIMILARITY

Do "birds of a feather flock together," or do "opposites attract?" Research offers far more support for the first adage than for the second (Berscheid & Reis, 1998). Despite the increasing diversity in the United States, similarity continues to play a key role in attraction (Macionis, 1997). And the similarity principle operates in friendships and in romantic relationships regardless of sexual orientation (Boyden, Carroll, & Maier, 1984; Aubé & Koestner, 1995). Heterosexual married and dating couples tend to be similar in *age, race, religion, socioeconomic status, education, intelligence, physical attractiveness,* and *attitudes* (Brehm, 1992; Hendrick & Hendrick, 1992). We've already explored similarity in physical attractiveness. Now, let's consider personality and attitudes.

Regarding *personality,* researchers report that males and females who identify strongly with traditional gender-role characteristics are more likely to be attracted to each other than to those who identify less strongly with stereotypic gender roles (Pursell & Banikiotes, 1978). Similarly, Type A individuals—those who tend to be hard-driving workaholics—are attracted to each other (Morell, Twillman, & Sullaway, 1989). In married couples, personality similarity appears to be associated with greater marital happiness (Caspi & Herbener, 1990).

Similarity in *attitudes* also causes liking (Byrne, 1971; Byrne, Clore, & Smeaton, 1986). In laboratory experiments, subjects who have previously provided information on their own attitudes are led to believe that they will be meeting a stranger. They are given information about the stranger's views that has been manipulated to show various degrees of similarity to their own views. As attitude similarity increases, subjects' ratings of the likability of the stranger increase (see Figure 8.5). This evidence supports the notion that similarity promotes attraction. More recent evidence suggests that liking is influenced by both similarity and dissimilarity in attitudes (Singh & Tan, 1992; Smeaton, Byrne, & Murnen, 1989). According to Donn Byrne's two-stage model, people first "sort" for dissimilarity, avoiding those who appear to be different. Then, among the remaining group, individuals are attracted to those who are most similar (Byrne, Clore, & Smeaton, 1986).

Relationship Satisfaction and Commitment

How do individuals gauge their satisfaction in a relationship? What determines whether a person will stay in or get out of a relationship? Let's examine these important questions. **Social exchange theory postulates that interpersonal relationships are governed by perceptions of the rewards and costs exchanged in interactions.** Basically, this model predicts that interactions between acquaintances, friends, and lovers will continue as long as the participants feel that the benefits they derive from the relationship are reasonable in comparison to the costs of being in the relationship. Harold Kelley and John Thibaut's (Kelley & Thibaut, 1978; Thibaut & Kelley, 1959) social exchange theory is based on B. F. Skinner's principle of reinforcement, which assumes that individuals try to maximize their rewards in life and minimize their costs (see Chapter 2).

FIGURE 8.5.
Attitude similarity and attraction. When asked to rate the likability of a hypothetical stranger, subjects give progressively higher ratings to people who share more attitudes with them. (Data from Gonzales et al., 1983)

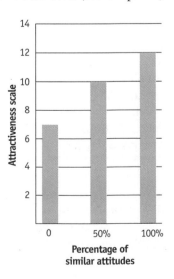

Rewards include such things as emotional support, status, and sexual gratification (in romantic relationships); costs are such things as the time and energy that a relationship requires, emotional conflicts, and the inability to engage in other rewarding activities because of relationship obligations. According to social exchange theory, people assess a relationship by its *outcome*—their subjective perception of the rewards of the relationship minus its costs (see Figure 8.6).

Individuals gauge their *satisfaction* with a relationship by comparing the relationship outcomes (rewards minus costs) to their subjective expectations. **This personal standard of what constitutes an acceptable balance of rewards and costs in a relationship is called the *comparison level*.** It is based on the outcomes you have experienced in previous relationships and the outcomes you have seen others experience in their relationships. Your comparison level may also be influenced by your exposure to fictional relationships, such as those you have read about or seen on television. Consistent with the predictions of exchange theory, research indicates that relationship satisfaction is higher when rewards are perceived to be high and costs, low.

To understand the role of *commitment* in relationships, we need to look at two additional factors. The first is the ***comparison level for alternatives*, or one's estimation of the available outcomes from alternative relationships.** In using this standard, individuals assess their current relationship outcomes in comparison to the potential outcomes of other similar relationships that are actually available to them. This principle helps explain why many unsatisfying relationships are not terminated until another love interest actually appears.

The second factor that figures in relationship commitment is ***investments*, or things that people contribute to a relationship that they can't get back if the relationship ends.** Investments include past costs (time, money) that they can never recover if the

relationship fails. Understandably, putting investments into a relationship strengthens one's commitment to it.

But what happens if individuals feel that they have invested a lot in a relationship that starts to feel bad? Because they're unwilling to forfeit their investments, some people put even *more* into such a relationship. Others decide that they will probably have to forfeit their investment sooner or later so they choose not to wait—especially if an attractive alternative comes into the picture.

We'll use a hypothetical example to illustrate how social exchange theory works. If both people in a romantic relationship feel that they are getting a lot out of the relationship (lots of strokes, high status) compared to its costs (a few arguments, occasionally giving up preferred activities), the relationship will probably be perceived as satisfactory and will be maintained. However, if either person begins to feel that the ratio of rewards to costs is falling below his or her comparison level, dissatisfaction is likely to occur. The dissatisfied person may attempt to alter the balance of costs and rewards or try to ease out of the relationship. The likelihood of ending the relationship depends on the number of important investments a person has in the relationship and whether the person believes that an alternative relationship is available that could yield greater satisfaction.

Social exchange theory principles seem to operate in a similar fashion regardless of a couple's sexual orientation (Peplau, 1991). Moreover, heterosexual and homosexual couples seem quite similar with regard to important aspects of relationships. For example, studies of heterosexual males and females, gay males, and lesbians found that all groups report high satisfaction with their relationships (Duffy & Rusbult, 1986; Kurdek & Schmitt, 1986), as well as moderately high investments in their relationships, moderately poor alternatives, and strong commitment (Duffy & Rusbult, 1986).

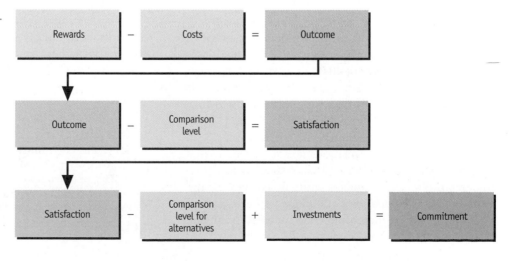

FIGURE 8.6.

The key elements of social exchange theory and their effects on a relationship. According to social exchange theory, relationship *outcome* is determined by the rewards minus the costs of a relationship. Relationship *satisfaction* is based on the outcome matched against comparison level (expectations). *Commitment* to a relationship is determined by one's satisfaction minus one's comparison level for alternatives plus one's investments in the relationship. (Based on Brehm & Kassin, 1993)

This theory of an "interpersonal marketplace" provides a useful model for analyzing many types of relationships. Nonetheless, many people resist the idea that close relationships operate according to an economic model. Much of this resistance probably stems from discomfort with the idea that self-interest plays such an important role in the maintenance of relationships. Some of this resistance may also be due to a feeling that the principles of social exchange theory don't apply well to close relationships. In fact, there is some empirical support for this position. Margaret Clark and her colleagues (Clark & Bennett, 1992) distinguish between *exchange relationships* (with strangers, acquaintances, co-workers) and *communal relationships* (with close friends, lovers, family members). Research suggests that in exchange relationships, the usual principles of social exchange dominate. Social exchange principles also operate in communal relationships, but people seem to apply these principles differently. For example, in communal relationships, rewards are usually given freely, without any expectation of prompt reciprocation (Clark & Mills, 1993). Also, individuals pay more attention to the needs of a partner in a communal relationship than in an exchange relationship. In other words, when people close to you are in need, you help them without stopping to calculate whether and when they will reward you in kind.

Now that we have explored initial attraction, acquaintanceship, and relationship development, let's zero in on two types of established associations: friendships and romantic relationships.

Friendship

LEARNING OBJECTIVES

- *Summarize the research on what makes a good friend.*
- *Describe gender differences in friendships.*

It's hard to overestimate the importance of friends. They provide help in times of need, advice in times of confusion, consolation in times of failure, and praise in times of achievement. The importance of friends was underscored in a survey of 40,000 readers of *Psychology Today* magazine. In the survey, 51% of the respondents indicated that in a crisis they were more likely to turn to friends than to family for help (Parlee et al., 1979).

Studies comparing same-gender friendships with heterosexual romantic relationships have found that qualities such as acceptance, trust, respect, confidence, understanding, spontaneity, mutual assistance, and happiness are valued in both kinds of relationships (Davis, 1985). The main difference appeared to be that romantic relationships also involve fascination and

Men's friendships are often based on doing things together.

exclusiveness. In addition, friendships were perceived to be more stable than romantic relationships among those who were unmarried. Another study found that friends report higher levels of contentment and commitment than dating partners do (Winn, Crawford & Fischer, 1991). Let's explore what makes a good friend and how gender affects patterns of friendship.

What Makes a Good Friend?

The most intriguing aspect of the *Psychology Today* survey was its investigation of what makes a "good friend." Figure 8.7 lists the most frequently endorsed qualities. The results suggest that loyalty is the heart and soul of friendship. As you can see, the top two qualities in Figure 8.7 are keeping confidences (an aspect of loyalty) and loyalty itself. Not surprisingly, the next most important ingredients of friendship are warmth/affection and supportiveness. The high ratings of candor (frankness) and a sense of humor are interesting and well worth keeping in mind.

These results generally coincide with those of another survey on friendship, although one other important factor emerged in this second survey (Block, 1980). That additional factor was a willingness to let friends be themselves. Block points out that people often put others under pressure to behave in ways that are consistent with their own expectations. Such

Web Link 8.2

SUNY Buffalo Counseling Center: Relationships Page
The Counseling Center at the State University of New York, Buffalo, is recognized for its excellent guides to interpersonal relationships and to improving communication among college students. Particularly helpful are the online materials that focus on questions and issues about intimate relationships.

"conditional" expectations would appear to resemble those held by many parents for their children. As discussed in Chapter 2, Carl Rogers believed that conditional affection contributes to distortions in people's self-concepts, therefore he advocated unconditional acceptance in child-rearing. Consistent with Roger's theory, Block's respondents emphasized the importance of unconditional acceptance from their friends.

A slightly different way of looking at what is important in friendship comes from a cross-cultural study of students in England, Italy, Japan, and Hong Kong (Argyle & Henderson, 1984). The investigators wanted to see whether they could find enough agreement on how friends should conduct themselves to permit the formulation of some informal rules governing friendships. For a behavior to qualify as a rule, subjects had to agree that the behavior was important in a friendship, that failure to behave this way could destroy the friendship, and that the behavior could differentiate between current and former friends and between intimate and nonintimate friends. On the basis of the students' responses, the authors identified six informal rules. As Figure 8.8 shows, the common thread running through these rules seems to be providing emotional and social support to friends. Hence we can conclude that loyalty, emotional support, and letting friends be themselves appear to be the most important expectations for friendship.

Gender Differences in Friendship

Men's and women's same-gender friendships have a lot in common, but there are some interesting differences that appear rooted in traditional gender roles and socialization. For one thing, men's friendships are often based on shared interests and doing things together (Hays, 1985; Sherrod, 1989). In contrast, women's friendships are more likely to focus on talking and emotional intimacy. Men seem to view their friends as serving specific functions (one may be a fishing partner; another, a traveling companion). Women seem to react to their friends in a more "global" way (Wright, 1982). Also, many men seem willing to tolerate and work around sources of tension in friendships, whereas women are more likely to confront friends about conflicts to resolve them (Wright, 1982).

We can also compare men's and women's friendships on preferred topics of conversation. Women are far more likely than men to discuss personal problems, feelings, and people (Caldwell & Peplau, 1982; Davidson & Duberman, 1982). Men who don't adhere to traditional gender roles are an exception to this rule. That is, these men appear to divulge as much to their best male friend as most women do to their best female friend (Lavine & Lombardo, 1984).

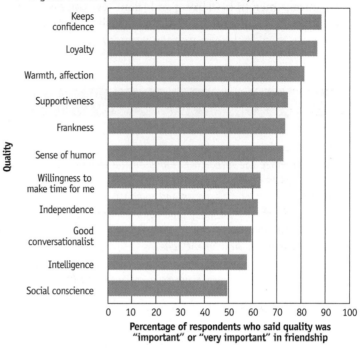

FIGURE 8.7.

Important qualities in a friend. The traits listed here are those that subjects cited most often when asked what makes a good friend. (Based on Parlee et al., 1979)

Percentage of respondents who said quality was "important" or "very important" in friendship

Friendships between men tend to be regulated by social roles. That is, men usually relate to each other as business partners, as tennis rivals, or as baseball fans. Moreover, men generally rate their same-gender friendships as less intimate than women rate theirs. Men also perceive less emotional support to be available from their friends than most women do (Sherrod, 1989). Nonetheless, men and women report essentially the same level of satisfaction with their friendships (Mazur, 1989).

There are several likely reasons for these gender differences in friendships (Berndt, 1982; Reis, Senchak, & Solomon, 1985). First, men and women appear to have different pathways to intimacy (shared activities versus self-disclosure, respectively). Second, men may have less need for intimacy than women do. Third, fear

The Rules of Friendship

Share news of success with a friend

Show emotional support

Volunteer help in time of need

Strive to make a friend happy when in each other's company

Trust and confide in each other

Stand up for a friend in his or her absence

FIGURE 8.8.

Vital behaviors in friendship. A cross-cultural inquiry into the behaviors that are vital to friendship identified the six rules of friendship listed here. (Adapted from Argyle & Henderson, 1984)

of homosexuality, which is stronger in males than females, is cited as a barrier to intimacy between male friends. Finally, traditional gender-role expectations encourage men to be "strong and silent." As you saw in Chapter 7, when self-disclosure is socially acceptable for men, they disclose more than women.

Romantic Love

LEARNING OBJECTIVES

- Discuss four myths about romantic love.
- Summarize the research findings on the experience of love in gay and straight couples.
- Discuss gender differences and romanticism.
- Define passion, intimacy, and commitment, and describe Sternberg's eight types of love.
- Discuss adult attachment styles.
- Discuss the course of romantic love over time, why relationships fail, and what couples can do to help relationships last.

Wander through a bookstore and you'll see an overwhelming array of titles such as *Love Can Be Found, Men Who Can't Love, Women Who Love Too Much*, and *How to Survive the Loss of a Love*. Turn up your radio and you'll hear the refrains of "Love Is a Wonderful Thing," "It's Your Love," "I Will Always Love You," and "Endless Love." Although there are other forms of love, such as parental love and platonic love, these books and songs are all about *romantic love*, a subject of consuming interest for almost everyone.

Although people have always been interested in love and romance, the scientific study of love has a short history that dates back only to the 1970s. Love is difficult to define, difficult to measure, and frequently difficult to understand. Nonetheless, psychologists have conducted hundreds of studies and developed a number of interesting theories on love and romantic relationships. Before exploring these, though, we'll first debunk some myths about love.

Myths About Love

Romantic love is a highly idealized concept in our culture. Some interesting as well as troublesome myths have been nurtured by this idealism—as well as by American television and movies. Accordingly, our first task is to take a realistic look at love and dispel some of these problematic notions. Most of our discussion will be based on the writings of Elaine Hatfield (formerly Walster) and Ellen Berscheid (Berscheid, 1988; Berscheid & Walster, 1978; Hatfield, 1988; Walster & Berscheid, 1974), who have probably conducted more

research on love than anyone else. Although they're rigorous researchers, they have also been willing to offer down-to-earth, practical insights about love.

Myth 1: When you fall in love, you'll know it. People often agonize over whether they are experiencing true love or mere infatuation. When individuals consult others about their doubts, they're often cautioned, "If it's true love, you'd know it." This assertion, which amounts to replying, "You must not really be in love," simply isn't accurate. Studies show that dating couples engage in increased attributional guesswork at transition points in their relationships to figure out their feelings (Fletcher et al., 1987). Thus, confusion about a romantic relationship is not the least bit unusual, and it does not mean that you aren't really in love.

Ellen Berscheid

Myth 2: When love strikes, you have no control over it. This myth suggests that love is so powerful that people are totally incapable of behaving wisely once they are under its spell. While it may be comforting to tell yourself that you have no control when you're in love, this rationalization encourages people to act irresponsibly in matters of the heart. But irresponsible behavior can result in tragic outcomes—sexually transmitted diseases (including AIDS), unwanted pregnancy, and unhappy marriages, to name a few. In the early stages of romantic relationships, it's especially hard to sort out the many intense feelings. However, as a result people need to proceed cautiously in making important decisions about sexual involvements and long-term commitments.

Elaine Hatfield

Myth 3: True love lasts forever. Love may last forever, but unfortunately, you can't count on it. People perpetuate this myth in an interesting way. If their love relationship disintegrates, they conclude that it was never genuine love, only infatuation or comfortable compatibility. This rationalization allows people to continue their search for the one, great, idealized lover who will supposedly bring them complete happiness. It's more realistic to view love as a sometimes wonderful, sometimes frustrating experience that might be encountered a number of times in one's life.

Myth 4: Love can conquer all problems. This myth is the basis for many unsuccessful marriages. Numerous couples, fully aware of problems in their relationship (such as poor communication or disagreement about gender roles) forge ahead into marriage anyway. Well-intentioned but naive, they declare, "As long as we love each other, we can work it out." While authentic love certainly helps in tackling marital problems, it does not guarantee success. In fact, how much you like your lover may be more important than how much you love your lover. When researchers correlated a host of variables with a measure of the "successfulness" of romantic relationships, liking for one's partner was more highly correlated (.62) with relationship success than was love (.50) of one's partner (Sternberg & Grajek, 1984). Of course, this small difference in just one study is hardly definitive. However, it raises the possibility that liking may conquer problems more effectively than love.

Sexual Orientation and Love

Sexual orientation **refers to a person's preference for emotional and sexual relationships with individuals of the same gender, the other gender, or either gender.** *Heterosexuals* seek emotional-sexual relationships with members of the other gender. *Homosexuals* seek emotional-sexual relationships with members of the same gender. *Bisexuals* seek emotional-sexual relationships with members of both genders. In recent years, the terms *gay* and *straight* have become widely used to refer to homosexuals and heterosexuals, respectively. *Gay* can refer to homosexuals of either gender, but most homosexual women prefer to call themselves *lesbians.*

Most studies of romantic love and relationships suffer from **heterosexism, or the assumption that all individuals and relationships are heterosexual.** For instance, most questionnaires on romantic love and romantic relationships fail to ask subjects about their sexual orientation. This means that when data are analyzed, there is no way to know whether subjects are referring to same- or other-gender romantic partners. Assuming that their subjects are all heterosexuals, researchers proceed to describe their findings without any mention of homosexuals. Because many more people identify themselves as heterosexual, heterosexism in research isn't likely to distort conclusions about heterosexuals. The problem with heterosexism is that it renders homosexual relationships invisible. Consequently, psychologists don't know as much about the role of sexual orientation as they would like to. Currently, researchers are devoting more attention to the experience of being homosexual. Where evidence is available, we'll mention it.

In the experience of love relationships, gender and identification with traditional or nontraditional gender roles seem to be more critical factors than sexual

The experience of romantic love seems to be the same regardless of a person's sexual orientation.

orientation. According to Linda Garnets and Greg Kimmel (1991), two psychologists well known for their research and writing on gay and lesbian issues, "Many similarities are found between heterosexual and homosexual couples, indicating commonality in dynamics within the relationship and a similar range of diversity among relationships" (p. 170). Both heterosexual and homosexual couples say they want their partners to have characteristics similar to theirs, hold similar values about relationships, report similar levels of relationship satisfaction, and perceive their relationships to be loving and satisfying. For these reasons, our discussion of love will presume that the *experience of love* is similar regardless of a person's sexual orientation.

Gender Differences Regarding Love

The differences in how males and females are socialized affect their attitudes toward love. The traditional stereotype holds that women are more romantic than men. Nonetheless, much of the research evidence suggests just the opposite—men are the more romantic gender (Dion & Dion, 1988). For example, men hold more romantic beliefs than women (Peplau, Hill, & Rubin, 1993). In addition, men fall in love more easily than women, whereas women fall out of love more easily than men (Hill, Rubin, & Peplau, 1976; Rubin, Peplau, & Hill, 1981). Furthermore, women seem to experience less emotional turmoil than men when romantic relationships break up.

Thus, as a whole, the evidence suggests that men are more romantic than women. However, we should note that women do seem more romantic with regard to *expressions* of love. That is, women are more willing to verbalize and display their affection (Balswick & Avertt, 1977). There is also evidence that women may be more sensitive than men to problems that occur in relationships (Blumstein & Schwartz, 1983). These gender differences seem in line with the observation in Chapter 5 that men tend to have independent self-views while women are more likely to have interdependent self-perceptions. Of course, without empirical data, this possible connection is only a thought-provoking speculation.

Another explanation for the finding that men appear to be more romantic than women is based on economics. Heterosexual women are still more economically dependent on their partners than vice versa. This situation means that choosing a potential partner solely for romantic reasons may be a luxury that men (gay or straight) can more easily afford than heterosexual women. Support for this perspective comes from a previously mentioned cross-cultural study that reported that a woman's interest in physically attractive men increased with her economic power (Gangestad, 1993). We are unaware of research on this question

Web Link 8.3

Love Page
James Park, an existentialist philosopher and advocate of freedom and authenticity in relationships, offers a distinctive challenge to more traditional notions of romantic love. He provides bibliographies on a host of topics, such as jealousy, sexual scripts, and the decision to have children.

with homosexual subjects so we don't know whether this principle holds for all women and, if it does, whether the reasons for it are similar.

Theories of Love

Can the experience of love be broken down into certain key components? How are romantic love relationships similar to other types of close relationships? These are the kinds of questions that some of the newer theories of love address. Let's take a look at two such theories.

TRIANGULAR THEORY OF LOVE

Robert Sternberg's (1986, 1988) *triangular theory of love* posits that all love experiences have three components: intimacy, passion, and commitment. Each of these components is represented as a point of a triangle, from which the theory derives its name (see Figure 8.9).

Passion **refers to the intense feelings (both positive and negative) experienced in love relationships, including sexual desire.** Passion is related to drives that lead to romance, physical attraction, and sexual consummation. Although sexual needs may be dominant in many close relationships, other needs also figure in the experience of passion, including the needs for affiliation, self-esteem, dominance, submission, and self-actualization. For example, self-esteem is threatened when one experiences jealousy.

Intimacy **refers to warmth, closeness, and sharing in a relationship.** Signs of intimacy include giving and receiving emotional support, wanting to promote the welfare of the loved one, and sharing one's self and one's possessions with another. As we've already discussed, self-disclosure is necessary to achieve and maintain feelings of intimacy in a relationship.

Commitment **involves the decision and intent to maintain a relationship in spite of the difficulties and costs that may arise.** According to Sternberg, commitment has a short-term and a long-term aspect. The short-term aspect concerns the conscious decision to love someone. The long-term aspect reflects the determination to make a relationship endure. Although the decision to love someone usually comes before commitment, this is not always the case (in arranged marriages, for instance).

Sternberg has described eight types of relationships that can result from the presence or absence of each of

FIGURE 8.9.

Sternberg's triangular theory of love. According to Robert Sternberg (1986), love includes three components: intimacy, passion, and commitment. These components are portrayed here as points on a triangle. The possible combinations of these three components yield the seven types of relationships mapped out here. The absence of all three components is called nonlove, which is not shown in the diagram.

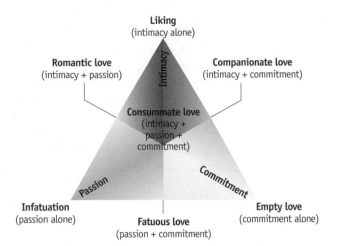

the three components of love (see Figure 8.9). One of these relationship types, nonlove, is not pictured in the diagram because it is defined as the absence of any of the three components. Most interpersonal relationships—casual interactions—are of this type. When all three components are present, *consummate love* is said to exist.

Sternberg's model has generated a great deal of interest and some research. In support of his theory, researchers have demonstrated that Sternberg's three components characterize not only how people think about love in general but also how they personally experience love (Aron & Westbay, 1996). Also, measures of commitment and intimacy were found to be among the best predictors of whether dating couples continued their relationships (Hendrick, Hendrick, & Adler, 1988). On the negative side, one study found little support for the idea that the various types of love can be accounted for by different weightings of intimacy, passion, and commitment (Hendrick & Hendrick, 1989).

ROMANTIC LOVE AS ATTACHMENT

In another groundbreaking theory of love, Cindy Hazan and Phillip Shaver (1987) assert that romantic love can be conceptualized as an attachment process, with similarities to the bond between infants and their caregivers. According to these theorists, adult romantic love and infant attachment share a number of features: intense fascination with the other person, distress at separation, and efforts to stay close and spend time together.

Hazan and Shaver's ideas build on earlier work in attachment theory by John Bowlby and Mary Ainsworth. Researchers who study attachment are keenly interested in the nature and development of **attachment styles, or typical ways of interacting in close relationships.** Their interest is fueled by the belief that attachment styles develop during the first year of life and strongly influence individuals' interpersonal interactions from then on.

Cindy Hazan

Infant attachment. Based on actual observations of infants and their primary caregivers, earlier researchers identified three attachment styles (Ainsworth, et al., 1978). Most infants develop a *secure attachment style* (see Figure 8.10 on the next page). However, other infants develop insecure attachments. Some infants are very anxious when separated from their caretaker, a response characterized as an *anxious-ambivalent attachment style*. A third group of infants never connect very well with their caretaker and are classified in the *avoidant attachment style*. How do attachments in infancy develop? As you can see in Figure 8.10, three parenting styles have been identified as likely determinants of attachment quality. A *warm/responsive* approach seems to promote secure attachments, while a *cold/rejecting* style is associated with avoidant attachments. An *ambivalent/inconsistent* style seems to result in anxious-ambivalent attachments.

Phillip Shaver

Adult Attachment. What do these attachment styles look like in adulthood? To answer this question, we'll summarize the findings of a number of studies (Shaver & Hazan, 1993). You can also see capsule summaries of adult attachment styles in Figure 8.10.

• *Secure adults* (55%). These people trust others, find it easy to get close to them, and are comfortable with mutual dependence. They rarely worry about being abandoned by their partner. Secure adults have the longest-lasting relationships and the fewest divorces. They describe their parents as behaving warmly to them and to each other.

• *Avoidant adults* (25%). These individuals both fear and feel uncomfortable about getting close to others. They are reluctant to trust others and prefer to maintain emotional distance from others. They have the lowest incidence of positive relationship experiences of the three groups. Avoidant adults describe their parents as less warm than secure adults do and see their mothers as cold and rejecting.

• *Anxious-ambivalent or preoccupied adults* (20%). These adults are obsessive and preoccupied with their relationships. They want more relationship closeness than their partners do and suffer extreme feelings of jealousy, based on fears of abandonment. Their relationships have the shortest duration of the three groups. Ambivalent adults describe their relationship with their parents as less warm than secure adults do and feel that their parents had unhappy marriages.

Cross-cultural studies in Australia and Israel have confirmed that people are distributed across the three styles with similar percentages in those countries (Feeney & Noller, 1990; Mikulincer, Florian, & Tolmacz, 1990). Also, males and females are distributed similarly across the three styles.

In an interesting development, Kim Bartholomew (Bartholomew & Horowitz, 1991) has proposed a four-category model of adult attachment styles. Her model is based on Bowlby's (1980) idea that individuals form abstract images about both the self and others, based on interactions with the primary caregiver. Thus, people develop perceptions (positive or negative) of their own self-worth as well as perceptions (positive or negative) of others' trustworthiness and reliability. Depending on where people fall on these two dimensions, they are classified into one of four attachment styles: secure, preoccupied (anxious-ambivalent), fearful, or dismissing (see Figure 8.11). The main difference between the Bartholomew and the Hazan/Shaver models is that Bartholomew's delineates two avoidant attachment styles. Individuals of both types avoid close relationships to protect themselves against disappointment; however, fearful avoidants have negative self-views, whereas *dismissing* avoidants have positive self-views. Whereas the former group needs others to bolster self-validation, the latter group does not. (The dismissing avoidant style emerged in Bartholomew's research, but not in Hazan and Shaver's because of

FIGURE 8.10.

Infant attachment and romantic relationships. According to Hazan and Shaver (1987), romantic relationships in adulthood are similar in form to attachment patterns in infancy, which are determined in part by parental caregiving styles. The theorized relations between parental styles, attachment patterns, and intimate relations are outlined here. Hazan and Shaver's (1987) study sparked a flurry of follow-up research, which has largely supported the basic premises of their groundbreaking theory, although the links between infant experiences and close relationships in adulthood appear to be somewhat more complex than those portrayed here (Shaver & Hazan, 1992). (Based on Hazan and Shaver, 1986, 1987; Shaffer, 1989)

Parents' caregiving style	Infant attachment	Adult attachment style
Warm/responsive—She/he was generally warm and responsive; she/he was good at knowing when to be supportive and when to let me operate on my own; our relationship was almost comfortable, and I have no major reservations or complaints about it.	**Secure attachment**—An infant/caregiver bond in which the child welcomes contact with a close companion and uses this person as a secure base from which to explore the environment.	**Secure**—I find it relatively easy to get close to others and am comfortable depending on them and having them depend on me. I don't often worry about being abandoned or about someone getting too close to me.
Cold/rejecting—She/he was fairly cold and distant, or rejecting, not very responsive; I wasn't her/his highest priority, her/his concerns were often elsewhere; it's possible that she/he would just as soon not have had me.	**Avoidant attachment**—An insecure infant/caregiver bond, characterized by little separation protest and a tendency of the child to avoid or ignore the caregiver.	**Avoidant**—I am somewhat uncomfortable being close to others; I find it difficult to trust them, difficult to allow myself to depend on them. I am nervous when anyone gets too close, and often love partners want me to be more intimate than I feel comfortable being.
Ambivalent/Inconsistent—She/he was noticeably inconsistent in her/his reactions to me, sometimes warm and sometimes not; she/he had her/his own agenda, which sometimes got in the way of her/his receptiveness and responsiveness to my needs; she/he definitely loved me but didn't always show it in the best way.	**Anxious/ambivalent attachment**—An insecure infant/caregiver bond, characterized by strong separation protest and a tendency of the child to resist contact initiated by the caregiver, particularly after a separation.	**Anxious/ambivalent**—I find that others are reluctant to get as close as I would like. I often worry that my partner doesn't really love me or won't want to stay with me. I want to merge completely with another person, and this desire sometimes scares people away.

differences in the methodology used to classify subjects: Bartholomew uses a structured interview; Hazan and Shaver use a self-report.) Bartholomew's model has been lauded by many researchers, including Hazan and Shaver.

Correlates of Attachment Styles. The idea of adult attachment styles has triggered an avalanche of research. Among other findings, it has been shown that securely attached individuals have more committed, satisfying, interdependent, and well-adjusted relationships compared to people with either anxious-ambivalent or avoidant attachment styles (Collins & Read, 1990; Simpson, 1990). Studies have also found that an anxious-ambivalent style is associated with not being in a relationship and with being in relationships of shorter duration, and that an avoidant style is associated with shorter relationships (Feeney & Noller, 1990; Shaver & Brennan, 1992).

There is widespread agreement that individuals in the two insecure attachment styles are more vulnerable to a number of problems and symptoms, including low self-esteem (Feeney & Noller, 1990), loneliness (Hazan & Shaver, 1987), and anxiety, depression, and physical symptoms (Hazan & Shaver, 1990).

Attachment patterns may exert influence beyond romantic relationships. For instance, correlations have been found between attachment styles and job satisfaction, attitudes about work, gender roles, and religious beliefs (Shaver & Hazan, 1993, 1994).

Stability of Attachment Styles. A number of studies have demonstrated that adult attachment styles parallel

Web Link 8.4

Phillip R. Shaver's Homepage
Phillip Shaver of the University of California, Davis, has done pioneering research on adult attachment and its relationship to romantic relationships. His homepage details his findings, provides online access to some of his more important papers, and introduces net surfers to the current work in his Adult Attachment Lab.

those in infancy (Shaver & Hazan, 1993). This pattern suggests that early bonding experiences do produce relatively enduring relationship styles. However, to conclude that there is an actual causal link between infant and adult attachment styles, we need longitudinal evidence. One such study has found consistency on some dimensions through midadolescence (Elicker, Englund, & Sroufe, 1992). Still, this finding doesn't mean that attachment styles are set in stone. Some people can revise their attachment styles in response to relationship experiences (Baldwin & Fehr, 1995; Scharfe & Bartholomew, 1994). For example, one study reported that about 30% of individuals had changed their attachment style over a period of four years (Kirkpatrick & Hazan, 1994).

To conclude, attachment styles play a significant role in relationships. Because the brisk pace of research in this area is likely to continue, we can expect many more insights to emerge on this fascinating topic.

The Course of Romantic Love

Most people find being in love exhilarating and wish the experience could last forever. Must passion fade? Regrettably, the answer to this question appears to be yes. Several theorists suggest that the intense attraction and arousal one feels for a lover seem destined to subside. Sternberg (1986) hypothesizes that passion reaches its peak early in a relationship and then declines in intensity. In contrast, both intimacy and commitment increase as time progresses, although they develop at different rates (see Figure 8.12 on the next page).

Berscheid and Hatfield's research also leads them to conclude that passionate love tends to peak early and then fights a difficult battle against the erosion of time. At first, love is "blind," so individuals usually develop an idealized picture of their lover (often a projection of their own needs). However, as time passes, the intrusion of reality undermines this idealized view.

Does the decline of passion mean the demise of a relationship? Not necessarily. Some relationships do dissolve when passion fades. However, many others evolve into different, but deeply satisfying, phases such as companionate love. Let's examine the research on why some romantic relationships endure while others do not.

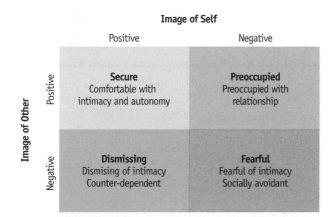

Image of Self

	Positive	Negative
Positive (Image of Other)	**Secure** Comfortable with intimacy and autonomy	**Preoccupied** Preoccupied with relationship
Negative (Image of Other)	**Dismissing** Dismissing of intimacy Counter-dependent	**Fearful** Fearful of intimacy Socially avoidant

FIGURE 8.11.

Bartholomew's model of adult attachment. Drawing on Bowlby's (1980) pioneering work on attachment, Bartholomew conceptualizes adult attachment as rooted in abstract images of oneself (as worthy of love and support or not) and of others (as trustworthy and available versus unreliable and rejecting). Adults' self-views and views of others are assessed with a structured interview. Based on their responses, people are categorized into one of four attachment styles. (Adapted from Bartholomew & Horowitz, 1991)

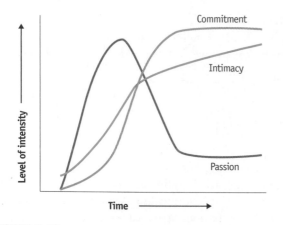

FIGURE 8.12.

The course of love over time. According to Sternberg (1986), the three components of love typically progress differently over time. He theorizes that passion peaks early in a relationship and then declines. In contrast, intimacy and commitment build gradually.

WHY RELATIONSHIPS FAIL

Not surprisingly, the issue that has drawn the most attention in relationship research is understanding why some relationships last and others fail (Berscheid & Reis, 1998). Yet because of the complexity of the issues involved, easy answers have not been forthcoming (Berscheid & Reis, 1998). Let's see what light researchers can shed on this crucial question.

A longitudinal study of undergraduate dating couples revealed that 42% of couples who had designated their relationship as their closest interpersonal relationship had split up within nine months (Berscheid, Snyder, & Omoto, 1989). Similarly, the Boston Couples Study, a longitudinal study of dating couples in the Boston area, reported that almost half (45%) of the relationships had dissolved at the end of two years (Hill, Rubin, & Peplau, 1976). A 15-year follow-up to this study reported that 32% of the initial dating couples had married and that 64% of them had not (Peplau, Hill, & Rubin, 1993). Among the couples who had married at some time during the study, 68% were still together at the time of the follow-up.

To identify the reasons that some relationships stand the test of time and some do not, let's take a closer look at the Boston Couples Study. Here, 200 couples (predominantly college students) were followed over a period of two years. To participate in the study, couples had to be "going steady" and believe that they were in love. If couples split, researchers asked them to give their reasons (see Figure 8.13). The results of this and other studies (Brehm, 1992; Buss, 1989) suggest that four prominent factors contribute to romantic breakups:

1. *Premature commitment.* Virtually all the reasons for breakups involved things that could only be known after some sharing of personal information over time. Hence, it seems that many couples make romantic commitments without taking the time to really get to know each other. These individuals may find out later that they don't really like each other or that they have little in common. For these reasons, "whirlwind courtships" are risky. Intimacy needs to be combined with commitment if relationships are to survive (Hendrick et al., 1988).

2. *Ineffective conflict management skills.* The vast majority of couples report having disagreements. Not surprisingly, the likelihood of disagreements increases as couples learn more about each other and become more interdependent (Buss, 1989). Unfortunately, as we discussed in Chapter 7, many people do not know how to deal with conflict constructively. This inability to manage conflicts appears to be a key factor in romantic breakups (Brehm, 1992).

3. *Availability of a more attractive relationship.* Whether a deteriorating relationship actually ends depends, in great part, on the availability of a more attractive alternative (Felmlee, Sprecher, & Bassin, 1990). We all know of individuals who bided their time in unsatisfying relationships only until they met someone new.

HELPING RELATIONSHIPS LAST

Are there things couples can do to ensure that their love relationships will last? Amazingly, only recently have researchers addressed this critical question. Still, there is enough research to support a few suggestions:

1. *Take plenty of time to get to know the other person before you make a long-term commitment.* Research based on Sternberg's theory found that the best predictors of whether dating couples' relationships would continue were their levels of intimacy and commitment (Hendrick, et al., 1988). Regarding intimacy, we have already noted that self-disclosures that lead individuals to feel understood, validated, and cared for are crucial (Reis & Patrick, 1996). Other advice comes from long-married couples who were asked why they thought their relationship had lasted (Lauer & Lauer, 1985). The most frequently cited responses of 351 couples who had been married for 15 years or more were (1) friendship ("I like my spouse as a person"); (2) commitment to the relationship ("I want the relationship to succeed"); (3) similarity in values and relationship issues ("We agree on how and how often to show affection"); and (4) positive feelings about each other ("My spouse has grown more interesting"). Thus, early attention to the intimacy foundations of a relationship and ongoing, mutual efforts to build a commitment can foster more enduring love.

2. *Emphasize the positive qualities in your partner and relationship.* It is essential to communicate more

FIGURE 8.13.

Factors contributing to breakups. Couples who broke up after dating steadily were asked why by Hill, Rubin, and Peplau (1976). The factors most commonly cited are listed here. The researchers distinguished between interactive factors, which consisted of problems that emerged out of the partners' ways of relating to each other, and noninteractive factors.

What Causes Couples to Break Up?		
Factors	Women's reports (%)	Men's reports (%)
Interactive factors		
Becoming bored with relationship	77	77
Differences in interests	73	61
Differences in backgrounds	44	47
Differences in intelligence	20	10
Conflicting sexual attitudes	48	43
Conflicting marriage ideas	43	29
Noninteractive factors		
Woman's desire to be independent	74	50
Man's desire to be independent	47	61
Woman's interest in someone else	40	31
Man's interest in someone else	18	29
Living too far apart	28	41
Pressure from woman's parents	18	13
Pressure from man's parents	10	9

positive feelings than negative ones to your partner. Early in a relationship, people find this easy to do, but it gets harder as relationships continue. For one thing, once the initial glow of the relationship wears off, a common attributional error comes into play. **The *actor-observer effect* is the tendency to attribute one's own behavior to situational factors and the behavior of others to personal factors.** This tendency can set up the destructive habit of chronically blaming the other person for problems and not taking responsibility when one should. Ironically, married couples generally make more negative and fewer positive statements to their spouse than to strangers, and we presume this holds for those in other types of committed relationships as well (Koren, Carlton, & Shaw, 1980; Miller, 1991). This tendency is more prevalent among distressed than among nondistressed couples (Bradbury & Fincham, 1990; Halford & Sanders, 1990). Unfortunately, when one partner engages in this behavior, the other usually responds in kind, which can set in motion a pattern of reciprocal negativity that makes things worse. Hence, as the old song advises, it's a good idea to "accentuate the positive and eliminate the negative."

3. *Develop effective conflict management skills.* Conflicts arise in all relationships, so it's important to handle them well. For one thing, it's helpful to distinguish between minor annoyances and significant problems. You need to learn to see minor irritations in

perspective and recognize how little they matter. With big problems, however, it's usually best to avoid the temptation to sweep them under the rug in the hope that they'll disappear. Important issues rarely disappear on their own, and if you postpone the inevitable discussion, the "sweepings" will have accumulated, making it harder to sort out the various issues and feelings. An interaction pattern common to dissatisfied couples is "demand-withdraw" (Roberts & Krokoff, 1990). Typically, this pattern involves the woman pressing the man to discuss a relationship problem and the man avoiding or withdrawing from the interaction. This pattern is associated with the "closeness versus separateness dilemma," in which one partner wants more intimacy and closeness and the other wants more privacy and independence (Christensen & Heavey, 1990). For more specific suggestions, refer to our discussion of conflict in Chapter 7.

Loneliness

LEARNING OBJECTIVES

- Describe three kinds of loneliness identified by Young.
- Discuss the prevalence and consequences of loneliness.
- Explain how current social trends and negative attitudes can contribute to loneliness.
- Describe how shyness, poor social skills, negative self-talk, and self-defeating attributions can contribute to loneliness.
- Give some suggestions for coping with loneliness.

Although individuals vary in their need for affiliation, friendship and love play important roles in people's lives. What happens when this fundamental need for these social relations is thwarted? For many people, the result is loneliness. **Loneliness occurs when a person has fewer interpersonal relationships than desired or when these relationships are not as satisfying as desired.** *Loneliness is not the same as spending time alone.* People can feel lonely even when surrounded by others (at a party or concert, for instance). Conversely, some people cherish solitude and are content with less social interaction than most others prefer. Thus, loneliness is a highly subjective and personal feeling.

Jeffrey Young (1982) has identified three kinds of loneliness. *Chronic loneliness* is a condition that affects people who have been unable to develop a satisfactory interpersonal network over a period of years. *Transitional loneliness* occurs when people who have had satisfying social relationships in the past become lonely because of a specific disruption of their social network (the death of a loved one, say, or divorce, or moving to a new locale). One study reported that 75% of new college students reported experiencing loneliness in their first few weeks on campus (Cutrona, 1982). *Transient loneliness* involves brief and sporadic feelings of loneliness, which many people may experience even when their social lives are reasonably adequate.

Loneliness may not occur in all areas of a person's life. For instance, you might be highly satisfied with your friendship network but feel frustrated about not having a suitable romantic relationship. Research suggests that loneliness can be attributed to perceived deficits in four types of relationships: (1) romantic/sexual relationships, (2) friendship relationships, (3) family relationships, and (4) community relationships (Schmidt & Sermat, 1983). Because it is likely that each problem would have different solutions, it's important to pinpoint the exact nature of your social deficits to better understand how to cope with loneliness.

Prevalence and Consequences of Loneliness

How many people are chronically tormented by severe loneliness? Although we don't have a precise answer to this question, anecdotal evidence suggests that the number of people plagued by severe loneliness is substantial. Telephone hotlines for troubled people report that complaints of loneliness dominate their calls.

Interestingly, the prevalence of loneliness in specific age groups contradicts stereotypes: (1) adolescents and young adults are the loneliest age group and (2) loneliness decreases with age, at least until the much later years of adulthood when one's friends begin to die (Rubenstein & Shaver, 1982). Gay and lesbian adolescents are particularly likely to be lonely (Bohan, 1996). Women are found to be lonelier than men, but only on measures that use words such as "lonely" or "loneliness" (Borys & Perlman, 1985). Thus, it is likely that there is no actual gender difference, but rather a reluctance by men to admit to feeling lonely. Friendships are particularly important to gay and lesbian individuals (Bryant & Demian, 1994).

The *personal* consequences of loneliness can be overwhelming. Painful thoughts of one's plight can dominate one's consciousness. As might be expected, studies have found a strong correlation between feelings of loneliness and feelings of depression (Anderson & Harvey, 1988). Similarly, researchers have reported a relationship between loneliness and poor physical and psychological health (Rubenstein & Shaver, 1982).

Unfortunately, loneliness seems to have *social* consequences, too. Several studies have found that when a hypothetical target person was characterized as socially isolated and lonely, participants rated that person as less well adjusted, less achieving and intellectually competent, and less socially competent than a nonlonely target person (Lau & Gruen, 1992; Rotenberg & Kmill, 1992). In addition, the lonely person was less preferred as a friend by others and was rated as weaker, more passive, less attractive, and less sincere compared to a nonlonely target. Lonely men were evaluated more negatively than lonely women. Of course, we need to be careful about generalizing too much from just a few studies, but it does seem that poor social skills are evaluated negatively by others. The good news is that effective social skills can be learned (see Chapter 7).

The Roots of Loneliness

A number of factors can contribute to feelings of loneliness. Because any event that ruptures the social fabric of a person's life may lead to loneliness, no one is immune. Social trends and personal qualities are among the prominent causes of loneliness.

CONTRIBUTING SOCIAL TRENDS

Social commentators and psychologists are increasingly concerned about social trends that seem to be undermining social connections in our culture (Flanders, 1982; Keyes, 1980; Kraut et al., 1998). Because of busy schedules, social interactions at home are reduced as family members eat on the run, on their own, or in front of the TV. And the fact that people watch television so much tends to diminish meaningful family conversation. While technology makes life easier in some respects, it can also have negative effects. For example, superficial social interactions become prevalent as people order their meals at drive-up windows, do their banking at drive-through facilities, and so forth. Finally, people are spending more time alone at computer terminals in their offices and homes. One study found that high levels of Internet use were associated with small but statistically significant declines in communication with family members as well as in the size of one's social circle and with increases in loneliness (Kraut et al., 1998).

As you might expect, individuals whose parents have been divorced report feeling more lonely than those from intact families do (Rubenstein & Shaver, 1982). Moreover, the earlier in their lives the divorce occurred, the stronger the feelings of loneliness experienced in adulthood. In contrast, no differences in loneliness were noted between individuals who had lost a parent through death and those from intact families. Interestingly, research does not support two intuitive expectations regarding loneliness: Loneliness doesn't correlate with the nature of residential setting (urban or rural) or with the frequency of changes in location.

NEGATIVE ATTITUDES ABOUT ONESELF AND OTHERS

A key factor that promotes loneliness is low self-esteem

and related negative attitudes about the self. Lonely people often have cynical and pessimistic attitudes and believe that life is uncontrollable (Anderson & Riger, 1991). Lonely people seem to selectively attend to negative information about themselves, thereby reinforcing an already negative self-concept (Frankel & Prentice-Dunn, 1990). Those who have unfavorable opinions of themselves often do not feel worthy of others' affection and may make little effort to pursue close relationships. This lack of confidence probably has a spiraling effect, as low self-esteem begets loneliness and loneliness begets still lower self-esteem.

Lonely individuals also seem to hold more negative attitudes toward others than nonlonely people do. Research has found that those who describe themselves as lonely evaluate others negatively (Wittenberg & Reis, 1986), don't trust others very much (Vaux, 1988), and expect to be evaluated negatively by others (Jones, Sansone, & Helm, 1983). As with self-esteem and loneliness, negative attitudes about others and loneliness probably interact.

FIGURE 8.14.

The situational determinants of shyness. Zimbardo (1977) asked subjects about the people and circumstances that made them feel shy. The results of his survey showed that shyness depends to a large degree on situational factors.

"What Makes You Shy?"	
	Percentage of shy students
Other people	
Strangers	70
Opposite sex	64
Authorities by virtue of their knowledge	55
Authorities by virtue of their role	40
Relatives	21
Elderly people	12
Friends	11
Children	10
Parents	8
Situations	
Where I am focus of attention—large group (as when giving a speech)	73
Large groups	68
Of lower status	56
Social situations in general	55
New situations in general	55
Requiring assertiveness	54
Where I am being evaluated	53
Where I am focus of attention—small group	52
Small social groups	48
One-to-one different-sex interactions	48
Of vulnerability (need help)	48
Small task-oriented groups	28
One-to-one same-sex interactions	14

SHYNESS AND POOR SOCIAL SKILLS

Shyness is commonly associated with loneliness (Marangoni & Ickes, 1989). **Shyness refers to discomfort, inhibition, and excessive caution in interpersonal relations.** Specifically, shy people tend to (1) be timid about expressing themselves, (2) be overly self-conscious about how others are reacting to them, (3) embarrass easily, and (4) experience physiological symptoms of their anxiety, such as a racing pulse, blushing, or an upset stomach. In pioneering research on shyness, Philip Zimbardo (1977, 1990) and his associates report that 60% of shy people indicated that their shyness was *situationally specific.* That is, shyness is triggered only in certain social contexts, such as asking someone for help or interacting with a large group of people (see Figure 8.14). You can learn more about shyness and how to cope with it in Zimbardo's *Shyness* (see the Recommended Reading).

Interpersonal skills, although not particularly difficult to develop, do have to be acquired. Poor social skills prevent many people from experiencing rewarding social interactions. A common finding is that lonely people show lower responsiveness to their conversational partners and are more self-focused (Rook, 1998). Similarly, researchers report that lonely people are relatively inhibited, speaking less than nonlonely people and disclosing less about themselves than those who are not lonely. This (often unconscious) tendency has the effect of keeping people at an emotional distance and limits interactions to a relatively superficial level. Anxiety about social skills is also correlated with loneliness (Anderson & Harvey, 1988).

NEGATIVE SELF-TALK AND SELF-DEFEATING ATTRIBUTIONS

Ultimately, what underlies many of the factors just discussed is *negative self-talk.* Lonely people are prone to irrational thinking about their social skills, the probability of their achieving intimacy, the likelihood of being rejected, and so forth. Young (1982) points out that lonely people engage in negative self-talk that prevents them from pursuing intimacy in an active and positive manner. He has identified some clusters of ideas that foster loneliness. Figure 8.15 gives examples of typical thoughts from six of these clusters of cognitions and the overt behaviors that result.

Several of the cognitions in Figure 8.15 are stable, internal self-attributions. The tendency to attribute loneliness to stable, internal causes constitutes a *self-defeating attributional style* (Anderson et al., 1994). In other words, lonely people tell themselves that they're lonely because they're basically unlovable individuals. Not only is this a devastating belief, it is also self-defeating because it offers no way to change the situation. Recall from Chapter 5 that there are *other* attributions a lonely person could make and that these explanations point to solutions. If a person says, "My conversational skills are weak" (unstable, internal cause), the solution would be: "I'll try to find out how to improve them." Or, if a person tells herself, "It always takes time to meet people when you move to a new location" (unstable, external cause), this suggests the solution of trying harder to develop new relationships and giving them time to work. The attribution "I've really searched, but I just can't find enough compatible people at my workplace" (stable, external cause) may lead to the decision, "It's time to look for a new job." As you can see, the last three attributions lead to active modes of coping.

Coping with Loneliness

For those who suffer from loneliness, there are no simple solutions, but there are some effective ones. A major reason that people have difficulty overcoming loneliness is that they tend to withdraw socially. One study that asked people what they did when they felt lonely

Web Link 8.5

The Shyness Homepage
The Shyness Institute (Portola Valley, CA) offers a "gathering of network resources for people seeking information and services for shyness." The Institute is co-directed by psychologists Lynne Henderson and Philip Zimbardo.

found the top responses to be "read" and "listen to music" (Rubenstein & Shaver, 1982). If used only occasionally, reading and listening to music can be constructive ways of dealing with loneliness. However, as long-term strategies, they do nothing to help a lonely person acquire new friends. This may be a particular problem for those with an avoidant attachment style.

Effective self-help strategies for overcoming loneliness include engaging in positive self-talk, avoiding the temptation to withdraw from social situations, and working on your conversational skills (Brehm, 1992). The importance of staying active socially cannot be overemphasized. Recall that proximity is a powerful factor in the development of close relationships. You have to be around people in order to make friends.

For those who seek professional help for their loneliness, there is good news: Both poor social skills and the negative perceptions that often underlie loneliness can be changed relatively easily and quickly (Young, 1982). Most college counseling centers have professionals who are skilled in *social skills training*. Over a series of sessions, individuals learn to change their negative views of themselves ("I'm boring") and others ("They're cold and unfriendly"). In addition, they watch videotapes of socially skilled models demonstrating appropriate social behavior in a variety of settings. They then practice these behaviors in the therapist's office. Sometimes these practice sessions are taped so individuals can actually see how they are coming across.

In the Application, we'll address an increasingly common mishap in relationships: date rape.

FIGURE 8.15.
Patterns of thinking underlying loneliness.
According to Young (1982), negative self-talk contributes to loneliness. Six clusters of irrational thoughts are illustrated here. Each cluster of cognitions leads to certain patterns of behavior (right) that promote loneliness.

Clusters of Cognitions Typical of Lonely Clients		
Clusters	**Cognitions**	**Behaviors**
A	1. I'm undesirable. 2. I'm dull and boring.	Avoidance of Friendship
B	1. I can't communicate with other people. 2. My thoughts and feelings are bottled up inside.	Low self-disclosure
C	1. I'm not a good lover in bed. 2. I can't relax, be spontaneous, and enjoy sex.	Avoidance of sexual relationships
D	1. I can't seem to get what I want from this relationship. 2. I can't say how I feel, or he/she might leave me.	Lack of assertiveness in relationships
E	1. I won't risk being hurt again. 2. I'd screw up any relationship.	Avoidance of potentially intimate relationships
F	1. I don't know how to act in this situation. 2. I'll make a fool of myself.	Avoidance of other people

Understanding Date Rape

LEARNING OBJECTIVES

- *Distinguish between date rape and seduction.*
- *Discuss the incidence and consequences of rape.*
- *Explain how alcohol and drugs, violent pornography, and adversarial attitudes contribute to date rape.*
- *Discuss how gender differences in sexual standards and communication problems contribute to date rape.*
- *List some suggestions for reducing the incidence of date rape.*

Answer the following "true" or "false."

_____ **1.** Rape is an aggressive act, not a sexual one.

_____ **2.** Most rapes are committed by acquaintances, not strangers.

_____ **3.** Violent pornography heightens sexual aggression in viewers.

_____ **4.** Men are more likely than women to perceive friendly behavior as having sexual intent.

Does it surprise you to learn that all of the above statements are true? We'll begin by addressing the first point. Rape is *not* an expression of sexuality, but rather an act of aggression. Sex is the means by which the rapist expresses power and hostility (Browne & Williams, 1993). Date rape is also an act of aggression, despite widespread reluctance to acknowledge this fact. Many people seem stuck on the idea that rape occurs only if a stranger leaps out of the bushes and attacks you; if someone you know forces you to have sex, it isn't rape. This denial of reality surrounding date rape causes women who have been raped to doubt themselves and allows men to deny responsibility for their behavior (Koss, 1985). (Because the vast majority of rapes are committed by men, our discussion will center on women as the victims of rape.)

Date rape refers to forced and unwanted intercourse in the context of dating. Date rape can occur on a first date, with someone you've dated for a while, or with someone to whom you're engaged. A broader term, *acquaintance rape,* involves a woman being forced to have unwanted intercourse with someone she knows. Thus, acquaintance rape includes not only date rape but also rape committed by nonromantic acquaintances ("friends," co-workers, neighbors, relatives).

Many people confuse date rape with seduction. The latter occurs when a woman is persuaded *and agrees* to have sex. Date rape often occurs when seduction fails and the man goes on to have sex with the woman without her consent. The force used in date rape is typically verbal or physical coercion, but sometimes it involves a weapon. A study of 190 male undergraduates at a Southern university reported that men used the following tactics to coerce dates into having sex: verbal persuasion (70%), ignoring a woman's protests (35%), physical restraint (11%), threats of physical aggression (3%), and physical aggression (3%) (Rappaport & Burkhart, 1982).

Incidence of Rape

It is difficult to obtain accurate information about the prevalence of any form of rape (it is believed that 90% of all rapes are never reported). Experts estimate that the chances of a woman being raped at some time in her life range between 14% and 25% (Koss, 1993). Contrary to popular belief, the vast majority—80%— of rapes are committed by acquaintances: Most rape victims are between the ages of 15 and 25.

Although almost all rape survivors are women, about 5% of rape survivors are men. Male rape usually occurs in prison settings, where sex is used to establish dominance. While rare, there are instances of women raping men (since men don't have total voluntary control over erections) (Sarrel & Masters, 1982). Obviously, the experience of rape is traumatic, regardless of one's gender. While sexual aggression is typically discussed in a heterosexual context, it also occurs among homosexual couples, although not much research is available (Lobel, 1986; Rozee, Bateman, & Gilmore, 1991).

Consequences of Rape

All rape is traumatic, but it is particularly shattering when a woman is raped by someone she has trusted and cared for. In addition, because most women are not used to the idea that rape can occur with someone they know, it is particularly difficult for a victim of date or acquaintance rape to deal with her feelings of betrayal, rage, and shame (Katz, 1991). During a rape, it is not uncommon for people to respond sexually (females with lubrication and orgasm; males with erection and orgasm) (Bancroft, 1980; Sarrel & Masters, 1982). Because these physiological responses are diametrically opposed to a person's actual feelings (terror, humiliation), this experience can add to the confusion, shame, and distress.

Rape survivors typically experience the same symptoms as others coping with posttraumatic stress disorder, as we noted in Chapter 4 (Koss, 1993). Although not all women are affected by rape in the same way, most rape survivors go through three stages: trauma, denial, and resolution.

- *Trauma.* Women experience a variety of emotional reactions to rape, including fear of being alone, fear of men, fear of retaliation (especially if charges are filed), and fear of trusting subsequent dating partners. Feelings of depression, anger, helplessness, guilt, pain, shame, and anxiety are also common. Many rape victims show signs of stress-related physical problems. Emotional reactions can be exacerbated if the woman's family and friends are not supportive—particularly if family or friends blame the victim for the attack. And, as you saw in Chapter 6, it is common for people to blame victims for their misfortune (defensive attribution).

• *Denial.* In this stage—which may last for months or years—rape victims try to put the trauma behind them and get on with their lives. During this period, women avoid talking about their rape as they try to deny that it took place. This strategy generally fails as a long-term solution because the powerful and painful emotions don't just go away.

• *Resolution.* To move beyond the experience, a woman needs to deal with her feelings by talking with someone who is supportive and understanding: a friend, a counselor, or a member of the clergy. Once she has worked through her feelings and fears, she may be able to put the trauma in the past and begin to feel in control of her life again. Still, she will probably always be haunted by the experience.

In addition to the trauma of the rape, survivors also have to cope with the possibilities of pregnancy and sexually transmitted disease. Rape victims often drop out of school because of the trauma and lack of social support. Other consequences of rape can affect both the survivor and the attacker. If they are students, the grades of both may suffer because of emotional distress and inability to concentrate on their studies. Moreover, if the rape survivor presses charges against her attacker, he faces criminal proceedings. If he is a student, he may be suspended from school whether or not the woman takes the case to court. And both may have to deal with negative publicity and social stigma.

Factors Contributing to Date Rape

To understand the phenomenon of date rape, it's essential to know something about the factors that contribute to it, which include alcohol and drugs, violent pornography, adversarial beliefs, gender and sexual standards, and communication problems.

ALCOHOL AND DRUGS

It probably comes as no surprise to learn that alcohol is involved in a majority of sexually aggressive incidents (Cate & Lloyd, 1992). What you might find surprising, however, is that the mere *belief* that one has drunk alcohol increases sexual arousal and sexual interest even if none has been consumed (Baron & Richardson, 1994). Both men and women report that men are more likely to engage in sexually coercive behavior if they have been drinking (Poppen & Segal, 1986).

Increasingly, so-called "date rape drugs" are a cause for concern. Rohypnol ("roofies") and gamma hydroxybutyrate (GHB) are two drugs used to subdue dates. Although these drugs are colorless, odorless, and tasteless, their effects are anything but benign. Victims typically pass out and have no recall of what happened while they were under the influence of the drug. To make it easier to spike a drink, predators typically look for individuals who are already intoxicated.

Men and women who drink heavily or take drugs on dates are likely to have impaired judgment and to be less inhibited. Unfortunately, alcohol and drugs make some men more willing to use force ("liquor courage") and women more vulnerable to the use of force (Shotlund & Hunter, 1995). If a woman passes out, she is easy prey for anyone who is willing to take advantage of her.

VIOLENT PORNOGRAPHY

A number of laboratory studies on the effects of aggressive pornography (depicting rape and other sexual violence against women) suggest that such material elevates some men's tendency to behave aggressively toward women (Donnerstein, Linz, & Penrod, 1987). Furthermore, men who have viewed sexually violent films report greater acceptance of rape myths as well as greater acceptance of interpersonal violence against women (Malamuth & Check, 1981). (See Figure 8.16 for selected items from two scales often used to measure rape-supportive attitudes.) Related research has shown that exposure to such material can increase male viewers' willingness to say that they would commit a rape, while decreasing their sensitivity to rape and the plight of rape victims (Donnerstein & Linz, 1984). Taken as a whole, research does not support the idea that violent pornography *directly* induces men to commit rape. Rather, viewed repeatedly, it works *indirectly* by fostering callous attitudes toward women and promoting perceptions of women as sexual objects to be manipulated by males (Mosher & Anderson, 1986).

How many men actually watch violent pornography? According to one survey, 36% of male college students reported having viewed material during the preceding year that featured forced sexual acts against

Web Link 8.6

Sexual Assault Information Page
Since 1995, Chris Bartley has offered a valuable group of resources relating to sexual assault, including information on date and acquaintance rape. This site offers detailed discussions of factors that contribute to sexual assault, such as defective communication.

Measuring Attitudes Toward Sexual Aggression

Rape Myth Acceptance Scale

1. When women go around braless or wearing short skirts and tight tops, they are just asking for trouble.

2. If a girl engages in necking or petting and she lets things get out of hand, it is her own fault if her partner forces sex on her.

3. Many women have an unconscious wish to be raped and may then unconsciously set up a situation in which they are likely to be attacked.

Scoring: People who score high on this scale agree with all of the above items.

Acceptance of Interpersonal Violence Scale

1. Being roughed up sexually is stimulating to many women.

2. Sometimes the only way a man can get a cold woman turned on is to use force.

3. A man is never justified in hitting his wife.

Scoring: People who score high on this scale agree with items 1 and 2 and disagree with item 3.

FIGURE 8.16.

Assessing attitudes about sexual aggression. Researchers use carefully constructed scales to assess individuals' attitudes about sexual aggression. Sample items from two such scales are shown here. (Adapted from Burt, 1980)

women, and 25% said that they had looked at materials depicting rape (Demaré, Lips, & Briere, 1993).

ADVERSARIAL BELIEFS

Males are more likely than females to perceive friendly behavior as a sexual invitation (Kowalski, 1993; Muehlenard, 1988; Shotland, 1989). This tendency is heightened in men who endorse traditional attitudes toward women and who hold rape-supportive beliefs (for instance, "women are manipulative in sexual relationships") (Kowalski, 1993). Such men also fail to distinguish between assertiveness and hostility (Murphy, Coleman, & Haynes, 1986).

On the basis of these and related findings, Neil Malamuth and Lisa Brown (1994) hypothesize that sexual aggressors may have a *suspicious schema* regarding women's communications about romantic or sexual interest. This schema includes the belief that women don't tell the truth about sex and the perception of hostile intent behind women's friendly or assertive rejections of sexual overtures. Thus, a man who holds such beliefs can think a woman has communicated sexual interest (and act accordingly) when, in fact, she has not. If a man doesn't make an effort to clarify a woman's intentions, he can easily let himself feel that he has been "led on." He may then use his anger as an excuse to force the woman to have sex. Because social norms support game playing as part of flirting, such interactions between couples in which the man holds a suspicious schema can lead to tragic consequences. We have summarized the characteristics associated with men who are likely to engage in date rape in Figure 8.17.

GENDER AND SEXUAL STANDARDS

Gender-based differences in sexual standards set up conflicts between men and women and put women at a

FIGURE 8.17.

Date rapists: warning signs. According to Rozee, Bateman, and Gilmore (1991), four factors appear to distinguish date rapists: feelings of sexual entitlement, a penchant for exerting power and control, high hostility and anger, and acceptance of interpersonal violence. The presence of more than one of these characteristics is an important warning sign (Malamuth, 1986). The possibility for date rape increases when sexual entitlement is coupled with any other factor.

Typical Characteristics of Date Rapists

Sexual entitlement	Power and control	Hostility and anger	Acceptance of interpersonal violence
Touching women with no regard for their wishes	Interrupting people, especially women	Showing a quick temper	Using threats in displays of anger
Sexualizing relationships that are appropriately not sexual	Being a bad loser	Blaming others when things go wrong	Using violence in borderline situations
Engaging in conversation that is inappropriately intimate	Exhibiting inappropriate competitiveness	Tending to transform other emotions into anger	Approving observed violence
Telling sexual jokes at inappropriate times or places	Using intimidating body language		Justifying violence
Making inappropriate comments about women's bodies, sexuality, and so on	Game playing		

disadvantage. For instance, society still encourages a double standard for males and females when it comes to sexual behavior. Men are encouraged to have sexual feelings, to act on them, and to "score," whereas women are discouraged from being sexual unless they are "carried away" by passion. This double standard promotes hidden norms that condone sexual aggression by men in dating relationships. Relatedly, some men still believe that if they spend money on a woman, she owes them sex (Shotland, 1989).

Also, traditional norms for dating and sexual behavior dictate that males should initiate sex and be persistent and that females should resist these advances (Check & Malamuth, 1983). Another problem area concerns beliefs about when sexual intercourse is appropriate in a relationship. Not surprisingly, we see gender differences here, too. In one survey, 50% of the men felt sexual intercourse was appropriate by the fifth date, but only 23% of the women felt this way (Knox & Wilson, 1981). Such gender-based standards can promote sex-related conflict.

COMMUNICATION PROBLEMS

When social norms encourage game playing as part of flirting, dating partners may not always say what they mean or mean what they say. Whereas the majority of women say "no" (in words or in nonverbal behavior) and mean it, some women may say "no" to sexual activity when they actually mean "maybe" or "yes." Studies surveying the extent of "token resistance" among college women report that approximately 38% of them have engaged in this behavior (Muehlenhard & McCoy, 1991; Shotland & Hunter, 1995).

Why do some women engage in token resistance? Researchers have grouped college women's responses into three categories: (1) *practical reasons* (fear of pregnancy), (2) *inhibition-related reasons* (emotional, religious, and moral worries), and (3) *manipulative reasons* (being in control, getting the man more aroused) (Muehlenhard & Hollabaugh, 1988). Carefully inspecting these reasons, other researchers reasoned that practical and inhibition-related concerns seemed to explain sexual refusal but not token resistance (Shotland & Hunter, 1995). And, although manipulative reasons could explain token resistance, the number of women who cite these reasons is relatively small (23%).

Thus, these researchers hypothesized that token resistance reflects women's changing sexual intentions as relationships develop over time. In other words, as dating proceeds, pressure to have sex as well as sexual arousal usually increase. In addition, some of the woman's concerns may diminish. Consequently, she may change her intentions to have sex. Several findings seem to support this view. First, sexual refusals occurred before the 11th date, while token resistant behavior occurred after this time. Second, on a given date, refusals occurred earlier and token resistance, later. Third, 83% of women who used token resistance reported having more than one sexual intention during a date, while only 34% of women who said "no" and meant it reported having multiple sexual intentions. Note that neither the patterning of token resistant behavior nor a change in sexual intentions is consistent with a "manipulative" explanation.

Of course, some women do engage in token resistance for manipulative purposes. This behavior occurs more often among women who are already involved in a sexual relationship than among those who are not, and it is often related to the woman's dissatisfaction with sexual practices in the relationship. The most frequently given "manipulative" reason for token resistance was "I wanted to be in control—the one to say when," a reflection of women's role as regulators of sexual activity and its timing (Shotland & Hunter, 1995). Relatively few women gave patently manipulative reasons, such as "I was angry with him and wanted to get back" or "I wanted him to beg." These findings are important because research has demonstrated that men who believe that women are sexually manipulative are likely to be sexually aggressive and may rape their partners (Koss et al., 1985; Muehlenhard & Linton, 1988). It is essential that men recognize that most women do not engage in token resistance for manipulative reasons.

On a related issue, the double standard presents women with an avoidance-avoidance conflict. If a woman openly acknowledges her interest in sex (doesn't use token resistance), she risks being perceived as "easy" by men who believe in the double standard. But if a woman uses token resistance as a tactic for coping with her dates' standards, she also puts herself at risk, because using token resistance sets the stage for miscommunication—and sometimes for tragedy (Kowalski, 1993).

Reducing the Incidence of Date Rape

What can be done to reduce the incidence of date rape? For one thing, rape prevention programs are on the increase. These programs target women, men, and mixed-gender audiences. Those for women strive to increase participants' awareness of rape and reduce their vulnerability. Those directed at men stress responsibility and the ability to empathize with women. Programs for mixed-gender audiences usually focus on communication issues and dating expectations. When well designed, such programs can be successful. Still, they focus on attitudinal changes, which don't automatically translate into noncoercive sexual behavior (Lonsway, 1996). Nonetheless, education remains a promising vehicle for addressing this problem.

Recommended Reading

Recovering from Rape by Linda E. Ledray (Henry Holt, 1994)

Rape survivors and their loved ones will find both emotional support and practical guidance in overcoming the trauma of rape in this comprehensive handbook. Each chapter contains a section addressed to the survivor and to the significant other. The author, a nurse/clinical psychologist who has worked with rape survivors for 20 years, guides the reader through the painful and complex initial emotional reactions toward recovery. The book also offers expert advice for the many practical issues that must be confronted: coping with the police, getting medical attention, getting tested for sexually transmitted diseases and pregnancy, telling other people (who, when, and how), and deciding whether to prosecute the rapist. Other chapters address such topics as childhood sexual assault, rapists and their motives, and rape prevention. At the end of the book, the author provides suggested readings as well as a list of resources and victim services, by state. The following excerpt addresses the importance of social support in the recovery process:

> *Numerous reports, books, and articles resulting from years of study and research in all types of crises, including rape, show that next to your own resilience, the key factor in your recovery is support from family and friends. Their support and understanding are important in helping you better deal with the emotional trauma and resolve the fear, anxiety, and depression. It's much easier to take risks and face what you see as potentially dangerous, uncomfortable, frightening situations with someone beside you. Although social support cannot make up for feeling that you lack control over your life and surroundings, it certainly can give you the extra confidence necessary to take calculated risks, face your fears, and overcome the immobilizing effects of anxiety and depression. [p. 105]*

To conclude, we offer the following suggestions for reducing date rape: (1) Recognize date rape for what it is: an act of sexual aggression. (2) Familiarize yourself with the characteristics of men who are likely to engage in date rape (see Figure 8.17) and be cautious about dating men who exhibit more than one of them. (3) Beware of excessive alcohol and drug use, which may deprive you of control. (4) Exercise control over your environment: Agree to go only to *public* places (not apartments) until you know someone very well, and always carry enough money for transportation back home. (5) Think through your feelings, values, and intentions about sexual relations *before* the question of having sex arises. (6) Communicate your feelings and expectations about sex by engaging in appropriate self-disclosure. (7) Listen carefully and respect the other's wishes. (8) Be prepared to act *aggressively* if assertive refusals fail to stop unwanted advances.

We hope that our discussion of date rape has increased your awareness of this serious problem and given you some suggestions for dealing with it in your own life. For survivors of date and acquaintance rape, we recommend *Recovering from Rape* (see Recommended Reading).

Key Ideas

PERSPECTIVES ON CLOSE RELATIONSHIPS

● Close relationships are those that are important, interdependent, and long-lasting. They include friendships as well as work, family, and romantic relationships. People in individualistic cultures believe that romantic love is a prerequisite for marriage, whereas those in collectivist cultures prefer arranged marriages.

INITIAL ATTRACTION AND RELATIONSHIP DEVELOPMENT

● People are initially drawn to others who are nearby, who are seen often, and who are physically attractive. Although physical attractiveness plays a key role in initial attraction, people also seek other desirable characteristics, such as kindness and intelligence. People often match up on looks, but sometimes men trade status for physical attractiveness in women, and vice versa.

● As people get acquainted, they prefer others who like them and those who have desirable personality characteristics. Similarity is a key factor in relationship development. Couples tend to be similar in age, race, religion, education, attitudes, and even some personality traits.

● Social exchange theory uses principles of reinforcement to predict relationship satisfaction and commitment. Whether individuals apply social exchange principles depends on whether they are in exchange or communal relationships.

FRIENDSHIP

● The key ingredients of friendship are loyalty, emotional support, and letting friends be themselves. Women's same-gender friendships tend to be characterized by intimacy and self-disclosure, whereas men's same-gender friendships typically involve doing things together.

ROMANTIC LOVE

● Myths about romantic love include the idea that when people fall in love they know it and the notion that people have no control over themselves when love strikes. Other myths are that love lasts forever and that it can conquer all problems. Research indicates that the experience of romantic love is the same for heterosexual and homosexual individuals. Contrary to stereotypes, men may be more romantic than women.

● Sternberg's triangular theory of love proposes that passion, intimacy, and commitment combine into eight different types of love. Hazan and Shaver theorize that love relationships follow the form of attachments in infancy, falling into three categoreies: secure, avoidant, and anxious-ambivalent. Bartholomew has proposed an alternative, four-category model of adult attachment styles. Although attachment styles show stability over time, it is possible for them to change.

● Initially, romantic love is usually characterized by passion, but strong passion appears to fade over time. In relationships that continue, passionate love evolves into a less intense, more mature form of love.

● The chief causes of relationship failure are the tendency to make premature commitments, ineffective conflict management skills, and the availability of a more attractive relationship. To help relationships last, couples should take the time to know each other very well, emphasize the positive qualities in their partner and relationship, and develop effective conflict management skills.

LONELINESS

● Loneliness involves discontent with the extent and quality of one's interpersonal network. A surprisingly large number of people in our society are troubled by loneliness, which is often associated with depression, as well as with poor physical and psychological health.

● Although loneliness is promoted by a number of social trends, it appears to result mainly from personal factors such as negative attitudes about oneself and others, shyness and poor social skills, and negative self-talk and self-defeating attributions. The keys to coping with loneliness are engaging in positive self-talk, avoiding the temptation to withdraw from social situations, and working on one's communication skills.

APPLICATION: UNDERSTANDING DATE RAPE

● The vast majority of rapes are committed by acquaintances, often on dates. Estimates suggest that the chances of a woman being raped at some time in her life range from 14% to 25%. Rape is a traumatic experience that has many serious consequences.

● Alcohol and drug use, violent pornography, adversarial beliefs, and gender-based sexual standards all contribute to date rape. Miscommunication revolving around token resistance is particularly important. Rape education programs have been successful in changing rape-relevant attitudes in the desired direction.

Key Terms

Actor-observer effect
Attachment styles
Close relationships
Commitment
Comparison level
Comparison level for alternatives
Date rape
Heterosexism
Intimacy
Investments
Loneliness
Mere exposure effect
Matching hypothesis
Passion
Proximity
Reciprocal liking
Sexual orientation
Shyness
Social exchange theory

Key People

Ellen Berscheid and Elaine Hatfield (Walster)
Cindy Hazan and Phillip Shaver
Harold Kelley and John Thibaut
Robert Sternberg

Practice Test

1. Arranged marriages are most common in:
   a. individualistic cultures.
   b. collectivist cultures.
   c. unrequited cultures.
   d. industrialized cultures.

2. The mere exposure effect refers to an increase in positive feelings due to :
   a. seeing someone often.
   b. interacting with someone often.
   c. communicating via e-mail often.
   d. having similar attitudes.

3. The matching hypothesis suggests that people match up on the basis of :
   a. religion.
   b. personality.
   c. socioeconomic status.
   d. looks.

4. An individual's personal standard of what constitutes an acceptable balance of rewards and costs in a relationship is termed:
   a. social exchange.
   b. comparison level for alternatives.
   c. comparison level.
   d. relationship satisfaction.

5. Women's same-gender friendships are based on _____; men's are based on _____.
   a. shopping together; hunting together
   b. attending sports events; attending sports events
   c. shared activities; intimacy and self-disclosure
   d. intimacy and self-disclosure; shared activities

6. If a researcher fails to determine the sexual orientation of her research participants and reports her findings without any mention of homosexuals, her study suffers from
   a. homosexism.
   b. social exchange.
   c. heterosexism.
   d. romantic bias.

7. The finding that men are more likely than women to choose partners for romantic reasons is probably due to the fact that men:
   a. have better vision than women.
   b. have more economic power than women.
   c. are more superficial than women.
   d. have fewer domestic skills than women.

8. Adults who have positive views of themselves but negative views of others would be categorized in which of the following attachment styles?
   a. Secure
   b. Preoccupied
   c. Dismissive avoidant
   d. Fearful avoidant

9. A self-defeating attributional style associated with loneliness involves attributing loneliness to
   a. internal, stable factors.
   b. internal, unstable factors.
   c. external, stable factors.
   d. external, unstable factors.

10. Which of the following is a major contributor to date rape?
    a. Alcohol and drug use
    b. Adversarial beliefs
    c. Communication problems
    d. Negative self-talk

Answers

1. b pages 217–218
2. a page 219
3. d pages 221–222
4. c page 225
5. d page 227
6. c page 229
7. b page 230
8. c pages 236–237
9. a page 238
10. d pages 240–242

INFOTRAC COLLEGE EDITION

Go to the Wadsworth Psychology Study Center (http://psychology.
wadsworth.com/) for quiz questions, research updates, hot topics, interactive exercises, and suggested readings in INFOTRAC related to this chapter.

Marriage and Intimate Relationships

"*My hands are shaky. I want to call her again but I know it is no good. She'll only yell and scream. It makes me feel lousy. I have work to do but I can't do it. I can't concentrate. I want to call people up, go see them, but I'm afraid they'll see that I'm shaky. I just want to talk. I can't think about anything besides this trouble with Nina. I think I want to cry.*"—A recently separated man quoted in Marital Separation [Weiss, 1975, p. 48]

This man is describing his feelings a few days after he and his wife broke up. He is still hoping for a reconciliation. In the meantime, he feels overwhelmed by anxiety, remorse, and depression. He feels very alone and is scared at the prospect of remaining alone. His emotional distress is so great that he can't think straight or work effectively. His reaction to the loss of an intimate relationship is not all that unusual. Marital breakups are devastating for most people—a reality that illustrates the enormous importance of intimate relationships in people's lives.

In this chapter we will take a look at marriage and other intimate relationships. We will discuss why people marry and how they progress toward the selection of a mate. To shed light on marital adjustment, we will describe the life cycle of the family, highlighting key vulnerable spots in marital relations. We will also address issues related to divorce, cohabitation, remaining single, and being gay. Finally, in the Application we will examine the tragic problem of violence in family relationships. Let's begin by discussing recent challenges to the traditional concept of marriage.

Challenges to the Traditional Model of Marriage

LEARNING OBJECTIVES

• *Discuss recent trends relating to the acceptance of singlehood and cohabitation, and changing views on the permanence of marriage.*

• *Discuss how transitions in gender roles, increased childlessness, and the decline of the nuclear family have affected the institution of marriage.*

Marriage is the legally and socially sanctioned union of sexually intimate adults. Traditionally, the marital relationship has included economic interdependence, common residence, sexual fidelity, and shared responsibility for children. Although the institution of marriage remains popular, it sometimes seems to be under assault from shifting social trends. This assault has prompted many experts to ask whether marriage is in serious trouble (Rodman & Sidden, 1992). Although it appears that marriage will weather the storm, it's worth looking at some of the social trends that are shaking the traditional model of marriage:

1. *Increased acceptance of singlehood.* An increasing proportion of the adult population under age 35 is remaining single (Stein, 1989). In part, this trend reflects longer postponement of marriage than before. The median age at which people marry has been increasing gradually since the mid-1960s, as Figure 9.1 shows. Thus, remaining single is becoming a more viable lifestyle. Furthermore, the negative stereotype of people who remain single, which pictures them as lonely, frustrated, and unchosen, is gradually evaporating.

2. *Increased acceptance of cohabitation.* **Cohabitation is living together in a sexually intimate relationship without the legal bonds of marriage.** Negative attitudes toward couples "living together" appear to be declining, although many people continue to disapprove of the practice. It is difficult to get accurate information on the number of couples who cohabit. However, various sources suggest that cohabitation has

FIGURE 9.1.

Median age at first marriage. The median age at which people in the United States marry for the first time has been creeping up for both males and females since the mid–1960s. This trend indicates that more people are postponing marriage. (Source: U.S. Bureau of the Census)

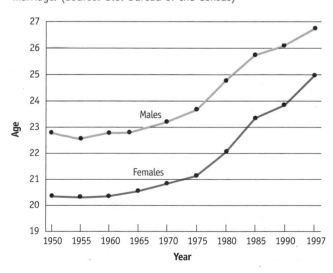

increased dramatically in recent decades (Wilhelm, 1998). Census data, for instance, indicate that the number of couples living together increased almost eightfold between 1970 and 1997.

3. *Reduced premium on permanence.* Most people still view marriage as a permanent commitment, but many are also strongly committed to their own personal growth. Marriage is often seen as just one context in which such growth can occur. Thus, an increasing number of people regard divorce as justifiable if their marriage fails to foster their interests as individuals (Popenoe, 1993). Accordingly, the social stigma associated with divorce has lessened, and divorce rates have risen. Some experts estimate that roughly two of every three marriages will ultimately result in separation or divorce (Wisensale, 1992).

4. *Transitions in gender roles.* The women's movement and economic pressures have led to substantial changes in the expectations of many people entering marriage today. The traditional breadwinner and homemaker roles for the husband and wife are being discarded by many couples, as more and more married women enter the workforce (see Figure 9.2). Role expectations for husbands and wives are becoming more varied, more flexible, and more ambiguous (Fine, 1992). Many people regard this trend as a step in the right direction (see Chapter 10). However, changing gender roles create new potential for conflict between marital partners.

5. *Increased voluntary childlessness.* In the past two decades, the percentage of women without children has climbed in all age groups (see Figure 9.3) as an increasing number of married couples have chosen not to have children (Seccombe, 1991). This trend is probably a result of new career opportunities for women, the tendency to marry at a later age, and changing attitudes. Since 1962, the percentage of American mothers who agree that "all couples should have children" has declined from 84% to 43% (Thornton, 1989).

6. *Decline of the traditional nuclear family.* Thanks to television shows like *Leave It to Beaver, Ozzie and Harriet,* and *Father Knows Best,* in the eyes of most American adults, the normal family should consist of a husband and wife married for the first time, rearing two or more children, with the man serving as the sole breadwinner and the woman filling the homemaker role (Coontz, 1992). As Demo (1992) notes, "This ideal continues to serve as the reference point against which contemporary families are judged, despite the fact that many families did not conform to these ideals even during the nostalgic 1950s and early 1960s" (p. 105). Today, it is estimated that only a small minority of American families match this idealized image of the "normal" family. The increasing prevalence of single-parent households, stepfamilies, childless marriages, unwed parents, and working wives have conspired to make the traditional nuclear family a highly deceptive mirage that does not reflect the diversity of family structures in America.

In summary, the norms that mold marital and intimate relationships have been restructured in fundamental ways in recent decades. Traditional values have eroded as people have increasingly embraced more individualistic values (Popenoe, 1993; Thornton, 1989). Thus, the institution of marriage is in a period of transition, creating new adjustment challenges for modern couples. Support for the concept of monogamy remains strong, but changes in the society

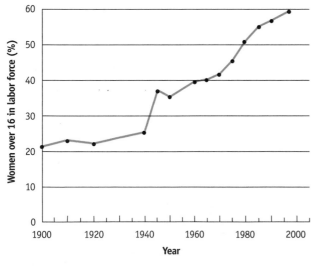

FIGURE 9.2.

Women in the workforce. The percentage of women in the United States (over age 16) who work outside the home has been rising steadily throughout this century. Even among women with children under six years of age, about 57% are employed. (Source: U.S. Bureau of Labor Statistics)

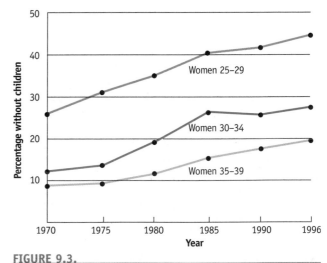

FIGURE 9.3.

Percentage of women without children by age group. The proportion of adult women in the United States who have never had a child has been increasing gradually over the last three decades. (Source: U.S. Bureau of the Census)

Thanks in part to television portrayals of the family, such as that seen on the popular Donna Reed Show, people cling to an idealized image of the traditional nuclear family, despite the fact that only a small minority of American families match this stereotype.

are altering the traditional model of marriage. The impact of these changes will be seen throughout this chapter as we discuss various facets of married life.

Moving Toward Marriage

LEARNING OBJECTIVES

- Discuss several factors influencing the selection of a mate.
- Outline Murstein's stage theory of mate selection.
- Summarize evidence on predictors of marital success.

"I'm ashamed of being single, I have to admit it. I have grown to hate the word. The worst thing someone can say is, 'How come you're still not married?' It's like saying, 'What's wrong with you?' I look at women who are frumpy and physically undesirable and they're monochromatic and uninteresting and they don't seem unselfish and giving and I wonder, 'How did they become such an integral part of a man's life that he wanted to marry them and spend his life with them?' I'm envious. They're married and I date."—A woman quoted in Tales from the Front *[Kavesh & Lavin, 1988, p. 91]*

This woman desperately wants to be married. The intensity of her motivation for marriage may be a bit unusual, but otherwise she is fairly typical. Like most people, she has been socialized to believe that her life isn't complete until she finds a mate. Although alternatives to marriage are more viable than ever, experts project that over 90% of Americans will marry at least once. Some will do it several times! But why? What motivates people to marry? And how do individuals choose their partners? We'll address these questions as we discuss the factors that influence the movement toward marriage.

The Motivation to Marry

A great variety of motivational factors propel people into marriage. Foremost among them is the desire to participate in a socially sanctioned, mutually rewarding, intimate relationship. Another key factor is the social pressure exerted on people to marry. Getting married is still the norm in our society. Your parents, relatives, and friends expect you to marry eventually, and they often make this expectation abundantly clear with their comments and inquiries.

The popular view in our culture is that people marry because they have fallen in love. Although partially accurate, this view is oversimplified. A multitude of motivational factors are involved in the decision to marry. Peter Stein (1975, 1976) interviewed single men and women ages 22 to 45 who were judged to be neither unattractive nor socially inept. As you can see in Figure 9.4 (on the next page), he learned that many forces push and pull people toward marriage or singlehood.

Selecting a Mate

Modern Western cultures are somewhat unusual in permitting free choice of one's marital partner. Most societies rely on parental arrangements and severely restrict the range of acceptable partners along religious and class lines (Bumiller, 1989). Mate selection in American culture is a gradual process that begins with dating and moves on to sometimes lengthy periods of courtship. In this section, we will look at the impact of endogamy, homogamy, and gender on marital choice. We'll also discuss Bernard Murstein's S-V-R theory, which provides a good overview of the process of mate selection.

ENDOGAMY

***Endogamy* is the tendency of people to marry within their own social group.** Buss (1985) reviews extensive evidence indicating that people tend to marry others of the same race, religion, ethnic background, and social class. This endogamy is promoted by cultural norms and by the way proximity and similarity influence interpersonal attraction (see Chapter 8). Although endogamy appears to be gradually declining, it's likely to remain influential for the foreseeable future (Surra, 1990).

HOMOGAMY

***Homogamy* is the tendency of people to marry others who have similar personal characteristics.** Among other things, marital partners tend to be similar in age and education (Mare, 1991; Schoen & Woolredge, 1989), physical attractiveness (Feingold, 1988), attitudes and values (Honeycutt, 1986; Kilby, 1993), and even in vulnerability to psychological disorders

FIGURE 9.4.

The decision to marry. Stein (1975) interviewed single people between 22 and 45 to ascertain the motivational factors that influence the decision to marry. *Pushes toward marriage* involve deficits supposedly felt by single persons. *Pushes toward single-hood* involve deficits felt by married people. *Pulls* are positive factors associated with marriage or being single. Not everyone weighs all these factors, but this list illustrates the complexity of the decision to marry.

The Decision to Marry			
Pushes toward marriage	**Pulls toward marriage**	**Pushes toward singlehood**	**Pulls toward singlehood**
Economic security	Influence of parents	Restrictions	Career opportunities
Influence from mass media	Desire for family	Suffocating one-to-one relationships, feeling trapped	Variety of experiences
Pressure from parents	Example of peers	Obstacles to self-development	Self-sufficiency
Need to leave home	Romanticization of marriage	Boredom, unhappiness, anger	Sexual availability
Interpersonal and personal reasons	Love	Role playing and conformity to expectations	Exciting lifestyle
Fear of independence	Physical attraction	Poor communication with mate	Freedom to change and experiment
Loneliness	Emotional attachment	Sexual frustration	Mobility
Alternative did not seem feasible	Security, social status, prestige	Lack of friends, isolation, loneliness	Sustaining frendships
Cultural expectations, socialization		Limitations on mobility and available experience	Supportive groups
Regular sex		Influence of and participation in women's movement	Men's and women's groups
Guilt over singlehood			Group living arrangements
			Specialized groups

(McLeod, 1995). Interestingly, homogamy *is* associated with longer-lasting and more satisfying marital relations (Houts, Robins, & Huston, 1996).

Deviations from homogamy in age and education do not tend to be symmetric, as husbands are usually older and better educated than their wives (South, 1991). The typical age gap is about 3–4 years (Surra, 1990). Cultural norms that discourage women from dating younger men may contribute to a "marriage squeeze" for women. Without the freedom to date younger men, women are likely to find their pool of potential partners dwindling more rapidly than men of similar age do (Oppenheimer, 1988).

People tend to marry others who are similar in race, religion, social class, education, and other personal characteristics—a phenomenon called homogamy.

GENDER AND MATE SELECTION PREFERENCES

Research reveals that males and females exhibit both similarities and differences in what they look for in a marital partner. Many characteristics, such as kindness, emotional stability, dependability, and a pleasant disposition, are rated highly by both sexes (Buss, 1989; Kenrick et al., 1993). However, a few crucial differences between men's and women's priorities have been found and these differences appear to be nearly universal across cultures. As we saw in Chapter 8, women tend to place a higher value than men on potential partners' socioeconomic status, intelligence, character, ambition, and financial prospects (Buss, 1996; Feingold, 1992a). In contrast, men consistently show more interest than women in potential partners' youthfulness, physical attractiveness, and interest in raising a family (Buss, 1994; Kenrick et al., 1993).

Most theorists explain these gender disparities in terms of evolutionary concepts (Buss, 1996; Feingold, 1992a). According to evolutionary theories, all organisms, including humans, are motivated to enhance their chances of passing on their genes to subsequent generations. Human females supposedly accomplish this end not by seeking larger or stronger partners, as in the animal kingdom, but by seeking male partners who possess or are likely to acquire more material resources that can be invested in children. Men, on the other hand, are assumed to maximize their reproductive outlook by seeking female partners with good breeding potential. Thus, men are thought to look for youth, attractiveness, good health, and other characteristics presumed to be associated with higher fertility. These evolutionary analyses of gender differences in mating are speculative and there are alternative explanations (see chapter 8), but they fit with the evidence quite well.

STIMULUS-VALUE-ROLE THEORY

A number of theories have attempted to shed light on the process of mate selection and the development of premarital relationships (see Berg & McQuinn, 1986; Cate, Huston, & Nesselrode, 1986; Stephen, 1985). We'll focus on one particularly prominent model, Bernard Murstein's (1976, 1986) *stimulus-value-role (S-V-R) theory.* According to Murstein, couples generally proceed through three stages—the stimulus, value, and role stages—as they move toward marriage.

During the first stage, a person's attraction to members of the other sex depends mainly on their *stimulus value.* At this point, the individual focuses on relatively superficial and easily identifiable characteristics of the other person. Especially the person's physical attractiveness, social status, occupational success, and reputation. Murstein borrows from *social exchange theory* (see Chapter 8) and argues that progress to the next stage depends on the pair's having relatively similar stimulus value, so as to produce an "even" exchange. The two persons may derive their stimulus value from different characteristics—one from wealth, say, and the other from beauty. However, progress to stage 2 is thought to depend on the couple's subjective perception that they possess similar stimulus value.

If a couple makes it to the second stage, involving *value comparison,* the significance of stimulus variables may be reduced. Further progress now depends on compatibility in values. Typically, the pair will begin to explore each other's attitudes about religion, politics, sex, gender roles, leisure activities, and so forth. If fundamental incompatibilities are uncovered, the relationship may stall at stage 2, or it may come to an end. However, if the two persons discover similarity in values, they are more likely to progress to stage 3.

In the *role stage,* people begin to think about getting married. Hence, they start evaluating whether the other person does a satisfactory job in the role of intimate companion. At this point, individuals focus on the distribution of power in their relationship, the reliability of emotional support, and the quality of their sexual liaison (if they have formed one). Although some people may marry after progressing through only the first two stages, Murstein maintains that marriage is generally delayed until couples are comfortable with role enactments in stage 3.

Murstein's theory has been questioned on the grounds that courtship relationships do not really evolve through distinct stages. Critics argue that individuals in romantic relationships acquire information about each other's stimulus characteristics, values, and roles continuously rather than in discrete stages (Leigh, Holman, & Burr, 1984, 1987). Although there is some merit to this criticism, S-V-R theory provides a useful overview of the factors that influence whether romantic relationships progress toward marriage.

Predictors of Marital Success

Are there any factors that reliably predict marital success? A great deal of research has been devoted to this question. This research has been plagued by one obvious problem: How do you measure "marital success"? Some researchers have simply compared divorced and intact couples in regard to premarital characteristics. The problem with this strategy is that many intact couples obviously do not have happy or successful marriages. Other researchers have used elaborate questionnaires to measure couples' marital satisfaction. Unfortunately, these scales are plagued by a number of problems. Among other things, they appear to measure complacency and lack of conflict more than satisfaction (Fowers et al., 1994). Although our measures of marital quality are rather crude, some predictors of marital success have been found. The relations are all statistically weak, but they are intriguing nonetheless.

Family Background. The marital adjustment of partners is correlated with the marital satisfaction of their parents. People whose parents were divorced are more likely than others to experience divorce themselves (White, 1990). For a number of reasons, marital instability appears to run in families (Teachman, Polonko, & Scanzoni, 1987).

Age. The ages of the bride and groom are also related to the likelihood of success. Couples who marry young have higher divorce rates (London & Wilson, 1988; White, 1990), as Figure 9.5 on the next page shows. Surprisingly, couples who marry late also have a higher propensity to divorce. Because they are selected from a smaller pool of potential mates, older newlyweds are more likely to differ in age, religion, social status, and education (Bitter, 1986). Such differences may make marriage more challenging regardless of age.

Length of Courtship. Longer periods of courtship are associated with a greater probability of marital success (Cate & Lloyd, 1988). Longer courtships may allow couples to evaluate their compatibility more accurately. Alternatively, the correlation between courtship length

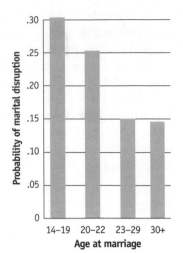

FIGURE 9.5.

Age at marriage and probability of marital disruption in the first five years. Martin and Bumpass (1989) estimated the likelihood of marital disruption (either divorce or separation) within five years for various groups. The data summarized here, based on people who married between 1980 and 1985, show that the probability of marital disruption is substantially higher among those who marry young.

and marital success may exist because people who are cautious about marriage have attitudes and values that promote marital stability.

Socioeconomic Class. The frequency of divorce is higher in the working and lower classes than in the upper and middle classes. There are probably many reasons, but a key one appears to be the greater financial stress in lower socioeconomic strata (Conger et al., 1990).

Personality. Generally, studies have found that partners' specific personality traits are not very predictive of marital success. However, the presence of psychological distress and emotional disorders in one or both partners is associated with marital problems (Larson & Holman, 1994; Mastekaasa, 1994). One interesting study (Long & Andrews, 1990) found an association between a trait called *perspective taking* and marital adjustment. *Perspective taking* **is a component of empathy that involves the tendency to put oneself in another person's place.** For both husbands and wives, high scores in perspective taking were found to be positively correlated with marital adjustment. Thus, individuals who work to understand their partner's viewpoint appear to have a better chance of marital success.

In summary, there are some thought-provoking correlations between couples' premarital characteristics and marital adjustment. However, many of the relevant studies are getting rather dated, given the shifting landscape of modern marriage (Cate & Lloyd, 1992), and most of the correlations are relatively small. Thus, there are no proven, reliable premarital predictors of marital success. However, researchers have found some stronger correlations when they have investigated the relationship between marital adjustment and the family life cycle. We'll examine this research next.

Marital Adjustment Across the Family Life Cycle

LEARNING OBJECTIVES

- Describe the relationship between the family life cycle and marital satisfaction.
- Discuss the factors couples weigh in deciding to have children.
- Discuss the dynamics of the transition to parenthood.
- Identify common problems that surface as a family's children reach adolescence.
- Discuss the transitions that occur in the later stages of the family life cycle.

"Jennifer has taken a lot of time away from us, the time that we normally spend doing things together or talking. It seems like maybe on a weekend when we would normally like to sleep in, or just have lazy sex, Jennifer wakes up and needs to be fed. . . . But I'm sure that will pass as soon as Jennifer gets a little older. We're just going through a phase."—A new mother quoted in American Couples [Blumstein & Schwartz, 1983, p. 205]

"We're just going through a phase." That statement highlights an important point: There are predictable patterns of development for families, just as there are for individuals. These patterns make up the *family life cycle,* **an orderly sequence of developmental stages that families tend to progress through.** The institutions of marriage and family are inevitably intertwined. With the advent of marriage, two persons add a new member to their existing families and create an entirely new family. Typically, this new family forms the core of one's life as an adult.

Sociologists have proposed a number of models to describe family development (Mattessich & Hill, 1987). Our discussion will be organized around a six-stage model of family development outlined by Carter and McGoldrick (1988; McGoldrick & Carter, 1989). Figure 9.6 provides an overview of their model. It spells out the developmental tasks during each stage of the life cycle for families that eventually have children and remain intact. Although Carter and McGoldrick have described variations on this basic pattern that are associated with remaining childless or going through a divorce, we will focus primarily on the basic pattern in this section.

Research suggests that the family life cycle is an important determinant of marital satisfaction. Numerous studies have measured spouses' overall satisfaction in different stages of the family life cycle and found a U-shaped relationship like the one shown in Figure 9.7 (Belsky, 1990a; Glenn, 1990; Orbuch et al., 1996). This U-shaped relationship reflects the fact that satisfaction tends to be greatest at the beginning and at the end of the family life cycle, with a noticeable decline

FIGURE 9.6.

Stages of the family life cycle. The family life cycle can be divided into six stages, as shown here (based on Carter & McGoldrick, 1988). The family's key developmental task during each stage is identified in the second column. The third column lists additional developmental tasks at each stage.

The Family Life Cycle		
Family life cycle stage	Emotional process of transition: Key developmental task	Additional changes in family status required to proceed developmentally
1. Between families: The unattached young adult	Accepting parent/offspring separation	a. Differentiation of self in relation to family of origin b. Development of intimate peer relationships c. Establishment of self in work
2. The joining of families through marriage: The newly married couple	Commitment to new system	a. Formation of marital system b. Realignment of relationships with extended families and friends to include spouse
3. The family with young children	Accepting new members into the system	a. Adjusting marital system to make space for child(ren) b. Taking on parenting roles c. Realignment of relationships with extended family to include parenting and grandparenting roles
4. The family with adolescents	Increasing flexibility of family boundaries to include children's independence	a. Shifting of parent-child relationships to permit adolescent to move in and out of system b. Refocus on midlife marital and career issues c. Beginning shift toward concerns for older generation
5. Launching children and moving on	Accepting a multitude of exits from and entries into the family system	a. Renegotiation of marital system as a dyad b. Development of adult-to-adult relationships between grown children and their parents c. Realignment of relationships to include in-laws and grandchildren d. Dealing with disabilities and death of parents (grandparents)
6. The family in later life	Accepting the shifting of generational roles	a. Maintaining own and/or couple functioning and interests in face of physiological decline; exploration of new familial and social role options b. Support for a more central role for middle generation c. Making room in the system for the wisdom and experience of the elderly; supporting the older generation without overfunctioning for them d. Dealing with loss of spouse, siblings, and other peers and preparation for own death; life review and integrations

occurring in the middle. The conventional explanation for this pattern is that the burdens of child-rearing undermine couples' satisfaction, which gradually begins to climb back up again as children grow up and the burden eases. This explanation is plausible, but alternative explanations can also account for the U-shaped pattern (Glenn, 1998). For example, the decline in satisfaction after the first few years of marriage could simply reflect the normal erosion of passionate love that is frequently seen in couples whether or not they are married or have children (see Chapter 8). Consistent with this analysis, a number of studies have shown that marital satisfaction tends to decline in the early stages of marriage even when there are no children (Bradbury, 1998). The increase in satisfaction in the later stages of the family life cycle could be due to diminishing demands and stresses from spouses' work roles, which often have a deleterious effect on marital interactions. Although the exact reasons for the U-shaped pattern in marital satisfaction are not yet clear, most potential explanations are based on the assumption that marital adjustment is influenced by the nature of the challenges that couples confront at various points in the family life cycle. Let's look at the challenges that arise at each stage.

Between Families: The Unattached Young Adult

As young adults become independent of their parents, they go through a transitional period during which they are "between families" until they form a new family through marriage. What is interesting about this stage is that it is being prolonged by more and more people. The percentage of young adults who are postponing marriage until their late twenties or early thirties has risen dramatically (Sporakowski, 1988). The extension of this stage is probably due to a number of factors, including the availability of new career options for women, increased educational requirements in the world of work, and increased emphasis on personal autonomy.

Joining Together: The Newly Married Couple

This phase begins when the unattached adult becomes attached. The newly married couple gradually settle into their roles as husband and wife. This phase can be quite troublesome, as the early years of marriage are often marred by numerous problems and disagreements (Johnson et al., 1986). *In general, however, this stage tends to be characterized by great happiness—the proverbial "marital bliss."* Spouses' satisfaction with their relationship tends to be relatively high early in marriage, before the arrival of the first child.

This prechildren phase used to be rather short for most newly married couples, as they quickly went about the business of having their first child. Traditionally, couples simply *assumed* that they would proceed to have children. Remaining childless by choice used to be virtually unthinkable. In recent decades, however, ambivalence about the prospect of having children has clearly increased, and the percentage of childless couples has doubled since 1960 (Groat, et al., 1997; Somers, 1993). Thus, more and more couples find themselves struggling to *decide* whether to have children. Often, this decision occurs after numerous postponements, when the couple finally acknowledges that "the right time" is never going to arrive (Crane, 1985).

Couples who choose to remain childless cite the great costs incurred in raising children. In addition to the financial burdens, they mention costs such as giving up educational or career opportunities, loss of time for leisure activities and each other, loss of privacy and autonomy, and worry about the responsibility associated with child-rearing (Bram, 1985; Seccombe, 1991).

The evidence suggests that these concerns are legitimate, as the social and economic burdens of parenting do lead to increased distress (Bird, 1997). In contrast, couples who decide to have children cite many reasons for this choice, including the responsibility to procreate, the joy of watching youngsters mature, the sense of purpose that children create, and the satisfaction associated with emotional nurturance and the challenges of child-rearing (Goetting, 1986). In spite of the costs involved in raising children, most parents report no regret about their choice. The vast majority of parents rate parenthood as a very positive and satisfying experience (Demo, 1992).

Family with Young Children

Although most parents are happy with their decision to have children, the arrival of the first child represents a major transition, and the disruption of routines can be extremely stressful (Lavee, Sharlin, & Katz, 1996). The new mother, already physically exhausted by the birth process, is particularly prone to postpartum distress (Hock et al., 1995). The transition to parenthood tends to be more difficult for older women and for working wives. Women who have to shoulder the major burden of infant care and those whose babies have difficult temperaments are also especially vulnerable to distress (Kalmuss, Davidson, & Cushman, 1992).

Crisis during the transition to first parenthood is far from universal, however (Ruble et al., 1988). Couples who have high levels of intimacy, closeness, and commitment prior to the first child's birth are likely to maintain a high level of satisfaction after the child's birth (Lewis, 1988). Interestingly, older males who father their first child relatively late tend to experience a smoother transition to parenthood than younger men (Cooney et al., 1993). The key to making this

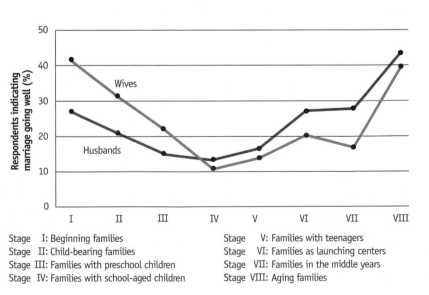

FIGURE 9.7.

Marital satisfaction across the family life cycle. This graph depicts the percentage of husbands and wives studied by Rollins and Feldman (1970) who said their marriage was going well "all the time" at various stages of the family life cycle. Rollins and Feldman (1970) broke the family life cycle into eight stages instead of six. The U-shaped relationship shown here has been found in many other studies as well.

Stage   I: Beginning families
Stage   II: Child-bearing families
Stage   III: Families with preschool children
Stage   IV: Families with school-aged children
Stage   V: Families with teenagers
Stage   VI: Families as launching centers
Stage   VII: Families in the middle years
Stage   VIII: Aging families

Although children can be unparalleled sources of joy and satisfaction, the transition to parenthood can be extremely stressful, especially for mothers.

transition less stressful may be to have *realistic expectations* about parental responsibilities (Belsky, 1985; Kalmuss et al., 1992). Studies find that stress tends to be greatest in new parents who have overestimated the benefits and underestimated the costs of their new role. Reactions to parenthood may also depend on how a couple's marriage is going. Satisfaction with parenting tends to be higher when marital quality is higher (Erel & Burnham, 1995; Rogers & White, 1998).

Although children bring their share of trials and tribulations to a marriage, evidence suggests that they should not have to shoulder all the blame for their parents' sagging marital satisfaction. Studies that have compared young married couples with children to similar couples without children have found that the early years of marriage typically bring a decline in marital satisfaction for both groups (Glenn, 1990; Kurdek, 1993). This decline may be somewhat steeper for parents because of the stress associated with raising children (Belsky, 1990a), but some of the negative effects attributed to parenthood may be due to other processes that unfold as marriages evolve over the years.

In any case, parenting is a complex topic to which many entire books have been devoted. Diverse styles of parenting tend to yield different results (Baumrind, 1991). We will consider this topic in earnest in the Chapter 11 Application.

Family with Adolescent Children

Although the adolescent years have long been viewed as a period of great stress and turmoil, research from the past decade has led to the conclusion that adolescence is not as turbulent or difficult as once believed (Offer et al., 1988; see Chapter 11). Ironically, though, studies indicate that it is an especially stressful period for the parents, who overwhelmingly rate adolescence as the most difficult stage of parenting (Gecas & Seff, 1990).

As adolescent children seek to establish their own identities, parental influence tends to decline while the influence of their peer groups tends to increase. Parents tend to retain more influence than peers over important matters, such as educational goals and career plans, but peers gradually gain more influence over less critical matters, such as style of dress and recreational plans (Gecas & Seff, 1990). Thus, conflicts between adolescent children and their parents tend to involve everyday matters such as chores and dress more than substantive issues such as sex and drugs (Barber, 1994). Conflict is particularly likely to surface between adolescents (of both sexes) and their mothers. Moreover, when conflict does occur, mothers are more adversely affected than fathers (Steinberg & Silverberg, 1987). This may be because women's self-esteem has tended to be more closely tied than men's to the quality of their family relationships.

In addition to worrying about their adolescent children, middle-aged couples often worry about the care of their parents. Thanks to increased longevity and decreased family size, today's average married couple has more parents than children, and an increasing number of adults provide care to their aging parents (Starrels et al., 1997; Wisensale, 1992). Females tend to assume most of the responsibility for elderly relatives, and it is estimated that in the future women can expect to spend more years caring for their aging parents than for their dependent children (Bromley & Blieszner, 1997; Brubaker, 1990). Many theorists are concerned that these multigenerational caregiving responsibilities may prove burdensome. However, the available evidence to date suggests that this shift in family responsibilities has had relatively little impact on caregivers' well-being (Loomis & Booth, 1995).

Launching Children into the Adult World

When children begin to reach their twenties, the family has to adapt to a multitude of exits and entries, as children leave and return, sometimes with their own

Web Link 9.1

American Academy of Child and Adolescent Psychiatry (AACAP): Facts for Families
Parents often need help coping with emerging problems in their children. The brochures available here (and in Spanish, too) cover a wide range of psychological problems and psychiatric conditions in children and adolescents.

spouses. This period, during which children normally progress from dependence to independence, brings a host of transitions. In many instances, conflict subsides and parent-child relations become closer and more supportive (Aquilino, 1997).

One might argue that launching children into the adult world tends to be a lengthier and more difficult process today than it once was (Goldscheider & Goldscheider, 1994). The percentage of 18- to 29-year-olds who live with their parents has climbed in recent decades (Aquilino, 1990; Glick & Lin, 1986). The rapidly rising cost of a college education and the shrinking job market have probably led many young adults to linger in their parents' homes. Moreover, crises such as separation, divorce, job loss, and pregnancy out of wedlock are forcing children who have ventured out on their own to return to their parents. The repercussions of these new trends are the subject of current research. Preliminary data suggest that living with one's parents during adulthood has a modest negative impact on parent-child relations (White & Rogers, 1997).

When parents do manage to get all their children launched into the adult world, they find themselves faced with an "empty nest." This period was formerly thought to be a difficult transition for many parents, especially mothers who were familiar only with the maternal role. Today, however, more women have experience with other roles outside the home, and most look forward to their "liberation" from child-rearing responsibilities (Reinke et al., 1985).

The Family in Later Life

Marital satisfaction tends to climb in the postparental period as couples find that they have more time to devote attention to each other (Brubaker, 1990). Whether this trend is the result of reduced parental responsibilities, reduced work responsibilities, or other considerations remains unclear (Lee, 1988). In any case, many couples take advantage of their newfound freedom, traveling or developing new leisure interests. For many people this can be a period of increased intimacy. Spouses do have to adapt to spending more time with

Couples often have more time to enjoy leisure activities together once their parental and work responsibilities decline. These joint activities can lead to increased intimacy.

each other, but most seem to make the adjustment without major problems (Treas, 1983). Of course, age-related considerations that are independent of the relationship, such as the increased likelihood of physical illness, can make the later years stressful. In general, however, the trend is for couples to report fairly high satisfaction until one of the spouses (usually the husband) dies.

Vulnerable Areas in Marital Adjustment

LEARNING OBJECTIVES

- Discuss how gaps in role expectations may affect marital adjustment.
- Summarize how spouses' work affects their marital satisfaction and their children.
- Discuss how financial issues are related to marital adjustment.
- Summarize evidence on the relationship between communication quality and marital adjustment.

"When we first got married, the first six months of conflicts were all about getting him to take account of what I had planned for him at home.... He would come waltzing in an hour and a half late for dinner, or cancel an evening with friends, because he had to close a deal.... We would argue and argue . . . not because I didn't want him to make a living . . . but because I thought he had to be more considerate."—A wife quoted in American Couples [Blumstein & Schwartz, 1983, p. 174]

Web Link 9.2

The Whole Family Center
This lively site features reasonable advice and useful links for issues that arise in families, such as raising children and coping with family crises. Two licensed psychologists—a married couple with broad training in marriage and family therapy—serve as the experts at the Center.

An unavoidable reality of marriage is that couples must confront a legion of problems together. During courtship, couples tend to focus on pleasurable activities. But once couples are married, they deal with a variety of problems, such as arriving at acceptable role compromises, paying bills, and raising a family. There is no such thing as a problem-free marriage. Successful marriages depend on couples' ability to handle their problems. In this section we will analyze the major kinds of difficulties that are likely to emerge. We can't offer simple solutions for these problems. However, in navigating your way through life, it helps to know where you're likely to encounter the most perilous reefs.

Gaps in Role Expectations

When a couple marry, they assume new roles—those of husband and wife. Each role comes with it certain expectations that the partners hold about how wives and husbands should behave. These expectations may vary greatly from one person to another. Gaps between partners in their role expectations appear to have a negative effect on couples' marital satisfaction (Lye & Biblarz, 1993). Unfortunately, substantial differences in role expectations seem particularly likely in this era of transition in gender roles.

Individuals' marital role expectations are shaped significantly by exposure to their parents' relationship. The traditional role expectations passed on by parents used to be fairly clear. A husband was supposed to act as the principal breadwinner, make the important decisions, and take care of certain household chores, such as car or yard maintenance. A wife was supposed to raise the children, cook, clean, and follow the leadership of her husband. Spouses had different spheres of influence. The working world was the domain of the husband, the home the domain of the wife.

In recent decades, however, the women's movement and other forces of social change have led to new expectations about marital roles. Young adults no longer blindly follow the traditions of their elders. Today, there are *options* from which to choose, so prospective mates can't assume that they share the same views on the appropriate responsibilities of spouses. Modern couples need to negotiate and renegotiate role responsibilities throughout the family life cycle (Zvonkovic et al., 1996). Interestingly, husbands and wives with nontraditional attitudes about gender roles in marriage report somewhat lower marital satisfaction than others, probably because they view alternatives to married life more favorably and because they place greater emphasis on personal fulfillment (Lye & Biblarz, 1993).

Women may be especially vulnerable to ambivalence and confusion about shifting marital roles. Surveys of college women (Baber & Monaghan, 1988; Machung, 1989) show that more women than ever are aspiring to demanding professional careers. At the same time, virtually all these women plan to marry and have children. Most expect to marry a man who will assume equal responsibility for child-rearing and domestic chores. Clearly, these women want to "have it all." Yet, research shows that husbands' career demands continue to take priority over their wives' vocational ambitions. It is wives who are expected to interrupt their career to raise young children, stay home when children are sick, and abandon their jobs when husbands' careers require relocation (Silberstein, 1992). Moreover, even when both spouses are employed, many husbands maintain traditional role expectations about housework, child care, and decision making (Blair, 1993), and many wives continue to see housework as a central feature of their family responsibilities (Robinson & Milkie, 1998).

Reflective of this reality, studies indicate that wives are still doing the bulk of the household chores in America, even when they work outside the home. For example, Blair and Johnson (1992) found that working wives devoted an average of 31 hours per week to housework (not including child care), while their husbands contributed only 15 hours on the average. The gap was even greater for nonemployed wives, who averaged 42 hours per week of housework in comparison to 12 hours per week for their husbands. Moreover, Blair and Johnson found that wives still do the vast

majority of "women's work," such as cooking, cleaning, and laundry, while men continue to do mostly traditional "male chores," such as auto maintenance and outdoor tasks (see Figure 9.8).

Wives who work outside of the home and also shoulder the bulk of household and child-rearing duties are likely to suffer from *role overload,* **which occurs when the prescribed activities for various roles are greater than the individual can comfortably handle.** Research indicates that women tend to report higher levels of role overload throughout the family life cycle (Higgins, Duxbury, & Lee, 1994). Women who are committed to their careers are also likely to experience a great deal of *inter-role conflict—***uncomfortable dissonance experienced when the demands of two or more roles are contradictory or incompatible.** Inter-role conflict occurs when competition exists between the role responsibilities associated with being a parent, spouse, and worker.

Role overload and inter-role conflict are less problematic for wives when couples have equitable role responsibilities. Men tend to do more housework when they have lighter work demands, when their wives earn a larger portion of the family income or work longer hours, and when they or their wives hold less traditional beliefs about gender roles (Almeida, Maggs, & Galambos, 1993; Coltrane & Ishii-Kuntz, 1992). A study by McHale and Crouter (1992) suggests that housework arrangements are most likely to be a source of discontent when spouses' expectations and preferences clash with reality. They found lower marital satisfaction when wives with nontraditional attitudes about gender roles had to live with a traditional division of household labor and when husbands with traditional attitudes had to adapt to a more equal division of labor. Obviously, women's and men's varied expectations about housework roles create considerable potential for conflict (Kluwer, Heesink, & Van De Vliert, 1997; Stohs, 1995).

In light of this reality, it is imperative that couples discuss role expectations in depth before marriage. If they discover that their views are divergent, they need to take the potential for problems seriously. Many people casually dismiss gender-role disagreements, thinking they can "straighten out" their partner later on. But assumptions about marital roles, whether traditional or not, may be deeply held and not easily changed.

Work and Career Issues

The possible interactions between one's occupation and one's marriage are numerous and complex. Individuals' job satisfaction and involvement can affect their own marital satisfaction, their partner's marital satisfaction, and their children's development.

HUSBANDS' WORK AND MARITAL ADJUSTMENT

Work has traditionally played a central role in men's lives. Hence, a host of studies have investigated the relationship between husbands' job satisfaction and their marital adjustment. We could speculate that these two variables might be either positively or negatively related. On the one hand, if a husband is highly committed to a satisfying career, he may have less time and energy to devote to his marriage and family. On the other hand, the frustration and stress of an unsatisfying job might spill over to contaminate one's marriage.

The research on this question suggests that both scenarios are realistic possibilities. Husbands who try to balance a high commitment to work with a strong commitment to parenting report more role strain than husbands who have a low commitment to their work (O'Neil & Greenberger, 1994). Moreover, studies find that husbands' stress at work can have a substantial negative effect on their wives' emotional health and marital satisfaction (Rook, Dooley, & Catalano, 1991; Small & Riley, 1990).

FIGURE 9.8.

Who does the housework?
Blair and Johnson (1992) studied the proportion of housework done by husbands and wives. These charts, based on employed wives, show that even working women continue to do a highly disproportionate share of most household tasks and that the division of labor still meshes with traditional gender roles.

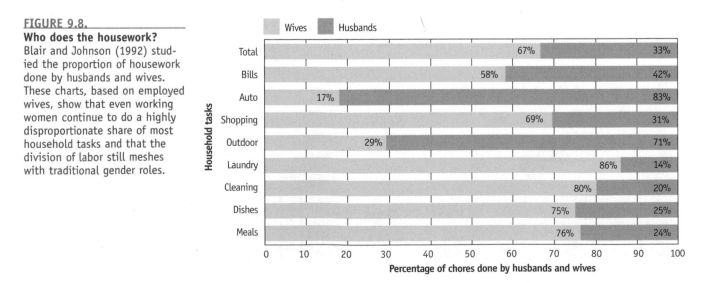

WIVES' WORK AND MARITAL ADJUSTMENT

Although few studies have looked at the impact of wives' work on their own marital satisfaction, many have examined the effect of wives' work on their husband's well-being or the couple's marital adjustment. This slant arises from traditional views that regard men's *lack of* employment, but women's *employment*, as departures from the norm. Typically, these studies simply categorize women as working or nonworking and compare the husbands' (or couples') marital satisfaction.

Most of these studies find no consistent differences in the marital adjustment of male-breadwinner versus dual-career couples (Barnett & Rivers, 1996; Spitze, 1988). Recently, some investigators have begun to study the mediating influence of spouses' *attitudes* toward married women's employment, with enlightening results. It appears that marital satisfaction tends to be highest when partners share similar gender-role expectations and when the wife's employment status matches her own (and her husband's) preference about it (Menaghan & Parcel, 1990). In summary, although dual-career couples do face special problems in negotiating career priorities, child-care arrangements, and other practical matters, their marriage need not be negatively affected.

PARENTS' WORK AND CHILDREN'S DEVELOPMENT

Another issue of concern has been the potential impact of parents' employment on their children. Virtually all of the research in this area has focused on the effects of mothers' employment outside the home. This research has been guided by two implicit assumptions: (1) The more time mothers spend with their children, the better off the children are, and (2) full-time housewives of previous generations devoted more time to their children than today's employed wives. Both assumptions have been questioned (Hoffman, 1987). Extremely high levels of mother-child interaction can backfire, contributing to excessive dependency in children. Furthermore, yesterday's full-time mothers did not have modern, time-saving household conveniences, and they had more children. Thus, they may not have devoted any more time to each individual child than today's working mothers. Furthermore, when mothers work outside the home, fathers tend to devote more time to child care, so that the combined time that both parents spend with their children is about the same as in traditional male breadwinner families (Gilbert, 1994).

What does the research on maternal employment show? Although most Americans believe that maternal employment is detrimental to children's development (Greenberger et al., 1988), a host of empirical studies have found that a mother's employment is not harmful to her children (Demo, 1992; Etaugh, 1993; Greenstein,

Web Link 9.3

American Association of Marriage and Family Therapy (AAMFT)

This well-designed site maintained by the American Association of Marriage and Family Therapy (AAMFT) not only offers Web surfers an understanding of how professional therapists can help couples and families in trouble, but also offers links to important family and marriage-related resources.

1993; MacEwen & Barling, 1991). For instance, studies generally have not found a link between mothers' employment status and the quality of infant-mother emotional attachment (Easterbrooks & Goldberg, 1985; Etaugh, 1993). Clearly, a child *can* form a strong attachment to a working mother. Furthermore, the *attitudes* of both parents are important. Families in which both the wife and husband are satisfied with the wife's role (whether she is employed or not) tend to have the best adjusted offspring (Easterbrooks & Goldberg, 1985).

Some researchers even suggest that maternal employment can have *positive* effects on children (Demo, 1992). For instance, studies have found that children of working mothers tend to be especially self-reliant and responsible. This advantage appears to be particularly pronounced for girls. Daughters of working mothers also tend to exhibit higher than average academic competence and career aspirations (Hoffman, 1987).

Financial Difficulties

How do couples' financial resources affect their marital adjustment? Neither financial stability nor wealth can ensure marital satisfaction. However, poverty can produce serious problems (Conger et al, 1990; Voydanoff, 1990). Without money, families live in constant dread of financial drains such as illness, layoffs, or broken appliances. Husbands tend to view themselves as poor providers and become hostile and irritable. Their hostility can undermine the warm, supportive exchanges that help sustain relationships. This problem is sometimes aggravated by disappointed wives who criticize their husbands. Spontaneity in communication may be impaired by an understandable reluctance to talk about financial concerns. It is thus clear that poverty can have negative effects on married couples and their children (Klebanov, Brooks-Gunn, & Duncan, 1994).

Even when financial resources are plentiful, money can be a source of marital strain. Quarrels about how to spend money are common and potentially damaging at all income levels. Pittman and Lloyd (1988), for instance, found that perceived financial stress (regardless of a family's actual income) was associated with

decreased marital satisfaction. Another study examined how happily married couples handled their money in comparison to couples that eventually divorced (Schaninger & Buss, 1986). In comparison to the divorced couples, the happy couples engaged in more joint decision making on finances. Thus, the best way to avoid troublesome battles over money is probably to engage in extensive planning of expenditures together.

Inadequate Communication

Effective communication is crucial to the success of a marriage. The damaging role that poor communication can play was clearly demonstrated in a study by Fowers and Olson (1989). They identified areas of marital functioning that differentiated between satisfied and dissatisfied couples. Of the three most important areas of functioning, two involved communication: spouses' comfort in sharing information with each other, and their willingness to recognize and resolve conflicts between them. (The third area was the quality of their sexual relationship.) Similarly, in a study of couples getting a divorce (Cleek & Pearson, 1985), communication difficulties were the most frequently cited problem among both husbands and wives (see Figure 9.9).

Spouses' strategies for resolving conflicts may be particularly crucial to marital satisfaction (Crohan, 1992). Many partners respond to conflict by withdrawing and refusing to communicate—a pattern associated with deteriorating marital satisfaction over time (Kurdek, 1995).

A number of studies have compared communication patterns in happy and unhappy marriages. This research indicates that unhappily married spouses (1) find it difficult to convey positive messages, (2) misunderstand each other more often, (3) are less likely to recognize that they have been misunderstood, (4) use more frequent, and more intense, negative messages, and (5) often differ in the amount of self-disclosure they prefer in the relationship (Noller & Fitzpatrick, 1990; Noller & Gallois, 1988 ; Sher & Baucom, 1993). Moreover, gender differences in approaches to communication (see the Chapter 10 Application) are frequently exaggerated in unhappily married couples (Gottman & Levenson, 1988).

The importance of marital communication was underscored in a widely cited study that attempted to predict the likelihood of divorce in a sample of 52 married couples (Buehlman, Gottman, & Katz, 1992). Each couple provided an oral history of their relation-

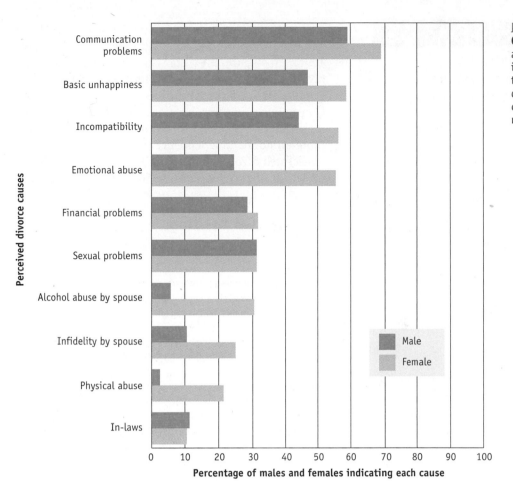

FIGURE 9.9.

Causes of divorce. When Cleek and Pearson (1985) asked divorcing couples about their perceptions about the causes of their divorce, both men and women cited communication difficulties more than any other cause.

ship and a 15-minute sample of their interaction style, during which they discussed two problem areas in their marriage. The investigators rated the spouses on a variety of factors that mostly reflected the subjects' ways of relating to each other. Based on these ratings, they were able to predict which couples would divorce within three years, with 94% accuracy!

In recent years, investigators have increasingly turned to attribution theory to better understand marital miscommunication (Fincham & Bradbury, 1992). As explained in Chapters 5 and 6, *attributions* are inferences that people draw about the causes of events, others' behavior, and even their own behavior. Attributing events to internal versus external factors, or stable versus unstable factors, can make all the difference in the world in how one relates to other people. Married people routinely make attributions to explain each other's behavior. For example, if a wife forgets her husband's birthday, he might conclude that she's self-centered and inconsiderate (an internal, stable attribution). Or he might conclude that she's drained by work overload at the office (an external, unstable attribution). Obviously, these attributions don't have the same implications for their relationship.

Research by Frank Fincham and his colleagues indicates that distressed spouses (usually defined as those seeking marital therapy) tend to explain their partners' negative behavior with internal, stable attributions that have global implications for their marriage ("she doesn't love me"). In contrast, they tend to explain their partners' positive behaviors with external, unstable attributions that have specific implications ("she was nice because she made a big sale today"). Patterns of attribution in happily married couples tend to be just the opposite (Bradbury & Fincham, 1988; Karney et al., 1994). Thus, in comparison to happy couples, distressed spouses blame their problems on each other and view good behavior as a temporary aberration. Unhappy spouses' biases in attribution could be either a cause or an effect of marital distress, but their biases clearly aren't a promising foundation for marital bliss.

Given the importance of good communication, many approaches to marital therapy emphasize the development of better communication skills in partners (O'Donohue & Crouch, 1996). However, poor marital communication is not simply due to poor communication *skills* (Burleson & Denton, 1997). In many instance, spouses may have adequate or even excellent communication ability but be *unwilling* to make communication a priority, avoid unnecessary criticism, share in decision making, and so forth.

Divorce

LEARNING OBJECTIVES

- Summarize evidence on changing divorce rates.
- Summarize evidence on the effects of divorce on spouses and their children.
- Discuss how men and women adjust to divorce.
- Summarize data on the frequency and success of remarriage and its impact on children.

"In the ten years that we were married I went from twenty-four to thirty-four and they were a very significant ten years. I started a career, started to succeed, bought my first house, had a child, you know, very significant years. And then all of a sudden, every goddamn thing, I'm back to zero. I have no house. I don't have a child. I don't have a wife. I don't have the same family. My economic position has been shattered. And nothing recoverable. All these goals which I had struggled for, every goddamn one of them, is gone."—A recently divorced man quoted in Marital Separation *[Weiss, 1975, p. 75]*

The dissolution of a marriage tends to be a bone-jarring event for most people, as this bitter quote illustrates. Any of the problems discussed in the previous section might lead a couple to consider divorce. However, people appear to vary in their threshold for divorce, just as they do in their threshold for marriage. Some couples will tolerate a great deal of disappointment and bickering without seriously considering divorce. Other couples are ready to call their attorney as soon as it becomes apparent that their expectations for marital bliss were somewhat unrealistic. Typically, however, divorce is the culmination of a gradual disintegration of the relationship brought about by an accumulation of many interrelated problems.

Increasing Rate of Divorce

Although relatively accurate statistics are available on divorce rates, it is still difficult to estimate the percentage of marriages ending in divorce. The usually cited ratio of marriages in a year to divorces in the same year is highly misleading. It would be more instructive to follow people married in a particular year over a period of time, but little research of this type has been done. In any case, it is clear that divorce rates have increased substantially in recent decades, as Figure 9.10 shows. The most widely cited recent estimates of future divorce risk are around 50% (Bumpass, Raley, & Sweet, 1995). Martin and Bumpass (1989) project that if you include couples who separate permanently but never bother to file for divorce, *two-thirds* of today's marriages in the United States will result in marital dissolution.

Divorce rates are higher among blacks than whites, among lower-income couples, among people who marry at a relatively young age, and among those whose parents divorced (Cherlin, 1992; Kurdek, 1993; White, 1991). As Figure 9.11 shows, the vast majority of divorces occur during the first few years of a marriage (Hiedemann, SuhomLinova, & O'Rand, 1998). Conventional wisdom assumes that divorce rates are higher among wives who earn more income and have more economic independence. A recent study *did* find an elevated divorce rate among nontraditional couples in which the wives earned 50–75% of the family

● Recommended Reading

Love Is Never Enough by Aaron T. Beck (Harper & Row, 1988)

Innumerable books attempt to tell couples how to make it all work. Aaron Beck's entry in this market appears to be superior to most of the others. Beck is the founder of cognitive therapy (see Chapter 16) and a renowned expert on the distorted thought patterns that promote anxiety and depression. He makes a compelling case that many married couples (especially those in distress) engage in the same errors of thinking as depressed and anxious people—namely, negativity, rigidity, and selectivity. If each spouse thinks about the other in such a distorted manner, then disillusionment, miscommunication, and frustration are inevitable.

Most of the chapters include one or more questionnaires readers can use to probe their own relationships. In addition, Beck provides a great deal of practical advice about how to identify and change the distorted thought patterns that undermine the marital satisfaction of so many couples. A unique feature of Beck's book is its inclusion of many actual conversations of troubled couples, along with the unspoken thoughts that lie behind each line of dialogue.

The following interchange occurred when Marjorie wanted to hang a picture but had difficulty driving the nail into the wall:

KEN: *[She's having a problem. I'd better help her.] Let me do it for you.*
MARJORIE: *[He has no confidence in my ability.] That's all right. I can do it myself [angrily].*
KEN: *What's the matter with you? I was only trying to help.*
MARJORIE: *That's all you ever do. You don't think I can do anything.*
KEN: *Well, you can't even drive a nail straight [laughs].*
MARJORIE: *There you go again—always putting me down.*
KEN: *I was just trying to help.*

The spouses had completely different versions of Ken's intervention. Marjorie's goal of hanging the picture was to assure herself that she could handle manual tasks; in fact, she was looking forward to Ken's praise for her demonstration of competence and independence. His intrusion, though, brought her sense of incompetence to the surface. While each was correct in the belief that Ken lacked confidence in Marjorie's manual ability, Ken perceived himself as kind and considerate, while Marjorie viewed him as intrusive and patronizing. What started as an innocent gesture of helpfulness on his part led to hurt feelings and antagonism. [p. 59]

FIGURE 9.10.

Increasing divorce rates. As this graph shows, the percentage of marriages ending in a divorce or permanent separation has been going up steadily for over 100 years. Today, experts *estimate* that about 50% of marriages eventually will end in divorce. (Source: Cherlin, 1981; Martin & Bumpass, 1989)

income (Heckert, Nowak, & Snyder, 1998), but the overall evidence on this point remains mixed (Ono, 1998). What types of specific marital problems are predictive of divorce? Amato and Rogers (1997) found that infidelity, jealousy, foolish spending behavior, and drinking and drug problems were the most consistent predictors of divorce.

A wide variety of social trends have probably contributed to increasing divorce rates (Raschke, 1987; White, 1990). The stigma attached to divorce has gradually eroded. Many religious denominations are becoming more tolerant of divorce, and marriage has thus lost some of its sacred quality. The declining fertility rate and the consequent smaller families probably make divorce a more viable possibility. The entry of more women into the work force has made many wives less financially dependent on the continuation of their marriage. New attitudes emphasizing individual fulfillment seem to have counterbalanced older attitudes that encouraged dissatisfied spouses to suffer in silence. Reflecting all these trends, the legal barriers to divorce have also diminished.

Deciding on a Divorce

Divorces are often postponed repeatedly, and they are rarely executed without a great deal of forethought. Indecision is common, as roughly two out of five divorce petitions are eventually withdrawn (Donovan & Jackson, 1990). The decision to divorce is not usually a singular event, but rather the outcome of a long series of smaller decisions that may take years to unfold (Morrison & Cherlin, 1995).

It is difficult to generalize about the relative merits of divorce as opposed to remaining in an unsatisfactory marriage. There is evidence that people who are currently divorced suffer a higher incidence of both

physical and psychological maladies and are less happy than those who are currently married (Frank, 1985; Kitson & Morgan, 1990). Furthermore, the process of getting divorced is usually stressful for both spouses. We might guess that as divorce becomes more commonplace, it should also become less stressful and traumatic, but available evidence does not support this supposition (Kitson, 1992). As painful as marital dissolution may be, remaining in an unhappy marriage is also potentially detrimental. Studies have found an association between marital distress and elevated rates of anxiety, depressive, and drug disorders in both men and women, although it's hard to tell what's causing what in many of these studies (Gotlib & McCabe, 1990).

Decisions about divorce must take into account the impact on a couple's children. Weighing this consideration is difficult, however, because divorces have highly

FIGURE 9.11.

Divorce rate as a function of years married. This graph shows the distribution of divorces in relation to how long couples have been married. As you can see, the vast majority of divorces occur in the early years, with divorce rates peaking between the fifth and tenth years of marriage. (Source: National Center for Health Statistics)

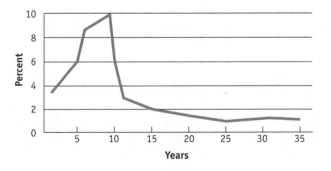

The high divorce rate has led to some novel ways of dealing with its worrisome legal aspects. Attorney Robert Nordyke discovered that the drive-up window at his new office—a former savings and loan branch in Salem, Oregon—was perfect for serving legal papers on his clients' spouses

in many children after a couple of years (Hetherington, 1991), divorce can have a lasting impact that may extend into adulthood. Amato and Keith (1991a) studied *adults* whose parents had divorced when they were children and found elevated rates of maladjustment, antisocial behavior, and marital instability, and lower educational and occupational attainments in comparison to adults whose parents had stayed married.

Children have more adjustment problems when their parents go through a particularly bitter, acrimonious, and conflict-dominated divorce (Tschann et al., 1989, 1990). Divorce also tends to be especially tough on boys whose mothers have sole custody and who therefore are denied a stable male role model

varied effects on children that depend on a complex constellation of interacting factors (Furstenberg & Cherlin, 1991; Hines, 1997). There has been much debate about whether children benefit if parents persevere and keep an unhappy marriage intact. Children whose parents divorce often exhibit quite a variety of adjustment problems that may continue for years (Amato & Keith, 1991b). However, so do children from intact homes characterized by persistent marital discord (Amato, 1993; Grych & Fincham, 1990). All in all, the weight of evidence suggests that in the long run it is less damaging to the children if unhappy parents divorce than if the children grow up in an intact but dissension-ridden home (Demo & Acock, 1988; Hines, 1997). However, this assertion is based on the assumption that the parents' divorce brings their bickering to an end. Unfortunately, the conflicts between divorcing spouses often continue unabated for many years after they part ways. Goldberg (1985), for instance, describes a case history in which a man's ex-wife was still calling him 10 to 15 times a day to disturb and berate him three years after their divorce.

In any case, we should not underestimate the trauma that most children go through when their parents divorce. After a divorce, children may exhibit depression, anxiety, nightmares, dependency, aggression, withdrawal, distractibility, lowered academic performance, reduced physical health, and precocious sexual behavior and substance abuse (Bray & Hetherington, 1993; Guidubaldi, Perry, & Nastasi, 1987; Hines, 1997). Although these effects begin to dissipate

● Recommended Reading

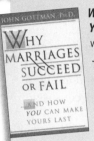

Why Marriages Succeed or Fail . . . and How You Can Make Yours Last by John Gottman, with Nan Silver (Simon & Schuster, 1994)

This book is about communication in intimate relationships—a subject that Gottman has studied intensively for over 20 years. A psychology professor at the University of Washington, Gottman is justifiably famous for his landmark research on the prediction of divorce. He has demonstrated that he can predict which couples will divorce with remarkable accuracy based on careful examination of the couples' communication patterns. According to Gottman, the marriages that last are not those that appear to be free of conflict, but those in which couples are able to resolve the conflicts that inevitably arise in intimate relationships. Gottman categorizes couples into three types based on their style of conflict resolution. In *validating marriages*, couples compromise often and work out their disagreements calmly. In *conflict-avoiding marriages*, couples rarely confront their disagreements openly. In *volatile marriages*, couples have frequent and passionate disputes. For all three types, the crucial consideration according to Gottman, is the relative balance of positive versus negative interactions. In this practical, readable analysis of marital communication, the authors provide plenty of case histories to make their ideas come alive. The book also includes many thought-provoking scales that readers can take to evaluate their own communication styles and tendencies. For example, there are scales to measure stonewalling, defensiveness, and how critical one is. *Why Marriages Succeed or Fail* is an outstanding book loaded with exercises, quizzes, and tips that should help readers improve their marital communication.

My laboratory conducts what amounts to the most intensive studies of couples interacting ever attempted, something akin to an X ray or CAT scan of a living relationship. My research teams have compared, microsecond to microsecond, how couples talk to one another. We've examined their facial expressions, monitored how much they fidget, and how they gesture. We've asked what happens to partners' heart rates when they try to work out their conflicts together. . . .What's more, gathering such information has allowed us to identify the specific processes that lead to the dissolution of a marriage, and those that weld it more firmly together. (p. 20)

Web Link 9.4

Divorce Central
Divorce Central is one of a number of excellent sites that provide information and advice on legal, emotional, and financial issues for individuals contemplating or going through a divorce. Annotated links to the other outstanding divorce-related sites can also be found here.

(Hetherington, 1991). The children's recovery and subsequent adjustment seem to depend primarily on the quality of their relationship with the custodial parent, on the quality of the child-rearing skills exhibited by the custodial parent, and on how well the custodial parent is adjusting to the divorce (Amato, 1993).

Adjusting to Divorce

It is clear that divorce is an exceedingly stressful life event (Buehler & Langenbrunner, 1987). It often combines all four major sources of stress described in Chapter 3: frustration, conflict, pressure, and change. In most respects, divorce appears to be more difficult and disruptive for women than for men (Clarke-Stewart & Bailey, 1990). Women are more likely to assume the responsibility of raising the children, whereas fathers tend to reduce their contact with their children (Albiston, Maccoby, & Mnookin, 1990). After divorce, over one-third of children see their father only a few times a year or not at all (Seltzer, 1991).

Another key consideration is that divorced women are less likely than their ex-husbands to have adequate income or a satisfying job. Research shows that after a divorce, the wife's income declines considerably more than her husband's does, although both tend to decline (Peterson, 1996; Smock, 1993). Paradoxically, although divorced women experience greater stress and feel more financially strapped than divorced men (Weitzman, 1989), women tend to experience serious mental health problems less often and to have more positive feelings about their divorce than men do (Kitson & Morgan, 1990). The reasons for these perplexing gender differences are not clear, although Arendell (1995) speculates that divorced women may benefit from stronger social support networks than divorced men. Among both men and women, high preoccupation with one's ex-spouse is associated with poorer adjustment to divorce (Masheter, 1997).

Remarriage

Evidence that adequate courtship opportunities exist for the divorced is provided by the statistics on remarriage. Roughly three-quarters of divorced women and five-sixths of divorced men eventually remarry

(Glick, 1984). About half of these remarriages occur within three years of the divorce. Among women, lesser education and lower income are associated with more rapid remarriage. In contrast, men who are better educated and financially well-off tend to remarry more quickly. The greater one's age at the time of divorce, the lower the likelihood of remarriage, especially among women (Bumpass, Sweet, & Martin, 1990).

How successful are second marriages? The answer depends on your standard of comparison. Divorce rates *are* higher for second than for first marriages (Martin & Bumpass, 1989). However, this statistic may simply indicate that this group of people see divorce as a reasonable alternative to an unsatisfactory marriage. Nonetheless, studies of marital adjustment suggest that second marriages are slightly less successful than first marriages and that marital satisfaction in remarriages is somewhat lower for women than for men (Vemer et al., 1989). Of course, if you consider that in this pool of people *all* the first marriages ran into serious trouble, then the second marriages look rather good by comparison. On the up side, remarried couples report more open communication, more willingness to confront conflict, and more egalitarian housekeeping and child rearing roles than couples in their first marriage do (Furstenberg, 1990; Giles-Sims, 1987; Hetherington & Clingempeel, 1992).

Another major issue related to remarriage is its effect on children. When children from stepfamilies are compared to children from first marriages, investigators find no differences in the youngsters' self-esteem or academic achievement (Pasley, Ihinger-Tallman, &

Although remarried couples tend to have more open communication, the evidence suggests that second marriages are slightly less successful than first marriages, on the average.

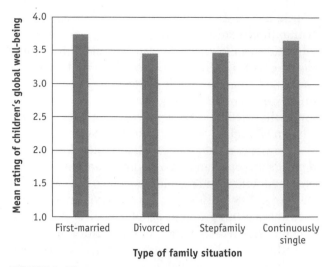

FIGURE 9.12.

Children's adjustment in four types of families. Acock and Demo (1994) assessed children's adjustment in four types of family structures: first marriages, divorced single-parent homes, stepfamilies, and families in which the mother never married. The comparisons of 2457 families did turn up some statistically significant differences, as children's overall well-being was highest in intact first marriages and lowest in divorced homes. However, as you can see, the differences were rather small and the authors conclude that "family structure has a modest effect on children's well-being" (p. 183).

Lofquist, 1994). However, adaptation to remarriage can be difficult. On the average, interaction in stepfamilies appears to be somewhat less cohesive and warm than in first-marriage families, and stepparent-stepchild relations tend to be more negative and distant than parent-child relations in first marriages (Bray & Hetherington, 1993). However, most studies find modest differences between stepfamilies and other types of families in the adjustment of their children. For example, Figure 9.12 highlights some representative results from one large-scale study (Acock & Demo, 1994).

Alternatives to Marriage

LEARNING OBJECTIVES

- *Describe stereotypes of single life and summarize evidence on the adjustment of single people.*
- *Discuss the prevalence of cohabitation and whether it improves the probability of marital success.*
- *Discuss the stability and dynamics of intimate relationships among homosexual couples.*
- *Describe five misconceptions about gay couples.*

We noted at the beginning of the chapter that the traditional model of marriage has been undermined by a variety of social trends. More and more people are choosing alternatives to marriage. In this section we examine some of these alternatives, including remaining single, cohabitation, and gay relationships.

Remaining Single

The pressure to marry is substantial in our society. People are socialized to believe that they are not complete until they have found their "other half" and have entered into a partnership for life (Shostak, 1987). We also refer to people's "failure" to marry. In spite of this pressure, an increasing proportion of young adults are remaining single, as Figure 9.13 shows.

Does the increased number of single adults mean that people are turning away from the institution of marriage? Perhaps a little, but for the most part, no. A variety of factors have contributed to the growth of the single population. Much of this growth is a result of the increase in the median age at which people marry and the increased rate of divorce. The vast majority of single, never-married people *do* hope to marry eventually. In one study of never-married men and women (South, 1993), 87.4% of the 926 respondents aged 19 to 25 agreed with the statement "I would like to get married someday."

FIGURE 9.13.

The proportion of young people who remain single. This graph shows the percentage of single men and women, aged 20–24 or 25–29, in 1997 as compared to 1960 (based on U.S. Census data). The proportion of people remaining single has increased substantially for both sexes, in both age brackets. Single men continue to outnumber single women in these age brackets.

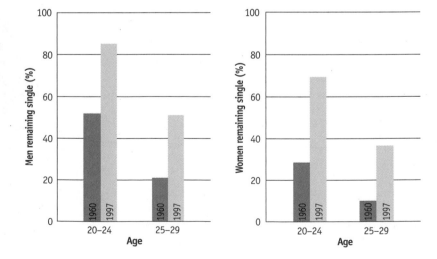

"That's right, Phil. A separation will mean—among other things—watching your own cholesterol."

Singlehood has been plagued by two disparate stereotypes (Keith, 1986). On the one hand, single people are sometimes portrayed as carefree swingers who are too busy enjoying the fruits of promiscuity to shoulder marital responsibilities. On the other hand, they are seen as losers who have not succeeded in snaring a mate; they may be portrayed as socially inept, maladjusted, frustrated, lonely, and bitter. These stereotypes do a great injustice to the diversity that exists among those who are single.

The "swinging single" stereotype appears to be a media-manufactured illusion designed to lure singles' spending power into nightclubs and bars. In reality, the singles bar circuit is usually described as an experience in alienation and disappointment. In comparison to married people, single people do have sex with more partners. However, they have sex less frequently, and they rate their sexual relations as less satisfying than their married counterparts (Cargan & Melko, 1982).

As for the "maladjusted, bitter" stereotype, it is true that single people exhibit poorer mental and physical health than married people (Gotlib & McCabe, 1990; Joung et al., 1997; Waite, 1995; Wyke & Ford, 1992), and they rate themselves as less happy than their married counterparts (Ross, 1995; Stack & Eshleman, 1998). However, the differences are modest, and the happiness gap has shrunk in recent years, especially among women (Glenn & Weaver, 1988). Although popular stereotypes suggest that being single is more difficult for women than for men, the empirical data are mixed. The physical health benefits of being married *are* greater for men than women (Lillard & Waite, 1995; Murphy, Glaser, & Grundy, 1997). But most studies find that single women are more satisfied with their lives and less distressed than comparable single men, and various lines of evidence suggest that women get along without men better than men get along without women (Davies, 1995; Marker, 1996).

Why is being married associated with greater health and happiness? The *health benefits* of marriage may result because spouses provide emotional and social support that buffers the negative effects of stress, because they discourage their partners' unhealthy habits, and because married people have higher income, which is associated with better health (Joung et al., 1997; Murphy et al., 1997). The *greater happiness* of married people has been attributed to the advantages they enjoy in social support, financial well-being, and physical health (Stack & Eshleman, 1998). Of course, the correlation between being married and health/happiness may be due in part to the effects of health and happiness on marital status. That is, it is likely that healthier and happier people are better able to attract and retain marital partners.

Cohabitation

As we noted earlier in the chapter, *cohabitation* refers to living together in a sexually intimate relationship outside of marriage. Recent years have witnessed a tremendous increase in the number of cohabiting couples (see Figure 9.14 on the next page). In 1997, there were slightly over 4.1 million unmarried couples living together in the United States. They represented about 7% of all couples (married and unmarried) sharing living quarters at that time. However, the percentage of couples living together at any one time does not accurately convey how widespread this phenomenon has become, because cohabiting unions tend to be short—about half of cohabiting couples either get married or break up within 18 months (Bumpass & Sweet, 1989). It is more instructive to study people getting married for the first time and determine what percentage of them have cohabited prior to their marriage (either with their spouse-to-be or someone else). Studies indicate that this percentage has increased dramatically, from around 11% in 1970 to nearly 50% in the 1990s (Bumpass, Sweet & Cherlin, 1991). Among previously divorced people getting married, the percentage who have cohabited is over 50% (Ganong & Coleman, 1994). Increasing rates of cohabitation are not unique to the United States and are even higher in some other countries, such as Denmark and Great Britain (Coleman & Salt, 1992).

Cohabitation tends to conjure up images of college students or other well-educated young couples without children, but these images are misleading. In reality, cohabitation rates have always been higher in the less-educated segments of the population. Moreover, almost half of cohabitants have been married previously, and one study found that 40% of cohabiting couples had

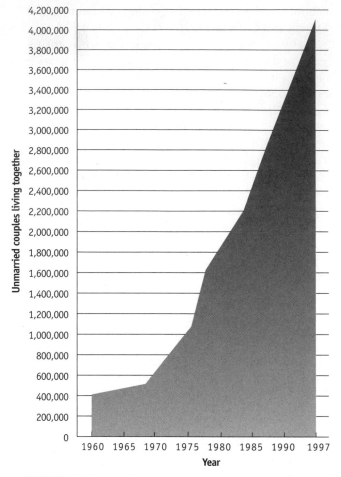

FIGURE 9.14.

Cohabitation in the United States. The number of unmarried couples living together has been increasing rapidly since 1970 (based on U.S. Census data). This increase shows no signs of leveling off.

children, mostly from previous marriages (Bumpass et al., 1991).

The principal motivations for cohabitation (as opposed to marriage) include more individualism, greater freedom, no need to divorce, the advantage of sharing living expenses, and the opportunity to check compatibility before marriage (Bumpass et al., 1991; Kotkin, 1985). Those who choose cohabitation tend to be relatively liberal in values, nonreligious, and nontraditional about intimate relationships (Booth & Amato, 1994; Macklin, 1983; Tanfer, 1987).

Although many people see cohabitation as a threat to the institution of marriage, most theorists see it as a new stage in the courtship process—a sort of trial marriage. Consistent with this view, about three-quarters of cohabitants expect to marry their current partner (Bumpass et al., 1991). In spite of these expectations, however, cohabitants report that they are less satisfied with their relationships than married couples (Brown & Booth, 1996; Nock, 1995), and cohabitating relationships are notably less stable than marital relationships

(Bumpass et al., 1991). Cohabiting couples are more likely to stay together if they have a child together (Wu, 1995).

In discussing the pros and cons of cohabitation, White (1987) points out that it may provide an opportunity for young people to experiment with marital-like responsibilities. As a prelude to marriage, it should reduce the likelihood of entering marriage with unrealistic expectations. Living together may also permit people to identify incompatible mates more effectively than a traditional courtship would. These considerations suggest that couples who cohabit before they marry should go on to more successful marriages than those who do not.

Although White's analyses seem plausible, researchers have *not* found that premarital cohabitation increases the likelihood of subsequent marital success. In fact, studies have found an association between premarital cohabitation and *higher* divorce rates in Canada, Sweden, and the United States (DeMaris & Rao, 1992; Krishnan, 1998; Schoen, 1992). What accounts for this finding? Most theorists argue that it's because this nontraditional lifestyle has historically attracted a liberal and unconventional segment of the population with a weak commitment to the institution of marriage and relatively few qualms about getting divorced. There is some empirical support for this explanation (Glenn, 1990; Hall, 1996; Thomson & Colella, 1992), but the evidence is mixed (DeMaris & MacDonald, 1993). If this explanation is accurate, the elevated divorce rates among cohabitants should gradually shrink to normal as cohabitation becomes more common, because the population of cohabitants will increasingly resemble the general population (McRae, 1997). A trend in this direction is already apparent (Schoen, 1992), as you can see in Figure 9.15.

Gay Relationships

Up until this point, we have, for purposes of simplicity, focused our attention on *heterosexuals,* those who seek emotional-sexual relationships with members of the other sex. However, we have been ignoring a significant minority group: *homosexual* men and women, who seek emotional-sexual relationships with members of the same sex. (In everyday language, the term *gay* is used to refer to homosexuals of both sexes, although many homosexual women prefer the term *lesbian* for themselves.) How large is this minority group? It's difficult to say, because negative attitudes about homosexuality continue to prevent many gays from "coming out of the closet" (Gonsiorek & Weinrich, 1991). A frequently cited estimate of the percentage of people who are homosexual is 10%. If homosexuals and bisexuals are lumped together, recent studies *suggest* that this figure is reasonably accurate for males, but an overestimate for females (Ellis & Ames, 1987; Janus & Janus, 1993).

Devoting a separate section to gay couples may seem to imply that the dynamics of their close relationships are different from those seen in heterosexual couples. Actually, this appears to be much less true than widely assumed, even though gays' close relationships unfold in a radically different social context than heterosexuals' marital relationships. As Garnets and Kimmel (1991) point out, gay relationships "develop within a social context of societal disapproval with an absence of social legitimization and support; families and other social institutions often stigmatize such relationships and there are no prescribed roles and behaviors to structure such relationships" (p. 170). Attitudes about gay relationships have become more liberal in recent years, but over half of Americans still condemn homosexual relations as morally wrong, and gays continue to be victims of employment and housing discrimination, not to mention verbal and physical abuse (Herek, 1991; Herek et al., 1997; Salholz, 1993). Gay couples cannot legally formalize their unions by getting married, and in fact, laws prohibiting same-gender sexual relations are still on the books in many states. Gay couples are also denied many economic benefits available to married couples (Rivera, 1991). For example, they can't file joint tax returns, and gay individuals generally can't obtain employer-provided health insurance for their partner.

FIGURE 9.15.

Cohabitation and marital instability. Comparisons of people who cohabit before marriage and those who do not have generally found higher rates of marital dissolution among the cohabiters. The data summarized here compare rates of marital disruption (either divorce or separation) in the first four years of marriage for cohorts of women born in various periods, based on research by Schoen (1992). These data suggest that the differences between cohabiters and non-cohabiters in marital instability are shrinking.

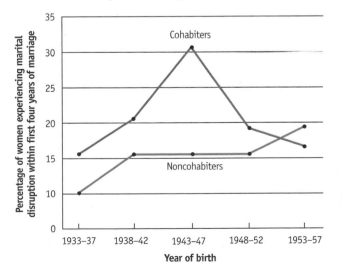

Despite the common stereotype that homosexuals rarely form long-term relationships, the fact is that they are similar to heterosexual couples in their attitudes and behaviors, and many enjoy long-term commitments in marriage-like arrangements.

COMPARISONS TO HETEROSEXUAL COUPLES

Given the lack of moral, social, legal, and economic supports for gay relationships, are gay unions less stable than marital unions? Researchers have not yet been able to collect adequate data on this question, but the limited data available suggest that gay couples' relationships *are* somewhat briefer and more prone to breakups than heterosexual marriages (Kurdek, 1998; Peplau, 1991). Insofar as this may be true, it's probably because gay relationships face fewer barriers to dissolution—that is, fewer practical problems that make breakups difficult or costly (Kurdek, 1998; Peplau & Cochran, 1990). Married couples considering divorce often face a variety of such barriers—attorneys' fees, concerns about children, wrangling over joint investments, and the disapproval of their families—that may motivate them to salvage their deteriorating relationship. In contrast, gay couples do not have to wrestle with the legal formalities of divorce, and they are less likely to have children, joint investments, or family opposition to worry about.

Although gay relationships evolve in a different social context than marital relationships, recent studies have documented striking commonalities between heterosexual and homosexual couples. Both types of couples report similar levels of love and commitment in their relationships, similar levels of overall satisfaction with their relationships, and similar levels of sexual satisfaction (Kurdek, 1998; Peplau, 1991). Resemblance is also apparent when researchers study what gays and heterosexuals want out of their relationships (Peplau, 1988; see Figure 9.16) and what they look for in a prospective partner (Laner, 1988). Homosexual and heterosexual couples are also similar in terms of the factors that predict relationship satisfaction (Kurdek & Schmitt, 1988) and the problems that contribute to breakups (Blumstein & Schwartz, 1983). Moreover, recent studies indicate that both types of couples generally wrestle with the same sources of conflict in their relationships and that their patterns of conflict resolution are largely the same (Kurdek, 1994a, 1994b).

MISCONCEPTIONS ABOUT GAY RELATIONSHIPS

Although research indicates a considerable continuity between homosexual and heterosexual relationships, basic misconceptions about the nature of gay relationships remain widespread. Let's look at some of these inaccurate stereotypes.

First, many people assume that most gay couples adopt traditional masculine and feminine roles in their relationships, with one partner behaving in a cross-sexed manner. This appears to be true in only a small minority of cases. In fact, on the whole, gay couples appear to be more flexible about role expectations than heterosexuals (Marecek, Finn, & Cardell, 1988; Zacks, Green, & Marrow, 1988). In comparison to married couples, gay couples display a more equitable balance of power in their relationships and are less likely to adhere to traditional gender roles.

Web Link 9.5

Partners Task Force for Gay and Lesbian Couples
Reflecting the belief that "same-gender couples deserve the same treatment as all other couples," this Web page offers resources that address a wide range of issues, including relationships, parenting, domestic partnership, ceremonial marriage, and legal and civil rights matters.

Second, it is widely believed that gays are characterized by exceptionally high levels of sexual activity and that they engage in casual sex with many partners. In reality, high levels of sexual activity are characteristic only in certain segments of the gay male population, are decidedly uncommon among lesbians, and have become less common among males since the advent of the AIDS epidemic (Blumstein & Schwartz, 1990; Isensee, 1990; Nichols, 1990). Regardless of their sexual orientation (gay or straight), males tend to have somewhat different motivations than females for engaging in sex. Women are more likely to regard sexual activity as an expression of affection and commitment, whereas men tend to attach more importance to sexual pleasure and conquest (Leigh, 1989). Their socialization is more likely than women's to stress the desirability of varied and frequent sexual activity. The gay male, being free of the strictures of marriage and having his choice of like-minded partners, has simply been in a better position than his heterosexual counterpart to act on this masculine socialization (Blasband & Peplau, 1985).

FIGURE 9.16

Comparing priorities in intimate relationships. Peplau (1981) asked heterosexual men and women and homosexual men and women to rate the significance (9 = high importance) of various aspects of their intimate relationships. As you can see, all four groups returned fairly similar ratings. Peplau concludes that gays and heterosexuals largely want the same things out of their relationships.

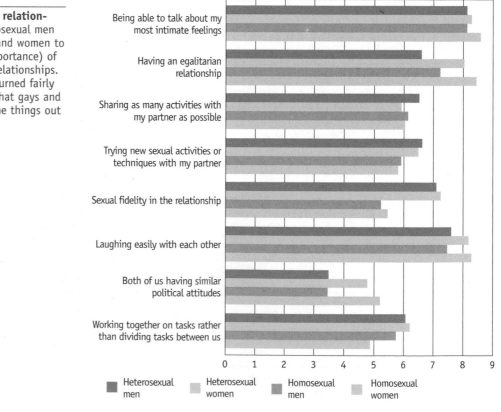

Third, popular stereotypes suggest that gays only rarely get involved in long-term intimate relationships. In reality, most homosexual men, and nearly all homosexual women, prefer stable, long-term relationships, and at any one time roughly half of gay males and three-quarters of lesbians are involved in committed relationships (Macklin, 1987; Peplau, 1991). Lesbian relationships are generally sexually exclusive. About half of committed male couples have "open" relationships, allowing for the possibility of sexual activity (but not affection) with outsiders. While intimate relationships among gays appear to be less stable than marriages among straights, they may compare favorably with heterosexual cohabitation, which would be a more appropriate baseline for comparison. Both gays and heterosexual cohabitants may face opposition to their relationship from their families and from society in general, and neither enjoys the legal and social sanctions of marriage.

Fourth, lesbians and gay men tend to be thought of as individuals rather than as members of families. This thinking reflects a society-wide bias that homosexuality and family just don't mesh (Allen & Demo, 1995). In reality, gays are very much involved in families as sons and daughters, as parents and stepparents, as aunts, uncles, and grandparents. Although exact data are not available, far more are parents than most people realize. Many of these parental responsibilities are left over from previous marriages, as about one-fifth of gay men and one-third of lesbians have been heterosexually married (Harry, 1983). But an increasing number of homosexuals are opting to have children in the context of their gay relationships (Barret & Robinson, 1994; Falk, 1994). Unfortunately, researchers have largely neglected gays' family life (Allen & Demo, 1995), so we know virtually nothing about gay fathers and only little about lesbian mothers. The preliminary evidence on gay parents suggests that they are similar to their heterosexual counterparts and that their children do not experience any unique ill effects and are no more likely than others to become homosexual (Falk, 1994; Flaks et al., 1995; Patterson, 1992).

Finally, an inevitable fate for any stereotyped group is that its members are lumped together and simplistically assumed to be identical. In reality, there is as much diversity among gays as there is among straights, dooming to failure any attempt to classify gays into "types" (Harry, 1990; Tripp, 1987). To identify an individual as "homosexual" is to say nothing more about that person's unique lifestyle, personality, or values than to describe someone as "heterosexual."

Understanding Intimate Violence

LEARNING OBJECTIVES

- *Summarize data on the prevalence of partner abuse.*
- *Summarize the characteristics of batterers and battered women.*
- *Discuss why women stay in abusive relationships.*
- *Discuss the incidence, causes, and effects of physical abuse in childhood.*
- *Discuss the incidence, causes, and effects of child sexual abuse.*

Answer the following statements "true" or "false."

____ **1.** Most women in abusive relationships are attracted to violent men.

____ **2.** Most men who have witnessed domestic violence as children will batter their intimate partners.

____ **3.** Severe child abuse is more often inflicted by strangers than by parents.

____ **4.** Incest usually develops out of an already close father-daughter relationship.

All of these statements are false and are myths that many people believe. Most of us assume that we will be safe with those whom we love and trust. Unfortunately, some individuals live with the terrible irony that they fear individuals to whom they feel closest. **Intimate violence is aggression toward those who are in close relationship to the aggressor.** Intimate violence takes many forms: psychological, physical, and sexual abuse of intimate partners and children. Tragically, sometimes violence against partners and children ends in homicide. In this Application, we'll focus on three of these serious social problems: partner abuse, child abuse, and child sexual abuse.

Partner Abuse

The O. J. Simpson trial dramatically heightened public awareness of partner violence, particularly wife battering and homicide. People found it difficult to reconcile the image of the smiling sports hero with the fact that he was a convicted wife batterer with a history of terrorizing his former spouse. *Physical abuse* can include kicking, biting, punching, choking, pushing, slapping, hitting with an object, threatening with a weapon, using a weapon, and rape. Examples of *psychological abuse* include humiliation, name calling, controlling what the partner does and whom the partner socializes with, refusing to communicate, unreasonable withholding of money, and questioning of the partner's sanity. We will focus primarily on physical abuse of partners, or *battering*.

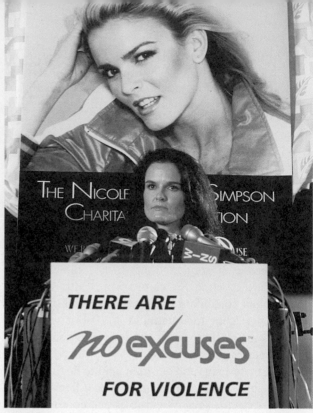

The murder of Nicole Brown Simpson and the exposure of the abuse that preceded it increased public awareness of intimate violence.

As with other taboo topics, obtaining accurate estimates of physical abuse is difficult. Research suggests that about 28% of all married couples experience some form of physical aggression (slapping, beating) over the life of their marriage (Straus & Gelles, 1990). Studies of gay and lesbian couples find that this problem occurs at about the same rate among them as well (Renzetti, 1995). Thus, domestic violence is not limited to heterosexual couples. These figures don't include the battering that goes on among cohabiting heterosexual couples, and some estimate that violence is even more common in these relationships (Stets, 1991). Moreover, this estimate excludes the physical abuse found in some dating relationships (see the discussion of date rape in the Application for Chapter 8). We also know that domestic violence is underreported because of the stigma attached to it.

Wives batter their husbands more than most people realize (Hampton, Gelles, & Harrop, 1989; Straus & Gelles, 1986), but much of wives' aggression appears to be in self-defense, and women inflict far less physical damage than men (Brush, 1990). Thus, women are the principal victims of severe, dangerous abuse. Wives are much more likely than husbands to suffer serious injuries and death as a result of physical assaults (Browne, 1993; Koss et al., 1994). A woman is the victim in 92% of nonfatal violent crimes committed by spouses and in 70% of murders by spouses. Battering by a partner is the single most common cause of injury to women in the United States, accounting for about 35% of females' visits to hospital emergency rooms (Novello, 1992).

The effects of battering reverberate beyond the obvious physical injuries. Victims of partner abuse tend to suffer from severe anxiety, depression, feelings of helplessness and humiliation, and stress-induced illness (Gelles & Conte, 1991; Lloyd & Emery, 1993). Children who witness marital violence also experience ill effects, such as anxiety and depression (O'Keefe, 1994).

CHARACTERISTICS OF BATTERERS

Research shows that characteristics of the batterer are much better predictors of violence than characteristics of the battered woman (Hotaling & Sugarman, 1986). Nonetheless, men who batter women are a diverse group, so a single profile has not emerged. Batterers typically have self-esteem problems (Walker, 1984) and are overly jealous and possessive (Okun, 1985). They are also likely to have been beaten as children or to have witnessed their mothers being beaten (Hotaling & Sugarman, 1986). One well-sampled study found that men who had observed violence between their parents were nearly three times as likely to hit their wives as were men whose parents had not been violent (Strauss et al., 1980). It's important to note, however, that most men who grow up in these difficult circumstances do not become batterers (Pagelow, 1992).

Abuse is more likely among men in the military (where aggression is encouraged), when men are unemployed (a serious threat to masculinity and self-esteem), and among men who have problems with alcohol or drugs (which impair judgment) (Koss & Gaines, 1993; McKenry, Julian & Gavazzi, 1995; Okun, 1985). Batterers often deny the seriousness of their behavior and deny responsibility for it. Battering appears to be slightly more common in families of lower socioeconomic status, but no social class is immune (Fineman & Mykitiuk, 1994; Schuller & Vidmar, 1992). Ethnicity doesn't appear to be related to abuse when groups are equated for socioeconomic status and employment (Gondolf, 1988).

CHARACTERISTICS OF BATTERED WOMEN

Although some characteristics of battered women have been identified, it isn't clear whether these traits contribute to the likelihood of abuse or whether they are the result of the abuse. For example, it is easy to understand why an abused woman might begin to feel that she is worthless. Battered women typically have low self-esteem, blame themselves, change their own behavior to minimize the abuse rather than trying to change that of their partner, and often deny what is really going on (Walker, 1984). Understandably, physical abuse often results in the *learned helplessness* syndrome (see Chapter 4), which involves passive coping, fatalism, and resignation to one's setbacks (Walker, 1993). Battered women are more likely to have a feminine or undifferentiated gender-role identity and are less likely to be androgynous (Mattley & Schwartz, 1990).

WHY DO WOMEN STAY IN ABUSIVE RELATIONSHIPS?

Why do some women remain in abusive relationships? One reason is that a woman may love her husband and truly believe that his behavior will change. Battered women tend to naively cling to the hope that their husbands will change (Herbert, Silver, & Ellard, 1991). And even if a woman is convinced that her husband won't change, she may remain in the relationship to avoid the social stigma of being divorced or to avoid disapproval from her family and friends, who are likely to fall into the trap of blaming the victim.

Economic realities are often important barriers to leaving an abusive husband. That is, an abused woman probably has children and will need to support both them and herself. If they are young, she may not want to leave them to go to work, and even if she does want to work, she will probably have difficulty obtaining a job that would pay for child care on top of other living expenses. A related problem is that abused women and their families often have nowhere to go (McHugh, Frieze, & Browne, 1993). Furthermore, there is evidence that trying to leave an abusive relationship may precipitate brutal attacks or murder. Despite the many difficulties of leaving abusive relationships (see Figure 9.17 on the next page), attention is still focused on why women stay rather than on why men batter and on what interventions will prevent women from being brutalized or killed when they do leave (Koss et al., 1994).

Child Abuse

Child abuse consists of intentional actions that result in harm to a child's physical or psychological well-being. It may include beatings, verbal abuse, neglect, and sexual abuse. As hard as it is to believe, estimates of the number of children abused in the U.S. annually range as high as 3 million (Emery & Laumann-Billings, 1998). Sadly, most physical abuse of children is inflicted by family members and caregivers. And younger children are at greater risk for abuse than older ones.

According to a 1994 Gallup poll, one in eight Americans reported having been punched, kicked, or choked by a parent or adult guardian, and one in twenty suffered even more severe physical punishment during childhood (Moore, 1994). Mothers are more likely than fathers to physically abuse their children (Strauss et al., 1980), but fathers are more likely to engage in sexual abuse (Russell, 1984). Boys are more likely to suffer from physical abuse, whereas girls are

FIGURE 9.17.

Perceived reasons for returning to abusive relationships. Shelters for battered wives generally report that the majority of their clients return to their partners. In one study (Johnson, Crowley, & Sigler, 1992), workers at ten shelters in Alabama were asked to rate the reasons *why* women returned to abusive relationships. The most frequently cited reasons are listed here in order of rated importance. As you can see, a diverse host of factors appear to propel women back into abusive relationships.

Perceived Reasons for Returning to Abusive Relationship	
Reasons	Mean Rating
Give the abuser one more chance	10.0
Lack of financial resources	9.1
Emotional dependency on the abuser	9.0
Lack of housing resources	8.7
Lack of job opportunities	7.7
Denial of cycle of violence	7.6
Lack of support or follow-through by the legal system	7.6
Lack of child-care resources	7.1
Lack of transportation	6.7
Fear that the abuser will find her and do her harm	6.7
Lack of support from other family members	6.6
Fear that the abuser will get custody of the children	5.8
Fear that the abuser will kidnap the children	5.8
Children miss the absent parent	5.6
Lack of professional counseling	5.1
Fear that the abuser will harm the children	4.6

more likely to be victimized by sexual abuse (Solomon, 1992). Because child abuse generally takes place behind closed doors, it is probably underreported to authorities. When people *suspect* that a child is being abused, they face an awkward and difficult situation. As they become increasingly sensitized to the seriousness of child abuse, more seem willing to try to stop it, but inaction is also common (see Figure 9.18).

CAUSES

What leads parents to engage in child abuse? A number of factors appear to play a role (Belsky, 1993; Emery & Laumann-Billings, 1998). A factor that is frequently cited is acceptance of violence as a legitimate disciplinary technique. Also, parents who have substance abuse problems or who are under heavy stress are more likely to abuse their children. Child abuse is also more prevalent in families that are large and poor, but it's important to note that the vast majority of poor parents do not abuse their children. Elevated rates of child abuse are also seen among parents who themselves were abused as children (Emery, 1989; Malinosky-Rummell & Hansen, 1993). Steele (1980) has suggested that four conditions appear necessary for child abuse to occur:

• A caregiver who is predisposed to abuse because of a history of neglect or abuse in his or her own life.

• A crisis that places extra stress on the caregiver.

• Lack of sources of support for the caregiver, either because he or she is unable to reach out, or because facilities are unavailable.

• A child who is perceived as being unsatisfactory in some way.

EFFECTS

The short- and long-term effects of child abuse vary depending on a variety of factors, including the age of the child when abuse was experienced, whether abuse occurred rarely or repeatedly, and the severity of the abuse. Those who experience repeated, severe abuse—especially at ages younger than 3 years—are more likely to have emotional difficulties (Kinard, 1982). Common effects of abuse in children include increased aggressiveness, low self-esteem, depression, and poor academic achievement (Gelles & Conte, 1991; Mullen et al., 1996). Childhood abuse has been found to be linked, in adulthood, to aggressiveness toward dating partners, spouses, and children; substance abuse; emotional problems; and self-injurious and suicidal behaviors (Bagley, 1995; Malinosky-Rummell & Hansen, 1993).

Child Sexual Abuse

The idea of sexual abuse of any kind is abhorrent to most people. The sexual abuse of children is viewed as particularly despicable because it involves helpless victims and is frequently perpetrated by individuals who are supposed to be the protectors of children (Densen-Gerber, 1984). *Child sexual abuse consists of coerced or tricked sexual interaction between a young person (usually defined as under 18) and an older person (usually defined as at least five years older than the victim).* The unwanted sexual interactions may include kissing, fondling of the breasts and genitals, oral sex, and intercourse. The most common form of sexual abuse is fondling (Haugaard & Reppucci, 1988). As is true of other forms of intimate violence, it is difficult to get accurate data regarding the prevalence of child sexual abuse, but it appears to be much more common than widely believed. In one widely cited national survey, 27% of women and 16% of men reported that they had been sexually abused as children (Finkelhor et al., 1990). In the United States, about 400,000 children are victims of sexual abuse each year (Finkelhor & Dziuba-Leatherman, 1994). The vast majority are female (Trickett & Putnam, 1993).

INCEST

Incest is a particular form of child sexual abuse. *Incest (also called intrafamilial sexual abuse) is sexual activity between close relatives, including steprelatives.* Traditionally, incest referred to sexual activities between

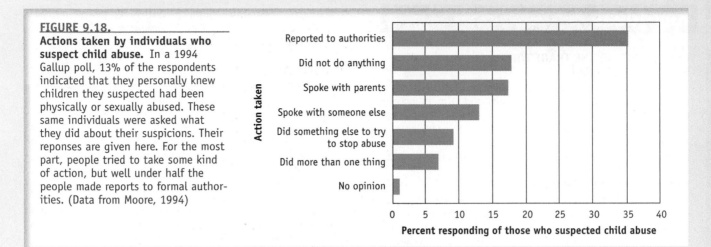

FIGURE 9.18.

Actions taken by individuals who suspect child abuse. In a 1994 Gallup poll, 13% of the respondents indicated that they personally knew children they suspected had been physically or sexually abused. These same individuals were asked what they did about their suspicions. Their responses are given here. For the most part, people tried to take some kind of action, but well under half the people made reports to formal authorities. (Data from Moore, 1994)

blood relatives, but the term now usually includes sexual activities between nonblood relatives as well (for instance, between stepfathers and stepdaughters). For reasons we have already mentioned, it is difficult to obtain accurate estimates of the prevalence of incest. Victims of incest are usually girls who are abused by their father, stepfather, or an older brother (Adler & Schultz, 1995; Canavan, Meyer, & Higgs, 1992). Sexual activity between stepfather and stepdaughter occurs more frequently than between daughters and their biological fathers. For example, in a study of 930 sexually abused women, 1 in 6 had been molested by a stepfather compared to 1 in 40 by a biological father (Stark, 1984). Although most victims of incest are girls, boys are also abused by relatives (Watkins & Bentovim, 1992).

Incestuous relationships between fathers and daughters typically start when the daughter is between 6 and 11 years of age, and they continue for at least two years. Most encounters don't involve intercourse; among prepubescent girls, they consist of fondling, masturbation, and oral sex (Burkhardt & Rotatori, 1995; Stark, 1984).

Incest occurs in families across all socioeconomic levels. Its causes are not entirely understood, but mental health professionals believe that it occurs most frequently in families (1) that are socially isolated, (2) that are controlled by strong, domineering fathers, and (3) in which the wife is either financially and emotionally dependent on the husband or sick, absent, alcoholic, or mentally ill. Frequently, the oldest daughter has taken over the household and child-care responsibilities, and the sexual relationship with her father evolves as an extension of the "little mother" role (Stark, 1984).

Contrary to popular stereotype, incest doesn't usually develop out of a loving father-daughter relationship that has gone too far. The abuser's motives are complex and usually combine sexuality with power, hostility, and the need for a dependent "partner." Daughters usually cooperate with their father's sexual advances, so physical force is seldom used. For this reason, victims of sexual abuse usually suffer considerable guilt and shame, making it difficult for them to seek help. Although some victims cooperate with their fathers because they are desperate for any kind of affection, many others do so and remain silent because they believe that they are keeping the family together, that their father will go to jail, or that there isn't anyone who can help them (Stark, 1984).

EFFECTS OF CHILD SEXUAL ABUSE

As with physical abuse, the long-term effects of sexual abuse vary depending on how frequently it occurred, whether physical abuse was also involved, the nature of the relationship between the victim and the abuser, and the availability of nonabusing caregivers. Victims of childhood sexual abuse often suffer from depression, anxiety, guilt, anger, helplessness, eating disorders, substance abuse problems, sexual problems, reckless behavior, and suicidal tendencies (Haugaard & Reppucci, 1988; Mullen et al., 1996; Trickett & Putnam, 1993; Wiehe, 1996). About one-third of sexually abused youngsters develop symptoms of *posttraumatic stress disorder* (see Chapter 3), such as nightmares, flashbacks, and emotional numbing (McNew & Abell, 1995). Many victims also have understandable difficulty trusting others (Cole & Putnam, 1992). In spite of this lengthy and intimidating list of negative consequences, perhaps as many as one-half of sexually abused children have the resilience to survive without serious long-term problems (Bagley, 1995; Kilpatrick, 1992).

Although most of us would prefer not to think about this darker side of relationships, intimate violence is a reality we can ill-afford to ignore. It deeply touches the lives of millions of individuals. Hopefully, increased public awareness of intimate violence will help reduce its incidence and its tragic effects.

Key Ideas

CHALLENGES TO THE TRADITIONAL MODEL OF MARRIAGE

● The traditional model of marriage is being challenged by the increasing acceptability of singlehood, the increasing popularity of cohabitation, the reduced premium on permanence, changes in gender roles, the increasing prevalence of voluntary childlessness, and the decline of the traditional nuclear family. Nonetheless, marriage remains quite popular.

MOVING TOWARD MARRIAGE

● A multitude of factors influence an individual's motivation to marry. Mate selection is influenced by endogamy, homogamy, and gender. Women place more emphasis on potential partners' character and financial prospects, whereas men are more interested in a partner's youthfulness and physical attractiveness.

● According to Murstein, the process of mate selection goes through three stages, which emphasize the stimulus value of the potential partner, value compatibility, and adequacy of role enactments. There are some premarital predictors of marital success, such as family background, age, length of courtship, social class, and personality, but the relations are weak.

MARITAL ADJUSTMENT ACROSS THE FAMILY LIFE CYCLE

● When marital satisfaction is mapped across the family life cycle, researchers find a U-shaped curve reflecting lower satisfaction in the middle stages. Newly married couples tend to be very happy before the arrival of children. Today more couples are struggling with the decision about whether to have children. The arrival of children is a major transition that is handled best by parents who have realistic expectations about the difficulties inherent in raising a family.

● As children reach adolescence, parents should expect more conflict as their influence declines. They must learn to relate to their children as adults and help launch them into the adult world. Once the children have struck out on their own, marital satisfaction tends to rise once again (although the causal relations underlying this association are open to debate).

VULNERABLE AREAS IN MARITAL ADJUSTMENT

● Gaps in expectations about marital roles may create marital stress. Disparities in expectations about gender roles and the distribution of housework may be especially common and problematic. Work concerns can clearly spill over to influence marital functioning, but the links between parents' employment and marital adjustment are complex.

● Wealth does not ensure marital happiness, but a lack of money can produce marital problems. Inadequate communication is a commonly reported marital problem, which is increasingly analyzed from an attributional perspective.

DIVORCE

● Divorce rates are increasing for a variety of reasons. Unpleasant as divorce may be, the evidence suggests that toughing it out in an unhappy marriage is often worse. Divorce can create problems for children, but so does a strife-ridden intact home.

● Divorce is quite stressful and may lead to a variety of emotional and practical problems associated with the crisis of change. A substantial majority of divorced people remarry. These second marriages have a somewhat lower probability of success than first marriages.

ALTERNATIVES TO MARRIAGE

● An increasing proportion of the young population are remaining single, but this does not mean that people are turning away from marriage. Single people are often stereotyped as carefree swingers or unhappy losers. Both pictures are largely inaccurate. Although singles generally have the same adjustment problems as married couples, evidence suggests that singles tend to be somewhat less happy and less healthy.

● The prevalence of cohabitation has increased dramatically. Logically, one might expect cohabitation to facilitate marital success, but research has consistently found an association between cohabitation and marital instability.

● Gay relationships develop in a starkly different social context than marital relationships. Nonetheless, studies have found that heterosexual and homosexual couples are similar in many ways. Gay relationships are characterized by great diversity. It is not true that gay couples usually assume traditional masculine and feminine roles, nor is it true that they rarely get involved in long-term intimate relationships or family relations.

APPLICATION: UNDERSTANDING INTIMATE VIOLENCE

● Intimate violence is a serious social problem that involves the emotional, physical, and sexual abuse of partners and children. Research suggests that physical abuse may occur in 28% of marriages and that it is at least as frequent among cohabiting couples, whether they are heterosexual or homosexual. Women are the principal victims of serious, dangerous abuse.

● Men who batter their partners typically have self-esteem problems, are possessive of their partners, and deny responsibility for their behavior. Battered women also have low self-esteem, but it isn't clear whether this is a cause or a result of abuse. Women stay in abusive relationships for a variety of compelling, practical reasons, including economic realities.

● One in eight Americans report having been physically abused in childhood. A history of abuse as a child combined with stress and deprivation predispose individuals to abusiveness. Childhood physical abuse can have serious short- and long-term effects.

● Estimates suggest that about 400,000 children experience sexual abuse in the United States each year. Victims of incest are usually girls who are abused by their father, stepfather, or an older brother. Sexual abuse occurs in families across all socioeconomic levels. The effects of incest can be quite serious for survivors.

Key Terms

Child abuse	Homogamy	Marriage
Child sexual abuse	Incest	Perspective taking
Cohabitation	Inter-role conflict	Role overload
Endogamy	Intimate violence	
Family life cycle	Intrafamilial sexual abuse	

Key People

Bernard Murstein   Letitia Anne Peplau

Practice Test

1. Which of the following is not one of the social trends undermining the traditional model of marriage?
   a. Increased acceptance of singlehood
   b. Increased voluntary childlessness
   c. Increased acceptance of cohabitation
   d. Increased premium on permanence in marriage

2. Endogamy refers to
   a. the tendency to marry within one's social group.
   b. the tendency to marry someone with similar characteristics.
   c. the final marriage in serial monogamy.
   d. norms that promote marriage outside one's social unit.

3. Research on the family life cycle has shown that marital satisfaction is highest at the:
   a. beginning.
   b. middle.
   c. end.
   d. both a and c.
   e. both b and c.

4. New-parent stress is greatest when:
   a. the newborn child wasn't planned for.
   b. parenting costs are underestimated and benefits are overestimated.
   c. the new parents are relatively young.
   d. the father is expected to be heavily involved in child care.

5. Most research suggests that maternal employment is:
   a. very harmful to children.
   b. moderately harmful to children.
   c. generally not harmful to children.
   d. extremely beneficial to young male children.

6. When financial resources are plentiful in a marriage, arguments about money:
   a. may still be a problem.
   b. don't occur.
   c. occur if the wife doesn't work.
   d. don't threaten marital satisfaction.

7. The preponderance of data suggests that sticking it out in an unhappy, contentious marriage tends to:
   a. be best for the children.
   b. be better than getting a divorce.
   c. be counterproductive for spouses and their children.
   d. build character.

8. What is the most probable cause for the increase in the proportion of young people who remain single?
   a. Loss of faith in the institution of marriage
   b. More cohabitation and greater personal autonomy
   c. An increase in the median age at which people get married
   d. Unwilling to undertake the financial burdens of marriage and family

9. Research on cohabitation indicates that:
   a. most cohabitants believe the institution of marriage is obsolete.
   b. most cohabitants would eventually like to marry.
   c. cohabitation is declining.
   d. cohabitation experience improves the chances that one's marriage will be successful.

10. Which of the following has been supported by research on intimate relationships among gays?
    a. Gay couples adopt traditional male/female sex roles.
    b. Gays rarely become involved in long-term relationships.
    c. Lesbian women are extremely promiscuous.
    d. Gays want the same things out of intimate relationships that heterosexuals want.

Answers

1. d pages 247–248
2. a page 249
3. d pages 249–250
4. b pages 254–255
5. c page 259

6. a pages 259–260
7. c pages 263–264
8. c pages 266–267
9. b pages 267–268
10. d pages 270–271

INFOTRAC
COLLEGE EDITION

Go to the Wadsworth Psychology Study Center (http://psychology. wadsworth.com/) for quiz questions, research updates, hot topics, interactive exercises, and suggested readings in INFOTRAC related to this chapter.

CHAPTER 10

Gender and Behavior

"*In classes, I experienced myself as a person to be taken lightly. In one seminar, I was never allowed to finish a sentence. There seemed to be a tacit understanding that I never had anything to say."—A woman quoted in* The Classroom Climate: A Chilly One for Women *(Hall & Sandler, 1982, p. 7)*

"*I get a feeling, like I want to say "I love you" or just put my arms around my girlfriend. But then, for some reason, I just shut down and I don't do anything. It seems like I am going to give up too much by getting too close. Maybe she'll want more than I have to give. This way I can cover myself. But I wind up feeling guilty about not showing her I care." (Rabinowitz & Cochran, 1994, p. 55)*

The woman and man quoted here feel boxed in by gender roles. They're struggling with the limitations placed on their behavior because of their gender. They aren't unique or unusual. Think about the times *you* have changed *your* behavior to bring it in line with society's concepts of masculinity and femininity.

Before going on, we need to clarify some terms. Some scholars prefer to use the term *gender* to refer to male-female differences that are learned and *sex* to designate biologically based differences between males and females. However, as well-respected authority Janet Shibley Hyde (1996) points out, making this sharp distinction between *sex* and *gender* fails to recognize that biology and culture may interact. Following this reasoning, we'll use **gender to mean the state of being male or female.** (When we use the term *sex*, we're referring to sexual behavior.) It's important to note that, as *we* use the term, *gender* says nothing about the *causes* of behavior. In other words, if we say that there are gender differences in aggressive behavior, we are simply stating that males and females differ in this area; we are saying

nothing about what might cause this difference. Because there are visible physical differences between males and females, you might be tempted to leap to the conclusion that biological differences are responsible for gender differences in aggression. Nonetheless, this would be incorrect. Figure 10.1 defines a number of gender-related terms for easy comparison.

In this chapter, we'll take up some intriguing and controversial questions. Are there genuine behavioral differences between males and females? If so, what are their origins? Are traditional gender-role expectations healthy or unhealthy? Why are gender roles in our society changing, and what does the future hold? In the Application, we'll explore gender and communication styles.

Gender Stereotypes

LEARNING OBJECTIVES

- Explain the nature of gender stereotypes.
- Discuss three important points about gender stereotypes.

Obviously, males and females differ biologically—in their genitals and other aspects of anatomy, and in their physiological functioning. These readily apparent physical disparities between males and females lead people to expect other differences as well. Recall from Chapter 6 that *stereotypes* are widely held beliefs that people possess certain characteristics simply because of their membership in a particular group. *Gender stereotypes* **are widely shared beliefs about males' and females'**

FIGURE 10.1.

Terminology related to gender. The topic of gender includes many closely related ideas that are easily confused. The gender-related concepts introduced in this chapter are summarized here for easy comparison.

Gender-Related Concepts	
Gender	The state of being male or female
Gender identity	An individual's perception of himself or herself as male or female
Gender stereotypes	Widely held and often inaccurate beliefs about males' and females' abilities, personality traits, and social behavior
Gender differences	Actual disparities in behavior between males and females, based on research observations
Gender roles	Culturally defined expectations about appropriate behavior for males and females
Gender-role identity	A person's identification with the traits regarded as masculine or feminine (one's sense of being masculine or feminine)
Sexual orientation	A person's preference for sexual partners of the other gender (heterosexual), the same gender (homosexual), or both genders (bisexual)

abilities, personality traits, and social behavior. Research indicates that there is a great deal of consensus on *supposed* behavioral differences between men and women (Bergen & Williams, 1991). For example, a survey of gender stereotypes in 25 countries revealed considerable similarity of views (Williams & Best, 1990). Because of the widespread gains in educational and occupational attainment by American women since the 1970s, you might expect to find changes in gender stereotypes from then to now. In fact, however, gender stereotypes in this country have largely remained stable since the early 1970s (Spence & Buchner, 1998).

Gender stereotypes are too numerous to summarize here. Instead, you can examine Figure 10.2, which lists a number of behavioral characteristics thought to be associated with femininity and masculinity. This list is based on a study in which subjects were asked to indicate the extent to which various traits were characteristic of each gender (Ruble, 1983). Although the list may contain a few surprises, you have probably encountered most of these stereotypes before. After all, everyone knows that women are more dependent, emotional, irrational, and talkative than men. Or are they?

Before we launch into the actual evidence on gender differences in behavior, we need to make several additional points. First, although there is general agreement on a number of gender stereotypes, there are variations as well (Williams & Best, 1990). The characteristics in Figure 10.2 represent the prototypic American male or female: white, middle-class, heterosexual, and Christian (Basow, 1992). Obviously, however, not everyone fits this set of characteristics. For those who differ from the prototype, there are also variations in some gender stereotypes. For example, the stereotypes of African American males and females are more similar on the dimensions of competence and expressiveness than those for white American males and females (Smith & Midlarsky, 1985). Also, African American women are viewed as less passive, dependent, emotional, intelligent, vain, and warm than white American women (Landrine, 1985; Romer & Cherry, 1980).

A second thing to keep in mind is that the traditional male stereotype is more complimentary than the conventional female stereotype. This fact is related to **androcentrism** or the belief that the male is the norm (Bem, 1993). In other words, our society is organized in a way that favors "masculine" characteristics and behavior. Figure 10.3 depicts androcentrism in the workplace. Of course, male gender-role stereotypes also have some negative aspects.

FIGURE 10.2.

Traditional gender stereotypes. This is a partial list of the characteristics that college students associate with a typical man and a typical woman. (Adapted from Ruble, 1983)

Elements of Traditional Gender Stereotypes	
Masculine	**Feminine**
Active	Aware of others' feelings
Adventurous	Considerate
Aggressive	Creative
Ambitious	Cries easily
Competitive	Devotes self to others
Dominant	Emotional
Independent	Enjoys art and music
Leadership qualities	Excitable in a crisis
Likes math and science	Expresses tender feelings
Makes decisions easily	Feelings hurt
Mechanical aptitude	Gentle
Not easily influenced	Home oriented
Outspoken	Kind
Persistent	Likes children
Self-confident	Neat
Skilled in business	Needs approval
Stands up under pressure	Tactful
Takes a stand	Understanding

FIGURE 10.3.

Male bias on the job. In the world of work, women who exhibit traditional "masculine" characteristics are often perceived negatively. Thus, a man and a woman may display essentially the same behavior but elicit very different reactions.

Androcentrism in the Workplace	
He's good on details.	She's picky.
He follows through.	She doesn't know when to quit.
He's assertive.	She's pushy.
He stands firm.	She's rigid.
He's a man of the world.	She's been around.
He's not afraid to say what he thinks.	She's outspoken.
He's close-mouthed.	She's secretive.
He exercises authority.	She's power-mad.
He climbed the ladder of success.	She slept her way to the top.
He's a stern taskmaster.	She's difficult to work for.

A final point about gender stereotypes is that since the 1980s, the boundaries between male and female stereotypes seem to have become less rigid (Deaux & Lewis, 1983, 1984). Earlier, the male and female stereotypes were perceived to be separate and distinct categories (for example, men are strong and women are weak). Now it seems that people see gender stereotypes as two overlapping categories. That is, when participants are asked to estimate the probability that a hypothetical man or woman is strong, estimates for a hypothetical man are .66 and for a hypothetical woman, .44 (Deaux & Lewis, 1983, 1984).

Now let's shift from gender stereotypes to the *actual behavior* of males and females. Keep in mind that we'll be looking at modern Western societies. The story may be different in other cultures.

Gender Similarities and Differences

L E A R N I N G   O B J E C T I V E S

- *Summarize the research findings on gender similarities and differences in verbal, mathematical, and spatial abilities.*
- *Summarize the research on gender differences in personality and social behavior.*
- *Summarize the research on gender and psychological disorders.*
- *Summarize the situation regarding overall behavioral differences between males and females.*

Are men more aggressive than women? Are women at greater risk than men for depression? Vast numbers of studies have attempted to answer these and related questions about gender and behavior. Moreover, new evidence is pouring in constantly, and many researchers report conflicting findings. Thus, it is almost an overwhelming task to keep up with trends in the field. Thankfully, a new research technique has come to the rescue. *Meta-analysis* **is a statistical technique that evaluates the results of many studies on the same question.** This technique yields two critical pieces of information: (1) the size of a gender difference (if one is found to exist), and (2) which group scores higher (males or females).

Although meta-analysis has been a great boon to researchers in this area, it is not a magic bullet that can reconcile the many contradictory and controversial findings. Two questions currently under hot debate are (Eagly, 1995): How large are gender differences? How important are such differences? We'll do our best to thread our way through the available research. We'll examine three areas: cognitive abilities, personality traits and social behavior, and psychological disorders.

Cognitive Abilities

Perhaps we should first point out that gender differences have *not* been found in *overall* intelligence. Of course, this fact shouldn't be surprising, because intelligence tests are intentionally designed to minimize differences between the scores of males and females.

But what about gender differences in *specific* cognitive skills? Let's look at *verbal ability* first. Until about the 1980s, it was agreed that females scored higher than males on measures of verbal ability and that this gap opened up during early adolescence (Hyde, 1981; Maccoby & Jacklin, 1974). Then, in the 1980s, a meta-analysis

Janet Shibley Hyde

of 165 studies altered the thinking on this issue. Janet Shibley Hyde and Marcia Linn (1988) found no gender differences (or differences so small as to be unimportant) across all types of verbal tests and within several specific verbal areas (vocabulary and reading comprehension, for instance). A little later, other researchers concluded that there are some important gender differences in the verbal area (Eagly, 1995; Halpern, 1992, 1997). Among the findings worth noting are the fact that girls usually start speaking a little earlier, have larger vocabularies and better reading scores in grade school, and are more verbally fluent (on tests of writing, for instance) (Halpern, 1997). Boys seem to fare better on verbal analogies. However, they are 3 to 4 times more likely than girls to be stutterers (Skinner & Shelton,

1985) and five to ten times more likely than girls to be dyslexic (Vandenberg, 1987). These complex and sometimes conflicting findings make it hard to draw simple and sweeping conclusions. The best we can say is that, on the whole, gender differences in verbal ability seem to be small; however, there do seem to be a few noteworthy differences that favor girls.

Hyde and her colleagues performed another major meta-analysis on tests of *mathematical ability* (Hyde, Fennema, & Lamon, 1990). Again, the conclusion reversed earlier thinking on the question: Gender differences in mathematical ability in the general population are essentially nil. However, there are several exceptions to this general rule. In mathematical *problem-solving*, boys start to slightly outperform girls when they reach high school. A likely reason for this, according to Hyde and her colleagues, is that boys are more likely to elect high school math courses. Still, because problem-solving ability is essential for success in scientific courses and careers (arenas currently underpopulated by women), this finding is a concern. Males also outperform females at the high end of the mathematical ability distribution. For instance, when gifted seventh- and eighth-graders take the Math subtest of the SAT, boys outnumber girls 17 to 1 in the group scoring over 700 (Benbow, 1988). To summarize, when all students are compared, gender differences in mathematical ability are small, except in the area of problem solving; however, many more boys than girls are precocious in mathematics.

In the cognitive area, the most compelling evidence for gender differences is in *spatial ability*. A meta-analysis showed that males clearly outperformed females in one type of spatial ability: mental rotation (Linn & Petersen, 1986). This is the ability to mentally rotate a figure in three dimensions, a skill that is important in occupations such as engineering. Because the gender difference here is relatively large and has been found repeatedly, it is worth noting (Halpern, 1992, 1997; Masters & Sanders, 1993). Apparently, experience and training can improve spatial ability. For example, one study that trained girls and boys on action video games reported gains in spatial ability, although boys still scored higher than girls (Subrahmanyam & Greenfield, 1994).

Has the societal push to reduce sexism produced any changes in these gender patterns in cognitive abilities over the past 25 years? There is evidence on both sides of the question (Feingold, 1988; Hyde et al., 1990; Halpern, 1997). To further complicate the issue, there have been other changes during the same period—for instance, testing companies eliminated items that showed large gender differences (Halpern, 1997). As we assess the findings to date, the bulk of the research seems to favor a no-change position.

Web Link 10.1

Women's Studies Database
Established in 1992, this database at the University of Maryland has been recognized as one of the premier Internet guides to issues related to women's and gender studies.

To summarize, males and females in the general population seem to be basically similar regarding mental abilities. The differences that do exist are relatively few—although some would argue that they are important differences (Halpern, 1997). We'll examine the possible causes of these differences after we examine gender comparisons in some additional areas.

Personality Traits and Social Behavior

In regard to personality and social behavior, research findings support some gender differences that are reasonably well documented.

SELF-CONFIDENCE

Many studies support the conclusion that, on the average, males are more self-confident than females. Low self-confidence in females most often appears in endeavors that are stereotyped as "masculine," such as math, spatial tasks, technical problems, and computers (Beyer & Bowden, 1997). This finding holds for both African American and white girls and women (Mednick & Thomas, 1993). Even when they receive the same grades in math and science courses as males, females perceive themselves as less competent than males consider themselves.

Women's self-confidence seems to fluctuate depending on the situation. When women perform tasks that they view as gender-neutral or gender-appropriate, when they get clear and direct feedback on their task performance, and when they work alone, their performance estimates are similar to men's (Mednick & Thomas, 1993).

AGGRESSION

Aggression **involves behavior that is intended to hurt someone, either physically or verbally** (see Chapter 4). As a rule, males are more aggressive than females, although the size of this difference is moderate (Hyde, 1984; Knight, Fabes, & Higgins, 1996). Gender differences in aggression are greater in neutral situations. When people are clearly provoked (by insult, frustration, threat), these differences shrink considerably (Bettencourt & Miller, 1996).

As usual, the picture gets more complex if we look more closely. For example, it seems that boys engage in more physical aggression, while girls engage in more verbal aggression (Coie & Dodge, 1997). Also,

females—even at a young age—are more likely than males to use relational aggression in their same-gender peer groups: spreading rumors, gossiping, talking behind another's back, and trying to get others to dislike someone (Crick & Grotpeter, 1995). This form of aggression is a potent weapon because close relationships are particularly important to girls (Crick, 1995). Too, because relational aggression is indirect, it is difficult to identify the aggressor or even to know that aggression has occurred.

Still, there is no getting around the fact that men commit a grossly disproportionate share of violent crimes (Kenrick, 1987). Figure 10.4 shows the stark gender differences in aggressive crimes such as assault, armed robbery, rape, and homicide.

SEXUAL ATTITUDES AND BEHAVIOR

In the sexual domain, a meta-analysis found men to have more permissive attitudes than women about casual, premarital, and extramarital sex (Oliver & Hyde, 1993). Similarly, in a survey of college students, 84% of the men reported having had sexual relationships without any emotional involvement, but only 42% of the women had done so (Carroll, Volk, & Hyde, 1985). Researchers have also found that males are more sexually active and more likely to engage in certain forms of sexual behavior (masturbation, for example) than females are (Eagly, 1995).

CONFORMITY

Conformity **involves yielding to real or imagined social pressure.** Traditional beliefs hold that females are more conforming than males, who are viewed as more independent-minded. Nonetheless, research has demonstrated that females *don't* conform to peer standards more than males *unless* there is group pressure to do so (Becker, 1986; Eagly & Carli, 1981; Hyde & Frost, 1993). As we noted earlier, race and gender often interact. For example, African American females seem to be less easily influenced and more assertive than either African American males or white females (Adams, 1980, 1983). The traditional explanation for gender differences in conformity is that women are more gullible than men, but there are alternative explanations as well: Women typically hold lower status in groups than do men, and women may be more concerned about preserving social harmony than men (Eagly, 1987).

COMMUNICATION

Popular stereotypes have it that females are much more talkative than males. In fact, the opposite is true: Men talk more than women (Aries, 1987). Men also

Type of offense	Percentage of arrests by gender (1997)		
Murder and nonnegligent manslaughter	90.5	9.5	
Forcible rape	98.8	1.2	
Robbery	90.7	9.3	
Aggravated assault	82.3	17.7	
All violent crimes	90.6	9.4	

Males Females   0   25   50   75   100

FIGURE 10.4.

Gender differences in violent crimes. Males are arrested for violent crimes far more often than females, as these statistics show. These data support the findings of laboratory studies indicating that males tend to be more physically aggressive than females. (Data from U.S. Bureau of the Census, 1997)

interrupt women more than women interrupt men (Hall, 1984) and also more than they interrupt other men (Smith-Lovin & Brody, 1989). Still, when women have more power in a relationship, they talk more than men (Kollock, Blumstein, & Schwartz, 1985). Thus, this supposed gender difference is probably better seen as a status difference (Johnson, 1994).

Another gender difference in verbal communication is tentativeness. Linda Carli (1990) looked for gender differences in three types of tentative language (see Figure 10.5). She found that women are more likely than men to use *hedges* ("kind of" or "you know") or *disclaimers* ("I may be wrong" or "I'm not sure"). Also, women are twice as likely to use *tag questions* at the ends of sentences (Carli, 1990; Lakoff, 1973; McMillan et al., 1977). For example, a woman might say, "Let's go to a movie, *OK?*" or "That was a terrific concert, *wasn't it?*" This gender difference has been attributed both to women's greater insecurity and to their greater interpersonal sensitivity (Wood, 1994). For more communication differences, see this chapter's Application.

Researchers have also studied how the genders compare in the realm of *non*verbal communication. Women appear to be more sensitive to nonverbal cues (Hall, 1990), but it is quite likely that status differences are responsible for these findings (Snodgrass, 1992).

Psychological Disorders

In terms of the *overall* incidence of mental disorders, no gender differences have been found. It seems that about one out of every three people will develop a psychological disorder at one time or another and that this is true for both males and females (Robins & Regier, 1991).

When researchers assess the prevalence of *specific* disorders, they *do* find gender differences (Regier et al., 1988; Russo & Green, 1993). Antisocial behavior, alcoholism, and other drug-related disorders are more prevalent among men. Women, on the other hand, are more likely to suffer from depression and anxiety disorders (phobias, for example). They also show higher rates of eating disorders (see the Chapter 15 Application). In addition, women *attempt* suicide more often than men, but men *complete* suicides (actually kill themselves) more frequently than women (Strickland, 1988).

What accounts for these gender differences in mental illnesses? For one thing, there is a relatively obvious connection between the symptoms of "male" and "female" disorders and traditional gender roles (Katz, Boggiano, & Silvern, 1993). That is, women's disorders seem to reflect a turning *inward*—negative, hostile, anxious feelings and conflicts are directed against the self. In men, these same feelings and conflicts are typically directed *outward*—against either other individuals or society. (Suicide is one obvious exception.)

Putting Gender Differences in Perspective

Although there are some genuine gender differences in behavior, remember that these are *group* differences. That is, they tell us nothing about individuals. Essentially, we are comparing the "average man" with the "average woman." Furthermore, the differences between these groups are relatively small. Figure 10.6 shows how scores on a trait might be distributed for men and women. Although the group averages are detectably different, you can see that there is great variability within each group (gender) and huge overlap between the two group distributions. Thus, a gender difference that shows up on the average does not by itself tell us anything about you or any other unique individual. This is why such differences should not be used to restrict *individual* choices.

A second essential point is that gender accounts for a very minute proportion of the differences between individuals. Using complicated statistical procedures, it is possible to gauge the influence of gender on behavior. These tests show that gender accounts for a minute proportion of the variation among people. Thus, factors other than gender are far more important determinants of differences between individuals.

Another point to keep in mind is that when gender differences are found, they do not mean that one gender is better than the other. When certain traits or

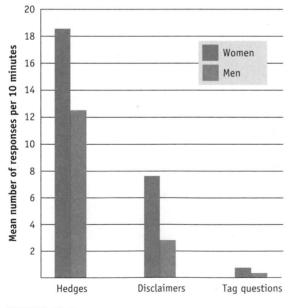

FIGURE 10.5.

Gender differences in the use of tentative language in mixed-gender groups. When men and women talked together for 10 minutes, it was found that women used significantly more hedges, disclaimers, and tag questions than men did. (Data from Carli, 1990)

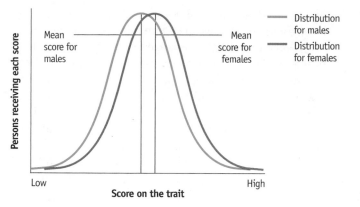

Mean score for males

Mean score for females

Persons receiving each score

Low — Score on the trait — High

Distribution for males
Distribution for females

FIGURE 10.6.

The nature of group differences. Gender differences are group differences that tell us little about individuals because of the great overlap between the groups. For a given trait, one gender may score higher on the average, but as you can see there is far more variation within each gender than between the genders.

abilities are deemed superior to others by a particular society or group, the tendency is to perceive the group that performs less well in these areas as deficient, rather than as different. As Diane Halpern humorously notes, "It is about as meaningful to ask 'Which is the smarter sex?'... as it is to ask 'Which has the better genitals?' (1997, p. 1092). The problem is not with gender differences, but with how these differences are evaluated by the larger society.

To conclude, the behavioral differences between males and females are relatively few in number and small in size. Moreover, gender-relevant behavior often appears and disappears as gender-role expectations become more or less salient (Deaux & LaFrance, 1998). *Ultimately, the similarities between women and men greatly outweigh the differences.*

Although gender differences in personality and behavior are relatively few and modest, sometimes it seems otherwise. How come? One explanation focuses on gender-based differences in social roles. Alice Eagly's (1987) *social role theory* asserts that minor gender differences are exaggerated by the different social roles that males and females occupy. For example, because women are assigned the role of caregiver, they learn to behave in nurturing ways. Moreover, people come to associate such role-related behaviors with individuals of a given gender, not the actual roles they play. In other words, people come to see nurturing as a female trait rather than a characteristic that anyone in a nurturing role would demonstrate. This is one way that stereotypes develop and persist.

Alice Eagly

Another explanation for discrepancies between beliefs and reality is that the differences actually reside in the eye of the beholder, not the beholdee. *Social constructionism* asserts that individuals construct their own reality based on societal expectations, conditioning, and self-socialization. According to social constructionists, the tendency to look for gender differences as well as specific beliefs about gender are rooted in the "gendered" messages and conditioning that permeate people's socialization experiences. To better understand these issues, we need to explore the role of biological and environmental factors as likely sources of gender differences.

Biological Origins of Gender Differences

LEARNING OBJECTIVES

- Summarize evolutionary explanations for gender differences.
- Review the evidence linking gender differences in cognitive abilities to brain organization.
- Review the evidence relating hormones to gender differences.

Are the few gender differences that *do* exist acquired through learning, or are they biologically built in? Until now, we have deferred tackling this controversial question. Essentially, it represents the age-old issue of nature versus nurture. The "nature" theorists concentrate on how biological disparities between the genders contribute to differences in behavior. "Nurture" theorists, on the other hand, emphasize the role of learning and environment. Although we will discuss biological and environmental influences separately, keep in mind that the distinctions between nature and nurture are less sharp today than they once were. A number of contemporary researchers and theorists in this area are interested in how biological and environmental factors interact. In this section, we'll look at evolutionary explanations of gender differences, as well as two other biologically based lines of inquiry in this area: brain organization and hormonal influences.

Evolutionary Explanations

Evolutionary psychologists suggest that gender differences in behavior reflect different natural selection pressures operating on the genders over the course of human history.

That is, natural selection favors behaviors that maximize the chances of passing on genes to the next generation (reproductive success).

To support their assertions, evolutionary psychologists look for gender differences that are consistent across cultures (Kenrick & Trost, 1993). Is there consistency across cultures for the better-documented gender differences? Despite some fascinating exceptions, gender differences in cognitive abilities, aggression, and sexual behavior *are* found in many cultures (Beller & Gafni, 1996; Halpern, 1997). According to evolutionary psychologists, these consistent differences have emerged because males and females have been confronted with different adaptive demands. For example, males supposedly are more *sexually active and permissive* because they invest less than females in the process of procreation and can maximize their reproductive success by seeking many sexual partners (Buss, 1996).

The gender gap in *aggression* is also explained in terms of reproductive fitness. Because females are more selective about mating than males are, males have to engage in more competition for sexual partners than females do. Greater aggressiveness is thought to be adaptive for males in this competition for sexual access because it should foster social dominance over other males and facilitate the acquisition of the material resources emphasized by females when they evaluate potential partners (Kenrick & Trost, 1997). Evolutionary theorists assert that gender differences in *spatial ability* reflect the division of labor in ancestral hunting-and-gathering societies in which males typically handled the hunting and females the gathering. Males' superiority on most spatial tasks has been attributed to the adaptive demands of hunting (Eals & Silverman, 1994).

Evolutionary analyses of gender differences are interesting, but controversial. While it is eminently plausible that evolutionary forces could have led to some divergence between males and females in typical behavior, evolutionary hypotheses are highly speculative and difficult to test empirically (Fausto-Sterling, 1992; Halpern, 1997). For example, it is quite a leap to infer that modern paper-and-pencil tests of spatial ability assess a talent that would have made high scorers superior hunters million of years ago. In addition, evolutionary theory can be used to claim that the status quo in society is the inevitable outcome of evolutionary forces (Lewontin, Rose, & Kamin, 1984). Thus, if males have dominant status over females, natural selection must have favored this arrangement. The crux of the problem is that evolutionary analyses can be used to explain almost anything. For instance, if the situation regarding spatial ability were reversed—if females scored higher than males—evolutionary theorists might attribute females' superiority to the adaptive demands of gathering food, weaving baskets, and making clothes—and it would be difficult to prove otherwise.

Brain Organization

Some theorists propose that male and female brains are organized differently, which might account for gender

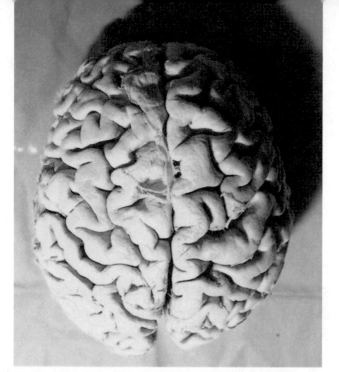

Studies have shown that the brain's cerebral hemispheres, shown here, are somewhat specialized in the kinds of cognitive tasks they handle and that such specialization is more pronounced in males than in females. Whether this difference bears any relation to gender differences in behavior is yet to be determined.

differences in some cognitive abilities. As you may know, the human brain is divided into two halves. **The cerebral hemispheres are the right and left halves of the cerebrum, which is the convoluted outer layer of the brain.** The largest and most complicated part of the human brain, the cerebrum is responsible for most complex mental activities.

Some evidence suggests that the right and left cerebral hemispheres are specialized to handle different cognitive tasks (Sperry, 1982; Springer & Deutsch, 1993). For example, it appears that the *left hemisphere* is more actively involved in *verbal and mathematical processing*, while the *right hemisphere* is specialized to handle *visual-spatial and other nonverbal processing*. This pattern is generally seen in both right-handed and left-handed people, although it is less consistent among those who are left-handed.

After these findings on hemispheric specialization surfaced, some theorists began to wonder whether a connection might exist between this division of labor in the brain and the then-observed gender differences in verbal and spatial skills. Consequently, researchers began looking for disparities between male and female brain organization.

Some thought-provoking findings *have* been reported. For instance, males exhibit more cerebral specialization than females (Bryden, 1988; Hines, 1990). In other words, males tend to depend more heavily than females on the left hemisphere in verbal processing and

on the right hemisphere in spatial processing. Gender differences have also been found in the size of the corpus callosum, the band of fibers connecting the two hemispheres of the brain (Steinmetz et al., 1995). More specifically, some studies suggest that females tend to have a larger corpus callosum. This might allow for better interhemispheric transfer of information, which, in turn, might underlie the more bilateral organization of female brains (Innocenti, 1994). Thus, some theorists have argued that these differences in brain organization are responsible for gender differences in verbal and spatial ability (Kimura & Hampson, 1993). Based on these findings, the popular press has often touted the idea that there are "male brains" and "female brains" that are fundamentally different (Bleier, 1984).

This idea is intriguing, but psychologists have a long way to go before they can attribute gender differences in verbal and spatial ability to right brain/left brain specialization. First, studies have not consistently found that males have more specialized brain organization than females (Fausto-Sterling, 1992; Halpern, 1992), and the finding of a larger corpus callosum in females does not always show up (Halpern, 1992; Hines, 1990). Second, it seems peculiar that strong lateralization would produce an advantage for males on one kind of task (spatial) and a disadvantage on another kind of task (verbal). Third, because a significant amount of brain development occurs over the first five to ten years after birth, during which time males and females are socialized differently, it is possible that different life experiences may accumulate to produce slight differences in brain organization (Hood et al., 1987). Finally, it's important to remember that male and female brains are much more similar than they are different. Thus, the notion that cerebral specialization is linked to gender differences in mental abilities is still under debate.

Hormonal Influences

Biological explanations of gender differences have also focused on the possible role of hormones. **Hormones are chemical substances released into the bloodstream by the endocrine glands.** We'll examine the effect of hormones on sexual differentiation and on sexual and aggressive behavior.

PRENATAL GENDER DIFFERENTIATION

We know that hormones play a key role in gender differentiation during *prenatal* development. Biological gender is determined by sex chromosomes. An XX pairing produces a female, and an XY pairing produces a male. However, both male and female embryos are essentially the same until about 8 to 12 weeks after conception. Around this time, male and female gonads (sex glands) begin to produce different hormonal secretions. The high level of *androgens* (male hormones) in males and the low level of androgens in females leads to the differentiation of male and female genital organs.

The influence of prenatal hormones on gender differentiation becomes apparent when something interferes with normal prenatal hormonal secretions. About a half dozen endocrine disorders can cause overproduction or underproduction of specific gonadal hormones during prenatal development. Scientists have also studied children born to mothers given an androgen-like drug to prevent miscarriage. Two trends have been noted in this research (Collaer & Hines, 1995). First, females exposed prenatally to abnormally high levels of androgens exhibit more male-typical behavior than other females do. Second, males exposed prenatally to abnormally low levels of androgens exhibit more female-typical behavior than other males. For example, girls with *congenital adrenal hyperplasia* tend to show "tomboyish" interests in vigorous outdoor activities and in "male" toys and have elevated scores on measures of aggressiveness and spatial ability.

The findings suggest that prenatal hormones shape gender differences in humans. But there are a few problems with this evidence (Basow, 1992; Fausto-Sterling, 1992). First, there is much more and much stronger evidence for females than for males. Second, it's always dangerous to draw conclusions about the general population based on small samples of people who have abnormal conditions. Third, most of the endocrine disorders studied have multiple effects (besides altering hormone level) that make it difficult to isolate actual causes. Fourth, most of the research is necessarily correlational, and it is always risky to draw causal conclusions from correlational data.

SEXUAL AND AGGRESSIVE BEHAVIOR

The hormone testosterone plays an important role in *sexual desire* for both men and women (Everitt & Bancroft, 1991). That is, when testosterone is reduced or eliminated, both men and women show decreases in sexual drive. A handful of studies have also reported associations between levels of male and female hormones and specific traits. So far, however, the results of these studies are equivocal and inconsistent (Fausto-Sterling, 1992; Hines, 1982). For instance, testosterone has been linked with higher levels of *aggression* in humans (Inoff-Germain et al., 1988), but the picture is complicated because it has also been found that aggressive behavior can produce increases in testosterone (Dabbs, 1992).

To summarize, hormones probably do play a role in some aspects of sexual and aggressive behavior, although the nature of the connections is not well understood. Also, hormones have less influence on human behavior than they do on animal behavior, because humans are more susceptible to environmental influences. We still have much to learn about the complicated ways in which hormones interact with social and psychological factors.

The overall evidence suggests that biological factors play a relatively minor role in gender differences, creating predispositions that are largely shaped by experience. In contrast, efforts to link gender differences to disparities in the way males and females are reared have proved more fruitful. We'll consider this perspective next.

Environmental Origins of Gender Differences

LEARNING OBJECTIVES

- *Define socialization and gender roles, and describe Margaret Mead's findings on the variability of gender roles and their implications.*
- *Explain how reinforcement and punishment, observational learning, and self-socialization operate in gender-role socialization.*
- *Describe how parents and peers influence gender-role socialization.*
- *Describe how schools and the media influence gender-role socialization.*

Socialization **is the acquisition of the norms and roles expected of people in a particular society.** This process includes all the efforts made by a society to ensure that its members learn to behave in a manner that's considered appropriate. Teaching children about gender roles is an important aspect of the socialization process. *Gender roles* **are cultural expectations about what is appropriate behavior for each gender.** For example, in our culture women have been expected to rear children, cook meals, clean house, and do laundry. On the other hand, men have been expected to be the family breadwinner, do yardwork, and tinker with cars.

Are gender roles in other cultures similar to those seen in our society? Generally, yes—but not necessarily. Despite a fair amount of cross-cultural consistency in gender roles, there is some dramatic variability as well (Munroe & Munroe, 1975). For instance, anthropologist Margaret Mead (1950) conducted a now-classic study of three tribes in New Guinea. She found one tribe in which *both* genders followed our masculine role expectations (the Mundugumor). She found another tribe in which *both* genders approximated our feminine role (the Arapesh). And she found one tribe in which the male and female roles were roughly the *reverse* of our own (the Tchambuli). Such remarkable discrepancies between cultures existing within 100 miles of one another demonstrate that gender roles are not a matter of biological destiny. Instead, like other roles, gender roles are acquired through socialization.

As we noted earlier, Eagly's social role theory suggests that gender differences occur because males and females are guided by different role expectations. In the next section, we'll discuss how society teaches individuals about gender roles.

Processes in Gender-Role Socialization

How do people acquire gender roles? Several key learning processes come into play, including reinforcement and punishment, observational learning, and self-socialization.

REINFORCEMENT AND PUNISHMENT

In part, gender roles are shaped by the power of rewards and punishment—the key processes in operant conditioning (see Chapter 2). Parents, teachers, peers, and others often reinforce (usually with tacit approval) "gender-appropriate" behavior and respond negatively to "gender-inappropriate behavior" (Fagot & Leinbach, 1987; Fagot, Leinbach, & O'Boyle, 1992). For example, a young boy who has hurt himself may be told that "big boys don't cry." If he succeeds in inhibiting his crying, he may get a pat on the back or a warm smile—both potent reinforcers. Over time, a consistent pattern of such reinforcement will strengthen the boy's tendency to "act like a man" and suppress emotional displays.

Most parents take gender-appropriate behavior for granted and don't go out of their way to reward it. On the other hand, they usually react negatively to gender-inappropriate behavior, especially in boys. For instance, a 10-year-old boy who enjoys playing with dollhouses will probably elicit strong disapproval. Fathers are especially likely to punish gender-inappropriate behavior in their sons (Lytton & Romney, 1991). Paternal reactions usually involve ridicule or verbal reprimands rather than physical punishment.

OBSERVATIONAL LEARNING

Younger children commonly imitate the behavior of a parent or an older sibling. This imitation, or *observational learning,* occurs when a child's behavior is influenced by observing others, who are called *models.* Parents serve as models for children, as do siblings, teachers, relatives, and others who are important in children's lives. Note that models are not limited to real people; TV actors, movie stars, and cartoon characters can also serve as models.

According to *social learning theory* (see Chapter 2), young children are more likely to imitate people who are nurturant, powerful, and similar to them (Bussey & Bandura, 1984). Children imitate both genders, but most children are prone to imitate same-gender models. Thus, observational learning often leads young girls to play with dolls, dollhouses, and toy stoves. By contrast, young boys are more likely to tinker with toy trucks, miniature gas stations, and tool kits. Interestingly, same-gender peers may be even more influential models than parents are (Maccoby, 1990).

SELF-SOCIALIZATION

Children are not merely passive recipients of gender-role socialization. Rather, they play an active role in this process (Bem, 1993; Cross & Markus, 1993). Self-socialization entails three steps. First, children learn to classify themselves as male or female and to recognize their gender as a permanent quality (around ages 5 or 6). Second, this self-categorization motivates them to value those characteristics and behaviors that are associated with their gender. Third, they strive to bring their behavior in line with what is considered gender-appropriate in their culture. In other words, children get involved in their own socialization, working diligently to discover the rules that are supposed to govern their behavior. Once gender stereotypes are internalized, they probably continue to influence behavior throughout life. Too, most people strive to behave in ways that are consistent with their own and others' expectations (Geis, 1993).

Sources of Gender-Role Socialization

Four major sources of gender-role messages are parents, peers, schools, and the media. Because researchers have focused on white, middle-class children, our discussion of gender-role socialization will primarily reflect these experiences (Reid & Paludi, 1993). Thus, you should keep in mind that individuals who have grown up in different types of households may have had different experiences. For example, traditional gender roles are relatively rigidly defined in Hispanic families (Comas-Diaz, 1987). Also, gender roles are changing, so the generalizations that follow may say more about how you were socialized than about how your children will be.

PARENTS

A great deal of gender-role socialization takes place in the home. Nonetheless, a meta-analysis of 172 studies of parental socialization practices suggests that parents don't treat girls and boys as differently as one might expect (Lytton & Romney, 1991). Still, there are some important distinctions. For one thing, there is a strong and consistent tendency for both mothers and fathers to emphasize and encourage *play activities* that are "gender-appropriate." Other studies have found that boys and girls are encouraged to play with different

Children learn behaviors appropriate to their gender roles very early in life. According to social learning theory, boys tend to follow in their father's footsteps, while girls tend to do the sorts of things their mother does.

types of toys (Etaugh & Liss, 1992). As Figure 10.7 shows, substantial gender differences are found in toy preferences. Generally, boys have less leeway to play with "feminine" toys than girls do with "masculine" toys. As children grow older, their leisure activities often vary by gender: Johnny plays in Little League and Mary gets dancing lessons.

A second way parents emphasize gender is in the assignment of *household chores* (Lytton & Romney, 1991). Tasks are doled out on the basis of gender stereotypes: Girls usually do laundry and dishes, whereas boys mow the lawn and sweep the garage.

Parents' attitudes about gender roles have been shown to influence the gender roles their children acquire (Weisner & Wilson-Mitchell, 1990). For example, middle-class parents may allow their children to deviate more from traditional gender roles than lower-class parents do (Reid & Paludi, 1993). Also, African

American families seem to place less emphasis on traditional gender roles than white American families (Binion, 1990). By contrast, Asian American families typically encourage subservience in their daughters (Tsai & Uemera, 1988), and Hispanic families usually encourage traditional gender-role behavior. Several studies report that only mothers with nontraditional views of gender roles seem to encourage their daughters to be independent (Brooks-Gunn, 1986; Carr & Mednick, 1988).

PEERS

Peers form an important network for learning about gender-role stereotypes, as well as gender-appropriate and gender-inappropriate behavior. Between the ages of 4 and 6, children seem to separate into same-gender groups. A longitudinal study showed that the ratio of time spent with same-gender playmates versus

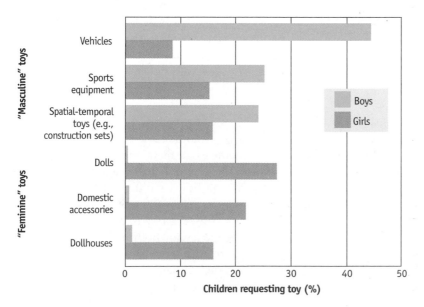

FIGURE 10.7.

Toy preferences and gender. This graph depicts the percentage of boys and girls asking for various types of toys in letters to Santa Claus (adapted from Richardson & Simpson, 1982). Boys and girls differ substantially in their toy preferences, which probably reflect the effects of gender-role socialization.

other-gender playmates rose from 3:1 to 11:1 between these ages (Maccoby, 1990; Maccoby & Jacklin, 1987). It would seem, then, that during these ages, same-gender peers are the most powerful instruments of such learning (Fagot, 1985; Harris, 1995).

Play among same-gender peers takes different forms for boys and girls. Boys play in larger groups and roam farther away from home, whereas girls prefer smaller groups and stay near the house (Feiring & Lewis, 1987). In addition, high status in boys' groups is achieved by engaging in dominant behavior (telling others what to do and enforcing orders). In contrast, girls usually express their wishes as suggestions rather than demands (Maltz & Borker, 1983). Also, boys engage in rough-and-tumble play much more frequently than girls do (Maccoby, 1988).

Peers seem to play a different and more important role for boys than for girls. For boys, male peers seem to assume more importance than adult models relatively early in life, for several reasons. First, adult males are relatively invisible to male children because they are at work and don't typically work in settings where children are present. Also, boys spend much of their time in the presence of females (mothers and female teachers). Thus, it has been suggested that males use the male peer group for information about the male role in the absence of adult male models and to resist female influence (Maccoby & Jacklin, 1987). Because girls have easy access to information about the female role and feel at ease with female adults, they don't need to rely on same-gender peers in the same way boys do. Research seems to support such an interpretation. For example, male peers appear to play a particularly important role for African American males, who are more likely to be reared in a female-headed home than white males are (Coates, 1987; Rashid, 1989). By contrast, African American girls report that they feel close both to family members and to male and female peers.

SCHOOLS

The school environment figures importantly in socializing gender roles (American Association of University Women, 1994; Sadker & Sadker, 1994). The *books* that children use in learning to read can influence their ideas about what is suitable behavior for males and females (Schau & Scott, 1984). Traditionally, males have been more likely to be portrayed as clever, heroic, and adventurous in these books, whereas females have been more often shown performing domestic chores. Although the depiction of stereotypical gender roles has declined considerably since the 1970s, researchers still find significant differences in how males and females are portrayed (Kortenhous & Demarest, 1993). Many high school and college textbooks also contain gender bias. The most common problems are the use of

generic masculine language ("policeman" versus "police officer" and so forth) and portraying males and females in stereotypic roles. You might review your textbooks for instances of gender bias.

Gender bias in schools also shows up in *teachers' behaviors.* Preschool and grade-school teachers often reward gender-appropriate behavior in their pupils (Fagot et al., 1985). Teachers also tend to pay greater attention to males—helping them, praising them, and scolding them more than females (AAUW Educational Foundation, 1992; Sadker & Sadker, 1994). By contrast, girls tend to be relatively invisible in the classroom and receive little encouragement for academic achievement from teachers. A recent national report concluded that girls' self-esteem is gradually eroded through such experiences as (1) teachers paying less attention to girls, (2) sexual harassment by male peers, (3) the stereotyping and invisibility of females in textbooks, and (4) test bias that restricts girls' chances of getting into college and obtaining scholarships (AAUW, 1994). Figure 10.8 depicts the development of this gender gap in self-esteem.

Gender bias also shows up in *academic and career counseling.* Despite the fact that females obtain higher grades in all subjects from elementary school through college than males do (Eccles, 1989), many counselors still encourage male students to be physicians and engineers and guide female students toward teaching, nursing, and homemaking (Read, 1991).

THE MEDIA

Television is yet another source of gender-role socialization (Luecke-Aleksa et al., 1995). American youngsters spend a lot of time watching TV (see Figure 10.9 on the next page). Children between the ages of 3 and 11 watch an average of 2 to 4 hours of TV per day (Huston et al., 1990). African American children and

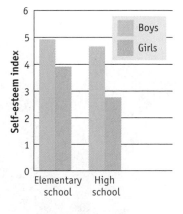

FIGURE 10.8.

The gender gap in self-esteem between elementary school and high school. Girls experience a significant drop in self-esteem between elementary school and high school whereas boys do not. In this study, self-esteem was measured by responses to five statements: "I like the way I look," "I like most things about myself," "I'm happy the way I am," "Sometimes I don't like myself that much, " and "I wish I were somebody else." (AAUW, 1994)

youth spend more time in front of the tube than their white peers (Brown et al., 1990).

An analysis of male and female TV *characters* showed that males outnumber females 2 to 1, the same ratio that existed in the 1950s (D. Davis, 1990). Although people of color are more visible on TV now than in the past, they are often segregated from whites (Zillman, Bryant, & Huston, 1994). Television *programs* have traditionally depicted men and women in highly stereotypic ways (Signorelli, 1993; Zillman et al., 1994). On prime-time programs today, more women are portrayed as having jobs. Still, most characters have professional jobs such as lawyers, whereas most real women work in lower-paying, lower-status jobs. The "up" side of this unbalanced portrayal is that professional TV characters can serve as positive role models for girls and women, but the "down" side is that viewers are led to underestimate the degree of inequity in the workplace (Basow, 1992).

Television *commercials* are even more gender stereotyped than programs are (Bretl & Cantor, 1988; Lovdal, 1989). Women are shown worrying about the ring around their husbands' collars, how white "their" laundry is, and how to use expensive cosmetics to "snare" a man. On the positive note, one study of children's toy commercials reported that boys and girls were equally represented (Rajecki et al., 1993).

Most *video games* push a hypermasculine stereotype featuring search-and-destroy missions, fighter pilot battles, and male sports (Lips, 1997). Of the few video games directed at girls, the great majority of them are highly stereotypic (shopping and Barbie games). Also, music videos frequently portray women as sex objects and men as dominating and aggressive (Sommers Flanagan et al., 1993), and these portrayals

Boys are under more pressure than girls to behave in gender-appropriate ways. Little boys who show an interest in dolls are likely to be chastised by both parents and peers.

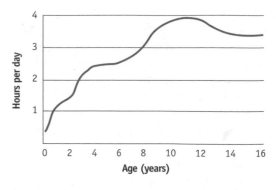

FIGURE 10.9.

Television viewing habits. As children grow up, they spend more and more time watching TV until viewing time begins to decline slightly at around age 12. Research shows that children's conceptions of gender roles are influenced to a considerable degree by what they watch on television. (Data from Liebert & Sprafkin, 1988)

appear to influence viewers' attitudes about sexual conduct (Hansen & Hansen, 1988).

A clear link exists between the number and type of television programs children watch and the acquisition of gender-stereotyped beliefs: Children who watch a lot of television hold more stereotyped beliefs about gender than children who watch less TV (Signorielli & Lears, 1992). Still, this study is correlational, so it is quite likely that other factors—such as parental values—come into play as well. Nonetheless, once gender stereotypes are learned, they are difficult to change.

Another manifestation of gender bias is television's inordinate *emphasis on physical attractiveness in women.* Males on television may or may not be good-looking, but the vast majority of females are young, attractive, and sexy (D. Davis, 1990). Exposure to such role models means that females experience much more pressure to be youthful, thin, and physically attractive than males do (Feingold, 1990). As you'll see in the Chapter 15 Application, these cultural expectations have been cited as a cause of the disproportionately high incidence of eating disorders in females (Levenkron, 1982; Polivy & Thomsen, 1988).

Traditional Gender Roles

LEARNING OBJECTIVES

- List five elements of the traditional male role.
- Describe three common problems associated with the traditional male role.
- List two major expectations of the traditional female role.
- Describe three common problems associated with the traditional female role.
- Describe two ways in which women are victimized by sexism.

The social norms that characterize traditional gender roles are based on several assumptions: that all members of the same gender have basically the same traits, that the traits of one gender are different from the traits of the other gender, and that masculine traits are more highly valued. And because traditional gender roles assume that everyone is heterosexual (heterosexism), they say nothing about homosexual individuals. This fact and the relative invisibility of gay males and lesbians mean that young homosexuals are deprived of positive role models. Thus, it is difficult for them to sort through the interrelated issues of identity, gender-role identity, and sexual orientation. Let's look at traditional gender-role expectations.

Role Expectations for Males

A number of psychologists have characterized the traditional male role (Brannon, 1976; Doyle, 1989; Levant, 1996; Pleck, 1995). According to James Doyle and Michele Paludi (1998), this role contains five key elements.

The antifeminine element. As we have seen, "real men" shouldn't act in any way that might be perceived as feminine. As Robert Brannon (1976) puts it, "No sissy stuff."

The success element. To prove their masculinity, men need to beat out other men at sports and at work. Having a high-status job, driving an expensive car, and making lots of money are aspects of this element.

The aggressive element. Men are expected to fight for what they believe is right and to aggressively defend themselves against threats. Aggression may take the form of verbal or physical force, even violence.

The sexual element. "Real men" should be the initiators and controllers of sexual activity.

The self-reliant element. Being "in control" and remaining cool and calm under pressure are aspects of this element.

Gender-role expectations for boys have remained relatively stable for years. However, it appears that the male role may be undergoing some changes. According to Joseph Pleck (1995), who has written extensively on this issue, in the *traditional male role*, masculinity is validated by individual physical strength, aggressiveness, and emotional inexpressiveness. In the *modern male role*, masculinity is validated by economic achievement, organizational power, emotional control (even over anger), and emotional sensitivity and self-expression, but only with women.

The traditional role exists along with the new expectations, so males are experiencing role inconsistencies and pressures to behave in ways that conflict with traditional masculinity. These include pressures to communicate personal feelings, to nurture children and share in housework, to integrate sexuality with love, and to curb aggression and violence (Levant, 1996). Some psychologists think that these pressures have shaken traditional masculine norms sufficiently that many men are experiencing a masculinity crisis (Levant, 1996). That is, they are feeling bewildered and confused, and their pride in being a man has been diminished. The rise in popularity of men's groups and organizations such as the Promise Keepers reflects this frustration. The good news is that boys and men are beginning to get more attention from psychological theorists, researchers, and clinicians (see the Recommended Reading).

Problems with the Male Role

It is a common misconception that only women suffer from narrow gender roles. Not so. Increasingly, the costs of the male role are a cause for concern (Doyle, 1989; Levant, 1996; Pleck, 1995).

PRESSURE TO SUCCEED

Most men are socialized to believe that job success is everything. They are encouraged to be highly competitive and are taught that a man's masculinity is measured by the size of his paycheck and job status (Doyle, 1989; Levant, 1996). As Christopher Kilmartin (1994) notes, "There is always another man who has more money, higher status, a more attractive partner, or a bigger house. The traditional man . . . must constantly work harder and faster " (p. 13). Small wonder, then, that so many men pursue success with a fervor that is sometimes dangerous to their health. The extent of this danger is illustrated by men's life expectancy, which is about six years shorter than women's (of course, factors besides gender roles contribute to this difference).

The majority of men who have internalized this success ethic are unable to realize their dreams. How does this "failure" affect them? Although many are able to adjust to it, many are not. The latter group are likely to suffer from poor self-esteem and a diminished sense of virility (Doyle, 1989). Men's obsession with success also creates problems for women. For instance, many men want to "keep women in their place" because their self-esteem is threatened when a woman earns more than they do (Astrachan, 1992; Blumstein & Schwartz, 1983). Men's emphasis on success also makes it more likely that they will spend long hours on the job. This pattern in turn decreases the amount of time families can spend together and increases the amount of time wives spend on housework and child care.

● Recommended Reading

The Masculine Self by Christopher T. Kilmartin (MacMillan, 1994)

This small paperback, written for college courses on gender, is highly readable. Kilmartin's major purpose is to help readers "understand the difference between being male and being a generic human being," (p.v). The implication is that androcentrism may render invisible the uniqueness of the male experience.

Kilmartin does an excellent job of blending classic and contemporary research findings to shed light on important questions. About half of the book is devoted to a thorough and research-based discussion of current problem areas for men: emotions, physical health, work, sexuality, violence, relationships, and mental health. He also addresses the important issues of race, ethnicity, sexual orientation, and age. In addition, he integrates male gender-role theory into the major perspectives on personality—psychoanalytic, social learning, humanistic, and biological.

The book closes with an enlightening discussion of contemporary men's movements, including the mythopoetic movement (Robert Bly and Sam Keen), profeminism, and the men's rights movement (Robert Farrell). Also included is an interesting discussion of men's studies, an emerging area of scholarly work.

In the following excerpt, Kilmartin discusses three costs of being a "real man."

The expectations that men compete, achieve, are "on top," and always look for more have left many men feeling driven, empty, disillusioned, and angry. . . . The traditional man can never get enough, and thus he can never really enjoy what he has. . . . Such a lifestyle often results in stress-related physical and psychological symptoms. . . . To strip a man of his emotional life is to take away one of the most basic aspects of human existence. . . . The damage that male gender roles do to the quality of connectedness to other people and to feelings about the self can hardly be overestimated. Many men feel alienated from their partners, children, and other men, and these feelings are often mutual. . . . The most serious result of unconnectedness to others is its influence on men's willingness to do physical and psychological harm to others. . . . The disproportionate participation of men in war, violence, damage to the planet, the oppression of marginalized social groups, and psychological cruelty must (at least partly) be laid at the doorstep of traditional masculinity. [1994, p. 13]

THE EMOTIONAL REALM

Most young boys are trained to believe that men should be strong, tough, cool, and detached. Also, men learn to direct negative and anxious feelings toward others, as we noted in our discussion of gender differences in psychological disorders. These experiences increase the tendency for males to behave aggressively and, sometimes, violently (Tavris, 1989). Intimate violence and sexual assaults are almost exclusively perpetrated by males, and almost 90% of violent crimes in the United States are committed by men (U.S. Bureau of the Census, 1997).

In contrast, males learn early to hide emotions such as love, joy, and sadness because they believe that such feelings are "feminine" and imply weakness. Over time, some men become strangers to their own emotional lives and are unable even to identify their emotions (Levant, 1996). This condition is termed *alexithymia* ("no words for emotions"). This difficulty with "tender" emotions has serious consequences. First, men's emotional inexpressiveness causes problems in their relationships with partners and children (Levant, 1996). Second, as we saw in Chapter 3, suppressed emotions contribute to many stress-related disorders.

SEXUAL PROBLEMS

Men often experience sexual problems that derive partly from their gender-role socialization, which gives them a "macho" sexual image to live up to. There are few things that men fear more than a sexual encounter in which they are unable to achieve an erection (Doyle, 1989). Unfortunately, these very fears often *cause* the impotence that men dread (see Chapter 13). The upshot is that men's obsession with sexual performance often produces anxiety that may interfere with their sexual responsiveness.

Another problem is that many men learn to confuse feelings of intimacy and sex. In other words, if a man experiences strong feelings of connectedness, he is likely to interpret them as sexual feelings. This confusion has a number of consequences (Kilmartin, 1994). For one thing, sex may be the only way some men can allow themselves to feel intimately connected to

Web Link 10.4

SPSMM (Society for the Psychological Study of Men and Masculinity)

The SPSMM is among the newest divisions of the American Psychological Association. Its site offers an introduction to contemporary psychological approaches to masculinity and a guide to other resources focusing on men and their identity.

another. Thus, men's keen interest in sex may be driven, in part, by strong needs for emotional intimacy that don't get satisfied in other ways. The confusion of intimacy and sex also explains why some men misperceive a woman's friendly touch as a sexual invitation, as we noted in our discussion of date rape. Finally, the sexualization of intimate feelings causes inappropriate anxiety when men feel affection for another man and is related to the problem of homophobia.

Homophobia **is the intense fear and intolerance of homosexuality.** Because homosexuality is still largely unaccepted, fear of being labeled homosexual keeps many people, but especially males, adhering to traditional gender roles who might otherwise be more flexible. One reason that homophobia is more prevalent among males is that the male role is rooted in the fear of appearing feminine—and feminine characteristics are mistakenly associated with gay males (McCreary, 1994; Thompson & Pleck, 1986). Second, homophobia is much more common in men than in women because males feel more pressure to avoid any behavior characteristic of the other gender (Herek, 1988; Levant, 1996). Although they will tolerate "tomboyism" in girls, parents (especially fathers) are highly intolerant of any "sissy" behavior exhibited by their sons. This intense pressure against appearing feminine contributes not only to homophobia among heterosexual males but also to negative attitudes toward females (Friedman, 1989).

Role Expectations for Females

The traditional female role consists of two major expectations (Doyle & Paludi, 1998).

The marriage mandate. "Real women" attain adult status when they get married. In marriage, women are expected to be responsible for housework and cooking. That a large number of lesbians have previously been married indicates the power of the marriage mandate (Chapman & Brannock, 1987).

The motherhood mandate. The imperative of the female role is to have children. This expectation has been termed the "motherhood mandate" by Nancy Felipe Russo (1979). Preferably, a woman should have at least two children, and at least one of them should be a son. Moreover, it is important that she be a "good" mother.

Although women are increasingly opting for jobs and careers, the expectation for a career is still not widespread enough to be called a "mandate" except among African American women (Dickson, 1993). In fact, the traditional female role is incompatible with achievement in traditionally masculine areas (Hyde, 1996).

The marriage and motherhood mandates fuel women's intense focus on *heterosexual success*—learning how to attract and interest males as prospective mates. The resulting emphasis on dating and marriage causes most women to feel ambivalent about a challenging career so as not to drive away a prospective mate who might be threatened by a high-achieving woman. If career opportunities for women continue to open up, increasing numbers of heterosexual women will experience conflicts between family responsibilities and career (a conflict most heterosexual men don't currently face).

Problems with the Female Role

Early writers in the feminist movement generated some compelling analyses of the problems associated with the traditional female role (Friedan, 1964; Millett, 1970). Since then, research has shown that many of these concerns are justified.

DIMINISHED ASPIRATIONS

Despite recent efforts to increase women's opportunities for achievement, young women continue to have lower aspirations than young men with comparable backgrounds and abilities (Mednick & Thomas, 1993). Higher intelligence and grades are generally associated with higher career aspirations, but this trend is less likely to hold true for girls than for boys (Kelly & Cobb, 1991). This discrepancy between women's abilities and their level of achievement has been termed the *ability-achievement gap* (Hyde, 1996). As we noted, the roots of this gap seem to lie in the conflict between achievement and femininity that is built into the traditional female role (Earle & Harris, 1985). Some women worry that they will be seen as unfeminine if they boldly strive for success.

JUGGLING MULTIPLE ROLES

Another problem with the female role is that role expectations and societal institutions have not kept pace with the reality of women's lives. Traditional gender roles dictate that husbands go to work and wives and mothers stay home and take care of the house and children. Today, however, 63% of married women with children under the age of six work outside the home (U.S. Bureau of the Census, 1997). This gap between roles and reality means that women who want to "have it all" experience burdens and conflicts that men do not (Eccles, 1994). That is, men's roles include worker, spouse, and parent with relatively little competition among these roles. This is because men typically have major day-to-day responsibilities in only *one* role (worker), which is also a high-status role. Most women, on the other hand, have day-to-day responsibilities as *both* spouse and parent. Furthermore, when women decide to work, they have major responsibilities in all *three* areas.

It's important to note that multiple roles, themselves, are not the problem. In fact, there is evidence that multiple roles can be beneficial for mental health, as you'll see in Chapter 12. Rather, the problem stems from unequal sharing of role responsibilities (women usually do more work). In addition, some women may experience psychological conflicts related to multiple roles that are fueled by the husband's negative attitudes about his wife's working outside the home or from her own attitudes about working, if she has been reared according to traditional gender roles (Basow, 1992).

Subsidized child-care programs and the equal participation of fathers in child-rearing and household tasks would go a long way toward alleviating women's stress in this area.

AMBIVALENCE ABOUT SEXUALITY

Like men, women may have sexual problems that stem, in part, from their gender-role socialization. For many women, the problem is difficulty in enjoying sex. Why is this? For one thing, girls are taught to suppress or deny their sexual feelings (Crooks & Baur, 1996). For another, they are told that a woman's role in sex is a passive one. In addition, girls are encouraged to focus on romance rather than on gaining sexual experience (Simon & Gagnon, 1977). As a result, many women feel uncomfortable (guilt, shame) about sex. The experience of menstruation (and its association with blood and pain) and the fear of pregnancy add another dimension of negativity to sex. And females' concerns about sexual exploitation and rape also foster negative emotions. Thus, when it comes to sex, women typically carry more "emotional baggage" than men. As a result, they are likely to have ambivalent feelings about sex instead of the largely positive feelings that men have (Hyde, 1996).

Sexism: A Special Problem for Females

Intimately intertwined with the topic of gender roles is the issue of sexism. *Sexism* **is discrimination against people on the basis of their gender.** (Using our terminology, the term should probably be "genderism," but we'll stick with standard terminology for the sake of clarity.) Sexism usually refers to discrimination by men against women. However, sometimes *women* discriminate against other women and sometimes *men* are the victims of gender-based discrimination. In this section, we'll mention two specific problems for women: economic discrimination and aggression toward them.

Economic Discrimination. This type of discrimination usually takes the form of differential access to jobs and differential treatment once on the job. Concerning *job access,* the problem is that women still don't have the same employment opportunities as men. For example, in 1996, only 17% of architects were women and only 26% of physicians and 11% of Congresspersons were women (U.S. Bureau of the Census, 1997). Ethnic minority women were even less likely than white women to work in these occupations. On the other hand, women are over-represented in such "pink-collar ghetto" occupations as secretary and preschool and kindergarten teacher (see Figure 10.10).

The second aspect of economic discrimination is women being *treated differently* on the job. Examples include lower job evaluations for women whose performance is equal to men's (Dobbins, Cardy, & Truxillo, 1986, 1988) and lower salaries for women employed in the same jobs as men (see Figure 10.11 on the next page). There also appears to be a "glass ceiling" that prevents most women and ethnic minorities from advancing beyond middle-management positions (U.S. Department of Labor, 1992).

Aggression Toward Females. Examples of aggression toward girls and women include rape, intimate violence, sexual harassment, sexual abuse, incest, and violent pornography. We've discussed a number of these problems elsewhere, so we'll make only a few points here. *Sexual harassment* is being recognized as a widespread problem that occurs not only on the job but also at home (obscene telephone calls), while walking outside (catcalls and whistles), and in medical and psychotherapy settings. It also takes place in schools and colleges. Figure 10.12 (on the next page) reports the results of a survey on the most common forms of sexual harassment in grades 2 through 12. Teachers and professors who pressure students for sexual favors in

Web Link 10.5

Feminist Majority Foundation
A massive set of resources dealing with issues from a feminist perspective have been brought together here.

exchange for grades have been singled out for strong criticism (Dziech & Weiner, 1990; Riggs, Murrell, & Cutting, 1993). When it comes to *intimate violence*, 4 women are killed every day by men who batter (Walker, 1989). In a nationwide survey of college women on 32 campuses, 32% reported that they had experienced physical aggression from a date or other intimate partner (White & Koss, 1991).

Although there are costs associated with traditional roles for both males and females, sexism causes particularly serious problems in the lives of girls and women. In addition, when prejudice and discrimination prevent talented individuals from making contributions from which all could benefit, society as a whole suffers.

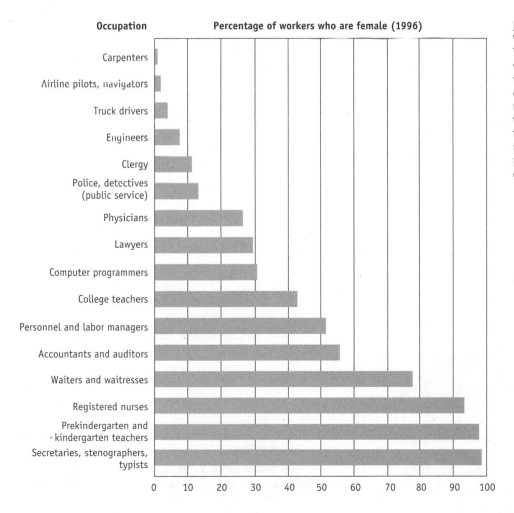

Occupation — **Percentage of workers who are female (1996)**

Carpenters
Airline pilots, navigators
Truck drivers
Engineers
Clergy
Police, detectives (public service)
Physicians
Lawyers
Computer programmers
College teachers
Personnel and labor managers
Accountants and auditors
Waiters and waitresses
Registered nurses
Prekindergarten and kindergarten teachers
Secretaries, stenographers, typists

0 10 20 30 40 50 60 70 80 90 100

FIGURE 10.10.

Women in the world of work. The percentage of women who work outside the home has been increasing steadily over the past century. Nonetheless, women remain underrepresented in many traditionally masculine occupations and overrepresented in many traditionally feminine occupations. (Data from U.S. Bureau of the Census, 1997)

FIGURE 10.11.

FIGURE 10.11.

The gender gap in weekly wages. Women continue to earn less than men in all occupational categories, as these 1996 data for selected occupations make clear. (Data from U.S. Bureau of Labor Statistics, 1997)

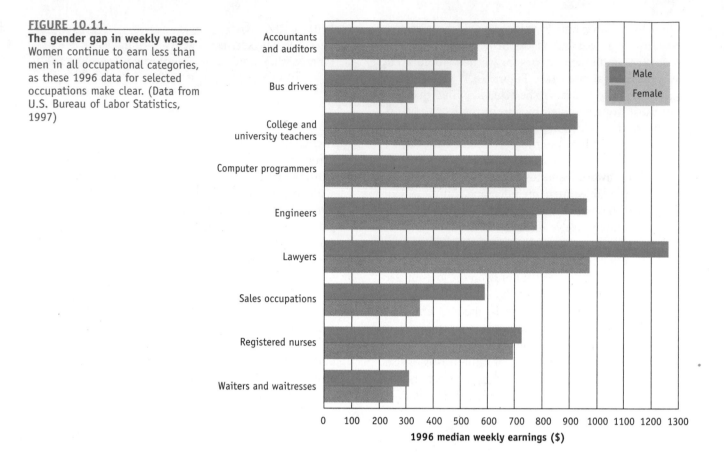

1996 median weekly earnings ($)

FIGURE 10.12.

Reported incidence of sexual harassment in the schools. This figure depicts common forms of sexual harassment in grades 2 through 12 and the percentage of girls reporting them. (Adapted from Stein, Marshall, & Tropp, 1993)

Type of harassment	Percentage reporting
Received suggestive gestures, looks, comments, or jokes	89
Touched, pinched, or grabbed	83
Leaned over or cornered	47
Received sexual notes or pictures	28
Pressured to do something sexual	27
Forced to do something sexual	10
Other form of harassment	7

Note: Percentages do not add to 100 because readers could indicate more than one type of harassment.

Gender in the Past and in the Future

LEARNING OBJECTIVES

● *Explain the basis for traditional gender roles and why they are changing.*

● *Define gender-role identity and discuss two alternatives to traditional gender roles.*

Until now, we have focused largely on *traditional* gender roles and some of the difficulties they tend to generate. In Western society, however, gender roles are in a state of transition. In fact, sweeping changes have already occurred. It's hard to imagine today, but less than 100 years ago, women were not allowed to vote or to manage their own finances. Only a few decades ago, it was virtually unheard of for a woman to initiate a date, manage a corporation, or run for public office. In this section, we'll discuss *why* gender roles are changing and what the future might hold.

Why Are Gender Roles Changing?

Many people are baffled as to why gender roles are changing. They can't understand why age-old traditions are being flouted and discarded. A number of theories attempt to explain why gender roles are in transition. Basically, these theories look at the past to explain the present and the future. A key consideration is that gender roles have always constituted a division of labor. In earlier societies, the division of labor according to gender was a natural outgrowth of some simple realities. In most hunting-and-gathering societies, as well as most herding societies, an economic premium was put on physical strength. Men tend to be stronger physically than women, so they were better equipped to handle such jobs as hunting and farming. In most societies they got those assignments, whereas women were responsible for gathering, home maintenance, and child-rearing (Nielsen, 1990). Another consideration was that women had to assume responsibility for nursing young children. Thus, although people might have worked out other ways of doing things (and some cultures did), there were some basic reasons for dividing labor according to gender in premodern societies.

Today's traditional gender roles are a carryover from the past. Once traditions are established, they have a way of perpetuating themselves. Moreover, males have had a vested interest in maintaining these traditions, since the arrangements made them a privileged class. Over the past century or so in Western society, these divisions of labor have become increasingly antiquated. Therein lies the prime reason for changes in gender roles. *Traditional gender roles no longer make economic sense!* The widespread use of machines to do work has rendered physical strength relatively unimportant. Furthermore, as we move toward a service economy, physical strength is even less relevant.

The future is likely to bring even more dramatic shifts in gender roles. We can see the beginnings of some of these changes now. For example, although women still bear children, nursing responsibilities are now optional. Moreover, as women become more economically independent, they will have less need to get married solely for economic reasons. The possibility of developing a fetus outside the uterus may seem farfetched now, but some experts predict that it is only a matter of time. If so, both men and women could be "mothers."

Traditional gender roles used to be an accepted fact of life. As you have seen, however, there are relatively few differences between males and females. In addition, most of the gender differences that do exist can be traced to differences in socialization. Consequently, social scientists are now more aware of the social and political bases for gender roles (Tavris, 1992). This awareness has focused attention and public debate on the prejudices that underlie unequal treatment of females (and sometimes males). This attention will likely add momentum to the movement toward non-traditional gender roles. It is safe to conclude that gender roles will remain in flux for some time to come.

Alternatives to Traditional Gender Roles

Gender-role identity is a person's identification with the traits regarded as masculine or feminine. Initially, gender-role identity was conceptualized as either "masculine" or "feminine." All males were expected to develop masculine gender-role identities and females, feminine gender-role identities. Individuals who did

not identify with the gender-role expectations for their gender or who identified with the characteristics for the other gender were judged to be few in number and to have psychological problems.

In the 1970s, psychologists began to rethink their ideas about gender-role identity. One assumption that was called into question is that males should be "masculine" and females should be "feminine." For one thing, it appears that the number of people who don't conform to gender-role norms is relatively high, as is the amount of strain that accompanies trying to conform to gender-role stereotypes (Pleck, 1981a, 1995). Also, research suggests that strong identification with traditional gender-role expectations can be problematic. For example, high femininity in females is associated with low self-esteem (Whitley, 1983) and increased psychological distress (Helgeson, 1994). High masculinity in males has been linked to increased Type A behavior (see Chapter 14), poor health care (Helgeson, 1994), greater likelihood of committing physical and sexual aggression in relationships (Mosher, 1991), and psychopathology (Evans & Dinning, 1982). Furthermore, heterosexual couples

● Recommended Reading

The Mismeasure of Woman by Carol Tavris (Simon & Schuster, 1992)

The title and thesis of this book refer to Protagoras's statement that "Man is the measure of all things." Tavris, a social psychologist, has written this book for the nonprofessional audience, and uses her natural wit and humor to excellent advantage. She points out the fallacy of using a male-centered standard for evaluating "what is normal" for both men and women. Using research findings, she exposes numerous myths about men and women that are the source of misunderstanding and frustration for many.

Tavris is not interested in replacing a male-centered view with a female-dominant view but rather in expanding one's view of what it means to be human. She urges readers to move away from the tendency to think in "us-them" terms about gender issues. Instead, she suggests that men and women need to work together and rethink how they need to be in order to have relationships and work that are life enhancing. In the following excerpt, she explains how gender-based attributions of behavior can be triggered by situational factors.

. . . men and women do not have a set of fixed masculine or feminine traits; the qualities and behaviors expected of women and men vary, depending on the situation the person is in. A token woman in a group of men will feel highly aware of her femaleness and so will the group. Almost everything she does will be attributed to her gender, which is why she is likely to be accused of being too feminine (thus not "one of the boys") or too masculine ("trying to be something she's not")—but what's really at issue is her visible difference from the majority. A token man in a group of women will have the comparable experience. [p. 292]

A division of labor based on gender no longer makes economic sense in our society. Relatively few jobs require great physical strength; the rest call for skills possessed by both men and women.

with traditional gender-role identities appear to have unsatisfying relationships when compared to less gender-typed couples (Ickes, 1993). (Problems seem to stem from the masculine emphasis on dominance and low self-disclosure.) Thus, contrary to earlier thinking, the evidence suggests that "masculine" males and "feminine" females are not particularly well-adjusted.

As people have become aware of the costs of traditional gender roles, there has been a lot of debate about moving beyond them. A big question in these discussions has been: What should we move toward? To date, two ideas have received the most attention: (1) androgyny and (2) gender-role transcendence. Let's examine these options.

ANDROGYNY

Like masculinity and femininity, androgyny is a type of gender-role identity. **Androgyny refers to the coexistence of both masculine and feminine personality traits in a single person.** In other words, an androgynous person is one who scores above average on measures of *both* masculinity and femininity.

To help you fully appreciate the nature of androgyny, we need to briefly review other kinds of gender identity (see Figure 10.13). Males who score high on masculinity and low on femininity, and females who score high on femininity and low on masculinity, are said to be

gender-typed. Males who score high on femininity but low on masculinity, and females who score high on masculinity but low on femininity, are said to be *cross-gender-typed.* Finally, males and females who score low on both masculinity and femininity are characterized as *gender-role undifferentiated.*

Keep in mind that we are referring to individuals' descriptions of themselves in terms of personality traits traditionally associated with each gender (dominance, nurturance, and so on). People sometimes confuse gender-role identity with sexual orientation, but they are not the same thing. A person can be homosexual, heterosexual, or bisexual (sexual orientations) and be androgynous, gender-typed, cross-gender-typed, or gender-role undifferentiated (gender-role identities).

In groundbreaking research, Sandra Bem (1975) challenged the then-prevailing view that males who scored high in masculinity and females who scored high in femininity are better adjusted than "masculine" women and "feminine" men. She argued that traditionally masculine men and feminine women feel compelled to adhere to rigid and narrow gender roles that unnecessarily restrict their behavior. In contrast, androgynous individuals ought to be able to function more flexibly. She also advanced the idea that androgynous people are psychologically healthier than those who are gender-typed.

Sandra Bem

What about Bem's ideas? First, androgynous people do seem more flexible than others (Bem, 1975). That is, they can be nurturing ("feminine") or independent ("masculine"), depending on the situation. In contrast, gender-typed males have difficulty behaving nurturantly, while gender-typed females have trouble with independence. Also, individuals whose partners

FIGURE 10.13.

Possible gender-role identities. This diagram summarizes the relations between subjects' scores on measures of masculinity and femininity and four possible gender identities.

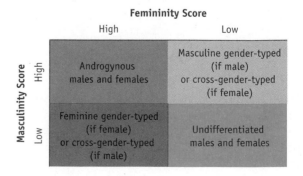

are either androgynous or feminine (but not masculine or undifferentiated) report higher relationship satisfaction (Antill, 1983). This finding holds for cohabiting heterosexuals, as well as for lesbian and gay couples (Kurdek & Schmitt, 1986b). Furthermore, a study of married couples revealed that the happiest couples were those in which both partners were androgynous (Zammichieli, Gilroy, & Sherman, 1988). Thus, in these areas, androgyny seems to be advantageous.

Bem's second assertion (that androgynous people are psychologically healthier than gender-typed individuals) requires a more complicated response. Since 1976, over a hundred studies have been conducted to try to answer this question. Some early studies *did* find a positive correlation between androgyny and mental health. Ultimately, however, the weight of the evidence did not support Bem's hypothesis that androgyny is especially healthy. In fact, several comprehensive surveys of the research reported that *masculine* traits (in either gender) were more strongly associated with psychological health than androgyny was (Hyde & Frost, 1993; Whitley, 1984). (Because most tests of self-esteem measure traits consistent with the male role—achievement and independence, for example—one would expect to find a positive relationship between masculinity and self-esteem [Whitley, 1988b].) These findings, as well as some problems with the concept of androgyny, have led Bem and other psychologists to take a different view of gender roles, as you'll see next.

GENDER-ROLE TRANSCENDENCE

As psychologists thought more about androgyny, they realized that the concept had some problems. For one thing, androgyny requires people to develop both masculine and feminine characteristics, rather than one or the other. Although it can be argued that androgyny is less restrictive than traditional gender roles, it may also lead people to feel that they have two sources of inadequacy to contend with, as opposed to only one (Bem, 1993).

More important, the idea that people should have both masculine and feminine traits reinforces the assumption that gender is an integral part of human behavior (Bem, 1983). In other words, the androgyny perspective presupposes that masculine and feminine traits actually exist within people. Another way of putting it is that our current system sets up self-fulfilling prophecies. That is, if we use gender-based labels ("masculine" and "feminine") to identify certain human characteristics and behavior, then we'll always, but wrongly, associate these traits with one gender or the other.

Many gender theorists maintain that masculinity and femininity are really only arbitrary labels that we have learned to impose on certain traits through societal conditioning. This assertion is the foundation for the *gender-role transcendence* perspective (Bem, 1983, 1993; Spence, 1983). **Gender-role transcendence means that to be fully human, people need to move beyond gender roles as a way of organizing the world and of perceiving themselves and others.** This goal requires that instead of dividing human characteristics into masculine and feminine categories (and then combining them, as the androgyny perspective suggests), we should dispense with the artificially constructed gender categories and labels altogether. How would this work? Instead of the labels "masculine" and "feminine," we would use gender-neutral terms such as "instrumental" and "expressive" to describe personality traits and behaviors. This "decoupling" of traits and gender would eliminate the self-fulfilling prophecy problem.

The advocates of gender-role transcendence argue that this practice would help us break our current habits of "projecting gender into situations irrelevant to genitalia" (Bem, 1985, p. 222) and hasten the advent of a gender-free society. They believe that if gender were to be eliminated (or even reduced) as a means of categorizing traits, each individual's unique capabilities and interests would assume greater importance, and individuals would be more free to develop their own unique potentials.

A Gender-Free Society?

Although many social scientists find the concept of a gender-free society appealing, some social critics are concerned about the decline of traditional gender roles (Davidson, 1988; Gilder, 1986). For instance, George F. Gilder (1986) maintains that conventional gender roles provide a fundamental underpinning for our economic and social order. Furthermore, he asserts that changes in gender roles will damage intimate relationships between women and men and have a devastating impact on family life. Gilder argues that women are needed in the home in their traditional homemaker role to provide for the socialization of the next generation. Without this traditional socialization, he predicts that our moral fabric will decay, leading to an increase in crime, violence, and drug abuse. Given these starkly contrasting projections, it will be most interesting to see what developments unfold in the next few decades.

Meanwhile, in the Application we'll take a look at how gender affects communication styles.

Bridging the Gender Gap in Communication

LEARNING OBJECTIVES

● Describe how the different socialization experiences of males and females contribute to communication problems between men and women.

● Describe expressive and instrumental styles of communication.

● Describe some common mixed-gender communication problems.

Answer the following questions "true" or "false."

_____ 1. Men talk much more than women in mixed-gender groups.

_____ 2. Women are more likely to ask for help than men.

_____ 3. Women are more willing to initiate confrontations in relationships than men.

_____ 4. Men talk more about nonpersonal issues with their friends than women do.

If you answered "true" to all of these statements, you were correct. They are just some of the observed differences in communication styles between males and females. While not characteristic of all men and women or of all mixed-gender conversations, these style differences appear to be the source of many misunderstandings between the genders.

When confronted with one of these distressing encounters in their personal or work relationships, people often attribute them to the other person's individual quirks or "failings." Instead, it seems that some of these frustrating experiences may result from gender differences in style. That is, men and women learn to speak different "languages" in social interactions, but don't realize it. In this Application, we'll explore the nature of these gender-based style differences, how they develop, and how they can contribute to interpersonal conflicts. We'll also offer some suggestions for dealing more effectively with these style differences.

The Clash of Two "Cultures"

According to sociolinguist Deborah Tannen (1990), males and females are typically socialized in different "cultures." That is, males are likely to learn a language of "status and independence," while females learn a language of "connection and intimacy" (p. 42). Tannen likens male/female communications to other "cross-cultural" communications—full of opportunities for misunderstandings to develop.

These differences in communication styles develop in childhood and are fostered by traditional gender stereotypes and the socializing influences of parents,

teachers, media, and childhood social interactions—usually with same-gender peers. As we noted earlier, boys play in larger groups, usually outdoors, and farther away from home than girls (Feiring & Lewis, 1987). Thus, boys are less under the scrutiny of adults and are therefore more likely to engage in activities that encourage exploration and independence. Also, boys' groups are often hierarchically organized (structured in terms of high- and low-status roles).

Deborah Tannen

Boys achieve high status in their groups by engaging in dominant behavior (telling others what to do and enforcing compliance). The games that boys play often result in winners and losers, and boys frequently bid for dominance by interrupting each other, calling each other names, boasting to each other about their abilities, and refusing to cooperate with each other (Maltz & Borker, 1983).

In contrast, girls usually play in small groups or in pairs, often indoors, and gain high status through popularity—the key to which is intimacy with peers. Many of the games girls play do not have winners or losers. And, while it is true that girls vary in abilities and skills, to call attention to oneself as better than others is frowned upon. Girls are likely to express their wishes as suggestions rather than as demands or orders (Maltz & Borker, 1983). Similarly, dominance is gained by verbal persuasion rather than by the direct bids for power characteristic of boys' social interactions (Charlesworth & Dzur, 1987). These two cultures shape the functions of speech in different ways. According to Eleanor Maccoby (1990), among boys, "speech serves largely egoistic functions and is used to establish and protect an individual's turf. Among girls, conversation is a more socially binding process" (p. 516).

These different styles carry over into adult social interactions. According to Tannen, because of different socialization experiences, many males learn to see the social world as hierarchical. To maintain independence and avoid failure (in their own eyes and in the eyes of other men), they have to jockey for high status. Hence, she says, men tend to approach conversations as "negotiations in which people try to achieve and maintain the upper hand if they can and protect themselves from others' attempts to put them down and push them around" (p. 25). Females, on the other hand, learn to see the social order as a community in which individuals are connected to others and one where the task is to preserve these connections. Consequently, women tend to approach conversations as "negotiations for closeness in which people try to seek and give confirmation and support, and to reach consensus. They try to

protect themselves from others' attempts to push them away" (p. 25). These different views of the social order are the root of the oft-heard complaint, "You just don't understand"—the title of Tannen's book (see the Recommended Reading above).

Instrumental and Expressive Styles

While not true of all men and women, there is evidence that men are more likely to use an "instrumental" style of communication and women, an "expressive" one (Block, 1973; Tannen, 1990). Interestingly, this gender difference has been found across a number of cultures (D'Andrade, 1966). **An *instrumental style* focuses on reaching practical goals and finding solutions to problems; an *expressive style* is characterized by being able to express tender emotions easily and being sensitive to the feelings of others.** (Obviously, many individuals use both styles, depending on the situation.)

As we mentioned, men tend to use instrumental communication styles more often than women. For example, research has shown that, in conflict situations, husbands are more likely to stay calm and problem-oriented (Gottman et al., 1979) and to make more efforts to find compromise solutions to problems (Rausch et al., 1974). However, an instrumental style can have a "darker" side. When the instrumental behav-

ior of calmness changes to coldness and unresponsiveness, it becomes negative. Research has shown that this emotional unresponsiveness is characteristic of many men and that it seems to figure importantly in marital dissatisfaction (Kilmartin, 1994).

A large number of studies indicate that women, on the average, are more skilled than men in *nonverbal* communication—a key component of the expressive style. For example, they are better at reading and sending nonverbal messages (J. A., Hall, 1990). Regarding verbal communication, women are better listeners (Miller, Berg, & Archer, 1983) and better at consoling individuals in emotional distress (Burleson, 1982). On the other hand, besides the already mentioned "positive" behaviors associated with the expressive style, women have been found to engage in some "negative" expressive behaviors as well (Brehm, 1992). For example, research has shown that, during relationship conflicts, women are more likely to (1) display strong negative emotions (Noller, 1985, 1987); (2) use psychologically coercive tactics (guilt, verbal attack, power plays) (Barnes & Buss, 1985); (3) reject attempts at reconciliation (Barnes & Buss, 1985); and (4) send double messages (such as making a negative verbal statement while smiling) (Noller, 1985, 1987). Women's greater use of such tactics may be attributable to their greater interest in changing relationships (Christensen & Heavey, 1990).

The idea that there are "two cultures" founded on gender-based communication styles has intuitive appeal because it confirms people's stereotypes and reduces complex issues to simple explanations. But, there's an important caveat here. As we have often noted, research shows that status and power differences sometimes lurk behind what seem to be gender differences. That is, because power and biological gender are often linked (males typically have more status; females have less), and because biological gender is a more visible factor than status, people often attribute behavioral differences to gender rather than to power. Also, there are individual differences in preferred styles: Some women prefer the "male style," and some men prefer the "female style"; many use either style, depending on the situation. Therefore, we caution you not to reduce *all* communication problems between males and females to "two cultures" and gender-based style differences.

Common Mixed-Gender Communication Problems

In this section, we'll briefly review some common mixed-gender communication problems noted by Tannen. To keep things simple, we'll use "she" and "he" to illustrate various scenarios, but you should interpret these labels loosely for the reasons mentioned above.

MISMATCHES

People expect their friends and partners to support and reassure them. When a mismatch occurs between their expectations and reality, they become confused and frustrated. Sometimes individuals are hurt or angry as well. Consider a woman who tells her partner about a recurring problem she is having at work because she wants some sympathy. Thinking that she is seeking a solution to the problem, he gives her advice. Not receiving the consolation she seeks, she believes he doesn't care. He, for his part, is frustrated about her repeated complaining, because after all he has offered her the same advice in the past. In this scenario, neither wants to frustrate the other, but that's exactly what happens because they are talking at cross-purposes. She wants him to commiserate with her, but he thinks she wants him to help her solve a problem. Each assumes the other knows what each wants, and neither does. These mismatches crop up quite frequently between couples.

RAPPORT TALK AND REPORT TALK

Tannen suggests that most women engage in *rapport talk* (displaying similarities and matching experiences with others), whereas many men seem to be more comfortable with *report talk* (exhibiting knowledge and skill to get and keep the attention of others). Also, men and women often have different ideas about what is important to talk about. She wants to talk about the personal details of her life and her feelings. He wants to talk about activities—things they do together or politics or sports. In this situation, his failure to talk about personal things confirms her worst expectations (the relationship is falling apart). He fears that if he says anything about emotions that might be fleeting—especially negative ones—they'll get blown out of proportion and create a problem where one doesn't exist. Again, these differences are rooted in childhood experiences.

TALKING ABOUT PEOPLE VERSUS THINGS

Women's conversations frequently involve sharing the details of their personal lives or "talking *about* people." It's important to understand that "talking about people" isn't necessarily destructive (although it can be if it turns into "talking *against* people"). As they did in childhood, women share secrets with one another as a way of being close. Men are interested in details, too, but those of a different kind: politics, news, and sports. Women fear being left out by not knowing what is going on in friends' lives; men fear being left out by not knowing what is going on in the world. Interestingly, Tannen notes that exchanging information about public events (men's style) has an advantage over sharing private information (women's style): It doesn't make men personally vulnerable.

Tannen suggests that frustrations can be reduced if men and women understand how their style differences operate here. That is, men need to understand why many women like to talk about the details of their personal lives, and women need to understand that most men don't have this need. In addition, she says that both women and men need to extend their communication strategies by adding aspects of the other style to their own. Thus, some men may need to learn to be more comfortable talking about their personal lives, whereas some women could benefit by talking more about impersonal topics and talking in a more assertive manner.

LECTURING AND LISTENING

In many mixed-gender conversations, particularly those in public settings, women often end up playing the listener to the man's "lecture." Although this fact illustrates that women often don't get the same attention as men, Tannen suggests that we look more closely here. How does this situation come about? Are men self-centered big-mouths? Are women meek, passive creatures? Instead of these interpretations, Tannen suggests that men and women are playing different games that are rooted in childhood experiences. Men are playing "Do you respect me?" and women, "Do you like me?"

As we noted, boys and men use words to jockey for status and challenge the authority of others—both men and women. Women who lack experience defending themselves against these challenges can easily misinterpret an assertive man's style as an attack on her credibility. Similarly, women have been taught to "hand off" the conversational ball and expect that others will do the same. While most women reciprocate, many men don't. When this happens, some women may feel awkward drawing the focus of the conversation back to themselves, because this style was frowned on during their childhood play with other girls.

To improve this kind of mixed-gender communication problem, Tannen suggests that women who tire of listening need to be more assertive and take some control of the conversation. Also, some men might be relieved to learn that they don't always have to talk. As you saw in Chapter 7, effective listening is a much-underrated communication skill.

THE WOMAN'S DOUBLE-BIND

According to Tannen, mixed-gender communication situations often place women at a disadvantage because the "male style" of communication is likely to predominate. If this were the only consideration, it wouldn't present much of a difficulty for women—they would just need to be proficient in the "male style." The problem arises because the male style is used as the norm against which both women's and men's speech is evaluated (recall androcentrism). This fact means that a woman will be evaluated negatively regardless of which style (male or female) she adopts. The female style is devalued, and a woman using a male style is also evaluated negatively. Women in positions of authority experience a special version of this double-bind. According to Tannen, "If they speak in ways expected of women, they are seen as inadequate leaders. If they speak in ways expected of leaders, they are seen as inadequate women" (p. 244).

Research supports this contention. When women failed to offer support for their arguments or used tag questions, subjects judged them to be less intelligent and less knowledgeable than men who behaved in an identical manner (Bradley, 1981). Similarly, students judged female professors as incompetent when they generated classroom discussion but did not negatively evaluate male professors who did the same thing (Macke, Richardson, & Cook, 1980).

Toward a "Shared Language"

Tannen asserts that many frustrations in personal and work relationships could be avoided if men and women were more aware of gender-based differences in communication styles. Many people misperceive style differences as the other's personal failings. If individuals could see the style differences for what they are, they could eliminate a lot of blaming and negative feelings. As Tannen says, "Nothing hurts more than being told your intentions are bad when you know they are good, or being told that you are doing something wrong when you know you're just doing it your way" (pp. 297–298). People need to understand that there are different ways of listening, talking, and of having conversations, not just their own way. For some hints on how to improve gender-based communication, see Figure 10.14.

FIGURE 10.14

Hints to improve communication. To have productive personal and work relationships in today's world demands that people be knowledgeable about gender and communication styles. Males and females may be able to benefit from the suggestions listed here. (Compiled by the authors based on insights from Tannen, 1990)

Hints for Men	Hints for Women
1. Notice whether or not you have a tendency to interrupt women. If you do, work on breaking this habit. When you catch yourself interrupting, say, "I'm sorry, I interrupted you. Go ahead with what you were saying."	**1.** When others interrupt you, politely but firmly redirect the conversation back to you. You can say, for example, "Excuse me, I haven't finished my point."
2. Avoid responding to a woman's questions in monosyllables ("Yep," "Nope," "Uh-huh"). Give her more details about what you did and explain why.	**2.** Look the person you're talking with directly in the eye.
3. Learn the art of conversational give and take. Ask women questions about themselves. And listen carefully when they respond.	**3.** A lower-pitched voice gets more attention and respect than a higher-pitched one, which is associated with little girls. Keeping your abdominal muscles firm as you speak will help keep your voice low.
4. Don't order women around. For example, don't say, "Get me the newspaper." First, notice whether it might be an inconvenience for her to do something for you. If it isn't, say, "Would you mind giving me the newspaper?" or "Would you please give me the newspaper?" If she's busy, get it yourself!	**4.** Learn to be comfortable claiming more space (without becoming a space hog). If you want your presence to be noted, don't fold yourself up into an unobtrusive object.
5. Don't be a space hog. Be more aware of the space you take up when you sit with others (especially women). Watch that you don't make women feel crowded out.	**5.** Talk more about yourself and your accomplishments. This isn't offensive as long as others are doing the same and the circumstances are appropriate. If the conversation turns to photography and you know a lot about the topic, it's perfectly OK to share your expertise.
6. Learn to open up about personal issues. Talk about your feelings, interests, hopes, and relationships. Talking about personal things helps others know who you are (and probably helps you clarify your self-perceptions, too).	**6.** Make a point of being aware of current events so you'll be knowledgeable about what others are discussing and have an opinion to contribute.
7. Learn to convey enthusiasm about things in addition to the victories of your favorite sports teams.	**7.** Resist the impulse to be overly apologetic. Although many women say "I'm sorry" to convey sympathy or concern (not apology), these words are likely to be interpreted as an apology. Because apologizing puts one in a lower-power position, women who use apologetic words inappropriately put themselves at a disadvantage.
8. Don't be afraid to ask for help if you need it.	

Key Ideas

GENDER STEREOTYPES

● Many stereotypes have developed around behavioral differences between the genders, although the distinctions between the male and female stereotypes are less rigid than they used to be. Gender stereotypes may vary depending on ethnicity, and they typically favor males.

GENDER SIMILARITIES AND DIFFERENCES

● There are no gender differences in general intelligence. When it comes to verbal ability, gender differences are small, and they generally favor females. Gender differences in mathematical ability are typically small as well, and they favor males. Males perform better than females on mental rotation tasks, an aspect of spatial ability.

● Research shows that males are typically more self-confident and more physically aggressive than females. Males have more permissive attitudes about casual sex and are more sexually active than females. Women seem to conform to group pressure a little more than men. They also talk less than males do and display more tentativeness in their speech. Women are more sensitive to nonverbal cues. The genders are similar in overall mental health, but they differ in prevalence rates for specific psychological disorders.

● All in all, the gender differences that do exist are quite small. Moreover, they are group differences that tell us little about individuals. Nonetheless, some people still believe that psychological differences between the genders are larger. Social role theory and social constructionism provide two explanations for this phenomenon.

BIOLOGICAL ORIGINS OF GENDER DIFFERENCES

● Biological explanations of gender differences include those based on evolution, brain organization, and hormones. Evolutionary psychologists explain gender differences on the basis of their evolutionary value. These analyses are speculative and difficult to test empirically.

● Regarding brain organization, some studies suggest that males exhibit more cerebral specialization than females. However, linking this finding to gender differences in cognitive abilities is questionable for a number of reasons.

● Efforts to tie hormone levels to gender differences have also been troubled by interpretive problems. Nonetheless, there probably is some hormonal basis for gender differences in aggression and some aspects of sexual behavior. Most experts believe that socialization plays a more important role than biology in most behavioral disparities between the genders.

ENVIRONMENTAL ORIGINS OF GENDER DIFFERENCES

● The socialization of gender roles appears to take place through the processes of (1) reinforcement and punishment, (2) observational learning, and (3) self-socialization. These processes operate through many social institutions, but parents, peers, schools, and the media are the primary sources of gender-role socialization.

TRADITIONAL GENDER ROLES

● The five elements of the traditional male role include the antifeminine element, the success element, the aggressive element, the sexual element, and the self-reliant element.

Problems associated with the traditional male role include excessive pressure to succeed, difficulty dealing with emotions, and sexual problems. Homophobia is a particular problem for men.

● The traditional role expectations for females include the "motherhood mandate" and the "marriage mandate." Among the principal costs of the traditional female role are diminished aspirations, juggling of multiple roles, and ambivalence about sexuality. In addition to these psychological problems, women also face sexist hurdles in the economic domain and may be victims of aggression.

GENDER IN THE PAST AND IN THE FUTURE

● Gender roles have always represented a division of labor. They are changing today, and they seem likely to continue changing because they no longer mesh with economic reality. Consequently, an important question is how to move beyond traditional gender roles. The perspectives of androgyny and gender-role transcendence provide two possible answers to this question.

APPLICATION: BRIDGING THE GENDER GAP IN COMMUNICATION

● Because of different socialization experiences, males and females usually learn different communication styles. These differences in experience and style seem to underlie a number of mixed-gender communication problems. Men and women need to understand these style differences to reduce interpersonal conflicts and the frustrations they cause.

● Men are more likely to use an instrumental style of communication, whereas women tend toward an expressive style. Common mixed-gender communication problems include mismatches in expectations, disparities in the tendency to engage in rapport-talk versus report-talk, differences in the tendency to talk about people versus things, falling into the lecture and listen trap, and the double-bind that women are often placed in.

Key Terms

Aggression	Gender-role tran-	Sexism
Androcentrism	scendence	Social construc-
Androgyny	Gender roles	tionism
Cerebral	Gender	Social role
hemispheres	stereotypes	theory
Conformity	Homophobia	Socialization
Expressive style	Hormones	
Gender	Instrumental	
Gender-role	style	
identity	Meta-analysis	

Key People

Sandra Bem	Joseph Pleck
Alice Eagly	Deborah Tannen
Janet Shibley Hyde	

Practice Test

1. Taken as a whole, gender differences in verbal ability are
   a. small and favor females.
   b. large and favor females.
   c. nonexistent.
   d. small and favor males.

2. The most compelling evidence for gender differences in cognitive ability is found in
   a. verbal ability.
   b. mathematical ability.
   c. spatial ability.
   d. all of the above.

3. Which of the following statements about gender differences is *false*?
   a. Males are more self-confident than females.
   b. Males are more physically aggressive than females.
   c. Females are more likely to yield to group pressure.
   d. Women talk more than men.

4. Of the three biologically based explanations for gender differences, which has the strongest support?
   a. Evolutionary theory
   b. Brain organization
   c. Hormonal influences
   d. Social constructionism

5. When children watch others and then imitate them, what is taking place?
   a. Self-socialization
   b. Observational learning
   c. Operant conditioning
   d. Androcentric bias

6. Two areas in which parents emphasize "gender-appropriate" behavior are
   a. dress and household chores.
   b. play activities and household chores.
   c. play activities and career choices.
   d. dress and career choices.

7. Which of the following statements about peer socialization is *true*?
   a. Male peer groups help provide information about the male role.
   b. Boys play in smaller groups and girls in larger groups.
   c. High status in boys' groups is achieved by making suggestions to others.
   d. Peers have relatively little impact on gender-role socialization.

8. Which of the following is *not* a problem with the male role?
   a. Pressure to succeed
   b. Emotional inexpressiveness
   c. Sexual problems
   d. Androgyny

9. Which of the following is *not* a problem with the female role?
   a. Social constructionism
   b. Diminished aspirations
   c. Juggling multiple roles
   d. Ambivalence about sexuality

10. According to Deborah Tannen, exhibiting knowledge and skill to get and keep the attention of others is _____, whereas displaying similarities and matching experiences with others is
    _____.
    a. rapport talk; report talk
    b. report talk; rapport talk
    c. self-talk; other-talk
    d. other-talk; self-talk

Answers

1. a page 281
2. c page 282
3. d page 283
4. c pages 285–288
5. b page 289
6. b pages 289–290
7. a page 291
8. d pages 293–295
9. a page 296
10. b page 304

INFOTRAC COLLEGE EDITION

Go to the Wadsworth Psychology Study Center (http://psychology. wadsworth.com/) for quiz questions, research updates, hot topics, interactive exercises, and suggested readings in INFOTRAC related to this chapter.

CHAPTER 11

Development in Adolescence and Adulthood

"My mother always complains that I spend too much time on the telephone. She thinks that I'm just gossiping with my friends and feels that my time would be better spent studying. She can't seem to understand that my friends and I help each other through some pretty rough situations. She thinks that way because she doesn't believe that anything a teenager does besides homework is important. My Mom tells me to learn in school, but she doesn't realize that I'm actually trying to learn to survive school. Attending school is like a tryout for life. I know that it sounds silly to adults, but at times getting a date, being invited to a certain party, or being chosen to work on the school's newspaper can mean more than getting an A on a test." —"Tracy," quoted in Teenagers Talk About School (Landau, 1988, p. 31)

Do Tracy's—or her mother's—complaints sound familiar? Have you ever been frustrated by your parents' or your child's inability to understand your point of view? Psychologists attribute these contrasting perspectives to differences in development. In the above scenario, Tracy and her mother are at different levels of development in a number of areas: physical, cognitive, personality, and social. Thus, they have different perspectives on themselves and the world.

Until the 1970s, it was widely assumed that psychological development slowed to a crawl as people reached adulthood. Now, however, psychologists realize that important developmental changes continue throughout adult life. As a result, they are probing into these changes to identify crucial patterns and trends. In this chapter, we'll review the major changes that take place during adolescence and adulthood. We'll also examine the topics of dying and death. In the Application, we'll offer some suggestions for effective parenting.

The Transition of Adolescence

LEARNING OBJECTIVES

- Define and discuss pubescence and secondary sex characteristics.
- Define and discuss puberty and primary sex characteristics.
- Summarize the findings on early and late maturation in boys and girls.
- Describe the cognitive changes that occur during adolescence.
- Explain Erikson's psychosocial crisis of adolescence and Marcia's four identity statuses.

- Discuss whether adolescence is a period of emotional turmoil.
- Summarize recent trends in adolescent suicide.

Adolescence is a transitional period between childhood and adulthood. Its age boundaries are not exact, but in our society adolescence begins at around age 13 and ends at about age 22. In some ways, adolescents resemble the children they were, yet the many changes they undergo during this stage ensure that they will be different from children in many respects. Similarly, we see glimpses of the adults that adolescents will become, but more often we observe that they don't behave much like adults. As adolescents mature, we see fewer resemblances to children and more similarities to adults.

Although most societies have at least a brief period of adolescence, this phenomenon is *not* universal across cultures (Schlegel & Barry, 1991). In some cultures, young people move directly from childhood to adulthood. A protracted period of adolescence is seen primarily in industrialized nations. In these societies, rapid technological progress has made lengthy education, and therefore prolonged economic dependence, the norm. Thus, in our own culture, junior high school, high school, and college students often have a "marginal" status. They are capable of reproduction and so are physiologically mature, yet they have not achieved the emotional and economic independence from their parents that are the hallmarks of adulthood.

As they mature, adolescents look increasingly like adults, although boys typically lag two years behind girls in physical development.

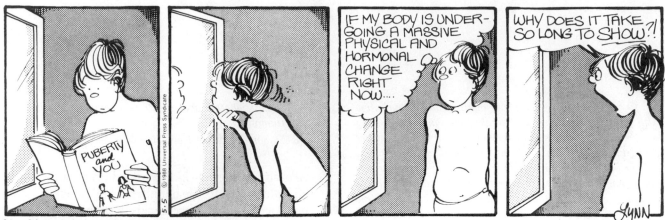

© Lynn Johnston Productions Inc./Distributed by United Feature Syndicate, Inc.

Let's begin our discussion of adolescent development with its most visible aspect: the physical changes that transform the body of a child into that of an adult.

Physical Changes

Do you remember your junior high school days when your body grew so fast that your clothes just couldn't "keep up"? This phase of rapid growth in height and weight is called the *adolescent growth spurt*—"spurt" because of the relatively sudden increases in body height and weight. Brought on by hormonal changes, It typically starts at about age 11 in girls and about two years later in boys (Malina, 1990). (Technically, this spurt should be called the *pre*adolescent growth spurt because it actually occurs *prior* to puberty, which is generally recognized as the beginning of adolescence.)

Psychologists use the term *pubescence* to describe the two-year span preceding puberty during which the changes leading to physical and sexual maturity take place. Besides growing taller and heavier during pubescence, children begin to take on the physical features that characterize adults of their respective genders. These bodily changes are termed *secondary sex characteristics*—physical features that distinguish one gender from the other but that are not essential for reproduction. For example, boys go through a voice change, develop facial hair, and experience greater skeletal and muscle growth in the upper torso, leading to broader shoulders and enhanced upper body strength. Females experience breast growth and a widening of the pelvic bones, plus increased fat deposits in this area, resulting in wider hips (Litt & Vaughan, 1992). Figure 11.1 details these physical changes in boys and girls.

The physical changes we've been describing are triggered by the pituitary gland. This "master gland" of the endocrine system sends signals to the adrenal glands (on top of the kidneys) and gonads (ovaries and testes), which in turn secrete the hormones responsible for the changes in physical characteristics that differentiate males and females.

Note that the capacity to reproduce is not attained in pubescence. This ability develops during *puberty,* **the stage that marks the beginning of adolescence and during which sexual functions reach maturity.** During puberty, the *primary sex characteristics*—**the structures necessary for reproduction**—develop fully. In the male, these structures include the testes, penis, and related internal structures; in females, they include the ovaries, vagina, uterus, and other internal reproductive structures (see Figure 11.1).

In females, the onset of puberty is typically signaled by *menarche*—**the first occurrence of menstruation.** American girls typically reach menarche at about age 13, with further sexual maturation continuing until approximately age 16 (Malina, 1990). Most girls are sterile for 12 to 18 months following menarche. (Pregnancy is a possibility for *some* girls at this age, so any girl who has begun to menstruate should assume that she can become pregnant.) Breast development and the presence of pubic hair serve as important social criteria of adolescence for girls in the absence of visible external genitals.

In males, there is no clear-cut marker of the onset of sexual maturity, although the capacity to ejaculate is used as an index of puberty (the onset of sperm production not being a visible event). The first ejaculation usually occurs through masturbation, rather than nocturnal emissions (Hyde, 1994). (In the latter, also called "wet dreams," ejaculation occurs during sleep and is sometimes accompanied by erotic dreams.) Experts note that ejaculation may not be a valid index of actual maturity, as early ejaculations may contain seminal fluid but not active sperm. American boys begin to produce sperm and ejaculate between ages 12 and 14, with complete sexual maturation occurring at about 18 (Brooks-Gunn & Reiter, 1990; Tanner, 1978).

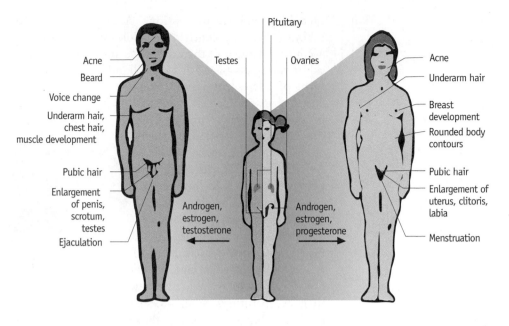

FIGURE 11.1.
Physical development during pubescence and puberty. During pubescence, the two years prior to puberty, a growth spurt occurs and secondary sex characteristics develop. During puberty, the primary sex characteristics mature. These various physical changes are caused by hormonal secretions.

Acne
Beard
Voice change
Underarm hair, chest hair, muscle development
Pubic hair
Enlargement of penis, scrotum, testes
Ejaculation
Testes
Pituitary
Ovaries
Androgen, estrogen, testosterone
Androgen, estrogen, progesterone
Acne
Underarm hair
Breast development
Rounded body contours
Pubic hair
Enlargement of uterus, clitoris, labia
Menstruation

As we have noted, puberty arrives about two years later in boys than in girls. Indeed, the major reason that adult males are taller than adult females is that males typically experience two additional years of development before the onset of the growth spurt (Brooks-Gunn & Reiter, 1990). Interestingly, *a secular trend*—generational changes in the timing of puberty—has been observed, at least in industrialized countries (Chumlea, 1982). That is, today's adolescents begin puberty earlier, and complete it more rapidly, than their counterparts in earlier generations. This trend apparently reflects improvements in nutrition and medical care. In the United States and some other industrialized countries, this trend appears to have leveled off, probably because of the high standard of living. Thus, the onset of sexual maturation may have a genetically predetermined age "floor."

Puberty also brings important changes in other body organs. For instance, the heart and lungs increase considerably in size, and the heart rate drops. These changes are more marked for boys than for girls and are responsible, in part, for the superior performance of males in certain physical activities relative to females. Before about age 12, boys and girls are similar in physical strength, speed, and endurance. After puberty, boys have clear advantage in all three areas (Smoll & Schutz, 1990).

After sexual maturation has been attained, adolescents continue to mature physically until their secondary sex characteristics are fully developed and their body has reached adult height and proportions. In girls, such growth continues until about 17 years of age; in boys, it goes on until about age 20 (Brooks-Gunn & Reiter, 1990).

Variation in the onset of pubescence and puberty is normal. Still, the timing of these physical changes

figures importantly in adjustment. More specifically, research suggests that girls who mature early and boys who mature late seem to feel particularly anxious and self-conscious about their changing bodies (Siegel, 1982). The early-maturing girl is taller and heavier than most of the girls and nearly all of the boys her age. The late-maturing boy is shorter and slighter than most of the boys and nearly all of the girls his age. To make matters worse, both groups have body types that are at odds with the cultural ideals of extreme slenderness for females and muscular physique for males.

Research has shown that early maturation in girls is correlated with poorer school performance, earlier experience of intercourse, and more unwanted pregnancies (Stattin & Magnusson, 1990). They also have more negative body images (Petersen, 1988) and are more likely to be depressed (Rierdan & Koff, 1991). Late-maturing boys have been found to feel more inadequate, to feel more insecure, and to think less of themselves than other boys do (Siegel, 1982). Optimal adjustment for girls is associated with puberty coming "on time," whereas optimal adjustment for boys is related to puberty arriving early. Also, girls' and boys' *perceptions* of the timing of their puberty and their feelings of attractiveness follow this same pattern (see Figure 11.2 on the next page).

Web Link 11.1

Adolescence Directory Online
Browsers will find guides to resources that cover many of the health, mental health, safety, personal, and parenting issues important to adolescence. This site is sponsored by the University of Indiana Center for Adolescence Studies.

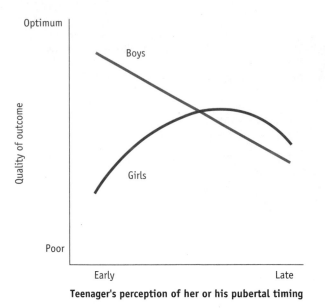

FIGURE 11.2.

Perceived timing of puberty and optimal adjustment. For girls, feelings of attractiveness and a positive body image are associated with the perception that puberty arrives "on time"; for boys, these feelings are associated with the perception that puberty arrives early. (Adapted from Tobin-Richards, Boxer, & Petersen, 1983)

Cognitive Changes

Around the time of early adolescence, major changes take place in thinking and problem solving (Keating, 1990). Compared to those who are younger, adolescents can think abstractly (not merely concretely) and more efficiently. They also become more self-aware and self-reflective and can view problems from several perspectives rather than only one. Thus, the thinking of adolescents is qualitatively different from that of younger children. Whereas children go about solving problems on a trial-and-error basis, most adolescents are capable of solving problems by generating a number of possible hypotheses and systematically testing these.

One of the significant outcomes of these cognitive changes is that adolescents are freed from the cognitive limitations of concrete reality. This means that they can apply their logical skills to such abstract concepts as love, justice, and truth and can contemplate heady social and political issues that would never occur to a younger child. The ability to engage in abstract thinking also frees adolescents from existing solely in the present. This newly developed ability to conceive of future events is one reason they spend so much time fantasizing, planning, and worrying about their lives-to-be.

A particularly interesting aspect of cognitive development is egocentrism. Jean Piaget, an early theorist of cognitive development, used the term **egocentrism to refer to the tendency to view reality in line with one's**

own idiosyncratic perceptions. According to David Elkind (1988), egocentrism in adolescence appears to account for much of the experience and behavior typical of young people of this age. Elkind aptly labels one form of adolescent egocentrism the *imaginary audience*. Because adolescents are so focused on themselves, they wrongly assume that they are the center of others' attention as well. Hence, adolescents often act as if they are performing for an audience. Examples of the imaginary audience at work include adolescents' excessive self-consciousness (both unwarranted self-criticism or self-admiration) and their fantasies about how others will react to the news of their death (others recall—too late of course—what a good person they really were).

David Elkind

A second form of adolescent egocentrism is the *personal fable*. In this case, adolescents believe that they are unique and, therefore, that others (especially parents) can't comprehend their special experiences. Familiar examples of the personal fable come readily to mind: the ecstasy of one's first romantic love experience (no one else has ever loved as deeply) and the utter devastation of one's first "breakup" (no one else has ever suffered so much).

Elkind suggests that much of the high-risk behavior of some adolescents is a result of the personal fable. For example, the high incidence of injury and death by accident in this group is likely based in adolescents' belief that they are immortal (even though others are not). Also, the high incidence of pregnancy that results from the failure to use birth control probably reflects the personal fable that "other girls can get pregnant, but not me."

Egocentrism seems to disappear as adolescents learn more about others through social interactions and intimate relationships characterized by mutual self-disclosure. That is, when individuals learn that others often have views that differ from their own, they replace the imaginary audience with a more realistic sense of the beliefs of others. Similarly, the ideas of the personal fable are eventually overcome as adolescents come to see that their own experiences are not so different from those of others (Lapsley et al., 1988).

Personality Changes

Adolescents are faced with a number of challenges in the realm of personality. They must grapple with identity questions, cope with changes in gender-role expectations, and deal with the stresses of moving from childhood to adulthood.

FIGURE 11.3.
Overview of Erikson's stages. Building on earlier work by Freud, Erik Erikson (1963) divided the life span into eight stages. Each stage involves a psychosocial crisis (column 2) that is played out in certain social relationships (column 3). If a crisis is handled effectively, the outcome is favorable (column 4).

Erikson's Stages of Psychosocial Development

Stage	Psychosocial crisis	Significant social relationships	Favorable outcome
1. First year of life	Trust versus mistrust	Mother or mother substitute	Trust and optimism
2. Second and third years	Autonomy versus doubt	Parents	A sense of self-control and adequacy
3. Fourth through sixth years	Initiative versus guilt	Basic family	Purpose and direction; ability to initiate one's own activities
4. Age 6 through puberty	Industry versus inferiority	Neighborhood school	Competence in intellectual, social, and physical skills
5. Adolescence	Identity versus diffusion	Peer groups and outgroups; models of leadership	An integrated image of oneself as a unique person
6. Early adulthood	Intimacy versus isolation	Partners in friendship and sex; competition, cooperation	An ability to form close and lasting relationships, to make career commitments
7. Middle adulthood	Generativity versus stagnation	Divided labor and shared household	Concern for family, society, and future generations
8. The aging years	Integrity versus despair	"Humankind," "my kind"	A sense of fulfillment and satisfaction with one's life; willingness to face death

THE SEARCH FOR IDENTITY

Erik Erikson (1963) devised a theory of personality development that views adolescence as a period of pivotal importance. (Figure 11.3 depicts all eight of Erikson's stages, although we will focus on only the last four in this chapter.) According to Erikson (1968), the premiere challenge of adolescence is developing a clear sense of identity. Doing so involves wrestling with such important issues as "Who am I?" "What do I stand for?" and "What kind of work do I want to do?" Gender, ethnicity, and sexual orientation are also important aspects of identity development.

As we explained in Chapter 5, it has been hypothesized that the psychosocial crisis of adolescence has four possible outcomes instead of just the two shown in Figure 11.3. Each of these "identity statuses" represents a different way of dealing with the identity crisis. *Foreclosure* is a premature commitment to visions, values, and roles prescribed by one's parents (identity crisis bypassed). *Moratorium* involves delaying commitment for a while to experiment with alternative ideologies (currently experiencing identity crisis). *Identity diffusion* is an inability to make identity commitments (unresolved identity crisis). Finally, *identity achievement* is arriving at a sense of self and direction after some consideration of alternative possibilities (resolved identity crisis).

A sense of identity usually evolves gradually as a result of innumerable daily decisions: whether to date a particular person, to take a particular course, to use drugs, to become sexually active, to become politically involved, to go to college, and so forth. At the end of this period of questioning (identity crisis), adolescents typically feel committed to an occupational direction and a system of values they can embrace as their own (Marcia, 1991). Certain parenting styles are associated with different identity statuses, as you'll see in the Application. Nonetheless, as they formulate their identity, adolescents gradually achieve psychological distance from their parents, becoming autonomous individuals with their own consciously chosen values and goals.

Erik Erikson

Although the struggle for a sense of identity neither begins nor ends in adolescence, it does tend to be especially intense during this period. Why? First, the physical changes of puberty force adolescents to revise their self-image and confront their sexuality. Second, the advent of formal operations promotes self-reflection. Third, faced with the end of mandatory schooling, adolescents must contemplate occupational choices and make decisions about their future.

Erikson and many other theorists believe that identity achievement is a cornerstone of sound psychological health. Identity diffusion can interfere with important developmental transitions that should unfold during the adult years.

TIME OF TURMOIL?

Is adolescence a period of emotional upheaval and turmoil? G. Stanley Hall (1904), one of the first psychologists to study adolescence, thought so. In fact, he specifically characterized adolescence as a period of "storm and stress." Hall attributed this turmoil to the conflicts between the physical changes of puberty and society's demands for social and emotional maturity.

Does research support the idea that adolescence is a period especially marked by emotional turbulence? There is evidence that adolescents do seem to experience more stress and more negative emotions than younger children (Larson & Asmussen, 1991; Larson & Ham, 1993). There is also a modest increase in parent-adolescent conflict (Eccles et al., 1993). Still, parent-adolescent relations are not as difficult or contentious as advertised (Lerner & Galambos, 1998). On the whole, the evidence indicates that a majority of teenagers make it through adolescence without any more turmoil than an individual is likely to encounter in other periods of life. Based on her extensive studies of adolescents, Anne Petersen (1987) has concluded, "The adolescent's journey toward adulthood is inherently marked by change and upheaval, but need not be fraught with chaos or deep pain" (p. 34).

No doubt because of popular expectations that the adolescent period will be filled with "storm and stress," many parents, teachers, and counselors view the onset of the teenage years with anxiety and dread. Young people, caught up in their own experiences and lacking a broader perspective, may perceive their conflicts and frustrations as an indication of serious psychological disturbance rather than as normal responses to adolescent transitions.

As young people progress through adolescence, the differences between the vast majority who can cope with the transition to adulthood and the small minority who cannot become increasingly obvious. Symptoms of those in the latter group include depression, suicidal behavior, drug and alcohol abuse, and chronic delinquency (Petersen, 1988; Takanishi, 1993). Because the incidence of such problems is relatively low, they should be given attention when they do appear (Petersen, 1988). Well-intentioned adults make a serious mistake by passing off problems as "normal adolescent turmoil" that will be "outgrown." Early professional attention in such cases can often forestall more serious difficulties.

Although the number of adolescents with serious problems remains relatively small, recent years have seen an alarming increase in the incidence of some of these psychological and social problems. For example, homicide accounts for 33% of the deaths among 15- to 19-year-old African American males and is the leading cause of death in this group (Millstein & Litt, 1990). Youth who live in poor, high-density metropolitan areas are most at risk. Still, the recent school shootings at Denver's Columbine High and elsewhere show that suburban youth are not free from risk. In the next section, we'll look at the problem of adolescent suicidal behavior.

Adolescent Suicide

Recent years have seen a surge in adolescent suicide. This trend is apparent in Figure 11.4a, which shows that suicide among 15- to 24-year-olds has increased dramatically since 1960, whereas it rose only slightly in the general population during this time. Despite these increases, only a small minority of adolescents commit suicide (Meehan et al., 1992). Figure 11.4b plots suicide rates as a function of age. Here you can see that, even with this steep increase, the incidence of suicide in the 15-24 age group is about the same or lower than that for any older age group.

FIGURE 11.4.

Adolescent suicide. (a) In recent decades the suicide rate for adolescents and young adults (ages 15–24) has increased far more than the suicide rate for the population as a whole. (b) Nonetheless, the suicide rate for this age group remains relatively low in comparison to that for other age groups. (Data from *Monthly Vital Statistics Report*, October 23, 1995)

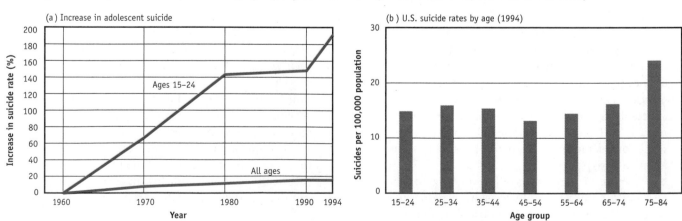

Actually, the suicide crisis among teenagers involves *attempted suicide* more than *completed* suicide. Experts estimate that when all age groups are lumped together, suicide attempts outnumber actual suicidal deaths by a ratio of about 8 to 1 (Cross & Hirschfeld, 1986). However, the ratio of attempted to completed suicides among adolescents is much higher than for any other age group: anywhere from 50:1 to 200:1 (Garland & Zigler, 1993). According to David Curran (1987), suicide attempts by adolescents tend to be a "communicative gesture designed to elicit caring" (p. 12). Put another way, they are desperate cries for attention, help, and support.

What drives an adolescent to such a dramatic, but dangerous, gesture? Research suggests that the "typical" suicidal adolescent has a long history of stress and personal problems extending back into childhood (de Wilde et al., 1992). Unfortunately, for some teenagers these problems—conflicts with parents, difficulties in school, problems with girlfriends and boyfriends—escalate during adolescence. As their efforts to cope with these problems fail, many teenagers rebel against parental authority, withdraw from social relationships, and make dramatic gestures such as running away from home. These actions often lead to progressive social isolation.

For a person who feels socially isolated, a pressing problem with great emotional impact can precipitate an attempted suicide. The problem—a poor grade in school, not being allowed to go somewhere or buy something special—may seem trivial to an objective observer. It may nevertheless serve as the final thread in a tapestry of frustration and distress.

The Expanse of Adulthood

LEARNING OBJECTIVES

- Explain Erikson's psychosocial crises of young, middle, and late adulthood.
- Summarize the key developmental transitions in early adulthood.
- Summarize the key developmental transitions in middle adulthood.
- Summarize the key developmental transitions in late adulthood.

As people progress through adulthood, they periodically ask themselves, "How am I doing for my age?" In pondering this question, they are likely to be influenced by their social clocks. A *social clock* is a person's notion of a developmental schedule that specifies what he or she should have accomplished by certain points in life. For example, if you feel that you should be married

by the time you're 30, that belief creates a marker on your social clock. Although social clocks are very much a product of socialization, they do show individual variations.

Social clocks can exert considerable influence over decisions concerning education, career moves, marriage, parenting, and other life choices. Adhering to a social clock based on prevalent age norms brings social approval and is thus a way to evaluate one's own development. Important life events that come too early or too late according to one's social clock produce more stress than transitions that occur "on time" (Chiriboga, 1987). It is easy to imagine how an early marriage, delayed career promotion, or premature retirement might be especially stressful. In particular, it seems that lagging behind one's personal schedule for certain achievements results in psychological distress (Rook, Catalano, & Dooley, 1989). In short, most people listen carefully to their social clocks ticking in the background as they proceed through adulthood. With this thought in mind, let's explore development in adulthood.

Erikson's View of Adulthood

Erik Erickson's (1963) theory offers some clues about the nature of personality changes people can expect during the adult years. Recall that each of Erikson's eight stages is characterized by a psychosocial crisis involving transitions in social relationships (see Figure 11.3).

STAGE SIX: INTIMACY VERSUS ISOLATION

During young adulthood, Erikson's sixth stage, the psychosocial crisis centers on whether a person can develop the capacity to share intimacy with others. Erikson was not concerned simply with the young adult's need to find a marriage partner. Rather, he was concerned with more subtle issues, such as whether one can learn to open up to others, truly commit to others, and give of oneself unselfishly. The person who can experience genuine intimacy is thought to be more likely to develop a mature and successful long-term relationship. Failure to resolve this psychosocial crisis

Web Link 11.2

Erik Erikson Tutorial Homepage
Profesor Margaret Anderson, who teaches at Cortland College in New York, has developed a set of tutorials on major figures of importance to educational psychology. Her Erik Erikson tutorial includes a summary of his eight stages of development, biographical details, discussion of some controversies regarding his theories, and links to other online sources.

favorably leads to difficulties in relating to others in a genuine fashion. The resulting sense of isolation can foster competitive interactions with friends and troublesome committed relationships.

Jacob Orlofsky and his colleagues (1973) found support for five different intimacy statuses, based on the quality of a person's relationships with others:

Intimate. Individuals in this status are capable of forming open and close relationships with both male and female friends and are involved in a committed relationship.

Preintimate. Although people in this category are capable of mature, reciprocal relationships, they haven't yet experienced a committed relationship because they are ambivalent about making commitments.

Stereotyped. Men and women in this status have relationships that are superficial and not very close. They often see others as objects to manipulate rather than to share with.

Pseudointimate. These individuals are typically involved in a relatively permanent relationship, but it resembles the stereotyped relationship in quality.

Isolate. Isolates avoid social situations and appear to be loners whose social interactions consist of casual conversations with a few acquaintances.

According to Erikson, the ability to establish and maintain intimate relationships depends on having successfully weathered the identity crisis of adolescence. In line with this prediction, at least one study has found that identity precedes intimacy rather than vice versa (Dyk & Adams, 1990). Also, researchers have found that college males and females in the more advanced identity statuses (achievement and moratorium) are most likely to be in the more advanced intimacy statuses (intimate and preintimate) (Fitch & Adams, 1983). Similarly, foreclosures and diffusions are predominantly in the less advanced intimacy statuses (stereotyped, pseudointimate, and isolate). A similar pattern has been found in adults up to 35 years of age (Raskin, 1986; Tesch & Whitbourne, 1982).

Additional support for Erikson's hypothesis comes from a study on identity status and marriage, with an interesting gender difference (Kahn et al., 1985). This study found that men who had achieved a stable sense of identity were more likely to be married earlier than those who had not done so. Also, those men who had not achieved a stable sense of identity tended to remain single. In contrast, women's likelihood of marrying was not affected by their identity status. This is no doubt because women experience stronger pressure to marry (recall our discussion of the "marriage mandate" in Chapter 10). However, women who lacked a strong sense of identity were more likely to experience marital breakups. Thus, this study showed that a stable sense of identity is related to men's *entering* committed relationships and to women's *remaining* in them.

STAGE SEVEN: GENERATIVITY VERSUS STAGNATION

Next up, in middle adulthood, is the challenge of acquiring generativity, or a concern for the welfare of future generations. Adults demonstrate generativity when they provide unselfish guidance to younger people. The recipients of this guidance are often one's own children, but not necessarily. For example, a middle-aged college professor may gain great satisfaction from working with students. Or a 50-year-old attorney might take on the role of "mentor" for a younger woman in her law firm. Thus, generativity and its opposite, stagnation, do not hinge on whether a person has children. Stagnation is characterized by self-absorption and self-indulgent preoccupation with one's own needs.

STAGE EIGHT: INTEGRITY VERSUS DESPAIR

During the retirement years—Erikson's last stage—the challenge is to achieve ego integrity. People who achieve integrity are able to look back on their lives with a sense of satisfaction and to find meaning and purpose there. The opposite, despair, is the tendency to dwell on the mistakes of the past, bemoan paths not chosen, and contemplate with bitterness the approach of death. Erikson suggests that it is better to face the future in a spirit of acceptance than to wallow in regret and resentment.

To test aspects of Erikson's theory, researchers studied male and female adults over a 20-year span (Whitbourne et al., 1992). By using a complex research design, the authors were able to demonstrate support for several of Erikson's propositions. For example, they found that psychosocial development proceeds in an orderly sequence of stages and that favorable resolutions of earlier stages lead to favorable resolutions of later stages.

Erikson's theory provides a useful and relatively accurate view of the key psychosocial issues confronting adults. Still, a single stage theory can't possibly characterize everyone's experiences. Furthermore, each of Erikson's three stages of adulthood offers additional developmental challenges. We'll address these major personal and social transitions next.

Early Adulthood (From About Age 20 to 40)

Between the ages of about 20 and 30, adults must learn a number of new and important roles. Take Jack, for

● Recommended Reading

Necessary Losses: The Loves, Dependencies and Impossible Expectations That All of Us Have to Give Up in Order to Grow by Judith Viorst (Ballantine/Fawcett gold medal, 1986)

Author Judith Viorst views personal loss as an inevitable fact of life. And, although loss is painful and often depressing, she strongly believes that unavoidable losses can help us grow. For Viorst, loss encompasses a much broader range of experiences than the traditional loss of loved ones through death. She discusses losses as a result of leaving and being left; changing, letting go, and moving on; and giving up romantic dreams, impossible expectations, and illusions of freedom, power, and safety. She also addresses the loss of one's own younger self, the self one always believed would be unwrinkled, invulnerable, and immortal.

The author is a popular writer who has had a number of years of psychoanalytic training and experience as a therapist. In keeping with this background, she emphasizes the role of past experiences and unconscious forces in shaping lives. She, like Freud, believes that becoming aware of these forces can help people become more self-directing. In writing this book, she wants to help readers understand how losses and growth are intricately intertwined as well as how readers have reacted to their own losses. She believes that this experience will enable readers to increase their self-awareness, which in turn will foster important personal growth. In the following excerpt, Viorst examines the experience of loss in marriage.

. . . the contrast between the marriage we wanted and the marriage we got spans more than romantic and sexual disappointment. For even when we marry with an earthier vision of what a good marriage should be, the married state—and the person with whom we are sharing it—may fail to meet some, sometimes all, of our expectations: That we will always be there for each other. That we will always be faithful and loyal to each other. That we will accept each other's imperfections. That we will never consciously hurt each other. That although we expect to disagree on many minor matters, we surely will be in agreement on major matters. That we will be open and honest with each other. That we will always go to bat for each other. That our marriage will be our sanctuary, our refuge, our "haven in a heartless world."

Not necessarily. Certainly, not all the time. [p. 210]

example: He graduated from college at age 22, then left his family and moved to Atlanta to start work as a management trainee. Shortly thereafter, he got involved in a serious relationship (which later broke up). Then, at age 25, Jack got engaged and married; at 26, he changed jobs; and at age 28, he and his wife had their first child. It's easy to see why the years from 20 to 30 have been described as "demographically dense," referring to the fact that more role changes occur during this period than any other (Rindfuss, 1991). For some, early adulthood is additionally stressful because it is a time for

sorting out sexual orientation. As we discuss in Chapter 13, gay males and lesbians take longer than heterosexuals to recognize their sexual orientation (Garnets & Kimmel, 1991).

To cope successfully with all these developmental challenges, young adults must have developed certain psychological and social competencies, including a set of personal values to guide their life decisions and enough self-control to reach their goals. In addition, they must have a sense of the kind of work they want to do, the job skills necessary for the position they want, and social skills by which to develop and maintain relationships at work and with friends and partners or mates. Also, most young adults are still struggling to become fully independent of their parents.

ADJUSTING TO THE WORLD OF WORK

Young adults are confronted with major challenges in their work lives (Super, 1957, 1985, 1988). To start, individuals need to complete their schooling and secure their first job. At this point in career development, many people are still only tentatively committed to their chosen occupational area. If their first experiences are not rewarding, they may shift to another area, where they continue to explore their work options. Ideally, people are able to find work that is gratifying. When that happens, they typically commit to an occupational area. Once individuals make a commitment to a particular kind of work, their future job moves usually take place within this area. During early adulthood, workers learn new skills and develop work attitudes that affect their job success. On the average, people in their twenties change jobs every two years (Seligman, 1994).

ADJUSTING TO MARRIAGE AND FAMILY LIFE

At the same time that young adults are launching their careers, most are beginning committed relationships. As noted in Chapter 9, the first few years of married life tend to be very happy (Aron & Henkemeyer, 1995; Tucker & Aron, 1993). The early years of committed gay and lesbian relationships also follow this pattern (Kurdek & Schmitt, 1988). Although an increasing number of people are choosing not to have children, the vast majority of married couples plan to do so. Still, the arrival of the first child represents a major transition. Postpartum depression can be a problem for new mothers, especially those who have to shoulder the major burden of infant care (Kalmuss, Davidson, & Cushman, 1992). In dual-earner families, women typically bear greater responsibilities in the realms of child-care and housework. Thus, mothers experience more work-family conflicts than fathers do (Higgins, Duxbury, & Irving, 1992). After the youngest child enters school, some women decide to return to school. Other major life events—a divorce, widowhood, job loss—can also trigger such a decision (Bradburn, Moen, & Dempster-McClain, 1995). After the arrival of children, marital satisfaction typically declines and continues to be low until middle adulthood, when it rises again (Tucker & Aron, 1993).

Middle Adulthood (From About Age 40 to 65)

Compared to early adulthood, which requires learning so many new roles, middle adulthood is an easier period. Nonetheless, middle adulthood has its share of challenges.

CONFRONTING THE AGING PROCESS

Chief among the challenges of middle adulthood is coming to terms with the aging process. Middle-aged adults notice a number of physical transformations: changes in vision that often require glasses or bifocals for reading, the onset of wrinkles and sagging skin, and more bodily aches and pains and general "creakiness." In addition, people are forced to acknowledge their mortality as they witness the deaths of parents, colleagues, and friends.

TRANSITIONS IN THE PARENTING ROLE

As children grow up, parental influence tends to decline, and the early years of parenting—which once seemed so difficult—are often recalled with fondness. When children reach adolescence and seek to establish their own identities, gradual realignment occurs in parent-child relationships. As we saw earlier in this chapter, parent-adolescent relations generally are not as bitter or contentious as widely assumed. Nonetheless, conflicts over values are common, and power struggles frequently ensue (Silverberg, Tennenbaum, & Jacob, 1992). When conflict does occur, mothers are often more adversely affected than fathers (Steinberg & Silverberg, 1987). This may be because women's self-esteem tends to be more closely tied to the quality of their family relationships.

Ironically, although recent studies have shown that adolescence is not as turbulent or difficult for youngsters as once believed, their parents *are* stressed out. Parents overwhelmingly rate adolescence as the most difficult stage of child-rearing (Gecas & Seff, 1990). Still, on balance, most parents seem to have little regret about their decision to have children and rate parenthood as a positive experience (Demo, 1992). A related challenge for most middle-aged adults is learning the grandparent role. In addition, some individuals (typically women) may assume responsibility for the care of their aging parents and relatives.

Although "emptying of the nest" is widely believed to be a traumatic event for parents, especially mothers, few seem to experience it as such (Birchler, 1992; Levinson, 1985). The postparental period often provides couples with new freedom to devote attention to each other. Many couples take advantage of this opportunity by traveling or developing new leisure interests. As offspring strike out on their own, couples' marital satisfaction tends to start climbing to higher levels once again (Brubaker, 1990). It tends to remain fairly high until one of the spouses (usually the husband) dies.

TRANSITIONS IN THE WORK ROLE

At midlife, workers seem to follow one of two patterns (Papalia & Olds, 1995). Those in the *stable career pattern* are at the peak of their careers. They have more responsibility, earn more money, and wield more influence than their younger co-workers. Some workers in this group continue to work at a frantic pace, struggling to accomplish their goals as they hear their social clocks ticking. Others seem content with their work achievements and begin to shift some of their attention and energy to family and leisure activities.

Workers in the *changing careers pattern* comprise a more varied group. Whereas all are seeking to begin a different type of work, their reasons for doing so may be quite different. Some are looking for a new line of work because they have been forced out of a job by cutbacks. Others are seeking new careers because they want new work challenges at this time in their lives. A third group is composed of women who are entering or reentering the workforce because family concerns now occupy less of their time and energy.

IS THERE A MIDLIFE CRISIS?

Much has been made about whether most people go through a *midlife crisis*. Two influential studies of adult development in the 1970s both concluded that a midlife crisis is a normal transition experienced by a majority of people. Daniel Levinson and his colleagues (1978) found that most of their subjects (all men) went through a midlife crisis around the ages of 40 to 45. This transition was marked by reappraisal of one's life and emotional turmoil. Roger Gould (1978) found that people tended to go through a midlife crisis between the ages of 35 and 45. His subjects reported feeling pressed by time. They heard their social clocks ticking loudly as they struggled to achieve their life goals.

Since the landmark studies of Levinson and Gould, many other researchers have questioned whether the midlife crisis is a normal developmental transition. A host of studies have failed to detect an increase in emotional turbulence at midlife (Baruch, 1984; Eisler & Ragsdale, 1992; Roberts & Newton, 1987). How can this discrepancy be explained? Levinson and Gould both depended primarily on interview and case study methods to gather their data. As we noted in Chapter 2, when knitting together impressionistic case studies, it is easy for investigators to see what they expect to see. Given that the midlife crisis has long been a part of developmental folklore, Levinson and Gould may have interpreted their case study data in this light (McCrae & Costa, 1984). In any case, investigators relying on more objective measures of emotional stability have found signs of midlife crises in only a tiny minority (2%–5%) of subjects (Chiriboga, 1989; McCrae & Costa, 1990). Thus, it's clear that the fabled midlife crisis is not universal, and it probably isn't even typical.

Of course, this doesn't mean that people don't make major changes in midlife. Nearly everyone knows someone who has embarked on a new career or committed relationship during middle age. Nonetheless, researchers find that such changes in direction are more often caused by unexpected events (divorce, job transfers, serious illness) than by midlife events such as menopause or becoming a grandparent (Baruch, 1984).

Late Adulthood (After Age 65)

Late adulthood also has its share of developmental transitions. These challanges include adjusting to retirement, adapting to changes in one's support network, coping with health problems, and confronting death.

RETIREMENT

As retirement looms near, people prepare to leave the workplace. Although 65 is the age typically associated with retirement, today individuals are leaving the workplace earlier (Clark, 1988). More men and women retire between the ages of 60 and 65 than later. This decrease in the age of retirement is occurring both in the United States and in other industrialized countries (Inkeles & Usui, 1989).

Individuals approach retirement with highly variable attitudes (Atchley, 1991). Chief concerns include having adequate retirement income and being able to fill the hours previously devoted to paid work. Happily, many studies have shown that retirement has no adverse effect on overall health or life satisfaction (Bossé, Spiro, & Kressin, 1996). Retirement can pose a problem, however, for those whose incomes are inadequate or who are forced to leave work because of ill health, mandatory retirement policies, or job elimination (Herzog, House, & Morgan, 1991). Retirement can also be stressful if it comes at the same time as other life changes, such as widowhood (Stull & Hatch, 1984). Although retirement may result in decreased income, it also provides more time for travel, hobbies, meaningful volunteer work, and friends (Cutler & Hendricks, 1990). Retirees who make the best adjustment have an adequate income and an extended social network of friends and family. In addition, they were satisfied with life before retirement and are healthy, active, and better educated than less-adjusted retirees (Palmore et al., 1985).

CHANGES IN SUPPORT NETWORKS

As we noted, relationship satisfaction starts rising later in life and remains fairly high until one of the spouses or partners dies. In addition, most older adults maintain their ties to their children and grandchildren. In one large study of over 11,000 adults aged 65 and over, 63% of the participants reported that they saw at least one of their children once a week or more often, and another 16% saw a child one to three times a month. Only 20% indicated that they saw their children once a month or less (Crimmins & Ingegneri, 1990). Surprisingly, elderly parents who see their children regularly or who report positive interactions with them don't describe themselves as happier than those who see their children less often or who have less positive relationships with their offspring (Seccombe, 1987; Markides & Krause, 1985).

Older adults report that siblings become more important than they were earlier and play an important role in adjustment at this age, but this finding appears to be limited to sisters (Cicirelli, 1989). A few studies have explored this issue in ethnic minority families. This research indicates that Hispanics have extensive family relationships, with frequent visiting and exchanges not only with the immediate family but also with grandparents and cousins (Keefe, 1984). There is also evidence that Italian American and African American siblings have closer relationships than siblings from nonethnic families, although the number of these intimate relationships appears to be relatively small (Gold, 1990; Johnson, 1982).

For older adults, friendships provide companionship and opportunities for shared activities.

Friends seem to play a more significant role in life satisfaction for older adults than family members do, at least for most white Americans. This situation is especially true for those who are unmarried, but it also holds true to some degree for those who are still married (Antonucci, 1990; Lee & Shehan, 1989). Friendships provide companionship, as well as opportunities for sharing activities and reflecting on common experiences. The gender differences in friendships we noted in Chapter 8 continue throughout adulthood. Thus, older men may have a larger network of friends than women do, but women's friendships are more intimate (Wright, 1989). Men rely heavily on their wives for emotional support, whereas women derive support from children and friends, along with their spouse (Antonucci & Akiyama, 1987). This difference in social support appears to place husbands at higher risk than wives for health and adjustment problems when a spouse dies.

For African American elders, *fictive kin* are an important component of social support networks. In these relationships, certain neighbors or peers acquire the status of a close family member and render mutual aid and support (Taylor et al., 1990). Also, for elderly African Americans, participation in church activities plays a central role in psychological adjustment (Bryant & Rakowski, 1992).

Other significant challenges for older adults include coping with health problems, dealing with the deaths of friends and partners, and confronting one's own mortality. We'll address these issues in the last two sections of the chapter.

Aging: A Gradual Process

LEARNING OBJECTIVES

- Discuss age-related changes in appearance and their psychological significance.
- Describe the sensory and neurological changes that accompany aging.
- Describe the endocrine changes that accompany aging.
- Discuss health changes as people age and two things people can do to maintain health.
- Describe age-related changes in intelligence and memory.
- Discuss age-related changes in learning and problem solving.
- Summarize evidence on personality change and stability in adulthood.

As an alternative to the ages-and-stages approach to adult development, many psychologists have simply set out to identify changes in physical, cognitive, and personality functioning that occur across the expanse of adulthood. Whereas some of these age-related developments are quite obvious, others are very subtle. In either case, the changes take place gradually.

Physical Changes

The physical changes that occur in adulthood affect appearance, the nervous system, vision and hearing, hormone functioning, and health. Unless we indicate otherwise, the following summary of trends is based on the work of Susan Krauss Whitbourne (1996), a leading researcher in adult psychology and aging.

CHANGES IN APPEARANCE

Height is stable in adulthood, although it does tend to decline by an inch or so after age 55, as the spinal column "settles." Weight is more variable and tends to increase in most adults up through the mid-50s, when a gradual decline typically begins. Although weight often goes down late in life, the percentage of body weight that is fat tends to increase throughout adulthood, much to the chagrin of many. The skin of the face and body tends to wrinkle and sag. The appearance of the face may change, as the nose and ears tend to become longer and wider, and the jaw appears to shrink. Hair tends to thin out and become gray in both genders, and many males have to confront receding hairlines and baldness.

The net impact of these changes is that many older people view themselves as less attractive. This unfortunate reality is probably aggravated by the media's obsession with youthful attractiveness. Older women suffer more than older men as a result of the decline in physical attractiveness. For example, one study showed that attractiveness ratings declined with age when the subject was a woman, but not when the subject was a man (Mathes et al., 1985). Some refer to this phenomenon as a "double standard" of aging (Bell, 1989). That is, because much of a woman's worth is determined by her physical attractiveness to men, her social status declines along with her attractiveness. In contrast, older men don't have to rely on their looks for social status; instead, they can use their occupational achievements and money.

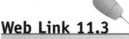

Web Link 11.3

SeniorNet
Research on Internet use has demonstrated an increasingly significant presence by older adults online. Perhaps some of that presence has been aided by this excellent site, which links seniors (age 50 and up) to technology and many age-related resources, especially discussion groups and educational opportunities.

CHANGES IN VISION AND HEARING

The proportion of people with 20/20 vision declines steadily as age increases. From about age 30 to the mid-60s, most people become increasingly farsighted. After the mid-60s, the trend is toward greater nearsightedness. Older people commonly have difficulty adapting to darkness, experience poor recovery from glare, and have reduced peripheral vision. Depth perception begins to decline in the mid-40s. These changes in vision may be responsible for accidents in and outside the home, but they most seriously affect driving ability (particularly at night). Drivers over 65 have a high proportion of accidents, which are typically caused by failing to obey traffic signs, not yielding the right of way, and making improper turns, rather than speeding (Kline et al., 1992).

Noticeable hearing losses do not usually show up until people reach their 50s. Whereas the vast majority of the elderly require corrective treatment for visual losses, only about a third of older adults suffer hearing losses that require corrective treatment. In addition, small sensory losses in touch, taste, and smell have been detected, usually after age 50. These losses generally have little impact on day-to-day functioning, although older people often complain that their food is somewhat tasteless. In contrast, visual and hearing losses often make interpersonal interaction more awkward and difficult, thus promoting social withdrawal in some.

NEUROLOGICAL CHANGES

The nervous system is composed of **neurons, individual cells that receive, integrate, and transmit information.** The number of active neurons in the brain declines steadily during adulthood. As neurons die, the brain decreases in both weight and volume, especially after age 50. Although this progressive neuronal loss sounds alarming, it is a normal part of the aging process. Its functional significance is the subject of some debate, but it doesn't appear to contribute to any of the age-related dementias. **Dementia is an abnormal condition marked by multiple cognitive deficits that include memory impairment.** Dementia can be caused by quite a variety of disorders, such as Alzheimer's disease, Parkinson's disease, and AIDS, to name just a few. Because some of these diseases are more prevalent in older adults, dementia is seen in about 15% of people over age 65 (Elias, Elias, & Elias, 1990). However, it is important to emphasize that dementia and "senility" are not part of the normal aging process. As Cavanaugh (1993) notes, "The term *senility* has no valid medical or psychological meaning, and its continued use simply perpetuates the myth that drastic mental decline is a product of normal aging" (p. 85).

Although the precise causes of Alzheimer's disease are not yet known, it is associated with changes in brain

The spotlight fell on Alzheimer's disease when former President Ronald Reagan announced that he was suffering from the condition.

chemistry (Albert & Moss, 1992) and structure (Hyman, et al., 1984). Alzheimer's disease is a vicious affliction that can strike during middle age (40–65) or later in life (after 65). The disease is one of progressive deterioration, ending in death, and it may take from one to 10 years to run its course. Tragically, there is not yet a cure for the disease.

The beginnings of Alzheimer's disease are so subtle that they are difficult to detect (Biegel, Sales, & Schulz, 1991). Individuals often forget common words, may report reduced energy, and may lose their temper. Later, obvious problems begin to emerge, including difficulties in speaking, comprehending, and performing complicated tasks. Individuals don't seem to have trouble with familiar activities.

From this point, profound memory loss develops, especially for recent events. For example, patients may forget the time, date, current season of the year, and where they are. They may also fail to recognize familiar people, something particularly devastating to family and friends. Sometimes, they experience hallucinations, delusions, and paranoid thoughts. Later, victims become completely disoriented and lose control of bladder and bowel functions (Biegel et al., 1991). At this point, they are unable to care for themselves at all. The disease is eventually fatal.

HORMONAL CHANGES

Although age-related changes occur in hormonal functioning, their significance is not well understood. They do *not* appear to be the chief cause of declining sexual activity during the later years. Rather, this decline reflects the acceptance of social norms that older people don't have sexual desires and that sexual activity in the elderly is "inappropriate." For women, decreased sexual activity may simply reflect lack of opportunity, since the proportion of widows increases dramatically with age. The vast majority of older adults remain physically capable of engaging in rewarding sexual encounters right on through their 70s, although arousal tends to be somewhat slower and less intense.

Among women, menopause is a rather dramatic transition that typically occurs in the early 50s. ***Menopause* is the time when menstruation ceases.** Not so long ago, menopause was almost universally associated with severe emotional strain. However, it is now clear that women's reactions to menopause vary greatly, depending on their expectations (Matthews, 1992). Most women suffer little psychological distress (McKinlay, McKinlay, & Brambilla, 1987). Episodes of moderate physical discomfort ("hot flashes" and "night sweats") during the transitional phase are fairly common but are typically no more troublesome than menstruation itself. The loss of fertility that accompanies menopause is not usually traumatic, since it comes at an age when few women would realistically plan to have more children. Women who experience emotional distress more often attribute their distress to a perceived loss of physical attractiveness than to a loss of reproductive capacity.

Although the idea of a "male menopause," has generated much discussion in recent years, there really is no equivalent experience among men. Significant endocrine changes do occur in males in their later years, but these changes are gradual and are largely unrelated to physical or psychological distress.

CHANGES IN HEALTH STATUS

The quality of health diminishes with increasing age. There are many reasons for this trend. Vital organ systems lose some of their functional capacity. Vulnerability to some diseases (such as heart disease) increases with age. For other diseases (such as pneumonia), the vulnerability may remain unchanged, but their effects may be more serious. In any case, there is a clear trend in the direction of declining health. The proportion of people with a chronic health problem climbs steadily with age. As you can see in Figure 11.5, common chronic health problems among those over 65 are arthritis, heart conditions, hypertension, and hearing impairment. Women over 65 have a 1 in 5 chance of breaking a hip (Brody, 1992).

Factors such as lifestyle differences and access to and affordability of health care obviously play an important role in maintaining good health. Among the elderly, the affluent have better health than the poor, and whites are healthier than African Americans (Gelfand, 1994). The health of elderly Hispanics seems to fall between that of whites and African Americans. Native Americans fare the worst.

Only a few elderly Americans live in nursing homes at any one time, although these numbers do increase with age. That is, only about 2% of individuals aged 65 to 74 live in nursing homes, whereas 22% of those over 85 do so (U.S. Bureau of the Census, 1992). However, with "the graying of America" due to the aging of the baby boomer generation, the number of elderly individuals needing nursing home care is expected to soar (Kunkel & Appelbaum, 1992). Nursing home use varies across ethnic groups, typically because of the availability of family members to care for the frail elderly (Doty, 1992). For instance, African American and Asian American families are more likely to care for the elderly at home than white families are.

Although it's a given that everyone ages, there are a few things people can do to improve their health regardless of age. For one thing, those who exercise tend to be healthier and live longer than those who do not (Rakowski & Mor, 1992). Regular exercise during adulthood has been shown to protect against hypertension, heart disease, and osteoporosis (Hill, Storandt, & Malley, 1993). Because exercise increases the strength and flexibility of joints and muscles, it also reduces the chance of injuries. Regular exercise also seems to play a role in ameliorating anxiety and mild depression (Blumenthal et al., 1991). Eating a healthy diet is

FIGURE 11.5.

Chronic health problems in those over age 65. Although most people over age 65 are in good health, they suffer from a number of chronic conditions. Note: These data refer only to noninstitutionalized individuals. (Source: U.S. Bureau of the Census, 1995)

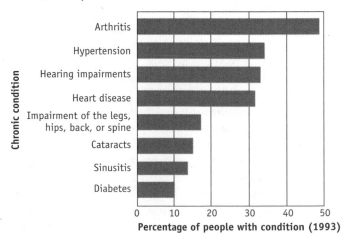

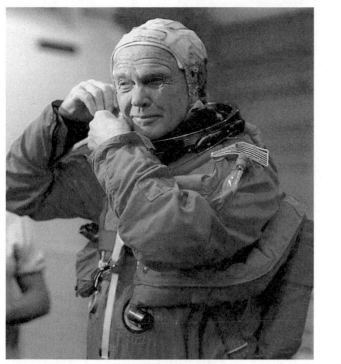

Many people, such as former Senator and astronaut John Glenn and former First Lady Betty Ford, remain active and productive in their 70s, 80s, and even beyond.

another habit that helps maintain health. The topics of exercise and nutrition are discussed more fully in Chapter 14.

Cognitive Changes

It is commonly believed that intelligence drops during middle age and that memory lapses become more frequent in the later years. Are these common conceptions correct? Let's review the evidence.

INTELLIGENCE

Researchers have long been interested in whether general intelligence, as measured by IQ tests, remains stable throughout the adult years. The current evidence suggests that IQ is fairly stable throughout most of adulthood. However, a small decline often begins after age 60 (Hertzog & Schaie, 1988; Schaie, 1990). This post-60 decline appears to be associated with failing health (Field, Schaie, & Leino, 1988) and with problems in focusing attention (Stankov, 1988). These studies also indicate that large individual differences exist in IQ fluctuations. Although some people experience a modest decline during middle age, many others actually show an *increase* in IQ as late as their 50s.

It does appear that people's IQ scores decline markedly and steadily as they approach death (Berg, 1987). This phenomenon is referred to as "terminal drop." It probably reflects the effects of declining health in those who are about to die.

MEMORY

Many elderly people feel that their memory "isn't what it used to be." In support of this perception, numerous studies report declines in the proficiency of long-term memory in older adults (Baltes & Kliegl, 1992; Hultsch & Dixon, 1990). However, most of these studies have been based on artificial laboratory tasks that bear little resemblance to the memory challenges that people encounter in everyday life. Thus, it's hard to say whether the memory losses seen in these studies have much practical significance.

Investigators have only recently begun to study age-related changes in memory for more meaningful, realistic content. These newer studies indicate that some modest declines seem to occur in memory for prose, television shows, conversations, past activities, and personal plans (Kausler, 1985). Such memory impairments could conceivably interfere with older adults' daily activities. However, the memory losses associated with aging are moderate in size and are not

Web Link 11.4

Adult Development and Aging (APA Division 20)
Psychological researchers interested in adulthood and aging form a distinct division within the American Psychological Association. The division's homepage contains a wide range of educational, instructional, and clinical resources and references for this area of concern.

universal. According to Salthouse (1991), age-related decreases in the capacity of short-term or working memory are the crucial factor underlying older adults' poorer performance on memory tasks and other changes in their cognitive functioning. Some older people, especially those who remain mentally active, suffer little memory impairment.

Cultural attitudes about aging have been shown to affect memory in the elderly. In an interesting study, researchers looked at memory performance in younger people (20s) and older people (late 50s to 90s). The participants were selected from three cultural groups with differing views of older people: hearing Americans (who hold negative views about aging), deaf Americans (who have generally positive views about aging), and hearing Chinese (who hold positive views about aging). As you can see in Figure 11.6, there were basically no differences in memory among the younger participants from the three different cultures. In contrast, older Chinese participants performed significantly better than older hearing and deaf Americans. Thus, as we noted in Chapter 6, stereotypes (in this case, about the elderly) can produce self-fulfilling prophecies, for better and for worse.

FIGURE 11.6.

The effect of cultural attitudes about aging on memory performance in older persons. Levy and Langer (1994) found that the memory performance of older mainland Chinese, whose culture has positive attitudes about aging, was significantly better than that of older hearing and deaf Americans. Although the differences were not statistically significant, older deaf Americans, whose culture generally has positive views about aging, performed better than older hearing Americans, whose culture has more negative attitudes about aging. The memory performance of young people from these three groups did not differ. (Graph adapted from Baron & Byrne, 1997).

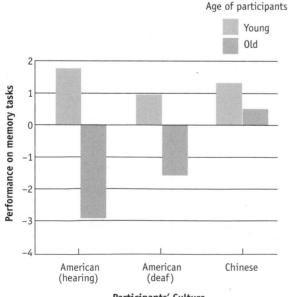

A popular misconception is that older people have vivid recollections of events in the distant past while being forgetful about recent events. In actuality, there is no evidence that the elderly have more numerous, or more vivid, early memories (Rabbitt & McGinnis, 1988). Their memories of events long ago may be loose reconstructions that are less accurate than people assume.

LEARNING AND PROBLEM SOLVING

Although intelligence and memory are more stable during adulthood than widely believed, some significant cognitive changes *do* take place. These changes are most apparent in specific aspects of learning and problem solving.

There is ample evidence that the ability to narrow one's focus of attention diminishes somewhat with increasing age, as does the ability to handle simultaneous multiple inputs (Hartley & McKenzie, 1991; Kausler, 1994). These changes may be due to decreased efficiency in filtering out irrelevant stimuli. Most of the studies have simply compared extreme age groups (very young participants against very old participants). Thus, it's not clear at what age these changes tend to emerge.

In the cognitive domain, age seems to take its toll on *speed* first. Many studies indicate that speed in learning, solving problems, retrieving memories, and processing information tends to decline with age, probably beginning in middle adulthood (Drachman, 1986; Salthouse & Babcock, 1991). The general nature of this trend (across differing tasks) suggests that it may be a result of age-related changes in neurological functioning (Birren & Fisher, 1995).

Overall success on both practical and laboratory problem-solving tasks appears to decrease as people grow older (Sinnott, 1989). For the most part, problem-solving ability is unimpaired if older people are given adequate time to compensate for their reduced speed in cognitive processing. Furthermore, many of the age-related decrements in cognitive functioning can be partly compensated for by increases in older adults' knowledge.

It should be emphasized that many people remain capable of great intellectual accomplishment well into their later years (Simonton, 1990). This reality was verified in a study of scholarly, scientific, and artistic productivity that examined lifelong patterns of work among 738 men who lived at least through the age of 79 (Dennis, 1966). Figure 11.7 plots the percentage of professional works completed by these men in their 20s, 30s, 40s, 50s, 60s, and 70s. As you can see, in most professions the 40s decade was the most productive. However, in many areas productivity was remarkably stable through the 60s and even the 70s. Other researchers have focused on the *quality*, rather than the

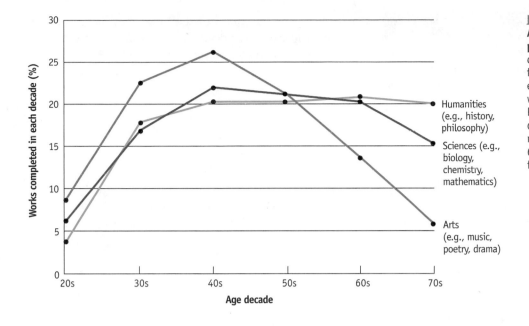

FIGURE 11.7.

Age trends in professional productivity. Dennis (1966) compiled the percentage of professional works completed in each decade of life by 738 men who lived to at least age 79. Productivity peaked in the 40s decade, but professional output remained strong through the 60s, and even through the 70s for the humanities and sciences.

quantity, of output. They typically find that "master-pieces" occur at the same relative frequency among the works of creators of all ages (Simonton, 1990).

Personality Changes

At midlife, Jerry Rubin went from having been an outraged, radical political activist to being a subdued, conventional Wall Street businessman. His transformation illustrates that major personality changes sometimes occur during adulthood. But how common are such changes? Is a grouchy 20-year-old destined to be a grouchy 40-year-old and a grouchy 65-year-old? Or can the grumpy young adult become a mellow senior citizen?

Psychologists have engaged in lively debate about whether personality remains stable in adulthood, and both sides have been able to cite supportive research. On the one hand, a number of large-scale longitudinal studies using objective assessments of personality traits provide evidence for long-term stability in personality. The general conclusion that emerges from these longitudinal studies is that personality tends to be quite stable over periods of 20 to 40 years (Costa & McCrae, 1994). For example, Paul Costa and Robert McCrae (1988) conducted a six-year longitudinal study of 983 men and who were ages 21 to 76 at the time of the first testing. Over this six-year period, the researchers looked at the stability of the traits in their five-factor model of personality (see Chapter 2). The stability of the participants' self-ratings on these five traits over six years is quite high. (Correlation coefficients for men and women were essentially the same.) Costa and McCrae also asked the spouses of the participants to rate the subjects over the same six-year interval. They found that the stability of the spousal ratings closely matched that of the participants' self-ratings.

On the other hand, some studies suggest that substantial personality changes continue to occur throughout the life span (Haan, Millsap, & Hartka, 1986; Helson & Moane, 1987; Whitbourne et al., 1992). For example, in a study of women graduates of Mills College, few personality changes were found between the ages of 21 and 27; however, between the ages of 27 and 43, the women increased in dominance (including confidence) and independence (Helson and Moane, 1987; Helson, Mitchell, & Moane, 1984). According to Susan Krauss Whitbourne and her colleagues (1992), "there is a growing body of evidence indicating the existence of adult personality changes on a variety of . . . variables" (p. 268).

Susan Krauss Whitbourne

In sum, researchers assessing the stability of personality in adulthood have reached contradictory conclusions. How can they be reconciled? This appears to be one of those debates in which researchers are eyeing the same findings from different perspectives. Hence, some conclude that the glass is half full, whereas others conclude that it's half empty. In his discussion of this controversy, Lawrence Pervin (1994) concludes that personality is characterized by *both* stability and change. Thus, some personality traits (such as emotional stability, extraversion, and assertiveness) tend to remain stable, while others (such as masculinity and femininity) tend to change as people grow older (Helson & Stewart, 1994).

Death and Dying

LEARNING OBJECTIVES

● *Discuss cultural and individual attitudes about death.*
● *Describe Kübler-Ross's five stages of dying and research findings about the dying process.*
● *Discuss the grieving process and what helps people cope with bereavement.*

Dealing with the deaths of close friends and loved ones is an increasingly frequent adjustment problem as people move through adulthood. Moreover, the final challenge of life is to confront one's own death.

Attitudes About Death

Because death is a taboo topic in modern Western society, the most common strategy for dealing with it is *avoidance.* There is plentiful evidence of Americans' inability to confront death comfortably. People often use euphemisms such as "passed away" to avoid even the word itself. To minimize exposure to the specter of death, individuals sometimes unnecessarily quarantine the dying in hospitals and nursing homes. These are all manifestations of what Kastenbaum (1986) calls a **death system—the collection of rituals and procedures used by a culture to handle death.** Death systems vary from one culture to another. Ours happens to be rather negative and evasive.

Negativism and avoidance are *not* universal features of death systems. In Mexican culture, death is discussed frequently and is even celebrated on a national feast day, the Day of the Dead (DeSpelder & Strickland, 1983). Also, the Amish view death as a natural transition rather than a dreaded adversary (Bryer, 1979). Thus, some cultures and subcultures display less fear of death than the majority culture.

American attitudes about death are wide ranging. There are conflicting findings about whether *preoccupation* with thoughts about death peaks in middle or old age. However, the evidence is fairly clear that *fear* of death tends to decline after middle age (Rasmussen & Johnson, 1994). Elderly adults are more likely to fear the period of uncertainty that comes before death than death itself. Thus, they are concerned about where they will live, who will take care of them, and how they will cope with the loss of control and independence they may experience before death.

To reduce death anxiety, it seems more important to have a well-formulated personal philosophy of death than a particular religious affiliation. For instance, one study found that both devout Christians and devout atheists were less anxious about death than those with ambivalent religious views (Moore, 1992). Individuals who haven't accomplished all that they had hoped are more likely to fear death, as are those who are anxious and depressed (Neimeyer & Van Brunt, 1995).

The Process of Dying

Pioneering research on the experience of dying was conducted by Elisabeth Kübler-Ross (1969, 1970) during the 1960s. At first, her project met with immense resistance. Fellow physicians at the hospital where she worked were initially unresponsive to her requests to interview dying patients. Gradually, however, it became apparent that many such patients were enthusiastic about the discussions. They were frustrated by the "conspiracy of silence" that surrounds death and relieved to get things out in the open.

Elisabeth Kübler-Ross

Eventually, Kübler-Ross interviewed over 200 terminally ill patients and developed a model of the process of dying. According to her model, people evolve through a series of five stages as they confront their own death. Huyck and Hoyer (1982) provide a succinct description of these reactions:

Stage 1: Denial. Denial, shock, and disbelief are the first reactions to being informed of a serious, life-terminating illness. According to Kübler-Ross, few patients maintain this stance to the end.

Stage 2: Anger. After denial, the patient often becomes nasty, demanding, difficult, and hostile. Asking and resolving the question "Why me?" can help the patient reduce resentment.

Stage 3: Bargaining. In this stage the patient wants more time and asks for favors to postpone death. The bargaining may be carried out with the physician or, more frequently, with God.

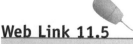

Web Link 11.5

The End of Life: Exploring Death in America
Since late 1997, National Public Radio (NPR) has regularly aired a range of programs relating to dying and death as experienced in American culture. This companion website at NPR offers not only printed and audio transcripts of each program but many bibliographical and organizational resources as well.

Stage 4: Depression. Depression is a signal that the acceptance process has really begun. Kübler-Ross has referred to this stage as *preparatory grief*—the sadness of anticipating an impending loss.

Stage 5: Acceptance. The person who achieves acceptance has taken care of unfinished business. The patient has relinquished the unattainable and is now ready to die. He or she will want to be with close family members, usually a wife or husband and children; dying children want to be with their parents. Although patients desire the presence of someone warm, caring, and accepting at this time, verbal communication may be totally unnecessary.

There is no question that Kübler-Ross greatly improved our understanding of the process of dying and stimulated research that continues to add to our knowledge. Nonetheless, her views have been heavily criticized (Kastenbaum, 1986). The strongest objections have focused on her belief that the dying process is stage-based. Systematic studies of dying patients have not always observed the same five emotions or the same progression of emotions she described (Baugher et al., 1989–90). Instead of progressing though a common, five-stage process, dying people seem to show "a jumble of conflicting or alternating reactions running the gamut from denial to acceptance, with tremendous variation affected by age, sex, race, ethnic group, social setting, and personality" (Butler & Lewis, 1982, p. 370).

Bereavement and Grieving

When a friend, spouse, or relative dies, individuals must cope with **bereavement, or the painful loss of a loved one through death.** The death of someone close typically brings forth the painful and complex emotions of grief. Cultural and religious rituals are designed to help survivors adjust to and cope with their loss. **These formal practices of an individual and a community in response to a death are termed** *mourning.*

CULTURAL VARIATIONS

Considerable variation exists among and within cultures as to how this major life event is acknowledged. In America, the bereaved are typically encouraged to break their emotional ties with the deceased relatively quickly and to return to their regular routines. In contrast, in Japan the bereaved are encouraged to maintain emotional ties to their dead loved ones. Almost all Japanese homes have altars dedicated to family ancestors, and family members routinely talk to the deceased and offer them food (Stroebe et al., 1992). Regardless of the particular form that mourning takes, all such rituals are designed to make death meaningful and to help

Millions of people mourned the untimely and tragic death of Princess Diana.

the bereaved cope with the pain and disruption of death (Marshall & Levy, 1990).

THE GRIEVING PROCESS

The common view of bereavement asserts that distress is an inevitable response to loss and that failure to experience distress is a sign that the individual has not grieved "properly" (Stroebe et al., 1992). As a result, the person is expected to suffer negative consequences later. According to respected theorist John Bowlby (1980), grieving is a four-stage process:

Stage 1: Numbness. In this initial phase, survivors are typically dazed and confused. They may experience physical reactions such as nausea or tightness in the chest or throat. This phase may last several days or, in cases when death has been unexpected, several weeks.

Stage 2: Yearning. In this phase, survivors try to recover the lost person. Individuals may report that they see the deceased and may wander as if they are searching for the loved one. They often feel frustration, anger, and guilt. In addition, they may experience intense feelings of sadness and may cry and sob uncontrollably. They may also suffer loss of appetite and insomnia.

Stage 3: Disorganization and despair. Searching for the loved one ceases as the loss is accepted as real. However, accepting the loss brings feelings of helplessness, despair, and depression. Survivors often experience extreme fatigue and a need to sleep much more than usual.

Stage 4: Reorganization. Individuals are able to resume their normal routines at home and at work. Depression lifts, regular sleeping habits return, and energy increases. Thoughts of the loved one may bring sadness, but these feelings are no longer overwhelming.

Although Bowlby's model is certainly plausible, research suggests that grief does not necessarily follow this straightforward path. Just as people react differently to the experience of dying, they also show variable responses to bereavement. For instance, Camille Wortmann and Roxane Silver (1990) summarized the findings of four studies that looked at the amount of distress widows experienced both one month after the death of their husbands and a year or two later. Four distinct patterns of grieving were evident. The *normal* pattern, is characterized by a high level of immediate distress and a low level of distress later on. In the *chronic* pattern, high levels of distress occur both immediately after the death and later on. In the *delayed* pattern, low immediate distress is followed by high distress later on. Finally, the *absent* pattern is characterized by low levels of distress both shortly after the husband died and later as well.

As you can see in Figure 11.8, the least common pattern was delayed grief—only 1% to 5% of mourners were in this category. Also, absent grief appears to be relatively common—30% to 78% of widows showed this pattern. Thus, Wortmann and Silver found little support for the traditional view of grieving. Instead, they suggest that many individuals are able to handle bereavement without significant distress.

Still, these researchers looked only at the experiences of widows. They would probably have obtained quite different findings if the subjects had been parents who had lost a child, the most difficult type of death adults must cope with (Stillion, 1995). One study compared the grief reactions of 255 middle-aged women who had experienced the death of either a spouse, a parent, or a child in the two years preceding the study (Leahy, 1993). As you might expect, mothers who had lost children had the highest levels of depression. And women whose husbands had died were significantly more depressed than women who had lost a parent. Other studies of bereaved persons (including men) have also found that they score higher on depression than the nonbereaved (Wortmann & Silver, 1990). They also score lower on life satisfaction and are at greater risk for illness. Thus, the death of an intimate is an adjustment challenge for most people, even though individual's reactions to the experience may vary.

COPING WITH BEREAVEMENT

To cope with loss, people need the sympathy and support of family and friends as well as the passage of time. In the case of a child's death, parents may find it helpful to talk with others who have been through this experience (Lieberman, 1993).

A particularly difficult bereavement situation occurs when a child or an adolescent loses a parent to death. In these cases, grieving typically involves frequent crying, trouble concentrating at school, and sleep problems. These symptoms may last from several months to a year (Silverman & Worden, 1992). It is important for adults to take the time to talk with grieving children. In particular, children need to be assured that the parent did not leave out of anger and that the remaining parent will not disappear (Furman, 1984). Groups for bereaved children and adolescents can be particularly helpful (Bacon, 1996).

In the upcoming Application, we'll look at some ways parents can facilitate their children's development by providing optimal combinations of affection and discipline.

FIGURE 11.8.

Four patterns of grieving. Using data from four different studies, Camille Wortman and Roxane Silver (1990) divided widows according to their levels of distress a month after their husbands had died (immediate distress) and one to two years later (later distress). This arrangement of data produced four patterns of grieving. Within each category, we have given the lowest and highest percentages reported among the four studies. Although the traditional view of grief holds that the "normal" pattern is the only healthy response to loss, these data show that other adaptive patterns of grieving are common.

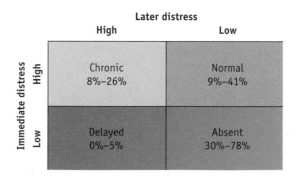

Becoming an Effective Parent

LEARNING OBJECTIVES

- Describe Ainsworth's three attachment styles and how caregivers can promote secure attachment in their infants.
- Summarize the research on the effects of day care on infants and children.
- Discuss Baumrind's parenting styles and their effects on children's development.
- Discuss issues related to the effective parenting of adolescents.
- List five suggestions for more effective parenting.
- List five suggestions for the effective use of punishment.

Are the following statements true or false?

_____ 1. Infant-mother emotional attachments are natural and formed readily.

_____ 2. Placing infants and children in day care negatively affects their development.

_____ 3. Extensive use of punishment is the key to effective discipline.

_____ 4. Parents shouldn't have to explain their reasons for punishing their children.

All these statements are false. All represent popular myths about child-rearing that you will encounter in this discussion of effective parenting. Many parents are eager to learn all they can about children's development. They search to find new and better ways to ensure optimal social, emotional, and cognitive development in their children. In this Application, we'll explore some key issues in modern parenting.

Maternal Behavior and Infant-Mother Attachment

During the first few months of life, infants rely on built-in behaviors such as crying, cooing, and smiling to initiate and maintain contact with adult caregivers. Before long, infants start to recognize their most frequent caregiver (typically, the mother) and are more easily soothed by that person. By the age of 8 months, most babies develop a strong emotional connection to a single familiar caregiver (hereafter assumed to be the mother, to simplify our discussion). **This emotional bond between infant and mother is termed** *infant attachment.*

Contrary to popular belief, infants' attachment to their mothers is not automatic. Indeed, as we noted in Chapter 8, not all infants develop a secure attachment to their mothers. Sometimes, mothers are insensitive or inconsistent in responding to their infants' needs (Isabella & Belsky, 1991). Problems with attachment

may also arise with "difficult" infants. For instance, some babies are prone to distress, spit up most of their food, make bathing a major battle, refuse to go to sleep, and rarely smile. It is easy to see that such behavior could undermine a mother's responsiveness to an infant (Mangelsdorf et al., 1990).

After extensive study, Mary Ainsworth and her colleagues (1978) concluded that infants could be classified into one of three attachment styles by about 8 months of age. These different styles develop out of parent-infant interactions during the early months of life. Babies with an *avoidant* attachment style tend to ignore their mothers. Those with an *anxious-ambivalent* style seem to desire contact with the mother, yet they actively resist her when she comes near. Fortunately, the majority of infants are *securely attached* and welcome contact with their mothers. A secure attachment to a caregiver during infancy is important because it seems to provide a basis for successful social relationships later in life (Elicker, Englund, & Sroufe, 1992). In Erik Erikson's terms, the securely attached baby has developed a sense of basic trust in the mother and toward the world at large.

Some researchers are studying a fourth—*disorganized/disoriented*—attachment style, in which infants are both drawn to their caregivers and fear them because of past negative interactions (Main & Solomon, 1990). This style appears to be common among abused children (Carlson et al., 1989). A recently published longitudinal study suggests that this attachment style is associated with dissociative disorders (see Chapter 15) in childhood and adolescence (Carlson, 1998).

How can caregivers promote a secure attachment in infants? Ainsworth and her associates reported that the mothers of securely attached infants were perceptive about the baby's needs, responded to those needs relatively quickly, and enjoyed physical contact with the baby. The implication is that these are among the key attributes of effective parenting of infants.

Day Care and Attachment

The impact of day care on attachment is a hotly debated topic these days. The crucial question is whether daily infant-mother separations might disrupt the attachment process. The issue is an important one, given that 58% of mothers with an infant under the age

Web Link 11.6

National Parent Information Network (NPIN)
Parents constantly face all sorts of questions about development; the NPIN site describes many guides to online and other resources to answer those questions.

of 1 work outside the home (U.S. Bureau of the Census, 1994). Research by Jay Belsky (1988, 1990b, 1992) suggests that babies who receive nonmaternal care for more than 20 hours per week have an increased risk of developing insecure attachments to their mothers. Belsky's findings have raised many eyebrows, but they need to be put in perspective. First, the data suggest that the proportion of day-care infants who exhibit insecure attachment is only slightly higher than the norm in American society and even lower than the norm in some other societies (Lamb, Sternberg, & Prodromidis, 1992). Second, many studies have found that maternal employment is not harmful to children (Demo, 1992), and some studies have even found that day care can have beneficial effects on youngsters' intellectual and social development (Andersson, 1992; Caldwell, 1993). Third, the effects of day care appear to depend on the *quality* of the care provided. Negative effects seem minimal and may even be outweighed by positive effects when children are cared for in spacious, well-equipped, adequately staffed facilities that provide lots of individual attention and carefully planned activities (Howes, Philipps, & Whitebook, 1992; Scarr et al., 1993).

Dimensions of Child-Rearing

As children move from infancy into toddlerhood, the role of parenting broadens. The manner in which parents react to a child's actions communicates their standards of appropriate and inappropriate behavior. Parents fulfill this role with varying degrees of conscious awareness.

Two major dimensions underlie parenting behavior (Maccoby & Martin, 1983). The first, and most important, is *parental acceptance.* Although most parents are at least moderately accepting of their children, some are indifferent or even hostile and rejecting. Parental acceptance and warmth appear to influence the degree to which children internalize the standards and expectations of their parents (Greenberger & Goldberg, 1989). Children whose parents hold them in high regard develop high self-esteem and self-control (behave appropriately even if the parents are not present). In contrast, children whose parents are less accepting may develop lower self-esteem and less self-control. Thus, they may behave when the parents are around (out of fear of punishment) but misbehave when on their own.

The second dimension of parenting behavior is *parental control,* or strictness of parental standards. For example, a parent who is moderately controlling sets high performance standards and expects increasingly mature behavior. A parent who is uncontrolling expects little of the child. The absence of control is associated with maladjustment and high levels of aggression.

Diana Baumrind

Diana Baumrind (1967, 1971, 1978) has looked at specific parenting styles as interactions between the two dimensions of acceptance and control. In addition, she wanted to know effects of these parenting styles on children's social and intellectual competence. In her initial study, Baumrind observed a sample of preschool children and their parents and rated both groups on a number of dimensions. Additional data were obtained through interviews with the parents. Baumrind was able to identify four distinct parenting styles: authoritarian, permissive, authoritative, and neglectful (see Figure 11.9).

Authoritative parents (high acceptance, high control) set high goals for their children but are also very accepting of their children and responsive to their needs. They encourage verbal give-and-take and allow their children to question parental requests. They also provide age-appropriate explanations that emphasize the consequences of "good" and "bad" behavior. Authoritative parents maintain firm control but take into account each child's unique and changing needs. They are willing to negotiate with their children, setting new and less restrictive limits when appropriate, particularly as children mature.

Authoritarian parents (low acceptance, high control) are highly demanding and controlling and use physical punishment or the threat of it with their children. By virtue of their higher status, they issue commands that are to be obeyed without question ("Do it because I said so"). These parents rigidly maintain tight control even as their children mature. They also tend to be somewhat emotionally distant and may be rejecting.

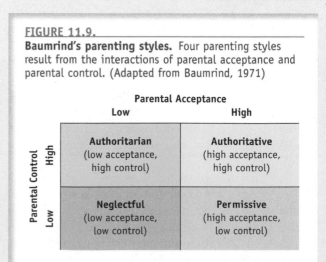

FIGURE 11.9.

Baumrind's parenting styles. Four parenting styles result from the interactions of parental acceptance and parental control. (Adapted from Baumrind, 1971)

	Parental Acceptance	
	Low	High
Parental Control — High	Authoritarian (low acceptance, high control)	Authoritative (high acceptance, high control)
Parental Control — Low	Neglectful (low acceptance, low control)	Permissive (high acceptance, low control)

Permissive parents (high acceptance, low control) make few or no demands of their children. They allow children free expression of impulses and set few limits on appropriate behavior. Permissive parents are responsive and warmly accepting and indulge their children's desires.

Neglectful parents (low acceptance, low control) provide for the basic physical and emotional needs of their children, but not much else. They convey the impression that they don't particularly care for their children: They are not particularly involved with or supportive of their children (no help with homework, minimal supervision, little time spent together).

Effects of Parenting Styles

Baumrind and others have found that parenting styles are associated with different traits in children. As you might expect, authoritative parenting is associated with the most positive outcomes. Children whose parents use this style do the best in school and are self-reliant, friendly, and cooperative. In contrast, the children of authoritarian parents tend to do less well in school and have lower self-esteem and poorer social skills. Permissive parents often have children whose grades are lower and who are undisciplined, impulsive, and easily frustrated. Children of neglectful parents have low self-esteem and are moody, impulsive, and aggressive (Maccoby & Martin, 1983).

Of course, these data are correlational and do *not* establish that the parenting style is the *cause* of the children's traits. The direction of influence probably goes both ways. For instance, parents may become increasingly authoritarian *in response to* their child's increasing resentment and irritability. Even so, Baumrind's results imply that authoritative parenting is most likely to foster social and cognitive competence in children.

Rearing Adolescents

As noted earlier, parent-adolescent relations are not as bitter or contentious as widely assumed, although conflicts over values are common and power struggles frequently ensue (Silverberg, Tennenbaum, & Jacob, 1992). Adolescents' emerging cognitive abilities enable them to question parental values and to formulate a personal philosophy to guide their own behavior.

One of the undercurrents in parent-adolescent relationships is that the balance of power between parent and child is shifting. Younger children accept their parents' power as a legitimate source of authority, especially if they have a warm relationship. The increasing autonomy of adolescents, however, requires a more equal parent-child relationship. While this is a neces-

sary step on the road to autonomous adulthood, negotiating such shifts in power can sometimes be difficult. Authoritative parents who are willing to respond to their teenagers' input are most likely to avoid such turmoil. Authoritarian parents who are unwilling to relinquish their control promote hostility and rebellion in adolescents. Permissive and neglectful parents, who never exercised much control over their children, may find themselves faced with adolescents whose behavior is completely out of hand.

Researchers who have studied parenting styles in adolescence have found essentially the same pattern of outcomes we noted earlier although the differences among the four groups are not always dramatic (Baumrind, 1989; Lamborn, et al., 1991). Authoritatively reared adolescents show the highest competence and adjustment, while neglectfully reared adolescents generally show the lowest. Adolescents reared with authoritarian or permissive styles generally fall between the other two groups. Figure 11.10, depicts the high school grades and school misconduct of adolescents in these four groups. These findings are consistent across a number of ethnic groups, including African American, Hispanic, and Asian American.

Toward Effective Parenting

Are there some "basic rules" for effective parenting? We offer five key principles here. Of course, it's essential to tailor these suggestions to the age and developmental level of a specific child. (For additional perspectives, see Figure 11.11, which lists ten good books on parenting.)

1. *Set high, but reasonable standards.* Children should be expected to behave in a socially appropriate manner for their age and to do as well as they can in school and in other activities. Parents who don't expect much from their children are teaching them not to expect much from themselves.

2. *Stay alert for "good" behavior and reward it.* Most parents pay attention to children when they are misbehaving and ignore them when they're being good. This

is backward! Develop the habit of praising good behavior so a child knows what you want.

3. *Explain your reasons when you ask a child to do something.* Don't assume that a child can read your mind. Explaining the purpose of a request can transform what might appear to be an arbitrary request into a reasonable one. It also encourages self-control in a child.

4. *Encourage children to take the perspective of others.* Talk to children about the effects of their behavior on others ("How would you feel if Keisha did that to you?"). This role-playing approach fosters moral development and empathy in children.

5. *Enforce rules consistently.* Children need to have a clear idea about what is expected of them and to know that there will be consequences when they fail to meet your standards. This practice also fosters self-control in children.

Parents often wonder how punishment can be used more effectively in disciplinary efforts. We'll take up this topic in the next section.

Using Punishment Effectively

To use punishment effectively, parents should use it less

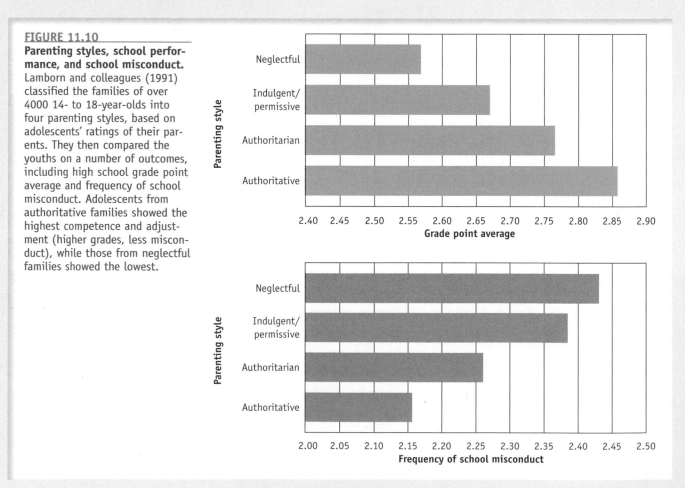

FIGURE 11.10

Parenting styles, school performance, and school misconduct. Lamborn and colleagues (1991) classified the families of over 4000 14- to 18-year-olds into four parenting styles, based on adolescents' ratings of their parents. They then compared the youths on a number of outcomes, including high school grade point average and frequency of school misconduct. Adolescents from authoritative families showed the highest competence and adjustment (higher grades, less misconduct), while those from neglectful families showed the lowest.

FIGURE 11.11.

FIGURE 11.11.
Top-rated self-help books on parenting. Based on a national survey of over 500 clinical and counseling psychologists, Santrock, Minnet, and Campbell (1994) compiled a list of the 25 most highly recommended self-help books. The ten books listed here deal with parenting or children. The other 15 self-help books, which deal with a variety of topics, are listed in Chapter 1.

Top-Rated Self-Help Books on Parenting

Infants and Mothers
by T. Barry Brazelton

What Every Baby Knows
by T. Barry Brazelton

Dr. Spock's Baby and Child Care
by Benjamin Spock and Michael Rothenberg

To Listen to a Child
by T. Barry Brazelton

The Boys and Girls Book About Divorce
by Richard Gardner

Toddlers and Parents
by T. Barry Brazelton

Between Parent and Teenager
by Haim Ginott

The First Three Years of Life
by Burton White

Between Parent and Child
by Haim Ginott

Children: The Challenge
by Rudolph Dreikurs

often. That's because punishment often has unintended, negative effects (Newsom, Favell, & Rincover, 1983; Van Houten, 1983). One of these side effects is that punishment often triggers *strong negative emotional responses,* including fear, anxiety, anger, and resentment. These emotional reactions can create a variety of problems, including hostility toward parents. A second side effect is that heavy punishment can result in the *general suppression of behavior.* In other words, children who are strongly and frequently punished may become withdrawn and inhibited because they fear that any behavior will be punished. Finally, studies show that harsh physical punishment often leads to an *increase in aggressive behavior* (Weiss et al., 1992). Children who are subjected to a lot of physical punishment tend to become more aggressive than the average youngster. Thus, the truckload of side effects associated with punishment make it less than ideal as a disciplinary procedure.

Although parents probably overuse punishment as a means of behavioral control, it does have a role to play in disciplinary efforts. The following guidelines summarize research evidence on how to make punishment effective while minimizing its side effects (Berkowitz, 1993).

1. *Punishment should not damage the child's self-esteem.* To be effective, punishment should get across the message that it is the *behavior* that is undesirable, not the child. Unduly harsh physical punishment, derogatory accusations, and other hurtful words erode the child's self-esteem.

2. *Punishment should be swift.* A delay in delivering punishment undermines its impact. A parent who says, "Wait until your father (or mother) gets home . . ." is making a fundamental mistake. (He or she is also unfairly setting up the other parent as the "heavy.") Quick punishment highlights the connection between the prohibited behavior and its negative outcome.

3. *Punishment should be consistent.* If you want to eliminate an undesirable behavior, you should punish it every time it occurs. When parents are inconsistent about punishing a particular behavior, they only create confusion in the child.

4. *Punishment should be explained.* When children are punished, the reason for their punishment should be explained as fully as possible, given the constraints of their age. The more children understand the reason they are punished, the more effective the punishment tends to be. These explanations, characteristic of the authoritative style, also foster the development of self-control.

5. *Point out alternative, positive ways for your child to behave and reinforce these actions.* One shortcoming of punishment is that it only tells a child what *not* to do. A better strategy is to punish an undesirable response *and* reward a positive alternative behavior. Children usually engage in undesirable behavior for a reason. Suggest another response that serves the same purpose and reward a child for doing it. For example, many troublesome behaviors exhibited by children are primarily attention-seeking devices. Punishment of these responses will be more effective if you can provide a child with more acceptable ways to gain attention.

Key Ideas

THE TRANSITION OF ADOLESCENCE

● During pubescence, the adolescent growth spurt takes place and secondary sex characteristics develop. During puberty, which begins a few years later, the primary sex characteristics mature. The onset of puberty marks the beginning of adolescence. Girls typically mature two years earlier than boys. Boys who mature late and girls who mature early may find puberty particularly stressful. During adolescence, cognitive changes also occur, including development of the ability to apply logic to hypothetical situations.

● In the realm of personality, adolescents must develop a clear sense of identity and cope with intensified gender-role expectations. Some theorists assert that adolescence is a period of turmoil; however, research does not support this view. For this reason, careful attention should be paid to youth who display symptoms of serious problems such as depression, suicidal behavior, drug and alcohol abuse, and chronic delinquency. Suicide among adolescents has been increasing, but fewer than 1% of young people actually take their lives.

THE EXPANSE OF ADULTHOOD

● Erikson's theory of personality development focuses on psychosocial crises in each of eight successive stages, centering on transitions in social relations. In adulthood, these crises are intimacy versus isolation, generativity versus stagnation, and integrity versus despair.

● During early adulthood, individuals make more major role changes than in any other developmental stage. These changes typically include leaving one's family, entering the workplace and developing a career, finding a mate, having and rearing children, and adjusting to family life.

● In middle adulthood, people must come to terms with the fact that their bodies are aging. In addition, they must deal with transitions in the parental role as children mature and leave home. Coping with the "empty nest" seems to be less of a problem than popular wisdom suggests.

● Workers at midlife seem to fall into one of two paths: the stable career pattern or the changing careers pattern. Very few individuals seem to experience a midlife crisis. Older adults must adjust to retirement, adapt to changes in their social networks, cope with health problems, and confront death.

AGING: A GRADUAL PROCESS

● Physical development during adulthood leads to many obvious changes in physical appearance and sensory acuity. After age 30 there is a steady loss of active brain cells; however, this loss has not been clearly related to reductions in cognitive functioning. Similarly, hormonal changes appear to be only modestly related to midlife distress or declining sexual activity. Unfortunately, health does tend to decline with increasing age for a variety of reasons. Engaging in regular exercise and eating a healthful diet can help maintain health.

● Intelligence seems to remain fairly stable during most of adulthood. Memory processes probably deteriorate less than believed. Attentional capacity, speed of learning, and success in problem solving all tend to decline slightly during old age. However, most people remain capable of sound intellectual functioning in their later years. The adult personality seems to be characterized by both stability and change.

DEATH AND DYING

● Attitudes about death vary from one culture to another. Attitudes in this culture are characterized by negativism, avoidance, and fear. Kübler-Ross's research on the process of dying indicated that individuals progress through a sequence of five stages. Later research has called into question the idea that people's reactions to dying follow such a straightforward path.

● There is wide variation between and within cultures regarding how death is acknowledged. Research has revealed several different patterns of grieving, calling into question traditional views of the process of mourning. The loss of a child is the most difficult type of death adults must cope with. In coping with bereavement, people need the support of family and friends. Support groups can also be helpful.

APPLICATION: BECOMING AN EFFECTIVE PARENT

● Attachment between infants and their primary caregivers develops very early in life. According to Mary Ainsworth, infants develop one of three attachment styles with their caregivers: secure, anxious-ambivalent, and avoidant. Of Diana Baumrind's four parenting styles, authoritative parenting is associated with the most positive outcomes in children. Although rearing adolescents presents parents with some special challenges, parent-adolescent relations are not nearly as problematic as many suppose. Effective parenting involves following five key principles, as well as knowing how to use punishment effectively.

Key Terms

Bereavement	Menarche	Puberty
Death system	Menopause	Pubescence
Dementia	Mourning	Secondary sex
Egocentrism	Neurons	characteristics
Infant	Primary sex char-	Secular trend
attachment	acteristics	Social clock

Key People

Mary Ainsworth	Erik Erikson
Diana Baumrind	Elisabeth Kübler-Ross
David Elkind	

Practice Test

1. Primary sex characteristics develop during:
   a. menarche.
   b. puberty.
   c. the adolescent growth spurt.
   d. pubescence.

2. Optimal adjustment is associated with puberty arriving _____ for girls and _____ for boys.
   a. late; on time
   b. early; on time
   c. on time; early
   d. late; early

3. High-risk behavior seen in some adolescents is probably caused by:
   a. the personal fable.
   b. the imaginary audience.
   c. puberty.
   d. identity achievement.

4. The idea that adolescence is the most stressful phase of development:
   a. has not yet been researched.
   b. has been researched, but not in the United States.
   c. is supported by research.
   d. is not supported by research.

5. According to Erikson, the psych social conflict of middle adulthood is:
   a. identity versus identity diffusion.
   b. intimacy versus isolation.
   c. generativity versus stagnation.
   d. integrity versus despair.

6. The life stage that involves more role changes than any other is:
   a. adolescence.
   b. early adulthood.
   c. middle adulthood.
   d. later adulthood.

7. Which of the following is a *false* statement about retirement?
   a. Retirement typically has a negative impact on overall health and life satisfaction.
   b. The best-adjusted retirees are those who were satisfied with life before retirement.
   c. Most older adults maintain their ties to their children.
   d. For African American elders, fictive kin play a key role in social support.

8. With regard to whether personality changes with age, it can be concluded that:
   a. a pattern of change is most typical.
   b. a pattern of stability is most typical.
   c. some traits change over time and some traits remain stable.
   d. no pattern can be discerned.

9. *Less* anxiety about death is found among those who:
   a. feel they haven't accomplished all that they had hoped.
   b. have a particular religious affiliation.
   c. have ambivalent religious views.
   d. have a well-formulated philosophy of death.

10. Baumrind's authoritative parenting style is characterized by:
    a. high acceptance and high control.
    b. low acceptance and high control.
    c. high acceptance and low control.
    d. low acceptance and low control.

Answers

1. b page 310
2. c pages 311–312
3. a page 312
4. d page 314
5. c pages 313, 316

6. b page 317
7. a page 319
8. c page 325
9. d page 326
10. a page 330

INFOTRAC
COLLEGE EDITION

Go to the Wadsworth Psychology Study Center (http://psychology.wadsworth.com/) for quiz questions, research updates, hot topics, interactive exercises, and suggested readings in INFOTRAC related to this chapter.

CHAPTER 12 | Careers and Work

"The [telephone] dictates. This crummy little machine with buttons on it—you've just got to answer it . . . Your job doesn't mean anything. Because you're just a little machine. A monkey could do what I do. . . .

"Until recently, I'd cry in the morning. I didn't want to get up. I'd dread Fridays because Monday was always looming over me. Another five days ahead of me . . .

"I'll be at home and the telephone will ring and I get nervous. It reminds me of the telephone at work . . ."—A receptionist quoted in Working *(Terkel, 1985)*

"Piano tuning is not really business. It's a dedication. There's such a thing as piano tuning, piano rebuilding, and antique restoration. There's such a thing as scale designing and engineering, to produce the highest sound quality possible. I'm in all of this and I enjoy every second of it. . . . I don't see any possibility of separating my life from my work. . . . There seems something mystic about music, about piano tuning. There's so much beauty comes out of music. There's so much beauty comes out of piano tuning."—A piano tuner quoted in Working *(Terkel, 1985)*

These quotations attest to the pivotal role of work in adult life. They speak poignantly of the tremendous impact, either positive or negative, that jobs can have on the quality of life. Perhaps the significant role of work shouldn't be so surprising, given that many people's sense of identity is determined by the nature of their work. When adults meet for the first time, their initial "How do you do?" is often followed by the more crucial question, "What do you do for a living?" The answer may convey information not only about one's occupation but also about one's social status, lifestyle, personality, interests, and aptitudes.

Because work plays such an important role in life, psychologists take a great interest in it. Those who study human behavior in work settings are *industrial/organizational psychologists.* Among other things, they examine the workplace and its effects on worker productivity and psychological adjustment. They are also becoming increasingly interested in how individuals balance work, family life, and leisure activities.

We'll begin this chapter by reviewing some important considerations in choosing a career. Then we'll explore two models of career development and discuss women's career issues. Next, we'll examine how the workplace and workforce are changing and look at some occupational hazards such as job stress and sexual harassment. We'll conclude with the important issue of balancing work, relationships, and leisure. In the

Application, we'll offer some concrete suggestions for enhancing your chances of landing a desirable job.

Choosing a Career

LEARNING OBJECTIVES

- Describe family and personal influences on job choice.
- Cite several helpful sources of career information.
- List some aspects of potential occupations that are important to know about.
- Explain the role of occupational interest inventories in career decisions.
- List five important considerations in choosing an occupation.

One of your biggest decisions in life is choosing a career. The importance of this decision is enormous. It may determine whether you are employed or unemployed, financially secure or insecure, happy or unhappy. Given our rapidly advancing technology and the increased training and education required to break into most fields, it is more important than ever to choose thoughtfully. In theory, what's involved in making a successful career choice is pretty straightforward. You need to have a clear grasp of your personal characteristics and realistic information about potential careers. From there, it's just a matter of selecting an occupation that is a good match with your personal characteristics. In reality, of course, the process is a lot more complicated. Let's take a closer look.

Examining Family Influences and Personal Characteristics

People who have limited job skills and qualifications have limited job options. Thus, they usually must take whatever job is available rather than a job that is well suited for them. Unfortunately, actually *choosing* a career is a luxury usually limited to the middle and upper classes. For those who are able to choose a career, family influences and personal characteristics come into play.

FAMILY INFLUENCES

Individuals' career choices are strongly influenced by their family background (Statt, 1994). That is, the jobs that appeal to people tend to be like those of their parents (Mortimer & Borman, 1988). For instance, people who grow up in middle-class homes are likely to aspire to high-paying professions in law, medicine, or engineering. On the other hand, individuals from low-income families often lean toward blue-collar jobs in construction work, office work, and food services.

Family background influences career choice for several reasons. For one thing, the single best predictor of occupational status is the number of years of education an individual has completed (Featherman, 1980). And, because parents and children often attain similar levels of education, they are likely to have similar jobs. Second, access to career information and useful career contacts is related to socioeconomic status. For instance, children from middle-class homes typically receive more useful information about work from their parents and teachers than children from poorer families do. Moreover, middle-class parents more often have connections with high-status job contacts (Grotevant & Cooper, 1988).

Finally, parenting practices come into play. As we noted in Chapter 11's Application on parenting, parenting styles are correlated with socioeconomic status. They also shape work-related values. Thus, children from middle-class homes are encouraged to be curious and independent, qualities that are essential to success in many high-status occupations. By contrast, children from lower-status families are taught to conform and obey. This means that they have less opportunity to develop the qualities demanded in high-status jobs. As we noted in Chapter 10, parents' gender-role expectations also influence their children's aspirations and sometimes interact with socioeconomic status and ethnicity.

PERSONAL CHARACTERISTICS

Although intelligence does not necessarily predict occupational success, it does predict the likelihood of entering particular occupations. That's because intelligence is related to the academic success that is necessary to enter many fields. Certain professions, such as law and medicine, are open only to people who can meet increasingly selective criteria as they move from high school to college to graduate education and professional training.

Other aptitudes and abilities are important as well. In many occupations, special talents are more important than general intelligence. Specific aptitudes that might make a person well suited for certain occupations include creativity, artistic or musical talent, mechanical ability, clerical skill, mathematical ability, and persuasive talents.

As you meander through life, you acquire interests in various kinds of activities. Are you intrigued by the business world? the academic world? international

Family background plays an important role in children's later career choices.

affairs? agriculture? the outdoors? physical sciences? music? athletics? human services? The list of potential interests is virtually infinite. Interests tend to stabilize in the late teens and remain constant afterward (Lowman, 1991). They underlie your motivation for work and your job satisfaction. Thus, they should definitely be considered in your career planning.

Psychologists agree that it is important to choose an occupation that is compatible with your personality (Lowman, 1991). In assessing your personality, you should pay special attention to your dominant traits, needs, and values. A particularly crucial characteristic is how socially skilled you are, as some jobs require much more social dexterity than others.

Researching Job Characteristics

The second step in selecting an occupation is seeking out information about jobs. There are over 20,000 occupations listed in the U.S. Department of Labor's *Dictionary of Occupational Titles.* Their sheer number is overwhelming. Obviously, you have to narrow down the scope of your search before you can start gathering information.

SOURCES OF CAREER INFORMATION

Once you have selected some jobs that might interest you, the next question is, Where do you get information on them? This is not a simple matter. The first step is usually to read some occupational literature. A general reference is the *Occupational Outlook Handbook,* available in most libraries and on the World Wide Web (see Web Link 12.1). This government document, published every two years by the U.S. Bureau of Labor Statistics, is a comprehensive guide to occupations. It includes job descriptions, education and training requirements, advancement possibilities, salaries, and employment outlooks for 250 occupations. In addition, it describes other sources of career education, training, and financial aid information, as well as resources for special groups such as youth, the handicapped, veterans, women, and minorities. Another helpful book is *The Where Am I Now? Where Am I Going Career Manual* by William Lareau (1997).

Besides these general books, you can often get more detailed information on particular occupations from government agencies, trade unions, and professional organizations. For example, if you're interested in a career in psychology, you can obtain a number of pamphlets or books from the American Psychological Association (APA). Also, the APA Web site provides links to other sites describing at least 50 subfields in psychology, many of which provide useful career information. Related professions (social work, school psychology, and so on) also have Web pages. You will find the addresses of these pages on Marky Lloyd's Careers in Psychology Web site (Web Link 12.3).

After you've read the available literature about an occupation, it's often a good idea to talk to some individuals working in that area. People in the field can provide you with more down-to-earth information than you can get by reading. Keep in mind, though, that the people you talk to may not be a representative sample of those who work in an occupation. Don't make the mistake of rejecting a potentially satisfying career just because one person hates it.

ESSENTIAL INFORMATION ABOUT OCCUPATIONS

When you examine occupational literature and interview people, what kinds of information should you seek? To some extent, the answer depends on your

Web Link 12.1

Occupational Outlook Handbook (OOH) Online
Every two years the U.S. Bureau of Labor Statistics publishes the *Occupational Outlook Handbook,* now available via the Internet. This handbook is a guide to every occupation in the United States. It includes descriptions of the nature of each job and its working conditions, educational requirements, future employment and earnings prospects, and sources of further information.

unique values and needs. However, some things are of concern to virtually anyone. For instance, when asked to rate the importance of various aspects of their jobs, the respondents in a 1991 Gallup poll gave the highest ratings to good health insurance, interesting work, and job security (see Figure 12.1). The issues you need to know about include:

The nature of the work. What would your duties and responsibilities be on a day-to-day basis?

Working conditions. Is the work environment pleasant or unpleasant, low key or high pressure?

Job entry requirements. What education and training are required to break into this occupational area?

Potential earnings. What are entry-level salaries, and how much can you hope to earn if you're exceptionally successful? What does the average person earn? What are the fringe benefits?

FIGURE 12.1.

Workers' evaluation of job characteristics. A 1991 Gallup Poll asked workers to rate the importance of various aspects of their jobs and to rate their level of satisfaction with these aspects of their present jobs. Workers rated good health insurance and job security very high, no doubt reflecting concerns about corporate downsizing and layoffs. (Data taken from Hugick & Leonard, 1991a; based on Rathus & Nevid, 1995)

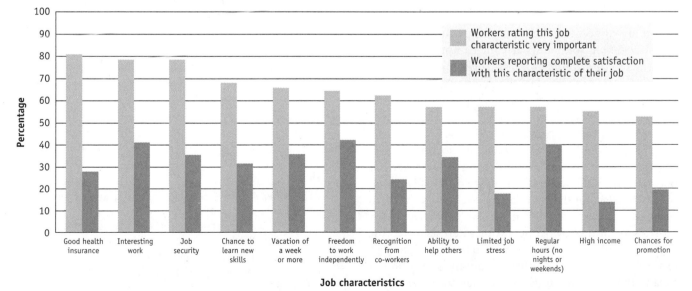

Potential status. What is the social status associated with this occupation? Is it personally satisfactory for you?

Opportunities for advancement. How do you move up in this field? Are there adequate opportunities for promotion and advancement?

Intrinsic job satisfaction. Apart from money and formal fringe benefits, what can you derive in the way of personal satisfaction from this job? Will it allow you to have fun, to help people, to be creative, or to shoulder responsibility?

Future outlook. What is the projected supply and demand for this occupational area?

By the way, if you're wondering whether your college education will be worth the effort in terms of job opportunities and salary, the answer generally is yes. Almost all the experts agree that the future belongs to those who are better educated (Church, 1993). On the other hand, a college diploma is no guarantee of a great job. In fact, many college graduates are underemployed. **Underemployment is settling for a job that does not fully utilize one's skills, abilities, and training.** Furthermore, this problem is not going to disappear soon. Between now and 2005, experts estimate that 30% of new college graduates will be underemployed (Shelley, 1994). Also, while it's true that the jobs you can obtain with a college degree do pay more than those requiring less education, the higher-paying jobs go to college graduates with *college-level* reading and quantitative skills. Those who graduate without these skills more often end up in high-school-level jobs (Pryor & Schaffer, 1997).

Using Psychological Tests for Career Decisions

If you are undecided about an occupation, you might consider taking some tests at your campus counseling center. **Occupational interest inventories** measure **your interests as they relate to various jobs or careers.** The most widely used tests of this type are the Strong-Campbell Interest Inventory (SCII) and the Kuder Occupational Interest Survey (KOIS).

Occupational interest inventories do not attempt to predict whether you would be successful in various occupations. Rather, they focus more on the likelihood of job *satisfaction* than job *success*. When you take an occupational interest inventory, you receive many scores indicating how similar your interests are to the typical interests of people in various occupations. For example, a high score on the accountant scale of a test means that your interests are similar to those of the

average accountant. This correspondence in interests does not ensure that you would enjoy a career in accounting, but it is a moderately good predictor of job satisfaction (Swaney & Prediger, 1985).

Interest inventories like the SCII can provide worthwhile food for thought about possible careers. The results may confirm your subjective guesses about your interests and strengthen already existing occupational preferences. Additionally, the test results may inspire you to investigate career possibilities that you had never thought of before. Unexpected results may stimulate you to rethink your career plans.

Although interest inventories can be helpful in working through career decisions, several cautions are worth noting. First, you may score high on some occupations that you're sure you would hate. Given the sheer number of occupational scales on the tests, this can easily happen by chance. However, you shouldn't dismiss the remainder of the test results just because you're sure that a few specific scores are "wrong." Second, don't let the test make career decisions for you. Some students naively believe that they should pursue whatever occupation yields their highest score. This is not how the tests are meant to be used. They merely provide information for you to consider. Ultimately, you have to think things out for yourself.

Third, you should be aware that most occupational interest inventories have a lingering gender bias. Many of these scales were originally developed 30 to 40 years ago when outright discrimination or more subtle discouragement prevented women from entering many traditionally "male" occupations. Critics assert that interest inventories have helped channel women into gender-typed careers, such as nursing and secretarial work, while guiding them away from more prestigious "male" occupations, such as medicine and engineering (Betz, 1993; Betz & Fitzgerald, 1987). Undoubtedly, this was true in the past. Recently, progress has been made toward reducing gender bias in occupational tests, but it has not been eliminated. Thus, in interpreting interest inventory results, be wary of letting gender stereotypes limit your career options. A good career counselor should be able to help women—as well as

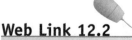

Web Link 12.2

The Riley Guide: Employment Opportunities and Job Resources on the Internet
This site, maintained by the well-regarded career expert Margaret F. Dikel, complements a fine career-planning book with the same title. The site contains hundreds of annotated links regarding almost any topic related to employment and careers.

men—sort through the effects of gender bias on their test results.

Taking Important Considerations into Account

As you contemplate your career options, keep the following points in mind.

1. *You have the potential for success in a variety of occupations.* Career counselors stress that people have multiple potentials (Carney & Wells, 1999). As we have noted, you have over 20,000 occupations to choose from. Considering the huge variety in job opportunities, it's foolish to believe that only one career would be right for you. If you expect to find one job that fits you perfectly, you may spend your entire lifetime searching for it.

2. *Be cautious about choosing a career solely on the basis of salary.* Because of the tremendous emphasis on material success in America, people are often tempted to choose a career solely on the basis of salary or status. According to experts, this is not a good idea (Lowman, 1991). When people ignore personal characteristics in choosing a career, they risk being mismatched. Such job mismatching can result in boredom, frustration, and unhappiness with one's work, and these negative feelings can also spill over into other spheres of life.

3. *There are limits on your career options.* Entry into a particular occupation is not simply a matter of choosing what you want to do. It's a two-way street. You get to make choices, but you also have to persuade schools and employers to choose you. Your career options will be limited to some extent by factors beyond your control, including fluctuations in the economy and the job market (Lock, 1996).

4. *Some career decisions are not easily undone.* Although it's never too late to strike out in new career directions, it is important to recognize that many decisions are not readily reversed. Once you invest time, money, and effort in moving along a particular career path, it may not be easy to change paths. This potential problem highlights why it is important to devote systematic thought to your occupational choice.

5. *Career choice is a developmental process that extends throughout life.* Occupational choice involves not a single decision but a series of decisions. Although this process was once believed to extend only from prepuberty to one's early 20s, it is now recognized that the process often continues throughout life. In a 1993 Gallup Poll, 48% of American workers said that they were either "very" or "somewhat likely" to switch careers during their working life (Moore & McAneny, 1993). Nonetheless, many middle-aged people tend to underestimate the options available to them and therefore miss opportunities to make constructive changes.

We want to emphasize that making occupational choices is not limited to youth.

In the next section, we'll explore in greater detail how personal characteristics are related to career choice and career development.

Models of Career Choice and Development

LEARNING OBJECTIVES

- *Summarize Holland's hexagonal model of career choice.*
- *Summarize Super's five-stage model of career development.*
- *Discuss women's career development.*

Psychologists have long been interested in understanding how individuals make career choices and how their careers evolve over time. Theorists have developed several different approaches to these issues. We'll examine two influential models: Holland's and Super's.

Holland's Trait Measurement and Matching Model

The most influential trait model of career choice is that developed by John Holland (1985, 1996). According to Holland, career choice is related to an individual's personality characteristics, which are assumed to be relatively stable over time. In Holland's system, people can be classified into one of six personality types, called *personal orientations.* Similarly, occupations can be classified into six ideal *work environments.* For obvious reasons, this model is often called the *hexagonal model.* According to Holland, people flourish when their personality type is matched with a work environment that is congruent with their abilities, interests, and self-beliefs. A good match typically results in career satisfaction, achievement, and stability, and the reverse is also true. Here are the six personal orientations and their optimal work environments:

Realistic people describe themselves as good at mechanical tasks and weak in social skills. They prefer jobs with tasks that are physical or mechanical and that are clearly defined, such as farming, auto mechanics, and engineering. They tend to avoid tasks that involve social skills, abstract thinking, subjectivity, or verbal skill.

Investigative people enjoy abstract thinking and logical analysis, preferring understanding to action. They like working with ideas rather than with things or people. Investigative individuals can often be found working in research laboratories or libraries.

Artistic people see themselves as imaginative and independent. They tend to be impulsive and creative and are socially aloof. These individuals dislike structured tasks, preferring instead to rely on their subjective impressions in dealing with the environment. They have a high need for emotional expression and often seek careers in art, music, or drama.

Social people describe themselves as being understanding and wanting to help others. They prefer to interact with people, and they have the necessary social skills to do so comfortably. They typically have greater verbal ability than mathematical ability. Social types are often found in the helping professions, such as teaching, nursing, and social work.

Enterprising people perceive themselves as happy, self-confident, sociable, and popular. They like to use their social skills to lead or persuade others. They prefer sales or supervisory positions, in which they can express these characteristics.

Conventional people are conforming, systematic, and orderly. They typically have greater clerical and mathematical ability than verbal ability. They prefer working environments that are structured and predictable and may be well suited to occupations in the business world.

Holland has developed several tests to measure the six basic personal orientations. One of them, the Self-Directed Search (SDS), is a self-scoring test. Once individuals identify their personality type on the SDS, they can match it with various relevant occupations. Studies have shown that the SDS has helped students reduce career indecision and select occupations consistent with their personality traits (McGowan, 1977; Tay, Ward, & Hill, 1993).

Obviously, these six personal orientations are ideal types, and no one person will fit perfectly into any one type. In fact, most people are a combination of two or three types (Holland, 1996). You can take a rough stab at categorizing your own personal orientation by studying Figure 12.2. Look at the matching work environments to get some ideas for possible career options.

Holland's hexagonal model has prompted considerable research, and much of it supports his theory

FIGURE 12.2.

Overview of Holland's theory of occupational choice. According to John Holland, people can be categorized into six personality types (personal orientations) that prefer different work environments. (Adapted from Holland, 1985)

Holland's Personal Orientations and Related Work Environments

Themes	Personal orientations	Work environments
Realistic	Values concrete and physical tasks. Perceives self as having mechanical skills and lacking social skills.	*Settings:* concrete, physical tasks requiring mechanical skills, persistence, and physical movement *Careers:* machine operator, truck driver, draftsperson, barber
Investigative	Wants to solve intellectual, scientific, and mathematical problems. Sees self as analytical, critical, curious, introspective, and methodical.	*Settings:* research laboratory, diagnostic medical case conference, work group of scientists *Careers:* marine biologist, computer programmer, clinical psychologist, architect, dentist
Artistic	Prefers unsystematic tasks or artistic projects: painting, writing, or drama. Perceives self as imaginative, expressive, and independent.	*Settings:* theater, concert hall, library, radio or TV studio *Careers:* sculptor, actor, designer, musician, author, editor
Social	Prefers educational, helping, and religious careers. Enjoys social involvement, church, music, reading, and dramatics. Is cooperative, friendly, helpful, insightful, persuasive, and responsible.	*Settings:* school and college classrooms, psychiatrist's office, religious meetings, mental institutions, recreational centers *Careers:* counselor, nurse, teacher, social worker, judge, minister, sociologist
Enterprising	Values political and economic achievements, supervision, and leadership. Enjoys leadership control, verbal expression, recognition, and power. Perceives self as extroverted, sociable, happy, assertive, popular, and self-confident.	*Settings:* courtroom, political rally, car sales room, real estate firm, advertising company *Careers:* realtor, politician, attorney, salesperson, manager
Conventional	Prefers orderly, systematic, concrete tasks with verbal and mathematical data. Sees self as conformist and having clerical and numerical skills.	*Settings:* bank, post office, file room, business office, Internal Revenue office *Careers:* banker, accountant, timekeeper, financial counselor, typist, receptionist

(Tracey & Rounds, 1993). For instance, people in occupations that are well matched to their personality are more satisfied with their jobs and are likely to remain in these jobs for a longer time than individuals who are not so well matched (Holland, 1985). Also, an individual's personal orientation has been found to be a much better predictor than other personal characteristics (age, gender, length of time on the job) of teachers' job satisfaction (Wiggins et al., 1983). Moreover, retirees typically choose work and volunteer activities that closely match their earlier careers (Milletti, 1984).

As we noted, one of the assumptions of trait models is that occupational interests remain stable during adulthood. The research evidence is mixed on this issue. On the positive side, one study found that the interests underlying career choices remain stable after about age 17 (Hansen & Campbell, 1985). It has also been found that when people change occupations, they frequently choose new jobs that correspond to the same personal orientation in Holland's model (Gottfredson, 1977). On the negative side, at least one study has found that accountants differed significantly in their needs and work attitudes at different life stages and also in the extent to which they fit Holland's conventional orientation (Adler & Aranya, 1984).

Thus, although the trait approach is useful, it fails to take into account the fact that people's interests, skills, motivations, aspirations, and situations change over time. By contrast, stage theories view occupational choice as a developmental process rather than a specific event (Crites, 1980; Osipow, 1987).

Super's Developmental Model

The most influential developmental model of career choice is one outlined by Donald Super (1957, 1985, 1988). He views occupational development as a process that begins in childhood, unfolds gradually across most of the life span, and ends with retirement. Super asserts that the person's *self-concept* is the critical factor in this process. In other words, decisions about work and career commitments reflect people's attempts to express their changing views of themselves. To map these changes, Super breaks the occupational life cycle into five major stages and a variety of substages (see Figure 12.3).

GROWTH STAGE

The growth stage encompasses childhood, during which youngsters fantasize about exotic jobs they would enjoy. Generally, they imagine themselves as detectives, airplane pilots, and brain surgeons rather

Stages of Occupational Development		
Stage	**Approximate ages**	**Key events and transitions**
Growth stage	**0–14**	**A period of general physical and mental growth**
Prevocational substage	0–3	No interest or concern with vocations
Fantasy substage	4–10	Fantasy is basis for vocational thinking
Interest substage	11–12	Vocational thought is based on individual's likes and dislikes
Capacity substage	13–14	Ability becomes the basis for vocational thought
Exploration stage	**15–24**	**General exploration of work**
Tentative substage	15–17	Needs, interests, capacities, values, and opportunities become bases for tentative occupational decisions
Transition substage	18–21	Reality increasingly becomes basis for vocational thought and action
Trial substage	22–24	First trial job is entered after the individual has made an initial vocational commitment
Establishment stage	**25–44**	**Individual seeks to enter a permanent occupation**
Trial substage	25–30	Period of some occupational change due to unsatisfactory choices
Stabilization substage	31–44	Period of stable work in a given occupational field
Maintenance stage	**45–65**	**Continuation in one's chosen occupation**
Decline stage	**65+**	**Adaptation to leaving workforce**
Deceleration substage	65–70	Period of declining vocational activity
Retirement substage	71+	A cessation of vocational activity

FIGURE 12.3.

Overview of Super's theory of occupational development.
According to Donald Super, people go through five major stages (and a variety of substages) of occupational development over the life span.

than plumbers, grocers, and bookkeepers. Until the very end of this period, children are largely oblivious to realistic considerations such as the abilities or education required for specific jobs. Instead, they base their fantasies purely on their likes and dislikes.

EXPLORATION STAGE

Pressures from parents, teachers, and peers to develop a general career direction begin to intensify during high school. By the end of high school, individuals are expected to have narrowed a general career direction into a specific one. Whether through studying about it or through part-time work, young people try to get a real taste of the projected occupation. During the later part of this stage, individuals typically attempt to enter the world of work on a full-time basis. Many people in this phase are still only tentatively committed to their chosen occupation. If their initial work experiences are gratifying, their commitment will be strengthened. However, if their first experiences are not rewarding, they may shift to another occupation, where they will continue the exploration process.

ESTABLISHMENT STAGE

Vacillation in career commitment continues to be common during the first part of the establishment stage. For some, doubts begin to surface for the first time as they reappraise the match between their personal attributes and their current position. Others simply carry earlier doubts into this stage. If a person's career choice turns out to be gratifying, however, the individual firmly commits to an occupation. With few exceptions, future job moves will take place *within* this occupational area. Having made a commitment, the person's task is now to demonstrate the ability to function effectively in the chosen occupation. To succeed, individuals must utilize previously acquired skills, learn new skills as necessary, and display flexibility in adapting to organizational changes.

MAINTENANCE STAGE

As the years go by, opportunities for further career advancement and occupational mobility decline. Around their mid-40s, many people cross into the maintenance stage, during which they worry more about *retaining* their achieved status than *improving* it. Rapidly changing technology may compel middle-aged employees to enhance and update their skills as they face competition from younger, more recently educated workers. The primary goal in this stage, however, is simply to protect the security, power, advantages, and perks that one has attained. With decreased emphasis on career advancement, many people shift energy and attention away from work concerns in favor of family concerns or leisure activities.

DECLINE STAGE

Deceleration involves a decline in work activity during one's later years as retirement looms near. People redirect their energy and attention toward planning for this major transition. In his original formulation, which was based on research in the 1950s, Super projected that deceleration ought to begin at around age 65. Since the 1970s, however, slowed economic growth and the entry of the large baby boom cohort into the workforce have combined to create an oversupply of skilled labor and professional talent. This social change has created pressures that promote early retirement. Because of these conditions, deceleration often begins earlier than Super initially indicated.

Retirement brings work activity to a halt. People approach this transition with highly varied attitudes. Many individuals look forward to it eagerly. Others approach it with apprehension, unsure about how they will occupy themselves and worried about their financial viability. Still others approach retirement with a combination of hopeful enthusiasm and anxious concern. Although anxiety about the unknown is understandable, many studies have shown that retirement typically has no adverse effect on overall health or life satisfaction (Bossé, Spiro, & Kressin, 1996). Although retirement may mean less income, it can also mean more time to spend with friends and on hobbies, travel, and meaningful volunteer work (Chambré, 1993).

As a stage theorist, Super deserves credit for acknowledging that people follow different patterns in their career development. He identified several patterns for both men and women that do not coincide with the conventional pattern we have described. In support of Super's model, it has been found that self-esteem and career maturity are positively correlated (Crook, Healy, & O'Shay, 1984). On the other hand, a study of adolescents reported that identity status was a stronger predictor of career maturity than was self-esteem (Wallace-Broscious, Serafica, & Osipow, 1994).

Finally, some experts predict that dramatic changes in the workplace, which we'll describe shortly, may mean that careers will cease to be a major source of life satisfaction for many (Howard, 1995). Job compatibility will fall by the wayside in the rush to obtain *any* job, and neither Holland's nor Super's models will be of much practical use.

Women's Career Development

Until fairly recently, most of the theories and research on career development have focused on men's careers. One reason for this situation was that relatively few women worked. Today, however, it is estimated that 62% of women (versus 73% of men) are in the labor force (U.S. Bureau of the Census, 1997). Once women began entering the workforce, it was simply taken for granted that the theories and concepts used to explain men's vocational development would apply equally well to women. However, experts in this area assert that men and women have different patterns of career development (Betz, 1993; Thornborrow & Sheldon, 1995). Why might this be? For one thing, most women still subordinate their career goals to their husbands.' If a married man wants or needs to move to another job, his wife typically follows him and takes the best job she can find in the new location. This is even the case with couples in which both are professional psychologists (Gutek, 1989). Hence, married women usually have less control over their careers than married men do.

Another reason for gender differences in career paths is that women are more likely to interrupt their careers to concentrate on child-rearing or family crises. Historically, women's participation in the labor force has shown a sharp rise as women take their first jobs, then a sharp dip as they leave the labor force to concentrate on rearing children, and finally a second sharp rise when they return to work, usually after the children are grown. Interestingly, this pattern has been labeled the *M-curve*—both for its shape on the graph and for "mother" (Farley, 1980), However, as we've mentioned, more and more mothers are returning to work when their children are small. In fact, the majority of wives with children one year old or younger now work (Thornborrow & Sheldon, 1995). As women's participation in the labor force increasingly resembles that of men, the M-curve is disappearing.

Still, many women do leave the labor force, even if for increasingly brief periods of time. This hiatus in employment is termed *labor force discontinuity*. Does labor force discontinuity pose any problems for women? Definitely. In fact, dropping out of the workforce is an important, but not the only, cause of the gender gap in salaries and employment status (Felmlee, 1995). Moreover, when women want to return to the workplace, they are unlikely to find the welcome mat out for any but entry-level positions (Treiman, 1985). Studies show that women who do not have children remain in the labor force and have a pattern of career advancement, whereas women who have children typically drop out of the workforce and show downward mobility in their career paths (Felmlee, 1995). An implication of this finding is that economic hardship is likely if married women with children become single parents. One study reported that after a divorce, the woman's standard of living drops 27% (Weitzman, 1996). Changes in the family and the work setting are needed to accommodate to the changing roles of women and men.

The Changing World of Work

LEARNING OBJECTIVES

● List six work-related trends.
● Describe the relationship between education and salary.
● Summarize important demographic changes that are transforming the workforce.
● Cite some of the problems that women and minorities face in today's workplace.
● Describe some challenges presented by workforce diversity to organizations and workers.

Before we plunge into the world of work, let's take a look at several important background issues: contemporary trends in the workplace, the relationship between education and earnings, and diversity in the workforce.

Workplace Trends

We'll define **work as an activity that produces something of value for others.** For some people, work is just a way to earn a living; for others, work is a way of life. For both types of workers, the nature of work is undergoing dramatic changes. Because trends in the workplace can affect your future job prospects, you need to be aware of six important trends:

1. *Most jobs will be in the service sector.* The United States, like many other industrialized nations, is shifting away from a manufacturing, or "goods producing," economy to a service-producing one (U.S. Bureau of Labor Statistics, 1998). Whereas the bulk of yesterday's jobs were in manufacturing, construction, agriculture, and mining, the jobs of the next decade will be in industries that provide services, such as health care, education, social work, communication, and

The growth of technology is significantly changing the nature of work, with both positive and negative effects.

computers. Figure 12.4 depicts 25 specific occupations expected to grow the most and pay the most between now and 2006.

2. *Technology is changing the nature of work.* Computers have dramatically transformed the workplace. From the worker's point of view, these changes are having both positive and negative effects. On the positive side, computer technology makes it possible for workers to work at home and to communicate with others in distant offices and while traveling. On the negative side, computers have been used to automate many jobs that people perform, reducing the need for workers.

3. *Temporary employment is increasing.* In 1988, temporary workers represented about 24% of the labor force; by the year 2000, some experts predict that part-time or contingent workers will grow to 50% of the workforce (Morrow, 1993). Although 50% is probably an overestimate (Fierman, 1994), there is no doubt that the number of part-time or contingent workers will increase. Corporations are downsizing and restructuring to cope with the changing economy and to be competitive globally. In doing so, they are eliminating large numbers of permanent jobs and doling out the work to temporary employees—clerical workers as well as professionals. By reducing the number of core (regular) workers, companies are able to dramatically cut their expenditures on payroll, health insurance, and pension

FIGURE 12.4.

High-growth, high-salary occupations for the 21st century.
According to the U.S. Department of Labor (1998), these 25 occupations will show fast growth, provide high pay and low unemployment, and have the largest number of job openings over the next decade.

Twenty-five "Best Bet" Occupations	
Computer systems analysts	Engineering, mathematical, and computer systems managers
General managers and top executives	Licensed practical nurses
Registered nurses	Financial managers
Secondary school teachers	Marketing, advertising, and public relations managers
Clerical supervisors and managers	Computer programmers
Database administrators and computer support specialists	Instructors and coaches, sports and physical training
Maintenance repairers, general utility	Lawyers
Special education teachers	Physicians
Computer engineers	Electrical and electronics engineers
Social workers	Corrections officers
Food service and lodging managers	Securities and financial services sales workers
College and university faculty	Physical therapists
	Artists and commercial artists

plans, as temporary employees don't typically receive such benefits. A leaner workforce also enables organizations to respond quickly to fast-changing markets. Many professionals thrive on temporary work; they have freedom, flexibility, and high incomes. Those who want only part-time work like the increased opportunities for contingent employment. The majority of temporary workers, however, are struggling to survive—with multiple jobs, low wages, unusual schedules, no benefits, and high anxiety (Morrow, 1993). If this trend continues, it will mean an almost unimaginable transformation of the relationship between Americans and their jobs (Kennedy & Laramore, 1993; Morrow, 1993).

4. *New work attitudes are required.* Yesterday's workers could usually count on job security. Thus, many could afford a somewhat passive attitude in shaping their careers. In contrast, today's workers have job security only as long as they can add value to a company. This situation means that workers must take a more active role in shaping their careers by viewing themselves as "free agents," ensuring that they have valuable skills, and by skillfully marketing themselves to prospective employers (Carney & Wells, 1999). Employees will be expected to perform a variety of functions and to increase both the productivity and quality of their work. Thus, in the new work environment, the keys to job success will be self-direction, self-management, knowledge, flexibility, and mobility (Lock, 1996).

5. *The boundaries between work and home are breaking down.* Computer technology is one force driving this change because people can work at home and stay in touch with the office via modem, telephone, and fax machine. Working at home is convenient—workers save time (no need to commute) and money (on gas, parking, clothes), and experience fewer work-related interruptions. Still, there may be more interruptions from family members and friends, necessitating setting rules to protect work time. The advent of on-site day care in some large companies means that a traditional home function has moved to the office. This development is largely a response to increases in the number of dual-earner households and in the number of single-parent families. The availability of quality on-site day care is obviously a big draw to these workers, because it allows parents to interact with their children during the day.

6. *Lifelong learning is a necessity.* Experts predict that today's jobs are changing so rapidly that in many cases, work skills will become obsolete over a 10- to 15-year period (Lock, 1996). Thus lifelong learning and training will become essential for employees. In some cases, job retraining will occur on the job; community colleges and technical institutes will provide continuing education (Lock, 1996). Workers who know "how to learn" will be able to keep pace with the rapidly changing workplace and will be highly valued. Those who cannot will be left behind.

Education and Earnings

Although a college education is certainly not a requirement for everyone, the ability to read, write, and do basic mathematical computations is essential to be competitive in the workplace. Ironically, as the number of years of education completed by the average American have increased, so have the problems of illiteracy and innumeracy. For example, a national survey of 3,600 young people aged 21–25 conducted by the Educational Testing Service found that only 34% of whites, 20% of Hispanics, and 8% of African Americans could calculate the tip and change for a two-item restaurant meal (Hamilton, 1988). Hence, it is not surprising that companies are having difficulty recruiting qualified entry-level workers.

Consider two chilling examples of what can happen when workers can't do basic math or read (Kennedy and Laramore, 1993): (1) an insurance clerk paid $2,200 on a dental claim that should have been only $22 (she didn't understand decimals); (2) a plant worker nearly killed several co-workers by fitting the wrong heavy piece of machinery onto a machine (he couldn't read). To prevent such errors, many organizations are having to invest in costly programs to educate new workers in the basic skills they should have learned in school (Hamilton, 1988).

Although jobs do exist for individuals with less than a college degree, these jobs usually offer the lowest pay and benefits. As new jobs develop, they will require more education and higher skill levels. In fact, occupations that require a bachelor's degree are projected to grow the fastest (U.S. Bureau of Labor Statistics, 1998). Clearly, then, a good basic education will enhance a person's prospects for existing and future jobs, and computer literacy is an essential complement to a good basic education (Broida, 1995). To summarize, the more education, the higher the income (see Figure 12.5). This relationship holds for both males and females. However, as you can see, men are paid from approximately $5,000 to $23,000 more than women.

The Changing Workforce

The *labor force* consists of all those who are employed as well as those who are currently unemployed but are looking for work. In this section, we'll look at some of the changes in the workforce and consider how women and other minorities fare in the workplace.

DEMOGRAPHIC CHANGES

The workforce is becoming increasingly diverse, with regard to both gender and ethnicity. In 1996, 67% of married women worked, compared to 44% in 1975 (U.S. Bureau of the Census, 1997). This increase holds even for women with very young children. For instance, in 1975 only 33% of women with children under the age of 3 worked outside the home. By 1994, this number had practically doubled to 61% (U.S. Bureau of the Census, 1997). These changes have implications not only for work and family life but also for men's and women's roles.

The workforce is also becoming more ethnically diverse (see Figure 12.6 on the next page), with Hispanic and Asian workers showing the greatest increases (U.S. Bureau of Labor Statistics, 1998). A number of these workers have been reared in families at or below the poverty level (Horowitz & O'Brien, 1989). Because family income typically determines the quality of schools a person attends, many of these new workers

FIGURE 12.5.

Education and income. This graph shows the median incomes of year-round, full-time workers aged 25 and over, by gender and educational attainment. As you can see, the more education people have, the higher their income tends to be. However, women earn less than men with comparable education. (Data from U.S. Bureau of the Census, 1998)

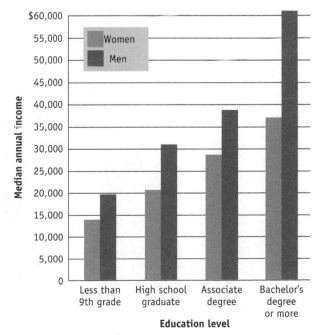

have not had the benefit of an adequate education. Consequently, they are at a disadvantage when it comes to competing for the better jobs.

TODAY'S WORKPLACE FOR WOMEN AND MINORITIES

Recent years have seen a dramatic upsurge in the number of females and minorities in the workplace. Is today's workplace essentially the same for these groups as it is for white males? In many respects, the answer appears to be no. Although job discrimination on the basis of race and gender has been illegal for more than 25 years, women and minority group members continue to face subtle obstacles to occupational success. Foremost among these is *job segregation*. Jobs are simultaneously typed by gender and by race (Amott & Matthaei, 1991; Green & Russo, 1993). Consider the occupation of railroad porter or skycap. Most such jobs are held by African American males.

Most white women and people of color have been concentrated in low-paying jobs with little opportunity for advancement or increase in salary (see Figure 10.10 on p. 297). Employees in female-dominated fields typically earn less than employees in male-dominated fields, even when the jobs require similar levels of training, skill, and responsibility (Betz, 1993) (see Figure 10.11 on p. 298).

Nonetheless, more women and minorities are entering higher-status occupations, even if at a low rate. Unfortunately, they still face discrimination because they are frequently *passed over for promotion* in favor of white men (Morrison & Von Glinow, 1990). This seems to be a problem especially at higher levels of management. For example, the 1995 report of the U.S. government's Glass Ceiling Commission reported that 95% of the senior-level managers of Fortune 1000 industries

Today's workforce is becoming increasingly diverse.

and Fortune 500 companies are men and that 97% are white (Swoboda, 1995). There appears to be a "glass ceiling" that prevents most women and ethnic minorities from advancing beyond middle-management positions (see Figure 12.7). Largely because of these reduced opportunities for career advancement, almost twice as many female corporate managers as males quit their jobs (Stroh, Brett, & Reilly, 1996).

When there is only one woman or minority person in an office, that person becomes a **token—or a symbol of all the members of that group.** Tokens are more distinctive than members of the dominant majority. And, as we discussed in Chapter 6, distinctiveness makes a person's actions subject to intense scrutiny, stereotyping, and judgments. Thus, if a white male makes a mistake, it is explained as an *individual* problem. When a token woman or minority person makes a mistake, it is seen as evidence that *all* members of that group are

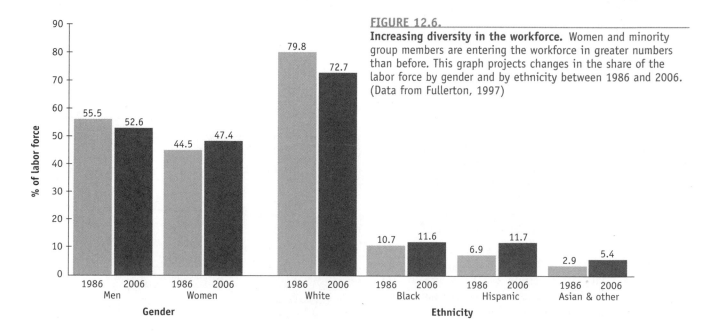

FIGURE 12.6.

Increasing diversity in the workforce. Women and minority group members are entering the workforce in greater numbers than before. This graph projects changes in the share of the labor force by gender and by ethnicity between 1986 and 2006. (Data from Fullerton, 1997)

FIGURE 12.7

The glass ceiling for women and minorities. A government survey of Fortune 1000 corporations found that women and minorities are underrepresented in management and executive positions. (U.S. Department of Labor, 1992)

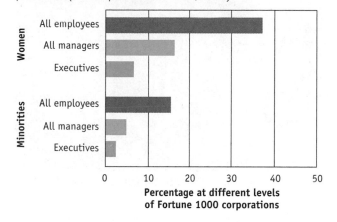

Percentage at different levels of Fortune 1000 corporations

incompetent. Hence, tokens experience a great deal of *performance pressure.* Interestingly, if tokens are perceived as being "too successful," they may be labeled "workaholics" or may be accused of trying to "show up" members of the dominant majority. These unfavorable perceptions may be reflected in performance appraisals. The performance of successful white men is less likely to be interpreted in these negative ways.

Another way the world of work is different for women and minorities is that they have *less access to same-gender or same-group role models and mentors* (Betz, 1993). Finally, *sexual harassment,* a topic we'll take up later, is much more likely to be a problem for working women than for working men.

In sum, women and minority individuals must contend with discrimination on the job in a number of forms. Often, to escape these negative experiences in the workplace, many women leave organizations to start their own businesses (Mergenhagen, 1996).

The Challenges of Change

The increasingly diverse workforce presents challenges to both organizations and workers. Important cultural differences exist in managing time and people, in identification with work, and in making decisions (Matsumoto, 1996). These differences can contribute to conflict. Another challenge is that some individuals feel that they are personally paying the price of prejudice in the workplace, and this perception causes resentment. Recognizing the problem, some corporations offer diversity training programs for their employees. Ironically, these programs can make the problem worse if they take a blaming stance toward white males or if they stir up workers' feelings but provide no ongoing

support for dealing with them (Baker, 1996). Thus, it is important that such programs be well designed.

Many who advocate abandoning affirmative action programs argue that these programs promote "reverse discrimination" through the use of unfair hiring and promotion practices (Fish, 1993). They also argue that affirmative action undercuts the role of merit in employment decisions and sets up (supposedly) underprepared workers for failure (Sowell, 1994). Negative feelings about affirmative action prompt some to automatically assume that *all* women and ethnic minority co-workers have been hired *only* because of their gender or ethnicity. Obviously, these assumptions can be quite harmful to an employee's success. For instance, several studies have demonstrated that attaching an affirmative action label to an employee results in negative attributions and perceptions of incompetence (Heilman, Block, & Lucas, 1992; Summers, 1991). Another study showed that African American subjects who believed that they received positive feedback because of their race experienced a loss of self-esteem (Crocker & Major, 1989).

To minimize conflict and to maintain worker productivity and satisfaction, companies can provide well-designed diversity programs and managers can educate themselves about the varied values and needs of their workers. Similarly, both majority and minority employees must be willing to learn to work comfortably with those who come from different backgrounds.

Coping with Occupational Hazards

LEARNING OBJECTIVES

- List some important sources of job stress.
- Describe four conditions that seem to predict whether stress will develop.
- Summarize the effects of job stress on physical and mental health.
- Describe actions organizations are taking to reduce job stress.
- Describe the prevalence and consequences of sexual harassment.
- Explain how organizations are addressing sexual harassment.
- Describe some causes and effects of unemployment.

Work can bring people deep satisfaction, but it can also be a source of frustration and conflict. In this section, we'll explore three challenges to today's workers: job stress, sexual harassment, and unemployment.

Job Stress

You saw in Chapter 3 that stress can emerge from any corner of your life. However, many theorists suspect that the workplace is the primary source of stress in modern society. Let's examine job stress and what employers and workers can do about it.

SOURCES OF STRESS ON THE JOB

Common job stressors include unusual hours (such as rotating shifts), the pressure of deadlines and work overload, perceived inequities at work, and lack of control over one's work (Buunk et al., 1998). High-pressure jobs such as air traffic controller or surgeon demand virtually perfect performance, as errors can have disastrous consequences. Firefighters and coal miners face frequent threats to their physical safety. Workers who must adapt to computers and automated offices experience "technostress" (Brod, 1988). Others sources of occupational stress include office politics and conflict with supervisors, subordinates, and co-workers. The list of stressful job conditions is practically endless.

Women may experience certain workplace stressors, such as sex discrimination and sexual harassment, at higher rates than men (Fitzgerald, 1993; Roby, 1995). African Americans and ethnic minorities must cope with racism and other types of discrimination on the job (Keita & Jones, 1990). Workers from lower socioeconomic groups typically work in more dangerous jobs than workers from higher socioeconomic status do.

According to Lennart Levi (1990), a well-known researcher in the area of job-related stress, four factors play a critical role in whether stress reactions develop:

1. *The degree of match between a worker and job.* A good match occurs when a person has the abilities needed to be successful at the job and when a job meets the worker's needs. When the employee and the job environment are compatible, stress is usually low. The greater the mismatch, the greater the worker's stress.

2. *The degree of control over working conditions.* Robert Karasek has proposed an intriguing model of

The jobs of emergency medical technicians are highly stressful.

occupational stress that supports this idea (Karasek, 1979; Karasek & Theorell, 1990). He suggests that the *psychological demands* made on a worker and a worker's amount of *decision control* are the two key factors in occupational stress. Psychological demands are measured by asking employees questions such as "Is there excessive work?" and "Must you work fast (or hard)?" To measure decision control, employees are asked such questions as "Do you have a lot of say in your job?" and "Do you have freedom to make decisions?" According to Karasek, *stress is greatest in jobs characterized by high psychological demands and low decision control.* Based on survey data obtained from workers, he has tentatively mapped out where various jobs fall on these two key dimensions of job stress, as shown in Figure 12.8. The jobs thought to be most stressful are those in the lower right area of this diagram.

3. *A worker's coping skills.* Some of the personal qualities that may moderate the effects of job stress include physical stamina, tolerance for ambiguity, excellent job-related skills, and the ability to cope with change (Matteson & Ivancevich, 1987). The impact of work stress may also be reduced by other factors that

CATHY © Cathy Guisewite. Reprinted with permission of UNIVERSAL PRESS SYNDICATE. All rights reserved.

moderate the effects of stress in general, such as hardiness, optimism, sensation seeking, and autonomic reactivity (see Chapter 3).

4. *Social support.* As we noted in Chapter 3, supportive friends and family members figure importantly in both physical and psychological health.

Those who develop work-related stress reactions respond in a variety of ways, as we'll see next.

EFFECTS OF JOB STRESS

As with other forms of stress, occupational stress is associated with a host of negative effects. In the work arena itself, job stress has been linked to an increased number of industrial accidents, increased absenteeism (Allegro & Veerman, 1998), poor job performance, and higher turnover rates (Buunk et al., 1998). Experts estimate that stress-related reductions in workers' productivity may cost American industry about $300 billion per year (Karasek & Theorell, 1990).

When job stress is temporary, as when important deadlines loom, workers usually suffer only minor and brief effects of stress, such as sleeplessness or anxiety. Prolonged and high levels of stress are more problematic, as those who work in people-oriented jobs such as human services, education, and health care can attest (Maslach & Goldberg, 1998). As we noted in Chapter 3,

prolonged stress can lead to *burnout,* characterized by exhaustion, frustration, cynicism, and poor job performance.

Of course, the negative effects of occupational stress extend beyond the workplace. Foremost among these adverse effects are those on employees' *physical* health (Buunk et al., 1998). Work stress has been related to a variety of physical maladies, including heart disease, high blood pressure, stroke, ulcers, and arthritis. In a test of Karasek's model of work stress, more symptoms of heart disease were more prevalent among Swedish men whose jobs were high in psychological demands and low in decision control (Karasek et al., 1981; see Figure 12.9 on the next page). Job stress can also have a negative impact on workers' *psychological* health (Buunk et al., 1998). Occupational stress has been related to decreased self-esteem, frequent anxiety, bouts of depression, and abuse of alcohol or drugs (Maslach & Goldberg, 1998). Experts estimate that the health care costs arising from occupational stress in the United States may run as high as $150 billion per year (Karasek & Theorell, 1990).

DEALING WITH JOB STRESS

There are essentially three avenues of attack for dealing with occupational stress (Ivancevich et al., 1990). The

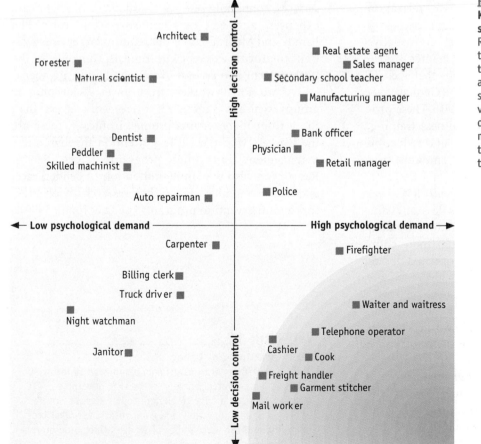

FIGURE 12.8.

Karasek's model of occupational stress as related to specific jobs.
Robert Karasek theorizes that occupational stress is greatest in jobs characterized by high psychological demands and low decision control. Based on survey data, this chart shows where various familiar jobs fall on these two dimensions. According to Karasek's model, the most stressful jobs are those that fall in the shaded area on the lower right.

FIGURE 12.9.

Job characteristics in Karasek's model and heart disease prevalence. Karasek et al. (1981) interviewed 1,621 Swedish men about their work and assessed their cardiovascular health. The vertical bars show the percentage of the men with symptoms of heart disease as a function of the characteristics of their jobs. The highest incidence of heart disease was found among men who had jobs high in psychological demands and low in decision control, just as Karasek's model of occupational stress predicts.

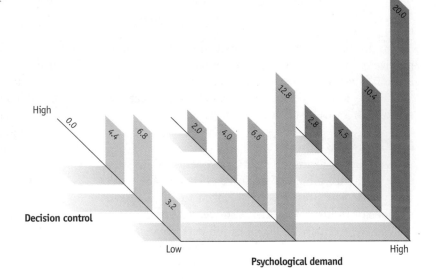

first is to intervene at the *individual* level by modifying workers' ways of coping with job stress. The second is to intervene at the *organizational* level by redesigning the work environment itself. The third is to intervene at the *individual-organizational interface* by improving the fit between workers and their companies.

Interventions at the *individual* level are the most widely used strategy for managing work stress (Maslach & Goldberg, 1998). Many companies have instituted programs designed to improve their employees' coping skills. These programs usually focus on relaxation training, time management, cognitive approaches to reappraising stressful events, and other constructive coping strategies that we discussed in Chapter 4. Also popular are *workplace wellness programs* that seek to improve employees' physical health (Gebhardt & Crump, 1990; Offerman & Gowing, 1990). These programs usually focus on exercise and fitness training, health screening, nutritional education, and reduction of health-impairing habits, such as smoking and overeating.

Interventions at the *organizational* level are intended to make work environments less stressful. Some companies have attempted to reduce occupational stress by making the surroundings more comfortable and attractive and by giving workers different tools or responsibilities. The key is to give adequate decision control to people in jobs that have high psychological demands (Karasek and Theorell, 1990). Decentralizing management and giving workers greater participation in decision making may help to reduce occupational stress (Wilpert, 1995).

Interventions at the *individual-organizational* interface can take many forms. In future years, the biggest challenge will probably be to accommodate the changing nature of the workforce, which is now dominated by dual-earner couples rather than married men

who are the sole wage earners in their families. Another 6% of workers are single parents (Friedman, 1987). What kinds of accommodations are companies making in response to the changing needs of their workers? A number of interesting innovations are being tried (Zedeck & Mosier, 1990). The more common options are flextime, flexible leave time, voluntary part-time work, job sharing, and working at home (see Figure 12.10). Other, less frequently offered benefits include flexible leave time, child-care information or referral services, counseling services, assistance with child care expenses, and employer-sponsored day care. The Family and Medical Leave Act requires larger organizations to provide workers with time off (unpaid) for the birth of a child or serious illness of a family member.

As we noted, workers from lower socioeconomic groups typically experience more work stress than those from higher status groups. Ironically, these are the workers who receive less attention through stress management and other programs (Ilgen, 1990). Researchers also pay limited attention to gender, race, and socioeconomic status in their research on job stressors and intervention programs (Keita & Jones, 1990).

Web Link 12.4

U.S. Department of Labor
The Labor Department has primary responsibility for many job- and work-related matters in the U.S. government. Its site can serve as a base to explore topics such as unsafe working conditions, wages and compensation, worker productivity, and the legal rights of workers (including protection from sexual harassment).

Worker-Responsive Innovations in the Workplace		
Benefit	Percentage of employers providing benefits	
	Private sector	Government
Flexible leave time	42.9	43.7
Flextime	43.6	37.5
Voluntary part-time work	35.3	26.7
Job sharing	15.0	23.5
Counseling services	4.2	18.2
Child-care information or referral services	4.3	15.8
Work at home	8.5	4.0
Employer-sponsored day care	1.6	9.4
Assistance with child-care expenses	3.1	2.9

FIGURE 12.10.

Worker-responsive innovations in the workplace. Increasingly, employers are recognizing that they have to address the needs of the changing labor force by providing new benefits that help employees meet family and leisure needs, as well as work demands. Among innovative benefits, flextime and flexible leave time have been the most widely offered. (Data from *Statistical Abstract of the United States,* 1990)

Sexual Harassment

Sexual harassment burst into the American consciousness in the fall of 1991 during the televised confirmation hearings for the nomination of Clarence Thomas as a Justice of the U.S. Supreme Court. Although Justice Thomas survived the confirmation process, many would argue that his reputation was damaged by Anita Hill's public allegations of sexual harassment. Allegations of sexual harassment have also caused problems for President Clinton. And Robert Packwood resigned his Senate seat in 1995 after multiple accusations of sexual harassment surfaced. These public examples have served as a wake-up call to individuals and companies, showing that they can be sued for harassment (regulations were instituted in 1980). Moreover, as workers recognize that they need to take the problem seriously, they also realize that they are relatively ignorant about what constitutes sexual harassment.

Sexual harassment occurs when employees are subjected to unwelcome sexually oriented behavior. According to law, there are two types of sexual harassment. The first is *quid pro quo* (from the Latin expression that translates as "something given or received in exchange for something else"). In the context of sexual harassment, quid pro quo involves making submission to unwanted sexual advances a condition of hiring, advancement, or not being fired. In other words, the worker's survival on the job depends on agreeing to engage in unwanted sex. The second type of harassment is *environmental.* This refers to any type of unwelcome sexual behavior that creates a hostile work environment, which can inflict psychological harm and interfere with job performance.

Sexual harassment can take a variety of forms: unsolicited and unwelcome flirting, sexual advances, or propositions; insulting comments about an employee's appearance, dress, or anatomy; unappreciated dirty jokes and sexual gestures; intrusive or sexual questions about an employee's personal life; explicit descriptions of the harasser's own sexual experiences; abuse of familiarities such as "honey" and "dear"; unnecessary and unwanted physical contact such as touching, hugging, pinching, or kissing; catcalls; exposure of genitals; physical or sexual assault; and rape. As experts have pointed out, sexual harassment is an abuse of power by a person in authority. Figure 12.11 details the frequency of seven types of harassing behaviors of various severity reported

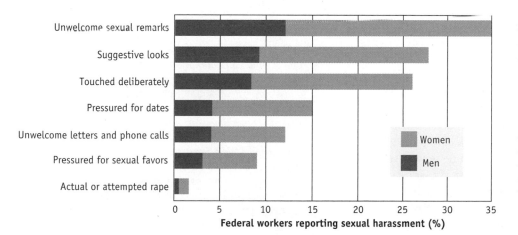

FIGURE 12.11.

Types of sexual harassment women workers report. A stratified random sample of 8,523 male and female federal workers were surveyed about seven types of harassing behaviors. As you can see, less severe types of sexual harassment occurred more frequently than the more severe forms, but sexual harassment in the workplace appears to be distressingly common. (Data from U.S. Merit Systems Protection Board, 1988)

Some people believe that President Clinton's behavior with Monica Lewinsky constituted sexual harassment because she was a young White House employee; others disagree because his advances were not unwelcome.

by male and female federal workers in a 1987 survey (U.S. Merit Systems Protection Board, 1988).

PREVALENCE AND CONSEQUENCES

Sexual harassment in the workplace is more widespread than most people realize. A review of 18 studies suggested that approximately 42% of female workers in the United States report having been sexually harassed (Gruber, 1990). A liberal estimate for male workers is 15% (Gutek, 1993). The typical female victim is young and unmarried, has had several years of technical training or college, and works in a male-dominated field (Tangri, Burt, & Johnson, 1982). Women in blue-collar jobs are particularly at risk, but sexual harassment also occurs in the professions. For example, in a survey of United Methodist clergywomen, 77% reported that they had experienced sexual harassment—41% of these by colleagues and other ministers ("Women Clerics," 1990).

A review of research on the consequences of sexual harassment reported that women experienced stress-related physical symptoms such as stomach disorders, inability to sleep, and weight loss (Gutek & Koss, 1993). Problematic emotional reactions include lower self-esteem, depression, anxiety, and anger. In addition, victims have reported difficulties in their personal relationships and in sexual adjustment (loss of desire, for example). Sexual harassment can also produce fallout

on the job: Women who are harassed may be less productive, less satisfied with their jobs, and less committed to their work and employer (Gutek, 1985).

STOPPING SEXUAL HARASSMENT

To predict the occurrence of sexual harassment, researchers have developed a two-factor model based on the person (prospective harasser) and the social situation (Pryor, Giedd, & Williams (1995). According to this model, individuals vary in their proclivity for sexual harassment, and organizational norms regarding the acceptability of sexual harassment also vary. Research suggests that sexual harassment is most likely to occur when individual proclivity is high and organizational norms are accepting. Thus, it follows that organizations can reduce the incidence of sexual harassment by promoting norms that are intolerant of sexual harassment.

Acknowledging the prevalence and negative impact of sexual harassment, many organizations have taken steps to educate and protect their workers. Managers are publicly speaking out against sexual harassment, supporting programs designed to increase employees' awareness of the problem, issuing policies expressly forbidding harassment, and implementing formal grievance procedures for handling allegations of

● Recommended Reading

Sexual Harassment on the Job: What It Is and How to Stop It by William Petrocelli and Barbara Kate Repa (Nolo Press, 1998)

People and employers now recognize that they need to know what constitutes sexual harassment and what does not. In addition, those who believe that they are being sexually harassed want to know how to stop it. As the title of this book indicates, it addresses both issues. The authors clearly define the varieties of sexual harassment and provide illustrative examples from the workplace and from court cases to reinforce their points. Petrocelli and Repa view the alternatives to ending sexual harassment as a series of escalating steps, and they helpfully guide readers through their various options. For employers, there is a chapter on workplace policies and programs to reduce occurrences of sexual harassment.

One common misconception about sexual harassment is that the laws prohibiting it restrict normal socializing between men and women at work. The truth is that sexual harassment consists of unwelcome conduct of a sexual nature—and it in no way affects ordinary social contact between employees. The oft-repeated fear of many people—mostly men—that sexual harassment laws prevent them from complimenting a women or asking her out for a date is simply misplaced. Nothing in the law prevents dating, as long as it is done in a reasonable manner that respects a co-worker's dignity and wishes. Office romances are not unlawful, as long as both employees involved welcome the relationship. [p. 1/4]

harassment. In the Recommended Reading box on page 354, we describe a book that both employers and employees should find helpful in this regard.

Unemployment

Despite record job growth, unemployment rates remain relatively high. If you include discouraged workers—those who want jobs but have given up looking—the figure is around 10%; without them, the figure is closer to 5%. People with little education and training have always been vulnerable to unemployment. In today's economic market, however, even those with a good education and excellent job skills are not immune to unemployment. What's going on?

CAUSES OF UNEMPLOYMENT

Unemployment today is caused primarily by the dramatic economic changes we have already discussed. The shift from a manufacturing to a service economy has resulted in dramatic transformations in the nature of work. On the positive side, this means that many new jobs are being created; on the down side, it means that workers in high-paying manufacturing jobs are being laid off (robots are now assembling cars, for instance). A second economic change is the globalization of the marketplace. For corporations, this means restructuring and downsizing to increase efficiency and profits—at the expense of workers, including those in white-collar jobs. Thus, a major consequence of these economic upheavals is *displaced workers*—**individuals who are unemployed because their jobs have disappeared.** Between 1991 and 1993, a total of 4.5 million workers with three or more years of experience were displaced (Gardner, 1994).

EFFECTS OF UNEMPLOYMENT

Losing one's job is difficult at best and devastating at worst. Not only can it cause economic distress, it can also cause health problems and such psychological difficulties as loss of self-esteem, depression, and anxiety (Sheeran & Abraham, 1994). Also, the rate of attempted and completed suicides increases with unemployment. The amount of distress experienced as the result of job loss is not affected by gender (Leana & Feldman, 1991).

While losing a job at any age is highly stressful, those who are laid off in middle age seem to find the experience most difficult, for several reasons. First, middle-aged workers have been on the job for a number of years. Because they typically feel highly involved in their work, being cut off from this important source of life satisfaction is very painful (Broomhall & Winefield, 1990). Second, older workers typically remain out of work for a longer time than younger workers do. Thus, economic hardship can be a real

possibility and can threaten quality of life not only for the worker but for the entire family. Of course, not all middle-aged workers are affected negatively by loss of work (Leana & Feldman, 1992). Individuals who are in their 50s and close to retirement and those who are motivated to try their hand at something new seem least affected.

Sometimes the stress of job loss leads to violence. Occasionally, such violent episodes occur in the workplace. As you can see in Figure 12.12, the overriding cause of on-the-job homicides is robbery and crimes (85%). Of the remaining causes, the next highest is business disputes (9%). These situations often involve a displaced worker who lashes out in rage and desperation at a supervisor or co-workers. Employees who lose their jobs because of downsizing—instead of poor job performance—are likely to believe they have been treated arbitrarily and unfairly—a situation found to be associated with increased aggression (Catalano, Novaco, McConnell, 1997). Job loss can also generate anger among people who are dependent on the displaced workers. For example, a study of over 800 employed individuals and their partners reported that job loss led partners to withdraw social support from each other and to be increasingly critical, insulting, and angry (Vinokur, Price, & Caplan, 1996).

COPING WITH UNEMPLOYMENT

Support from friends and family is essential in coping with unemployment. When a person is out of work for

FIGURE 12.12.

Violence at work. Business-related disputes with work colleagues, such as retaliation for being fired, account for a relatively small portion of homicides at work, even though they are the second leading cause of on-the-job homicides. Homicides in the workplace are not the largest source of fatalities in the workplace (accidents are); nonetheless, they occur often enough to be a source of concern to workers. (Data from U.S. Bureau of Labor Statistics, 1997)

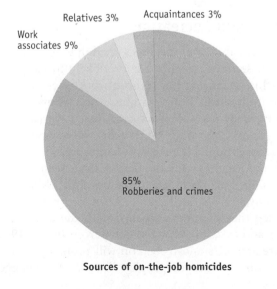

Relatives 3%   Acquaintances 3%
Work associates 9%
85% Robberies and crimes

Sources of on-the-job homicides

an extended period of time or has little social support, counseling may also be helpful. Some companies offer programs for laid-off workers. These programs typically teach employees how to search for jobs, manage stress, and cultivate social support. One such program was found to be successful in alleviating depression (Price, Ryn, & Vinokur, 1992).

Balancing Work and Other Spheres of Life

LEARNING OBJECTIVES

● *List several types of leisure activities and summarize the benefits of such activities.*

● *Summarize current perspectives on workaholism.*

● *Explain the scarcity hypothesis and the enhancement hypothesis.*

● *Summarize the findings on the effects of multiple roles.*

A major challenge for workers today is balancing work, family, and leisure activities in ways that are personally satisfying. We noted that dual-earner families are becoming increasingly common and that the traditional boundaries between family and paid work life are breaking down. These two developments are related. Historically, traditional gender roles assigned women's work to the home and men's work outside the home. This division of labor created boundaries between family and work life. As more women enter the workforce, these boundaries are becoming blurred. The technology-based changes in the workplace are also eroding these distinctions between family and work life. Let's examine three issues related to balancing various life roles.

Leisure and Recreation

Computers and other machines are doing more of our work these days, and this trend is likely to continue. Does this mean that the 40-hour work week is on its way out? It seems not. The number of hours people work typically affects how much money they make, and most Americans would rather work more hours and make more money (Kennedy & Laramore, 1993). Still, awareness of the need for leisure time seems to be increasing, according to a Gallup Poll (Moore & McAneny, 1993). In 1993, 67% of workers polled reported that they were satisfied with the amount of leisure and free time available, down from 76% in 1963. Leisure activities and recreation will probably assume greater importance in people's lives, as the changes

sweeping the workplace are causing people to become alienated from their work (Holland, 1996).

We'll define *leisure* as **unpaid activities people choose to engage in because the activities are personally meaningful.** How might we distinguish activities that are meaningful from those that aren't? Although people frequently lounge in front of the TV set for hours at a time, most would also acknowledge that an important difference exists between this use of time and, say, going outside and taking photographs of dazzling spring flowers. While one activity merely provides respite from a boring or exhausting day (which you sometimes need), the other can be genuinely revitalizing. Being a couch potato will probably contribute nothing to your state of mind and may even contribute to your feeling apathetic and depressed (Kubey & Csikszentmihalyi, 1990). On the other hand, participating in activities that are truly meaningful (photography, for example) does contribute to one's feeling of well-being (Ragheb, 1993).

TYPES OF LEISURE ACTIVITIES

The types of leisure activities that people prefer are quite diverse (see Figure 12.13). Popular leisure pursuits include:

Hobbies. People pursue such hobbies as photography; acting; music (playing and listening); gardening; knitting; drawing; collecting stamps, autographs, and so forth; hiking; camping; fishing; and birdwatching.

Reading. Although fewer individuals read now than in the past, plenty of people still love to curl up with a good book. Books allow readers to escape from daily cares, solve mysteries, travel to real or imaginary places, learn useful information, and find inspiration. Mysteries, romances, science fiction, historical novels, biographies, and self-help books—the variety of books is truly astounding.

Surfing the Internet. A relatively new entry into the world of leisure, the Internet offers an amazing array of activities: e-mailing friends and relatives, visiting chat rooms on topics of interest, playing multiuser games, listening to music, visiting world-class museums, and taking tours through ancient historic sites, to mention just a few options.

Travel. Many choose their destinations spontaneously, but others are more systematic in their travel plans. For example, some individuals want to travel to all the U.S. national parks or all the major Civil War battlefields. Those who can afford it may travel to other countries— to get a taste of real French cooking or a firsthand look at what remains of ancient Egyptian civilization.

Games. Some individuals enjoy playing bridge for relaxation; others like to play board games such as Scrabble or chess. Computerized and video games are highly popular.

Sports. Many people like to play team sports such as bowling or softball, enjoying the benefits of both physical exercise and social interaction. Others enjoy individual sports such as jogging, swimming, surfing, ice skating, or skiing.

Volunteer activities. Helping others appeals to individuals in almost all age groups. Moreover, you can use your skills to help others in an incredibly diverse array of settings: homeless shelters, hospitals, schools, battered women's shelters, boys' and girls' clubs, and sports teams, for example.

Being aware of the broad range of leisure activities heightens your chances of selecting those that are most meaningful to you.

BENEFITS OF LEISURE ACTIVITIES

The idea that a satisfying balance of work, relationships, and leisure activities will lead to a more rewarding and healthy life has intuitive appeal. Happily, research generally supports this notion. For example, college students who participate at high levels in a variety of leisure activities report higher rates of perceived

physical, mental, and social health than students who are less involved (Caldwell, Smith & Weissinger, 1992). In a study of senior police officers in the United Kingdom, researchers reported that those who exercised showed higher levels of job satisfaction and better mental and physical health than officers who did not (Kirkcaldy et al., 1994). As you'll see in Chapter 14, regular exercise can also reduce the effects of stress and improve one's mood and self-concept. Among adults aged 55 and older, regular participation in a variety of leisure activities is positively correlated with psychological well-being and negatively related to depression (Dupuis & Smale, 1995). Interestingly, this study found that one leisure activity was *negatively* related to perceived well-being: viewing television. Additional research is needed on the actual (versus perceived) benefits of leisure.

As we noted, using the Internet is a relatively new leisure activity; thus, researchers are currently debating the impact of the Internet on frequent users. On the positive side, the Internet provides entertainment and facilitates communication among people with common interests who may be thousands of miles apart. Yet there may be some downsides to Internet use, especially for heavy users (Kraut et al., 1998). In a recent study, researchers reported that greater use of the Internet was associated with declines in users' communication with family members at home as well as declines in the size of their social circle. In addition, greater use of the

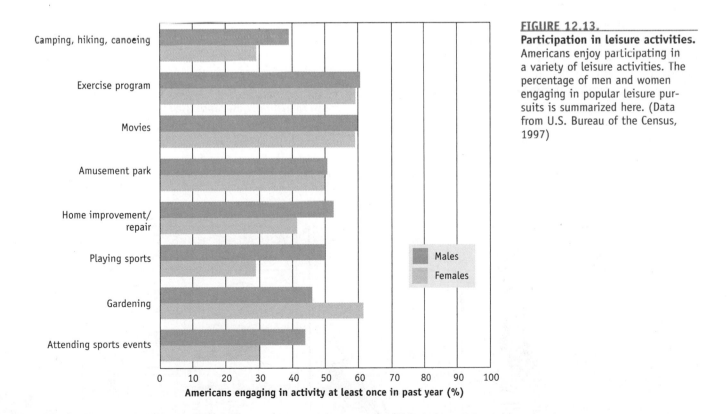

FIGURE 12.13.

Participation in leisure activities. Americans enjoy participating in a variety of leisure activities. The percentage of men and women engaging in popular leisure pursuits is summarized here. (Data from U.S. Bureau of the Census, 1997)

Internet was associated with increases in depression and loneliness. Because more and more people will have access to the Internet, this important issue merits further study.

Workaholism

Most people cherish their leisure activities and relationships with their families and friends. However, a small minority of people devote nearly all their time and energy to their jobs. These individuals tend to avoid nonwork activities. They put in considerable overtime, take few vacations, regularly bring work home from the office, and think about work most of the time. They are energetic, intense, and overly ambitious. In short, they are workaholics.

Psychologists are divided on the issue of whether workaholism is problematic. Should workaholics be praised for their dedication and encouraged in their single-minded pursuit of fulfillment through work? Or is workaholism a form of "addiction," a sign that an individual is driven by compulsions he or she cannot control? In support of the former view, Machlowitz (1980) found that workaholics tend to be highly satisfied with their jobs and with their lives. They work hard simply because work is the most meaningful activity they know. Yet other evidence suggests that workaholics may have a pathological need to exercise rigid control over themselves and their environments (Schwartz, 1982).

How can these conflicting findings be reconciled? Naughton (1987) has suggested that there may be two types of workaholics. One type, the job-involved workaholic, works for the pure joy of it. Such people derive immense satisfaction from work and generally perform well in highly demanding jobs. The other type, the compulsive workaholic, is neither well adjusted nor an asset to an employer. Compulsive workaholics are addicted to work. Their devotion to work reflects a rigid, overcontrolling personality. They approach their jobs in a ritualized manner and cannot deviate from their set routines. They often alienate their supervisors and co-workers with their rigidity. Interestingly, compulsive workaholics are not necessarily satisfied with their jobs, and they may be prone to develop *burnout*. Thus, it appears that workaholism may be either constructive or problematic, depending on the motivation underlying a particular individual's dedication to work.

Multiple Roles

The biggest recent change in the labor force has been the emergence of the dual-earner family, which is now the dominant family form in the United States (Hayghe, 1990). Dual-earner couples are struggling to work out new ways of balancing family life and the demands of work (see the Recommended Reading on page 359). These changes in work and family life have sparked the interest of researchers in many disciplines, including psychology.

An important fact of life for dual-earner couples is that two workers juggle three jobs: two paid jobs and one unpaid job at home. (In truth, if a couple has children, it is probably more realistic to describe them as having *four* jobs: two paid jobs and two unpaid jobs—housework and child care.) Most researchers have taken the tack that what goes on at work can spill over to affect family life, and vice versa. These *spillover* effects can be either positive or negative. For example, if you have a great day at the office, you'll probably come home in a good mood. But if your children are ill, your worry about them might undermine your concentration at work.

Most of the burdens associated with dual-earner households are borne by wives (Crosby & Jaskar, 1993). Women's unpaid work at home after her paid workday ends has been termed "the second shift" (Hochschild, 1989). Sometimes multiple roles are incompatible and cause *role conflict*. Because the division of labor in many homes is still based on traditional gender roles, wives are more likely to experience role conflict than husbands are. Let's say that a woman is scheduled to make a major presentation at work on Tuesday morning and

Recommended Reading

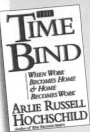

The Time Bind: When Work Becomes Home and Home Becomes Work by Arlie Russell Hochschild (Metropolitan Books, 1997)

Sociologist Hochschild addresses the difficulties of balancing work and family life. She makes the disturbing claim that many adult workers are spending more time at work than at home because they actually prefer it that way. For the children of these parents, it means spending more time in day care or after-school activities.

Hochschild's unsettling thesis is based on a case study of an anonymous Fortune 500 corporation ("Americo"). In three summers of field research, she interviewed employers and employees, attended business meetings, and shadowed working parents and their children. She observed that although Americo offered a number of "family friendly" programs (flextime, paternity leave), employees rarely made use of them. For many workers, lack of participation was rooted in concerns about career advancement and fears about job security in the age of downsizing. The shocker was that many workers actually preferred office life to home life! In other words, workers saw the office as a structured, supportive refuge compared to the conflicts, hassles, and pressures of home life.

To address the problem, the author urges parents to start a "time movement" by organizing to reduce work hours. Ironically, her data give little reason to believe that working parents would want to join such a movement. Moreover, she fails to address the really significant implication of her findings—namely, that Americans really need to reconsider what a satisfying adult life encompasses. Despite such weaknesses in her analysis, the findings are provocative and well worth thinking about.

> "I always tell people that I come to work to relax. I know to some people this sounds mean, but to me it's eight hours of relaxation. I can to go work and the kids aren't right in front of me to worry about. Mario, too, will tell you it's relaxing to work. At work, I can do more of what I want. At home, I have to do what the kids want" [p. 186].

her 2-year-old son wakes up with a fever and can't go to day care. If her husband can stay home with the baby, all is well. If he can't, then she either has to find someone else to care for him or do so herself. Either way, she feels guilt, conflict, and stress. To date, more women than men juggle multiple roles; thus, most of the research on this topic has used women as subjects.

What are the effects of juggling multiple roles? There are two competing perspectives on this question (Baruch, Biener, & Barnett, 1987). The *scarcity hypothesis* assumes that everyone has a finite amount of energy. Thus, the more roles a person has, the more energy will be used. The more energy expended, the greater the stress and other negative consequences. In contrast, the *enhancement hypothesis* asserts that people's energy resources are not limited. Psychologists who espouse this view use the analogy of those who exercise (expend energy) yet say they actually feel less tired and more energetic. The more roles one has, the greater the opportunities for stimulation, social status, and self-esteem. Also, multiple roles should serve as a buffer against the assaults of painful experiences, as negative events in one role can be balanced by the positive aspects of other roles.

Both hypotheses are supported by research. In support of the scarcity hypothesis, employed women report that the competing demands of work and family life are a major source of stress (Duxbury & Higgins, 1991). A study of 232 professional women (attorneys, physicians, and professors) reported that the majority of women often experienced career-family conflicts (Gray, 1983). For obvious reasons, the presence of young children reduces women's satisfaction with their professional work (Amaro, Russo, & Johnson, 1987). If working mothers can't find (or can't afford) high-quality care for their children, combining work and motherhood is stressful (Ross & Mirowsky, 1988). A high income can ease the strains and increase work satisfaction, but most women don't have high-paying jobs.

In support of the enhancement hypothesis, it has been found that working women are happier and healthier than full-time homemakers, except when their children are infants (Amatea & Fong, 1991; Helson, Elliott, & Leigh, 1990; Walker & Best, 1991). Still, because much of this research is correlational, it isn't clear whether paid work makes women happier and healthier or whether they would be happier and healthier than homemakers even if they didn't work. Also, these studies haven't looked at whether the positive effects of working may be the result of some other factor, such as salary, rather than work per se. However, in one study that looked at a number of possible correlates of self-esteem (employment, income, education, marital status, and developmental status), the researchers found that employment was the *only* significant predictor of self-esteem in midlife women (Coleman & Antonucci, 1983). Thus, although there is no definitive proof of the positive benefits of work for women, the evidence points strongly toward this conclusion. Again, the availability of high-quality child care and the involvement of the father in child care are key factors in the adjustment of working mothers (Ross & Mirowsky, 1988). Most of the research on multiple roles has focused on women with high-paying jobs. Additional research is needed on women in lower-paying jobs and on the effects of multiple roles on men.

To summarize, meaningful work, rewarding family interactions and friendships, and revitalizing leisure pursuits are three components of a rewarding life. Maintaining a satisfying balance among these life components is a major challenge in contemporary times.

In the Application, we'll describe how to conduct an effective job search and offer a few interviewing tips.

Getting Ahead in the Job Game

- *Summarize the guidelines for putting together an effective résumé.*
- *Discuss strategies for targeting companies you would like to work for.*
- *Describe several strategies for landing a job interview.*
- *List some factors that can influence an interviewer's rating of a job candidate.*
- *List the do's and don'ts of interviewing for jobs.*

Answer the following statements "true" or "false."

_____ **1.** The most common and effective job search method is answering classified ads.

_____ **2.** Your technical qualifications are the most important factor in determining the success of your job search.

_____ **3.** Employment agencies are a good source of leads to high-level professional jobs.

_____ **4.** You should make sure that your résumé is very thorough and includes everything you have ever done.

_____ **5.** It's a good idea to inject some humor into your job interviews. It will help both you and your interviewer relax.

Most career counselors would agree that all these statements are generally false. Although there isn't a single "tried and true" method for obtaining desirable jobs, experts do have guidelines that can increase your chances of success. Their insights are summarized in this Application.

Above all else, it is important to conduct a job search that is well-organized, thorough, and systematic. Sending out a hastily written résumé to a few randomly selected companies is a waste of effort. An effective job search requires lots of time and careful planning. People who are desperate for a job tend to behave in ways that cause prospective employers to see them as bad risks. Thus, it is crucial that you begin your search well in advance of the time when you will need a job. The best time to look for a job is when you don't need one. Then you can select an employer, rather than seeking an employer who will select you.

Of course, no amount of planning and effort can guarantee favorable results in a job search. Luck is definitely a part of the picture. Success may hinge on being in the right place, or meeting the right person at the right time. Moreover, becoming a top candidate for a position will depend on factors other than your technical competence. This is not to say that technical competence isn't necessary; it is. But given the realities of today's job market, employers are often inundated with applicants who have all of the required training and experience. The one who is ultimately selected often is not the one with the best technical qualifications. Rather, hiring decisions are made on the basis of subjective impressions gleaned from résumés, telephone conversations, and face-to-face interviews. These impressions are based on perceptions of personality, appearance, social skills, and body language. Knowing this, you can practice certain strategies that may increase the odds in your favor.

No matter what type of job you're looking for, successful searches have certain elements in common. First, you must prepare a résumé. Next, you need to target specific companies or organizations you would like to work for. Then, you must inform these companies of your interest in such a way as to get them interested in you.

Putting Together a Résumé

No matter what your job search strategy, an excellent résumé is a critical ingredient. The purpose of a résumé is not to get you a job. Rather, it is to get you an interview. To do so, it must communicate to the reader that you have at least the minimum technical qualifications for the position, know the standard conventions of the work world, and are a person who is on the fast track to success. Furthermore, it must achieve these goals without being flashy or gimmicky.

Your résumé will project the desired positive, yet conservative, image if you follow these guidelines (Carney & Wells, 1999):

1. Use white, ivory, or beige (*never* any other color) paper high in rag content.

2. Make sure it contains not a single typographical error.

3. Use the best professional printing service available.

4. Keep it short. One side of an 8.5" x 11" sheet of paper will suffice for most college students; do not go over 2 pages.

5. Don't write in full sentences, and avoid using the word *I*. Instead, begin each statement with an "action" word that describes a specific achievement, as in "Supervised a staff of fifteen" or "Handled all customer complaints."

6. Avoid giving any personal information that is superfluous to the job. It is an unnecessary distraction and may give the reader cause to dislike you and therefore reject your application.

An effective résumé will generally contain the following information, laid out in an easy-to-read format (Figure 12.14 shows an attractively prepared résumé).

```
                    TERESA M. MORGAN

Campus Address                              Permanent Address
1252 River St., Apt. 808                        1111 W. Franklin
East Lansing, MI 48823                        Jackson, MI 49203
(517) 332-6086                                  (517) 782-0819

OBJECTIVE        To pursue a career in interior design, or a related field, in which I
                 can utilize my design training. Willing to relocate after June 1996.

EDUCATION        Michigan State University, East Lansing, MI 48825.
Sept. 1994–      Bachelor of Arts–Interior Design, with emphasis in Design
June 1996        Communication and Human Shelter. Courses include Lighting,
                 Computers, Public Relations and History of Art.
                 (F.I.D.E.R. accredited) 3.0 GPA (4.0 5 A).

July 1995–       Michigan State University overseas study, England and France,
Aug. 1995        Decorative Arts and Architecture. 4.0 GPA (4.0 5 A).

Sept. 1992–      Jackson Community College, Jackson, MI 49201.
June 1994        Associate's Degree. 3.5 GPA (4.0 5 A).

EMPLOYMENT       Food Service and Maintenance, Owen Graduate Center, Michigan
Sept. 1995–      State University.
June 1996        • Prepared and served food.
                 • Managed upkeep of adjacent Van Hoosen Residence Hall.

Dec. 1994–       Food Service and Maintenance, McDonel Residence Hall.
June 1995        • Served food and cleaned facility.
                 • General building maintenance.

June 1993–       Waitress, Charlie Wong's Restaurant, Jackson, MI.
Dec. 1993        • Served food, dealt with a variety of people on a personal level.
                 • Additional responsibilities: cashier, hostess, bartender, and
                   employee trainer.

                 • Community College Transfer scholarship from MSU.
HONORS           • American Society of Interior Design Publicity Chairman;
AND                Executive board, MSU Chapter.
ACTIVITIES       • Sigma Chi Little Sisters.
                 • Independent European travel, summer 1995.
                 • Stage manager and performer in plays and musicals.

               REFERENCES and PORTFOLIO available upon request.
```

FIGURE 12.14.

Example of an attractively formatted résumé. The physical appearance of a résumé is very important. This example shows what a well-prepared résumé should look like. (Adapted from Lock, 1996)

Heading. At the top of the page, give your name, address, and phone number. This is the only section of the résumé that is not given a label.

Objective. State a precise career goal, remembering to use action words and to avoid the use of *I*. An example might be "Challenging, creative position in the communication field requiring extensive background in newspaper, radio, and television."

Education. List any degrees you've earned, giving major field of study, date, and granting institution for each. (List the highest degree you received first. If you have a college degree, you don't need to mention your high school diploma.) If you have received any *academic* honors or awards, mention them in this section.

Experience. This section should be organized chronologically, beginning with your most recent job and working backward. For each position, describe your responsibilities and your achievements. Be specific, and make sure your most recent position is the one with the greatest achievements. Never pad your résumé by listing trivial accomplishments. Readers find this annoying. Moreover, it just calls attention to the fact that you don't have more important items to list.

If you are currently a student or are a recent graduate, your schooling will provide the basis for both your experience and your qualifications. You can give yourself a boost over the competition by taking part-time or summer jobs in the field in which you plan to work. If this option isn't feasible, do some volunteer work in this area and list it under an "Honors and Activities" section on your résumé.

Technology is changing a number of aspects of the job search process, including the preparation and screening of résumés. Increasingly, companies are likely to electronically scan résumés for key words that match job specifications (Lock, 1996). Thus, it's helpful to know how to create an electronic résumé in addition to the traditional paper version; you can get information about doing so at your campus Career Services office. The World Wide Web is an excellent source of career-related information. Most of the Web Links in this chapter contain information that can help you prepare an effective résumé and cover letter.

Finding Companies You Want to Work For

Initially, you need to determine what general type of organization will best suit your needs. Do you want to work in a school? a hospital? a small business? a large corporation? a government agency? a human services agency? If you want to select an appropriate work environment, you need an accurate picture of your personal qualities and knowledge of various occupations and their characteristics.

Once you've decided on a setting, you need to target specific companies. That's easy; you simply look for companies that have advertised openings in your field, right? Not necessarily. If you restrict yourself to this approach, you may miss many valuable opportunities. Experts estimate that up to 80% of all vacancies, especially those above entry level, are never advertised (Bolles, 1997).

How should you proceed? Certainly you should check the classified section in newspapers to identify the many positions that are advertised. If you are willing to relocate anywhere, a good source for business

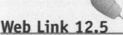

Web Link 12.5

Careers.wsj.com

Compiled by an editorial team using Dow Jones & Co. information sources (including the *Wall Street Journal*), this site contains both daily updates on employment issues and more than 1,000 job-seeking and employment articles. Students can find an extraordinary wealth of tips and strategies on résumé and cover letter preparation, effective interviewing, and similar practical matters.

and professional jobs is the *National Business Employment Weekly*. You should also consult any trade or professional newspapers, magazines, or journals in your field. The Internet is also a good place to search for job openings (see several of the Web Links in this chapter).

You could also go to an employment agency, but keep in mind that these agencies generally handle only entry-level, hourly wage jobs. In addition, they can cost you thousands of dollars (Lareau, 1997). If you're interested in professional jobs, you might consider contacting executive recruiters, widely known as "headhunters." Executive recruiters work on commission for organizations that have vacancies to fill. They earn their livelihood by actively looking for people who have the qualifications being sought by the hiring organization. You can locate headhunters nationwide by consulting *The Directory of Executive Recruiters*.

What about that 80% of openings that are not advertised? Actually, this statistic is somewhat misleading. It includes a large number of vacancies that are filled by promotions within organizations (Lareau, 1985). Nonetheless, many organizations do have openings that are not accessible through traditional channels. If you have targeted companies that haven't advertised any vacancies, you may want to initiate the contact yourself. In support of this approach, a survey by the Bureau of the Census indicated that "direct application to an employer" was both the most commonly used and the most effective job search method (Bolles, 1997). Richard Bolles, author of *What Color Is Your Parachute?*, suggests the following strategy. First, identify a specific problem that the organization has, then develop a strategy to solve it. Next, find out who has the power to hire and fire (either through library research or a network of personal contacts). Finally, approach this person directly to convince him or her of your unique capability to help.

Landing an Interview

No one is going to hire you without first "checking out the goods." This inspection process typically involves one or more formal interviews. How do you go about getting yourself invited for an interview? If you are applying for an advertised vacancy, the traditional approach is to mail a résumé with a cover letter to the hiring organization. If your letter and résumé stand out from the crowd, you may be invited for an interview. One way to increase your chances is to persuade the prospective employer that you are interested enough in the company to have done some research on the organization. By taking the time to learn something about a company, you should be in a better position to make a convincing case about the ways in which your expertise will be particularly useful to the organization.

If you are approaching an organization in the absence of a known position opening, your strategy may be somewhat different. You may still opt to send a résumé, along with a more detailed cover letter explaining why you have selected this particular company. Another option, suggested by Bolles (1997), is to introduce yourself (by phone or in person) directly to the person in charge of hiring and request an interview. You can increase your chances of success by using your network of personal contacts to identify some acquaintance that you and the person in charge have in common. Then, you can use this person's name to facilitate

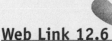

Web Link 12.6

The Catapult on JOBWEB
The National Association of Colleges and Employers has assembled a comprehensive set of resources for both students and career guidance professionals. The site includes information on job searching, employment listings, educational updating, and college- and university-based resources.

To be successful on a job interview, candidates need to dress appropriately and convey confidence, enthusiasm, and interest in the job.

your approach. Once you do have that interview with a potential employer, you should follow up with a thank-you note and a résumé that will jog the employer's memory about your training and talents.

Polishing Your Interview Technique

The final, and most crucial, step in the process of securing a job is the face-to-face interview. If you've gotten this far, the employer already knows that you have the requisite training and experience to do the job. Now your challenge is to convince the employer that you're the kind of person who would fit in well in the organization. Your interviewer will attempt to verify that you have the intangible qualities that will make you a good team player. Even more important, the interviewer will attempt to identify any "red flag" behaviors, attitudes, or traits that mark you as an unacceptable risk.

Because interviews are so important, you would think that interviewers' ratings of job applicants are heavily based on job-relevant considerations. Unfortunately, research shows that this is not usually the case. For one thing, confirmation bias (Chapter 6) can operate in interview situations. That is, interviewers who have formed positive expectations about a job candidate (based on the résumé, letters of recommendation, and the like) before meeting the person often display interview behaviors that tend to confirm these expectations, and vice versa (Dipboye, 1992). In addition, researchers have found that more attractive candidates are usually rated higher than less attractive ones, as are those who dress in a manner consistent with the dress norms in an organization (Forsythe, Drake, & Cox, 1985). It has also been found that job candidates who are overweight are rated lower (especially if they are women) than those of average weight (Pingitore et al., 1994). Finally, it has been found that interviewees who emit positive nonverbal cues—leaning forward, smiling, and nodding—are rated higher than those who do not (Riggio & Throckmorton, 1988). Thus, to do your best in an interview, you should brush up on your nonverbal communication skills (Chapter 7) and your impression management tactics (Chapter 5).

To create the right impression, you must come across as confident, enthusiastic, and ambitious. Your demeanor should be somewhat formal and reserved, and you should avoid any attempts at humor—you never know what might offend your interviewer (Lareau, 1997). Above all, never give more information than the interviewer requests, especially negative information. If asked directly what your weaknesses are—a common ploy—respond with a "flaw" that is really a positive, as in "I tend to work too hard at times." Don't interrupt or contradict your interviewer. And don't ever blame or criticize anyone, especially previous employers, even if you feel that the criticism is justified (Carney & Wells, 1999).

Developing an effective interview technique requires practice. Many experts suggest that you never turn down an interview, because you can always benefit from the practice even if you don't want the job. Advance preparation is also crucial. Never go into an interview cold. Find out all you can about the company before you go. Try to anticipate the questions that will be asked and have some answers ready. In general, you will not be asked simply to reiterate information from your résumé. Remember, it is your personal qualities that are being assessed at this point. A final word of advice: If possible, avoid any discussion of salary in an initial interview. The appropriate time for salary negotiation is *after* a firm offer of employment has been extended. You can find additional tips on interviewing by visiting many of the Web Links in this chapter.

Key Ideas

CHOOSING A CAREER
● Ideally, people look for jobs that are compatible with their personal characteristics. Thus, individuals need to have a sense of their abilities, personality, and interests, as well as information about potential careers.
● A variety of resources are available to individuals who want to learn about possible career options. In researching prospective careers, it is important to find out about the nature of the work, working conditions, entry requirements, potential earnings, potential status, opportunities for advancement, intrinsic satisfactions, and the future outlook for jobs.
● Individuals who have trouble making career decisions may find it helpful to take an occupational interest inventory. People have the potential for success in a variety of occupations, and they need to keep this and other considerations in mind as they make career decisions.

MODELS OF CAREER CHOICE AND DEVELOPMENT
● John Holland's hexagonal model of career development asserts that people select careers based on their own personality characteristics. Holland has identified six personal orientations and matching work environments.
● Super's stage theory holds that self-concept development is the basis for career choice. According to this model, there are five stages in the occupational life cycle: growth, exploration, establishment, maintenance, and decline.
● Models of career development in women are still being developed. Women's career paths are often less orderly and predictable than men's because of the need to juggle multiple roles and because many women interrupt their careers to devote time to child-rearing.

THE CHANGING WORLD OF WORK
● Work is an activity that produces something of value for others. A number of contemporary trends are changing the world of work. Generally, the more education individuals obtain, the higher their salaries will be.
● Between now and the year 2005, more women and minorities will join the labor force. Although women and minorities are participating in the workforce at all occupational levels, they tend to be concentrated in the lower-paying and lower-status positions. Furthermore, women and minorities face discrimination in a number of areas. Increasing diversity in the workforce presents challenges to both organizations and workers.

COPING WITH OCCUPATIONAL HAZARDS
● Major hazards in the workplace include job stress, sexual harassment, and unemployment. The negative effects of stress affect both employers and employees. Interventions to manage stress in the workplace can be made at the individual level, the organizational level, and the individual-organizational interface.
● Victims of sexual harassment often develop physical and psychological symptoms of stress that can lead to decreased work motivation and productivity. Many organizations are taking steps to educate their workers about this problem.
● Because of dramatic changes in the economy, unemployment is a problem for both unskilled and skilled workers. Job loss is highly stressful; middle-aged workers are most distressed by the experience. Unemployed workers who believe that they have been treated unfairly and arbitrarily typically feel angry; a few of these individuals may resort to violence in the workplace. In coping with unemployment, social support is critical. Some companies teach their laid-off workers how to cope with their situation.

BALANCING WORK AND OTHERS SPHERES OF LIFE
● A major challenge for workers today is balancing work, family, and leisure activities in ways that are personally satisfying. Leisure seems to play an important role in psychological and physical health. Workaholism may be constructive or problematic, depending on a person's underlying motives for work. As dual-earner families have become the family norm, juggling multiple roles has emerged as a challenge, especially for women.

APPLICATION: GETTING AHEAD IN THE JOB GAME
● Career counselors are in agreement about the essential elements of a successful job search. The key factors include (1) determining the type of organization that will best suit one's needs, (2) constructing an effective résumé, (3) winning a job interview, and (4) developing an effective interview technique.
● Before interviewing with a company, it is wise to do some research on the company to demonstrate your interest in the organization. Nonverbal communication skills can be crucial in job interviews. You should try to appear confident and enthusiastic. If possible, try to avoid salary discussions in your initial interview.

Key Terms

Displaced workers
Labor force
Leisure
Occupational interest inventories
Sexual harassment
Token
Underemployment
Work

Key People

Nancy Betz
John Holland
Robert Karasek
Donald Super

Practice Test

1. Individuals' career choices are often:
   a. much higher in status than those of their parents.
   b. similar to those of their parents.
   c. much lower in status than those of their parents.
   d. unrelated to their family background.

2. According to a Gallup poll, which of the following aspects of jobs did workers rate highest?
   a. Good health insurance, interesting work, and job security
   b. Regular hours, chances for promotion, and high income
   c. Freedom to work independently, recognition from co-workers, and vacation of a week or more
   d. Chance to learn new skills, ability to help others, and limited job stress

3. Occupational interest inventories are designed to predict:
   a. how successful an individual is likely to be in a job.
   b. how long a person will stay in a career.
   c. how satisfied a person is likely to be in a job.
   d. all of the above.

4. Holland's hexagonal theory of occupational choice emphasizes:
   a. the role of self-esteem in job choice.
   b. the unfolding of career interests over time.
   c. parental influences and job choice.
   d. matching personality traits and job environments.

5. Which of the following is *not* a work-related trend?
   a. Technology is changing the nature of work.
   b. New work attitudes are required.
   c. Temporary employment is on the decline.
   d. Lifelong learning is a necessity.

6. Findings on education and earnings show that:
   a. there is no relationship between education and earnings.
   b. at all levels of education, men earn more than women.
   c. at all levels of education, women earn more than men.
   d. there are no gender differences in education and earnings.

7. When there is only one woman or minority person in a workplace setting, that person becomes a symbol of his or her group and is referred to as a _____.
   a. protected species
   b. derisive symbol
   c. sex object
   d. token

8. Job stress has been found to lead to all but which the following negative effects?
   a. Burnout
   b. Bipolar disorder
   c. High blood pressure
   d. Anxiety

9. According to recent research, spending a lot of time on the Internet:
   a. is associated with increased depression and reduced social contacts.
   b. is associated with benefits to mental health and social relationships.
   c. is associated with higher self-esteem, but reduced social interactions.
   d. is associated with neither positive nor negative outcomes.

10. Which of the following is a good tip in preparing an effective résumé?
    a. Make your résumé as long as possible.
    b. Use complete sentences.
    c. Use white, ivory, or beige paper.
    d. Provide a lot of personal information.

Answers

1. b pages 337–338
2. a page 339
3. c page 340
4. d page 341
5. c pages 345–347
6. b page 347
7. d pages 348–349
8. b page 351
9. a pages 357–358
10. c page 360

INFOTRAC COLLEGE EDITION

Go to the Wadsworth Psychology Study Center (http://psychology.wadsworth.com/) for quiz questions, research updates, hot topics, interactive exercises, and suggested readings in INFOTRAC related to this chapter.

Development and Expression of Sexuality

Sex. For some people it's a source of great intimacy and pleasure. For others it is a source of extraordinary anxiety and frustration. To some, it's a sport; to others, an oppressive duty. Whatever the case, sexuality plays a central role in people's lives. Americans sometimes seem obsessed with sex. People joke and gossip about it constantly. Movies and TV shows, magazines and novels are saturated with sex. The advertising business uses sex to sell everything from automobiles to toothpaste. People voraciously consume books to help them improve their sex lives. Yet many couples find it excruciatingly difficult to talk to each other about sex, and misconceptions about sexuality abound.

In this chapter we'll consider sexuality and adjustment. Specifically, we'll look at the development of sexuality and the interpersonal dynamics of sexual relationships. Then, we'll discuss sexual arousal and the varieties of sexual expression. We'll also address the important topics of contraception and sexually transmitted diseases. In the Application, we'll offer some suggestions for enhancing sexual relationships.

Before we begin we should point out that sex research is subject to some unique problems. For one thing, researchers have a particularly difficult time getting representative samples of subjects. Most studies of American sexuality are overrepresented with white, middle-class volunteers. Also, many people are understandably reluctant to discuss their sex lives. Thus people who are willing to volunteer information appear to be more liberal and more sexually experienced than the general population (Clement, 1990). Furthermore, given the difficulties in doing direct observation, sex researchers have depended mostly on interviews and questionnaires. Unfortunately, people may respond less than truthfully about their sex lives because of shame, embarrassment, boasting, or wishful thinking (Catania, McDermott, & Pollack, 1986). Thus, you need to evaluate the results of sex research with more than the usual caution.

Becoming a Sexual Person

LEARNING OBJECTIVES

- List four key aspects of sexual identity.
- Discuss how hormones influence sexual differentiation and sexual behavior.

- Discuss how families, peers, schools, and the media shape sexual attitudes and behavior.
- Discuss gender differences in sexual socialization and how they affect individuals.
- Summarize current thinking on the origins of sexual orientation.
- Discuss the adjustment and identity development of lesbians and gay males.

People vary greatly in how they express their sexuality. While some eagerly reveal the intimate details of their sex lives, others can't even use sexual words without embarrassment. Some people need to turn the lights out before they can have sex; others would like to be on camera with spotlights shining. To understand this diversity, we need to examine developmental influences on human sexual behavior.

Key Aspects of Sexual Identity

Identity refers to a stable sense of who one is and what one stands for (see Chapter 5). We'll use the term **sexual identity to refer to the complex of personal qualities, self-perceptions, attitudes, values, and preferences that guide one's sexual behavior.** In other words, your sexual identity consists of your sense of yourself as a sexual person. It includes four key features: sexual orientation, body image, sexual values and ethics, and erotic preferences.

1. *Sexual orientation.* Sexual orientation is an individual's preference for emotional and sexual relationships with individuals of one gender or the other. **Heterosexuals seek emotional-sexual relationships with members of the other gender. Homosexuals seek emotional-sexual relationships with members of the same gender. Bisexuals seek emotional-sexual relationships with members of both genders.** In recent years, the terms *gay* and *straight* have become widely used to refer to homosexuals and heterosexuals, respectively. Male homosexuals are called *gay,* whereas female homosexuals prefer to be called *lesbians.* As a social issue, sexual orientation has only recently come out of the closet. Because many people are ignorant about this issue, we'll give it a closer look a little later.

2. *Body image.* Your body image is how you see yourself physically. Your view of your physical self definitely affects how you feel about yourself in the sexual domain. A positive body image is correlated with greater sexual activity and higher sexual satisfaction (Hatfield & Rapson, 1996). The increasing popularity of plastic surgery for breast enhancements, tummy tucks, and face-lifts testifies to the importance people place on body image.

3. *Sexual values and ethics.* All cultures impose constraints on how people are expected to behave sexually. People are taught that certain expressions of sexuality are "right" while others are "wrong." The nature of these sexual messages varies depending on gender, race, ethnicity, and socioeconomic status. For example, the double standard encourages sexual experimentation in males, but not females. Individuals are faced with the daunting task of sorting through these often-conflicting messages to develop their own sexual values and ethics.

4. *Erotic preferences.* Within the limits imposed by sexual orientation and values, people still differ in what they find enjoyable. Your erotic preferences encompass your attitudes about self-stimulation, oral sex, styles of foreplay and intercourse, and other sexual activities. They develop through a complex interplay of physiological and psychosocial influences—issues we'll take up next.

Physiological Influences

Among the various physiological factors involved in sexual behavior, hormones have been of particular interest to researchers.

HORMONES AND SEXUAL DIFFERENTIATION

During prenatal development, a number of biological developments result in a fetus that is a male or a female. Hormones play an important role in this process, which is termed *sexual differentiation.* Around the third month of prenatal development, different hormonal secretions begin to be produced by male and female **gonads—the sex glands.** In males, the testes produce **androgens, the principal class of male sex hormones.** Testosterone is the most important of the androgens. In females, the ovaries produce **estrogens, the principal class of female sex hormones.** Actually, both classes of hormones are present in both genders, but in different proportions. During prenatal development, the differentiation of the genitals depends primarily on the level of testosterone produced—high in males, low in females.

At puberty, hormones reassert their influence on sexual development (Brooks-Gunn & Reiter, 1990). As you saw in Chapter 11, adolescents attain reproductive capacity as hormonal changes trigger the maturation of the *primary sex characteristics* (sex organs). Hormonal shifts also regulate the development of *secondary sex characteristics* (physical features that distinguish the genders but are not directly involved in reproduction). In females, more estrogen leads to breast development, widened hips, and more rounded body contours. In males, more androgen results in developing facial hair, a deeper voice, and angular body contours.

HORMONES AND SEXUAL BEHAVIOR

Hormonal fluctuations clearly regulate sex *drive* in many species of animals. Hormones also play a role in human sexuality, but their influence is much more modest. *Androgen* does seem related to sexual motivation in *both* men and women, although the effect is less strong in women (Everitt & Bancroft, 1991; Sherwin, 1991). Also, high levels of testosterone in female and male subjects correlate with higher rates of sexual activity (Knussmann, Christiansen, & Couwenbergs, 1986). Curiously, *estrogen* levels among women do not correlate well with sexual interest. There does appear to be an association between females' sex drive and their ovulation/menstruation cycles, but the hormonal basis for this association is yet to be determined (Stanislaw & Rice, 1988).

In summary, physiological factors have important effects on sexual development. Their influence on *anatomy,* however, is much greater than their influence on sexual *activity.*

Psychosocial Influences

The principal psychosocial influences on sexual identity are essentially the same as the main sources of gender-role socialization discussed in Chapter 10. Sexual identity is shaped by families, peers, schools, and the media.

FAMILIES

Parents and the home environment are significant influences on sexual identity in the early years. Before they reach school age, children usually engage in some sex play and exploration, often under the guise of "playing doctor." They also display curiosity about sexual matters, asking questions such as "Where do babies come from?" Parents frequently punish innocent, exploratory sex play and squirm when kids ask sexual questions. These sorts of reactions tend to convey the idea that sex is "dirty." As a result, children may begin to feel guilty about their sexual urges and curiosity. Thus, parents who are uncomfortable with their sexuality can pass on that discomfort to their children at early ages.

When it comes time for more systematic sex instruction, many parents have difficulty talking with their children. One survey found that 31% of American teenagers have never talked to their parents about sex and that 42% were anxious about bringing up the topic with their parents (Harris et al., 1986). The issue of homosexuality is an especially difficult one to broach, as we'll discuss later. Not surprisingly, open communication about sexual topics in the home correlates with better sexual adjustment among college students (Lewis & Janda, 1988). Furthermore, adolescents who receive most of their sex education from a parent are less likely to be sexually active, and they are more likely to use contraceptives if they *are* sexually active (Baker, Thalberg, & Morrison, 1988; Milan & Kilmann, 1987).

Ultimately, parents who make sex a taboo topic end up reducing their influence on their kids' evolving sexual identity, as the children turn elsewhere for information about sexuality. Thus, a conspiracy of silence about sex in the home can backfire by increasing the influence of peers, schools, and the media.

PEERS

As you can see in Figure 13.1, friends are, by far, the principal source of sex information for both males and females. Of course, this is the proverbial case of "the blind leading the blind." Peers can be a source of highly misleading information. Furthermore, they often champion sexual ethics at odds with parents' views.

However, peers can be a highly effective force for sexually responsible behavior, as innovative sex education programs such as Atlanta's Postponing Sexual Involvement demonstrate (Howard & McCabe, 1990). In this program, selected high school seniors are trained to educate younger students to postpone sexual involvement until they are mature enough to be sexually responsible. Among other things, students practice effective responses to the "lines" teens encounter. Teens who participate in such programs are less likely to have sex, and when they do have sex, they are more likely to use contraceptives.

SCHOOLS

To allay parents' fears that sex education will encourage sexual behavior, many sex education programs are nothing more than "an organ recital—what is connected to what in the body with no discussion of how or why two bodies might connect with each other" (Zellman & Goodchilds, 1983, p. 53). Unfortunately, these courses ignore the important psychological and social aspects of sexuality.

Web Link 13.1

Sex Education Resources on the World Wide Web: Recommended Sites
In writing a 1997 article for the *Journal of Sex Education and Therapy*, David A. Gotlib and Peter Fagan of Johns Hopkins University surveyed the Web for the best online resources about sexuality. Here are their recommendations, last updated in the fall of 1998.

FIGURE 13.1.

Main sources of sexual information in childhood. When questioned about where they got their information about sex during childhood, adult respondents cited friends as their most frequent source of information. (Adapted from Reinisch, 1990)

Main Sources of Sexual Information in Childhood	
Sources of information	Percentage using source*
Friend	42
Mother	29
Books	22
Boyfriend or girlfriend	17
Sex education	14
Magazines	13
Father	12
Sister	8
Movies	6
Brother	6
Other relative	6
Television	5
Teacher	5

*Respondents could choose up to three sources.

Research on the effectiveness of sex education programs suggests that they lead to neither the experimentation that parents worry about nor the restraint that the programs advocate (Jacobs & Wolf, 1995). On a positive note, programs that encourage youth to personalize sexual information and to use it in decision making do lead to more effective contraceptive practices (Barth, Petro, & Leland, 1992). Most teenagers would prefer to receive sex education in school (McKay & Holoway, 1997). Yet in 1995, fewer than half of the states required comprehensive sex education programs (National Abortion Rights Action League, 1995).

THE MEDIA

Increasingly, television is becoming a source of information about sex. A 1998 Time/CNN poll reported that TV is the main source of sex information for 29% of teens, as opposed to 11% of teens in 1986 (Stodghill, 1998). American teenagers see nearly 14,000 sexual encounters a year on TV alone (Cole, Emery, & Horowitz, 1993). And, television portrayals of sexual relationships are likely to influence young people's emerging sexual values (Strouse & Fabes, 1985). Unfortunately, one rarely sees TV characters taking steps to avoid pregnancy or sexually transmitted diseases (Braverman & Strasburger, 1994).

Sex is found in cyberspace as well. Newsgroups with sexually explicit images are very popular, especially among males. At one American university, 13 of the 40 most frequently visited newsgroups had titles that were sex-related (Elmer-Dewitt, 1995). Many parents are understandably alarmed about young children having easy access to sexually explicit material.

Books and magazines are another major source of information on sex. Unfortunately, many of these publications perpetuate myths about sex and miseducate their young readers. The lyrics of rock music also contain extensive references to sexual behavior and norms of sexual conduct (Ray, Soares, & Tolchinsky, 1988). Some rap music has come under fire because it portrays women as sex objects and advocates sexual violence against women.

Exposure to erotic materials appears to elevate the likelihood of sexual behavior for only a few hours (Cattell, Kawash, & DeYoung, 1972). Nonetheless, such material may have long-term effects on attitudes that eventually influence sexual behavior. For instance, one study found that participants who were exposed to a large dose of (nonaggressive) pornography developed more liberal attitudes about acceptable sexual practices (Zillmann and Bryant, 1984). As we noted in the Chapter 8 Application, viewing *aggressive* pornography may strengthen the myth that women enjoy being raped (Malamuth, 1984) and may increase men's aggressive behavior toward women (Malamuth & Donnerstein, 1982).

In summary, sexual identities are shaped by a host of intersecting influences. Given the multiplicity of factors at work, it should be obvious that people bring highly diverse expectations to their sexual relationships. As you'll see, this diversity can complicate sexual interactions.

Gender Differences in Sexual Socialization

In our culture, sex typically means different things to men than to women. According to John DeLamater (1987), women are taught to take a "person-centered" orientation to sexuality, while men are taught to take a recreational, or "body-centered," approach toward sex. In other words, women typically equate love, commitment, intimacy, and sex; men usually separate sex and love (Hatfield & Rapson, 1996). By contrast, Swedish men and women tend to equate love and sex to a greater degree than most Americans do (Foa et al., 1987).

Societal values obviously come into play here. American males are encouraged to experiment sexually, to initiate sexual activities, and to enjoy sex without emotional involvement (Fracher & Kimmel, 1987). They also get the message to be conquest-oriented regarding sex ("scoring"). Adolescent males also use sex

Because of gender differences in sexual socialization, females tend to begin seeing themselves as sexual persons at a later age than males.

as a vehicle for validating their social status with other males (Garnets & Kimmel, 1991). Consequently, sex has a variety of meanings for men: They may emphasize "sex for fun" in casual relationships and reserve "sex with love" for committed relationships (Oliver & Hyde, 1993). Despite the stereotypes of men always being ready for sex, men often report feeling pressured to pursue sex even when they're not interested, for fear of being perceived as unmasculine or gay (Crooks & Baur, 1996).

Girls are typically taught to view sex in the context of a loving relationship (Hatfield & Rapson, 1996). They learn about romance and the importance of physical attractiveness and catching a mate. It isn't until women actually begin having sexual experiences that they begin to see themselves as sexual persons.

Sexual socialization takes longer for females than for males. One reason is *sexual guilt* (Lott, 1987). Whereas social norms encourage males to be sexually active, these norms discourage such behavior in females—sexually active women may be looked on as "loose" or "easy lays." Thus, women learn to feel guilty about having sexual feelings and wanting to act on them. Second, women typically develop *negative associations about their genitals and sex* that males don't experience: blood and pain associated with menstruation, fears of pregnancy, and fears of penetration. Girls also hear negative messages about sex and men ("Men only want one thing") from their mothers, siblings, and female peers. They are also aware of rape and incest. All these negative associations with sex are combined with the positive rewards of dating and emotional intimacy. Hence, it's no surprise that many women feel ambivalent about sex (Hyde, 1996). These feelings can tilt in the negative direction if early sexual partners are unskilled, impatient, or selfish.

With differing views of sexuality and relationships, males and females are likely to be out of sync with each other—particularly in adolescence and early adulthood. A metaanalysis of studies on gender differences in sexuality found men to be much more accepting of casual sex ("one-night stands") than women (Oliver & Hyde, 1993). Not until adulthood do women become more comfortable with themselves as sexual persons, and males more comfortable with emotional intimacy and commitment. These gender differences mean that communication is essential for mutually satisfying sexual relationships.

How do these gender differences in sexual socialization operate in *homosexual* relationships? Because both members of homosexual couples have been socialized similarly, they are less likely than straight couples to have "incompatibility problems." Like heterosexual women, lesbians typically experience emotional attraction to their partners before experiencing sexual feelings (Garnets & Kimmel, 1991). By contrast, gay men (like heterosexual men) place much more importance on physical appearance and sexual compatibility in selecting partners (Blumstein & Schwartz, 1983) and develop emotional relationships out of sexual ones (Harry, 1983).

Sexual Orientation

Gay, straight, or in-between? In this section, we'll explore the intriguing and controversial topic of sexual orientation.

KEY CONSIDERATIONS

Most people view heterosexuality and homosexuality as two distinct categories: you're either one or the other. However, many individuals who define themselves as heterosexuals have had homosexual experiences, and vice versa (Kinsey, 1948, 1953; Laumann et al., 1994). Thus, experts believe that it is more accurate to view heterosexuality and homosexuality as end points on a continuum. Indeed, Alfred Kinsey devised a seven-point scale, shown in Figure 13.2, to characterize sexual orientation.

Alfred Kinsey

How are people distributed on this scale? No one knows for sure, because it's hard to get accurate data. Furthermore, there's some debate about where to draw the lines between heterosexuality, bisexuality, and homosexuality on the Kinsey scale. A frequently cited estimate of the number of people who are predominantly homosexual is 10%; however, several recent surveys have all reported lower estimates (ACFS Investigators, 1992; Johnson et al., 1992; Laumann et al., 1994). If homosexuals and bisexuals are lumped together, the 10% figure is probably reasonably accurate for males but is an overestimate for females.

Now let's complicate things a little more. Using Kinsey's model, how would you characterize a person who was married for 10 years, has children, got a divorce, and is now involved in a committed homosexual relationship? And what about a person who is married but who has homosexual fantasies and feels strongly drawn to members of the same gender? Other theorists have proposed more elaborate models to accommodate these complex realities. One thought-provoking model portrays sexual orientation as a cluster of seven factors that can be rated along Kinsey's seven-point scale: sexual behavior; emotional preference; sexual fantasies; sexual attraction; social

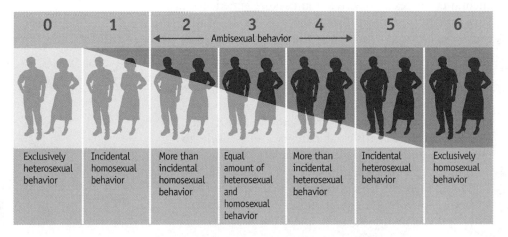

FIGURE 13.2.

Heterosexuality and homosexuality as end points on a continuum. Kinsey and other sex researchers view heterosexuality and homosexuality as ends of a continuum rather than as all-or-none distinctions. Kinsey created this seven-point scale (from 0 to 6) for describing sexual orientation. He used the term *ambisexual* to describe those falling in the middle of the scale, but *bisexual* is more widely used today.

0	1	2	3	4	5	6
		←	Ambisexual behavior	→		
Exclusively heterosexual behavior	Incidental homosexual behavior	More than incidental homosexual behavior	Equal amount of heterosexual and homosexual behavior	More than incidental heterosexual behavior	Incidental heterosexual behavior	Exclusively homosexual behavior

Both biological and environmental factors appear to contribute to homosexuality, although its precise developmental roots remain obscure.

preference; lifestyle, social world, and community; and self-identification (Klein, Sepekoff, & Wolff, 1986). According to this view, individuals' ratings on the seven factors may or may not be congruent. Moreover, these ratings may change over time to match shifts in people's understanding of their sexual orientation. As this model shows, sexual orientation is a complex concept that we need to know a lot more about.

ORIGINS

Why do some people become straight and others, gay? We will focus on possible causes of homosexuality because relatively little has been written about the causes of heterosexuality (a reflection of heterosexism). A number of *environmental explanations* have been suggested as causes of homosexuality. Freud believed that the combination of a "binding" mother and distant father contributed to the development of male homosexuality. Sociologists propose that homosexuality develops because of poor relationships with same-gender peers or because being labeled a homosexual sets up a self-fulfilling prophecy. Learning theorists assert that homosexuality results from early negative heterosexual encounters or early positive homosexual experiences. Surprisingly, the most comprehensive study of the causes of sexual orientation found no compelling support for *any* of these leading environmental explanations of homosexuality (Bell, Weinberg, & Hammersmith, 1981). On a related issue, no evidence has been found that parents' sexual orientation is linked to that of their children (Bozett, 1987; Falk, 1989). That is, heterosexual parents are as likely to produce homosexual (or heterosexual) offspring as homosexual parents are.

Some theorists have speculated that *biological factors* may be involved in the development of homosexuality, because many gay men and some lesbians can

trace their homosexual leanings back to their childhood years (Bell, Weinberg, & Hammersmith, 1981; Garnets & Kimmel, 1991). Several lines of research suggest that hormonal secretions during prenatal development may shape sexual development, organize the brain in a lasting manner, and influence subsequent sexual orientation (Berenbaum & Snyder, 1995). To date, however, the research is inconclusive, so this theory must be viewed with caution. Other theorists have explored possible hormonal differences between adult heterosexuals and homosexuals. Again, however, there is no convincing evidence linking hormonal patterns to sexual orientation, although this possibility can't be ruled out. If hormones shape sexual orientation, their effects must be complex and subtle (Garnets & Kimmel, 1991; Gladue, 1987).

Genetic factors are also possible determinants of sexual orientation. In one study, researchers identified gay and bisexual men who had a twin brother (identical or fraternal) or an adopted brother (Bailey & Pillard, 1991). It was found that the concordance rates for homosexuality were substantially higher for identical twins than for fraternal twins or adopted siblings (see Figure 13.3). These researchers found a similar pattern of results in a study of lesbian women with twin or adopted sisters (Bailey et al., 1993). The concordance rates findings clearly point to a genetic contribution to

FIGURE 13.3.

Genetics and sexual orientation. A concordance rate indicates the percentage of twin pairs or other pairs of relatives that exhibit the same characteristic. If relatives who share more genetic relatedness show higher concordance rates than relatives who share less genetic overlap, this evidence suggests a genetic predisposition to the characteristic. Recent studies of both gay men and lesbian women have found higher concordance rates among identical twins than fraternal twins, who, in turn, exhibit more concordance than adoptive siblings. These findings are consistent with the hypothesis that genetic factors influence sexual orientation. If only genetic factors were responsible for sexual orientation, the identical twin concordance rates would be 100%; because they are much lower, environmental factors must also play a role. (Data from Bailey & Pillard, 1991; Bailey et. al., 1993)

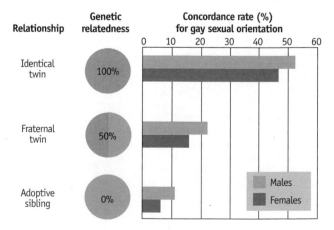

sexual orientation. However, if only genetic factors determined sexual orientation, we would see 100% concordance for the identical twin pairs. However, the fact that these concordance rates were 52% for gay men and 48% for lesbians indicates that environmental factors also play a role in sexual orientation. Finally, there is evidence for a genetic marker for homosexuality in men (Hamer, et al., 1993; Hu et al., 1995) but not in women (Hu et al., 1995). Researchers speculate that a gene or genes on the X chromosome might somehow contribute to male homosexuality. Thus, studying possible genetic links to homosexuality appears to be a promising line of inquiry.

The bottom line is that it isn't yet clear what determines sexual orientation. This issue is an exceedingly complex one and research is still in its infancy. The best we can say is that the explanation must lie in some complex interaction of biological and environmental factors (Byne & Parsons, 1993; Gladue, 1994).

ATTITUDES TOWARD HOMOSEXUALITY

News stories spotlight gay couples at high school proms, and television programs now feature homosexual characters. Clearly, homosexuals are much more visible today than they were in the past. Still, Americans' attitudes toward homosexuality are predominantly negative, especially among men. A 1996 survey reported that about 60% of all Americans believe that sex between two adults of the same gender is always wrong (Yang, 1997). On the other hand, attitudes vary widely depending on the issue (see Figure 13.4).

Homophobia **is the intense fear and intolerance of homosexuality.** Characteristics associated with homophobia include being older, having conservative religious beliefs, endorsing traditional gender roles, having less education, and coming from a rural area (Kite & Deaux, 1986; Seltzer, 1992). Unfortunately, negative attitudes sometimes translate into hate crimes, such as the brutal murder of Matthew Shepard, a gay college student, in Wyoming (see photo).

Attitudes about homosexuality are becoming more positive, but most Americans still disapprove of it. Unfortunately, negative attitudes can result in hate crimes, as in the case of Matthew Shepard, a Wyoming college student who was beaten to death.

Not all societies view homosexuality negatively. A review of anthropological studies of 294 societies reported that 59 societies had a clear opinion of homosexuality; within this group, 69% approved of it and 31% condemned it (Gregerson, 1982).

ADJUSTMENT

The mental health community initially classified homosexuality as a psychological disorder. The pioneering research of Evelyn Hooker (1957) and others, however, demonstrated that view to be a myth: Gays and straights do not differ on overall measures of psychological adjustment (Bell & Weinberg, 1978; Rosen, 1974). The results of these studies, changes in public attitudes, and political lobbying contributed to the

Prejudice Toward Homosexuals			
Poll Question	Yes	No	Depends/ No opinion
Should homosexuals have equal rights in terms of job opportunities?	84%	12%	4%
Should homosexual relations between consenting adults be legal?	44%	47%	9%
Should homosexuals be allowed to marry and have the same rights as traditionally married couples?	27%	68%	5%

FIGURE 13.4.
Attitudes toward homosexuals. According to 1996 Gallup polls, Americans' attitudes toward gays are highly variable, depending on the specific issue. Women generally have more accepting attitudes than men. (Adapted from Moore, 1996; Saad, 1996)

deletion of homosexuality from the official list of psychological disorders in 1973 (Rothblum, Solomon, & Albee, 1986).

Researchers have also examined the adjustment of children from homosexual families. A study that compared children from lesbian and heterosexual families reported no differences in peer group relationships, popularity, or social adjustment (Green, 1982).

IDENTITY DEVELOPMENT

Homosexuals seem to take longer to recognize their sexual orientation than heterosexuals do, for several reasons (Garnets & Kimmel, 1991; McDonald, 1982; Vance & Green, 1984). For one thing, the widespread *assumption that heterosexuality is universal* means that some individuals never even consider the possibility that they might be homosexual until they have pretty strong evidence that they are. A second reason is tied to the *stigma* associated with homosexuality: Even when individuals suspect they are homosexual, they may try to deny this fact for fear of social rejection. Third, homosexuals report both same- and other-gender erotic arousal and sexual behavior during adolescence and early adulthood. Some experts speculate that *sexual experiences with the other gender* may cause gay men and lesbians to misclassify themselves as heterosexuals, thus delaying their awareness of their true sexual orientation (Hencken, 1984).

Clarity about sexual orientation seems to take longer in lesbians than in gay men. Possible reasons include the fact that lesbians are more likely than gay men to engage in heterosexual sex, less likely to be involved in same-gender erotic activity, more likely to continue other-gender sexual activities after questioning their sexual identity, and more likely to get married than gay men (Garnets & Kimmel, 1991; Chapman & Brannock, 1987).

Linda Garnets and Greg Kimmel (1991) have summarized the research on homosexual identity development. Developmental milestones in this process include the following:

Web Link 13.2

Queer Resources Directory (QRD)
In its 1994 mission statement, the Queer Resources Directory described itself as "an electronic research library specifically dedicated to sexual minorities—groups which have traditionally been labeled as 'queer' and systematically discriminated against." Consisting of more than 22,000 files and still growing, QRD offers a rich array of resources.

1. *Initial awareness of same-gender erotic desires.* Individuals become aware of strong emotional and sexual attractions to members of the same gender. This recognition in turn triggers a "developmental transition in which individuals report feeling different and being off course" (p. 154).

2. *Reconciling sexual orientation with negative societal attitudes.* Over time, individuals transform the category of "gay" or "lesbian" from a negative (societal stereotype) to a positive one and accept, by degrees, that the label applies to themselves. Individuals use a number of cognitive strategies to reconcile negative societal attitudes with their own sexual orientation.

3. *Exploring gay and lesbian subcultures.* Contact with these subcultures is available in most cities, by newspaper subscription, and by toll-free information services. Such contact provides a range of role models and diminishes feelings of isolation.

4. *Disclosing sexual orientation to others.* Over time, homosexuals usually feel the need to disclose their identity to other people. Communicating one's sexual orientation to others appears to be a prerequisite for the emergence of a positive gay male or lesbian identity. Nevertheless, individuals need to balance the psychological and social benefits of doing so against the costs (being fired from their jobs, losing friends, losing custody of their children, falling victim to hate crimes). A pragmatic solution to this conflict is *rational outness*—being "as open as possible, because it feels healthy to be honest, and as closed as necessary to protect against discrimination" (Bradford & Ryan, 1987, p. 77). Homosexual individuals are more likely to disclose their sexual orientation to close heterosexual friends and siblings than to parents, co-workers, or employers.

Coming to terms with one's homosexuality in a hostile environment is understandably difficult. A survey of 165 15- to 21-year-old gay and bisexual youth reported that over half feared disclosing their sexual orientation to their parents (D'Augelli & Hershberger, 1993). This same study reported that, among parents who knew about their children's homosexuality, 12% of mothers were perceived by their children to be rejecting and 8% to be intolerant but not rejecting; comparable figures for fathers were 18% and 10%, respectively. Finally, these researchers found that a third of the survey participants feared rejection from peers, and 46% reported that they had actually lost friends over the issue. These painful circumstances contribute to high rates of depression, suicide, substance abuse, and high-risk sexual behavior among this group (Hershberger & D'Augelli, 1995). Clearly, gay youth (and adults) need more emotional support and positive messages about being gay (see the Recommended Reading box on the next page).

Loving Someone Gay by Don Clark
(Celestial Arts, 1997)

Now in its twentieth anniversary edition, this book speaks both to those who are gay and to those who know someone gay. The author, a clinical psychologist who is gay, writes in a personal and informal style that draws the reader in. He also easily weaves in real-life examples to illustrate his points. The first two sections address questions of special interest to homosexuals. For example, Clark discusses the impact of invisibility and oppression on one's self-concept, as well as the rewards of being gay. Other topics include coming out, meeting other gay people, the emotional and sexual aspects of relationships, and dealing with break-ups. The third section, "Loving Someone Gay," contains advice for people who know someone gay: parents, wives, husbands, sons, daughters, other relatives, friends, and neighbors. In "Professional Help," the fourth section, Clark provides suggestions for those who interact, often unknowingly, with gays (teachers, librarians, physicians, nurses, clergy, counselors, police, judges, legislators, and researchers).

Another excellent book in this area is *Positively Gay: New Approaches to Gay and Lesbian Life* edited by Betty Berzon (Celestial Arts, 1992). In this book, experts explore a variety of topics of interest to gay individuals: special issues in same-gender relationships, family relationships, children, aging, religion, work, people of color, and AIDS. For a book that deals specifically with gays and their parents, try *Coming Out to Parents: A Two-Way Survival Guide for Lesbians and Gay Men and Their Parents* by Mary Borhek (Pilgrim Press, 1993).

Most of all, I suppose, from the long list that could be drawn of the rewards of that come with being gay, I like being able to be myself. Being gay has given me a self that is respectful of differences in people. It has granted me the ability to look on the human world with a greater sense of compassion. [p. 69]

Interaction in Sexual Relationships

LEARNING OBJECTIVES

- *Describe five common sexual motives.*
- *Describe four common barriers in communicating about sex.*

Because of their importance, sexual relationships stir up intense emotions. When things are going well, you feel on top of the world; when they're not, you feel in the grip of despair. In this section, we'll briefly discuss the interpersonal dynamics of sexual relationships.

Motives Underlying Sexual Interactions

What motivates individuals to engage in sexual encounters? As you might surmise, sexual motives are quite diverse (Nass, Libby, and Fisher, 1981). We'll mention only a few:

Affection. Longing for love, closeness, and physical and emotional union.

Lust. Having passion for intensifying and then gratifying sexual desires with a focus on sensual arousal, fantasies, and delight in touching and being touched.

Duty. Feeling obligated to have sex on schedule or to keep a partner from being uncomfortably frustrated. A woman often feels that she can't leave a man unsatisfied. The notion that he could masturbate or that she might feel equally uncomfortable if highly aroused but not satisfied is missing from this picture.

Boredom. Using sex to enhance a dull environment or routine activities.

Self-affirmation. Acting out one's perceived sexual identity so that the other will notice and approve of it.

Consistent with the gender differences we discussed earlier, men and women usually have different motives for sex (Carroll, Volk, & Hyde, 1985; Taris & Semin, 1997). In one study, college students were asked, "What was your most important reason for having sexual intercourse on the most recent occasion?" Lust and pleasure motives were cited by 51% of the men but only 9% of the women. Love and emotional reasons were cited by 51% of the women but only 24% of the men (Whitley, 1988). Similar gender differences have been found in a community survey that looked at a broader sample of subjects than just college students (Leigh, 1989). Furthermore, these gender differences appear to transcend sexual orientation, as they are observed in gays as well as straights. Some experts speculate that these differences are due to gender-role socialization (Carroll et al., 1985); others believe that they are a product of biological influences (Knoth, Boyd, & Singer, 1988).

Communicating About Sex

Because individuals differ in sexual motives, attitudes, and appetites, disagreements about sex are commonplace (Laumann et al., 1994). Couples have to negotiate whether, how often, and when they will have sex. They also have to decide what kinds of erotic activities will take place and what sexual behavior means to their relationship. This negotiation process may not be explicit, but it's there. Many people find it difficult to talk to their partner about sex, yet unresolved disparities are likely to be an ongoing source of frustration in a relationship. Experts have identified four common barriers to sexual communication:

1. *Fear of appearing ignorant.* According to a Kinsey Institute/Roper poll, most Americans are woefully ignorant about sex (Reinisch, 1990). Specifically, 55% of a statistically representative sample of American adults failed an 18-item test of basic sexual knowledge (could answer correctly only 50% or fewer of the questions). Another 27% received D's (could answer only 56–66% of the questions correctly). (You can test your own knowledge about some aspects of sex by responding to the questions in Figure 13.5.) Because most people feel that they should be experts about sex and know that they are not, they feel ashamed. To hide their ignorance, they avoid talking about sex.

2. *Concern about partner's response.* Both men and women say they want their partners to tell them exactly what they want sexually (see Figure 13.6). Ironically, neither feels comfortable doing so (Hatfield & Rapson, 1996). People usually hold back because they're afraid of hurting the other's feelings. Or, they fear that their partner won't respect and love them if they say what they really want. Still, when people keep their preferences to themselves, they are likely to be frustrated and unsatisfied.

3. *Conflicting attitudes about sex.* Many people, particularly women, are burdened with the negative sexual messages they learned as children. Also, most individuals have contradictory beliefs about sex ("Sex is 'beautiful'" and "Sex is 'dirty'"), and this dissonance produces psychological conflicts. It may also cause individuals to feel uncomfortable with themselves as sexual persons and to have difficulty talking about sex.

4. *Early negative sexual experiences.* Some people have had negative sexual experiences that inhibit their enjoyment of sex. If these experiences are due to ignorant or inconsiderate sexual partners, subsequent positive sexual interactions will usually resolve the problem over time. If earlier sexual experiences have been

FIGURE 13.5.

How knowledgeable about sex are you? Check your basic sexual knowledge by answering 5 of the 18 questions on the Kinsey Institute's test. Information about each of the questions is discussed in this chapter. (Based on Reinisch, 1990)

How Knowledgeable About Sex Are You?

1. Petroleum jelly, Vaseline Intensive Care, baby oil, and Nivea are not good lubricants to use with a condom or diaphragm.

_____ True _____ False _____ Don't know

2. More than one out of four (25%) American men have had a sexual experience with another male during their teens or adult years.

_____ True _____ False _____ Don't know

3. It is usually difficult to tell whether people are or are not homosexual just by their appearance or gestures.

_____ True _____ False _____ Don't know

4. A woman or teenage girl can get pregnant during her menstrual flow (her "period").

_____ True _____ False _____ Don't know

5. A woman or teenage girl can get pregnant even if the man withdraws his penis before he ejaculates (before he "comes").

_____ True _____ False _____ Don't know

Scoring: 1. True. (Oil-based creams, lotions, and jellies can produce microscopic holes in rubber products within 60 seconds of their application.) 2. True. (A Kinsey Institute review of research estimated that at least 25% of American males have had at least one same-sex experience.) 3. True. (Gay males can be extremely masculine, average, or effeminate in their appearance and gestures. Lesbians can be extremely feminine, average, or masculine in their appearance and gestures.) 4. True. (While the chance of a woman's becoming pregnant during her menstrual period is lower than at other times, pregnancy can occur if she has unprotected sex during her period. Sperm can live for up to 8 days in a woman's reproductive tract, and if the menstrual cycle is irregular, as it is likely to be in adolescence, sperm may still be present in the reproductive tract a week later to fertilize a new egg.) 5. True. (The pre-ejaculatory fluid secreted from the tip of the penis during arousal may contain enough sperm to fertilize an egg.)

FIGURE 13.6.

What men and women want more of during sex. Dating and married couples were asked which sexual activities they wanted more of in their relationships. Men and women all agreed that they wanted more instructions from their partners. They also generally agreed that they wanted warmer, more involved sexual relationships and more experimentation. In terms of gender differences, men wanted their partners to take the initiative and to be wilder and sexier; women wanted more emotional reassurance. (Based on Hatfield & Rapson, 1993)

What Men and Women Want More of During Sex.

Dating Couples	
Men	**Women**
Wish their partners would:	
Be more experimental	Talk more lovingly
Initiate sex more often	Be more seductive
Try more oral-genital sex	Be warmer and more involved
Give more instructions	Give more instructions
Be warmer and more involved	Be more complimentary

Married Couples	
Men	**Women**
Wish their partners would:	
Be more seductive	Talk more lovingly
Initiate sex more	Be more seductive
Be more experimental	Be more complimentary
Be wilder and sexier	Be more experimental
Give more instructions	Give more instructions
	Be warmer and more involved

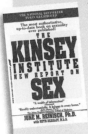
traumatic, as in the case of rape or incest, counseling may be required to help the individual view sex positively and enjoy it.

It's unfortunate that couples have difficulty talking about sex. Studies show that open communication is associated with greater relationship satisfaction and greater sexual satisfaction (Cupach & Comstock, 1990). Most of the advice in Chapter 7 on how to improve verbal and nonverbal communication can be applied to sexual relationships. Assertive communication and constructive conflict-resolution strategies can keep sexual negotiations healthy. A basic rule is to accentuate the positive ("I like it when you . . .") rather than the negative ("I don't like it when you . . .").

The Human Sexual Response

LEARNING OBJECTIVES

● Describe the four phases of the human sexual response cycle.
● Discuss gender differences in patterns of orgasm and some reasons for them.

When people engage in sexual activity, exactly how does the body respond? Surprisingly, until William Masters and Virginia Johnson conducted their groundbreaking research in the 1960s, very little was known about the physiology of the human sexual response. Masters and Johnson used physiological recording devices to monitor the bodily changes of volunteers engaging in sex. Their observations and interviews with their subjects yielded a detailed description of the human sexual response that has won them widespread acclaim.

William Masters and Virginia Johnson

The Sexual Response Cycle

Masters and Johnson's (1966, 1970) description of the sexual response cycle is a general one, outlining typical rather than inevitable patterns. You should keep in mind that people vary considerably. Figure 13.7 on the next page shows how the intensity of sexual arousal changes as women and men progress through the four phases of the sexual response cycle.

EXCITEMENT PHASE

During the initial phase of excitement, the level of arousal usually escalates rapidly. In both sexes, muscle tension, respiration rate, heart rate, and blood pressure increase quickly. In males **vasocongestion—engorgement of blood vessels**—produces penile erection, swollen testes, and the movement of the scrotum (the sac containing the testes) closer to the body. In females, vasocongestion leads to a swelling of the clitoris and vaginal lips, vaginal lubrication, and enlargement of the uterus. Most women also experience nipple erection and a swelling of the breasts.

PLATEAU PHASE

The name given to the "plateau" stage is misleading because physiological arousal does not level off. Instead, it continues to build, but at a much slower pace. In women, further vasocongestion produces a tightening of the lower third of the vagina and a "ballooning" of the upper two-thirds. This lifts the uterus and cervix away from the end of the vagina. In men, the

FIGURE 13.7.

The human sexual response cycle. There are similarities and differences between men and women in patterns of sexual arousal. Pattern A, which culminates in orgasm and resolution, is the most typical sequence for both sexes. Pattern B, which involves sexual arousal without orgasm followed by a slow resolution, is also seen in both genders, but it is more common among women. Pattern C, which involves multiple orgasms, is seen almost exclusively in women, as men go through a refractory period before they are capable of another orgasm. (Based on Masters & Johnson, 1966)

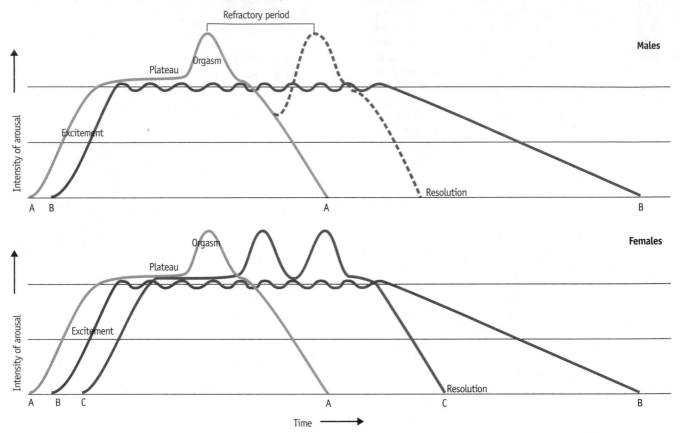

head of the penis may swell, and the testicles typically enlarge and move closer to the body. Many men secrete a bit of pre-ejaculatory fluid from the tip of the penis that may contain sperm.

Distractions during the plateau phase can delay or stop movement to the next stage. These include ill-timed interruptions like a telephone call, the doorbell ringing, or a child's knocking—or not!—on the bedroom door. Equally distracting can be such things as physical discomfort, pain, guilt, frightening thoughts, feelings of insecurity or anger toward one's partner, and anxiety about being able to have an orgasm.

ORGASM PHASE

Orgasm occurs when sexual arousal reaches its peak intensity and is discharged in a series of muscular contractions that pulsate through the pelvic area. Heart rate, respiration rate, and blood pressure increase sharply during this exceedingly pleasant spasmodic response. The male orgasm is usually accompanied by ejaculation of seminal fluid. Interestingly, some women report that they ejaculate some kind of fluid at orgasm. How common this is and the source and nature of the

fluid are matters still under debate (Darling, Davidson, & Conway-Welch, 1990). The subjective experience of orgasm appears to be essentially the same for men and women.

RESOLUTION PHASE

During the resolution phase, the physiological changes produced by sexual arousal subside. If one has not had an orgasm, the reduction in sexual tension may be relatively slow and sometimes unpleasant. After orgasm, men generally experience a *refractory period,* **a time following male orgasm during which males are largely unresponsive to further stimulation.** The refractory period varies from a few minutes to a few hours and increases with age.

Gender Differences in Patterns of Orgasm

As a whole, the sexual responses of women and men parallel each other fairly closely. The similarities clearly outweigh the differences. Nonetheless, there are some interesting differences between the genders in their patterns of experiencing orgasm. During *intercourse*, women are somewhat less likely than men to reach orgasm (that is, they are more likely to follow pattern B in Figure 13.7). According to a recent survey of American sexual behavior (Laumann et al., 1994), about 63% of women reported that they "always" or "usually" reached orgasm in their primary sexual relationships, compared to 95% of men (see Figure 13.8). Apparently, about 10% of American women have never had an orgasm by any means (Spector & Carey, 1990).

In their laboratory, Masters and Johnson found that the men they studied took about 4 minutes to reach a climax with their partners. Women took about 10–20 minutes to reach orgasm with their partners, but they reached orgasm in about 4 minutes when they masturbated. Clearly, then, women are capable of reaching orgasm more quickly than they typically do. Our point here is not that men and women should race each other to the finish line, but that physiological factors are not the likely cause of gender differences related to orgasm.

How do we account for these disparities? First, although most women report that they enjoy intercourse, it is not the optimal mode of stimulation for them. This is because intercourse provides rather indirect stimulation to the clitoris, the most sexually sensitive genital area in most women. Thus, more lengthy foreplay, including manual or oral stimulation of the clitoris, is usually the key to enhancing women's sexual pleasure (Darling, Davidson, & Cox, 1991). Unfortunately, many couples are locked into the idea that orgasms should be achieved only through intercourse. (Even the word foreplay suggests that any other form of sexual stimulation is merely preparation for the "main event.")

Web Link 13.3

SIECUS (Sexuality Information and Education Council of the United States)
This site is produced by one of the oldest organizations in the U.S. devoted to educating the public about matters of sexuality. It contains not only SIECUS-related information but an excellent annotated set of links to many topics related to sexuality.

Orgasmic inconsistency in women can also be caused by intercourse that is too brief or too mechanical to be satisfying. Because most women associate sex and affection, they want to hear some tender words during a sexual encounter. Men who can verbally express their love and affection will usually find their partners more sexually responsive.

The incidence of orgasm among lesbians also supports a socialization-based explanation of gender differences in orgasmic consistency. Kinsey (1953) found that lesbians who had been sexually active for five years reached orgasm more consistently than heterosexual women who had been married for the same length of time. He suggested that this was because female partners know more about women's sexuality and techniques for optimizing women's sexual satisfaction than male partners do. Also, female partners are more likely to emphasize the emotional aspects of lovemaking than male partners (Blumstein & Schwartz, 1983).

Because women reach orgasm through intercourse less consistently than men, they are more likely than men to fake an orgasm (Darling & Davidson, 1986). Surveys reveal that both genders do this, but women do it more often. More than half of all adult women have faked orgasm (Wiederman, 1997)—although not usually in a restaurant as in the movie *When Harry Met*

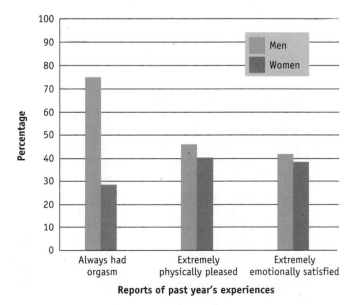

FIGURE 13.8.

Sexual satisfaction with primary partner. A recent major survey of American sexual behavior showed large gender differences in the consistency of orgasm, a physical measure of sexual satisfaction. Men's and women's subjective evaluations of physical and emotional sexual satisfaction are much more similar. These data indicate that not everyone who has an orgasm every time has a blissful sex life and that factors other than orgasm contribute to a satisfying sex life. (From Laumann et al., 1994)

Sally! People typically fake orgasms to bring sexual activity to an end when they're tired or to make their partners feel better. Frequent faking is not a good idea, because it can undermine communication about sex.

Sexual Expression

LEARNING OBJECTIVES

- *Discuss fantasy as well as kissing and touching as aspects of sexual expression.*
- *Discuss the prevalence of self-stimulation and attitudes about it.*
- *Discuss oral and anal sex as forms of sexual expression.*
- *Discuss intercourse and the preferred sexual activities of gay males and lesbians.*

People experience and express sexuality in myriad ways. *Erogenous zones* **are areas of the body that are sexually sensitive or responsive.** The genitals and breasts usually come to mind when people think of erogenous zones, as they are particularly sensitive areas for most people. But it's worth noting that many individuals fail to appreciate the potential that lies in other areas of the body. Virtually any area of the body can function as an erogenous zone.

Indeed, the ultimate erogenous zone may be the mind. By this we mean that an individual's mental set is extremely important to sexual arousal. Skillful genital stimulation by a partner may have absolutely no impact if a person is not in the mood. Yet fantasy in the absence of any other stimulation can produce great arousal. In this section, we'll consider the most common forms of sexual expression.

Fantasy

Have you ever fantasized having sex with someone other than your partner? If so, you've had one of the most commonly reported fantasies (see Figure 13.9). There's no need to feel guilty about this; more than 90% of men and women have fantasies during sexual activities with another person (Leitenberg & Henning, 1995). As you might expect, women's fantasies tend to be more romantic, while men's tend to contain more explicit imagery. Most sex therapists view sexual fantasies as harmless ways to enhance sexual excitement and achieve orgasm (Davidson, 1985).

As you can see in Figure 13.9, dominance and submission fantasies are not uncommon. Still, people's fantasizing about a particular encounter, such as forced sex, doesn't mean that they really want to have such an experience. Only one-tenth of 1% of women say that they enjoy forced sex, and only one-third of 1% of men say that they enjoy forcing a partner to have sex (Laumann et al., 1994).

Kissing and Touching

Most two-person sexual activities begin with kissing. Kissing usually starts with the lips but may be extended to almost any area of the partner's body. Mutual caressing is also an integral element of sexual stimulation for most couples. Like kissing, this tactile stimulation may be applied to any area of the body. Manual and oral stimulation of the other partner's genitals are related sexual practices. As with any type of sexual activity, specific techniques are not as important as good communication about one's preferences.

Men often underestimate the importance of kissing and touching (including clitoral stimulation). It is not surprising, therefore, that heterosexual women commonly complain that their partners are in too much of a hurry (Denny, Field, & Quadagno, 1984). Partners who seek to learn about each other's preferences and who try to accommodate each other are much more likely to have mutually satisfying sexual experiences than those who don't.

● Recommended Reading

Human Sexuality Today by Bruce M. King (Prentice Hall, 1999)

College courses on sexuality are gradually appearing all over the country, and a host of new books to serve these courses are now available. If you can't enroll in a course on sexuality, you may want to read one of the better textbooks. If so, *Human Sexuality Today* by Bruce King is an outstanding candidate. King's text is accurate, thorough, up-to-date, well organized, and written in an engaging, highly readable manner. Lots of first-person accounts are also sprinkled throughout the text. The author is sensitive to readers' personal needs; he discusses the interpersonal aspects of sex without getting bogged down in physiology. Moreover, the book is a paperback and thus more manageable than most heavy, hardcover texts on the topic. There is also positive coverage of homosexuality.

Other sexuality texts of similar quality include *Our Sexuality* by Robert Crooks and Karla Baur (Brooks/Cole, 1996) and *Understanding Human Sexuality* by Janet Shibley Hyde and John D. DeLamater (McGraw-Hill, 1996). Any of these books can provide you with an excellent introduction to the realities of human sexual expression.

Unfortunately, many men take the attitude that what feels good to the gander must also feel good for the goose—if it feels good to the man to have his penis in his partner's vagina, then it must also feel equally good to the woman to have his penis in her vagina. The stimulation provided by the vaginal walls to the penis during intercourse is similar to that experienced by men during masturbation, but the reverse is not true for women. [p. 333]

Self-Stimulation

Masturbation, or the stimulation of one's own genitals, has traditionally been condemned as immoral because it is nonreproductive. Disapproval and suppression of masturbation were truly intense in the 19th and early 20th centuries, when people believed that the practice was harmful to physical and mental health. Because the term *masturbation* has acquired negative connotations, many modern experts prefer to use *self-stimulation* or *autoeroticism.*

Kinsey discovered over four decades ago that most people masturbate with no ill effects. Sexologists now recognize that self-stimulation is normal and healthy. In fact, sex therapists often prescribe masturbation to treat both male and female sexual problems (see this Chapter's Application). Nonetheless, nearly half of those who engage in the practice feel guilty about it (Laumann et al., 1994).

Self-stimulation is common in our society: By adulthood, nine out of ten males and eight out of ten females report having masturbated at least once (Atwood & Gagnon, 1987). Masturbation is less common among those with less education (Laumann et al., 1994). African American males masturbate less than Asian, white, and Hispanic men.

Among married couples, 57% of husbands and 37% of wives report engaging in self-stimulation (Laumann et al., 1994). In fact, masturbation in marriage is often associated with a greater degree of marital and sexual satisfaction (Hurlbert & Whittaker, 1991). However, marital partners usually don't talk to each other about their masturbation, probably for fear that their partner might view it as a sign of sexual discontent.

Web Link 13.4

American Sexual Behavior

Tom W. Smith, of the National Opinion Research Center at the University of Chicago, has assembled one of the most complete compendiums of statistics relating to "trends, socio-demographic differences, and risk behavior" in the sexual behavior of Americans that can be found anywhere. It can be downloaded from the NORC's library site simply by clicking on the name of the report (users must have Adobe Acrobat Reader installed on their computer to read the document).

Oral and Anal Sex

Oral sex refers to oral stimulation of the genitals. ***Cunnilingus* is oral stimulation of the female genitals; *fellatio* is oral stimulation of the penis.** Partners may stimulate each other simultaneously, or one partner may stimulate the other without immediate reciprocation. Oral-genital sex may be one of several activities in a sexual encounter, or it may be the main event. Oral sex is a major source of orgasms for many heterosexual couples, and it plays a central role in homosexual relationships. A positive aspect of oral sex is that it does not result in pregnancy. However, it is possible to contract AIDS through mouth-genital stimulation, especially if semen is swallowed (in fellatio).

Fantasies During Intercourse

Theme	Subjects reporting fantasy (%) Males	Subjects reporting fantasy (%) Females
A former lover	42.9	41.0
An imaginary lover	44.3	24.3
Oral-genital sex	61.2	51.4
Group sex	19.3	14.1
Being forced or overpowered into a sexual relationship	21.0	36.4
Others observing you engage in sexual intercourse	15.4	20.0
Others finding you sexually irresistible	55.2	52.8
Being rejected or sexually abused	10.5	13.2
Forcing others to have sexual relations with you	23.5	15.8
Others giving in to you after resisting you at first	36.8	24.3
Observing others engaging in sex	17.9	13.2
A member of the same sex	2.8	9.4
Animals	0.9	3.7

Note: For comparison, the responses of "frequently" and "sometimes" were combined for both males and females to obtain these percentages. The number of respondents answering for a specific fantasy ranged from 103 to 106 for males and from 105 to 107 for females.

FIGURE 13.9.
Common sexual fantasies. The percentage of men and women reporting various sexual fantasies during intercourse is shown here. Sue (1979) concluded that people fantasize about experiences they wouldn't seek out in real life.

There is a residue of negative attitudes about oral sex, particularly among African Americans, Hispanics, religious conservatives, and those with less education (Laumann et al., 1994). However, the prevalence of oral sex appears to have increased dramatically since the Kinsey studies of the late 1940s and early 1950s (Gagnon & Simon, 1987). About 80% of men and 70% of women (both gay and straight) report that they have either given or received oral sex at least once (Laumann et al., 1994). It appears that oral sex is now a component in most couples' sexual relationships (Blumstein & Schwartz, 1983; Wyatt, Peters, & Guthrie, 1988).

Anal intercourse **involves insertion of the penis into a partner's anus and rectum.** Legally, it is termed sodomy (and is still considered illegal in some states). About 25% of men and women report that they have practiced anal sex at least once (Laumann et al., 1994). Anal intercourse is more popular among homosexual male couples than among heterosexual couples. However, even among gay men it ranks behind oral sex and mutual masturbation in prevalence. AIDS is easily transmitted by anal sex as rectal tissues are easily torn, allowing the virus to pass through the membrane.

Intercourse

Vaginal intercourse, known more technically as *coitus,* **is inserting the penis into the vagina and (typically) pelvic thrusting.** It is the most widely endorsed and widely practiced sexual act in our society. In the recent American sex survey, 95% of heterosexual respondents said that they had practiced vaginal sex the last time they had sex (Laumann et al., 1994). Inserting the penis generally requires adequate vaginal lubrication, or intercourse may be difficult and painful for the woman. This is another good reason for couples to spend plenty of time on mutual kissing and touching. In the absence of adequate lubrication, partners may choose to use artificial lubricants such as K-Y jelly.

Couples use a variety of positions in intercourse. Many use more than one position in a single encounter. The man-above, or "missionary," position is the most common, but the woman-above, side-by-side, and rear-entry positions are also popular. Each position has its advantages and disadvantages, according to Masters and Johnson (1970). Although people are fascinated by the relative merits of various positions, specific positions may not be as important as the tempo, depth, and angle of movements in intercourse. As with other aspects of sexual relations, the crucial consideration is that partners talk to each other about their preferences.

What kinds of sexual activities do homosexuals prefer in the absence of coitus (which is, by definition, a heterosexual act)? Gay men engage in fellatio, mutual masturbation, and anal intercourse, in that order

(Lever, 1994). Lesbians engage in cunnilingus, mutual masturbation, and *tribadism,* in which one partner lies on top of the other and makes thrusting movements so that both receive genital stimulation at the same time. Contrary to stereotype, a dildo (an artificial penis) is rarely used by lesbian couples (Jay & Young, 1979).

Patterns of Sexual Behavior

LEARNING OBJECTIVES

- Describe how the fear of contracting AIDS has influenced sexual attitudes and practices.
- Summarize attitudes toward and prevalence of "premarital" sex.
- Summarize the findings on sex patterns in dating couples and married couples.
- Compare and contrast sexual behavior in married versus committed homosexual couples.
- Summarize the evidence on infidelity in committed relationships.

In this section we'll consider whether fears of contracting acquired immune deficiency syndrome (AIDS) have influenced sexual attitudes and behaviors. Then we'll see how age, gender, and type of relationship are related to sexual behavior.

Sex in the Age of AIDS

American sexual attitudes and behaviors have become more liberal over the past 30 years. Although the media have labeled these changes a "sexual revolution," it is probably more accurate to characterize them as an evolution in attitudes and behavior. This trend toward more permissive sexual expression appears to be continuing (Hyde, 1994).

While heralded by some, these changes have had several serious downsides. Two troublesome problems in the 1980s and 1990s were increases in teenage pregnancy and sexually transmitted diseases (Byrne, Kelley, & Fisher, 1993; Hatcher et al., 1998). The spread of human immunodeficiency virus (HIV) infection that leads to AIDS was, and remains, a special concern. Has public awareness of AIDS put the brakes on these liberal trends?

In Figure 13.10, you can see that the incidence of premarital intercourse was just as high in 1985 as it had been in 1980, and higher than it had been in 1975. Thus, the results of this survey show no reduction in premarital sex since the early 1980s. While there is some evidence that college students' *attitudes* toward casual sex are becoming more disapproving (Robinson, et al., 1991), these attitudes aren't necessarily translating into more conservative sexual *behavior* (Hyde, 1994).

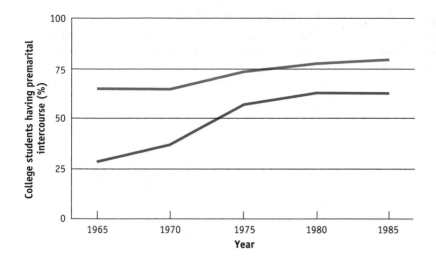

FIGURE 13.10.

Premarital sex among college students. The percentage of college students who report engaging in premarital intercourse did not decline between 1980 and 1985, indicating that concerns about AIDS have not affected this aspect of their sexual behavior. The graph also shows that premarital sex has increased among college students since 1965. Males are still more likely to engage in premarital sex than females, but the gap has been closing. (Data from Robinson et al., 1991)

Has AIDS had any impact on safer sex practices such as using condoms and having only a few sexual partners? Among teens, this doesn't appear to be the case, for reasons we'll discuss a little later (Murstein & Mercy, 1994). However, among adults, the percentage using condoms the first time they had sex rose from 48% in the beginning of the 1980s to 65% by the end of the 1980s (Forrest & Singh, 1990). Finally, post-college-age gay and straight adult men are reducing their number of sex partners and increasing their condom use, although younger gay men are not (Ehrhardt, Yingling, & Warne, 1991). Thus, there is evidence that concerns about contracting AIDS are affecting sexual practices; however, older individuals are more likely to practice safer sex than younger people.

"Premarital" Sex

The term *premarital sex* conjures up images of furtive sex among teenagers. Obviously, with more people delaying marriage, premarital sex increasingly involves relationships between mature adults. Clearly, the emotional implications of sex between a pair of 15-year-olds living with their parents and a pair of independent 30-year-olds are likely to be quite different. Another problem with the term premarital is that it doesn't apply to homosexuals, who aren't permitted to marry under the law. Although the term "premarital sex" is becoming dated, many contemporary researchers continue to use the term to refer to early, youthful sexual encounters.

ATTITUDES

Compared to a generation ago, more people believe that sex before marriage is acceptable, as long as the two people are emotionally committed to each other (Michael et al., 1994). Although a meta-analysis of gender differences in sexuality found that males were more accepting than females of premarital sex under casual

circumstances (Oliver & Hyde, 1993), a study of college students reported that only 33% of the men and 3% of the women endorsed premarital sex with a "casual acquaintance" (Earle & Perricone, 1986). Thus, the casual one-night stands that get so much attention in the media appear to be less frequent than commonly believed.

PREVALENCE

It is clear that the prevalence of premarital sex has increased since the 1960s (Robinson et al., 1991), as Figure 13.10 shows. Roughly 75% of Americans engage in premarital sex (Hyde, 1994). A survey of Los Angeles adolescents and young adults reported that the average age of first intercourse was between 15 and 16. Moreover, there were no striking age differences among ethnic groups (see Figure 13.11). Thus, most people no longer enter committed relationships as virgins. Some of the increase in premarital sex is attributable to later marriages, but premarital sex among teenagers *has* become more frequent as well

FIGURE 13.11.

Ethnicity and premarital intercourse. A survey of 16- to 25-year-olds from different ethnic groups in the Los Angeles area revealed that the average age for first having sex was relatively similar between males and females and among the ethnic groups. (Adapted from Moore & Erickson, 1985)

Subgroup	Mean age of first intercourse
Males (all ethnic groups combined)	14.9
Females (all ethnic groups combined)	15.9
Whites	16.2
Blacks	14.4
Hispanics	15.3
Asians	16.4

(Braverman & Strasburger, 1993). Teenagers who engage in premarital sex are typically less religious and less concerned about academic achievement; they also place a greater value on independence and report being more influenced by peers than by parents (Jessor et al., 1983). Interestingly, adult homosexuals report rates of *heterosexual* premarital intercourse that are nearly identical to those reported by heterosexuals (Saghir & Robbins, 1973). Among other things, these findings support the view that adolescence is an important period for working out answers to questions about sexual orientation.

Males and females have different reactions to their first experience with sexual intercourse (Coles & Stokes, 1985). For instance, three times as many males as females report feeling glad (60% to 23%). Also, girls are more likely to feel sadness, disappointment, guilt, and ambivalence. Surprisingly, the girl's partner is not usually aware of her negative feelings. In a study that asked college women to rate their first coital experience on a scale ranging from 1 (no pleasure at all) to 7 (strongly experienced pleasure), the average pleasure rating was 3.9 (Weis, 1983). Women whose first experiences are positive and minimally painful have had a history of sex play in childhood and adolescence, have positive feelings about these experiences, and had their first intercourse in a safe environment (no fear of discovery) with a caring partner (Weis, 1985).

Sex in Committed Relationships

Sex is an important element in most committed, romantic relationships. In this section, we'll examine patterns of sexual activity in dating couples, married couples, and gay couples.

SEX BETWEEN DATING PARTNERS

At some point, couples confront the question of whether or when they should have sex. For some, the decision is easy; for others, it's not. Some worry that sex might adversely affect the relationship; others fear that having sex will cause trouble. Is there evidence to support either view? Research suggests that dating couples who have sex are more likely to be dating the same person three months later than couples who don't have sex (Simpson, 1987). Of course, this was a correlational study, so it's possible that couples who were sexually active started out with closer relationships. If this were so, relationship satisfaction might be more significant than sexual activity. However, when the researchers took this factor into account, the relationships of the sexually active couples still lasted longer. It would be interesting to see whether this same pattern of results was obtained 6 months or a year later.

MARITAL SEX

There is ample evidence that couples' overall marital satisfaction is highly related to their satisfaction with their sexual relationship (Henderson-King & Veroff, 1994; Kurdek, 1991). Thus, good sex and a good marriage tend to go hand in hand. Of course, it is difficult to tell whether this is a matter of good sex promoting good marriages or good marriages promoting good sex. In all probability, it's a two-way street. It seems likely that marital closeness is conducive to sexual pleasure and that sexual satisfaction increases marital satisfaction.

Married couples vary greatly in how often they have sex (see Figure 13.12). *On the average,* couples in their 20s and 30s engage in sex about two or three times a week (Blumstein & Schwartz, 1990). The frequency of sex among married couples tends to decrease as the

FIGURE 13.12.

Frequency of sex among married men and women. A recent well-sampled survey asked Americans, "How often have you had sex in the past 12 months?" Married individuals' responses to the question were wide ranging. The most frequent response was "a few times per month" followed by "2 to 3 times a week." (Data from Michael et al., 1994)

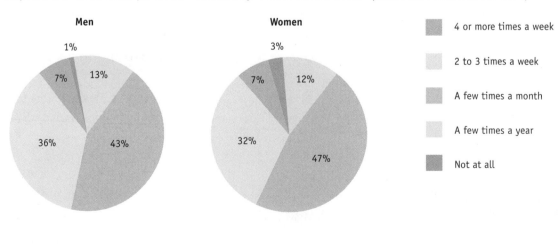

years wear on (Laumann et al., 1994). Biological changes play some role in this trend, but social factors seem more compelling. Most couples attribute this decline to increasing fatigue from work and child-rearing and to growing familiarity with their sexual routine.

As men and women age, sexual arousal tends to build more slowly and orgasms tend to diminish in frequency and intensity. Males' refractory periods lengthen, and females' vaginal lubrication and elasticity decrease. Nevertheless, people over 60 remain capable of rewarding sexual encounters. In a study of healthy 80- to 102-year-olds, 62% of the men and 30% of the women reported that they still engaged in sexual intercourse (Bretschneider & McCoy, 1988). About 80% of couples over the age of 60 continue to engage in intercourse every week or two (Brecher, 1984).

SEX IN HOMOSEXUAL RELATIONSHIPS

On the average, homosexual couples have sex about as often as heterosexual couples of similar ages—two or three times a week (Blumstein & Schwartz, 1983). Similarly, homosexual individuals vary widely in their desire for sex. One well-known survey reported that about 45% of lesbian couples wished that they had sex more often than they actually did, whereas only 5% preferred a lower frequency. Among gay males, some 37% expressed a desire for sex more often and 21% preferred a lower frequency (Blumstein & Schwartz, 1983).

Gay and lesbian couples are more likely to have egalitarian relationships than are heterosexual couples (Blumstein & Schwartz, 1983; Kurdek & Schmitt, 1986b; Peplau, 1988). This fact may account for some interesting differences between homosexual and heterosexual couples that Masters and Johnson (1979) discovered based on their observations and interviews.

First, both male and female homosexual couples seemed to have a *non-goal-oriented view* of their sexual activities. Gay and lesbian couples enjoyed a variety of mutually pleasurable sexual activities and didn't get focused on reaching orgasm. They took their time on preliminaries such as holding and kissing, and they communicated a lot with each other. In contrast, heterosexual couples were likely to spend just 30 seconds on preliminary activities before they shifted to genital stimulation. The latest sex surveys suggest that heterosexual couples are spending more time on foreplay, however (Laumann et al., 1994).

A second finding was that, compared to heterosexual couples, homosexual couples rated higher on the *subjective quality* of their sexual experiences—that is, total body contact, enjoyment of each aspect of the sexual experience, psychological involvement, and responsiveness to the needs and desires of the partner. Communication was a key factor in this difference. Masters and Johnson believed that homosexual couples

communicated their sexual feelings pretty well, but they criticized the "persistent neglect" of sexual communication in straight couples.

Infidelity in Committed Relationships

The public disclosure of the Clinton-Lewinsky affair propelled the issue of sexual infidelity into the national spotlight. Sexual infidelity occurs when a person who is in a committed relationship engages in erotic activity with someone other than his or her partner. Among married couples, this behavior is also called "adultery" or "extramarital sex." Precisely what kind of erotic activity qualifies as "cheating" is debatable, especially between men and women, as you can see in Figure 13.13. The vast majority of people (75%) in our society strongly disapprove of extramarital sex (Laumann et al., 1994). Generally, gay male couples are more permissive about sexual activity with other individuals than lesbian and married couples are (Blumstein & Schwartz, 1988; Kurdek, 1991).

Does a deep emotional involvement without sex with someone other than your partner constitute infidelity? No doubt many people would say "yes." One researcher found that emotional affairs were about half as common as sexual affairs (Thompson, 1984). Such affairs often occur over the telephone or the Internet—as depicted in the movie *You've Got Mail* (Shaw, 1997).

PREVALENCE

Despite the fact that a majority of people disapprove of infidelity, a substantial number of people get involved in it. Because of the associated stigma and secrecy,

FIGURE 13.13.

What constitutes infidelity? A 1998 *Time*/CNN poll asked 397 married men and 431 married women whether various actions constituted cheating in a marriage. Men's responses were more liberal than women's, especially regarding "kissing someone else." (From Handy, 1998)

What Constitutes Infidelity		
Does this constitute cheating in a marriage?	Answered Yes Married Men	Married Women
Kissing someone else	59%	75%
Having a sexually explicit conversation on the phone	64%	74%
Having a sexually explicit conversation on the Internet	62%	72%
Holding hands with someone else	40%	49%
Fantasizing about having sex with someone else	39%	43%
Casually flirting with someone else	32%	38%

accurate estimates of infidelity are difficult to come by. One review of research on the topic suggested that about 40%–50% of husbands and about 25%–35% of wives engage in extramarital activity at least once (Thompson, 1983). Much more conservative estimates were reported in several recent surveys on sex: about 25% for men and about 10% for women (Laumann et al., 1994; Wiederman, 1997). Some experts speculate that widespread concerns about AIDS and genital herpes are behind this trend toward increased sexual fidelity.

MOTIVATIONS

Why do people pursue extramarital sexual encounters? Common reasons include anger toward a partner, dissatisfaction with a relationship (Thompson, 1983), desire for new and different sexual experiences (Buunk, 1980), a need to confirm that one is still desirable to members of the other gender, and a means of triggering the end of an unsatisfying relationship (Brown, 1988). Sometimes extramarital sexual activity occurs simply because two persons are attracted to each other. Erotic reactions to people other than one's partner do not cease when one makes a permanent commitment. Most people suppress these sexual desires because they disapprove of adultery.

The gender differences in motivations for infidelity parallel gender differences in sexual socialization: Men's motivations are tied to sex and women's, to emotions. When a man has an extramarital affair, it doesn't necessarily mean that he is unhappy with his marriage. On the other hand, when a woman has an affair, it may suggest that she is unhappy with her relationship (Glass & Wright, 1985; Thompson, 1984).

IMPACT

The impact of extramarital sexual activity on marriages has not been investigated extensively. Experts speculate that approximately 20% of all divorces are caused by infidelity (Reinisch, 1990). Still, it's hard to know in these cases whether extramarital sex is a symptom of a disintegrating relationship or its cause. Occasionally, extramarital affairs may have a positive effect on a marriage. Some participants report experiencing a sense of self-discovery and self-recognition as a result of extramarital sexual experiences (Atwater, 1982).

The findings on the impact of infidelity in gay relationships are contradictory. One investigator reported no differences in the perceived quality of "open" versus "closed" relationships in males (Kurdek, 1988). On the other hand, another study found that male couples in closed relationships reported greater feelings of closeness, more favorable attitudes toward their relationship, and lower tension than couples in open relationships (Kurdek & Schmitt, 1986a).

Practical Issues in Sexual Activity

LEARNING OBJECTIVES

● Describe common barriers to effective contraception and discuss the merits of the pill and condoms.
● Describe the various types of STDs and discuss their prevalence and means of transmission.
● List six suggestions for safer sexual practices.

Regardless of the context of sexual activity, two practical issues are often matters of concern: contraception and sexually transmitted diseases. These topics are more properly the concern of medicine than of psychology, but birth control and sex-related diseases certainly do have their behavioral aspects.

Contraception

Most people want to control whether and when they will conceive a child, so they need reliable contraception. Despite the availability of effective contraceptive methods, however, many people fail to exercise much control.

BARRIERS TO EFFECTIVE CONTRACEPTION

Effective contraception requires that intimate couples negotiate their way through a complex sequence of steps. First, they must define themselves as sexually active. Second, they must have accurate knowledge about fertility and conception. Third, their chosen method of contraception must be readily accessible. Finally, they must have the motivation and skill to use the method correctly and consistently. Failure to meet even one of these conditions can result in an unintended pregnancy.

Despite the threat of AIDS, about a third to a half of sexually active American teenagers do not use contraception or use it only on occasion (Braverman & Strasburger, 1993). Why is this? First, many adolescents believe that if they aren't gay, aren't intravenous drug users, and don't have frequent sex, they don't need to take precautions (Tucker & Cho, 1991). Second, many harbor the illusion that pregnancy or sexually transmitted diseases "could never happen to me" (Braverman & Strasburger, 1994). Third, girls who feel guilty about planned sex often fail to use contraception; they then rationalize their sexual behavior by telling themselves that "we got carried away" (Cassell, 1984). Finally, ready access to contraceptive devices is often a problem for adolescents.

Like their younger peers, college students engage in risky sexual practices for a variety of reasons. A key factor is conflicting norms about gender and sexual

© 1986, *The Boston Globe*. Distributed by Los Angeles Times Syndicate. Reprinted with permission.

behavior. Although men are socialized to be the initiators of sexual activity, when it comes to birth control, men frequently rely on women to take charge (Geis & Gerrard, 1984). It is difficult for a woman to maintain an image of sexual naiveté and also be responsible for contraception. Telling her partner that she is "on the pill" or whipping out a condom conveys quite a different message. Studies have shown that when college women believe that their sexual partners are not supportive of contraception, couples are less likely to practice protected sex (Whitley & Hern, 1991).

Another contributing factor is alcohol, which doesn't increase sexual desire but does typically impair judgment. Many college students drink as a socially acceptable way to avoid potentially embarrassing discussions about sex. Also, women who experience higher guilt and lower self-esteem are more likely to engage in unprotected sex than those with lower guilt and higher self-esteem (Gerrard, 1987; Whitley & Schofield, 1986).

SELECTING A CONTRACEPTIVE METHOD

If a couple is motivated to control their fertility, how should they go about selecting a technique? A rational choice requires accurate knowledge of the effectiveness, benefits, costs, and risks of the various methods. Figure 13.14 (on the next page) summarizes information on most of the methods currently available. The *ideal failure rate* estimates the probability of conception when the technique is used correctly and consistently. The *actual failure rate* is what occurs in the real world, when users' negligence is factored in.

Besides being informed about the various types of contraceptive methods, couples must also put this information to use. Contraception is a joint responsibility. Hence, it's essential for partners to discuss their preferences for contraception, to decide what method(s) they are going to use, and to *act* on their decision.

Let's look in more detail at the two most widely used birth control methods in the Western world: oral contraceptives and condoms (Calderone & Johnson, 1989; Hatcher et al., 1998).

Oral contraceptives are pills taken daily by mouth. They contain synthetic forms of two hormones: estrogen and progesterone. "The pill" actually refers to over 50 different oral contraceptive products that inhibit ovulation in women. Oral contraception is preferred by many couples because it is the only widely available method that is separated in time from the sex act itself. No other method (except for the intrauterine device, which is rarely prescribed today, and implants, which are more expensive that the pill) permits a similar degree of sexual spontaneity.

Despite much worrisome publicity, use of oral contraceptives does not appear to increase a woman's overall risk for cancer (Collaborative Group on Hormonal Factors in Breast Cancer, 1997). In fact, the likelihood of certain forms of cancer (such as uterine cancer) is reduced in women who use low-dosage oral contraceptives. The pill does slightly increase the risk of certain cardiovascular disorders, such as heart disease and stroke. Thus, alternative methods of contraception should be considered by smokers over age 35 and women with any suspicion of cardiovascular disease.

A *condom* is a sheath worn over the penis during intercourse to collect ejaculated semen. The condom is the only widely available contraceptive device for use by males. It can be purchased in any drugstore without a

Web Link 13.5

Office of Population Research

Since 1936, this research endeavor at Princeton University has studied population issues from many perspectives. This site includes extensive links and guides to the topics of pregnancy prevention (including emergency contraception) and reproductive choice.

FIGURE 13.14.

A comparison of widely used contraceptive techniques. Couples can choose from a variety of contraceptive methods. This chart summarizes the advantages and disadvantages of each method. Note that the typical failure rate is much higher than the ideal failure rate for all methods, because couples do not use contraceptive techniques consistently and correctly. (Based on Hatcher et al., 1998; Masters, Johnson, & Kolodny, 1994)

Contraceptive Methods

Method	Ideal failure rate (%)	Actual failure rate (%)	Advantages	Disadvantages
Birth control pills (combination)	0.1	5	Highly reliable; coitus-independent; has some health benefits	Side effects; daily use; continual cost; health risks for some women; no protection against STDs
Minipill (progestin only)	0.5	5	Thought to have low risk of side effects; coitus-independent; has some health benefits	Breakthrough bleeding; daily use; continual cost; health risks for some women; no protection against STDs
IUD	1–2	1–2	No memory or motivation required for use; very reliable	Cramping, bleeding, expulsion; risk of pelvic inflammatory disease; no protection against STDs
Diaphragm with spermicidal cream or jelly	6	20	No major health risks; inexpensive	Aesthetic objections
Condom (male)	3	14	Protects against STDs; simple to use; male responsibility; no health risks; no prescriptions required	Unaesthetic to some; requires interruption of sexual activity; continual cost
Sponge	9	20	24-hour protection; simple to use; no taste or odor; inexpensive; effective with several acts of intercourse	Aesthetic objections; continual cost; no protection against STDs
Cervical cap with cream or jelly	9	20	Can wear for weeks at a time; coitus-independent; no major health risks	May be difficult to insert; may irritate cervix
Spermicides	6	26	No major health risks; no prescription required; some protect against AIDS	Unaesthetic to some; must be properly inserted; continual cost
Rhythm	1–9	25	No cost; acceptable to Catholic church	Requires high motivation and periods of abstinence; unreliable; no protection against STDs
Withdrawal	4	19	No cost or health risks	Reduces sexual pleasure; unreliable; requires high motivation
Implants	.05	.05	Highly reliable; continuous protection for up to 5 years; easily reversible; low risk of side effects; some health benefits	Slightly visible; costly; minor surgery required for insertion and removal; possible side effects; no protection against STDs
No contraception	85	85	No immediate monetary cost	High risk of pregnancy and STDs

Note: STDs = Sexually transmitted diseases

prescription. If used correctly, the condom is highly effective in preventing pregnancy (Hatcher et al., 1998). It must be placed over the penis after erection but before any contact with the vagina, and space must be left at the tip to collect the ejaculate. The man should withdraw before completely losing his erection, and hold the rim of the condom during withdrawal to prevent any semen from spilling into the vagina.

Condoms are generally made of latex rubber but are occasionally made from animal membranes ("skin"). Polyurethane condoms, introduced in 1994, are thinner and stronger than latex condoms. The use of rubber and polyurethane condoms can reduce the chances of contracting or passing on various sexually transmitted diseases. However, oil-based creams and lotions (petroleum jelly, hand creams, and baby oil, for example) should not be used as lubricants with *rubber* condoms (or diaphragms). Within 60 seconds, these products can make microscopic holes in the rubber membrane that are large enough to allow passage of the AIDS virus and organisms produced by other sexually transmitted diseases (Reinisch, 1990). Water-based lubricants such as K-Y jelly don't cause this problem. Polyurethane condoms are impervious to oils. Skin condoms do *not* offer protection against sexually transmitted diseases.

In closing, we'll mention that the Federal Drug Administration announced in 1997 that high doses of ordinary birth control pills taken within 72 hours after intercourse can prevent pregnancy (Painter, 1997). (A specific number of pills must be taken at prescribed intervals, depending on the brand of pill.) Although no substitute for regular birth control, this approach is particularly helpful in cases of rape. The main side effects seem to be nausea and vomiting.

Sexually Transmitted Diseases

A *sexually transmitted disease* (STD) is an illness that is transmitted primarily through sexual contact. When people think of STDs, they typically think of syphilis and gonorrhea, but these diseases are only the tip of the iceberg. There are actually about 20 sexually transmitted diseases. Some of them—for instance, pubic lice—are minor nuisances that can readily be treated. Others, however, are severe afflictions that are difficult to treat. For instance, if it isn't detected early, syphilis can cause heart failure, blindness, and brain damage, and AIDS is eventually fatal. (We'll discuss AIDS in detail in Chapter 14.)

PREVALENCE AND TRANSMISSION

No one is immune to sexually transmitted diseases. Even monogamous partners can develop some STDs (yeast infections, for instance). Sexually transmitted diseases occur more frequently than widely realized, and most STDs are increasing in prevalence. Health authorities estimate that there are about 13 million new cases in the United States each year (Hatcher et al., 1994). If you are between the ages of 15 and 55, you have about a one in four chance of developing a sexually transmitted disease—not including AIDS—during your lifetime (Centers for Disease Control and Prevention, 1992). The highest incidence of STDs is seen in the under-25 age group (Hatcher et al., 1998).

The principal types of sexually transmitted diseases are listed in Figure 13.15 (on the next page), along with their symptoms and modes of transmission. Most of these are spread from one person to another through intercourse, oral-genital contact, or anal-genital contact. Concerning the transmission of STDs, six points are worth emphasizing:

1. You should consider *any* activity that exposes you to blood, semen, vaginal secretions, menstrual blood, urine, feces, or saliva as high-risk behavior *unless* you and your partner are in a mutual, sexually exclusive relationship and neither of you is infected.

2. The more sexual partners you have, the higher your chances of exposure to a sexually transmitted disease.

3. Don't assume that the labels people attach to themselves (heterosexual or homosexual) accurately describe their actual sexual behavior. According to the director of the Kinsey Institute, "Studies of men from the general population show that more than 30% (1 out of 3) have had at least one sexual experience with another male since puberty" (Reinisch, 1990).

4. People can often be carriers of sexually transmitted diseases without being aware of it. For instance, in its early stages gonorrhea may cause no readily apparent symptoms in women, who may unknowingly transmit the disease to their partners.

5. Even when people know they have a sexually transmitted disease, they may fail to refrain from sex or inform their partners. Guilt and embarrassment cause many people to ignore symptoms of sexually transmitted diseases and continue their normal sexual activities. Close to half of the subjects in one study admitted that they had told dates that they had had fewer sexual partners than was actually the case (Reinisch, 1990). People are even more likely to lie about homosexual activity, sex with prostitutes, and drug use (Reinisch, 1990). So don't assume that sexual partners will warn you that they may be contagious.

6. Engaging in anal intercourse (especially being the receiving partner) puts one at very high risk for AIDS. Rectal tissues are delicate and easily torn, thus letting the virus pass through the membrane. Oral-genital sex may also transmit AIDS, particularly if semen is swallowed.

PREVENTION

Abstinence is the best way to minimize the risk of acquiring sexually transmitted diseases. However, this is not an appealing or realistic option for most people. Short of abstinence, the best strategy is to engage in sexual activity only in the context of a long-term relationship, where you have an opportunity to know your partner reasonably well. Sexual interactions with casual acquaintances greatly increase your risk for STDs, including AIDS.

Along with being judicious about sexual relations, it's also essential that you talk openly about safer sexual practices with your partner. Still, if you don't carry the process one step further and practice what you preach,

Web Link 13.6

AIDS HIV AEGIS
This is the largest and probably most important Web-based resource dealing with HIV and AIDS. This site offers an extraordinary collection of information sources, both printed and online.

FIGURE 13.15.

Overview of common sexually transmitted diseases (STDs). This chart summarizes the symptoms and modes of transmission of 11 STDs. Note that intercourse is not required to transmit all STDs—many STDs can be contracted through oral-genital contact or other forms of physical intimacy. (Adapted from Hatcher et al., 1998; Hyde, 1994)

Sexually Transmitted Diseases (STDs)

STD	Transmission	Symptoms
Acquired immune deficiency syndrome (AIDS)	The AIDS virus is spread by coitus or anal intercourse. There is a chance the virus may also be spread by oral-genital sex, particularly if semen is swallowed. (AIDS can also be spread by non-sexual means: contaminated blood, contaminated hypodermic needles, and transmission from an infected woman to her baby during pregnancy or childbirth.)	Most people infected with the virus show no immediate symptoms; antibodies usually develop in the blood 2–8 weeks after infection. People with the virus may remain symptom-free for 5 years or more. No cure for the disease has yet been found.
Candidiasis (yeast infection)	The *Candida albicans* fungus may accelerate growth when the chemical balance of the vagina is disturbed; it may also be transmitted through sexual interaction.	White, "cheesy" discharge; irritation of vaginal and vulvar tissue.
Chlamydial infection	The *Chlamydia trichomatis* bacterium is transmitted primarily through sexual contact. It may also be spread by fingers from one body site to another.	In men, chlamydial infection of the urethra may cause a discharge and burning during urination. Chlamydia-caused epidymitis may produce a sense of heaviness in the affected testicle(s), inflammation of the scrotal skin, and painful swelling at the bottom of the testicle. In women, pelvic inflammatory disease caused by chlamydia may disrupt menstrual periods, elevate temperature, and cause abdominal pain, nausea, vomiting, and headache.
Genital warts (venereal warts)	The virus is spread primarily through genital, anal, or oral-genital interaction.	Warts are hard and yellow-gray on dry skin areas, soft pinkish red and cauliflowerlike on moist areas.
Gonorrhea ("clap")	The *Neisseria gonorrhoeae* bacterium (gonococcus) is spread through genital, oral-genital, or genital-anal contact.	Most common symptoms in men are a cloudy discharge from the penis and burning sensations during urination. If the disease is untreated, complications may include inflammation of the scrotal skin and swelling at the base of the testicle. In women, some green or yellowish discharge is produced, but the disease commonly remains undetected. At a later stage, pelvic inflammatory disease may develop.
Herpes	The genital herpes virus (HSV-2) appears to be transmitted primarily by vaginal, oral-genital, or anal-sexual intercourse. The oral herpes virus (HSV-1) is transmitted primarily by kissing.	Small red, painful bumps (papules) appear in the region of the genitals (genital herpes) or mouth (oral herpes). The papules become painful blisters that eventually rupture to form wet, open sores.
Pubic lice ("crabs")	*Phthirus pubis,* the pubic louse, is spread easily through body contact or through shared clothing or bedding.	Persistent itching. Lice are visible and may often be located in pubic hair or other body hair.
Syphilis	The *Treponema pallidum* bacterium (spirochete) is transmitted from open lesions during genital, oral-genital, or genital-anal contact.	*Primary stage:* A painless chancre appears at the site where the spirochetes entered the body. *Secondary stage:* The chancre disappears and a generalized skin rash develops. *Latent stage:* There may be no observable symptoms. *Tertiary stage:* Heart failure, blindness, mental disturbance, and many other symptoms may occur. Death may result.
Trichomoniasis	The protozoan parasite *Trichomonas vaginalis* is passed through genital sexual contact or less frequently by towels, toilet seats, or bathtubs used by an infected person.	White or yellow vaginal discharge with an unpleasant odor; vulva is sore and irritated.
Viral hepatitis	The hepatitis B virus may be transmitted by blood, semen, vaginal secretions, and saliva. Manual, oral, or penile stimulation of the anus is strongly associated with the spread of this virus. Hepatitis A seems to be spread primarily via the fecal-oral route. Oral-anal sexual contact is a common mode of sexual transmission for hepatitis A.	Vary from nonexistent to mild, flulike symptoms to an incapacitating illness characterized by high fever, vomiting, and severe abdominal pain.

you remain at risk. Unfortunately, there is evidence that many people are still engaging in risky sexual behavior—a practice they can ill afford while we are in the grip of the deadly AIDS epidemic. A government-sponsored, nationwide survey of 10,630 heterosexuals between the ages of 18 and 75 found that condoms were always used by only 17% of those with multiple partners, by only 13% of those with risky sex partners (partners who were HIV-positive, intravenous drug users, nonmonogamous, transfusion recipients, or hemophiliacs), and by only 11% of untested transfusion recipients (Catania et al., 1992).

Safer sex practices have increased dramatically among older gay and bisexual males (Stall, Coates, & Hoff, 1988), but younger gay males may still be taking sexual risks (Griggs, 1990). Lesbians have the lowest rates of syphilis and gonorrhea among sexually active individuals, as well as extremely low rates of AIDS (Reinisch, 1990). Lesbian sexual behaviors don't typically involve penetration, so there is little risk of exposure to infectious organisms from breaks in oral, vaginal, or anal tissues. Lesbians also tend to have fewer sexual partners than other sexually active women or men. All the same, for reasons we have already mentioned, lesbians should still follow "safer sex" guidelines.

We offer the following suggestions for safer sex (Hyde, 1994; King, 1999):

- Because the AIDS virus is easily transmitted through anal intercourse, it's a good idea to avoid this type of sex.
- If you are not involved in a sexually exclusive relationship, always use rubber or polyurethane condoms. They have a good track record of preventing STDs and offer effective protection against the AIDS virus. (As mentioned earlier, never use oil-based lubricants with rubber condoms; use water-based lubricants instead.)
- Wash your genitals with soap and warm water before and after sexual contact.
- Urinate soon after intercourse.
- Don't have sex with someone who has had lots of previous partners. People won't always be honest about this, so it's important to know whether you can trust a prospective partner's word.
- Watch for sores, rashes, or discharge around the vulva or penis, or elsewhere on your body, especially the mouth. If you have cold sores, avoid kissing or oral sex.

If you have several sexual partners in a year, you should have regular STD checkups. You will have to ask for them, as most doctors and health clinics won't perform STD tests unless they're asked to. Also, if you have any reason to suspect that you have an STD, find a good health clinic and get tested *as soon as possible*. It's normal to be embarrassed or afraid of getting bad news, but don't delay. Health professionals are in the business of helping people, not judging them.

Remember that the symptoms of some STDs disappear as the disease progresses. Don't make the mistake of thinking that you really don't have an STD when you might. To make really sure, have yourself tested twice. If both tests are negative, you can stop worrying. If your test results are positive, it's essential to get the proper treatment *right away*. Notify your sexual partner(s) so they can be tested immediately, too. In addition, it's important to avoid sexual intercourse and oral sex until you and your partner(s) are fully treated and a physician or clinic says you are no longer infectious.

In the Application, we'll focus on enhancing sexual satisfaction and how to treat common sexual problems.

Enhancing Sexual Relationships

LEARNING OBJECTIVES

- List six general suggestions for enhancing sexual relationships.
- Discuss the nature, prevalence, and causes of common sexual dysfunctions.
- Describe strategies for coping with erectile difficulties, premature ejaculation, and orgasmic difficulties.

Answer the following statements "true" or "false."

_____ **1.** Sexual problems are unusual.

_____ **2.** Sexual problems belong to couples rather than individuals.

_____ **3.** Sexual problems are highly resistant to treatment.

_____ **4.** Sex therapists sometimes recommend masturbation as a treatment for certain types of problems.

The answers are (1) false, (2) true, (3) false, and (4) true. If you answered several of the questions incorrectly, you have misconceptions about sexual difficulties that may affect your sexual relations, but you are by no means unusual. As you saw in our earlier discussion of the results of the Kinsey Institute poll, misconceptions about sexuality are the norm rather than the exception. Fortunately, there are plenty of useful ideas on how to improve sexual relationships.

For the sake of simplicity, our advice is directed to heterosexual couples, but much of what we have to say is also relevant to homosexual couples. For advice aimed specifically at homosexual couples, we recommend *Permanent Partners: Building Gay and Lesbian Relationships That Last* by Betty Berzon (1990).

General Suggestions

Let's begin with some general ideas about how to enhance sexual relationships, drawn from several excellent books on sexuality (Crooks & Baur, 1996; Hyde, 1994; King, 1999). Even if you are satisfied with your sex life, these ideas may be useful as "preventive medicine."

1. *Pursue adequate sex education.* A surprising number of people are ignorant about the realities of sexual functioning. So the first step in promoting sexual satisfaction is to acquire accurate information about sex. The shelves of most bookstores are bulging with popular books on sex, but many of them are loaded with inaccuracies. A good bet is to pick up a college textbook on human sexuality. The Recommended Readings in this chapter describe books that we think are excellent. Enrolling in a course on sexuality is also a good idea. Most colleges offer such courses today.

2. *Review your sexual values system.* Many sexual problems stem from a negative sexual values system that associates sex with immorality. The guilt feelings caused by such an orientation can interfere with sexual functioning. Thus, sex therapists often encourage adults to examine the sources and implications of their sexual values.

3. *Communicate about sex.* As children, people often learn that they shouldn't talk about sex. Many people carry this edict into adulthood and have great difficulty discussing sex, even with their partner. Good communication is extremely important in a sexual relationship. Figure 13.16 lists common problems in sexual relations reported by a sample of 100 couples (Frank, Anderson, & Rubenstein, 1978). Many of the problems reported by the couples—such as choosing an inconvenient time, too little erotic activity before intercourse, and too little tenderness afterward—are traceable largely to poor communication. Your partner is not a mind reader. You have to share your thoughts and feelings to promote mutual satisfaction. If you are unsure about your partner's preferences, ask. Provide candid (but diplomatic) feedback when your partner asks about your reactions.

4. *Avoid goal setting.* Sexual encounters are not tests or races. Sexual relations usually work out best when people relax and enjoy themselves. People often get overly concerned about orgasms or about both

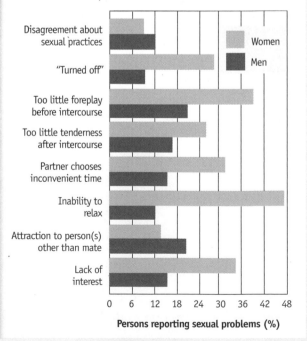

FIGURE 13.16.

Common problems in sexual relations. The percentage of men and women reporting various types of problems in their sexual relationships is shown here, based on a sample of 100 couples. (Data from Frank, Anderson, & Rubenstein, 1978)

partners reaching orgasm simultaneously. A grim determination to climax typically makes it harder to do so. This mental set can lead to disruptive habits like *spectatoring* or stepping outside the sexual act to judge one's performance. It's better to adopt the philosophy that getting there is at least half the fun.

5. *Enjoy your sexual fantasies.* As we noted earlier, the mind is the ultimate erogenous zone. Although Freudian theory originally saw sexual fantasy as an unhealthy byproduct of sexual frustration and immaturity, the modern view is that not having sexual fantasies is a sign of pathology (Leitenberg & Henning, 1995). Men and women both report that their sexual fantasies increase their excitement. So don't be afraid to use fantasy to enhance your sexual arousal.

6. *Be selective about sex.* Sexual encounters generally work out better when you have privacy and a relaxed atmosphere, when you are well rested, and when you are enthusiastic. If you consistently have sex in bad situations, your sex life probably won't be very rewarding. Of course, you can't count on (or insist on) having ideal situations all the time, but you should be aware of the value of being selective. If your heart isn't in it, it may be wise to wait. Partners often differ about when, where, and how often they should have sex (Gagnon & Simon, 1987). Such differences are normal and should not be a source of resentment. Couples simply need to work toward reasonable compromises—through open communication.

Understanding Sexual Dysfunction

Many people struggle with **sexual dysfunctions—impairments in sexual functioning that cause subjective distress.** Figure 13.17 shows the prevalence of some of the sexual problems we will discuss (Laumann et al., 1994).

Traditionally, people have assumed that a sexual problem lies in one partner. Although it is convenient to refer to a man's erectile difficulties or a woman's orgasmic difficulties, research indicates that most sexual problems emerge out of partners' unique ways of relating to each other. In other words, sexual problems belong to couples rather than to individuals.

Both physiological and psychological factors can contribute to sexual problems (Bancroft, 1980). Some medications can interfere with sexual functioning, as can alcohol and drugs. Fears about pregnancy or STDs, negative attitudes about sex, unresolved relationship issues, and prior sexual abuse can also interfere with one's sex life. In this section, we examine the symptoms and causes of three common sexual dysfunctions: erectile difficulties, premature ejaculation, and orgasmic difficulties.

Erectile difficulties occur when a man is persistently unable to achieve or maintain an erection

adequate for intercourse. Impotence is the traditional name for this problem, but sex therapists have discarded the term because of its demeaning connotation. A man who has never had an erection sufficient for intercourse is said to have *primary erectile difficulties.* A man who has had intercourse in the past but who is currently having problems achieving erections is said to have *secondary erectile difficulties.* The latter problem is more common and easier to overcome.

Some 30 million American men are estimated to suffer from erectile difficulties if a broad criterion (the inability to get an erection adequate for satisfactory sexual performance) is used (Handy, 1998). Erectile difficulties affect about 1 in 20 men age 40 and over, and about 1 in 4 over age 65.

Experts now estimate that organic factors may contribute to as many as 50% of all cases of erectile dysfunction (Buvat et al., 1990). A host of common diseases (such as diabetes) can produce erectile problems as a side effect (Melman & Leiter, 1983). So can many of the medications used to treat physical illnesses (Buffum et al., 1981).

Many temporary conditions, such as fatigue, worry about work, an argument with one's partner, a depressed

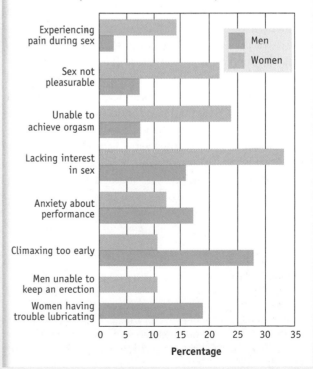

FIGURE 13.17.

Sexual difficulties in normal couples. This graph shows the prevalence of various sexual problems during a year in a probability sample of American men and women. The most common problems among men are premature ejaculation and anxiety about performance; in women, they are lack of interest in sex and orgasmic difficulties. (From Laumann et al., 1994)

mood, or too much alcohol can cause such incidents. The most common psychological cause of erectile difficulties is anxiety about sexual performance. Common causes of anxiety include doubts about virility and conflict about the morality of sexual desires. If either partner turns the incident into a major catastrophe, the man may begin to get unduly concerned about his sexual response, and the seeds of anxiety may be sown.

Premature ejaculation **occurs when sexual relations are impaired because a man consistently reaches orgasm too quickly.** What is "too quickly"? Obviously, any time estimate is hopelessly arbitrary. The critical consideration is the subjective feelings of the partners. If either partner feels that the ejaculation is persistently too fast for sexual gratification, they have a problem.

What causes premature ejaculation? Although a few men may have a low threshold to stimulation and be prone to quick ejaculation (Strassberg, 1994), psychological factors are the typical cause. Some men simply don't exert much effort to prolong intercourse. Most of these men do not view their ejaculations as premature, even if their partners do. Other causes can include depression or anger at one's partner. Many therapists believe that this problem is rooted in early sexual experiences in which a rapid climax was advantageous. Furtive sex in the backseat of a car, quick efforts at masturbation, and experiences with prostitutes are situations in which men typically attempt to achieve orgasm quickly. A pattern of rapid ejaculation established by these formative experiences can become entrenched.

Orgasmic difficulties **occur when people experience sexual arousal but have persistent problems in achieving orgasm.** When this problem occurs in men, it is often called *retarded ejaculation.* The traditional name for this problem in women, *frigidity,* is no longer used because of its derogatory implications. Since this problem is much more common among women, we'll limit our discussion to them. As with erectile difficulties, it is useful to distinguish between primary and secondary orgasmic difficulties. A woman who has never experienced an orgasm through any kind of stimulation is said to have *primary orgasmic difficulties.* Women who formerly experienced orgasms but are currently unable to do so are said to have *secondary orgasmic difficulties.* Women who seek treatment because they experience orgasm only through noncoital techniques (oral, manual, and self-stimulation) also fall into this category. Although primary orgasmic difficulties would seem to be the more severe problem, they are actually more responsive to treatment than secondary orgasmic difficulties.

Physical causes of orgasmic difficulties are rare (occasionally, medications are a problem). One of the leading psychological causes is a negative attitude toward sex. Women who have been taught that sex is dirty or sinful are likely to approach it with shame and guilt. These feelings can inhibit sexual expression, undermine arousal, and impair orgasmic responsiveness.

A lack of authentic affection for one's partner seems to undermine sexual arousal in women more than in men. Thus, women may have orgasmic difficulties when the emotional closeness in their relationship deteriorates (Hurlbert & Whittaker, 1991). Arousal may also be inhibited by fear of pregnancy or excessive concern about achieving orgasm. Some women have orgasmic difficulties because intercourse is too brief or because their partners are unconcerned about their needs and preferences. Some women do not experience orgasms simply because they (and their partners) haven't explored sexual activities that they might find more rewarding than intercourse.

Coping with Specific Problems

With the advent of modern sex therapy, sexual problems no longer have to be chronic sources of frustration and shame. *Sex therapy* **involves the professional treatment of sexual dysfunctions.** Masters and Johnson have reported high success rates for their treatments of specific problems, as Figure 13.18 shows. Some critics argue that the cure rates reported by Masters and Johnson are overly optimistic in comparison with those reported by other investigators (Zilbergeld & Evans, 1980). Nonetheless, there is a consensus that sexual dysfunctions can be overcome with encouraging regularity (McConaghy, 1993). If you're in the market for a sex therapist, be sure to get someone who is qualified to work in this specialized field. One professional credential to look for is that provided by the American Association of Sex Educators, Counselors, and Therapists (AASECT).

Of course, sex therapy isn't for everyone. It can be expensive and time-consuming. In some areas, it is difficult to find. However, many people can benefit from ideas drawn from the professional practice of sex therapy (Hartman & Fithian, 1994; Masters et al., 1994).

ERECTILE DIFFICULTIES

Viagra, the much-touted pill for treating erectile disorders, is about 80% effective (Handy, 1998). Still, it is not

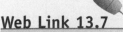

Web Link 13.7

Sexual Health Network
The health professionals who staff this Connecticut-based site have assembled a comprehensive set of information resources related to all aspects of human sexual health. Especially notable here are materials discussing sexual functioning for persons with physical injuries or disabilities.

without its drawbacks—some of them life threatening. Moreover, many therapists argue that taking only a medical approach to this problem fails to address coexisting psychological causes (Schover, & Leiblum, 1994).

To overcome psychologically based erectile difficulties, the key is to decrease the man's performance anxiety. It is a good idea for a couple to discuss the problem openly. The woman should be reassured that the difficulty does not reflect lack of affection. Obviously, it is crucial for her to be emotionally supportive rather than hostile and demanding.

Masters and Johnson use a procedure called sensate focus in the treatment of erectile difficulties and other dysfunctions. **Sensate focus is an exercise in which partners take turns pleasuring each other while giving guided verbal feedback and in which certain kinds of stimulation are temporarily forbidden.** One partner stimulates the other, who simply lies back and enjoys it while giving instructions and feedback about what feels good. Initially, the partners are not allowed to touch each other's genitals or to attempt intercourse. This prohibition should free the man from feelings of pressure to perform. Over a number of sessions, the couple gradually include genital stimulation in their sensate focus, but intercourse is still banned. With the pressure to perform removed, many men spontaneously get erections. Repeated arousals should begin to restore the man's confidence in his sexual response. As his confidence returns, the couple can move on gradually to attempts at intercourse.

PREMATURE EJACULATION

Men troubled by premature ejaculation range from those who climax almost instantly to those who cannot last the time that their partner requires. In the latter case, simply slowing down the tempo of intercourse may help. Sometimes the problem can be solved indirectly by discarding the traditional assumption that orgasms should come through intercourse. If the female partner enjoys oral or manual stimulation, these techniques can be used to provide her with an orgasm either before or after intercourse. This strategy can reduce the

performance pressure for the male partner, and couples may find that intercourse starts to last longer.

For the problem of instant ejaculation, two treatments are very effective: the *stop-start method* (Semans, 1956) and the *squeeze technique* (Masters & Johnson, 1970). With both of these, the woman brings the man to the verge of orgasm through manual stimulation. Then, she either stops stimulating him (stop-start technique) or squeezes the end of his penis firmly for 3–5 seconds (squeeze technique) until he calms down. She repeats this procedure three or four times before bringing him to orgasm. These exercises can help a man recognize preorgasmic sensations and teach him that he can delay ejaculation.

ORGASMIC DIFFICULTIES

Since orgasmic difficulties among women are often the result of negative attitudes about sex, a restructuring of values is often the key to conquering the problem. Therapeutic discussions may be geared toward helping nonorgasmic women reduce their ambivalence about sexual expression. Sex therapists often suggest that women who have never had an orgasm try to have one through masturbation. Many women achieve orgasms in intercourse after an initial breakthrough with self-stimulation (Hurlbert & Whjittaker, 1991).

As we noted, a woman's orgasmic difficulties may stem from not feeling close to her partner. Thus, treatment sometimes focuses on couples' relationship problems more than on sexual functioning per se. Particular efforts are made to improve partners' communication skills.

For reasons we discussed earlier, it is not uncommon for women to be troubled by orgasmic difficulties only in the context of intercourse. This is particularly true for sexually inexperienced women. If partners don't assume that orgasms must come through coitus, this need not be a problem. However, many couples want the woman to experience orgasm during intercourse. Sensate focus exercises can help them realize this goal. The guided verbal feedback from the woman can greatly improve her partner's appreciation of her unique erotic preferences.

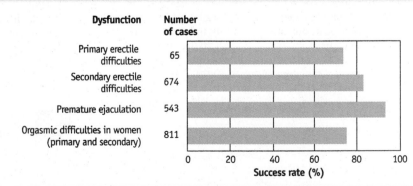

FIGURE 13.18.
Success rates reported by Masters and Johnson in their treatment of sexual dysfunctions. This figure shows the success rates for cases treated between 1959 and 1985. Treatment was categorized as successful only if the change in sexual function was clear and enduring. The minimum follow-up period was two years, and in many cases follow-up was five years later. (Adapted from Masters, Johnson, & Kolodny, 1988)

Dysfunction	Number of cases
Primary erectile difficulties	65
Secondary erectile difficulties	674
Premature ejaculation	543
Orgasmic difficulties in women (primary and secondary)	811

Key Ideas

BECOMING A SEXUAL PERSON

● One's sexual identity is made up of sexual orientation, body image, sexual values and ethics, and erotic preferences. Physiological factors such as hormones influence sexual differentiation, maturation, and anatomy more than they do sexual activity. Psychosocial factors appear to have more impact on sexual behavior. Sexual identity is shaped by families, peers, schools, and the media. Because of differences in sexual socialization, sexuality usually has different meanings for males and females.

● Many experts believe that sexual orientation is best viewed as a continuum, with end points of heterosexuality and homosexuality. The determinants of sexual orientation are not yet known but appear to be a complex interaction of biological and environmental factors. Although attitudes toward homosexuals are still largely negative, gay and straight people do not differ in adjustment. Homosexuals take longer to recognize their sexual orientation than heterosexuals do.

INTERACTION IN SEXUAL RELATIONSHIPS

● People frequently enter into sexual interactions with differing motivations. Men tend to be motivated more by physical gratification, whereas women are more likely to have emotional motives. Variations among people in erotic preferences are also shaped by their attitudes.

● Disparities between partners in sexual interest and erotic preferences understandably lead to conflicts that necessitate negotiation. Effective communication plays an important role in satisfaction with one's sex life and with the relationship in general.

THE HUMAN SEXUAL RESPONSE

● The physiology of the human sexual response was elucidated by Masters and Johnson. They analyzed the sexual response cycle into four phases: excitement, plateau, orgasm, and resolution. Women reach orgasm less consistently than men in intercourse, usually because foreplay and intercourse are too brief and because of gender differences in sexual socialization.

SEXUAL EXPRESSION

● Sexual fantasies are normal and are an important aspect of sexual expression. Kissing and touching are important erotic activities, but their importance is often underestimated by heterosexual males. Despite the strongly negative attitudes about masturbation that are traditional in our society, this practice is quite common, even among married people. Oral-genital sex has become a common element in most couples' sexual repertoires.

● Coitus is the most widely practiced sexual act in our society. Four coital positions are commonly used, each with its advantages and disadvantages. Sexual activities between gay males include mutual masturbation, fellatio, and, less often, anal intercourse. Lesbians engage in mutual masturbation, cunnilingus, and tribadism.

PATTERNS OF SEXUAL BEHAVIOR

● American sexual attitudes and behavior have become more liberal over the past 20 years. The awareness of AIDS has resulted in more conservative attitudes toward casual sex but has not had much impact on actual sexual behavior. The acceptability and prevalence of premarital sex have increased since the 1960s.

● Satisfaction with the sexual aspect of a relationship is correlated with the overall satisfaction with the relationship. Younger married couples tend to have sex about two or three times a week; this frequency declines with age. Homosexual couples appear to spend more time on mutual sexual activities before moving to orgasm and to communicate more with each other, compared to heterosexual couples.

● Most Americans strongly disapprove of extramarital sex. Infidelity is uncommon among married couples and lesbians and more common among gay male couples. People become involved in extramarital relationships for a variety of reasons.

PRACTICAL ISSUES IN SEXUAL ACTIVITY

● Contraception and sexually transmitted diseases are two practical issues that concern many couples. Many people who do not want to conceive a child fail to use contraceptive procedures effectively, if at all. Contraceptive methods differ in effectiveness and have various advantages and disadvantages.

● STDs are increasing in prevalence, especially among teenagers. The danger of contracting STDs is higher among those who have had more sexual partners. Using condoms with spermicides decreases the risk of contracting STDs. Early treatment of STDs is important.

APPLICATION: ENHANCING SEXUAL RELATIONSHIPS

● To enhance their sexual relationships, individuals need to have adequate sex education and positive values about sex. They also need to be able to communicate with their partners about sex and avoid goal setting in sexual encounters. Enjoying sexual fantasies and being selective about their sexual encounters are also important.

● Common sexual dysfunctions include erectile difficulties, premature ejaculation, and orgasmic difficulties. Treatments designed for specific sexual problems are extremely effective.

Key Terms

Anal intercourse	Gonads	Sensate focus
Androgens	Heterosexuals	Sex therapy
Bisexuals	Homophobia	Sexual
Coitus	Homosexuals	dysfunctions
Cunnilingus	Orgasm	Sexual identity
Erectile	Orgasmic	Sexually
difficulties	difficulties	transmitted
Erogenous zones	Premature	disease (STD)
Estrogens	ejaculation	Vasocongestion
Fellatio	Refractory period	

Key People

Alfred Kinsey	William Masters and Virginia Johnson

Practice Test

1. Young men typically feel _____ about sex; young women typically feel _____ about sex.
   a. positive; positive
   b. positive; negative
   c. ambivalent; ambivalent
   d. positive; ambivalent

2. Which of the following statements about sexual orientation is *true*?
   a. Heterosexuality and homosexuality are best viewed as two distinct categories.
   b. Heterosexuality and homosexuality are best viewed as end points on a continuum.
   c. Biological factors alone probably determine sexual orientation.
   d. Environmental factors alone probably determine sexual orientation.

3. Which of the following describes the correct order of the four phases of the sexual response cycle?
   a. Resolution, plateau, excitement, orgasm
   b. Plateau, excitement, orgasm, resolution
   c. Excitement, plateau, orgasm, resolution
   d. Excitement, orgasm, plateau, resolution

4. Sexual fantasies:
   a. are signs of abnormality.
   b. are quite normal.
   c. rarely include having sex with someone other than one's partner.
   d. are an excellent indication of what people want to experience in reality.

5. Which of the following is a result of public awareness of AIDS?
   a. More conservative attitudes about casual sex
   b. More liberal attitudes about casual sex
   c. No changes in attitudes about casual sex
   d. Dramatic reductions in sexual activity

6. Regarding overall marital satisfaction and sexual satisfaction, research indicates there is:
   a. a strong relationship.
   b. a weak relationship.
   c. no relationship.
   d. a strong relationship, but only in the first year of marriage.

7. About what percent of Americans strongly disapprove of sexual infidelity?
   a. 15%
   b. 35%
   c. 55%
   d. 75%

8. Which of the following statements about condom use is *false*?
   a. It's okay to use oil-based lubricants with polyurethane condoms.
   b. It's okay to use oil-based lubricants with rubber condoms.
   c. Skin condoms do not protect against STDs.
   d. It's okay to use water-based lubricants with rubber or polyurethane condoms.

9. Sexually transmitted diseases:
   a. are all very serious.
   b. always cause symptoms right away.
   c. are most common among people under age 25.
   d. are most common among people between 25 and 40.

10. Which of the following is a *not* one of the text's suggestions for enhancing your sexual relationships?
    a. Pursue adequate sex education
    b. Review your sexual values system
    c. Communicate about sex
    d. Set clear goals for each sexual encounter

Answers

1. d pages 370–371
2. b pages 371–373
3. c pages 377–378
4. b page 380
5. a pages 382–383
6. a page 384
7. d page 385
8. b pages 387–388
9. c page 389
10. d pages 392–393

INFOTRAC
COLLEGE EDITION

Go to the Wadsworth Psychology Study Center (http://psychology. wadsworth.com/) for quiz questions, research updates, hot topics, interactive exercises, and suggested readings in INFOTRAC related to this chapter.

CHAPTER 14

Psychology and Physical Health

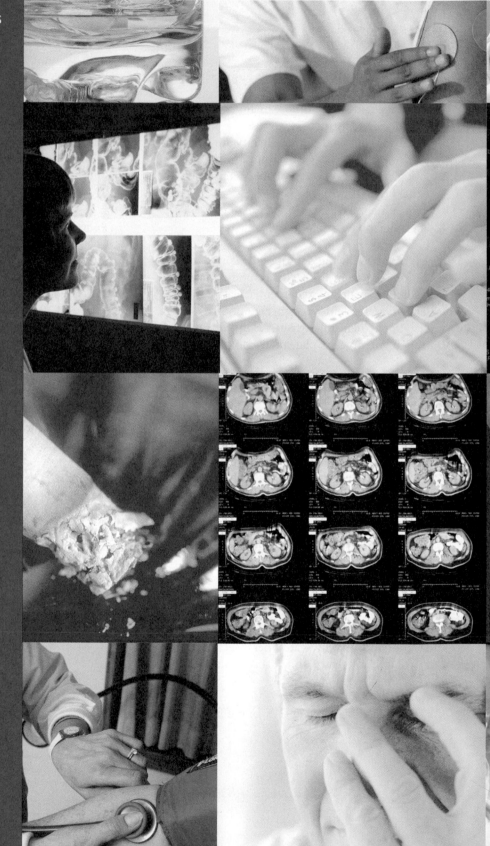

The patterns of illness found in a society tend to fluctuate over time. In our society, some interesting trends have occurred during the last century or so. Before the 20th century, the principal threats to health were *contagious diseases* caused by specific infectious agents. Because such diseases can be transmitted readily from one person to another, people used to live in fear of epidemics. The leading causes of death were diseases such as the plague, smallpox, typhoid fever, influenza, diphtheria, yellow fever, malaria, cholera, tuberculosis, polio, and scarlet fever. Today, the incidence of these diseases has declined to the point where none of them is among the leading killers in the United States (see Figure 14.1).

What neutralized these dreaded diseases? The general public tends to attribute the conquest of contagious diseases to advances in medical treatment. Although progress in medicine certainly played a role, Grob (1983) marshals evidence that the significance of such progress has been overrated. Of greater signifi-

cance, according to Grob, have been (1) improvements in nutrition, (2) improvements in public hygiene and sanitation (water filtration, treatment of sewage, and so forth), and (3) evolutionary changes in human immune resistance to the diseases. Whatever the causes, infectious diseases are no longer the major threat to physical health in the industrialized nations of the world (although many remain quite prevalent in Third World countries).

Unfortunately, the void left by contagious diseases has been filled all too quickly by various *chronic diseases*—illnesses that develop gradually over several years (refer to Figure 14.1). Psychosocial factors, such as lifestyle and stress, play a much larger role in the development of chronic diseases than they do in contagious diseases. Today, the three leading chronic diseases (heart disease, cancer, and stroke) account for nearly two-thirds of the deaths in the United States and these mortality statistics reveal only the tip of the iceberg. Many other, less serious illnesses (such as headaches,

FIGURE 14.1.

Changing patterns of illness. Trends in the death rates for various diseases during the 20th century reveal that contagious diseases (shown in blue) have declined as a threat to health. However, the death rates for stress-related chronic diseases (shown in red) have remained quite high. The pie chart (inset), which depicts the percentage of deaths caused by the leading killers today, shows the results of these trends: Three chronic diseases (heart disease, cancer, and stroke) account for over 62% of all deaths.

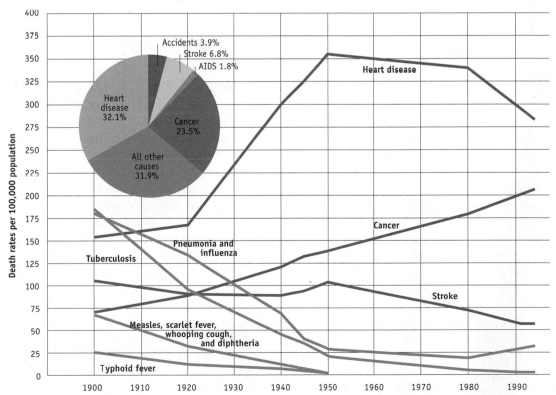

backaches, skin disorders, asthma, and ulcers) are also influenced by psychosocial factors.

In light of these dramatic trends, it is not surprising that the way we think about illness is changing. Traditionally, illness has been thought of as a purely biological phenomenon produced by an infectious agent or some internal physical breakdown. However, the shifting patterns of disease and new findings relating stress to physical illness have rocked the foundation of this biological model. In its place a new model is gradually emerging. The *biopsychosocial* **model holds that physical illness is caused by a complex interaction of biological, psychological, and sociocultural factors.** This new model does not suggest that biological factors are unimportant. Rather, it simply asserts that biological factors operate in a psychosocial context that can also be highly influential.

The growing recognition that psychological factors influence physical health led to the development of a new specialty within psychology. *Health psychology* **is concerned with how psychosocial factors relate to the promotion and maintenance of health, and with the causation, prevention, and treatment of illness.** This specialty is relatively young, having emerged in the late 1970s. Our focus in this chapter will be on this exciting new domain of health psychology.

Psychological factors can influence physical health in three general ways:

1. *Direct effects of stress.* The most basic way in which psychological functioning can affect physical health is through the direct effects of stress on physiological processes. As we discussed in Chapter 3, stress tends to elicit wide-ranging physiological arousal, which can lead to bodily changes that may be damaging in the long run.

2. *Health-impairing habits.* Many habitual patterns of behavior can increase vulnerability to various kinds of illnesses. For instance, there is ample evidence that the likelihood of developing heart disease is influenced by cigarette smoking, physical inactivity, poor diet, and other aspects of lifestyle.

3. *Reactions to illness.* Behavioral response to symptoms of illness can have a decided impact on one's health. Many people delay seeking needed medical consultation, thus increasing their risk of serious illness. Furthermore, a surprisingly large number of people ignore their doctors' advice or are unable to comply successfully with their doctors' instructions.

The three ways in which behavior can influence physical health will serve as our organizing scheme in this chapter. The chapter's first section analyzes the link between stress and illness. The second section examines common health-impairing habits, such as smoking and overeating. The third section discusses how people's reactions to illness can affect their health. In the Application we will expand on one particular type of health-impairing habit: the use of recreational drugs.

Stress, Personality, and Illness

LEARNING OBJECTIVES

- Describe the Type A personality and its link to heart disease.
- Discuss possible explanations for the link between Type A personality and heart disease.
- Summarize evidence relating emotional reactions and depression to heart disease.
- Summarize evidence linking stress and personality to cancer.
- Summarize evidence linking stress to a variety of diseases and immune functioning.
- Discuss the strength of the relationship between stress and illness.

As we noted in Chapter 3, during the 1970s health researchers began to uncover new links between stress and a variety of diseases previously believed to be purely physiological in origin. In this section, we'll look at the evidence on the apparent link between stress and physical illness and discuss how personality factors contribute to this relationship. We'll begin with heart disease, which is far and away the leading cause of death in North America.

Type A Personality, Emotions, and Heart Disease

Heart disease accounts for nearly 40% of the deaths in the United States every year. *Coronary heart disease* **results from a reduction in blood flow through the coronary arteries, which supply the heart with blood.** This type of heart disease causes about 90% of heart-related deaths. Atherosclerosis is the principal cause of coronary disease. *Atherosclerosis* **is a gradual narrowing of the coronary arteries,** usually caused by a buildup of fatty deposits and other debris on the inner walls (see Figure 14.2). Atherosclerosis progresses slowly over several years. Narrowed coronary arteries may eventually lead to situations in which the heart is temporarily deprived of adequate blood flow, causing a condition known as *myocardial ischemia*. This ischemia may be accompanied by brief chest pain, called *angina*. If a coronary artery is blocked completely (by a blood clot, for instance), the abrupt interruption of blood flow can produce a full-fledged heart attack, or *myocardial infarction*.

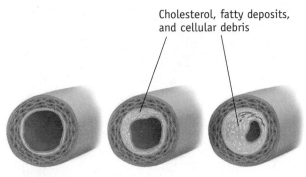

Cholesterol, fatty deposits, and cellular debris

FIGURE 14.2.

Atherosclerosis. Atherosclerosis, a narrowing of the coronary arteries, is the principal cause of coronary disease. (a) A normal artery. (b) Fatty deposits, cholesterol, and cellular debris on the walls of the artery have narrowed the path for blood flow. (c) Advanced atherosclerosis. In this situation, a blood clot might suddenly block the flow of blood through the artery.

In the 1960s and 1970s a pair of cardiologists, Meyer Friedman and Ray Rosenman (1974), were investigating the causes of coronary disease. Originally, Friedman and Rosenman were interested in the usual factors thought to produce a high risk of heart attack: smoking, obesity, physical inactivity, and so forth. Although they found these factors to be important, they eventually recognized that a piece of the puzzle was missing. Many people who smoked constantly, got little exercise, and were severely overweight still managed to avoid the ravages of heart disease. Meanwhile, other people who seemed to be in much better shape with regard to these risk factors experienced the misfortune of a heart attack. Gradually, Friedman and Rosenman unraveled the riddle. What was their explanation for these perplexing findings? Stress! Specifically, they found a connection between coronary risk and a pattern of behavior they called the *Type A*

personality, which involves self-imposed stress and intense reactions to stress.

ELEMENTS OF THE TYPE A PERSONALITY

Friedman and Rosenman divided people into two basic types (Friedman, 1996; Rosenman, 1993). **The *Type A personality* includes three elements: (1) a strong competitive orientation, (2) impatience and time urgency, and (3) anger and hostility.** In contrast, **the *Type B personality* is marked by relatively relaxed, patient, easygoing, amicable behavior.**

Type A's are ambitious, hard-driving perfectionists who are exceedingly time-conscious. They routinely try to do several things at once. Thus, a Type A person may watch TV, talk on the phone, work on a report, and eat dinner all at the same time. Type A's are so impatient that they frequently finish others' sentences for them! They fidget frantically over the briefest delays. They tend to be highly competitive, achievement-oriented workaholics who drive themselves with many deadlines. They speak rapidly and emphatically. They are cynical about life and hostile toward others. They are easily aggravated and get angry quickly. Type B's are less hurried, less competitive, and less easily angered than Type A's. The strength of one's Type A tendencies can be measured with either structured interviews or questionnaires. The checklist in Figure 14.3 lists some questions that are representative of those used in measurements of Type A behavior.

Which aspects of Type A behavior are most strongly related to increased coronary risk? Are competitiveness, time urgency, and hostility equally important? These are questions of current interest in research on the Type A syndrome. Based on recent studies, many researchers believe that hostility may be more important for coronary risk than other elements of the Type

FIGURE 14.3.

The Type A personality. The ten questions shown here highlight some of the behavioral traits associated with the Type A personality.

Measuring the Type A Personality

You can use the checklist below to estimate the likelihood that you might be a Type A personality. However, the checklist should be regarded as providing only a rough estimate, because Friedman and Rosenman (1974) emphasize that how you answer certain questions in their interview is often more significant than the answers themselves. Nonetheless, if you answer "yes" to a majority of the items below, you may want to consider reading their book *Type A Behavior and Your Heart*.

_____ 1. Do you find it difficult to restrain yourself from hurrying others' speech (finishing their sentences for them)?

_____ 2. Do you often try to do more than one thing at a time (such as eat and read simultaneously)?

_____ 3. Do you often feel guilty if you use extra time to relax?

_____ 4. Do you tend to get involved in a great number of projects at once?

_____ 5. Do you find yourself racing through yellow lights when you drive?

_____ 6. Do you need to win in order to derive enjoyment from games and sports?

_____ 7. Do you generally move, walk, and eat rapidly?

_____ 8. Do you agree to take on too many responsibilities?

_____ 9. Do you detest waiting in lines?

_____ 10. Do you have an intense desire to better your position in life and impress others?

A personality (Adams, 1994; Burg, 1995; Miller et al., 1996). In particular, investigators have been impressed by the apparent relationship between *cynical hostility* and coronary disease, hypertension, and early mortality. People high in cynical hostility are moody, suspicious, resentful, and distrusting. They are quick to anger and to criticize others. When they get upset, they tend to show relatively strong physiological reactions. In comparison to others, they exhibit elevated heart rate and blood pressure reactivity (Smith & Brown, 1991) and elevated secretions of stress hormones (Pope & Smith, 1991). More research is needed, and the evidence is far from conclusive (Rosenman, 1991), but cynical hostility may prove to be the most toxic element of the Type A syndrome.

EVALUATING THE RISK

How strong is the link between Type A personality and coronary risk? Based on preliminary data, Friedman and his associates originally estimated that Type A's were *six* times more prone to heart attack than Type B's. At the other extreme, some studies have failed to find an association between Type A behavior and coronary risk (Ragland & Brand, 1988; Shekelle et al., 1985). What can we make of these inconsistent findings? Miller and his associates (1991) have demonstrated convincingly that most of the studies that have failed to find a link between Type A behavior and coronary disease have been characterized by one or more of several methodological limitations (chief among them, poor

© 1987 Mike Twohy.

"While you've been learning to relax, Tom, I'm afraid a less enlightened 'Type A' personality got your job."

sample selection). Nonetheless, the mixed findings suggest that the relationship between Type A behavior and coronary risk is more modest than originally believed. Taken as a whole, the data suggest that the increased coronary risk for Type A's is perhaps double that for Type B's (Lyness, 1993; Weaver & Rodnick, 1986). The modest nature of this relationship probably means that Type A behavior increases coronary risk for only a portion of the population.

EXPLAINING THE CONNECTION

Why is Type A behavior associated with increased coronary risk? Research on the Type A syndrome has uncovered a number of possible explanations (see Figure 14.4).

FIGURE 14.4.

Mechanisms that may link Type A personality to heart disease. Explanations for the apparent link between Type A behavior and heart disease are many and varied. Four widely discussed possibilities are summarized in the middle column of this diagram.

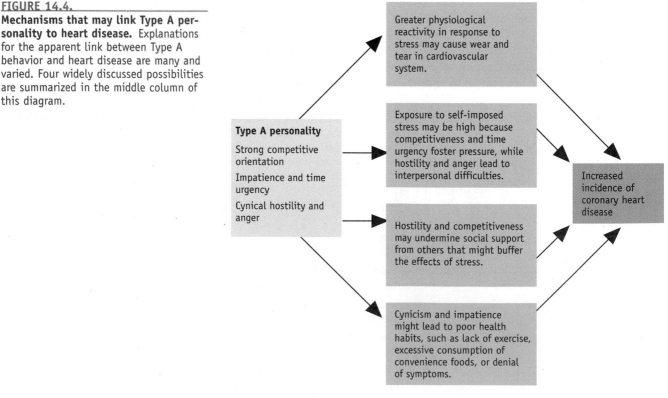

First, Type A individuals appear to exhibit greater physiological reactivity than Type B's (Lyness, 1993; Smith & Brown, 1991). The frequent ups and downs in heart rate and blood pressure may create wear and tear in their cardiovascular systems.

Second, Type A's probably create additional stress for themselves. For example, their competitiveness may lead them to put themselves under a lot of pressure, and their hostility may provoke many arguments and conflicts with others. Consistent with this line of thinking, Smith and colleagues (1988) found that subjects high in hostility reported more hassles, more negative life events, more marital conflict, and more work-related stress than subjects who were lower in hostility.

Third, thanks to their antagonistic ways of relating to others, Type A personalities tend to have less social support than others (Smith & Christensen, 1992). As we noted in Chapter 3, research suggests that social support may be an important coping resource that promotes health and buffers the effects of stress (Leppin & Schwarzer, 1990; Spiegel, 1993).

Fourth, perhaps because of their cynicism and their tendency to push themselves to work hard, Type A's tend to exhibit health habits that may contribute to the development of cardiovascular disease. For example, in comparison to Type B's, they drink more alcohol, get less exercise, and ignore symptoms of fatigue more often (Houston & Vavak, 1991; Leiker & Hailey, 1988).

In sum, there are a variety of plausible explanations for the connection between the Type A syndrome and heart disease. With all these mechanisms at work, it's not surprising that Type A behavior is associated with increased coronary risk. What's surprising is that the association isn't stronger.

EMOTIONAL REACTIONS AND HEART DISEASE

Although the Type A personality syndrome has dominated research on how psychological functioning contributes to heart disease, recent studies suggest that emotional reactions may also be critical. *One line of research has supported the hypothesis that transient mental stress and the resulting emotions can tax the heart.* Based on anecdotal evidence, cardiologists and laypersons have long voiced suspicions that strong emotional reactions might trigger heart attacks in individuals with coronary disease, but it has been difficult to document this connection. However, advances in cardiac monitoring have facilitated investigation of the issue. As suspected, laboratory experiments with cardiology patients have shown that brief periods of mental stress can trigger acute symptoms of heart disease, such as myocardial ischemia and angina (Gottdiener et al., 1994). Researchers have also examined this issue by having patients keep a diary of their emotions while their cardiac functioning is monitored continuously for

48 hours as they go about their business. The investigators found that the likelihood of myocardial ischemia increased two- or three-fold when people reported negative emotions, such as tension, frustration, and sadness (Gullette et al., 1997). Consistent with this evidence, another study of cardiology patients showed that stress management training can reduce the likelihood of a second heart attack (Blumenthal et al., 1997). Taken together, these studies suggest that emotional reactions to stressful events may precipitate heart attacks in people with coronary disease and that learning to better manage one's emotions may reduce one's coronary risk.

Another line of research has recently implicated depression as a major risk factor for heart disease. *Depressive disorders,* which are characterized by persistent feelings of sadness and despair, are a fairly common form of mental illness (see Chapter 15). Many studies have found elevated rates of depression among patients suffering from heart disease, but most theorists have explained this correlation by asserting that being diagnosed with heart disease makes people depressed. Recent evidence, however, suggests that the causal relations may be just the opposite—*that the emotional dysfunction of depression may cause heart disease.* For example, Pratt and colleagues (1996) examined a large sample of people 13 years after they were screened for depression. They found that participants who had been depressed at the time of the original study were four times more likely than others to experience a heart attack during the intervening 13 years. Because the participants' depressive disorders preceded their heart attacks, one cannot argue that their heart disease caused their depression.

Given that there is a correlation between depression and smoking (Breslau, Kilbey, & Andreski, 1993), we might argue that increased smoking is responsible for the elevated incidence of heart disease among people suffering from depression. However, several studies have shown that the predictive link between depression and heart disease remains even after controlling for the effects of smoking (Glassman & Shapiro, 1998). Although the physiological mechanisms that underlie this connection remain obscure (Appels, 1997), it appears that depression may make people more vulnerable to heart disease.

Stress and Cancer

If there is a single word that can strike terror into most people's hearts, it is probably *cancer*. People generally view cancer as the most sinister, tragic, loathsome, and unbearable of diseases. In reality, cancer is actually a *collection* of over 100 closely related diseases that vary in their characteristics and amenability to treatment. **Cancer refers to malignant cell growth, which may occur in many organ systems in the body.** The core problem in cancer is that cells begin to reproduce in a rapid, disorganized fashion. As this reproduction process lurches out of control, the teeming new cells clump together to form tumors. If this wild growth continues unabated, the spreading tumors cause tissue damage and begin to interfere with normal functioning in the affected organ systems.

The research linking psychological factors to the *onset* of cancer is relatively weak. A few retrospective studies have found evidence that high stress precedes the development of cancer (Cohen, Kunkel, & Levenson, 1998), but many others have failed to find any connection, and there is no convincing evidence that stress contributes to the causation of cancer (Cooper, 1984; Newell, 1991). Investigators have also attempted to ascertain whether there is a *cancer-prone*

personality, which might reflect unsuccessful patterns of coping with stress. These studies have yielded some intriguing threads of consistency, suggesting that lonely, depressed people who have difficulty expressing anger may have an elevated risk for cancer (Eysenck, 1988, 1993; LeShan, 1966; Temoshok, 1987). However, this research must be viewed with caution, given the possibility that one's personality may change after the discovery that one has cancer (Scherg, 1987).

Although efforts to link psychological factors to the onset of cancer have largely failed, there is more convincing evidence that stress and personality influence the *course* of the disease. The onset of cancer frequently sets off a chain reaction of stressful events. Patients typically have to grapple with fear of the unknown; difficult and aversive treatment regimens; nausea, fatigue, and other treatment side effects; dislocations in intimate relationships; career disruptions; job discrimination; and financial worries. Such stressors may often contribute to the progress of the disease, perhaps by impairing certain aspects of immune system functioning (Andersen, Kiecolt-Glaser, & Glaser, 1994). The impact of all this stress may depend in part on one's personality. Research suggests that mortality rates are higher among patients who respond with depression, repressed anger, and other negative emotions (Friedman, 1991). In contrast, prospects appear to be better for patients who can maintain their emotional stability and enthusiasm.

Stress and Other Diseases

The development of questionnaires to measure life stress has allowed researchers to look for correlations between stress and a variety of diseases. These researchers have uncovered many connections between stress and illness. For example, Thomason et al. (1992) found an association between life stress and the course of rheumatoid arthritis. Working with a sample of female students, Williams and Deffenbacher (1983) found that life stress was correlated with the number of vaginal (yeast) infections the women reported in the past year. Other studies have connected stress to the development of genital herpes (VanderPlate, Aral, &

Magder, 1988) and periodontal disease (Marcenes & Sheiham, 1992). Researchers have also found an association between high stress and flareups of inflammatory bowel disease (Olden, 1998) and asthma (Sriram & Silverman, 1998).

These are just a handful of representative examples of studies relating stress to physical diseases. Figure 14.5 provides a longer list of health problems that have been linked to stress. Many of these stress-illness connections are based on tentative or inconsistent findings, but the sheer length and diversity of the list is remarkable. Why should stress increase the risk for so many kinds of illness? A partial answer may lie in immune functioning.

Stress and Immune Functioning

The apparent link between stress and many types of illness raises the possibility that stress may undermine the body's immune functioning. **The *immune response* is the body's defensive reaction to invasion by bacteria, viral agents, or other foreign substances.** The human immune response works to protect the body from many forms of disease. Immune reactions are multifaceted, but they depend heavily on actions initiated by specialized white blood cells, called *lymphocytes*.

A wealth of studies indicate that experimentally induced stress can impair immune functioning *in animals* (Ader & Cohen, 1984, 1993; Moynihan & Ader, 1996). That is, stressors such as crowding, shock, and restraint reduce various aspects of lymphocyte reactivity in laboratory animals.

Studies by Janice Kiecolt-Glaser and her colleagues have also related stress to suppressed immune activity *in humans* (Kiecolt-Glaser & Glaser, 1995). In one study, medical students provided researchers with blood samples so that their immune response could be assessed at various points (Kiecolt-Glaser et al., 1984). The students provided the baseline sample a month before final exams and contributed the "high-stress" sample on the first day of their finals. The subjects also responded to the Social Readjustment Rating Scale (SRRS; see Chapter 3) as a measure of recent stress. Reduced levels of immune activity were found during the extremely stressful finals week. Reduced immune activity was also correlated with higher scores on the SRRS.

Janice Kiecolt-Glaser

Many other studies have also shown a link between stress and suppressed immune response (Herbert & Cohen, 1993). For example, when quarantined volunteers were exposed to respiratory viruses that cause the common cold, those under high stress were more likely to be infected by the viruses (Cohen, Tyrrell, & Smith, 1993). Other studies have found evidence of reduced immune activity among people who scored relatively high on a stress scale measuring daily hassles (Levy et al., 1989), among men who were recently divorced or separated (Kiecolt-Glaser et al., 1988), and among people recently traumatized by a hurricane (Ironson et al., 1997). Thus, scientists are beginning to assemble some impressive evidence that stress can temporarily suppress human immune functioning, which may make people more vulnerable to infections.

FIGURE 14.5.

Stress and health problems. The onset or progress of the health problems listed here *may* be affected by stress. The evidence is fragmentary in many instances, but the number and diversity of problems on this list are certainly cause for concern.

Health Problems That May Be Linked to Stress	
Health problem	**Representative evidence**
Common cold	Stone et al. (1992)
Ulcers	Ellard et al. (1990)
Asthma	Sriram & Silverman (1998)
Headaches	Ghaemi, Irizarry, & Joseph (1998)
Menstrual discomfort	Siegel, Johnson, & Sarason (1979)
Vaginal infections	Williams & Deffenbacher (1983)
Genital herpes	VanderPlate, Aral, & Magder (1988)
Skin disorders	Fava et al. (1989)
Rheumatoid arthritis	Thomason et al. (1992)
Chronic back pain	Craufurd, Creed, & Jayson (1990)
Female reproductive problems	Seibel & McCarthy (1993)
Diabetes	Gonder-Frederick et al. (1990)
Complications of pregnancy	Pagel et al. (1990)
Hernias	Rahe & Holmes (1965)
Glaucoma	Cohen & Hajioff (1972)
Hyperthyroidism	H. Weiner (1978)
Hemophilia	Buxton et al. (1981)
Tuberculosis	Wolf & Goodell (1968)
Leukemia	Greene & Swisher (1969)
Stroke	Harmsen et al. (1990)
Appendicitis	Creed (1989)
Multiple sclerosis	Grant et al. (1989)
Periodontal disease	Marcenes & Sheiham (1992)
Hypertension	Pickering et al. (1996)
Cancer	Holland & Lewis (1993)
Coronary heart disease	Rosengren, Tibblin, & Wilhelmsen (1991
AIDS	Ironson et al. (1994)
Inflammatory bowel disease	Olden (1998)
Epileptic seizures	Aird (1988)

Conclusions

In summary, a wealth of evidence suggests that stress influences physical health. However, virtually all of the relevant research is correlational, so it cannot demonstrate conclusively that stress *causes* illness (Brett et al., 1990; Watson & Pennebaker, 1989). The association between stress and illness could be due to a third variable. Perhaps some aspect of personality or some type of physiological predisposition makes people overly prone to interpret events as stressful *and* overly prone to interpret unpleasant physical sensations as symptoms of illness (see Figure 14.6). For instance, in the Chapter 3 Application we discussed how neuroticism might increase individuals' sensitivity to both stress and illness.

Moreover, critics of this research note that many of the studies used research designs that may have inflated the apparent link between stress and illness (Critelli & Ee, 1996; Schroeder & Costa, 1984). For example, researchers often have subjects make after-the-fact reports of how much stress and illness they endured during the last year or two. If some subjects have a tendency to recall more stress than others *and* to recall more illness than others, their better memories would artificially increase the correlation between stress and illness.

In spite of methodological problems favoring inflated correlations, the research in this area consistently indicates that the *strength* of the relationship between stress and health is modest. The correlations typically fall in the .20s and .30s. Clearly, stress is not an irresistible force that produces inevitable effects on health. Actually, this fact should come as no surprise. As we saw in Chapter 3, some people handle stress better than others. Furthermore, stress is only one actor on a crowded stage. A complex network of biopsychosocial

FIGURE 14.6.

The stress/illness correlation. Based on the evidence as a whole, most health psychologists would accept the assertion that stress often contributes to the causation of illness. However, some critics argue that the stress-illness correlation could reflect other causal processes. One or more aspects of personality, physiology, or memory might contribute to the correlation between high stress and high incidence of illness (see Chapter 3 for additional discussion of this complex issue).

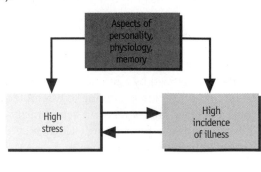

factors influence health, including genetic endowment, exposure to infectious agents and environmental toxins, nutrition, exercise, alcohol and drug use, smoking, use of medical care, and cooperation with medical advice. In the next section we'll look at some of these factors as we examine health-impairing habits and lifestyles.

Habits, Lifestyles, and Health

LEARNING OBJECTIVES

- *Give some reasons why people develop health-impairing habits.*
- *Discuss the health effects of smoking.*
- *Discuss the dynamics of giving up smoking.*

- Summarize data on patterns of alcohol use and the short-term risks of drinking.
- Summarize the major long-term health risks and social costs of drinking.
- Discuss the health risks and determinants of obesity.
- Discuss fad diets and the key elements in effective weight loss.
- Provide examples of links between nutrition and health and discuss the basis for poor nutrition.
- List three general goals intended to foster sound nutrition.
- Summarize evidence on the benefits and risks of exercise.
- List five guidelines for embarking on an effective exercise program.
- Describe AIDS and summarize evidence on the transmission of the HIV virus.
- Identify some common misconceptions about AIDS and discuss the prevention of AIDS.

Some people seem determined to dig an early grave for themselves. They do precisely those things they have been warned are particularly bad for their health. For example, some people drink heavily even though they know they're corroding their liver. Others eat all the wrong foods even though they know they're increasing their risk for a heart attack. Such downright self-destructive behavior is much more common than most people realize. In fact, research reveals that *chronic self-destructiveness* is a measurable personality trait that is related to a variety of potentially harmful behaviors, from driving recklessly (as reflected by traffic tickets) to postponing important medical tests (Kelley et al., 1985).

It may seem puzzling that people behave in self-destructive ways. Why do they do it? Several factors are involved. First, many health-impairing habits creep up on people slowly. For instance, drug use may grow imperceptibly over years, or exercise habits may decline ever so gradually. Second, many health-impairing habits involve activities that are quite pleasant at the time. Actions such as eating favorite foods, smoking cigarettes, and getting "high" are potent reinforcing events. Third, the risks associated with most health-impairing habits are chronic diseases such as cancer that usually take 10, 20, or 30 years to develop. It is relatively easy to ignore risks that lie in the distant future. Fourth, it appears that *people have a tendency to underestimate the risks associated with their own health-impairing habits* while viewing the risks associated with others' self-destructive behaviors much more accurately (van der Velde, van der Pligt, & Hooykaas, 1994; Weinstein, 1989). In other words, most people are aware of the dangers associated with certain habits, but they often engage in *denial* when it is time to apply this information to themselves.

In this section we'll discuss how health is affected by smoking, drinking, overeating and obesity, poor nutrition, and lack of exercise. We'll also look at behavioral factors that relate to AIDS. The health risks of recreational drug use are covered in the Application.

Smoking

The smoking of tobacco is widespread in our culture, with current consumption running around 2500 cigarettes a year per adult in the United States (Givovino et al., 1994). The percentage of people who smoke has declined noticeably since the mid-1960s. Nonetheless, about 28% of adult men and 23% of adult women in the United States continue to smoke regularly. Moreover, among those who continue to smoke, the proportion who smoke "heavily" has increased.

HEALTH EFFECTS

Suspicions about the health risks associated with tobacco use were voiced in some quarters early in the 20th century. However, the risks of smoking were not widely appreciated until the mid-1960s. Since then, accumulating evidence has clearly shown that smokers face a much greater risk of premature death than non-smokers (Schmitz, Jarvik, & Schneider, 1997; U.S.

Department of Health and Human Services, 1995). For example, a 25-year-old male who smokes two packs a day has an estimated life expectancy *8.3 years shorter* than that of a similar nonsmoker (Schlaadt & Shannon, 1994). The overall risk is positively correlated with the number of cigarettes smoked and their tar and nicotine content. Cigar and pipe smoking are also associated with elevated health risks, although they are less hazardous than cigarette smoking. The health costs of smoking can be put in perspective by noting that smoking accounts for roughly 60 times as many deaths per year as cocaine and heroin use combined (Jarvik & Schneider, 1992).

Why are mortality rates higher for smokers? Smoking increases the likelihood of developing a surprisingly large range of diseases. Many of these diseases are highly lethal, including 7 of the 14 leading causes of death among people over age 65 (Rimer et al., 1990). Lung cancer and heart disease kill the largest number of smokers. However, smokers also have an elevated risk for oral, bladder, and kidney cancer, as well as cancers of the larynx, esophagus, and pancreas (Newcomb & Carbone, 1992); for arteriosclerosis, hypertension, stroke, and other cardiovascular diseases (McBride, 1992); and for bronchitis, emphysema, and other pulmonary diseases (Sherman, 1992).

The dangers of smoking are not limited to smokers themselves. Family members and co-workers who spend a lot of time around smokers are exposed to second-hand smoke, which can increase their risk for a variety of illnesses, especially lung cancer (Byrd, 1992) and heart disease (Glantz & Parmley, 1995; Howard et al., 1998). One report estimates that passive smoking is the third leading cause of preventable deaths in the United States (Glantz & Parmley, 1991). Young children with asthma are particularly vulnerable to the effects of passive smoking (Stoddard & Miller, 1995).

GIVING UP SMOKING

Studies show that if people can give up smoking, their health risks decline reasonably quickly (Samet, 1992). Five years after people stop smoking, their health risk is already noticeably lower than that of people who continue to smoke. The health risks of people who give up tobacco continue to decline until they reach a normal level after about 15 years (see Figure 14.7). Evidence suggests that most smokers would like to quit, but they are reluctant to give up a major source of pleasure and they worry about craving cigarettes, gaining weight, and becoming tense and irritable (Grunberg, Bowen, & Winders, 1986; Orleans et al., 1991).

There are nearly 40 million ex-smokers in the United States. Collectively, they clearly demonstrate that it is possible to give up smoking successfully. But many didn't succeed until their third, fourth, or fifth

FIGURE 14.7.

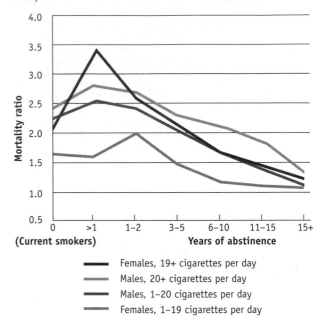

Quitting smoking and cancer risk. Research suggests that various types of health risks associated with smoking decline gradually after people give up tobacco. The data shown here, from the U.S. Surgeon General's report on smoking, illustrate the overall effects on mortality rates. (Data from: USDHHS, 1990)

— Females, 19+ cigarettes per day
— Males, 20+ cigarettes per day
— Males, 1–20 cigarettes per day
— Females, 1–19 cigarettes per day

attempt, and most would testify that quitting isn't easy. Research shows that long-term success rates for efforts to quit smoking are in the vicinity of only 25% (Cohen et al., 1989). However, light smokers (fewer than 20 cigarettes per day) are somewhat more successful at quitting than heavy smokers. The probability of a relapse after quitting is much greater among people who experience high levels of stress (Cohen & Lichtenstein, 1990) and those who drink alcohol (Schiffman et al., 1994). Discouragingly, people who enroll in formal smoking-cessation programs aren't any more successful than people who try to quit on their own (Cohen et al., 1989). In fact, it is estimated that 80–90% of the people who successfully give up smoking quit on their own, without professional help.

No single approach to quitting smoking is most effective for everyone. However, if you attempt to give

Web Link 14.2

The QuitNet Community
The Boston University School of Public Health sponsors an online community for individuals who want to quit smoking and tobacco use. A range of excellent resources, including an online support "community" available 24 hours a day, can help people make this behavioral health change.

up smoking on your own (without entering a formal treatment program), the self-modification techniques described in Chapter 4 can be invaluable. A good program should include careful monitoring of smoking habits, ample rewards for going without cigarettes, and control of antecedents to avoid situations that trigger smoking. It is also worth noting that people attempting to give up smoking often fail several times before eventually succeeding. Evidence suggests that the readiness to quit builds gradually as people cycle through periods of abstinence and relapse (Biener & Abrams, 1991; Prochaska et al., 1988). Hence, if your effort to quit smoking ends in failure, don't give up hope—try again in a few weeks or a few months.

In recent years attention has focused on the potential value of *nicotine substitutes*—nicotine gum and the newer nicotine skin patch, which releases a steady dose of nicotine into the body. The rationale for nicotine substitutes is that insofar as nicotine is addictive, it might be helpful to use a substitute during the period, when the person is trying to give up cigarettes. Do these substitutes work? The evidence is ambiguous. On the positive side, controlled studies have demonstrated that nicotine substitutes increase long-term rates of quitting in comparison to placebos (Schmitz, Jarvik, & Schneider, 1997). However, the increases are small and the success rates are still discouragingly low. For instance, in one study (Tonneson et al., 1991), the "increased" abstinence rates for subjects using the nicotine patch were only 24% after 6 months and 17% after 12 months. Clearly, nicotine substitutes are not a panacea, and they are not a substitute for a firm determination to quit.

Drinking

Alcohol rivals tobacco as one of the leading causes of health problems in American society. Alcohol encompasses a variety of beverages containing ethyl alcohol, such as beers, wines, and distilled spirits. The concentration of alcohol in these drinks varies from about 4% in most beers up to 40% in 80-proof liquor (or more in higher-proof liquors). Survey data indicate that around 100 million people in the United States drink alcoholic beverages. About two-thirds of the adult population drink, so drinkers outnumber abstainers about two to one. As Figure 14.8 shows, per capita consumption of alcohol in the United States declined in the 1980s, but this decrease followed decades of steady growth, and alcohol consumption remains relatively high, although certainly not the highest in the world (Williams et al., 1992).

Drinking is particularly prevalent on college campuses, according to a recent, large-scale survey by researchers at the Harvard School of Public Health (Wechsler et al., 1994). This survey of over 17,000 undergraduates at 140 schools found that 85% of the students drank. Moreover, 50% of the men and 39% of the women reported that they engage in binge drinking with the intention of getting drunk. Perhaps most telling, college students spend far more money on alcohol ($5.5 billion annually) than they do on their books.

WHY DO PEOPLE DRINK?

The effects of alcohol are influenced by the user's experience, motivation, and mood, as well as by the presence of food in the stomach, the proof of the beverage, and the rate of drinking. Thus, there is great variability

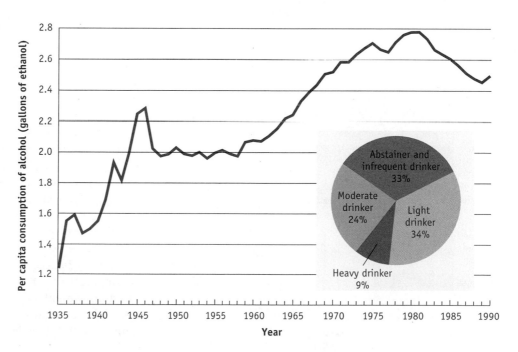

FIGURE 14.8.

Drinking in America. Drinking in the United States, as indexed by per capita consumption of ethanol in gallons, has risen steadily through most of the 20th century, although there was a modest decline during the 1980s. The inset shows the percentage of American adults who are abstainers or heavy, moderate, or light drinkers. Although only 9% of the population drinks heavily, drinkers outnumber abstainers by about two to one. (Data from: Edlin & Golanty, 1992; Williams et al., 1992)

Overindulging in alcohol is particularly widespread among college students.

in how alcohol affects different people on different occasions. Nonetheless, the central effect is a "Who cares?" brand of euphoria that temporarily boosts self-esteem as one's problems melt away. Negative emotions such as tension, worry, anxiety, and depression are dulled, and inhibitions may be loosened. Thus, when first-year college students are asked why they drink, they say it's to relax, to feel less tense in social situations, to keep friends company, and to forget their problems (see Figure 14.9). Of course, other factors are also at work. Many people drink largely out of habit. Drinking is a widely endorsed and encouraged social ritual in our culture. Its central role is readily apparent if you think about all the alcohol consumed at weddings, sports events, holiday parties, and so forth. Moreover, the

FIGURE 14.9.

Why students drink. Alcohol use among college students is higher than in the population as a whole. What motivates this drinking? A survey of 1669 first-year college students at 14 schools suggests that students drink primarily to relax and to ease tensions in social situations. (Data from: Williams & Knight, 1994)

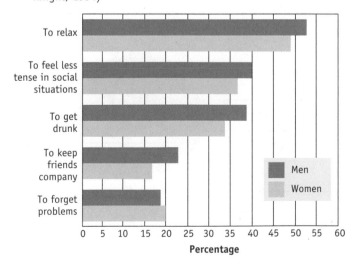

Web Link 14.3

Go Ask Alice!
One of the longest-standing and most popular sources of frank information on the Net has been Alice! from Columbia University's Health Education Program. Geared especially to the needs of undergraduate students, Alice! browsers will find direct answers to questions about relationships, sexuality and sexual health, fitness and nutrition, alcohol and drug consumption, emotional health, and general health.

alcohol industry spends hundreds of millions of dollars on advertising to convince us that drinking is cool, sexy, sophisticated, and harmless.

SHORT-TERM RISKS AND PROBLEMS

Alcohol has a variety of side effects, including some that can be very problematic. To begin with, there is that infamous source of regret, the "hangover," which may include headaches, dizziness, nausea, and vomiting. In the constellation of alcohol's risks, however, hangovers are downright trivial. For instance, life-threatening overdoses are more common than most people realize. Although it's possible to overdose with alcohol alone, a more common problem is overdosing on combinations of alcohol and sedative or narcotic drugs. These combinations result in about 140,000 emergency room visits annually in the United States.

In substantial amounts, alcohol has a decidedly negative effect on intellectual functioning and perceptual-motor coordination. The resulting combination of tainted judgment, slowed reaction time, and reduced coordination can be deadly when people attempt to drive after drinking. As Figure 14.10 shows, depending on body weight, it may take only a few drinks for driving to be impaired. It's estimated that alcohol contributes to 50% of all auto accidents. Drunk driving is a major social problem that costs about 20,000 lives every year and is the leading cause of death in young adults. Alcohol has also been implicated in about half of all home accidents and fire fatalities, and about 70% of drownings (Kinney & Leaton, 1987).

With their inhibitions released, some drinkers become argumentative and prone to aggression. In the Harvard survey of over 17,000 undergraduates, 34% of the students from "heavy drinking" schools reported that they had been insulted or humiliated by a drunken student, 20% had experienced serious arguments, and 13% had been pushed or assaulted (Wechsler et al., 1994). Worse yet, alcohol appears to contribute to about 90% of student rapes and 95% of violent crime on campus. In society at large, alcohol is associated with a host of violent crimes, including murder, assault, rape, child abuse, and spouse abuse (Maisto, Galizio, & Connors, 1995). Finally, alcohol can also contribute to

FIGURE 14.10.

Drinking and impaired driving.
This chart estimates how many
drinks it takes to impair driving
ability in people of various
weights. As you can see, as few
as three drinks in a two-hour
period can elevate blood alcohol
content (BAC) to a dangerous
level.

		BAC to .05% Be careful driving			.05–.09% Driving will be impaired			.10% & up Do not drive			

Weight (lbs)

100	1	2	3	4	5	6	7	8	9	10	11	12
120	1	2	3	4	5	6	7	8	9	10	11	12
140	1	2	3	4	5	6	7	8	9	10	11	12
160	1	2	3	4	5	6	7	8	9	10	11	12
180	1	2	3	4	5	6	7	8	9	10	11	12
200	1	2	3	4	5	6	7	8	9	10	11	12
220	1	2	3	4	5	6	7	8	9	10	11	12
240	1	2	3	4	5	6	7	8	9	10	11	12

Drinks (1½ oz liquor or 12 oz beer) in two-hour period

reckless sexual behavior, which may have ramifications for one's health. In the Harvard survey, 41% of the binge drinkers reported that they had unplanned sex due to drinking, and 22% indicated that their drinking had led to unprotected sex.

LONG-TERM HEALTH EFFECTS AND SOCIAL COSTS

Alcohol's long-term health risks are mostly (but not exclusively) associated with chronic, heavy consumption of alcohol. Estimates of the number of people at risk vary considerably. According to Winick (1992), approximately 19 million people in the United States have drinking problems, including about 8 million who should probably be characterized as *alcoholics*. **Alcoholism is a chronic, progressive disorder marked by a growing compulsion to drink and impaired control over drinking that eventually interfere with health and social behavior.** Whether alcoholism is best viewed as a disease or a self-control problem is the source of considerable debate, but there is a reasonable consensus about the warning signs of alcoholism. These include preoccupation with alcohol, drinking to relieve uncomfortable feelings, gulping drinks, clandestine drinking, and the other indicators listed in Figure 14.11.

Alcoholism and problem drinking are associated with an elevated risk for a wide range of serious health problems (Goodwin & Gabrielli, 1997), including cirrhosis of the liver, an irreversible scarring of the liver,

which is the ninth leading cause of death in the United States. Although there is some thought-provoking (albeit controversial) evidence that moderate drinking may reduce one's risk for coronary disease (Rimm et al., 1991), it is clear that heavy drinking increases the risk for heart disease, hypertension, and stroke (USDHHS, 1990). Excessive drinking is also correlated with an elevated risk for various types of cancer including oral, stomach, pancreatic, colon, and rectal cancer (Garro, Espina, & Lieber, 1992). Moreover, serious drinking problems can lead to malnutrition, pregnancy complications, brain damage and neurological disorders. Finally, alcoholism can produce severe psychotic states, characterized by delirium, disorientation, and hallucinations.

FIGURE 14.11.

Detecting a drinking problem. Experts estimate that as many as 19 million people in the United States may have a drinking problem (Winick, 1992). However, facing the reality that one has a problem with alcohol is always difficult. This list of the chief warning signs associated with problem drinking is intended to facilitate this process. (From Edlin & Golanty, 1992)

Warning Signs of Problem Drinking or Alcoholism
1. Gulping drinks.
2. Drinking to modify uncomfortable feelings.
3. Personality or behavioral changes after drinking.
4. Getting drunk frequently.
5. Experiencing "blackouts"—not being able to remember what happened while drinking.
6. Frequent accidents or illness as a result of drinking.
7. Priming—preparing yourself with alcohol before a social gathering at which alcohol is going to be served.
8. Not wanting to talk about the negative consequences of drinking (avoidance).
9. Preoccupation with alcohol.
10. Focusing social situations around alcohol.
11. Sneaking drinks or clandestine drinking.

Web Link 14.4

National Institute of Alcohol Abuse and Alcoholism
Just two of the many scientific research sources from this government agency include the entire collection of the bulletin *Alcohol Alert,* issued since 1988 on specific topics related to alcoholism ("Alcohol and Sleep," "Youth Drinking"), and the ETOH Database, a searchable repository of more than 100,000 records on alcoholism and alcohol abuse.

We have focused on the personal risks of alcohol abuse, but the enormous social costs of alcohol should also be emphasized. Drinking problems wreak havoc in millions of families. Children of alcoholics grow up in dysfunctional environments in which the risk of physical or sexual abuse is much higher than normal (Mathew et al., 1993). Homes of alcoholics tend to become tense battlegrounds as family members attempt to cope with the problem drinker's self-destructive behavior. Family members experience their own emotional crises as they struggle with feelings of frustration, anger, fear, pity, and resentment. Moreover, in the world of work, alcohol-related absenteeism and reduced efficiency on the job cost American industry billions of dollars annually. It is hard to put a dollar value on the diverse social costs of alcohol abuse, but experts estimate that alcohol costs the U.S. economy between $86 and $116 billion annually (National Institute on Alcohol Abuse and Alcoholism, 1991). Thus, the social costs of alcohol are staggering.

Overeating

Obesity, **the condition of being overweight,** is a common health problem. The criteria of obesity vary considerably. Typically, people are assumed to be obese if their weight exceeds their ideal body weight by 20%. Surveys suggest that about 24% of men and 27% of women in the United States are obese (Williamson, 1995). Obesity is similar to smoking in that it exerts a relatively subtle impact on health that is easy for many people to ignore. Nevertheless, the long-range effects of obesity can be quite dangerous. Overweight people have an increased risk of coronary disease, hypertension, stroke, respiratory problems, arthritis, diabetes, gall bladder disease, back problems, infertility, and at least four types of cancer (Pi-Sunyer, 1995; Willett & Manson, 1995). Figure 14.12 gives estimates of the

Obesity, which carries quite a number of health risks, is a product of many factors, including genetic predisposition.

extent to which obesity elevates the risk for some of these diseases.

DETERMINANTS OF OBESITY

A few decades ago it was widely believed that obesity is a function of personality. Obesity was thought to occur mostly in depressed, anxious, compulsive people who overeat to deal with their negative emotions. However, research eventually showed that there is no such thing as an "obese personality" (Rodin, Schank, & Striegel-Moore, 1989). Instead, research showed that a complex network of interacting factors determine whether people develop weight problems.

Heredity. Chief among these factors is *genetic predisposition* (Bouchard, 1995). In one influential study, adults raised by foster parents were compared with their biological and foster parents in regard to *body mass index—*

FIGURE 14.12.
Obesity and mortality. This graph shows the increased mortality risks for men who are either 20% or 40% above average weight for their age and height. Clearly, obesity is a significant health risk. (Data from VanItallie, 1979)

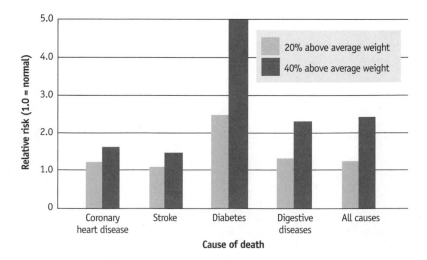

a measure of weight that controls for variations in height (Stunkard et al., 1986). The investigators found that the adoptees resembled their biological parents more than their adoptive parents. In a subsequent *twin study,* Stunkard and associates (1990) found that identical twins reared apart were far more similar in body mass index than fraternal twins reared together (see Chapter 2 for a discussion of the logic underlying twin studies). Based on a study of over 4000 twins, Allison and Colleagues (1994) estimate that genetic factors account for 61% of the variation in weight among men, and 73% among women. These genetic factors probably explain why some people can eat constantly without gaining weight, whereas other people grow chubby eating far less. Thus, it appears that some people inherit a genetic vulnerability to obesity.

Set point. People who lose weight on a diet have a rather strong (and depressing) tendency to gain back the weight they lose. The reverse is also true. People who have to work to put on weight often have trouble keeping it on. According to Richard Keesey (1995), these observations suggest that the body may have a *set point,* **which represents its natural point of stability in body weight.** According to set-point theory, the body monitors fat-cell levels to keep them fairly stable (Keesey, 1993; Keesey & Powley, 1986). When fat stores slip below a crucial set point, the body supposedly begins to compensate for this change. This compensation apparently leads to increased hunger and decreased metabolism. The processes hypothesized by set-point theory function to keep an individual's weight within a limited range (not at one precise weight, as the theory's name suggests).

Can your set point be changed? The evidence is not very encouraging. Studies suggest that long-term excessive eating can gradually increase one's set point, but decreasing it seems to be very difficult (Keesey, 1986). This finding does *not* mean that all obese people are doomed to remain obese forever. However, it does suggest that most overweight people must be prepared to make *permanent* changes in their eating and exercise habits if they expect to keep their weight down (Keesey, 1988).

Dietary restraint. Some investigators have proposed that vacillations in *dietary restraint* contribute to obesity (Herman & Polivy, 1988; Polivy & Herman, 1995). According to this theory, chronic dieters are *restrained eaters*—people who consciously work overtime to control their eating impulses and who feel guilty when they fail. To lose weight, restrained eaters go hungry much of the time, but they are constantly thinking about food. However, when their cognitive control is disrupted, they become *disinhibited* and eat to excess. The crux of

the problem is that restrained eaters assume "Either I am on a diet, or I am out of control." A variety of events, such as drinking alcohol or experiencing emotional distress, can disrupt restrained eaters' control. But for many, the most common source of disinhibition is simply the perception that they have cheated on their diet. "I've already blown it," they think to themselves after perhaps just one high-calorie appetizer, "so I might as well enjoy as much as I want." They then proceed to consume a large meal or to go on an eating binge for the remainder of the day.

Paradoxically, then, dietary restraint is thought to lead to frequent overeating and thus contribute to obesity. Research on the theory of dietary restraint is mixed. There is ample evidence to support the disinhibition hypothesis—the idea that restrained eaters often overeat after disruptions of self-control (Ruderman, 1986). And there is evidence that restrained eaters experience greater weight fluctuations than unrestrained eaters, as the theory would predict (Heatherton, Polivy, & Herman, 1991). However, some studies suggest that vacillations in dietary restraint may be just as common among people of normal weight as among obese people (Rodin, Schank, Striegel-Moore, 1989). Thus, there is plenty of room for argument about whether dietary restraint is a key factor contributing to the development of obesity.

LOSING WEIGHT

Whether out of concern about their health or just old-fashioned vanity, an ever-increasing number of people are trying to lose weight. At any given time, about 24% of men and 40% of women are dieting (Brownell & Rodin, 1994). Although concerns have been raised that dieting carries its own risks, the evidence clearly indicates that weight loss efforts involving moderate changes in eating and exercise are more beneficial than harmful to people's health (French & Jeffery, 1994). Recent research has provided some good news for those who need to lose weight. Studies have demonstrated that relatively modest weight reductions can significantly diminish many of the health risks associated with obesity (Blackburn, 1995). Thus, the traditional objective of obesity treatment—reducing to one's ideal weight—has been replaced by more modest and realistic goals (Wadden, 1998).

Although modest weight losses may be sufficient for health purposes, many people nonetheless pursue extreme dieting measures that can become dangerous. According to medical and nutritional experts, many of the popular fad diets promising large, rapid weight reductions can be perilous to one's health (Atkinson, 1989; Dwyer, 1995). For instance, an article in the *Journal of the American Medical Association* (Wadden et al., 1983) revealed that by the end of 1982 the U.S. Food

and Drug Administration had received 138 complaints of illness (including six deaths) from people following the Cambridge diet. The article also mentions that liquid-protein diets were thought to be associated with some 58 deaths before they faded from view. Thus, it is important to understand that faddish, extreme nutritional programs are money-making ventures for their developers. They usually have little genuine merit and may even be dangerous. What, by the way, do Wadden et al. (1983) recommend to achieve safe, durable weight loss? They advocate "behavior modification, nutrition counseling, and exercise" (p. 2834).

While there may be a number of causes of obesity, there is only one way to lose weight. You must change your ratio of energy intake (food consumption) to energy output (physical activities). To be quite specific, to lose one pound you need to burn up 3500 more calories than you consume. You have three options in trying to change your ratio of energy input to energy output: (1) You can sharply reduce your food consumption; (2) you can sharply increase your exercise output; (3) or you can simultaneously decrease your food intake and step up your exercise output in more moderate ways. Most experts recommend the third option, with an emphasis on reducing food intake. Although exercise clearly can contribute to weight loss, its effects are limited (Segal & Pi-Sunyer, 1989). Even a vigorous, hour-long workout will only burn off an extra 200–300 calories—a drop in the bucket in comparison to what most people could achieve by eating less. Nonetheless, Brownell (1995) emphasizes that exercise *is* an essential ingredient of an effective weight-loss regimen, which seems to play a key role in the long-term maintenance of reduced weight. (And exercise can yield many other benefits, which we will discuss momentarily.)

Although popular diet regimens promise rapid weight loss, experts agree that slow, gradual reductions in weight are more likely to be maintained than rapid reductions (Brownell, 1989). Self-modification techniques (see Chapter 4) can be helpful in achieving gradual weight loss. It is important to avoid "yo-yo dieting," the syndrome in which the same weight is lost and regained over and over in a cyclical manner (Bray, DeLany, & York, 1992). Yo-yo dieting appears to alter metabolism in ways that make it harder and harder to lose weight—and it may carry other risks as well.

Recent evidence suggests that dieters should monitor the *kinds* of calories that they consume as well as the *number* of calories. Foods with a high fat content are converted into body fat more readily than foods high in carbohydrates or protein (Gurin, 1989). Thus, people who want to "shape up" should consume low-fat diets (Rolls, 1995). This point highlights the importance of nutritional patterns, which we consider in the next section.

Poor Nutrition

Nutrition **is a collection of processes (mainly food consumption) through which an organism utilizes the materials (nutrients) required for survival and growth.** The term also refers to the *study* of these processes. Unfortunately, most of us don't study nutrition very much. Moreover, the cunning mass marketing of nutritionally worthless foods makes it more and more difficult to maintain sound nutritional habits.

NUTRITION AND HEALTH

Evidence is accumulating that patterns of nutrition influence susceptibility to a variety of diseases and health problems. In addition to the problems associated with obesity, which we have already discussed, other possible connections between eating patterns and health include the following:

1. Heavy consumption of foods that elevate serum cholesterol level (eggs, cheeses, butter, shellfish, sausage, and the like) appears to increase the risk of heart disease (Muldoon, Manuck, & Matthews, 1990). Eating habits are only one of several factors that influence serum cholesterol level, but they do make an important contribution. Unfortunately, recent studies have turned up disturbing—and baffling—evidence that lower cholesterol levels are associated with increases in depression and accidents (Kaplan, Manuck & Shumaker, 1992) and in suicide attempts (Golier et al., 1995).

2. High salt intake is thought to be a contributing factor in the development of hypertension (Kaplan, 1986), although there is still some debate about its exact role.

3. High caffeine consumption may elevate one's risk for hypertension (Lovallo et al., 1996) and for coronary disease (Grossarth-Maticek & Eysenck, 1991). However, the evidence is mixed, and a large-scale study found no association between caffeine consumption and cardiovascular risk (Grobbee et al., 1990). Given these inconsistent findings, more research is needed to settle the issue.

4. High-fat diets have been implicated as possible contributors to some forms of cancer, especially cancers of the colon, prostate, and breast (Levy, 1985). Some studies also suggest that high-fiber diets may reduce one's risk for colon and rectal cancer (Rosen, Nystrom, & Wall, 1988), but the evidence is far from conclusive.

5. Vulnerability to osteoporosis, an abnormal loss of bone mass observed most commonly in post-menopausal women, appears to be elevated by a life-long pattern of inadequate calcium intake (Fahey & Gallagher-Allred, 1990).

6. High intake of vitamin E may reduce one's risk for coronary disease (Rimm et al., 1993). Researchers emphasize that more studies should be conducted before medical authorities recommend widespread use of vitamin E supplements, but their findings are encouraging.

7. Nutritional patterns play a role in the *course and management* of a host of diseases. Prominent examples include gallstones, kidney stones, gout, peptic ulcers, and rheumatoid arthritis (Werbach, 1988). Eating habits may also contribute to the causation of some of these diseases, although the evidence is less compelling on this point.

Of course, nutritional habits interact with other factors—genetics, exercise, environment, and so on—to determine whether someone will develop a particular disease. Nonetheless, the examples just described indicate that eating habits *can* influence physical health.

THE BASIS FOR POOR NUTRITION

Nutritional deficiencies are more widespread in the United States than most people realize. One recent study found that 70% of men and 80% of women consumed a diet deficient in at least one of 15 essential nutrients (Murphy et al., 1992). For the most part, these deficiencies are not a result of low income or an inability to afford appropriate foods. Instead, most malnutrition in America is attributable to lack of knowledge about nutrition and lack of effort to ensure good nutrition (Quillin, 1987).

In other words, our nutritional shortcomings are due to ignorance and poor motivation. Americans are remarkably naive about the basic principles of nutrition. Schools tend to provide little education in this area, and most people are not highly motivated to make sure their food consumption is nutritionally sound. Instead, people approach eating very casually, guided not by nutritional needs but by convenience, palatability, and clever advertising.

For most people, then, the first steps toward improved nutrition involve changing attitudes and acquiring information. First and foremost, people need to recognize the importance of nutrition and commit themselves to making a real effort to regulate their eating patterns. Second, people should try to acquire a basic education in nutritional principles.

NUTRITIONAL GOALS

The most healthful approach to nutrition is to follow well-moderated patterns of food consumption that ensure nutritional adequacy while limiting the intake of certain substances that can be counterproductive. Here are some general guidelines for achieving these goals:

1. *Consume a balanced variety of foods.* Food is made up of a variety of components, six of which are essential to your physical well-being. These six *essential nutrients* are proteins, fats, carbohydrates, vitamins, minerals, and fiber. Proteins, fats, and carbohydrates supply the body with its energy. Vitamins and minerals help release that energy and serve other important functions as well. Fiber provides roughage that facilitates digestion. It is probably a bit unrealistic to expect most people to keep track of which nutrients are found in which foods. However, it is fairly easy to promote adequate intake of all essential nutrients. All you need do is consume a balanced diet in terms of the *basic food groups*, which are described in the food guide pyramid shown in Figure 14.13 on the next page.

2. *Avoid excessive consumption of fats, cholesterol, sugar, and salt.* These commodities are all overrepresented in the typical American diet. They are not inherently bad, but they can become problematic when consumed in excess. It is particularly prudent to limit the intake of saturated fats by eating less beef, pork, ham, hot dogs, sausage, lunch meats, whole milk, and fried foods. Consumption of many of these foods should also be limited to reduce cholesterol intake, which influences vulnerability to heart disease. In

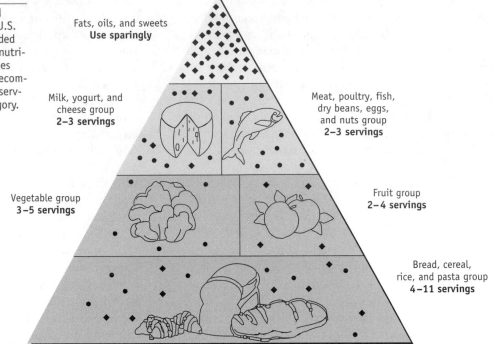

FIGURE 14.13.

The food guide pyramid. The food pyramid, endorsed in 1991 by the U.S. Department of Agriculture, is intended to provide a simple, easy guide to nutritionally balanced eating. It identifies key categories of food and makes recommendations about how many daily servings one should have in each category.

Fats, oils, and sweets
Use sparingly

Milk, yogurt, and cheese group
2–3 servings

Meat, poultry, fish, dry beans, eggs, and nuts group
2–3 servings

Vegetable group
3–5 servings

Fruit group
2–4 servings

Bread, cereal, rice, and pasta group
4–11 servings

KEY ●Fat (naturally occurring and added) ◆ Sugars (added)

particular, beef, pork, lamb, sausage, cheese, butter, and eggs are high in cholesterol. Refined (processed) sugar is believed to be grossly overconsumed. Hence, people should limit their dependence on soft drinks, chocolate, candies, pies, cakes, and jams. Finally, many people should cut down on their salt intake. This may require more than simply ignoring the salt shaker, as many prepackaged foods are loaded with salt.

3. *Increase consumption of complex carbohydrates, polyunsaturated fats, natural sugars, and foods with fiber.* If you're supposed to avoid all the foods mentioned in the preceding paragraph, you may be wondering what's left to eat. Please note, however, that the experts suggest only that you reduce *excessive consumption* of those foods while increasing consumption in other areas. In particular, fruits, vegetables, and whole grains contain complex carbohydrates, natural sugars, and ample fiber. To substitute polyunsaturated fats for saturated ones, you can eat more fish, chicken, turkey, and veal; trim meats of fat more thoroughly; use skim (nonfat) milk; and switch to vegetable oils that are high in polyunsaturated fats.

Lack of Exercise

In 1984, James Fixx, the noted author of several books touting the benefits of running, died from a heart attack while out jogging. All over the country, people who rarely exercise probably nodded their heads knowingly and made comments about exercise having little real value. Despite such rationalizations, there is

considerable evidence of a link between exercise and health. Research indicates that regular exercise is associated with increased longevity (Lee, Hsieh, & Paffenbarger, 1995). Moreover, one study showed that you don't have to be a dedicated athlete to benefit from exercise (Blair et al., 1989). It found that even a moderate level of fitness—a level that could be achieved by taking a brisk half-hour walk each day—was associated with lower mortality rates (see Figure 14.14).

BENEFITS AND RISKS OF EXERCISE

Exercise is correlated with greater longevity because it promotes a diverse array of specific benefits. First, an appropriate exercise program can enhance cardiovascular fitness and thereby reduce one's susceptibility to cardiovascular problems (Lakka et al., 1994). Fitness is associated with reduced risk for both coronary disease and hypertension (Froelicher, 1990; Hagberg, 1990). Second, regular physical activity can contribute to the avoidance of obesity (Epstein et al., 1995). Hence, fitness may indirectly reduce one's risk for a variety of obesity-related health problems, including diabetes, respiratory difficulties, arthritis, and back pain (Bray, 1990). Third, recent studies suggest that physical fitness is also associated with a decreased risk for colon cancer in men, and for breast and reproductive cancer in women (Marcus, Bock, & Pinto, 1997). The apparent link between exercise and reduced cancer risk has been a pleasant surprise for scientists, who are now scrambling to figure out the physiological mechanisms underlying this association. Fourth, exercise can serve

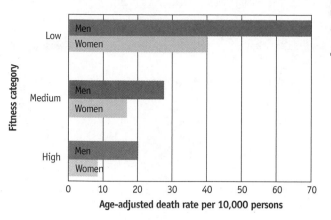

Participants were divided into five categories based on their fitness, ranging from least fit (group 1) to most fit (group 5).

Low fitness: Group 1

Medium fitness: Groups 2 and 3

High fitness: Groups 4 and 5

FIGURE 14.14.

Physical fitness and mortality. Blair et al. (1989) studied death rates among men and women who exhibited low, medium, or high fitness. As you can see, even medium fitness was associated with lower mortality rates in both sexes. The investigators note that one could achieve this level of fitness by taking a brisk half-hour walk each day.

as a buffer that reduces the potentially damaging effects of stress (Brown, 1991; Brown & Siegel, 1988). This buffering effect may occur because people high in fitness show less physiological reactivity to stress than those who are less fit. Fifth, successful participation in an exercise program can produce desirable personality changes that may promote physical wellness. Research suggests that fitness training can lead to improvements in one's mood, self-concept, and work efficiency, as well as reductions in tension, anxiety, and depression (D. R. Brown, 1990; Sacks, 1993).

It is important to note, however, that exercise programs have their own hazards. For example, jogging clearly elevates one's risk of muscular and skeletal injuries (it's especially hard on the knees) and can bring on heat stroke and possibly even a heart attack (Pate & Macera, 1994; Siscovick, 1990). The fact that exercise can both improve cardiovascular health and cause a heart attack may seem paradoxical. However, this contradiction was explained in a study by Siscovick and colleagues (1984). They found that men who participated in regular exercise activity lowered their cardiac risk. Vigorous exercise does temporarily (during the exercise) increase cardiac risk—but almost exclusively among those who do not exercise regularly. Although James Fixx's death appears inconsistent with the assertion that exercise decreases cardiac risk, Fixx took up jogging because he knew there was a history of heart problems in his family. In other words, he carried a hereditary vulnerability to heart attack that might have killed him 20 years earlier if it hadn't been for his regular exercise (his father had his first heart attack at age 35). In any case, an exercise program should be planned carefully to minimize the risks and maximize the benefits.

DEVISING AN EXERCISE PROGRAM

Putting together a good exercise program is difficult for many people. Exercise is time-consuming, and if you're out of shape, your initial attempts may be painful, aversive, and discouraging. To circumvent these problems, it is wise to heed the following advice (Greenberg, 1993):

1. *Look for an activity that you will find enjoyable.* You have a great many physical activities to choose from (see Figure 14.15). Shop around for one that you find intrinsically enjoyable. Doing so will make it much easier for you to follow through and exercise regularly.

2. *Increase your participation gradually.* Don't try to do too much too quickly. An overzealous approach can lead to frustration, not to mention injury. An exercise regimen should build gradually. If you do experience injuries, avoid the common tendency to ignore them. Consult your physician to see whether continuing your exercise program is advisable.

3. *Exercise regularly without overdoing it.* Sporadic exercise will not improve your fitness. A widely cited rule of thumb is that you should plan on exercising for a minimum of 30 minutes three times a week, or you will gain little benefit from your efforts. At the other extreme, don't try to become fit overnight by working out too vigorously and too frequently. Even highly trained athletes include days off in their schedules. These off-days are necessary to allow muscles to recover from their hard work.

4. *Reinforce yourself for your participation.* To offset the inconvenience or pain that may be associated with exercise, it is a good idea to reinforce yourself for your participation. The behavior modification procedures discussed in Chapter 4 can be helpful in devising a viable exercise program.

5. *Avoid the competition trap.* If you choose a competitive sport for your physical activity (for example, basketball or tennis), try to avoid becoming obsessed with victory. It is easy to get overly concerned with winning at games. When this happens, you put yourself under pressure. This situation is obviously self-defeating, since it adds another source of stress to your life.

FIGURE 14.15.

A scorecard on the benefits of 14 sports and exercises. Here is a summary of how seven experts rated the value of 14 sporting activities (the highest rating possible on any one item was 21). The ratings were based on vigorous participation four times per week.

How Beneficial Is Your Sport?														
	Jogging	Bicycling	Swimming	Skating (ice or roller)	Handball/ Squash	Skiing— Nordic	Skiing— Alpine	Basketball	Tennis	Calis- thenics	Walking	Golf	Softball	Bowling
Physical fitness														
Cardiorespiratory endurance (stamina)	21	19	21	18	19	19	16	19	16	10	13	8	6	5
Muscular endurance	20	18	20	17	18	19	18	17	16	13	14	8	8	5
Muscular strength	17	16	14	15	15	15	15	15	14	16	11	9	7	5
Flexibility	9	9	15	13	16	14	14	13	14	19	7	9	9	7
Balance	17	18	12	20	17	16	21	16	16	15	8	8	7	6
General well-being														
Weight control	21	20	15	17	19	17	15	19	16	12	13	6	7	5
Muscle definition	14	15	14	14	11	12	14	13	13	18	11	6	5	5
Digestion	13	12	13	11	13	12	9	10	12	11	11	7	8	7
Sleep	16	15	16	15	12	15	12	12	11	12	14	6	7	6
Total	148	142	140	140	140	139	134	134	128	126	102	67	64	51

Behavior and AIDS

Some of the most problematic links between behavior and health may be those related to AIDS. AIDS stands for **acquired immune deficiency syndrome, a disorder in which the immune system is gradually weakened and eventually disabled by the human immunodeficiency virus (HIV).** Being infected with the HIV virus is not equivalent to having AIDS. AIDS is the final stage of the HIV infection process, typically manifested about ten years after the original infection (Bartlett, 1993; Brettle & Leen, 1991). With the onset of AIDS, the body is left virtually defenseless against a host of opportunistic infectious agents. AIDS inflicts its harm indirectly by opening the door to other diseases. The symptoms of AIDS vary widely, depending on the specific constellation of diseases that an individual develops. Ultimately, AIDS is a fatal disorder, and there is no cure on the horizon. Unfortunately, the worldwide prevalence of this deadly disease continues to increase at an alarming rate.

Until recently, the average length of survival for people after the onset of the AIDS syndrome was about 18 to 24 months (Libman, 1992). Encouraging advances in the treatment of AIDS with drugs called *protease inhibitors* hold out promise for substantially longer survival, but these drugs have been rushed into service, and their long-term efficacy remains unknown (Cohen, 1997; Deeks et al., 1997). Spurred by findings linking stress to immune function, researchers have begun to explore whether stress might speed up the progression of AIDS. Some studies have found a modest association between stress and the course of the disease, but others have not (Kessler et al., 1991). Taken as a whole, current evidence suggests that stress is *not* a key factor modulating how rapidly AIDS progresses (Kalichman, 1995).

TRANSMISSION

As mentioned in chapter 13, the HIV virus is transmitted through person-to-person contact involving the exchange of bodily fluids, primarily semen and blood. The two principal modes of transmission in the United States have been sexual contact and the sharing of needles by intravenous (IV) drug users. In the United States, sexual transmission has occurred primarily among gay and bisexual men, but in the world as a whole, infection through heterosexual relations is much more common (Mann, Tarantola, & Netter, 1992; see Figure 14.16). In heterosexual relations, male-to-female transmission is more prevalent than female-to-male transmission (Ickovics & Rodin, 1992). The HIV virus can be found in the tears and saliva of infected individuals, but the concentrations are low, and there is no evidence that the infection can be spread through casual contact. Even most forms of noncasual contact, including kissing, hugging, and sharing food with infected individuals, appear safe (Kalichman, 1995).

MISCONCEPTIONS

Misconceptions about AIDS are widespread. Ironically,

FIGURE 14.16.

HIV transmission worldwide. In the United States, about 80% of HIV transmission thus far has occurred among gay men or intravenous drug users, However, in the world as a whole, heterosexual relations is the predominant mode of transmission, as these data show. (Data from Mann et al., 1992)

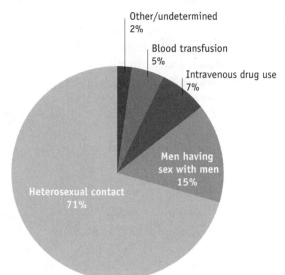

Other/undetermined
2%

Blood transfusion
5%

Intravenous drug use
7%

Men having
sex with men
15%

Heterosexual contact
71%

the people who hold these misconceptions fall into two polarized camps. On the one hand, a great many people have unrealistic fears that AIDS can be readily transmitted through casual contact with infected individuals. These people worry unnecessarily about contracting AIDS from a handshake, a sneeze, or an eating utensil. They tend to be paranoid about interacting with homosexuals, thus fueling discrimination against gays. Some people also believe that it is dangerous to donate blood when, in fact, blood donors are at no risk whatsoever.

On the other hand, many young heterosexuals who are sexually active with a variety of partners foolishly downplay their risk for HIV, naively assuming that they are safe as long as they avoid IV drug use and sexual relations with gay or bisexual men (Friedman & Goodman, 1992). They greatly underestimate the probability that their sexual partners may have previously used IV drugs or had unprotected sex with an infected individual. Also, because AIDS is usually accompanied by discernible symptoms, many young people believe that prospective sexual partners who carry the HIV virus will exhibit telltale signs of illness. However, as we have already noted, having AIDS and being infected with HIV are not the same thing, and HIV carriers often remain healthy and symptom-free for many years after they are infected. In sum, many myths about AIDS persist, in spite of extensive efforts to educate the public about this complex and controversial disease. Figure 14.17 contains a short quiz to test your knowledge of the facts about AIDS.

FIGURE 14.17

A quiz on knowledge of AIDS. Because misconceptions about AIDS abound, it may be wise to take this brief quiz to test your knowledge. (Adapted from Kalichman, 1995)

AIDS Risk Knowledge Test

Answer the following "true" or "false."

T	F	**1.** The AIDS virus cannot be spread through kissing.
T	F	**2.** A person can get the AIDS virus by sharing kitchens and bathrooms with someone who has AIDS.
T	F	**3.** Men can give the AIDS virus to women.
T	F	**4.** The AIDS virus attacks the body's ability to fight off diseases.
T	F	**5.** You can get the AIDS virus by someone sneezing, like a cold or the flu.
T	F	**6.** You can get AIDS by touching a person with AIDS.
T	F	**7.** Women can give the AIDS virus to men.
T	F	**8.** A person who got the AIDS virus from shooting up drugs cannot give the virus to someone by having sex.
T	F	**9.** A pregnant woman can give the AIDS virus to her unborn baby.
T	F	**10.** Most types of birth control also protect against getting the AIDS virus.
T	F	**11.** Condoms make intercourse completely safe.
T	F	**12.** Oral sex is safe if partners "do not swallow."
T	F	**13.** A person must have many different sexual partners to be at risk for AIDS.
T	F	**14.** It is more important to take precautions against AIDS in large cities than in small cities.
T	F	**15.** A positive result on the AIDS virus antibody test often occurs for people who do not even have the virus.
T	F	**16.** Only receptive (passive) anal intercourse transmits the AIDS virus.
T	F	**17.** Donating blood carries no AIDS risk for the donor.
T	F	**18.** Most people who have the AIDS virus look quite ill.

Answers: 1. T 2. F 3. T 4. T 5. F 6. F 7. T 8. F 9. T 10. F 11. F 12. F 13. F 14. F 15. F 16. F 17. T 18. F

PREVENTION

The behavioral changes that minimize the risk of developing AIDS are fairly straightforward, although making the changes is often much easier said than done. In all groups, the more sexual partners a person has, the higher the risk that one will be exposed to the HIV virus. Thus, people can reduce their risk by having sexual contacts with fewer partners and by using condoms to control the exchange of semen. It is also important to curtail certain sexual practices (in particular, anal sex) that increase the probability of semen/blood mixing. Intravenous drug users could greatly reduce their risk by abandoning their drug use, but their doing so is unlikely, since most are physically dependent on the drugs. Alternatively, they need to improve the sterilization of their needles and avoid sharing syringes with other users.

Reactions to Illness

LEARNING OBJECTIVES

- *Summarize evidence on patterns of treatment-seeking behavior.*
- *Discuss the factors that tend to undermine doctor-patient communication and how to improve it.*
- *Explain the appeal of the "sick role."*
- *Discuss the prevalence of nonadherence to medical advice and its causes.*

So far we have emphasized the psychosocial aspects of maintaining health and minimizing the risk of illness. Health is also affected by how individuals respond to physical symptoms and illnesses. Some people engage in denial and ignore early-warning signs of developing diseases. Others engage in active coping efforts to conquer their diseases. In this section, we discuss the decision to seek medical treatment, the sick role, and compliance with medical advice.

The Decision to Seek Treatment

Have you ever experienced nausea, diarrhea, stiffness, headaches, cramps, chest pains, or sinus problems? Of course you have; everyone experiences some of these problems periodically. However, whether you view these sensations as *symptoms* is a matter of individual interpretation. When two persons experience the same unpleasant sensations, one may shrug them off as a nuisance, while the other may rush to a physician. Studies suggest that depressed people and those who are relatively high in anxiety and neuroticism tend to report more symptoms of illness than others do (Larsen, 1992; Leventhal et al., 1996). Those who are extremely attentive to bodily sensations and health concerns also report more symptoms than the average person (Barsky, 1988).

Variations in the perception of symptoms help explain why people vary so much in their readiness to seek medical treatment (Cameron, Leventhal, & Leventhal, 1993). Generally, people are more likely to seek medical care when their symptoms are unfamiliar, frightening, or disruptive of their work or social activities (Bernard & Krupat, 1994). Another key

consideration is how friends and family react to the symptoms. Medical consultation is much more likely when friends and family view symptoms as serious and encourage the person to seek medical care (Sanders, 1982).

The biggest problem in regard to treatment seeking is the tendency of many people to delay the pursuit of needed professional consultation. Yet doing so is important, because early diagnosis and quick intervention can facilitate more effective treatment of many health problems. Unfortunately, procrastination is the norm even when people are faced with a medical emergency, such as a heart attack. Why do people dawdle in the midst of a crisis? Robin DiMatteo (1991) mentions a number of reasons, noting that people delay because they often (a) misinterpret and downplay the significance of their symptoms, (b) fret about looking silly if the problem turns out to be nothing, (c) worry about "bothering" their physician, (d) are reluctant to disrupt their plans (to go out to dinner, see a movie, and so forth), and (e) waste time on trivial matters (such as taking a shower, gathering personal items, or packing clothes) before going to a hospital emergency room.

Robin DiMatteo

The Sick Role

Although many people tend to delay medical consultations, some people are positively eager to seek medical care. These people have learned that potential benefits are to be had in adopting the "sick role" (Lubkin, 1990; Parsons, 1979). For instance, the sick role absolves people from responsibility for their incapacity and can be used to exempt them from many of their normal duties and obligations (Segall, 1997). Fewer demands are placed on sick people, who often can be selective in deciding which demands to ignore. Illness can provide a convenient, face-saving excuse for one's failures (Wolinksky, 1988). Sick people may also find themselves to be the center of attention from friends and relatives. This increased attention can be very rewarding, especially to those who received little attention

Web Link 14.5

healthfinder
Through the U.S. Department of Health and Human Services, the government has opened an ambitious online gateway to consumer-oriented information about health in all its aspects. Annotated descriptions are available for all resources identified in no-cost searches of this database.

previously. Moreover, much of this attention is favorable, in that the sick person is showered with affection, concern, and sympathy.

Thus, some people grow to *like* the sick role, although they may not be aware of it. Such people readily seek professional care, but they tend to behave in subtle ways that prolong their illness (Kinsman, Dirks, & Jones, 1982). For example, they may only pretend to go along with medical advice, a common problem that we discuss momentarily.

Communicating with Health Providers

When people seek help from physicians and other health care providers, many factors can undermine effective communication. About half of medical patients depart their doctors' offices not understanding what they have been told and what they are supposed to do (DiMatteo, 1991). This reality is most unfortunate, because good communication is a crucial requirement for sound medical decisions, informed choices about treatment, and appropriate follow-through by patients (Gambone, Reiter, & DiMatteo, 1994).

There are many barriers to effective provider-patient communication (Beisecker, 1990; DiMatteo, 1997). Economic realities dictate that medical visits are generally quite brief, allowing little time for discussion. Illness and pain are subjective matters that may be difficult to describe. Many providers use too much medical jargon and overestimate their patients' understanding of technical terms. Some providers are uncomfortable being questioned and discourage their patients' information seeking. Patients who are upset and worried about their illness may simply forget to report some symptoms or to ask questions they meant to ask. Other patients are evasive about their real concerns because they fear a serious diagnosis. Many patients are reluctant to challenge doctors' authority and are too passive in their interactions with providers.

What can you do to improve your communication with health care providers? The key is to not be a passive consumer of medical services (Ferguson, 1993; Kane, 1991). Arrive for an appointment on time, with your questions and concerns prepared in advance. Try to be accurate and candid in replying to your doctor's questions. If you don't understand something the doctor says, don't be embarrassed to ask for clarification. If you have doubts about the suitability or feasibility of your doctor's recommendations, don't be afraid to voice them.

Adherence to Medical Advice

Many patients fail to adhere to the instructions they receive from physicians and other health care professionals. Such nonadherence is not limited to people who have come to like the sick role, and it's a major problem in our medical care system. The evidence suggests that noncompliance with medical advice may occur 30% to 60% of the time (DiMatteo, 1994; Kaplan & Simon, 1990).

This point is not intended to suggest that you passively accept all professional advice from medical personnel. However, when you have doubts about a prescribed treatment, you should speak up. Passive resistance can backfire. For instance, if a physician sees no improvement in a patient who falsely insists that he has been taking his medicine, the physician may abandon an accurate diagnosis in favor of an inaccurate one. The inaccurate diagnosis could lead to inappropriate treatments that might be harmful to the patient.

Why don't people comply with the advice that they've sought out from highly regarded health care professionals? Physicians tend to attribute noncompliance to patients' personality traits, but research indicates that other factors are more important. Three considerations are especially prominent (DiMatteo & Friedman, 1982; Evans & Haynes, 1990):

1. *Frequently, noncompliance is due to a failure by the patient to understand the instructions as given.* Highly trained professionals often forget that what seems obvious and simple to them may be obscure and complicated to many of their patients.

2. *Another key factor is how aversive or difficult the instructions are.* If the prescribed regimen is unpleasant, compliance will tend to decrease. And the more that following instructions interferes with routine behavior, the less likely that the patient will cooperate successfully.

3. *If a patient has a negative attitude toward a physician, the probability of noncompliance will increase.* When patients are unhappy with their interactions with the doctor, they're more likely to ignore the medical advice provided.

In response to the noncompliance problem, some health psychologists are exploring ways to increase patients' adherence to medical advice. They've found that the communication process between the practitioner and the patient is of critical importance. Courtesy, encouragement, reassurance, taking time to answer questions, and decreased reliance on medical jargon can improve compliance (DiNicola & DiMatteo, 1984; Hall, Roter, & Katz, 1988).

Understanding the Effects of Drugs

LEARNING OBJECTIVES

● *Explain the concepts of tolerance, physical and psychological dependence, and overdose.*

● *Summarize the main effects and risks of narcotics.*

● *Summarize the main effects and risks of sedatives.*

● *Summarize the main effects and risks of stimulant drugs.*

● *Summarize the main effects and risks of hallucinogens.*

● *Summarize the main effects and risks of marijuana and designer drugs.*

Answer the following "true" or "false."

_____ **1.** Smoking marijuana can make men impotent and sterile.

_____ **2.** Overdoses caused by cocaine are relatively rare.

_____ **3.** It is well documented that LSD causes chromosome damage.

_____ **4.** Hallucinogens are addictive.

_____ **5.** Snorting cocaine is safer than smoking crack.

As you will learn in this Application, all of these statements are false. If you answered all of them accurately, you may already be well informed about drugs. If not, you *should* be. Intelligent decisions about drugs require an understanding of their effects and risks.

This Application focuses on the use of drugs for their pleasureable effects, commonly referred to as *drug abuse* or *recreational drug use*. Drug abuse reaches into every corner of our society, and it is a problematic health-impairing habit. Although small declines occurred in the abuse of certain drugs during the 1980s (Johnson & Muffler, 1992), it appears that recreational drug use is here to stay for the forseeable future.

Like other controversial social problems, recreational drug use often inspires more rhetoric than reason. For instance, a former president of the American Medical Association made headlines when he declared that marijuana "makes a man of 35 sexually like a man of 70." In reality, the research findings do not support this assertion. This influential physician later retracted his statement, admitting that he had made it simply to campaign against marijuana use (Leavitt, 1995). Unfortunately, such scare tactics can backfire by undermining the credibility of drug education efforts.

Recreational drug use involves personal, moral, political, and legal issues that are not matters for science to resolve. However, the more knowledgeable you are about drugs, the more informed your decisions and opinions about them will be. Accordingly, this Application is intended to provide you with nonjudgmental, realistic coverage of issues related to recreational drug use. We'll begin by reviewing key drug-related concepts. Then we'll examine the effects and risks of five types of widely abused drugs: narcotics, sedatives, stimulants, hallucinogens, and cannabis. We'll wrap up our coverage with a brief discussion of newer drugs that have surfaced in recent years.

Drug-Related Concepts

The drugs that people use recreationally are termed *psychoactive*. **Psychoactive drugs are chemical substances that modify a person's mental, emotional, or behavioral functioning.** Not all psychoactive drugs produce effects that lead to drug abuse. Generally, people prefer drugs that elevate their mood or produce pleasant alterations in consciousness. The principal types of recreational drugs are described in Figure 14.18. This table lists representative drugs in each of the five categories and indicates how the drugs are taken, their principal medical uses, their desired effects, and their common side effects.

Most drugs produce tolerance effects. **Tolerance is a progressive decrease in a person's responsiveness to a drug with continued use.** Tolerance effects usually lead people to consume larger and larger doses of a drug to attain the effects they desire. Tolerance builds more rapidly to some drugs than to others. The first column in Figure 14.19 indicates whether various categories of drugs tend to produce rapid or gradual tolerance.

Our society discourages some types of drug use more than others, but all drugs have side effects and carry risks.

FIGURE 14.18.

Major categories of abused drugs. This chart summarizes the methods of ingestion, chief medical uses, and principal effects of five major types of recreational drugs. Alcohol is covered in the main body of the chapter. (Based on Blum, 1984; Julien, 1995; Lowinson et al., 1997)

Comparison of Major Abused Drugs

Drugs	Methods of administration	Principal medical uses	Desired effects	Short-term side effects
Narcotics (opiates) Morphine Heroin	Injected, smoked, oral	Pain relief	Euphoria, relaxation, anxiety reduction, pain relief	Lethargy, drowsiness, nausea, impaired coordination, impaired mental functioning, constipation
Sedatives Barbiturates (e.g., Seconal) Nonbarbiturates (e.g., Quaalude)	Oral, injected	Sleeping pill, anticonvulsant	Euphoria, relaxation, anxiety reduction, reduced inhibitions	Lethargy, drowsiness, severely impaired coordination, impaired mental functioning, emotional swings, dejection
Stimulants Amphetamines Cocaine	Oral, sniffed, injected, freebased, smoked	Treatment of hyperactivity and narcolepsy; local anesthetic (cocaine only)	Elation, excitement, increased alertness, increased energy, reduced fatigue	Increased blood pressure and heart rate, increased talkativeness, restlessness, irritability, insomnia, reduced appetite, increased sweating and urination, anxiety, paranoia, increased aggressiveness, panic
Hallucinogens LSD Mescaline Psilocybin	Oral		Increased sensory awareness, euphoria, altered perceptions, hallucinations, insightful experiences	Dilated pupils, nausea, emotional swings, paranoia, jumbled thought processes, impaired judgment, anxiety, panic reaction
Cannabis Marijuana Hashish THC	Smoked, oral	Treatment of glaucoma; other uses under study	Mild euphoria, relaxation, altered perceptions, enhanced awareness	Bloodshot eyes, dry mouth, reduced memory, sluggish motor coordination, sluggish mental functioning, anxiety

Note: A major omission from this table is PCP (phencyclidine hydrochloride), which does not fit neatly into any of the listed categories. PCP has stimulant, hallucinogenic, and anesthetic effects. Its short-term side effects can be very dangerous. Common side effects include agitation, paranoia, confusion, and severe mental disorientation that has been linked to accidents and suicides.

In evaluating the potential problems associated with the use of specific drugs, a key consideration is the likelihood of either physical or psychological dependence. Although recent evidence indicates that there is a physiological basis for both forms of drug dependence (Koob & Bloom, 1988; Ray & Ksir, 1990), there are important differences between the two syndromes. *Physical dependence* **exists when a person must continue to take a drug to avoid withdrawal illness (which occurs when drug use is terminated).** The symptoms of withdrawal illness vary depending on the drug. Withdrawal from heroin and barbiturates can produce fever, chills, tremors, convulsions, seizures, vomiting, cramps, diarrhea, and severe aches and pains. The agony of withdrawal from these drugs virtually compels addicts to continue using them. Withdrawal from stimulants leads to a different and somewhat milder syndrome dominated by fatigue, apathy, irritability, depression, and disorientation.

Psychological dependence **exists when a person must continue to take a drug to satisfy intense mental and emotional craving for it.** Psychological dependence is more subtle than physical dependence, as it is not marked by a clear withdrawal reaction. However, psychological dependence can create a powerful, overwhelming need for a drug. Both types of dependence

FIGURE 14.19.

Specific risks for various categories of drugs. This chart shows estimates of the risk potential for tolerance, dependence, and overdose for the five major categories of drugs discussed in this Application.

Risks Associated with Abused Drugs

Drugs	Tolerance	Risk of physical dependence	Risk of psychological dependence	Fatal overdose potential
Narcotics (opiates)	Rapid	High	High	High
Sedatives	Rapid	High	High	High
Stimulants	Rapid	Moderate	High	Moderate to high
Hallucinogens	Gradual	None	Very low	Very low
Cannabis	Gradual	None	Low to moderate	Very low

are established gradually with repeated use of a drug. Drugs vary greatly in their potential for creating either physical or psychological dependence. The second and third columns in Figure 14.19 provide estimates of the risk of each kind of dependence for the drugs covered in our discussion.

An *overdose* is an excessive dose of a drug that can seriously threaten one's life. Any drug can be fatal if a person takes enough of it, but some drugs carry more risk of overdose than others. In Figure 14.19, column 4 estimates the risk of accidentally consuming a lethal overdose of various drugs. Drugs that are central nervous system (CNS) depressants—narcotics and sedatives—carry the greatest risk of overdose. It's important to understand that the effects of these drugs are additive. Many overdoses involve lethal *combinations* of CNS depressants. What happens when people overdose on these drugs? Their respiratory system usually grinds to a halt, producing coma, brain damage, and death within a brief period. In contrast, fatal overdoses with CNS stimulants (cocaine and amphetamines) usually involve a heart attack, stroke, or cortical seizure.

Now that our basic vocabulary is spelled out, we can begin to examine the effects and risks of major recreational drugs. Of course, we'll be describing the *typical* effects of each drug. Please bear in mind that the effects of any drug depend on the user's age, body weight, physiology, personality, mood, expectations, and previous experience with the drug. The dose and potency of the drug, the method of administration, and the setting in which the drug is taken also influence its effects (Leavitt, 1995). Our coverage is based largely on comprehensive books by Blum (1984), Julien (1995) and Lowinson and colleagues (1997), but we'll cite additional sources when discussing specific studies or controversial points.

Narcotics

Narcotics (or opiates) are drugs derived from opium that are capable of relieving pain. In legal regulations, the term *narcotic* is used in a haphazard way to refer to a variety of drugs besides opiates. Our discussion will focus on heroin and morphine, but many of the points would also apply to less potent opiates, such as codeine, demerol, and methadone.

EFFECTS

The most significant narcotics problem in modern, Western society is the use of heroin. Most users inject this drug intravenously with a hypodermic needle. The main effect is an overwhelming sense of euphoria. This euphoric effect has a "Who cares?" quality to it that makes the heroin high an attractive escape from reality.

Common side effects include nausea, lethargy, drowsiness, constipation, and slowed respiration.

RISKS

Narcotics carry a high risk for both *psychological and physical dependence* (Jaffe, Knapp, & Ciraulo, 1997). It is estimated that there are about a half-million heroin addicts in the United States (Winick, 1997). Although heroin withdrawal usually isn't life threatening, it can be terribly unpleasant, so that "junkies" have a desperate need to continue their drug use. Once dependence is entrenched, users tend to develop a *drug-centered lifestyle* that revolves around the need to procure more heroin. This happens because the drug is very expensive (up to $200 a day) and available only through highly undependable black market channels. Obviously, it is difficult to lead a productive life if one's existence is dominated by a desperate need to "score" heroin. The inordinate cost of the drug forces many junkies to resort to criminal activities to support their habit.

Overdose is also a very real danger with heroin (Jaffe, 1992). Part of the problem is difficulty in judging the purity of heroin obtained through black market sources. Opiates are additive with other CNS depressants, and most narcotic overdoses occur in combination with the use of sedatives or alcohol. Junkies also risk *contracting infectious disease* because they often share hypodermic needles and tend to be sloppy about sterilizing them. The most common of these diseases used to be hepatitis, but in recent years AIDS has been transmitted at an alarming rate through the population of intravenous drug users (Des Jarlais, Hagan, & Friedman, 1997).

Sedatives

Sedatives are sleep-inducing drugs that tend to decrease central nervous system activation and behavioral activity. In street jargon, they are often called "downers." Over the years, the most widely abused sedatives have been the barbiturates, which are compounds derived from barbituric acid. However, barbiturates have gradually become medically obsolete and diminished in availability, so sedative abusers have had to turn to drugs in the benzodiazepine family, such as Valium (Wesson et al., 1997).

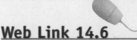

Web Link 14.6

Web of Addictions
From the earliest days of the World Wide Web, this page at The Well has been regularly recognized as a primary source for accurate and responsible information about alcoholism and other drug addictions.

EFFECTS

People abusing sedatives generally consume larger doses than are prescribed for medical purposes. These overly large doses have a euphoric effect similar to that produced by drinking large amounts of alcohol (Wesson, Smith, & Seymour, 1992). Feelings of tension, anxiety, and depression are temporarily replaced by a relaxed, pleasant state of intoxication, in which inhibitions may be loosened. Sedatives carry a truckload of dangerous side effects. Motor coordination suffers badly, producing slurred speech and a staggering walk, among other things. Intellectual functioning also becomes sluggish, and judgment is impaired. One's emotional tone may become unstable, with feelings of dejection often intruding on the intended euphoric mood.

RISKS

Sedatives have the potential to produce both psychological and physical dependence. They also are among the leading cause of overdoses in the United States (O'Brien & Woody, 1986) because of their additive interactions with other CNS depressants (especially alcohol) and because of the degree to which they impair judgment. In their drug-induced haze, sedative abusers are prone to take doses they would ordinarily recognize as dangerous. Also, with prolonged use, the dose of barbiturates needed to feel high increases more rapidly than the dose the body can handle. Thus, the margin of safety between an intoxicating dose and a lethal one gradually narrows. Sedative users also elevate their risk for *accidental injuries* because these drugs can have drastic effects on motor coordination. Many users trip down stairs, fall off bar stools, get into automobile accidents, and so forth.

Stimulants

Stimulants **are drugs that tend to increase central nervous system activation and behavioral activity.** They range from mild, widely available stimulants, such as caffeine and nicotine, to stronger, carefully regulated stimulants, such as cocaine and amphetamines ("speed"). We'll focus on the latter two drugs.

Cocaine is an organic substance extracted from the coca shrub, which grows most prominently in South America. It is usually consumed as a crystalline powder that is snorted through the nasal cavities. However, some users "freebase" cocaine. Freebasing is chemical treatment used to extract nearly pure cocaine concentrate from ordinary street cocaine. "Crack" is the most widely distributed byproduct of this process, consisting of little chips of pure cocaine that are usually smoked. Smoking crack is far more dangerous than snorting cocaine powder because of its greater purity. Also,

Recreational drug users come from all ages and all walks of life.

smoking leads to a more rapid absorption of the drug into the bloodstream (Gold & Miller, 1997).

Synthesized in a pharmaceutical laboratory, amphetamines are usually consumed orally. However, speed is also sold as a crystalline powder (called "crank") that may be snorted or injected intravenously. Recently, a smokable form of methamphetamine (called "ice") has been developed.

EFFECTS

Amphetamines and cocaine have almost indistinguishable effects, except that cocaine produces a very brief high (20–30 minutes unless more is taken), while a speed high can last many hours (Gold, Miller, & Jonas, 1992). Stimulants produce a euphoria very different from that created by narcotics or sedatives. They produce a buoyant, elated, enthusiastic, energetic, "I can conquer the world!" feeling accompanied by increased alertness. Common side effects include increased blood pressure, muscle tension, sweating, and restlessness. Some users experience unpleasant feelings of irritability, anxiety, and paranoia.

RISKS

Stimulants can cause physical dependence, but the physical distress caused by stimulant withdrawal is mild in comparison to that caused by narcotic or sedative withdrawal (Kleber & Gawin, 1986). Psychological dependence on stimulants is a more common problem. Cocaine can create an exceptionally powerful psychological dependence that compels the user to pursue the drug with a fervor normally seen only when physical dependence exists.

Both cocaine and amphetamines can suppress appetite and disrupt sleep. Thus, heavy use of stimulants may lead to poor eating, poor sleeping, and ultimately, a deterioration in physical health. Furthermore, stimulant use increases one's risk for stroke, heart attack, and other forms of cardiovascular disease, and crack smoking is associated with a host of respiratory problems (Gold, 1997).

Heavy stimulant use occasionally leads to the onset of a severe psychological disorder called *amphetamine* or *cocaine psychosis* (depending on the drug involved), which is dominated by intense paranoia (King & Ellinwood, 1997). All of the risks associated with stimulant use increase *greatly* when more potent forms of the drugs (crack and ice) are used. *Overdoses* on stimulants used to be relatively infrequent (Kalant & Kalant, 1979). However, in recent years, cocaine overdoses have increased sharply as more people experiment with freebasing, crack smoking, and other more dangerous modes of ingestion (Gold, 1992).

Hallucinogens

Hallucinogens **are a diverse group of drugs that have powerful effects on mental and emotional functioning, marked most prominently by distortions in sensory and perceptual experience.** The principal hallucinogens are LSD, mescaline, and psilocybin, which have similar effects, although they vary in potency. Mescaline comes from the peyote plant, psilocybin comes from a particular type of mushroom, and LSD is a synthetic drug.

EFFECTS

Hallucinogens intensify and distort perception in ways that are difficult to describe, and they temporarily impair intellectual functioning as thought processes become meteoric and jumbled. These drugs can produce awesome feelings of euphoria that sometimes include an almost mystical sense of "oneness" with the human race. This is why they have been used in religious ceremonies in various cultures. Unfortunately, at the other end of the emotional spectrum, they can also produce nightmarish feelings of anxiety, fear, and paranoia, commonly called a "bad trip."

RISKS

There is no potential for physical dependence on hallucinogens, and no deaths attributable to overdose are known to have occurred. Psychological dependence has been reported but appears to be very rare (Grinspoon & Bakalar, 1986). Research reports that LSD increases chromosome breakage were based on poor methodology (Dishotsky et al., 1971). However, like most drugs, hallucinogens may be harmful to a fetus if taken by a pregnant woman.

Although the dangers of hallucinogens have probably been exaggerated in the popular press, there are some significant risks (Pechnick & Ungerleider, 1997). Emotion is highly volatile with these drugs, so users can

never be sure that they won't experience *acute panic* from a terrifying bad trip. Generally, this disorientation subsides within a few hours, leaving no permanent emotional scars. However, in such a severe state of disorientation, *accidents and suicide* are possible. *Flashbacks* are vividly hallucinogenic experiences months after the original drug ingestion. Repetitious, frightening flashbacks can become troublesome. In a small minority of users, hallucinogens may contribute to the development of a variety of psychological disorders (psychoses, depressive reactions, paranoid states) that appear partially attributable to the drug (Ungerleider & Pechnick, 1992).

Marijuana

Cannabis **is the hemp plant from which marijuana, hashish, and THC are derived.** Marijuana is a mixture of dried leaves, flowers, stems, and seeds taken from the plant, while hashish comes from the plant's resin. THC, the active chemical ingredient in cannabis, can be synthesized for research purposes (for example, to give to animals).

EFFECTS

When smoked, cannabis has an almost immediate impact that may last several hours. The effects of the drug vary greatly, depending on the user's expectations and experience with it, the drug's potency, and the amount smoked. The drug has subtle effects on emotion, perception, and cognition (Grinspoon & Bakalar, 1997). Emotionally, the drug tends to create a mild, relaxed state of euphoria. Perceptually, it enhances the impact of incoming stimulation, thus making music sound better, food taste better, and so on. Cannabis tends to produce a slight impairment in cognitive functioning (especially short-term memory) and perceptual-motor coordination while the user is high. However, there are huge variations among users.

RISKS

Overdose and physical dependence are not problems, but as with any other drug that produces pleasant feelings, marijuana has the potential to produce psychological dependence (Grinspoon & Bakalar, 1992). There is no solid evidence that cannabis causes psychological disorders. However, marijuana can cause *transient problems with anxiety and depression* in some people. Some studies also suggest that cannabis may have a more negative effect on driving than has been widely believed (Moskowitz, 1985). Like tobacco, marijuana smoke carries carcinogens and impurities into the lungs, thus increasing one's chances for *respiratory and pulmonary diseases, as well as lung cancer* (Cohen, 1986; Gold, 1989). However, the evidence on other widely publicized risks remains controversial. Here is a brief overview of the evidence on some of these controversies.

- *Does marijuana cause brain damage?* The handful of studies linking marijuana to brain damage have been shown to be methodologically unsound (Kuehnle et al., 1977). Marijuana affects brain-wave activity (Heath, 1976), but there is no clear evidence that such changes in brain activity are permanent or pathological (Jenike, 1987).

- *Does marijuana reduce one's immune response?* Cannabis may suppress the body's natural immune response slightly (Nahas, 1976). However, infectious diseases are no more common among marijuana smokers than nonsmokers. Hence, this effect is apparently too small to have any practical importance (Relman, 1982).

- *Does marijuana impair reproductive functioning?* Cannabis does have some endocrine and reproductive effects that merit further investigation. Marijuana appears to produce a small, reversible decline in sperm count among male smokers and may have temporary effects on hormone levels (Bloodworth, 1987). The popular media have frequently implied that marijuana therefore makes men sterile and impotent. In reality, there is no evidence that marijuana produces any lasting effects on male smokers' fertility or sexual functioning (Grinspoon & Bakalar, 1997). Of greater concern are reports that marijuana—like tobacco—may be hazardous for pregnant women. Some studies suggest that marijuana use may be associated with an increased risk of premature birth and low birth weight (Day & Richardson, 1991; Fried, 1986).

Designer Drugs

Thus far, we have focused on the most commonly abused drugs in our culture. Most of these drugs have a history of abuse that goes back centuries, and even the newest have been around for many decades. In this section we'll briefly look at some newer, less widely abused drugs.

***Designer drugs* are illicitly manufactured variations on known recreational drugs.** Underground chemists typically make slight alterations in the chemical structure of opiates, amphetamines, or hallucinogens or assemble them into new combinations. Designer drugs were originally invented to circumvent legal restrictions. Reasoning that authorities couldn't restrict drugs that didn't exist yet, enterprising drug dealers figured that they couldn't be prosecuted successfully for selling their new compounds. Flexible regulations that outlawed such drugs were developed eventually. However, the market for designer drugs remains, and they continue to be manufactured.

The best known designer drug is MDMA, which is sold on the street as "ecstasy." This compound is related to amphetamines and hallucinogens (Grob & Poland, 1997). It produces a short-lived high (about 90 minutes). Users feel warm, friendly, sensual, and serene, but alert. Problematic side effects include increased blood pressure, heart arrhythmias, and transient anxiety. Fentanyl is another designer drug that has gained a following among narcotics users (Stanford, 1987). Known on the street as "China white," this synthetic opiate is much more potent than heroin. It carries a high risk of overdose.

Designer drugs probably account for only a small portion of the illicit drug use in the United States (Morgan, 1997), but the emergence of these drugs is alarming for two reasons. First, designer drugs haven't been studied much yet, and their long-term risks are unknown. Second, these drugs are manufactured by "kitchen chemists" whose quality control varies enormously. Designer drugs often contain potentially harmful impurities, contaminants, and toxic byproducts because of inadvertent errors in the manufacturing process.

Key Ideas

STRESS, PERSONALITY, AND ILLNESS

● The biopsychosocial model holds that physical health is influenced by a complex network of biological, psychological, and sociocultural factors. Stress is one of the psychological factors that can affect physical health. In particular, Type A behavior has been implicated as a contributing cause of coronary heart disease. This competitive, impatient, hostile pattern of behavior may double one's coronary risk. A number of mechanisms may contribute to this connection.

● Emotional reactions may also influence susceptibility to heart disease. Recent research has suggested that transient mental stress and the negative emotions that result may tax the heart. Yet another line of research has identified the emotional dysfunction of depression as a risk factor for heart diesase.

● The connection between psychological factors and the onset of cancer is not well documented, but stress and personality may influence the course of the disease. Researchers have found associations between stress and the onset of a variety of other diseases. Stress may play a role in a host of diseases because it can temporarily suppress immune functioning. While there's little doubt that stress can contribute to the development of physical illness, the link between stress and illness is modest.

HABITS, LIFESTYLES, AND HEALTH

● People commonly engage in health-impairing habits and lifestyles. These habits creep up slowly, and their risks are easy to ignore because the dangers often lie in the distant future. Smokers have much higher mortality rates than nonsmokers because they are more vulnerable to a variety of diseases. Giving up smoking is difficult in part because nicotine is addictive.

● Drinking rivals smoking as a source of health problems. In the short term, drinking can impair driving, cause various types of accidents, and increase the likelihood of aggressive interactions or reckless sexual behavior. In the long term, chronic, excessive alcohol consumption increases one's risk for a host of health problems, including cirrhosis of the liver, heart disease, hypertension, stroke, and cancer, among other things.

● Obesity elevates one's risk for many health problems. Body weight is influenced by genetic endowment, set point, and vacillations in dietary restraint. Weight loss is best accomplished by decreasing caloric consumption while increasing exercise.

● Poor nutritional habits have been linked to a host of health problems, although much of the evidence is tentative. One's health can best be served by following balanced food consumption patterns while limiting the intake of fats and sugars.

● Lack of exercise is associated with elevated mortality rates. Regular exercise can reduce one's risk for cardiovascular disease, cancer, and obesity-related diseases; buffer the effects of stress; and lead to desirable personality changes.

● Although misconceptions abound, HIV is transmitted almost exclusively by sexual contact and the sharing of needles by IV drug users. One's risk for HIV infection—and thus AIDS—can be reduced by avoiding IV drug use, having fewer sexual partners, using condoms, and curtailing certain sexual practices.

REACTIONS TO ILLNESS

● Everyone experiences physical symptoms, but people vary in how they respond to such symptoms. Variations in seeking treatment are influenced by the severity of the symptoms and by the reactions of friends and family. The biggest problem is the tendency of many people to delay needed medical treatment. At the other extreme, a minority of people learn to like the sick role because it earns them attention and allows them to avoid stress.

● Good communication is crucial to effective health services, but many factors undermine communication between patients and health providers, such as short visits, overuse of medical jargon, and patients' reluctance to ask questions. The key to improving communication with health care providers is to not be a passive consumer of medical services.

● Noncompliance with medical advice is a major problem. The likelihood of nonadherence is greater when instructions are difficult to understand, when recommendations are difficult to follow, and when patients are unhappy with their doctor.

APPLICATION: UNDERSTANDING THE EFFECTS OF DRUGS

● Recreational drugs vary in their potential for tolerance effects, psychological dependence, physical dependence, and overdose. The risks associated with narcotics use include both types of dependence, overdose, and the acquisition of infectious diseases.

● Sedatives can also produce both types of dependence, are subject to overdoses, and elevate one's risk for accidental injuries. Stimulant use can lead to psychological dependence, overdose, psychosis, and a deterioration in physical health.

● Hallucinogens can in some cases contribute to accidents, suicides, and psychological disorders, and they can cause flashbacks. The risks of marijuana use include psychological dependence, transient problems with anxiety and depression, and respiratory and pulmonary diseases. Marijuana use can also impair driving.

Key Terms

Acquired immune deficiency syndrome (AIDS)	Designer drugs	Psychoactive drugs
	Hallucinogens	
	Health psychology	Psychological dependence
Alcoholism	Immune response	Sedatives
Atherosclerosis		Set point
Biopsychosocial model	Narcotics	Stimulants
	Nutrition	Tolerance
Cancer	Obesity	Type A personality
Cannabis	Overdose	
Coronary heart disease	Physical dependence	Type B personality

Key People

Robin DiMatteo
Meyer Friedman and Ray Rosenman

Janice Kiecolt-Glaser

Practice Test

1. The greatest threats to health in our society today are:
   a. environmental toxins.
   b. accidents.
   c. chronic diseases.
   d. contagious diseases caused by specific infectious agents.

2. Which characteristic of Type A behavior seems most closely associated with coronary risk?
   a. Rapid talking
   b. Cynical hostility
   c. Competitiveness
   d. Time urgency

3. Why do people tend to act in self-destructive ways?
   a. Because many health-impairing habits creep up on them
   b. Because many health-impairing habits involve activities that are quite pleasant at the time
   c. Because the risks tend to lie in the distant future
   d. All of the above

4. Short-term risks of alcohol consumption include all but which of the following?
   a. Hangovers and life-threatening overdoses in combination with other drugs
   b. Poor perceptual coordination and driving drunk
   c. Increased aggressiveness and argumentativeness
   d. Transient anxiety from endorphin-induced flashbacks

5. George's objection to exercise is that the dangers of muscular and skeletal injuries, not to mention heart attacks, far outweigh the benefits. Given the research, what would you say?
   a. He's right and all he really needs to do is watch his diet.
   b. He's right and all he really needs to do is stop smoking and drinking alcohol.
   c. He's wrong because there are no such hazards associated with exercise.
   d. He's wrong because the dangers can easily be minimized by developing a workout regimen gradually and following it regularly.

6. Which of the following has *not* been found to be a mode of transmission for AIDS?
   a. Sexual contact among homosexual men
   b. Sharing of food
   c. Heterosexual contact
   d. The sharing of needles by intravenous drug users

7. Regarding the seeking of medical treatment, the biggest problem is:
   a. the tendency of many people to delay it.
   b. the tendency of many people to rush too quickly for medical care for minor problems.
   c. not having enough doctors to cover peoples' needs.
   d. the tendency of people in higher socioeconomic categories to delay it.

8. In which of the following cases are people most likely to follow the instructions they receive from health care professionals?
   a. When the instructions are complex and punctuated with impressive medical jargon
   b. When they do not fully understand the instructions but still feel the need to do something
   c. When they like and understand the health care professional
   d. All of the above

9. Which of the following risks is not typically associated with narcotics use?
   a. Overdose
   b. Flashbacks
   c. Physical dependence
   d. Infectious disease

10. The use of sedatives may result in personal injury because they:
    a. cause motor coordination to deteriorate.
    b. produce a strong physical dependence.
    c. suppress pain warnings of physical harm.
    d. trigger hallucinations, such as flying.

Answers

1. c page 399
2. b pages 401–402
3. d page 407
4. d page 410
5. d pages 416–417
6. b page 418
7. a page 420
8. c page 421
9. b page 424
10. a pages 424–425

INFOTRAC COLLEGE EDITION

Go to the Wadsworth Psychology Study Center (http://psychology.wadsworth.com/) for quiz questions, research updates, hot topics, interactive exercises, and suggested readings in INFOTRAC related to this chapter.

CHAPTER 15

Psychological Disorders

"*The government of the United States was overthrown more than a year ago! I'm the president of the United States of America and Bob Dylan is vice president!*" *So said Ed, the author of a prominent book on journalism, who was speaking to a college journalism class, as a guest lecturer. Ed also informed the class that he had killed both John and Robert Kennedy, as well as Charles de Gaulle, the former president of France. He went on to tell the class that all rock music songs were written about him, that he was the greatest karate expert in the universe, and that he had been fighting "space wars" for 2000 years. The students in the class were mystified by Ed's bizarre, disjointed "lecture," but they assumed that he was putting on a show that would eventually lead to a sensible conclusion. However, their perplexed but expectant calm was shattered when Ed pulled a hatchet from the props he had brought with him and hurled the hatchet at the class! Fortunately, he didn't hit anyone, as the hatchet sailed over the students' heads. At that point, the professor for the class realized that Ed's irrational behavior was not a pretense. The professor evacuated the class quickly while Ed continued to rant and rave about his presidential administration, space wars, vampires, his romances with female rock stars, and his personal harem of 38 "chicks." (Adapted from Pearce, 1974)*

Clearly, Ed's behavior was abnormal. Even *he* recognized that when he agreed later to be admitted to a mental hospital, signing himself in as the "President of the United States of America." What causes such abnormal behavior? Does Ed have a mental illness, or does he just behave strangely? What is the basis for judging behavior as normal versus abnormal? How common are such disorders? These are just a few of the questions that we will address in this chapter as we discuss psychological disorders and their complex causes.

Abnormal Behavior: Myths, Realities, and Controversies

LEARNING OBJECTIVES

- *Describe and evaluate the medical model of abnormal behavior.*
- *Explain the most commonly used critieria of abnormality.*
- *Discuss whether and how culture influences judgments of abnormality.*
- *Discuss the history of the DSM system and describe the five axes of DSM-IV.*
- *Discuss some controversial aspects of DSM-IV.*
- *Summarize data on the prevalence of various psychological disorders.*

Misconceptions about abnormal behavior are common. We therefore need to clear up some preliminary issues before we describe the various types of psychological disorders. In this section, we will discuss (1) the medical model of abnormal behavior, (2) the criteria of abnormal behavior, (3) the classification of psychological disorders, and (4) the prevalence of such disorders.

The Medical Model Applied to Abnormal Behavior

In Ed's case, there's no question that his behavior was abnormal. But does it make sense to view his unusual and irrational behavior as an illness? This is a controversial question. **The *medical model* proposes that it is useful to think of abnormal behavior as a disease.** This point of view is the basis for many of the terms used to refer to abnormal behavior, including mental *illness*, psychological *disorder*, and psychopathology (*pathology* refers to manifestations of disease). The medical model gradually became the dominant way of thinking about abnormal behavior during the 18th and 19th centuries, and its influence remains strong today.

The medical model clearly represented progress over earlier models of abnormal behavior. Prior to the 18th century, most conceptions of abnormal behavior were based on superstition. People who behaved strangely were thought to be possessed by demons, to be witches in league with the devil, or to be victims of God's punishment. Their disorders were "treated" with chants, rituals, exorcisms, and such. If the people's behavior was seen as threatening, they were candidates for chains, dungeons, torture, and death (see Figure 15.1 on the next page).

The rise of the medical model brought improvements in the treatment of those who exhibited abnormal behavior. As victims of an illness, they were viewed with more sympathy and less hatred and fear. Although living conditions in early asylums were often deplorable, gradual progress was made toward more humane care of the mentally ill. It took time, but ineffectual approaches to treatment eventually gave way to scientific investigation of the causes and cures of psychological disorders.

PROBLEMS WITH THE MEDICAL MODEL

In recent decades, critics have suggested that the medical model may have outlived its usefulness. A particularly vocal critic has been Thomas Szasz (1974, 1993). Szasz asserts that "strictly speaking, disease or illness can affect only the body; hence there can be no mental

FIGURE 15.1.

Historical conceptions of mental illness. Throughout most of history, psychological disorders were thought to be caused by demonic possession, and the mentally ill were candidates for chains and torture.

illness. . . . Minds can be 'sick' only in the sense that jokes are 'sick' or economies are 'sick'" (1974, p. 267). He further argues that abnormal behavior usually involves a deviation from social norms rather than an illness. He contends that such deviations are "problems in living" rather than medical problems. According to Szasz, the medical model's disease analogy converts moral and social questions about what is acceptable behavior into medical questions. Under the guise of "healing the sick," this conversion allegedly allows modern society to lock up deviant people and to enforce its norms of conformity.

Thomas Szasz

Other critics of the medical model are troubled because medical diagnoses of abnormal behavior pin potentially derogatory labels on people (Rothblum, Solomon, & Albee, 1986). Being labeled as psychotic, schizophrenic, or mentally ill carries a social stigma that can be difficult to shake. Even after a full recovery, someone who has been labeled mentally ill may have difficulty finding a place to live, getting a job, or making friends. Deep-seated prejudice against people who have been labeled mentally ill is commonplace (Mehta & Farina, 1997).

PUTTING THE MEDICAL MODEL IN PERSPECTIVE

So, what position should we take on the medical model? In this chapter, we will assume an intermediate position, neither accepting nor discarding the model entirely. There certainly are significant problems with the medical model, and the issues raised by its critics deserve serious attention. However, in its defense, the medical model *has* stimulated scientific research on abnormal behavior. Moreover, some of the problems that are blamed on the disease analogy are not unique to this conception of abnormality. People who displayed strange, irrational behavior were labeled and stigmatized long before the medical model came along.

Hence, we'll take the position that the disease analogy can be useful, as long as we remember that it is *only* an analogy. Medical concepts such as *diagnosis, etiology,* and *prognosis* have proven useful in the treatment and study of abnormality. **Diagnosis involves distinguishing one illness from another. *Etiology* refers to the apparent causation and developmental history of an illness. A *prognosis* is a forecast about the probable course of an illness.** These medically based concepts have widely shared meanings that permit clinicians, researchers, and the public to communicate more effectively in their discussions of abnormal behavior. So, flawed though it may be, we will use the disease analogy and will use terms such as *abnormal behavior, mental illness, psychopathology,* and *psychological disorders* interchangeably. Do keep in mind, however, that the medical model *is* only an analogy.

Criteria of Abnormal Behavior

If your next-door neighbor scrubs his front porch twice every day and spends virtually all his time cleaning and recleaning his house, is he normal? If your sister-in-law goes to one physician after another seeking treatment for ailments that appear imaginary, is she psychologically healthy? How are we to judge what's normal and what's abnormal? More important, who's to do the judging?

These are complex questions. In a sense, *all* people make judgments about normality in that they express opinions about others' (and perhaps their own) mental health and adjustment. Of course, formal diagnoses of psychological disorders are made by mental health professionals. In making these diagnoses, clinicians rely on an overlapping hodgepodge of criteria, which reflect the lack of scientific consensus on how to define the concept of mental disorder (Wakefield, 1992). Let's examine the three criteria that are most frequently used in judgments of abnormality. Although two or three criteria may apply in a particular case, people are often viewed as disordered when only one criterion is met.

Deviance. As Szasz has pointed out, people are often said to have a disorder because their behavior deviates from what their society considers acceptable. What constitutes normality varies somewhat from one culture to another, but all cultures have such norms. When individuals ignore these standards and expectations, they may be labeled mentally ill. Consider transvestites, for instance. **Transvestism is a sexual disorder in which a man achieves sexual arousal by dressing in women's clothing.** This behavior is regarded as disordered because a man who wears a dress, brassiere, and nylons is deviating from our culture's norms. The example of transvestism illustrates the arbitrary nature of cultural standards regarding normality, as it is considered normal for women in our society to dress in men's clothing, but not vice versa. Thus, the same overt behavior (cross-sex dressing) is acceptable for women and deviant for men.

Maladaptive behavior. In many cases, people are judged to have a psychological disorder because their everyday adaptive behavior is impaired. This is the key criterion in the diagnosis of substance use (drug) disorders. In and of itself, recreational drug use is not terribly unusual or deviant. However, when the use of cocaine, for instance, begins to interfere with a person's social or occupational functioning, a substance use disorder is said to exist. In such cases, it is the maladaptive quality of the behavior that makes it disordered.

Personal distress. Frequently, the diagnosis of a psychological disorder is based on an individual's report of great personal distress. This is usually the criterion met by people who are troubled by depression or anxiety disorders. Depressed people, for instance, may or may not exhibit deviant or maladaptive behavior. Such people are usually labeled as having a disorder when they describe their subjective pain and suffering to friends, relatives, and mental health professionals.

THE CULTURAL BOUNDS OF NORMALITY

The major categories of psychological disorders transcend culture, and researchers have found considerable continuity across cultures in regard to what is considered normal or abnormal (Butcher, Narikiyo, & Vitousek, 1993). Nonetheless, judgments of abnormality are influenced to some extent by cultural norms and values (Lewis-Fernandez & Kleinman, 1994). Behavior that is considered deviant or maladaptive in one society may be quite acceptable in another. For example, in modern Western society people who "hear voices" are assumed to be irrational and are routinely placed in mental hospitals. However, in some cultures, hearing voices is commonplace and hardly merits a raised eyebrow.

Cultural norms regarding acceptable behavior can also change over time. For example, consider how views of homosexuality have changed in our society. Reflecting the prejudices of the past, homosexuality used to be listed as a sexual disorder in the American Psychiatric Association's diagnostic system. However, in 1973 the association voted to delete homosexuality from the official list of psychological disorders. This long-overdue action occurred for several reasons (Rothblum, Solomon, & Albee, 1986). First, attitudes toward homosexuality in our society had become more accepting. Second, gay rights activists campaigned vigorously for the change. Third, research showed that gays and heterosexuals do not differ overall on measures of psychological health. Although scientific research helped pave the way for this change, it mostly reflected shifting attitudes in Western culture.

The key point is that diagnoses of psychological disorders involve *value judgments* about what represents normal or abnormal behavior. The criteria of mental illness are not nearly as value-free as the criteria of physical illness. In evaluating physical diseases, people can usually agree that a weak heart or a bad kidney is pathological, regardless of their personal values. However, judgments about mental illness reflect prevailing cultural values, social trends, and political forces, as well as scientific knowledge (Kirk & Kutchins, 1992).

NORMALITY AND ABNORMALITY AS A CONTINUUM

Antonyms such as normal versus abnormal and mental health versus mental illness imply that people can be divided neatly into two distinct groups: those who are normal and those who are not. In reality, it is often difficult to draw a line that clearly separates normality from abnormality. On occasion, everyone experiences personal distress. Everybody acts in deviant ways once in a while. And everyone displays some maladaptive behavior. People are judged to have psychological disorders only when their behavior becomes *extremely* deviant, maladaptive, or distressing. Thus, normality and abnormality exist on a continuum. It's a matter of degree, not an either-or proposition (see Figure 15.2).

For the most part, people with psychological disorders do *not* behave in bizarre ways that are very different from the behavior of normal people. At first glance, people

David Rosenhan

with psychological disorders usually are indistinguishable from those without disorders. A study by David Rosenhan (1973) showed that even mental health professionals may have difficulty distinguishing normality from abnormality. To study diagnostic accuracy,

FIGURE 15.2.

Normality and abnormality as a continuum. No sharp boundary exists between normal and abnormal behavior. Behavior is normal or abnormal in degree, depending on the extent to which it is deviant, personally distressing, or maladaptive.

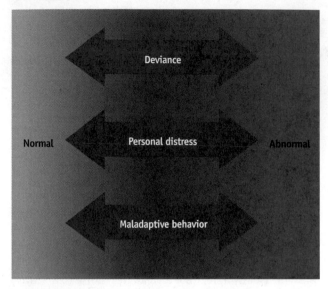

Rosenhan arranged for a number of normal people to seek admission to mental hospitals. These "pseudopatients" arrived at the hospitals complaining of one false symptom—hearing voices. Except for this single symptom, they acted as they normally would and gave accurate information when interviewed about their personal histories. *All* the pseudopatients were admitted, and the average length of their hospitalization was 19 days!

Why is it so hard to distinguish normality from abnormality? The pseudopatients' observations about life on the psychiatric wards offer a clue. They noted that the real patients acted normal most of the time and only infrequently acted in a deviant manner. As you might imagine, Rosenhan's study evoked quite a controversy about our diagnostic system for mental illness. Let's take a look at how this diagnostic system has evolved.

Psychodiagnosis: The Classification of Disorders

Obviously, we cannot lump all psychological disorders together without giving up all hope of understanding them better. A sound taxonomy of mental disorders can facilitate empirical research and enhance communication among scientists and clinicians (Adams & Cassidy, 1993). Thus, a great deal of effort has been invested in devising an elaborate system for classifying psychological disorders.

Guidelines for psychodiagnosis were vague and informal prior to 1952, when the American Psychiatric Association unveiled its *Diagnostic and Statistical Manual of Mental Disorders* (Grob, 1991). Known as DSM-I, this classification scheme described about 100 disorders. Revisions intended to improve the system were incorporated into the second edition (DSM-II) published in 1968, but the diagnostic guidelines were still pretty sketchy, and there was widespread dissatisfaction with the lack of consistency in psychiatric diagnosis (Wilson, 1993). All too often, several clinicians evaluating the same patient would arrive at different diagnoses. Thus, the revisions of the next two editions, DSM-III (1980) and DSM-III-R (1987), sought, first and foremost, to improve the consistency of psychodiagnosis. To achieve this end, diagnostic guidelines were made more explicit, concrete, and detailed. These revisions *did* lead to substantial increases in diagnostic consistency for many disorders, although there is still room for considerable improvement (Garfield, 1993). The current edition, DSM-IV, was introduced in 1994. More than ever before, the architects of the most recent DSM worked to base their revision on empirical research, as opposed to the consensus of experts (Widiger et al., 1991).

THE MULTIAXIAL SYSTEM

The publication of DSM-III in 1980 introduced a new multiaxial system of classification, which asks for judgments about individuals on five separate dimensions, or "axes." Figure 15.3 provides an overview of the entire system and the five axes. The diagnoses of disorders are made on Axes I and II. Clinicians record any major disorders that are apparent on Axis I (Clinical Syndromes). They use Axis II (Personality Disorders) to list milder, long-running personality disturbances, which often coexist with Axis I syndromes. People may receive diagnoses on both axes.

The remaining axes are used to record supplemental information. A patient's physical disorders are listed on Axis III (General Medical Conditions). On Axis IV (Psychosocial and Environmental Problems), the clinician makes notations regarding the types of stress experienced by the individual in the past year. On Axis V (Global Assessment of Functioning), estimates are made of the individual's current level of adaptive functioning (in social and occupational behavior, viewed as a whole) and of the individual's highest level of functioning in the past year.

Most theorists agree that the multiaxial system is a step in the right direction, because it recognizes the importance of information besides a traditional diagnostic label. However, the distinction between Axis I disorders and Axis II disorders is plagued by conceptual inconsistencies (Frances et al., 1991), and clinicians apparently make little use of Axis III (Maricle, Leung, & Bloom, 1987). Furthermore, Axes IV and V are poorly

FIGURE 15.3.

Overview of the DSM diagnostic system. Published by the American Psychiatric Association, the *Diagnostic and Statistical Manual of Mental Disorders* is the formal classification system used in the diagnosis of psychological disorders. It is a *multiaxial* system, which means that information is recorded on the five axes described here. (Adapted with permission from the *Diagnostic and Statistical Manual of Mental Disorders*, 4th ed., 1994; copyright 1994 American Psychiatric Association)

Axis I
Clinical Syndromes

1. *Disorders usually first diagnosed in infancy, childhood, or adolescence*
   This category includes disorders that arise before adolescence, such as attention deficit disorders, autism, mental retardation, enuresis, and stuttering.

2. *Organic mental disorders*
   These disorders are temporary or permanent dysfunctions of brain tissue caused by diseases or chemicals. Examples are delirium, dementia, and amnesia.

3. *Substance-related disorders*
   This category refers to the maladaptive use of drugs and alcohol. Mere consumption and recreational use of such substances are not disorders. This category requires an abnormal pattern of use, as with alcohol abuse and cocaine dependence.

4. *Schizophrenia and other psychotic disorders*
   The schizophrenias are characterized by psychotic symptoms (for example, grossly disorganized behavior, delusions, and hallucinations) and by over 6 months of behavioral deterioration. This category also includes delusional disorder and schizoaffective disorder.

5. *Mood disorders*
   The cardinal feature is emotional disturbance. Patients may, or may not, have psychotic symptoms. These disorders include major depression, bipolar disorder, dysthymic disorder, and cyclothymic disorder.

6. *Anxiety disorders*
   These disorders are characterized by physiological signs of anxiety (for example, palpitations) and subjective feelings of tension, apprehension, or fear. Anxiety may be acute and focused (panic disorder) or continual and diffuse (generalized anxiety disorder).

7. *Somatoform disorders*
   These disorders are dominated by somatic symptoms that resemble physical illnesses. These symptoms cannot be accounted for by organic damage. There must also be strong evidence that these symptoms are produced by psychological factors or conflicts. This category includes somatization and conversion disorders and hypochondriasis.

8. *Dissociative disorders*
   These disorders all feature a sudden, temporary alteration or dysfunction of memory, consciousness, identity, and behavior, as in dissociative amnesia and multiple personality.

9. *Sexual and gender-identity disorders*
   There are three basic types of disorders in this category: gender identity disorders (discomfort with identity as male or female), paraphilias (preference for unusual acts to achieve sexual arousal), and sexual dysfunctions (impairments in sexual functioning).

Axis II
Personality Disorders

These disorders are patterns of personality traits that are longstanding, maladaptive, and inflexible and involve impaired functioning or subjective distress. Examples include borderline, schizoid, and antisocial personality disorders.

Axis III
General Medical Conditions

Physical disorders or conditions are recorded on this axis. Examples include diabetes, arthritis, and hemophilia.

Axis IV
Psychosocial and Environmental Problems

Axis IV is for reporting psychosocial and environmental problems that may affect the diagnosis, treatment, and prognosis of mental disorders (Axis I and II). A psychosocial or environmental problem may be a negative life event, an environmental difficulty or deficiency, a familial or other interpersonal stress, an inadequacy of social support or personal resources, or another problem that describes the context in which a person's difficulties have developed.

Axis V
Global Assessment of Functioning (GAF) Scale

Code	Symptoms
100	Superior functioning in a wide range of activities
90	Absent or minimal symptoms, good functioning in all areas
80	Symptoms transient and expectable reactions to psychosocial stressors
70	Some mild symptoms or some difficulty in social, occupational, or school functioning, but generally functioning pretty well
60	Moderate symptoms or difficulty in social, occupational, or school functioning
50	Serious symptoms or impairment in social, occupational, or school functioning
40	Some impairment in reality testing or communication or major impairment in family relations, judgment, thinking, or mood
30	Behavior considerably influenced by delusions or hallucinations, serious impairment in communication or judgment, or inability to function in almost all areas
20	Some danger of hurting self or others, occasional failure to maintain minimal personal hygiene, or gross impairment in communication
10	Persistent danger of severely hurting self or others
1	

defined, and more evidence is needed regarding their validity (Goldman, Skodol, & Lave, 1992; Rey et al., 1988). It is hoped that research will lead to improvement of the supplementary axes in future editions of the DSM system.

CONTROVERSIES SURROUNDING THE DSM

Since the publication of the third edition in 1980, the DSM system has become the dominant classification scheme for mental disorders around the world (Maser, Kaelber, & Weise, 1991; Williams, 1994). Nonetheless, the DSM system has garnered its share of criticism. First, some critics argue that the heavy focus on improving the consistency of psychodiagnosis has drawn attention away from an equally basic issue—the *validity* of the diagnostic categories (Carson, 1991). Precise, detailed descriptions of disorders are of little value unless the descriptions mesh well with the constellations of problems that people actually experience. Some theorists have even questioned the wisdom of the DSM's *categorical approach* to describing disorders, which assumes (incorrectly, they argue) that people can reliably be placed in discontinuous (nonoverlapping) diagnostic categories (Clark, Watson, & Reynolds, 1995). These critics argue that too many people qualify for two or more diagnoses and that patients in the same diagnostic category exhibit too much diversity in their symptoms. Critics of the categorical approach also argue that it places too much emphasis on fitting patients into categories rather than on trying to understand their unique problems (Tucker, 1998).

Second, recent editions of the DSM sparked controversy by adding everyday problems that are not traditionally thought of as mental illnesses to the diagnostic system. For example, the DSM system includes a *developmental coordination disorder* (basically, extreme clumsiness in children), a *nicotine dependence disorder* (distress derived from quitting smoking), and a *pathological gambling disorder* (difficulty controlling one's gambling). Critics argue that this approach "medicalizes" everyday problems and casts the shadow of pathology on normal behavior (Kirk & Kutchins, 1992). In part, everyday problems were added to the

diagnostic system so that more people could bill their insurance companies for professional treatment of the conditions (Garfield, 1986). Many health insurance policies permit reimbursement only for the treatment of disorders on the official (DSM) list. There's merit in making it easier for more people to seek needed professional help. Nonetheless, the pros and cons of including everyday problems in DSM are complicated.

Shifting definitions of normality and abnormality inevitably affect estimates regarding the number of people who suffer from psychological disorders. The changes made in DSM-III stimulated a flurry of research on the prevalence of specific mental disorders that has continued through the present. Let's examine some of this research.

The Prevalence of Psychological Disorders

How common are psychological disorders? What percentage of the population is afflicted with mental illness? Is it 10%? Perhaps 25%? Could the figure range as high as 40% or 50%?

Such estimates fall in the domain of *epidemiology*—**the study of the distribution of mental or physical disorders in a population.** In epidemiology, *prevalence* **refers to the percentage of a population that exhibits a disorder during a specified time period.** In the case of mental disorders, the most interesting data are the estimates of *lifetime prevalence,* the percentage of people who endure a specific disorder at any time in their lives.

Estimates of lifetime prevalence suggest that psychological disorders are more common than most people realize. Prior to the advent of DSM-III, studies suggested that about *one-fifth* of the population exhibited clear signs of mental illness (Neugebauer, Dohrenwend, & Dohrenwend, 1980). However, the older studies did not assess drug-related disorders very effectively, because these disorders were vaguely described in DSM-I and DSM-II. More recent studies, using the explicit criteria for substance use disorders in recent editions of the DSM system, have found psychological disorders in roughly *one-third* of the population! This increase in mental illness is more apparent than real, as it is mostly a result of more effective tabulation of drug-related disorders. As Figure 15.4 shows, the most common disorders are (1) anxiety disorders, (2) substance (alcohol and drugs) use disorders, and (3) mood disorders (Robins, Locke, & Regier, 1991).

We are now ready to start examining the specific types of psychological disorders. Obviously, we cannot cover all of the multitudinous disorders listed in DSM-IV. However, we will introduce most of the major

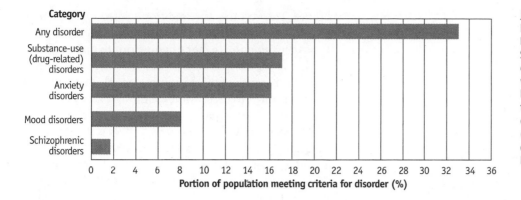

FIGURE 15.4.
Prevalence of common psycho-logical disorders in the United States. This graph shows the estimated percentage of people who have, at any time in their life, suffered from one of four types of psychological disorders or from a disorder of any kind (top bar). (Based on combined data from several chapters in Robins & Regier, 1991)

categories of disorders to give you an overview of the many forms abnormal behavior takes. In discussing each set of disorders, we will begin with brief descriptions of the specific syndromes or subtypes that fall in the category. Then we'll focus on the *etiology* of the disorders in that category. Although many paths can lead to specific disorders, some are more common than others. We'll highlight some of the common paths in order to enhance your understanding of the roots of abnormal behavior.

Anxiety Disorders

LEARNING OBJECTIVES

- *List and describe four types of anxiety disorders.*
- *Discuss the contribution of biological factors and conditioning to the etiology of anxiety disorders.*
- *Discuss the contribution of cognitive factors, personality traits, and stress to the etiology of anxiety disorders.*

Everyone experiences anxiety from time to time. It is a natural and common reaction to many of life's difficulties. For some people, however, anxiety becomes a chronic problem. These people experience high levels of anxiety with disturbing regularity. *Anxiety disorders are a class of disorders marked by feelings of excessive apprehension and anxiety.* There are four principal types of anxiety disorders: generalized anxiety disorders, phobic disorders, obsessive-compulsive disorders, and panic disorders. They are not mutually exclusive, since many people who develop one anxiety syndrome often suffer from another at some point in their lives (Massion, Warshaw, & Keller, 1993). People with anxiety disorders also exhibit elevated rates of depression (Clark, Beck, & Beck, 1994). Studies suggest that anxiety disorders are quite common, occurring in roughly 17% of the population (Robins & Regier, 1991). Most of these cases are generalized anxiety disorders or phobic disorders (Blazer et al., 1991; Eaton, Dryman, & Weissman, 1991).

Generalized Anxiety Disorder

The *generalized anxiety disorder* is marked by a chronic, high level of anxiety that is not tied to any specific threat. This anxiety is sometimes called "free-floating anxiety" because it is nonspecific. People with this disorder worry constantly about yesterday's mistakes and tomorrow's problems. In particular, they worry about minor matters related to family, finances, work, and personal illness (Sanderson & Barlow, 1990). They often dread decisions and brood over them endlessly. Their anxiety is frequently accompanied by physical symptoms, such as trembling, muscle tension, diarrhea, dizziness, faintness, sweating, and heart palpitations.

Phobic Disorder

In a phobic disorder, an individual's troublesome anxiety has a specific focus. **A *phobic disorder* is marked by a persistent and irrational fear of an object or situation that presents no realistic danger.** Although mild phobias are extremely common, people are said to have a phobic disorder only when their fears seriously interfere with their everyday behavior. The following case provides an example of a phobic disorder:

Hilda is 32 years of age and has a rather unusual fear. She is terrified of snow. She cannot go outside in the snow. She cannot even stand to see snow or hear about it on the weather report. Her phobia severely constricts her day-to-day behavior. Probing in therapy revealed that her phobia was caused by a traumatic experience at age 11. Playing at a ski lodge, she was buried briefly by a small avalanche of snow. She had no recollection of this experience until it was recovered in therapy. (Adapted from Laughlin, 1967, p. 227)

As Hilda's unusual snow phobia illustrates, people can develop phobic responses to virtually anything. Nonetheless, certain types of phobias are relatively common, as the data in Figure 15.5 show. Particularly common are acrophobia (fear of heights), claustrophobia

© 1990 by Sidney Harris.

(fear of small, enclosed places), brontophobia (fear of storms), hydrophobia (fear of water), and various animal and insect phobias (Eaton et al., 1991). People troubled by phobias typically realize that their fears are irrational, but they still are unable to calm themselves when confronted by a phobic object.

Panic Disorder and Agoraphobia

A *panic disorder* is characterized by recurrent attacks of overwhelming anxiety that usually occur suddenly and unexpectedly. These paralyzing attacks are accompanied by physical symptoms of anxiety. After a number of anxiety attacks, victims often become apprehensive, wondering when their next panic will occur. Their concern about exhibiting panic in public may escalate to the point where they are afraid to leave home. This creates a condition called *agoraphobia*, which is a common complication of panic disorders.

Agoraphobia **is a fear of going out to public places** (its literal meaning is "fear of the marketplace or open places"). Because of this fear, some people become prisoners confined to their homes, although many can venture out if accompanied by a trusted companion (Hollander, Simeon, & Gorman, 1994). As its name suggests, agoraphobia has traditionally been viewed as a phobic disorder. However, empirical research suggests that agoraphobia shares more kinship with panic disorders than with phobic disorders (Turner et al., 1986). Nonetheless, agoraphobia can occur independently of panic disorder, and some theorists question the wisdom of lumping panic and agoraphobia together in the DSM classification system (Noyes, 1988). The vast majority of people who suffer from panic disorder or agoraphobia are female (Rapee & Barlow, 1993).

Obsessive-Compulsive Disorder

Obsessions are *thoughts* that repeatedly intrude on one's consciousness in a distressing way. Compulsions are *actions* that one feels forced to carry out. Thus, **an obsessive-compulsive disorder** (OCD) **is marked by persistent, uncontrollable intrusions of unwanted thoughts (obsessions) and urges to engage in senseless rituals (compulsions).** To illustrate, let's examine the bizarre behavior of a man once reputed to be the wealthiest person in the world:

The famous industrialist Howard Hughes was obsessed with the possibility of being contaminated by germs. This led him to

FIGURE 15.5.
Common phobias. Frequently reported phobias are listed here, along with their typical age of onset and information on gender differences. (From Marks, 1969)

Common Phobias		Percent of all phobias	Gender difference	Typical age of onset
Agoraphobia (fear of places of assembly, crowds, open spaces)		10–50%	Large majority are women	Early adulthood
Social phobia (fear of being observed doing something humiliating)		10%	Majority are women	Adolescence
Specific phobias				
Animals		5–15%	Vast majority are women	Childhood
Cats (ailurophobia)	Dogs (cynophobia)			
Insects (insectophobia)	Spiders (arachnophobia)			
Birds (avisophobia)	Horses (equinophobia)			
Snakes (ophidiophobia)	Rodents (rodentophobia)			
Inanimate objects		20%	None	Any age
Dirt (mysophobia)	Storms (brontophobia)			
Heights (acrophobia)	Darkness (nyctophobia)			
Closed spaces (claustrophobia)				
Illness-injury (nosophobia)		15–25%	None	Middle age
Death (thanatophobia)				
Cancer (cancerophobia)				
Venereal disease (venerophobia)				

Repeatedly cleaning things that are already clean is an example of compulsive behavior.

devise extraordinary rituals to minimize the possibility of such contamination. He would spend hours methodically cleaning a single telephone. He once wrote a three-page memo instructing assistants on exactly how to open cans of fruit for him. The following is just a small portion of the instructions that Hughes provided for a driver who delivered films to his bungalow. "Get out of the car on the traffic side. Do not at any time be on the side of the car between the car and the curb. . . . Carry only one can of film at a time. Step over the gutter opposite the place where the sidewalk dead-ends into the curb from a point as far out into the center of the road as possible. Do not ever walk on the grass at all, also do not step into the gutter at all. Walk to the bungalow keeping as near to the center of the sidewalk as possible." (Adapted from Barlett & Steele, 1979, pp. 227–237)

The typical age of onset for OCD is early adulthood (Sturgis, 1993). Obsessions often center on fear of contamination, inflicting harm on others, suicide, or sexual acts. Compulsions usually involve stereotyped rituals that temporarily relieve anxiety. Common examples include constant handwashing, repetitive cleaning of things that are already clean, and endless rechecking of locks, faucets, and such (Foa & Kozak, 1995). Specific types of obsessions tend to be associated with specific types of compulsions. For example, obsessions about contamination tend to be paired with cleaning compulsions, and obsessions about symmetry tend to be paired with ordering and arranging compulsions (Leckman et al., 1997). Although many of us can be compulsive at times, full-fledged obsessive-compulsive disorders occur in roughly 2%–4% of the population (Karno & Golding, 1991). The prevalence of obsessive-compulsive disorder seems to be increasing, but this trend may simply reflect changes in clinicians' and researchers' diagnostic tendencies (Stein et al., 1997; Stoll, Tohen, & Baldessarini, 1992).

Etiology of Anxiety Disorders

Like most psychological disorders, anxiety disorders develop out of complicated interactions among a variety of factors. Conditioning and learning appear especially important, but biological factors may also contribute to anxiety disorders.

BIOLOGICAL FACTORS

Recent studies suggest that there may be a weak genetic predisposition to anxiety disorders (Kendler et al., 1992; Pauls et al., 1995). These findings are consistent with the idea that inherited differences in temperament might make some people more vulnerable than others to anxiety disorders. Kagan and his colleagues (1992) have found that about 15%–20% percent of infants display an *inhibited temperament,* characterized by shyness, timidity, and wariness, which appears to have a strong genetic basis. Research suggests that this temperament is a risk factor for the development of anxiety disorders (Rosenbaum, Lakin, & Roback, 1992).

One recent theory holds that *anxiety sensitivity* may make people vulnerable to anxiety disorders (Reiss, 1991; Schmidt, Lerew, & Jackson, 1997). According to this notion, some people are very sensitive to the internal physiological symptoms of anxiety and are prone to overreact with fear when they experience these symptoms. Anxiety sensitivity may fuel an inflationary spiral in which anxiety breeds more anxiety, which eventually spins out of control in the form of an anxiety disorder.

Recent evidence suggests that a link may exist between anxiety disorders and neurochemical activity in the brain. **Neurotransmitters are chemicals that carry signals from one neuron to another.** Therapeutic drugs (such as Valium) that reduce excessive anxiety appear to alter activity at synapses for a neurotransmitter called GABA. This finding and other lines of evidence suggest that disturbances in the neural circuits using GABA may play a role in some types of anxiety disorders (Lloyd, Fletcher, & Minchin, 1992). Abnormalities in other neural circuits using the transmitter serotonin have recently been implicated in panic and obsessive-compulsive disorders (Stein & Uhde, 1995). Thus, scientists are beginning to unravel the neurochemical bases for anxiety disorders.

CONDITIONING AND LEARNING

Many anxiety responses may be *acquired through classical conditioning* and *maintained through operant conditioning* (see Chapter 2). According to Mowrer (1947), an originally neutral stimulus (the snow in Hilda's case, for instance) may be paired with a frightening event (the avalanche) so that it becomes a conditioned stimulus eliciting anxiety (see Figure 15.6). Once a fear is acquired through classical conditioning, the

The Consumer's Guide to Psychotherapy
by Jack Engler and Daniel Goleman (Simon & Schuster, 1992)

Written by a clinical psychologist at the Harvard Medical School (Engler) and a psychologist who writes on the behavioral sciences for the *New York Times* (Goleman). This remarkably thorough handbook provides advice on many aspects of therapy. It covers how to decide whether you need therapy, how to find the right therapist, what to realistically expect out of therapy, how to get the most out of therapy, and how to tell when therapy isn't working.

A unique strength of the book is its lengthy discussion of various types of pathology and how they are generally treated. For each type of pathology, such as anxiety disorders, eating disorders, schizophrenia, depression, substance abuse, alcoholism, somatoform disorders, and so forth, the authors discuss (a) signs to look for, (b) variations and complications, (c) what therapists recommend, and (d) what you should know about therapy (for that disorder). The book also includes a chapter on psychiatric drugs and appendixes that list self-help groups, therapist referral sources, and other sources of information on mental health care.

Obsessions and compulsions are symptoms of the same disorder. Obsessions are thoughts that completely preoccupy a person, while compulsions are actions that people feel they must perform.

Often obsessions take the form of a single, circumscribed worry, such as believing that no matter how often you wash your hands, they are still dirty. Compulsions are frequently ordinary acts repeated over and over, such as checking appliances to see that they are off.

Many people have a few minor habits that are obsessive or compulsive. Some people like to count things, such as telephone poles they pass. Others like to check their door several times to make sure it is locked. And children normally develop compulsive habits for a time as they grow up.

A bit of obsessiveness—being well organized and neat, for example—is not a problem. A compulsive attention to detail can even be an advantage in life.

But when obsessions or compulsions start interfering with living your life spontaneously, then they become a problem that needs treatment. So it is all right to be very neat, but if you spend all your time straightening up your house and never get around to other important things, your neatness has become a compulsion.

Many people who suffer from obsessions or compulsions manage to keep them secret from those around them. They may wait until they are alone to indulge the compulsion or never mention that they are utterly preoccupied by some thought that won't leave them alone.

At their most serious, obsessions and compulsions can be so overwhelming that they completely dominate a person's life. In these extreme cases, they almost always occur together. [p. 531]

person may start avoiding the anxiety-producing stimulus. The avoidance response is negatively reinforced because it is followed by a reduction in anxiety. This process involves operant conditioning (also shown in Figure 15.6). Thus, separate conditioning processes may create and then sustain specific anxiety responses (Levis, 1989). Consistent with this view, one study of people suffering from two types of social phobia found that 44% of the subjects could identify a traumatic conditioning experience that probably contributed to their anxiety disorder (Stemberger et al., 1995).

The tendency to develop phobias of certain types of objects and situations may be explained by Martin Seligman's (1971) concept of *preparedness*. Like many theorists, Seligman believes that classical conditioning creates most phobic responses. *However, he suggests that people are biologically prepared by their evolutionary history to acquire some fears much more easily than others.* His theory would explain why people develop phobias of ancient sources of threat (such as snakes and spiders) much more readily than modern sources of threat (such as electrical outlets or hot irons). Some laboratory studies of conditioned fears have yielded evidence consistent with Seligman's theory. For example, Cook and Mineka (1989) found that monkeys acquired conditioned fears of stimuli that they should be prepared

FIGURE 15.6.

Conditioning as an explanation for phobias. Many phobias appear to be acquired through classical conditioning when a neutral stimulus is paired with an anxiety-arousing stimulus. Once acquired, a phobia may be maintained through operant conditioning because avoidance of the phobic stimulus leads to a reduction in anxiety, resulting in negative reinforcement.

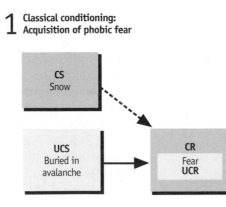

1 Classical conditioning: Acquisition of phobic fear

CS
Snow

UCS
Buried in avalanche

CR
Fear
UCR

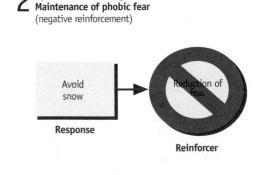

2 Operant conditioning: Maintenance of phobic fear (negative reinforcement)

Avoid snow

Response

Reduction of fear

Reinforcer

to fear, such as snakes, with relative ease in comparison to other stimuli, such as flowers. As a whole, however, research has provided only modest support for the role of preparedness in the acquisition of phobias (McNally, 1987; Ohman & Soares, 1993).

There are a number of problems with conditioning models of phobias (Rachman, 1990). For instance, many people with phobias cannot recall or identify a traumatic conditioning experience that led to their phobia. Conversely, many people endure extremely traumatic experiences that should create a phobia but do not. To provide better explanations for these complexities, conditioning models of anxiety disorders are currently being revised to include a larger role for cognitive factors.

COGNITIVE FACTORS

Cognitive theorists maintain that certain styles of thinking make some people particularly vulnerable to anxiety disorders. According to these theorists, some people are prone to suffer from problems with anxiety because they tend to (a) misinterpret harmless situations as threatening, (b) focus excessive attention on perceived threats, and (c) selectively recall information that seems threatening (Beck, 1988a; McNally, 1990, 1994). In one intriguing test of the cognitive view, anxious and nonanxious subjects were asked to read 32 sentences that could be interpreted in either a threatening or a nonthreatening manner (Eysenck et al., 1991). For instance, one such sentence was "The doctor examined little Emma's growth," which could mean that the doctor checked her height or the growth of a tumor. As Figure 15.7 shows, the anxious subjects interpreted the sentences in a threatening way more often than the nonanxious subjects did. Thus, the cognitive view holds that some people are prone to anxiety disorders because they see threat in every corner of their lives (Williams et al., 1997).

PERSONALITY

Certain personality traits appear to be related to the likelihood of developing anxiety disorders. Foremost among them is *neuroticism,* one of the "Big Five" traits described in Chapter 2. People who score high in neuroticism tend to be self-conscious, nervous, jittery, insecure, guilt prone, and gloomy. Neuroticism is correlated with an elevated prevalence of anxiety disorders and a poorer prognosis for recovery (Clark, Watson, & Mineka, 1994). The mechanisms underlying this association are the subject of debate. One possibility is that the correlation between neuroticism and anxiety disorders may reflect the operation of a third variable—a genetic predisposition to both (Carey & DiLalla, 1994). This explanation appears plausible given the evidence for a genetic component in both neuroticism and

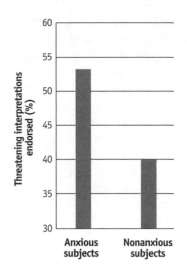

FIGURE 15.7.
Cognitive factors in anxiety disorders. Eysenck and his colleagues (1991) compared how subjects with anxiety problems and nonanxious subjects tended to interpret sentences that could be viewed as threatening or nonthreatening. Consistent with cognitive models of anxiety disorders, anxious subjects were more likely to interpret the sentences in a threatening light.

anxiety disorders, but more research is needed to rule out other explanations.

STRESS

Finally, recent studies have supported the long-held suspicion that anxiety disorders are stress related. For instance, Blazer, Hughes, and George (1987) found an association between stress and the development of generalized anxiety disorders. Men who experienced high stress were 8.5 times more likely to develop these disorders than men under low stress. In another study, Faravelli and Pallanti (1989) found that patients with panic disorder had experienced a dramatic increase in stress in the month prior to the onset of their disorder. Thus, there is reason to believe that high stress often helps precipitate the onset of anxiety disorders.

Somatoform Disorders

LEARNING OBJECTIVES

● *Distinguish somatoform disorders from psychosomatic disorders and describe three types of somatoform disorders.*

● *Summarize what is known about the causes of somatoform disorders.*

Chances are, you have met people who always seem to be complaining about aches, pains, and physical maladies of doubtful authenticity. You may have thought to yourself, "It's all in his head" and concluded that the person exhibited a "psychosomatic" condition. However, as we discussed in Chapter 14, the term *psychosomatic* is widely misused. **Psychosomatic diseases are genuine physical ailments caused in part by psychological factors, especially emotional distress.** These diseases, which include maladies such as ulcers, asthma, and high blood pressure, have a genuine organic basis and are not imagined ailments. They are recorded on the DSM axis for physical problems (Axis III). When physical illness appears entirely psychological in origin, we are dealing with somatoform disorders, which are recorded on Axis I. *Somatoform disorders are physical ailments with no authentic organic basis that are due to psychological factors.* Although their symptoms are more imaginary than real, victims of somatoform disorders are *not* simply faking illness. Deliberate feigning of illness for personal gain is another matter altogether, called *malingering*.

People with somatoform disorders typically seek treatment from physicians practicing neurology, internal medicine, or family medicine, instead of from psychologists or psychiatrists. Making accurate diagnoses of somatoform disorders can be difficult, because the causes of physical ailments are sometimes hard to identify. In some cases, a problem is misdiagnosed as a somatoform disorder when a genuine organic cause for a person's physical symptoms goes undetected despite extensive medical examinations and tests (Rubin, Zorumski, & Guze, 1986).

We will discuss three specific types of somatoform disorders: somatization disorders, conversion disorders, and hypochondriasis. Diagnostic difficulties make it hard to obtain sound data on the prevalence of somatoform disorders. Hypochondriasis seems to be fairly common, with somatization and conversion disorders less frequent (Barsky, 1989).

Somatization Disorder

Individuals with somatization disorders are often said to "cling to ill health." *A somatization disorder is marked by a history of diverse physical complaints that appear to be psychological in origin.* Somatization disorders occur mostly in women (Martin & Yutzy, 1994) and often in conjunction with depression or generalized anxiety disorder (Gureje et al., 1997). Victims report an endless succession of minor physical ailments. They usually have a long and complicated history of medical treatment from many doctors. The distinguishing feature of this disorder is the diversity of victims' physical complaints. Over the years, they report a mixed bag of cardiovascular, gastrointestinal, pulmonary, neurological, and genitourinary symptoms. The unlikely nature of such a smorgasbord of symptoms occurring together often alerts a physician to the possible psychological basis for the patient's problems.

Conversion Disorder

Conversion disorder is characterized by a significant loss of physical function (with no apparent organic basis), usually in a single organ system. Common symptoms include partial or complete loss of vision, partial or complete loss of hearing, partial paralysis, severe laryngitis or mutism, and loss of feeling or function in limbs, such as that seen in the following case:

Mildred was a rancher's daughter who lost the use of both of her legs during adolescence. Mildred was at home alone one afternoon when a male relative attempted to assault her. She screamed for help, and her legs gave way as she slipped to the floor. She was found on the floor a few minutes later when her mother returned home. She could not get up, so she was carried to her bed. Her legs buckled when she made subsequent attempts to walk on her own. Due to her illness, she was waited on hand and foot by her family and friends. Neighbors brought her homemade things to eat or to wear. She became the center of attention in the household. (Adapted from Cameron, 1963, pp. 312–313)

People with conversion disorders are usually troubled by more severe ailments than people with somatization disorders. In some cases of conversion disorder, there are telltale clues about the psychological origins of the illness because the patient's symptoms are not consistent with medical knowledge about their apparent disease. For instance, the loss of feeling in one hand that is seen in "glove anesthesia" is inconsistent with the known facts of neurological organization (see Figure 15.8).

Hypochondriasis

Hypochondriacs constantly monitor their physical condition, looking for signs of illness. Any tiny alteration from their physical norm leads them to conclude that they have contracted a disease. *Hypochondriasis (more widely known as hypochondria) is characterized by excessive preoccupation with health concerns and incessant worry about developing physical illnesses.* The following case illustrates the nature of hypochondria:

Jeff is a middle-aged man who works as a clerk in a drug store. He spends long hours describing his health problems to anyone who will listen. Jeff is an avid reader of popular magazine articles on medicine. He can tell you all about the latest medical discoveries. He takes all sorts of pills and vitamins to ward off possible illnesses. He's the first to try every new product on the market. Jeff is constantly afflicted by new symptoms of illness. His most recent problems were poor digestion and a heartbeat that he thought was irregular. He frequently goes to physicians who can find nothing wrong with him physically. They tell him that he is healthy. He thinks they use "backward techniques." He suspects that his illness is too rare to be diagnosed successfully. (Adapted from Suinn, 1984, p. 236)

FIGURE 15.8.

Glove anesthesia. In conversion disorders, the physical complaints are sometimes inconsistent with the known facts of physiology. Such is the case in *glove anesthesia*, in which the patient complains of losing feeling in a hand. Given the patterns of nerve distribution in the arm shown in (a), a loss of feeling in the hand exclusively (as shown in b) is a physical impossibility, indicating that the patient's problem is psychological in origin.

(a)　　(b)

When hypochondriacs are assured by their physician that they do not have any real illness, they often are skeptical and disbelieving. As in Jeff's case, they frequently assume that the physician must be incompetent, and they go shopping for another doctor. Hypochondriacs don't subjectively suffer from physical distress as much as they *overinterpret* every conceivable sign of illness. Hypochondria frequently appears alongside other psychological disorders, especially anxiety disorders and depression (Simon & VonKorff, 1991). For example, Howard Hughes's obsessive-compulsive disorder was coupled with profound hypochondria. Indeed, hypochondria coexists with other disorders so often, some theorists have raised doubts about whether it should be viewed as a separate diagnostic category (Iezzi & Adams, 1993).

Etiology of Somatoform Disorders

Inherited aspects of physiological functioning, such as a highly reactive autonomic nervous system, may predispose some people to somatoform disorders (Weiner, 1992). However, available evidence suggests that these disorders are largely a function of personality and learning.

PERSONALITY FACTORS

People with certain types of personality traits seem to be particularly prone to develop somatoform disorders. The prime candidates appear to be people with *histrionic* personality characteristics (Nemiah, 1985; Slavney, 1990). The histrionic personality tends to be self-centered, suggestible, excitable, highly emotional, and overly dramatic. Such people thrive on the attention that they get when they become ill. The personality trait of *neuroticism* also seems to elevate individuals' susceptibility to somatoform disorders (Kirmayer, Robbins, & Paris, 1994).

THE SICK ROLE

As we discussed in Chapter 14, some people grow fond of the role associated with being sick (Lubkin, 1990; Pilowsky, 1978). Their complaints of physical symptoms may be reinforced by indirect benefits derived from their illness. One payoff is that becoming ill is a superb way to avoid having to confront life's challenges. Many people with somatoform disorders are avoiding facing up to marital problems, career frustrations, family responsibilities, and the like. After all, when you're sick, others cannot place great demands on you. Another benefit is that physical problems can provide a convenient excuse when people fail, or worry about failing, in endeavors that are critical to their self-esteem (Organista & Miranda, 1991).

Attention from others is another payoff that may reinforce complaints of physical illness. When people become ill, they command the attention of family, friends, co-workers, neighbors, and doctors. The sympathy that illness often brings may strengthen the person's tendency to feel ill. This clearly occurred in Mildred's case of conversion disorder. Her illness paid handsome dividends in terms of attention, consolation, and kindhearted assistance from others.

Dissociative Disorders

LEARNING OBJECTIVES

- Describe three dissociative disorders.
- Summarize what is known about the causes of dissociative disorders.

Dissociative disorders are among the more unusual syndromes that we will discuss. **Dissociative disorders are a class of disorders in which people lose contact with portions of their consciousness or memory, resulting in disruptions in their sense of identity.** We'll describe three dissociative syndromes: dissociative amnesia, dissociative fugue, and multiple-personality disorder, all of which are relatively uncommon.

Reprinted by permission of Edgar Argo.

"THE WAY HE MOANS AND GROANS WHEN HE GETS A LITTLE COLD... I CAN'T DECIDE WHETHER HE SHOULD CALL A DOCTOR OR A DRAMA CRITIC."

Dissociative Amnesia and Fugue

Dissociative amnesia and fugue are overlapping disorders characterized by serious memory deficits. *Dissociative amnesia* **is a sudden loss of memory for important personal information that is too extensive to be due to normal forgetting.** Memory losses may occur for a single traumatic event (such as an automobile accident) or for an extended period of time surrounding the event. Cases of amnesia have been observed after people have experienced disasters, accidents, combat stress, physical abuse, and rape, or after they have witnessed the violent death of a parent, among other things (Arrigo & Pezdek, 1997; Lowenstein, 1996). **In *dissociative fugue,* people experience extensive amnesia and confusion about their identity, coupled with unexpected travel away from their customary home.** These people forget their name, their family, where they live, and where they work! In spite of this wholesale forgetting, they usually remember matters unrelated to their identity, such as how to drive a car and how to do math.

Multiple-Personality Disorder

Multiple-personality disorder **(MPD) involves the coexistence in one person of two or more largely complete, and usually very different, identities or personalities.** The formal name for this disorder was changed to *dissociative identity disorder* in the recent revision of the DSM system, but it remains more widely known by its traditional name. In multiple-personality disorders, the divergences in behavior go far beyond those that people normally display in adapting to different roles in life. People with multiple personalities feel that they have more than one identity. Each personality has his or her own name, memories, traits, and physical mannerisms. Although rare, this "Dr. Jekyl and Mr. Hyde" syndrome is frequently portrayed in novels, movies, and television shows. In popular media portrayals, the syndrome is often mistakenly called *schizophrenia.* As you will see later, schizophrenic disorders are entirely different.

In a multiple-personality disorder, the various personalities are often unaware of each other (Eich et al., 1997). In other words, the experiences of a specific personality are only recalled by that personality and not the other personalities. The alternate personalities commonly display traits that are quite foreign to the original personality. For instance, a shy, inhibited person might develop a flamboyant, extraverted alternate personality. Transitions between identities often occur suddenly. The disparities between identities can be bizarre, as different personalities may assert that they are different in age, race, gender, and sexual orientation (Kluft, 1996).

The 1980s saw a dramatic increase in the diagnosis of multiple-personality disorders (Ross et al., 1991). Some theorists believe that these disorders used to be underdiagnosed—that is, they often went undetected (Saxe et al., 1993). However, it appears more likely that a handful of clinicians have begun overdiagnosing the condition (Frankel, 1990; Thigpen & Cleckley, 1984). Consistent with this view, a survey of all the psychiatrists in Switzerland (Modestin, 1992) found that 90% of them had never seen a case of MPD, whereas three of the psychiatrists had each seen more than 20 MPD patients. The data from this study suggest that six psychiatrists (out of 655 surveyed) accounted for two-thirds of the MPD diagnoses in Switzerland.

Etiology of Dissociative Disorders

Dissociative amnesia and fugue are usually attributed to excessive stress. However, relatively little is known about why this extreme reaction to stress occurs in a tiny minority of people but not in the vast majority who are subjected to similar stress. There is speculation that certain personality traits—fantasy proneness and a tendency to become intensely absorbed in personal experiences—may make some people more susceptible to dissociative disorders, but adequate evidence on this line of thought is lacking (Kihlstrom, Glisky, & Angiulo, 1994).

The causes of multiple-personality disorders are particularly obscure. Some skeptical theorists, such as Nicholas Spanos (1994, 1996) believe that people with multiple personalities are engaging in intentional role playing to use mental illness as a face-saving excuse for their personal failings. He also argues that a small minority of therapists help to create MPD in their patients by subtly encouraging the emergence of alternate personalities. According to Spanos, multiple-personality disorder is a creation of modern North American culture, much as demonic possession was a creation of early Christianity. To bolster his argument, he discusses how MPD patients' symptom presentations seem to have been influenced by popular media. For example, the typical MPD patient used to report

Web Link 15.2

International Society for the Study of Dissociation
Dissociative disorders, including multiple personality disorder, form the focus of this organization of research and clinical professionals. In addition to a selective bibliography and a set of treatment guidelines, the site offers an impressive set of links to other professional groups involved in studying and treating dissociation.

having two or three personalities, but since the publication of *Sybil* (Schreiber, 1973) and other books describing patients with many personalities, the average number of alternate personalities has climbed to about 15. In a similar vein, there has been a dramatic upsurge in the number of MPD patients reporting that they were victims of ritual satanic abuse during childhood in the years since the publication of *Michelle Remembers* (Smith & Padzer, 1980), a book about an MPD patient who purportedly was tortured by a satanic cult.

In spite of these troubling concerns, many clinicians are convinced that multiple-personality disorder is an authentic disorder (Gleaves, 1996; Kihlstrom, Tataryn, & Hoyt, 1993). They argue that neither patients nor therapists have incentives to manufacture cases of MPD, which are often greeted with skepticism and outright hostility. They maintain that most cases of MPD are rooted in severe emotional trauma that occurred during childhood. A substantial majority of people with multiple-personality disorder report a history of disturbed home life, beatings and rejection from parents, and sexual abuse (Lewis et al., 1997; Scroppo et al., 1998). In the final analysis, however, very little is known about the causes of multiple-personality disorder, which remains a controversial diagnosis.

Mood Disorders

LEARNING OBJECTIVES

● *Describe the two major mood disorders and discuss their prevalence.*

● *Explain how genetic and neurochemical factors may be related to the development of mood disorders.*

● *Explain how cognition and attributions may contribute to mood disorders.*

● *Explain how interpersonal behavior and stress may contribute to mood disorders.*

What did Abraham Lincoln, Marilyn Monroe, Ernest Hemingway, Winston Churchill, Janis Joplin, and Leo Tolstoy have in common? Yes, they all achieved great prominence, albeit in different ways at different times. But, more pertinent to our interest, they all suffered from severe mood disorders. Although mood disorders can be terribly debilitating, people with mood disorders may still achieve greatness, because such disorders tend to be *episodic*. In other words, emotional disorders often come and go. Thus, episodes of disturbance are interspersed among periods of normality. These episodes of disturbance can vary greatly in length, but they typically last several months (Coryell & Winokur, 1992).

Of course, we all have our ups and downs in terms of mood. Life would be dull indeed if emotional tone were constant. Everyone experiences depression occasionally and has other days that bring an emotional high. Such emotional fluctuations are natural, but some people are prone to extreme distortions of mood. **Mood disorders are a class of disorders marked by emotional disturbances that may spill over to disrupt physical, perceptual, social, and thought processes.**

There are two basic types of mood disorders: unipolar and bipolar (see Figure 15.9). People with *unipolar disorders* experience emotional extremes at just one end of the mood continuum—depression. People with *bipolar disorders* experience emotional extremes at both ends of the mood continuum, going

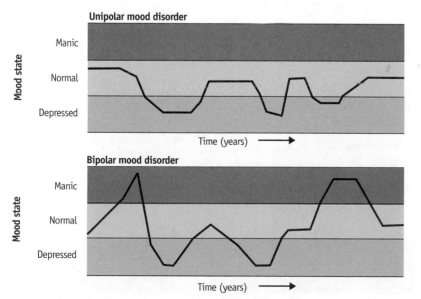

FIGURE 15.9.

Episodic patterns in mood disorders. Episodes of emotional disturbance come and go unpredictably in mood disorders. People with unipolar disorders suffer from bouts of depression only, while people with bipolar disorders experience both manic and depressed episodes. The time between episodes of disturbance varies greatly.

through periods of both *depression* and *mania* (excitement and elation). The mood swings in bipolar disorders can be patterned in many ways.

Depressive Disorder

The line between normal and abnormal depression can be difficult to draw (Grove & Andreasen, 1992; Kendler & Gardner, 1998). Ultimately, a subjective judgment is required. Crucial considerations in this judgment include the duration of the depression and its disruptive effects. When a depression significantly impairs everyday adaptive behavior for more than a few weeks, there is reason for concern.

In *depressive disorders* **people show persistent feelings of sadness and despair and a loss of interest in previous sources of pleasure.** In Figure 15.10 the most common symptoms of depressive disorders are summarized and compared to the symptoms of mania. Negative emotions form the heart of the depressive syndrome, but many other symptoms may also appear. Depressed people often give up activities that they used to find enjoyable. For example, a depressed person might quit going bowling or give up a favorite hobby like photography. Reduced appetite and insomnia are common. People with depression often lack energy. They tend to move sluggishly and talk slowly. Anxiety, irritability, and brooding are frequently observed. Self-esteem tends to sink as the depressed person begins to feel worthless. Depression plunges people into feelings of hopelessness, dejection, and boundless guilt. The severity of abnormal depression varies considerably. The onset of unipolar disorder can occur at any point in the life span and is *not* strongly related to age (Lewinsohn et al., 1986).

Web Link 15.3

Dr. Ivan's Depression Central
Psychiatrist Ivan Goldberg has constructed a site that might be better titled "Everything You Ever Wanted to Know About Depression." He offers a wealth of resources regarding depression and mood disorders.

How common are depressive disorders? Very common. Studies in the 1980s suggested that about 7% of Americans endure a depressive disorder at some time (Weissman et al., 1991). However, a recent, large-scale study using more probing interview techniques estimated that the lifetime prevalence of depression may be as high as 17% (Blazer et al., 1994). Moreover, evidence suggests that the prevalence of depression is increasing, as it is higher in more recent age cohorts (Lewinsohn et al., 1993). In particular, age cohorts born since World War II appear to have an elevated risk for depression (Smith & Weissman, 1992). The factors underlying this rise in depression are not readily apparent, and researchers are scrambling to collect data that might shed light on this unanticipated trend. Researchers also find that the prevalence of depression is about twice as high in women as it is in men (Culbertson, 1997). This gender gap in depression opens up during middle to late adolescence (Hankin et al., 1998). Theorists have proposed many possible explanations for this gender gap, creating considerable debate (Nolen-Hoeksema & Girgus, 1994).

Bipolar Disorder

Bipolar disorders **(formerly known as manic-depressive disorders) are marked by the experience of both**

Mood disorders are common and have afflicted many successful, well-known people, such as media entrepreneur Ted Turner and legendary author Ernest Hemingway. Mood disorders do not preclude great achievement because they are episodic.

depressed and manic periods. The symptoms seen in manic periods generally are the opposite of those seen in depression (see Figure 15.10 for a comparison). In a manic episode, a person's mood becomes elevated to the point of euphoria. Self-esteem skyrockets as the person bubbles over with optimism, energy, and extravagant plans. People become hyperactive and may go for days without sleep. They talk rapidly and shift topics wildly as their minds race at breakneck speed. Judgment is often impaired. Some people in manic periods gamble impulsively, spend money frantically, or become sexually reckless. Like depressive disorders, bipolar disorders vary considerably in severity.

You may be thinking that the euphoria in manic episodes sounds appealing. If so, you are not entirely wrong. In their milder forms, manic states can seem attractive. The increases in energy, self-esteem, and optimism can be deceptively seductive. Because of the increase in energy, many bipolar patients report temporary surges of productivity and creativity (Goodwin & Jamison, 1990).

Although there may be some positive aspects to manic episodes, bipolar disorders ultimately prove to be troublesome for most victims. Manic periods often have a paradoxical negative undertow of uneasiness and irritability (Rehm & Tyndall, 1993). Moreover, mild manic episodes usually escalate to higher levels that become scary and disturbing. Impaired judgment leads many victims to do things that they greatly regret later, as illustrated in the following case:

Robert, a dentist, awoke one morning with the idea that he was the most gifted dental surgeon in his tri-state area. He decided that he should try to provide services to as many people as possible, so that more people could benefit from his talents. Thus, he decided to remodel his two-chair dental office, installing 20 booths so that he could simultaneously attend to 20 patients. That same day he drew up plans for this arrangement, telephoned a number of remodelers, and invited bids for the work. Later that day, impatient to get going on his remodeling, he rolled up his sleeves, got himself a sledgehammer, and began to knock down the walls in his office. Annoyed when that didn't go

Web Link 15.4

Suicide ... Read This First
For those thinking about or dealing with suicidal issues in themselves or others, this site speaks directly and helpfully about suicide and suicidal feelings. It also includes suggestions for good resources and links to more information.

so well, he smashed his dental tools, washbasins, and X-ray equipment. Later, Robert's wife became concerned about his behavior and summoned two of her adult daughters for assistance. The daughters responded quickly, arriving at the family home with their husbands. In the ensuing discussion, Robert—after bragging about his sexual prowess—made advances toward his daughters. He had to be subdued by their husbands. (Adapted from Kleinmuntz, 1980, p. 309)

Although not rare, bipolar disorders are much less common than unipolar depression. Bipolar disorders affect a little under 1% of the population (Weissman et al., 1991). Unlike depressive disorders, bipolar disorders are seen equally often in men and women (Tohen & Goodwin, 1995). As Figure 15.11 (on the next page) shows, onset of bipolar disorders is age-related, with the peak of vulnerability occurring between the ages of 20 and 29 (Goodwin & Jamison, 1990).

Etiology of Mood Disorders

We know quite a bit about the etiology of mood disorders, although the puzzle hasn't been assembled completely. There appear to be a number of routes into these disorders, involving intricate interactions between psychological and biological factors.

GENETIC VULNERABILITY

The evidence strongly suggests that genetic factors influence the likelihood of developing major depression or a bipolar mood disorder. In studies that assess the impact of heredity on psychological disorders, investigators look at *concordance rates*. **A *concordance***

Comparison of Manic and Depressive Symptoms		
Characteristics	**Manic episode**	**Depressive episode**
Emotional	Elated, euphoric, very sociable, impatient at any hindrance	Gloomy, hopeless, socially withdrawn, irritable
Cognitive	Characterized by racing thoughts, flight of ideas, desire for action, and impulsive behavior; talkative, self-confident; experiencing delusions of grandeur	Characterized by slowness of thought processes, obsessive worrying, inability to make decisions, negative self-image, self-blame, and delusions of guilt and disease
Motor	Hyperactive, tireless, requiring less sleep than usual, showing increased sex drive and fluctuating appetite	Less active, tired, experiencing difficulty in sleeping, showing decreased sex drive and decreased appetite

FIGURE 15.10.
Common symptoms in manic and depressive episodes. The emotional, cognitive, and motor symptoms exhibited in manic and depressive illnesses are largely the opposite of each other.

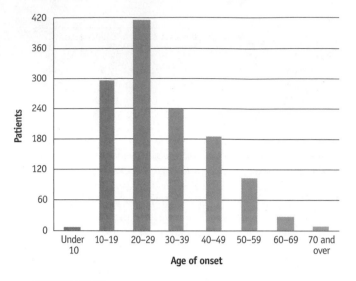

FIGURE 15.11.

Age of onset for bipolar mood disorder. The onset of bipolar disorder typically occurs in adolescence or early adulthood. The data graphed here, which were combined from ten studies, show the distribution of age of onset for 1304 bipolar patients. As you can see, bipolar disorder emerges most frequently during the 20s. (Data from Goodwin & Jamison, 1990)

rate **indicates the percentage of twin pairs or other pairs of relatives that exhibit the same disorder.** If relatives who share more genetic similarity show higher concordance rates than relatives who share less genetic overlap, this finding supports the genetic hypothesis. Twin studies, which compare identical and fraternal twins (see Chapter 2), suggest that genetic factors *are* involved in mood disorders (Rieder, Kaufmann, & Knowles, 1994). Concordance rates average around 67% for identical twins but only 15% for fraternal twins, who share less genetic similarity. Thus, evidence suggests that heredity can create a *predisposition* to mood disorders. Environmental factors probably determine whether this predisposition is converted into an actual disorder. The influence of genetic factors appears to be stronger for bipolar disorders than for unipolar disorders (Nurnberger & Gershon, 1992).

NEUROCHEMICAL FACTORS

Heredity may influence susceptibility to mood disorders by creating a predisposition toward certain types of neurochemical activity in the brain. Correlations have been found between mood disorders and the levels of two neurotransmitters in the brain: norepinephrine and serotonin (Delgado et al., 1992; Nemeroff, 1998). The details remain elusive, but it seems clear that a neurochemical basis exists for at least some mood disorders. A variety of drug therapies are fairly effective in the treatment of severe mood disorders. Most of these drugs are known to affect the availability (in the brain) of the neurotransmitters that have been related to

mood disorders (Nathan et al., 1995). Since this effect is unlikely to be a coincidence, it bolsters the plausibility of the idea that neurochemical changes produce mood disturbances.

If alterations in neurotransmitter activity are the basis for many mood disorders, what causes the alterations in neurotransmitter activity? These neurochemical changes probably depend on the body's reactions to environmental events. Thus, a number of psychological factors have been implicated in the etiology of mood disorders. We'll examine evidence on patterns of thinking, interpersonal style, and stress.

COGNITIVE FACTORS

A variety of theories emphasize how cognitive factors contribute to depressive disorders (Abramson, Metalsky, & Alloy, 1988; Beck, 1987; Ellis, 1984; Seligman, 1992). In recent years, theories that focus on people's patterns of *attribution* have generated a great deal of research on the cognitive roots of depression. As noted in Chapter 5, **attributions are inferences that people draw about the causes of events, others' behavior, and their own behavior.** People routinely make attributions because they want to *understand* their personal fates and the events that take place around them. For example, if your boss criticizes your work, you will probably ask yourself why. Was your work really that sloppy? Was your boss just in a grouchy mood? Was the criticism a manipulative effort to motivate you to work harder? Each of these potential explanations is an attribution.

Attributions can be analyzed along a number of dimensions. Three important dimensions are illustrated in Figure 15.12. The most prominent dimension is the degree to which people attribute events to *internal, personal factors versus external, situational factors*. For instance, if you performed poorly on a standardized mathematics test, you might attribute your poor showing to your lack of intelligence (an internal attribution) or to the horrible heat and humidity in the exam room (an external attribution).

Another key dimension is the degree to which people attribute events to factors that are *stable or unstable over time*. Thus, you might blame your poor test performance on exhaustion (an internal but unstable factor that could change next time) or on your poor math skills (an internal but stable factor). Some theories are also interested in the degree to which attributions have *global versus specific implications*. Thus, you might attribute your low test score to the unfairness of standardized tests (which has very general, global implications) or to distractions in the room (the specific test taking situation). Figure 15.12 provides additional examples of attributions that might be made for poor test performance.

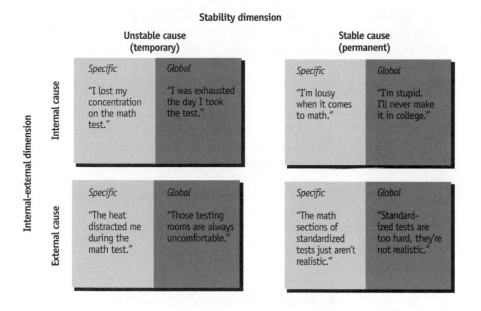

Stability dimension

	Unstable cause (temporary)		Stable cause (permanent)	
	Specific	Global	Specific	Global
Internal cause	"I lost my concentration on the math test."	"I was exhausted the day I took the test."	"I'm lousy when it comes to math."	"I'm stupid. I'll never make it in college."
External cause	"The heat distracted me during the math test."	"Those testing rooms are always uncomfortable."	"The math sections of standardized tests just aren't realistic."	"Standardized tests are too hard, they're not realistic."

Internal-external dimension

FIGURE 15.12.
Attributional style and depression. Possible attributions for poor performance on a standardized math exam are shown here. Note how these explanations vary in terms of whether causes are seen as internal-external, stable-unstable, and specific-global. People who consistently explain their failures with attributions that are internal, stable, and global are particularly vulnerable to depression.

Theories that link attribution to depression focus on the *attributional style* that people display, especially when they are trying to explain failures, setbacks, and other negative events. Studies suggest that *people who tend to make internal, stable, and global attributions for negative events are more vulnerable to depression* than other people (Robins & Hayes, 1995; Sweeney, Anderson, & Bailey, 1986). Why? Because in making internal, stable, and global attributions, people blame their setbacks on personal inadequacies (internal) they see as unchangeable (stable), and they draw far-reaching (global) conclusions about their lack of worth. In other words, they draw depressing conclusions about themselves.

Thus, cognitive models of depression maintain that negative thinking is what makes many people feel helpless, hopeless, and dejected. One problem with cognitive models of depression is that the hypothesized mechanisms may not be unique to depression (Ralph & Mineka, 1998). Recent evidence suggests that negative thinking may foster anxiety and general distress as well. Another problem with cognitive theories is their difficulty in separating cause from effect (Barnett & Gotlib, 1988). Does negative thinking cause depression? Or does depression cause negative thinking? Could both be caused by a third variable, such as neurochemical changes (see Figure 15.13)? Evidence can be mustered to support all three of these possibilities, suggesting that negative thinking, depression, and neurochemical alterations may feed off of each other as a depression deepens.

Consistent with this line of thinking, Susan Nolen-Hoeksema (1991) and other researchers have found that depressed people who *ruminate* about their depression remain depressed longer than those who try to distract themselves (Just & Alloy, 1997;

Nolen-Hoeksema, Morrow, & Fredrickson, 1993). People who respond to depression with rumination repetitively focus their attention on their depressing feelings, thinking constantly about how sad, lethargic, and unmotivated they are. According to Nolen-Hoeksema, excessive rumination tends to extend and amplify individuals' episodes of depression. She believes that women are more likely to ruminate than men and that this disparity may be the primary reason why depression is more common in women.

Susan Nolen-Hoeksema

INTERPERSONAL ROOTS

Some theorists emphasize how inadequate social skills put people on the road to depressive disorders (Lewinsohn & Gotlib, 1995; Segrin & Abramson, 1994).

FIGURE 15.13.
Interpreting the correlation between negative thinking and depression. Cognitive theories of depression assert that consistent patterns of negative thinking cause depression. Although these theories are highly plausible, depression could cause negative thoughts, or both could be caused by a third factor, such as neurochemical changes in the brain.

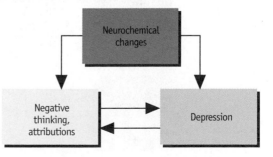

According to this notion, depression-prone people lack the social finesse needed to acquire many important kinds of reinforcers, such as good friends, top jobs, and desirable spouses. This paucity of reinforcers could understandably lead to negative emotions and depression (see Figure 15.14). Consistent with this theory, researchers have found correlations between poor social skills and depression (Dykman et al., 1991). For example, Joiner (1997) found that shyness was a risk factor for depression among people who had relatively little social support.

Another interpersonal consideration is that depressed people tend to be depressing (Joiner, 1994). Individuals suffering from depression are often irritable and pessimistic. They complain a lot, and they aren't very enjoyable companions. As a consequence, depressed people inadvertently court rejection from those around them (Joiner & Metalsky, 1995). In turn, rejection and lack of social support may aggravate and deepen a person's depression (Potthoff, Holahan, & Joiner, 1995). To compound these problems, recent evidence indicates that depressed people may gravitate to partners who view them unfavorably and hence reinforce their negative views of themselves (Giesler, Josephs, & Swann, 1996).

PRECIPITATING STRESS

Mood disorders sometimes appear mysteriously "out of the blue" in people who are leading benign, nonstressful lives. For this reason, experts used to believe that mood disorders are relatively uninfluenced by stress. However, recent advances in the measurement of personal stress have altered this picture. The evidence available today suggests a moderately strong link between stress and the onset of mood disorders

FIGURE 15.14.

Interpersonal factors in depression. Interpersonal theories about the etiology of depression emphasize how poor social skills may contribute to the development of the disorder.

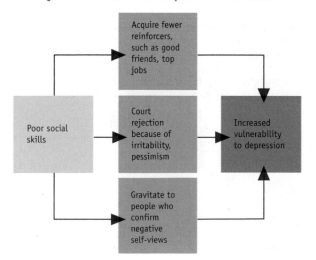

(Hammen & Gitlin, 1997; Kessler, 1997). Stress also appears to affect how people with mood disorders respond to treatment and whether they experience a relapse of their disorder (Monroe et al., 1996).

Of course, many people endure great stress without getting depressed. The impact of stress varies, in part because different people have different degrees of *vulnerability* to mood disorders (Monroe & Simons, 1991). Variations in vulnerability appear to depend primarily on one's biological makeup. Similar interactions between stress and vulnerability probably influence the development of many kinds of disorders, including those that are next on our agenda: the schizophrenic disorders.

Schizophrenic Disorders

LEARNING OBJECTIVES

- Describe the prevalence and general symptoms of schizophrenia.
- Describe four schizophrenic subtypes.
- Explain the distinction between positive and negative symptoms in schizophrenia.
- Discuss how the course of schizophrenia unfolds in three patterns and identify factors related to the prognosis for schizophrenic patients.
- Summarize how genetic vulnerability, neurochemical factors, and structural abnormalities in the brain may contribute to the etiology of schizophrenia.
- Summarize how communication deviance, expressed emotion, and stress may contribute to schizophrenia.

Literally, *schizophrenia* means "split mind." However, when Eugen Bleuler coined the term in 1911, he was referring to the fragmenting of thought processes seen in the disorder—not to a "split personality." Unfortunately, writers in the popular media often assume that the split-mind notion refers to the rare syndrome in which a person manifests two or more personalities. As you have already learned, this syndrome is actually called *multiple-personality disorder or dissociative identity disorder*. Schizophrenia is a much more common, and altogether different, type of disorder.

Schizophrenic disorders are a class of disorders marked by disturbances in thought that spill over to affect perceptual, social, and emotional processes. How common is schizophrenia? Prevalence estimates suggest that about 1% to 1.5% of the population may suffer from schizophrenic disorders (Keith, Regier, & Rae, 1991). That may not sound like much, but it means that in the United States alone there may be 4 million people troubled by schizophrenic disturbances. Moreover, schizophrenia is a severe, debilitating disorder that places a heavy burden on our mental health system. Flynn (1994) estimates that schizophrenia accounts for about three-quarters of the total U.S. tax dollars spent on the treatment of mental illness.

General Symptoms

There are a number of distinct schizophrenic syndromes, but they share some general characteristics that we will examine before looking at the subtypes. Many of these characteristics are apparent in the following case history (adapted from Sheehan, 1982).

Sylvia was first diagnosed as schizophrenic at age 15. She has been in and out of many types of psychiatric facilities since then. She has never been able to hold a job for any length of time. During severe flare-ups of her disorder, her personal hygiene deteriorates. She rarely washes, wears clothes that neither fit nor match, smears makeup on heavily but randomly, and slops food all over herself. Sylvia occasionally hears voices talking to her. Sylvia tends to be argumentative, aggressive, and emotionally volatile. Over the years, she has been involved in innumerable fights with fellow patients, psychiatric staff members, and strangers. Her thoughts can be highly irrational, as is apparent from the following quotation:

"Mick Jagger wants to marry me. If I have Mick Jagger, I don't have to covet Geraldo Rivera. Mick Jagger is St. Nicholas and the Maharishi is Santa Claus. I want to form a gospel rock group called the Thorn Oil, but Geraldo wants me to be the music critic on Eyewitness News, so what can I do? Got to listen to my boyfriend. Teddy Kennedy cured me of my ugliness. I'm pregnant with the son of God. I'm going to marry David Berkowitz and get it over with. Creedmoor is the headquarters of the American Nazi Party. They're eating the patients here. Archie Bunker wants me to play his niece on his TV show. I work for Epic Records. I'm Joan of Arc. I'm Florence Nightingale. The door between the ward and the porch is the dividing line between New York and California. Divorce isn't a piece of paper, it's a feeling. Forget about Zip Codes. I need shock treatment. The body is run by electricity. My wiring is all faulty. A fly is a teen-age wasp. I'm marrying an accountant. I'm in the Pentecostal Church, but I'm considering switching my loyalty to the Charismatic Church." (Sheehan, 1982, pp.104–105)

Sylvia's case clearly shows that schizophrenic thinking can be bizarre and that schizophrenia is a brutally serious, psychologically disfiguring disorder. Although no single symptom is inevitably present, the following symptoms are commonly seen in schizophrenia (Black & Andreasen, 1994; Grebb & Cancro, 1989).

IRRATIONAL THOUGHT

Disturbed, irrational thought processes are the central feature of schizophrenic disorders. Various kinds of delusions are common. **Delusions are false beliefs that are maintained even though they clearly are out of touch with reality.** For example, one patient's delusion that he is a tiger (with a deformed body) has persisted for 15 years (Kulick, Pope, & Keck, 1990). More typically, affected persons believe that their private thoughts are being broadcast to other people or that thoughts are being injected into their mind against their will (Maher & Spitzer, 1993). In *delusions of grandeur*, people maintain that they are extremely famous or important. Sylvia expressed an endless array of grandiose delusions, such as thinking that Mick Jagger wanted to marry her, that she dictated the hobbit stories to Tolkien, and that she was going to win the Nobel Prize for medicine.

In addition to delusions, the schizophrenic person's train of thought deteriorates. Thinking becomes chaotic rather than logical and linear. There is a "loosening of associations" as the schizophrenic shifts topics in disjointed ways. The quotation from Sylvia illustrates this symptom dramatically. The entire passage involves a wild flight of ideas, but at one point (beginning with the sentence "Creedmoor is the headquarters . . .") she rattles off ten consecutive sentences that have no apparent connection to the preceding sentence.

DETERIORATION OF ADAPTIVE BEHAVIOR

Schizophrenia usually involves a noticeable deterioration in the quality of one's routine functioning in work, social relations, and personal care. Friends will often make remarks such as "Hal just isn't himself anymore." This deterioration is readily apparent in Sylvia's inability to get along with others or function in the work world. It's also apparent in her neglect of personal hygiene.

DISTORTED PERCEPTION

A variety of perceptual distortions may occur in schizophrenia, with the most common being auditory hallucinations. **Hallucinations are sensory perceptions that occur in the absence of a real, external stimulus or that represent gross distortions of perceptual input.** Schizophrenics frequently report that they hear voices of nonexistent or absent people talking to them. Sylvia, for instance, heard messages from former Beatle Paul McCartney. These voices often provide an insulting running commentary on the person's behavior ("You're an idiot for shaking his hand"). The voices may be argumentative ("You don't need a bath"), and they may issue commands ("Prepare your home for visitors from outer space").

DISTURBED EMOTION

Normal emotional tone can be disrupted in schizophrenia in a variety of ways. Although it may not be an accurate indicator of their underlying emotional experience (Kring et al., 1993), some victims show little emotional responsiveness, a symptom referred to as "blunted or flat affect." Others show inappropriate emotional responses that don't jell with the situation or with what they are saying. For instance, a schizophrenic patient might cry over a Smurfs cartoon and then laugh about a news story describing a child's tragic death. People with schizophrenia may also become emotionally volatile. This pattern was displayed by Sylvia, who often overreacted emotionally in erratic, unpredictable ways.

Subtypes

Four subtypes of schizophrenic disorders are recognized, including a category for people who don't fit neatly into any of the first three categories (Black & Andreasen, 1994).

PARANOID TYPE

As its name implies, *paranoid schizophrenia* **is dominated by delusions of persecution, along with delusions of grandeur.** In this common form of schizophrenia, people come to believe that they have many enemies who want to harass and oppress them. They may become suspicious of friends and relatives, or they may attribute the persecution to mysterious, unknown persons. They are convinced that they are being watched and manipulated in malicious ways. To make sense of this persecution, they often develop delusions of grandeur. They believe that they must be enormously important people, often seeing themselves as great inventors or as great religious or political leaders. For example, in the case described at the beginning of the chapter, Ed's belief that he was president of the United States was a delusion of grandeur.

CATATONIC TYPE

Catatonic schizophrenia **is marked by striking motor disturbances, ranging from muscular rigidity to random motor activity.** Some catatonics go into an extreme form of withdrawal known as a catatonic stupor. They may remain virtually motionless and seem oblivious to the environment around them for long periods of time. Others go into a state of catatonic excitement. They become hyperactive and incoherent. Some alternate between these dramatic extremes. The catatonic subtype is not particularly common, and its prevalence seems to be declining.

DISORGANIZED TYPE

In *disorganized schizophrenia,* **a particularly severe deterioration of adaptive behavior is seen.** Prominent symptoms include emotional indifference, frequent incoherence, and virtually complete social withdrawal. Aimless babbling and giggling are common. Delusions often center on bodily functions ("My brain is melting out my ears").

UNDIFFERENTIATED TYPE

People who are clearly schizophrenic but who cannot be placed into any of the three previous categories are said to have *undifferentiated schizophrenia,* **which is marked by idiosyncratic mixtures of schizophrenic symptoms.** The undifferentiated subtype is fairly common.

POSITIVE VERSUS NEGATIVE SYMPTOMS

Some theorists are beginning to doubt the value of dividing schizophrenic disorders into these four subtypes (Nicholson & Neufeld, 1993). Critics note that the catatonic subtype is disappearing and that undifferentiated cases aren't a subtype so much as a hodgepodge of "leftovers." Critics also point out that the classic schizophrenic subtypes do not differ meaningfully in etiology, prognosis, or response to treatment. The absence of such differences casts doubt on the value of the current classification scheme.

Because of such problems, Nancy Andreasen (1990) and others (Carpenter, 1992; McGlashan & Fenton, 1992) have proposed an alternative approach to subtyping. This new scheme divides schizophrenic disorders into just two categories based on the predominance of negative versus positive symptoms (see Figure 15.15). *Negative symptoms* involve behavioral deficits, such as flattened emotions, social withdrawal, apathy, impaired attention, and poverty of speech. *Positive symptoms* involve behavioral excesses or peculiarities, such as hallucinations, delusions, bizarre behavior, and wild flights of ideas.

Nancy Andreasen

Theorists advocating this scheme hoped to find consistent differences between the two subtypes in etiology, prognosis, and response to treatment, and some progress along these lines *has* been made. For example, a predominance of positive symptoms is associated with better adjustment prior to the onset of schizophrenia and greater responsiveness to treatment (Cuesta, Peralta, & DeLeon, 1994; Fenton & McGlashan, 1994). However, the assumption that patients can be placed into discrete categories based on this scheme now seems untenable. Most patients exhibit both types of symptoms and vary only in the degree to which positive or negative symptoms dominate (Black & Andreasen, 1994). Moreover, there is some debate about which symptoms should be classified as positive and which should be regarded as

Positive and Negative Symptoms in Schizophrenia

Negative symptoms	Percent of patients	Positive symptoms	Percent of patients
Few friendship relationships	96	Delusions of persecution	81
Few recreational interests	95	Auditory hallucinations	75
Lack of persistence at work or school	95	Delusions of being controlled	46
Impaired grooming or hygiene	87	Derailment of thought	45
Paucity of expressive gestures	81	Delusions of grandeur	39
Social inattentiveness	78	Bizarre social, sexual behavior	33
Emotional nonresponsiveness	64	Delusions of thought insertion	31
Inappropriate emotion	63	Aggressive, agitated behavior	27
Poverty of speech	53	Incoherent thought	23

FIGURE 15.15.

Examples of positive and negative symptoms in schizophrenia. Some theorists believe that schizophrenic disorders should be classified into just two types, depending on whether patients exhibit mostly positive symptoms (behavioral excesses) or negative symptoms (behavioral deficits). Examples of negative symptoms seen in people with schizophrenic disorders are listed on the left, with examples of positive symptoms listed on the right. The percentages, based on a sample of 111 schizophrenic patients studied by Andreasen (1987), provide an indication of how common each specific symptom is.

negative, and some theorists have proposed a third category of symptoms reflecting *disorganization* of behavior (Toomey et al., 1997). Although it seems fair to say that the distinction between positive and negative symptoms is enhancing our understanding of schizophrenia, it has not yielded a classification scheme that can replace the traditional subtypes of schizophrenia.

Course and Outcome

Schizophrenic disorders usually emerge during adolescence or early adulthood and only rarely after age 45 (Murphy & Helzer, 1986). The emergence of schizophrenia may be either sudden or gradual. Once it clearly emerges, the course of schizophrenia is variable (Ciompi, 1980; Marengo et al., 1991), but patients tend to fall into three broad groups. Some patients, presumably those with milder disorders, are treated successfully and enjoy a full recovery. Other patients experience a partial recovery so that they can return to their normal life. However, they experience regular relapses and are in and out of treatment facilities for much of the remainder of their lives. Finally, a third group of patients endure chronic illness that sometimes results in permanent hospitalization. Overall, less than half of schizophrenic patients enjoy a significant recovery (Hegarty et al., 1994). For unknown reasons, gender is associated with the course and outcome of schizophrenia. The differences are modest, but in comparison to females, males tend to have an earlier onset of the disease, more hospitalizations, and higher relapse rates (Szymanski et al., 1995).

A number of factors are related to the likelihood of recovery from schizophrenic disorders (Ho, et al., 1998; Lehmann & Cancro, 1985). A patient has a relatively *favorable prognosis* when (1) the onset of the disorder

Recommended Reading

Surviving Schizophrenia: A Family Manual
by E. Fuller Torrey (Harper, 1988, 1995)

E. Fuller Torrey is a prominent psychiatrist who has specialized in the treatment and study of schizophrenia. He has conducted basic research and written technical articles on schizophrenia, as well as this practical book intended for the lay public. Torrey points out that many myths surrounding schizophrenia have added to the anguish of families that have been victimized by this illness. He explains that schizophrenia is not caused by childhood trauma, domineering mothers, or passive fathers. He discusses how genetic vulnerability, flawed brain chemistry, and other factors contribute to the development of schizophrenic disorders. Torrey discusses the treatment of schizophrenia at great length. He also explains the various ways in which the disease can evolve. Some of the best material is found in chapters on what the patient needs and what the family needs.

Throughout the book, Torrey writes with clarity, eloquence, and conviction. He's not reluctant to express strong opinions. For instance, in an appendix he lists the ten worst readings on schizophrenia (along with the ten best), and his evaluations are brutal. He characterizes one book as "absurd drivel" and dismisses another by saying, "If a prize were to be given to the book which has produced the most confusion about schizophrenia over the past 20 years, this book would win going away." Since scientists and academicians are usually reluctant to express such strong opinions, Torrey's candor is remarkably refreshing.

Psychoanalysis is to schizophrenia as Laetrile is to cancer. Both have enjoyed surprising popularity considering the fact that they lack scientific basis, are completely ineffective, may make the patient worse if administered in toxic doses, and still attract patients who are willing to pay vast sums of money in desperation for a cure. Freud himself recognized that schizophrenic patients "are inaccessible to the influence of psychoanalysis and cannot be cured by our endeavors," but that observation has not stopped his followers from trying. [1988, p. 220]

has been sudden rather than gradual, (2) the onset has occurred at a later age, (3) the patient's social and work adjustment were relatively good prior to the onset of the disorder, (4) the proportion of negative symptoms is relatively low, and (5) the patient has a relatively healthy, supportive family situation to return to. Most of these predictors are concerned with the etiology of schizophrenic illness, which is the matter we turn to next.

Etiology of Schizophrenia

Most of us can identify, at least to some extent, with people who suffer from mood disorders, somatoform disorders, and anxiety disorders. You can probably imagine events that might leave you struggling with depression, grappling with anxiety, or worrying about your physical health. But what could possibly have led Ed to believe that he had been fighting space wars and vampires? What could account for Sylvia thinking that she was Joan of Arc? Or that she had dictated the hobbit novels to Tolkien? As mystifying as these delusions may seem, you'll see that the etiology of schizophrenic disorders is not all that different from the etiology of other disorders.

GENETIC VULNERABILITY

Evidence is plentiful that hereditary factors play a role in the development of schizophrenic disorders (Rieder et al., 1994). For instance, in twin studies, concordance rates average around 48% for identical twins, in comparison to about 17% for fraternal twins (Gottesman, 1991). Studies also indicate that a child born to two schizophrenic parents has about a 46% probability of developing a schizophrenic disorder (as compared to the probability of about 1% for the population as a whole). These and other findings that demonstrate the genetic roots of schizophrenia are summarized in Figure 15.16. Overall, the picture is similar to that seen for mood disorders. Several converging lines of evidence indicate that people inherit a genetically transmitted *vulnerability* to schizophrenia (Fowles, 1992). Although genetic factors may account for more than two-thirds of the variability in susceptibility to schizophrenia, genetic mapping studies have made little progress in identifying the genes responsible (Levinson et al., 1998).

NEUROCHEMICAL FACTORS

Like mood disorders, schizophrenic disorders appear to be accompanied by changes in the activity of one or more neurotransmitters in the brain (Knable, Kleinman, & Weinberger, 1995). Excess *dopamine* activity has been implicated as a likely cause of schizophrenia (Abi-Dargham, et al., 1998). This hypothesis makes sense because most of the drugs that are useful in the treatment of schizophrenia are known to dampen dopamine activity in the brain (Marder & Van Putten, 1995). However, the evidence linking schizophrenia to high dopamine levels is riddled with inconsistencies, complexities, and interpretive problems (Carson & Sanislow, 1993). Perhaps some of these inconsistencies will be resolved by a new theory that links schizophrenia to abnormally high dopamine activity in subcortical areas of the brain, coupled with abnormally low dopamine activity in the prefrontal cortex (Davis et al.,

FIGURE 15.16.

Genetic vulnerability to schizophrenic disorders. Relatives of schizophrenic patients have an elevated risk for schizophrenia. This risk is greater among closer relatives. Although environment also plays a role in the etiology of schizophrenia, the concordance rates shown here suggest that there must be a genetic vulnerability to the disorder. These concordance estimates are based on pooled data from 40 studies conducted between 1920 and 1987. (Data from Gottesman, 1991)

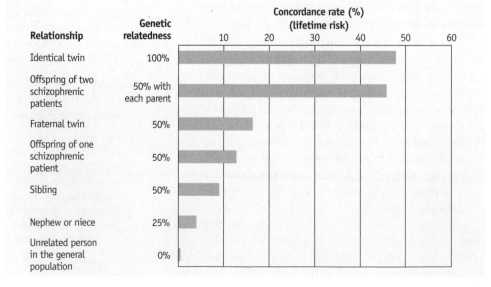

1991). Another new line of thought on the neurochemistry of schizophrenia emphasizes that neurotransmitter systems are not entirely independent. Researchers are currently exploring how interactions between the dopamine and serotonin neurotransmitter systems may contribute to schizophrenia (Kapur & Remington, 1996). Thus, investigators are gradually making progress in their search for the neurochemical bases of schizophrenia.

STRUCTURAL ABNORMALITIES IN THE BRAIN

Various studies have suggested that schizophrenic individuals have difficulty in focusing and switching their attention (Dawson et al., 1993; Smith et al., 1998). Some theorists believe that many bizarre aspects of schizophrenic behavior may be due mainly to an inability to filter out unimportant stimuli (Judd et al., 1992). This lack of selectivity supposedly leaves victims of the disorder flooded with overwhelming sensory input.

Such problems with attention suggest that schizophrenic disorders may be caused by neurological defects (Perry & Braff, 1994). Until recently, this theory was based more on speculation than on actual research. However, new advances in brain-imaging technology are beginning to yield some intriguing data. The findings suggest an association between enlarged brain ventricles (the hollow, fluid-filled cavities in the brain shown in Figure 15.17) and chronic schizophrenic disturbance, especially among male patients (Nopoulous, Flaum, & Andreasen, 1997; Raz, 1993).

The significance of enlarged brain ventricles is hotly debated, however. Enlarged ventricles are not unique to schizophrenia—they are a sign of many kinds of brain pathology. Furthermore, even if the association between enlarged ventricles and schizophrenia is replicated consistently, it will be difficult to sort out whether this brain abnormality is a cause or an effect of schizophrenia (Flaum et al., 1995). Researchers are currently more intrigued by the finding that the *thalamus* is smaller and shows less metabolic activity in schizophrenic patients than in normal control subjects (Buchsbaum et al., 1996). Given the crucial role of the thalamus as the brain's relay center, these previously undetected abnormalities could have great functional significance.

COMMUNICATION DEVIANCE

Over the years, hundreds of investigators have tried to relate patterns of family interaction to the development of schizophrenia. Popular theories have come and gone as empirical evidence has overturned once-plausible hypotheses (Goldstein, 1988). Vigorous research and debate in this area continue today. The current emphasis is on families' communication patterns and their expression of emotions.

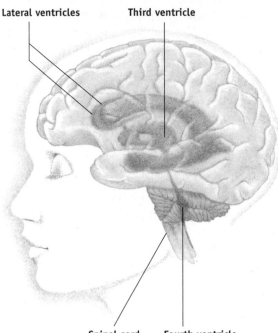

Lateral ventricles **Third ventricle**

Spinal cord **Fourth ventricle**

FIGURE 15.17.

Schizophrenia and the ventricles of the brain. Cerebrospinal fluid (CSF) circulates around the brain and spinal cord. The hollow cavities in the brain filled with CSF are called ventricles. This drawing shows the four ventricles in the human brain. Recent studies with new brain-imaging techniques suggest an association between enlarged ventricles in the brain and the occurrence of schizophrenic disturbance.

Various theorists assert that vulnerability to schizophrenia is increased by exposure to defective interpersonal communication during childhood. Studies have found a relationship between schizophrenia and *communication deviance* (Goldstein, 1987; Singer, Wynne, & Toohey, 1978). Communication deviance includes unintelligible speech, stories with no endings, heavy use of unusual words, extensive contradictions, and lack of attention to children's communication efforts. The evidence suggests that schizophrenia is more likely to develop when youngsters grow up in homes characterized by vague, muddled, fragmented communication. Researchers speculate that communication deviance gradually undermines a child's sense of reality and encourages youngsters to withdraw into their own private worlds, setting the stage for schizophrenic thinking later in life.

EXPRESSED EMOTION

Studies of expressed emotion have primarily focused on how this element of family dynamics influences the *course* of schizophrenic illness after the onset of the disorder (Leff & Vaughn, 1985). *Expressed emotion* reflects the degree to which a relative of a schizophrenic patient displays highly critical or emotionally overinvolved attitudes toward the patient. Audiotaped interviews are used to assess relatives' expressed emotion. The interviews are carefully evaluated for critical comments, resentment toward the patient, and excessive emotional involvement (overprotective, overconcerned attitudes).

Studies show that a family's expressed emotion is a good predictor of the course of a schizophrenic patient's illness (Kavanaugh, 1992; Parker & Hadzi-Pavlovic, 1990). After release from a hospital, schizophrenic patients who return to a family high in expressed emotion show relapse rates three or four times those of patients who return to a family low in expressed emotion. Part of the problem for patients returning to homes high in expressed emotion is that their families are probably sources of more stress than of social support. Interestingly, recent research suggests that the effects of expressed emotion may not be confined to schizophrenic patients. Patients suffering from *mood disorders* whose families are high in expressed emotion also show elevated relapse rates (Hinrichsen & Pollack, 1997; Simoneau, et al., 1998).

PRECIPITATING STRESS

Most theories of schizophrenia assume that stress plays a key role in triggering schizophrenic disorders (Fowles, 1992; Zubin, 1986). According to this notion, various biological and psychological factors influence individuals' *vulnerability* to schizophrenia. High stress may then serve to precipitate a schizophrenic disorder in someone who is vulnerable. At least one study has shown that high stress can also trigger relapses in schizophrenic patients who have made progress toward recovery (Ventura et al., 1989).

Understanding Eating Disorders

LEARNING OBJECTIVES

- Describe the symptoms and medical complications of anorexia nervosa and bulimia nervosa.
- Discuss the history, prevalence, and gender distribution of eating disorders.
- Explain how genetic factors, personality, and culture may contribute to eating disorders.
- Explain how family dynamics, disturbed thinking, and dieting may contribute to eating disorders.

Answer the following "true" or "false."

_____ 1. Although they have attracted attention only in recent years, eating disorders have a long history and have always been fairly common.

_____ 2. Eating disorders are universal problems found in virtually all cultures.

_____ 3. People with anorexia nervosa are much more likely to recognize their eating behavior as pathological than people suffering from bulimia nervosa.

_____ 4. The prevalence of eating disorders is twice as high in women as it is in men.

_____ 5. The binge-and-purge syndrome seen in bulimia nervosa is not common in anorexia nervosa.

_____ 6. Normal dieting is not a risk factor for eating disorders.

All six of these statements are false, as you will see in this Application. The psychological disorders that we discussed in the main body of the chapter have largely been recognized for centuries and generally are found in one form or another in all cultures and societies. Eating disorders present a sharp contrast to this picture: They have only been recognized in recent decades, and they have largely been confined to affluent, Westernized cultures (Russell, 1995; Szmukler & Patton, 1995). In spite of these fascinating differences, eating disorders have much in common with traditional forms of pathology.

Eating disorders are severe disturbances in eating behavior characterized by preoccupation with weight and unhealthy efforts to control weight. The vast majority of cases consist of two sometimes overlapping syndromes: *anorexia nervosa* and *bulimia nervosa*.

Anorexia Nervosa

Anorexia nervosa involves intense fear of gaining weight, disturbed body image, refusal to maintain normal weight, and dangerous measures to lose weight. Two subtypes have been observed (Garfinkel, 1995). In *restricting type anorexia nervosa*, people drastically reduce their intake of food, sometimes literally starving themselves. In *binge-eating/purging type anorexia nervosa*, victims attempt to lose weight by forcing themselves to vomit after meals, by misusing laxatives and diuretics, and by engaging in excessive exercise.

Both types entail a disturbed body image. No matter how frail and emaciated the victims become, they insist that they are too fat. Their morbid fear of obesity means that they are never satisfied with their weight. If they gain a pound or two, they panic. The only thing that makes them happy is to lose more weight. The common result is a relentless decline in body

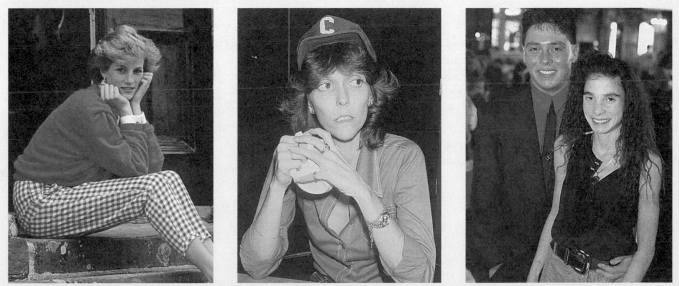

Eating disorders have become common and have been seen in many prominent women, such as Princess Diana (left), singer Karen Carpenter (middle), and gymnast Christy Henrich (right).

weight—patients entering treatment for anorexia nervosa are typically 25%–30% below their normal weight (Hsu, 1990). Because of their disturbed body image, people suffering from anorexia generally do *not* appreciate the maladaptive quality of their behavior and rarely seek treatment on their own. They are typically coaxed or coerced into treatment by friends or family members who are alarmed by their appearance.

Anorexia nervosa eventually leads to a cascade of medical problems, including *amenorrhea* (a loss of menstrual cycles in women), gastrointestinal problems, low blood pressure, *osteoporosis* (a loss of bone density), and metabolic disturbances that can lead to cardiac arrest or circulatory collapse (Fairburn, 1995; Goldbloom & Kennedy, 1995). Anorexia is a debilitating illness that leads to death in 2%–10% of patients (Slade, 1995; Treasure & Szmukler, 1995). Anorexia often coexists with other psychological disorders, especially depression and anxiety disorders (P. Cooper, 1995).

Bulimia Nervosa

Bulimia nervosa involves habitually engaging in out-of-control overeating followed by unhealthy compensatory efforts, such as self-induced vomiting, fasting, abuse of laxatives and diuretics, and excessive exercise. The eating binges are usually carried out in secret and are followed by intense guilt and concern about gaining weight. These feelings motivate ill-advised strategies to undo the effects of the overeating. However, vomiting only prevents the absorption of about half of recently consumed food, and laxatives and diuretics have negligible impact on caloric intake, so people suffering from bulimia nervosa typically maintain a reasonably normal weight (Beumont, 1995; Kaye et al., 1993).

Medical problems associated with bulimia nervosa include amenorrhea, dental problems, and metabolic deficiencies and gastrointesinal problems (Mitchell, 1995). Bulimia often coexists with other psychological disturbances, including depression, anxiety disorders, and substance abuse (P. Cooper, 1995; G. Wilson, 1993).

Obviously, bulimia nervosa shares many features with anorexia nervosa, such as a morbid fear of becoming obese, preoccupation with food, and rigid, maladaptive approaches to controlling weight that are grounded in naive all-or-none thinking. However, the syndromes also differ in crucial ways. First and foremost, bulimia is a less life-threatening condition. Second, although their weight and appearance usually is more "normal" than that seen in anorexia, people with bulimia are much more likely to recognize that their eating behavior is pathological and are more

prone to cooperate with treatment (Striegel-Moore, Silberstein, & Rodin, 1993).

History and Prevalence

Historians have been able to track down descriptions of anorexia nervosa that date back centuries, so the disorder is *not* entirely new, but anorexia nervosa did not become a common affliction until the middle part of the 20th century (Russell, 1995). Although bingeing and purging have a long history in some cultures, they were not part of a pathological effort to control weight, and bulimia nervosa appears to be an entirely new syndrome that emerged gradually in the middle of the 20th century and was first recognized in the 1970s (Parry-Jones & Parry-Jones, 1995; Russell, 1997).

Both disorders are a product of modern, affluent, Western culture, where food is generally plentiful and the desirability of being thin is widely endorsed. Until recently, these problems were not seen in developing nations where access to adequate food was often precarious (Hoek, 1995). However, now that advances in communication have exported Western culture to farflung corners of the globe, eating disorders have started showing up in developing nations (Wilfley & Rodin, 1995).

There is a huge gender gap in the likelihood of developing eating disorders. About 90%–95% of individuals with anorexia nervosa and bulimia nervosa are female (Hoek, 1995). This staggering discrepancy appears to be a result of cultural pressures rather than biological factors (Striegel-Moore, 1995). Western standards of attractiveness emphasize being slender more for females than for males, and women generally experience heavier pressure to be physically attractive than men do (Sobal, 1995). The prevalence of eating disorders is also elevated in certain groups that place an undue emphasis on thinness, such as fashion models, dancers, actresses, and athletes. Eating disorders mostly afflict *young* women. The typical age of onset for anorexia is 14–18, and for bulimia it is 15–21 (see Figure 15.18).

How common are eating disorders in Western societies? The prevalence of these disorders has increased

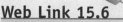

Web Link 15.6

Eating Disorders Shared Awareness (EDSA)
When rhythms of hunger and eating no longer function normally, a person may begin to experience an eating disorder that can eventually become life-threatening. EDSA and its closely related sites provide a vast range of information about anorexia, bulimia, and other forms of eating disorders.

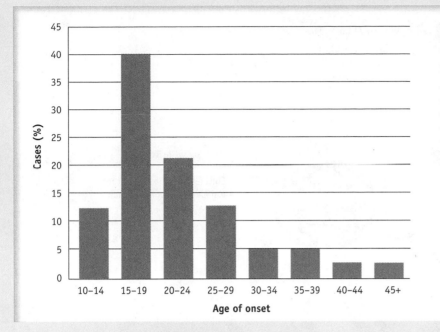

FIGURE 15.18.

Age of onset for anorexia nervosa. Eating disorders mostly emerge during adolescence, as these data for anorexia nervosa show. This graph shows how age of onset was distributed in a sample of 166 female patients from Minnesota. As you can see, over half the patients experienced the onset of their illness before the age of 20, with vulnerability clearly peaking between the ages of 15 and 19. (Data adapted from Lucas et al., 1991)

dramatically in recent decades, although this escalation may be leveling off. Studies of young women suggest that about 1% to 1.5% develop anorexia nervosa (Walters & Kendler, 1995) and about 2% to 3% develop bulimia nervosa (Hoek et al., 1995). These figures may seem small, but they mean that millions of young women are wrestling with serious eating problems.

Etiology of Eating Disorders

Like other types of psychological disorders, eating disorders are caused by multiple determinants that work interactively. Figure 15.19 on the next page provides an overview of the factors that contribute to the emergence of anorexia nervosa and bulimia nervosa.

GENETIC VULNERABILITY

The evidence is not nearly as strong or complete as it is for many other types of psychopathology (such as anxiety, mood, and schizophrenic disorders), but some people may inherit a genetic vulnerability to eating disorders. Studies show that relatives of patients with eating disorders have elevated rates of anorexia nervosa and bulimia nervosa (Strober, 1995). And studies of female twins report higher concordance rates for identical twins than fraternal twins, suggesting that a genetic predisposition may be at work (Kendler et al., 1991; Walters & Kendler, 1995).

PERSONALITY FACTORS

Strober (1995) has suggested that genetic factors may exert their influence indirectly by fostering certain personality traits that make people more vulnerable to eating disorders. Although there are innumerable exceptions, victims of anorexia nervosa tend to be

obsessive, rigid, neurotic, and emotionally restrained, whereas victims of bulimia nervosa tend to be impulsive, overly sensitive, and low in self-esteem (Wonderlich, 1995). Most of these personality traits *are* influenced by genetics, making Strober's hypothesis plausible. Nonetheless, personality-based explanations of eating disorders remain speculative.

CULTURAL VALUES

The contribution of cultural values to the increased prevalence of eating disorders can hardly be overestimated (Abramson & Valene, 1991; Striegel-Moore, 1995). In Western society, young women are socialized to believe that they must be attractive, and to be attractive they must be thin. Women's magazines are filled with articles on dieting and exercise. The actresses and fashion models who dominate the media and serve as role models for millions of women tend to be remarkably slender. As Figure 15.20 on page 461 shows, the increased premium on being thin is reflected in statistics on Miss America contestants and Playboy centerfolds, whose average weight declined gradually between 1959 and 1988 (Garner et al., 1980; Wiseman et al., 1992). Thanks to this cultural milieu, the vast majority of young women are dissatisfied with their weight and feel that they need to diet (Hunicutt & Newman, 1993). Unfortunately, in a small portion of these women, the pressure to be thin, in combination with genetic vulnerability, family pathology, and other factors, leads to unhealthy efforts to control weight.

THE ROLE OF THE FAMILY

Quite a number of theorists emphasize how family dynamics often contribute to the development of anorexia nervosa and bulimia nervosa in young women

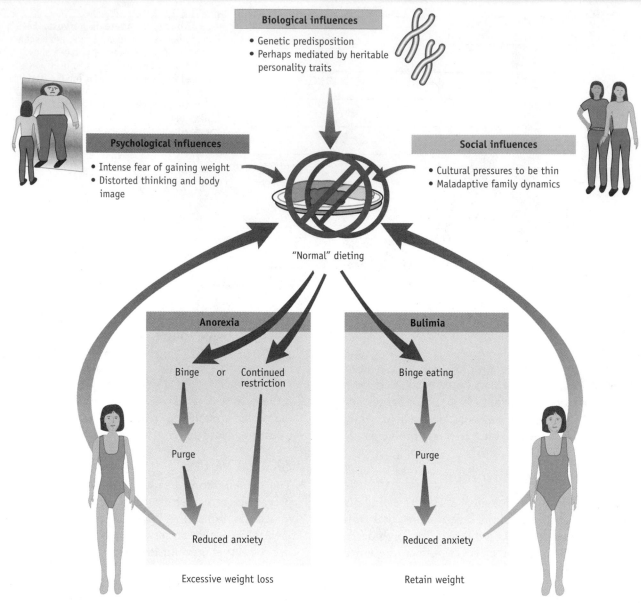

Biological influences
- Genetic predisposition
- Perhaps mediated by heritable personality traits

Psychological influences
- Intense fear of gaining weight
- Distorted thinking and body image

Social influences
- Cultural pressures to be thin
- Maladaptive family dynamics

"Normal" dieting

Anorexia

Binge   or   Continued restriction

Purge

Reduced anxiety

Excessive weight loss

Bulimia

Binge eating

Purge

Reduced anxiety

Retain weight

FIGURE 15.19.

The etiology of eating disorders. The causes of eating disorders are complex and multifaceted. Psychological, biological, and social factors often lead people into "normal" dieting, which sometimes spins out of control. Maladaptive weight control efforts temporarily relieve individuals' pathological fear of gaining weight, but this reduced anxiety has a tremendous cost, as anorexia nervosa and bulimia nervosa are dangerous illnesses. (Adapted from Barlow & Durand, 1999)

(Eisler, 1995). Some theorists suggest that parents who are overly involved in their children's lives turn the normal adolescent push for independence into an unhealthy struggle (Minuchin, Rosman, & Baker, 1978). Needing to assert their autonomy, some adolescent girls seek extreme control over their body, leading to pathological patterns of eating (Bruch, 1978). Other theorists argue that parents of adolescents with eating disorders tend to define their children's needs for them instead of allowing them to define their own needs, thus making the youngsters insensitive to their internal needs (Bruch, 1973; Steiner et al., 1991). In contrast, Pike and Rodin (1991) maintain that some mothers contribute to eating disorders simply by endorsing society's message that "you can never be too thin" and by modeling unhealthy dieting behaviors of their own. Although more research is needed to better understand the role of family dynamics in eating pathology, it appears that families can contribute to eating disorders in a variety of ways.

COGNITIVE FACTORS

Cognitive theorists emphasize the role of disturbed thinking in the etiology of eating disorders (Butow, Beumont, & Touyz, 1993; de Silva, 1995). For example, anorexic patients' typical belief that they are fat when

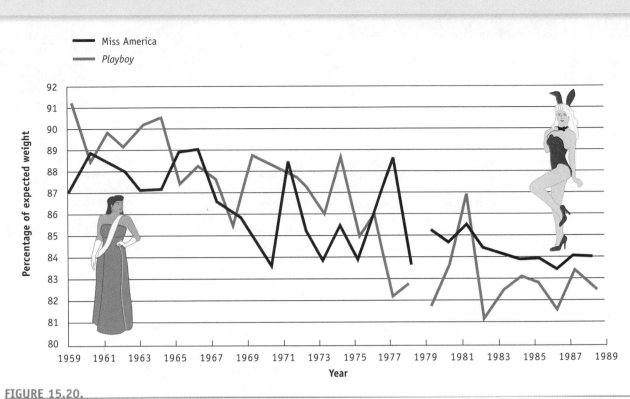

FIGURE 15.20.

Weight trends among *Playboy* centerfolds and Miss America contestants. This graph charts how the average weight of *Playboy* centerfolds and Miss America contestants changed over the course of 30 years (from 1959 to 1989). To control for age and height, each woman's weight was compared to the average weight for a woman of her age and height and expressed as a percentage of the expected weight. Given the small samples, the figures are a little erratic, but overall, the data show a clear downward trend. (Data from Garner et al., 1980; Wiseman et al., 1992; graphic from Barlow & Durand, 1999)

they are really wasting away is a dramatic illustration of how thinking goes awry. Patients with eating disorders display rigid, all-or-none thinking and many maladaptive beliefs, such as "I must be thin to be accepted," "If I am not in complete control, I will lose all control," and "If I gain one pound, I'll go on to gain enormous weight." Additional research is needed to determine whether distorted thinking is a *cause* or merely a *symptom* of eating disorders.

THE ROLE OF DIETING

People who develop eating disorders typically start with relatively "normal" *dieting* efforts that gradually escalate into abnormal weight-control measures (Polivy & Herman, 1995). Thus, a history of dieting is viewed as a risk factor for eating disorders. Indeed, some theorists have argued that eating disorders ought to be thought of as dieting disorders (Beumont, Garner, & Touyz, 1994). The pivotal role of dieting was apparent in one study of adolescent girls, which found that dieters were eight times more likely to develop an eating disorder over the course of the next year than non-dieters were

(Patton et al., 1990). Of course, the vast majority of young women who diet do *not* go on to develop eating disorders, so dieting is only important in conjuction with other factors, such as vulnerability and stress (Z. Cooper, 1995; Wilson, 1995).

Course and Outcome

Virtually all of the psychotherapies that we will discuss in the next chapter—such as insight therapy, group therapy, behavior therapy, and drug therapy—have been used in the treatment of eating disorders. How successful are these therapeutic interventions for eating disorders? The picture is mixed. About 40%–50% of patients experience a full recovery, while treatment is largely a failure for about 20%–25% of patients (Hsu, 1995; Steinhausen, 1995). The remaining patients fall somewhere in between, experiencing modest improvement along with continued struggles. The prognosis is somewhat better for bulimia nervosa than for anorexia nervosa.

Key Ideas

ABNORMAL BEHAVIOR: MYTHS, REALITIES, AND CONTROVERSIES

● The medical model assumes that it is useful to view abnormal behavior as a disease. There are serious problems with the medical model, but the disease analogy is useful if one remembers that it is only an analogy. Three criteria are used in deciding whether people suffer from psychological disorders: deviance, personal distress, and maladaptive behavior. Often, it is difficult to draw a clean line between normality and abnormality.

● DSM-IV is the official psychodiagnostic classification system in the United States. This system describes over 200 disorders and asks for information about patients on five axes. Psychological disorders are more common than widely believed, affecting roughly one-third of the population.

ANXIETY DISORDERS

● The anxiety disorders include generalized anxiety disorder, phobic disorder, panic disorder, and obsessive-compulsive disorder. These disorders have been linked to genetic predisposition, temperament, anxiety sensitivity, and neurochemical abnormalities in the brain.

● Many anxiety responses, especially phobias, may be caused by classical conditioning and maintained by operant conditioning. Cognitive theorists maintain that some people are vulnerable to anxiety disorders because they see threat everywhere. The personality trait of neuroticism and encounters with stress may also contribute to the onset of these disorders.

SOMATOFORM DISORDERS

● Somatoform disorders include somatization disorder, conversion disorder, and hypochondriasis. These disorders often emerge in people with highly suggestible, histrionic personalities. Somatoform disorders may be learned avoidance strategies reinforced by attention and sympathy.

DISSOCIATIVE DISORDERS

● Dissociative disorders include dissociative amnesia, dissociative fugue, and multiple-personality (dissociative identity) disorder. These disorders appear to be uncommon, although there is some controversy about the prevalence of multiple-personality disorder. Stress and childhood trauma may contribute to multiple-personality disorder, but overall, the causes of dissociative disorders are not well understood.

MOOD DISORDERS

● The principal mood disorders are major (unipolar) depression and bipolar disorder. People vary in their genetic vulnerability to mood disorders, which are accompanied by changes in neurochemical activity in the brain. Cognitive models posit that an attributional style emphasizing internal, stable, and global attributions contributes to depression.

● Rumination may also foster depression, but cognitive models have difficulty sorting out cause and effect. Depression is often rooted in interpersonal inadequacies, since people who lack social finesse often have difficulty acquiring life's reinforcers. Mood disorders are sometimes stress related.

SCHIZOPHRENIC DISORDERS

● Schizophrenic disorders are characterized by deterioration of adaptive behavior, irrational thought, distorted perception, and disturbed mood. Schizophrenic disorders are classified as paranoid, catatonic, disorganized, or undifferentiated. The distinction between positive and negative symptoms has proven useful, but it has not yielded an effective new classification scheme.

● Research has linked schizophrenia to genetic vulnerability, changes in neurotransmitter activity, and enlarged ventricles in the brain. Precipitating stress and communication deviance may also contribute to the emergence of schizophrenia. Patients who return to homes high in expressed emotion tend to have elevated relapse rates.

APPLICATION: UNDERSTANDING EATING DISORDERS

● The principal eating disorders are anorexia nervosa and bulimia nervosa. Both reflect a morbid fear of gaining weight. Anorexia and bulimia are both associated with other psychopathology, and both lead to a cascade of medical problems. Easting disorders appear to be a product of modern, affluent, Westernized culture.

● Females account for 90%–95% of eating disorders. The typical age of onset is roughly 15 to 20. There appears to be a genetic vulnerability to eating disorders, which may be mediated by heritable personality traits. Cultural pressures on young women to be thin clearly help foster eating disorders. Some theorists emphasize how family dynamics, disturbed thinking, and "normal" dieting can contribute to the development of eating disorders.

Key Terms

Agoraphobia
Anorexia nervosa
Anxiety disorders
Attributions
Bipolar disorder
Bulimia nervosa
Catatonic schizophrenia
Concordance rate
Conversion disorder
Delusions
Depressive disorder
Diagnosis
Disorganized schizophrenia
Dissociative amnesia

Dissociative disorders
Dissociative fugue
Dissociative identity disorder
Eating disorders
Epidemiology
Etiology
Generalized anxiety disorder
Hallucinations
Hypochondriasis
Medical model
Mood disorders
Multiple-personality disorder
Neurotransmitters

Obsessive-compulsive disorder
Panic disorder
Paranoid schizophrenia
Phobic disorder
Prevalence
Prognosis
Psychosomatic diseases
Schizophrenic disorders
Somatization disorder
Somatoform disorders
Transvestism
Undifferentiated schizophrenia

Key People

Nancy Andreasen
Susan Nolen-Hoeksema
David Rosenhan

Martin Seligman
Thomas Szasz

Practice Test

1. A term referring to the apparent causation and developmental history of an illness is:
   a. prognosis.
   b. etiology.
   c. chronology.
   d. concordance.

2. Although Sue always feels high levels of dread, worry, and anxiety, she still meets her daily responsibilities. Sue's behavior:
   a. should not be considered abnormal, since her adaptive functioning is not impaired.
   b. should not be considered abnormal, since everyone sometimes experiences worry and anxiety.
   c. can still be considered abnormal, since she feels great personal distress.
   d. both a and b.

3. Recent epidemiological studies, which have included drug-related disorders, have found psychological disorders in about _____ of the population.
   a. one-fifth
   b. one-fourth
   c. one-third
   d. one-half

4. People who repeatedly perform senseless rituals to overcome their anxiety are said to have a(n):
   a. generalized anxiety disorder.
   b. obsessive-compulsive disorder.
   c. manic disorder.
   d. phobic disorder.

5. If a woman has a paralyzed arm for which no organic basis can be found, she probably has:
   a. a conversion disorder.
   b. paralytic hypochondriasis.
   c. a dissociative disorder.
   d. a schizophrenic disorder.

6. Which of the following is a mood disorder?
   a. Schizophrenia
   b. Phobic disorder
   c. Bipolar disorder
   d. All of the above

7. A concordance rate indicates:
   a. the percentage of twin pairs or other close relatives that exhibit the same disorder.
   b. the percentage of people with a given disorder that are currently receiving treatment.
   c. the prevalence of a given disorder in the general population.
   d. the rate of cure for a given disorder.

8. Delusions of grandeur and persecution are features that characterize the _____ subtype of schizophrenia.
   a. catatonic
   b. disorganized
   c. undifferentiated
   d. paranoid

9. The finding that many schizophrenics have difficulty focusing their attention implies that schizophrenia may be caused by:
   a. neurological defects.
   b. exposure to deviant communication patterns.
   c. a specific recessive gene.
   d. traumatic childhood experiences.

10. About _____ of patients with eating disorders are female.
    a. 40%
    b. 50%–60%
    c. 75%
    d. 90%–95%

Answers

1. b   page 432
2. c   pages 432–433
3. c   page 436
4. b   pages 438–439
5. a   page 442
6. c   pages 445–447
7. a   pages 447–448
8. d   page 452
9. a   pages 454–456
10. d   page 458

INFOTRAC COLLEGE EDITION

Go to the Wadsworth Psychology Study Center (http://psychology.wadsworth.com/) for quiz questions, research updates, hot topics, interactive exercises, and suggested readings in INFOTRAC related to this chapter.

CHAPTER 16

Psychotherapy

What do you picture when you hear the term *psychotherapy*? If you're like most people, you probably envision a troubled patient lying on a couch in a therapist's office, with the therapist asking penetrating questions and providing sage advice. Typically, people believe that psychotherapy is only for those who are "sick" and that therapists have special powers that allow them to "see through" their clients. It is also widely believed that therapy requires years of deep probing into a client's innermost secrets. Many people further assume that therapists routinely tell their patients how to lead their lives. Like most stereotypes, this picture of psychotherapy is a mixture of fact and fiction, as you'll see in the upcoming pages.

In this chapter, we'll take a down-to-earth look at the complex process of psychotherapy. We'll start by discussing some general questions about the provision of therapy. Who seeks therapy? What kinds of professionals provide therapy? How many different types of therapy are there? After we've considered these general issues, we'll examine some of the more widely used approaches to psychotherapy, analyzing their goals, techniques, and effectiveness. In the Application at the end of the chapter, we focus on practical issues in case you ever have to advise someone about seeking psychotherapy.

The Elements of Psychotherapy: Treatments, Clients, and Therapists

LEARNING OBJECTIVES

- *Identify the three major categories of therapy.*
- *Discuss why people do or do not seek psychotherapy.*
- *Describe the various types of mental health professionals involved in the provision of therapy.*

Today people have a bewildering array of approaches to psychotherapy to choose from. In fact, the immense diversity of therapeutic treatments makes it difficult to define the concept of *psychotherapy*. After organizing an unprecedented conference that brought together many of the world's leading authorities on psychotherapy, Jeffrey Zeig (1982) commented, "I do not believe there is any capsule definition of psychotherapy on which

the 26 presenters could agree" (p. xix). In lieu of a definition, we can identify a few basic elements that the various approaches to therapy have in common. All psychotherapies involve a helping relationship (the treatment) between a professional with special training (the therapist) and another person in need of help (the client). As we look at each of these three elements, you'll see the diverse nature of modern psychotherapy.

Treatments: How Many Types Are There?

In their efforts to help people, psychotherapists use many methods of treatment, including discussion, emotional support, persuasion, conditioning procedures, relaxation training, role playing, prescription of drugs, biofeedback, and group therapy. Some therapists also use a variety of less conventional procedures, such as rebirthing, poetry therapy, and primal therapy. No one knows exactly how many approaches to treatment there are. One expert (Kazdin, 1994) estimates that there may be over 400 distinct types of psychotherapy! Fortunately, we can impose some order on this chaos. As varied as therapists' procedures are, approaches to treatment can be classified into three major categories:

1. *Insight therapies.* Insight therapy is "talk therapy" in the tradition of Freud's psychoanalysis. This is probably the approach to treatment that you envision when you think of psychotherapy. In insight therapies, clients engage in complex, often lengthy verbal interactions with their therapists. The goal in these discussions is to pursue increased insight regarding the nature of the client's difficulties and to sort through possible solutions. Insight therapy can be conducted with an individual or with a group.

2. *Behavior therapies.* Behavior therapies are based on the principles of learning and conditioning, which were introduced in Chapter 2. Instead of emphasizing personal insights, behavior therapists make direct efforts to alter problematic responses (phobic behaviors, for instance) and maladaptive habits (drug use, for instance). Behavior therapists work on changing clients' overt behaviors. They use different procedures for different kinds of problems. Most of their procedures involve either classical conditioning or operant conditioning.

3. *Biomedical therapies.* Biomedical approaches to therapy involve interventions into a person's biological functioning. The most widely used procedures are prescription of drugs and electroconvulsive therapy. As the name bio*medical* therapies suggests, these treatments have traditionally been provided only by physicians with a medical degree (usually psychiatrists). This situation may change, however, as psychologists have begun to campaign for prescription privileges (DeLeon & Wiggins, 1996; Pachman, 1996). They have made some progress toward this goal, even though many psychologists have argued against pursuing the right to prescribe medication (DeNelsky, 1996; Hayes & Heiby, 1996).

In this chapter we examine approaches to therapy that fall into each of these three categories. Although different methods are used in each, the three major classes of treatment are not entirely incompatible. For example, a client being seen in insight therapy may also be given medication.

Clients: Who Seeks Therapy?

In the therapeutic triad (treatments, therapists, clients), the greatest diversity is seen among the clients. They bring to therapy the full range of human problems: anxiety, depression, unsatisfactory interpersonal relations, troublesome habits, poor self-control, low self-esteem, marital conflicts, self-doubt, a sense of emptiness, and feelings of personal stagnation. Therapy is sought by people who feel troubled, but the nature and severity of the trouble varies greatly from one person to another. The two most common presenting problems are excessive anxiety and depression (Narrow et al., 1993). Interestingly, people often delay for many years before finally seeking treatment for their psychological disorders (Kessler, Olfson, & Berglund, 1998).

A client in treatment does *not* necessarily have an identifiable psychological disorder. Some people seek professional help for everyday problems (career decisions, for instance) or vague feelings of discontent (Strupp, 1996). Thus, therapy includes efforts to foster clients' personal growth as well as to provide professional interventions for mental disorders.

People vary in their willingness to seek psychotherapy. As you can see in Figure 16.1, women are more likey than men to receive therapy. Treatment is also more likely when people have medical insurance and when they have more education (Olfson & Pincus, 1996). *Unfortunately, it appears that many people who need therapy don't receive it* (Pekarik, 1993). As Figure 16.2 shows for specific types of disorders, only a portion of the people who need treatment receive it (Regier et al., 1993). People who could benefit from therapy do not seek it for a variety of reasons. Some are unaware of its availability, and some believe that it is always expensive. The biggest roadblock is that many people equate being in therapy with admitting personal weakness.

Therapists: Who Provides Professional Treatment?

Friends and relatives may provide excellent advice about personal problems, but their assistance does not qualify as therapy. Psychotherapy refers to *professional* treatment by someone with special training. However, a common source of confusion about psychotherapy is the variety of "helping professions" available to offer assistance. Psychology and psychiatry are the principal professions involved in psychotherapy, providing the lion's share of mental health care (see Figure 16.3 on page 468). However, therapy is also provided by psychiatric social workers, psychiatric nurses, and counselors, as outlined in Figure 16.4.

PSYCHOLOGISTS

Two types of psychologists may provide therapy, although the distinction between them is more theoretical than real. *Clinical psychologists* and *counseling psychologists* specialize in the diagnosis and treatment of psychological disorders and everyday behavioral problems. In theory, the training of clinical psychologists emphasizes treatment of full-fledged disorders, whereas the training of counseling psychologists is slanted toward treatment of everyday

● Recommended Reading

The Psychotherapy Maze by Otto Ehrenberg and Miriam Ehrenberg (Aronson, 1994)

This book is billed as a "consumer's guide to the ins and outs of therapy." The Ehrenbergs provide a frank, down-to-earth discussion of practical issues relating to psychotherapy. Most books on therapy are devoted to explaining various theoretical approaches. The Ehrenbergs go far beyond that in their book. They tackle practical issues such as how to select a therapist, how to help make therapy work for you, and how to judge whether therapy is doing you any good. They also discuss mundane but important details such as fees, insurance, missed sessions, and emergency phone calls. The Ehrenbergs' goal is to make therapy less intimidating and mysterious. They succeed handsomely in this endeavor.

Even without the cultural barriers, it's not easy to get started in psychotherapy. To begin with, there is the uncertainty about how to go about doing it: how do you pick a therapist, what do you say when you go to one, and what do you have to do once you're in therapy? If you are thinking of therapy for yourself, you probably feel anxious about starting off on a new experience in which a lot is at stake and the outcome is uncertain. You are not sure what is going to happen to you and how you are going to take to it. You might be worried about what other people are going to think of you. On top of all this, you have to overcome a certain amount of lethargy. Getting started means putting in time and effort, it means planning and committing yourself to a new routine, and it usually means having to make financial sacrifices. [p. 26]

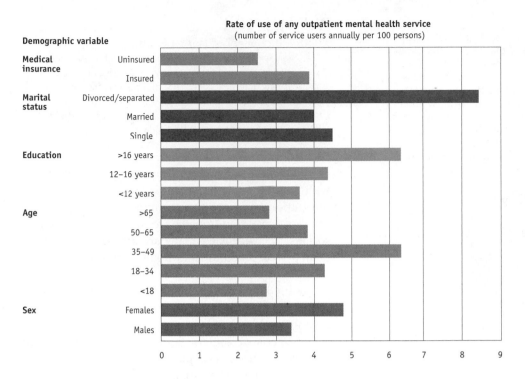

Rate of use of any outpatient mental health service
(number of service users annually per 100 persons)

Demographic variable

Medical insurance: Uninsured, Insured

Marital status: Divorced/separated, Married, Single

Education: >16 years, 12–16 years, <12 years

Age: >65, 50–65, 35–49, 18–34, <18

Sex: Females, Males

FIGURE 16.1.

Therapy utilization rates.
Olfson and Pincus (1996) gathered data on the use of non-hospital outpatient mental health services in the United States in relation to various demographic variables. As you can see, people are more likely to enter therapy if they have medical insurance than if they do not. In regard to marital status, utilization rates are particularly high among those who are divorced or separated. The use of therapy is greater among those who have more education and, when it comes to age, utilization peaks in the 35–49 age bracket. Finally, females are more likely to pursue therapy than males are.

adjustment problems in normal people. In practice, however, there is great overlap between clinical and counseling psychologists in training, in skills, and in the clientele they serve.

Both types of psychologists must earn a doctoral degree (Ph.D., Psy.D., or Ed.D.). A doctorate in psychology requires five to seven years of training beyond a bachelor's degree. The process of gaining admission to a Ph.D. program in clinical psychology is highly competitive (about as competitive as for medical school). Psychologists receive most of their training on university campuses, although they also serve a one- to two-year internship in a clinical setting, such as a hospital.

In providing therapy, psychologists use either insight or behavioral approaches. In comparison to psychiatrists, they are more likely to use behavioral techniques and less likely to use psychoanalytic methods. Clinical and counseling psychologists do psychological testing as well as psychotherapy, and many also conduct research.

PSYCHIATRISTS

Psychiatrists **are physicians who specialize in the treatment of psychological disorders.** Many psychiatrists also treat everyday behavioral problems. However, in comparison to psychologists, psychiatrists devote more time to relatively severe disorders (schizophrenia, mood disorders) and less time to everyday marital, family, job, and school problems. Psychiatrists have an M.D. degree. Their graduate training requires four years of course work in medical school and a four-year apprenticeship in a residency at an approved hospital. Their psychotherapy training occurs during their residency, since the required course work in medical school is essentially the same for all students, whether they are going into surgery, pediatrics, or psychiatry.

In their provision of therapy, psychiatrists tend to emphasize biomedical treatments that have historically been their exclusive province (drug therapy, for instance). Psychiatrists use a variety of insight therapies, but psychoanalysis and its descendants remain

FIGURE 16.2.

The likelihood of treatment among people with various disorders. Not everyone who has a psychological disorder receives professional treatment. This graph shows the percentage of people with specific disorders who obtained mental health treatment during a one-year period. As you can see, for most types of disorders only a minority of afflicted people receive treatment. (Data based on Regier et al., 1993)

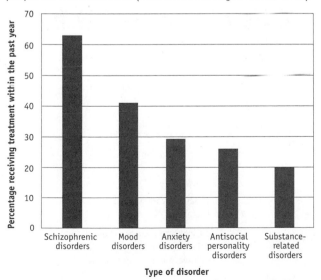

FIGURE 16.3.

Who people see for therapy. Based on a national survey, Olfson and Pincus (1994) estimated that in 1987 Americans made 79.5 million outpatient psychotherapy visits. Information on the therapist's profession was missing for 11% of these visits. The pie chart shows how the remaining visits were distributed among psychologists, psychiatrists, other mental health professionals (social workers, counselors, and such) and general medical professionals (typically physicians specializing in family practice, internal medicine, or pediatrics). As you can see, psychologists and psychiatrists account for about 62% of outpatient treatment.

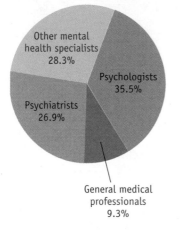

Online Dictionary of Mental Health
This thematically arranged "dictionary" assembles diverse links related to many forms of psychotherapy, the treatment of psychological disorders, and general issues of mental health. It is sponsored by the Centre for Psychotherapeutic Studies at the University of Sheffield's Medical School in the United Kingdom.

generally have a master's degree and typically work with patients and their families to ease the patient's integration back into the community. Although social workers have traditionally worked in hospitals and social service agencies, many are licensed as independent, private practitioners who provide a wide range of therapeutic services.

Many kinds of *counselors* also provide therapeutic services. Counselors are usually found working in schools, colleges, and human service agencies (youth centers, geriatric centers, family planning centers, and so forth). Counselors typically have a master's degree. They often specialize in particular types of problems, such as vocational counseling, marital counseling, rehabilitation counseling, and drug counseling.

Although there are clear differences among the helping professions in education and training, their roles in the treatment process overlap considerably. In this chapter, we will refer to psychologists or psychiatrists as needed, but otherwise we'll use the terms clinician, *therapist*, and *mental health professional* to refer to psychotherapists of all kinds, regardless of their professional degree.

Now that we have discussed the basic elements in psychotherapy, we can examine specific approaches to treatment in terms of their goals, procedures, and effectiveness. We'll begin with a few representative insight therapies.

dominant. In comparison to psychologists, psychiatrists are less likely to use group therapies or behavior therapies.

OTHER MENTAL HEALTH PROFESSIONALS

Several other mental health professions provide psychotherapy services. In hospitals and other institutions, psychiatric social workers and psychiatric nurses often work as part of a treatment team with a psychologist or psychiatrist. Psychiatric nurses, who may have a bachelor's or master's degree in their field, play a large role in hospital inpatient treatment. Psychiatric social workers

FIGURE 16.4.

The principal mental health professions. Psychotherapists come from a variety of professional backgrounds. This chart provides an overview of various types of therapists' education and typical professional activities.

Types of Therapists

Title	Degree	Years beyond bachelor's degree	Typical roles and activities
Clinical or counseling psychologist	Ph.D. Psy.D. Ed.D.	5–7	Diagnosis, psychological testing, insight and behavior therapy
Psychiatrist	M.D.	8	Diagnosis; insight, behavior, and biomedical therapy
Social worker	M.S.W.	2	Insight and behavior therapy, family therapy, helping patients return to the community
Psychiatric nurse	B.S., B.A., M.A.	0–2	Inpatient care, insight and behavior therapy
Counselor	M.A., M.S.	2	Insight and behavior therapy, working primarily with everyday adjustment and marital and career issues

Insight Therapies

Many schools of thought exist as to how to do insight therapy. Therapists with different theoretical orientations use different methods to pursue different kinds of insights. What these varied approaches have in common is that *insight therapies involve verbal interactions intended to enhance clients' self-knowledge and thus promote healthful changes in personality and behavior.* Although there may be hundreds of insight therapies, the leading eight or ten approaches appear to account for the lion's share of treatment. In this section, we'll delve into psychoanalysis, client-centered therapy, and cognitive therapy. We'll also discuss how insight therapy can be done with groups as well as individuals.

Psychoanalysis

Sigmund Freud worked as a psychotherapist for almost 50 years in Vienna. Through a painstaking process of trial and error, he developed innovative techniques for the treatment of psychological disorders and distress. His system of *psychoanalysis* came to dominate psychiatry for many decades. Although the dominance of psychoanalysis has eroded in recent decades (Reiser, 1989), a diverse array of psychoanalytic approaches to therapy continue to evolve and to remain influential today (Eagle & Wolitzky, 1992).

Sigmund Freud

Psychoanalysis is an insight therapy that emphasizes the recovery of unconscious conflicts, motives, and defenses through techniques such as free association, dream analysis, and transference. To appreciate the logic of psychoanalysis, we have to look at Freud's thinking about the roots of mental disorders. Freud treated mostly anxiety-dominated disturbances, such as phobic, panic, obsessive-compulsive, and conversion disorders, which were then called *neuroses.* He believed that neurotic problems are caused by unconscious conflicts left over from early childhood. As explained in Chapter 2, he thought that these inner conflicts involve battles among the id, ego, and superego, usually over sexual and aggressive impulses. Freud theorized that people depend on defense mechanisms to avoid confronting these conflicts, which remain hidden in the depths of the unconscious. However, he noted that defensive maneuvers often lead to self-defeating behavior. Furthermore, he asserted that defenses tend to be only partially successful in alleviating anxiety, guilt, and other distressing emotions. With this model in mind, let's take a look at the therapeutic procedures used in psychoanalysis.

PROBING THE UNCONSCIOUS

Given Freud's assumptions, we can see that the logic of psychoanalysis is very simple. The analyst attempts to probe the murky depths of the unconscious to discover the unresolved conflicts causing the client's neurotic behavior. In a sense, the analyst functions as a psychological detective. In this effort to explore the unconscious, the therapist relies on two techniques: free association and dream analysis.

In *free association,* clients spontaneously express their thoughts and feelings exactly as they occur, with as little censorship as possible. Clients lie on a couch so they will be better able to let their minds drift freely. In free associating, clients expound on anything that comes to mind, regardless of how trivial, silly, or embarrassing it might be. Gradually, most clients begin to let everything pour out without conscious censorship. The analyst studies these free associations for clues about what is going on in the unconscious.

In *dream analysis,* the therapist interprets the symbolic meaning of the client's dreams. For Freud, dreams were the "royal road to the unconscious," the most direct means of access to patients' innermost conflicts, wishes, and impulses. Clients are encouraged and trained to remember their dreams, which they describe in therapy. The therapist then analyzes the symbolism in these dreams to interpret their meaning.

To better illustrate these matters, let's look at an actual case treated through psychoanalysis (adapted from Greenson, 1967, pp. 40–41). Mr. N was troubled by an unsatisfactory marriage. He claimed to love his wife, but he preferred sexual relations with prostitutes. Mr. N reported that his parents also endured lifelong marital difficulties. His childhood conflicts about their relationship appeared to be related to his problems. Both dream analysis and free association can be seen in the following description of a session in Mr. N's treatment:

In psychoanalysis, the therapist encourages the client to reveal thoughts, feelings, dreams, and memories which can then be interpreted in relation to the client's current problems.

Mr. N reports a fragment of a dream. All that he can remember is that he is waiting for a red traffic light to change when he feels that someone has bumped into him from behind. . . . The associations led to Mr. N's love of cars, especially sports cars. He loved the sensation, in particular, of whizzing by those fat, old, expensive cars. . . . His father always hinted that he had been a great athlete, but he never substantiated it. . . . Mr. N doubted whether his father could really perform. His father would flirt with a waitress in a cafe or make sexual remarks about women passing by, but he seemed to be showing off. If he were really sexual, he wouldn't resort to that.

As is characteristic of free association, Mr. N's train of thought meanders about with little direction. Nonetheless, clues about his unconscious conflicts are apparent. What did Mr. N's therapist extract from this session? The therapist saw sexual overtones in the dream fragment, where Mr. N was bumped from behind. The therapist also inferred that Mr. N had a competitive orientation toward his father, based on the free association about whizzing by fat, old, expensive cars. As you can see, analysts must *interpret* their clients' dreams and free associations. This is a critical process throughout psychoanalysis.

INTERPRETATION

Interpretation **involves the therapist's attempts to explain the inner significance of the client's thoughts, feelings, memories, and behaviors.** Contrary to popular belief, analysts do not interpret everything, and they generally don't try to dazzle clients with startling revelations. Instead, analysts move forward inch by inch, offering interpretations that should be just out of the client's own reach. Mr. N's therapist eventually offered the following interpretations to his client:

I said to Mr. N near the end of the hour that I felt he was struggling with his feelings about his father's sexual life. He seemed to be saying that his father was sexually not a very potent man. . . . He also recalls that he once found a packet of condoms under his father's pillow when he was an adolescent and he thought "My father must be going to prostitutes." I then intervened and pointed out that the condoms under his father's pillow seemed to indicate more obviously that his father used the condoms with his mother, who slept in the same bed. However, Mr. N wanted to believe his wish-fulfilling fantasy: mother doesn't want sex with father and father is not very potent. The patient was silent and the hour ended.

As you may already have guessed, the therapist has concluded that Mr. N's difficulties are rooted in an Oedipal complex (see Chapter 2). Mr. N has unresolved sexual feelings toward his mother and hostile feelings about his father. These unconscious conflicts, which are rooted in his childhood, are distorting his intimate relations as an adult.

RESISTANCE

How would you expect Mr. N to respond to his therapist's suggestion that he was in competition with his father for the sexual attention of his mother? Obviously, most clients would have great difficulty accepting such an interpretation. Freud fully expected clients to display some resistance to therapeutic efforts. *Resistance* **involves largely unconscious defensive maneuvers intended to hinder the progress of therapy.** Why do clients try to resist the helping process? Because they don't want to face up to the painful, disturbing conflicts that they have buried in their unconscious. Although they have sought help, they are reluctant to confront their real problems.

Resistance may take many forms. Patients may show up late for their sessions, merely pretend to engage in free association, or express hostility toward the therapist. For instance, Mr. N's therapist noted that after the session just described, "The next day he began by telling me that he was furious with me. . . ." Analysts use a variety of strategies to deal with their clients' resistance. Often, a key consideration is the handling of *transference*, which we consider next.

TRANSFERENCE

Transference **occurs when clients start relating to their therapists in ways that mimic critical relationships in their lives.** Thus, a client might start relating to a therapist as if the therapist were an overprotective mother, rejecting brother, or passive spouse. In a sense, the client *transfers* conflicting feelings about important people onto the therapist. For instance, in his treatment, Mr. N transferred some of the competitive hostility he felt toward his father onto his analyst.

Psychoanalysts often encourage transference such that clients begin to reenact relations with crucial people in the context of therapy. These reenactments can help bring repressed feelings and conflicts to the surface, allowing the client to work through them. The therapist's handling of transference is complicated and difficult because transference may arouse confusing, highly charged emotions in the client.

Undergoing psychoanalysis is not easy. It can be a slow, painful process of self-examination that routinely requires three to five years of hard work. Ultimately, if resistance and transference can be handled effectively, the therapist's interpretations should lead the client to profound insights. For instance, Mr. N eventually admitted, "The old boy is probably right, it does tickle me to imagine that my mother preferred me and I could beat out my father. Later, I wondered whether this had something to do with my own screwed-up sex life with my wife." According to Freud, once clients recognize the unconscious sources of their conflicts, they can resolve these conflicts and discard their neurotic defenses.

Though still available, classical psychoanalysis as done by Freud is not widely practiced anymore. Freud's psychoanalytic method was geared to a particular kind of clientele that he was seeing in Vienna many years ago. As his followers fanned out across Europe and America, many found that it was necessary to adapt psychoanalysis to different cultures, changing times, and new kinds of patients. Thus, many variations on Freud's original approach to psychoanalysis have developed over the years. These descendants of psychoanalysis are collectively known as *psychodynamic approaches* to therapy.

Some of these adaptations, such as those by Carl Jung (1917) and Alfred Adler (1927), were sweeping revisions based on fundamental differences in theory. Other variations, such as those devised by Melanie Klein (1948) and Heinz Kohut (1971), involved more subtle changes in theory. Still other revisions (Alexander, 1954; Stekel, 1950) simply involved efforts to modernize and streamline psychoanalytic techniques (rather than theory), as outlined in Figure 16.5. Hence, today we have a rich diversity of psychodynamic approaches to therapy (Ursano & Silberman, 1994).

Client-Centered Therapy

You may have heard of people going into therapy to "find themselves" or to "get in touch with their real feelings." These now-popular phrases emerged out of the human potential movement, which was stimulated in part by Carl Rogers's work (Rogers, 1951, 1986). Taking a humanistic perspective, Rogers devised *client-centered therapy* (also known as *person-centered therapy*) in the 1940s and 1950s.

Client-centered therapy is an insight therapy that emphasizes providing a supportive emotional climate for clients, who play a major role in determining the pace and direction of their therapy. You may wonder why the troubled, untrained client is put in charge of the pace and direction of the therapy. Rogers (1961) provides a compelling justification:

Carl Rogers

It is the client who knows what hurts, what directions to go, what problems are crucial, what experiences have been deeply buried. It began to occur to me that unless I had a need to demonstrate my own cleverness and learning, I would do better to rely upon the client for the direction of movement in the process. (pp. 11–12)

Rogers's theory about the principal causes of neurotic anxieties is quite different from the Freudian explanation. As discussed in Chapter 2, Rogers maintained that most personal distress is due to inconsistency, or "incongruence," between a person's

FIGURE 16.5.
Comparing classical and modern psychoanalysis. Contemporary psychoanalytic therapists continue to practice in the tradition established by Freud, but there are a number of differences, as pointed out by Baker (1985). Baker divides contemporary psychodynamic therapies into three subgroups. "Modern psychoanalysis," profiled in the right column, refers to the group that has remained most loyal to Freud's ideas while modifying clinical techniques.

Some Differences Between Classical and Modern Psychoanalysis

Classical psychoanalysis	Modern psychoanalysis
Frequency of treatment is usually four to five times per week.	Frequency of treatment is typically one to two times per week.
Patient is treated "on the couch."	Patient is typically seen "face to face."
Treatment goals emphasize character reconstruction.	Treatment emphasizes problem resolution, enhanced adaptation, and support of ego functions with limited character change.
Treatment approach emphasizes the neutrality and nonintrusion of the analyst.	Therapist assumes an active and direct stance.
Technique emphasizes "free association," uncovering, interpretation, and analysis of transference and resistance.	A wide range of interventions are used, including interpretive, supportive, and educative techniques. Transference is typically kept less intense.

self-concept and reality. According to his theory, incongruence makes people prone to feel threatened by realistic feedback about themselves from others. For example, if you inaccurately viewed yourself as a hardworking, dependable person, you would feel threatened by contradictory feedback from friends or co-workers. According to Rogers, anxiety about such feedback often leads to reliance on defense mechanisms, distortions of reality, and stifled personal growth. Excessive incongruence is thought to be rooted in clients' overdependence on others for approval and acceptance.

Given Rogers's theory, client-centered therapists stalk insights that are quite different from the repressed conflicts that psychoanalysts try to track down. Client-centered therapists help clients to realize that they do not have to worry constantly about pleasing others and winning acceptance. They encourage clients to respect their own feelings and values. They help people restructure their self-concept to correspond better to reality. Ultimately, they try to foster self-acceptance and personal growth.

THERAPEUTIC CLIMATE

In client-centered therapy, the *process* of therapy is not as important as the emotional *climate* in which the therapy takes place. According to Rogers, it is critical for the therapist to provide a warm, supportive, accepting climate. This creates a safe environment in which clients can confront their shortcomings without feeling threatened. The lack of threat should reduce clients' defensive tendencies and thus help them to open up. To create this atmosphere of emotional support, Rogers believed that client-centered therapists must provide three conditions:

1. *Genuineness.* The therapist must be genuine with the client, communicating in an honest and spontaneous manner. The therapist should not be phony or defensive.

2. *Unconditional positive regard.* The therapist must also show complete, nonjudgmental acceptance of the client as a person. The therapist should provide warmth and caring for the client with no strings attached. This does not mean that the therapist must approve of everything that the client says or does. A therapist can disapprove of a particular behavior while continuing to value the client as a human being.

3. *Empathy.* Finally, the therapist must provide accurate empathy for the client. This means that the therapist must understand the client's world from the client's point of view. Furthermore, the therapist must be articulate enough to communicate this understanding to the client.

Rogers firmly believed that a supportive emotional climate was the major force promoting healthy changes in therapy. However, in recent years some client-centered therapists have begun to place more emphasis on therapeutic process (Rice & Greenberg, 1992).

THERAPEUTIC PROCESS

In client-centered therapy, the client and therapist work together as equals. The therapist provides relatively little guidance and keeps interpretation and advice to a minimum. So, just what does the client-centered therapist do, besides creating a supportive climate? Primarily, the therapist provides feedback to help clients sort out their feelings. The therapist's key task is *clarification.* Client-centered therapists try to function like a human mirror, reflecting statements back to their clients, but with enhanced clarity. They help clients become more aware of their true feelings by highlighting themes that may be obscure in the clients' rambling discourse. The reflective nature of client-centered therapy can be seen in the following exchange between a client and therapist:

CLIENT: *I really feel bad today . . . just terrible.*
THERAPIST: *You're feeling pretty bad.*
CLIENT: *Yeah, I'm angry and that's made me feel bad, especially when I can't do anything about it. I just have to live with it and shut up.*
THERAPIST: *You're very angry and feel like there's nothing you can safely do with your feelings.*
CLIENT: *Uh-huh. I mean . . . if I yell at my wife she gets hurt. If I don't say anything to her I feel tense.*
THERAPIST: *You're between a rock and a hard place—no matter what you do, you'll wind up feeling bad.*
CLIENT: *I mean she chews ice all day and all night. I feel stupid saying this. It's petty, I know. But when I sit there and try to concentrate, I hear all these slurping and crunching noises. I can't stand it . . . and I yell. She feels hurt—I feel bad—like I shouldn't have said anything.*
THERAPIST: *So when you finally say something you feel bad afterward.*
CLIENT: *Yeah, I can't say anything to her without getting mad and saying more than I should. And then I cause more trouble than it's worth. (Duke & Nowicki, 1979, p. 565)*

By working with clients to clarify their feelings, client-centered therapists hope to gradually build toward more far-reaching insights. In particular, they try to help clients become more aware of and comfortable about their genuine selves. Obviously, these are ambitious goals. Client-centered therapy resembles psychoanalysis in that both seek to achieve a major reconstruction of a client's personality. We'll see more limited and specific goals in cognitive therapy, which we consider next.

Cognitive Therapy

In Chapter 3 we saw that people's cognitive interpretations of events make all the difference in the world in how well they handle stress. In Chapter 15 we learned that cognitive factors play a key role in the development of depressive disorders. Citing the importance of findings such as these, two former psychoanalysts—Aaron Beck (1976, 1987) and Albert Ellis (1973, 1989)—independently devised cognitive-oriented therapies that became highly influential (Arnkoff & Glass, 1992). Since we covered the main ideas

Aaron Beck

underlying Ellis's *rational-emotive therapy* in our discussion of coping strategies in Chapter 4, we'll focus on Beck's system of *cognitive therapy* here. **Cognitive therapy is an insight therapy that emphasizes recognizing and changing negative thoughts and maladaptive beliefs.**

In recent years cognitive therapy has been applied fruitfully to a wide range of disorders (Beck, 1991; Hollon & Beck, 1994), but it was originally devised as a treatment for depression. According to Beck, depression is caused by "errors" in thinking (see Figure 16.6). He asserts that depression-prone people tend to (1) blame their setbacks on personal inadequacies without considering circumstantial explanations, (2) focus selectively on negative events while ignoring positive ones, (3) make unduly pessimistic projections about the future, and (4) draw negative conclusions about their worth as persons based on insignificant events. For instance, imagine that you earned a poor score on a minor quiz in a class. If you made the kinds of errors in thinking just described, you might blame the score on your woeful stupidity, dismiss comments from a classmate that it was an unfair test, hysterically predict that you will surely flunk the course, and conclude that you are not genuine college material.

GOALS AND TECHNIQUES

The goal of cognitive therapy is to change the way clients think. To begin, clients are taught to detect their automatic negative thoughts. These are self-defeating statements that people are prone to make when analyzing problems. Examples might include "I'm just not smart enough," "No one really likes me," and "It's all my fault." Clients are then trained to subject these automatic thoughts to reality testing. The therapist helps them to see how unrealistically negative the thoughts are.

The therapist's goal is not to promote unwarranted optimism, but rather to help the client use more reasonable standards of evaluation. For example, a cognitive therapist might point out that a client's failure to get a desired promotion at work may be attributable to many factors and that this setback doesn't mean that the client is incompetent. Gradually, the therapist digs deeper, looking for the unrealistic assumptions that underlie clients' constant negative thinking. These, too, have to be changed.

Unlike client-centered therapists, cognitive therapists are actively involved in determining the pace and direction of treatment. They usually talk extensively in the therapy sessions. They may argue openly with clients as they try to persuade them to alter their patterns of thinking.

KINSHIP WITH BEHAVIOR THERAPY

Cognitive therapy borrows heavily from behavioral approaches to treatment, which we will discuss shortly. Specifically, cognitive therapists often use "homework

Cognitive Errors That Promote Depression	
Cognitive error	**Description**
Overgeneralizing	If it is true in one case, it applies to any case that is even slightly similar.
Selective abstraction	The only events that matter are failures, deprivation, and so on. I should measure myself by errors, weaknesses, etc.
Excessive responsibility (assuming personal causality)	I am responsible for all bad things, failures, and so on.
Assuming temporal causality (predicting without sufficient evidence)	If it has been true in the past, then it is always going to be true.
Self-references	I am the center of everyone's attention, especially when it comes to bad performances or personal attributes.
"Catastrophizing"	Always think of the worst. It is most likely to happen to you.
Dichotomous thinking	Everything is either one extreme or another (black or white; good or bad).

FIGURE 16.6.

Beck's cognitive theory of depression. According to Aaron Beck (1976, 1987), depression is caused by certain patterns of negative thinking. This chart lists some of the particularly damaging cognitive errors that can foster depression. (Adapted from Beck, 1976)

assignments" that focus on changing clients' overt behaviors (Wright & Beck, 1994). Clients may be instructed to engage in overt responses on their own, outside of the clinician's office. For example, one shy, insecure young man in cognitive therapy was told to go to a singles bar and engage three different women in conversations for up to five minutes each (Rush, 1984). He was instructed to record his thoughts before and after each of the conversations. This assignment elicited various maladaptive patterns of thought that gave the young man and his therapist plenty to talk about in subsequent sessions. As this example illustrates, cognitive therapy is a creative blend of "talk therapy" and behavior therapy, although it is primarily an insight therapy.

Cognitive therapy was originally designed as a treatment for individuals. However, it has recently been adapted for use with groups (Covi & Primakoff, 1988). Most insight therapies can be conducted on either an individual or group basis (Kaplan & Sadock, 1993), so let's take a look at the dynamics of group therapy.

Group Therapy

Although it dates back to the early part of the 20th century, group therapy came of age during World War II and its aftermath in the 1950s (Rosenbaum, Lakin, & Roback, 1992). During this period, the expanding demand for therapeutic services forced clinicians to use group techniques (Scheidlinger, 1993). **Group therapy is the simultaneous treatment of several or more clients in a group.** Most major insight therapies have been adapted for use with groups. In fact, the ideas underlying Rogers's client-centered therapy spawned the much-publicized encounter group movement. Although group therapy can be conducted in a variety of ways, we can provide a general overview of the process as it usually unfolds (see Fuchs, 1984; Vinogradov & Yalom, 1994; Yalom, 1995).

PARTICIPANTS' ROLES

A therapy group typically consists of about five to ten participants. The therapist usually screens the participants, excluding anyone who seems likely to be disruptive. Some theorists maintain that judicious selection of participants is crucial to effective group treatment (Salvendy, 1993). There is some debate about whether or not it is best to have a homogeneous group (people who are similar in age, gender, and presenting problem). Practical necessities usually dictate that groups are at least somewhat diversified.

In group treatment, the therapist's responsibilities include selecting participants, setting goals for the group, initiating and maintaining the therapeutic process, and protecting clients from harm (Weiner,

Group therapies have proven particularly helpful when members share similar problems, such as alcoholism, overeating, or depression.

1993). The therapist often plays a relatively subtle role in group therapy, staying in the background and focusing mainly on promoting group cohesiveness. The therapist always retains a special status, but the therapist and clients are on much more equal footing in group therapy than in individual therapy. The leader in group therapy expresses emotions, shares feelings, and copes with challenges from group members. In other words, group therapists participate in the group's exchanges and "bare their own souls" to some extent.

In group therapy, participants essentially function as therapists for one another. Group members describe their problems, trade viewpoints, share experiences, and discuss coping strategies. Most important, they provide acceptance and emotional support for each other. In this supportive atmosphere, group members work at peeling away the social masks that cover their insecurities. Once their problems are exposed, members work at correcting them. As members come to value one another's opinions, they work hard to display healthy changes to win the group's approval.

ADVANTAGES OF THE GROUP EXPERIENCE

Group therapies obviously save time and money, which can be critical in understaffed mental hospitals and other institutional settings. Therapists in private practice usually charge less for group than individual therapy, making therapy affordable for more people. However, group therapy is *not* just a less costly substitute for individual therapy. For many types of patients and problems, group therapy can be just as effective as individual treatment (Piper, 1993). Moreover, group therapy has unique strengths of its own. Irwin Yalom (1995), who has studied group therapy extensively, has described some of these advantages:

1. *In group therapy, participants often come to realize that their misery is not unique.* Clients often enter therapy feeling very sorry for themselves. They think that they alone have a burdensome cross to bear. In the group situation, they quickly see that they are not unique. They are reassured to learn that many other people have similar or even worse problems.

2. *Group therapy provides an opportunity for participants to work on their social skills in a safe environment.* Many personal problems essentially involve difficulties in relating effectively to people. Group therapy can provide a workshop for improving interpersonal skills that cannot be matched by individual therapy.

3. *Certain kinds of problems are especially well suited to group treatment.* Specific types of problems and clients respond especially well to the social support that group therapy can provide. Peer self-help groups illustrate this advantage. In peer self-help groups, people who have a problem in common get together regularly to help one another out. The original peer self-help group was Alcoholics Anonymous. Today, there are similar groups made up of former psychiatric patients, single parents, drug addicts, and so forth.

Whether therapy is conducted on a group or an individual basis, clients usually invest considerable time, effort, and money in insight therapies. Are they worth the investment?

Evaluating Insight Therapies

In 1952, Hans Eysenck shocked mental health professionals by reporting that there was no sound evidence that insight therapy actually helped people. What was the basis for this startling claim? When Eysenck (1952) reviewed numerous studies of therapeutic outcome for clients suffering from neurotic problems, he found that about two-thirds of the clients recovered. A two-thirds recovery rate sounds reasonable, except that Eysenck found a similar recovery rate among *untreated* neurotics. As we noted in Chapter 15, psychological disorders sometimes clear up on their own. **A *spontaneous remission* is a recovery from a disorder that occurs without formal treatment.** Based on his estimate of the

spontaneous remission rate for neurotic disorders, Eysenck concluded that the therapeutic effects of insight therapy are small or nonexistent.

In the ensuing years, critics pounced on Eysenck's article looking for flaws (Jacobson & Christensen, 1996). They found a variety of shortcomings in his data. For instance, Eysenck used different time frames in comparing the recovery rates of treated and untreated neurotics. The two-thirds recovery rate in the untreated groups was based on a *two-year* time period, whereas the two-thirds recovery rate for the treated groups occurred in a *two-month* time frame (Strupp & Howard, 1992). Moreover, the treated and untreated groups were not matched in terms of the severity of their disorders, their attitudes and expectations about therapy, or any other relevant variables that might influence therapeutic outcomes. Eysenck also made many arbitrary judgments about "recoveries" that were consistently favorable to the untreated groups. After taking a close look at Eysenck's data, Bergin (1971) argued that the data really suggested a spontaneous remission rate for neurotic disorders in the vicinity of 30%–40%. Although Eysenck's conclusions were unduly pessimistic, he made an important contribution to the mental health field by sparking debate and research on the effectiveness of insight therapy.

Hans Eysenck

Evaluating the effectiveness of any approach to psychotherapy is a complicated matter (Howard et al., 1996; Roth & Fonagy, 1996). This is especially true for insight therapies. If you were to undergo insight therapy, how would you judge its effectiveness? By how you felt? By looking at your behavior? By asking your therapist? By consulting your friends and family? What would you be looking for? People enter therapy with different problems and needs. Different schools of thought seek to realize entirely different goals. Thus, measures of therapeutic outcome tend to be subjective, with little consensus about the best way to assess therapeutic progress (Lambert & Hill, 1994). Moreover,

Web Link 16.2

The Effectiveness of Psychotherapy: The *Consumer Reports* Study

In 1995, *Consumer Reports* concluded that psychotherapy is indeed effective in the treatment of psychological problems and disorders. Researcher Martin Seligman reviews the methods of the study's authors and compares their approach to other ways of judging psychotherapy's effects.

people enter therapy with diverse problems of varied severity, so the efficacy of treatment can be evaluated meaningfully only for specific clinical problems (Elliott, Stiles, & Shapiro, 1993).

Another problem is that both therapists and clients are biased strongly in the direction of evaluating therapy favorably (Rachman & Wilson, 1980). Why? Therapists want to see improvement because it reflects on their professional competence. Obviously, they hope to see clients getting better as a result of their work. Clients are slanted toward a favorable evaluation because they want to justify their effort, their heartache, their expense, and their time.

In spite of these difficulties, hundreds of therapy outcome studies have been conducted since Eysenck prodded researchers into action. These studies have examined a broad range of specific clinical problems and used diverse methods to assess therapeutic outcomes, including scores on psychological tests and ratings by family members, as well as therapists' and clients' ratings. Although Eysenck (1993) remains skeptical, these studies consistently indicate that insight therapy *is* superior to no treatment or to placebo treatment and that the effects of therapy are reasonably durable (Barlow, 1996; Lambert & Bergin, 1994; Lipsey & Wilson, 1993). In one recent, widely discussed study that focused on patients' self-reports, the vast majority of the respondents subjectively felt that they had derived considerable benefit from their therapy (Seligman, 1995).

Admittedly, this outcome research does not indicate that insight therapy leads to miraculous results. The superiority of therapy over no treatment is usually characterized as modest. Moreover, when professional therapy is compared to paraprofessional interventions (mostly peer self-help groups), the differences in efficacy are often negligible (Christensen & Jacobson, 1994; Lambert & Bergin, 1994). Nonetheless, many studies suggest that insight therapies can be cost-effective interventions (Gabbard et al., 1997).

Therapy and the Recovered Memories Controversy

While debate about the efficacy of insight therapy has simmered for four decades, the 1990s brought an entirely new controversy that has rocked the psychotherapy profession like never before. The subject of this emotionally charged debate is the recent spate of prominent reports involving the recovery of repressed memories of sexual abuse and other childhood trauma through therapeutic techniques that some critics characterize as questionable. In recent years the media have been flooded with stories of people—including some celebrities—who have recovered long-lost recollections

of sexual abuse, typically with the help of their therapists. For example, in 1991 TV star Roseanne Barr suddenly recalled years of abuse by her parents, and a former Miss America remembered having been sexually assaulted by her father (Wielawski, 1991). These recovered memories have led to a rash of lawsuits in which adult plaintiffs have sued their parents, teachers, neighbors, pastors, and so forth for alleged child abuse 20 or 30 years earlier (even the Archbishop of Chicago has been sued, although the suit was soon dropped). For the most part, these parents, teachers, and neighbors have denied the allegations. Many of them have seemed genuinely befuddled by the accusations, which have torn some previously happy families apart. In an effort to make sense of the charges, many accused parents have argued that their children's recollections are false memories created inadvertently by well-intentioned therapists through the power of suggestion.

The crux of the debate is that child abuse usually takes place behind closed doors, and in the absence of corroborative evidence, there isn't any way to reliably distinguish genuine recovered memories from those that are false. Some recovered memories have been substantiated by independent witnesses or belated admissions of guilt from the accused (for example, see Horn, 1993). But in the vast majority of cases, the allegations of abuse have been vehemently denied, and independent corroboration has not been available (Loftus, 1993). Recovered recollections of sexual abuse have become so common, a support group has been formed for people who feel that they have been victimized by "false memory syndrome." Thousands of families have sought help from the False Memory Syndrome Foundation. By 1996, over 800 lawsuits had been filed against therapists who were accused of creating false memories in their patients (Taub, 1996).

Psychologists are sharply divided on the issue of recovered memories, leaving the public understandably confused. Many psychologists, especially therapists in clinical practice, accept most recovered memories at face value (Briere & Conte, 1993; Herman, 1992, 1994; Terr, 1994; Whitfield, 1995). They assert that it is

Web Link 16.3

Narrative Psychology: Therapeutic Recovery of Memory
At this site devoted to narrative and other interpretive approaches to psychology, Professor Vincent Hevern has gathered a balanced set of resources relating to the therapeutic recovery of memories (also called "The Memory Wars"). Both sides of the controversy are represented by extensive bibliographical, video, and Internet-based resources.

common for patients to bury traumatic incidents in their unconscious. Citing new evidence that sexual abuse in childhood is far more widespread than most people realize, they argue that most repressed memories of abuse are probably genuine. They attribute the recent upsurge in reports of recovered memories to therapists' and clients' increased sensitivity to an issue that people used to be reluctant to discuss.

In contrast, many other psychologists, especially memory researchers, have expressed skepticism about the recent flood of recovered memories (Frankel, 1993; Lindsay & Poole, 1995; Loftus, 1993; Lynn & Nash, 1994). These psychologists do not argue that people are lying about their repressed memories. Rather, they maintain that some suggestible, confused people struggling to understand profound personal problems have been convinced by persuasive therapists that their emotional problems must be the result of abuse that occurred years ago. Critics blame a small minority of therapists who presumably have good intentions but operate under the dubious assumption that virtually all psychological problems are attributable to childhood sexual abuse (Lindsay & Read, 1994; Spanos, 1994). Using hypnosis, dream interpretation, and leading questions, they supposedly prod and probe patients until they inadvertently create the memories of abuse that they are searching for. Consistent with this view,

Yapko (1994) reviews evidence that some therapists are (1) overly prone to see signs of abuse where none has occurred, (2) unsophisticated about the extent to which memories can be distorted, and (3) naive about how much their expectations and beliefs can influence their patients' efforts to achieve self-understanding.

Psychologists who doubt the authenticity of repressed memories support their analysis by pointing to discredited cases of recovered memories. For example, with the help of a church counselor, one woman recovered memories of how her minister father repeatedly raped her, got her pregnant, and then aborted the pregnancy with a coat-hanger, but subsequent evidence revealed that the woman was still a virgin and that her father had had a vasectomy years before (Testa, 1996). The skeptics also point to published case histories that clearly involved suggestive questioning and to cases in which patients have recanted recovered memories of sexual abuse (see Figure 16.7 on the next page) after realizing that these memories were implanted by their therapists (Goldstein & Farmer, 1993; Loftus, 1994). Those who question recovered memories also point to several lines of carefully controlled laboratory research that demonstrate that it is not all that difficult to create "memories" of events that never happened (Belli & Loftus, 1994). For example, studies have shown that subtle suggestions made to hypnotized subjects can be

FIGURE 16.7

False memory syndrome.
Recovered memories of sexual abuse are viewed with skepticism in some quarters. One reason is that some people who have recovered previously repressed recollections of childhood abuse have subsequently realized that their "memories" were the product of suggestion. A number of case histories, such as the one summarized here (from Jaroff, 1993) have demonstrated that therapists who relentlessly search for memories of abuse in their patients sometimes create the memories they are seeking.

A Case History of False Memory Syndrome

Suffering from a prolonged bout of depression and desperate for help, Melody Gavigan, 39, a computer specialist from Long Beach, California, checked herself into a local psychiatric hospital. As Gavigan recalls the experience, her problems were just beginning. During five weeks of treatment there, a family and marriage counselor repeatedly suggested that her depression stemmed from incest during her childhood. While at first Gavigan had no recollection of any abuse, the therapist kept prodding. "I was so distressed and needed help so desperately, I latched on to what he was offering me," she says. "I accepted his answers."

When asked for details, she wrote page after page of what she believed were emerging repressed memories. She told about running into the yard after being raped in the bathroom. She incorporated into another lurid rape scene an actual girlhood incident, in which she had dislocated a shoulder. She went on to recall being molested by her father when she was only a year old—as her diapers were being changed—and sodomized by him at five. Following what she says was the therapist's advice, Gavigan confronted her father with her accusations, severed her relationship with him, moved away, and formed an incest survivors' group.

But she remained uneasy. Signing up for a college psychology course, she examined her newfound memories more carefully and concluded that they were false. Now Gavigan has begged her father's forgiveness and filed a lawsuit against the psychiatric hospital for the pain that she and her family suffered.

converted into "memories" of things they never saw (Sheehan, Green, & Truesdale, 1992).

Of course, psychologists who believe in recovered memories have mounted rebuttals to these arguments. For example, Gleaves (1994) argues that a recantation of a recovered memory of abuse does not prove that the memory was false. He points out that individuals with a history of sexual abuse often vacillate between denying and accepting that the abuse occurred. Olio (1994) argues that laboratory demonstrations showing how easy it is to create false memories have involved trivial memory distortions that are a far cry from the vivid, emotionally wrenching recollections of sexual abuse that have generated the recovered memories controversy. She concludes, "The possibility of implanting entire multiple scenarios of horror that differ markedly from the individual's experience, such as memories of childhood abuse in an individual who does not have a trauma history, remains an unsubstantiated hypothesis" (p. 442). Moreover, even if one accepts the assertion that therapists *can* create false memories of abuse in their patients, Pope and Brown (1996) note that there is virtually no direct evidence on how often this occurs and no empirical basis for the claim that there has been an *epidemic* of such cases.

Although both sides seem genuinely concerned about the welfare of the people involved, the debate about recovered memories of sexual abuse has grown increasingly bitter. Those who are skeptical about repressed memories argue that thousands of innocent families are being ripped to shreds by unquestioned acceptance of recovered memories of sexual abuse. The other camp raises an equally disturbing concern that the recent suspicions about repressed memories will turn the clock back to a time when women and children were reluctant to report abuse because they were often ignored, ridiculed, or made to feel guilty.

So, what can we conclude about the recovered memories controversy? It seems pretty clear that therapists can unknowingly create false memories in their patients and that a significant portion of recovered memories of abuse are the product of suggestion. But it also seems likely that some cases of recovered memories are authentic. At this point, we don't have adequate data to estimate what proportion of recovered memories of abuse fall in each category (Brown, Scheflin, & Hammond, 1998). Thus, the matter needs to be addressed with great caution. On the one hand, people should be extremely careful about accepting recovered memories of abuse in the absence of convincing corroboration. On the other hand, recovered memories of abuse cannot be summarily dismissed, and it would be tragic if the repressed memories controversy made people overly skeptical about the all-too-real problem of childhood sexual abuse.

Behavior Therapies

LEARNING OBJECTIVES

- Summarize the general approach and principles of behavior therapies.
- Describe the three steps in systematic desensitization and the logic underlying the treatment.
- Describe the use of aversion therapy and social skills training.
- Summarize evidence on the efficacy of behavior therapies.

Behavior therapy is different from insight therapy in that behavior therapists make no attempt to help clients achieve grand insights about themselves. Why not? Because behavior therapists believe that such insights

aren't necessary to produce constructive change. For example, consider a client troubled by compulsive gambling. The behavior therapist doesn't care whether this behavior is rooted in unconscious conflicts or parental rejection. What the client needs is to get rid of the maladaptive behavior. Consequently, the therapist simply designs a program to eliminate the compulsive gambling. Actually, behavior therapists may work with clients to attain some limited insights about how environmental factors evoke troublesome behaviors (Franks & Barbrack, 1983). This information can be helpful in designing a behavioral therapy program.

The crux of the difference between insight therapy and behavior therapy lies in how each views symptoms. Insight therapists treat pathological symptoms as signs of an underlying problem. In contrast, behavior therapists think that the symptoms *are* the problem. Thus, **behavior therapies involve the application of the principles of learning to direct efforts to change clients' maladaptive behaviors.**

Behaviorism has been an influential school of thought in psychology since the 1920s. But behaviorists devoted little attention to clinical issues until the 1950s, when behavior therapy emerged out of three independent lines of research fostered by B. F. Skinner and his colleagues (1953) in the United States, Hans Eysenck (1959) and his colleagues in Britain, and Joseph Wolpe (1958) and his colleagues in South Africa (Glass & Arnkoff, 1992). Since then, there has been an explosion of interest in behavioral approaches to psychotherapy.

General Principles

Behavior therapies are based on certain assumptions (Agras & Berkowitz, 1994). *First, it is assumed that behavior is a product of learning.* No matter how self-defeating or pathological a client's behavior might be, the behaviorist believes that it is the result of past conditioning. *Second, it is assumed that what has been learned can be unlearned.* The same learning principles that explain how the maladaptive behavior was acquired can be used to get rid of it. Thus, behavior therapists attempt to change clients' behavior by applying the principles of classical conditioning, operant conditioning, and observational learning.

Behavior therapies are close cousins of the self-modification procedures described in the Chapter 4 Application. Both use the same principles of learning to alter behavior directly. In discussing *self-modification*, we examined some relatively simple procedures that people can apply to themselves to improve everyday self-control. In our discussion of *behavior therapy* we will examine more complex procedures used by mental health professionals in the treatment of more severe problems.

Like self-modification, behavior therapy requires that clients' vague complaints ("My life is filled with frustration") be translated into specific, concrete behavioral goals ("I need to increase my use of assertive responses in dealing with colleagues"). Once the troublesome behaviors have been targeted, the therapist designs a program to alter these behaviors. The nature of the therapeutic program depends on the types of problems identified. Specific procedures are designed for specific types of problems, as you'll see in our discussion of systematic desensitization.

Systematic Desensitization

Devised by Joseph Wolpe (1958, 1987), systematic desensitization revolutionized psychotherapy by giving therapists their first useful alternative to traditional "talk therapy" (Fishman & Franks, 1992). *Systematic desensitization is a behavior therapy used to reduce clients' anxiety responses through counterconditioning.* The treatment assumes that most anxiety responses are acquired through classical conditioning (as we discussed in Chapter 15). According to this model, a harmless stimulus (for instance, a bridge) may be paired with a frightening event (lightning strikes it), so it becomes a conditioned stimulus elicit-

Joseph Wolpe

ing anxiety. The goal of systematic desensitization is to weaken the association between the conditioned stimulus (the bridge) and the conditioned response of anxiety. Systematic desensitization involves three steps.

First, the therapist helps the client build an anxiety hierarchy. The hierarchy is a list of anxiety-arousing stimuli centering on the specific source of anxiety, such as flying, academic tests, or snakes. The client ranks the stimuli from the least anxiety arousing to the most anxiety arousing. This ordered list of related, anxiety-provoking stimuli constitutes the anxiety hierarchy. An example of an anxiety hierarchy for one woman's fear of heights is shown in Figure 16.8.

The second step involves training the client in deep muscle relaxation. This second phase may begin during early sessions while the therapist and client are still constructing the anxiety hierarchy. Different therapists use different relaxation training procedures. Whatever procedures are used, the client must learn to engage in deep and thorough relaxation on command from the therapist.

FIGURE 16.8.

Example of an anxiety hierarchy. Systematic desensitization requires the construction of an anxiety hierarchy like the one shown here, which was developed for a woman with a fear of heights who had a penchant for hiking in the mountains.

An Anxiety Hierarchy for Systematic Desensitization	
Degree of fear	
5	I'm standing on the balcony of the top floor of an apartment tower.
10	I'm standing on a stepladder in the kitchen to change a light bulb.
15	I'm walking on a ridge. The edge is hidden by shrubs and treetops.
20	I'm sitting on the slope of a mountain, looking out over the horizon.
25	I'm crossing a bridge 6 feet above a creek. The bridge consists of an 18-inch-wide board with a handrail on one side.
30	I'm riding a ski lift 8 feet above the ground.
35	I'm crossing a shallow, wide creek on an 18-inch-wide board, 3 feet above water level.
40	I'm climbing a ladder outside the house to reach a second-story window.
45	I'm pulling myself up a 30-degree wet, slippery slope on a steel cable.
50	I'm scrambling up a rock, 8 feet high.
55	I'm walking 10 feet on a resilient, 18-inch-wide board, which spans an 8-foot-deep gulch.
60	I'm walking on a wide plateau, 2 feet from the edge of a cliff.
65	I'm skiing an intermediate hill. The snow is packed.
70	I'm walking over a railway trestle.
75	I'm walking on the side of an embankment. The path slopes to the outside.
80	I'm riding a chair lift 15 feet above the ground.
85	I'm walking up a long, steep slope.
90	I'm walking up (or down) a 15-degree slope on a 3-foot-wide trail. On one side of the trail the terrain drops down sharply; on the other side is a steep upward slope.
95	I'm walking on a 3-foot-wide ridge. The slopes on both sides are long and more than 25 degrees steep.
100	I'm walking on a 3-foot-wide ridge. The trail slopes on one side. The drop on either side of the trail is more than 25 degrees.

In the third step, the client tries to work through the hierarchy, learning to remain relaxed while imagining each stimulus. Starting with the least anxiety-arousing stimulus, the client imagines the situation as vividly as possible while relaxing. If the client experiences strong anxiety, he or she drops the imaginary scene and concentrates on relaxation. The client keeps repeating this process until being able to imagine a scene with little or no anxiety. Once a particular scene is conquered, the client moves on to the next stimulus situation in the anxiety hierarchy. Gradually, over a number of therapy sessions, the client progresses through the hierarchy, unlearning troublesome anxiety responses.

As clients conquer *imagined* phobic stimuli, they may be encouraged to confront the *real* stimuli. Although desensitization to imagined stimuli *can* be effective by itself, contemporary behavior therapists usually follow it up with direct exposures to the real anxiety-arousing stimuli (Emmelkamp & Scholing, 1990). Indeed, behavioral interventions emphasizing direct exposures to anxiety-arousing situations have become behavior therapists' treatment of choice for phobic and other anxiety disorders (Goldfried, Greenberg, & Marmar, 1990). Usually, these real-life confrontations prove harmless, and individuals' anxiety responses decline.

According to Wolpe (1958, 1990), the principle at work in systematic desensitization is simple. Anxiety and relaxation are incompatible responses. The trick is to recondition people so that the conditioned stimulus elicits relaxation instead of anxiety. This is *counterconditioning*—an attempt to reverse the process of classical conditioning by associating the crucial stimulus with a new conditioned response. Although Wolpe's explanation of how systematic desensitization works has been questioned, the technique's effectiveness in eliminating specific anxieties has been well documented (Spiegler & Guevremont, 1998).

Aversion Therapy

Aversion therapy is far and away the most controversial of the behavior therapies. It's not something that you would sign up for unless you were pretty desperate. Psychologists usually suggest it only as a treatment of last resort, after other interventions have failed. What's so terrible about aversion therapy? The client has to endure decidedly unpleasant stimuli, such as shock or drug-induced nausea.

Aversion therapy is a behavior therapy in which an aversive stimulus is paired with a stimulus that elicits an undesirable response. For example, alcoholics have had drug-induced nausea paired with their favorite drinks during therapy sessions (Nathan, 1993). By pairing an *emetic drug* (one that causes vomiting) with alcohol, the therapist hopes to create a conditioned aversion to alcohol (see Figure 16.9).

Aversion therapy takes advantage of the automatic nature of responses produced through classical conditioning. Admittedly, alcoholics treated with aversion therapy know that they won't be given an emetic outside of their therapy sessions. However, their reflex response to the stimulus of alcohol may be changed so that they respond to it with nausea and distaste. Obviously, this response should make it much easier to resist the urge to drink.

Troublesome behaviors treated successfully with aversion therapy include drug abuse, sexual deviance, gambling, shoplifting, stuttering, cigarette smoking, and overeating (Sandler, 1975; Wolpe, 1990). Typically, aversion therapy is only one element in a larger treatment program. Of course, this procedure should only be used with willing clients when other options have failed (Rimm & Cunningham, 1985).

Social Skills Training

Many psychological problems grow out of interpersonal difficulties. Behavior therapists point out that humans are not born with social finesse. People acquire their social skills through learning. Unfortunately, some people have not learned how to be friendly, how to make conversation, how to express anger appropriately, and so forth. Social ineptitude can contribute to anxiety, feelings of inferiority, and various kinds of disorders. In light of these findings, therapists are increasingly using social skills training in efforts to improve clients' social abilities (Liberman, Mueser, & DeRisi, 1989). This approach to therapy has yielded promising results in the treatment of depression, shyness, social anxiety, and even schizophrenia (Becker, 1990; Penn & Mueser, 1996; Wixted, Bellack, & Hersen, 1990).

Social skills training **is a behavior therapy designed to improve interpersonal skills that emphasizes shaping, modeling, and behavioral rehearsal.** This type of behavior therapy can be conducted with individual clients or in groups. Social skills training depends on the principles of operant conditioning and observational learning. The therapist makes use of *modeling* by encouraging clients to watch socially skilled friends and colleagues, so that responses (eye contact, active listening, and so on) can be acquired through observation.

In *behavioral rehearsal,* the client tries to practice social techniques in structured role-playing exercises. The therapist provides corrective feedback and uses approval to reinforce progress. Eventually, clients try their newly acquired skills in real-world interactions. Usually, they are given specific homework assignments. *Shaping* is used in that clients are gradually asked to handle more complicated and delicate social situations. For example, a nonassertive client may begin by working on making requests of friends. Only much later will the client be asked to tackle standing up to his or her boss.

Evaluating Behavior Therapies

Behavior therapists have historically placed more emphasis than insight therapists have on the importance of measuring therapeutic outcomes. As a result, there is ample evidence regarding the effectiveness of behavior therapy (Liberman & Bedell, 1989; Rachman & Wilson, 1980). How does the effectiveness of behavior therapy compare to that of insight therapy? In direct comparisons, the differences between the therapies are usually small (Smith, Glass, & Miller, 1980). However, these modest differences tend to favor behavioral approaches for certain types of disorders (Lambert & Bergin, 1992). Of course, behavior therapies are not well suited to the treatment of some types of problems (vague feelings of discontent, for instance). Furthermore, it's misleading to make global statements about the effectiveness of behavior therapies, because they include many different procedures designed for different purposes. For example, the value of systematic desensitization for phobias has no bearing on the value of aversion therapy for sexual deviance.

For our purposes, it is sufficient to note that there is favorable evidence on the efficacy of most of the widely used behavioral interventions (Wixted et al., 1990). Behavior therapies seem to be particularly effective in the treatment of anxiety problems, phobias, obsessive-compulsive disorders, sexual dysfunction, schizophrenia, drug-related problems, eating disorders, hyperactivity, autism, and mental retardation (Emmelkamp, 1994; Liberman & Bedell, 1989).

Many of these problems would not be amenable to treatment with the biomedical therapies, which we consider next. To some extent, the three major approaches to treatment have different strengths. Let's see where the strengths of the biomedical therapies lie.

FIGURE 16.9.

Aversion therapy. Aversion therapy uses classical conditioning to create an aversion to a stimulus that has elicited problematic behavior. For example, in the treatment of drinking problems, alcohol may be paired with a nausea-inducing drug to create a conditioned aversion to alcohol.

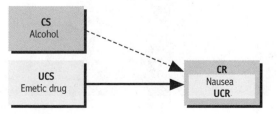

Biomedical Therapies

In the 1950s, a French surgeon was looking for a drug that would reduce patients' autonomic response to surgical stress. The surgeon noticed that chlorpromazine produced a mild sedation. Based on this observation, Delay and Deniker (1952) decided to give chlorpromazine to hospitalized schizophrenic patients to see whether it would have a calming effect on them. Their experiment was a dramatic success. Chlorpromazine became the first effective antipsychotic drug—and a revolution in psychiatry was begun. Hundreds of thousands of severely disturbed patients—patients who had appeared doomed to lead the remainder of their lives in mental hospitals—were gradually sent home thanks to the therapeutic effects of antipsychotic drugs (see Figure 16.10). Today, biomedical therapies, such as drug treatment, lie at the core of psychiatric practice.

Biomedical therapies **are physiological interventions intended to reduce symptoms associated with psychological disorders.** These therapies assume that psychological disorders are caused, at least in part, by biological malfunctions. As we discussed in the previous chapter, this assumption clearly has merit for many disorders, especially the more severe ones. We will discuss two biomedical approaches to psychotherapy: drug therapy and electroconvulsive therapy.

Treatment with Drugs

Psychopharmacotherapy **is the treatment of mental disorders with medication.** We will refer to this kind of treatment more simply as *drug therapy*. Therapeutic drugs for psychological problems fall into three major groups: (1) antianxiety drugs, (2) antipsychotic drugs, and (3) antidepressant drugs. Another important drug that does not fit neatly into any of these categories is lithium, which is used in the treatment of bipolar mood disorders. Of these drugs, the antianxiety agents are the most widely prescribed (see Figure 16.11). Surprisingly, only about 17% of the prescriptions for drugs used in the treatment of psychological problems are written by psychiatrists (Beardsley et al., 1988). Instead, the vast majority of these prescriptions are written by primary care physicians.

ANTIANXIETY DRUGS

Most of us know someone who pops pills to relieve anxiety. The drugs involved in this common coping strategy are *antianxiety drugs,* **which relieve tension, apprehension, and nervousness.** The most popular of these drugs are Valium and Xanax. These are the trade names (the proprietary names that pharmaceutical companies use in marketing drugs) for diazepam and alprazolam, respectively.

Valium, Xanax, and other drugs in the benzodiazepine family are often called *tranquilizers*. These drugs are routinely prescribed for people with anxiety disorders. They are also given to millions of people who simply suffer from chronic nervous tension. In the mid-1970s, pharmacists in the United States were filling nearly *100 million* prescriptions each year for Valium and similar antianxiety drugs. Many critics characterized this level of use as excessive (Lickey & Gordon, 1991).

Antianxiety drugs exert their effects almost immediately. They can be fairly effective in alleviating

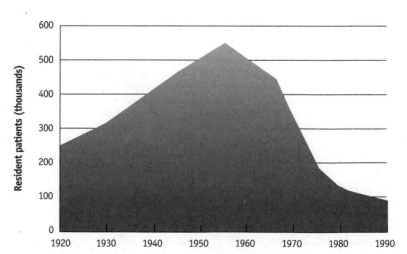

FIGURE 16.10.

The declining inpatient population in mental hospitals. The number of inpatients in public mental hospitals has declined dramatically since the late 1950s. In part, this decline has been due to "deinstitutionalization"—a philosophy that emphasizes outpatient care whenever possible. However, above all else, the decline was made possible by the development of effective antipsychotic medications.

FIGURE 16.11.

Expenditures on drugs used in the treatment of psychological problems. Hundreds of millions of dollars are spent on psychopharmacotherapy in the United States each year. Of the three categories of therapeutic drugs, the antianxiety drugs are the most frequently prescibed, as these data on outpatient expenditures reflect. (Data based on Zorc et al., 1991)

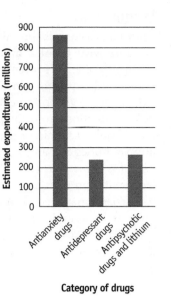

feelings of anxiety (Ballenger, 1995). However, their effects are measured in hours, so their impact is relatively short-lived. Common side effects of antianxiety drugs include drowsiness, depression, nausea, and confusion. These drugs also have some potential for abuse, dependency, and overdose problems (Taylor, 1995). Another drawback is that patients who have been on antianxiety drugs for a while often experience withdrawal symptoms when their drug treatment is stopped (Lader, 1990). The existence of these and related problems led to a moderate decline in the prescription of Valium and similar drugs in the 1980s. Currently, clinicians and researchers are experimenting with a new antianxiety drug called BuSpar (buspirone). It appears to have little potential for abuse or dependence (Cole & Yonkers, 1995). Unlike Valium, BuSpar is slow-acting, exerting its effects in one to three weeks, but with fewer sedative side effects (Norman & Burrows, 1990).

ANTIPSYCHOTIC DRUGS

Antipsychotic drugs are used primarily in the treatment of schizophrenia. They are also given to people with severe mood disorders who become delusional. The trade names (and generic names) of some prominent drugs in this category are Thorazine (chlorpromazine), Mellaril (thioridazine), and Haldol (haloperidol). *Antipsychotic drugs* **are used to gradually reduce psychotic symptoms, including hyperactivity, mental confusion, hallucinations, and delusions.**

Studies suggest that about 70%–90% of psychotic patients respond favorably (albeit in varied degrees) to antipsychotic medication (Buckley & Meltzer, 1995). When antipsychotic drugs are effective, they work their magic gradually, as shown in Figure 16.12. Patients usually begin to respond within two days to a week. Further improvement may occur for several months. Many

schizophrenic patients are placed on antipsychotics indefinitely because these drugs can reduce the likelihood of a relapse into an active schizophrenic episode.

Antipsychotic drugs undeniably make a major contribution to the treatment of severe mental disorders, but they are not without problems. They have many unpleasant side effects (Lader & Herrington, 1990). Drowsiness, constipation, and cotton mouth are common. Patients may also experience tremors, muscular rigidity, and impaired coordination. After being released from a hospital, many schizophrenic patients, supposedly placed on antipsychotics indefinitely, discontinue their drug regimen because of the disagreeable side effects. Unfortunately, relapse into another schizophrenic episode often occurs in about two-thirds of patients after they stop taking antipsychotic medication (Marder & Van Putten, 1995). In addition to minor side effects, antipsychotics may cause a severe and lasting problem called *tardive dyskinesia*. **Tardive dyskinesia is a neurological disorder marked by chronic tremors and involuntary spastic movements.** This debilitating syndrome resembles Parkinson's disease, and there is no cure, although spontaneous remission is possible (Gardos et al., 1994).

Psychiatrists are currently experimenting with a new class of antipsychotic agents, called *atypical antipsychotic drugs*. Three drugs in this category have been released thus far (clozapine, risperidone, olanzapine), and even more promising versions are undergoing clinical trials. Although these drugs are not risk-free, they seem to produce fewer side effects than traditional antipsychotics (Apter, 1996). Moreover, they appear to help a significant portion of the patients who do not respond to conventional antipsychotic medications

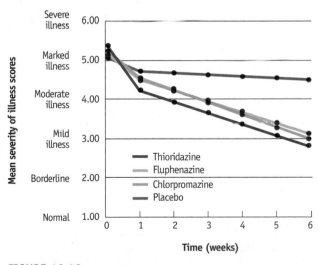

FIGURE 16.12.

The time course of antipsychotic drug effects.
Antipsychotic drugs reduce psychotic symptoms gradually, over a span of weeks, as graphed here. In contrast, patients given placebo pills show little improvement. (Data from Cole, Goldberg, & Davis, 1966; J. M. Davis, 1985)

(Conley, Carpenter, & Tamminga, 1997), and they may carry less risk for tardive dyskinesia (Tollefson et al., 1997). Some experts have predicted that the atypical antipsychotics will almost completely replace conventional antipsychotic medications in the near future (Pickar et al., 1996).

ANTIDEPRESSANT DRUGS

As their name suggests, **antidepressant drugs gradually elevate mood and help bring people out of a depression.** Prior to 1987, there were two principal classes of antidepressants: *tricyclics* (such as Elavil) and *MAO inhibitors* (such as Nardil). These two sets of drugs affect neurochemical activity in different ways and tend to work with different patients. Overall, they are beneficial for about 80% of depressed patients (Potter, Manji, & Rudorfer, 1995). The tricyclics have fewer problematic side effects than the MAO inhibitors (Charney et al., 1995). Like antipsychotic drugs, antidepressants exert their effects gradually over a period of weeks.

Today, psychiatrists are more likely to prescribe a newer class of antidepressants, called *selective serotonin reuptake inhibitors (SSRIs)*, which slow the reuptake process at serotonin synapses. The drugs in this class, which include Prozac (fluoxetine), Paxil (paroxetine), and Zoloft (sertraline), seem to yield rapid therapeutic gains in the treatment of depression (Jann, Jenike, & Lieberman, 1994). SSRIs also have proven valuable in the treatment of obsessive-compulsive disorders and panic disorders (Ballenger et al., 1998; Cartwright & Hollander, 1997). However, Prozac and the other SSRIs are not "miracle drugs," as suggested by some popular magazines. Like all drugs for psychological disorders, the SSRIs have side effects and risks that must be carefully weighed against their benefits (Tollefson, 1995). Although early reports blaming SSRIs for incidents of suicide and homicide have not been substantiated (Slaby, 1997), the drugs do have negative effects on sexual functioning, and patients do experience withdrawal symptoms if treatment is terminated abruptly (Balon, 1997; D' Mello, Fernandes, & Colenda, 1997).

Web Link 16.4

Dr. Bob's Psychopharmacology Tips
Psychopharmacology is the use of medications to treat psychological disorders. University of Chicago physician and pharmacology specialist Robert Hsiang provides both broad and specific references about drugs and the human mind, including a searchable archive of professional information and tips about the field.

LITHIUM

Lithium **is a chemical used to control mood swings in patients with bipolar mood disorders.** Lithium has excellent value in preventing *future* episodes of both mania and depression in patients with bipolar illness (Maj et al., 1998; Tondo et al., 1998). Lithium can also be used in efforts to bring patients with bipolar illness out of *current* manic or depressive episodes. However, antipsychotics and antidepressants are more frequently used for these purposes. On the negative side of the ledger, lithium does have some dangerous side effects if its use isn't managed skillfully (Lenox & Manji, 1995). Lithium levels in the patient's blood must be monitored carefully, because high concentrations can be highly toxic and even fatal. Kidney and thyroid gland complications are the major problems associated with lithium therapy (Post, 1989).

EVALUATING DRUG THERAPIES

Drug therapies can produce clear therapeutic gains for many kinds of patients. What's especially impressive is that they can be effective in severe disorders that otherwise defy therapeutic endeavors. Nonetheless, drug therapies are controversial. Critics of drug therapy have raised a number of issues (Breggin, 1990, 1991; Cohen & McCubbin, 1990; Lickey & Gordon, 1991). First, some critics argue that drug therapies often produce superficial curative effects. For example, Valium does not really solve problems with anxiety—it merely provides temporary relief from an unpleasant symptom. Moreover, this temporary relief may lull patients into complacency about their problem and prevent them from working toward a more lasting solution. Second, critics charge that many drugs are overprescribed and many patients overmedicated. According to these critics, many physicians habitually hand out prescriptions without giving adequate consideration to more complicated and difficult interventions. This problem is compounded by the fact that drugs calm patients and make it easier for hospital staff to run their wards. Thus, critics argue that there is a tendency in some institutions to overmedicate patients to minimize disruptive behavior. Third, some critics charge that the side effects of therapeutic drugs are worse than the illnesses the drugs are supposed to cure. Citing problems such as tardive dyskinesia, lithium toxicity, and addiction to antianxiety agents, these critics argue that the risks of therapeutic drugs aren't worth the benefits.

In their relatively even-handed evaluation of psychiatric drugs, Lickey and Gordon (1991) acknowledge that the issues raised by the critics of drug therapy are legitimate sources of concern, but after reviewing the evidence they defend the value of therapeutic drugs. They argue that drug therapies were never touted as *cures* and that "the relief of symptoms is a genuine benefit that must not be dismissed as trivial" (p. 358). They agree that some drugs are overprescribed and that most drugs have potentially serious side effects, but they conclude that, overall, the benefits of drug therapy far exceed any harm done.

Obviously, drug therapies have stirred up some debate. However, this controversy pales in comparison to the furious debates inspired by electroconvulsive (shock) therapy (ECT). ECT is so controversial that the residents of Berkeley, California, voted to outlaw ECT in their city. However, in subsequent lawsuits the courts ruled that scientific questions cannot be settled through a vote, and they overturned the law. What makes ECT so controversial? You'll see in the next section.

Electroconvulsive Therapy (ECT)

In the 1930s, a Hungarian psychiatrist named Ladislas Meduna speculated that epilepsy and schizophrenia could not coexist in the same body. On the basis of this observation, which turned out to be inaccurate, Meduna theorized that it might be useful to induce epileptic-like seizures in schizophrenic patients. Initially, a drug was used to trigger these seizures. However, by 1938, a pair of Italian psychiatrists (Cerletti & Bini, 1938) demonstrated that it was safer to elicit the seizures with electric shock. Thus, modern electroconvulsive therapy was born.

Electroconvulsive therapy (ECT) is a biomedical treatment in which electric shock is used to produce a cortical seizure accompanied by convulsions. In ECT, electrodes are attached to the skull over the temporal lobes of the brain (see the photo below). A light anesthesia is induced, and the patient is given a variety of drugs to minimize the likelihood of complications, such as spinal fractures. An electric current is then applied for about a second. The current should trigger a brief (5–20 seconds) convulsive seizure, during which the patient usually loses consciousness. Patients normally awaken in an hour or two. People typically receive between 6 and 20 treatments as inpatients at a hospital (Fink, 1992).

The clinical use of ECT peaked in the 1940s and 1950s, before effective drug therapies were widely available. ECT has long been controversial, and its use did decline in the 1960s and 1970s. Nonetheless, there has been a resurgence in the use of ECT, and it is *not* a rare form of therapy. Although only about 8% of psychiatrists administer ECT (Hermann et al., 1998), estimates suggest that about 100,000 people receive ECT treatments each year in the United States (Hermann et al., 1995). Some critics argue that ECT is overused because it is a lucrative procedure that boosts psychiatrists' income while consuming relatively little of their time in comparison to insight therapy (Frank, 1990).

Conversely, some ECT advocates argue that ECT is underutilized because the public harbors many misconceptions about its risks and side effects (Farah, 1997).

Controversy about ECT is also fueled by patients' reports that the treatment is painful, dehumanizing, and terrifying. Although improvements in the administration of ECT have made it less disagreeable than it once was, many patients continue to report that they find the treatment extremely aversive (Breggin, 1991).

EFFECTIVENESS OF ECT

The evidence on the effectiveness of ECT is open to varied interpretations, and the therapeutic efficacy of the treatment is hotly debated. Ardent proponents maintain that it is a remarkably effective treatment (Abrams, 1992; Fink, 1992; Swartz, 1993). However, equally ardent opponents argue that it is no more effective than a placebo (Breggin, 1991; Friedberg, 1976). Reported improvement rates for ECT treatment range from negligible to very high (Small, Small, & Milstein, 1986). The findings on relapse rates after treatment are also inconsistent (Frank, 1990; Weiner, 1984).

In light of these problems, conclusions about the value of ECT must be tentative. Although ECT was once considered appropriate for a wide range of disorders, in recent decades it has primarily been recommended for the treatment of depression. Accumulating evidence suggests that it may also have value for manic patients (Mukherjee, Sackeim, & Schnur, 1994). Overall, there does seem to be enough favorable evidence to justify *conservative* use of ECT in treating severe mood disorders (Rudorfer & Goodwin, 1993; Weiner & Coffey, 1988). Curiously, to the extent that

This patient is being prepared for electroconvulsive therapy. The mouthpiece keeps the patient from biting her tongue during the electrically induced seizures.

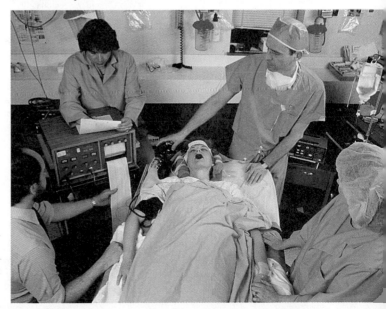

ECT may be effective, no one is sure why. The discarded theories about how ECT works could fill several books.

The debate about whether ECT works and how it works does *not* make ECT unique among approaches to psychotherapy. Controversies exist regarding the effectiveness of most psychotherapies. However, this controversy is especially problematic because ECT may carry substantial risks.

RISKS ASSOCIATED WITH ECT

Even ECT proponents acknowledge that memory losses, impaired attention, and other cognitive deficits are common short-term side effects of electroconvulsive therapy (Sobin et al., 1995). However, ECT proponents assert that these deficits are mild and usually disappear within six months (Calev et al., 1993). In contrast, ECT critics maintain that these cognitive losses are significant and often permanent (Breggin, 1991; Frank, 1990). The physiological bases of these cognitive deficits are not well understood, but the evidence indicates that ECT does not cause any structural damage in the brain (Devanand et al., 1994).

So, what can be concluded about ECT and cognitive deficits? The truth probably lies somewhere between the positions staked out by the proponents and opponents of ECT. In a relatively dispassionate review of the ECT controversy, Small and associates (1986) asserted that "there is little doubt that ECT produces both short- and long-term intellectual impairment." However, they concluded that this impairment isn't inevitable and that it isn't permanent in the vast majority of cases. Nonetheless, given the concerns about the risks of electroconvulsive therapy, it appears that its use will remain controversial for some time to come.

Blending Approaches to Psychotherapy

LEARNING OBJECTIVES

- Discuss the merits of blending approaches to therapy.
- Explain the two approaches to eclecticism in therapy.

We have examined several approaches to therapy, which are summarized and compared in Figure 16.13. However, there is no mandate that a client must be treated with just one approach. Often, a clinician will use several approaches in working with a client. For example, a depressed person might receive cognitive therapy (an insight therapy), social skills training (a behavior therapy), and antidepressant medication (a biomedical therapy). Multiple approaches are particularly likely when a treatment *team* provides therapy.

FIGURE 16.13.

Comparison of psychotherapy approaches. This chart compares behavior therapies, biomedical therapies, and three leading approaches to insight therapy.

Major Approaches to Psychotherapy				
Type of psychotherapy	Primary founders	Origin of disorder	Therapeutic goals	Therapeutic techniques
Psychoanalysis	Freud	Unconscious conflicts resulting from fixations in earlier development	Insights regarding unconscious conflicts and motives; personality reconstruction	Free association, dream analysis, interpretation, catharsis, transference
Client-centered therapy	Rogers	Incongruence between self-concept and actual experience; dependence on acceptance from others	Congruence between self-concept and experience; acceptance of genuine self; self-determination, personal growth	Genuineness, empathy, unconditional positive regard, clarification, reflecting back to client
Cognitive therapy	Beck Ellis	Irrational assumptions and negative, self-defeating thinking about events related to self	Detection of negative thinking; substitution of more realistic thinking	Thought stopping, recording automatic thoughts, refuting negative thinking, reattribution, homework assignments
Behavior therapies	Wolpe Skinner Eysenck	Maladaptive patterns of behavior acquired through learning	Elimination of symptomatic, maladaptive behaviors; acquisition of more adaptive responses	Classical and operant conditioning, reinforcement, punishment, extinction, shaping, aversive conditioning, systematic desensitization, social skills training
Biomedical therapies		Physiological malfunction, primarily abnormal neurotransmitter activity	Elimination of symptoms; prevention of relapse	Antipsychotic, antianxiety, and antidepressant drugs; lithium; electroconvulsive therapy (ECT)

Studies suggest that combining approaches to treatment has significant merit (Frank, 1991; Klerman et al., 1994). One representative study compared the value of insight therapy alone, drug therapy alone, and a combination of insight and drug therapy for unipolar depression (Weissman et al., 1979). The subjects were treated on an outpatient basis. The groups treated only with antidepressant medication or only with interpersonal therapy both responded well. However, the greatest improvement was found in the group treated with both. Interestingly, the two treatments complemented each other nicely. The drug therapy was particularly effective in relieving certain symptoms, while the insight therapy was especially effective in relieving others. Thus, there is much to be said for combining approaches to treatment.

The value of multiple approaches may explain why a significant trend seems to have crept into the field of psychotherapy: a movement away from strong loyalty to individual schools of thought and a corresponding move toward integrating various approaches to therapy (Arkowitz, 1992; Norcross & Goldfried, 1992). Most clinicians used to depend exclusively on one system of therapy while rejecting the utility of all others. This era of fragmentation may be drawing to a close. In recent surveys of psychologists' theoretical orientations, researchers have been surprised to find that the greatest proportion of respondents describe themselves as *eclectic* in approach (Garfield & Bergin, 1994; see Figure 16.14).

Eclecticism in the practice of therapy involves drawing ideas from two or more systems of therapy, instead of committing to just one system. Therapists can be eclectic in a number of ways (Arkowitz, 1992). Two common approaches are theoretical integration and technical eclecticism. In *theoretical integration,* two or more systems of therapy are combined or blended to take advantage of the strengths of each. Paul Wachtel's (1977, 1991) efforts to blend psychodynamic and behavioral therapies is a prominent example. *Technical eclecticism* involves borrowing ideas, insights, and techniques from a variety of sources while tailoring one's intervention strategy to the unique needs of each client. Advocates of technical eclecticism, such as Arnold Lazarus (1976, 1989), maintain that therapists should ask themselves, "What is the best approach for this specific client, problem, and situation?" and then adjust their strategy accordingly.

● Recommended Reading

Am I Crazy, Or Is It My Shrink? by Larry E. Beutler, Bruce Bongar, and Joel N. Shurkin (Oxford University Press, 1998)

This is a stellar, new addition to the rather large stable of books dealing with the provision of psychotherapy. The irreverent title, which is suggestive of a relatively simplistic, lightweight look at therapy, is a little misleading. In reality, this book is a serious, sophisticated work that may be more thoroughly grounded in scientific research than any of the many competing books. The character of the book is consistent with the fact that Larry Beutler is one of the leading researchers on the efficacy of psychotherapy. That is *not* to say that this is a research treatise. It is a pragmatic, readable discussion of everyday issues, such as what to look for in choosing a therapist, what questions to ask when you have doubts about your therapy, what role you play in the success of your treatment, how to recognize and deal with unprofessional or unethical behavior on the part of a therapist, and how to recognize when therapy is not working. The greatest strength of the book is its analysis of what research says about the effectiveness of specific therapies for particular problems. The authors carefully summarize the findings on what works with what problems.

As the assigned healers and priest-confessors for a host of created and real societal and personal ills, modern mental health practitioners have sought to develop interventions for alleviating these ills. These interventions are each based on a particular conception or model of how people function and change.

No single model of behavior is true or effective for treating all problems and individuals. Treatments from each model are effective for some problems and situations, and ineffective or less effective for others. [p. 185]

FIGURE 16.14.

The leading approaches to therapy among psychologists.
The pooled data from a survey of 415 clinical and counseling psychologists (D. Smith, 1982) and another survey of 479 clinical psychologists (Norcross & Prochaska, 1982) indicate that the most widely employed approaches to therapy are (in order) the eclectic, psychodynamic, behavioral, cognitive, and client-centered approaches.

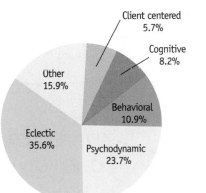

Client centered
5.7%

Cognitive
8.2%

Other
15.9%

Behavioral
10.9%

Eclectic
35.6%

Psychodynamic
23.7%

Looking for a Therapist

- *Discuss when and where to seek therapy.*
- *Discuss the potential importance of a therapist's gender and professional background.*
- *Discuss whether therapists' theoretical approach influences their effectiveness.*
- *Summarize what one should look for in a prospective therapist and what one should expect out of therapy.*

Answer the following "true" or "false."

____ 1. Psychotherapy is an art as well as a science.

____ 2. The type of professional degree that a therapist holds is relatively unimportant.

____ 3. Psychotherapy can be harmful or damaging to a client.

____ 4. Psychotherapy does not have to be expensive.

____ 5. It is a good idea to shop around when choosing a therapist.

All of these statements are true. Do any of them surprise you? If so, you're in good company. Many people know relatively little about the practicalities of selecting a therapist.

The task of finding an appropriate therapist is no less complex than shopping for any other major service. Should you see a psychologist or a psychiatrist? Should you opt for individual therapy or group therapy? Should you see a client-centered therapist or a behavior therapist? The unfortunate part of this complexity is that people seeking psychotherapy often feel overwhelmed by personal problems. The last thing they need is to be confronted by yet another complex problem.

Nonetheless, the importance of finding a good therapist cannot be overestimated. Therapy can sometimes have harmful rather than helpful effects. We have already discussed how drug therapies and ECT can sometimes be damaging, but problems are not limited to these interventions. Talking about your problems with a therapist may sound pretty harmless, but studies indicate that insight therapies can also backfire

(Lambert & Bergin, 1994; McGlashan et al., 1990). Although a great many talented therapists are available, psychotherapy, like any other profession, has incompetent practitioners as well. Therefore, you should shop for a skilled therapist, just as you would for a good attorney or a good mechanic.

In this application, we'll go over some information that should be helpful if you ever have to look for a therapist for yourself or for a friend or family member (based on Amada, 1985; Bruckner-Gordon, Gangi, & Wallman, 1988; Ehrenberg & Ehrenberg, 1986; Pittman, 1994).

When Should You Seek Professional Treatment?

There is no simple answer to this question. Obviously, people *consider* the possibility of professional treatment when they are psychologically distressed. However, they have other options besides psychotherapy. There is much to be said for seeking advice from family, friends, the clergy, and so forth. Insights about personal problems do not belong exclusively to people with professional degrees.

So, when should you turn to professionals for help? You should begin to think seriously about therapy when (1) you have no one to lean on, (2) the people you lean on indicate that they're getting tired of it, (3) you feel helpless and overwhelmed, or (4) your life is seriously disrupted by your problems. Of course, you do not have to be falling apart to justify therapy. You may want to seek professional advice simply because you want to get more out of life.

Where Do You Find Therapeutic Services?

Psychotherapy can be found in a variety of settings. Contrary to general belief, most therapists are not in private practice. Many work in institutional settings such as community mental health centers, hospitals, and human service agencies. The principal sources of therapeutic services are described in Figure 16.15. The

FRANK & ERNEST reprinted by permission of Newspaper Enterprise Association, Inc.

Principal Sources of Therapeutic Services	
Source	**Comments**
Private practitioners	Self-employed therapists are listed in the Yellow Pages under their professional category, such as psychologists or psychiatrists. Private practitioners tend to be relatively expensive, but they also tend to be highly experienced therapists.
Community mental health centers	Community mental health centers have salaried psychologists, psychiatrists, and social workers on staff. The centers provide a variety of services and often have staff available on weekends and at night to deal with emergencies.
Hospitals	Several kinds of hospitals provide therapeutic services. There are both public and private mental hospitals that specialize in the care of people with psychological disorders. Many general hospitals have a psychiatric ward, and those that do not will usually have psychiatrists and psychologists on staff and on call. Although hospitals tend to concentrate on inpatient treatment, many provide outpatient therapy as well.
Human service agencies	Various social service agencies employ therapists to provide short-term counseling. Depending on your community, you may find agencies that deal with family problems, juvenile problems, drug problems, and so forth.
Schools and workplaces	Most high schools and colleges have counseling centers where students can get help with personal problems. Similarly, some large businesses offer in-house counseling to their employees.

exact configuration of therapeutic services available will vary from one community to another. To find out what your community has to offer, it is a good idea to consult your friends, your local phone book, or your local community mental health center.

Is the Therapist's Profession Important?

Psychotherapists may be trained in psychology, psychiatry, social work, counseling, psychiatric nursing, or marriage and family therapy. Researchers have *not* found any reliable associations between therapists' professional background and therapeutic efficacy (Beutler, Machado, & Neufeldt, 1994), probably because many talented therapists can be found in all of these professions. Thus, the kind of degree that a therapist holds doesn't need to be a crucial consideration in your selection process. It *is* true that only a psychiatrist can prescribe drugs for disorders that merit drug therapy. However, some critics argue that many psychiatrists are too quick to use drugs to solve problems (Breggin, 1991). In any case, other types of therapists can refer you to a psychiatrist if they think that drug therapy would be helpful. If you have a health insurance policy that covers psychotherapy, you may want to check to see whether it carries any restrictions about the therapist's profession.

Is the Therapist's Gender Important?

This depends on your attitude. If *you* feel that the therapist's gender is important, then for you it is. The therapeutic relationship must be characterized by trust and rapport. Feeling uncomfortable with a therapist of one gender or the other could inhibit the therapeutic process. Hence, you should feel free to look for a male or female therapist if you prefer to do so. This point is probably most relevant to female clients whose troubles may be related to the extensive sexism in our society (A. G. Kaplan, 1985). It is entirely reasonable for women to seek a therapist with a feminist perspective if that would make them feel more comfortable.

You should also be aware that sexual exploitation is an occasional problem in the context of therapy. Studies indicate that a small minority of therapists take advantage of their clients sexually (Pope, Keith-Spiegel, & Tabachnick, 1986). These incidents almost always involve a male therapist making advances to a female client. The available evidence indicates that these sexual liaisons are usually harmful to clients (Williams, 1992). There are absolutely no situations in which therapist-client sexual relations are an ethical therapeutic practice. If a therapist makes sexual advances, the client should terminate treatment.

Is Therapy Always Expensive?

Psychotherapy does not have to be prohibitively expensive. Private practitioners tend to be the most expensive, charging between $25 and $100 per (50-minute) hour. These fees may seem high, but they are in line with those of similar professionals, such as dentists and attorneys. Community mental health centers and social service agencies are usually supported by tax dollars. Hence, they can charge lower fees than most therapists in private practice. Many of these organizations use a sliding

Web Link 16.5

How to Find Help with Life's Problems (APA Brochure)
This online brochure from the American Psychological Association provides guidance for seeking out the best type of assistance for various human issues and difficulties.

scale, so that clients are charged according to how much they can afford to pay. Thus, most communities have inexpensive opportunities for psychotherapy. Moreover, many health insurance plans provide at least partial reimbursement for the cost of psychotherapy.

Is the Therapist's Theoretical Approach Important?

Logically, you might expect that the diverse approaches to therapy vary in effectiveness. For the most part, this is *not* what researchers find, however. After reviewing the evidence, Jerome Frank (1961) and Lester Luborsky and his colleagues (1975) both quote the dodo bird who has just judged a race in *Alice in Wonderland:* "Everybody has won, and *all* must have prizes." Improvement rates for various theoretical orientations usually come out pretty close in most studies (Lambert & Bergin, 1994; Wampold et al., 1997). In their landmark review of outcome studies, Smith and Glass (1977) estimated the effectiveness of many major approaches to therapy. As Figure 16.16 shows, the estimates cluster together closely.

However, these findings are a little misleading, as they have been averaged across many types of patients and many types of problems. Most experts seem to think that *for certain types of problems, some approaches to therapy are more effective than others* (Crits-Christoph, 1997; Norcross, 1995). For example, Martin

Seligman (1995) asserts that panic disorders respond best to cognitive therapy, that specific phobias are most amenable to treatment with systematic desensitization, and that obsessive-compulsive disorders are best treated with behavior therapy or medication. Thus, for a specific type of problem, a therapist's theoretical approach *may* make a difference.

It is also important to point out that the finding that various approaches to therapy are roughly equal in overall efficacy does not mean that all *therapists* are created equal. Some therapists unquestionably are more effective than others. However, these variations in effectiveness appear to depend on individual therapists' personal skills rather than on their theoretical orientation (Beutler et al., 1994). Good, bad, and mediocre therapists are found within each school of thought.

The key point is that effective therapy requires skill and creativity. Arnold Lazarus, who devised multimodal therapy, emphasizes that therapists "straddle the fence between science and art." Therapy is scientific in that interventions are based on extensive theory and empirical research (Forsyth & Strong, 1986). Ultimately, though, each client is a unique human being, and the therapist has to creatively fashion a treatment program that will help that individual.

What Should You Look for in a Prospective Therapist?

Some clients are timid about asking prospective therapists questions about their training, approach, fees, and so forth. However, these are reasonable questions, and the vast majority of therapists will be most accommodating in providing answers. Usually, you may ask your preliminary questions over the phone. If things seem promising, you may decide to make an appointment for an interview (you will probably have to pay for the interview). In this interview, the therapist will gather

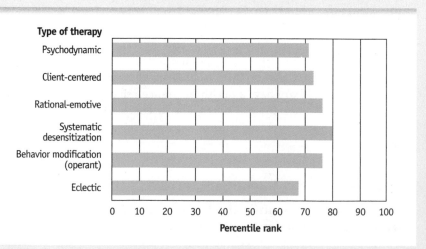

FIGURE 16.16.
Efficacy of different approaches to therapy.
Smith and Glass (1977) reviewed nearly 400 studies in which clients who were treated with a specific type of therapy were compared with a control group made up of people with similar problems who went untreated. The bars indicate the percentile rank (on outcome measures) attained by the average client treated with each type of therapy when compared to control subjects. The higher the percentile, the more effective the therapy was. As you can see, the different approaches were fairly close in their apparent effectiveness.

more information to determine the likelihood of being able to help you, given the therapist's training and approach to treatment. At the same time, you should be making a similar judgment about whether *you* believe the therapist could help you with your problems.

What should you look for? First, you should look for personal warmth and sincere concern. Try to judge whether you will be able to talk to this person in a candid, nondefensive way. Second, look for empathy and understanding. Is the person capable of appreciating your point of view? Third, look for self-confidence. Self-assured therapists will communicate a sense of competence without trying to intimidate you with jargon or boasting needlessly about what they can do for you. When all is said and done, you should *like* your therapist. Otherwise, it will be difficult to establish the needed rapport.

What If There Isn't Any Progress?

If you feel that your therapy isn't going anywhere, you should probably discuss these feelings with your therapist. Don't be surprised, however, if the therapist suggests that it may be your own fault. Freud's concept of

FIGURE 16.17.

Signs of resistance. Resistance in therapy may be subtle, but Ehrenberg and Ehrenberg (1986) have identified some telltale signs to look for.

Signs of Resistance in Therapy

If you're dissatisfied with your progress in therapy, resistance may be the problem when:

1. You have nothing specific or concrete to complain about.

2. Your attitude about therapy changes suddenly just as you reach the truly sensitive issues.

3. You've had the same problem with other therapists in the past.

4. Your conflicts with the therapist resemble those that you have with other people.

5. You start hiding things from your therapist.

resistance has some validity. Some clients *do* have difficulty facing up to their problems. Thus, if your therapy isn't progressing, you may need to consider whether your resistance may be slowing progress. This self-examination isn't easy, as you are not an unbiased observer. Some common signs of resistance identified by Ehrenberg and Ehrenberg (1986) are listed in Figure 16.17.

Given the very real possibility that poor progress may be due to resistance, you should not be too quick to leave therapy when dissatisfied. However, it *is* possible that your therapist isn't sufficiently skilled or that the two of you are incompatible. Thus, after careful and deliberate consideration, you should feel free to terminate your therapy.

What Is Therapy Like?

It is important to have realistic expectations about therapy, or you may be unnecessarily disappointed. Some people expect miracles. They expect to turn their life around quickly with little effort. Others expect their therapist to run their lives for them. These are unrealistic expectations.

Therapy is usually a slow process. Your problems are not likely to melt away quickly. Moreover, therapy is hard work, and your therapist is only a facilitator. Ultimately, *you* have to confront the challenge of changing your behavior, your feelings, or your personality. This process may not be pleasant. You may have to face up to some painful truths about yourself. As Ehrenberg and Ehrenberg (1986) point out, "Psychotherapy takes time, effort, and courage."

Key Ideas

THE ELEMENTS OF PSYCHOTHERAPY: TREATMENTS, CLIENTS, AND THERAPISTS

● Psychotherapy involves three elements: treatments, clients, and therapists. Approaches to treatment are diverse, but they can be grouped into three categories: insight therapies, behavior therapies, and biomedical therapies. People vary considerably in their willingness to seek psychotherapy, and many people who need therapy do not receive it.

● Therapists come from a variety of professional backgrounds. Clinical and counseling psychologists, psychiatrists, clinical social workers, psychiatric nurses, and counselors are the principal providers of therapeutic services.

INSIGHT THERAPIES

● Insight therapies involve verbal interactions intended to enhance self-knowledge. In psychoanalysis, free association and dream analysis are used to explore the unconscious. When an analyst's probing hits sensitive areas, resistance can be expected. The transference relationship may be used to overcome this resistance. Classical psychoanalysis is not widely practiced anymore, but Freud's legacy lives on in a rich diversity of modern psychodynamic therapies.

● The client-centered therapist tries to provide a supportive climate in which clients can restructure their self-concepts. The process of therapy emphasizes clarification of the client's feelings and self-acceptance. Cognitive therapy concentrates on changing the way clients think about events in their lives. Most theoretical approaches to insight therapy have been adapted for use with groups. Group therapy has unique advantages in comparison to individual therapy.

● Eysenck's work in the 1950s raised doubts about the effectiveness of insight therapy and stimulated research on its efficacy. The weight of the evidence suggests that insight therapies can be effective. Repressed memories of childhood sexual abuse recovered through therapy are a new source of controversy in the mental health field. Although many recovered memories of abuse may be the product of suggestion, some probably are authentic.

BEHAVIOR THERAPIES

● Behavior therapies use the principles of learning in direct efforts to change specific aspects of behavior. Systematic desensitization is a treatment for phobias. It involves the construction of an anxiety hierarchy, relaxation training, and step-by-step movement through the hierarchy.

● In aversion therapy, a stimulus associated with an unwanted response is paired with an unpleasant stimulus in an effort to eliminate the maladaptive response. Social skills training can improve clients' interpersonal skills through shaping, modeling, and behavioral rehearsal. Ample evidence shows that behavior therapies are effective.

BIOMEDICAL THERAPIES

● Biomedical therapies involve physiological interventions for psychological problems. Two examples of biomedical treatments are drug therapy and electroconvulsive therapy. A great variety of disorders are treated with drugs. The principal types of therapeutic drugs include antianxiety drugs, antipsychotic drugs, antidepressant drugs, and lithium. Drug therapies can be very effective, but they have their pitfalls. Many drugs produce problematic side effects, and some are overprescribed.

● Electroconvulsive therapy (ECT) is used to trigger a cortical seizure that is believed to have therapeutic value for mood disorders, especially depression. There is contradictory evidence and heated debate about the effectiveness of ECT and about possible risks associated with its use.

BLENDING APPROACHES TO PSYCHOTHERAPY

● Combinations of insight, behavioral, and biomedical therapies are often used fruitfully in the treatment of psychological disorders. Many modern therapists are eclectic, using specific ideas, techniques, and strategies gleaned from a number of theoretical approaches.

APPLICATION: LOOKING FOR A THERAPIST

● Many practical considerations are relevant to the task of seeking professional treatment. Therapeutic services are available in many settings, and such services do not have to be expensive. Excellent therapists and mediocre therapists can be found in all of the mental health professions, using the full range of therapeutic approaches. Thus, therapists' personal skills are more important than their professional degree or their theoretical orientation.

● In selecting a therapist, warmth, empathy, confidence, and likability are desirable traits, and it is reasonable to insist on a therapist of one gender or the other. If progress is slow, your own resistance may be the problem. Therapy requires time, hard work, and the courage to confront your problems.

Key Terms

Antianxiety drugs	Clinical	Psychiatrists
Antidepressant	psychologists	Psychoanalysis
drugs	Cognitive therapy	Psychopharmaco-
Antipsychotic	Counseling	therapy
drugs	psychologists	Resistance
Aversion therapy	Dream analysis	Social skills
Behavior	Electroconvulsive	training
therapies	therapy (ECT)	Spontaneous
Biomedical	Free association	remission
therapies	Group therapy	Systematic
Client-centered	Insight therapies	desensitization
therapy	Interpretation	Tardive
	Lithium	dyskinesia
		Transference

Key People

Aaron Beck	Sigmund Freud	Joseph Wolpe
Hans Eysenck	Carl Rogers	

Practice Test

1. Which of the following approaches to psychotherapy is based on the theories of Sigmund Freud and his followers?
   a. Behavior therapies
   b. Client-centered therapy
   c. Biomedical therapies
   d. Psychoanalytic therapy

2. If a client in psychoanalysis leads the therapist away from sensitive material, the client is displaying:
   a. stupidity.
   b. resistance.
   c. free association.
   d. transference.

3. Because Suzanne has an unconscious sexual attraction to her father, she behaves seductively toward her therapist. Suzanne's behavior is most likely a form of:
   a. resistance.
   b. transference.
   c. misinterpretation.
   d. spontaneous remission.

4. Client-centered therapy emphasizes:
   a. interpretation.
   b. probing the unconscious.
   c. clarification.
   d. all of the above.

5. With regard to psychological disorders, spontaneous remission refers to a:
   a. recovery from a disorder that occurs without formal treatment.
   b. recovery from a disorder that occurs as a result of formal treatment.
   c. sudden reoccurrence of a disorder in a client who had apparently been cured.
   d. failure to recover despite extensive treatment.

6. According to behavior therapists, pathological behaviors:
   a. are signs of an underlying emotional or cognitive problem.
   b. should be viewed as the expression of an unconscious sexual or aggressive conflict.
   c. can be modified directly through the application of established principles of conditioning.
   d. both a and b.

7. A stimulus that elicits an undesirable response is paired with a noxious stimulus in:
   a. aversion therapy.
   b. cognitive therapy.
   c. systematic desensitization.
   d. psychoanalysis.

8. A schizophrenic would most likely be treated with what type of drug?
   a. Antianxiety
   b. Antipsychotic
   c. Antidepressant
   d. Lithium

9. Drug therapies have been criticized on the grounds that:
   a. they are ineffective in most patients.
   b. they temporarily relieve symptoms without addressing the real problem.
   c. many drugs are overprescribed and many patients are overmedicated.
   d. both b and c.

10. A therapist's theoretical approach is not nearly as important as his or her:
    a. age.
    b. appearance.
    c. personal characteristics and skills.
    d. type of professional training.

Answers

1. d page 469
2. b page 470
3. b pages 470–471
4. c pages 471–472
5. a page 475
6. c pages 478–479
7. a pages 480–481
8. b page 483
9. d pages 484–485
10. c page 490

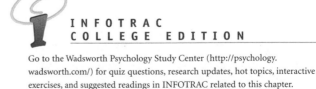

INFOTRAC COLLEGE EDITION

Go to the Wadsworth Psychology Study Center (http://psychology.wadsworth.com/) for quiz questions, research updates, hot topics, interactive exercises, and suggested readings in INFOTRAC related to this chapter.

Appendix: URLs for Recommended Web Sites

The recommended Web Links sprinkled throughout the chapters in this text are intended to spark your interest in further exploration of adjustment issues on the World Wide Web. We chose to not include the addresses (URLs) in the annotated Web Links because the Web is a fluid, dynamic medium where change is the only constant. Many of the URLs for suggested sites will change before this book makes it off the printing press.

If you are interested in accessing some of the recommended Web sites, we suggest that you do so through the *Psychology Applied to Modern Life* homepage at the Wadsworth Psychology Study Center Web site (http://psychology.wadsworth.com/). Links to all of the recommended Web sites will be maintained there, and the Wadsworth Webmaster will periodically update the URLs.

Nonetheless, recognizing that you may want to go directly to a specific site or to give a suggested URL to a friend, we have compiled a list of the current URLs for all the recommended Web sites in this Appendix. They are organized by chapter and are listed in the order of their appearance in the book.

Web Site	Web Address (URL)
Chapter 1: Adjusting to Modern Life	
Psychological Self-Help: An On-Line Text	http://www.cmhc.com/psyhelp/
Assessing the Quality of Psychological Health Care Sites Available on the Internet	http://www.cmhc.com/perspectives/articles/art12982.htm
The Critical Thinking Community	http://www.sonoma.edu/cthink/
Research Methods Tutorials	http://trochim.human.cornell.edu/tutorial/TUTORIAL.HTM
American Psychological Association (APA)	http://www.apa.org/
CalRFN Project Study Tips	http://128.32.89.153/CalRENHP.html
Chapter 2: Theories of Personality	
Sigmund Freud Museum, Vienna, Austria	http://freud.t0.or.at/
C. G. Jung, Analytical Psychology and Culture	http://www.cgjung.com/cgjung/homepage.html
Behavior Analysis	http://server.bmod.athabascau.ca/html/aupr/ba.htm
Personality Theories	http://www.ship.edu/~cgboeree/perscontents.html
Great Ideas in Personality	http://galton.psych.nwu.edu/greatideas.html
Chapter 3: Stress and Its Effects	
Stress and Workstress Directory	http://web.inter.nl.net/hcc/T.Compernolle/strescat.htm
Stress, Anxiety, Fears, and Psychosomatic Disorders	http://www.cmhc.com/psyhelp/chap5/
Stress Management and Peak Performance	http://www.unl.edu/stress/
Stress and You: History of Chronic Fatigue	http://www.chronicfatigue.org/History.html
The Road to Burnout	http://helping.apa.org/stress6.html
David Baldwin's Trauma Information Pages	http://www.trauma-pages.com/
Chapter 4: Coping Processes	
The Albert Ellis Institute	http://www.rebt.org/
Mind Tools	http://www.mindtools.com/index.html

Web Site	Web Address (URL)
American Self-Help Clearinghouse Sourcebook	http://www.cmhc.com/selfhelp/
The Anxiety-Panic Internet Resource: Relaxation	http://www.algy.com/anxiety/relax.html

Chapter 5: The Self

Web Site	Web Address (URL)
Research Sources: Concepts of Person, Self, and Personal Identity	http://www.canisius.edu/~gallaghr/pi.html
Identity and Self	http://www.massey.ac.nz/~ALock/virtual/identity.htm
Classic Theories of Child Development	http://idealist.com/children/cdw.html
Distinctions between Self-Esteem and Narcissism: Implications for Practice	http://ericeece.org/pubs/books/selfe.html
Impression Management & Dramaturgy	http://www.nwmissouri.edu/nwcourses/martin/socialpsych/impmanag/index.htm

Chapter 6: Person Perception and Social Influence

Web Site	Web Address (URL)
Social Psychology Network	http://www.wesleyan.edu/spn/
Social Cognition Paper Archive and Information Center	http://www.psych.purdue.edu/~esmith/scarch.html
Persuasion Theory and Research	http://www.as.wvu.edu/~sbb/comm221/comm221.htm
The Stanford Prison Experiment: Still Powerful After All These Years	http://www2.stanford.edu/dept/news/relaged/970108prisonexp.html
Influence at Work	http://www.influenceatwork.com/index.html

Chapter 7: Interpersonal Communication

Web Site	Web Address (URL)
Nonverbal Communication Research Page	http://198.199.133.62/nonverbal.html
Facial Recognition Homepage	http://www.cs.rug.nl/~peterkr/FACE/face.html
UCSC Perceptual Science Laboratory	http://mambo.ucsc.edu/
The Web of Culture	http://www.webofculture.com/home/home.html
Effective Presentations	http://www.kumc.edu/SAH/OTEd/jradel/effective.html

Chapter 8: Friendship and Love

Web Site	Web Address (URL)
The Student Counseling Virtual Pamphlet Collection	http://uhs.bsd.uchicago.edu/scrs/vpc/virtulets.html
SUNY Buffalo Counseling Center: Relationships Page	http://ub-counseling.buffalo.edu/Relationships/
Love Page	http://www.tc.umn.edu/nlhome/g296/parkx032/LVindex.html
Philip R. Shaver's Homepage	http://psychology.ucdavis.edu/Shaver/default.html
The Shyness Homepage	http://www.shyness.com/
Sexual Assault Information Page	http://www.cs.utk.edu/~bartley/saInfoPage.html

Chapter 9: Marriage and Intimate Relationships

Web Site	Web Address (URL)
American Academy of Child and Adolescent Psychiatry (AACAP): Facts for Families	http://www.aacap.org/web/aacap/factsFam/
The Whole Family Center	http://www.wholefamily.com/
American Association of Marriage and Family Therapy (AAMFT)	http://www.aamft.org/
Divorce Central	http://www.divorcecentral.com/
Partners Task Force for Gay and Lesbian Couples	http://www.buddybuddy.com/toc.html

Chapter 10: Gender and Behavior

Web Site	Web Address (URL)
Women's Studies Database	http://www.inform.umd.edu/EdRes/Topic/WomensStudies/
Great Ideas in Personality: Sociobiology	http://galton.psych.nwu.edu/greatideas/sociobiology.html
Gender and Race in Media	http://www.uiowa.edu/~commstud/resources/GenderMedia/index.html
SPSMM (Society for the Psychological Study of Men and Masculinity)	http://web.indstate.edu:80/spsmm/
Feminist Majority Foundation	http://www.feminist.org/

Chapter 11: Development in Adolescence and Adulthood

Web Site	Web Address (URL)
Adolescence Directory Online	http://education.indiana.edu/cas/adol/adol.html

Web Site	Web Address (URL)
Erik Erikson Tutorial Homepage	http://snycorva.cortland.edu/~ANDERSMD/ ERIK/WELCOME.HTML
SeniorNet	http://www.seniornet.com/
Adult Development and Aging (APA Division 20)	http://www.iog.wayne.edu/apadiv20/apadiv20.htm
The End of Life: Exploring Death in America	http://www.npr.org/programs/death/
National Parent Information Network (NPIN)	http://npin.org/
Chapter 12: Work and Career Development	
Occupational Outlook Handbook (OOH) Online	http://stats.bls.gov/ocohome.htm
The Riley Guide: Employment Opportunities and Job Resources on the Internet	http://www.dbm.com/jobguide/
Marky Lloyd's Careers in Psychology Page	http://www.psywww.com/careers/index.htm
U.S. Department of Labor	http://www.dol.gov/
Careers.wsj.com	http://careers.wsj.com/
The Catapult on JOBWEB	http://www.jobweb.org/catapult/catapult.htm
Chapter 13: Development and Expression of Sexuality	
Sex Education Resources on the World Wide Web: Recommended Sites	http://www.jagunet.com/~dgotlib/meanstreets.htm
Queer Resources Directory (QRD)	http://www.qrd.org/QRD/
SIECUS (Sexuality Information and Education Council of the United States)	http://www.siecus.org/
American Sexual Behavior	http://www.norc.uchicago.edu/library/
Office of Population Research	http://opr.princeton.edu/
AIDS HIV AEGIS	http://www.aegis.com/
Sexual Health Network	http://www.sexualhealth.com/
Chapter 14: Psychology and Physical Health	
Centers for Disease Control & Prevention (CDC)	http://www.cdc.gov/
The QuitNet Community	http://www.quitnet.org/
Go Ask Alice!	http://www.alice.columbia.edu/
National Institute of Alcohol Abuse and Alcoholism	http://www.niaaa.nih.gov/
healthfinder	http://www.healthfinder.gov/
Web of Addictions	http://www.well.com/user/woa/
Chapter 15: Psychological Disorders	
Mental Health Net	http://www.cmhc.com/
International Society for the Study of Dissociation	http://www.issd.org/
Dr. Ivan's Depression Central	http://www.psycom.net/depression.central.html
Suicide ... Read This First	http://www.metanoia.org/suicide/
Doctor's Guide to the Internet: Schizophrenia	http://www.pslgroup.com/SCHIZOPHR.HTM
Eating Disorders Shared Awareness (EDSA)	http://www.eating-disorder.com/
Chapter 16: Psychotherapy	
Online Dictionary of Mental Health	http://www.shef.ac.uk/~psysc/psychotherapy/index.html
The Effectiveness of Psychotherapy: The *Consumer Reports* Study	http://www.apa.org/journals/seligman.html
Narrative Psychology: Therapeutic Recovery of Memory	http://maple.lemoyne.edu/~hevern/nr-mem.html
Dr. Bob's Psychopharmacology Tips	http://uhs.bsd.uchicago.edu/~bhsiung/tips/tips.html
How to Find Help with Life's Problems (APA Brochure)	http://helping.apa.org/brochure/index.html

Glossary

acquired immune deficiency syndrome (AIDS) A disorder in which the immune system is gradually weakened and eventually disabled by the human immunodeficiency virus (HIV).

actor-observer effect The tendency to attribute one's own behavior to situation factors and others' behavior to personal factors.

adjustment The psychological processes through which people manage or cope with the demands and challenges of everyday life.

aggression Any behavior intended to hurt someone, either physically or verbally.

agoraphobia A fear of going out to public places.

alcoholism A chronic, progressive disorder marked by a growing compulsion to drink and impaired control over drinking that eventually interfere with health and social behavior.

ambient stress Chronic environmental conditions that, although not urgent, are negatively valued and place adaptive demands on people.

anal intercourse The insertion of the penis into a partner's anus and rectum.

androcentrism The belief that the male is the norm.

androgens The principal class of male sex hormones.

androgyny The coexistence of both masculine and feminine personality traits in an individual.

anorexia nervosa An eating disorder characterized by intense fear of gaining weight, disturbed body image, refusal to maintain normal weight, and dangerous methods to lose weight.

antecedents In behavior modification, events that typically precede a target response.

antianxiety drugs Drugs that relieve tension, apprehension, and nervousness.

antidepressant drugs Drugs that gradually elevate mood and help to bring people out of a depression.

antipsychotic drugs Drugs used to gradually reduce psychotic symptoms, including hyperactivity, mental confusion, hallucinations, and delusions.

anxiety disorders A class of psychological disorders marked by feelings of excessive apprehension and anxiety.

approach-approach conflict A conflict in which a choice must be made between two attractive goals.

approach-avoidance conflict A conflict in which a choice must be made about whether to pursue a single goal that has both attractive and unattractive aspects.

archetypes Emotionally charged images and thought forms that have universal meaning.

assertiveness Acting in one's own best interest by expressing one's feelings and thoughts honestly and directly.

atherosclerosis A disease characterized by gradual narrowing of the coronary arteries.

attachment styles Typical ways of interacting in close relationships.

attitudes Beliefs and feelings about people, objects, and ideas.

attributional style The tendency to use similar causal explanations for a wide variety of events in one's life.

attributions Inferences that people draw about the causes of events, others' behavior, and their own behavior.

autonomic nervous system (ANS) That portion of the peripheral nervous system made up of the nerves that connect to the heart, blood vessels, smooth muscles, and glands.

aversion therapy A behavior therapy in which an aversive stimulus is paired with a stimulus that elicits an undesirable response.

avoidance-avoidance conflict A conflict in which a choice must be made between two unattractive goals.

basking in reflected glory The tendency to enhance one's image by publicly announcing one's association with those who are successful.

behavior Any overt (observable) response or activity by an organism.

behavior modification A systematic approach to changing behavior through the application of the principles of conditioning.

behavior therapies The application of the principles of learning to direct efforts to change clients' maladaptive behaviors.

behavioral contract A written agreement outlining a promise to adhere to the contingencies of a behavior modification program.

behaviorism A theoretical orientation based on the premise that scientific psychology should study observable behavior.

bereavement The painful loss of a loved one through death.

biomedical therapies Physiological interventions intended to reduce symptoms associated with psychological disorders.

biopsychosocial model The idea that physical illness is caused by a complex interaction of biological, psychological, and sociocultural factors.

bipolar disorders Psychological disorders marked by the experience of both depressed and manic periods.

bisexuals People who seek emotional-sexual relationships with members of both genders.

brainstorming Generating as many ideas as possible while withholding criticism and evaluation.

bulimia nervosa An eating disorder characterized by habitual out-of-control overeating followed by unhealthy compensatory efforts, such as self-induced vomiting, fasting, abuse of laxatives and diuretics, and excessive exercise.

burnout Physical, mental, and emotional exhaustion that is attributable to work-related stress.

bystander effect The social phenomenon in which individuals are less likely to provide needed help when others are present than when they are alone.

cancer Malignant cell growth, which may occur in many organ systems in the body.

cannabis The hemp plant from which marijuana, hashish, and THC are derived.

case study An in-depth investigation of an individual subject.

catastrophic thinking Unrealistic appraisals of stress that exaggerate the magnitude of one's problems.

catatonic schizophrenia A type of schizophrenia marked by striking motor disturbances, ranging from muscular rigidity to random motor activity.

catharsis The release of emotional tension.

cerebral hemispheres The right and left halves of the cerebrum, which is the convoluted outer layer of the brain.

channel The medium through which a message reaches the receiver.

child abuse Intentional actions that result in harm to a child's physical or psychological well-being.

child sexual abuse Coerced or tricked sexual interaction between a young person (under age 18) and another person (at least five years older than the victim).

classical conditioning A type of learning in which a neutral stimulus acquires the capacity to evoke a response that was originally evoked by another stimulus.

client-centered therapy An insight therapy that emphasizes providing a supportive emotional climate for clients, who play a major role in determining the pace and direction of their therapy.

clinical psychologists Psychologists who specialize in the diagnosis and treatment of psychological disorders and everyday behavioral problems.

clinical psychology The branch of psychology concerned with the diagnosis and treatment of psychological problems and disorders.

close relationships Relatively long-lasting relationships in which frequent interactions occur in a variety of settings and in which the impact of the interactions is strong.

cognition The thought processes involved in acquiring knowledge.

cognitive therapy An insight therapy that emphasizes recognizing and changing negative thoughts and maladaptive beliefs.

cohabitation Living together in a sexually intimate relationship without the legal bonds of marriage.

coitus The insertion of the penis into the vagina and (typically) pelvic thrusting.

collective unconscious According to Jung, a storehouse of latent memory traces inherited from people's ancestral past that is shared with the entire human race.

collectivism Putting group goals ahead of personal goals and defining one's identity in terms of the groups to which one belongs.

collusion The situation that occurs when two people have an unspoken agreement to deny some problematic aspect of reality in order to sustain their relationship.

commitment The decision and intent to maintain a relationship in spite of the difficulties and costs that may arise.

communication apprehension The anxiety caused by having to talk with others.

comparison level One's standard of what constitutes an acceptable balance of rewards and costs in a relationship.

comparison level for alternatives One's estimation of the available outcomes from alternative relationships.

compensation A defense mechanism characterized by efforts to overcome imagined or real inferiorities by developing one's abilities.

compliance Yielding to social pressure in one's public behavior, even though one's private beliefs have not changed.

concordance rate A statistic indicating the percentage of twin pairs or other pairs of relatives that exhibit the same disorder.

conditioned response (CR) A learned reaction to a conditioned stimulus that occurs because of previous conditioning.

conditioned stimulus (CS) A previously neutral stimulus that has, through conditioning, acquired the capacity to evoke a conditioned response.

confirmation bias The tendency to behave toward others in ways that confirm your expectations about them.

conflict The struggle that occurs when two or more incompatible motivations or behavioral impulses compete for expression.

conformity Yielding to real or imagined social pressure.

conscientiousness The tendency to be diligent, punctual, and dependable.

conscious According to Freud, whatever one is aware of at a particular point in time.

constructive coping Efforts to deal with stressful events that are judged to be relatively healthful.

context The environment in which communication takes place.

control group Subjects in an experiment who do not receive the special treatment given to the experimental group.

conversion disorders Psychological disorders characterized by a significant loss of physical function (with no apparent organic basis), usually in a single organ system.

cooperative interdependence See superordinate goals

coping Active efforts to master, reduce, or tolerate the demands created by stress.

coronary heart disease A chronic disease characterized by a reduction in blood flow from the coronary arteries, which supply the heart with blood.

correlation The extent to which two variables are related to each other.

correlation coefficient A numerical index of the degree of relationship that exists between two variables.

counseling psychologists Psychologists who specialize in the treatment of everyday behavioral problems.

cunnilingus The oral stimulation of the female genitals.

date rape Forced and unwanted intercourse with someone in the context of dating.

death system The collection of rituals and procedures used by a culture to handle death.

defense mechanisms Largely unconscious reactions that protect a person from unpleasant emotions such as anxiety and guilt.

defensive attribution The tendency to blame victims for their misfortune, so that one feels less likely to be victimized in a similar way.

delusions False beliefs that are maintained even though they clearly are out of touch with reality.

dementia An abnormal condition marked by multiple cognitive defects that include memory impairment.

dependent variable In an experiment, the variable that is thought to be affected by manipulations of the independent variable.

depressive disorder Psychological disorders characterized by persistent feelings of sadness and despair and a loss of interest in previous sources of pleasure.

designer drugs Illicitly manufactured variations of known recreational drugs.

diagnosis Distinguishing one illness from another.

diffusion of responsibility The expectation that others who are present will take responsibility for action.

discrimination Behaving differently, usually unfairly, toward members of a group.

disorganized schizophrenia A type of schizophrenia characterized by a particularly severe deterioration of adaptive behavior.

displaced workers Individuals who are unemployed because their jobs have disappeared.

displacement Diverting emotional feelings (usually anger) from their original source to a substitute target.

display rules Norms that govern the appropriate display of emotions.

dissociative amnesia A sudden loss of memory for important personal information that is too extensive to be due to normal forgetting.

dissociative disorders A class of psychological disorders characterized by loss of contact with portions of one's consciousness or memory, resulting in disruptions in one's sense of identity.

dissociative fugue A loss of memory for one's entire past life, along with one's sense of personal identity.

dissociative identity disorder See multiple-personality disorder.

door-in-the-face technique Making a very large request that is likely to be turned down to increase the chance that people will agree to a smaller request later.

downward social comparison The defensive tendency to compare oneself with someone whose troubles are more serious than one's own.

dream analysis A psychotherapeutic technique in which the therapist interprets the symbolic meaning of the client's dreams.

eating disorders Severe disturbances in eating behavior characterized by preoccupation with weight and unhealthy efforts to control weight.

ego According to Freud, the decision-making component of personality that operates according to the reality principle.

egocentrism The tendency to view reality in line with one's own idiosyncratic perceptions.

elaboration likelihood model The idea that an individual's thoughts about a persuasive message (rather than the message itself) determine whether attitude change will occur.

electroconvulsive therapy (ECT) A biomedical treatment in which electric shock is used to produce a cortical seizure accompanied by convulsions.

emotions Powerful, largely uncontrollable feelings, accompanied by physiological changes.

empathy Adopting another's frame of reference to understand his or her point of view.

empiricism The premise that knowledge should be acquired through observation.

endocrine system Glands that secrete chemicals called hormones into the bloodstream.

endogamy The tendency of people to marry within their own social group.

epidemiology The study of the distribution of mental or physical disorders in a population.

erectile difficulties The male sexual dysfunction characterized by the persistent inability to achieve or maintain an erection adequate for intercourse.

erogenous zones Areas of the body that are sexually sensitive or responsive.

estrogens The principal class of female sex hormones.

etiology The apparent causation and developmental history of an illness.

experiment A research method in which the investigator manipulates an (independent) variable under carefully controlled conditions and observes whether there are changes in a second (dependent) variable as a result.

experimental group The subjects in an experiment who receive some special treatment in regard to the independent variable.

expressive style A style of communication characterized by the ability to express tender emotions easily and to be sensitive to the feelings of others.

external attributions Ascribing the causes of behavior to situational demands and environmental constraints.

extinction The gradual weakening and disappearance of a conditioned response tendency.

extraverts Those who tend to be interested in the external world of things and people.

family life cycle An orderly sequence of developmental stages that families tend to progress through.

fellatio The oral stimulation of the penis.

fight-or-flight response A physiological reaction to threat that mobilizes an organism for attacking (fight) or fleeing (flight) an enemy.

fixation In Freud's theory, a failure to move forward from one stage to another as expected.

foot-in-the-door technique Getting people to agree to a small request to increase the chances that they will agree to a larger request later.

free association A psychotherapeutic technique in which clients spontaneously express their thoughts and feelings exactly as they occur, with as little censorship as possible.

frustration The feelings that occur in any situation in which the pursuit of some goal is thwarted.

fundamental attribution error The tendency to explain others' behavior as a result of personal rather than situational factors.

games Manipulative interactions progressing toward a predictable outcome, in which people conceal their real motivations.

gay See homosexuals.

gender The state of being male or female.

gender identity The ability to correctly classify oneself as male or female.

gender-role identity A person's identification with the traits regarded as masculine or feminine.

gender-role transcendence The idea that to be fully human, people need to move beyond gender roles as a way of organizing the world and of perceiving themselves and others.

gender roles Cultural expectations about what is appropriate behavior for each gender.

gender stereotypes Widely shared beliefs about males' and females' abilities, personality traits, and social behavior.

general adaptation syndrome A model of the body's stress response, consisting of three stages: alarm, resistance, and exhaustion.

generalized anxiety disorder A psychological disorder marked by a chronic high level of anxiety that is not tied to any specific threat.

gonads The sex glands.

group therapy The simultaneous treatment of several or more clients in a group.

hallucinogens A diverse group of drugs that have powerful effects on mental and emotional functioning, marked most prominently by distortions in sensory and perceptual experience.

hardiness A personality syndrome marked by commitment, challenge, and control that is purportedly associated with strong stress resistance.

health psychology The subfield of psychology concerned with the relation of psychosocial factors to the promotion and maintenance of health, and with the causation, prevention, and treatment of illness.

heterosexism The assumption that all individuals and relationships are heterosexual.

heterosexuals People whose sexual desires and erotic behaviors are directed toward the other gender.

hierarchy of needs A systematic arrangement of needs, according to priority, in which basic needs must be met before less basic needs are aroused.

homogamy The tendency of people to marry others who have similar personal characteristics.

homophobia The intense fear and intolerance of homosexuality.

homosexuals People who seek emotional-sexual relationships with members of the same gender.

hormones Chemical substances released into the bloodstream by the endocrine glands.

humanism A theoretical orientation that emphasizes the unique qualities of humans, especially their free will and their potential for personal growth.

hypochondriasis (hypochondria) Excessive preoccupation with health concerns and incessant worry about developing physical illnesses.

id In Freud's theory, the primitive, instinctive component of personality that operates according to the pleasure principle.

identification Bolstering self-esteem by forming an imaginary or real alliance with some person or group.

identity A relatively clear and stable sense of who one is and what one stands for.

immune response The body's defensive reaction to invasion by bacteria, viral agents, or other foreign substances.

impression management Usually conscious efforts to influence the way others think of one.

incest Sexual activity between close relatives.

incongruence The disparity between one's self-concept and one's actual experience.

independent variable In an experiment, a condition or event that an experimenter varies in order to see its impact on another variable.

individualism Putting personal goals ahead of group goals and defining one's identity in terms of personal attributes rather than group memberships.

infant attachment The strong emotional bond that infants usually develop with their caregivers during the first year of their lives.

ingratiation Efforts to make oneself likable to others.

insight therapies A group of psychotherapies in which verbal interactions are intended to enhance clients' self-knowledge and thus promote healthful changes in personality and behavior.

instrumental style A style of communication that focuses on reaching practical goals and finding solutions to problems.

interfamilial sexual abuse *See* intimate violence.

interference Forgetting information because of competition from other learned material.

internal attributions Ascribing the causes of behavior to personal dispositions, traits, abilities, and feelings rather than to external events.

Internet addiction Spending an inordinate amount of time on the Internet and inability to control online use.

interpersonal communication An interactional process whereby one person sends a message to another.

interpersonal conflict Disagreement among two or more people.

interpretation A therapist's attempts to explain the inner significance of the client's thoughts, feelings, memories, and behaviors.

inter-role conflict Uncomfortable dissonance experienced when the demands of two or more roles are contradictory or incompatible.

intimacy Warmth, closeness, and sharing in a relationship.

intimate violence Aggression toward those who are in close relationships to the aggressor.

introvert A person who tends to be preoccupied with the internal world of his or her own thoughts, feelings, and experiences.

investments Things that people contribute to a relationship that they can't get back if the relationship ends.

kinesics The study of communication through body movements.

labor force All people who are employed as well as those who are currently unemployed but are looking for work.

learned helplessness Passive behavior produced by exposure to unavoidable aversive events.

leisure Unpaid activities one chooses to engage in because they are personally meaningful.

life changes Any noticeable alterations in one's living circumstances that require readjustment.

lithium A chemical used to control mood swings in patients with bipolar mood disorders.

loneliness The emotional state that occurs when a person has fewer interpersonal relationships than desired or when these relationships are not as satisfying as desired.

lowball technique Getting people to commit themselves to an attractive proposition before its hidden costs are revealed.

marriage The legally and socially sanctioned union of sexually intimate adults.

matching hypothesis The idea that people of similar levels of physical attractiveness gravitate toward each other.

medical model The idea that it is useful to think of abnormal behavior as a disease.

meditation A family of mental exercises in which a conscious attempt is made to focus attention in a nonanalytical way.

menarche The first occurrence of menstruation.

menopause The cessation of menstruation.

mere exposure effect An increase in positive feelings toward a novel stimulus (such as a person) based on frequent exposure to it.

message The information or meaning that is transmitted from one person to another.

meta-analysis A statistical technique that evaluates the results of many studies on the same question.

mnemonic devices Strategies for enhancing memory.

mood disorders A class of disorders marked by emotional disturbances that may spill over to disrupt physical, perceptual, social, and thought processes.

mourning Formal practices of an individual and a community in response to a death.

multiple-personality disorders Dissociative disorders involving the coexistence in one person of two or more largely complete, and usually very different, personalities. *Also called* dissociative identity disorder.

narcotics (opiates) Drugs derived from opium that are capable of relieving pain.

naturalistic observation An approach to research in which the researcher engages in careful observation of behavior without intervening directly with the subjects.

need for self-actualization The need to fulfill one's potential; the highest need in Maslow's motivational hierarchy.

negative reinforcement The strengthening of a response because it is followed by the removal of a (presumably) unpleasant stimulus.

neurons Individual cells that receive, integrate, and transmit information.

neuroticism A broad personality trait associated with chronic anxiety, insecurity, and self-consciousness.

neurotransmitters Chemicals that carry signals from one neuron to another.

noise Any stimulus that interferes with accurately expressing or understanding a message.

nonverbal communication The transmission of meaning from one person to another through means or symbols other than words.

nutrition A collection of processes (mainly food consumption) through which an organism uses the materials (nutrients) required for survival and growth.

obedience A form of compliance that occurs when people follow direct commands, usually from someone in a position of authority.

obesity The condition of being overweight.

observational learning Learning that occurs when an organism's responding is influenced by observing others, who are called models.

obsessive-compulsive disorder A psychological disorder marked by persistent uncontrollable intrusions of unwanted thoughts (obsessions) and by urges to engage in senseless rituals (compulsions).

occupational interest inventories Tests that measure one's interests as they relate to various jobs or careers.

Oedipal complex According to Freud, a child's erotically tinged desires for the other-sex parent, accompanied by feelings of hostility toward the same-sex parent.

operant conditioning A form of learning in which voluntary responses come to be controlled by their consequences.

optimism A general tendency to expect good outcomes.

orgasm The release that occurs when sexual arousal reaches its peak intensity and is discharged in a series of muscular contractions that pulsate through the pelvic area.

orgasmic difficulties Sexual disorders characterized by an ability to experience sexual arousal but persistent problems in achieving orgasm.

overcompensation Making up for frustration in one area by seeking overgratification in another area.

overdose An excessive dose of a drug that can seriously threaten one's life.

overlearning The continued rehearsal of material after one first appears to have mastered it.

panic disorder Recurrent attacks of overwhelming anxiety that usually occur suddenly and unexpectedly.

paralanguage All vocal cues other than the content of the verbal message itself.

paranoid schizophrenia A type of schizophrenia dominated by delusions of persecution, along with delusions of grandeur.

passion The intense feelings (both positive and negative) experienced in love relationships, including sexual desire.

person perception The process of forming impressions of others.

personal space A zone of space surrounding a person that is felt to "belong" to that person.

personality An individual's unique constellation of consistent behavioral traits.

personality trait A durable disposition to behave in a particular way in a variety of situations.

perspective taking A component of empathy that involves the tendency to put oneself in another person's place.

persuasion The communication of arguments and information intended to change another person's attitudes.

phobic disorders Anxiety disorders marked by a persistent and irrational fear of an object or situation that presents no realistic danger.

physical dependence The need to continue to take a drug to avoid withdrawal illness.

pleasure principle According to Freud, the principle according to which the id operates, demanding immediate gratification of its urges.

polygraph A device that records fluctuations in physiological arousal as a person answers questions.

positive reinforcement The strengthening of a response because it is followed by the arrival of a (presumably) pleasant stimulus.

possible selves One's conceptions about the kind of person one might become in the future.

posttraumatic stress disorder Disturbed behavior that emerges sometime after a major stressful event is over.

preconscious According to Freud, material just beneath the surface of awareness that can be easily retrieved.

prejudice A negative attitude toward members of a group.

premature ejaculation Impaired sexual relations because a man consistently reaches orgasm too quickly.

pressure Expectations or demands that one behave in a certain way.

prevalence The percentage of a population that exhibits a disorder during a specified time period.

primacy effect The fact that initial information tends to carry more weight than subsequent information.

primary appraisal An initial evaluation of whether an event is (1) irrelevant to one, (2) relevant, but not threatening, or (3) stressful.

primary sex characteristics The structures necessary for reproduction.

procrastination The tendency to delay tackling tasks until the last minute.

prognosis A forecast about the probable course of an illness.

projection Attributing one's own thoughts, feelings, or motives to another person.

projective tests Personality tests that ask subjects to respond to vague, ambiguous stimuli in ways that may reveal the subjects' needs, feelings, and personality traits.

proxemics The study of people's use of interpersonal space.

proximity Geographic, residential, and other forms of spatial closeness.

psychiatrists Physicians who specialize in the treatment of psychological disorders.

psychoactive drugs Chemical substances that modify a person's mental, emotional, or behavioral functioning.

psychoanalysis An insight therapy that emphasizes the recovery of unconscious conflicts, motives, and defenses through techniques such as free association, dream analysis, and transference.

psychodynamic theories All the diverse theories descended from the work of Sigmund Freud that focus on unconscious mental forces.

psychological dependence The need to continue to take a drug to satisfy intense mental and emotional craving for it.

psychological test A standardized measure of a sample of a person's behavior.

psychology The science that studies behavior and the physiological and mental processes that underlie it and the profession that applies the accumulated knowledge of this science to practical problems.

psychopharmacotherapy The treatment of mental disorders with medication.

psychosexual stages In Freud's theory, developmental periods with a characteristic sexual focus that leave their mark on adult personality.

psychosomatic diseases Genuine physical ailments caused in part by psychological factors, especially emotional distress.

puberty The stage during which sexual functions reach maturity and that marks the beginning of adolescence.

pubescence The two-year span preceding puberty during which the changes leading to physical and sexual maturity take place.

public self An image or facade presented to others in social interactions.

punishment The weakening (decrease in frequency) of a response because it is followed by the arrival of a (presumably) unpleasant stimulus.

rational-emotive therapy An approach to therapy that focuses on altering clients' patterns of irrational thinking to reduce maladaptive emotions and behavior.

rationalization Creating false but plausible excuses to justify unacceptable behavior.

reactance The response that occurs when a person's freedom to behave in a certain way is impeded, thus leading to efforts to restore the threatened freedom.

reaction formation Behaving in a way that is exactly the opposite of one's true feelings.

reality principle According to Freud, the principle by which the ego seeks to delay gratification of the id's urges until appropriate outlets and situations can be found.

receiver The person to whom a message is targeted.

reciprocal liking Liking those who show they like you.

reciprocity norm The rule that one should pay back in kind what one receives from others.

reference group A set of people against whom one compares oneself.

refractory period A time after orgasm during which males are unable to experience another orgasm.

regression A reversion to immature patterns of behavior.

reliability The measurement consistency of a test.

repression Keeping distressing thoughts and feelings buried in the unconscious.

resistance Largely unconscious defensive maneuvers intended to hinder the progress of therapy.

role overload Stress that occurs when the prescribed activities for various roles are greater than the individual can comfortably handle.

schizophrenic disorders A class of disorders marked by disturbances in thought that spill over to affect perceptual, social, and emotional processes.

secondary appraisal An evaluation of one's coping resources and options for dealing with stress.

secondary sex characteristics The physical features that distinguish one gender from the other but are not essential for reproduction.

secular trend Generational changes in the timing of puberty.

sedatives Sleep-inducing drugs that tend to decrease central nervous system activation and behavioral activity.

self-actualization *See* need for self-actualization.

self-attributions Inferences that people draw about the causes of their own behavior.

self-complexity How simple or elaborate one's self-concept is.

self-concept A collection of beliefs about one's basic nature, unique qualities, and typical behavior.

self-disclosure The voluntary act of verbally communicating private information about oneself to another person.

self-discrepancy The mismatching of self-perceptions.

self-efficacy One's belief about one's ability to perform behaviors that should lead to expected outcomes.

self-enhancement The tendency to maintain positive views of oneself.

self-esteem One's overall assessment of one's worth as a person; the evaluative component of the self-concept.

self-fulfilling prophecy The process whereby expectations about a person cause the person to behave in ways that confirm the expectations.

self-handicapping The tendency to sabotage one's performance to provide an excuse for possible failure.

self-monitoring The degree to which people attend to and control the impressions they make on others.

self-regulation Directing and controlling one's behavior.

self-report inventories Personality scales that ask individuals to answer a series of questions about their characteristic behavior.

self-serving bias The tendency to attribute one's successes to personal factors and one's failures to situational factors.

self-verification theory The idea that people prefer to receive feedback from others that is consistent with their own self-views.

sensate focus A sex-therapy exercise in which partners take turns pleasuring each other with guided verbal feedback while certain kinds of stimulation are temporarily forbidden.

sensation seeking A generalized preference for high or low levels of sensory stimulation.

set point A natural point of stability in body weight, thought to involve the monitoring of fat cell levels.

sex therapy The professional treatment of sexual dysfunctions.

sexism Discrimination against people on the basis of their sex.

sexual dysfunctions Impairments in sexual functioning that cause subjective distress.

sexual harassment The subjection of individuals to unwelcome sexually oriented behavior.

sexual identity The complex of personal qualities, self-perceptions, attitudes, values, and preferences that guide one's sexual behavior.

sexual orientation A person's preference for emotional and sexual relationships with individuals of the same gender, the other gender, or either gender.

sexually transmitted disease (STD) An illness that is transmitted primarily through sexual contact.

shaping Modifying behavior by reinforcing closer and closer approximations of a desired response.

shyness Discomfort, inhibition, and excessive caution in interpersonal relations.

social clock A person's notion of a developmental schedule that specifies what the person should have accomplished by certain points in life.

social comparison theory The idea that people need to compare themselves with others in order to gain insight into their own behavior.

social constructionism The assertion that individuals construct their own reality based on societal expectations, conditioning, and self-socialization.

social exchange theory The idea that interpersonal relationships are governed by perceptions of the rewards and costs exchanged in interactions.

social role theory The assertion that minor gender differences are exaggerated by the different social roles that males and females occupy.

social skills training A behavior therapy designed to improve interpersonal skills that emphasizes shaping, modeling, and behavioral rehearsal.

social support Aid and succor provided by members of one's social networks.

socialization The process by which individuals acquire the norms and roles expected of people in a particular society.

somatization disorder A psychological disorder marked by a history of diverse physical complaints that appear to be psychological in origin.

somatoform disorders A class of psychological disorders involving physical ailments that have no authentic organic basis but are due solely to psychological factors.

source The person who initiates, or sends, a message.

spontaneous remission A recovery from a disorder that occurs without formal treatment.

SQ3R A study system designed to promote effective reading that includes five steps: survey, question, read, recite, and review.

standardization The uniform procedures used to administer and score a test.

stereotypes Widely held beliefs that people have certain characteristics simply because of their membership in a particular group.

stimulants Drugs that tend to increase central nervous system activation and behavioral activity.

stress Any circumstances that threaten or are perceived to threaten one's well-being and thereby tax one's coping abilities.

subliminal persuasion Persuasion via messages presented below the level of conscious awareness.

superego According to Freud, the moral component of personality that incorporates social standards about what represents right and wrong.

superordinate goals Requiring two groups to work together to achieve a mutual goal.

surveys Structured questionnaires designed to solicit information about specific aspects of subjects' behavior.

systematic desensitization A behavior therapy used to reduce clients' anxiety responses through counterconditioning.

test norms Statistics that provide information about where a score on a psychological test ranks in relation to other scores on that test.

token A symbol of all the members of a group.

token economy A system for doling out symbolic reinforcers that are exchanged later for a variety of genuine reinforcers.

tolerance A progressive decrease in responsiveness to a drug with continued use.

transference A phenomenon that occurs when clients start relating to their therapist in ways that mimic critical relationships in their lives.

transvestism A sexual disorder in which a man achieves sexual arousal by dressing in women's clothing.

twin studies Studies in which researchers assess hereditary influence by comparing the resemblance of identical twins and fraternal twins on a trait.

Type A personality A personality style marked by a competitive orientation, impatience and urgency, and anger and hostility.

Type B personality A personality style marked by relatively relaxed, patient, easygoing, amicable behavior.

unconditioned response (UCR) An unlearned reaction to an unconditioned stimulus that occurs without previous conditioning.

unconditioned stimulus (UCS) A stimulus that evokes an unconditioned response without previous conditioning.

unconscious According to Freud, thoughts, memories, and desires that are well below the surface of conscious awareness but that nonetheless exert great influence on our behavior.

underemployment Settling for a job that does not make full use of one's skills, abilities, and training.

undifferentiated schizophrenia A type of schizophrenia marked by idiosyncratic mixtures of schizophrenic symptoms.

validity The ability of a test to measure what it was designed to measure.

variables *See* dependent variable; independent variable.

vasocongestion Engorgement of blood vessels.

work An activity that produces something of value for others.

References

AAUW Educational Foundation (1992). *How schools shortchange girls.* Washington, DC: AAUW.

Abel, M. H. (1998). Interaction of humor and gender in moderating relationships between stress and outcomes. *Journal of Psychology, 132,* 267–276.

Abi-Dargham, A., Gil, R., Krystal, J., Baldwin, R. M., Seibyl, J. P., Bowers, M., van Dyck, C. H., Charney, D. S., Innis, R. B., & Laruelle, M. (1998). Increased striatal dopamine transmission in schizophrenia: Confirmation in a second cohort. *American Journal of Psychiatry, 155,* 761–767.

Abrams, R. (1992). *Electroconvulsive therapy.* New York: Oxford University Press.

Abramson, E. E., & Valene, P. (1991). Media use, dietary restraint, bulimia and attitudes towards obesity: A preliminary study. *British Review of Bulimia Anorexia Nervosa, 5,* 73–76.

Abramson, L. Y., Metalsky, G. I., & Alloy, L. B. (1988). The hopelessness theory of depression: Does the research test the theory? In L. Y. Abramson (Ed.), *Social cognition and clinical psychology: A synthesis.* New York: Guilford Press.

Abramson, L. Y., Seligman, M. E. P., & Teasdale, J. D. (1978). Learned helplessness in humans: Critique and reformulation. *Journal of Abnormal Psychology, 87,* 49–74.

Acock, A. C., & Demo, D. H. (1994). *Family diversity and well-being.* Thousand Oaks, CA: Sage Publications.

ACSF investigators (1992, December). AIDS and sexual behaviour in France. *Nature, 360,* 407–409.

Adams, H. E., & Cassidy, J. F. (1993). The classification of abnormal behavior: An overview. In P. B. Sutker & H. E. Adams (Eds.), *Comprehensive textbook of psychopathology* (2nd ed.). New York: Plenum.

Adams, H. E., Wright, L. W., Jr., & Lohr, B. A. (1996). Is homophobia associated with homosexual arousal? *Journal of Abnormal Psychology, 105,* 440–445.

Adams, K. A. (1980). Who has the final word? Sex, race, and dominance behavior. *Journal of Personality and Social Psychology, 38,* 1–8.

Adams, K. A. (1983). Aspects of social context as determinants of black women's resistance to challenges. *Journal of Social Issues, 39,* 69–78.

Adams, S. H. (1994). Role of hostility in women's health during midlife: A longitudinal study. *Health Psychology, 13,* 488–495.

Ader, R., & Cohen, N. (1984). Behavior and the immune system. In W. D. Gentry (Ed.), *Handbook of behavioral medicine.* New York: Guilford Press.

Adler, A. (1917). *Study of organ inferiority and its psychical compensation.* New York: Nervous and Mental Diseases Publishing.

Adler, A. (1927). *Practice and theory of individual psychology.* New York: Harcourt, Brace & World.

Adler, N. A., & Schultz, J. (1995). Sibling incest offenders. *Child Ause and Neglect, 19,* 811–819.

Adler, R., & Towne, N. (1987). *Looking out/looking in.* New York: Holt, Rinehart & Winston.

Adler, S., & Aranya, N. (1984). A comparison of the work needs, attitudes, and preferences of professional accountants at different career stages. *Journal of Vocational Behavior, 25,* 45–57.

Adorno, T. W., Frenkel-Brunswik, E., Levinson, D. J., & Sanford, B. W. (1950). *The authoritarian personality.* New York: Harper & Row.

Affleck, G., Tennen, H., Urrows, S., & Higgins, P. (1994). Person and contextual features of daily stress reactivity: Individual differences in relations of undesirable daily events with mood disturbance and chronic pain intensity. *Journal of Personality and Social Psychology, 66(2),* 329–340.

Agras, W. S., & Berkowitz, R. (1994). Behavior therapy. In R. E. Hales, S. C. Yudofsky, & J. A. Talbott (Eds.), *The American Psychiatric Press textbook of psychiatry* (2nd ed.). Washington, DC: American Psychiatric Press.

Ainsworth, M. D. S., Blehar, M. C., Waters, E., & Wall, S. (1978). *Patterns of attachment: A psychological study of the strange situation.* Hillsdale, NJ: Erlbaum.

Aird, R. B. (1988). The importance of seizure-inducing factors in youth. *Brain Development, 10,* 73.

Albert, M. S., & Moss, M. B. (1992). The assessment of memory disorders in patients with Alzheimer's disease. In L. R. Squire & N. Butters (Eds.), *Neuropsychology of memory* (2nd ed.). New York: Guilford Press.

Alberti, R. E., & Emmons, M. L. (1995). *Your perfect right: A guide to assertive living.* San Luis Obispo, CA: Impact.

Albiston, C. R., Maccoby, E. E., & Mnookin, R. R. (1990, Spring). Does joint legal custody matter? *Stanford Law and Policy Review,* 167–179.

Alexander, C. N., Chandler, H. M., Langer, E. J., Newman, R. I., & Davies J. L. (1989). Transcendental meditation, mindfulness, and longevity: An experimental study with the elderly. *Journal of Personality and Social Psychology, 57,* 950–964.

Alexander, C. N., Davies, J. L., Dixon, C. A., Dillbeck, M. C., Druker, S. M., Oetzel, R. M., Muehlman, J. M., & Orme-Johnson, D. W. (1990). Growth of higher states of consciousness: The Vedic psychology of human development. In C. N. Alexander & E. J. Langer (Eds.), *Higher stages of human development: Perspectives on adult growth.* New York: Oxford University Press.

Alexander, C. N., Rainfourth, M. V., & Gelderloos, P. (1991). Transcendental Meditation, self-actualization, and psychological health: A conceptual overview and statistical meta-analysis. *Journal of Social Behavior and Personality, 6,* 189–247.

Alexander, F. (1954). Psychoanalysis and psychotherapy. *Journal of the American Psychoanalytic Association, 2,* 722–733.

Alicke, M. D., Smith, R. H., & Klotz, J. L. (1986). Judgments of personal attractiveness: The role of faces and bodies. *Personality and Social Psychology Bulletin, 12,* 381–389.

Allegro, J. T., & Veerman, T. J. (1998). Sickness absence. In P. J. D. Drenth, H. Thierry, & C. J. de Wolff (Eds.), *Handbook of work and organizational psychology.* East Sussex, UK: Psychology Press.

Allen, K. M., Blascovich, J., Tomaka, J., & Kelsey, R. M. (1991). Presence of human friends and pet dogs as moderators of autonomic responses to stress in women. *Journal of Personality and Social Psychology, 61,* 582–589.

Allen, K. R., & Demo, D. H. (1995). The families of lesbians and gay men: A new frontier in family research. *Journal of Marriage and the Family, 57,* 111–127.

Allison, D. B., Heshka, S., Neale, M. C., Lykken, D. T., & Heymsfield, S. B. (1994). A genetic analysis of relative weight among 4,020 twin pairs, with an emphasis on sex effects. *Health Psychology, 13,* 362–365.

Allison, S. T., Messick, D. M., & Goethals, G. R. (1989). On being better but not smarter than others: The Muhammad Ali effect. *Social Cognition, 7,* 275–295.

Alloy, L. B., & Abramson, L. Y. (1988). Depressive realism: Four theoretical perspectives. In L. B. Alloy (Ed.), *Cognitive processes in depression.* New York: Guilford Press.

Alloy, L. B., Clements, C., & Kolden, G. (1985). The cognitive diathesis-stress theories of depression: Therapeutic implications. In S. Reiss & R. R. Bootzin (Eds.), *Theoretical issues in behavior therapy.* Orlando, FL: Academic Press.

Allport, G. W. (1937). *Personality: A psychological interpretation.* New York: Holt.

Allport, G. W. (1961). *Pattern and growth in personality.* New York: Holt, Rinehart & Winston.

Almeida, D. M., Maggs, J. L., & Galambos, N. L. (1993). Wives' employment hours and spousal participation in family work. *Journal of Family Psychology, 7,* 233–244.

Altemeyer, B. (1988a). *Enemies of freedom: Understanding right-wing authoritarianism.* San Francisco: Jossey-Bass.

Altemeyer, B. (1988b). The good soldier, marching in step: A psychological explanation of state terror. *Sciences, March/April,* 30–38.

Altman, I., Vinsel, A., & Brown, B. A. (1981). Dialectic conceptions in social psychology: An application to social penetration and privacy regulation. In L. Berkowitz (Ed.), *Advances in experimental social psychology* (Vol. 14). New York: Academic Press.

Amada, G. (1985). *A guide to psychotherapy.* Lanham, MD: Madison Books.

Amaro, H., Russo, N. F., & Johnson, J. (1987). Family and work predictors of psychological well-being among Hispanic women professionals. *Psychology of Women Quarterly, 11,* 523–532.

Amatea, E. S., & Fong, M. L. (1991). The impact of role stressors and personal resources on the stress experience of professional women. *Psychology of Women Quarterly, 15,* 419–430.

Amato, P. R. (1993). Children's adjustment to divorce: Theories, hypotheses, and empirical support. *Journal of Marriage and the Family, 55,* 23–28.

Amato, P. R., & Keith, B. (1991a). Parental divorce and adult well-being: A meta-analysis. *Journal of Marriage and the Family, 53*, 43–58.

Amato, P. R., & Keith, B. (1991b). Parental divorce and the well-being of children: A meta-analysis. *Psychological Bulletin, 110*, 26–46.

Amato, P. R., & Rogers, S. J. (1997). A longitudinal study of marital problems and subsequent divorce. *Journal of Marriage and the Family, 59*, 612–624.

Ambady, N., & Rosenthal, R. (1992). Thin slices of expressive behavior as predictors of interpersonal consequences: A meta-analysis. *Psychological Bulletin, 111*, 256–274.

American Association of University Women. (1994). *Shortchanging girls, shortchanging America*. Washington, DC: Author.

American Psychiatric Association. (1994). *Diagnostic and statistical manual of mental disorders* (4th ed.). Washington, DC: Author.

Amott, T., & Matthaei, J. (1991). *Race, gender, and work: A multicultural economic history of women in the United States*. Boston, MA: South End Press.

Andersen, B. L., Kiecolt-Glaser, J. K., & Glaser, R. (1994). A biobehavioral model of cancer stress and disease course. *American Psychologist, 49*, 389–404.

Anderson, C. A., & Harvey, R. J. (1988). Discriminating between problems in living: An examination of depression, loneliness, shyness, and social anxiety. *Journal of Social and Clinical Psychology, 6*, 482–491.

Anderson, C. A., & Riger, A. L. (1991). A controllability attributional model of problems in living: Dimensional and situational interactions in the prediction of depression and loneliness. *Social Cognition, 9*, 149–181.

Anderson, C. A., Miller, R. S., Riger, A. L., Dill, J. C., & Sedikides, C. (1994). Behavioral and characterological attributional styles as predictors of depression and loneliness: Review, refinement, and test. *Journal of Personality and Social Psychology, 66*, 549–558.

Anderson, D. M., & Christenson, G. M. (1991). Ethnic breakdown of AIDS-related knowledge and attitudes from the National Adolescent Student Health Survey. *Journal of Health Education, 2*, 30–34.

Anderson, J. R. (1980). *Cognitive psychology and its implications*. New York: Freeman.

Anderson, K. J. (1990). Arousal and the inverted-U hypothesis: A critique of Neiss's "reconceptualizing arousal." *Psychological Bulletin, 107*, 96–100.

Anderson, S. C. (1994). A critical analysis of the concept of codependency. *Social Work, 39*, 677–685.

Andersson, B. E. (1992). Effects of day-care on cognitive and socioemotional competence of thirteen-year-old Swedish schoolchildren. *Child Development, 63*, 20–36.

Andre, R. (1991). *Positive solitude: A practical program for mastering loneliness and achieving self-fulfillment*. New York: HarperCollins.

Andreasen, N. C. (1987). The diagnosis of schizophrenia. *Schizophrenia Bulletin, 13*, 9–22.

Andreasen, N. C. (1990). Positive and negative symptoms: Historical and conceptual aspects. In N. C. Andreasen (Ed.), *Modern problems of pharmacopsychiatry: Positive and negative symptoms and syndromes*. Basel: Karger.

Ankey, C. D. (1992). Sex differences in relative brain size: The mismeasure of woman, too? *Intelligence, 16*, 329–336.

Antill, J. K. (1983). Sex-role complementarity versus similarity in married couples. *Journal of Personality and Social Psychology, 45*, 145–155.

Antonucci, T. C. (1990). Social supports and social relationships. In R. H. Binstock & L. K.

George (Eds.), *Handbook of aging and the social sciences* (3rd ed.). San Diego: Academic Press.

Antonucci, T. C., & Akiyama, H. (1987). Social networks in adult life and a preliminary examination of the convoy model. *Journal of Gerontology, 42*, 519–527.

Appels, A. (1997). Depression and coronary heart disease: Observations and questions. *Journal of Psychosomatic Research, 43*, 443–452.

Apter, J. T. (1996). A new generation of antipsychotics emerges: A guide for the practicing physician. *Primary Psychiatry, 3*, 22–23.

Aquilino, W. S. (1990). The likelihood of parent-adult child coresidence: Effects of family structure and parental characteristics. *Journal of Marriage and the Family, 52*, 405–419.

Aquilino, W. S. (1997). From adolescent to young adult: A prospective study of parent-child relations during the transition to adulthood. *Journal of Marriage and the Family, 59*, 670–686.

Archer, S. L. (1982). The lower age boundaries of identity development. *Child Development, 53*, 1551–1556.

Arendell, T. (1995). *Fathers and divorce*. New York: Sage Publications.

Argyle, M. (1987). *The psychology of happiness*. London: Metheun.

Argyle, M., & Henderson, M. (1984). The rules of friendship. *Journal of Social and Personal Relationships, 1*, 211–237.

Argyle, M., Henderson, M., Bond, M. H., Iizuka, Y., & Contarello, A. (1986). Cross-cultural variations in relationship rules. *International Journal of Psychology, 21*, 287–315.

Argyle, M. (1991). *Intercultural communication: A reader*. Belmont, CA: Wadsworth.

Aries, E. (1987). Gender and communication. In P. Shaver & C. Hendrick (Eds.), *Sex and gender*. Newbury Park, CA: Sage Publications.

Arkowitz, H. (1992). Integrative theories of therapy. In D. K. Freedheim (Ed.), *History of psychotherapy: A century of change*. Washington, DC: American Psychological Association.

Arnett, J. J. (1996). Sensation seeking, aggressiveness, and adolescent reckless behavior. *Personality & Individual Differences, 20*, 693–702.

Arnkoff, D. B., & Glass, C. R. (1992). Cognitive therapy and psychotherapy. In D. K. Freedheim (Ed.), *History of psycho-therapy: A century of change*. Washington, DC: American Psychological Association.

Aron, A. (1988). The matching hypothesis reconsidered again: Comment on Kalick and Hamilton. *Journal of Personality and Social Psychology, 54*, 441–446.

Aron, A., & Henkmeyer, L. (1995). Marital satisfaction and passionate love. *Journal of Social and Personal Relationships, 12*, 139–146.

Aron, A., & Westbay, L. (1996). Dimensions of the prototype of love. *Journal of Personality and Social Psychology, 70*, 535–551.

Aronson, E., Stephan, C., Sikes, J., Blaney, N., & Snapp, M. (1978). *The jigsaw classroom*. Beverly Hills, CA: Sage.

Arrigo, J. M., & Pezdek, K. (1997). Lessons from the study of psychogenic amnesia. *Current Directions in Psychological Science, 6*, 148–152.

Asch, S. E. (1955). Opinions and social pressures. *Scientific American, 193(5)*, 31–35.

Asch, S. E. (1956). Studies of independence and conformity: A minority of one against a unanimous majority. *Psychological Monographs, 70* (9, Whole No. 416).

Asendorpf, J. B. (1986). Shyness in middle and late childhood. In W. H. Jones, J. M. Cheek, & S. R. Briggs (Eds.), *Shyness: Perspectives on research and treatment*. New York: Plenum.

Asendorpf, J. B., & Ostendorf, F. (1998). Is self-enhancement healthy? Conceptual, psychometric, and empirical analysis. *Journal of Personality and Social Psychology, 74*, 955–966.

Aspinwall, L. G., & Taylor, S. E. (1992). Modeling cognitive adaptation: A longitudinal investigation of the impact of individual differences and coping on college adjustment and performance. *Journal of Personality and Social Psychology, 63*, 989–1003.

Astrachan, A. (1992). Men and the new economy. In M. S. Kimmel & M. A. Messner (Eds.), *Men's lives* (2nd ed.). New York: Macmillan.

Atchley, R. C. (1982). The process of retirement: Comparing women and men. In M. Szinovacz (Ed.), *Women's retirement*. Newbury Park, CA: Sage Publications.

Atchley, R. C. (1991). *Social forces and aging*. Belmont, CA: Wadsworth.

Atkinson, R. L. (1989). Low and very low calorie diets. *Medical Clinics of North America, 73*, 203–215.

Atwater, L. (1982). *The extramarital connection: Sex, intimacy, and identity*. New York: Irvington.

Atwood, J. D., & Gagnon, J. H. (1987). Masturbatory behavior in college youth. *Journal of Sex Education and Therapy, 13(2)*, 35–42.

Aubé, J., & Koestner, R. (1995). Gender characteristics and relationship adjustment: Another look at similarity-complementarity hypotheses. *Journal of Personality, 63*, 879–904.

Avery, D., & Winokur, G. (1978). Suicide, attempted suicide, and relapse rates in depression. *Archives of General Psychiatry, 35*, 749–753.

Babcock, M. (1995). Critiques of codependency: History and background issues. In M. Babcock & C. McKay (Eds.), *Challenging codependency: Feminist critiques*. Toronto: University of Toronto Press.

Baber, K. M., & Monaghan, P. (1988). College women's career and motherhood expectations: New options, old dilemmas. *Sex Roles, 19*, 189–203.

Bacon, J. B. (1996). Support groups for bereaved children. In C. A. Corr & D. M. Corr (Eds.), *Handbook of childhood death and bereavement*. New York: Springer-Verlag.

Bagley, C. (1995). *Child sexual abuse and mental health in adolescents and adults*. Aldershot, UK: Ashgate.

Bailey, J. M., & Pillard, R. C. (1991). A genetic study of male sexual orientation. *Archives of General Psychiatry, 48*, 1089–1096.

Bailey, J. M., Pillard, R. C., Neale, M. C., & Agyei, Y. (1993). Heritable factors influence sexual orientation in women. *Archives of General Psychiatry, 50*, 217–223.

Bailey, J. M., Willerman, L., & Parks, C. (1991). A test of maternal stress theory of human male homosexuality. *Archives of Sexual Behavior, 20*, 277–294.

Baker, E. L. (1985). Psychoanalysis and psycho-analytic therapy. In S. J. Lynn & J. P. Garske (Eds.), *Contemporary psychotherapies: Models and methods*. Columbus, OH: Merrill.

Baker, L. A., & Daniels, D. (1990). Nonshared environmental influences and personality differences in adult twins. *Journal of Personality and Social Psychology, 58*, 103–110.

Baker, O. (1996). Managing diversity: Implications for white managers. In B. P. Bowser & R. G. Hunt (Eds.), *Impacts of racism on white Americans*. Newbury Park, CA: Sage.

Baker, S., Thalberg, S., & Morrison, D. (1988). Parents' behavioral norms as predictors of adolescent sexual activity and contraceptive use. *Adolescence, 23*, 278–281.

Baldwin, M., & Fehr, B. (1995). On the instability of attachment style ratings. *Personal Relationships, 2*, 247–261.

Ballenger, J. C. (1995). Benzodiazepines. In A. F. Schatzberg & C. B. Nemeroff (Eds.), *The American Psychiatric Press textbook of psychopharmacology*. Washington, DC: American Psychiatric Press.

Ballenger, J. C., Wheadon, D. E., Steiner, M., Bushnell, W., & Gergel, I. P. (1998). Double-blind, fixed-dose, placebo-controlled study of paroxetine in the treatment of panic disorder. *American Journal of Psychiatry, 155*, 36–42.

Balon, R. (1997). Serotonin reuptake inhibitors and sexual dysfunction. *Primary Psychiatry, 4*, 28–33.

Balswick, J., & Avertt, C. P. (1977). Differences in expressiveness: Gender, interpersonal orientation, and perceived expressiveness as contributing factors. *Journal of Marriage and the Family, 39*, 121–127.

Baltes, P. B., & Kleigl, R. (1992). Further testing of limits of cognitive plasticity: Negative age differences in a mnemonic skill are robust. *Developmental Psychology, 28* 121–125.

Bancroft, J. (1980). Psychophysiology of sexual dysfunction. In M. Dekker (Ed.), *Handbook of biological psychiatry*. New York: Dekker.

Bandura, A. (1973). *Aggression: A social learning analysis*. Englewood Cliffs, NJ: Prentice-Hall.

Bandura, A. (1977). *Social learning theory*. Englewood Cliffs, NJ: Prentice-Hall.

Bandura, A. (1986). *Social foundations of thought and action: A social-cognitive theory*. Englewood Cliffs, NJ: Prentice-Hall.

Bandura, A. (1989). Human agency in social cognitive theory. *American Psychologist, 44*, 1175–1184.

Bandura, A. (1990a). Perceived self-efficacy in the exercise of personal agency. *Journal of Applied Sport Psychology, 2*, 128–163.

Bandura, A. (1990b). Self-regulation of motivation through goal systems. In R. A. Dienstbier (Ed.), *Nebraska symposium on motivation* (Vol. 38). Lincoln: University of Nebraska Press.

Bandura, A. (1992). Self-efficacy mechanism in psychobiologic functioning. In R. Schwarzer (Ed.), *Self-efficacy: Thought control of action*. Washington, DC: Hemisphere.

Bandura, A. (1993). Perceived self-efficacy in cognitive development and functioning. *Educational Psychologist, 28*, 117–148.

Bandura, A. (1997). *Self-efficacy: The exercise of control*. New York: W. H. Freeman.

Barber, B. K. (1994). Cultural, family, and personal contexts of parent-adolescent conflict. *Journal of Marriage and the Family, 56*, 375–386.

Barlett, D. L., & Steele, J. B. (1979). *Empire: The life, legend and madness of Howard Hughes*. New York: Norton.

Barlow, D. H., & Duvand, V. M. (1999). *Abnormal psychology: An investigative approach*. Belmont, CA: Wadsworth.

Barlow, D. H. (1996). Health care policy, psychotherapy research, and the future of psychotherapy. *American Psychologist, 50*, 1050–1058.

Barnes, M. L., & Buss, D. M. (1985). Sex differences in the interpersonal behavior of married couples. *Journal of Personality and Social Psychology, 48*, 654–661.

Barnett, P. A., & Gotlib, I. H. (1988). Psychosocial functioning and depression: Distinguishing among antecedents, concomitants, and consequences. *Psychological Bulletin, 104*, 97–126.

Barnett, R. C., & Rivers, C. (1996). *She works/He works: How two-income families are happier, healthier, and better off*. New York/San Francisco: Harper Collins.

Barnlund, D. C. (1989). *Communicative styles of Japanese and Americans*. Belmont, CA: Wadsworth.

Baron, R. A., & Byrne, D. (1997). *Social psychology*. Boston: Allyn & Bacon.

Baron, R. A., & Richardson, D. R. (1994). *Human aggression* (2nd ed.). New York: Plenum.

Baron, R. S., Cutrona, C. E., Hicklin, D., Russell, D. W., & Lubaroff, D. M. (1990). Social support and immune function among spouses of cancer patients. *Journal of Personality and Social Psychology, 59*, 344–352.

Barret, R. L., & Robinson, B. E. (1994). Gay dads. In A. E. Gottfried & A. W. Gottfried (Eds.), *Redefining families: Implications for children's development*. New York: Plenum.

Barsky, A. J. (1988). The paradox of health. *New England Journal of Medicine, 318*, 414–418.

Barsky, A. J. (1989). Somatoform disorders. In H. I. Kaplan & B. J. Sadock (Eds.), *Comprehensive textbook of psychiatry/V*. Baltimore: Williams & Wilkins.

Barth, R. P., Petro, J. V., & Leland, N. (1992). Preventing adolescent pregnancy with social and cognitive skills. *Journal of Adolescent Research, 7*, 208–222.

Bartholomew, K., & Horowitz, L. M. (1991). Attachment styles among young adults: A test of a four-category model. *Journal of Personality and Social Psychology, 61*, 226–244.

Bartlett, J. G. (1993). *The Johns Hopkins Hospital guide to medical care of patients with HIV infection* (3rd ed.). Baltimore, MD: Williams & Wilkins.

Baruch, G. K. (1984). The psychological well-being of women in the middle years. In G. K. Baruch & J. Brooks-Gunn (Eds.), *Women in midlife*. New York: Plenum.

Baruch, G. K., Biener, L., & Barnett, R. C. (1987). Women and gender in research on stress. *American Psychologist, 42*, 130–136.

Basow, S. A. (1992). *Gender stereotypes and roles* (3rd ed.). Pacific Grove, CA: Brooks/Cole.

Baugher, R. J., Burger, C., Smith, R., & Wallston, K. (1989–1990). A comparison of terminally ill persons at various time periods to death. *Omega, 20*, 103–115.

Baum, A. (1990). Stress, intrusive imagery, and chronic distress. *Health Psychology, 9*, 653–675.

Baum, A., & Paulus, P. B. (1987). Crowding. In D. Stokols & I. Altman (Eds.), *Handbook of environmental psychology* (Vol. 1). New York: Wiley-Interscience.

Baumeister, R. F. (1984). Choking under pressure: Self-consciousness and paradoxical effects of incentives on skillful performance. *Journal of Personality and Social Psychology, 46*, 610–620.

Baumeister, R. F. (1989). The optimal margin of illusion. *Journal of Social and Clinical Psychology, 8*, 176–189.

Baumeister, R. F. (1991). On the stability of variability: Retest reliability of metatraits. *Personality and Social Psychology Bulletin, 17*, 633–639.

Baumeister, R. F. (1995). Disputing the effects of championship pressures and home audiences. *Journal of Personality and Social Psychology, 68*, 644–648.

Baumeister, R. F. (1997). Esteem threat, self-regulatory breakdown, and emotional distress as factors in self-defeating behavior. *Review of General Psychology, 1*, 145–174.

Baumeister, R. F. (1998). The Self. In D. T. Gilbert, S. T. Fiske, & G. Lindzey (Eds.), *The Handbook of Social Psychology*. Boston: Mcgraw-Hill.

Baumeister, R. F., & Steinhilber, A. (1984). Paradoxical effects of supportive audiences on performance under pressure: The home field disadvantage in sports championships. *Journal of Personality and Social Psychology, 47*, 85–93.

Baumeister, R. F., Smart, L., & Boden, J. M. (1996). Relation of threatened egotism to violence and aggression: The dark side of high self-esteem. *Psychological Review, 103*, 5–33.

Baumeister, R. F., Tice, D. M., & Hutton, D. G. (1989). Self-presentational motivations and personality differences in self-esteem. *Journal of Personality, 57*, 547–579.

Baumgarder, A. H., & Brownlee, E. A. (1987). Strategic failure in social interaction: Evidence for expectancy disconfirmation process. *Journal of Personality and Social Psychology, 52*, 525–535.

Baumrind, D. (1964). Some thoughts on the ethics of reading Milgram's "Behavioral study of obedience." *American Psychologist, 19*, 421–423.

Baumrind, D. (1967). Child care practices anteceding three patterns of preschool behavior. *Genetic Psychology Monographs, 75*, 43–88.

Baumrind, D. (1971). Current patterns of parental authority. *Developmental Psychology Monographs, 4* (1, Part 2).

Baumrind, D. (1978). Parental disciplinary patterns and social competence in children. *Youth and Society, 9*, 239–276.

Baumrind, D. (1989). Rearing competent children. In W. Damon (Ed.), *Child development today and tomorrow*. San Francisco: Jossey-Bass.

Baumrind, D. (1991). Effective parenting during the early adolescent transition. In P. A. Cowan & M. Hetherington (Eds.), *Family transitions*. Hillsdale, NJ: Erlbaum.

Baxter, L. A. (1988). A dialectical perspective on communication strategies in relationship development. In S. Duck (Ed.), *Handbook of personal relationships*. New York: Wiley.

Beardsley, R. S., Gardocki, G. J., Larson, D. B., & Hidalgo, J. (1988). Prescribing of psychotropic medication by primary care physicians and psychiatrists. *Archives of General Psychiatry, 45*, 1117–1119.

Beattie, M. (1987). *Co-dependent no more*. New York: HarperCollins.

Beattie, M. (1989). *Beyond codependency: And getting better all the time*. New York: HarperCollins.

Beattie, M. (1993). *The language of letting go: Daily meditations for codependents*. San Francisco: Harper.

Beck, A. T. (1976). *Cognitive therapy and the emotional disorders*. New York: International Universities Press.

Beck, A. T. (1987). Cognitive therapy. In J. K. Zeig (Ed.), *The evolution of psychotherapy*. New York: Brunner/Mazel.

Beck, A. T. (1988a). Cognitive approaches to panic disorder: Theory and therapy. In S. Rachman & J. Maser (Eds.), *Panic: Psychological perspectives*. Hillsdale, NJ: Erlbaum.

Beck, A. T. (1988b). *Love is never enough*. New York: Harper &Row.

Beck, A. T. (1991). Cognitive therapy: A 30 year retrospective. *American Psychologist, 46*, 368–375.

Beck, J., & Morgan, P. A. (1986). Designer drug confusion: A focus on MDMA. *Journal of Drug Education, 16*, 287–302.

Becker, B. J. (1986). Influence again: Another look at gender differences in social influence. In J. S. Hyde & M. C. Linn (Eds.), *The psychology of gender: Advances through meta-analysis*. Baltimore: Johns Hopkins University Press.

Becker, R. E. (1990). Social skills training. In A. S. Bellack & M. Hersen (Eds.), *Handbook of comparative treatments for adult disorders*. New York: Wiley.

Bednar, R. L., & Peterson, S. R. (1995). *Self-esteem: Paradoxes and innovations in clinical theory and practice*. Washington, DC.: American Psychological Association.

Beer, J. M., Arnold, R. D., & Loehlin, J. C. (1998). Genetic and environmental influences on MMPI factor scale: Joint model fitting to twin and adoption data. *Journal of Personality and Social Psychology, 74*, 818–827.

Behar, R. (1991, May 6). The thriving cult of greed and power. *Time*, pp. 50–77.

Beisecker, A. E. (1990). Patient power in doctor-patient communication: What do we know? *Health Communication, 2*, 105–122.

Bell, A. P., & Weinberg, M. S. (1978). *Homosexualities: A study of diversity among men and women.* New York: Simon & Schuster.

Bell, A. P., Weinberg, M. S., & Hammersmith, K. S. (1981). *Sexual preference—Its development in men and women.* Bloomington: Indiana University Press.

Bell, I. P. (1989). The double standard: Age. In J. Freeman (Ed.), *Women: A feminist perspective* (4th ed.). Mountain View, CA: Mayfield.

Bell, P. A., Greene, T. C., Fisher, J. D., & Baum, A. (1996). *Environmental psychology* (4th ed.). Fort Worth: Harcourt Brace.

Beller, M., & Gafni, N. (1996). The 1991 international assessment of educational progress in mathematics and sciences: The gender differences perspective. *Journal of Educational Psychology, 88*, 365–377.

Belli, R. F., & Loftus, E. F. (1994). Recovered memories of childhood abuse: A source monitoring perspective. In S. J. Lynn & J. W. Rhue (Eds.), *Dissociation: Clinical and theoretical perspectives.* New York: Guilford Press.

Belsky, J. (1985). Exploring differences in marital change across the transition to parenthood: The role of violated expectations. *Journal of Marriage and the Family, 47*, 1037–1044.

Belsky, J. (1988). The "effects" of infant day care reconsidered. *Early Childhood Research Quarterly, 3*, 235–272.

Belsky, J. (1990a). Children and marriage. In F. D. Fincham & T. N. Bradbury (Eds.), *The psychology of marriage: Basic issues and applications.* New York: Guilford Press.

Belsky, J. (1990b). Infant day care, child development, and family policy. *Society, 27*, 10–12.

Belsky, J. (1992). Consequences of child care for children's development: A deconstructionist view. In A. Booth (Ed.), *Child care in the 1990s.* Hillsdale, NJ: Erlbaum.

Belsky, J. (1993). Etiology of child maltreatment: A developmental-ecological analysis. *Psychological Bulletin, 114*, 413–434.

Bem, S. L. (1975, September). Androgyny vs. the tight little lives of fluffy women and chesty men. *Psychology Today*, pp. 58–62.

Bem, S. L. (1983). Gender schema theory and its implications for child development: Raising gender-aschematic children in a gender-schematic society. *Signs, 8*, 598–616.

Bem, S. L. (1985). Androgyny and gender schema theory: A conceptual and empirical integration. In T. B. Sonderegger (Ed.), *Nebraska symposium on motivation 1984: Psychology and gender* (Vol. 32). Lincoln: University of Nebraska Press.

Bem, S. L. (1993). The lenses of gender: *Transforming the debate on sexual inequality.* New Haven, CT: Yale University Press.

Benbow, C. P. (1988). Sex differences in mathematical reasoning ability in intellectually talented preadolescents: Their nature, effects, and possible causes. *Behavioral and Brain Sciences, 11*, 169–232.

Bendis, D. (1997, May). A dose of moral adrenaline from Dr. Laura. *The Christian Century*, 476–478.

Benet, V., & Waller, N. G. (1995). The big seven factor model of personality description: Evidence for its cross-cultural generality in a Spanish sample. *Journal of Personality and Social Psychology, 69*, 701–718.

Benjamin, L. T., Jr., Cavell, T. A., & Shallenberger, W. R., III. (1984). Staying with initial answers on objective tests: Is it a myth? *Teaching of Psychology, 11*, 133–141.

Benson, H. (1975). *The relaxation response* (1st ed.). New York: Morrow.

Benson, H. (1984). *Beyond the relaxation response.* Times Books.

Benson, H., & Klipper, M. Z. (1988). *The relaxation response* (2nd ed.). New York: Avon.

Berenbaum, S. A., & Snyder, E. (1995). Early hormonal influences on childhood sex-typed activity and playmate preferences: Implications for the development of sexual orientation. *Developmental Psychology, 31*, 31–42.

Berg, J. H., & McQuinn, R. D. (1986). Attraction and exchange in continuing and noncontinuing dating relationships. *Journal of Personality and Social Psychology, 50*, 942–952.

Berg, S. (1987). Intelligence and terminal decline. In G. L. Maddox & E. W. Busse (Eds.), *Aging: The universal human experience.* New York: Springer.

Bergen, D. J., & Williams, J. E. (1991). Sex stereotypes in the United States revisited: 1972–1988. *Sex Roles, 24*, 413–423.

Bergin, A. E. (1971). The evaluation of therapeutic outcomes. In A. E. Bergin & S. L. Garfield (Eds.), *Handbook of psychotherapy and behavior change: An empirical analysis.* New York: Wiley.

Berglas, S., & Jones, E. E. (1978). Drug choice as a self-handicapping strategy in response to noncontingent success. *Journal of Personality and Social Psychology, 36*, 405–417.

Berkowitz, L. (1969). The frustration-aggression hypothesis revisited. In L. Berkowitz (Ed.), *Roots of aggression: A reexamination of the frustration-aggression hypothesis.* New York: Atherton.

Berkowitz, L. (1989). Frustration-aggression hypothesis: Examination and reformulation. *Psychological Bulletin, 106*, 59–73.

Berkowitz, L. (1993). *Aggression: Its causes, consequences, and control.* New York: McGraw-Hill.

Bernard, L. C., & Krupat, E. (1994). *Health psychology: Biopsychosocial factors in health and illness.* Fort Worth, TX: Harcourt Brace.

Berndt, T. J. (1982). The features and effects of friendship in early adolescence. *Child Development, 53*, 1447–1460.

Berne, E. (1961). *Transactional analysis in psychotherapy.* New York: Ballantine.

Berne, E. (1964). *Games people play.* New York: Grove Press.

Berne, P. H., & Savary, L. M. (1993). *Building self-esteem in children.* New York: Continuum.

Berry, D. S., & McArthur, L. Z. (1985). Some components and consequences of a babyface. *Journal of Personality and Social Psychology, 48*, 312–323.

Berscheid, E. (1988). Some comments on love's anatomy: Or, whatever happened to old-fashioned lust? In R. J. Sternberg & M. L. Barnes (Eds.), *The psychology of love.* New Haven, CT: Yale University Press.

Berscheid, E., & Reis, H. T. (1998). Attraction and close relationships. In D. T. Gilbert, S. T. Fiske, & G. Lindzey (Eds.), *The handbook of social psychology* (Vol. 2). Boston: McGraw-Hill.

Berscheid, E., & Walster, E. (1978). *Interpersonal attraction.* Reading, MA: Addison-Wesley.

Berscheid, E., Dion, K., Walster, E., & Walster, G. W. (1971). Physical attractiveness and dating choice: A test of the matching hypothesis. *Journal of Experimental Social Psychology, 7*, 173–189.

Berscheid, E., Snyder, M., & Omoto, A. M. (1989). The relationship closeness inventory: Assessing the closeness of interpersonal relationships. *Journal of Personality and Social Psychology, 57*, 792–807.

Berzon, B. (1990) *Permanent partners: Building gay and lesbian relationships that last.* New York: E. P. Dutton.

Bettelheim, B. (1943). Individual and mass behavior in extreme situations. *Journal of Abnormal and Social Psychology, 38*, 417–452.

Bettencourt, B. A., & Miller, N. (1996). Gender differences in aggression as a function of provocation: A meta-analysis. *Psychological Bulletin, 119*, 422–447.

Betz, N. E. (1993). Women's career development. In F. L. Denmark & M. A. Paludi (Eds.), *Psychology of women: A handbook of issues and theories.* Westport, CT: Greenwood Press.

Betz, N. E., & Fitzgerald, L. E. (1987). *The career psychology of women.* New York: Academic Press.

Betz, N. E., & Hackett, G. (1986). Applications of self-efficacy theory to understanding career choice behavior. *Journal of Social and Clinical Psychology, 4*, 279–289.

Beumont, P. J. V., Garner, D. M., & Touyz, S. W. (1994). Diagnosis of eating or dieting disorders: What may we learn from past mistakes? *International Journal of Eating Disorders, 16*, 349–362.

Beumont, P. J. V. (1995). The clinical presentation of anorexia and bulimia nervosa. In K. D. Brownell & C. G. Fairburn (Eds.), Eating disorders and obesity: *A comprehensive handbook.* New York: Guilford Press.

Beutler, L. E., Bongar, B., & Shurkin, J. N. (1998). *Am I crazy, or is it my shrink?* New York: Oxford University Press.

Beutler, L. E., Machado, P. P. P., & Neufeldt, S. A. (1994). Therapist variables. In A. E. Bergin & S. L. Garfield (Eds.), *Handbook of psychotherapy and behavior change* (4th ed.). New York: Wiley.

Beyer, S., & Bowden, E. M. (1997). Gender differences in self-perceptions: Convergent evidence from three measures of accuracy and bias. *Personality and Social Psychology Bulletin, 23*, 157–172.

Biegel, D. E., Sales, E., & Schulz, R. (1991). *Family caregiving in chronic illness.* Newbury Park, CA: Sage Publications.

Biener, L., & Abrams, D. B. (1991). The contemplation ladder: Validation of a measure of readiness to consider smoking cessation. *Health Psychology, 10*, 360–365.

Bierly, M. M. (1985). Prejudice toward contemporary outgroups as a generalized attitude. *Journal of Applied Social Psychology, 15*, 189–199.

Binion, V. (1990). Psychological androgyny: A black female perspective. *Sex Roles, 22*, 487–507.

Birchler, G. R. (1992). Marriage. In V. B. Van Hasselt & M. Hersen (Eds.), *Handbook of social development: A lifespan perspective.* New York: Plenum.

Bird, C. E. (1997). Gender difference in the social and economic burdens of parenting and psychological distress. *Journal of Marriage and the Family, 59*, 809–823.

Birren, J. E., & Fisher, L. M. (1995). Aging and speed of behavior: Possible consequences for psychological functioning. *Annual Review of Psychology, 46*, 329–353.

Bitter, R. G. (1986). Late marriage and marital instability: The effects of heterogeneity and inflexibility. *Journal of Marriage and the Family, 48*, 631–640.

Black, D. W., & Andreasen, N. C. (1994). Schizophrenia, schizophreniform disorder, and delusional (paranoid) disorder. In R. E. Hales, S. C. Yudofsky, & J. A. Talbott (Eds.), *The American Psychiatric Press textbook of psychiatry* (2nd ed.). Washington, DC: American Psychiatric Press.

Black, D. W., & Winokur, G. (1990). Suicide and psychiatric diagnosis. In S. J. Blumenthal & D. J. Kupfer (Eds.), *Suicide over the life cycle: Risk factors, assessment, and treatment of suicidal patients*. Washington, DC: American Psychiatric Press.

Blackburn, G. L. (1995). Effects of weight loss on weight-related risk factors. In K. D. Brownell & C. G. Fairburn (Eds.), Eating disorders and obesity: *A comprehensive handbook*. New York : Guilford Press.

Blair, S. L. (1993). Employment, family, and perceptions of marital quality among husbands and wives. *Journal of Family Issues, 14,* 189–212.

Blair, S. L., & Johnson, M. P. (1992). Wives' perceptions of the fairness of the division of household labor: The intersection of housework and ideology. *Journal of Marriage and the Family, 54,* 570–581.

Blair, S. N., Kohl, H. W., Paffenbarger, R. S., Clark, D. G., Cooper, K. H., & Gibbons, L. W. (1989). Physical fitness and all-cause mortality: A prospective study of healthy men and women. *Journal of the American Medical Association, 262,* 2395–2401.

Blasband, D., & Peplau, L. A. (1985). Sexual exclusivity versus openness in gay male couples. *Archives of Sexual Behavior, 14,* 395–412.

Blascovich, J., & Katkin, E. S. (1993). Cardiovascular reactivity to psychological stress and disease: Conclusions. In J. Blascovich & E. S. Katkin (Eds.), *Cardiovascular reactivity to psychological stress & disease*. Washington, DC: American Psychological Association.

Blazer, D. G., Hughes, D., & George, L. K. (1987). Stressful life events and the onset of generalized anxiety syndrome. *American Journal of Psychiatry, 144,* 1178–1183.

Blazer, D. G., Hughes, D., George, L. K., Swartz, M., & Boyer, R. (1991). Generalized anxiety disorder. In L. N. Robins & D. A. Regier (Eds.), *Psychiatric disorders in America: The epidemiologic catchment area study*. New York: Free Press.

Blazer, D. G., Kessler, R. C., McGonagle, K. A., & Swartz, M. S. (1994). The prevalence and distribution of major depression in a national community sample: The national comorbidity survey. *American Journal of Psychiatry, 151,* 979–986.

Bleier, R. (1984). *Science and gender: A critique of biology and its theories on women*. New York: Pergamon Press.

Block, J.D. (1980). *Friendship: How to give it; how to get it*. New York: Macmillan.

Block, J. H. (1973). Conceptions of sex role: Some cross-cultural and longitudinal perspectives. *American Psychologist, 28,* 512–526.

Bloodworth, R. C. (1987). Major problems associated with marijuana abuse. *Psychiatric Medicine, 3,* 173–184.

Bloomfield, H. H., & Kory, R. B. (1976). *Happiness: The TM program, psychiatry, and enlightenment*. New York: Simon & Schuster.

Blum, K. (1984). *Handbook of abusable drugs*. New York: Gardner Press.

Blumenthal, J. A., Emery, C. F., Madden, D. J., Schniebolk, S., Walsh-Riddle, M., George, L. K., McKee, D. C., Higginbotham, M. B., Cobb, F. R., & Coleman, R. E. (1991). Long-term effects of exercise on psychological functioning in older men and women. *Journal of Gerontology, 46,* 352–361.

Blumenthal, J. A., Jiang, W., Babyak, M. A., Krantz, D. S., Frid, D. J., Coleman, R. E.,

Waugh, R., Hanson, M., Applebaum, M., O'Connor, C., & Morris, J. J. (1997). Stress management and exercise training in cardiac patients with myocardial ischemia: Effects on prognosis and evaluation of mechanisms. *Archives of Internal Medicine, 157,* 2213–2223.

Blumstein, P., & Schwartz, P. (1983). *American couples: Money, work, sex*. New York: Morrow.

Blumstein, P., & Schwartz, P. (1989). Intimate relationships and the creation of sexuality. In B. Risman & P. Schwartz (Eds.), *Gender in intimate relationships: A microstructural approach*. Belmont, CA: Wadsworth.

Blumstein, P., & Schwartz, P. (1990). Intimate relationships and the creation of sexuality. In D. P. McWhirter, S. A. Sanders, & J. M. Reinisch (Eds.), *Homosexuality/heterosexuality: Concepts of sexual orientation*. New York: Oxford University Press.

Bobo, L. (1988). Group conflict, prejudice, and the paradox of contemporary racial attitudes. In P. A. Katz, & D. A. Taylor (Eds.), *Eliminating racism: Profiles in controversy*. New York: Plenum Press.

Bohan, J. S. (1996). *Psychology and sexual orientation coming to terms*. New York and London: Routledge.

Bolger, N. (1990). Coping as a personality process: A prospective study. *Journal of Personality and Social Psychology, 59,* 525–537.

Bolles, R. N. (1997). *What color is your parachute: A practical manual for job-hunters and career-changers*. Berkeley, CA: Ten Speed Press.

Bond, R., & Smith, P. B. (1994). Culture and conformity: A meta-analysis of studies using the Asch-type perceptual judgement task. *British Psychological Society 1994 Proceedings,* 41.

Booth, A., & Amato, P. R. (1994). Parental gender role nontraditionalism and offspring outcomes. *Journal of Marriage and the Family, 56,* 865–877.

Bores-Rangel, E., Church, A. T., Szendre, D., & Reeves, C. (1990). Self-efficacy in relation to occupational consideration and academic performance in high school equivalency students. *Journal of Counseling Psychology, 37,* 407–418.

Bornstein, R. F., & D'Agostino, P. R. (1992). Stimulus recognition and the mere exposure effect. *Journal of Personality and Social Psychology, 63,* 545–552.

Borys, S., & Perlman, D. (1985). Gender differences in loneliness. *Personality and Social Psychology Bulletin, 11,* 63–74.

Boskind-White, M. (1985). Bulimarexia: A sociocultural perspective. In S. W. Emmett (Ed.), *Theory and treatment of anorexia nervosa and bulimia: Biomedical, sociocultural, and psychological perspectives*. New York: Brunner/Mazel.

Bossé, R., Spiro, A., & Kressin, N. R. (1996). The psychology of retirement. In R. T. Woods (Ed.), *Handbook of the clinical psychology of aging*. Chicester, UK: Wiley.

Bouchard, C. (1995). Genetic influences on body weight and shape. In K. D. Brownell & C. G. Fairburn (Eds.), *Eating disorders and obesity: A comprehensive handbook*. New York: Guilford Press.

Bower, G. H. (1970). Organizational factors in memory. *Cognitive Psychology, 1,* 18–46.

Bower, G. H., & Clark, M. C. (1969). Narrative stories as mediators of serial learning. *Psychonomic Science, 14,* 181–182.

Bower, S. A., & Bower, G. H. (1991). *Asserting yourself: A practical guide for positive change* (2nd ed.). Reading, MA: Addison-Wesley.

Bowers, J. W., Metts, S. M., & Duncanson, W. T. (1985). Emotion and interpersonal communication. In M. L. Knapp & G. R. Miller (Eds.), *Handbook of interpersonal communication*. Newbury Park, CA: Sage Publications.

Bowlby, J. (1980). *Attachment and loss: Vol. 3. Loss: Sadness and depression*. New York: Basic Books.

Boyden, T., Carroll, J. S., & Maier, R. A. (1984). Similarity and attraction in homosexual males: The effects of age and masculinity-femininity. *Sex Roles, 10,* 939–948.

Bozett, F. W. (1987). Children of gay fathers. In F. W. Bozett (Ed.), *Gay and lesbian parents*. New York: Praeger.

Bradburn, E. M., Moen, P., & Dempster-McClain, D. (1995). Women's return to school following the transition to motherhood. *Social Forces, 73,* 1517–1551.

Bradbury, T. N., & Fincham, F. D. (1988). Individual difference variables in close relationships: A contextual model of marriage as an integrative framework. *Journal of Personality and Social Psychology, 54,* 713–721.

Bradbury, T. N., & Fincham, F. D. (1990). Attributions in marriage: Review and critique. *Psychological Bulletin, 107,* 3–33.

Bradbury, T. N. (1998). *The developmental course of marital dysfunction*. New York: Cambridge University Press.

Bradford, J., & Ryan, C. (1987). *National lesbian health care survey: Mental health implications*. Washington, DC: National Lesbian and Gay Health Foundation.

Bradley, P. H. (1981). The folk-linguistics of women's speech: An empirical examination. *Communications Monographs, 48,* 73–90.

Bradshaw, J. (1988). *Healing the shame that binds you*. Pompano Beach, FL: Health Communications.

Bram, S. (1985). Childlessness revisited: A longitudinal study of voluntarily childless couples, delayed parents, and parents. *Lifestyles: A Journal of Changing Patterns, 8,* 46–66.

Brannon, R. (1976). The male sex role: Our culture's blueprint of manhood, and what's done for us lately. In D. David & R. Brannon (Eds.), *The forty-nine percent majority*. Reading, MA: Addison-Wesley.

Branscombe, N. R., & Wann, D. L. (1994). Collective self-esteem consequences of out-group derogation when a valued social identity is on trial. *European Journal of Social Psychology, 24,* 641–657.

Branscombe, N. R., Wann, D. L., Noel, J. G., & Coleman, J. (1993). In-group or out-group extremity: Importance of the threatened social identity. *Personality and Social Psychology Bulletin, 19,* 381–388.

Braverman, P. K., & Strasburger, V. C. (1993). Adolescent sexual activity. *Clinical Pediatrics, 32,* 658–668.

Braverman, P. K., & Strasburger, V. C. (1994). Sexually transmitted diseases. *Clinical Pediatrics, 33,* 26–37.

Bray, G. A. (1990). Exercise and obesity. In C. Bouchard, R. J. Shephard, T. Stephens, J. R. Sutton, & B. D. McPherson (Eds.), *Exercise, fitness and health: A consensus of current knowledge*. Champaign, IL: Human Kinetics Books.

Bray, G. A., York, B., & DeLany, J. (1992). A survey of the opinions of obesity experts on the causes and treatment of obesity. *American Journal of Clinical Nutrition, 55,* 151S–154S.

Bray, J. H., & Hetherington, E. M. (1993). Families in transition: Introduction and overview. *Journal of Family Psychology, 7,* 3–8.

Brecher, E. M. (1984). *Love, sex, and aging*. Boston: Little, Brown.

Breggin, P. R. (1990). Brain damage, dementia and persistent cognitive dysfunction associated with neuroleptic drugs: Evidence, etiology, implications. *The Journal of Mind and Behavior, 11,* 425–464.

Breggin, P. R. (1991). *Toxic psychiatry*. New York: St. Martin's Press.

Brehm, J. W. (1966). *A theory of psychological reactance*. New York: Academic Press.

Brehm, S. S. (1992). *Intimate relationships* (2nd ed.). New York: McGraw-Hill.

Brehm, S. S., & Kassin, S. M. (1993). *Social psychology*. Boston: Houghton Mifflin.

Brehm, S. S., & Kassin, S. M. (1993). *Social psychology* (2nd ed.). Boston: Houghton Mifflin.

Brent, D. A., & Kolko, D. J. (1990). The assessment and treatment of children and adolescents at risk for suicide. In S. J. Blumenthal & D. J. Kupfer (Eds.), *Suicide over the life cycle: Risk factors, assessment, and treatment of suicidal patients*. Washington, DC: American Psychiatric Press.

Breslau, N., Kilbey, M. M., & Andreski, P. (1993). Nicotine dependence and major depression: New evidence from a prospective investigation. *Archives of General Psychiatry, 50*, 31–35.

Bretl, D. J., & Cantor, J. (1988). The portrayal of men and women in U.S. television commercials: A recent content analysis and trends over 15 years. *Sex Roles, 18*, 595–609.

Bretschneider, J. G., & McCoy, N. L. (1988). Sexual interest and behavior in healthy 80- to 102-year-olds. *Archives of Sexual Behavior, 17*, 109–130.

Brett, J. F., Brief, A. P., Burke, M. J., George, J. M., & Webster, J. (1990). Negative affectivity and the reporting of stressful life events. *Health Psychology, 9*, 57–68.

Brettle, R. P., & Leen, L. S. (1991). The natural history of HIV and AIDS in women. *AIDS, 5*, 1283–1292.

Brewer, M. B. (1988). A dual process model of impression formation. In T. K. Srull & R. S. Wyer, Jr. (Eds.), *Advances in social cognition* (Vol. 1). Hillsdale, NJ: Erlbaum.

Brewer, M. B., & Brown, R. J. (1997). Intergroup relations. In D. T. Gilbert, S. T. Fiske, & G. Lindzey (Eds.), *The handbook of social psychology* (Vol. 2). Boston: McGraw-Hill.

Bridges, K. R., & Roig, M. (1997). Academic procrastination and irrational thinking: A re-examination with context controlled. *Personality & Individual Differences, 22*, 941–944.

Briere, J., & Conte, J. R. (1993). Self-reported amnesia for abuse in adults molested as children. *Journal of Traumatic Stress, 6*, 21–31.

Brockner, J. (1983). Low self-esteem and behavioral plasticity: Some implications. In L. Wheeler & P. Shaver (Eds.), *Review of personality and social psychology* (Vol. 4). Newbury Park, CA: Sage Publications.

Brod, C. (1988). *Technostress: Human cost of the computer revolution*. Reading, MA: Addison-Wesley.

Brody, J. E. (1992, December 9). Hip fracture: A potential killer that can be avoided. *The New York Times*, C16.

Brody, N., & Crowley, M. J. (1995). Environmental (and genetic) influences on personality and intelligence. In D. H. Saklofske & M. Zeidner (Eds.), *International handbook of personality and intelligence*. New York: Plenum Press.

Broida, R. (1995, Winter). Tea and Tennyson. *Career Woman*, 34–36.

Bromage, B. K., & Mayer, R. E. (1986). Quantitative and qualitative effects of repetition on learning from technical text. *Journal of Educational Psychology, 78*, 271–278.

Bromley, M., & Blieszner, R. (1997). Planning for long-term care: Filial behavior and relationship quality of adult children with independent parents. *Family Relations*, 155–162.

Brooks-Gunn, J. (1986). The relationship of maternal beliefs about sex typing to maternal and young children's behavior. *Sex Roles, 14*, 21–35.

Brooks-Gunn, J., & Reiter, E. O. (1990). The role of pubertal processes. In S. S. Feldman & G. R. Elliott (Eds.), *At the threshold: The developing adolescent*. Cambridge, MA: Harvard University Press.

Broomhall, H. S., & Winefield, A. H. (1990). A comparison of the affective well-being of young and middle-aged unemployed men matched for length of employment. *British Journal of Medical Psychology, 63*, 43–52.

Brown, B. B., Lohr, M. J., & McClenahan, E. L. (1986). Early adolescents' perceptions of peer pressure. *Journal of Early Adolescence, 6*, 139–154.

Brown, D. R. (1990). Exercise, fitness, and mental health. In C. Bouchard, R. J. Shephard, T. Stephens, J. R. Sutton, & B. D. McPherson (Eds.), *Exercise, fitness, and health: A consensus of current knowledge*. Champaign, IL: Human Kinetics Books.

Brown, D., Scheflin, A. W., & Hammond, D. C. (1998). *Memory, trauma treatment, and the law*. New York: W. W. Norton.

Brown, E. (1994). Affairs: The hidden meanings have major impact on therapeutic approach. *Behavior Today*, 3–4.

Brown, J. D. (1990). Evaluating one's abilities: Shortcuts and stumbling blocks on the road to self-knowledge. *Journal of Experimental Social Psychology, 26*, 149–167.

Brown, J. D. (1991). Staying fit and staying well: Physical fitness as a moderator of life stress. *Journal of Personality and Social Psychology, 60*, 555–561.

Brown, J. D., & McGill, K. L. (1989). The cost of good fortune: When positive life events produce negative health consequences. *Journal of Personality and Social Psychology, 57*, 1103–1110.

Brown, J. D., & Rogers, R. J. (1991). Self-serving attributions: The role of physiological arousal. *Personality and Social Psychology Bulletin, 17*, 501–506.

Brown, J. D., & Siegel, J. M. (1988). Exercise as a buffer of life stress: A prospective study of adolescent health. *Health Psychology, 7*, 341–353.

Brown, J., Childers, K. W., Bauman, K. E., & Koch, G. G. (1990). The influence of new media and family structure on young adolescents' television and radio use. *Communication Research, 17*, 65–82.

Brown, S., & Booth, A. (1996). Cohabitation versus marriage: A comparison of relationship quality. *Journal of Marriage and the Family*, 668–678.

Browne, A. (1993). Violence against women by male partners: Prevalence, outcomes, and policy implications. *American Psychologist, 48*, 1077–1087.

Browne, A., & Williams, K. R. (1993). Gender, intimacy, and lethal violence: Trends from 1976 through 1987. *Gender & Society, 7*, 78–98.

Brownell, K. D. (1989, June). When and how to diet. *Psychology Today*, pp. 40–46.

Brownell, K. D. (1995). Exercise in the treatment of obesity. In K. D. Brownell & C. G. Fairburn (Eds.), *Eating disorders and obesity: A comprehensive handbook*. New York: Guilford Press.

Brownell, K. D., & Rodin, J. (1994). The dieting maelstrom. *American Psychologist, 49*, 781–791.

Brubaker, T. (1990). Families in later life: A burgeoning research area. *Journal of Marriage and the Family, 52*, 959–982.

Bruch, H. (1973). *Eating disorders: Obesity, anorexia nervosa and the person within*. New York: Basic Books.

Bruch, H. (1978). *The golden cage: The enigma of anorexia nervosa*. Cambridge, MA: Harvard University Press.

Bruckner-Gordon, F., Gangi, B. K., & Wallman, G. U. (1988). *Making therapy work: Your guide to choosing, using, and ending therapy*. New York: HarperCollins.

Brush, L. D. (1990). Violent acts and injurious outcomes in married couples: Methodological issues in the national survey of families and households. *Gender and Society, 4*, 56–67.

Bryan, J. H., & Test, M. A. (1967). Models and helping: Naturalistic studies in aiding behavior. *Journal of Personality and Social Psychology, 6*, 400–407.

Bryant, S. S., & Demian. (1994). Relationship characteristics of American gay and lesbian couples: Findings from a national survey. *Journal of Gay and Lesbian Social Services, 1*, 101–117.

Bryant, S., & Rakowski, W. (1992). Predictors of mortality among elderly African-Americans. *Research on Aging, 14*, 50–67.

Bryden, M. P. (1988). An overview of the dichotic listening procedure and its relation to cerebral organization. In K. Hugdahl (Ed.), *Handbook of dichotic listening*. Chichester, England: Wiley.

Bryer, K. B. (1979). The Amish way of death: A study of family support systems. *American Psychologist, 34*, 255–261.

Buchsbaum, M. S., Someya, T., Teng, C. Y., Abel, L., Chin, S., Najafi, A., Haier, R. J., Wu, J., & Bunney, W. E., Jr. (1996). PET and MRI of the thalamus in never-medicated patients with schizophrenia. *American Journal of Psychiatry, 153*, 191–199.

Buck, E. B., Newton, B. J., & Mura-matsu, Y. (1984). Independence and obedience in the U.S. and Japan. *International Journal of Intercultural Relations, 8*, 279–300.

Buckley, P. F., & Meltzer, H. Y. (1995). Treatment of schizophrenia. In A. F. Schatzberg & C. B. Nemeroff (Eds.), *The American Psychiatric Press textbook of psychopharmacology*. Washington, DC: American Psychiatric Press.

Buda, M., & Tsuang, M. T. (1990). The epidemiology of suicide: Implications for clinical practice. In S. J. Blumenthal & D. J. Kupfer (Eds.), *Suicide over the life cycle: Risk factors, assessment, and treatment of suicidal patients*. Washington, DC: American Psychiatric Press.

Buehler, C., & Langenbrunner, M. (1987). Divorce-related stressors: Occurrence, disruptiveness, and area of life change. *Journal of Divorce, 11*, 25–50.

Buehlman, K. T., Gottman, J. M., & Katz, L. F. (1992). How a couple views their past predicts their future: Predicting divorce from an oral history interview. *Journal of Family Psychology, 5*, 295–318.

Buffum, J., Pharm, D., Smith, D. E., Moser, C., Apter, M., Buxton, M., & Davison, J. (1981). Drugs and sexual function. In H. I. Lief (Ed.), *Sexual problems in medical practice*. Chicago: American Medical Association.

Bull, R., & Rumsey, N. (1988). *The social psychology of facial appearance*. New York: Springer-Verlag.

Bullock, W. A., & Gilliland, K. (1993). Eysenck's arousal theory of introversion-extraversion: A converging measures investigation. *Journal of Personality and Social Psychology, 64*, 113–123.

Bumiller, E. (1989). First comes marriage—Then, maybe, love. In J. M. Henslin (Ed.), *Marriage and family in a changing society* (3rd ed.). New York: Free Press.

Bumpass, L. L., & Sweet, J. A. (1989). National estimates of cohabitation: Cohort levels and union stability. *Demography, 25*, 615–625.

Bumpass, L. L., Raley, R. K., & Sweet, J. (1995). The changing character of stepfamilies: Implications of cohabitation and nonmarital childbearing. *Demography, 32,* 425–436.

Bumpass, L. L., Sweet, J. A., & Cherlin, A. (1991). The role of cohabitation in declining rates of marriage. *Journal of Marriage and the Family, 53,* 913–927.

Bumpass, L. L., Sweet, J. A., & Martin, T. C. (1990). Changing patterns of remarriage. *Journal of Marriage and the Family, 52,* 747–756.

Burg, M. W. (1995). Anger, hostility, and coronary heart disease: A review. *Mind/Body Medicine, 1,* 159–172.

Burger, J. M. (1989). Negative reactions to increases in perceived personal control. *Journal of Personality and Social Psychology, 56,* 246–256.

Burger, J. M. (1993). *Personality.* Pacific Grove, CA: Brooks/Cole.

Burger, J. M., & Petty, R. E. (1981). The low-ball compliance technique: Task or person commitment? *Journal of Personality and Social Psychology, 40,* 492–500.

Burgoon, J. K., Buller, D. B., & Woodall, W. G. (1989). *Nonverbal communication: The unspoken dialogue.* New York: Harper & Row.

Burhans, K. K., & Dweck, C. S. (1995). Helplessness in early childhood: The role of contingent worth. *Child Development, 66,* 1719–1738.

Buri, J. R., Louiselle, P. A., Misukanis, T. M., & Mueller, R. A. (1988). Effects of parental authoritarianism and authoritativeness on self-esteem. *Personality and Social Psychology Bulletin, 14,* 271–282.

Burkhardt, S. A., & Rotatori, A. F. (1995). *Treatment and prevention of childhood sexual abuse: A child-generated model.* Washington, DC: Taylor & Francis.

Burleson, B. R. (1982). The development of comforting communication skills in childhood and adolescence. *Child Development, 53,* 1578–1588.

Burleson, B. R., & Denton, W. H. (1997). The relationship between communication skill and marital satisfaction: Some moderating effects. *Journal of Marriage and the Family, 59,* 884–902.

Burt, M. R. (1980). Cultural myths and supports for rape. *Journal of Personality and Social Psychology, 38,* 217–230.

Buscaglia, L. (1982). *Living, loving and learning.* Thorofare, NJ: Charles B. Slack.

Buss, D. M. (1985). Human mate selection. *American Scientist, 73,* 47–51.

Buss, D. M. (1988). The evolution of human intrasexual competition: Tactics of mate attraction. *Journal of Personality and Social Psychology, 54,* 616–628.

Buss, D. M. (1989). Sex differences in human mate preferences: Evolutionary hypotheses tested in 37 cultures. *Behavioral and Brain Sciences, 12,* 1–14.

Buss, D. M. (1994). Mate preferences in 37 cultures. In W. J. Lonner & R. S. Malpass (Eds.), *Psychology and culture.* Boston: Allyn & Bacon.

Buss, D. M., & Barnes, M. (1986). Preferences in human mate selection. *Journal of Personality and Social Psychology, 50,* 559–570.

Buss, D. M. (1995). Evolutionary psychology: A new paradigm for psychological science. *Psychological Inquiry, 6,* 1–30.

Buss, D. M. (1996). The evolutionary psychology of human social strategies. In E. T. Higgins & A. W. Kruglanski (Eds.), *Social psychology: Handbook of basic principles.* New York: Guilford Press.

Buss, D. M. (1997). Evolutionary foundation of personality. In R. Hogan, J. Johnson, & S. Briggs (Eds.), *Handbook of personality psychology.* San Diego, CA: Academic Press.

Buss, D. M. (1991). Evolutionary personality psychology. *Annual Review of Psychology, 42,* 459–491.

Bussey, K., & Bandura, A. (1984). Influence of gender constancy and social power on sex-linked modeling. *Journal of Personality and Social Psychology, 47,* 1292–1302.

Butcher, J. N., Narikiyo, T., & Vitousek, K. B. (1993). Understanding abnormal behavior in cultural context. In P. B. Sutker & H. E. Adams (Eds.), *Comprehensive handbook of psychopathology.* New York: Plenum.

Butler, R., & Lewis, M. (1982). *Aging and mental health* (3rd ed.). St. Louis: Mosby.

Butow, P., Beumont, P., & Touyz, S. (1993). Cognitive processes in dieting disorders. *International Journal of Eating Disorders, 14,* 319–330.

Buunk, B. (1980). Extramarital sex in the Netherlands: Motivations in social and marital context. *Alternative Lifestyles, 3,* 11–39.

Buunk, B. P., Collins, R. L., Taylor, S. E., VanYperen, N. W., & Dakof, G. A. (1990). The affective consequences of social comparison: Either direction has its ups and downs. *Journal of Personality and Social Psychology, 59,* 1238–1249.

Buunk, B. P., de Jonge, J., Ybema, J. F., & de Wolff. C. J. (1998). Psychosocial aspects of occupational stress. In P. J. D. Drenth, H. Thierry, & C. J. de Wolff (Eds.), *Handbook of work and organizational psychology.* East Sussex, UK: Psychology Press.

Buvat, J., Buvat-Herbaut, M., Lemaire, A., & Marcolin, G. (1990). Recent developments in the clinical assessment and diagnosis of erectile dysfunction. *Annual Review of Sex Research, 1,* 265–308.

Buxton, M. N., Arkel, Y., Lagos, J., Deposito, F., Lowenthal, H., & Simring, S. (1981). Stress and platelet aggregation in hemophiliac children and their family members. *Research Communications in Psychology, Psychiatry and Behavior, 6,* 21–48.

Byne, W., & Parsons, B. (1993). Human sexual orientation: The biologic theories reappraised. *Archives of General Psychiatry, 50,* 228–238.

Byrd, J. C. (1992). Environmental tobacco smoke: Medical and legal issues. *Medical Clinics of North America, 76,* 377–398.

Byrne, D. (1971). *The attraction paradigm.* New York: Academic Press.

Byrne, D., Clore, G. L., & Smeaton, G. (1986). The attraction hypothesis: Do similar attitudes affect anything? *Journal of Personality and Social Psychology, 51,* 1167–1170.

Byrne, D., Kelley, K., & Fisher, W. A. (1993). Unwanted teenage pregnancies: Incidence, interpretation, and intervention. *Applied and Preventive Psychology, 2,* 101–113.

Calderone, M. S., & Johnson, E. W. (1989). *The family book about sexuality.* New York: Harper & Row.

Caldwell, B. M. (1993). Impact of day care on the child. *Pediatrics, 91,* 225–228.

Caldwell, L. L., Smith, E. A., & Weissinger, E. (1992). The relationship of leisure activities and perceived health of college students. *Society and Leisure, 15,* 545–556.

Caldwell, M. A., & Peplau, L. A. (1982). Sex differences in same-sex friendship. *Sex Roles, 8,* 721–732.

Calev, A., Phil, D., Pass, H. L., Shapira, B., Fink, M., Tubi, N., & Lerer, B. (1993). ECT and memory. In C. E. Coffey (Ed.), *The clinical science of electroconvulsive therapy.* Washington, DC: American Psychological Press.

Cameron, L., Leventhal, E. A., & Leventhal, H. (1993). Symptom representations and affect as determinants of care seeking in a community-dwelling, adult sample population. *Health Psychology, 12,* 171–179.

Cameron, N. (1963). *Personality development and psychopathology.* Boston: Houghton Mifflin.

Campbell, E. Q., & Pettigrew, T. F. (1959). Racial and moral crisis: The role of Little Rock ministers. *American Journal of Sociology, 64,* 509–516.

Campbell, J. D. (1986). Similarity and uniqueness: The effects of attribute type, relevance, and individual differences in self-esteem and depression. *Journal of Personality and Social Psychology, 50,* 281–294.

Campbell, J. D., & Lavallee, L. F. (1993). Who am I? The role of self-concept confusion in understanding the behavior of people with low self-esteem. In R. Baumeister (Ed.), *Self-esteem: The puzzle of low self-regard.* New York: Plenum.

Campbell, J. D., Chew, B., & Scratchley, L. S. Cognitive and emotional reactions to daily events: The effects of self-esteem and self-complexity. *Journal of Personality, 59,* 473–505.

Canavan, M. M., Meyer, I. W. J., & Higgins, D. C. (1992). The female experience of sibling incest. *Journal of Marital and Family Therapy, 18,* 129–142.

Cannon, W. B. (1932). *The wisdom of the body.* New York: Norton.

Cantor, N. (1990). Social psychology and sociobiology: What can we leave to evolution? *Motivation and Emotion, 14,* 245–254.

Carey, G., & DiLalla, D. L. (1994). Personality and psychopathology: Genetic perspectives. *Journal of Abnormal Psychology, 103,* 32–43.

Cargan, L., & Melko, M. (1982). *Singles: Myths and realities.* Newbury Park, CA: Sage Publications.

Carli, L. J. (1990). Gender, language, and influence. *Journal of Personality and Social Psychology, 59,* 941–951.

Carlson, E. A. (1998). A prospective longitudinal study of attachment disorganization/disorientation. *Child Development, 69,* 1107–1128.

Carlson, R. (1997). *Don't sweat the small stuff ... and it's all small stuff: Simple ways to keep the little things from taking over your life.* New York: Hyperion.

Carlson, V., Cicchetti, D., Barnett, D., & Braunwald, K. (1989). Disorganized/disoriented attachment relationships in maltreated infants. *Developmental Psychology, 25,* 525–531.

Carney, C. G., & Wells, C. F. (1999). *Working well, living well: Discover the career within you.* Pacific Grove, CA: Brooks/Cole.

Carpenter, W. T. (1992). The negative symptom challenge. *Archives of General Psychiatry, 49,* 236–237.

Carr, P. G., & Mednick, M. T. (1988). Sex role socialization and the development of achievement motivation in black preschool children. *Sex Roles, 18,* 169–180.

Carrington, P. (1987). Managing meditation in clinical practice. In M. A. West (Ed.), *The psychology of meditation.* Oxford: Clarendon Press.

Carrington, P. (1993). Modern forms of meditation. In P. M. Lehrer & R. L. Woolfolk (Eds.), *Principles and practice of stress management* (2nd ed.). New York: Guilford Press.

Carroll, J. L., Volk, K. D., & Hyde, J. S. (1985). Differences between males and females in motives for engaging in sexual intercourse. *Archives of Sexual Behavior, 14,* 131–139.

Carson, R. C. (1991). Dilemmas in the pathway of the DSM-IV. *Journal of Abnormal Psychology, 100,* 302–307.

Carson, R. C., & Sanislow, C. A., III. (1993). The schizophrenias. In P. B. Sutker & H. E.

Adams (Eds.), *Comprehensive handbook of psychopathology* (2nd ed.). New York: Plenum.

Carter, E. A., & McGoldrick, M. (1988). Overview: The changing family life cycle—A framework for family therapy. In E. A. Carter & M. McGoldrick (Eds.), *The changing family life cycle: A framework for family therapy* (2nd ed.). New York: Gardner Press.

Carter, R. J., & Myerowitz, B. E. (1984). Sex-role stereotypes: Self-reports of behavior. *Sex Roles, 10,* 293–306.

Cartwright, C., & Hollander, E. (1997). Pharmacotherapy of obsessive-compulsive disorder-experience with the SSRIs. *Primary Psychiatry, 4,* 38–45.

Carver, C. S., & Scheier, M. F. (1994). Situational coping and coping dispositions in a stressful transaction. *Journal of Personality and Social Psychology, 66,* 184–195.

Carver, C. S., Pozo, C., Harris, S. D., Noriega, V., Scheier, M. F., Robinson, D. S., Ketcham, A. S., Moffat, F. L., Jr., & Clark, K. C. (1993). How coping mediates the effect of optimism on distress: A study of women with early stage breast cancer. *Journal of Personality and Social Psychology, 65,* 375–390.

Carver, C. S., Scheier, M. F., & Weintraub, J. K. (1989). Assessing coping strategies: A theoretically based approach. *Journal of Personality and Social Psychology, 56,* 267–283.

Cashmore, J. A., & Goodnow, J. J. (1986). Influences on Australian parents' values: Ethnicity versus sociometric status. *Journal of Cross-Cultural Psychology, 17,* 441–454.

Caspi, A., & Herbener, E. S. (1990). Continuity and change: Assortative marriage and the consistency of personality in adulthood. *Journal of Personality and Social Psychology, 58,* 250–258.

Caspi, A., Bolger, N., & Eckenrode, J. (1987). Linking person and context in the daily stress process. *Journal of Personality and Social Psychology, 52,* 184–195.

Cassell, C. (1984). *Swept away: Why women fear their own sexuality.* New York: Simon & Schuster.

Catalano, R., Novaco, R., & McConnell, W. (1997). A model of the net effect of job loss on violence. *Journal of Personality and Social Psychology, 72,* 1440–1447.

Catania, J. A., Coates, T. J., Stall, R., Turner, H., Peterson, J., Hearst, N., Dolcini, M. M., Hudes, E., Gagnon, J., Wiley, J., & Groves, R. (1992). Prevalence of AIDS-related risk factors and condom use in the United States. *Science, 258,* 1101–1106.

Catania, J. A., McDermott, L. J., & Pollack, L. M. (1986). Questionnaire response bias and face-to-face interview sample bias in sexuality research. *The Journal of Sex Research, 22,* 52–72.

Cate, R. M., & Lloyd, S. A. (1988). Courtship. In S. Duck (Ed.), *Handbook of personal relationships.* New York: Wiley.

Cate, R. M., & Lloyd, S. A. (1992). *Courtship.* Newbury Park, CA: Sage Publications.

Cate, R. M., Huston, T. L., & Nesselroade, J. R. (1986). Premarital relationships: Toward the identification of alternative pathways to marriage. *Journal of Social and Clinical Psychology, 4,* 3–22.

Cattell, R. B. (1950). *Personality: A systematic, theoretical and factual study.* New York: McGraw-Hill.

Cattell, R. B. (1966). *The scientific analysis of personality.* Chicago: Aldine.

Cattell, R. B. (1990). Advances in Cattellian personality theory. In L. A. Pervin (Ed.), *Handbook of personality: Theory and research.* New York: Guilford Press.

Cattell, R. B., Eber, H. W., & Tatsuoka, M. M. (1970). *Handbook of the Sixteen Personality Factor Questionnaire* (16PF). Champaign, IL: Institute for Personality and Ability Testing.

Cattell, R. B., Kawash, G. F., & DeYoung, G. E. (1972). Validation of objective measures of ergic tension: Response of the sex urge to visual stimulation. *Journal of Experimental Research in Personality, 6,* 76–83.

Cavanaugh, J. C. (1993). *Adult development and aging* (2nd ed.). Pacific Grove, CA: Brooks/Cole.

Cegala, D. J., & Sillars, A. L. (1989). Further examination of nonverbal manifestations of interaction involvement. *Communication Reports, 2,* 39–47.

Centers for Disease Control and Prevention. (1992). *Sexually transmitted disease surveillance.* Atlanta: CDC.

Cerletti, U., & Bini, L. (1938). Un nuevo metodo di shockterapie "L'elettro-shock." Boll. Acad. Med. Roma, 64, 136–138.

Cermak, T. L. (1986). Diagnostic criteria for codependency. *Journal of Psychoactive Drugs, 18,* 15–20.

Chaiken, S. (1979). Communicator's physical attractiveness and persuasion. *Journal of Personality and Social Psychology, 37,* 1387–1397.

Chambré, S. M. (1993). Voluntarism by elders: Past trends and future prospects. *Gerontologist, 33,* 221–228.

Chang, E. C. (1996). Cultural differences in optimism, pessimism, and coping: Predictors of subsequent adjustment in Asian American and Caucasian American college students. *Journal of Counseling Psychology, 43,* 113–123.

Chang, E. C. (1998). Dispositional optimism and primary and secondary appraisal of a stressor: Controlling for confounding influences and relations to coping and psychological and physical adjustment. *Journal of Personality and Social Psychology, 74,* 1109–1120.

Chang, R. Y., & Kelly, P. K. (1993). *Step-by-step problem solving: A practical guide to ensure problems get (and stay) solved.* Irvine, CA: Richard Chang Associates.

Chapman, B. E., & Brannock, J. C. (1987). A proposed model of lesbian identity development: An empirical investigation. *Journal of Homosexuality, 14,* 69–80.

Charlesworth, W. R., & Dzur, C. (1987). Gender comparisons of preschoolers' behavior and resource utilization in group problem-solving. *Child Development, 58,* 191–200.

Charney, D. S., Miller, H. L., Licinio, J., & Salomon, R. (1995). Treatment of depression. In A. F. Schatzberg & C. B. Nemeroff (Eds.), *The American Psychiatric Press textbook of psychopharmacology.* Washington, DC: American Psychiatric Press.

Check, J., & Malamuth, N. (1983). Sex role stereotyping and reactions to depictions of stranger versus acquaintance rape. *Journal of Personality and Social Psychology, 45,* 344–356.

Chehrazi, S. (1986). Female psychology. *Journal of the American Psychoanalytic Association, 34,* 111–162.

Cherlin, A. J. (1981). *Marriage, divorce, remarriage.* Cambridge, MA: Harvard University Press.

Cherlin, A. (1992). *Marriage, divorce, remarriage.* Cambridge, MA: Harvard University Press.

Chiriboga, D. A. (1987). Personality in later life. In P. Silverman (Ed.), *The elderly as modern pioneers.* Bloomington: Indiana University Press.

Chiriboga, D. A. (1989). Mental health at the mid-point: Crisis, challenge, or relief? In S. Hunter & M. Sundel (Eds.), *Mid-life myths: Issues, findings, and practical implications.* Thousand Oaks, CA: Sage.

Chodorow, N. (1978). *The reproduction of mothering.* Berkeley, CA: University of California Press.

Chopra, D. (1993). *Ageless body, timeless mind.* New York: Crown.

Christensen, A., & Heavey, C. L. (1990). Gender and social structure in the demand/withdraw pattern of marital conflict. *Journal of Personality and Social Psychology, 59,* 73–81.

Christensen, A., & Jacobson, N. S. (1994). Who (or what) can do psychotherapy: The status and challenge of nonprofessional therapies. *Psychological Science, 5,* 8–14.

Chumlea, W. C. (1982). Physical growth in adolescence. In B. B. Wolman (Ed.), *Handbook of developmental psychology.* Englewood Cliffs, NJ: Prentice-Hall.

Church, A. T., & Burke, P. J. (1994). Exploratory and confirmatory tests of the Big Five and Tellegen's three- and four-dimensional models. *Journal of Personality and Social Psychology, 66,* 93–114.

Church, A. T. (1994). Relating to Tellegen and five-factor models of personality structure. *Journal of Personality and Social Psychology, 67,* 898–909.

Church, G. J. (1993, November 22). Jobs in an age of insecurity. *Time,* pp. 32–39.

Cialdini, R. B. (1993). *Influence: Science and practice* (3rd ed.). Glenview, IL: HarperCollins.

Cialdini, R. B., Borden, R. J., Thorne, A., Walker, M. R., Freeman, S., & Sloan, L. R. (1976). Basking in reflected glory: Three (football) field studies. *Journal of Personality and Social Psychology, 34,* 366–375.

Cicirelli, V. G. (1989). Feelings of attachment to siblings and well-being in later life. *Psychology and Aging, 4,* 211–216.

Ciompi, L. (1980). Catamnestic long-term study on the course of life and aging in schizophrenics. *Schizophrenia Bulletin, 6,* 607–618.

Clark, D. A., Beck, A. T., & Beck, J. S. (1994). Symptom differences in major depression, dysthymia, panic disorder, and generalized anxiety disorder. *American Journal of Psychiatry, 151,* 205–209.

Clark, L. A., Watson, D., & Mineka, S. (1994). Temperament, personality, and the mood and anxiety disorders. *Journal of Abnormal Psychology, 103,* 103–116.

Clark, L. A., Watson, D., & Reynolds, S. (1995). Diagnosis and classification of psychopathology: Challenges to the current system and future directions. *Annual Reviews of Psychology, 46,* 121–153.

Clark, L. F. (1993). Stress and the cognitive-conversational benefits of social interaction. *Journal of Social and Clinical Psychology, 12,* 25–55.

Clark, M. S., & Bennett, M. E. (1992). Research on relationships: Implications for mental health. In D. N. Ruble, R. R. Costanzo, & M. E. Oliveri (Eds.), *The social psychology of mental health.* New York: Guilford Press.

Clark, M. S., & Mills, J. (1993). The difference between communal and exchange relationships: What it is and is not. *Journal of Personality and Social Psychology Bulletin, 19,* 684–691.

Clark, M. S., Mills, J., & Powell, M. C. (1986). Keeping track of needs in communal and exchange relationships. *Journal of Personality and Social Psychology, 51,* 333–338.

Clark, R. L. (1988). The future of work and retirement. *Research on Aging, 10,* 169–193.

Clarke-Stewart, K. A., & Bailey, B. L. (1989). Adjusting to divorce: Why do men have it easier? *Journal of Divorce, 13,* 75–94.

Cleary, P. J. (1980). A checklist for life event research. *Journal of Psychosomatic Research, 24,* 199–207.

Cleek, M. G., & Pearson, T. A. (1985). Perceived causes of divorce: An analysis of interrelationships. *Journal of Marriage and the Family, 47,* 179–183.

Clement, U. (1990). Surveys of heterosexual behavior. *Annual Review of Sex Research, 1,* 45–74.

Coates, D. L. (1987). Gender differences in the structure and support characteristics of black adolescents' social networks. *Sex Roles, 17,* 667–687.

Cocks, J. (1991, July 1). A nasty jolt for the top pops. *Time,* pp. 78–79.

Cocores, J. (1987). Co-addiction: A silent epidemic. *Psychiatry Letter, 5,* 5–8.

Cohen, C. E. (1981). Person categories and social perception: Testing some boundaries of the processing effects of prior knowledge. *Journal of Personality and Social Psychology, 40,* 441–452.

Cohen, D., & McCubbin, M. (1990). The political economy of tardive dyskinesia: Asymmetries in power and responsibility. *The Journal of Mind and Behavior, 11,* 465–488.

Cohen, F. (1979). Personality, stress and the development of physical illness. In G. C. Stone, F. Cohen, N. E. Adler, & associates (Eds.), *Health psychology—A handbook.* San Francisco: Jossey-Bass.

Cohen, J. (1997). Advances painted in shades of gray at a D.C. conference. *Science, 275,* 615–616.

Cohen, M. J. M., Kunkel, E. S., & Levenson, J. L. (1998). Associations between psychosocial stress and malignancy. In J. R. Hubbard & E. A. Workman (Eds.), *Handbook of stress medicine: An organ system approach.* Boca Raton: CRC Press.

Cohen, R. L., & Borsoi, D. (1996). The role of gestures in description-communication: A cross-sectional study of aging. *Journal of Nonverbal Behavior, 20,* 45–64.

Cohen, S. (1986). Marijuana. In A. J. Frances & R. E. Hales (Eds.), *Psychiatry Update: Annual Review* (Vol. 5). Washington, DC: American Psychiatric Press.

Cohen, S. (1988). Psychosocial models of the role of social support in the etiology of physical disease. *Health Psychology, 7,* 269–297.

Cohen, S., & Hajioff, A. (1972). Life events and the onset of acute closed-angle glaucoma. *Journal of Psychosomatic Research, 16,* 335–341.

Cohen, S., & Lichtenstein, E. (1990). Perceived stress, quitting smoking, and smoking relapse. *Health Psychology, 9,* 466–478.

Cohen, S., & Syme, S. L. (Eds.). (1985). *Social support and health.* New York: Academic Press.

Cohen, S., Evans, G. W., Krantz, D. S., & Stokols, D. (1980). Physiological, motivational, and cognitive effects of aircraft noise on children: Moving from the laboratory to the field. *American Psychologist, 35,* 231–243.

Cohen, S., Kamarck, T., & Mermelstein, R. (1983). A global measure of perceived stress. *Journal of Health and Social Behavior, 24,* 385–396.

Cohen, S., Lichtenstein, E., Prochaska, J. O., Rossi, J. S., Gritz, E. R., Carr, C. R., Orleans, C. T., Schoenbach, V. J., Biener, L., Abrams, D., DiClemente, C., Curry, S., Marlatt, G. A., Cummings, K. M., Emont, S. L., Giovino, A., & Ossip-Klein, D. (1989). Debunking myths about self-quitting: Evidence from 10 prospective studies of persons who attempt to quit smoking by themselves. *American Psychologist, 44,* 1355–1365.

Cohen, S., Tyrrell, D. A., & Smith, A. P. (1993). Negative life events, perceived stress, negative affect, and susceptibility to the common cold. *Journal of Personality and Social Psychology, 64,* 131–140.

Cohn, L. D., & Adler, N. E. (1992). Female and male perceptions of ideal body shapes: Distorted views among Caucasian college students. *Psychology of Women Quarterly, 16,* 69–79.

Coie, J. D., & Doddge, K. A. (1997). Aggression and antisocial behavior. In W. Damon & N. Eisenberg (Eds.), *Handbook of child psychology* (Vol. 3). New York: Wiley.

Cole, J. O., & Yonkers, K. A. (1995). Nonbenzodiazepine anxiolytics. In A. F. Schatzberg & C. B. Nemeroff (Eds.), *The American Psychiatric Press textbook of psychopharmacology.* Washington, DC: American Psychiatric Press.

Cole, P. M., & Putnam, F. W. (1992). Effect of incest on self and social functioning: A developmental psychopathology perspective. *Journal of Consulting and Clinical Psychology, 60,* 174–184.

Cole, S. W., Kemeny, M. E., Taylor, S. E., & Visscher, B. R. (1996). Elevated physical health risk among gay men who conceal their homosexual identity. *Health Psychology, 15,* 243–251.

Cole, W., Emery, M., & Horowitz, J. M. (1993, May 24). What should we teach our children about sex? *Time,* pp. 60–66.

Coleman, D., & Salt, J. (1991). *The British population: Patterns, trends, processes.* Oxford: Oxford University Press.

Coleman, L. M., & Antonucci, T. C. (1983). Impact of work on women at midlife. *Developmental Psychology, 19,* 290–294.

Coles, R., & Stokes, G. (1985). *Sex and the American teenager.* New York: Harper.

Colgrove, M., Bloomfield, H., & McWilliams, P. (1991). *How to survive the loss of a love.* Los Angeles, CA: Prelude Press.

Collaborative Group on Hormonal Factors in Breast Cancer. (1997). Breast cancer and hormone replacement therapy: Collaborative reanalysis of data from 51 epidemiological studies of 52,705 women with breast cancer and 108,411 women without breast cancer. *Lancet, 350,* 1047–1059.

Collaer, M. L., & Hines, M. (1995). Human behavioral sex differences: A role for gonadal hormones during early development? *Psychological Bulletin, 118,* 55–107.

Collins, R. G. (1993). Reconstruing codependency using self-in-relation theory: A feminist perspective. *Social Work, 38,* 470–476.

Collins, N. L., & Miller, L. C. (1994). Self-disclosure and liking: A meta-analytic review. *Psychological Bulletin, 116,* 457–475.

Collins, N. L., & Read, S. J. (1990). Adult attachment, working models, and relationship quality in dating couples. *Journal of Personality and Social Psychology, 58,* 644–663.

Coltrane, S., & Ishii-Kuntz, M. (1992). Men's housework: A life course perspective. *Journal of Marriage and the Family, 54,* 43–57.

Colvin, C. R., & Block, J. (1994). Do positive illusions foster mental health? An examination of the Taylor and Brown formulation. *Psychological Bulletin, 116,* 3–20.

Colvin, C. R., Block, J., & Funder, D. C. (1995). Overly positive self-evaluations and personality: Negative implications for mental health. *Journal of Personality and Social Psychology, 68,* 1152–1162.

Comas-Diaz, L. (1987). Feminist therapy with mainland Puerto Rican women. *Psychology of Women Quarterly, 11,* 461–474.

Comas-Diaz, L. (1991). Feminism and diversity in psychology: The case of women of color. *Psychology of Women Quarterly, 15,* 597–609.

Conger, R., Elder, G., Lorenz, F., Conger, K., Simons, R., Whitbeck, L., Huck, S., & Melby, J. (1990). Linking economic hardship to marital quality and instability. *Journal of Marriage and the Family, 52,* 643–656.

Conley, R. R., Carpenter, W. T., & Tamminga, C. A. (1997). Time to clozapine response in a standardized trial. *American Journal of Psychiatry, 154,* 1243–1247.

Cook, M., & Mineka, S. (1989). Observational conditioning of fear to fear-relevant versus fear-irrelevant stimuli in Rhesus monkeys. *Journal of Abnormal Psychology, 98,* 448–459.

Cooney, T. M., Pedersen, F. A., Indelicato, S., & Palkovitz, R. (1993). Timing of fatherhood: Is "on-time" optimal? *Journal of Marriage and the Family, 55,* 205–215.

Coontz, S. (1992). *The way we never were: American families and the nostalgia trap.* New York: Basic Books.

Cooper, C. L. (1984). The social-psychological precursors to cancer. *Journal of Human Stress, 10,* 4–11.

Cooper, H., Okamura, L., & Gurka, V. (1992). Social activity and subjective well-being. *Personality and Individual Differences, 13,* 573–583.

Cooper, K. (1970). *The new aerobics.* New York: Bantam.

Cooper, P. J. (1995). Eating disorders and their relationship to mood and anxiety disorders. In K. D. Brownell & C. G. Fairburn (Eds.), *Eating disorders and obesity: A comprehensive handbook.* New York: Guilford Press.

Cooper, Z. (1995). The development and maintenance of eating disorders. In K. D. Brownell & C. G. Fairburn (Eds.), *Eating disorders and obesity: A comprehensive handbook.* New York: Guilford Press.

Coopersmith, S. (1967). *The antecedents of self-esteem.* San Francisco: Freeman.

Coopersmith, S. (1975). Studies in self-esteem. In R. C. Atkinson (Ed.), *Psychology in progress: Readings from Scientific American.* San Francisco: Freeman.

Coryell, W., & Winokur, G. (1992). Course and outcome. In E. S. Paykel (Ed.), *Handbook of affective disorders* (2nd ed.). New York: Guilford Press.

Costa, P. T., Jr., & McCrae, R. R. (1988). Personality in adulthood: A six-year longitudinal study of self-reports and spouse ratings on the NEO Personality Inventory. *Journal of Personality and Social Psychology, 54,* 853–863.

Costa, P. T., Jr., & McCrae, R. R. (1994). Set like plaster? Evidence for the stability of adult personality. In T. F. Heatherton & J. L. Weinberger (Eds.), *Can personality change?* Washington, DC: American Psychological Association.

Costa, P. T., Jr., & McCrae, R. R. (1985). *NEO Personality Inventory.* Odessa, FL: Psychological Assessment Resources.

Costa, P. T., Jr., & McCrae, R. R. (1992). *Revised NEO Personality Inventory: NEO PI and NEO Five-Factor Inventory (Professional Manual).* Odessa, FL: Psychological Assessment Resources.

Costa, P. T., Jr., McCrae, R. R., & Dye, D. A. (1991). Facet scales for agreeableness and conscientiousness: A revision of the NEO Personality Inventory. *Personality and Individual Differences, 12,* 887–898.

Covi, L., & Primakoff, L. (1988). Cognitive group therapy. In A. J. Frances & R. E. Hales (Eds.), *Review of psychiatry* (Vol. 7). Washington, DC: American Psychiatric Association.

Crane, P. T. (1985). Voluntary childlessness: Some notes on the decision-making process. In D. B. Gutknecht & E. W. Butler (Eds.), *Family, self, and society: Emerging issues, alternatives, and interventions* (2nd ed.). New York: UPA.

Craufurd, D. I. O., Creed, F., & Jayson, M. D. (1990). Life events and psychological disturbance in patients with low-back pain. *Spine, 15,* 490–494.

Creed, F. (1989). Appendectomy. In G. W. Brown & T. O. Harris (Eds.), *Life events and illness*. New York: Guilford Press.

Creed, F. (1993). Stress and psychosomatic disorders. In L. Goldberger & S. Breznitz (Eds.), *Handbook of stress: Theoretical and clinical aspects* (2nd ed.). New York: Free Press.

Crick, N. R., & Grotpeter, J. K. (1995). Relational aggression, gender, and social-psychological adjustment. *Child Development, 66,* 710–722.

Crick, N. R. (1995). Relational aggression: The role of intent attributions, feeling of distress, and provocation type. *Development and Psychopathology, 7,* 313–322.

Crimmins, E. M., & Ingegneri, D. G. (1990). Interaction and living arrangements of older parents and their children. *Research on Aging, 12,* 3–35.

Critelli, J. W., & Ee, J. S. (1996). Stress and physical illness: Development of an integrative model. In T. W. Miller (Ed.), *Theory and assessment of stressful life events*. Madison, CT: International Universities Press.

Crites, J. O. (1980). Career development. In J. F. Adams (Ed.), *Understanding adolescence: Current developments in adolescent psychology* (4th ed.). Boston: Allyn & Bacon.

Crits-Christoph, P. (1997). Limitations of the dodo bird verdict and the role of clinical trials in psychotherapy research: Comment on Wampold, et al. (1997). *Psychological Bulletin, 122,* 216–220.

Crocker, J., & Luhtanen, R. (1990). Collective self-esteem and ingroup bias. *Journal of Personality and Social Psychology, 58,* 60–67.

Crocker, J., & Major, B. (1989). Social stigma and self-esteem: The self-protective properties of stigma. *Psychological Review, 96,* 608–630.

Crocker, J., & McGraw, K. M. (1984). What's good for the goose is not good for the gander: Solo status as an obstacle to occupational achievement for males and females. *American Behavioral Scientist, 27,* 357–370.

Crockett, L. J. (1990). Sex role and sex typing in adolescence. In R. M. Lerner, A. C. Petersen, & J. Brooks-Gunn (Eds.), *The encyclopedia of adolescence* (Vol. 2). New York: Garland.

Crohan, S. E. (1992). Marital happiness and spousal consensus on beliefs about marital conflict: A longitudinal investigation. *Journal of Social and Personal Relationships, 9,* 89–102.

Crook, R. H., Healy, C. C., & O'Shay, D. W. (1984). The linkage of work achievement to self-esteem, career maturity, and college achievement. *Journal of Vocational Behavior, 25,* 70–79.

Crooks, R., & Baur K. (1996). *Our sexuality* (6th ed.). Pacific Grove, CA: Brooks/Cole.

Crosby, F. J., & Jaskar, K. L. (1993). Women and men at home and at work: Realities and illusions. In S. Oskamp & M. Costanzo (Eds.), *Gender issues in contemporary society*. Newbury Park, CA: Sage Publications.

Cross, C. K., & Hirschfeld, R. M. A. (1986). Epidemiology of disorders in adulthood: Suicide. In G. L. Klerman, M. M. Weissman, P. S. Appelbaum, & L. H. Roth (Eds.), *Psychiatry: Vol. 5. Social, epidemiologic, and legal psychiatry*. New York: Basic Books.

Cross, S. E., & Markus, H. R. (1993). Gender in thought, belief, and action: A cognitive approach. In A. E. Beall & R. J. Sternberg (Eds.), *The psychology of gender*. New York: Guilford Press.

Crouter, A. C., Manke, B. A., & McHale, S. M. (1995). The family context of gender intensification in early adolescence. *Child Development, 66,* 317–329.

Crovitz, H. F. (1971). The capacity of memory loci in artificial memory. *Psychonomic Science, 24,* 187–188.

Cuesta, M. J., Peralta, B., & DeLeon, J. (1994). Schizophrenic syndromes associated with treatment response. *Progress in Neurology, Psychopharmacology, and Biological Psychiatry, 18,* 87–99.

Culbertson, F. M. (1997). Depression and gender: An international review. *American Psychologist, 52,* 25–31.

Cunningham, J. A., Strassberg, D. S., & Haan, B. (1986). Effects of intimacy and sex-role congruency on self-disclosure. *Journal of Social and Clinical Psychology, 4,* 393–401.

Cunningham, M. R. (1986). Measuring the physical in physical attractiveness: Quasi-experiments on the sociobiology of female facial beauty. *Journal of Personality and Social Psychology, 50,* 925–935.

Cunningham, M. R., Barbee, A. P., & Pike, C. L. (1990). What do women want? Facialmetric assessment of multiple motives in the perception of male facial physical attractiveness. *Journal of Personality and Social Psychology, 59,* 61–72.

Cunningham, M. R., Roberts, A. R., Wu, C., Barbee, A. P., & Druen, P. B. (1995). "Their ideas of beauty are, on the whole, the same as ours": Consistency and variability in the cross-cultural perception of female physical attractiveness. *Journal of Personality and Social Psychology, 68,* 261–279.

Cupach, W. R., & Comstock, J. (1990). Satisfaction with sexual communication in marriage: Links to sexual satisfaction and dyadic adjustment. *Journal of Social and Personal Relationships, 7,* 179–186.

Curran, D. K. (1987). *Adolescent suicidal behavior*. Washington, DC: Hemisphere.

Curtis, R. C., & Miller, K. (1986). Believing another likes or dislikes you: Behaviors making the beliefs come true. *Journal of Personality and Social Psychology, 51,* 284–290.

Cutler, S. J., & Hendricks, J. (1990). Leisure and time use across the life course. In R. Binstock & L. George (Eds.), *Aging and the social sciences* (3rd ed.). New York: Academic Press.

Cutrona, C. E. (1982). Transition to college: Loneliness and the process of social adjustment. In L. A. Peplau & D. Perlman (Eds.), *Loneliness: A sourcebook of current theory, research, and therapy*. New York: Wiley.

Dabbs, J. M., Jr. (1992). Testosterone measurements in social and clinical psychology. *Journal of Social and Clinical Psychology, 11,* 302–321.

D'Andrade, R. G. (1966). Sex differences and cultural institutions. In E. Maccoby (Ed.), *The development of sex differences*. Stanford, CA: Stanford University Press.

Dantzer, R., & Mormede, P. (1995). Psychoneuroimmunology of stress. In B. E. Leonard & K. Miller (Eds.), *Stress, the immune system and psychiatry*. New York: Wiley.

Darley, J. M., & Gilbert, D. T. (1985). Social psychological aspects of environmental psychology. In G. Lindzey & E. Aronson (Eds.), *Handbook of social psychology* (3rd ed., Vol. 2). New York: Random House.

Darling, C. A., Davidson, J. K., & Conway-Welch, C. (1990). Female ejaculation: Perceived origins, the Grafenberg spot/area, and sexual responsiveness. *Archives of Sexual Behavior, 19,* 29–47.

Darling, C. A., Davidson, J. K., & Cox, R. P. (1991). Female sexual response and the timing of partner orgasm. *Journal of Sex and Marital Therapy, 17,* 3–21.

Darling, C. A., Davidson, J. K. (1986). Enhancing relationships: Understanding the feminine mystique of pretending orgasm. *Journal of Sex and Marital Therapy, 12,* 182–196.

D'Augelli, A. R., & Hershberger, S. L. (1993). Lesbian, gay, and bisexual youth in community settings: Personal challenges and mental health problems. *American Journal of Community Psychology, 21,* 421–448.

Davidson, J. (1985). The utilization of sexual fantasies by sexually experienced university students. *Journal of American College Health, 34,* 24–32.

Davidson, J. (1988). *The agony of it all*. Los Angeles: Tarcher.

Davidson, J. K., & Moore, N. B. (1994). Masturbation and premarital sexual intercourse among college women: Making choices for sexual fulfillment. *Journal of Sex and Marital Therapy, 20,* 178–199.

Davidson, N. (1988). *The failure of feminism*. Buffalo: Prometheus.

Davies, L. (1995). A closer look at gender and distress among the never married. *Women and Health, 23,* 13–30.

Davis, D. M. (1990). Portrayals of women in prime-time network television: Some demographic characteristics. *Sex Roles, 23,* 325–332.

Davis, J. A., & Smith, T. (1991). *General social surveys, 1972–1991*. Storrs, CT: University of Connecticut, Roper Center for Public Opinion Research.

Davis, J. M. (1985). Antipsychotic drugs. In H. I. Kaplan & B. J. Sadock (Eds.), *Comprehensive textbook of psychiatry/IV*. Baltimore: Williams & Wilkins.

Davis, K. E. (1985, February). Near and dear: Friendship and love compared. *Psychology Today*, pp. 22–30.

Davis, K. L., Kahn, R. S., Ko, G., & Davidson, M. (1991). Dopamine in schizophrenia: A review and reconceptualization. *American Journal of Psychiatry, 148,* 1474–1486.

Davis, L. (1990). *The courage to heal workbook for women and men survivors of child sexual abuse*. New York: HarperCollins.

Davis, M. H., Morris, M. M., & Kraus, L. A. (1998). Relationship-specific and global perceptions of social support: Associations with well-being and attachment. *Journal of Personality and Social Psychology, 74,* 468–481.

Dawod, N. (1995). Stressors encountered by junior high school students and their relation to grade point average, sex and grade. *Dirasat, 22A(Supplement),* 3671–3706.

Dawson, M. E., Hazlett, E. A., Filion, D. L., Neuchterlein, K. H., & Schell, A. M. (1993). Attention and schizophrenia: Impaired modulation of the startle reflex. *Journal of Abnormal Psychology, 102,* 633–641.

Day, N. L., & Richardson, G. A. (1991). Prenatal marijuana use: Epidemiology, methodological issues, and infant outcome. *Chemical Dependency and Pregnancy, 18,* 77–91.

Deaux, K., & Hanna, R. (1984). Courtship in the personals column: The influence of gender and sexual orientation. *Sex Roles, 11,* 363–375.

Deaux, K., & La France, M. (1998). Gender. In D. T. Gilbert, S. T. Fiske, & G. Lindzey (Eds.), *The handbook of social psychology*. Boston: McGraw-Hill.

Deaux, K., & Lewis, L. L. (1983). Components of gender stereotypes. *Psychological Documents, 13,* Ms. No. 2583.

Deaux, K., & Lewis, L. L. (1984). Structure of gender stereotypes: Interrelationships among components and gender label. *Journal of Personality and Social Psychology, 46,* 991–1004.

De Beni, R., Mo, A., & Cornoldi, C. (1997). Learning from texts or lectures: Loci mnemonics can interfere with reading but not with listening. *European Journal of Cognitive Psychology, 9,* 401–415.

De Brabander, B., Hellemans, J., Boone, C., & Gerits, P. (1996). Locus of control, sensation seeking, and stress. *Psychological Reports, 79,* 1307–1312.

Deeks, S. G., Smith, M., Holodniy, M., & Kahn, J. O. (1997). HIV-1 protease inhibitors: A review for clinicians. *Journal of the American Medical Association, 277,* 145–154.

Defrank, R., & Ivancevich, J. M. (1986). Job loss: An individual level review and model. *Journal of Vocational Behavior, 19,* 1–20.

Deikman, A. J. (1990). *The wrong way home: Uncovering the patterns of cult behavior in American society.* Boston: Beacon Press.

DeJong, W., & Musilli, L. (1982). External pressure to comply: Handicapped versus nonhandicapped requesters and the foot-in-the-door phenomenon. *Personality and Social Psychology Bulletin, 8,* 522–527.

DeLamater, J. (1987). A sociological perspective. In J. H. Geer & W. T. O'Donohue (Eds.), *Theories of human sexuality.* New York: Plenum.

Delay, J., & Deniker, P. (1952). *Trente-huit cas de psychoses traitees par la cure prolongee et continue de 4560 RP.* Paris: Masson et Cie.

DeLeon, P. H., & Wiggins, J. G., Jr. (1996). Prescription privileges for psychologists. *American Psychologist, 51,* 225–229.

Delgado, P. L., Price, L. H., Heninger, G. R., & Charney, D. S. (1992). Neurochemistry. In E. S. Paykel (Ed.), *Handbook of affective disorders* (2nd ed.). New York: Guilford Press.

DeLongis, A., Folkman, S., & Lazarus, R. S. (1988). The impact of daily stress on health and mood: Psychological and social resources as mediators. *Journal of Personality and Social Psychology, 54,* 486–495.

Demaré, D., Lips, H. M., & Briere, J. (1993). Sexually violent pornography, anti-women attributes, and sexual aggression: A structural equation model. *Journal of Research in Personality, 27,* 285–300.

DeMaris, A., & MacDonald, W. (1993). Premarital cohabitation and marital instability: A test of the unconventionality hypothesis. *Journal of Marriage and the Family, 55,* 399–407.

DeMaris, A., & Rao, K. V. (1992). Premarital cohabitation and subsequent marital stability in the United States: A reassessment. *Journal of Marriage and the Family, 54,* 178–190.

Demo, D. H. (1992). Parent-child relations: Assessing recent changes. *Journal of Marriage and the Family, 54,* 104–117.

Demo, D. H., & Acock, A. C. (1988). The impact of divorce on children. *Journal of Marriage and the Family, 50,* 619–648.

Dempsey, C. (1994). Health and social issues of gay, lesbian, and bisexual adolescents. *Families in Society: The Journal of Contemporary Human Services,* 160–167.

DeNelsky, G. Y. (1996). The case against prescription privileges for psychologists. *American Psychologist, 51,* 207–212.

Dennis, W. (1966). Creative productivity between the ages of 20 and 80 years. *Journal of Gerontology, 21,* 1–8.

Denny, N., Field, J., & Quadagno, D. (1984). Sex differences in sexual needs and desires. *Archives of Sexual Behavior, 13,* 233–245.

Densen-Gerber, J. (1984). Sexual abuse of children: Emerging issues. *New York Pediatrician, 2,* 3–6.

DePaulo, B. M. (1992). Nonverbal behavior and self-presentation. *Psychological Bulletin, 111,* 203–243.

DePaulo, B. M., & Friedman, H. (1998). Nonverbal communication. In D. T. Gilbert, S. T. Fiske, & G. Lindzey (Eds.), *The handbook of social psychology* (Vol. 2). Boston: McGraw-Hill.

DePaulo, B. M., Kenny, D. A., Hoover, C. W., Webb, W., & Oliver, P. (1987). Accuracy of person perception: Do people know what kinds of impressions they convey? *Journal of Personality and Social Psychology, 52,* 303–315.

DePaulo, B. M., Lanier, K., & Davis, T. (1983). Detecting the deceit of the motivated liar. *Journal of Personality and Social Psychology, 45,* 1096–1103.

DePaulo, B. M., LeMay, C. S., & Epstein, J. A. (1991). Effects of importance of success and expectations for success on effectiveness at deceiving. *Personality and Social Psychology Bulletin, 17,* 14–24.

DePaulo, B. M., Stone, J., & Lassiter, G. D. (1985). Deceiving and detecting deceit. In B. R. Schlenker (Ed.), *The self and social life.* New York: McGraw-Hill.

Derlega, V. J., Winstead, B. A., Wong, P. T. P., & Hunter, S. (1985). Gender effects in an initial encounter: A case where men exceed women in disclosure. *Journal of Social and Personal Relationships, 2,* 25–44.

Derogatis, L. R. (1982). Self-report measures of stress. In L. Goldberger & S. Breznitz (Eds.), *Handbook of stress: Theoretical and clinical aspects.* New York: Free Press.

Derogatis, L. R. (1987). The Derogatis Stress Profile (DSP): Quantification of psychological stress. *Advances in Psychosomatic Medicine, 17,* 30–54.

Derogatis, L. R., & Coons, H. L. (1993). Self-report measures of stress. In L. Goldberger & S. Breznitz (Eds.), *Handbook of stress: Theoretical and clinical aspects* (2nd ed.). New York: Free Press.

de Silva, P. (1995). Cognitive-behavioral models of eating disorders. In G. Szmukler, C. Dare, & J. Treasure (Eds.), *Handbook of eating disorders: Theory, treatment and research.* New York: Wiley.

Des Jarlais, D. C., Hagan, H., & Friedman, S. R. (1997). Epidemiology and emerging public health perspectives. In J. H. Lowinson, P. Ruiz, R. B. Millman, & J. G. Langrod (Eds.), *Substance abuse: A comprehensive textbook* (3rd ed.). Baltimore: Williams & Wilkins.

DeSpelder, L. A., & Strickland, A. L. (1983). *The last dance: Encountering death and dying.* Palo Alto, CA: Mayfield.

Deutsch, M., & Gerard, H. B. (1955). A study of normative and informational social influences upon individual judgment. *Journal of Abnormal and Social Psychology, 51,* 629–636.

Devanand, D. P., Dwork, A. J., Hutchinson, E. R., Bolwig, T. G., & Sackeim, H. A. (1994). Does ECT alter brain structure? *American Journal of Psychiatry, 151,* 957–970.

Devine, P. G. (1989). Stereotypes and prejudice: Their automatic and controlled components. *Journal of Personality and Social Psychology, 56,* 5–18.

DeVito, J. A. (1992). *The interpersonal communication book.* New York: HarperCollins.

de Wilde, E. J., Kienhorst, I. C. W. M., Diekstra, R. F. W., & Wolters, W. H. G. (1992). The relationship between adolescent suicidal behavior and life events in childhood and adolescence. *American Journal of Psychiatry, 149,* 45–51.

Dickson, L. (1993). The future of marriage and the family in Black America. *Journal of Black Studies, 23,* 472–491.

DiClemente, C. C. (1986). Self-efficacy and the addictive behaviors. *Journal of Social and Clinical Psychology, 4,* 302–315.

Diener, E. (1984). Subjective well-being. *Psychological Bulletin, 93,* 542–575.

Diener, E., & Diener, C. (1996). Most people are happy. *Psychological Science, 7,* 181–185.

Diener, E., Diener, M., & Diener, C. (1995). Factors predicting the subjective well-being of nations. *Journal of Personality and Social Psychology, 69,* 851–864.

Diener, E., Sandvik, E., Seidlitz, L., & Diener, M. (1993). The relationship between income and subjective well-being: Relative or absolute? *Social Indicators Research, 28,* 195–223.

Diener, E., Suh, E., Smith, H., & Shao, L. (1995). National differences in reported subjective well-being: Why do they occur? *Social Indicators Research, 34,* 7–32.

Diener, E., Wolsic, B., & Fujita, F. (1995). Physical attractiveness and subjective well-being. *Journal of Personality and Social Psychology, 69,* 120–129.

DiMatteo, M. R. (1991). *The psychology of health, illness, and medical care: An individual perspective.* Pacific Grove, CA: Brooks/Cole.

DiMatteo, M. R. (1994). Enhancing patient adherence to medical recommendations. *Journal of the American Medical Association, 271,* 79–83.

DiMatteo, M. R. (1997). Health behaviors and care decisions: An overview of professional-patient communication. In D. S. Gochman (Ed.), *Handbook of health behavior research II: Provider determinants.* New York: Plenum Press.

DiMatteo, M. R., & Friedman, H. S. (1982). *Social psychology and medicine.* Cambridge, MA: Oelgeschlager, Gunn & Hain.

Dimsdale, J. E. (1988). A perspective on Type A behavior and coronary disease. *New England Journal of Medicine, 318,* 110–112.

Dindia, K., & Allen, M. (1992). Sex differences in self-disclosure: A meta-analysis. *Psychological Bulletin, 112,* 106–124.

DiNicola, D. D., & DiMatteo, M. R. (1984). Practitioners, patients, and compliance with medical regimens: A social psychological perspective. In A. Baum, S. E. Taylor, & J. E. Singer (Eds.), *Handbook of psychology and health: Vol. 4. Social psychological aspects of health.* Hillsdale, NJ: Erlbaum.

Dion, K. K. (1986). Stereotyping based on physical attractiveness: Issues and conceptual perspectives. In C. P. Herman, M. P. Zanna, & E. T. Higgins (Eds.), *Appearance, stigma and social behavior: The Ontario symposium on personality and social psychology* (Vol. 3). Hillsdale, NJ: Erlbaum.

Dion, K. K., & Dion, K. L. (1993). Individualistic and collectivistic perspectives on gender and the cultural context of love and intimacy. *Journal of Social Issues, 49,* 53–69.

Dion, K. K., Berscheid, E., & Walster, E. (1972). What is beautiful is good. *Journal of Personality and Social Psychology, 24,* 285–290.

Dion, K. L., & Dion, K. K. (1988). Romantic love: Individual and cultural perspectives. In R. J. Sternberg & M. L. Barnes (Eds.), *The psychology of love.* New Haven, CT: Yale University Press.

Dipboye, R. L. (1992). *Selection interviews: Process perspectives.* Cincinnati: South-Western.

Dishotsky, N. I., Loughman, W. D., Mogar, R. E., & Lipscomb, W. R. (1971). LSD and genetic damage: Is LSD chromosome damaging, carcinogenic, mutagenic, or teratogenic? *Science, 172,* 431–440.

Dixon, N. F. (1980). Humor: A cognitive alternative to stress? In I. G. Sarason & C. D. Spielberger (Eds.), *Stress and anxiety* (Vol. 7). Washington, DC: Hemisphere.

D'Mello, D. A., Fernandes, C. L., & Colenda, C. C. I. (1997). Serotonin reuptake inhibitor antidepressant withdrawal syndromes. *Primary Psychiatry, 4,* 51–56.

Dobbins, G. H., Cardy, R. L., & Truxillo, D. M. (1986). Effects of rated sex and purpose of appraisal on the accuracy of performance evaluations. *Basic and Applied Social Psychology, 7,* 225–241.

Dobbins, G. H., Cardy, R. L., & Truxillo, D. M. (1988). The effects of purpose of appraisal and individual differences in stereotypes of women on sex differences in performance ratings: A laboratory and field study. *Journal of Applied Psychology, 73,* 551–558.

Dohrenwend, B. P., Raphael, K. G., Schwartz, S., Stueve, A., & Skodol, A. (1993). The structured event probe and narrative rating method for measuring stressful life events. In L. Goldberger & S. Breznitz (Eds.), *Handbook of stress: Theoretical and clinical aspects* (2nd ed.). New York: Free Press.

Dohrenwend, B. S., & Dohrenwend, B. P. (1981). Life stress and illness: Formulation of the issues. In B. S. Dohrenwend & B. P. Dohrenwend (Eds.), *Stressful life events and their contexts.* New York: Prodist.

Dollard, J., Doob, L. W., Miller, N. E., Mowrer, O. H., & Sears, R. R. (1939). *Frustration and aggression.* New Haven, CT: Yale University Press.

Donnerstein, E., & Linz, D. (1984, January). Sexual violence in the media: A warning. *Psychology Today,* pp. 14–15.

Donnerstein, E., Linz, D., & Penrod, S. (1987). *The question of pornography.* New York: Free Press.

Donovan, P. (1997). Confronting a hidden epidemic: The Institute of Medicine's report on sexually transmitted diseases. *Family Planning Perspectives, 29,* 87–89.

Donovan, R. L., & Jackson, B. L. (1990). Deciding to divorce: A process guided by social exchange, attachment and cognitive dissonance theories. *Journal of Divorce, 13,* 23–35.

Doty, P. J. (1992). The oldest old and the use of institutional long-term care from an international perspective. In R. M. Suzman, D. P. Willis, & K. G. Manton (Eds.), *The oldest old.* New York: Oxford University Press.

Douglass, M. E., & Douglass, D. N. (1993). *Manage your time, your work, yourself.* New York: American Management Association.

Douvan, E., & Adelson, J. (1966). *The adolescent experience.* New York: Wiley.

Dovidio, J. F., & Gaertner, S. L. (Eds.). (1986). *Prejudice, discrimination, and racism.* New York: Academic Press.

Dovidio, J. F., & Gaertner, S. L. (1991). Changes in the expression of racial prejudice. In H. J. Knopke, R. J. Norrell, & R. W. Rogers (Eds.), *Opening doors: Perspectives in race relations in contemporary America.* Tuscaloosa: University of Alabama Press.

Dovidio, J. F., Ellyson, S. L., Keating, C. F., Heltman, K., & Brown, C. E. (1988). The relationship of social power to visual display of dominance between men and women. *Journal of Personality and Social Psychology, 54,* 233–242.

Doyle, J. A. (1989). *The male experience.* Dubuque, IA: William C. Brown.

Doyle, J. A., & Paludi, M. A. (1991). *Sex and gender.* Dubuque, IA: William C. Brown.

Doyle, J. A., & Paludi, M. A. (1998). *Sex and gender: The human experience* (4th ed.). McGraw-Hill.

Drachman, D. A. (1986). Memory and cognitive function in normal aging. *Developmental Neuropsychology, 2,* 277–285.

Driskell, J. E., Willis, R. P., & Copper, C. (1992). Effect of overlearning on retention. *Journal of Applied Psychology, 77,* 615–622.

Duck, S. (1994). *Meaningful relationships: Talking, sense, and relating.* Thousand Oaks, CA: Sage.

Duffy, S. M., & Rusbult, C. E. (1986). Satisfaction and commitment in homosexual and heterosexual relationships. *Journal of Homosexuality, 12,* 1–23.

Duke, M., & Nowicki, S., Jr. (1979). *Abnormal psychology: Perspectives on being different.* Pacific Grove, CA: Brooks/Cole.

Dunning, D., Perie, M., & Story, A. L. (1991). Self-serving prototypes of social categories. *Journal of Personality and Social Psychology, 61,* 957–968.

Dupuis, S. L., & Smale, B. J. A. (1995). An examination of the relationship between psychological well-being and depression and leisure activity participation among older adults. *Society and Leisure, 18,* 67–92.

Dusek, J. B. (1987). Sex roles and adjustment. In D. B. Carter (Ed.), *Current conceptions of sex roles and sex typing.* New York: Praeger.

Duxbury, L. E., & Higgins, C. A. (1991). Gender differences in work-family conflict. *Journal of Applied Psychology, 76,* 60–74.

Dwyer, J. (1995). Popular diets. In K. D. Brownell & C. G. Fairburn (Eds.), *Eating disorders and obesity.* New York: Guilford Press.

Dyer, W. W. (1976). *Your erroneous zones.* New York: Crowell.

Dyk, P. H., & Adams, G. R. (1990). Identity and intimacy: An initial investigation of three theoretical models using cross-lag panel correlations. *Journal of Youth and Adolescence, 19,* 91–110.

Dykman, B. M., Horowitz, L. M., Abramson, L. Y., & Usher, M. (1991). Schematic and situational determinants of depressed and nondepressed students' interpretation feedback. *Journal of Abnormal Psychology, 100,* 45–55.

Dziech, B. W., & Weiner, L. (1990). *The lecherous professor: Sexual harassment on campus.* Urbana: University of Illinois Press.

D'Zurilla, T. J., & Sheedy, C. F. (1991). Relation between social problem-solving ability and subsequent level of psychological stress in college students. *Journal of Personality and Social Psychology, 61,* 841–846.

Eagle, M. N., & Wolitzky, D. L. (1992). Psychoanalytic theories of psychotherapy. In D. K. Freedheim (Ed.), *History of psychotherapy: A century of change.* Washington, DC: American Psychological Association.

Eagly, A. H. (1987). *Sex differences in social behavior: A social-role interpretation.* Hillsdale, NJ: Erlbaum.

Eagly, A. H. (1995). The science and politics of comparing women and men. *American Psychologist, 50,* 145–158.

Eagly, A. H., & Carli, L. L. (1981). Sex of researchers and sex-typed communications as determinants of sex differences in influenceability: A meta-analysis of social influence studies. *Psychological Bulletin, 90,* 1–20.

Eagly, A. H., Ashmore, R. D., Makhijani, M. G., & Longo, L. C. (1991). What is beautiful is good, but . . . : A meta-analytic review of research on the physical attractiveness stereotype. *Psychology Bulletin, 110,* 107–128.

Eals, M., & Silverman, I. (1994). The hunter-gatherer theory of spatial sex differences: Proximate factors mediating the female advantage in recall of object arrays. *Ethology and Sociobiology, 15,* 95–115.

Earle, J. R., & Harris, C. T. (1985). Modern women and the dynamics of social psychological ambivalence. *Psychology of Women Quarterly, 9,* 65–80.

Earle, J. R., & Perricone, P. J. (1986). Premarital sexuality: A ten-year study of attitudes and behavior on a small university campus. *Journal of Sex Research, 22,* 304–310.

Easterbrooks, M. A., & Goldberg, W. A. (1985). Effects of early maternal employment on toddlers, mothers, and fathers. *Developmental Psychology, 21,* 774–783.

Eaton, W. W., Dryman, A., & Weissman, M. M. (1991). Panic and phobia. In L. N. Robins & D. A. Regier (Eds.), *Psychiatric disorders in America: The epidemiologic catchment area study.* New York: Free Press.

Ebbinghaus, H. (1885/1964). *Memory: A contribution to experimental psychology.* (H. A. Ruger & E. R. Bussemius, Trans.). New York: Dover. (Original work published 1885)

Eccles, J. S. (1989). Bringing young women to math and science. In M. Crawford & M. Gentry (Eds.), *Gender and thought.* New York: Springer-Verlag.

Eccles, J. S., Midgley, C., Wigfield, A., Buchanan, C. M., Reuman, D., Flanagan, C., & MacIver, D. (1993). Development during adolescence: The impact of stage-environment fit on young adolescents' experiences in schools and in families. *American Psychologist, 48,* 90–101.

Eccles, J. S. (1994). Understanding women's educational and occupational choices: Applying the Eccles et al. model of achievement-related choices. *Psychology of Women Quarterly, 18,* 585–610.

Edlin, G., & Golanty, E. (1992). *Health and wellness: A holistic approach.* Boston: Jones and Bartlett.

Edwards, K., & Smith, E. E. (1996). A disconfirmation bias in the evaluation of arguments. *Journal of Personality and Social Psychology, 71,* 5–24.

Egan, G. (1990). *The skilled helper: A systematic approach to effective helping.* Pacific Grove, CA: Brooks/Cole.

Egan, K. J., Kogan, H. N., Garber, A., & Jarrett, M. (1983). The impact of psychological distress on the control of hypertension. *Journal of Human Stress, 9,* 4–10.

Ehrenberg, O., & Ehrenberg, M. (1986). *The psychotherapy maze.* Northvale, NJ: Aronson.

Ehrenberg, O., & Ehrenberg, M. (1994). *The psychotherapy maze: A consumer's guide to getting in and out of therapy.* Northvale, NJ: Jason Aronson.

Ehrhardt, A. A., Yingling, S., & Warne, P. A. (1991). Sexual behavior in the era of AIDS: What has changed in the United States? *Annual Review of Sex Research, 2,* 25–48.

Eich, E., Macaulay, D., Loewenstein, R. J., & Dihle, P. H. (1997). Memory, amnesia, and dissociative identity disorder. *Psychological Science, 8,* 417–422.

Eisler, I. (1995). Family models of eating disorders. In G. Szmukler, C. Dare, & J. Treasure (Eds.), *Handbook of eating disorders: Theory, treatment and research.* New York: Wiley.

Eisler, R. M., & Ragsdale, K. (1992). Masculine gender role and midlife transition in men. In V. B. Van Hasselt & M. Hersen (Eds.), *Handbook of social development: A lifespan perspective.* New York: Plenum.

Ekman, P. (1975, September). The universal smile: Face muscles talk every language. *Psychology Today,* pp. 35–39.

Ekman, P. (1992). Facial expressions of emotion: New findings, new questions. *Psychological Science, 3* 34–38.

Ekman, P. (1994). Strong evidence for universals in facial expressions: A reply to Russell's mistaken critique. *Psychological Bulletin, 115,* 268–287.

Ekman, P., & Friesen, W. V. (1984). *Unmasking the face.* Palo Alto, CA: Consulting Psychologists Press.

Ekman, P., Friesen, W. V., & Ellsworth, P. (1982). What emotion categories or dimensions can observers judge from facial behavior? In P. Ekman (Ed.), *Emotion in the human face* (2nd ed.). Cambridge, MA: Cambridge University Press.

Ekman, P., Friesen, W. V., O'Sullivan, M., Chan, A., Diacoyanni-Tarlatzis, I., Heider, K., Krause, R., LeCompte, W. A., Pitcairn, T., Ricci-Bitti, P. E., Scherer, K. R., Tomita, M., & Tzavaras, A. (1987). Universals and cultural differences in the judgments of facial expressions of emotion. *Journal of Personality and Social Psychology, 53,* 712–717.

Elias, M. F., Elias, J. W., & Elias, P. K. (1990). Biological and health influences on behavior. In J. E. Birren & K. W. Schaie (Eds.), *Handbook of the psychology of aging.* San Diego: Academic Press.

Elicker, J., Englund, M., & Sroufe, L. A. (1992). Predicting peer competence and peer relationships in childhood from early parent-child relation-ships. In R. D. Parke & G. W. Ladd (Eds.), *Family-peer relationships.* Hillsdale, NJ: Erlbaum.

Eliot, R. S., & Breo, D. L. (1989). *Is it worth dying for?* New York: Bantam Books.

Elkind, D. (1988). *The hurried child: Growing up too fast, too soon.* Reading, MA: Addison-Wesley.

Ellard, K., Beaurepaire, J., Jones, M., Piper, D., & Tennant, C. (1990). Acute chronic stress in duodenal ulcer disease. *Gastroenterology, 99,* 1628–1632.

Elliott, E. (1989). Stress and illness. In S. Cheren (Ed.), *Psychosomatic medicine: Theory, physiology, and practice* (Vol. 1). Madison, CT: International Universities Press.

Elliott, R., Stiles, W. B., & Shapiro, D. A. (1993). Are some therapies more equivalent than others? In T. R. Giles (Ed.), *Handbook of effective psychotherapy.* New York: Plenum.

Ellis, A. (1973). *Humanistic psychotherapy: The rational-emotive approach.* New York: Julian Press.

Ellis, A. (1977). *Reason and emotion in psychotherapy.* Seacaucus, NJ: Lyle Stuart.

Ellis, A. (1984). *Reason and emotion in psychotherapy.* Seacaucus, NJ: Lyle Stuart.

Ellis, A. (1985). *How to live with and without anger.* New York: Citadel Press.

Ellis, A. (1987). The evolution of rational-emotive therapy (RET) and cognitive behavior therapy (CBT). In J. K. Zeig (Ed.), *The evolution of psychotherapy.* New York: Brunner/Mazel.

Ellis, A. (1989). Rational-emotive therapy. In R. J. Corsini & D. Wedding (Eds.), *Current Psychotherapies.* Itasca, IL: Peacock.

Ellis, A. (1993). The advantages and disadvantages of self-help therapy materials. *Professional Psychology: Research and Practice, 24,* 335–339.

Ellis, A. (1994). *Reason and emotion in psychotherapy.* Seacaucus, NJ: Birch Lane Press.

Ellis, A. (1995). Thinking processes involved in irrational beliefs and their disturbed consequences. *Journal of Cognitive Psychotherapy, 9,* 105–116.

Ellis, A. (1996). How I learned to help clients feel better and get better. *Psychotherapy, 33,* 149–151.

Ellis, L., & Ames, M. A. (1987). Neurohormonal functioning and sexual orientation: A theory of homosexuality heterosexuality. *Psychological Bulletin, 101,* 233–258.

Elmer-Dewitt, P. (1995, July 3). Cyberporn. *Time,* 38–43, 45.

Emanuel, H. M. (1987). Put time on your side. In A. D. Timpe (Ed.), *The management of time.* New York: Facts On File.

Emery, R. E. (1989). Family violence. *American Psychologist, 44,* 321–328.

Emery, R. E., & Lauman-Billings, L. (1998). An overview of the nature, causes, and consequences of abusive family relationships: Toward differentiating maltreatment and violence. *American Psychologist, 53,* 121–135.

Emmelkamp, P. M. G. (1994). Behavior therapy with adults. In A. E. Bergin & S. L. Garfield (Eds.), *Handbook of psychotherapy and behavior change* (4th ed.). New York: Wiley.

Emmelkamp, P. M. G., & Scholing, A. (1990). Behavioral treatment for simple and social phobias. In R. Noyes, Jr., M. Roth, & G. D. Burrows (Eds.), *Handbook of anxiety: The treatment of anxiety* (Vol. 4). Amsterdam: Elsevier.

Engel, J. W., & Saracino, M. (1986). Love preferences and ideals: A comparison of homosexual, bisexual, and heterosexual groups. *Contemporary Family Therapy, 8,* 241–250.

Engler, J., & Goleman, D. (1992). *The consumer's guide to psychotherapy.* New York: Simon & Schuster.

Eppley, K., Abrams, A., & Shear, J. (1989). The differential effects of relaxation techniques on trait anxiety: A meta-analysis. *Journal of Clinical Psychology, 45,* 957–974.

Epstein, L. H., Valoski, A. M., Vara, L. S., McCurley, J., Wisniewski, L., Kalarchian, M. A., Klein, K. R., & Shrager, L. R. (1995). Effects of decreasing sedentary behavior and increasing activity on weight change in obese children. *Health Psychology, 14,* 109–115.

Epstein, S. P. (1990). Cognitive-experiential self-theory. In L. A. Pervin (Ed.), *Handbook of personality: Theory and research.* New York: Guilford Press.

Epstein, S. P., & Katz, L. (1992). Coping ability, stress, productive load, and symptoms. *Journal of Personality and Social Psychology, 62,* 813–825.

Epstein, S. P., & Meier, P. (1989). Constructive thinking: A broad coping variable with specific components. *Journal of Personality and Social Psychology, 57,* 332–350.

Epstein, S., & Brodsky, A. (1993). *You're smarter than you think.* New York: Simon & Schuster.

Erel, O., & Burnham, B. (1995). Interrelatedness of marital relations and parent-child relations: A meta-analytic review. *Psychological Bulletin, 118,* 108–132.

Erickson, S. J., Feldman, S. S., & Steiner, H. (1996). Defense mechanisms and adjustments in normal adolescents. *American Journal of Psychiatry, 153,* 826–828.

Erikson, E. H. (1963). *Childhood and society.* New York: Norton.

Erikson, E. H. (1968). *Identity: Youth and crisis.* New York: Norton.

Esterling, B. A., Antoni, M. H., Fletcher, M. A., Margulies, S., & Schniederman, N. (1994a). Emotional disclosure through writing or speaking modulates latent Epstein-Barr virus antibody titers. *Journal of Consulting and Clinical Psychology, 62,* 130–140.

Esterling, B. A., Kiecolt-Glaser, J. K., Bodnar, J. D., & Glaser, R. (1994b). Chronic stress, social support, and persistent alterations in the natural killer cell response to cytokines in older adults. *Health Psychology, 13,* 291–298.

Esterson, A. (1993). *Seductive mirage: An exploration of the work of Sigmund Freud.* Chicago: Open Court.

Etaugh, C. (1993). Maternal employment: Effects on children. In J. Frankel (Ed.), *The employed mother and the family context.* New York: Springer.

Etaugh, C., & Liss, M. B. (1992). Home, school, and playroom: Training grounds for adult gender roles. *Sex Roles, 26,* 129–147.

Eutsch, M., & Gerard, H. B. (1955). A study of normative and informational social influences upon individual judgment. *Journal of Abnormal and Social Psychology, 51,* 629–636.

Evans, C. E., & Haynes, R. B. (1990). Patient compliance. In R. E. Rakel (Ed.), *Textbook of family practice.* Philadelphia: Saunders.

Evans, G. W., Hygge, S., & Bullinger, M. (1995). Chronic noise and psychological stress. *Psychological Science, 6,* 333–338.

Evans, G. W., Lepore, S. J., & Schroeder, A. (1996). The role of interior design elements in human responses to crowding. *Journal of Personality and Social Psychology, 70,* 41–46.

Evans, R. G., & Dinning, W. D. (1982). MMPI correlates of the Bem Sex Role Inventory and Extended Personal Attributes Questionnaire in a male psychiatric sample. *Journal of Clinical Psychology, 38,* 811–815.

Everitt, B. J., & Bancroft, J. (1991). Of rats and men: The comparative approach to male sexuality. *Annual Review of Sex Research, 2,* 77–118.

Eysenck, H. J. (1952). The effects of psychotherapy: An evaluation. *Journal of Consulting Psychology, 16,* 319–324.

Eysenck, H. J. (1959). Learning theory and behaviour therapy. *Journal of Mental Science, 195,* 61–75.

Eysenck, H. J. (1967). *The biological basis of personality.* Springfield, IL: Charles C Thomas.

Eysenck, H. J. (1982). *Personality, genetics and behavior: Selected papers.* New York: Praeger.

Eysenck, H. J. (1988, December). Health's character. *Psychology Today,* pp. 28–35.

Eysenck, H. J. (1990). Biological dimensions of personality. In L. A. Pervin (Ed.), *Handbook of personality: Theory and research.* New York: Guilford Press.

Eysenck, H. J. (1991). Dimensions of personality: 16, 5, or 3?—Criteria for a taxonomic paradigm. *Personality and Individual Differences, 12,* 773–790.

Eysenck, H. J. (1992). Four ways five factors are not basic. *Personality and Individual Differences, 13,* 667–673.

Eysenck, H. J. (1993a). Forty years on: The outcome problem in psychotherapy revisited. In T. R. Giles (Ed.), *Handbook of effective psychotherapy.* New York: Plenum.

Eysenck, H. J. (1993b). Prediction of cancer and coronary heart disease: Mortality by means of a personality inventory: Results of a 15-year follow-up study. *Psychological Reports, 72,* 499–516.

Eysenck, H. J., & Eysenck, S. B. G. (1969). *Personality structure and measurement.* San Diego, CA: EDITS.

Eysenck, M. W., Mogg, K., May, J., Richards, A., & Mathews, A. (1991). Bias in interpretation of ambiguous sentences related to threat in anxiety. *Journal of Abnormal Psychology, 100,* 144–150.

Fagley, N. S. (1987). Positional response bias in multiple-choice tests of learning: Its relation to testwiseness and guessing strategy. *Journal of Educational Psychology, 79,* 95–97.

Fagot, B. I. (1985). Changes in thinking about early sex role development. *Developmental Review, 5,* 83–98.

Fagot, B. I., & Leinbach, M. D. (1987). Socialization of sex roles within the family. In B. Carter (Ed.), *Current conceptions of sex roles and sex typing: Theory and research.* New York: Praeger.

Fagot, B. I., Hagan, R., Leinbach, M. D., & Kronsberg, S. (1985). Differential reactions to assertive and communicative acts of toddler boys and girls. *Child Development, 56,* 1499–1505.

Fagot, B. I., Leinbach, M. D., & O'Boyle, D. (1992). Gender labeling, gender stereotyping, and parenting behaviors. *Developmental Psychology, 28,* 225–230.

Fahey, P. J., & Gallagher-Allred, C. (1990). Nutrition. In R. E. Rakel (Ed.), *Textbook of family practice* (4th ed.). Philadelphia: Saunders.

Fairburn, C. G. (1995). Physiology of anorexia nervosa. In K. D. Brownell & C. G. Fairburn (Eds.), *Eating disorders and obesity: A comprehensive handbook.* New York: Guilford Press.

Falk, P. (1989). Lesbian mothers: Psychosocial assumptions in family law. *American Psychologist, 44,* 941–947.

Falk, P. (1994). The gap between psychological assumptions and empirical research in lesbian-mother child custody cases. In A. E. Gottfried & A. W. Gottfried (Eds.), *Redefining families: Implications for children's development.* New York: Plenum.

Falsetti, S. A., & Ballenger, J. C. (1998). Stress and anxiety disorders. In J. R. Hubbard & E. A. Workman (Eds.), *Handbook of stress medicine: An organ system approach.* New York: CRC Press.

Fancher, R. E. (1979). *Pioneers of psychology.* New York: Norton.

Farah, A. (1997). An overview of ECT. *Primary Psychiatry, 4,* 58–62.

Faravelli, C., & Pallanti, S. (1989). Recent life events and panic disorders. *American Journal of Psychiatry, 146,* 622–626.

Farina, A., Burns, G. L., Austad, C., Bugglin, C., & Fischer, E. H. (1986). The role of physical attractiveness in the readjustment of discharged psychiatric patients. *Journal of Abnormal Psychology, 95,* 139–143.

Farley, J. (1980). Worklife problems for both women and men. In D. A. Neugarten & J. M. Shafritz (Eds.), *Sexuality in occupations: Romantic and coercive behavior at work.* Oak Park, IL: Moore.

Fausto-Sterling, A. (1992). *Myths of gender: Biological theories about women and men* (2nd ed.). New York: Basic Books.

Fava, G. A., Perini, G. I., Santonastaso, P., & Fornasa, C. V. (1989). Life events and psychological distress in dermatologic disorders: Psoriasis, chronic urticaria, and fungal infections. In T. W. Miller (Ed.), *Stressful life events.* Madison, CT: International Universities Press.

Featherman, D. (1980). Schooling and occupational careers: Constancy and change in worldly success. In O. Brim, Jr. & J. Kagan (Eds.), *Constancy and change in human development.* Cambridge, MA: Harvard University Press.

Federal Bureau of Investigation (1995). *Uniform crime reports: Crime in the United States.* Washington, DC: U.S. Government Printing Office.

Feeney, J. A., & Noller, P. (1990). Attachment style as a predictor of adult romantic relationships. *Journal of Personality and Social Psychology, 58,* 281–291.

Feingold, A. (1988). Matching for attractiveness in romantic partners and same-sex friends: A meta-analysis and theoretical critique. *Psychological Bulletin, 104,* 226–235.

Feingold, A. (1990). Gender differences in effects of physical attractiveness on romantic attraction: A comparison across five research paradigms. *Journal of Personality and Social Psychology, 59,* 981–993.

Feingold, A. (1992a). Gender differences in mate selection preferences: A test of the parental investment model. *Psychological Bulletin, 112,* 125–139.

Feingold, A. (1992b). Good-looking people are not what we think. *Psychological Bulletin, 111,* 304–341.

Feiring, C., & Lewis, M. (1987). The child's social network: Sex differences from three to six years. *Sex Roles, 17,* 621–636.

Feldman, R. S., Philippot, P., & Custrini, R. J. (1991). Social competence and nonverbal behavior. In R. S. Feldman & B. Rime (Eds.), *Fundamentals of nonverbal behavior.* Cambridge: Cambridge University Press.

Felker, B., & Hubbard, J. R. (1998). Influence of mental stress on the endocrine system. In J. R. Hubbard & E. A. Workman (Eds.), *Handbook of stress medicine: An organ system approach.* New York: CRC Press.

Felmlee, D. H. (1995). Causes and consequences of women's employment discontinuity, 1967–1973. *Work and Occupation, 22,* 167–187.

Felmlee, D., Sprecher, S., & Bassin, E. (1990). The dissolution of intimate relationships: A hazard model. *Social Psychology Quarterly, 513–30.*

Felson, R. B. (1989). Parents and the reflected appraisal process: A longitudinal analysis. *Journal of Personality and Social Psychology, 56,* 965–971.

Fenton, W. S., & McGlashan, T. H. (1994). Antecedents, symptom progression, and long-term outcome of the deficit syndrome in schizophrenia. *American Journal of Psychiatry, 151,* 351–356.

Fenwick, P. (1987). Meditation and the EEG. In M. A. West (Ed.), *The psychology of meditation.* Oxford: Clarendon Press.

Fenz, W. D., & Epstein, S. (1967). Gradients of physiological arousal, skin conductance, heart rate, and respiration rate as a function of experience. *Psychosomatic Medicine, 29,* 33–51.

Ferguson, T. (1993). Working with your doctor. In D. Goleman & J. Gurin (Eds.), *Mind-body medicine: How to use your mind for better health.* Yonkers, NY: Consumer Reports Books.

Ferrari, J. R. (1992). Psychometric validation of two adult measures of procrastination: Arousal and avoidance measures. *Journal of Psychopathology & Behavioral Assessment, 14,* 97–100.

Ferrari, J. R., Johnson, J. L., & McCown, W. G. (1995). *Procrastination and task avoidance: Theory research and treatment.* New York: Plenum Press.

Ferree, M. M., & Hall, E. J. (1990). Visual images of American society: Gender and race in introductory sociology textbooks. *Gender and Society, 4,* 500–533.

Festinger, L. (1954). A theory of social comparison processes. *Human Relations, 7,* 117–140.

Festinger, L., Schachter, S., & Back, K. (1950). *Social pressures in informal groups: A study of human factors in housing.* Stanford, CA: Stanford University Press.

Field, D., Schaie, K. W., & Leino, E. V. (1988). Continuity in intellectual functioning: The role of self-reported health. *Psychology and Aging, 3,* 385–392.

Fierman, J. (1994, January 24). The contingency work force. *Fortune,* 30–36.

Fincham, F. D., & Bradbury, T. N. (1992). Assessing attributions in marriage: The relationship attribution measure. *Journal of Personality and Social Psychology, 62,* 457–468.

Fincham, F. D., Beach, S. R., & Baucom, D. H. (1987). Attribution processes in distressed and nondistressed couples: 4. Self-partner attribution differences. *Journal of Personality and Social Psychology, 52,* 739–748.

Fine, M. A. (1992). Families in the United States: Their current status and future prospects. *Family Relations, 41,* 430–435.

Fine, R. (1990). *The history of psychoanalysis.* New York: Continuum.

Fineman, M. A., & Mykitiuk, R. (1994). *The public nature of private violence: The discovery of domestic abuse.* New York: Routledge.

Fink, M. (1992). Electroconvulsive therapy. In E. S. Paykel (Ed.), *Handbook of affective disorders* (2nd ed.). New York: Guilford Press.

Finkelhor, D., & Dziuba-Leatherman, J. (1994). Victimization of children. *American Psychologist, 49,* 173–183.

Finkelhor, D., Hotaling, G., Lewis, I. A., & Smith, C. (1990). *Missing, abducted, runaway, and throwaway children in America.* Washington, DC: U.S. Department of Justice.

Fish, S. (1993, November). Reverse racism of how the pot got to call the kettle black. *Atlantic Monthly, 272,* 128–136.

Fisher, S., & Greenberg, R. P. (1985). *The scientific credibility of Freud's theories and therapy.* New York: Columbia University Press.

Fisher, S., & Greenberg, R. P. (1996). *Freud scientifically reappraised: Testing the theories and therapy.* New York: Wiley.

Fishman, D. B., & Franks, C. M. (1992). Evolution and differentiation within behavior therapy: A theoretical epistemological review. In D. K. Freedheim (Ed.), *History of psychotherapy: A century of change.* Washington, DC: American Psychological Association.

Fiske, S. T. (1993). Social cognition and social perception. *Annual Review of Psychology, 44,* 155–194.

Fiske, S. T., & Taylor, S. E. (1991). *Social cognition.* New York: McGraw-Hill.

Fitch, S. A., & Adams, G. R. (1983). Ego identity and intimacy status: Replication and extension. *Developmental Psychology, 19,* 839–845.

Fitzgerald, L. F. (1993). Sexual harassment: Violence against women in the workplace. *American Psychologist, 48,* 1070–1076.

Flaks, D. K., Ficher, I., Masterpasqua, M., & Joseph, G. (1995). Lesbians choosing motherhood: A comparative study of lesbians and heterosexual parents and their children. *Developmental Psychology, 31,* 105–114.

Flanders, J. P. (1982). A general systems approach to loneliness. In L. A. Peplau & D. Perlman (Eds.), *Loneliness: A source-book of current theory, research and therapy.* New York: Wiley.

Flaum, M., Swayze, V. W., O'Leary, D. S., Yuh, W. T. C., Ehrhardt, J. C., Arndt, S. V., & Andreasen, N. C. (1995). Effects of diagnosis, laterality, and gender on brain morphology in schizophrenia. *American Journal of Psychiatry, 152,* 704–714.

Fletcher, G. J. O., & Fitness, J. (1990). Occurrent social cognition in close relationship interaction: The role of proximal and distal variables. *Journal of Personality and Social Psychology, 59,* 464–474.

Fletcher, G. J. O., Fincham, F. D., Cramer, L., & Heron, N. (1987). The role of attributions in the development of dating relationships. *Journal of Personality and Social Psychology, 53,* 481–489.

Flett, G. L., Hewitt, P. L., & Martin, T. R. (1995). Dimensions of perfectionism and procrastination. In J. R. Ferrari, J. L. Johnson, & W. G. McCown (Eds.), *Procrastination and task avoidance: Theory, research, and treatment.* New York: Plenum Press.

Florian, V., Mikulincer, M., & Taubman, O. (1995). Does hardiness contribute to mental health during a stressful real-life situation? The roles of appraisal and coping. *Journal of Personality and Social Psychology, 68,* 687–695.

Flynn, L. M. (1994). Schizophrenia from a family point of view: A social economic perspective. In N. C. Andreasen (Ed.), *Schizophrenia: From mind to molecule.* Washington, DC: American Psychiatric Press.

Foa, E. B., & Kozak, M. J. (1995). DSM-IV field trial: Obsessive-compulsive disorder. *American Journal of Psychiatry, 152,* 90–96.

Foa, E. B., & Riggs, D. S. (1995). Posttraumatic stress disorder following assault: Theoretical considerations and empirical findings. *Current Directions in Psychological Science, 4,* 61–65.

Foa, U. G., Anderson, B., Converse, J, Jr., Urbansky, W. A., Cawley, M. J. I., Muhlhausen, S. M., & Tornblom, K. Y. (1987). Gender-related sexual attitudes: Some cross-cultural similarities and differences. *Sex Roles, 16,* 511–519.

Folkman, S., Lazarus, R. S., Gruen, R. J., & DeLongis, A. (1986). Appraisal, coping, health status, and psychological symptoms. *Journal of Personality and Social Psychology, 50,* 571–579.

Forrest, J. D., & Singh, S. (1990). The sexual and reproductive behavior of American women, 1982–1988. *Family Planning Perspectives, 22,* 206–214.

Forsyth, D. R., & Strong, S. R. (1986). The scientific study of counseling and psychotherapy: A unificationist view. *American Psychologist, 41,* 113–119.

Forsythe, S., Drake, M. F., & Cox, C. E. (1985). Influence of applicant's dress on interviewer's selection decisions. *Journal of Applied Psychology, 70,* 374–378.

Foss, R. D., & Dempsey, C. B. (1979). Blood donation and the foot-in-the-door technique. *Journal of Personality and Social Psychology, 37,* 580–590.

Fowers, B. J., & Olson, D. H. (1989). ENRICH Marital Inventory: A discriminant validity and cross-validation assessment. *Journal of Marital and Family Therapy, 15,* 65–79.

Fowers, B. J., Applegate, B., Olson, D. H., & Pomerantz, B. (1994). Marital conventionalization as a measure of marital satisfaction: A confirmatory factor analysis. *Journal of Family Psychology, 8,* 98–103.

Fowles, D. C. (1992). Schizophrenia: Diathesis-stress revisited. *Annual Review of Psychology, 43,* 303–336.

Fracher, J. C., & Kimmel, M. S. (1987). Hard issues and soft spots: Counseling men about sexuality. In M. Scher, M. Stevens, G. Good, & G. A. Eichenfield (Eds.), *Handbook of counseling and psychotherapy with men.* Newbury Park, CA: Sage Publications.

Frances, A. J., First, M. B., Widiger, T. A., Miele, G. M., Tilly, S. M., Davis, W. W., & Pincus, H. A. (1991). An A to Z guide to DSM-IV conundrums. *Journal of Abnormal Psychology, 100,* 407–412.

Francis, M. E., & Pennebaker, J. W. (1992). Putting stress into words: The impact of writing on psychological, absentee and self-reported emotional well-being measures. *American Journal of Health Promotion, 6,* 280–287.

Franco, S. E., Hubbard, J. R., & Martin, P. R. (1998). Stress and addiction. In J. R. Hubbard & E. A. Workman (Eds.), *Handbook of stress medicine: An organ system approach.* New York: CRC Press.

Frank, E. (1991). Interpersonal psychotherapy as a maintenance treatment for patients with recurrent depression. *Psychotherapy, 28,* 259–266.

Frank, E., Anderson, C., & Rubinstein, D. (1978). Frequency of sexual dysfunction in "normal" couples. *New England Journal of Medicine, 299,* 111–115.

Frank, H. B. (1985). Gender differences in postmarital adjustment. In D. C. Goldberg (Ed.), *Contemporary marriage: Special issues in couples therapy.* Homewood, IL: Dorsey Press.

Frank, J. D. (1961). *Persuasion and healing.* Baltimore: John Hopkins University Press.

Frank, L. R. (1990). Electroshock: Death, brain damage, memory loss, and brainwashing. *The Journal of Mind and Behavior, 11,* 489–512.

Frankel, A., & Prentice-Dunn, S. (1990). Loneliness and the processing of self-relevant information. *Journal of Social and Clinical Psychology, 9,* 303–315.

Frankel, F. H. (1990). Hypnotizability and dissociation. *American Journal of Psychiatry, 147,* 823–829.

Frankel, F. H. (1993). Adult reconstruction of childhood events in the multiple personality literature. *American Journal of Psychiatry, 150,* 954–958.

Franken, R. E., Gibson, K. J., & Rowland, G. L. (1992). Sensation seeking and the tendency to view the world as threatening. *Personality and Individual Differences, 13,* 31–38.

Frankl, V. (1984). *Man's search for meaning.* New York: Pocket Books.

Franks, C. M., & Barbrack, C. R. (1983). Behavior therapy with adults: An integrative perspective. In M. Hersen, A. E. Kazdin, & A. S. Bellack (Eds.), *The clinical psychology handbook.* New York: Pergamon.

Franzoi, S. L., & Herzog, M. E. (1987). Judging personal attractiveness: What body aspects do we use? *Personality and Social Psychology Bulletin, 13,* 19–33.

Freedman, J. (1978). *Happy people.* New York: Harcourt Brace Jovanovich.

Freedman, J. L., & Fraser, S. C. (1966). Compliance without pressure: The foot-in-the-door technique. *Journal of Personality and Social Psychology, 4,* 195–202.

Fremouw, W. J., de Perczel, M., & Ellis, T. E. (1990). *Suicide risk: Assessment and response guidelines.* New York: Pergamon.

French, S. A., & Jeffery, R. W. (1994). Consequences of dieting to lose weight: Effects on physical and mental health. *Health Psychology, 13,* 195–212.

Freud, S. (1901/1960). *The psychopathology of everyday life* (Standard ed., Vol. 6). London: Hogarth. (Original work published 1901)

Freud, S. (1920/1924). *A general introduction to psychoanalysis.* New York: Boni and Liveright. (Original work published 1920)

Freud, S. (1923). *The ego and the id* (Standard ed., Vol. 19.) London: Hogarth.

Fried, P. A. (1986). Marijuana and human pregnancy. In I. J. Chasnoff (Ed.), *Drug use in pregnancy: Mother and child.* Lancaster, PA: MTP Press.

Fried, S. B., & Schultis, G. A. (1995). *The best self-help and self-awareness books: A topic-by-topic guide to quality information.* Chicago: American Library Association.

Friedan, B. (1964). *The feminine mystique.* New York: Dell.

Friedberg, J. (1976). *Shock treatment is not good for your brain.* San Francisco: Glide Publications.

Friedman, D. E. (1987). Work vs. family: War of the worlds. *Personnel Administrator, 32,* 36–39.

Friedman, H. S. (1983). Social perception and face-to-face interaction. In D. Perlman & D. C. Cozby (Eds.), *Social psychology.* New York: Holt, Rinehart & Winston.

Friedman, H. S. (1991). *The self-healing personality: Why some people achieve health and others succumb to illness.* New York: Holt.

Friedman, H. S., & Miller-Herringer, T. (1991). Nonverbal display of emotion in public and private: Self-monitoring, personality, and expressive cues. *Journal of Personality and Social Psychology, 61,* 766–775.

Friedman, H. S., Tucker, J. S., Schwartz, J. E., Martin, L. R., Tomlinson-Keasey, C., Wingard, D. L., & Criqui, M. H. (1995). Childhood conscientiousness and longevity: Health behaviors and cause of death. *Journal of Personality and Social Psychology, 68,* 696–703.

Friedman, H. S., Tucker, J. S., Tomlinson-Keasey, C., Schwartz, J. E., Wingard, D. L., & Criqui, M. H. (1993). Does childhood personality predict longevity? *Journal of Personality and Social Psychology, 65,* 176–185.

Friedman, J. (1989). The impact of homophobia on male sexual development. *Siecus Report, 17,* 8–9.

Friedman, L. S., & Goodman, E. (1992). Adolescents at risk for HIV infection. *Primary Care, 19,* 171–190.

Friedman, M., & Rosenman, R. F. (1974). *Type A behavior and your heart.* New York: Knopf.

Friedman, M. (1996). *Type A behavior: Its diagnosis and treatment.* New York: Plenum Press.

Friedrich-Cofer, L., & Huston, A. C. (1986). Television violence and aggression: The debate continues. *Psychological Bulletin, 100,* 364–371.

Froelicher, V. F. (1990). Exercise, fitness, and coronary heart disease. In C. Bouchard, R. J. Shephard, T. Stephens, J. R. Sutton, & B. D. McPherson (Eds.), *Exercise, fitness, and health: A consensus of current knowledge.* Champaign, IL: Human Kinetics Books.

Fromm, E. (1963). *Escape from freedom.* New York: Holt.

Fromm, E. (1981). *Sane society.* New York: Fawcett.

Fuchs, R. M. (1984). Group therapy. In T. B. Karasu (Ed.), *The psychiatric therapies.* Washington, DC: American Psychiatric Association.

Fullerton, H. N., Jr. (1997). Labor force 2006: Slowing down and changing composition. *Monthly Labor Review, 120,* 23–38.

Funk, S. C. (1992). Hardiness: A review of theory and research. *Health Psychology, 11,* 335–345.

Furman, E. (1984). Children's patterns in mourning the death of a loved one. In H. Wass & C. A. Corr (Eds.), *Childhood and death.* Washington, DC: Hemisphere.

Furnham, A. F. (1984). Value systems and anomie in three cultures. *International Journal of Psychology, 19,* 565–579.

Furstenberg, F. F., Jr. (1990). Divorce and the American family. *Annual Review of Sociology, 16,* 379–403.

Furstenberg, F. F., Jr., & Cherlin, A. J. (1991). *Divided families: What happens to children when parents part.* Cambridge, MA: Harvard University Press.

Gabbard, G. O., Lazar, S. G., Hornberger, J., & Spiegel, D. (1997). The economic impact of psychotherapy: A review. *American Journal of Psychiatry, 154,* 147–155.

Gaertner, S. L., & Dovidio, J. F. (1986). The aversive form of racism. In J. F. Dovidio & S. L. Gaertner (Eds.), *Prejudice, discrimination, and racism: Theory and research.* Orlando, FL: Academic Press.

Gagnon, J. H., & Simon, W. (1987). The sexual scripting of oral genital contacts. *Archives of Sexual Behavior, 16,* 1–25.

Galambos, N. L., Almeida, D. M., & Petersen, A. C. (1990). Masculinity, femininity, and sex role attitudes in early adolescence: Exploring gender intensification. *Child Development, 61,* 1905–1914.

Galanter, H. (1989). *Cults: Faith, healing, and coercion.* New York: Oxford University Press.

Gambone, J. C., Reiter, R. C., & DiMatteo, M. R. (1994). *The PREPARED provider: A guide for improved patient communication.* Beaverton, OR: Mosybl Great Performance.

Gangestad, S. W. (1993). Sexual selection and physical attractiveness: Implications for mating dynamics. *Human Nature, 4,* 205–235.

Ganong, L., & Coleman, M. (1986). A comparison of clinical and empirical literature on children in stepfamilies. *Journal of Marriage and the Family, 48,* 309–318.

Ganong, L., & Coleman, M. (1994). *Remarried family relationships.* Newbury Park, CA: Sage.

Gantt, W. H. (1975, April 25). Unpublished lecture, Ohio State University. Cited in D. Hothersall (1984), *History of psychology*. New York: Random House.

Gardner, J. M. (1994). *Worker displacement during the early 1990's*. Washington, DC: U.S. Department of Labor.

Gardos, G., Casey, D. E., Cole, J. O., Perenyi, A., Kocsis, E., Arato, M., Samson, J. A., & Conley, C. (1994). Ten-year outcome of tardive dyskinesia. *American Journal of Psychiatry, 151,* 836–841.

Garfield, S. L. (1986). Problems in diagnostic classification. In T. Millon & G. L. Klerman (Eds.), *Contemporary directions in psychopathology: Toward the DSM-IV*. New York: Guilford Press.

Garfield, S. L. (1993). Methodological problems in clinical diagnosis. In P. B. Sutker & H. E. Adams (Eds.), *Comprehensive handbook of psychopathology*. New York: Plenum.

Garfield, S. L., & Bergin, A. E. (1994). Introduction and historical overview. In A. E. Bergin & S. L. Garfield (Eds.), *Handbook of psychotherapy and behavior change* (4th ed.). New York: Wiley.

Garfinkel, P. E. (1995). Classification and diagnosis of eating disorders. In K. D. Brownell & C. G. Fairburn (Eds.), *Eating disorders and obesity: A comprehensive handbook*. New York: Guilford Press.

Garland, A. F., & Zigler, E. (1993). Adolescent suicide prevention: Current research and social policy implications. *American Psychologist, 48,* 169–182.

Garner, D. M., Garfinkel, P. E., Schwartz, D., & Thompson, M. (1980). Cultural expectations of thinness in women. *Psychological Reports, 47,* 483–491.

Garnets, L., & Kimmel, D. (1991). Lesbian and gay male dimensions in the psychological study of human diversity. In J. D. Goodchilds (Ed.), *Psychological perspectives on human diversity in America*. Washington, DC: American Psychological Association.

Garro, A. J., Espina, N., & Lieber, C. S. (1992). Alcohol and cancer. *Alcohol Health and Research World, 16,* 81–86.

Gebhard, P. H. (1966). Factors in marital orgasm. *Journal of Social Issues, 22,* 88–95.

Gebhardt, D. L., & Crump, C. E. (1990). Employee fitness and wellness programs in the workplace. *American Psychologist, 45,* 262–272.

Gecas, V., & Schwalbe, M. L. (1986). Parental behavior and adolescent self-esteem. *Journal of Marriage and the Family, 48,* 37–46.

Gecas, V., & Seff, M. A. (1990). Families and adolescents: A review of the 1980s. *Journal of Marriage and the Family, 52,* 941–958.

Geis, B. D., & Gerrard, M. (1984). Predicting male and female contraceptive behavior: A discriminant analysis of groups high, moderate, and low in contraceptive effectiveness. *Journal of Personality and Social Psychology, 46,* 669–680.

Geis, F. L. (1993). Self-fulfilling prophecies: A social psychological view of gender. In A. E. Beall & R. J. Sternberg (Eds.), *The psychology of gender*. New York: Guilford Press.

Geiser, R. L., Rarick, D. L., & Soldow, G. F. (1977). Deception and judgment accuracy: A study in person perception. *Personality and Social Psychology Bulletin, 3,* 446–449.

Gelderloos, P., Walton, K. G., Orme-Johnson, D. W., & Alexander, C. N. (1991). Effectiveness of the transcendental meditation program in preventing and treating substance misuse: A review. *The International Journal of Addictions, 26,* 293–325.

Gelfand, D. E. (1994). *Aging and ethnicity*. New York: Springer.

Gelles, R. J., & Conte, J. R. (1991). Domestic violence and sexual abuse of children: A review of research in the eighties. In A. Booth (Ed.), *Contemporary families: Looking forward, looking back*. Minneapolis: National Council on Family Relations.

Genuis, S., & Genuis, S. (1995). Adolescent sexual involvement: Time for primary prevention. *The Lancet, 345,* 240–241.

Gerbner, G., Gross, L., Morgan, M., & Signorielli, N. (1986). Living with television: The dynamics of the cultivation process. In J. Bryant & D. Zillmann (Eds.), *Perspectives on media effects*. Hillsdale, NJ: Erlbaum.

Gerrard, M. (1987). Emotional and cognitive barriers to effective contraception: Are males and females really different? In K. Kelley (Ed.), *Females, males, and sexuality: Theories and research*. Albany: SUNY Press.

Gerzon, R. (1997). *Finding serenity in the age of anxiety*. New York: Macmillan.

Ghaemi, S. N., Irizarry, M. C., & Joseph, A. B. (1998). The effect of psychological stress on neurological disorders. In J. R. Hubbard & E. A. Workman (Eds.), *Handbook of stress medicine: An organ system approach*. New York: CRC Press.

Ghosh, T. B., & Victor, B. S. (1994). Suicide. In R. E. Hales, S. C. Yudofsky, & J. A. Talbott (Eds.), *The American Psychiatric Press textbook of psychiatry* (2nd ed.). Washington, DC: American Psychiatric Press.

Gibbs, N. (1989, July 31). Sick and tired. *Time,* pp. 48–53.

Gibbs, N. (1993, May 3). Oh, my God, they're killing themselves. *Time,* pp. 27–43.

Giesler, R. B., Josephs, R. A., & Swann, W. B., Jr. (1996). Self-verification in clinical depression: The desire for negative evaluation. *Journal of Abnormal Psychology, 105,* 358–368.

Gilbert, D. A. (1988). *Compendium of American public opinion*. New York: Facts On File.

Gilbert, L. A. (1993). *Two careers/one family*. Newbury Park, CA: Sage Publications.

Gilbert, L. A. (1994). Current perspectives on dual-career families. *Current Directions in Psychological Science, 3,* 101–104.

Gilder, G. F. (1986). *Men and marriage*. New York: Pelican.

Giles-Sims, J. (1987). Social exchange in remarried families. In K. Pasley & M. Ihinger-Tallman (Eds.), *Remarriage and stepparenting: Current research and theory*. New York: Guilford Press.

Gillis, J. S. (1993). Effects of life stress and dysphoria on complex judgments. *Psychological Reports, 72,* 1355–1363.

Givovino, G. A., Schooley, M. W., Zhu, B., Chrisman, J. H., Tomar, S. L., Peddicord, J. P., Merritt, R. K., Housten, C. G., & Eriksen, M. P. (1994). Surveillance for selected tobacco-use behaviors: United States, 1990–1994. *Morbidity and Morality Weekly Report, 43,* No. SS-3.

Gladue, B. A. (1987). Psychobiological contributions. In L. Diamant (Ed.), *Male and female homosexuality: Psychological approaches*. Washington, DC: Hemisphere.

Gladue, B. A. (1994). The biopsychology of sexual orientation. *Current Directions in Psychological Science, 3,* 150–154.

Glantz, S. A., & Parmley, W. W. (1991). Passive smoking and heart disease: Epidemiology, physiology, and biochemistry. *Circulation, 83,* 1–12.

Glantz, S. A., & Parmley, W. W. (1995). Passive smoking and heart disease: Mechanisms and risk. *Journal of the American Medical Association, 273,* 1047–1053.

Glass, C. R., & Arnkoff, D. B. (1992). Behavior therapy. In D. K. Freedheim (Ed.), *History of psychotherapy: A century of change*. Washington, DC: American Psychological Association.

Glass, S. P., & Wright, T. L. (1985). Sex differences in type of extramarital involvement and marital dissatisfaction. *Sex Roles, 12,* 1101–1120.

Glassman, A. H., & Shapiro, P. A. (1998). Depression and the course of coronary artery disease. *American Journal of Psychiatry, 155,* 4–11.

Glazer, M. P., & Glazer, P. M. (1990). *The whistleblowers: Exposing corruption in government and industry*. New York: Basic Books.

Gleaves, D. H. (1994). On "The reality of repressed memories." *American Psychologist, 49,* 440–441.

Gleaves, D. H. (1996). The sociocognitive model of dissociative disorder: A reexamination of the evidence. *Psychological Bulletin, 120,* 42–59.

Glenberg, A. M. (1992). Disturbed practice effects. In L. R. Squire (Ed.), *Encyclopedia of learning and memory*. New York: Macmillan.

Glenn, N. D. (1990). Quantitative research on marital quality in the 1980s: A critical review. *Journal of Marriage and the Family, 52,* 818–831.

Glenn, N. D. (1998). The course of marital success and failure in five American 10-year marriage cohorts. *Journal of Marriage and the Family, 60,* 569–576.

Glenn, N. D., & Weaver, C. N. (1988). The changing relationship of marital status to reported happiness. *Journal of Marriage and the Family, 50,* 317–324.

Glick, P. C. (1984). Marriage, divorce, and living arrangements: Prospective changes. *Journal of Family Issues, 5,* 7–26.

Glick, P. C., & Lin, S. (1986). More young adults are living with their parents: Who are they? *Journal of Marriage and the Family, 48,* 107–112.

Goetting, A. (1986). Parental satisfaction: A review of research. *Journal of Family Issues, 7,* 83–109.

Gold, D. T. (1990). Late-life sibling relationships: Does race affect typological distribution? *The Gerontologist, 30,* 741–748.

Gold, M. S. (1989). *Marijuana*. New York: Plenum.

Gold, M. S. (1992). Cocaine (and crack): Clinical aspects. In J. H. Lowinson, P. Ruiz, & R. B. Millman (Eds.), *Substance abuse: A comprehensive textbook* (2nd ed.). Baltimore: Williams & Wilkins.

Gold, M. S., & Miller, N. S. (1997). Cocaine (and crack): Neurobiology. In J. H. Lowinson, P. Ruiz, R. B. Millman, & J. G. Langrod (Eds.), *Substance abuse: A comprehensive textbook* (3rd ed.). Baltimore: Williams & Wilkins.

Gold, M. S., Miller, N. S., & Jonas, J. M. (1992). Cocaine (and crack): Neurobiology. In J. H. Lowinson, P. Ruiz, & R. B. Millman (Eds.), *Substance abuse: A comprehensive textbook* (2nd ed.). Baltimore: Williams & Wilkins.

Gold, M. S. (1997). Cocaine (and crack): Clinical aspects. In J. H. Lowinson, P. Ruiz, R. B. Millman, & J. G. Langrod (Eds.), *Substance abuse: A comprehensive textbook* (3rd ed.). Baltimore: Williams & Wilkins.

Goldberg, L. R. (1993). The structure of phenotypic personality traits. *American Psychologist, 48,* 26–34.

Goldberg, M. (1985). Remarriage: Repetition versus new beginnings. In D. C. Goldberg (Ed.), *Contemporary marriage: Special issues in couples therapy*. Homewood, IL: Dorsey Press.

Goldberger, L. (1993). Sensory deprivation and overload. In L. Goldberger & S. Breznitz (Eds.), *Handbook of stress: Theoretical and clinical aspects* (2nd ed.). New York: Free Press.

Goldbloom, D. S., & Kennedy, S. H. (1995). Medical complications of anorexia nervosa. In

K. D. Brownell & C. G. Fairburn (Eds.), *Eating disorders and obesity: A comprehensive handbook*. New York: Guilford Press.

Goldfried, M. R., Greenberg, L. S., & Marmar, C. (1990). Individual psychotherapy: Process and outcome. *Annual Review of Psychology, 41,* 659–688.

Goldman, H. H., Skodol, A. E., & Lave, T. R. (1992). Revising axis V for DSM-IV: A review of measures of social functioning. *American Journal of Psychiatry, 149,* 1148–1156.

Goldscheider, F., & Goldscheider, C. (1994, March). Leaving and returning home in 20th century America. *Population Bulletim, 48* (4).

Goldstein, E., & Farmer, K. (Eds.). (1993). *True stories of false memories*. Boca Raton, FL: Sirs Publishing.

Goldstein, M. J. (1987). Family interaction patterns that antedate the onset of schizophrenia and related disorders: A further analysis of data from a longitudinal prospective study. In K. Hahlweg & M.J. Goldstein (Eds.), *Understanding major mental disorder: The contribution of family interaction research.* New York: Family Process Press.

Goldstein, M. J. (1988). The family and psychopathology. *Annual Review of Psychology, 39,* 283–300.

Goleman, D. (1979, November). Interview with Richard S. Lazarus, Positive denial: The case for not facing reality. *Psychology Today,* pp. 44–60.

Goleman, D. (1995). *Emotional intelligence.* New York: Bantam Books.

Golier, J. A., Marzuk, P. M., Leon, A. C., Weiner, C., & Tardiff, K. (1995). Low serum cholesterol level and attempted suicide. *American Journal of Psychiatry, 152,* 419–423.

Gonder-Frederick, L. A., Carter, W. R., Cox, D. J., & Clarke, W. L. (1990). Environmental stress and blood glucose change in insulin-dependent diabetes mellitus. *Health Psychology, 9,* 503–515.

Gondolf, E. W. (1988). *Battered women as survivors.* Lexington, MA: Lexington Books.

Gonsiorek, J. C., & Weinrich, J. D. (1991). The definition and scope of sexual orientation. In J. C. Gonsiorek & J. D. Weinrich (Eds.), *Homosexuality: Research implications for public policy.* Newbury Park, CA: Sage Publications.

Gonzales, M. H., & Meyers, S. A. (1993). "Your mother would like me": Self-presentation in the personals ads of heterosexual and homosexual men and women. *Personality and Social Psychology Bulletin, 19,* 131–142.

Gonzales, M. H., Davis, J. M., Loney, G. L., Lukens, C. K., & Junghans, C. H. (1983). Interactional approach to interpersonal attraction. *Journal of Personality and Social Psychology, 44,* 1192–1197.

Goodall, K. (1972, November). Field report: Shapers at work. *Psychology Today,* pp. 53–63, 132–138.

Goodwin, D. W., & Gabrielli, W. F. (1997). Alcohol: Clinical aspects. In J. H. Lowinson, P. Ruiz, R. B. Millman, & J. G. Langrod (Eds.), *Substance abuse: A comprehensive textbook* (3rd ed.). Baltimore: Williams & Wilkins.

Goodwin, F. K., & Jamison, K. R. (1990). *Manic-depressive illness.* New York: Oxford University Press.

Goodwin, R. (1990). Sex differences among partner preferences: Are the sexes really very similar? *Sex Roles, 23,* 501–513.

Gorman, J. M., & Davis, J. M. (1989). Antianxiety drugs. In H. I. Kaplan & B. J. Sadock (Eds.), *Comprehensive textbook of psychiatry/V.* Baltimore: Williams & Wilkins.

Gotlib, I. H., & McCabe, S. B. (1990). Marriage and psychopathology. In F. D. Fincham & T. N. Bradbury (Eds.), *The psychology of marriage: Basic issues and applications.* New York: Guilford Press.

Gottdiener, J. S., Krantz, D. S., & Howell, R. H., Hecht, G. M., Klein, J., Falconer, J. J., & Rozanski, A. (1994). Induction of silent myocardial ischemia with mental stress testing: Relationship to the triggers of ischemia during daily life activities and to ischemic functional severity. *Journal of the American College of Cardiology, 24,* 1645–1651.

Gottesman, I. I. (1991). *Schizophrenia genesis: The origins of madness.* New York: Freeman.

Gottfredson, G. D. (1977). Career stability and redirection in adulthood. *Journal of Applied Psychology, 62,* 436–445.

Gottman, J. M. (1979). *Marital interaction.* New York: Academic Press.

Gottman, J. M., & Levenson, R. S. (1988). The social psychophysiology of marriage. In P. Noller & M. A. Fitzpatrick (Eds.), *Perspectives on marital interaction.* Clevedon, England, and Philadelphia: Multilingual Matters.

Gottman, J., & Silver, N. (1994). *Why marriages succeed or fail . . . and how you can make it last.* New York: Simon & Schuster.

Gould, R. L. (1978). *Transformations: Growth and change in adult life.* New York: Simon & Schuster.

Graham, J. W. (1986). Principle organizational dissent: A theoretical essay. *Research in Organizational Behavior, 8,* 1–52.

Graig, E. (1993). Stress as a consequence of the urban physical environment. In L. Goldberger & S. Breznitz (Eds.), *Handbook of stress: Theoretical and clinical aspects* (2nd ed.). New York: Free Press.

Grant, I., McDonald, W. I., Patterson, T., & Trimble, M. R. (1989). Multiple sclerosis. In G. W. Brown & T. O. Harris (Eds.), *Life events and illness.* New York: Guilford Press.

Gray, J. D. (1983). The married professional woman: An examination of her role conflicts and coping strategies. *Psychology of Women Quarterly, 7,* 235–243.

Gray, J. (1992). *Men are from mars, women are from venus: A practical guide for improving communication and getting what you want in your relationship.* New York: HarperCollins.

Graziano, W. G., & Eisenberg, N. H. (1997). Agreeableness: A dimension of personality. In R. Hogan, J. Johnson, & S. Briggs (Eds), *Handbook of personality psychology.* San Diego, CA: Academic Press.

Grebb, J. A., & Cancro, R. (1989). Schizophrenia: Clinical features. In H. I. Kaplan & B. J. Sadock (Eds.), *Comprehensive textbook of psychiatry/V.* Baltimore: Williams & Wilkins.

Green, B. L., & Russo, N. F. (1993). Work and family roles: Selected issues. In F. L. Denmark & M. A. Paludi (Eds.), *Psychology of women: A handbook of issues and theories.* Westport, CT: Greenwood Press.

Green, R. (1982). The best interests of the child with a lesbian mother. *American Academy of Psychiatry and the Law Bulletin, 10,* 7–15.

Green, S. K., Buchanan, D. R., & Heuer, S. K. (1984). Winners, losers, and choosers: A field investigation of dating initiation. *Personality and Social Psychology Bulletin, 10,* 502–511.

Greenberg, J. S. (1993). *Comprehensive stress management.* Dubuque, IA: William C. Brown.

Greenberg, M. A., Wortman, C. B., & Stone, A. A. (1996). Emotional expression and physical health: Revising traumatic memories or fostering self-regulation? *Journal of Personality and Social Psychology, 71,* 588–602.

Greenberger, E., & Goldberg, W. A. (1989). Work, parenting, and the socialization of children. *Developmental Psychology, 25,* 22–35.

Greenberger, E., Goldberg, W. A., Crawford, T., & Granger, J. (1988). Beliefs about the consequences of maternal employment for children. *Psychology of Women Quarterly, 12,* 35–59.

Greene, R. L. (1992). *Human memory: Paradigms and paradoxes.* Hillsdale, NJ: Erlbaum.

Greene, W. A., & Swisher, S. N. (1969). Psychological and somatic variables associated with the development and course of monozygotic twins discordant for leukemia. *Annals of the New York Academy of Sciences, 164,* 394–408.

Greenson, R. R. (1967). *The technique and practice of psychoanalysis* (Vol. 1). New York: International Universities Press.

Greenstein, T. N. (1993). Maternal employment and child behavioral outcomes. *Journal of Family Issues, 14,* 323–354.

Greenwald, A. G., Spangenberg, E. R., Pratkanis, A. R., & Eskenazi, J. (1991). Double-blind tests of subliminal self-help audiotapes. *Psychological Science, 2,* 119–122.

Gregersen, E. (1982). *Sexual practices.* New York: Franklin Watts.

Griggs, L. (1990, July 2). A losing battle with AIDS. *Time,* pp. 41–43.

Grinspoon, L., & Bakalar, J. B. (1992). Marihuana. In J. H. Lowinson, P. Ruiz, & R. B. Millman (Eds.), *Substance abuse: A comprehensive textbook* (2nd ed.). Baltimore: Williams & Wilkins.

Grinspoon, L., & Bakalar, J. B. (1997). Marihuana. In J. H. Lowinson, P. Ruiz, R. H. Millman, & J. G. Langrod (Eds.), *Substance abuse: A comprehensive textbook* (3rd ed.). Baltimore: Williams & Wilkins.

Groat, H. T., Giordano, P. C., Cernkovich, S. A., Pugh, M. D., & Swinford, S. P. (1997). Attitudes toward childbearing among young parents. *Journal of Marriage and the Family, 59,* 568–581.

Grob, C. S., & Poland, R. E. (1997). MDMA. In J. H. Lowinson, P. Ruiz, R. B. Millman, & J. G. Langrod (Eds.), *Substance abuse: A comprehensive textbook* (3rd ed.). Baltimore: Williams & Wilkins.

Grob, G. N. (1983). Disease and environment in American history. In D. Mechanic (Ed.), *Handbook of health, health care, and the health professions.* New York: Free Press.

Grob, G. N. (1991). Origins of DSM-I: A study in appearance and reality. *American Journal of Psychiatry, 148,* 421–431.

Grobbee, D. E., Rimm, E. B., Giovannucci, E., Colditz, G., Stampfer, M., & Willett, W. (1990). Coffee, caffeine, and cardiovascular disease in men. *New England Journal of Medicine, 323,* 1026–1032.

Grolnick, W. S., & Ryan, R. M. (1989). Parent styles associated with children's self-regulation and competence in school. *Journal of Educational Psychology, 81,* 143–154.

Gross, J. J. (1998). Antecedent- and response-focused emotion regulation: Divergent consequences for experience, expression, and physiology. *Journal of Personality and Social Psychology, 74,* 224–237.

Gross, J. J., & Levenson, R. W. (1997). Hiding feelings: The acute effects of inhibiting negative and positive emotion. *Journal of Abnormal Psychology, 106,* 95–103.

Grossarth-Maticek, R., & Eysenck, H. J. (1991). Coffee-drinking and personality as factors in the genesis of cancer and coronary heart disease. *Neuropsychobiology, 23,* 153–159.

Grotevant, H. D., & Cooper, C. R. (1988). The role of family experience in career exploration during adolescence. In P. Baltes, D. Feartherman, & R. Lerner (Eds.), *Life-span development and behavior* (Vol. 8). Hillsdale, NJ: Erlbaum.

Grove, W. M., & Andreasen, N. C. (1992). Concepts, diagnosis and classification. In E. S. Paykel (Ed.), *Handbook of affective disorders* (2nd ed.). New York: Guilford Press.

Gruber, J. E. (1990). Methodological problems and policy implication in sexual harassment research. *Population Research and Policy Review, 9*, 235–254.

Gruen, R. J. (1993). Stress and depression: Toward the development of integrative models. In L. Goldberger & S. Breznitz (Eds.), *Handbook of stress: Theoretical and clinical aspects.* New York: Free Press.

Grunberg, N. E., & Straub, R. O. (1992). The role of gender and taste class in the effects of stress on eating. *Health Psychology, 11*, 97–100.

Grunberg, N. E., Bowen, D. J., & Winders, S. E. (1986). Effects of nicotine on body weight and food consumption in female rats. *Psychopharmacology, 90*, 101–105.

Grynch, J. H., & Fincham, F. D. (1990). Marital conflict and children's adjustment: A cognitive-contextual framework. *Psychological Bulletin, 108*, 267–290.

Guidubaldi, J., Perry, J. D., & Nastasi, B. K. (1987). Growing up in a divorced family: Initial and long-term perspectives on children's adjustment. In S. Oskamp (Ed.), *Family processes and problems: Social psychological aspects* (Vol. 7, Applied Social Psychology Annual). Newbury Park, CA: Sage Publications.

Gullette, E. C. D., Blumenthal, J. A., Babyak, M., Jiang, W., Waugh, R. A., Frid, D. J., O'Connor, C. M., Morris, J. J., & Krantz, D. S. (1997). Effects of mental stress on myocardial ischema during daily life. *Journal of the American Medical Association, 277*, 1521–1526.

Gupta, G. R. (1992). Love, arranged marriage, and the Indian social structure. In J. J. Macionis & N. V. Benokraitis (Eds.), *Seeing ourselves: Classic, contemporary and cross-cultural reading in sociology.* Englewood Cliffs, NJ: Prentice-Hall.

Gupta, U., & Singh, P. (1982). Exploratory study of love and liking type of marriages. Indian *Journal of Applied Psychology, 19*, 92–97.

Gureje, O., Simon, G. E., Ustun, T. B., & Goldberg, D. P. (1997). Somatization in cross-cultural perspective: A world health organization study in primary care. *American Journal of Psychiatry, 154*, 989–995.

Gurin, J. (1989, June). Leaner, not lighter. *Psychology Today*, pp. 32–36.

Gutek, B. (1993). Responses to sexual harassment. In S. Oskamp & M. Costanzo (Eds.), *Gender issues in contemporary society.* Newbury Park, CA: SagePublications.

Gutek, B. A. (1985). *Sex and the workplace: Impact of sexual behavior and harassment on women, men and organizations.* San Francisco: Jossey-Bass.

Gutek, B. A. (1989). Relocation, family, and the bottom line: Results from the Division 35 survey. *Psychology of Women Quarterly, 16*, 5–7.

Gutek, B., & Koss, M. P. (1993). Changed women and changed organizations: Consequences of and coping with sexual harassment. *Journal of Vocational Behavior, 42*, 28–48.

Haaken, J. (1990). A critical analysis of the co-dependence construct. *Psychiatry, 53*, 396–406.

Haaken, J. (1993). From Al-Anon to ACOA: Codependence and the reconstruction of care-giving. *Signs, 18*, 321–345.

Haan, N., Millsap, R., & Hartka, E. (1986). As time goes by: Change and stability in personality over 50 years. *Psychology of Aging, 1*, 220–232.

Haas, A., & Haas, K. (1993). *Understanding sexuality.* St. Louis: Times Mirror/Mosby.

Hagberg, J. M. (1990). Exercise, fitness, and hypertension. In C. Bouchard, R. J. Shephard, T. Stephens, J. R. Sutton, & B. D. McPherson (Eds.), *Exercise, fitness, and health: A consensus of current knowledge.* Champaign, IL: Human Kinetics Books.

Halford, W. K., & Sanders, M. R. (1990). The relationship of cognition and behavior during marital interaction. *Journal of Social and Clinical Psychology, 9*, 489–510.

Hall, D. R. (1996). Marriage as a pure relationship: Exploring the link between premarital cohabitation and divorce in Canada. *Journal of Comparative Family Studies, 27*, 1–12.

Hall, E. T. (1966) *The hidden dimension.* Garden City, NY: Doubleday.

Hall, G. S. (1904). *Adolescence.* New York: Appleton.

Hall, J. A. (1984). *Nonverbal sex differences: Communication accuracy and expressive style.* Baltimore: Johns Hopkins University Press.

Hall, J. A. (1990). *Nonverbal sex differences: Communication accuracy and expressive style* (2nd ed.). Baltimore: Johns Hopkins University Press.

Hall, J. A., & Veccia, E. M. (1990). More "touching" observations: New insights on men, women, and interpersonal touch. *Journal of Personality and Social Psychology, 59*, 1155–1162.

Hall, J. A., & Veccia, E. M. (1991). Touch asymmetry between the sexes. In C. L. Ridgeway (Ed.), *Gender, interaction, and inequality.* New York: Springer-Verlag.

Hall, J. A., Roter, D. L., & Katz, N. R. (1988). Meta-analysis of correlates of provider behavior in medical encounters. *Medical Care, 26*, 1–19.

Hall, R. M., & Sandler, B. R. (1982). *The classroom climate: A chilly one for women?* Washington, DC: Association of American Colleges.

Halpern, D. F. (1992). *Sex differences in cognitive abilities* (2nd ed.). Hillsdale, NJ: Erlbaum.

Halpern, D. F. (1997). Sex differences in intelligence: Implications for education. *American Psychologist, 52*, 1091–1102.

Halverson, C. F., Jr., & Wampler, K. S. (1997). Family influences on personality development. In R. Hogan, J. Johnson, & S. Briggs (Eds), *Handbook of personality psychology.* San Diego, CA: Academic Press.

Hamachek, D. (1992). *Encounters with the self.* Fort Worth: Harcourt Brace Jovanovich.

Hamer, D. H., Hu, S., Magnuson, V. L., Hu, N., & Pattatucci, A. M. L. (1993). A linkage between DNA markers on the X chromosome and male sexual orientation. *Science, 261*, 321–327.

Hamilton, M. H. (1988, July 10). Employing new tools to recruit workers. *Washington Post*, pp. H1, H3.

Hammen, C., & Gitlin, M. (1997). Stress reactivity in bipolar patients and its relation to prior history of disorder. *American Journal of Psychiatry, 154*, 856–857.

Hampton, R. L., Gelles, R. J., & Harrop, J. W. (1989). Is violence in black families increasing? A comparison of 1975 and 1985 national survey rates. *Journal of Marriage and the Family, 51*, 969–980.

Handy, B. (1998a, May 4). The Viagra craze. *Time*, 50–57.

Handy, B. (1998b, August 31). How we really feel about fidelity. *Time*, 52–54.

Hankin, B. L., Abramson, L. Y., Moffitt, T. E., Silva, P. A., McGee, R., & Angell, K. E. (1998). Development of depression from preadolescence to young adulthood: Emerging gender differences in a 10-year longitudinal study. *Journal of Abnormal Psychology, 107*, 128–140.

Hansen, C. H., & Hansen, R. D. (1988). How rock music videos can change what is seen when boy meets girl: Priming stereotypic appraisal of social interations. *Sex Roles, 19*, 287–316.

Hansen, J. C., & Campbell, D. P. (1985). *Manual for the SVIB-SCII* (4th ed.). Stanford, CA: Stanford University Press.

Hansen, J. E., & Schuldt, W. J. (1984). Marital self-disclosure and marital satisfaction. *Journal of Marriage and the Family, 46*, 923–926.

Harmsen, P., Rosengren, A., Tsipogianni, A., &Wilhelmsen, L. (1990). Risk factors for stroke in middle-aged men in Goteborg, Sweden. *Stroke, 21*, 23–29.

Harper, J., & Capdevila, C. (1990). Codependency: A critique. *Journal of Psychoactive Drugs, 22*, 285–292.

Harrigan, J. A., Lucic, K. S., Kay, D., McLaney, A., & Rosenthal, R. (1991). Effect of expresser role and type of self-touching on observers' perceptions. *Journal of Applied Psychology, 21*, 585–609.

Harriott, J., & Ferrari, J. R. (1996). Prevalence of procrastination among samples of adults. *Psychological Reports, 78*, 611–616.

Harris, J. R. (1995). Where is the child's environment? A group socialization theory of development. *Psychological Review, 102*, 458–189.

Harris, L., & Associates (1986). *American teens speak: Sex, myths, TV and birth control.* New York: Planned Parenthood.

Harris, M. B., Harris, R. J., & Bochner, S. (1982). Fat, four-eyed, and female: Stereotypes of obesity, glasses, and gender. *Journal of Applied Social Psychology, 12*, 503–516.

Harris, T. (1967). *I'm OK—you're OK.* New York: HarperCollins.

Harrison, A. A., & Saeed, I. (1977). Let's make a deal: An analysis of revelations and stipulations in lonely heart advertisements. *Journal of Personality and Social Psychology, 35*, 257–264.

Harry, J. (1983). Gay male and lesbian relationships. In E. D. Macklin & R. H. Rubin (Eds.), *Contemporary families and alternative lifestyles: Handbook on research and theory.* Newbury Park, CA: Sage Publications.

Harry, J. (1990). A probability sample of gay males. *Journal of Homosexuality, 19*, 89–104.

Harter, S. (1990). Self and identity development. In S. S. Feldman & G. R. Elliott (Eds.), *The developing adolescent.* Cambridge, MA: Harvard University Press.

Harter, S. (1993). Causes and consequences of low self-esteem in children and adolescents. In R. Baumeister (Ed.), *Self-esteem: The puzzle of low self-regard.* New York: Plenum.

Hartley, A. A., & McKenzie, C. R. M. (1991). Attentional and perceptual contributions to the identification of extrafoveal stimuli: Adult age comparisons. *Journal of Gerontology, 46*, P202–P206.

Hartman, W. E., & Fithian, M. A. (1994). *Treatment of sexual dysfunction: A bio-psycho-social approach.* New York: Aronson.

Hartmann, E. (1993). Nightmares. In M. A. Carskadon (Ed.), *Encyclopedia of sleep and dreaming.* New York: Macmillan.

Harvey, J. H., Town, J. P., & Yarkin, K. L. (1981). How fundamental is "the fundamental attribution error"? *Journal of Personality and Social Psychology, 40*, 346–349.

Hatcher, R. A., Trussell, J., Stewart, F., Cates, W. Jr., Stewart, G., Guest, F., & Kowal, D. (1998). *Contraceptive technology* (17th ed.). New York: Ardent Media.

Hatcher, R. A., Trussell, J., Stewart, F., Stewart, G. K., Kowal, D., Guest, F., Cates, W., Jr., & Policar, M. S. (1994). *Contraceptive technology* (16th ed.). New York: Irvington.

Hatfield, E. (1988). Passionate and companionate love. In R. J. Sternberg & M. L. Barnes (Eds.), *The psychology of love.* New Haven, CT: Yale University Press.

Hatfield, E., & Rapson, R. L. (1993). *Love, sex, and intimacy: Their psychology, biology, and history*. New York: HarperCollins.

Hatfield, E., & Rapson, R. L. (1996). *Love and sex: Cross-cultural perspectives*. Boston: Allyn & Bacon.

Haugaard, J. J., & Reppucci, N. D. (1988). *The sexual abuse of children*. San Francisco: Jossey-Bass.

Haycock, L. A., McCarthy, P., & Skay, C. L. (1998). Procrastination in college students: The role of self-efficacy and anxiety. *Journal of Counseling & Development, 76,* 317–324.

Hayes, S. C., & Heiby, E. (1996). Psychology's drug problem: Do we need a fix or should we just say no? *American Psychologist, 51,* 198–206.

Hayghe, H. V. (1990, March). Family members in the work force. *Monthly Labor Review,* pp. 14–19.

Hays, R. B. (1985). A longitudinal study of friendship development. *Journal of Personality and Social Psychology, 48,* 909–924.

Hazan, C., & Shaver, P. (1986). *Parental caregiving style questionnaire*. Unpublished questionnaire.

Hazan, C., & Shaver, P. (1987). Romantic love conceptualized as an attachment process. *Journal of Personality and Social Psychology, 52,* 511–524.

Hazan, C., & Shaver, P. R. (1990). Love and work: An attachment-theoretical perspective. *Journal of Personality and Social Psychology, 59,* 270–280.

Heady, B., & Wearing, A. (1989). Personality, life events, and subjective well-being: Toward a dynamic equilibrium model. *Journal of Personality and Social Psychology, 57,* 731–739.

Healy, J. M., Stewart, A. J., & Copeland, A. P. (1993). The role of self-blame in children's adjustment to parental separation. *Personality and Social Psychology Bulletin, 19,* 279–289.

Hearold, S. (1986). A synthesis of 1,043 effects of television on social behavior. In G. Comstock (Ed.), *Public communications and behavior* (Vol. 1). New York: Academic Press.

Heath, R. G. (1976). Cannabis sativa derivatives: Effects on brain function of monkeys. In G.G. Nahas (Ed.), *Marijuana: Chemistry, biochemistry and cellular effects*. New York: Springer.

Heatherton, T. F., & Ambady, N. (1993). Self-esteem, self-prediction, and living up to commitments. In R. Baumeister (Ed.), *Self-esteem: The puzzle of low self-regard*. New York: Plenum.

Heatherton, T. F., Polivy, J., & Herman, C. P. (1991). Restraint, weight loss, and variability of body weight. *Journal of Abnormal Psychology, 100,* 78–83.

Heckert, D. A., Nowak, T. C., & Snyder, K. A. (1998). The impact of husbands' and wives' relative earnings on marital disruption. *Journal of Marriage and the Family, 60,* 690–703.

Hegarty, J. D., Baldessarini, R. J., Tohen, M., Waternaux, C., & Oepen, G. (1994). One hundred years of schizophrenia: A meta-analysis of the outcome literature. *American Journal of Psychiatry, 151,* 1409–1416.

Heider, F. (1958). *The psychology of interpersonal relations*. New York: Wiley.

Heilman, M. E., Block, C. J., & Lucas, J. A. (1992). Presumed incompetent? Stigmatization and affirmative action efforts. *Journal of Applied Psychology, 77,* 536–544.

Helgeson, V. S. (1994). Relation of agency and communion to well-being: Evidence and potential explanations. *Psychological Bulletin, 116,* 412–428.

Helson, R., Elliott, T., & Leigh, J. (1990). Number and quality of roles. *Psychology of Women Quarterly, 14,* 83–101.

Helson, R., & Moane, G. (1987). Personality change in women from college to midlife. *Journal of Personality and Social Psychology, 53,* 176–186.

Helson, R., & Stewart, A. (1994). Personality change in adulthood. In T. F. Heatherton & J. L. Weinberger (Eds.), *Can personality change?* Washington, DC: American Psychological Association.

Helson, R., Mitchell, V., & Moane, G. (1984). Personality and patterns of adherence and non-adherence to the social clock. *Journal of Personality and Social Psychology, 46,* 1079–1096.

Hembre, R. (1988). Correlates, causes, effects, and treatment of test anxiety. *Review of Educational Research, 58,* 47–77.

Hencken, J. (1984). Conceptualizations of homosexual behavior which preclude homosexual self-labeling. *Journal of Homosexuality, 9,* 53–63.

Henderson, C. W. (1975). *Awakening: Ways to psychospiritual growth*. Englewood Cliffs, NJ: Prentice-Hall.

Henderson-King, D. H., & Veroff, J. (1994). Sexual satisfaction and marital well-being in the first years of marriage. *Journal of Social and Personal Relationships, 11,* 509–534.

Hendrick, C., & Hendrick, S. S. (1989). Research on love: Does it measure up? *Journal of Personality and Social Psychology, 56,* 784–794.

Hendrick, S. S., & Hendrick, C. (1992). *Liking, loving, and relating* (2nd ed.). Pacific Grove, CA: Brooks/Cole.

Hendrick, S. S., Hendrick, C., & Adler, N. L. (1988). Romantic relationships: Love, satisfaction, and staying together. *Journal of Personality and Social Psychology, 54,* 980–988.

Henley, N. M. (1977). *Body politics: Power, sex and nonverbal communication*. Englewood Cliffs, NJ: Prentice-Hall.

Henley, N. M. (1986). *Body politics: Power, sex, and nonverbal communication* (2nd ed.). New York: Simon & Schuster.

Henley, N. M., & Freeman, J. (1981). The sexual politics of interpersonal behavior. In S. Cox (Ed.), *Female psychology: The emerging self*. New York: St. Martin's Press.

Henshaw, S. K. (1997). Teenage abortion and pregnancy statistics by state. *Family Planning Perspectives, 29,* 115–122.

Herbert, T. B., & Cohen, S. (1993). Stress and immunity in humans: A meta-analytic review. *Psychosomatic Medicine, 5,* 364–379.

Herbert, T. B., Silver, R. C., & Ellard, J. H. (1991). Coping with an abusive relationship: I. How and why do women stay? *Journal of Marriage and the Family, 53,* 311–325.

Herek, G. M. (1988). Heterosexuals' attitudes toward lesbians and gay men: Correlates and gender differences. *Journal of Sex Research, 25,* 451–477.

Herek, G. M. (1991). Stigma, prejudice, and violence against lesbians and gay men. In J. C. Gonsiorek & J. D. Weinrich (Eds.), *Homosexuality: Research implications for public policy*. Newbury Park, CA: Sage Publications.

Herek, G. M., Gillis, J. R., Cogan, J. C., & Glunt, E. K. (1997). Hate crime victimization among lesbian, gay, and bisexual adults. *Journal of Interpersonal Violence, 12,* 195–215.

Herman, C. P., & Polivy, J. (1988). Studies of eating in normal dieters. In B. T. Walsh (Ed.), *Eating behavior in eating disorders*. Washington, DC: American Psychiatric Press.

Herman, J. L. (1992). *Trauma and recovery*. New York: Basic Books.

Herman, J. L. (1994). Presuming to know the truth. *Nieman Reports, 48,* 43–45.

Hermann, R. C., Dorwart, R. A., Hoover, C. W., & Brody, J. (1995). Variation in ECT use in the United States. *American Journal of Psychiatry, 152,* 869–875.

Hermann, R. C., Ettner, S. L., Dorwart, R. A., Hoover, C. W., & Yeung, E. (1998). Characteristics of psychiatrists who perform ECT. *American Journal of Psychiatry, 155,* 889–894.

Hershberger, S. L., & D'Augelli, A. R. (1995). The impact of victimization on the mental health and suicidality of lesbian, gay, and bisexual youths. *Developmental Psychology, 31,* 65–74.

Hertzog, C., & Schaie, K. W. (1988). Stability and changes in adult intelligence: 2. Simultaneous analysis of longitudinal means and covariance structures. *Psychology and Aging, 3,* 122–130.

Herzog, A. R., House, J. S., & Morgan, J. N. (1991). Relation of work and retirement to health and well-being in older age. *Psychology and Aging, 6,* 202–211.

Heszen-Niejodek, I. (1997). Coping style and its role in coping with stressful encounters. *European Psychologist, 2,* 342–351.

Hetherington, E. M. (1991). The role of individual differences and family relationships in children's coping with divorce and remarriage. In P. A. Cowan & M. Hetherington (Eds.), *Family transitions*. Hillsdale, NJ: Erlbaum.

Hetherington, E. M., & Clingempeel, W. G. (1992). Coping with marital transitions: A family systems perspective. *Monographs of the Society for Research in Child Development, 227* (whole No. 57, Nos. 2–3).

Hettich, P. I. (1998). *Learning skills for college and career*. Pacific Grove, CA: Brooks/Cole.

Hewstone, M. (1990). The ultimate attribution error? A review of the literature on intergroup causal attribution. *European Journal of Social Psychology, 20,* 311–335.

Iliedemann, B., Suhomlinova, O., & O'Rand, A. M. (1998). Economic independence, economic status, and empty nest in midlife marital disruption. *Journal of Marriage and the Family, 60,* 219–231.

Higgins, C. A., Duxbury, L. E., & Irving, R. H. (1992). Work-family conflict in the dual-career family. *Organizational Behavior and Human Decision Processes, 51,* 51–75.

Higgins, C. A., Duxbury, L. E., & Lee, C. (1994). Impact of lifecycle stages and gender on ability to balance work and family responsibilities. *Family Relations,* 144–150.

Higgins, E. T. (1989). Self-discrepancy theory: What patterns of self-beliefs cause people to suffer? In L. Berkowitz (Ed.), *Advances in experimental social psychology* (Vol. 22). New York: Academic Press.

Higgins, E. T., Bond, R. N., Klein, R., & Strauman, T. (1986). Self-discrepancies and emotional vulnerability: How magnitude, accessibility, and type of discrepancy influence affect. *Journal of Personality and Social Psychology, 51,* 5–15.

Hilgard, E. R. (1987). *Psychology in America: A historical survey*. San Diego: Harcourt Brace Jovanovich.

Hill, C. T., Rubin, Z., & Peplau, L. A. (1976). Breakups before marriage: The end of 103 affairs. *Journal of Social Issues, 32,* 147–168.

Hill, R. D., Storandt, M., & Malley, M. (1993). The impact of exercise training on psychological function in older adults. *Journal of Gerontology, 48,* 12–17.

Hilton, J. L., & Darley, J. M. (1985). Constructing other persons: A limit on the effect. *Journal of Experimental Social Psychology, 21,* 1–18.

Hilton, J. L., Fein, S., & Miller, D. T. (1993). Suspicion and dispositional inference. *Personality and Social Psychology Bulletin, 19,* 501–512.

Hines, A. M. (1997). Divorce-related transitions, adolescent development, and the role of the parent-child relationship: A review of the literature. *Journal of Marriage and the Family, 59,* 375–388.

Hines, M. (1990). Gonadal hormones and human cognitive development. In J. Balthazart (Ed.), *Hormones, brain and behavior in vertebrates: 1. Sexual differentiation, neuroanatomical aspects, neurotransmitters and neuropeptides.* Basel: Karger.

Hinrichsen, G. A., & Pollack, S. (1997). Expressed emotion and the course of late-life depression. *Journal of Abnormal Psychology, 106,* 336–340.

Hiroto, D. S., & Seligman, M. E. P. (1975). Generality of learned helplessness in man. *Journal of Personality and Social Psychology, 31,* 311–327.

Hirschfeld, R. M. A., & Davidson, L. (1988). Risk factors for suicide. In A. J. Frances & R. E. Hales (Eds.), *Review of psychiatry* (Vol. 7). Washington, DC: American Psychiatric Press.

Hirt, E. R., Deppe, R. K., & Gordon, L. J. (1991). Self-reported versus behavioral self-handicapping: Empirical evidence for a theoretical distincion. *Journal of Personality and Social Psychology, 61,* 981–991.

Ho, B. C., Nopoulos, P., Flaum, M., Arndt, S., & Andreasen, N. C. (1998). Two-year outcome in first-episode schizophrenia: Predictive value of symptoms for quality of life. *American Journal of Psychiatry, 155,* 1196–1201.

Hobfoll, S. E., & Vaux, A. (1993). Social support: Resources and context. In L. Goldberger & S. Breznitz (Eds.), *Handbook of stress: Theoretical and clinical aspects* (2nd ed.). New York: Free Press.

Hochschild, A. (1989). *The second shift: Working parents and the revolution at home.* New York: Viking Penguin.

Hochschild, A. R. (1997). *The time bind.* New York: Metropolitan Books.

Hochswender, W. (1990, June 17). For today's fathers, their holiday seems a bit set in its ways. *New York Times,* pp. 1, 22.

Hock, E., Schirtzinger, M. B., Lutz, W. J., & Widaman, K. (1995). Maternal depressive symptomatology over the transition to parenthood: Assessing the influence of marital satisfaction and marital sex role traditionalism. *Journal of Family Psychology, 9,* 79–88.

Hodges, B. H. (1974). Effects of valence on relative weighting in impression formation. *Journal of Personality and Social Psychology, 30,* 378–381.

Hoek, H. W. (1995). The distribution of eating disorders. In K. D. Brownell & C. G. Fairburn (Eds.), *Eating disorders and obesity: A comprehensive handbook.* New York: Guilford Press.

Hoek, H. W., Bartelds, A. I. M., Bosveld, J. J. F., van der Graaf, Y., Limpens, V. E. L., Maiwald, M., & Spaaij, C. J. K. (1995). Impact of urbanization on detection rates of eating disorders. *American Journal of Psychiatry, 152,* 1272–1278.

Hoffman, E. (1994). *The drive for self: Alfred Adler and the founding of individual psychology.* Reading, MA: Addison-Wesley.

Hoffman, L. (1987). The effects on children of maternal and paternal employment. In N. Gerstel & H. Gross (Eds.), *Families and work.* Philadelphia: Temple University Press.

Hofstede, G. (1980). *Culture's consequences: International differences in work-related values.* Newbury Park, CA: Sage Publications.

Hofstede, G. (1983). Dimensions of national cultures in fifty countries and three regions. In J. Deregowski, S. Dziurawiec, & R. Annis (Eds.), *Explications in cross-cultural psychology.* Lisse: Swets and Zeitlinger.

Hogan, J., & Ones, D. S. (1997). Conscientiousness and integrity at work. In R. Hogan, J. Johnson, & S. Briggs (Eds), *Handbook of personality psychology.* San Diego, CA: Academic Press.

Hokanson, J. E., & Burgess, M. (1962). The effects of three types of aggression on vascular processes. *Journal of Abnormal and Social Psychology, 65,* 446–449.

Holahan, C. J. (1986). Environmental psychology. *Annual Review of Psychology, 37,* 381–407.

Holahan, C. J., & Moos, R. H. (1985). Life stress and health: Personality, coping, and family support in stress resistance. *Journal of Personality and Social Psychology, 49,* 739–747.

Holahan, C. J., & Moos, R. H. (1990). Life stressors, resistance factors, and improved psychological functioning: An extension of the stress resistance paradigm. *Journal of Personality and Social Psychology, 58,* 909–917.

Holahan, C. J., & Moos, R. H. (1994). Life stressors and mental health: Advances in conceptualizing stress resistance. In W. R. Avison & I. H. Gotlib (Eds.), *Stress and mental health: Contemporary issues and prospects for the future.* New York: Plenum.

Holland, J. C., & Lewis, S. (1993). Emotions and cancer: What do we really know? In D. Goleman & J. Gurin (Eds.), *Mind/body medicine: How to use your mind for better health.* Yonkers, NY: Consumer Reports Books.

Holland, J. L. (1985). *Making vocational choices: A theory of vocational personalities and work environments.* Englewood Cliffs, NJ: Prentice-Hall.

Holland, J. L. (1996). Exploring careers with a typology: What we have learned and some new directions. *American Psychologist, 51,* 397–406.

Hollander, E., Simeon, D., & Gorman, J. M. (1994). Anxiety disorders. In R. E. Hales, S. C. Yudofsky & J. A. Talbott (Eds.), *The American Psychiatric Press textbook of psychiatry* (2nd ed.). Washington, DC: American Psychiatric Press.

Hollon, S. D., & Beck, A. T. (1994). Cognitive and cognitive-behavioral therapies. In A. E. Bergin & S. L. Garfield (Eds.), *Handbook of psychotherapy and behavior change* (4th ed.). New York: Wiley.

Holmes, D. S. (1984). Meditation and somatic arousal reduction: A review of the experimental evidence. *American Psychologist, 39,* 1–10.

Holmes, D. S. (1987). The influence of meditation versus rest on physiological arousal: A second examination. In M.A. West (Ed.), *The psychology of meditation.* Oxford: Clarendon Press.

Holmes, T. H., & Rahe, R. H. (1967). The Social Readjustment Rating Scale. *Journal of Psychosomatic Research, 11,* 213–218.

Honeycutt, J. M. (1986). A model of marital functioning based on an attraction paradigm and social-penetration dimensions. *Journal of Marriage and the Family, 48,* 651–667.

Hood, K. E., Draper, P., Crockett, L. J., & Petersen, A. C. (1987). The ontogeny and phylogeny of sexual differences in development: A biopsychosocial synthesis. In B. Carter (Ed.), *Current conceptions of sex roles and sex typing: Theory and research.* New York: Praeger.

Hooker, E. (1957). The adjustment of the male overt homosexual. *Journal of Projective Techniques, 21,* 18–31.

Horn, M. (1993, November 29). Memories lost and found. *U.S. News & World Report,* pp. 52–63.

Horowitz, F. D., & O'Brien, M. (1989). In the interest of the nation: A reflective essay on the state of our knowledge and the challenges before us. *American Psychologist, 44,* 441–445.

Hotaling, G. T., & Sugarman, D. B. (1986). An analysis of risk markers in husband to wife violence: The current state of knowledge. *Violence and Crimes, 1,* 101–124.

House, J. S., Landis, K. R., & Umberson, D. (1988). Social relationships and health. *Science, 241,* 540–545.

Houston, B. K., & Vavak, C. R. (1991). Hostility: Developmental factors, psychosocial correlates, and health behaviors. *Health Psychology, 10,* 9–17.

Houts, R. M., Robins, E., & Huston, T. L. (1996). Compatibility and the development of premarital relationships. *Journal of Marriage and the Family, 58,* 7–20.

Howard, A. (1995). *The changing nature of work.* San Francisco: Jossey-Bass.

Howard, G., Wagenknecht, L. E., Burke, G. L., Diez-Roux, A., Evans, G. W., McGovern, P., Nieto, J., & Tell, G. S. (1998). Cigarette smoking and progression of atherosclerosis: The atherosclerosis risk in communities (ARIC) study. *Journal of the American Medical Association, 279,* 119–124.

Howard, K. I., Moras, K., Brill, P. L., Martinovich, Z., & Lutz, W. (1996). Evaluation of psychotherapy: Efficacy, effectiveness, and patient progress. *American Psychologist, 51,* 1059–1064.

Howard, M., & McCabe, J. B. (1990). Helping teenagers postpone sexual involvement. *Family Planning Perspectives, 22,* 21–26.

Howes, C., Phillips, D. A., & White-brook, M. (1992). Thresholds of quality: Implications for the social development of children in center-based child care. *Child Development, 63,* 449–460.

Hsu, L. K. G. (1990). *Eating disorders.* New York: Guilford Press.

Hsu, L. K. G. (1995). Outcome of bulimia nervosa. In K. D. Brownell & C. G. Fairburn (Eds.), *Eating disorders and obesity: A comprehensive handbook.* New York: Guilford Press.

Hu, S., Pattatucci, A. M. L., Patterson, C., Li, L., Fulker, D. W., Cherny, S. S., Kuglyak, L., & Hamer, D. (1995). Linkage between sexual orientation and chromosome Xq28 in males but not in females. *Nature Genetics, 11,* 248–256.

Hubbard, J. A., & Coie, J. D. (1994). Emotional correlates of social competence in children's peer relationships. *Merrill-Palmer Quaterly, 40,* 1–20.

Hubbard, J. R., & Workman, E. A. (1998). *Handbook of stress medicine: An organ system approach.* New York: CRC Press.

Hubbard, L. R. (1989). *Scientology: The fundamentals of thought.* Los Angeles: Bridge.

Huesmann, L. R., & Eron, L. D. (1986). *Television and the aggressive child: A cross-national comparison.* Hillsdale, NJ: Erlbaum.

Huesmann, L. R., & Morikawa, S. (1985). Learned helplessness and depression: Cognitive factors in treatment and inoculation. In S. Reiss & R. R. Bootzin (Eds.), *Theoretical issues in behavior therapy.* Orlando, FL: Academic Press.

Hugick, L., & Leonard, J. (1991a, September). Job dissatisfaction grows. *Gallup Poll Monthly,* pp. 2–15.

Hugick, L., & Leonard, J. (1991b, October). Sex in America. *The Gallup Poll Monthly,* pp. 60–73.

Hull, J. G., & Young, R. D. (1983). Self-consciousness, self-esteem, and success-failure as determinants of alcohol consumption in male social drinkers. *Journal of Personality and Social Psychology, 44,* 1097–1109.

Hull, J. G., Young, R. D. & Jouriles, E. (1986). Applications of the self-awareness model of alcohol consumption: Predicting patterns of use and abuse. *Journal of Personality and Social Psychology, 51*, 790–796.

Hultsch, D. F., & Dixon, R. A. (1990). Learning and memory in aging. In J. E. Birren & K. W. Schaie (Eds.), *Handbook of the psychology of aging* (3rd ed.). San Diego: Academic Press.

Hunicutt, C. P., & Newman, I. A. (1993). Adolescent dieting practices and nutrition knowledge: Health values. *The Journal of Health Behavior, Education, and Promotion, 17*, 35–40.

Hunt, J. M., Smith, M. F., & Kernan, J. B. (1985). The effects of expectancy disconfirmation and argument strength on message processing level: An application to personal selling. In E. C. Hirschman & M. B. Holbrook (Eds.), *Advances in consumer research* (Vol. 12). Provo, UT: Association for Consumer Research.

Hunt, M. (1974). *Sexual behavior in the 1970s.* Chicago: Playboy Press.

Hurlbert, D. F., & Whittaker, K. E. (1991). The role of masturbation in marital and sexual satisfaction: A comparative study of female masturbators and nonmasturbators. *Journal of Sex Education and Therapy, 17*, 272–282.

Huston, A. C., & Wright, J. C. (1982). Effects of communications media on children. In C. B. Kopp & J. B. Krakow (Eds.), *The child: Development in a social context.* Reading, MA: Addison-Wesley.

Huston, A. C., Donnerstein, E., Fairchild, H., Feshbach, N. D., Katz, P. A., Murray, J. P., Rubinstein, E. A., Wilcox, B. L., & Zuckerman, D. (1992). *Big world, small screen: The role of television in American society.* Lincoln: University of Nebraska Press.

Huston, A. C., Wright, J. C., Rice, M. L., Kerkman, D., & St. Peters, M. (1990). Development of television viewing patterns in early childhood: A longitudinal investigation. *Developmental Psychology, 26*, 409–420.

Huyck, M. H., & Hoyer, W. J. (1982). *Adult development and aging.* Belmont, CA: Wadsworth.

Hyde, J. S. (1981). How large are cognitive gender differences? *American Psychologist, 36*, 892–901.

Hyde, J. S. (1984). How large are gender differences in aggression? A developmental meta-analysis. *Developmental Psychology, 20*, 722–736.

Hyde, J. S. (1994). *Understanding human sexuality* (5th ed.). New York: McGraw-Hill.

Hyde, J. S. (1996). *Half the human experience: The psychology of women* (5th ed.). Lexington, MA: Heath.

Hyde, J. S. (1996). *The psychology of women: Half the human experience.* Lexington, MA: D. C. Heath.

Hyde, J. S., Fennema, E., & Lamon, S. J. (1990). Gender differences in mathematics performance: A meta-analysis. *Psychological Bulletin, 107*, 139–155.

Hyde, J. S., & Frost, L. A. (1993). Meta-analysis in the psychology of women. In F. L. Denmark & M. A. Paludi (Eds.), *Psychology of women: A handbook of issue and theories.* Westport, CT: Greenwood Press.

Hyde, J. S., & Linn, M. C. (1988). Gender differences in verbal ability: A meta-analysis. *Psychological Bulletin, 104*, 53–69.

Hyman, B. T., Van Hoesen, G. W., Damasio, A. R., & Barnes, C. L. (1984). Alzheimer's disease: Cell-specific pathology isolates the hippocampal formation. *Science, 225*, 1168–1170.

Iaccino, J. F. (1996). A further examination of the bizarre imagery mnemonic: Its effectiveness with mixed context and delayed testing. *Perceptual & Motor Skills, 83*, 881–882.

Ickes, W. (1993). Traditional gender roles: Do they make and then break our relationships? *Journal of Social Issues, 3*, 71–85.

Ickovics, J. R., & Rodin, J. (1992). Women and AIDS in the United States: Epidemiology, natural history, and mediating mechanisms. *Health Psychology, 11*, 1–16.

Iezzi, A., & Adams, H. E. (1993). Somatoform and factitious disorders. In P. B. Sutker & H. E. Adams (Eds.), *Comprehensive handbook of psychopathology* (2nd ed.). New York: Plenum.

Ilgen, D. R. (1990). Health issues at work: Opportunities for industrial/organization psychology. *American Psychologist, 45*, 252–261.

Inglehart, R. (1990). *Culture shift in advanced industrial society.* Princeton, NJ: Princeton University Press.

Inkeles, A., & Usui, C. (1989). Retirement patterns in cross-national perspective. In D. I. Kertzer & K. W. Schaie (Eds.), *Age structuring in comparative perspective.* Hillsdale, NJ: Erlbaum.

Innocenti, G. M. (1994). Some new trends in the study of the corpus callosum. *Behavioral and Brain Research, 64*, 1–8.

Inoff-Germain, G., Arnold, G. S., Nottelmann, E. D., Susman, E. J., Cutler, G. B., Jr., & Chrousos, G. P. (1988). Relations between hormone levels and observational measures of aggressive behavior of young adolescents in family interactions. *Developmental Psychology, 24*, 129–139.

Ironson, G., Klimas, N. G., Antoni, M., Friedman, A., Simoneau, J., LaPerriere, A., Baggett, L., August, S., Arevalo, F., Schneiderman, N., & Fletcher, M. A. (1994). Distress, denial, and low adherence to behavioral interventions predict faster disease progression in gay men infected with human immunodeficiency virus. *International Journal of Behavioral Medicine, 1*, 90–98.

Ironson, G., Wynings, C., Sschneiderman, N., Baum, A., Rodriguez, M., Greenwood, D., Benight, C., Antoni, M., LaPerriere, A., Huang, H. S., Klimas, N., & Fletcher, M. A. (1997). Post-traumatic stress symptoms, intrusive thoughts, loss, and immune function after Hurricane Andrew. *Psychosomatic Medicine, 59*, 128–141.

Isabella, R. A., & Belsky, J. (1991). Interactional synchrony and the origins of infant-mother attachment: A replication study. *Child Development, 62*, 373–384.

Isensee, R. (1990). *Love between men: Enhancing intimacy and keeping your relationship alive.* New York: Prentice Hall.

Iwao, S. (1993). *The Japanese woman: Traditional image and changing reality.* New York: Free Press.

Jacobs, C., & Wolf, E. (1995). School sexuality education and adolescent risk-taking behavior. *Journal of School Health, 65*, 91–95.

Jacobson, E. (1938). *Progressive relaxation.* Chicago: University of Chicago Press.

Jacobson, N. S., & Christensen, A. (1996). Studying the effectiveness of psychotherapy: How well can clinical trials do the job? *American Psychologist, 51*, 1031–1039.

Jaffe, J. H. (1992). Opiates: Clinical aspects. In J. H. Lowinson, P. Ruiz, & R. B. Millman (Eds.), *Substance abuse: A comprehensive textbook* (2nd ed.). Baltimore: Williams & Wilkins.

Jaffe, J. H., Knapp, C. M., & Ciraulo, D. A. (1997). Opiates: Clinical aspects. In. J. H. Lowinson, P. Ruiz, R. B. Millman, & J. G. Langrod (Eds.), *Substance abuse: A comprehensive textbook* (3rd ed.). Baltimore: Williams & Wilkins.

Jahoda, M. (1958). *Current concepts of positive mental health.* New York: Basic Books.

Janis, I. L. (1958). *Psychological stress.* New York: Wiley.

Janis, I. L. (1993). Decision making under stress. In L. Goldberger & S. Breznitz (Eds.), *Handbook of stress: Theoretical and clinical aspects* (2nd ed.). New York: Free Press.

Jann, M. W., Jenike, M. A., & Lieberman, J. A. (1994). The new psychopharmaceuticals. *Patient Care, 28*, 47–61.

Janus, S. S., & Janus, C. L. (1993). *The Janus report on sexual behavior.* New York: Wiley.

Jaroff, L. (1993, November 29). Lies of the mind. *Time*, pp. 52–59.

Jarvik, M. E., & Schneider, N. G. (1992). Nicotine. In J. H. Lowinson, P. Ruiz, & R. B. Millman (Eds.), *Substance abuse: A comprehensive textbook* (2nd ed.). Baltimore: Williams & Wilkins.

Jaskiewicz, J. A., & McAnarney, E. R. (1994). Pregnancy during adolescence. *Pediatrics in Review, 15*, 32–38.

Jay, K., & Young, A. (1979). *The gay report.* New York: Summit Books.

Jefferson, J. W., & Greist, J. H. (1994). Mood disorders. In R. E. Hales, S. C. Yudofsky, & J. A. Talbott (Eds.), *The American Psychiatric Press textbook of psychiatry* (2nd ed.). Washington, DC: American Psychiatric Press.

Jemmott, J. B., III, & Magloire, K. (1988). Academic stress, social support, and secretory Immunoglobin A. *Journal of Personality and Social Psychology, 55*, 803–810.

Jenike, M. A. (1987). Drug abuse. In E. Rubenstein & D. D. Federman (Eds.), *Scientific American medicine.* New York: Scientific American Press.

Jennison, K. M. (1992). The impact of stressful life events and social support on drinking among older adults: A general population survey. *International Journal of Aging and Human Development, 35*, 99–123.

Jepson, C., & Chaiken, S. (1986). *The effect of anxiety on the systematic processing of persuasive communications.* Washington, DC: Paper presented at the annual meeting of the American Psychological Association.

Jessor, R., Costa, F., Jessor, L., & Donovan, J. E. (1983). Time of first intercourse: A prospective study. *Journal of Personality and Social Psychology, 44*, 608–626.

Johnson, A. M., Wadsworth, J., Wellings, K., Bradshaw, S., & Field, J. (1992). Sexual lifestyles and HIV risk. *Nature, 360*, 410–412.

Johnson, B. D., & Muffler, J. (1992). Sociocultural aspects of drug use and abuse in the 1990s. In J. H. Lowinson, P. Ruiz, & R. B. Millman (Eds.), *Substance abuse: A comprehensive textbook* (2nd ed.). Baltimore: Williams & Wilkins.

Johnson, B. T. (1991). Insights about attitudes: Meta-analytic perspectives. *Personality and Social Psychology Bulletin, 17*, 289–299.

Johnson, C. L. (1982). Sibling solidarity: Its origin and functioning in Italian-American families. *Journal of Marriage and the Family, 44*, 155–167.

Johnson, C. (1994). Gender, legitimate authority, and leader-subordinate conversations. *American Sociological Review, 59*, 122–135.

Johnson, D. R., White, L. K., Edwards, J. N., & Booth, A. (1986). Dimensions of marital quality: Toward methodological and conceptual refinement. *Journal of Family Issues, 7*, 31–49.

Johnson, D. W., & Johnson, F. (1994). *Joining together* (5th ed.). Englewood Cliffs, NJ: Prentice-Hall.

Johnson, I. M., Crowley, J., & Sigler, R. T. (1992). Agency response to domestic violence: Services provided to battered women. In E. C. Viano (Ed.), *Intimate violence: Interdisciplinary perspectives.* Washington, DC: Hemisphere.

Johnson, J. G., & Bornstein, R. F. (1991). Does daily stress independently predict psychopathology? *Journal of Social and Clinical Psychology, 10,* 58–74.

Johnson, J. G., & Sherman, M. F. (1997). Daily hassles mediate the relationship between major life events and psychiatric symptomatology: Longitudinal findings from an adolescent sample. *Journal of Social and Clinical Psychology, 16,* 389–404.

Johnson, R. D., & Downing, L. L. (1979). Deindividuation and valence of cues: Effects on prosocial and antisocial behavior. *Journal of Personality and Social Psychology, 37,* 1532–1538.

Joiner, T. E. (1994). Contagious depression: Existence, specificity to depressed symptoms, and the role of reassurance seeking. *Journal of Personality and Social Psychology, 67,* 287–296.

Joiner, T. E., Jr. (1997). Shyness and low social support as interactive diatheses, with loneliness as mediator: Testing an interpersonal-personality view of vulnerability to depressive symptoms. *Journal of Abnormal Psychology, 106,* 386–394.

Joiner, T. E., Jr., & Metalsky, G. I. (1995). A prospective test of an integrative interpersonal theory of depression: A naturalistic study of college students. *Journal of Personality and Social Psychology, 69,* 778–788.

Jonah, B. A. (1997). Sensation seeking and risky driving: A review and synthesis of the literature. *Accident Analysis & Prevention, 29,* 651–665.

Jones, E. E. (1990). *Interpersonal perception.* New York: Freeman.

Jones, E. E., & Davis, K. (1965). From acts to dispositions: The attribution process in person perception. In L. Berkowitz (Ed.), *Advances in experimental social psychology* (Vol. 2). New York: Academic Press.

Jones, E. E., Rhodewalt, F., Berglas, S., & Skelton, J. A. (1981). Effects of strategic self-presentation on subsequent self-esteem. *Journal of Personality and Social Psychology, 41,* 407–421.

Jones, E. E. (1990). *Interpersonal perception.* New York: W. H. Freeman.

Jones, L., & Petruzzi, D. C. (1995). Test anxiety: A review of theory and current treatment. *Journal of College Student Psychotherapy, 10,* 3–15.

Jones, M. (1993, July 5). Getting away from the "R" word. *Publishers Weekly,* pp. 42–45.

Jones, R. A., & Brehm, J. W. (1970). Persuasiveness of one- and two-sided communications as a function of awareness there are two sides. *Journal of Experimental Social Psychology, 6,* 47–56.

Jones, W. H., Sansome, C., & Helm, B. (1983). Loneliness and interpersonal judgments. *Personality and Social Psychology Bulletin, 9,* 437–442.

Jorgensen, R. S., Johnson, B. T., Kolodziej, M. E., & Schreer, G. E. (1996). Elevated blood pressure and personality: A meta-analytic review. *Psychological Bulletin, 120,* 293–320.

Joung, I. M. A., Stronks, K., Van De Mheen, H., Van Poppel, F. W. A., Van Der Meer, J. B. W., & Mackenbach, J. P. (1997). The contribution of intermediary factors to marital status differences in self-reported health. *Journal of Marriage and the Family, 59,* 476–490.

Jourard, S. M. (1971). *The transparent self.* New York: Van Nostrand Reinhold.

Jourard, S. M., & Landsman, T. (1980). *Healthy personality: An approach from the viewpoint of humanistic psychology.* New York: Macmillan.

Judd, L. L., McAdams, L. A., Budnick, B., & Braff, D. L. (1992). Sensory gating effects in schizophrenia: New results. *American Journal of Psychiatry, 149,* 488–493.

Julien, R. M. (1995). *A primer of drug action* (7th ed.). New York: W. H. Freeman.

Jung, C. G. (1917). On the psychology of the unconscious. In *Collected Works* (Vol. 7). Princeton, NJ: Princeton University Press.

Jung, C. G. (1921). Psychological types. In *Collected Works* (Vol. 6). Princeton, NJ: Princeton University Press.

Jung, C. G. (1933). *Modern man in search of a soul.* New York: Harcourt, Brace & World.

Just, N., & Alloy, L. B. (1997). The response styles theory of depression: Tests and an extension of the theory. *Journal of Abnormal Psychology, 106,* 221–229.

Kagan, J., Snidman, N., & Arcus, D. M. (1992). Initial reactions to unfamiliarity. *Current Directions in Psychological Science, 1,* 171–174.

Kahle, L. R., & Homer, P. M. (1985). Physical attractiveness of the celebrity endorser: A social adaptation perspective. *Journal of Consumer Research, 11,* 954–961.

Kahn, S., Zimmerman, G., Csikszentmihalyi, M., & Getzels, J. W. (1985). Relations between identity in young adulthood and intimacy at midlife. *Journal of Personality and Social Psychology, 49,* 1316–1322.

Kalant, H., & Kalant, O. J. (1979). Death in amphetamine users: Causes and rates. In D. E. Smith (Ed.), *Amphetamine use, misuse and abuse.* Boston: G. K. Hall.

Kalichman, S. C. (1995). *Understanding AIDS: A guide for mental health professionals.* Washington, DC: American Psychological Association.

Kalick, S. M., & Hamilton, T. E., III. (1986). The matching hypothesis reexamined. *Journal of Personality and Social Psychology, 51,* 673–682.

Kalmuss, D., Davidson, A., & Cushman, L. (1992). Parenting expectations, experiences, and adjustment to parenthood: A test of the violated expectations framework. *Journal of Marriage and the Family, 52,* 516–526.

Kaminer, W. (1995). Chances are you're codependent too. In M. Babcock & C. McKay (Eds.), *Challenging codependency: Feminist critiques.* Toronto: University of Toronto Press.

Kane, J. (1991). *Be sick well: A healthy approach to chronic illness.* Oakland, CA: New Harbinger.

Kanner, A. D., Coyne, J. C., Schaefer, C., & Lazarus, R. S. (1981). Comparison of two modes of stress measurement: Daily hassles and uplifts versus major life events. *Journal of Behavioral Medicine, 4,* 1–39.

Kaplan, A. G. (1985). Female or male therapists for women patients: New formulations. *Psychiatry, 48,* 111–121.

Kaplan, H. I. (1989). History of psychosomatic medicine. In H. I. Kaplan & B. J. Sadock (Eds.), *Comprehensive textbook of psychiatry/V* (Vol. 2) (5th ed.). Baltimore: Williams & Wilkins.

Kaplan, H. I., & Sadock, B. J. (Eds.). (1993). *Comprehensive group psychotherapy.* Baltimore: Williams & Wilkins.

Kaplan, N. M. (1986). Dietary aspects of the treatment of hypertension. In L. Breslow, J. E. Fielding, & L. B. Lave (Eds.), *Annual review of public health* (Vol. 7). Palo Alto, CA: Annual Reviews.

Kaplan, R. M., & Simon, H. J. (1990). Compliance in medical care: Reconsideration of self-predictions. *Annals of Behavioral Medicine, 12,* 66–71.

Kaplan, R. M., Manuck, S. B., & Shumaker, S. (1992). Does lowering cholesterol cause increases in depression, suicide, and accidents? In H. S. Freidman (Ed.), *Hostility coping and health.* Washington, DC: American Psychological Association.

Kapur, S., & Remington, G. (1996). Serotonin-dopamine interaction and its relevance to schizophrenia. *American Journal of Psychiatry, 153,* 466–476.

Karasek, R. A., Jr. (1979). Job demands, job decision latitude, and mental strain: Implications for job redesign. *Administrative Science Quarterly, 24,* 285–308.

Karasek, R. A., Jr., Baker, D., Marxer, F., Ahlbom, A., & Theorell, T. (1981). Job decision latitude, job demands, and cardiovascular disease: A prospective study of Swedish men. *American Journal of Public Health, 71,* 694–705.

Karasek, R. A., Jr., & Theorell, T. (1990). *Healthy work: Stress, productivity, and the reconstruction of working life.* New York: Basic Books.

Karney, B. R., Bradbury, T. N., Fincham, F. D., & Sullivan, K. T (1994). The role of negative affectivity in the association between attributions and marital satisfaction. *Journal of Personality and Social Psychology, 66,* 413–424.

Karno, M., & Golding, J. M. (1991). Obsessive compulsive disorder. In L. N. Robins & D. A. Regier (Eds.), *Psychiatric disorders in America: The epidemiologic catchment area study.* New York: Free Press.

Kass, F., Spitzer, R. L., Williams, J. B. W., & Widiger, T. (1989). Self-defeating personality disorder and DSM-III-R: Development of the diagnostic criteria. *American Journal of Psychiatry, 146,* 1022–1026.

Kassler, J. (1994). *Bitter medicine.* New York: Birch Lane Press.

Kastenbaum, R. (1985). Dying and death: A life-span approach. In J. E. Birren & K. W. Schaie (Eds.), *Handbook of the psychology of aging.* New York: Van Nostrand Reinhold.

Kastenbaum, R. (1986). *Death, dying, and human experience.* Columbus, OH: Charles E. Merrill.

Katz, B. L. (1991). The psychological impact of stranger versus nonstranger rape on victims' recovery. In A. Parrot & L. Bechhofer (Eds.), *Acquaintance rape: The hidden crime.* New York: Wiley.

Katz, I., Wackenhut, J., & Hass, G. (1986). Racial ambivalence, value duality, and behavior. In J. F. Dovidio & S. L. Gaertner (Eds.), *Prejudice, discrimination, and racism: Theory and research.* Orlando, FL: Academic Press.

Katz, L., & Epstein, S. (1991). Constructive thinking and coping with laboratory-induced stress. *Journal of Personality and Social Psychology, 81,* 789–800.

Katz, P. A., Boggiano, A., & Silvern, L. (1993). Theories of female personality. In F. L. Denmark & M. A. Paludi (Eds.), *Psychology of women: A handbook of issues and theories.* Westport, CT: Greenwood Press.

Kausler, D. H. (1985). Episodic memory: Memorizing performance. In N. Charness (Ed.), *Aging and human performance.* Chichester, England: Wiley.

Kausler, D. H. (1994). *Learning and memory in normal aging.* San Diego: Academic Press.

Kavanagh, D. J. (1992). Recent developments in expressed emotion in schizophrenia. *British Journal of Psychiatry, 160,* 601–620.

Kavesh, L., & Lavin, C. (1988). *Tales from the front.* New York: Doubleday.

Kaye, W. H., Weltzin, T. E., Hsu, L. K. G., McConaha, C. W., & Bolton, B. (1993). Amount of calories retained after binge eating and vomiting. *American Journal of Psychiatry, 150,* 969–971.

Kazdin, A. E. (1982). History of behavior modification. In A. S. Bellack, M. Hersen, & A. E. Kazdin (Eds.), *International handbook of behavior modification and behavior therapy.* New York: Plenum.

Kazdin, A. E. (1994). Methodology, design, and evaluation in psychotherapy research. In A. E.

Bergin & S. L. Garfield (Eds.), *Handbook of psychotherapy and behavior change* (4th ed.). New York: Wiley.

Keating, D. P. (1990). Adolescent thinking. In S. S. Feldman & G. R. Elliott (Eds.), *At the threshold: The developing adolescent*. Cambridge, MA: Harvard University Press.

Keefe, S. E. (1984). Real and ideal extended familism among Mexican Americans and Anglo Americans: On the meaning of "close" family ties. *Human Organization, 43,* 65–70.

Keesey, R. E. (1986). A set-point theory of obesity. In K. D. Brownell & J. P. Foreyt (Eds.), *Handbook of eating disorders: Physiology, psychology, and treatment of obesity, anorexia, and bulimia.* New York: Basic Books.

Keesey, R. E. (1988). The body-weight set point. *Postgraduate Medicine, 83,* 114–127.

Keesey, R. E. (1993). Physiological regulation of body energy: Implications for obesity. In A. J. Stunkard & T. A. Wadden (Eds.), *Obesity: Theory and therapy.* New York: Raven Press.

Keesey, R. E. (1995). A set-point model of body weight regulation. In K. D. Brownell & C. G. Fairburn (Eds.), *Eating disorders and obesity: A comprehensive handbook.* New York: Guilford Press.

Keesey, R. E., & Powley, T. L. (1986). The regulation of body weight. *Annual Review of Psychology, 37,* 109–133.

Kegan, R. (1994). *In over our heads: The mental demands of modern life.* Cambridge, MA: Harvard University Press.

Keinan, G. (1987). Decision making under stress: Scanning of alternatives under controllable and uncontrollable threats. *Journal of Personality and Social Psychology, 52,* 639–644.

Keita, G. P., & Jones, J. M. (1990). Reducing adverse reaction to stress in the workplace. *American Psychologist, 45,* 1137–1141.

Keith, P. M. (1986). The social context and resources of the unmarried in old age. *International Journal of Aging and Human Development, 23,* 81–96.

Keith, S. J., Regier, D. A., & Rae, D. S. (1991). Schizophrenic disorders. In L. N. Robins & D. A. Regier (Eds.), *Psychiatric disorders in America: The epidemiologic catchment area study.* New York: Free Press.

Kelley, H. H. (1950). The warm-cold dimension in first impressions of persons. *Journal of Personality, 18,* 431–439.

Kelley, H. H. (1967). Attribution theory in social psychology. In D. Levine (Ed.), *Nebraska Symposium on Motivation* (Vol. 15). Lincoln: University of Nebraska Press.

Kelley, H. H., & Thibaut, J. W. (1978). *Interpersonal relations: A theory of interdependence.* New York: Wiley-Interscience.

Kelley, K., Byrne, D., Przybyla, D. P. J., Eberly, C., Eberly, B., Greendlinger, V., Wan, C. K., & Gorsky, J. (1985). Chronic self-destructiveness: Conceptualization, measurement and initial validation of the construct. *Motivation and Emotion, 9,* 135–151.

Kelly, K. R., & Cobb, S. J. (1991). A profile of the career development characteristics of young gifted adolescents: Examining gender and multicultural differences. *Roeper Review, 13,* 202–206.

Kelsey, R. M. (1993). Habituation of cardiovascular reactivity to psychological stress: Evidence and implications. In J. Blascovich & E. S. Katkin (Eds.), *Cardiovascular reactivity to psychological stress and disease.* Washington, DC: American Psychological Association.

Kendler, K. S., & Gardner, C. O., Jr. (1998). Boundaries of major depression: An evaluation of DSM-IV criteria. *American Journal of Psychiatry, 155,* 172–177.

Kendler, K. S., MaClean, C., Neale, M., Kessler, R., Heath, A., & Eaves, L. (1991). The genetic epidemiology of bulimia nervosa. *American Journal of Psychiatry, 148,* 1627–1637.

Kendler, K. S., Neale, M. C., Kessler, R. C., Heath, A. C., & Eaves, L. J. (1992). Generalized anxiety disorder in women: A population-based twin study. *Archives of General Psychiatry, 49,* 267–272.

Kennedy, J. L., & Laramore, D. (1993). *Joyce Lain Kennedy's career book* (2nd ed.). Lincolnwood, IL: VGM Career Horizons.

Kenny, D. A., & DePaulo, B. M. (1993). Do people know how others view them? An empirical and theoretical account. *Psychological Bulletin, 114,* 145–161.

Kenny, D. A. (1994). Using the social relations model to understand relationships. In R. Erber & R. Gilmour (Eds.), *Theoretical frameworks for personal relationships.* Hillsdale, NJ: Erlbaum.

Kenrick, D. T. (1987). Gender, genes, and the social environment. In P. C. Shaver & C. Hendrick (Eds.), *Review of Personality and Social Psychology* (Vol. 8). Newbury Park, CA: Sage Publications.

Kenrick, D. T., Groth, G. E., Trost, M. R., & Sadalla, E. K. (1993). Integrating evolutionary and social exchange perspectives on relationships: Effects of gender, self-appraisal, and involvement level on mate selection criteria. *Journal of Personality and Social Psychology, 64,* 951–969.

Kenrick, D. T., & Keefe, R. C. (1992). Age preferences in mates reflect sex differences in human reproductive strategies. *Behavioral and Brain Sciences, 15,* 75–133.

Kenrick, D. T., & Trost, M. R. (1993). The evolutionary perspective. In A. E. Beall & R. J. Sternberg (Eds.), *The psychology of gender.* New York: Guilford Press.

Kessler, R. C. (1997). The effects of stressful life events on depression. *Annual Review of Psychology, 48,* 191–214.

Kessler, R. C., Foster, C., Joseph, J., Ostrow, D., Wortman, C., Phair, J., & Chmiel, J. (1991). Stressful life events and symptom onset in HIV infection. *American Journal of Psychiatry, 148,* 733–738.

Kessler, R. C., Olfson, M., & Berglund, P. A. (1998). Patterns and predictors of treatment contact after first onset of psychiatric disorders. *American Journal of Psychiatry, 155,* 62–69.

Kessler, R. C., Sonnega, A., Bromett, E., Hughes, M., & Nelson, C. B. (1995). Post-traumatic stress disorder in the National Comorbidity Survey. *Archives of General Psychiatry, 52,* 1048–1060.

Keyes, R. (1980). We, the lonely people. In J. Hartog, J. R. Audy, & Y. A. Cohen (Eds.), *The anatomy of loneliness.* New York: International Universities Press.

Keyes, R. (1991). *Timelock: How life got so hectic and what you can do about it.* New York: HarperCollins.

Kiecolt-Glaser, J. K., Garner, W., Speicher, C., Penn, G. M., Holliday, J., & Glaser, R. (1984). Psychosocial modifiers of immunocompetence in medical students. *Psychosomatic Medicine, 46,* 7–14.

Kiecolt-Glaser, J. K., & Glaser, R. (1995). Measurement of immune response. In S. Cohen, R. C. Kessler, & L. U. Gordon (Eds.), *Measuring stress: A guide for health and social scientists.* New York: Oxford University Press.

Kiecolt-Glaser, J. K., Glaser, R., Williger, D., Stout, J., Messick, G., Sheppard, S., Ricker, D., Romisher, S. C., Briner, W., Bonnell, G., & Donnerberg, R. (1985). Psychosocial enhancement of immunocompetence in a geriatric population. *Health Psychology, 4,* 25–42.

Kiecolt-Glaser, J. K., Kennedy, S., Malkoff, S., Fisher, L., Speicher, C. E., & Glaser, R. (1988). Marital discord and immunity in males. *Psychosomatic Medicine, 50,* 213–229.

Kihlstrom, J. F. (1990). The psychological unconscious. In L. A. Pervin (Ed.), *Handbook of personality: Theory and research.* New York: Guilford Press.

Kihlstrom, J. F., Glisky, M. L., & Angiulo, M. J. (1994). Dissociative tendencies and dissociative disorders. *Journal of Abnormal Psychology, 103,* 117–124.

Kihlstrom, J. F., Tataryn, D. J., & Hoyt, I. P. (1993). Dissociative disorders. In P. B. Sutker & H. E. Adams (Eds.), *Comprehensive handbook of psychopathology* (2nd ed.). New York: Plenum.

Kilby, R. W. (1993). *The study of human values.* Lanham, MD: University Press of America.

Kilmartin, C. T. (1994). *The masculine self.* New York: Macmillan.

Kilpatrick, A. (1992). *Long-range effects of child and adolescent sexual experiences: Myths, mores, and menaces.* Hillsdale, NJ: Erlbaum.

Kimura, D. (1987). Are men's and women's brains really different? *Canadian Psychology, 28,* 133–147.

Kimura, D., & Hampson, E. (1993). Neural and hormonal mechanisms mediating sex differences in cognition. In P. A. Vernon (Ed.), *Biological approaches to the study of human intelligence.* Norwood, NJ: Ablex.

Kinard, E. M. (1982). Experiencing child abuse: Effects on emotional adjustment. *American Journal of Orthopsychiatry, 52,* 82–91.

Kinder, D. R., & Sears, D. O. (1981). Prejudice and politics: Symbolic racism versus racial threats to the good life. *Journal of Personality and Social Psychology, 40,* 414–431.

King, B. M. (1999). *Human sexuality today* (3rd ed.). Upper Saddle River, NJ: Prentice Hall.

King, G. R., & Ellinwood, E. H. (1992). Amphetamines and other stimulants. In J. H. Lowinson, P. Ruiz, & R. B. Millman (Eds.), *Substance abuse: A comprehensive textbook* (2nd ed.). Baltimore: Williams & Wilkins.

King, G. R., & Ellinwood, E. H. Jr. (1997). Amphetamines and other stimulants. In J. H. Lowinson, P. Ruiz, R. B. Millman, & J. G. Langrod (Eds.), *Substance abuse: A comprehensive textbook* (3rd ed.). Baltimore: Williams & Wilkins.

King, L. A., & Emmons, R. A. (1990). Conflict over emotional expression: Psychological and physical correlates. *Journal of Personality and Social Psychology, 58,* 864–877.

King, L. A., & Emmons, R. A. (1991). Psychological, physical, and interpersonal correlates of emotional expressiveness, conflict and control. *European Journal of Personality, 5,* 131–150.

King, L. A., King, D. W., Fairbank, J. A., Keane, T. M., & Adams, G. A. (1998). Resilience-recovery factors in post-traumatic stress disorder among female and male Vietnam veterans: Hardiness, postwar social support, and additional stressful life events. *Journal of Personality and Social Psychology, 74,* 420–434.

Kinney, J., & Leaton, G. (1987). *Loosening the grip: A handbook of alcohol information* (3rd ed.). St. Louis: Times Mirror/Mosby.

Kinsey, A. C., Pomeroy, W. B., & Martin, C. E. (1948). *Sexual behavior in the human male.* Philadelphia: Saunders.

Kinsey, A. C., Pomeroy, W. B., Martin, C. E., & Gebhard, P. H. (1953). *Sexual behavior in the human female.* Philadelphia: Saunders.

Kinsman, R. A., Dirks, J. F., & Jones, N. F. (1982). Psychomaintenance of chronic physical illness: Clinical assessment of personal styles affecting medical management. In T. Millon, C.

Green, & R. Meagher (Eds.), *Handbook of clinical health psychology.* New York: Plenum.

Kirk, S. A., & Kutchins, H. (1992). *The selling of DSM: The rhetoric of science in psychiatry.* New York: Aldine de Gruyter.

Kirkcaldy, B. D., Cooper, C. L., Shephard, R. J., & Brown, J. S. (1994). Exercise, job satisfaction, and well-being among superintendent police officers. *European Review of Applied Psychology, 44*, 117–123.

Kirkpatrick, L. A., & Hazan, C. (1994). Attachment styles and close relationships: A four-year prospective study. *Personal Relationships, 1*, 123–142.

Kirmayer, L. J., Robbins, J. M., & Paris, J. (1994). Somatoform disorders: Personality and the social matrix of somatic distress. *Journal of Abnormal Psychology, 103*, 125–136.

Kite, M. E., & Deaux, K. (1986). Attitudes toward homosexuality: Assessment and behavioral consequences. *Basic and Applied Social Psychology, 7*, 137–162.

Kite, M. E., & Whitley, B. E., Jr. (1996). Sex differences in attitudes toward homosexual persons, behaviors, and civil rights: A meta-analysis. *Personality and Social Psychology Bulletin, 22*, 336–353.

Kitson, G. C. (1992). *Portrait of divorce: Adjustment to marital breakdown.* New York: Guilford Press.

Kitson, G. C., & Morgan, L. A. (1990). The multiple consequences of divorce: A decade review. *Journal of Marriage and the Family, 52*, 913–924.

Klassen, M. (1987). How to get the most out of your time. In A. D. Timpe (Ed.), *The management of time.* New York: Facts On File.

Klebanov, P. K., Brooks-Gunn, J., & Duncan, G. J. (1994). Does neighborhood and family poverty affect mothers' parenting, mental health, and social support? *Journal of Marriage and the Family, 56*, 441–455.

Kleber, H. D., & Gawin, F. H. (1986). Cocaine. In A. J. Frances & R. E. Hales (Eds.), *Psychiatric Update: Annual Review* (Vol. 5). Washington, DC: American Psychiatric Press.

Klein, D. N., & Rubovits, D. R. (1987). The reliability of subjects' reports of life events inventories: A longitudinal study. *Journal of Behavioral Medicine, 10*, 501–512.

Klein, F., Sepekoff, B., & Wolf, T. J. (1985). Sexual orientation: A multivariable dynamic process. *Journal of Homosexuality, 11*, 35–49.

Klein, M. (1948). *Contributions to psychoanalysis.* London: Hogarth.

Kleininna, P. R., & Kleininna, A. M. (1988). Current trends toward convergence of the behavioristic, functional, and cognitive perspectives in experimental psychology. *The Psychological Record, 38*, 369–392.

Kleinke, C. L. (1986). Gaze and eye contact: A research review. *Psychological Bulletin, 100*, 78–100.

Kleinke, C. L. (1991). *Coping with life challenges.* Pacific Grove, CA: Brooks/Cole.

Kleinke, C. L., Meeker, F. B., & Staneski, R. A. (1986). Preference for opening lines: Comparing ratings by men and women. *Sex Roles, 15*, 585–600.

Kleinke, C. L., & Staneski, R. A. (1980). First impressions of female bust size. *Journal of Social Psychology, 110*, 123–134.

Kleinmuntz, B. (1980). *Essentials of abnormal psychology.* San Francisco: Harper & Row.

Kleinmuntz, B., & Szucko, J. J. (1984). Lie detection in ancient and modern times: A call for contemporary scientific study. *American Psychologist, 39*, 766–776.

Klerman, G. L., Weissman, M. M., Markowitz, J. C., Glick, I., Wilner, P. J., Mason. B., & Shear,

M. K. (1994). Medication and psychotherapy. In A. E. Bergin & S. L. Garfield (Eds.), *Handbook of psychotherapy and behavior change* (4th ed.). New York: Wiley.

Kline, D. W., Kline, T. J. B., Fozard, J. L., Kosnik, W., Schieber, F., & Sekuler, R. (1992). Vision, aging, and driving: The problems of older drivers. *Journal of Gerontology, 42*, P27–P34.

Kline, P. (1995). A critical review of the measurement of personality and intelligence. In D. H. Saklofske & M. Zeidner (Eds.), *International handbook of personality and intelligence.* New York: Plenum Press.

Kluft, R. P. (1996). Dissociative identity disorder. In L. K. Michelson & W. J. Ray (Eds.), *Handbook of dissociation: Theoretical, empirical, and clinical perspectives.* New York: Plenum Press.

Kluwer, E. S., Heesink, J. A. M., & Van de Vliert, E. (1997). The marital dynamics of conflict over the division of labor. *Journal of Marriage and the Family, 59*, 635–653.

Knable, M. B., Kleinman, J. E., & Weinberger, D. R. (1995). Neurobiology of schizophrenia. In A. F. Schatzberg & C. B. Nemeroff (Eds.), *The American Psychiatric Press textbook of psychopharmacology.* Washington, DC: American Psychiatric Press.

Knight, G. P., Fabes, R. A., & Higgins, D. A. (1996). Concerns about drawing causal inference from meta-analysis: An example in the study of gender differences in aggression. *Psychological Bulletin, 119*, 410–421.

Knoth, R., Boyd, K., & Singer, B. (1988). Empirical tests of sexual selection theory: Predictions of sex differences in onset, intensity, and time course of sexual arousal. *Journal of Sex Research, 24*, 73–89.

Knox, D., & Wilson, K. (1981). Dating behaviors of university students. *Family Relations, 30*, 255–258.

Knussman, R., Christiansen, K., & Couwenbergs, C. (1986). Relations between sex hormone levels and sexual behavior in men. *Archives of Sexual Behavior, 15*, 429–445.

Kobak, R. R., & Sceery, A. (1988). Attachment in late adolescence: Working models, affect regulation, and representations of self and others. *Child Development, 59*, 135–146.

Kobasa, S. C. (1979). Stressful life events, personality, and health: An inquiry into hardiness. *Journal of Personality and Social Psychology, 37*, 1–11.

Kobasa, S. C. (1984, September). How much stress can you survive? *American Health*, pp. 64–77.

Kogan, N. (1990). Personality and aging. In J. E. Birren & K. W. Schaie (Eds.), *Handbook of the psychology of aging.* San Diego: Academic Press.

Kohn, P. M., Lafreniere, K., & Gurevich, M. (1991). Hassles, health, and personality. *Journal of Personality and Social Psychology, 61*, 478–482.

Kohut, H. (1971). *Analysis of the self.* New York: International Universities Press.

Kokin, M., & Walker, I. (1995). Coependency is a misleading concept. In M. Babcock & C. McKay (Eds.), *Challenging codependency: Feminist critiques.* Toronto: University of Toronto Press.

Kollock, P., Blumstein, P., & Schwartz, P. (1985). Sex and power in interaction: Conversational privileges and duties. *American Sociological Review, 50*, 34–46.

Koob, G. F., & Bloom, F. E. (1988). Cellular and molecular mechanisms of drug dependence. *Science, 242*, 715–723.

Koopman, C., Classen, C., & Spiegel, D. (1994). Predictors of posttraumatic stress symptoms among survivors of the Oakland/Berkeley,

Calif., firestorm. *American Journal of Psychiatry, 151*, 888–894.

Koranyi, E. K. (1989). Physiology of stress reviewed. In S. Cheren (Ed.), *Psychosomatic medicine: Theory, physiology, and practice* (Vol. 1). Madison, CT: International Universities Press.

Koren, P., Carlton, K., & Shaw, D. (1980). Marital conflict: Relations among behaviors, outcomes, and distress. *Journal of Consulting and Clinical Psychology, 48*, 460–468.

Kortenhaus, C. M., & Demarest, J. (1993). Gender role stereotyping in children's literature: An update. *Sex Roles, 3*, 219–232.

Koss, M. P. (1985). The hidden rape victim: Personality, attitudinal, and situational characteristics. *Psychology of Women Quarterly, 9*, 193–212.

Koss, M. P. (1993). Rape: Scope, impact, interventions, and public policy. *American Psychologist, 48*, 1062–1069.

Koss, M. P., & Gaines, J. A. (1993). The prediction of sexual aggression by alcohol use, athletic participation and fraternity affiliation. *Journal of Interpersonal Violence, 8*, 94–108.

Koss, M. P., Goodman, L. A., Browne, A., Fitzgerald, L. F., Keita, G. P., & Russo, N. F. (1994). *No safe haven: Male violence against women at home, at work, and in the community.* Washington, DC: American Psychological Association.

Koss, M. P., Leonard, K. E., Beezley, D. A., & Oros, C. (1985). Nonstranger sexual aggression: A discriminant analysis of the psychological characteristics of undetected offenders. *Sex Roles, 12*, 981–992.

Kotkin, M. (1985). To marry or live together? Lifestyles: A *Journal of Changing Patterns, 7*, 156–170.

Kowalski, R. M. (1993). Inferring sexual interest from behavioral cues: Effects of gender and sexually relevant attitudes. *Sex Roles, 29*, 13–36.

Kramer, H. (1994). *Liberating the adult within.* New York: Simon & Schuster.

Kraut, R., Patterson, M., Lundmark, V., Kiesler, S., Mukopadhyay, T., & Scherlis, W. (1998). Internet paradox: A social technology that reduces social involvement and psychological well-being? *American Psychologist, 53*, 1017–1031.

Krestan, J., & Bepko, C. (1995). Codependency: The social reconstruction of female experience. In M. Babcock & C. McKay (Eds.), *Challenging codependency: Feminist critiques.* Toronto: University of Toronto Press.

Krilov, L. R. (1988, March). Sexually transmitted diseases in adolescents. *Medical Aspects of Human Sexuality*, pp. 67–77.

Kring, A. M., Kerr, S. L., Smith, D. A., & Neale, J. M. (1993). Flat affect in schizophrenia does not reflect diminished subjective experience of emotion. *Journal of Abnormal Psychology, 102(4)*, 507–517.

Krishnan, V. (1998). Premarital cohabitation and marital disruption. *Journal of Divorce & Remarriage, 28*, 157–170.

Kristiansen, C. M., & Giulietti, R. (1990). Perceptions of wife abuse: Effects of gender, attitudes toward women, and just-world beliefs among college students. *Psychology of Women Quarterly, 14*, 177–189.

Krueger, W. C. F. (1929). The effect of overlearning on retention. *Journal of Experimental Psychology, 12*, 71–78.

Kubey, R., & Csikszentmihalyi, M. (1990). *Leisure and the benefits of television.* Hillsdale, NJ: Erlbaum.

Kübler-Ross, E. (1969). *On death and dying.* New York: Macmillan.

Kübler-Ross, E. (1970). The dying patient's point of view. In O. G. Brim, Jr., H. E. Freeman, S. Levine, & N. A. Scotch (Eds.), *The dying patient.* New York: Russell Sage Foundation.

Kuehnle, J., Mendelson, J. H., Davis, K. R., & New, P. F. J. (1977). Computerized tomographic examination of heavy marijuana smokers. *Journal of the American Medical Association, 237,* 1231–1232.

Kulick, A. R., Pope, H. G., & Keck, P. E. (1990). Lycanthropy and self-identification. *Journal of Nervous and Mental Disease, 178,* 134–137.

Kunkel, S. R., & Applebaum, R. A. (1992). Estimating the prevalence of long-term disability for an aging society. *Journal of Gerontology, 47,* S253–260.

Kurdek, L. A. (1988). Perceived social support in gays and lesbians in cohabitating relationships. *Journal of Personality and Social Psychology, 54,* 504–509.

Kurdek, L. A. (1991). Sexuality in homosexual and heterosexual couples. In K. McKinney & S. Sprecher (Eds.), *Sexuality in close relationships.* Hillside, NJ: Erlbaum.

Kurdek, L. A. (1994a). Areas of conflict for gay, lesbian, and heterosexual couples: What couples argue about influences relationship satisfaction. *Journal of Marriage and the Family, 56,* 923–934.

Kurdek, L. A. (1994b). Conflict resolution styles in gay, lesbian, heterosexual nonparent, and heterosexual parent couples. *Journal of Marriage and the Family, 56,* 705–722.

Kurdek, L. A. (1995). Predicting change in marital satisfaction from husbands' and wives' conflict resolution styles. *Journal of Marriage and the Family, 57,* 153–164.

Kurdek, L. A. (1998). Relationship outcomes and their predictors: Longitudinal evidence from heterosexual married, gay cohabiting, and lesbian cohabiting couples. *Journal of Marriage and the Family, 30,* 553–568.

Kurdek, L. A., & Schmitt, J. P. (1986a). Early development of relationship quality in heterosexual married, heterosexual cohabiting, gay, and lesbian couples. *Developmental Psychology, 22,* 305–309.

Kurdek, L. A., & Schmitt, J. P. (1986b). Interaction of sex role self-concept with relationship quality and relationship beliefs in married, heterosexual cohabiting, gay, and lesbian couples. *Journal of Personality and Social Psychology, 51,* 365–370.

Kurdek, L. A., & Schmitt, J. P. (1988). Relationship quality of gay men in closed or open relationships. In J. P. De Cecco (Ed.), *Gay relationships.* New York: Harrington Park Press.

Kwan, V. S. Y., Bond, M. H., & Singelis, T. M. (1997). Pancultural explanations for life satisfaction: Adding relationship harmony to self-esteem. *Journal of Personality and Social Psychology, 73,* 1038–1051.

Lader, M. H. (1990). Benzodiazepine withdrawal. In R. Noyes, Jr., M. Roth, & G. D. Burrows (Eds.), *Handbook of anxiety: The treatment of anxiety* (Vol. 4). Amsterdam: Elsevier.

Lader, M. H., & Herrington, R. (1990). *Biological treatments in psychiatry.* New York: Oxford University Press.

Lakein, A. (1973). *How to get control of your time and your life.* New York: Wyden.

Lakein, A. (1996). *How to get control of your time and your life.* New York: New American Library.

Lakka, T. A., Venalainen, J. M., Rauramaa, R., Salonen, R., Tuomilehto, J., & Salonen, J. T. (1994). Relations of leisure-time physical activity and cardiorespiratory fitness to the risk of acute myocardial infarction in men. *New England Journal of Medicine, 330,* 1549–1554.

Lakoff, R. (1973). Language and woman's place. *Language and Society, 2,* 45–79.

Lalumiere, M. L., & Quinsey, V. L. (1996). Sexual deviance, antisociality, mating effort, and the use of sexually coercive behaviors. *Personality & Individual Differences, 21,* 33–48.

Lamb, M. E., Sternberg, K. J., & Prodromidis, M. (1992). Nonmaternal care and the security of infant-mother attachment: A reanalysis of the data. *Infant Behavior and Development, 15,* 71–83.

Lambert, M. J., & Bergin, A. E. (1992). Achievements and limitations of psychotherapy research. In D. K. Freedheim (Ed.), *History of psychotherapy: A century of change.* Washington, DC: American Psychological Association.

Lambert, M. J., & Bergin, A. E. (1994). The effectiveness of psychotherapy. In A. E. Bergin & S. L. Garfield (Eds.), *Handbook of psychotherapy and behavior change* (4th ed.). New York: Wiley.

Lambert, M. J., & Hill, C. E. (1994). Assessing psychotherapy outcomes and processes. In A. E. Bergin & S. L. Garfield (Eds.), *Handbook of psychotherapy and behavior change* (4th ed.). New York: Wiley.

Lamborn, S. D., Mounts, N. S., Steinberg, L., & Dornbusch, S. M. (1991). Patterns of competence and adjustment among adolescents from authoritative, authoritarian, indulgent, and neglectful families. *Child Development, 62,* 1049–1065.

Landau, E. (1988). *Teenagers talk about school.* Englewood Cliffs, NJ: Julian Messner.

Landrine, H. (1985). Race & class stereotypes of women. *Sex Roles, 13,* 65–75.

Laner, M. R. (1988). Permanent partner priorities: Gay and straight. In J. P. De Cecco (Ed.), *Gay relationships.* New York: Harrington Park Press.

Langer, E., Bashner, R., & Chanowitz, B. (1985). Decreasing prejudice by increasing discrimination. *Journal of Personality and Social Psychology, 49,* 113–120.

Langer, E. (1989). *Mindfulness.* New York: Addison-Wesley.

Langlois, J. H., & Roggman, L. A. (1990). Attractive faces are only average. *Psychological Science, 1,* 115–121.

Langone, J. (1988). *AIDS: The facts.* Boston: Little, Brown.

Lanyon, R. I., & Goodstein, L. D. (1997). *Personality assessment.* New York: Wiley.

Lapsley, D. K., Jackson, S., Rice, K., & Shadid, G. E. (1988). Self-monitoring and the "new look" at the imaginary audience and personal fable: An ego-developmental analysis. *Journal of Adolescent Research, 3,* 17–31.

Lareau, W. (1997). *The where am I now? Where am I going? career manual.* Clinton, NJ: New Win Publishing.

Larsen, K. S. (1990). The Asch conformity experiment: Replication and transhistorical comparisons. *Journal of Social Behavior and Personality, 5,* 163–168.

Larsen, R. J. (1992). Neuroticism and selective encoding and recall of symptoms: Evidence from a combined concurrent-retrospective study. *Journal of Personality and Social Psychology, 62,* 480–488.

Larson, J. H., & Holman, T. B. (1994). Premarital predictors of marital quality and stability. *Family Relations, 43,* 228–237.

Larson, R., & Asmussen, L. (1991). Anger, worry, and hurt in early adolescence: An enlarging world of negative emotions. In M. E. Colten & S. Gore (Eds.), *Adolescent stress: Causes and consequences.* New York: Aldine de Gruyter.

Larson, R., & Ham, M. (1993). Stress and "storm and stress" in early adolescence: The relationship of negative events with dysphoric affect. *Developmental Psychology, 29,* 130–140.

Lassner, J. B., Matthews, K. A., & Stoney, C. M. (1994). Are cardiovascular reactors to asocial stress also reactors to social stress? *Journal of Personality and Social Psychology, 66,* 69–77.

Latané, B., & Darley, J. M. (1970). *The unresponsive bystander: Why doesn't he help?* New York: Appleton-Century-Crofts.

Latané, B., & Nida, S. A. (1981). Ten years of research on group size and helping. *Psychological Bulletin, 89,* 308–324.

Lau, S., & Gruen, G. E. (1992). The social stigma of loneliness: Effect of target person's and perceiver's sex. *Personality and Social Psychology Bulletin, 18,* 182–189.

Lauer, J., & Lauer, R. (1985, June). Marriages made to last. *Psychology Today,* pp. 22–26.

Laughlin, H. (1967). *The neuroses.* Washington, DC: Butterworth.

Laughlin, H. (1979). *The ego and its defenses.* New York: Aronson.

Laumann, E. O., Gagnon, J. H., Michael, R. T., & Michaels, S. (1994). *The social organization of sexuality: Sexual practices in the United States.* Chicago: University of Chicago Press.

Lavee, Y., Sharlin, S., & Katz. R. (1996). The effect of parenting stress on marital quality: An integrated mother-father model. *Journal of Family Issues, 17,* 114–135.

La Via, M. F., & Workman, E. A. (1998). Stress-induced immunodepression in humans. In J. R. Hubbard & E. A. Workman (Eds.), *Handbook of stress medicine: An organ system approach.* New York: CRC Press.

Lavine, L. O., & Lombardo, J. P. (1984). Self-disclosure: Intimate and non-intimate disclosures to parents and best friends as a function of Bem sex-role category. *Sex Roles, 11,* 735–744.

Lay, C. H. (1992). Trait procrastination and the perception of person-task characteristics. *Journal of Social Behavior and Personality, 7,* 483–494.

Lay, C. H. (1995). Trait procrastination, agitation, dejection, and self-discrepancy. In J. R. Ferrari, J. L. Johnson, & W. G. McCown (Eds.), *Procrastination and task avoidance: Theory, research, and treatment.* New York: Plenum Press.

Lay, C. H., Edwards, J. M., Parker, J. D. A., & Endler, N. S. (1989). An assessment of appraisal anxiety, coping, and procrastination during an examination period. *European Journal of Personality, 3,* 195–208.

Lay, C. H., Kovacs, A., & Danto, D. (1998). The relation of trait procrastination to the big-five factor conscientiousness: An assessment with primary-junior school children based on self-report scales. *Personality & Individual Differences, 25,* 187–193.

Lazarus, A. A. (1976). *Multimodal behavior therapy.* New York: Springer.

Lazarus, A. A. (1987). The need for technical eclecticism: Science, breadth, depth, and specificity. In J. K. Zeig (Ed.), *The evolution of psychotherapy.* New York: Brunner/Mazel.

Lazarus, A. A. (1989). Multimodal therapy. In R. J. Corsini & D. Wedding (Eds.), *Current Psychotherapies.* Itasca, IL: Peacock.

Lazarus, R. S. (1991). *Emotion and adaptation.* New York: Oxford.

Lazarus, R. S. (1993). Why we should think of stress as a subset of emotion. In L. Goldberger & S. Breznitz (Eds.), *Handbook of stress: Theoretical and clinical aspects* (2nd ed.). New York: Free Press.

Lazarus, R. S., & Folkman, S. (1984). *Stress, appraisal and coping.* New York: Springer.

Leahy, J. M. (1993). A comparison of depression in women bereaved of a spouse, a child, or a parent. *Omega, 26,* 207–217.

Leana, C. R., & Feldman, D. C. (1991). Gender differences in responses to unemployment. *Journal of Vocational Behavior, 38,* 65–77.

Leana, C. R., & Feldman, D. C. (1992). *Coping with job loss.* New York: Lexington Books.

Leary, M. R., & Jones, J. L. (1993). The social psychology of tanning and sunscreen use: Self-presentational motives as a predictor of health risk. *Journal of Applied Social Psychology, 23,* 1390–1406.

Leary, M. R., & Kowalski, R. (1995). *Social anxiety.* New York: Guilford.

Leary, M. R., Tchividjian, L. R., & Kraxberger. B. E. (1994). Self-presentation can be hazardous to your health: Impression management and health risk. *Health Psychology, 13,* 461–470.

Leavitt, F. (1995). *Drugs and behavior* (3rd ed.). Thousand Oaks, CA: Sage Publications.

LeBoeuf, M. (1980, February). Managing time means managing yourself. *Business Horizons,* pp. 41–46.

Lebov, M. (1980). *Practical tools and techniques for managing time.* Englewood Cliffs, NJ: Prentice-Hall.

Leckman, J. F., Grice, D. E., Boardman, J., Zhang, H., Vitale, A., Bondi, C., Alsobrook, J., Peterson, B. S., Cohen, D. J., Rasmussen, S. A., Goodman, W. K., McDougle, C. J., & Pauls, D. L. (1997). Symptoms of obsessive-compulsive disorder. *American Journal of Psychiatry, 154,* 911–917.

Ledray, L. E. (1994). *Recovering from rape* (2nd ed.). New York: Henry Holt.

Lee, G. R. (1988). Marital satisfaction in later life: The effects of nonmarital roles. *Journal of Marriage and the Family, 50,* 775–783.

Lee, G. R., & Shehan, C. L. (1989). Retirement and marital satisfaction. *Journal of Gerontology, 44,* S226–230.

Lee, I. M., Hsieh, C., & Paffenbarger, R. S. Jr. (1995). Exercise intensity and longevity in men. *Journal of the American Medical Association, 273,* 1179–1184.

Lee, R. T., & Ashforth, B. E. (1996). A meta-analytic examination of the correlates of the three dimensions of job burnout. *Journal of Applied Psychology, 81,* 123–133.

Lefcourt, H. M., Davidson, K., Shepherd, R., Phillips, M., Prkachin, K., & Mills, D. (1995). Perspective-taking humor: Accounting for stress moderation. *Journal of Social and Clinical Psychology, 14,* 373–391.

Leff, J., & Vaughn, C. (1985). *Expressed emotion in families.* New York: Guilford Press.

Lehmann, H. E., & Cancro, R. (1985). Schizophrenia: Clinical features. In H. I. Kaplan & B. J. Sadock (Eds.), *Comprehensive textbook of psychiatry/IV.* Baltimore: Williams & Wilkins.

Lehrer, P. M., & Woolfolk, R. L. (1984). Are stress reduction techniques interchangeable, or do they have specific effects? A review of the comparative empirical literature. In R. L. Woolfolk & P. M. Lehrer (Eds.), *Principles and practice of stress management.* New York: Guilford Press.

Lehrer, P. M., & Woolfolk, R. L. (1993). Specific effects of stress management techniques. In P. M. Lehrer & R. L. Woolfolk (Eds.), *Principles and practice of stress management* (2nd ed.). New York: Guilford Press.

Leigh, B. C. (1989). Reasons for having and avoiding sex: Gender, sexual orientation, and relationship to sexual behavior. *Journal of Sex Research, 26,* 199–209.

Leigh, G. K., Holman, T. B., & Burr, W. R. (1984). An empirical test of sequence in Murstein's SVR Theory of mate selection. *Family Relations, 33* 225–231.

Leigh, G. K., Holman, T. B., & Burr, W. R. (1987). Some confusions and exclusions of the SVR theory of dyadic pairing: A response to Murstein. *Journal of Marriage and the Family, 49,* 933–937.

Leiker, M., & Hailey, B. J. (1988). A link between hostility and disease: Poor health habits. *Behavioral Medicine, 14,* 129–133.

Leitenberg, H., & Henning, K. (1995). Sexual fantasy. *Psychological Bulletin, 117,* 469–496.

Leiter, M. P., & Maslach, C. (1988). The impact of interpersonal environment on burnout and organizational commitment. *Journal of Organizational Behavior, 9,* 297–308.

Lemack, G. E., Uzzo, R. G., & Poppas, D. P. (1998). Effects of stress on male reproductive function. In J. R. Hubbard & E. A. Workman (Eds.), *Handbook of stress medicine: An organ system approach.* New York: CRC Press.

Lenox, R. H., & Manji, H. K. (1995). Lithium. In A. F. Schatzberg & C. B. Nemeroff (Eds.), *The American Psychiatric Press textbook of psychopharmacology.* Washington, DC: American Psychiatric Press.

Leo, J. (1987, January 12). Exploring the traits of twins. *Time,* p. 63.

Lepore, S. J. (1992). Social conflict, social support, and psychological distress: Evidence of cross-domain buffering effects. *Journal of Personality and Social Psychology, 63* 857–867.

Leppin, A., & Schwarzer, R. (1990). Social support and physical health: An updated meta-analysis. In L. R. Schmidt, P. Schwenkmezger, J. Weinman, & S. Maes (Eds.), *Theoretical and applied aspects of health psychology.* London: Harwood.

Lerner, M. J., & Miller, D. T. (1978). Just world research and the attribution process: Looking back and ahead. *Psychological Bulletin, 85,* 1030–1051.

Lerner, R. M., & Galambos, N. L. (1998). Adolescent development: Challenges and opportunities for research, programs, and policies. *Annual review of psychology, 49,* 413–446.

Lesage, A. D., Boyer, R., Grunberg, F., Vanier, C., Morissette, R., Menard-Buteau, C., & Loyer, M. (1994). Suicide and mental disorders: A case-control study of young men. *American Journal of Psychiatry, 151,* 1063–1068.

LeShan, L. (1966). An emotional life-history pattern associated with neoplastic disease. *Annals of the New York Academy of Sciences, 125,* 780–793.

Levant, R. F. (1996). The new psychology of men. *Professional Psychology: Research and Practice, 27,* 259–265.

LeVay, S. (1991). A difference in hypothalamic structure and homosexual men. *Science, 253* 1034–1037.

Levenkron, S. (1982). *Treating and overcoming anorexia nervosa.* New York: Scribner's.

Leventhal, E. A., Hansell, S., Diefenbach, M., Leventhal, H., & Glass, D. C. (1996). Negative affect and self-report of physical symptoms: Two longitudinal studies of older adults. *Health Psychology, 15,* 193–199.

Lever, J. (1994, August 24). Sexual revelations. *The Advocate,* 17–24.

Levi, L. (1990). Occupational stress: Spice of life or kiss of death? *American Psychologist, 45,* 1142–1145.

Levinson, D. F., Mahtani, M. M., Nancarrow, D. J., Brown, D. M., Kruglyak, L., Kirby, A., Hayward, N. K., Crowe, R. R., Andreasen, N. C., Black, D. W., Silverman, J. M., Endicott, J.,

Sharpe, L., Mohs, R. C., Siever, L. J., Walters, M. K., lennon, D. P., Jones, H. L., Nurs, B., Nertney, D. A., Daly, M. J., Gladis, M., & Mowry, B. J. (1998). Genome scan of schizophrenia. *American Journal of Psychiatry, 155,* 741–750.

Levinson, D. J. (1985). The life cycle. In H. I. Kaplan & B. J. Sadock (Eds.), *Comprehensive textbook of psychiatry/IV.* Baltimore: Williams & Wilkins.

Levinson, D. J., Darrow, C. M., Klein, E. G., Levinson, M. H., & McKee, B. (1978). *The seasons of a man's life.* New York: Knopf.

Levis, D. J. (1989). The case for a return to a two-factor theory of avoidance: The failure of non-fear interpretations. In S. B. Klein & R. R. Bowrer (Eds.), *Contemporary learning theories: Pavlovian conditioning and the status of traditional learning theory.* Hillsdale, NJ: Erlbaum.

Levy, B., & Langer, E. (1994). Aging free from negative stereotypes: Successful memory in China and among the American deaf. *Journal of Personality and Social Psychology, 66,* 989–997.

Levy, M. B., & Davis, K. E. (1988). Lovestyles and attachment styles compared: Their relations to each other and to various relationship characteristics. *Journal of Social and Personal Relationships, 5,* 439–471.

Levy, S. M. (1985). *Behavior and cancer.* San Francisco: Jossey-Bass.

Levy, S. M., Herberman, R. B., Simons, A., Whiteside, T., Lee, J., McDonald, R., & Beadle, M. (1989). Persistently low natural killer cell activity in normal adults: Immunological, hormonal and mood correlates. *Natural Immune Cell Growth Regulation, 8,* 173–186.

Lewin, K. (1935). *A dynamic theory of personality.* New York: McGraw-Hill.

Lewinsohn, P. M., & Gotlib, I. H. (1995). Behavioral theory and treatment of depression. In E. E. Beckham & W. R. Leber (Eds.), *Handbook of depression* (2nd ed.). New York: Guilford Press.

Lewinsohn, P. M., Duncan, E. M., Stanton, A. K., & Hautzinger, M. (1986). Age at first onset for nonbipolar depression. *Journal of Abnormal Psychology, 95,* 378–383.

Lewinsohn, P. M., Rohde, P., Seeley, J. R., & Fischer, S. A. (1993). Age-cohort changes in the lifetime occurrence of depression and other mental disorders. *Journal of Abnormal Psychology, 102,* 110–120.

Lewis, B. P., & Linder, D. E. (1997). Thinking about choking? Attentional processes and paradoxical performance. *Personality and Social Psychology Bulletin, 23,* 937–944.

Lewis, D. O., Yeager, C. A., Swica, Y., Pincus, J. H., & Lewis, M. (1997). Objective documentation of child abuse and dissociation in 12 murderers with dissociative identity disorder. *American Journal of Psychiatry, 154,* 1703–1710.

Lewis, J. M. (1988). The transition to parenthood: II. Stability and change in marital structure. *Family Process, 27,* 273–283.

Lewis, R. J., & Janda, L. H. (1988). The relationship between adult sexual adjustment and childhood experiences regarding exposure to nudity, sleeping in the parental bed, and parental attitudes toward sexuality. *Archives of Sexual Behavior, 17,* 349–362.

Lewis-Fernandez, R., & Kleinman, A. (1994). Culture, personality, and psychology. *Journal of Abnormal Psychology, 103* 67–71.

Lewontin, R. C., Rose, S., & Kamin, L. (1984). *Not in our genes: Biology, ideology and human nature.* New York: Pantheon.

Liberman, R. P., & Bedell, J.R. (1989). Behavior therapy. In H.I. Kaplan & B.J. Sadock (Eds.), *Comprehensive textbook of psychiatry/V.* Baltimore: Williams & Wilkins.

Liberman, R. P., Mueser, K. T., & DeRisi, W. J. (1989). *Social skills training for psychiatric patients.* New York: Pergamon.

Lichter, S. R., Lichter, L. S., Rothman, S., & Amundson, D. (1987, July-August). Prime-time prejudice: TV's images of blacks and Hispanics. *Public Opinion,* pp. 13–16.

Lickey, M. E., & Gordon, B. (1991). *Medicine and mental illness: The use of drugs in psychiatry.* New York: Freeman.

Lieberman, M. A. (1993). Bereavement self-help groups: A review of conceptual and methodological issues. In M. S. Stroebe, W. Stroebe, & R. O. Hansson (Eds.), *Handbook of bereavement.* New York: Cambridge University Press.

Liebert, R. M., & Spiegler, M. D. (1994). *Personality: Strategies and issues.* Pacific Grove, CA: Brooks/Cole.

Liebert, R. M., & Sprafkin, J. N. (1988). *The early window: Effects of television on children and youth.* New York: Pergamon.

Lightsey, O. R. (1994). "Thinking positive" as a stress buffer: The role of positive automatic cognitions in depression and happiness. *Journal of Counseling Psychology, 41,* 325–334.

Lillard, L. A., & Waite, L. J. (1995). "Till death do us part": Marital disruption and mortality. *American Journal of Sociology, 100,* 1131–1156.

Linden, W. (1993). The autogenic training method of J. H. Schultz. In P. M. Lehrer & R. L. Woolfolk (Eds.), *Principles and practice of stress management* (2nd ed.). New York: Guilford Press.

Lindgren, H. C. (1969). *The psychology of college success: A dynamic approach.* New York: Wiley.

Lindsay, D. S., & Poole, D. A. (1995). Remembering childhood sexual abuse in therapy: Psychotherapists' self–reported beliefs, practices, and experiences. *Journal of Psychiatry & Law, 23,* 461–476.

Lindsay, D. S., & Read, J. D. (1994). Psychotherapy and memories of childhood sexual abuse: A cognitive perspective. *Applied Cognitive Psychology, 8,* 281–338.

Linn, M. C., & Petersen, A. C. (1986). A meta-analysis of gender differences in spatial ability: Implications for mathematics and science achievement. In J. S. Hyde & M. C. Linn (Eds.), *The psychology of gender: Advances through meta-analysis.* Baltimore: Johns Hopkins University Press.

Linville, P. W. (1985). Self-complexity and affective extremity: Don't put all of your eggs in one cognitive basket. *Social Cognition, 3* 94–120.

Linville, P. W. (1987). Self-complexity as a cognitive buffer against stress-related illness and depression. *Journal of Personality and Social Psychology, 52,* 663–676.

Linville, P. W., & Fischer, G. W. (1991). Preferences for separating or combining events. *Journal of Personality and Social Psychology, 60,* 5–23.

Lippa, R. A. (1994). *Introduction to social psychology.* Pacific Grove, CA: Brooks/Cole.

Lips, H. M. (1997). *Sex and gender: An introduction.* Mountain View, CA: Mayfield.

Lipsey, M. W., & Wilson, D. B. (1993). The efficacy of psychological, educational, and behavioral treatment: Confirmation from meta-analysis. *American Psychologist, 48,* 1181–1209.

Litt, I. F., & Vaughan, V. C., III. (1992). Adolescence. In R. E. Behrman (Ed.), *Nelson textbook of pediatrics.* Philadelphia: Saunders.

Litwack, M., & Resnick, M. R. (1984). *The art of self-fulfillment.* New York: Simon & Schuster.

Lloyd, G. K., Fletcher, A., & Minchin, M. C. W. (1992). GABA agonists as potential anxiolytics. In G. D. Burrows, S. M. Roth, & R. Noyes, Jr. (Eds.), *Handbook of anxiety* (Vol. 5). Oxford: Elsevier.

Lloyd, M. A. (1985). *Adolescence.* New York: HarperCollins.

Lloyd, S. A., & Emery, B. C. (1993). Abuse in the family: An ecological, life-cycle perspective. In T. H. Brubaker (Ed.), *Family relations: Challenges for the future.* Newbury Park, CA: Sage Publications.

Lobel, K. (1986). *Naming the violence.* Seattle: Seal Press.

Lock, R. D. (1996a). *Job search.* Pacific Grove, CA: Brooks/Cole.

Lock, R. D. (1996b). *Taking charge of your career direction.* Pacific Grove, CA: Brooks/Cole.

Loehlin, J. C. (1992). *Genes and environment in personality development.* Newbury Park, CA: Sage.

Loewenstein, R. J. (1996). Dissociative amnesia and dissociative fugue. In L. K. Michelson & W. J. Ray (Eds.), *Handbook of dissociation: Theoretical, empirical, and clinical perspectives.* New York: Plenum Press.

Loftus, E. F. (1993). The reality of repressed memories. *American Psychologist, 48,* 518–537.

Loftus, E. F. (1994). The repressed memory controversy. *American Psychologist, 49,* 443–445.

London, K. A., & Wilson, B. F. (1988). Divorce. *American Demographics, 10,* 22–26.

Long, E. C. J., & Andrews, D. W. (1990). Perspective taking as a predictor of marital adjustment. *Journal of Personality and Social Psychology, 59,* 126–131.

Longman, D. G., & Atkinson, R. H. (1996). *College learning and study skills.* Belmont, CA: West/Wadsworth.

Lonsway, K. A. (1996). Preventing acquaintance rape through education. *Psychology of Women Quarterly, 20,* 229–265.

Loomis, L. S., & Booth, A. (1995). Multigenerational caregiving and well-being: The myth of the beleaguered sandwich generation. *Journal of Family Issues, 16,* 131–148.

Lott, B. (1987). *Women's lives: Themes and variations in gender learning.* Pacific Grove, CA: Brooks/Cole.

Loughead, T. A. (1991). Addictions as a process: Commonalities or codependence. *Contemporary Family Therapy: An International Journal, 13* 455–470.

Lovallo, W. R., a'Absi, M., Pincomb, G. A., Everson, S. A., Sung, B. E., Passey, R. B., & Wilson, M. F. (1996). Caffeine and behavioral stress effects on blood pressure in borderline hypertensive caucasian men. *Health Psychology, 15,* 11–17.

Lovdal, L. T. (1989). Sex role messages in television commercials: An update. *Sex Roles, 21,* 715–724.

Lowinson, J. H., Ruiz, P., Millman, R. B., & Langrod, J. G. (1997). *Substance abuse: A comprehensive textbook.* Baltimore: Williams & Wilkins.

Lowman, R. L. (1991). *The clinical practice of career assessment: Interests, abilities, and personality.* Washington, DC: American Psychological Association.

Lubkin, I. M. (1990). Illness roles. In I. M. Lubkin (Ed.), *Chronic Illness: Impact and interventions* (2nd ed.). Boston: Jones and Bartlett.

Luborsky, L., Singer, B., & Luborsky, L. (1975). Comparative studies of psychotherapies: Is it true that everyone has won and all must have prizes? *Archives of General Psychiatry, 32,* 995–1008.

Lucas, A. R., Beard, C. M., O'Fallon, W. M., & Kurland, L. T. (1991). 50-year trends in the incidence of anorexia nervosa in Rochester, Minn.: A population-based study. *American Journal of Psychiatry, 148,* 917–922.

Luecke-Aleska, D., Anderson, D. R., Collins, P. A., & Schmitt, K. L. (1995). Gender constancy and television viewing. *Developmental Psychology, 31,* 773–780.

Luhtanen, R., & Crocker, J. (1992). A collective self-esteem scale: Self-evaluation of one's social identity. *Personality and Social Psychology Bulletin, 18,* 302–318.

Lulofs, R. S. (1994). *Conflict: From theory to action.* Scottsdale, AZ: Gorsuch Scarisbuck Publishers.

Lye, D. N., & Biblarz, T. J. (1993). The effects of attitudes toward family life and gender roles on marital satisfaction. *Journal of Family Issues, 14,* 157–188.

Lykes, M. B. (1985). Gender and individualistic vs. collectivist bases for notions about the self. *Journal of Personality, 53* 356–383.

Lyness, S. A. (1993). Predictors of differences between Type A and Type B individuals in heart rate and blood pressure reactivity. *Psychological Bulletin, 114,* 266–295.

Lynn, D. J., & Vaillant, G. E. (1998). Anonymity, neutrality, and confidentiality in the actual methods of Sigmund Freud: A review of 43 cases, 1907–1939. *American Journal of Psychiatry, 155,* 163–171.

Lynn, M., & Mynier, K. (1993). Effects of server posture on restaurant tipping. *Journal of Applied Social Psychology, 23,* 678–685.

Lynn, M., & Shurgot, B. A. (1984). Responses to lonely hearts advertisements: Effects of reported physical attractiveness, physique, and coloration. *Personality and Social Psychology Bulletin, 10,* 349–357.

Lynn, S. J., & Nash, M. (1994). Truth in memory: Ramifications for psychotherapy and hypnotherapy. *American Journal of Clinical Hypnosis, 36,* 194–208.

Lyon, D., & Greenberg, J. (1991). Evidence of codependency in women with an alcoholic parent: Helping out Mr. Wrong. *Journal of Personality and Social Psychology, 61,* 435–439.

Lytton, H., & Romney, D. M. (1991). Parents' differential socialization of boys and girls: A meta-analysis. *Psychological Bulletin, 109,* 267–296.

Maccoby, E. E. (1988). Gender as a social category. *Developmental Psychology, 24,* 755–765.

Maccoby, E. E. (1990). Gender and relationships: A developmental account. *American Psychologist, 45,* 513–520.

Maccoby, E. E., & Jacklin, C. N. (1974). *The psychology of sex differences.* Stanford, CA: Stanford University Press.

Maccoby, E. E., & Jacklin, C. N. (1987). Gender segregation in childhood. In E. H. Reese (Ed.), *Advances in child development.* New York: Academic Press.

Maccoby, E. E., & Martin, J. A. (1983). Socialization in the context of the family: Parent-child interaction. In P. H. Mussen (Series Ed.) & E. M. Hetherington (Vol. Ed.), *Handbook of child psychology: Vol. 4. Socialization, personality, and social development.* New York: Wiley.

MacEwen, K. E., & Barling, J. (1991). Effects of maternal employment experiences on children's behavior via mood, cognitive difficulties, and parenting behavior. *Journal of Marriage and the Family, 53* 635–644.

Machlowitz, M. M. (1980). *Workaholics: Living with them, working with them.* Reading, MA: Addison-Wesley.

Machung, A. (1989). Talking career, thinking job: Gender differences in career and family expectations of Berkeley seniors. *Family Studies, 15*, 35–58.

Macionis, J. J. (1997). *Sociology* (6th ed.). Upper Saddle River, NJ: Prentice Hall.

Macke, A. S., Richardson, L. W., & Cook, J. (1980). *Sex-typed teaching styles of university professors and student reactions.* Columbus, OH: Ohio State University Research Foundation.

MacKenzie, R. A. (1997). *The time trap.* New York: AMACOM.

Mackie, D. M., Worth, L. T., & Asuncion, A. G. (1990). Processing of persuasive in-group messages. *Journal of Personality and Social Psychology, 58*, 812–822.

Macklin, E. D. (1983). Nonmarital hetero-sexual cohabitation: An overview. In E. D. Macklin & R. H. Rubin (Eds.), *Contemporary families and alternative lifestyles: Handbook on research and theory.* Newbury Park, CA: Sage Publications.

Macklin, E. D. (1987). Nontraditional family forms. In M. B. Sussman & S. K. Steinmetz (Eds.), *Handbook of marriage and the family.* New York: Plenum.

Macmillan, M. (1991). *Freud evaluated: The completed arc.* Amsterdam: North-Holland.

Maddi, S. R. (1989). *Personality theories: A comparative analysis.* Chicago, IL: Dorsey Press.

Maher, B. A., & Spitzer, M. (1993). Delusions. In P. B. Sutker & H. E. Adams (Eds.), *Comprehensive handbook of psychopathology* (2nd ed.). New York: Plenum.

Mahoney, M. J. (1979). *Self-change: Strategies for solving personal problems.* New York: Norton.

Main, M., & Solomon, J. (1990). Procedures for identifying infants as disorganized/disoriented during the Ainsworth Strange Situation. In M. T. Greenberg, D. Cicchetti, & E. M. Cummings (Eds.), *Attachment in the preschool years: Theory, research, and intervention.* Chicago: University of Chicago Press.

Maisto, S. A., Galizio, M., & Connors, G. J. (1995). *Drug use and abuse* (2nd ed.). Fort Worth, TX: Harcourt Press.

Maj, M., Pirozzi, R., Magliano, L., & Bartoli, L. (1998). Long-term outcome of lithium prophylaxis in bipolar disorder: A 5-year prospective study of 402 patients at a lithium clinic. *American Journal of Psychiatry, 155*, 30–35.

Major, B. (1981). Gender patterns in touching behavior. In C. Mayo & N. M. Henley (Eds.), *Gender and nonverbal behavior.* New York: Springer-Verlag.

Major, B., Schmidlin, A. M., & Williams, L. (1990). Gender patterns in social touch: The impact of setting and age. *Journal of Personality and Social Psychology, 58*, 634–643.

Malamuth, N. A. (1984). Violence against women: Cultural and individual cases. In N. M. Malamuth & E. Donnerstein, *Pornography and sexual aggression.* New York: Academic Press.

Malamuth, N. M., & Brown, L. M. (1994). Sexually aggressive men's perspective of women's communications: Testing three explanations. *Journal of Personality and Social Psychology, 67*, 699–712.

Malamuth, N. M., & Check, J. V. P. (1981). The effects of mass media exposure on acceptance of violence against women: A field experiment. *Journal of Research in Personality, 15*, 436–446.

Malamuth, N. M., & Donnerstein, E. (1982). The effects of aggressive-pornographic mass media stimuli. In L. Berkowitz (Ed.), *Advances in Experimental Social Psychology* (Vol. 15). New York: Academic Press.

Malina, R. M. (1990). Physical growth and performance during the transitional years (9–16). In G. R. Adams & T. P. Gullota (Eds.), *From*

childhood to adolescence: A transitional period? Newbury Park, CA: Sage Publications.

Malinosky-Rummell, R., & Hansen, D. J. (1993). Long-term consequences of childhood physical abuse. *Psychological Bulletin, 114*, 68–79.

Mallinckrodt, B., & Fretz, B. R. (1988). Social support and the impact of job loss on older professionals. *Journal of Counseling Psychology, 33*, 281–286.

Maltz, D. N., & Borker, R. A. (1983). A cultural approach to male-female miscommunication. In J. A. Gumperz (Ed.), *Language and social identity.* New York: Cambridge University Press.

Mandler, G. (1993). Thought, memory, and learning: Effects of emotional stress. In L. Goldberger & S. Breznitz (Eds.), *Handbook of stress: Theoretical and clinical aspects* (2nd ed.). New York: Free Press.

Mangelsdorf, S., Gunnar, M., Kestenbaum, R., Lang, S., & Andreas, D. (1990). Infant proneness-to-distress temperament, maternal personality, and mother-infant attachment: Associations and goodness of fit. *Child Development, 61*, 830–831.

Mann, J., Tarantola, D. J. M., & Netter, T. W. (1992). *A global report: AIDS in the world.* New York: Oxford University Press.

Manuck, S. B., Kamarck, T. W., Kasprowicz, A. S., & Waldstein, S. R. (1993). Stability and patterning of behaviorally evoked cardiovascular reactivity. In J. Blascovich & E. S. Katkin (Eds.), *Cardiovascular reactivity to psychological stress and disease.* Washington, DC: American Psychological Association.

Marangoni, C., & Ickes, W. (1989). Loneliness: A theoretical review with implications for measurement. *Journal of Social and Personal Relationships, 6*, 93–128.

Marcenes, W. G., & Sheiham, A. (1992). The relationship between work stress and oral health status. *Social Science and Medicine, 35*, 1511.

Marcia, J. E. (1980). Identity in adolescence. In J. Adelson (Ed.), *Handbook of adolescent psychology.* New York: Wiley.

Marcia, J. E. (1991). Identity and self-development. In R. M. Lerner, A. C. Petersen, & J. Brooks-Gunn (Eds.), *Encyclopedia of adolescence* (Vol. 1). New York: Garland.

Marcus, B. H., Bock, B. C., & Pinto, B. M. (1997). Initiation and maintenance of exercise behavior. In D. S. Gochman (Ed.), *Handbook of health behavior research II: Provider determinants.* New York: Plenum Press.

Marder, S. R., & Van Putten, T. (1995). Antipsychotic medications. In A. F. Schatzberg & C. B. Nemeroff (Eds.), *The American Psychiatric Press textbook of psychopharmacology.* Washington, DC: American Psychiatric Press.

Mare, R. D. (1991). Five decades of educational assortative mating. *American Sociological Review, 56*, 15–32.

Marecek, J., Finn, S. E., & Cardell, M. (1988). Gender roles in the relationships of lesbians and gay men. In J. P. De Cecco (Ed.), *Gay relationships.* New York: Harrington Park Press.

Marengo, J., Harrow, M., Sands, J., & Galloway, C. (1991). European versus U.S. data on the course of schizophrenia. *American Journal of Psychiatry, 148*, 606–611.

Maricle, R., Leung, P., & Bloom, J. D. (1987). The use of DSM-III axis III in recording physical illness in psychiatric patients. *American Journal of Psychiatry, 144*, 1484–1486.

Marker, N. F. (1996). Flying solo at midlife: Gender, marital status, and psychological well-being. *Journal of Marriage and the Family, 58*, 917–932.

Markides, K. S., & Krause, N. (1985). Intergenerational solidarity and psychological well-being among older Mexican Americans: A three-generations study. *Journal of Gerontology, 40*, 390–392.

Marks, I. M. (1987). *Fears, phobias, and rituals: Panic, anxiety, and their disorders.* New York: Oxford University Press.

Markus, H., & Cross, S. (1990). The interpersonal self. In L. A. Pervin (Ed.), *Handbook of personality: Theory and research.* New York: Guilford Press.

Markus, H., & Kitayama, S. (1991). Culture and the self: Implications for cognition, emotion, and motivation. *Psychological Review, 98*, 224–253.

Markus, H., & Nurius, P. (1986). Possible selves. *American Psychologist, 41*, 954–969.

Markus, H., & Ruvolo, A. (1989). Possible selves: Personalized representations of goals. In L. A. Pervin (Ed.), *Goal concepts in personality and social psychology.* Hillsdale, NJ: Erlbaum.

Markus, H., & Wurf, E. (1987). The dynamic self-concept: A social psychological perspective. *Annual Review of Psychology, 38*, 299–337.

Markus, I. M. (1969). *Fears and phobias.* New York: Academic Press.

Marsh, H. W., & Parker, J. W. (1984). Determinants of student self-concept: Is it better to be a relatively large fish in a small pond even if you don't learn to swim well? *Journal of Personality and Social Psychology, 47*, 213–231.

Marsh, P. (Ed.). (1988). *Eye to eye: How people interact.* Topsfield, MA: Salem House.

Marshall, V. W., & Levy, J. A. (1990). Aging and dying. In R. H. Binstock & L. K. George (Eds.), *Handbook of aging and the social sciences.* San Diego, CA: Academic Press.

Martin, R. A. (1996). The situational humor response questionnaire (SHRQ) and coping humor scale (CHS): A decade of research findings. *Humor: International Journal of Humor Research, 9*, 251–272.

Martin, R. A., & Lefcourt, H. M. (1983). Sense of humor as a moderator of the relation between stressors and moods. *Journal of Personality and Social Psychology, 45*, 1313–1324.

Martin, R. L., & Yutzy, S. H. (1994). Somatoform disorders. In R. E. Hales, S. C. Yudofsky, & J. A. Talbott (Eds.), *The American Psychiatric Press textbook of psychiatry* (2nd ed.). Washington, DC: American Psychiatric Press.

Martin, T. C., & Bumpass, L. L. (1989). Recent trends in marital disruption. *Demography, 26*, 37–51.

Maser, J. D., Kaelber, C., & Weise, R. E. (1991). International use and attitudes toward DSM-III and DSM-III-R: Growing consensus in psychiatric classification. *Journal of Abnormal Psychology, 100*, 271–279.

Masheter, C. (1997). Healthy and unhealthy friendship and hostility between ex-spouses. *Journal of Marriage and the Family, 59*, 463–475.

Maslach, C. (1982). Understanding burnout: Definitional issues in analyzing a complex phenomenon. In W. S. Paine (Ed.), *Job stress and burnout: Research, theory and intervention perspectives.* Newbury Park, CA: Sage Publications.

Maslach, C., & Goldberg, J. (1998). Prevention of burnout: New perspectives. *Applied and Preventive Psychology, 7*, 63–74.

Maslow, A. (1968). *Toward a psychology of being.* New York: Van Nostrand.

Maslow, A. (1970). *Motivation and personality.* New York: Harper & Row.

Massion, A. O., Warshaw, M. G., & Keller, M. B. (1993). Quality of life and psychiatric morbidity in panic disorder and generalized anxiety disorder. *American Journal of Psychiatry, 150,* 600–607.

Mastekaasa, A. (1994). Psychological well-being and marital dissolution. *Journal of Family Issues, 15,* 208–228.

Masters, M. S., & Sanders, B. (1993). Is the gender difference in mental rotation disappearing? *Behavior Genetics, 23,* 337–341.

Masters, W. H., & Johnson, V. E. (1966). *Human sexual response.* Boston: Little, Brown.

Masters, W. H., & Johnson, V. E. (1970). *Human sexual inadequacy.* Boston: Little, Brown.

Masters, W. H., & Johnson, V. E. (1979). *Homosexuality in perspective.* Boston: Little, Brown.

Masters, W. H., & Johnson, V. E. (1980). *Human sexual inadequacy* (2nd ed.). New York: Bantam Books.

Masters, W. H., Johnson, V. E., & Kolodny, R. C. (1988). *Human sexuality.* Glenview, IL: Scott, Foresman.

Masters, W. H., Johnson, V. E., & Kolodny, R. C. (1994). *Heterosexuality.* New York: HarperCollins.

Matarazzo, J. D. (1992). Psychological testing and assessment in the 21st century. *American Psychologist, 47,* 1007–1018.

Mathes, E. W., Brennan, S. M., Haugen, P. M., & Rice, H. B. (1985). Ratings of physical attractiveness as a function of age. *Journal of Social Psychology, 125,* 157–168.

Mathew, R., Wilson, W., Blazer, D., & George, L. (1993). Psychiatric disorders in adult children of alcoholics: Data from the epidemiologic catchment area project. *American Journal of Psychiatry, 150,* 793–796.

Matsumoto, D. (1994). *People: Psychology from a cultural perspective.* Pacific Grove, CA: Brooks/Cole.

Matsumoto, D. (1996). *Culture and psychology.* Pacific Grove, CA: Brooks/Cole.

Matteson, M. T., & Ivancevich, J. M. (1987). *Controlling work stress: Effective human resource and management strategies.* San Francisco: Jossey-Bass.

Mattessich, P., & Hill, R. (1987). Life cycle and family development. In M. B. Sussman & S. K. Steinmetz (Eds.), *Handbook of marriage and the family.* New York: Plenum.

Matthews, K. A. (1992). Myths and realities of menopause. *Psychosomatic Medicine, 54,* 1–9.

Matthews, K. A., & Rodin, J. (1989). Women's changing work roles: Impact on health, family, and public policy. *American Psychologist, 44,* 1389–1393.

Matthews, K. A., Scheier, M. F., Brunson, B. I., & Carducci, B. (1989). Why do unpredictable events lead to reports of physical symptoms? In T. W. Miller (Ed.), *Stressful life events.* Madison, CT: International Universities Press.

Matthews, K. A., Woodall, K. L., & Stoney, C. M. (1990). Changes in and stability of cardiovascular responses to behavioral stress. *Child Development, 61,* 1134–1144.

Mattley, C., & Schwartz, M. D. (1990). Emerging from tyranny: Using the battered woman scale to compare the gender identities of battered and non-battered women. *Symbolic Interaction, 13* 281–289.

Mayer, J. D., & Salovey, P. (1997). What is emotional intelligence? In P. Salovey & D. Sluyter (Eds.), *Emotional development and emotional intelligence: Educational implications.* New York: Basic Books.

Mazur, E. (1989). Predicting gender differences in same-sex friendships from affiliation motive and value. *Psychology of Women Quarterly, 13,* 277–291.

McBride, P. E. (1992). The health consequences of smoking: Cardiovascular diseases. *Medical Clinics of North America, 76,* 333–353.

McCann, C. D., & Hancock, R. D. (1983). Self-monitoring in communicative interactions: Social cognitive consequences of goal-directed message modification. *Journal of Experimental Social Psychology, 19,* 109–121.

McConaghy, N. (1993). *Sexual behavior: Problems and management.* New York: Plenum.

McConahay, J. B. (1986). Modern racism, ambivalence, and the modern racism scale. In J. F. Dovidio & S. L. Gaertner (Eds.), *Prejudice, discrimination, and racism: Theory and research.* Orlando FL: Academic Press.

McConahay, J. B., & Hough, J. C., Jr. (1976). Symbolic racism. *Journal of Social Issues, 32,* 23–45.

McCrae, R. R. (1984). Situational determinants of coping responses: Loss, threat and challenge. *Journal of Personality and Social Psychology, 46,* 919–928.

McCrae, R. R. (1996). Social consequences of experimental openness. *Psychological Bulletin, 120,* 323–337.

McCrae, R. R., & Costa, P. T., Jr. (1984). *Emerging lives, enduring dispositions: Personality in adulthood.* Boston: Little, Brown.

McCrae, R. R., & Costa, P. T., Jr. (1987). Validation of the five-factor model of personality across instruments and observers. *Journal of Personality and Social Psychology, 52,* 81–90.

McCrae, R. R., & Costa, P. T., Jr. (1990). *Personality in adulthood.* New York: Guilford Press.

McCrae, R. R., & Costa, P. T., Jr. (1997). Personality trait structure as a human universal. *American Psychologist, 52,* 509–516.

McCreary, D. R. (1994). The male role and avoiding femininity. *Sex Roles, 31,* 517–531.

McCroskey, J. C., & Beatty, M. J. (1986). Oral communication apprehension. In W. H. Jones, J. M. Cheek, & S. R. Briggs (Eds.), *Shyness: Perspectives on research and treatment.* New York: Plenum.

McDaniel, M. A., & Einstein, G. O. (1986). Bizarre imagery as an effective memory aid: The importance of distinctiveness. *Journal of Experimental Psychology: Learning, Memory & Cognition, 12,* 54–65.

McDaniel, M. A., Waddill, P. J., & Shakesby, P. S. (1996). Study strategies, interest, and learning from text: The application of material appropriate processing. In D. J. Herrmann, C. McEvoy, C. Hertzog, P. Hertel, & M. K. Johnson (Eds.), *Basic and applied memory research: Theory in context* (Vol. 1). Mahwah, NJ: Erlbaum.

McDonald, G. J. (1982). Individual differences in the coming out process of gay men: Implications for theoretical models. *Journal of Homosexuality, 8,* 47–60.

McDougle, L. G. (1987). Time management: Making every minute count. In A. D. Timpe (Ed.), *The management of time.* New York: Facts On File.

McFarland, C., & Buehler, R. (1995). Collective self-esteem as a moderator of the frog-pond effect in reactions to performance feedback. *Journal of Personality and Social Psychology, 68,* 1055–1070.

McFarlin, D. B., Baumeister, R. F., & Blascovich, J. (1984). On knowing when to quit: Task failure, self-esteem, advice, and non-productive persistence. *Journal of Personality, 52,* 138–155.

McGee-Cooper, A., & Trammell, D. (1994). *Time management for unmanageable people.* New York: Bantam Books.

McGinnies, E., & Ward, C. D. (1980). Better liked than right: Trustworthiness and expertise as factors in credibility. *Personality and Social Psychology Bulletin, 6,* 467–472.

McGlashan, T. H., & Fenton, W. S. (1992). The positive-negative distinction in schizophrenia: Review of natural history validators. *Archives of General Psychiatry, 49,* 63–72.

McGlashan, T. H., Mohr, D. C., Beutler, L. E., Engle, D., Shoham-Salomon, V., Bergan, J., Kaszniak, A. W., & Yost, E. B. (1990). Identification of patients at risk for nonresponse and negative outcome in psychotherapy. *Journal of Consulting and Clinical Psychology, 58,* 622–628.

McGoldrick, M., & Carter, E. A. (1989). The family life cycle—Its stages and dislocations. In J. M. Henslin (Ed.), *Marriage and family in a changing society.* New York: Free Press.

McGowan, A. S. (1977). Vocational maturity and anxiety among vocationally undecided and indecisive students. *Journal of Vocational Behavior, 10,* 196–204.

McGrath, J. E. (1977). Settings, measures and themes: An integrative review of some research on social-psychological factors in stress. In A. Monat & R. S. Lazarus (Eds.), *Stress and coping: An anthology.* New York: Columbia University Press.

McGuigan, F. J. (1993). Progressive relaxation: Origins, principles, and clinical applications. In P. M. Lehrer & R. L. Woolfolk (Eds.), *Principles and practice of stress management* (2nd ed.). New York: Guilford Press.

McHale, S. M., & Crouter, A. C. (1992). You can't always get what you want: Incongruence between sex-role attitudes and family work roles and its implications for marriage. *Journal of Marriage and the Family, 54,* 537–547.

McHugh, M. C., Frieze, I. H., & Browne, A. (1993). Research on battered women and their assailants. In F. L. Denmark & M. A. Paludi (Eds.), *Psychology of women: A handbook of issues and theories.* Westport, CT: Greenwood Press.

McKay, A., & Holowaty, P. (1997). Sexual health education: A study of adolescents' opinions, self-perceived needs, and current and preferred sources of information. *Canadian Journal of Human Sexuality, 6,* 29–38.

McKay, M., & Fanning, P. (1992). *Self-esteem.* Oakland, CA: New Harbinger.

McKay, M., & Fanning, P. (1994). *Self-esteem.* Oakland, CA: New Harbinger.

McKay, M., Davis, M., & Fanning, P. (1995). *Messages: The communication skills book.* Oakland, CA: New Harbinger.

McKenry, P. C., Julian, T. W., & Gavazzi, S. M. (1995). Toward a biopsychosocial model of domestic violence. *Journal of Marriage and the Family, 57,* 307–320.

McKinlay, J. B., McKinlay, S. M., & Brambilla, D. (1987). The relative contributions of endocrine changes and social circumstances to depression in mid-aged women. *Journal of Health and Social Behavior, 28,* 345–363.

McLean, D. E., & Link, B. G. (1994). Unraveling complexity: Strategies to refine concepts, measures, and research designs in the study of life events and mental health. In W. R. Avison & I. H. Gotlib (Eds.), *Stress and mental health: Contemporary issues and prospects for the future.* New York: Plenum Press.

McLeod, J. D. (1995). Social and psychological bases of homogamy for common psychiatric disorders. *Journal of Marriage and the Family, 57,* 201–214.

McMillan, J. R., Clifton, A. K., McGrath, D., & Gale, W. S. (1977). Women's language: Uncertainty or interpersonal sensitivity and emotionality? *Sex Roles, 3* 545–560.

McNally, R. J. (1987). Preparedness and phobias: A review. *Psychological Bulletin, 101,* 283–303.

McNally, R. J. (1990). Psychological approaches to panic disorder: A review. *Psychological Bulletin, 108,* 403–419.

McNally, R. J. (1994). Cognitive bias in panic disorder. *Current Directions in Psychological Science, 3,* 129–132.

McNew, J., & Abell, N. (1995). Posttraumatic stress symptomatology: Similarities and differences between Vietnam veterans and adult survivors of childhood sexual abuse. *Social Work, 40,* 115–126.

McRae, S. (1997). Cohabitation: A trial run for marriage? *Sexual and Marital Therapy, 12,* 259–273.

Mead, M. (1950). *Sex and temperament in three primitive societies.* New York: Mentor Books.

Mednick, M. T., & Thomas, V. G. (1993). Women and the psychology of achievement: A view from the eighties. In F. L. Denmark & M. A. Paludi (Eds.), *Psychology of women: A handbook of issues and theories.* Westport, CT: Greenwood Press.

Meehan, P. J., Lamb, J. A., Saltzman, L. E., & O'Carroll, P. W. (1992). Attempted suicide among young adults: Progress toward a meaningful estimate of prevalence. *American Journal of Psychiatry, 149,* 41–44.

Mehta, S., & Farina, A. (1997). Is being "sick" really better? Effect of the disease view of mental disorder on stigma. *Journal of Social and Clinical Psychology, 16,* 405–419.

Meichenbaum, D. (1993). Stress inoculation training: A 20-year update. In P. M. Lehrer & R. L. Woolfolk (Eds.), *Principles and practice of stress management* (2nd ed.). New York: Guilford Press.

Meilman, P. W. (1979). Cross-sectional age changes in ego identity status during adolescence. *Developmental Psychology, 15,* 230–232.

Meindl, J. R., & Lerner, M. J. (1984). Exacerbation of extreme responses to an outgroup. *Journal of Personality and Social Psychology, 47,* 71–84.

Mellers, B. A., Richards, V., & Birnbaum, M. H. (1992). Distributional theories of impression formation. *Organizational Behavior and Human Decision Processes, 51,* 313–343.

Melman, A., & Leiter, E. (1983). The urologic evaluation of impotence (male excitement phase disorder). In H. S. Kaplan (Ed.), *The evaluation of sexual disorders: Psychological and medical aspects.* New York: Brunner/Mazel.

Menaghan, E. G., & Parcel, T. L. (1990). Parental employment and family life: Research in the 1980s. *Journal of Marriage and the Family, 52,* 1079–1098.

Mendenhall, W. (1989). Co-dependency definitions and dynamics. *Alcoholism Treatment Quarterly, 6,* 3–17.

Merckelbach, H., De Ruiter, C., Van Den Hout, M. A., & Hoekstra, R. (1989). Conditioning experiences and phobias. *Behavior Research and Therapy, 27,* 657–662.

Mergenhagen, P. (1996). Her own boss. *American Demographics, 18,* 36–41.

Merikle, P., & Skanes, H. E. (1992). Subliminal self-help audiotapes: A search for placebo effects. *Journal of Applied Psychology, 77,* 772–776.

Merton, R. (1948). The self-fulfilling prophecy. *Antioch Review, 8,* 193–210.

Michael, R. T., Gagnon, J. H., Laumann, E. O., & Kolata, G. (1994). *Sex in America.* Boston: Little, Brown.

Mikulincer, M., Florian, V., & Tolmacz, R. (1990). Attachment styles and fear of personal death: A case study of affect regulation. *Journal of Personality and Social Psychology, 58,* 273–280.

Milan, R., & Kilmann, P. (1987). Interpersonal factors in premarital conception. *Journal of Sex Research, 23,* 289–321.

Milgram, N., Marshevsky, S., & Sadeh, C. (1995). Correlates of academic procrastination: Discomfort, task aversiveness, and task capability. *Journal of Psychology, 129,* 145–155.

Milgram, S. (1963). Behavioral study of obedience. *Journal of Abnormal and Social Psychology, 67,* 371–378.

Milgram, S. (1974). *Obedience to authority.* New York: Harper & Row.

Miller, A. G. (1986). *The obedience experiments: A case study of controversy in social science.* New York: Praeger.

Miller, B. C., & Sollie, D. L. (1986). Normal stresses during the transition to parenthood. In R. H. Moos (Ed.), *Coping with life crises: An integrated approach.* New York: Plenum.

Miller, D. T., & Ross, M. (1975). Self-serving biases in the attribution of causality: Fact or fiction? *Psychological Bulletin, 82,* 213–225.

Miller, G. P. (1978). *Life choices: How to make the critical decisions—about your education, career, marriage, family, life style.* New York: Thomas Y. Crowell.

Miller, J. G. (1984). Culture and the development of everyday social explanation. *Journal of Personality and Social Psychology, 46,* 961–978.

Miller, L. C., Berg, J. H., & Archer, R. L. (1983). Openers: Individuals who elicit intimate self-disclosure. *Journal of Personality and Social Psychology, 44,* 1234–1244.

Miller, M. L., & Thayer, J. F. (1988). On the nature of self-monitoring: Relationships with adjustment and identity. *Personality and Social Psychology Bulletin, 14,* 544–553.

Miller, N. E. (1944). Experimental studies of conflict. In J. McV. Hunt (Ed.), *Personality and the behavior disorders* (Vol. 1). New York: Ronald.

Miller, N. E. (1959). Liberalization of basic S-R concepts: Extension to conflict behavior, motivation, and social learning. In S. Koch (Ed.), *Psychology: A study of a science.* (Vol. 2). New York: McGraw-Hill.

Miller, R. S. (1991). On decorum in close relationships: Why aren't we polite to those we love? *Contemporary Social Psychology, 15,* 63–65.

Miller, T. Q., Smith, T. W., Turner, C. W., Guijarro, M. L., & Hallet, A. J. (1996). A meta-analytic review of research on hostility and physical health. *Psychological Bulletin, 119,* 322–348.

Miller, T. Q., Turner, C. W., Tindale, R. S., Posavac, E. J., & Dugoni, B. L. (1991). Reasons for the trend toward null findings in research on Type A behavior. *Psychological Bulletin, 110,* 469–485.

Miller, T. W. (Ed.). (1989). *Stressful life events.* Madison, CT: International Universities Press.

Millett, K. (1970). *Sexual politics.* Garden City, NY: Doubleday.

Milletti, M. A. (1984). *Voices of experience: 1500 retired people talk about retirement.* New York: Teachers Insurance Annuity Association/College Retirement Equity Fund.

Millstein, S. G., & Litt, I. F. (1990). At the threshold: The developing adolescent. In S. S. Feldman & G. R. Elliott (Eds.), *At the threshold: The developing adolescent.* Cambridge, MA: Harvard University Press.

Minuchin, S., Rosman, B. L., & Baker, L. (1978). *Psychosomatic families: Anorexia nervosa in context.* Cambridge, MA: Harvard University Press.

Mischel, W. (1973). Toward a cognitive social learning conceptualization of personality. *Psychological Review, 80,* 252–283.

Mischel, W. (1990). Personality dispositions revisited and revised: A view after three decades. In L. A. Pervin (Ed.), *Handbook of personality: Theory and research.* New York: Guilford Press.

Mischel, W., & Mischel, H. N. (1976). A cognitive social learning approach to morality and self-regulation. In T. Lickona (Ed.), *Moral development and behavior: Theory, research and social issues.* New York: Holt, Rinehart & Winston.

Mitchell, J. E. (1995). Medical complications of bulimia nervosa. In K. D. Brownell & C. G. Fairburn (Eds.), *Eating disorders and obesity: A comprehensive handbook.* New York: Guilford Press.

Mitchell, V. F. (1987). Rx for improving staff effectiveness. In A. D. Timpe (Ed.), *The management of time.* New York: Facts On File.

Modestin, J. (1992). Multiple personality disorder in Switzerland. *American Journal of Psychiatry, 149,* 88–92.

Moghaddam, F. M., Taylor, D. M., & Wright, S. C. (1993). *Social psychology in cross-cultural perspective.* New York: Freeman.

Monroe, S. M., & Kelley, J. M. (1995). Measurement of stress appraisal. In S. Cohen, R. C. Kessler, & L. U. Gordon (Eds.), *Measuring stress: A guide for health and social scientists.* New York: Oxford University Press.

Monroe, S. M., & McQuaid, J. R. (1994). Measuring life stress and assessing its impact on mental health. In W. R. Avison & I. H. Gotlib (Eds.), *Stress and mental health: Contemporary issues and prospects for the future.* New York: Plenum.

Monroe, S. M., & Simons, A. D. (1991). Diathesis-stress theories in the context of life stress research: Implications for the depressive disorders. *Psychological Bulletin, 110,* 406–425.

Monroe, S. M., Roberts, J. E., Kupfer, D., & Frank, I. Life stress and treatment of current depression. *Journal of Abnormal Psychology, 105,* 313–328.

Montepare, J. M., & Zebrowitz-McArthur, L. (1987). Perceptions of adults with childlike voices in two cultures. *Journal of Experimental Social Psychology, 23* 331–349.

Moore, D. S., & Erickson, P. I. (1985). Age, gender, and ethnic differences in sexual and contraceptive knowledge, attitudes, and behaviors. *Family and Community Health, 8(3),* 38–51.

Moore, D. W. (1993, April). Public polarized on gay issue. *The Gallup Poll Monthly,* pp. 30–34.

Moore, D. W. (1994, May). One in seven Americans victim of child abuse. *The Gallup Poll Monthly,* pp. 18–22.

Moore, D. W. (1996, April). Public opposes gay marriages. *The Gallop Poll Monthly,* 19–21.

Moore, D. W., & McAneny, L. (1993, May). Workers concerned they can't afford to retire. *The Gallup Poll Monthly,* pp. 16–25.

Moore, M. K. (1992). An empirical investigation of the relationship between religiosity and death concern. *Dissertation Abstracts International, 53,* 527.

Moore, N. B., & Davidson, J. K. (1997). Guilt about first intercourse: An antecedent of sexual dissatisfaction among college women. *Journal of Sex and Marital Therapy, 23,* 29–46.

Moore, T. E. (1982). Subliminal advertising: What you see is what you get. *Journal of Marketing, 46,* 38–47.

Moos, R. H., & Billings, A. G. (1982). Conceptualizing and measuring coping resources and processes. In L. Goldberger & S. Breznitz (Eds.), *Handbook of stress: Theoretical and clinical aspects.* New York: Free Press.

Moos, R. H., & Schaefer, J. A. (1993). Coping resources and processes: Current concepts and measures. In L. Goldberger & S. Breznitz (Eds.), *Handbook of stress: Theoretical and clinical aspects* (2nd ed.). New York: Free Press.

Morell, M. A., Twillman, R. K., & Sullaway, M. E. (1989). Would a Type A date another Type A? Influence of behavior type and personal attributes in the selection of dating partners. *Journal of Applied Social Psychology, 19,* 918–931.

Moretti, M. M., & Higgins, E. T. (1990). Relating self-discrepancy to self-esteem: The contribution of discrepancy beyond actual-self ratings. *Journal of Experimental Social Psychology, 26,* 108–123.

Morgan, H. J., & Janoff-Bulman, R. (1994). Victims' responses to traumatic life events: An unjust world or an uncaring world? *Social Justice Research, 7,* 47–68.

Morgan, J. P. (1992). Controlled substance analogues: Current clinical and social issues. In J. H. Lowinson, P. Ruiz, & R. B. Millman (Eds.), *Substance abuse: A comprehensive textbook* (2nd ed.). Baltimore: Williams & Wilkins.

Morgan, J. P. (1997). Designer drugs. In J. H. Lowinson, P. Ruiz, R. B. Millman, & J. G. Langrod (Eds.), *Substance abuse: A comprehensive textbook* (3rd ed.). Baltimore: Williams & Wilkins.

Morris, M. W., & Peng, K. (1994). Culture and cause: American and Chinese attributions for social and physical events. *Journal of Personality and Social Psychology, 67,* 949–971.

Morrison, A. M., & Von Glinow, M. A. (1990). Women and minorities in management. *American Psychologist, 45,* 200–208.

Morrison, D. R., & Cherlin, A. J. (1995). The divorce process and young children's well-being: A prospective analysis. *Journal of Marriage and the Family, 57,* 800–812.

Morrison, E. W., & Bies, R. J. (1991). Impression management in the feedback-seeking process: A literature review and research agenda. *Academy of Management Review, 16,* 322–341.

Morrow, L. (1993, March 29). The temping of America. *Time,* pp. 40–44, 46–47.

Morse, S., & Gergen, K. J. (1970). Social comparison, self-consistency, and the concept of self. *Journal of Personality and Social Psychology, 16,* 148–156.

Mortimer, J. T., & Borman, K. M. (1988). *Work experience and psychological development through the life span.* Boulder, CO: Westview Press.

Mosher, D. L. (1991). Macho men, machismo, and sexuality. *Annual Review of Sex Research, 2,* 199–248.

Mosher, D. L., & Anderson, R. D. (1986). Macho personality, sexual aggression, and reactions to guided imagery of realistic rape. *Journal of Research in Personality, 20,* 77–94.

Moskowitz, H. (1985). Marijuana and driving. *Accident Analysis & Prevention, 17,* 323–345.

Mowrer, O. H. (1947). On the dual nature of learning: A reinterpretaton of "conditioning" and "problem-solving." *Harvard Educational Review, 17,* 102–150.

Moynihan, J. A., & Ader, R. (1996). Psychoneuroimmunology: Animal models of disease. *Psychosomatic Medicine, 58,* 546–558.

Mrazek, P. B., & Mrazek, D. A. (1978). The effects of child sexual abuse. In R. S. Kempe & C. H. Kempe (Eds.), *Child abuse.* Cambridge, MA: Harvard University Press.

Muehlenhard, C. L. (1988). Misinterpreted dating behaviors and the risk of date rape. *Journal of Social and Clinical Psychology, 6,* 20–37.

Muehlenhard, C. L., & Hollabaugh, L. C. (1988). Do women sometimes say no when they mean yes? The prevalence and correlates of women's token resistance to sex. *Journal of Personality and Social Psychology, 54,* 872–879.

Muehlenhard, C. L., & Linton, M. A. (1987). Date rape and sexual aggression in dating situations: Incidence and risk factors. *Journal of Counseling Psychology, 34,* 186–196.

Muehlenhard, C. L., & McCoy, M. L. (1991). Double standard/double bind: The sexual double standard and women's communication about sex. *Psychology of Women Quarterly, 15,* 447–461.

Mukherjee, S., Sackeim, H. A., & Schnur, D. B. (1994). Electroconvulsive therapy of acute manic episodes: A review of 50 years' experience. *American Journal of Psychiatry, 151,* 169–176.

Muldoon, M. F., Manuck, S. B., & Matthews, K. A. (1990). Effects of cholesterol lowering on mortality: A quantitative review of primary prevention trials. *British Medical Journal, 301,* 309–314.

Mullen, B., & Baumeister, R. F. (1987). Group effects on self-attention and performance: Social loafing, social facilitation, and social impairment. In C. Hendrick (Ed.), *Group processes and intergroup relations* (Vol. 9). Newbury Park, CA: Sage Publications.

Mullen, B., & Felleman, B. (1990). Tripling in the dorms: A meta-analytic integration. *Basic and Applied Social Psychology, 11,* 33–44.

Mullen, P. E., Martin, J. L., Anderson, J. C., Romans, S. E., & Herbison, G. P. (1996). The long-term impact of the physical, emotional, and sexual abuse of children: A community study. *Child Abuse and Neglect, 20,* 7–21.

Mullis, R. L., Youngs, G. A., Mullis, A. K., & Rathge, R. (1993). Adolescent stress: Issues of measurement. *Adolescence, 28,* 267–279.

Munroe, R. L., & Munroe, R. H. (1975). *Cross-cultural human development.* Pacific Grove, CA: Brooks/Cole.

Murphy, J. M., & Helzer, J. E. (1986). Epidemiology of schizophrenia in adulthood. In G. L. Klerman, M. M. Weissman, P. S. Appelbaum, & L. H. Roth (Eds.), *Psychiatry: Vol. 5. Social, epidemiologic, and legal psychiatry.* New York: Basic Books.

Murphy, K., & Welch, F. (1989). Wage premiums for college graduates: Recent growth and possible explanations. *Educational Researcher, 18,* 17–26.

Murphy, M., Glaser, K., & Grundy, E. (1997). Marital status and long-term illness in Great Britain. *Journal of Marriage and the Family, 59,* 156–164.

Murphy, S. P., Rose, D., Hudes, M., & Viteri, F. E. (1992). Demographic and economic factors associated with dietary quality for adults in the 1987–88 nationwide food consumption theory. *Journal of the American Diet Association, 92,* 1352–1357.

Murphy, W. D., Coleman, E. M., & Haynes, M. R. (1986). Factors related to coercive sexual behavior in a nonclinical sample of males. *Violence and Victims, 1,* 255–278.

Murstein, B. I. (1976). *Who will marry whom? Theories and research in marital choice.* New York: Springer.

Murstein, B. I. (1986). *Paths to marriage.* Newbury Park, CA: Sage Publications.

Murstein, B., & Mercy, T. (1994). Sex, drugs, relationships, contraception, and fears of disease on a college campus over 17 years. *Adolescence, 29,* 303–322.

Myers, D. G. (1980). *Inflated self: Human illusions and the biblical call to hope.* New York: Seabury Press.

Myers, D. G. (1992). *The pursuit of happiness: Who is happy—and why.* New York: Morrow.

Myers, D. G., & Diener, E. (1995). Who is happy? *Psychological Science, 6,* 10–19.

Myers, D. G., & Diener, E. (1997). The pursuit of happiness. *Scientific American, Special Issue 7,* 40–43.

Nahas, G. G. (1976). *Marijuana: Chemistry, biochemistry and cellular effects.* New York: Springer.

Narrow, W. E., Regier, D. A., Rae, D. S., Manderscheid, R. W., & Locke, B. Z. (1993). Use of services by persons with mental and addictive disorders: Findings from the National Institute of Mental Health Epidemiologic Catchment Area Program. *Archives of General Psychiatry, 50,* 95–107.

Nass, G. D., Libby, R. W., & Fisher, M. P. (1981). *Sexual choices: An introduction to human sexuality.* Monterey, CA: Brooks/Cole.

Nathan, K. I., Musselman, D. L., Schatzberg A. F., & Nemeroff, C. B. (1995). Biology of mood disorders. In A. F. Schatzberg & C. B. Nemeroff (Eds.), *The American Psychiatric Press textbook of psychopharmacology.* Washington, DC: American Psychiatric Press.

Nathan, P. E. (1993). Alcoholism: Psychopathology, etiology, and treatment. In P. B. Sutker & H. E. Adams (Eds.), *Comprehensive handbook of psychopathology.* New York: Plenum Press.

National Abortion and Reproductive Rights Action League. (1995). *Sexuality education in America: A state-by-state review.* NARRAL.

National Institute on Alcohol Abuse and Alcoholism. (1991). *Alcohol alert 11: Estimating the economic cost of alcohol abuse.* Rockville, MD: Author.

Naughton, T. J. (1987). A conceptual view of workaholism and implications for career counseling and research. *The Career Development Quarterly, 35,* 180–187.

Naveh-Benjamin, M., Lavi, H., McKeachie, W. J., & Lin, Y. (1997). Individual differences in students' retention of knowledge and conceptual structures learned in university and high school courses: The case of test anxiety. *Applied Cognitive Psychology, 11,* 507–526.

Naylor, T. H., Willimon, W. H., & Naylor, M. R. (1994). *The search for meaning.* Nashville: Abingdon Press.

Neimeyer, R. A., & Van Brunt, D. (1995). Death anxiety. In H. Wass & R. A. Neimeyer (Eds.), *Dying: Facing the facts* (3rd ed.). Washington, DC: Taylor & Francis.

Neiss, R. (1988). Reconceptualizing arousal: Psychobiological states in motor performance. *Psychological Bulletin, 103,* 345–366.

Neiss, R. (1990). Ending arousal's reign of error: A reply to Anderson. *Psychological Bulletin, 107,* 101–105.

Nemeroff, C. B. (1998, June). The neurobiology of depression. *Scientific American,* 42–49.

Nemeth, C., & Chiles, C. (1988). Modelling courage: The role dissent in fostering independence. *European Journal of Social Psychology, 18,* 275–280.

Nemiah, J. C. (1985). Somatoform disorders. In H. I. Kaplan & B. J. Sadock (Eds.), *Comprehensive textbook of psychiatry/IV.* Baltimore: Williams & Wilkins.

Neugebauer, R., Dohrenwend, B. P., & Dohrenwend, B. S. (1980). Formulation about hypotheses about the true prevalence of functional psychiatric disorders among adults in the United States. In B. P. Dohrenwend, B. S. Dohrenwend, M. S. Gould, B. Link, R. Neugebauer, & R. Wunsch-Hitzig (Eds.), *Mental illness in the United States: Epidemiological estimates.* New York: Praeger.

Nevid, J. S. (1984). Sex differences in factors of romantic attraction. *Sex Roles, 11,* 401–411.

Newcomb, M. D. (1990). Social support and personal characteristics: A developmental and interactional perspective. *Journal of Social and Clinical Psychology, 9*, 54–68.

Newcomb, P. A., & Carbone, P. P. (1992). The health consequences of smoking: Cancer. *Medical Clinics of North America, 76*, 305–331.

Newell, G. R. (1991, May). Stress and cancer. *Primary Care and Cancer, 29–30*.

Newman, M., & Berkowitz, B. (1976). *How to be awake and alive*. Westminster, MD: Ballantine.

Newsom, C., Favell, J. E., & Rincover, A. (1983). Side effects of punishment. In S. Axelrod & J. Apsche (Eds.), *The effects of punishment on human behavior*. New York: Academic Press.

Nezu, A. M. (1986). Efficacy of a social-problem therapy approach for unipolar depression. *Journal of Consulting and Clinical Psychology, 54*, 196–202.

Nichols, M. (1990). Lesbian relationships: Implications for the study of sexuality and gender. In D. P. McWhirter, S. A. Sanders, & J. M. Reinisch (Eds.), *Homosexuality/heterosexuality: Concepts of sexual orientation*. New York: Oxford University Press.

Nicholson, I. R., & Neufeld, R. W. J. (1993). Classification of the schizophrenias according to symptomatology: A two-factor model. *Journal of Abnormal Psychology, 102*, 259–270.

Nielsen, J. M. (1990). *Sex and gender in society: Perspective on stratification* (2nd ed.). Prospect Heights, IL: Waveland.

Niemann, Y. F., Jennings, L., Rozelle, R. M., Baxter, J. C., & Sullivan, E. (1994). Use of free responses and cluster analysis to determine stereotypes of eight groups. *Personality and Social Psychology Bulletin, 20*, 379–390.

Nock, S. L. (1995). A comparison of marriages and cohabiting relationships. *Journal of Family Issues, 13*, 53–76.

Noel, J. G., Wann, D. L., & Branscombe, N. R. (1995). Peripheral ingroup membership status and public negativity toward outgroups. *Journal of Personality and Social Psychology, 68*, 127–137.

Noel, J. G., Wann, D. L., & Branscombe, N. R. (1995). Peripheral ingroup membership status and public negativity toward outgroups. *Journal of Personality and Social Psychology, 68*, 127–137.

Nolen-Hoeksema, S. (1991). Responses to depression and their effects on the duration of depressive episodes. *Journal of Abnormal Psychology, 100*, 569–582.

Nolen-Hoeksema, S., & Girgus, J. S. (1994). The emergence of gender differences in depression during adolescence. *Psychological Bulletin, 115*, 424–443.

Nolen-Hoeksema, S., Girgus, J. S., & Seligman, M. E. P. (1992). Predictors and consequences of childhood depressive symptoms: A 5-year longitudinal study. *Journal of Abnormal Psychology, 101*, 405–422.

Nolen-Hoeksema, S., & Morrow, J. (1991). A prospective study of depression and posttraumatic stress symptoms after a natural disaster: The 1989 Loma Prieta earthquake. *Journal of Personality and Social Psychology, 61*, 115–121.

Nolen-Hoeksema, S., Morrow, J., & Fredrickson, B. L. (1993). Response styles and the duration of episodes of depressed mood. *Journal of Abnormal Psychology, 102*, 20–28.

Noller, P. (1985). Negative communications in marriage. *Journal of Social and Personal Relationships, 2*, 289–301.

Noller, P. (1987). Nonverbal communication in marriage. In D. Perlman & S. Duck (Eds.), *Intimate relationships: Development, dynamics, and deterioration*. Newbury Park, CA: Sage Publications.

Noller, P., & Fitzpatrick, M. A. (1990). Marital communication in the eighties. *Journal of Marriage and the Family, 52*, 832–843.

Noller, P., & Gallois, C. (1988). Understanding and misunderstanding in marriage: Sex and marital adjustment differences in structured and free interaction. In P. Noller & M. A. Fitzpatrick (Eds.), *Perspectives on marital interaction*. Clevedon, England: Multilingual Matters.

Noller, P., & Guthrie, D. (1991). Studying communication in marriage: An integration and critical evaluation. In W. H. Jones, & D. Perlman (Eds.), *Advances in personal relationships* (Vol. 3). London: Jessica Kingsley.

Noller, P., Feeney, J. A., Bonnell, D., & Callan, V. (1994). A longitudinal study of conflict in early marriage. *Journal of Social and Personal Relationships, 11*, 233–252.

Nopoulos, P., Flaum, M., & Andreasen, N. C. (1997). Sex differences in brain morphology in schizophrenia. *American Journal of Psychiatry, 154*, 1648–1654.

Norcross, J. C., & Goldfried, M. R. (Eds.). (1992). *Handbook of psychotherapy integration*. New York: Basic Books.

Norcross, J. C., & Prochaska, J. O. (1982). National survey of clinical psychologists: Affiliations and orientations. *Clinical Psychologist, 35, 1*, 4–6.

Norcross, J. C. (1995). Dispelling the dodo bird verdict and the exclusivity myth in psychotherapy. *Psychotherapy, 32*, 500–504.

Norman, T. R., & Burrows, G. D. (1990). Buspirone for the treatment of generalized anxiety disorder. In R. Noyes, Jr., M. Roth, & G. D. Burrows (Eds.), *Handbook of anxiety: The treatment of anxiety* (Vol. 4). Amsterdam: Elsevier.

Novaco, R. W., Stokols, D., & Milanesi, L. (1990). Objective and subjective dimensions of travel impedance as determinants of commuting stress. *American Journal of Community Psychology, 18*, 231–257.

Novello, A. (1992, March 23). The domestic violence issue: Hear our voices. *American Medical News, 35*, 41–42.

Novello, A., Rosenberg, M., Saltzman, L., & Shosky, J. (1992). From the Surgeon General, U.S. Public Health Service. *The Journal of the American Medical Association, 267*, 3132.

Noyes, R. Jr. (1988). Revision of the DSM-III classification of anxiety disorders. In R. Noyes, Jr., M. Roth, & G. D. Burrows (Eds.), *Handbook of anxiety: Classification, etiological factors and associated disturbances* (Vol. 2). Amsterdam: Elsevier.

Nurnberger, J. I., & Gershon, E. S. (1992). Genetics. In E. S. Paykel (Ed.), *Handbook of affective disorders* (2nd ed.). New York: Guilford Press.

Nurnberger, J. I., & Zimmerman, J. (1970). Applied analysis of human behavior: An alternative to conventional motivational inferences and unconscious determination in therapeutic programming. *Behavior Therapy, 1*, 59–69.

Nye, R. D. (1992). *Three psychologies: Perspectives from Freud, Skinner, and Rogers*. Pacific Grove, CA: Brooks/Cole.

O'Brien, C. P., & Woody, G. E. (1986). Sedative-hypnotics and antianxiety agents. In A. J. Frances & R. E. Hales (Eds.), *Psychiatric Update: Annual Review* (Vol. 5). Washington, DC: American Psychiatric Press.

O'Brien, P. E., & Gaborit, M. (1992). Codependency: A disorder separate from chemical dependency. *Journal of Clinical Psychology, 48*, 129–136.

O'Donohue, W., & Crouch, J. L. (1996). Marital therapy and gender-linked factors in communication. *Journal of Marital and Family Therapy, 22*, 87–101.

Offer, D., Ostrov, E., Howard, K. I., & Atkinson, R. (1988). *The teenage world: Adolescents' self-image in ten countries*. New York: Plenum.

Offermann, L. R., & Gowing, M. K. (1990). Organizations of the future: Changes and challenges. *American Psychologist, 45*, 95–108.

Ohman, A., & Soares, J. J. F. (1993). On the automatic nature of phobic fear: Conditioned electrodermal responses to masked fear-relevant stimuli. *Journal of Abnormal Psychology, 102*, 121–132.

O'Keefe, D. J. (1990). *Persuasion: Theory and research*. Newbury Park, CA: Sage Publications.

O'Keefe, M. (1994). Adjustment of children from maritally violent homes. *Families in Society: The Journal of Contemporary Human Services, 75*, 403–415.

Okun, L. (1985). *Woman abuse*. Albany, NY: SUNY Press.

Olden, K. W. (1998). Stress and the gastrointestinal tract. In J. R. Hubbard & E. A. Workman (Eds.), *Handbook of stress medicine: An organ system approach*. New York: CRC Press.

Olfson, M., & Pincus, H. A. (1994). Outpatient psychotherapy in the United States, I: Volume, costs, and user characteristics. *American Journal of Psychiatry, 151*, 1281–1288.

Olfson, M., & Pincus, H. A. (1996). Outpatient mental health care in nonhospital settings: Distribution of patients across provider groups. *American Journal of Psychiatry, 153*, 1353–1356.

Olio, K. (1994). Truth in memory. *American Psychologist, 49*, 442–443.

Oliver, M. B., & Hyde, J. S. (1993). Gender differences in sexuality: A meta-analysis. *Psychological Bulletin, 114*, 29–51.

Olmstead, R. E., Guy, S. M., O'Malley, P. M., & Bentley, P. M. (1991). Longitudinal assessment of the relationship between self-esteem, fatalism, loneliness and substance use. *Journal of Social Behavior and Personality, 6*, 749–770.

O'Neil, R., & Greenberger, E. (1994). Patterns of commitment to work and parenting: Implications for role strain. *Journal of Marriage and the Family, 56*, 101–118.

Ono, H. (1998). Husbands' and wives' resources and marital dissolution. *Journal of Marriage and the Family, 60*, 674–689.

Oppenheimer, V. K. (1988). A theory of marriage timing. *American Journal of Sociology, 94*, 563–591.

Orbuch, T. L., House, J. S., Mero, R. P., & Webster, P. S. (1996). Marital quality over the life course. *Social Psychology Quarterly, 59*, 162–171.

Orenstein, P. (1994). *School girls: Young women, self-esteem, and the confidence gap*. New York: Doubleday.

Organista, P. B., & Miranda, J. (1991). Psychosomatic symptoms in medical outpatients: An investigation of self-handicapping theory. *Health Psychology, 10*, 427–431.

Orleans, C. T., Rimer, B. K., Cristinzio, S., Keintz, M. K., & Fleisher, L. (1991). A national survey of older smokers: Treatment needs of a growing population. *Health Psychology, 10*, 343–351.

Orlofsky, J. L., Marcia, J. E., & Lesser, I. M. (1973). Ego identity status and the intimacy versus isolation crisis of young adulthood. *Journal of Personality and Social Psychology, 27*, 211–219.

Orme-Johnson, D. W. (1987). Transcendental Meditation and reduced health care utilization. *Psychosomatic Medicine, 49*, 493–507.

Osipow, S. H. (1987). Counseling psychology: Theory, research, and practice in career counseling. *Annual Review of Psychology, 38*, 257–278.

Ouellette, S. C. (1993). Inquiries into hardiness. In L. Goldberger & S. Breznitz (Eds.), *Handbook of stress: Theoretical and clinical aspects* (2nd ed.). New York: Free Press.

Ozer, D. J., & Reise, S. P. (1994). Personality assessment. *Annual Review of Psychology, 45,* 357–388.

Ozer, E. M., & Bandura, A. (1990). Mechanisms governing empowerment effects: A self-efficacy analysis. *Journal of Personality and Social Psychology, 58,* 472–486.

Pachman, J. S. (1996). The dawn of a revolution in mental health. *American Psychologist, 51,* 213–215.

Packard, V. (1972). *A nation of strangers.* New York: David McKay.

Pagel, M. D., Erdly, W. W., & Becker, J. (1987). Social networks: We get by with (and in spite of) a little help from our friends. *Journal of Personality and Social Psychology, 53* 793–804.

Pagel, M.D., Smilkstein, G., Regen, H., & Montano, D. (1990). Psychosocial influences on newborn outcomes: A controlled prospective study. *Social Science Medicine, 30,* 597–604.

Pagelow, M. D. (1992). Adult victims of domestic violence: Battered women. *Journal of Interpersonal Violence, 7,* 87–120.

Painter, K. (1997, February 25). "Morning-after pill" receives FDA backing. *USA Today, 1.*

Paivio, A. (1986). *Mental representations: A dual coding approach.* New York: Oxford University Press.

Palkovitz, R. J., & Lore, R. K. (1980). Note taking and note review: Why students fail questions based on lecture material. *Teaching of Psychology, 7,* 159–161.

Pallak, S. R. (1983). Salience of a communicator's physical attractiveness and persuasion: A heuristic versus systematic processing interpretation. *Social Cognition, 2,* 158–170.

Palmore, E. B., Burchett, B. M., Fillenbaum, C. G., George. L. K., & Wallman, L. M. (1985). *Retirement: Causes and consequences.* New York: Springer.

Papalia, D. E., & Olds, C. W. (1994). *Human Development* (6th ed.). New York: McGraw-Hill.

Pardeck, J. T. (1991). Using books in clinical practice. *Psychotherapy in Private Practice, 9,* 105–119.

Park, C. C., & Shapiro, L. N. (1979). *You are not alone: Understanding and dealing with mental illness.* Boston: Little, Brown.

Park, C. L., Cohen, L. H., & Murch, R. L. (1996). Assessment and prediction of stress-related growth. *Journal of Personality, 64,* 71–105.

Park, C. W., & Young, S. M. (1986). Consumer response to television commercials: The impact of involvement and background music on brand attitude formation. *Journal of Marketing Research, 23* 11–24.

Parker, G., & Hadzi-Pavlovic, D. (1990). Expressed emotion as a predictor of schizophrenic relapse: An analysis of aggregated data. *Psychological Medicine, 20,* 961–965.

Parlee, M.B., & the editors of Psychology Today. (1979, September). The friendship bond: PT's survey report on friendship in America. *Psychology Today,* pp. 43–54, 113.

Parrott, W. G., & Smith, R. H. (1993). Distinguishing the experiences of envy and jealousy. *Journal of Personality and Social Psychology, 64,* 906–920.

Parry-Jones, B., & Parry-Jones, W. L. (1995). History of bulimia and bulimia nervosa. In K. D. Brownell & C. G. Fairburn (Eds.), *Eating disorders and obesity: A comprehensive handbook.* New York: Guilford Press.

Parsons, T. (1979). Definitions of health and illness in light of the American values and social structure. In E. G. Jaco (Ed.), *Patients, physicians and illness: A sourcebook in behavioral science and health.* New York: Free Press.

Pasley, K., Ihinger-Tallman, M., & Lofquist, A. (1994). Remarriage and stepfamilies: Making progress in understanding. In K. Pasley & M. Ihinger-Tallman (Eds.), *Stepparenting: Issues in theory, research, and practice.* Westport, CT: Greenwood Press.

Pate, R. R., & Macera, C. A. (1994). Risks of exercising: Musculoskeletal injuries. In C. Bouchard, R. J. Shepard, & T. Stephens (Eds.), *Physical activity, fitness, and health: International proceedings and consensus statement.* Champaign, IL: Human Kinetics.

Patterson, C. (1992). Children of lesbian and gay parents. *Child Development, 63,* 1025–1042.

Patterson, M. L. (1988). Functions of nonverbal behavior in close relationships. In S. Duck (Ed.), *Handbook of personal relationships: Theory, research, and interventions.* New York: Wiley.

Patton, G. C., Johnson-Sabine, E., Wood, K., Mann, A. H., & Wakeling, A. (1990). Abnormal eating attitudes in London schoolgirls—A prospective epidemiological study: Outcome at twelve month follow-up. *Psychological Medicine, 20,* 383–394.

Paulhus, D. L. (1989). Socially desirable responding: Some new solutions to old problems. In D. M. Buss & N. Cantor (Eds.), *Personality psychology: Recent trends and emerging directions.* New York: Springer-Verlag.

Paulhus, D. L. (1991). Measurement and control of response bias. In J. P. Robinson, P. Shaver, & L. S. Wrightsman (Eds.), *Measures of personality and social psychological attitudes.* San Diego: Academic Press.

Paulhus, D. L., Fridhandler, B., & Hayes, S. (1997). Psychological defense: Contemporary theory and research. In R. Hogan, J. Johnson, & S. Briggs (Eds), *Handbook of personality psychology.* San Diego, CA: Academic Press.

Pauls, D. L., Alsobrook, J. P., II, Goodman, W., Rasmussen, S., & Leckman, J. F. (1995). A family study of obsessive-compulsive disorder. *American Journal of Psychiatry, 152,* 76–84.

Pavlov, I. P. (1906). The scientific investigation of psychical faculties or processes in the higher animals. *Science, 24,* 613–619.

Payne, D. G., & Wenger, M. J. (1996). Practice effects in memory: Data, theory, and unanswered questions. In D. J. Herrmann, C. McEvoy, C. Hertzog, P. Hertel, & M. K. Johnson (Eds.), *Basic and applied memory research: Practical applications* (Vol. 2). Mahwah, NJ: Erlbaum.

Pearce, L. (1974). Duck! It's the new journalism. *New Times, 2,* 40–41.

Pechnick, R. N., & Ungerleider, J. T. (1997). Hallucinogens. In J. H. Lowinson, P. Ruiz, R. B. Millman, & J. G. Langrod (Eds.), *Substance abuse: A comprehensive textbook* (3rd ed.). Baltimore: Williams & Wilkins.

Peirce, R. S., Frone, M. R., Russell, M., & Cooper, M. L. (1996). Financial stress, social support, and alcohol involvement: A longitudinal test of the buffering hypothesis in a general population survey. *Health Psychology, 15,* 38–47.

Pekarik, G. (1993). Beyond effectiveness: Uses of consumer-oriented criteria in defining treatment success. In T. R. Giles (Ed.), *Handbook of effective psychotherapy.* New York: Plenum.

Penn, D. L., & Mueser, K. T. (1996). Research update on the psychosocial treatment of schizophrenia. *American Journal of Psychiatry, 153,* 607–617.

Pennebaker, J. W., Colder, M., & Sharp, L. K. (1990). Accelerating the coping process. *Journal of Personality and Social Psychology, 58,* 528–537.

Peplau, L. A. (1988). Research on homosexual couples: An overview. In J. P. De Cecco (Ed.), *Gay relationships.* New York: Harrington Park Press.

Peplau, L. A. (1991). Lesbian and gay relationships. In J. C. Gonsiorek & J. D. Weinrich (Eds.), *Homosexuality: Research implications for public policy.* Newbury Park, CA: Sage Publications.

Peplau, L. A., & Cochran, S. D. (1990). A relational perspective on homosexuality. In D. P. McWhirter, S. A. Sanders, & J. M. Reinisch (Eds.), *Homosexuality/heterosexuality: Concepts of sexual orientation.* New York: Oxford University Press.

Peplau, L. A., Hill, C. T., & Rubin, Z. (1993). Sex role attitudes in dating and marriage: A 15-year follow-up of the Boston couples study. *Journal of Social Issues, 49,* 31–52.

Perlman, D., & Oskamp, S. (1971). The effects of picture context and exposure frequency on evaluations of negroes and whites. *Journal of Experimental and Social Psychology, 7,* 503–514.

Perloff, R. M. (1993). *The dynamics of persuasion.* Hillsdale, NJ: Erlbaum.

Perry, W., & Braff, D. L. (1994). Information-processing deficits and thought disorder in schizophrenia. *American Journal of Psychiatry, 151,* 363–367.

Pervin, L. A. (1994). Personality stability, personality change, and the question of process. In T. F. Heatherton & J. L. Weinberger (Eds.), *Can personality change?* Washington, DC: American Psychological Association.

Petersen, A. C. (1987, September). Those gangly years. *Psychology Today,* pp. 28–34.

Petersen, A. C. (1988). Adolescent development. *Annual Review of Psychology, 39,* 583–607.

Petersen, A. C., Compas, B. E., Brooks-Gunn, J., Stemmler, M., Ey, S., & Grant, K. E. (1993). Depression in adolescence. *American Psychologist, 48,* 155–168.

Peterson, C., Maier, S. F., & Seligman, M. E. P. (1993). *Learned helplessness: A theory for the age of personal control.* New York: Oxford University Press.

Peterson, C., & Seligman, M. E. P. (1984). Causal explanations as a risk factor for depression: Theory and evidence. *Psychological Review, 91,* 347–374.

Peterson, C., Seligman, M. E. P., & Vaillant, G. E. (1988). Pessimistic explanatory style is a risk factor for physical illness: A thirty-five-year longitudinal study. *Journal of Personality and Social Psychology, 55,* 23–27.

Peterson, C., Seligman, M. E. P., Yurko, K. H., Martin, L. R., & Friedman, H. S. (1998). Catastrophizing and untimely death. *Psychological Science, 9,* 127–130.

Peterson, R. R. (1996). A reevaluation of the economic consequences of divorce. *American Sociological Review, 61,* 528–536.

Petras, R., & Petras, K. (1993). *The 776 stupidest things ever said.* New York: Doubleday.

Pettigrew, T. F. (1979). The ultimate attribution error: Extending Allport's cognitive analysis of prejudice. *Personality and Social Psychology Bulletin, 5,* 461–476.

Pettigrew, T. F., & Meertens, R. W. (1995). Subtle and blatant prejudice in Western Europe. *European Journal of Social Psychology, 25,* 57–75.

Petty, R. E., & Cacioppo, J. T. (1979). Effects of forewarning of persuasive intent and involvement on cognitive responses and persuasion. *Personality and Social Psychology Bulletin, 5,* 173–176.

Petty, R. E., & Cacioppo, J. T. (1986). The elaboration likelihood model of persuasion. In L.

Berkowitz (Ed.), *Advances in experimental social psychology* (Vol. 19). Orlando, FL: Academic Press.

Petty, R. E., & Cacioppo, J. T. (1990). Involvement and persuasion: Tradition versus integration. *Psychological Bulletin, 107,* 367–374.

Petty, R. E., Priester, J. R., & Wegener, D. T. (1994). Cognitive processes in attitude change. In R. S. Wyer & T. K. Srull (Eds.), *Handbook of social cognition* (Vol. 2). Hillsdale, NJ: Erlbaum.

Peyser, H. S. (1993). Stress, ethyl alcohol, and alcoholism. In L. Goldberger & S. Breznitz (Eds.), *Handbook of stress: Theoretical and clinical aspects* (2nd ed.). New York: Free Press.

Pfau, M., Kenski, H. C., Nitz, M., & Sorenson, J. (1990). Efficacy of inoculation strategies in promoting resistance to political attack messages: Application to direct mail. *Communication Monographs, 57,* 25–43.

Phelps, S., & Austin, N. (1997). *The assertive woman.* San Luis Obispo, CA: Impact.

Phinney, J. (1989). Stage of ethnic identity in minority group adolescents. *Journal of Early Adolescence, 9,* 34–49.

Phinney, J. (1990). Ethnic identity in adolescents and adults. *Psychological Bulletin, 108,* 499–514.

Pickar, D., Perkins, D. O., Ayuso-Gutierrez, J. L., Jeste, D. V., Wong, J., & Liberman, J. A. (1996). Atypical agents ready to replace older antipsychotics. *Primary Psychiatry, 3,* 18–23.

Pickering, T. G., Devereux, R. B., James, G. D., Gerin, W., Landsbergis, P., Schnall, P. L., & Schwartz, J. E. (1996). Environmental influences on blood pressure and the role of job strain. *Journal of Hypertension, 14,* S179–S185.

Pike, K. M., & Rodin, J. (1991). Mothers, daughters, and disordered eating. *Journal of Abnormal Psychology, 100,* 198–294.

Pillow, D. R., West, S. G., & Reich, J. W. (1991). Attributional style in relation to self-esteem and depression: Mediational and interactive models. *Journal of Research in Personality, 25,* 57–69.

Pillow, D. R., Zautra, A. J., & Sandler, I. (1996). Major life events and minor stressors: Identifying mediational links in the stress process. *Journal of Personality and Social Psychology, 70,* 381–394.

Pilowsky, I. (1978). A general classification of abnormal illness behaviors. *British Journal of Psychology, 51,* 131–137.

Pines, A. M. (1993). Burnout. In L. Goldberger & S. Breznitz (Eds.), *Handbook of stress: Theoretical and clinical aspects* (2nd ed.). New York: Free Press.

Pines, A. M., & Aronson, E. (1988). *Career burnout: Causes and cures.* New York: Free Press.

Pines, A. M., Aronson, E., & Kafry, D. (1981). *Burnout: From tedium to personal growth.* New York: Free Press.

Pingitore, R., Dugoni, B. L., Tindale, R. S., & Spring, B. (1994). Bias against overweight job applicants in a simulated employment interview. *Journal of Applied and Social Psychology, 79,* 909–917.

Piper, W. E. (1993). Group psychotherapy research. In H. I. Kaplan & B. J. Sadock (Eds.), *Comprehensive group psychotherapy.* Baltimore: Williams & Wilkins.

Pi-Sunyer, F. X. (1995). Medical complications of obesity. In K. D. Brownell & C. G. Fairburn (Eds.), *Eating disorders and obesity: A comprehensive handbook.* New York: Guilford Press.

Pittman, F., III. (1994, January/February). A buyer's guide to psychotherapy. *Psychology Today,* pp. 50–53, 74–81.

Pittman, J. F., & Lloyd, S. A. (1988). Quality of family life, social support, and stress. *Journal of Marriage and the Family, 50,* 53–67.

Platt, S. (1984). Unemployment and suicidal behaviour: A review of the literature. *Social Science and Medicine, 19,* 93–115.

Pleck, J. H. (1981). *The myth of masculinity.* Cambridge, MA: MIT Press.

Pleck, J. H. (1995). The gender role strain paradigm: An update. In R. F. Levant & W. S. Pollack (Eds.), *A new psychology of men.* New York: Basic Books.

Plomin, R. (1990). *Nature and nurture: An introduction to human behavioral genetics.* Pacific Grove, CA: Brooks/Cole.

Polivy, J., & Herman, C. P. (1995). Dieting and its relation to eating disorders. In K. D. Brownell & C. G. Fairburn (Eds.), *Eating disorders and obesity: A comprehensive handbook.* New York: Guilford Press.

Polivy, J., & Thomsen, L. (1988). Dieting and other eating disorders. In E. A. Blechman & K. D. Brownell (Eds.), *Handbook of behavioral medicine for women.* New York: Pergamon.

Poloma, M. M., & Pendleton, B. F. (1990). Religious domains and general well-being. *Social Indicators Research, 22,* 255–276.

Pope, K. S., & Brown, L. (1996). Recovered memories of abuse: Assessment, therapy, forensics. Washington, D.C.: *American Psychological Association.*

Pope, K. S., Keith-Spiegel, P., & Tabachnick, B. G. (1986). Sexual attraction to clients. *American Psychologist, 41,* 147–158.

Pope, M. K., & Smith, T. W. (1991). Cortisol excretion in high and low cynically hostile men. *Psychosomatic Medicine, 53* 386–392.

Popenoe, D. (1993). American family decline, 1960–1990: A review and appraisal. *Journal of Marriage and the Family, 55,* 527–555.

Poppen, P. J., & Segal, N. J. (1988). The influence of sex and sex role orientation on sexual coercion. *Sex Roles, 19,* 689–701.

Post, R. M. (1989). Mood disorders: Somatic treatment. In H. I. Kaplan & B. J. Sadock (Eds.), *Comprehensive textbook of psychiatry/V* (Vol. 2). Baltimore: Williams & Wilkins.

Potter, W. Z., Manji, H. K., & Rudorfer, M. V. (1995). Tricyclics and tetracyclics. In A. F. Schatzberg & C. B. Nemeroff (Eds.), *The American Psychiatric Press textbook of psychopharmacology.* Washington, DC: American Psychiatric Press.

Potthoff, J. G., Holahan, C. J., & Joiner, T. E., Jr. (1995). Reassurance-seeking, stress generation, and depressive symptoms: An integrative model. *Journal of Personality and Social Psychology, 68,* 664–670.

Pratkanis, A. R., & Aronson, E. (1992). *Age of propaganda: The everyday use and abuse of persuasion.* New York: Freeman.

Pratkanis, A. R., & Aronson, E. (1998). *Age of propaganda: The everyday use and abuse of persuasion.* New York: Freeman.

Pratt, L. A., Ford, D. E., Crum, R. M., Armenian, H. K., Gallo, J. J., & Eaton, W. W. (1996). Depression, psychotropic medication, and risk of myocardial infarction: Prospective data from the Baltimore ECA follow-up. *Archives of Internal Medicine, 94,* 3123–3129.

Prentice-Dunn, S., & Rogers, R. W. (1989). Deindividuation and the self-regulation of behavior. In P. B. Paulis (Ed.), *Psychology of group influence* (2nd ed.). Hillsdale, NJ: Erlbaum.

Pressman, S. (1993). *Outrageous betrayal: The real story of Werner Erhard, Est and the Forum.* New York: St. Martin's Press.

Prest, L. A., & Protinsky, H. (1993). Family systems theory: A unifying framework for code-pendence. *American Journal of Family Therapy, 21,* 352–360.

Price, R., Ryn, M., & Vinokur, A. (1992). Impact of a preventive job search intervention on the likelihood of depression among the unemployed. *Journal of Health and Social Behavior, 33,* 158–167.

Prochaska, J. O., Velicer, W. F., DiClemente, C. C., & Fava, J. (1988). Measuring processes of change: Applications to the cessation of smoking. *Journal of Consulting and Clinical Psychology, 56,* 520–528.

Pryor, F. L., & Schaffer, D. (1997, July). Wages and the university educated: A paradox resolved. *Monthly Labor Review,* 3–14.

Pryor, J. B., Giedd, J. L., & Williams, K. B. (1995). A social psychological model for predicting sexual harassment. *Journal of Social Issues, 51,* 69–84.

Punetha, D., Giles, H., & Young, L. (1987). Ethnicity and immigrant values: Religion and language choice. *Journal of Language and Social Psychology, 6,* 229–241.

Pursell, S. A., & Banikiotes, P. G. (1978). Androgyny and initial interpersonal attraction. *Personality and Social Psychology Bulletin, 4,* 235–243.

Putnam, L. L. (1990). Reframing integrative and distributive bargaining: A process perspective. In B. H. Sheppard, M. H. Bazerman, & R. J. Lewicki (Eds.), *Research on negotiation in organizations* (Vol. 2). Greenwich, CT: JAI Press.

Quillin, P. (1987). *Healing nutrients.* New York: Random House.

Rabbitt, P., & McGinnis, L. (1988). Do clever old people have earlier and richer first memories? *Psychology and Aging, 3* 338–341.

Rabey, S. (1996, April). Where is the Christian men's movement headed? Burgeoning Promise Keepers inspires look-alikes. *Christianity Today,* 46–50.

Rabinowitz, F. E., & Cochran, S. V. (1994). *Man alive: A primer of men's issues.* Pacific Grove, CA: Brooks/Cole.

Rabkin, J. G. (1993). Stress and psychiatric disorders. In L. Goldberger & S. Breznitz (Eds.), *Handbook of stress: Theoretical and clinical aspects* (2nd ed.). New York: Free Press.

Rabkin, J. G., & Streuning E. L. (1976). Life events, stress and illness. *Science, 194,* 1013–1020.

Rachman, S. J. (1990). *Fear and courage.* New York: Freeman.

Rachman, S. J. (1992). Behavior therapy. In L. R. Squire (Ed.), *Encyclopedia of learning and memory.* New York: Macmillan.

Rachman, S. J., & Wilson, G. T. (1980). *The effects of psychological therapy.* New York: Pergamon.

Ragheb, M. G. (1993). Leisure and perceived wellness: A field investigation. *Leisure Sciences, 12,* 13–24.

Ragland, D. R., & Brand, R. J. (1988). Type A behavior and mortality from coronary heart disease. *The New England Journal of Medicine, 318,* 65–69.

Rahe, R. H., & Arthur, R. H. (1978). Life change and illness studies. *Journal of Human Stress, 4,* 3–15.

Rahe, R. H., & Holmes, T. H. (1965). Social, psychologic and psychophysiologic aspects of inguinal hernia. *Journal of Psychosomatic Research, 8,* 487–491.

Rahim, M. A., & Magner, N. R. (1995). Confirmatory factor analysis of the styles of handling interpersonal conflict: First-order factor model and its invariance across groups. *Journal of Applied Psychology, 80,* 122–132.

Rajecki, D. W. (1990). *Attitudes.* Sunderland, MA.: Sinnauer Associates.

Rajecki, D. W., Dame, J. A., Creek, K. J., Barreckman, P. J., Reid, C. A., & Appleby, D. C. (1993) Gender casting in television toy advertisements. *Journal of Consumer Psychology, 2,* 307–327.

Rakowski, W., & Mor, V. (1992). The association of physical activity with mortality among older adults in the longitudinal study of aging (1984–1988). *Journals of Gerontology, 47(4),* 122–129.

Ralph, J. A., & Mineka, S. (1998). Attributional style and self-esteem: The prediction of emotional distress following a midterm exam. *Journal of Abnormal Psychology, 107,* 203–215.

Rapee, R. M., & Barlow, D. H. (1993). Generalized anxiety disorder, panic disorder, and the phobias. In P. B. Sutker & H. E. Adams (Eds.), *Comprehensive handbook of psychopathology* (2nd ed.). New York: Plenum.

Raphael, K. G., Cloitre, M., & Dohrenwend, B. P. (1991). Problems of recall and misclassification with checklist methods of measuring stressful life events. *Health Psychology, 10,* 62–74.

Raschke, H. J. (1987). Divorce. In M. B. Sussman & S. K. Steinmetz (Eds.), *Handbook of marriage and the family.* New York: Plenum.

Rashid, H. M. (1989). Divergent paths in the development of African-American males: A qualitative perspective. *Urban Research Review, 12,* 1–2, 12–13.

Raskin, P. M. (1986). The relationship between identity and intimacy in early adulthood. *Journal of Genetic Psychology, 147,* 167–181.

Rasmussen, C. H., & Johnson, M. E. (1994). Spirituality and religiosity: Relative relationships to death anxiety. *Omega, 29,* 313–318.

Rathus, S. A., & Nevid, J. S. (1995). *Adjustment and growth: The challenges of life.* Ft. Worth: Harcourt Brace.

Raush, H. L., Barry, W. A., Hertel, R. K., & Swain, M. A. (1974). *Communication, conflict and marriage.* San Francisco: Jossey-Bass.

Ray, L., Soares, E. J., & Tolchinsky, B. (1988). Explicit lyrics: A content analysis of top 100 songs from the '50s to the '80s. *The Speech Communication Annual, 2,* 43–56.

Ray, O., & Ksir, C. (1990). *Drugs, society & human behavior.* St. Louis: Times Mirror/Mosby.

Raz, S. (1993). Structural cerebral pathology in schizophrenia: Regional or diffuse? *Journal of Abnormal Psychology, 102,* 445–452.

Read, C. R. (1991). Achievement and career choices: Comparisons of males and females. *Roeper Review, 13* 188–193.

Regier, D. A., Boyd, J. H., Burke, J. D., Rea, D. S., Myers, J. K., Kramer, M., Robins, L. N., George, L. K., Karno, M., & Locke, B. Z. (1988). One-month prevalance of mental disorders in the United States. *Archives of General Psychiatry, 45,* 977–986.

Regier, D. A., Narrow, W. E., Rae, D. S., Manderscheid, R. W., Locke, B. Z., & Goodwin, F. K. (1993). The de facto U.S. Mental and Addictive Disorders Service System: Epidemiologic Catchment Area prospective 1-year prevalence rates of disorders in services. *Archives of General Psychiatry, 50,* 85–94.

Rehm, L. P., & Tyndall, C. I. (1993). Mood disorders: Unipolar and bipolar. In P. B. Sutker & H. E. Adams (Eds.), *Comprehensive handbook of psychopathology* (2nd ed.). New York: Plenum.

Reid, P. T., & Paludi, M. A. (1993). Developmental psychology of women: Conception to adolescence. In F. L. Denmark & M. A. Paludi (Eds.), *Psychology of women: A handbook of issues and theories.* Westport, CT: Greenwood Press.

Reinisch, J. M. (1990). *The Kinsey Institute new report on sex: What you must know to be sexually literate.* New York: St. Martin's.

Reinke, B. J., Ellicott, A. M., Harris, R. L., & Hancock, E. (1985). Timing of psychosocial changes in women's lives. *Human Development, 28,* 259–280.

Reis, H. T. (1998). Gender differences in intimacy and related behaviors: Context and processes. In D. Canary & K. Dindia (Eds.), *Sex and gender in communication: Similarities and differences.* Mahwah, NJ: Erlbaum.

Reis, H. T., & Patrick. B. C. (1996). Attachment and intimacy: Component processes. In E. T. Higgins & A. Kruglanski (Eds.), *Social psychology: Handbook of basic principles.* New York: Guilford.

Reis, H. T., Senchak, M., & Solomon, B. (1985). Sex differences in the intimacy of social interaction: Further examination of potential explanation. *Journal of Personality and Social Psychology, 48,* 1204–1217.

Reis, H. T., & Shaver, P. (1988). Intimacy as an interpersonal process. In S. W. Duck (Ed.), *Handbook of personal relationships.* New York: Wiley.

Reis, H. T., & Wheeler, L. (1991). Studying social interaction with the Rochester Interaction Record. *Advances in Experimental Social Psychology, 24,* 269–318.

Reis, T. J., Gerrard, M., & Gibbons, F. X. (1993). Social comparison and the pill: Reactions to upward and downward comparison of contraceptive behavior. *Personality and Social Psychology Bulletin, 19,* 13–21.

Reiser, M. F. (1989). The future of psychoanalysis in academic psychiatry: Plain talk. *Psychoanalytic Quarterly, 58,* 185–209.

Reiss, S. (1991). Expectancy model of fear, anxiety and panic. *Clinical Psychology Review, 11,* 141–154.

Relman, A. (1982). Marijuana and health. *New England Journal of Medicine, 306,* 603–604.

Renzetti, C. (1995). Violence in gay and lesbian relationships. In R. J. Gelles (Ed.), *Vision 2010: Families and violence, abuse and neglect.* Minneapolis: National Council on Family Relations.

Repetti, R. L. (1984). Determinants of children's sex-stereotyping: Parental sex-role traits and television viewing. *Personality and Social Psychology Bulletin, 10,* 457–468.

Repetti, R. L. (1992). Social withdrawal as a short-term coping response to daily stressors. In H. S. Friedman (Ed.), *Hostility coping and health.* Washington, DC: American Psychological Association.

Repetti, R. L. (1993). Short-term effects of occupational stressors on daily mood and health complaints. *Health Psychology, 12,* 125–131.

Revenson, T. A., & Felton, B. J. (1989). Disability and coping as predictors of psychological adjustment to rheumatoid arthritis. *Journal of Consulting and Clinical Psychology, 57,* 344–348.

Rey, J. M., Stewart, G. W., Plapp, J. M., Bashir, M. R., & Richards, I. N. (1988). DSM-III axis IV revisited. *American Journal of Psychiatry, 145,* 286–292.

Rhodewalt, F., & Agustsdottir, S. (1986). Effects of self-presentation on the phenomenal self. *Journal of Personality and Social Psychology, 50,* 47–55.

Rhodewalt, F., Morf, C., Hazlett, S., & Fairfield, M. (1991). Self-handicapping: The role of discounting and augmentation in the preservation of self-esteem. *Journal of Personality and Social Psychology, 61,* 122–131.

Rhodewalt, F., Sanbonmatsu, D. M., Tschanz, B., Feick, D. L., & Waller, A. (1995). Self-handicapping and interpersonal trade-offs: The effects of claimed self-handicaps on observers' performance evaluations and feedback. *Personality and Social Psychology Bulletin, 21,* 1042–1050.

Rice, L. N., & Greenberg, L. S. (1992). Humanistic approaches to psychotherapy. In D. K. Freedheim (Ed.), *History of psychotherapy: A century of change.* Washington, DC: American Psychological Association.

Richardson, J. G., & Simpson, C. H. (1982). Children, gender and social structure: An analysis of the contents of letters to Santa Claus. *Child Development, 53* 429–436.

Rieder, R. O., Kaufmann, C. A., & Knowles, J. A. (1994). Genetics. In R. E. Hales, S. C. Yudofsky, & J. A. Talbott (Eds.), *The American Psychiatric Press textbook of psychiatry* (2nd ed.). Washington, DC: American Psychiatric Press.

Rierdan, J., & Koff, E. (1991). Depressive symptomatology among very early maturing girls. *Journal of Youth and Adolescence, 20,* 415–425.

Rifkin, J. (1989). *Time wars: The primary conflict in human history.* New York: Simon & Schuster.

Riggio, R. E., & Throckmorton, B. (1988). The relative effect of verbal and nonverbal behavior, appearance, and social skills on valuations made in hiring interviews. *Journal of Applied Social Psychology, 18,* 331–348.

Riggs, R. O., Murrell, P. H., & Cutting, J. C. (1993). *Sexual harassment in higher education: From conflict to community.* Washington, DC: ERIC Clearinghouse on Higher Education.

Rimer, B. K., Orleans, C. T., Keintz, M. K., Cristinzio, S., & Fleisher, L. (1990). The older smoker: Status, challenges and opportunities for intervention. *Chest, 97,* 547–553.

Rimm, D. C., & Cunningham, H. M. (1985). Behavior therapies. In S. J. Lynn & J. P. Garske (Eds.), *Contemporary psychotherapies: Models and methods.* Columbus, OH: Merrill.

Rimm, E. B., Giovannucci, E. L., Willet, W. C., Coditz, G. A., Ascherio, A., Rosner, B., & Stampfer, M. J. (1991). Prospective study of alcohol consumption and risk of coronary disease in men. *The Lancet, 338,* 464–468.

Rimm, E. B., Stampfer, M. J., Ascherio, A., Giovannucci, E., Colditz, G. A., & Willett, W. C. (1993). Vitamin E consumption and the risk of coronary heart disease in men. *New England Journal of Medicine, 328,* 1450–1456.

Rindfuss, R. R. (1991). The young adult years: Diversity, structural change, and fertility. *Demography, 28,* 493–512.

Rindfuss, R. R., Morgan, S. P., & Swicegood, G. (1988). *First births in America.* Berkeley: University of California Press.

Ringer, R. J. (1978). *Winning through intimidation.* New York: Fawcett.

Rivera, R. R. (1991). Sexual orientation and the law. In J. C. Gonsiorek & J. D. Weinrich (Eds.), *Homosexuality: Research implications for public policy.* Newbury Park, CA: Sage Publications.

Road rage plagues drivers. (1997, November/December). *AAA Going Places,* 41–42.

Robbins, A. (1991). *Awaken the giant within: How to take immediate control of your mental, emotional, physical, and financial destiny.* New York: Simon & Schuster (Summit Books).

Roberts, L. J., & Krokoff, L. J. (1990). A time series analysis of withdrawal, hostility, and displeasure in satisfied and dissatisfied marriages. *Journal of Marriage and the Family, 52,* 95–105.

Roberts, P., & Newton, P. M. (1987). Levinsonian studies of women's adult development. *Psychology and Aging, 2,* 154–163.

Robins, C. J., & Hayes, A. H. (1995). The role of causal attributions in the prediction of depression. In G. M. Buchanan & M. E. P. Seligman (Eds.), *Explanatory style.* Hillsdale, NJ: Erlbaum.

Robins, E. (1990). The study of interdependence in marriage. In F. D. Fincham & T. N.

Bradbury (Eds.), *The psychology of marriage: Basic issues and applications.* New York: Guilford Press.

Robins, L. N., & Regier, D. A. (Eds.). (1991). *Psychiatric disorders in America: The epidemiologic catchment area study.* New York: Free Press.

Robins, L. N., Helzer, J. E., Weissman, M. M., Orvaschel, H., Gruenberg, E., Burke, J. D., & Regier, D. A. (1984). Lifetime prevalence of specific psychiatric disorders in three sites. *Archives of General Psychiatry, 41,* 949–958.

Robins, L. N., Locke, B. Z., & Regier, D. A. (1991). An overview of psychiatric disorders in America. In L. N. Robins & D. A. Regier (Eds.), *Psychiatric disorders in America: The epidemiologic catchment area study.* New York: Free Press.

Robinson, F. P. (1970). *Effective study* (4th ed.). New York: HarperCollins.

Robinson, I., Ziss, K., Ganza, B., & Katz, S. (1991). Twenty years of the sexual revolution, 1965–1985: An update. *Journal of Marriage and the Family, 53* 216–220.

Robinson, J. P., & Godbey, G. (1997). *Time for life: The surprising ways Americans use their time.* University Park, PA: Pennsylvania State University Press.

Robinson, J. P., & Milkie, M. A. (1998). Back to basics: Trends in and role determinants of women's attitudes toward housework. *Journal of Marriage and the Family, 60,* 205–218.

Robinson, L. A., Berman, J. S., & Neimeyer, R. A. (1990). Psychotherapy for the treatment of depression: A comprehensive review of controlled outcome research. *Psychological Bulletin, 108,* 30–49.

Roby, P. A. (1995). Becoming shop stewards: Perspectives on gender and race in ten trade unions. *Labor Studies Journal,* 65–82.

Rodin, J., Schank, D., & Striegel-Moore, R. H. (1989). Psychological features of obesity. *Medical Clinics of North America, 73* 47–66.

Rodman, H., & Sidden, J. (1992). A critique of pessimistic views about U.S. families. *Family Relations, 41,* 436–439.

Roediger, H. L., III. (1992). Retrieval processes in memory. In L. R. Squire (Ed.), *Encyclopedia of learning and memory.* New York: Macmillan.

Roehrs, T. A, Zorick, F., & Roth, T. (1994). Transient and short-term insomnia. In M. H. Kryger, T. Roth, & W. C. Dement (Eds.), *Principles and practice of sleep medicine* (2nd ed.). Philadelphia: Saunders.

Rogers, C. R. (1951). *Client-centered therapy: Its current practice, implications, and theory.* Boston: Houghton Mifflin.

Rogers, C. R. (1961). *On becoming a person: A therapist's view of psychotherapy.* Boston: Houghton Mifflin.

Rogers, C. R. (1977). *Carl Rogers on personal power.* New York: Delacorte.

Rogers, C. R. (1980). *A way of being.* Boston: Houghton Mifflin.

Rogers, C. R. (1986). Client-centered therapy. In I. L. Kutash & A. Wolf (Eds.), *Psychotherapist's casebook.* San Francisco: Jossey-Bass.

Rogers, S. J., & White, L. K. (1998). Satisfaction with parenting: The role of marital happiness, family structure, and parents' gender. *Journal of Marriage and the Family, 60,* 293–308.

Rollins, B., & Feldman, H. (1970). Marital satisfaction over the family life cycle. *Journal of Marriage and the Family, 32,* 20–28.

Rolls, B. J. (1995). Impact of sugar and fat substitutes on food intake. In K. D. Brownell & C. G. Fairburn (Eds.), *Eating disorders and obesity: A comprehensive handbook.* New York: Guilford Press.

Romer, N., & Cherry, D. (1980). Ethnic and social class differences in children's sex-role concepts. *Sex Roles, 6,* 245–263.

Romzek, B. S., & Dubnick, M. J. (1987). Accountability in the public sector: Lessons from the Challenger tragedy. *Public Administration Review, 47,* 227–238.

Rook, K. S. (1998). Investigating the positive and negative sides of personal relationships: Through a lens darkly? In B. H. Spitzberg & W. R. Cupach (Eds.), *The dark side of close relationships.* Mahwah, NJ: Lawrence Erlbaum.

Rook, K. S. (1990). Parallels in the study of social support and social strain. *Journal of Social and Clinical Psychology, 9,* 118–132.

Rook, K. S., Catalano, R., & Dooley, D. (1989). The timing of major life events: Effects of departing from the social clock. *American Journal of Community Psychology, 17,* 233–258.

Rook, K. S., Dooley, D., & Catalano, R. (1991). Stress transmission: The effects of husbands' job stressors on the emotional health of their wives. *Journal of Marriage and the Family, 53* 165–177.

Rosen, D. H. (1974). *Lesbianism: A study of female homosexuality.* Springfield, IL: Charles C Thomas.

Rosen, G. M. (1987). Self-help treatment books and the commercialization of psychotherapy. *American Psychologist, 42,* 46–51.

Rosen, M., Nystrom, L., & Wall, S. (1988). Diet and cancer mortality in the counties of Sweden. *American Journal of Epidemiology, 127,* 42–49.

Rosen, R. D. (1977). *Psychobabble.* New York: Atheneum.

Rosenbaum, J. F., Biederman, J., Bolduc, E. A., Hirschfeld, D. R., Faraone, S. V., & Kagan, J. (1992). Comorbidity of parental anxiety disorders as risk for childhood-onset anxiety in inhibited children. *American Journal of Psychiatry, 149,* 475–481.

Rosenbaum, M., Lakin, M., & Roback, H. B. (1992). Psychotherapy in groups. In D. K. Freedheim (Ed.), *History of psychotherapy: A century of change.* Washington, DC: American Psychological Association.

Rosenberg, E. L., & Ekman, P. (1994). Coherence between expressive systems in emotion. *Cognition and Emotion, 8,* 201–229.

Rosenberg, M. (1985). Self-concept and psychological well-being in adolescence. In R. L. Leahy (Ed.), *The development of the self.* Orlando, FL: Academic Press.

Rosenfeld, L. B., Civikly, J. M., & Herron, J. R. (1979). Anatomical and psychological sex differences. In G. J. Chelune & associates (Eds.), *Self-disclosure: Origins, patterns, and implications of openness in interpersonal relationships.* San Francisco: Jossey-Bass.

Rosengren, A., Tibblin, G., & Wilhelmsen, L. (1991). Self-perceived psychological stress and incidence of coronary artery disease in middle-aged men. *American Journal of Cardiology, 68,* 1171–1175.

Rosenhan, D. L. (1973). On being sane in insane places. *Science, 179,* 250–258.

Rosenman, R. H. (1991). Type A behavior pattern and coronary heart disease: The hostility factor? *Stress Medicine, 7,* 245–253.

Rosenman, R. H. (1993). Relationships of the Type A behavior pattern with coronary heart disease. In L. Goldberger & S. Breznitz (Eds.), *Handbook of stress: Theoretical and clinical aspects* (2nd ed.). New York: Free Press.

Rosenthal, H. (1988). *Not with my life I don't: Preventing your suicide and that of others.* Muncie, IN: Accelerated Development.

Rosenthal, R. (1985). From unconscious experimenter bias to teacher expectancy effects. In J. B. Dusek, V. C. Hall, & W. J. Meyer (Eds.), *Teacher expectancies.* Hillsdale, NJ: Erlbaum.

Rosenthal, R., Hall, J. A., DiMatteo, M. R., Rodgers, P. L., & Archer, D. (1979). *Sensitivity to non-verbal cues: The P Test.* Baltimore: Johns Hopkins University Press.

Roskos-Ewoldsen, D. R., & Fazio, R. H. (1992). The accessibility of source likability as a determinant of persuasion. *Personality and Social Psychology, 18,* 19–25.

Ross, C. A., Anderson, G., Fleisher, W. P., & Norton, G. R. (1991). The frequency of multiple personality disorder among psychiatric inpatients. *American Journal of Psychiatry, 148,* 1717–1720.

Ross, C. A., Miller, S. D., Reagor, P., Bjornson, L., Fraser, G. A., & Anderson, G. (1990). Structured interview data on 102 cases of multiple personality disorder from four centers. *American Journal of Psychiatry, 147,* 596–601.

Ross, C. E. (1995). Reconceptualizing marital status as a condition of social attachment. *Journal of Marriage and the Family, 57,* 129–140.

Ross, C. E., & Van Willigen, M. (1997). Education and the subjective quality of life. *Journal of Health & Social Behavior, 38,* 275–297.

Ross, C. W., & Mirowsky, J. (1988). Child care and emotional adjustment to wives' employment. *Journal of Health and Social Behavior, 29,* 127–138.

Ross, L. D. (1977). The intuitive psychologist and his shortcomings: Distortions in the attribution process. In L. Berkowitz (Ed.), *Advances in experimental social psychology* (Vol. 10). New York: Academic Press.

Ross, M., & Conway, M. (1986). Remembering one's own past: The construction of personal histories. In R. M. Sorrentino & E. T. Higgins (Eds.), *Handbook of motivation and cognition: Foundations of social behavior.* New York: Guilford Press.

Ross, M., McFarland, C., & Fletcher, G. J. O. (1981). The effect of attitude on the recall of personal histories. *Journal of Personality and Social Psychology, 10,* 627–634.

Rotenberg, K. J., & Kmill, J. (1992). Perception of lonely and non-lonely persons as a function of individual differences in loneliness. *Journal of Social and Personal Relationships, 9,* 325–330.

Roth, A., & Fonagy, P. (1996). *What works for whom? A critical review of psychotherapy research.* New York: Guilford Press.

Rothblum, E. D., Solomon, L. J., & Albee, G. W. (1986). A sociopolitical perspective of DSM-III. In T. Millon & G. L. Klerman (Eds.), *Contemporary directions in psychopathology: Toward the DSM-IV.* New York: Guilford Press.

Rotter, J. B. (1982). *The development and application of social learning theory.* New York: Praeger.

Rotton, J., & Frey, J. (1984). Psychological costs of air pollution: Atmospheric conditions, seasonal trends, and psychiatric emergencies. *Population and Environmental Behavior and Social Issues, 7,* 3–16.

Rowe, D. C. (1997). Genetics, temperament, and personality. In R. Hogan, J. Johnson, & S. Briggs (Eds), *Handbook of personality psychology.* San Diego, CA: Academic Press.

Rozee, P. D., Bateman, P., & Gilmore, T. (1991). The personal perspective of acquaintance rape prevention: A three-tier approach. In A. Parrot & L. Bechhofer (Eds.), *Acquaintance rape: The hidden crime.* New York: Wiley.

Rubenstein, C. M., & Shaver, P. (1982). The experience of loneliness. In L. A. Peplau & D. Perlman (Eds.), *Loneliness: A sourcebook of current theory, research and therapy.* New York: Wiley.

Rubin, E. H., Zorumski, C. F., & Guze, S. B. (1986). Somatoform disorders. In T. Millon &

G. L. Klerman (Eds.), *Contemporary directions in psychopathology: Toward the DSM-IV*. New York: Guilford Press.

Rubin, L. (1985). *Just friends: The role of friendship in our lives*. New York: HarperCollins.

Rubin, Z., Peplau, L. A., & Hill, C. T. (1981). Loving and leaving: Sex differences in romantic attachments. *Sex Roles, 7,* 821–835.

Ruble, D. N., Fleming, A. S., Hackel, L. S., & Stangor, C. (1988). Changes in the marital relationship during the transition to first time motherhood: Effects of violated expectations concerning division of household labor. *Journal of Personality and Social Psychology, 55,* 78–87.

Ruble, T. L. (1983). Sex stereotypes: Issues of change in the 1970s. *Sex Roles, 9,* 397–402.

Rubonis, A. V., & Bickman, L. (1991). Psychological impairment in the wake of disaster: The disaster-psychopathology relationship. *Psychological Bulletin, 109,* 384–399.

Ruderman, A. J. (1986). Dietary restraint: A theoretical and empirical review. *Psychological Bulletin, 99,* 247–262.

Rudorfer, M. V., & Goodwin, F. K. (1993). Introduction. In C. E. Coffey (Ed.), *The clinical science of electroconvulsive therapy*. Washington, DC: American Psychiatric Press.

Ruse, M. (1987). Sociobiology and knowledge: Is evolutionary epistemology a viable option? In C. Crawford, M. Smith, & D. Krebs (Eds.), *Sociobiology and psychology: Ideas, issues and applications*. Hillsdale, NJ: Erlbaum.

Rush, A. J. (1984). Cognitive therapy. In T. B. Karasu (Ed.), *The psychiatric therapies*. Washington, DC: American Psychiatric Association.

Rushton, J. P. (1992). Cranial capacity related to sex, rank, and race in a stratified random sample of 6,325 U.S. Military personnel. *Intelligence, 16,* 401–413.

Rushton, J. P., Fulker, D. W., Neale, M. C., Nias, D. K. B., & Eysenck, H. J. (1986). Altruism and aggression: The heritability of individual differences. *Journal of Personality and Social Psychology, 50,* 1192–1198.

Russell, D. E. H. (1984). *Sexual exploitation*. Newbury Park, CA: Sage Publications.

Russell, G. F. M. (1995). Anorexia nervosa through time. In G. Szmukler, C. Dare, & J. Treasure (Eds.), *Handbook of eating disorders: Theory, treatment, and research*. New York: Wiley.

Russell, G. F. M. (1997). The history of bulimia nervosa. In D. M. Garner & P. E. Garfinkel (Eds.), *Handbook of treatment for eating disorders* (2nd ed.). New York: Guilford Press.

Russo, N. F. (1979). Overview: Sex roles, fertility, and the motherhood mandate. *Psychology of Women Quarterly, 4,* 7–15.

Russo, N. F., & Green, B. L. (1993). Women and mental health. In F. L. Denmark & M. A. Paludi (Eds.), *Psychology of women: A handbook of issues and theories*. Westport, CT: Greenwood Press.

Saad, L. (1996, December). Americans growing more tolerant of gays. *The Gallup Poll Monthly,* 12–14.

Sabatelli, R. M. (1988). Exploring relationship satisfaction: A social exchange perspective on the interdependence between theory, research, and practice. *Family Relations, 37,* 217–222.

Sabini, J. (1992). *Social psychology*. New York: Norton.

Sacks, M. H. (1993). Exercise for stress control. In D. Goleman & J. Gurin (Eds.), *Mind/body medicine: How to use your mind for better health*. Yonkers, NY: Consumer Reports Books.

Sadker, M., & Sadker, D. (1985, March). Sexism in the schoolroom of the '80s. *Psychology Today,* pp. 54–57.

Sadker, M., & Sadker, D. (1994). *Failing at fairness: How America's schools cheat girls*. New York: Scribners.

Saghir, M. T., & Robins, E. R. (1973). *Male and female homosexuality: A comprehensive investigation*. Baltimore: Williams & Wilkins.

Salholz, E. (1990, March 12). The future of gay America. *Newsweek,* 20–25.

Salminen, S. (1992). Defensive attribution hypothesis and serious occupational accidents. *Psychological Reports, 70,* 1195–1199.

Salovey, P., & Mayer, J. D. (1990). Emotional intelligence. *Imagination, Cognition, and Personality, 9,* 185–211.

Salthouse, T. A. (1991). Mediation of adult age differences in cognition by reductions in working memory and speed of processing. *Psychological Science, 2,* 179–183.

Salthouse, T. A., & Babcock, R. L. (1991). Decomposing adult age differences in working memory. *Developmental Psychology, 27,* 763–776.

Salvendy, J. T. (1993). Selection and preparation of patients and organization of the group. In H. I. Kaplan & B. J. Sadock (Eds.), *Comprehensive group psychotherapy*. Baltimore: Williams & Wilkins.

Samet, J. M. (1992). The health benefits of smoking cessation. *Medical Clinics of North America, 76,* 399–414.

Samovar, L. A., & Porter, R. E. (1995). *Communication between cultures*. Belmont, CA: Wadsworth.

Sanders, G. S. (1982). Social comparison and perceptions of health and illness. In G. S. Sanders & J. Suls (Eds.), *Social psychology of health and illness*. Hillsdale, NJ: Erlbaum.

Sanderson, W. C., & Barlow, D. H. (1990). A description of patients diagnosed with DSM-III-R generalized anxiety disorder. *Journal of Nervous and Mental Disease, 178,* 588–591.

Sandler, J. (1975). Aversion methods. In F. H. Kanfer & A. P. Goldstein (Eds.), *Helping people change: A textbook of methods*. New York: Pergamon.

Santrock, J. W., Minnett, A. M., & Campbell, B. D. (1994). *The authoritative guide to self-help books*. New York: Guilford Press.

Sarason, I. G. (1984). Stress, anxiety and cognitive interference: Reactions to stress. *Journal of Personality and Social Psychology, 46,* 929–938.

Sarason, I. G., Johnson, J. H., & Siegel, J. M. (1978). Assessing the impact of life changes: Development of the Life Experiences Survey. *Journal of Consulting and Clinical Psychology, 46,* 932–946.

Sarason, I. G., Pierce, G. R., & Sarason, B. R. (1994). General and specific perceptions of social support. In W. R. Avison & I. H. Gotlib (Eds.), *Stress and mental health: Contemporary issues and prospects for the future*. New York: Plenum.

Sarrel, P., & Masters, W. (1982). Sexual molestation of men by women. *Archives of Human Sexuality, 11,* 117–131.

Saxe, G. N., van der Kolk, B. A., Berkowitz, R., Chinman, G., Hall, K., Lieberg, G., & Schwartz, J. (1993). Dissociative disorders in psychiatric inpatients. *American Journal of Psychiatry, 150,* 1037–1042.

Scarr, S. (1992). Developmental theories for the 1990s: Development and individual differences. *Child Development, 63,* 1–19.

Scarr, S., Phillips, D., McCartney, K., & Abbott-Shim, M. (1993). Quality of child care as an aspect of family and child care policy in the United States. *Pediatrics, 91,* 182–188.

Schachter, S. (1959). *The psychology of affiliation*. Stanford, CA: Stanford University Press.

Schaef, A. W. (1986). *Codependence misdiagnosed-mistreated*. Minneapolis: Winston Press.

Schaef, A. W. (1992). *Meditations for women who do too much*. San Francisco: Harper San Francisco.

Schaefer, J., & Moos, R. (1992). Life crises and personal growth. In B. Carpenter (Ed.), *Personal coping: Theory, research, and application*. Westport, CT: Praeger.

Schaeffer, M., Street, S., Singer, J., & Baum, A. (1988). Effects of control on the stress reactions of commuters. *Journal of Applied Social Psychology, 18,* 944–957.

Schaffer, D. R. (1989). *Developmental psychology: Childhood and adolescence*. Pacific Grove, CA: Brooks/Cole.

Schaie, K. W. (1990). Intellectual development in adulthood. In J. E. Birren & K. W. Schaie (Eds.), *Handbook of the psychology of aging* (3rd ed.). San Diego: Academic Press.

Schaninger, C. M., & Buss, W. C. (1986). A longitudinal comparison of consumption and finance handling between happily married and divorced couples. *Journal of Marriage and the Family, 48,* 129–136.

Scharfe, E., & Bartholomew, K. (1994). Reliability and stability of adult attachment patterns. *Personal Relationships, 1,* 23–43.

Schau, C. G., & Scott, K. P. (1984). Impact of gender characteristics of instructional materials: An integration of the research literature. *Journal of Educational Psychology, 76,* 183–193.

Scheidlinger, S. (1993). History of group psychotherapy. In H. I. Kaplan & B. J. Sadock (Eds.), *Comprehensive group psychotherapy*. Baltimore: Williams & Wilkins.

Scheier, M. F., & Carver, C. S. (1992). Effects of optimism on psychological and physical well-being: Theoretical overview and empirical update. *Cognitive Theory and Research, 16,* 201–228.

Scheier, M. F., & Carver, C. S. (1985). Optimism, coping, and health: Assessment and implications of generalized outcome expectancies. *Health Psychology, 4,* 219–247.

Scheier, M. F., Matthews, K. A., Owens, J. F., Magovern, G. J., Sr., Lefebvre, R. C., Abbott, R. A., & Carver, C. S. (1989). Dispositional optimism and recovery from coronary artery bypass surgery: The beneficial effects on physical and psychological well-being. *Journal of Personality and Social Psychology, 57,* 1024–1040.

Scherg, H. (1987). Psychosocial factors and disease bias in breast cancer patients. *Psychosomatic Medicine, 49,* 302–312.

Scheuer, E., & Epstein, S. (1997). Constructive thinking, reactions to a laboratory stressor, and symptoms in everyday life. *Anxiety, Stress & Coping: An International Journal, 10,* 269–303.

Schilit, W. K. (1987). Thinking about managing your time. In A. D. Timpe (Ed.), *The management of time*. New York: Facts On File.

Schlaadt, R. G., & Shannon, P. T. (1994). *Drugs: Use, misuse, and abuse* (4th ed.). Englewood Cliffs, NJ: Prentice-Hall.

Schlegel, A., & Barry, H., III. (1991). *Adolescence: An anthropological inquiry*. New York: Free Press.

Schlenger, W. E., Kulka, R. A., Fairbank, J. A., Hough, R. L., et al. (1992). The prevalence of post-traumatic stress disorder in the Vietnam generation: A multimethod, multisource assessment of psychiatric disorder. *Journal of Traumatic Stress, 5,* 333–363.

Schlenker, B. R., Phillips, S. T., Boniecki, K. A., & Schlenker, D. R. (1995). Championship pressures: Choking or triumphing in one's own territory? *Journal of Personality and Social Psychology, 68,* 632–643.

Schlenker, B. R., & Weigold, M. F. (1992). Interpersonal processes involving impression regulation and management. *Annual Review of Psychology, 43*, 133–168.

Schlenker, B. R., Weigold, M. F., & Hallam, J. R. (1990). Self-serving attributions in social context: Effects of self-esteem and social pressure. *Journal of Personality and Social Psychology, 58*, 855–863.

Schlessinger, L. C. (1995). *Ten stupid things women do to mess up their lives.* San Francisco: Harper Perennial Library.

Schmidt, N. B., Lerew, D. R., & Jackson, R. J. (1997). The role of anxiety sensitivity in the pathogenesis of panic: Prospective evaluation of spontaneous panic attacks during acute stress. *Journal of Abnormal Psychology, 106*, 355–364.

Schmidt, N., & Sermat, V. (1983). Measuring loneliness in different relationships. *Journal of Personality and Social Psychology, 44*, 1038–1047.

Schmitz, J. M., Jarvik, M. E., & Schneider, N. G. (1997). Nicotine. In J. H. Lowinson, P. Ruiz, R. B. Millman, & J. G. Langrod (Eds.), *Substance abuse: A comprehensive textbook* (3rd ed.). Baltimore: Williams & Wilkins.

Schoen, R. (1992). First unions and the stability of first marriages. *Journal of Marriage and the Family, 54*, 281–284.

Schoen, R., & Wooldredge, J. (1989). Marriage choices in North Carolina and Virginia, 1969–71 and 1979–81. *Journal of Marriage and the Family, 51*, 465–481.

Schor, J. (1991). *The overworked American.* New York: Basic Books.

Schover, L. R., & Leiblum, S. R. (1994). Commentary: The stagnation of sex therapy. *Journal of Pscyhology and Human Sexuality, 6*, 5–30.

Schreiber, F. R. (1973). *Sybil.* New York: Warner.

Schroeder, D. H., & Costa, P. T., Jr. (1984). Influence of life events stress on physical illness: Substantive effects or methodological flaws? *Journal of Personality and Social Psychology, 46*, 853–863.

Schuller, R. A., & Vidmar, N. (1992). Battered woman syndrome evidence in the courtroom: A review of the literature. *Law and Human Behavior, 16*, 273–291.

Schultz, J. H., & Luthe, W. (1969). *Autogenic therapy: Vol. 1. Autogenic methods.* New York: Grune & Stratton.

Schwartz, H. S. (1982). Job involvement as obsession. *Academy of Management Review, 7*, 429–432.

Schwarzer, R., & Fuchs, R. (1995). Changing risk behaviors and adopting health behaviors: The role of self-efficacy beliefs. In A. Bandura (Ed.), *Self-efficacy in changing societies.* New York: Cambridge University Press.

Scroppo, J. C., Drob, S. L., Weinberger, J. L., & Eagle, P. (1998). Identifying dissociative identity disorder: A self-report and projective study. *Journal of Abnormal Psychology, 107*, 272–284.

Seage, G. R., Landers, S., Lamb, G. A., & Epstein, A. M. (1990). Effect of changing patterns of care and duration of survival on the cost of treating the acquired immunodeficiency syndrome (AIDS). *American Journal of Public Health, 80*, 835–839.

Sears, D. O. (1987). Symbolic racism. In P. Katz & D. Taylor (Eds.), *Towards the elimination of racism: Profile in controversy.* New York: Plenum.

Sears, D. O., & Citrin, J. (1985). *Tax revolt: Something for nothing in California.* Cambridge: Harvard University Press.

Seccombe, K. (1987). Children: Their impact on the elderly in declining health. *Research on Aging, 9*, 312–326.

Seccombe, K. (1991). Assessing the costs and benefits of children: Gender comparisons among childfree husbands and wives. *Journal of Marriage and the Family, 53* 191–202.

Segal, K. R., & Pi-Sunyer, F. X. (1989). Exercise and obesity. *Medical Clinics of North America, 73* 217–236.

Segal, M. W. (1974). Alphabet and attraction: An unobtrusive measure of the effect of propinquity in a field setting. *Journal of Personality and Social Psychology, 30*, 654–657.

Segall, A. (1997). Sick role concepts and health behavior. In D. S. Gochman (Ed.), *Handbook of health behavior research I: Personal and social determinants.* New York : Plenum Press.

Segerstrom, S. C., Taylor, S. E., Kemeny, M. E., & Fahey, J. L. (1998). Optimism is associated with mood, coping and immune change in response to stress. *Journal of Personality and Social Psychology, 74*, 1646–1655.

Segrin, C., & Abramson, L. Y. (1994). Negative reactions to depressive behaviors: A communication theories analysis. *Journal of Abnormal Psychology, 103* 655–668.

Seibel, M. M., & McCarthy, J. A. (1993). Infertility, pregnancy, and the emotions. In D. Goleman & J. Gurin (Eds.), *Mind/body medicine: How to use your mind for better health.* Yonkers, NY: Consumer Reports Books.

Seidlitz, L., & Diener, E. (1993). Memory for positive versus negative life events: Theories for the differences between happy and unhappy persons. *Journal of Personality and Social Psychology, 64*, 654–664.

Seligman, L. (1994). *Developmental career conseling and assessment* (2nd ed.). Thousand Oaks, CA: Sage.

Seligman, M. E. P. (1971). Phobias and preparedness. *Behavior Therapy, 2*, 307–321.

Seligman, M. E. P. (1974). Depression and learned helplessness. In R. J. Friedman & M. M. Katz (Eds.), *The psychology of depression: Contemporary theory and research.* New York: Wiley.

Seligman, M. E. P. (1990). *Learned optimism: How to change your mind and your life.* New York: Pocket Books.

Seligman, M. E. P. (1992). *Helplessness: On depression, development, and death.* New York: Freeman.

Seligman, M. E. P. (1994). *What you can change and what you can't.* New York: Knopf.

Seligman, M. E. P. (1995). The effectiveness of psychotherapy. *American Psychologist, 50*, 965–974.

Seltzer, J. A. (1991). Relationships between fathers and children who live apart: The father's role after separation. *Journal of Marriage and the Family, 53* 79–101.

Seltzer, R. (1992). The social location of those holding antihomosexual attitudes. *Sex Roles, 26*, 391–398.

Selye, H. (1936). A syndrome produced by diverse nocuous agents. *Nature, 138*, 32.

Selye, H. (1956). *The stress of life.* New York: McGraw-Hill.

Selye, H. (1974). *Stress without distress.* New York: Lippincott.

Selye, H. (1982). History and present status of the stress concept. In L. Goldberger & S. Breznitz (Eds.), *Handbook of stress: Theoretical and clinical aspects.* New York: Free Press.

Semans, J. H. (1956). Premature ejaculation: A new approach. *Journal of Southern Medicine, 79*, 353–361.

Senecal, C., Lavoie, K., & Koestner, R. (1997). Trait and situational factors in procrastination: An interactional model. *Journal of Social Behavior and Personality, 12*, 889–903.

Seta, J. J., Seta, C. E., & Wang, M. A. (1991). Feelings of negativity and stress: An averaging-summation analysis of impressions of negative life experiences. *Personality and Social Psychology Bulletin, 17*, 376–384.

Shaffer, D. R. (1989). *Developmental psychology: Childhood and adolescence.* Pacific Grove, CA: Brooks/Cole.

Shapiro, D. H., Jr. (1984). Overview: Clinical and physiological comparison of meditation with other self-control strategies. In D. H. Shapiro, Jr. & R. N. Walsh (Eds.), *Meditation: Classic and contemporary perspectives.* New York: Aldine.

Shapiro, D. H., Jr. (1987). Implications of psychotherapy research for the study of meditation. In M. A. West (Ed.), *The psychology of meditation.* Oxford: Clarendon Press.

Shapiro, S., Skinner, E. A., Kessler, L. G., Von Korff, M., German, P. S., Tischler, G. L., Leaf, P. J., Benham, L., Cottler, L., & Regier, D. A. (1984). Utilization of health and mental health services. *Archives of General Psychiatry, 41*, 971–978.

Shavelson, R. J., Hubner, J. J., & Stanton, G. C. (1976). Self-concept: Validation of construct interpretations. *Review of Educational Research, 46*, 407–411.

Shaver, P. R., & Brennan, K. A. (1992). Attachment styles and the "Big Five" personality traits: Their connections with each other and with romantic relationship outcomes. *Personality and Social Psychology Bulletin, 18*, 536–545.

Shaver, P. R., & Hazan, C. (1992). Adult romantic attachment: Theory and evidence. In D. Perlman & W. Jones (Eds.), *Advances in personal relationships* (Vol. 4). Bristol, PA: Taylor & Francis.

Shaver, P. R., & Hazan, C. (1993). Adult attachment: Theory and research. In W. Jones & D. Perlman (Eds.), *Advances in personal relationships* (Vol. 4). London: Jessica Kingsley.

Shaver, P. R., & Hazan, C. (1994). Attachment. In A. L. Weber & J. H. Harvey (Eds.), *Perspectives on close relationships.* Boston: Allyn & Bacon.

Shaver, P. R., Wu, S., & Schwartz, J. C. (1991). Cross-cultural similarities and differences in emotion and its representation: A prototype approach. In M. S. Clark (Ed.), *Review of personality and social psychology* (Vol. 13). Newbury Park, CA: Sage Publications.

Shaw, J. (1997). Treatment rationale for Internet infidelity. *Journal of Sex Education and Therapy, 22*, 29–34.

Sheehan, P. W., Green, V., & Truesdale, P. (1992). Influence of rapport on hypnotically induced pseudomemory. *Journal of Abnormal Psychology, 101*, 690–700.

Sheehan, S. (1982). *Is there no place on earth for me?* Boston: Houghton Mifflin.

Sheeran, P., & Abraham, C. (1994). Unemployment and self-conception: A symbolic interactionist analysis. *Journal of Community and Applied Social Psychology, 4*, 115–129.

Shekelle, R. B., Hulley, S. B., Neaton, J. D., Billings, J. H., Borhani, N. O., Gerace, T. A., Jacobs, D. R., Lasser, N. L., Mittlemark, M. B., & Stamler, J. (1985). The MRFIT behavior pattern study: II. Type A behavior and incidence of coronary heart disease. *American Journal of Epidemiology, 122*, 559–570.

Shelley, K. J. (1994). More job openings—even more new entrants: The outlook for college graduates, 1992–2005. *Occupational Outlook Quarterly, 38*, 4–9.

Shenk, D. (1997). *Data smog: Surviving the information glut.* San Francisco: HarperEdge.

Shephard, R. J. (1986). Passive smoking: Attitudes, health, and performance. In T. Ney & A. Gale (Eds.), *Smoking and human behavior.* Chichester: Wiley.

Shepperd, J. A., & Arkin, R. M. (1989). Self-handicapping: The moderating roles of public self-consciousness and task importance. *Personality and Social Psychology Bulletin, 15,* 252–265.

Sher, T. G., & Baucom, D. H. (1993). Marital communication: Differences among maritally distressed, depressed, and nondistressed-non-depressed couples. *Journal of Family Psychology, 7,* 148–153.

Sherer, M., Maddox, J. E., Mercandante, B., Prentice-Dunn, S., Jacobs, B., & Rogers, R. W. (1982). The self-efficacy scale: Construction and validation. *Psychological Reports, 51,* 663–671.

Sherif, M., Harvey, L. J., White, B. J., Hood, W. R., & Sherif, C. W. (1988). *The robbers cave experiment: Intergroup conflict and cooperation.* Middletown, CT: Wesleyan University Press.

Sherif, M., & Hovland, C. I. (1961). *Social judgment: Assimilation and contrast effects in communication and attitude change.* New Haven, CT: Yale University Press.

Sherman, C. B. (1992). The health consequences of cigarette smoking: Pulmonary diseases. *Medical Clinics of North America, 76,* 355–375.

Sherrod, D. (1989). The influence of gender on same-sex friendships. In C. Hendrick (Ed.), *Review of personality and social psychology: Vol. 10. Close relationships.* Newbury Park, CA: Sage Publications.

Sherwin, B. B. (1991). The psychoendocrinology of aging and female sexuality. *Annual Review of Sex Research, 2,* 181–198.

Sherwood, A. (1993). Use of impedance cardiography in cardiovascular reactivity research. In J. Blascovich & E. S. Katkin (Eds.), *Cardiovascular reactivity to psychological stress and disease.* Washington, DC: American Psychological Association.

Shiffman, S., Fischer, L. A., Paty, J. A., Gnys, M., Hickcox, M., & Kassel, J. D. (1994). Drinking and smoking: A field study of their association. *Annals of Behavioral Medicine, 16,* 203–209.

Shneidman, E. S. (1985). *At the point of no return.* New York: Wiley.

Shore, T. H. (1992). Subtle gender bias in the assessment of managerial potential. *Sex Roles, 27,* 499–515.

Shostak, A. (1987). Singlehood. In M. B. Sussman & S. K. Steinmetz (Eds.), *Handbook of marriage and the family.* New York: Plenum.

Shotland, R. L. (1989). A model of the causes of date rape in developing and close relationships. In C. Hendrick (Ed.), *Review of personality and social psychology: Vol. 10. Close relationships.* Newbury Park, CA: Sage Publications.

Shotland, R. L., & Hunter, B. A. (1995). Women's "token resistant" and compliant sexual behaviors are related to uncertain sexual intentions and rape. *Personality and Social Psychology Bulletin, 21,* 226–236.

Showers, C. (1992). Compartmentalization of positive and negative self-knowledge: Keeping bad apples out of the bunch. *Journal of Personality and Social Psychology, 62,* 1036–1049.

Shuval, J. T. (1993). Migration and stress. In L. Goldberger & S. Breznitz (Eds.), *Handbook of stress: Theoretical and clinical aspects* (2nd ed.). New York: Free Press.

Siebert, A. (1995). *Student success: How to succeed in college and still have time for your friends.* Fort Worth, TX: Harcourt Brace.

Siegel, J. M. (1990). Stressful life events and use of physician services among the elderly. *Journal of Personality and Social Psychology, 58,* 1081–1086.

Siegel, J. M., Johnson, J. H., & Sarason, I. G. (1979). Life changes and menstrual discomfort. *Journal of Human Stress, 5,* 41–46.

Siegel, O. (1982). Personality development in adolescence. In B. B. Wolman (Ed.), *Handbook of developmental psychology.* Englewood Cliffs, NJ: Prentice-Hall.

Siegler, I. C., Nowlin, J. B., & Blumenthal, J. A. (1980). Health and behavior: Methodological considerations for adult development and aging. In L. W. Poon (Ed.), *Aging in the 1980s: Psychological issues.* Washington, DC: American Psychological Association.

Signorielli, N., & Lears, M. (1992). Children, television, and conceptions about chores: Attitudes and behaviors. *Sex Roles, 27,* 157–170.

Signorielli, N. (1993) Television, the portrayal of women, and children's attitudes. In G. L. Berry & J. K. Asamen (Eds.), *Children and television: Images in a changing sociocultural world.* Newbury Park, CA: Sage.

Silberstein, L. R. (1992). *Dual-career marriage, a system in transition.* Hillsdale, NJ: Erlbaum.

Silverberg, S. B., Tennenbaum, D. L., & Jacob, T. (1992). Adolescence and family interaction. In V. B. Van Hasselt & M. Hersen (Eds.), *Handbook of social development: A lifespan perspective.* New York: Plenum.

Silverman, P. R., & Worden, J. M. (1992). Children's reactions in the early months after the death of a parent. *American Journal of Orthopsychiatry, 62,* 93–104.

Simkins, L. (1994). Update on AIDS and sexual behavior of college students: Seven years later. *Psychological Reports, 74,* 208–210.

Simmons, C. H., von Kolke, A., & Shimizu, H. (1986). Attitudes toward romantic love among American, German, and Japanese students. *Journal of Social Psychology, 126,* 327–336.

Simon, G. E., & VonKorff, M. (1991). Somatization and psychiatric disorder in the NIMH epidemiologic catchment area study. *American Journal of Psychiatry, 148,* 1494–1500.

Simon, W., & Gagnon, J. (1977). Psychosexual development. In D. Byrne & L. A. Byrne (Eds.), *Exploring human sexuality.* New York: Crowell.

Simoneau, T. L., Miklowitz, D. J., & Saléem, R. (1998). Expressed emotion and interactional patterns in the families of bipolar patients. *Journal of Abnormal Psychology, 107,* 497–507.

Simonton, D. K. (1990). Creativity and wisdom in aging. In J. E. Birren & K. W. Schaie (Eds.), *Handbook of psychology of aging.* San Diego: Academic Press.

Simpson, J. A. (1987). The dissolution of romantic relationships: Factors involved in relationship stability and emotional distress. *Journal of Personality and Social Psychology, 53,* 683–692.

Simpson, J. A. (1990). Influence of attachment styles on romantic relationships. *Journal of Personality and Social Psychology, 59,* 971–980.

Singer, M. T., & Lalich, J. (1995). *Cults in our midst.* San Francisco: Jossey-Bass.

Singer, M. T., Wynne, L. C., & Toohey, M. L. (1978). Communication disorders and the families of schizophrenics. In L. C. Wynne, R. L. Cromwell, & S. Matthysse (Eds.), *The nature of schizophrenia: New approaches to research and treatment.* New York: Wiley Medical.

Singh, D. (1993). Adaptive significance of female physical attractiveness: Role of waist-to-hip ratio. *Journal of Personality and Social Psychology, 65,* 293–307.

Singh, D. (1995). Female judgment of male attractiveness and desirability for relationships: Role of waist-to-hip ratio and financial status.

Journal of Personality and Social Psychology, 69, 1089–1101.

Singh, R., & Tan, L. S. C. (1992). Attitudes and attraction: A test of the similarity-repulsion hypotheses. *British Journal of Social Psychology, 31,* 227–238.

Sinnott, J. D. (1989). A model for solution of ill-structured problems: Implications for everyday and abstract problem solving. In J. D. Sinnott (Ed.), *Everyday problem solving: Theory and application.* New York: Praeger.

Siscovick, D. S. (1990). Risks of exercising: Sudden cardiac death and injuries. In C. Bouchard, R. J. Shephard, T. Stephens, J. R. Sutton, & B. D. McPherson (Eds.), *Exercise, fitness, and health: A consensus of current knowledge.* Champaign, IL: Human Kinetics Books.

Siscovick, D. S., Weiss, N. S., Fletcher, R. H., & Lasky, T. (1984). The incidence of primary cardiac arrest during vigorous exercise. *New England Journal of Medicine, 311,* 874–877.

Skinner, B. F. (1953). *Science and human behavior.* New York: Macmillan.

Skinner, B. F. (1974). *About behaviorism.* New York: Knopf.

Skinner, B. F. (1987). Whatever happened to psychology as the science of behavior? *American Psychologist, 42,* 780–786.

Skinner, B. F. (1990). Can psychology be a science of mind? *American Psychologist, 45,* 1206–1210.

Skinner, P. H., & Shelton, R. L. (1985). *Speech, language, and hearing: Normal processes and disorders* (2nd ed.). New York: Wiley.

Slaby, A. E. (1997). Beyond reasonable doubt: The case for SSRI's. *Primary Psychiatry, 4,* 26–27.

Slade, P. (1995). Prospects for prevention. In G. Szmukler, C. Dare, & J. Treasure (Eds.), *Handbook of eating disorders: Theory, treatment, and research.* Chichester, England: Wiley.

Slavney, P. R. (1990). *Perspectives on hysteria.* Baltimore: John Hopkins University Press.

Small, I. F., Small, J. G., & Milstein, V. (1986). Electroconvulsive therapy. In P. A. Berger & H. K. H. Brodie (Eds.), *American handbook of psychiatry: Biological psychiatry* (Vol. 8) (2nd ed.). New York: Basic Books.

Small, S. A., & Riley, D. (1990). Toward a multidimensional assessment of work spillover into family life. *Journal of Marriage and the Family, 52,* 51–61.

Smeaton, G., Byrne, D., & Murnen, S. K. (1989). The repulsion hypothesis revisited: Similarity irrelevance or dissimilarity bias. *Journal of Personality and Social Psychology, 56,* 54–59.

Smith, A. L., & Weissman, M. M. (1992). Epidemiology. In E. S. Paykel (Ed.), *Handbook of affective disorders* (2nd ed.). New York: Guilford Press.

Smith, C. A., & Lazarus, R. S. (1993). Appraisal components, core relational themes, and the emotions. *Cognition and Emotion, 7,* 233–269.

Smith, D. (1982). Trends in counseling and psychotherapy. *American Psychologist, 37,* 802–809.

Smith, E. R., & Mackie, D. M. (1995). *Social psychology.* New York: Worth.

Smith, G. L., Large, M. M., Kavanagh, D. J., Karayanidis, F., Barrett, N. A., Michie, P. T., & O'Sullivan, B. T. (1998). Further evidence for a deficit in switching attention in schizophrenia. *Journal of Abnormal Psychology, 197,* 390–398.

Smith, J. C. (1993). *Understanding stress and coping.* New York: Macmillan.

Smith, K. (1991). Comments on "Teen suicide and changing cause-of-death certification, 1953–1987." *Suicidal Life-Threatening Behavior, 21,* 260–262.

Smith, M. (1985). *When I say no I feel guilty*. New York: Bantam Books.

Smith, M. L., & Glass, G. V. (1977). Meta-analysis of psychotherapy outcome studies. *American Psychologist, 32,* 752–760.

Smith, M. L., Glass, G. V., & Miller, R. L. (1980). *The benefits of psychotherapy.* Baltimore: Johns Hopkins University Press.

Smith, M., & Pazder, L. (1980). *Michelle remembers.* New York: Pocket Books.

Smith, P. A., & Midlarsky, E. (1985). Empirically derived conceptions of femaleness and maleness: A current view. *Sex Roles, 12,* 313–328.

Smith, R. E. (1989). Effects of coping skills training on generalized self-efficacy and locus of control. *Journal of Personality and Social Psychology, 56,* 228–233.

Smith, T. W., & Brown, P. C. (1991). Cynical hostility, attempts to exert social control, and cardiovascular reactivity in married couples. *Journal of Behavioral Medicine, 14,* 581–592.

Smith, T. W., & Christensen, A. J. (1992). Hostility, health, and social contexts. In H. S. Friedman (Ed.), *Hostility coping and health.* Washington, DC: American Psychological Association.

Smith, T. W., Pope, M. K., Sanders, J. D., Allred, K. D., & O'Keefe, J. L. (1988). Cynical hostility at home and work: Psychosocial vulnerability across domains. *Journal of Research in Personality, 22,* 525–548.

Smith, T. W., Turner, C. W., Ford, M. H., Hunt, S. C., Barlow, G. K., Stults, B. M., & Williams, R. R. (1987). Blood pressure reactivity in adult male twins. *Health Psychology, 6,* 209–220.

Smith-Lovin, L., & Brody, C. (1989). Interruptions in group discussions: The effects of gender and group composition. *American Sociological Review, 54,* 424–435.

Smock, P. J. (1993). The economic costs of marital disruption for young women over the past two decades. *Demography, 30,* 353–371.

Smoll, F. L., & Schutz, R. W. (1990). Quantifying gender differences in physical performance: A developmental perspective. *Developmental Psychology, 26,* 360–369.

Smollar, J., & Youniss, J. (1985). Adolescent self-concept development. In R. L. Leahy (Ed.), *The development of the self.* Orlando, FL: Academic Press.

Snelling, R. O., & Snelling, A. M. (1985). *Jobs! What they are . . . Where they are . . . What they pay!* New York: Simon & Schuster.

Snodgrass, S. E. (1992). Further effects of role versus gender on interpersonal sensitivity. *Journal of Personality and Social Psychology, 62,* 154–158.

Snyder, C. R., Lassegard, M., & Ford, C. E. (1986). Distancing after group success and failure: Basking in reflected glory and cutting off reflected failure. *Journal of Personality and Social Psychology, 51,* 382–388.

Snyder, M. (1979). Self-monitoring processes. In L. Berkowitz (Ed.), *Advances in experimental social psychology* (Vol. 12). New York: Academic Press.

Snyder, M. (1986). *Public appearances/Private realities: The psychology of self-monitoring.* New York: Freeman.

Snyder, M., & Campbell, B. (1982). Self-monitoring: The self in action. In J. Suls (Ed.), *Psychological perspectives on the self.* Hillsdale, NJ: Erlbaum.

Snyder, M., & Ickes, W. (1985). Personality and social behavior. In G. Lindzey & E. Aronson (Eds.), *Handbook of social psychology,* (Vol. 2). New York: Random House.

Snyder, M., Tanke, E. D., & Berscheid, E. (1977). Social perception and interpersonal behavior: On the self-fulfilling nature of social stereotypes. *Journal of Personality and Social Psychology, 35,* 655–666.

Sobal, J. (1995). Social influences on body weight. In K. D. Brownell & C. G. Fairburn (Eds.), *Eating disorders and obesity: A comprehensive handbook.* New York: Guilford Press.

Sobin, C., Sackeim, H. A., Prudic, J., Devanand, D. P., Moody, B. J., & McElhiney, M. C. (1995). Predictors of retrograde amnesia following ECT. *American Journal of Psychiatry, 152,* 995–1001.

Soloman, J. C. (1992). Child sexual abuse by family members: A radical feminist perspective. *Sex Roles, 27,* 473–485.

Solomon, S., & Canino, G. (1990). Appropriateness of the DSM-III-R criteria for posttraumatic stress disorder. *Comprehensive Psychiatry, 31,* 227–237.

Solomon, Z., Weisenberg, M., Schwarzwald, J., & Mikulincer, M. (1988). Combat stress reaction and posttraumatic stress disorder as determinants of perceived self-efficacy in battle. *Journal of Social and Clinical Psychology, 6,* 356–370.

Somers, M. D. (1993). A comparison of voluntarily childfree adults and parents. *Journal of Marriage and the Family, 55,* 653–650.

Sommers-Flanagan, R., Sommers-Flanagan, J., & Davis, B. (1993). What's happening on music television? A gender-role content analysis. *Sex Roles, 28,* 745–753.

Sotiriou, P. E. (1984). *Integrating college study skills: Reasoning in reading, listening and writing.* Belmont, CA: Wadsworth.

Sotiriou, P. E. (1996). *Integrating college study skills: Reasoning in reading, listening, and writing.* Belmont, CA: Wadsworth.

South, S. J. (1991). Sociodemographic differentials in mate selection preferences. *Journal of Marriage and the Family, 53* 928–940.

South, S. J. (1993). Racial and ethnic differences in the desire to marry. *Journal of Marriage and the Family, 55,* 357–370.

Sowell, T. (1994). *Race and culture: A world view.* New York: Basic Books.

Spanos, N. P. (1994). Multiple identity enactments and multiple personality disorder: A sociocognitive perspective. *Psychological Bulletin, 116,* 143–165.

Spanos, N. P. (1996). *Multiple identities and false memories.* Washington, DC: American Psychological Association.

Spector, I., & Carey, M. (1990). Incidence and prevalence of the sexual dysfunctions: A critical review of the empirical literature. *Archives of Sexual Behavior, 19,* 389–408.

Spence, J. T. (1983). Comment on Lubinski, Tellegen, and Butcher's "Masculinity, femininity, and androgyny viewed and assessed as distinct concepts." *Journal of Personality and Social Psychology, 44,* 440–446.

Spence, J. T., & Buckner, C. E. (1999). Instrumental and expressive traits, trait stereotypes, and sexist attitudes: What do they signify? *Psychology of Women Quarterly,* in press.

Sperry, R. W. (1982). Some effects of disconnecting the cerebral hemispheres. *Science, 217,* 1223–1226, 1250.

Spiegel, D. (1993). Social support: How friends, family, and groups can help. In D. Goleman & J. Gurin (Eds.), *Mind/body medicine: How to use your mind for better health.* Yonkers, NY: Consumer Reports Books.

Spiegel, D. (1994). Dissociative disorders. In R. E. Hales, S. C. Yudofsky, & J. A. Talbott (Eds.), *The American Psychiatric Press textbook of psychiatry* (2nd ed.). Washington, DC: American Psychiatric Press.

Spiegler, M. D., & Guevremont, D. C. (1993). *Contemporary behavior therapy.* Pacific Grove, CA: Brooks/Cole.

Spiegler, M. D., & Guevremont, D. C. (1998). *Contemporary behavior therapy.* Pacific Grove, CA: Brooks/Cole.

Spitze, G. (1988). Women's employment and family relations: A review. *Journal of Marriage and the Family, 50,* 595–618.

Spivey, C. B., & Prentice-Dunn, S. (1990). Assessing the directionality of deindividuated behavior: Effects of deindividuation, modeling, and private self-consciousness on aggressive and prosocial responses. *Basic and Applied Social Psychology, 11,* 387–403.

Sporakowski, M. J. (1988). A therapist's views on the consequences of change for the contemporary family. *Family Relations, 37,* 373–378.

Sprecher, S. (1989). The importance to males and females of physical attractiveness, earning potential and expressiveness in initial attraction. *Sex Roles, 21,* 591–607.

Sprecher, S., Sullivan, Q., & Hatfield, E. (1994). Mate selection preferences: Gender differences examined in a national sample. *Journal of Personality and Social Psychology, 66,* 1074–1080.

Springer, S. P., & Deutsch, G. (1993). *Left brain, right brain* (4th ed.). New York: Freeman.

Sriram, T. G., & Silverman, J. J. (1998). The effects of stress on the respiratory system. In J. R. Hubbard & E. A. Workman (Eds.), *Handbook of stress medicine: An organ system approach.* New York: CRC Press.

Stack, S., & Eshleman, J. R. (1998). Marital status and happiness: A 17-nation study. *Journal of Marriage and the Family, 60,* 527–536.

Stacy, A. W., Newcomb, M. D., & Bentler, P. M. (1993). Cognitive motivations and sensation seeking as long-term predictors of drinking problems. *Journal of Social and Clinical Psychology, 12,* 1–24.

Stall, R. D., Coates, T. J., & Hoff, C. (1988). Behavioral risk reduction for HIV infection among gay and bisexual men: A review of results from the United States. *American Psychologist, 43,* 878–885.

Stanford, M. W. (1987). Designer drugs: Medical aspects and clinical management. *Alcoholism Treatment Quarterly, 4,* 97–125.

Stanislaw, H., & Rice, F. J. (1988). Correlation between sexual desire and menstrual cycle characteristics. *Archives of Sexual Behavior, 17,* 499–508.

Stankov, L. (1988). Aging, attention, and intelligence. *Psychology and Aging,* 59–74.

Stark, E. (1984, May). The unspeakable family secret. *Psychology Today,* pp. 41–46.

Starker, S. (1990). Self-help books: Ubiquitous agents of health care. *Medical Psychotherapy: An International Journal, 3* 187–194.

Starker, S. (1992). Characteristics of self-help book readers among VA medical outpatients. *Medical Psychotherapy: An International Journal, 5,* 89–93.

Starrels, M. E., Ingersoll-Dayton, B., Dowler, D. W., & Neal, M. B. (1997). The stress of caring for a parent: Effects of the elder's impairment on an employed adult child. *Journal of Marriage and the Family, 59,* 860–872.

Statt, D. A. (1994). *Psychology and the world of work.* New York: New York University Press.

Stattin, H., & Magnusson, D. (1990). *Pubertal maturation in female development.* Hillsdale, NJ: Erlbaum.

Staw, B. M., & Ross, J. (1985). Stability in the midst of change: A dispositional approach to job attitudes. *Journal of Applied Psychology, 70,* 469–480.

Steele, B. (1980). Psychodynamic factors in child abuse. In C. H. Kempe & F. E. Helfer (Eds.), *The battered child*. Chicago: University of Chicago Press.

Stein, M. B., & Uhde, T. W. (1995). Biology of anxiety disorders. In A. F. Schatzberg & C. B. Nemeroff (Eds.), *The American Psychiatric Press textbook of psychopharmacology*. Washington, DC: American Psychiatric Press.

Stein, M. B., Forde, D. R., Anderson, G., & Walker, J. R. (1997a). Obsessive-compulsive disorder in the community: An epidemiologic survey with clinical reappraisal. *American Journal of Psychiatry, 154*, 1120–1126.

Stein, M. B., Walker, J. R., Hazen, A. L., & Forde, D. R. (1997b). Full and partial posttraumatic stress disorder: Findings from a community survey. *American Journal of Psychiatry, 154*, 1114–1119.

Stein, N., Marshall, N. L., & Tropp, L. R. (1993). *Secrets in public: Sexual harassment in our schools*. Wellesley, MA: Center for Research on Women at Wellesley College and the NOW Legal Defense and Education Fund.

Stein, P. J. (1975). Singlehood: An alternative to marriage. *Family Coordinator, 24*, 489–503.

Stein, P. J. (1976). *Single*. Englewood Cliffs, NJ: Prentice-Hall.

Stein, P. J. (1989). The diverse world of single adults. In J. M. Henslin (Ed.), *Marriage and family in a changing society* (3rd ed.). New York: Free Press.

Steinberg, L., & Silverberg, S. B. (1987). Influences on marital satisfaction during the middle stages of the family life cycle. *Journal of Marriage and the Family, 49*, 751–760.

Steiner, H., Smith, C., Rosenkranz, R. T., & Litt, I. (1991). The early care and feeding of anorexics. *Child Psychiatry and Human Development, 21*, 163–167.

Steinhausen, H. C. (1995). The course and outcome of anorexia nervosa. In K. D. Brownell & C. G. Fairburn (Eds.), *Eating disorders and obesity: A comprehensive handbook*. New York: Guilford Press.

Steinmetz, H., Staiger, J. F., Schluag, G., Huang, Y., & Jancke, L. (1995). Corpus callosum and brain volume in women and men. *Neuroreport, 3*, 1002–1004.

Stekel, W. (1950). *Techniques of analytical psychotherapy*. New York: Liveright.

Stemberger, R. T., Turner, S. M., Beidel, D. C., & Calhoun, K. S. (1995). Social phobia: An analysis of possible developmental factors. *Journal of Abnormal Psychology, 104*, 526–531.

Stephan, W. G. (1989). A cognitive approach to stereotyping. In D. Bartal, C. F. Graumann, A. W. Kruglanski, & W. Stroebe (Eds.), *Stereotyping and prejudice: Changing conceptions*. New York: Springer-Verlag.

Stephen, T. D. (1985). Fixed-sequence and circular-causal models of relationship development: Divergent views on the role of communication in intimacy. *Journal of Marriage and the Family, 47*, 955–963.

Stern, G. S., McCants, T. R., & Pettine, P. W. (1982). Stress and illness: Controllable and uncontrollable events' relative contributions. *Personality and Social Psychology Bulletin, 8*, 140–145.

Sternberg, R. J. (1986). A triangular theory of love. *Psychological Review, 93* 119–135.

Sternberg, R. J. (1988). Triangulating love. In R. J. Sternberg & M. L. Barnes (Eds.), *The psychology of love*. New Haven, CT: Yale University Press.

Sternberg, R. J., & Grajek, S. (1984). The nature of love. *Journal of Personality and Social Psychology, 47*, 312–329.

Stets, J. E. (1991). Cohabiting and marital aggression: The role of social isolation. *Journal of Marriage and the Family, 53*, 669–680.

Stevens, G., Owens, D., & Schaefer, E. C. (1990). Education and attractiveness in marriage choices. *Social Psychology Quarterly, 53* 62–70.

Stillion, J. M. (1995). Death in the lives of adults: Responding to the tolling of the bell. in H. Wass & R. A. Neimeyer (Eds.), *Dying: Facing the facts*. New York: Taylor & Francis.

Stoddard, J. J., & Miller, T. (1995). Impact of parental smoking on the prevalence of wheezing respiratory illness in children. *American Journal of Epidemiology, 141*, 96–102.

Stodghill, R. (1998, June 15). Where'd you learn that? *Time*, 52–59.

Stoffer, G. R., Davis, K. E., & Brown, J. B., Jr. (1977). The consequences of changing initial answers on objective tests: A stable effect and a stable misconception. *Journal of Educational Research, 70*, 272–277.

Stohs, J. H. (1995). Predictors of conflict over the household division of labor among women employed full time. *Sex Roles, 33*, 257–275.

Stoll, A. L., Tohen, M., & Baldessarini, R. J. (1992). Increasing frequency of the diagnosis of obsessive-compulsive disorder. *American Journal of Psychiatry, 149*, 638–640.

Stone, A. A., & Neale, J. M. (1984). New measure of daily coping: Development and preliminary results. *Journal of Personality and Social Psychology, 46*, 892–906.

Stone, A. A., Bovbjerg, D. H., Neale, J.M., Napoli, A., Valdimarsdottir,H., Cox, D., Hayden, F. G., & Gwaltney, J. M. (1992). Development of the common cold symptoms following experimental rhinovirus infection is related to prior stressful events. *Behavioral Medicine, 18*, 115–120.

Stone, L. (1977). *The family, sex and marriage in England 1500–1800*. New York: Harper & Row.

Strassberg, D. (1994). A physiologically based model of early ejaculation: A solution or a problem? *Journal of Sex Education & Therapy, 20*, 215–217.

Strauman, T. J., Vookles, J., Berenstein, V., Chaiken, S., & Higgins, E. T. (1991). Self-discrepancies and vulnerability to body dissatisfaction and disordered eating. *Journal of Personality and Social Psychology, 61*, 946–956.

Straus, M. A., & Gelles, R. J. (1986). Societal change and change in family violence from 1975 to 1985 as revealed by two national surveys. *Journal of Marriage and the Family, 48*, 465–479.

Straus, M. A., Gelles, R. J., & Steinmetz, S. K. (1980). *Behind closed doors: Violence in the American family*. New York: Doubleday.

Strickland, B. R. (1988). Sex-related differences in health and illness. *Psychology of Women Quarterly, 12*, 381–399.

Striegel-Moore, R. H. (1995). A feminist perspective on the etiology of eating disorders. In K. D. Brownell & C. G. Fairburn (Eds.), *Eating disorders and obesity: A comprehensive handbook*. New York: Guilford Press.

Striegel-Moore, R. H., Silberstein, L. R., & Rodin, J. (1993). The social self in bulimia nervosa: Public self-consciousness, social anxiety, and perceived fraudulence. *Journal of Abnormal Psychology, 102*, 297–303.

Strober, M. (1995). Family-genetic perspectives on anorexia nervosa and bulimia nervosa. In K. D. Brownell & C. G. Fairburn (Eds.), *Eating disorders and obesity: A comprehensive handbook*. New York: Guilford Press.

Stroebe, M., Gergen, M. M., Gergen, K. J., & Stroebe, W. (1992). Broken hearts or broken bonds: Love and death in historical perspective. *American Psychologist, 47*, 1205–1212.

Stroh, L. K., Brett, J. M., & Reilly, A. H. (1996). Family structure, glass ceiling, and traditional explanations for the differential rate of turnover of female and male managers. *Journal of Vocational Behavior, 49*, 99–118.

Strouse, J., & Fabes, R. A. (1985). Formal vs. informal sources of sex education: Competing forces in the sexual socialization of adolescents. *Adolescence, 78*, 251–263.

Strupp, H. H. (1996). The tripartite model and the *Consumer Reports* study. *American Psychologist, 51*, 1017–1024.

Strupp, H. H., & Howard, K. I. (1992). A brief history of psychotherapy research. In D. K. Freedheim (Ed.), *History of psychotherapy: A century of change*. Washington, DC: American Psychological Association.

Stull, D. E., & Hatch, L. R. (1984). Unraveling the effects of multiple life changes. *Research on Aging, 6*, 560–571.

Stunkard, A. J., Harris, J. R., Pederson, N. L., & McClearn, G. E. (1990). The body-mass index of twins who have been reared apart. *New England Journal of Medicine, 322*, 1483–1487.

Stunkard, A. J., Sorensen, T., Hanis, C., Teasdale, T. W., Chakraborty, R., Schull, W. J., & Schulsinger, F. (1986). An adoption study of human obesity. *New England Journal of Medicine, 314*, 193–198.

Sturgis, E. T. (1984). Obsessional and compulsive disorders. In H. E. Adams & P. B. Sutker (Eds.), *Comprehensive handbook of psychopathology*. New York: Plenum.

Sturgis, E. T. (1993). Obsessive-compulsive disorders. In P. B.Sutker & H. E. Adams (Eds.), *Comprehensive handbook of psychopathology* (2nd ed.). New York: Plenum.

Subrahmanyam, K., & Greenfield, P. M. (1994). Effect of video game practice on spatial skills in girls and boys [Special issue]. *Journal of Applied Developmental Psychology, 15*, 13–32.

Sue, D. (1979). Erotic fantasies of college students during coitus. *Journal of Sex Research, 15*, 299–305.

Suedfeld, P. (1979). Stressful levels of environmental stimulation. In I. G. Sarason & C. D. Spielberger (Eds.), *Stress and anxiety* (Vol. 6). Washington, DC: Hemisphere.

Suh, E., Diener, E., Oishi, S., & Triandis, H. C. (1998). The shifting basis of life satisfaction judgments across cultures: Emotions versus norms. *Journal of Personality and Social Psychology, 74*, 482–493.

Suinn, R. M. (1984). *Fundamentals of abnormal psychology*. Chicago: Nelson-Hall.

Sulloway, F. J. (1991). Reassessing Freud's case histories: The social construction of psychoanalysis. *ISIS, 82*, 245–275.

Summers, R. J. (1991). The influence of affirmative action on perceptions of a beneficiary's qualifications. *Journal of Applied Social Psychology, 21*, 1265–1276.

Super, D. E. (1957). *The psychology of careers*. New York: HarperCollins.

Super, D. E. (1985). Career and life development. In D. Brown & L. Brooks (Eds.), *Career choice and development*. San Francisco: Jossey-Bass.

Super, D. E. (1988). Vocational adjustment: Implementing a self-concept. *The Career Development Quarterly, 36*, 351–357.

Surra, C. A. (1990). Research and theory on mate selection and premarital relationships in the 1980s. *Journal of Marriage and the Family, 52*, 844–865.

Sussman, N. M., & Rosenfeld, H. M. (1982). Influence of culture, language, and sex on conversational distance. *Journal of Personality and Social Psychology, 42*, 66–74.

Swaney, K., & Prediger, D. (1985). The relationship between interest-occupation congruence and job satisfaction. *Journal of Vocational Behavior, 26,* 13–24.

Swann, W. B. (1987). Identity negotiation: Where two roads meet. *Journal of Personality and Social Psychology, 53,* 1038–1051.

Swann, W. B., Jr., & Ely, R. J. (1984). A battle of wills: Self-verification versus behavioral confirmation. *Journal of Personality and Social Psychology, 46,* 1287–1302.

Swann, W. B., Jr., Hixon, J. G., Stein-Seroussi, A., & Gilbert, D. T. (1990). The fleeting gleam of praise: Behavioral reactions to self-relevant feedback. *Journal of Personality and Social Psychology, 43* 59–66.

Swann, W. B., Jr., Pelham, B. W., & Krull, D. S. (1989). Agreeable fancy or disagreeable truth? How people reconcile their self-enhancement and self-verification needs. *Journal of Personality and Social Psychology, 57,* 782–791.

Swann, W. B., Jr., Stein-Seroussi, A., & Giesler, R. B. (1992). Why people self-verify. *Journal of Personality and Social Psychology, 62,* 392–401.

Swann, W. B., Jr., Stein-Seroussi, A., & McNulty, S. E. (1992). Outcasts in a white-lie society: The enigmatic worlds of people with negative self-conceptions. *Journal of Personality and Social Psychology, 62,* 618–624.

Swartz, C. M. (1993). Clinical and laboratory predictors of ECT response. In C. E. Coffey (Ed.), *The clinical science of electroconvulsive therapy.* Washington, DC: American Psychiatric Press.

Sweeney, P. D., Anderson, K., & Bailey, S. (1986). Attributional style in depression: A meta-analytic review. *Journal of Personality and Social Psychology, 50,* 974–991.

Swim, J. K., Aikin K. J., Wayne, S. H., & Hunter, B. A. (1995). Sexism and racism: Old-fashioned and modern prejudices. *Journal of Personality and Social Psychology, 68,* 199–214.

Swoboda, F. (1995, November 25). Law, education failing to break glass ceiling. *Washington Post,* C1, C2.

Szasz, T. S. (1974). *The myth of mental illness.* New York: HarperCollins.

Szasz, T. S. (1993). *A lexicon of lunacy: Metaphoric malady, moral responsibility, and psychiatry.* New Brunswick, NJ: Transaction.

Szmukler, G. I., & Patton, G. (1995). Sociocultural models of eating disorders. In G. Szmukler, C. Dare, & J. Treasure (Eds.), *Handbook of eating disorders: Theory, treatment and research.* New York: Wiley.

Szymanski, S., Lieberman, J. A., Alvir, J. M., Mayerhoff, D., Loebel, A., Geisler, S., Chakos, M., Koreen, A., Jody, D., Kane, J., Woerner, M., & Cooper, T. (1995). Gender differences in onset of illness, treatment response, course, and biologic indexes in first-episode schizophrenic patients. *American Journal of Psychiatry, 152,* 698–703.

Tajfel, H. (1982). *Social identity and intergroup relations.* London: Cambridge University Press.

Takanishi, R. (1993). The opportunities of adolescence—Research, interventions, and policy. *American Psychologist, 48,* 85–87.

Tanfer, K. (1987). Patterns of premarital cohabitation among never-married women in the United States. *Journal of Marriage and the Family, 49,* 483–497.

Tangri, S. S., Burt, M. R., & Johnson, L. B. (1982). Sexual harassment at work: Three explanatory models. *Journal of Social Issues, 38,* 33–54.

Tannen, D. (1990). *You just don't understand: Women and men in conversation.* New York: Ballantine.

Tannen, D. (1998). *The argument culture: Moving from debate to dialogue.* New York: Random House.

Tanner, J. M. (1978). *Fetus into man: Physical growth from conception to maturity.* Cambridge, MA: Harvard University Press.

Taris, T. W., & Semin, G. R. (1997). Gender as a narrative of the effects of the love motive and relational context on sexual experience. *Archives of Sexual Behavior, 26,* 159–180.

Taub, S. (1996). The legal treatment of recovered memories of child sexual abuse. *Journal of Legal Medicine, 17,* 183–214.

Tavris, C. (1982). *Anger: The misunderstood emotion.* New York: Simon & Schuster.

Tavris, C. (1989). *Anger: The misunderstood emotion* (2nd ed.). New York: Simon & Schuster.

Tavris, C. (1991). The mismeasure of woman: Paradoxes and perspectives in the study of gender. In J. D. Good-childs (Ed.), *Psychological perspectives on human diversity in America.* Washington, DC: American Psychological Association.

Tavris, C., & Sadd, S. (1977). *The Redbook report on female sexuality.* New York: Delacorte.

Tavris, C. (1992). *The mismeasure of woman.* New York: Simon & Schuster.

Tavris, C. (1995). Do codependency theories explain women's unhappiness—or exploit their insecurities? In M. Babcock & C. McKay (Eds.), *Challenging codependency: Feminist critiques.* Toronto: University of Toronto Press.

Tay, K. H., Ward, C. M., & Hill, J. A. (1993, August). *Holland's congruence and certainty of career aspirations in Asian graduate students.* Paper presented at the meeting of the American Psychological Association, Toronto, Canada.

Taylor, C. B. (1995). Treatment of anxiety disorders. In A. F. Schatzberg & C. B. Nemeroff (Eds.), *The American Psychiatric Press textbook of psychopharmacology.* Washington, DC: American Psychiatric Press.

Taylor, D. A., & Altman, I. (1987). Communication in interpersonal relationships: Social penetration processes. In M. E. Roloff & G. R. Miller (Eds.), *Interpersonal processes: New directions in communication research.* Newbury Park, CA: Sage Publications.

Taylor, R. J., Chatters, L. M., Tucker, M. B., & Lewis, E. (1990). Developments in research on black families: A decade review. *Journal of Marriage and the Family, 52,* 993–1014.

Taylor, S. E. (1989). *Positive illusions: Creative self-deception and the healthy mind.* New York: Basic Books.

Taylor, S. E., & Brown, J. D. (1988). Illusion and well-being: A social psychological perspective on mental health. *Psychological Bulletin, 103,* 193–210.

Taylor, S. E., & Brown, J. D. (1994). Positive illusions and well-being revisited: Separating fact from fiction. *Psychological Bulletin, 116,* 21–27.

Teachman, J. D., Polonko, K. A., & Scanzoni, J. (1987). Demography of the family. In M. B. Sussman & S. K. Steinmetz (Eds.), *Handbook of marriage and the family.* New York: Plenum.

Tedeschi, R. G., & Calhoun, L. G. (1996). The posttraumatic growth inventory: Measuring the positive legacy of trauma. *Journal of Traumatic Stress, 9,* 455–472.

Tellegen, A., Lykken, D. T., Bouchard, T. J., Jr., Wilcox, K. J., Segal, N. L., & Rich, S. (1988). Personality similarity in twins reared apart and together. *Journal of Personality and Social Psychology, 54,* 1031–1039.

Temoshok, L. (1987). Personality, coping style, emotion and cancer: Towards an integrative model. *Cancer Surveys, 6,* 545–567.

Terkel, S. (1985). *Working: People talk about what they do all day and how they feel about what they do.* New York: Pantheon.

Terpstra, D. E., & Baker, D. D. (1989). The identification and classification of reactions to sexual harassment. *Journal of Organizational Behavior, 10,* 1–14.

Terr, L. (1994). *Unchained memories: True stories of traumatic memories, lost and found.* New York: Basic Books.

Terry, D. J. (1994). Determinants of coping: The role of stable and situation factors. *Journal of Personality and Social Psychology, 66,* 895–910.

Tesch, S. A., & Whitbourne, S. K. (1982). Intimacy and identity status in young adults. *Journal of Personality and Social Psychology, 43,* 1041–1051.

Testa, K. (1996). Church to pay $1 million in false-memory case. *San Jose Mercury News,* 8A.

Thibaut, J. W., & Kelley, H. H. (1959). *The social psychology of groups.* New York: Wiley.

Thigpen, C. H., & Cleckley, H. M. (1984). On the incidence of multiple personality disorder: A brief communication. *International Journal of Clinical and Experimental Hypnosis, 32,* 63–66.

Thomas, K. W. (1988). The conflict-handling modes: Toward more precise theory. *Management Communication Quarterly, 1,* 430–436.

Thomas, M. H. (1982). Physiological arousal, exposure to a relatively lengthy aggressive film, and aggressive behavior. *Journal of Research in Personality, 16,* 72–81.

Thomason, B. T., Brantkey, P. J., Jones, G. N., Dyer, H. R., & Morris, J. L. (1992). The relation between stress and disease activity in rheumatoid arthritis. *Journal of Behavioral Medicine, 15,* 215–220.

Thompson, A. P. (1983). Extramarital sex: A review of the research literature. *Journal of Sex Research, 19,* 1–22.

Thompson, A. P. (1984). Emotional and sexual components of extramarital relations. *Journal of Marriage and the Family, 46,* 35–42.

Thompson, E. H., & Pleck, J. H. (1986). The structure of male role norms. *American Behavioral Scientist, 29,* 531–543.

Thompson, S. C., & Spacapan, S. (1991). Perceptions of control in vulnerable populations. *Journal of Social Issues, 47,* 1–21.

Thomson, E., & Colella, U. (1992). Cohabitation and marital stability: Quality or commitment? *Journal of Marriage and the Family, 54,* 259–267.

Thornborrow, N. M., & Sheldon, M. B. (1995). Women in the labor force. In J. Freeman (Ed.), *Women: A feminist perspective* (5th ed.). Mountain View, CA: Mayfield.

Thorndyke, P. W., & Hayes-Roth, B. (1979). The use of schemata in the acquisition and transfer of knowledge. *Cognitive Psychology, 11,* 83–106.

Thornquist, M. H., & Zuckerman, M. (1995). Psychopathy, passive-avoidance learning and basic dimensions of personality. *Personality & Individual Differences, 19,* 525–534.

Thornton, A. (1989). Changing attitudes toward family issues in the United States. *Journal of Marriage and the Family, 51,* 873–893.

Thornton, B. (1984). Defensive attribution of responsibility: Evidence for an arousal-based motivational bias. *Journal of Personality and Social Psychology, 46,* 721–734.

Thornton, B. (1992). Repression and its mediating influence on the defensive attribution of responsibility. *Journal of Research in Personality, 26,* 44–57.

Tice, D. M. (1991). Esteem protection or enhancement? Self-handicapping motives and attributions differ by trait self-esteem. *Journal of Personality and Social Psychology, 5,* 711–725.

Tice, D. M. (1993). The social motivations of people with low self-esteem. In R. Baumeister (Ed.), *Self-esteem: The puzzle of low self-regard.* New York: Plenum.

Tice, D. M., & Baumeister, R. F. (1997). Longitudinal study of procrastination, performance, stress, and health: The cost and benefits of dawdling. *Psychological Science, 8,* 454–458.

Tice, D. M., Butler, J. L., Muraven M. B., & Stillwell A. M. (1995). When modesty prevails: Differential favorability of self-presentation to friends and strangers. *Journal of Personality and Social Psychology, 69,* 1120–1138.

Ting-Toomey, S. (1991). Intimacy expressions in three cultures: France, Japan and the United States. *International Journal of Intercultural Relations, 15,* 29–46.

Tobin-Richards, M. H., Boxer, A. M., & Petersen, A. C. (1983). The psychological significance of pubertal change: Sex differences in perceptions of self during early adolescence. In J. Brooks-Gunn & A. C. Petersen (Eds.), *Girls at puberty: Biological and psychosocial perspectives.* New York: Plenum.

Toffler, A. (1970). *Future shock.* New York: Random House.

Toffler, A. (1980). *The third wave.* New York: Bantam Books.

Tohen, M., & Goodwin, F. K. (1995). Epidemiology of bipolar disorder. In M. T. Tsuang, M. Tohen, & G. E. P. Zahner (Eds.), *Textbook in psychiatric epidemiology.* New York: Wiley.

Tollefson, G. D. (1995). Selective serotonin reuptake inhibitors. In A. F. Schatzberg & C. B. Nemeroff (Eds.), *The American Psychiatric Press textbook of psychopharmacology.* Washington, DC: American Psychiatric Press.

Tollefson, G. D., Beasley, C. M., Jr., Tamura, R. N., Tran, P. V., & Potvin, J. H. (1997). Blind, controlled, long-term study of the comparative incidence of treatment-emergent tardive dyskinesia with olanzapine or haloperidol. *American Journal of Psychiatry, 154,* 1248–1254.

Tolstedt, B. E., & Stokes, J. P. (1984). Self-disclosure, intimacy, and the depenetration process. *Journal of Personality and Social Psychology, 46,* 84–90.

Tondo, L., Baldessarini, R. J., Hennen, J., & Floris, G. (1998). Lithium maintenance treatment of depression and mania in bipolar I and bipolar II disorders. *American Journal of Psychiatry, 155,* 638–645.

Toomey, R., Kremen, W. S., Simpson, J. C., Samson, J. A., Seidman, L. J., Lyons, M. J., Faraone, S. V., & Tsuang, M. T. (1997). Revisiting the factor structure for positive and negative symptoms: Evidence from a large heterogeneous group of psychiatric patients. *American Journal of Psychology, 154,* 371–377.

Torrey, E. F. (1992). *Freudian fraud: The malignant effect of Freud's theory on American thought and culture.* New York: Harper Perennial.

Tracey, T. J., & Rounds, J. (1993). Evaluating Holland's and Gati's vocational-interest models: A structural meta-analysis. *Psychological Bulletin, 113,* 229–246.

Travis, C. B. (1988). *Women and health psychology: Mental health issues.* Hillsdale, NJ: Erlbaum.

Treas, J. (1983). Aging and the family. In D. S. Woodruff & J. E. Birren (Eds.), *Aging: Scientific perspectives and social issues.* Pacific Grove, CA: Brooks/Cole.

Treasure, J., & Szmukler, G. I. (1995). Medical complications of chronic anorexia nervosa. In G. I. Szmukler, C. Dare, & J. Treasure (Eds.), *Handbook of eating disorders: Theory, treatment and research.* Chichester, England: Wiley.

Treiman, D. J. (1985). The work histories of women and men: What we know and what we need to find out. In A. S. Rossi (Ed.), *Gender and the life course.* New York: Aldine.

Triandis, H. C. (1989). Self and social behavior in differing cultural contexts. *Psychological Review, 96,* 269–289.

Triandis, H. C. (1994). *Culture and social behavior.* New York: McGraw-Hill.

Trickett, P. K., & Putnam, F. M. (1993). Impact of child sexual abuse on females: Toward a developmental, psychobiological interpretation. *Psychological Science, 4,* 81–87.

Tripp, C. A. (1987). *The homosexual matrix.* New York: Meridian.

Trovato, F., & Lauris, G. (1989). Marital status and mortality in Canada: 1951–1981. *Journal of Marriage and the Family, 51,* 907–922.

Tsai, M., & Uemera, A. (1988). Asian Americans: The struggles, the conflicts, and the successes. In P. Bronstein & K. Quina (Eds.), *Teaching a psychology of people.* Washington, DC: American Psychological Association.

Tsai, M., & Uemura, A. (1988). Asian Americans: The struggles, the conflicts, and the successes. In P. Bronstein & K. Quina (Eds.), *Teaching a psychology of people.* Washington, DC: American Psychological Association.

Tschann, J. M., Johnston, J. R., Kline, M., & Wallerstein, J. S. (1989). Family process and children's functioning during divorce. *Journal of Marriage and the Family, 51,* 431–444.

Tschann, J. M., Johnston, J. R., Kline, M., & Wallerstein, J. S. (1990). Conflict, loss, change and parent-child relationships: Predicting children's adjustment during divorce. *Journal of Divorce, 13* 1–22.

Tucker, G. J. (1998). Putting DSM-IV in perspective. *American Journal of Psychiatry, 155,* 159–161.

Tucker, P., & Aron, A. (1993). Passionate love and marital satisfaction at key transition points in the family life cycle. *Journal of Social and Clinical Psychology, 12,* 135–147.

Tucker, V., & Cho, C. (1991). AIDS and adolescents. *Postgraduate Medicine, 89,* 49–53.

Turner, J. C. (1987). *Rediscovering the social group: A self-categorization theory.* Oxford, England: Basil Blackwell.

Turner, J. R., & Wheaton, B. (1995). Checklist measurement of stressful life events. In S. Cohen, R. C. Kessler, & L. U. Gordon (Eds.), *Measuring stress: A guide for health and social scientists.* New York: Oxford University Press.

Turner, S. M., McCann, B. S., Beidel, D. C., & Mezzich, J. E. (1986). DSM-III classification of the anxiety disorders: A psychometric study. *Journal of Abnormal Psychology, 95,* 168–172.

Uchino, B. N., Cacioppo, J. T., & Kiecolt-Glaser, J. K. (1996). The relationship between social support and physiological processes: A review with emphasis on underlying mechanisms and implications for health. *Psychological Bulletin, 119,* 488–531.

Uhle, S. M. (1994). Codependence: Contextual variables in the language of social pathology. *Issues in Mental Health Nursing, 15,* 307–317.

Ungerleider, J. T., & Pechnick, R. (1992). Hallucinogens. In J. H. Lowinson, P. Ruiz, & R. B. Millman (Eds.), *Substance abuse: A comprehensive textbook* (2nd ed.). Baltimore: Williams & Wilkins.

Upshaw, H. S. (1969). The personal reference scale: An approach to social judgment. In L. Berkowitz (Ed.), *Advances in experimental social psychology* (Vol. 4). New York: Academic Press.

Ursano, R. J., & Silberman, E. K. (1994). Psychoanalysis, psychoanalytic psychotherapy, and supportive psychotherapy. In R. E. Hales, S. C. Yudofsky, & J. A. Talbott (Eds.), *The American Psychiatric Press textbook of psychiatry* (2nd ed.). Washington, DC: American Psychiatric Press.

U.S. Bureau of Labor Statistics. (1997). *National census of fatal occupational injuries, 1997.* U.S. Government Printing Office.

U.S. Bureau of Labor Statistics. (1998). *Occupational outlook handbook: 1998–1999.* Washington, DC: U.S. Government Printing Office.

U.S. Bureau of the Census. (1992). *Sixty-five plus in America (Current Population Reports, Special Studies, Series P23 178).* Washington, DC: U.S. Government Printing Office.

U.S. Bureau of the Census. (1994). *Statistical abstract of the United States: 1994* (114th ed.). Washington, DC: U.S. Government Printing Office.

U.S. Bureau of the Census. (1995). *Statistical abstract of the United States: 1995* (115th ed.). Washington, DC: U.S. Government Printing Office.

U.S. Bureau of the Census. (1997). *Statistical abstract of the United States.* Washington, DC: U.S. Government Printing Office.

U.S. Department of Health and Human Services. (1990). *The health benefits of smoking cessation: A report of the surgeon general.* Washington, DC: U.S. Government Printing Office.

U.S. Department of Health and Human Services. (1995). *Healthy people 2000 review, 1994.* Washington DC: U.S. Government Printing Office.

U.S. Department of Labor. (1992). *Pipelines of progress: An update on the glass ceiling initiative.* Washington, DC: U.S. Government Printing Office.

U.S. Merit Systems Protection Board. (1988). *Sexual harassment of federal workers: An update.* Washington, DC: U.S. Government Printing Office.

Vaillant, G. E. (1994). Ego mechanisms of defense and personality psychopathology. *Journal of Abnormal Psychology, 103,* 44–50.

Vance, B. K., & Green, V. (1984). Lesbian identities: An examination of sexual behavior and sex role acquisition as related to age of initial same-sex encounter. *Psychology of Women Quarterly, 8,* 293–307.

Vandenberg, S. G. (1987). Sex differences in mental retardation and their implications for sex differences in ability. In J. M. Reinisch, L. A. Rosenblum, & S. A. Sanders (Eds.), *Masculinity/Femininity: Basic perspectives.* New York: Oxford University Press.

van der Velde, F. W., van der Pligt, J., & Hooykaas, C. (1994). Perceiving AIDS-related risk: Accuracy as a function of differences in actual risk. *Health Psychology, 13,* 25–33.

VanderPlate, C., Aral, S. O., & Magder, L. (1988). The relationship among genital herpes simplex virus, stress, and social support. *Health Psychology, 7,* 159–168.

Van Houten, R. (1983). Punishment: From the animal laboratory to the applied setting. In S. Axelrod & J. Apsche (Eds.), *The effects of punishment on human behavior.* New York: Academic Press.

VanItallie, T. B. (1979). Obesity: Adverse effects on health and longevity. *American Journal of Clinical Nutrition, 32,* 2727.

Van Wormer, K. (1995). Codependency: Implications for women and therapy. In M. Babcock & C. McKay (Eds.), *Challenging codependency: Feminist critiques.* Toronto: University of Toronto Press.

Vaux, A. (1988). Social and personal factors in loneliness. *Journal of Social and Clinical Psychology, 6,* 462–471.

Veenhoven, R. (1993). *Happiness in nations.* Rotterdam, Netherlands: Risbo.

Vemer, E., Coleman, M., Ganong, L. H., & Cooper, H. (1989). Marital satisfaction in remarriage: A meta-analysis. *Journal of Marriage and the Family, 51,* 713–725.

Ventura, J., Nuechterlein, K. H., Lukoff, D., & Hardesty, J. P. (1989). A prospective study of stressful life events and schizophrenic relapse. *Journal of Abnormal Psychology, 98,* 407–411.

Verderber, R. F., & Verderber, K. S. (1998). *Interact: Using interpersonal communication skills.* Belmont, CA: Wadsworth.

Vernberg, E. M., La Greca, A. M., Silverman, W. K., & Prinstein, M. J. (1996). Prediction of posttraumatic stress symptoms in children after Hurricane Andrew. *Journal of Abnormal Psychology, 105,* 237–248.

Vernon, P. A., Jang, K. L., Harris, J. A., & McCarthy, J. M. (1997). Environmental predictors of personality differences: A twin and sibling study. *Journal of Personality and Social Psychology, 72,* 177–183.

Vinogradov, S., & Yalom, I. D. (1994). Group therapy. In R. E. Hales, S. C. Yu-dofsky, & J. A. Talbott (Eds.), *The American Psychiatric Press textbook of psychiatry* (2nd ed.). Washington, DC: American Psychiatric Press.

Vinokur, A. D., & van Ryn, M. (1993). Social support and undermining in close relationships: Their independent effects on the mental health of unemployed persons. *Journal of Personality and Social Psychology, 65,* 350–359.

Vinokur, A. D., Price, R. H., & Caplan, R. D. (1996). Hard times and hurtful partners: How financial strain affects depression and relationship satisfaction of unemployed persons and their spouses. *Journal of Personality and Social Psychology, 71,* 166–179.

Vitaliano, P. P., Katon, W., Maiuro, R. D., & Russo, J. (1989). Coping in chest pain patients with and without psychiatric disorders. *Journal of Consulting and Clinical Psychology, 57,* 338–343.

Vogt, T., Mullooly, J., Ernst, D., Pope, C., & Hollis, J. (1992). Social networks as predictors of ischemic heart disease, cancer, stroke and hypertension: Incidence, survival and mortality. *Journal of Clinical Epidemiology, 45,* 659–666.

Von Baeyer, C. L., Sherk, D. L., & Zanna, M. P. (1981). Impression management in the job interview: When the female applicant meets the male (chauvinist) interviewer. *Personality and Social Psychology Bulletin, 7,* 45–51.

Voydanoff, P. (1990). Economic distress and family relations: A review of the eighties. *Journal of Marriage and the Family, 52,* 1099–1115.

Wachtel, P. L. (1977). *Psychoanalysis and behavior therapy: Toward an integration.* New York: Basic Books.

Wachtel, P. L. (1989). *The poverty of affluence: A psychological portrait of the American way of life.* Philadelphia: New Society.

Wachtel, P. L. (1991). From eclecticism to synthesis: Toward a more seamless psychotherapeutic integration. *Journal of Psychotherapy Integration, 1,* 43–54.

Wadden, T. A., Stunkard, A. J., Brownell, K. D., & VanItallie, T. B. (1983). The Cambridge diet. *Journal of the American Medical Association, 250,* 2833–2834.

Wadden, T. A. (1998). New goals of obesity treatment: A healthier weight and other ideals. *Primary Psychiatry, 5,* 45–54.

Wade, C., & Tavris, C. (1990). *Learning to think critically: A handbook to accompany psychology.* New York: HarperCollins.

Waite, L. J. (1995). Does marriage matter? *Demography, 32,* 483–507.

Wakefield, J. C. (1992). The concept of mental disorder: On the boundary between biological facts and social values. *American Psychologist, 47,* 373–388.

Walker, L. (1984) *The battered woman.* New York: Springer Publishing.

Walker, L. (1993). The battered woman syndrome is a psychological consequence of abuse. In R. Gelles & D. Loseke (Eds.), *Current controversies in family violence.* Newbury Park, CA: Sage.

Walker, L. E. (1989). Psychology and violence against women. *American Psychologist, 44,* 695–702.

Walker, L. O., & Best, M. A. (1991). Well-being of mothers with infant children: A preliminary comparison of employed women and home-makers. *Women and Health, 17,* 71–89.

Wallace-Broscious, A., Serafica, F. C., & Osipow, S. H. (1994). Adolescent career development: Relationships to self-concept and identity status. *Journal of Research on Adolescence, 4,* 127–149.

Walster, E., & Berscheid, E. (1974). A little bit about love: A minor essay on a major topic. In T. L. Huston (Ed.), *Foundations of interpersonal attraction.* New York: Academic Press.

Walster, E., Aronson, E., Abrahams, D., & Rottman, L. (1966). Importance of physical attractiveness in dating behavior. *Journal of Personality and Social Psychology, 4,* 508–516.

Walters, E. E., & Kendler, K. S. (1995). Anorexia nervosa and anorexic-like syndromes in a population-based female twin sample. *American Journal of Psychiatry, 152,* 64–71.

Wampold, B. E., Mondin, G. W., Moody, M., Stich, F., Benson, K., & Ahn, H. N. (1997). A meta-analysis of outcome studies comparing bona fide psychotherapies: Empirically, "all must have prizes." *Psychological Bulletin, 122,* 203–215.

Ward, S. E., Leventhal, H., & Love, R. (1988). Repression revisited: Tactics used in coping with a severe health threat. *Personality and Social Psychology Bulletin, 14,* 735–746.

Warner, R. E. (1991). Bibliotherapy: A comparison of the prescription practices of Canadian and American psychologists. *Canadian Psychology, 32,* 529–530.

Warshaw, M. G., Fierman, E., Pratt, L., Hunt, M., Yonkers, K. A., Massion, A. O., & Keller, M. B. (1993). Quality of life and dissociation in anxiety disorder patients with histories of trauma or PTSD. *American Journal of Psychiatry, 150,* 1512–1516.

Watkins, W. G., & Bentovim, A. (1992). The sexual abuse of male children and adolescents: A review of current research. *Journal of Child Psychology & Psychiatry & Allied Disciplines, 33,* 197–248.

Watson, A., & Boundy, D. (1989). *Willpower's not enough.* New York: Harper & Row.

Watson, D. L., & Tharp, R. G. (1993). *Self-directed behavior: Self-modification for personal adjustment* (6th ed.). Pacific Grove, CA: Brooks/Cole.

Watson, D. L., & Tharp, R. G. (1997). *Self-directed behavior: Self-modification for personal adjustment.* Pacific Grove, CA: Brooks/Cole.

Watson, D., & Clark, L. A. (1997). Extraversion and its positive emotional core. In R. Hogan, J. Johnson, & S. Briggs (Eds), *Handbook of personality psychology.* San Diego, CA: Academic Press.

Watson, D., & Pennebaker, J. W. (1989). Health complaints, stress, and distress: Exploring the central role of negative affectivity. *Psychological Review, 96,* 234–254.

Watson, J. B. (1913). Psychology as the behaviorist views it. *Psychological Review, 20,* 158–177.

Wayne, S. J., & Ferris, G. R. (1990). Influence tactics, and exchange quality in supervisor-subordinate interactions: A laboratory experiment and field study. *Journal of Applied Psychology, 75,* 487–499.

Weaver, R. C., & Rodnick, J. E. (1986). Type-A behavior: Clinical significance, evaluation, and management. *Journal of Family Practice, 23,* 255–261.

Webb, S. L. (1991). *Step forward: Sexual harassment in the workplace—What you need to know!* New York: Mastermedia.

Wechsler, H., Davenport, A., Dowdall, G., Moeykens, B., & Castillo, S. (1994). Health and behavioral consequences of binge drinking in college. A national survey of students at 140 campuses. *Journal of the American Medical Association, 272,* 1672–1677.

Weil, M. M., & Rosen, L. D. (1997). *TechnoStress: Coping with technology @ home @ work @ play.* New York: Wiley.

Weinberg, C. (1979). *Self creation.* New York: Avon.

Weinberger, D. A. (1990). The construct validity of the repressive coping style. In J. L. Singer (Ed.), *Repression and dissociation.* Chicago: University of Chicago Press.

Weiner, B. (Ed.). (1974). *Achievement motivation and attribution theory.* Morristown, NJ: General Learning Press.

Weiner, B. (1985). "Spontaneous" causal thinking. *Psychological Bulletin, 97,* 74–84.

Weiner, B. (1986). *An attribution theory of emotion and motivation.* New York: Springer-Verlag.

Weiner, B., Frieze, I., Kukla, A., Reed, L., Rest, S., & Rosenbaum, R. M. (1972). Perceiving the causes of success and failure. In E. E. Jones, D. E. Kanouse, H. H. Kelley, R. E. Nisbett, S. Valins, & B. Weiner (Eds.), *Perceiving the causes of behavior.* Morristown, NJ: General Learning Press.

Weiner, H. (1978). Emotional factors. In S. C. Werner & S. H. Ingbar (Eds.), *The thyroid.* New York: HarperCollins.

Weiner, H. (1992). *Perturbing the organism: The biology of stressful experience.* Chicago: University of Chicago Press.

Weiner, H., & Fawzy, F. I. (1989). An integrative model of health, disease, and illness. In S. Cheren (Ed.), *Psychosomatic medicine: Theory, physiology, and practice* (Vol. 1). Madison, CT: International Universities Press.

Weiner, M. F. (1993). Role of the leader in group psychotherapy. In H. I. Kaplan & B.J. Sadock (Eds.), *Comprehensive group psychotherapy.* Baltimore: Williams &Wilkins.

Weiner, R. D. (1984). Does electroconvulsive therapy cause brain damage? *Behavioral and Brain Sciences, 7,* 1–22.

Weiner, R. D., & Coffey, C. E. (1988). Indications for use of electroconvulsive therapy. In A. J. Frances & R. E. Hales (Eds.), *Review of psychiatry* (Vol. 7). Washington, DC: American Psychiatric Press.

Weinstein, N. D. (1980). Unrealistic optimism about future life events. *Journal of Personality and Social Psychology, 39,* 806–820.

Weinstein, N. D. (1989). Perceptions of personal susceptibility to harm. In V. M. Mays, G. W. Albee, & S. F. Schneider (Eds.), *Primary prevention of AIDS: Psychological approaches.* Newbury Park, CA: Sage Publications.

Weis, D. L. (1983). Affective reactions of women to their initial experience of coitus. *Journal of Sex Research, 19,* 209–237.

Weis, D. L. (1985). The experience of pain during women's first sexual intercourse: Cultural mythology about female sexual initiation. *Archives of Sexual Behavior, 14,* 421–428.

Weisaeth, L. (1993). Disasters: Psychological and psychiatric aspects. In L. Goldberger & S. Breznitz (Eds.), *Handbook of stress: Theoretical and clinical aspects* (2nd ed.). New York: Free Press.

Weisner, T. S., & Wilson-Mitchell, J. E. (1990). Nonconventional family life-styles and sex typing in six-year-olds. *Child Development, 61,* 1915–1933.

Weiss, B., Dodge, K. A., Bates, J. E., & Petit, G. S. (1992). Some consequences of early harsh discipline: Child aggression and a maladaptive social information processing style. *Child Development, 63,* 1321–1335.

Weiss, R. S. (1975). *Marital separation.* New York: Basic Books.

Weissman, M. M., Bruce, M. L., Leaf, P. J., Florio, L. P., & Holzer, C., III. (1991). Affective disorders. In L. N. Robins & D. A. Regier (Eds.), *Psychiatric disorders in America: The epidemiologic catchment area study.* New York: Free Press.

Weissman, M. M., Prusoff, B. A., DiMascio, A., Neu, C., Goklaney. M., & Klerman, G. L. (1979). The efficacy of drugs and psychotherapy in the treatment of acute depressive episodes. *American Journal of Psychiatry, 136,* 555–558.

Weisz, J. R., Rothbaum, F. M., & Blackburn, T. C. (1984). Standing out and standing in: The psychology of control in America and Japan. *American Psychologist, 39,* 955–969.

Weiten, W. (1988). Pressure as a form of stress and its relationship to psychological symptomatology. *Journal of Social and Clinical Psychology, 6,* 127–139.

Weiten, W. (1998). Pressure, major life events, and psychological symptoms. *Journal of Social Behavior and Personality, 13,* 51–68.

Weitzman, L. J. (1985). *The divorce revolution: The unexpected social and economic consequences for women and children in America.* New York: Free Press.

Weitzman, L. J. (1989). The divorce revolution and the feminization of poverty. In J. M. Henslin (Ed.), *Marriage and the family in a changing society.* (3rd ed.). New York: Free Press.

Weitzman, L. (1996). The economic consequences of divorce are still unequal: Comment on Peterson. *American Sociological Review, 61,* 537–538.

Wekstein, L. (1979). *Handbook of suicidology.* New York: Brunner/Mazel.

Werbach, M. R. (1988). *Nutritional influences on illness: A sourcebook of clinical research.* Tarzana, CA: Third Line Press.

Weschler, H., Davenport, A., Dowdall, G., Moeykens, B., & Castillo, S. (1994). Health and behavioral consequences of binge drinking in college: A national survey of students at 140 campuses. *Journal of the American Medical Association, 272,* 1672–1677.

Wesson, D. R., Smith, D. E., & Seymour, R. B. (1992). Sedative-hypnotics and tricyclics. In J. H. Lowinson, P. Ruiz, & R. B. Millman (Eds.), *Substance abuse: A comprehensive textbook* (2nd ed.). Baltimore: Williams & Wilkins.

Wesson, D. R., Smith, D. E., Ling, W., & Seymour, R. B. (1997). Sedative-hypnotics and tricyclics. In J. H. Lowinson, P. Ruiz, R. B. Millman, & J. G. Langrod (Eds.), *Substance abuse: A comprehensive textbook* (3rd ed.). Baltimore: Williams & Wilkins.

Westefeld, J. S., & Furr, S. R. (1987). Suicide and depression among college students. *Professional Psychology: Research and Practice, 18,* 119–123.

Westen, D. (1990). Psychoanalytic approaches to personality. In L. A. Pervin (Ed.), *Handbook of personality: Theory and research.* New York: Guilford Press.

Wheaton, B. (1994). Sampling the stress universe. In W. R. Avison & I. H. Gotlib (Eds.), *Stress and mental health: Contemporary issues and prospects for the future.* New York: Plenum Press.

Whitbourne, S. K. (1996). *The aging individual: Physical and psychological perspectives.* New York: Springer.

Whitbourne, S. K., Zuschlag, M. K., Elliot, L. B., & Waterman, A. S. (1992). Psychosocial development in adulthood: A 22-year sequential study. *Journal of Personality and Social Psychology, 63,* 260–271.

White, J. M. (1987). Premarital cohabitation and marital stability in Canada. *Journal of Marriage and the Family, 49,* 641–647.

White, J. W., & Koss, M. P. (1991). Courtship violence: Incidence in a national sample of higher education students. *Violence and Victims, 6,* 247–256.

White, L. K. (1990). Determinants of divorce: A review of research in the eighties. *Journal of Marriage and the Family, 32,* 904–912.

White, L. K. (1991). Determinants of divorce: A review of research in the eighties. In A. Booth (Ed.), *Contemporary families: Looking forward, looking back.* Minneapolis: National Council on Family Relations.

White, L. K., & Booth, A. (1985). Stepchildren in remarriages. *American Sociological Review, 50,* 689–698.

White, L. K., & Rogers, S. J. (1997). Strong support but uneasy relationships: Coresident and adult children's relationships with their parents. *Journal of Marriage and the Family, 59,* 62–76.

Whitehead, W. E. (1994). Assessing the effects of stress on physical symptoms. *Health Psychology, 13,* 99–102.

Whitfield, C. L. (1991). *Co-dependence: Healing the human condition.* Deerfield Beach, FL: Health Communications.

Whitfield, C. L. (1993). *Boundaries and relationships: Knowing, protecting and enjoying the self.* Deerfield Beach, FL: Health Communications.

Whitfield, C. L. (1995). *Memory and abuse: Remembering and healing the effects of trauma.* Deerfield Beach, FL: Health Communications.

Whitley, B. E., Jr. (1983). Sex-role orientation and self-esteem: A critical meta-analytic review. *Journal of Personality and Social Psychology, 44,* 765–778.

Whitley, B. E., Jr. (1984). Sex-role orientation and psychological well-being: Two meta-analyses. *Sex Roles, 12,* 207–225.

Whitley, B. E., Jr. (1988a). *College students' reasons for sexual intercourse: A sex role perspective.* Paper presented at the 96th Annual Meeting of the American Psychological Association, Atlanta, GA.

Whitley, B. E., Jr. (1988b). Masculinity, femininity, and self-esteem: A multitrait-multimethod analysis. *Sex Roles, 18,* 419–432.

Whitley, B. E., Jr., & Hern, A. L. (1991). Perceptions of vulnerability to pregnancy and the use of effective contraception. *Personality and Social Psychology Bulletin, 17,* 104–110.

Whitley, B. E., Jr., & Schofield, J. W. (1986). A meta-analysis of research on adolescent contraceptive use. *Population and Environment, 8,* 173–203.

Widiger, T. A., Frances, A. J., Pincus, H. A., Davis, W. W., & First, M. B. (1991). Toward an empirical classification for the DSM-IV. *Journal of Abnormal Psychology, 100,* 280–288.

Wiebe, D. J. (1991). Hardiness and stress moderation: A test of proposed mechanisms. *Journal of Personality and Social Psychology, 60,* 89–99.

Wiederman, M. W. (1997). Extramarital sex: Prevalence and correlates in a national survey. *Journal of Sex Research, 34,* 167–174.

Wiehe, V. R. (1996). *Working with child abuse and neglect.* Thousand Oaks, CA: Sage.

Wielawski, I. (1991, October 3). *Unlocking the secrets of memory.* Los Angeles Times, p. 1.

Wiggins, J. D., Lederer, D. A., Salkowe, A., & Rys, G. S. (1983). Job satisfaction related to tested congruence and differentiation. *Journal of Vocational Behavior, 23,* 112–121.

Wiggins, J. S. (1992). Have model, will travel. *Journal of Personality, 60,* 527–532.

Wiggins, J. S., & Trapnell, P. D. (1997). Personality structure: The return of the big five. In R. Hogan, J. Johnson, & S. Briggs (Eds), *Handbook of personality psychology.* San Diego, CA: Academic Press.

Wilfley, D. E., & Rodin, J. (1995). Cultural influences on eating disorders. In K. D. Brownell & C. G. Fairburn (Eds.), *Eating disorders and obesity: A comprehensive handbook.* New York: Guilford Press.

Wilhelm, B. (1998). Changes in cohabitation across cohorts: The influence of political activism. *Social Forces, 77,* 289–313.

Willett, W. C., & Manson, J. E. (1995). Epidemiologic studies of health risks due to excess weight. In K. D. Brownell & C. G. Fairburn (Eds.), *Eating disorders: A comprehensive handbook.* New York: Guilford Press.

Williams, B. K., & Knight, S. M. (1994). *Healthy for life: Wellness and the art of living.* Pacific Grove, CA: Brooks/Cole.

Williams, G. D., Stinson, F. S., Clem, D., & Noble, J. (1992). *Surveillance report 23, Apparent per capita alcohol consumption: National, state, and regional trends, 1977–1990.* Rockville, MD: National Institute on Alcohol Abuse and Alcoholism.

Williams, J. B. W. (1994). Psychiatric classification. In R. E. Hales, S. C. Yudofsky, & J. A. Talbott (Eds.), *The American Psychiatric Press textbook of psychiatry* (2nd ed.). Washington, DC: American Psychiatric Press.

Williams, J. E., & Best, D. L. (1982). *Measuring sex stereotypes: A thirty-nation study.* Newbury Park, CA: Sage Publications.

Williams, J. E., & Best, D. L. (1990). *Measuring sex stereotypes: A multination study* (Rev. ed.). Newbury Park, CA: Sage Publications.

Williams, J. M. G., Watts, F. N., MacLeod, C., & Mathews, A. (1997). *Cognitive psychology and emotional disorders* (2nd ed.). Chichester, UK: Wiley.

Williams, L. B. (1991). Determinants of unintended childbearing among ever-married women in the United States. *Family Planning Perspectives, 23,* 212–221.

Williams, M. H. (1992). Exploitation and inference: Mapping the damage from therapist-patient sexual involvement. *American Psychologist, 47,* 412–421.

Williams, N. A., & Deffenbacher, J. L. (1983). Life stress and chronic yeast infections. *Journal of Human Stress, 9,* 26–31.

Williamson, D. F. (1995). Prevalence and demographics of obesity. In K. D. Brownell & C. G. Fairburn (Eds.), *Eating disorders and obesity: A comprehensive handbook.* New York: Guilford Press.

Wilpert, B. (1995). Organizational behavior. *Annual review of psychology, 46,* 59–90

Wilson, E. O. (1980). *Sociobiology.* Cambridge, MA: Harvard University Press.

Wilson, G. (1990). Personality, time of day and arousal. *Personality and Individual Differences, 11,* 153–168.

Wilson, G. T. (1993). Binge eating and addictive disorders. In C. G. Fairburn, & G. T. Wilson

(Eds.), *Binge eating: Nature, assessment, and treatment.* New York: Guilford Press.

Wilson, G. T. (1995). The controversy over dieting. In K. D. Brownell & C. G. Fairburn (Eds.), *Eating disorders and obesity: A comprehensive handbook.* New York: Guilford Press.

Wilson, M. (1993). DSM-III and the transformation of American psychiatry: A history. *American Journal of Psychiatry, 150,* 399–410.

Winick, C. (1992). Epidemiology of alcohol and drug abuse. In J. H. Lowinson, P. Ruiz, & R. B. Millman (Eds.), *Substance abuse: A comprehensive textbook* (2nd ed.). Baltimore, MD: Williams & Wilkins.

Winick, C. (1997). Epidemiology. In J. H. Lowinson, P. Ruiz, R. B. Millman, & J. G. Langrod (Eds.), *Substance abuse: A comprehensive textbook* (3rd ed.). Baltimore: Williams & Wilkins.

Winn, K. I., Crawford, D. W., & Fischer, J. (1991). Equity and commitment in romance versus friendship. *Journal of Social Behavior and Personality, 6,* 301–314.

Wiseman, C. V., Gray, J. J., Mosimann, J. E., & Ahrens, A. H. (1992). Cultural expectations of thinness in women: An update. *International Journal of Eating Disorders, 11,* 85–89.

Wisensale, S. K. (1992). Toward the 21st century: Family change and public policy. *Family Relations, 41,* 417–422.

Wittenberg, M. T., & Reis, H. T. (1986). Loneliness, social skills, and social perception. *Personality and Social Psychology Bulletin, 12,* 121–130.

Wixted, J. T., Bellack, A. S., & Hersen, M. (1990). Behavior therapy. In A. S. Bellack & M. Hersen (Eds.), *Handbook of comparative treatments for adult disorders.* New York: Wiley.

Wolf, S., & Goodell, H. (1968). *Stress and disease.* Springfield, IL: Charles C. Thomas.

Wolinsky, F. D. (1988). Sick role legitimation. In D. S. Gochman (Ed.), *Health behavior: Emerging research perspectives.* New York: Plenum Press.

Woll, S. (1986). So many to choose from: Decision strategies in videodating. *Journal of Social and Personal Relationships, 3,* 43–52.

Wolpe, J. (1958). *Psychotherapy by reciprocal inhibition.* Stanford, CA: Stanford University Press.

Wolpe, J. (1987). The promotion of scientific therapy: A long voyage. In J. K. Zeig (Ed.), *The evolution of psychotherapy.* New York: Brunner/Mazel.

Wolpe, J. (1990). *The practice of behavior therapy.* Elmsford, NY: Pergamon.

Women clerics find sexual harassment. (1990, December 1). *Washington Post,* C12.

Wonderlich, S. A. (1995). Personality and eating disorders. In K. D. Brownell & C. G. Fairburn (Eds.), *Eating disorders and obesity: A comprehensive handbook.* New York: Guilford Press.

Wood, J. M., Nezworski, M. T., & Stejskal, W. J. (1996). The comprehensive system for the Rorschach: A critical examination. *Psychological Science, 7,* 3–10.

Wood, J. T. (1994). *Gendered lives: Communication, gender, and culture.* Belmont, CA: Wadsworth.

Wood, J. T. (1993). Engendered relationships: Interaction, caring, power, and responsibility in close relationships. In S. Duck (Ed.), *Processes in close relationships: Contexts of close relationships* (Vol. 3). Beverly Hills, CA: Sage.

Wood, J. V. (1989). Theory and research concerning social comparisons of personal attributes. *Psychological Bulletin, 106,* 231–248.

Wood, W., & Kallgren, C. A. (1988). Communicator attributes and persuasion: Recipients' access to attitude-relevant information in memory. *Personality and Social Psychology Bulletin, 14,* 172–182.

Wooley, S. C., & Wooley, O. W. (1985). Intensive outpatient and residential treatment for bulimia. In D. M. Garner & P. E. Garfinkel (Eds.), *Handbook of psychotherapy for anorexia and bulimia.* New York: Guilford.

Woolfolk, R. L., & Richardson, F. C. (1978). *Stress, sanity and survival.* New York: Sovereign/Monarch.

Worthen, J. B. (1997). Resiliency of bizarreness effects under varying conditions of verbal and imaginal elaboration and list composition. *Journal of Mental Imagery, 21,* 167–194.

Wortman, C. B., & Silver, R. C. (1990). Successful mastery of bereavement and widowhood: A life-course perspective. In P. B. Baltes & M. M. Baltes (Eds.), *Successful aging.* Cambridge, MA: Cambridge University Press.

Wright, J. C., & Dawson, V. L. (1985). Distortion in control attributions for real life events. *Journal of Research in Psychology, 19,* 54–71.

Wright, J. H., & Beck, A. T. (1994). Cognitive therapy. In R. E. Hales, S. C. Yudofsky, & J. A. Talbott (Eds.), *The American Psychiatric Press textbook of psychiatry* (2nd ed.). Washington, DC: American Psychiatric Press.

Wright, P. H. (1982). Men's friendships, women's friendships, and the alleged inferiority of the latter. *Sex Roles, 8,* 1–20.

Wright, P. H. (1989). Gender differences in adults' same- and cross-gender friendships. In R. G. Adams & R. Blieszner (Eds.), *Older adult friendship.* Newbury Park, CA: Sage Publications.

Wright, P. H., & Wright, K. D. (1991). Codependency: Addictive love, adjustive relating, or both? *Contemporary Family Therapy: An International Journal, 13,* 435–454.

Wright, R. A., & Contrada, R. J. (1986). Dating selectivity and interpersonal attraction: Toward a better understanding of the "elusive phenomenon." *Journal of Social and Personal Relationships, 3,* 131–148.

Wu, Z. (1995). The stability of cohabitation relationships: The role of children. *Journal of Marriage and the Family, 57,* 231–236.

Wurman, R. S. (1989). *Information anxiety.* New York: Doubleday.

Wyatt, G. E., Peters, S. D., & Guthrie, D. (1988). Kinsey revisited, Part I: Comparison of the sexual socialization and sexual behavior of white women over 33 years. *Archives of Sexual Behavior, 17,* 201–239.

Wyke, S., & Ford, G. (1992). Competing explanations for associations between marital status and health. *Social Science and Medicine, 34,* 523–532.

Wyler, A. R., Masuda, M., & Holmes, T. H. (1971). Magnitude of life events and seriousness of illness. *Psychosomatic Medicine, 33,* 115–122.

Xiaohe, X., & Whyte, M. K. (1990). Love matches and arranged marriages: A Chinese replication. *Journal of Marriage and the Family, 52,* 709–722.

Yalom, I. D. (1995). *The theory and practice of group psychotherapy* (4th ed.). New York: Basic Books.

Yang, A. S. (1997). The polls—trends: Attitudes toward homosexuality. *Public Opinion Quarterly, 61,* 477–507.

Yapko, M. D. (1994). *Suggestions of abuse: True and false memories of childhood sexual trauma.* New York: Simon & Schuster.

Young, J. E. (1982). Loneliness, depression and cognitive therapy: Theory and application. In L. A. Peplau & D. Perlman (Eds.), *Loneliness: A sourcebook of current theory, research and therapy.* New York: Wiley.

Young, K. S. (1996, August). *Internet addiction: The emergence of a new clinical disorder.* Paper presented at the meeting of the American Psychological Association, Toronto, Ontario, Canada.

Young, K. S. (1998). *Caught in the net: How to recognize the signs of Internet addiction—and a winning strategy for recovery.* New York: Wiley.

Younkin, S. L., & Betz, N. E. (1996). Psychological hardiness: A reconceptualization and measurement. In T. W. Miller (Ed.), *Theory and assessment of stressful life events.* Madison, CT: International Universities Press.

Zacks, E., Green, R. J., & Marrow, J. (1988). Comparing lesbian and heterosexual couples on the Circumplex Model: An initial investigation. *Family Process, 27,* 471–484.

Zajonc, R. B. (1968). Attitudinal effects of mere exposure. *Journal of Personality and Social Psychology, 9,* 1–27.

Zammichieli, M. E., Gilroy, F. D., & Sherman, M. F. (1988). Relation between sex-role orientation and marital satisfaction. *Personality and Social Psychology Bulletin, 14,* 747–754.

Zanna, M. P., & Olson, J. M. (1982). Individual differences in attitudinal relations. In M. P. Zanna, E. T. Higgins, & C. P. Herman (Eds.), *Consistency in social behavior: The Ontario symposium, Vol. 2.* Hillsdale, NJ: Erlbaum.

Zechmeister, E. B., & Nyberg, S. E. (1982). *Human memory: An introduction to research and theory.* Pacific Grove, CA: Brooks/Cole.

Zedeck, S., & Mosier, K. L. (1990). Work in the family and employing organization. *American Psychologist, 45,* 240–251.

Zeig, J. K. (1987). Introduction: The evolution of psychotherapy—Fundamental issues. In J. K. Zeig (Ed.), *The evolution of psychotherapy.* New York: Brunner/Mazel.

Zellman, G. L., & Goodchilds, J. D. (1983). Becoming sexual in adolescence. In E. R. Allgeier & N. B. McCormick (Eds.), *Changing boundaries.* Palo Alto, CA: Mayfield.

Zilbergeld, B., & Evans, M. (1980, August). The inadequacy of Masters and Johnson. *Psychology Today,* pp. 28–34, 37–43.

Zillmann, D., & Bryant, J. (1984). Effects of massive exposure to pornography. In N. M. Malamuth & E. Donnerstein (Eds.), *Pornography and sexual aggression.* New York: Academic Press.

Zillmann, D., Bryant, J., & Huston, A. C. (1994). *Media, family, and children.* Hillsdale, NJ: Erlbaum.

Zimbardo, P. G. (1977). *Shyness: What it is, what to do about it.* Reading, MA: Addison-Wesley.

Zimbardo, P. G. (1990). *Shyness.* Reading, MA: Addison-Wesley.

Zimbardo, P. G. (1992). Cults in everyday life: Dependency and power. *Contemporary Psychology, 37,* 1187–1189.

Zimbardo, P. G. (1997, May). *What messages are behind today's cults?* APA Monitor.

Zimbardo, P. G., & Leippe, M. R. (1991). *The psychology of attitude change and social influence.* New York: McGraw-Hill.

Zimmerman, B. J. (1995). Self-efficacy and educational development. In A. Bandura (Ed.), *Self-efficacy in changing societies.* New York: Cambridge University Press.

Zorc, J. J., Larson, D. B., Lyons, J. S., & Beardsley, R. S. (1991). Expenditures for psychotropic medications in the United States in 1985. *American Journal of Psychiatry, 148,* 644–647.

Zubin, J. (1986). Implications of the vulnerability model for DSM-IV with special reference to schizophrenia. In T. Millon & G. L. Klerman (Eds.), *Contemporary directions in psychopathology: Toward the DSM-IV.* New York: Guilford Press.

Zuckerman, M. (1979). *Sensation seeking: Beyond the optimal level of arousal.* Hillsdale, NJ: Erlbaum.

Zuckerman, M. (1990). The psychophysiology of sensation seeking. *Journal of Personality, 58,* 313–345.

Zuckerman, M. (1991). *Psychobiology of personality.* New York: Cambridge University Press.

Zuckerman, M. (1995). Good and bad humors: Biochemical bases of personality and its disorders. *Psychological Science, 6,* 325–332.

Zuckerman, M. (1996). The psychological model for impulsive unsocialized sensation seeking: A comparative approach. *Neuropsychobiology, 34,* 125–129.

Zuckerman, M., Lazzaro, M. M., & Waldgeir, D. (1979). Undermining effects of the foot-in-the-door technique with extrinsic rewards. *Journal of Applied Social Psychology, 9,* 292–296.

Zuwerink, J. R., & Devine, P. G. (1996). Attitude importance and resistance to persuasion: It's not just the thought that counts. *Journal of Personality and Social Psychology, 70,* 931–944.

Zvonkovic, A. N., Greaves, K. M., Schmiege, C. J., & Hall, L. D. (1996). The marital construction of gender through work and family decisions: A qualitative analysis. *Journal of Marriage and the Family, 58, 1,* 91–100.

Credits

This page constitutes an extension of the copyright page. We have made every effort to trace the ownership of all copyrighted material and to secure permission from copyright holders. In the event of any question arising as to the use of any material, we will be pleased to make the necessary corrections in future printings. Thanks are due to the following authors, publishers, and agents for permission to use the material indicated.

Photo Credits

Contents
xiii: © David Young-Wolff/Photo Edit; xv: AP/Wide World Photos; xvi: © A. Ramey/Photo Edit; xvii: © Rhoda Sidney/Stock, Boston; xx: © Tom McCarthy/Photo Edit; xviii: AP/Wide World Photos; xxi: © Najlah Feanny/Saba; xxiii: Ragnar Sigurdsson/Tony Stone Images; xxiv: © David Harvey/Woodfin Camp & Associates, all rights reserved; xxv: AP/Wide World Photos; xxvi: Bob Daemmrich/Stock Boston; xxviii: © Bruce Ayres/Tony Stone Images.

Chapter 1
3: (left) AP/Wide World Photos; (center)© Les Stone/Sygma; (right) © Blake Little/Sygma; 7: © David Young-Wolff/Photo Edit; 20: (left) © Frank Siteman/Stock, Boston; (right) © Frank Siteman/Stock, Boston; 22: © Gary A. Conner/Photo Edit.

Chapter 2
33: (below) National Library of Medicine; (above) AP/Wide World Photos; 37: © Myrleen Ferguson/Photo Edit; 38: Culver Pictures, Inc.; 39: Culver Pictures, Inc.; 41: Sovfoto; 43: (above) Harvard University News Office; (below) Courtesy of the B.F. Skinner Foundation; 45: Courtesy of Albert Bandura; 48: Carl Rogers Memorial Library; 49: Courtesy of Abraham Maslow; 52: (left) © Michael Nichols/Magnum Photos; (right) Courtesy of Hans Eysenck, photo by Mark Gerson; 59: (left) © Laura Dwight/Photo Edit; (right) Reprinted by permission of the publishers from Henry A. Murray, *Thematic Apperception*, Cambridge, Mass., Harvard University Press, Copyright © 1943 by The President and Fellows of Harvard College, © 1971 by Henry A. Murray.

Chapter 3
64: Courtesy, Richard Lazarus; 65: (left) © Cameraman/The Image Works; (right)

Hiroyuki Matsumoto/Tony Stone Images; 67: Courtesy, Neal Miller; 70: (left) © David Woo/Stock, Boston; (right) © Kerbs/Monkmeyer Press Photos; 76: Corbis-Bettmann; 80: AP/Wide World Photos; 84: Courtesy, Suzanne C. Ouelette; 87: Craig Prentis/Allsport; 88: Courtesy, Eleanor Holmes Williams.

Chapter 4
98: Courtesy, Dr. Martin Seligman; 101: © David Young-Wolff/Photo Edit; 104: Courtesy, Shelley Taylor; 106: Courtesy, Albert Ellis; 117: (left) Andrew Errington/Tony Stone Images; (right) David Madison/Tony Stone Images; 118: © A. Ramey/Photo Edit; 123: (right) © M. Siluk/Picture Cube/Index Stock; (left) © Rob Crandall/Stock, Boston.

Chapter 5
129: Stanford University News Service, photo by L. A. Cicero; 133: © David Young-Wolff/Photo Edit; 134: Brooks/Cole Publishing Company; 135: © David Young-Wolff/Photo Edit; 138: © David Young-Wolff/Photo Edit; 139: Courtesy, Roy Baumeister; 142: © Rhoda Sidney/Stock, Boston; 146: Courtesy, Robert Cialdini; 148: Courtesy, Albert Bandura; 150: © K. Jordan/Sygma; 151: Courtesy, Mark Synder; 154: (left) Lisa Rose/Globe Photos, Inc. © 1999; (right) Rose Hartman/Globe Photos, inc. © 1999.

Chapter 6
159: © LeDuc/Monkmeyer Press Photo; 160: Courtesy, Susan Fiske; 164: Stanford University News Service; 165: © Lee Snider/The Image Works; 173: AP/Wide World Photos; 176: © Eric Kroll; 177: Photos copyright 1965 by Stanley Milgram. From the film Obedience, distributed by The Pennsylvania State University. Reprinted by permission of Alexandra Milgram.

Chapter 7
191: (above) © Donna Conner/Sygma; (below) From *Unmasking the Face*, © 1975 by Paul Ekman, photographs courtesy of Paul Ekman; 192: (right) © A. Ramey/Stock, Boston; (left) © W. Hill, Jr./The Image Works; 193: © Bob Daemmrich/The Image Works; 196: © Wolfgang Spunbarg/Photo Edit; 203: © Tom McCarthy/Photo Edit; 208: Photo by Sara Barrett, courtesy of Random House; 209: © Alan Carey/The Image Works.

Chapter 8
217: (left) © Brady/Monkmeyer Press Photo; (right) © Fujifotos/The Image Works; 222: © Tom McCarthy/Photo Edit; 223: © Tom McCarthy/The Image Works; 226: © Jeff Greenberg/The Image Works; 228: Courtesy, Ellen Berscheid; 229: (above) Courtesy, Elaine Hatfield; (below) © Bob Daemmrich/The Image Works; 231: (above) Photo by Bill Warren, *The Ithaca Journal;* (below) Photo supplied by Philip Shaver.

Chapter 9
249: Corbis-Bettmann; 250: © Tony Freemann/Photo Edit; 255: Bruce Ayers/Tony Stone Images; 256: © John Blaustein/Woodfin Camp & Associates, all rights reserved.; 264: © Matthew McVay/Saba Photos; 265: © Michael Newman/Photo Edit; 269: © Bob Daemmrich/Stock, Boston; 272: © Najlah Feanny/Saba.

Chapter 10
281: Courtesy, Janet Shibley Hyde; 285: Courtesy, Alice Eagly; 287: Brooks Cole Collection; 290: (right) © David Young-Wolff/Photo Edit; (left) © Tony Freeman/Photo Edit; 292: Goodwin/Monkmeyer Press Photos; 300: (left) Rashid/Monkmeyer Press Photos; (right) Brooks/Cole Collection; 302: Photo by Sara Barrett, courtesy of Random House.

Chapter 11
309: David Young Wolff/Tony Stone Images; 312: Courtesy, David Elkind; 313: Ted Streshinsky/Photo 20-20; 319: Ragnar Sigurdsson/Tony Stone Images; 321: Sygma; 323: (left) Sygma; (right) © Lara Jo Regan/Gamma Liaison; 325: Courtesy, Susan Whitbourne; 326: © Roos/Gamma Liaison; 327: Pacal Le Segretain/Austral/Sgyma; 330: Courtesy, Diane Baumrind.

Chapter 12
338: © Myrleen Ferguson/Photo Edit; 345: © Matthew Borkoski/Stock, Boston; 348: © Michael Newman/Photo Edit; 350: © David Harvey/Woodfin Camp & Associates, all rights reserved; 354: © Lawrence Schwartzwald/Gamma Liaison; 363: © B. Daemmrich/The Image Works.

Chapter 13
370: © Tom Prettyman/Photo Edit; 371: AP/Wide World Photos; 372: © Bob Daemmrich/Uniphoto; 373: AP/Wide

World Photos; **377:** © John Chaisson/Gamma Liaison.

Chapter 14
405: Courtesy, Janice Kiecott-Glaser; **410:** © Bob Daemmrich/Stock, Boston; **412:** © Mary Kate Denny/Photo Edit; **420:** Courtesy, Robin DiMatteo; **422:** © David Young-Wolff/Photo Edit; **425:** © Michael Newman/Photo Edit.

Chapter 15
432: (below) Courtesy, Thomas Szasz; **433:** Courtesy, David Rosenhan; **439:** © Bob Daemmrich/Stock, Boston; **446:** (left) © Evan Agostini/Gamma Liaison; (right) © Y. Karsh/Woodfin Camp & Associates. All rights reserved. **449:** Courtesy, Susan Nolen-Hoeksema; **452:** Courtesy, Nancy Andreasen; **457:** (left) © T. Grahm/Sgyma; (center) © Schiffman/Gamma Liaison; (right) © Kansas City Star/Gamma Liaison.

Chapter 16
469: National Library of Medicine; **470:** © Bruce Ayres/Tony Stone Images; **471:** Courtesy, Carl Rogers Memorial Library; **473:** Courtesy, Aaron T. Beck; **474:** © B. Daemmrich/The Image Works; **475:** Mark Gerson/Courtesy, H. J. Eysenck; **479:** Courtesy, Joseph Wolpe; **485:** © James Wilson/Woodfin Camp & Associates, all rights reserved.

Figure Credits

Contents
xv: Figure 3.1 adapted from R. S. Lazarus and S. Folkman, *Stress, Appraisal and Coping.* © Copyright 1984 Springer Publishing Company, Inc.; **xvii:** Figure 5.10 based on "Relation of Threatened Egotism to Violence and Aggression: The Dark Side of High Self-Esteem" by R. F. Baumeister, L. Smart, & J. M. Boden, 1996, *Psychological Review,* Vol. 103, No. 1, 5-33, Fig. 1, p. 12. Copyright © 1996 by the American Psychological Association, **xx:** Figure 8.9 from "A Triangular Theory of Love," by R. J. Sternberg, 1986, *Psychological Review, 93,* 119–135. Copyright 1986 by the American Psychological Association. Reprinted by permission; **xxiii:** Figure 11.9 table constructed from Diana Baumrind (1971). Current patterns of parental authority (Monograph). *Developmental Psychology, 4*(1, Part 2), 1–103. Copyright © 1971 by the American Psychological Association. Adapted by permission of the author; **xxv:** Figure 13.8 from *The Social Organization of Sexuality: Sexual Practices in the United States,* by E. O. Laumann, J. H. Gagnon, R. T. Michael, and S. Michaels. Copyright © 1994 University of Chicago Press. Reprinted by permission.

Chapter 1
7: Cover image from *I'm Dysfunctional, You're Dysfunctional,* by Wendy Kraminer. Cover design by Julie Metz. Copyright © 1992 Addison-Wesley Publishing Company. Reprinted by permission of J. Metz. **9:** Cover image from *What You Can Change & What You Can't,* by Martin E. P. Seligman. Copyright © 1994 Alfred A. Knopf, Inc. Reprinted by permission. **10:** Figure 1.2 from *Learning to Think Critically: A Handbook to Accompany Psychology,* by Carole Wade and Carol Tavris. Copyright © 1990 by Harper & Row Publishers, Inc. Reprinted by permission of HarperCollins, Publishers, Inc. **19:** Cover image from *The Pursuit of Happiness: Who is Happy—and Why?* by David G. Myers. Copyright © 1992 William Morrow & Co., Inc. Reprinted by permission. **20:** Figure 1.10 (based D. G. Myers & E. Diener (1995). "Who is happy?" *Psychological Science, 6,* 10–19) and adapted from "Marital status and personal happiness: An analysis of trend data" by G. R. Lee, K. Seccombe, & C. L. Shehan (1991). *Journal of Marriage and the Family, 53,* 839–844. **24:** Cover image from *Learning Skills for College and Career,* by Paul I. Hettich. Copyright © 1992 Brooks/Cole Publishing Company. **25:** Figure 1.13 adapted from *The Psychology of College Success: A Dynamic Approach,* by permission of H. C. Lindgren, 1969. **27:** Figure 1.14 adapted from "Narrative Stories as Mediators of Serial Learning," by G. H. Bower and M. C. Clark, 1969, *Psychonomic Science, 14,* 181–182. Copyright © 1969 by the Psychonomic Society. Adapted by permission of the Psychonomic Society; Figure 1.15 adapted from "Analysis of a Mnemonic Device," by G. H. Bower, 1970, American Scientist (September–October), 58, 496–499. Copyright © 1970 by American Scientist. Reprinted by permission.

Chapter 2
41: Figure 2.6 adapted from *Psychology,* Second Edition, by G. R. Lefrançois. Copyright © 1983 by Wadsworth, Inc. Reprinted by permission of Brooks/Cole Publishing Company. **48:** Figure 2.13 reproduced with permission of authors and publisher from M. Sherer, J. E. Maddox, B. Mercandante, S. Prentice-Dunn, B. Jacobs, and R. W. Rogers, "The Self-Efficacy Scale: Construction and Validation." *Psychological Reports,* 1982, 51, 663–671. Copyright © Psychological Reports 1982. **52:** Cover image from *Three Psychologies,* by Robert D. Nye. Copyright © 1992 Brooks/Cole Publishing Company; Figure 2.17 adapted from *Personality: Theory, Research and Application,* by C. R. Potkay and B. P. Allen, p. 246. Copyright © 1986 by Wadsworth, Inc. **54:** Figure 2.18 from H. J. Eysenck, *The Biological Basis of Personality* First Edition, p. 36, 1967. Courtesy of Charles C. Thomas, Publisher, Springfield, IL. **59:** Figure 2.22 adapted from *Personality Structure and Measurement,* by H. J. Eysenck and S. B. G. Eysenck. Copyright © 1969 by EdITS publishers. Reprinted by permission. **60:** Figure 2.23 from R. B. Cattell in *Psychology Today,* July 1973, 40–46. Reprinted with permission from Psychology Today Magazine. Copyright © 1973 (Sussex Publishers, Inc.).

Chapter 3
64: Figure 3.1 adapted from R. S. Lazarus and S. Folkman, *Stress, Appraisal and Coping.* © Copyright 1984 Springer Publishing Company, Inc.; Cover image from *Technostress: Coping with Technology @ Work @ Home @ Play* by Michelle M. Weil and Larry D. Rosen. © 1997 John Wiley & Sons. **65:** Figure 3.2 adapted from "Chronic Noise and Psychological Stress," by G. W. Evans, S. Hygge, and M. Bullinger, *Psychological Science, 6,* 333–338. Copyright © 1995 Cambridge University Press. **69:** Figure 3.5 from "The Social Readjustment Rating Scale," by T. H. Homes and R. H. Rahe, 1967, *Journal of Psychosomatic Research, 11,* 213–218. Copyright © 1967 by Pergamon Press, Inc. Adapted by permission. **71:** Figure 3.7 from W. D. Fenz and S. Epstein, "Gradients of Physiological Arousal, Skin Conductance, Heart Rate, and Respiration Rate as Function of Experience," *Psychosomatic Medicine, 29,* 33–51, © American Psychosomatic Society, 1967. Reprinted by permission. **76:** Figure 3.12 adapted from *The Stress of Life,* by Hans Selye, p. 121, 1956. Copyright © 1956 by McGraw-Hill Publishing Company. **79:** Figure 3.15 based on "Paradoxical Effects of Supportive Audiences on Performance Under Pressure: The Home Field Disadvantages in Sports Championships," by R. F. Baumeister & A. Steinhilber, 1984. *Journal of Personality and Social Psychology, 47*(1), 85–95. Copyright © 1984 by the American Psychological Association. Added data from "Championship Pressures: Choking or Triumphing on One's Own Territory?" by B. R. Schlenker, et. al., *Journal of Personality and Social Psycology, 68,* 632–643. **81:** Figure 3.16 adapted from "Full and partial posttraumatic stress disorder: Findings from a community survey," by M. B. Stein, J. R. Walker, A. L. Hazen & D. R. Forde, 1997. *American Journal of Psychiatry, 154,* 1114–1119. © 1997 American Psychiatric Publishing Group. **85:** Cover image from *Learned Optimism: How to Change Your Mind and Your Health,* by Martin E. P. Seligman. Copyright © 1990 Pocket Books. Reprinted by permission of Bob Silverman. **90:** Figure 3.21 from "Assessing the Impact of Life Changes," by I. G. Sarason, J. H. Johnson, and J. M. Siegel, 1978, *Journal of Consulting and Clinical Psychology, 46,* 932–946. Copyright © 1978 by the American Psychological Association. Reprinted by permission of the author. **93:** Figure 3.22 from "Assessing the Impact of Life Changes," by I. G. Sarason, J. H. Johnson, and J. M. Siegel,

1978, *Journal of Consulting and Clinical Psychology, 46,* 932–946. Copyright © 1978 by the American Psychological Association. Reprinted by permission of the author.

Chapter 4
98: Figure 4.1 from "Assessing Coping Strategies: A Theoretically Based Approach," by C. S. Carver, M. F. Scheier, and J. K. Weintraub, 1989, *Journal of Personality and Social Psychology, 56*(2), 267–283. Copyright 1989 by the American Psychological Association. Reprinted by permission. **100:** Cover image reprinted with the permission of Simon & Schuster from *Anger: The Misunderstood Emotion,* by Carol Tavris. Copyright © 1989 by Jackie Seow-Pracher; Figure 4.2 adapted from "The Effects of Three Types of Aggression on Vascular Processes," by J. E. Hokanson and M. Burgess, 1962, *Journal of Abnormal and Social Psychology, 65,* 446–449. Copyright 1962 by the American Psychological Association. Adapted by permission. **101:** Figure 4.3 from *Caught in the net: How to recognize the signs of Internet addiction—and a winning strategy for recovery* by K. S. Young, 1998. Copyright © 1998 John Wiley & Sons, New York. **103:** Figure 4.4 adapted from *Abnormal Psychology and Modern Life,* Eighth Edition, by R. C. Carson, J. N. Butcher, and J. C. Coleman, pp. 64–65, 1988. Copyright © 1988 by Scott, Foresman and Company. Adapted by permission. **105:** Cover image from *You're Smarter Than You Think,* by Seymour Epstein, with Archie Brodsky. Copyright © 1993 Simon & Schuster, Inc. **108:** Cover image from *How to Stubbornly Refuse to Make Yourself Miserable About Anything—Yes, Anything!* by Albert Ellis. Copyright © 1988 Carol Publishing Group. Reprinted by permission. **109:** Figure 4.7 adapted from "Sense of Humor as a Moderator of the Relation Between Stressors and Moods," by R. A. Martin and H. M. Lefcourt, 1983, *Journal of Personality and Social Psychology, 45*(6), 1313–1324. Copyright 1983 by the American Psychological Association. Adapted by permission. **111:** Figure 4.8 from Le Boeuf, "Managing Time Means Managing Yourself," Questionnaire, p. 45. Reprinted from *Business Horizons Magazine,* February 1980. Copyright by the Foundation for the School of Business at Indiana University. Used with permission. **113:** Cover image from *Timelock: How Life Got So Hectic and What You Can Do About It,* by Ralph Keyes. Copyright © 1991 HarperCollins Publishers, Inc. Reprinted by permission. **117:** Cover image from *Emotional Intelligence: Why It Can Matter More Than IQ* by Daniel Goleman. Copyright © 1995 Bantam Books. **118:** Figure 4.12 (based on illustration on p. 86 by Lorelle A. Raboni of *Scientific American, 226,* 85–90, February 1972) adapted from "The Psychology of

Meditation," by R. K. Wallace and H. Bensen. Copyright © 1972 by Scientific American, Inc. All rights reserved. Adapted by permission. **119:** Figure 4.13 adapted from figure on pp. 114–115 from *The Relaxation Response* by Herbert Benson with Miriam Z. Klipper. Copyright © 1975 by William Morrow and Company, Inc. By permission of William Morrow and Company, Inc. **122:** Figure 4.16 from *Self-Directed Behavior: Self-Modification for Personal Adjustment,* Fourth Edition, by D. L. Watson and R. L. Tharp, pp. 213–214. Copyright © 1972, 1977, 1981, 1985, 1993 by Brooks/Cole Publishing Company.

Chapter 5
131: Cover image from *Encounters with the Self,* by Don Hamachek. Copyright 1992 Harcourt, Brace, Jovanovich. **133:** Figure 5.4 from "Self-Consciousness, Self-Esteem, and Success-Failure as Determinants of Alcohol Consumption in Male Social Drinkers," by J. G. Hull and R. D. Young, 1983, *Journal of Personality and Social Psychology, 44*(6), 1097–1109. Copyright © 1983 American Psychological Association. Reprinted by permission of the author. **136:** Figure 5.6 adapted from "Culture and the Self: Implications for Cognition, Emotion, and Motivation," by H. R. Markus and Shinobu Kitayama, 1991, *Psychological Review, 98*(2), pp. 224–253. Copyright 1991 American Psychological Association. Reprinted by permission of the author. **140:** Figure 5.9 from *Social Psychology,* Second Edition, by S. S. Brehm and S. M. Kassin. Copyright © 1993 Houghton-Mifflin Company. Reprinted by permission. **141:** Figure 5.10 based on "Relation of Threatened Egotism to Violence and Aggression: The Dark Side of High Self-Esteem" by R. F. Baumeister, L. Smart, & J. M. Boden, 1996, *Psychological Review,* Vol. 103, No. 1, 5-33, Fig. 1, p. 12. Copyright © 1996 by the American Psychological Association. **144:** Figure 5.12 from "Perceiving the Causes of Success and Failure," by B. Weiner, I. Frieze, A. Kukla, L. Reed, and R. M. Rosenbaum. In E. E. Jones, D. E. Kanuouse, H. H. Kelly, R. E. Nisbett, S. Valins, and B. Weiner (Eds.), *Perceiving Causes of Behavior,* 1972, General Learning Press. Reprinted by permission of the author. **151:** Figure 5.15 based on Table 703, p. 198 of *Interpersonal Perception,* by E. E. Jones. © 1990, W. H. Freeman & Co., New York. **154:** Cover image from *Self-Esteem,* by Matthew McKay and Patrick Fanning. Copyright © 1993 New Harbinger Publications. Reprinted by permission.

Chapter 6
160: Figure 6.1 adapted from *Social Psychology,* Second Edition, by S. S. Brehm and S. M. Kassin, p. 137. Copyright © 1993 Houghton Mifflin Company. Reprinted by permission. **162:** Figure 6.2

adapted from *Social Psychology* by E. R. Smith and D. M. Mackie, p. 103. Copyright © 1995 Worth Publishing. Reprinted by permission. **169:** Figure 6.5 adapted from *Social Psychology* by S. S. Brehm and S. M. Kassin, fig. 4.4. Copyright © 1993 Houghton Mifflin Company. **170:** Cover image from *Age of Propaganda: The Everyday Use and Abuse of Persuasion* by Anthony R. Pratkanis & Elliot Aronson. Copyright © 1992 W. H. Freeman & Co. **174:** Figure 6.9 (adapted from illustrations by Sarah Love on p. 35, *Scientific American,* November 1955) from "Opinion and Social Pressure," by Solomon Asch. Copyright © 1955 by Scientific American, Inc. All rights reserved. Adapted by permission. **175:** Figure 6.10 (adapted from illustrations by Sarah Love on p. 32, *Scientific American,* November 1955) from "Opinion and Social Pressure," by Solomon Asch. Copyright © 1955 by Scientific American, Inc. All rights reserved. Adapted by permission. **177:** Figure 6.11 copyright 1965 by Stanley Milgram, from the film *Obedience,* distributed by the New York University Film Division and The Pennsylvania State University, PCR. By permission of the Estate of Stanley Milgram. **182:** Cover image from *Influence: Science and Practice,* Third Edition, by Robert B. Cialdini, 1993, HarperCollins Publishers, Inc. Cover photo by James H. Karales/Peter Arnold, Inc. Reprinted by permission of Peter Arnold, Inc.

Chapter 7
194: Figure 7.5 adapted from *Eye to Eye: How People Interact,* by Peter Marsh. Copyright © 1988 by Andromeda Oxford Ltd. Reprinted by permission of HarperCollins, Publishers, Inc. **198:** Cover image from *Messages: The Communication Skills Book,* by Matthew McKay, Martha Davis, and Patrick Fanning. Copyright © 1983 New Harbinger Publications. Reprinted by permission. **205:** Figure 7.9 adapted from *Conflict: From Theory to Action* by R. S. Lulofs, fig. 2.3, p. 42. Copyright © 1994 Gorsuch Scarisbrick Publishers. **208:** Cover image from *The Argument Culture: Moving From Debate to Dialogue* by Deborah Tannen, 1998. Copyright © 1998, Random House. **209:** Figure 7.13 from "Road rage plagues drivers," (1997, November, December). *AAA Going Places,* pp. 41–42. Copyright © 1997 American Automobile Association. **211:** Cover image from *Asserting Yourself: A Practical Guide for Positive Change,* by Sharon Anthony Bower and Gordon H. Bower. Cover design by Richard Rossiter. Copyright © 1991 Addison-Wesley Publishing Co. Reprinted by permission of R. Rossiter. **212:** Figure 7.12 based on Table of Rules for Assertive DESC Scripts on page 100 from *Asserting Yourself: A Practical Guide for Positive Change,* by Sharon Anthony Bower and Gordon H.

Bower. Copyright © 1991 Addison-Wesley Publishers. **213:** Figure 7.13 adapted from *Asserting Yourself: A Practical Guide for Positive Change, 2/E,* by Sharon Anthony Bower and Gordon H. Bower. Copyright © 1991 Addison-Wesley Publishers.

Chapter 8
218: Cover image from *Love and Sex: Cross-Cultural Perspectives,* by Elaine Hatfield and Richard L. Rapson. Copyright © 1996 by Allyn and Bacon. **220:** Figure 8.1 from "Sex Differences in Human Mate Preferences: Evolutionary Hypotheses Tested in 37 Cultures," by D. M. Buss, 1989, *Behavioral and Brain Sciences, 12,* 1–14. Copyright © 1989 by Cambridge University Press. Reprinted with the permission of Cambridge University Press. **222:** Figure 8.3 adapted from "The Evolution of Human Intrasexual Competition: Tactics of Mate Attraction," by D. M. Buss, 1988, *Journal of Personality and Social Psychology, 54*(4), 616–628. Copyright © 1988 by the American Psychological Association. Adapted by permission of the author. **224:** Figure 8.5 adapted from "Interactional Approach to Interpersonal Attraction," by M. H. Gonzales, J. M. Davis, G. L. Loeny, C. K. Lukens, and C. H. Junghans, 1983, *Journal of Personality and Social Psychology, 44,* 1191–1197. Copyright © 1983 by the American Psychological Association. Adapted by permission. **225:** Figure 8.6 adapted from Sharon S. Brehm and Saul M. Kassin, *Social Psychology,* Second Edition. Copyright © 1993 by Houghton Mifflin Company. Adapted with permission. **227:** Figure 8.7 from "The Friendship Bond," by Mary Brown Parlee and the Editors of *Psychology Today, 13*(4), 49. Reprinted with permission from Psychology Today Magazine. Copyright © 1979 (Sussex Publishers, Inc.); Figure 8.8 adapted from "The Rules of Friendship," by M. Argyle and M. Henderson, 1984, *Journal of Social and Personal Relationships, 1,* 211–237. **228:** Cover image from *Just Friends: The Role of Friendship In Our Lives,* by Lillian Rubin. Copyright © 1986 Harper & Row. Reprinted by permission. **231:** Figure 8.9 from "A Triangular Theory of Love," by R. J. Sternberg, 1986, *Psychological Review, 93,* 119–135. Copyright 1986 by the American Psychological Association. Reprinted by permission. **233:** Figure 8.11 adapted from "Attachment Styles Among Young Adults: A Test of a Four-Category Model" by K. Bartholomew & L. M. Horowitz, 1991, *Journal of Personality and Social Psychology,* Vol. 61, No. 2, 226–244, Fig. 1, p. 227. Copyright © 1991 by the American Psychological Association. **235:** Figure 8.13 adapted from "Breakups Before Marriage: The End of 103 Affairs," by C. T. Hill, Z. Rubin, and L. A. Peplau, 1976, *Journal of Social Issues, 32,* 147–168. Basic Books Publishing Co., Inc. Adapted by permission of the author. All rights

reserved. **237:** Cover image from P. Zimbardo, *Shyness,* © 1977 Phillip Zimbardo, Inc. Cover illustration © 1989 by Bart Goldman. Reprinted by permission of Addison-Wesley Publishing Company, Inc. and Bart Goldman; Figure 8.14 from P. Zimbardo, *Shyness,* © 1977 by Philip Zimbardo. Reprinted by permission of Addison-Wesley Publishing Company, Inc. **238:** Figure 8.15 from a paper presented at the annual convention of the American Psychological Association, September 2, 1979. An expanded version of this paper appears in *New Directions in Cognitive Therapy,* edited by Emery, Hollon, and Bedrosian, Guilford Press, 1981, and in *Loneliness: A Sourcebook of Current Theory, Research and Therapy,* by L. A. Peplau and D. Perlman (Eds.). Copyright © 1982 by John Wiley & Sons, Inc. Reprinted by permission of John Wiley & Sons, Inc., and Jeffrey Young. **241:** Figure 8.16 adapted from "Cultural Myths and Supports for Rape," by M. R. Burt, 1980, *Journal of Personality and Social Psychology, 38,* 217–230. Copyright © 1980 by the American Psychological Association. Adapted by permission of the author. **243:** Cover image from *Recovering from Rape,* by Linda Ledray. Copyright © 1994 by Henry Holt & Co. Inc. Reprinted by permission of Henry Holt and Co., Inc.

Chapter 9
247: Figure 9.1 data from U.S. Bureau of the Census, *Current Population Reports,* Series P-20, No. 412, "Households, Families, Marital Status and Living Arrangements," March 1986 (Advance Report), Washington, DC: U.S. Government Printing Office, p. 4. **248:** Figure 9.3 data from the National Center for Health Statistics, U.S. Bureau of the Census, 1991. **250:** Figure 9.4 adapted from Peter J. Stein, "Singlehood: An Alternative to Marriage," *The Family Coordinator, 24*(4), 500. Copyright © 1975 by the National Council on Family Relations, 3989 Central Ave. N. E., Suite 550, Minneapolis, MN 55421. Reprinted by permission. **254:** Figure 9.7 adapted from "Marital Satisfaction over the Family Life Cycle," by Boyd C. Rollins and Harold Feldman, J*ournal of Marriage and the Family, 32* (February 1970), 25. Copyright © 1975 by the National Council on Family Relations, 3989 Central Ave., N.E., Suite 550, Minneapolis, MN 55421. Reprinted by permission. **262:** Cover image from *Love Is Never Enough,* by Aaron T. Beck. Copyright © 1988 Harper & Row. Reprinted by permission. **264:** Cover image from *Why Marriages Succeed or Fail...and How You Can Make Yours Last,* by John Gottman, with Nan Silver. Copyright © 1994 Simon & Schuster Publishers. **268:** Figure 9.14 data from Glick & Norton, 1979. Population Reference Bureau, Washington, DC: U.S. Bureau of the Census. **270:** Figure 9.16 from "What Homosexuals Want," by L. A.

Peplau, March 1981, *Psychology Today, 3,* 28–38. Reprinted with permission from Psychology Today Magazine. Copyright © 1981 (Sussex Publishers, Inc.). **274:** Figure 9.17 adapted from "Agency response to domestic violence: Services provided to battered women," by I. M. Johnson, J. Crowley & R. T. Sigler. *Intimate violence: Interdisciplinary perspectives,* E. C. Viano (Ed.), 1992, 191-202. Copyright © 1992 Hemisphere Publishing, Washington, D.C.

Chapter 10
280: Figure 10.2 adapted from "Sex Stereotypes: Issues of Change in the 70s," by T. L. Ruble, 1983, *Sex Roles, 9,* 397–402. Copyright © 1983 Plenum Publishing Company. Adapted by permission. **283:** Figure 10.4 data from the U. S. Bureau of the Census, *Statistical Abstract of the United States: 1994* (114th edition), Washington, D.C., 1994. **286:** Cover image from *The New Our Bodies, Ourselves: A Book By and For Women,* by The Boston Women's Health Book Collective. Copyright © 1992 Simon & Schuster, Inc. Reprinted by permission. **290:** Figure 10.7 adapted from "Children, Gender and Social Structure: An Analysis of the Contents of Letters to Santa Claus," by J. G. Richardson and C. H. Simpson, 1982, *Child Development, 53,* 429–436. Copyright © 1982 by the Society for Research in Child Development, Inc. Adapted by permission. **292:** Figure 10.8 from Graph B on page 7 of the Executive Summary of the American Association of University Women's Report, *Shortchanging Girls, Shortchanging America,* Revised Edition, August 1994. Washington, D.C.: AAUW. Reprinted by permission; Figure 10.9 data from Robert M. Liebert and Joyce Sprafkin, *The Early Window: Effects of Television on Children and Youth,* Third Edition. Copyright © 1988. Reprinted by permission of Allyn and Bacon. **294:** Cover image from *The Masculine Self* by Christopher T. Kilmartin, 1994. Copyright © 1994 by Macmillan Publishing. **297:** Figure 10.10 data from U. S. Bureau of the Census, *Statistical Abstract of the United States: 1994* (114th edition). Washington D.C., 1994. **298:** Figure 10.11 data from U. S. Bureau of Labor Statistics, *Employment and Earnings, 42*(1), January, 1995, Table 39, pp. 209–213; Figure 10.12 adapted from *Secrets in Public: Sexual Harassment in Our Schools,* by N. Stein, N. L. Marshall, and L. R. Tropp, p. 4. Copyright © 1993 Center for Research on Women at Wellesley College and the NOW Legal Defense and Education Fund. **299:** Cover image reprinted with permission of Simon & Schuster from *The Mismeasure of Woman,* by Carol Tavris. Copyright © 1992 by Jackie Seow. **303:** Cover image from *You Just Don't Understand: Women and Men in Conversation,* by D. Tannen. Copyright © 1990 Ballantine Books. Reprinted by permission of William Morrow & Co., Inc. **305:** Figure 10.14

based on *You Just Don't Understand: Women and Men in Conversation*, by D. Tannen. Copyright © 1990 by William Morrow & Company, Inc. Reprinted by permission of William Morrow & Company, Inc.

Chapter 11
312: Figure 11.2 adapted from "The Psychological Significance of Pubertal Change: Sex Differences in Perceptions of Self During Early Adolescence," by M. H. Tobin-Richards, A. M. Boxer, and A. C. Petersen. In J. Brooks-Gunn and A. C. Petersen (Eds.), *Girls at Puberty: Biological and Psychosocial Perspectives*, p. 137. Copyright © 1983 Plenum Publishing Inc. Reprinted by permission. **313:** Figure 11.3 adapted from *Child-hood and Society*, Second Edition, by Erik H. Erikson. Copyright 1950, © 1963 by W. W. Norton & Co., Inc. Copyright renewed 1978, 1991 by Erik H. Erikson. **314:** Figure 11.4 data from U.S. Bureau of the Census, *Statistical Abstract of the United States: 1994* (114th edition), Washington, D.C., 1994. **317:** Cover image from *Necessary Losses*, by Judith Viorst. Copyright © 1986 Ballantine Books (A Fawcett Gold Medal Book). **322:** Figure 11.5 data from U. S. Bureau of the Census, *Statistical Abstract of the United States: 1994* (114th edition), Table 208, p. 140, Washington D.C., 1994. **324:** Figure 11.6 data from B. Levy & E. Langer "Aging Free From Negative Stereotypes: Successful Memory in China and Among the American Deaf," from the *Journal of Personality and Social Psychology*, Vol. 66, 989–997. Copyright © 1994 by the American Psychological Association, Inc. Adapted from figure 6.15, p. 228 of Baron & Byrne, *Social Psychology*. Copyright © 1997 Allyn & Bacon. **325:** Figure 11.7 based on data from "Creative Productivity between the Ages of 20 and 80 Years," by W. Dennis, 1966. *Journal of Gerontology, 2*(1), 1–8. Copyright © 1966 the Gerontological Society of America. Adapted by permission. **330:** Figure 11.9 table constructed from Diana Baumrind (1971). Current patterns of parental authority (Monograph). *Developmental Psychology, 4*(1, Part 2), 1–103. Copyright © 1971 by the American Psychological Association. Adapted by permission of the author. **331:** Cover image from *The Hurried Child: Growing Up Too Fast, Too Soon*, by D. Elkind. Copyright © 1988 David Elkind. Reprinted by permission of Addison-Wesley Publishing Company, Inc. **332:** Figure 11.10 from "Patterns of Competence and Adjustment among Adolescents from Authoritative, Authoritarian, Indulgent, and Neglectful Families," by S. D. Lamborn, N. S. Mounts, L. Steinberg, & S. M. Dornbusch, in *Child Development, 62*, 1049–1065. Copyright © 1991 by the Society for Research in Child Development, Inc.

Chapter 12
342: Figure 12.2 from John L. Holland, *Making Vocational Choices: A Theory of Vocational Personalities and Work Environments*, Second Edition. Copyright © 1985, pp. 19–23, 36–40. Adapted by permission of Prentice-Hall, Inc., Englewood Cliffs, NJ. **343:** Figure 12.3 adapted from *Theories of Occupational Choice and Vocational Development*, by J. Zaccaria, pp. 51–52. Copyright © 1970 by Time Share Corporation, New Hampshire. **348:** Figure 12.6 adapted from "Labor Force 2006: Slowing Down & Changing Composition," by H. N. Fullerton, Jr., 1997. *Monthly Labor Review, 120*, 23–38. Copyright ©1997 Bureau of Labor Statistics, U. S. Department of Labor. **349:** Figure 12.7 data from U. S. Department of Labor, *Pipelines of Progress: A Status Report on the Glass Ceiling*, 1992, Washington, D.C., U. S. Government Printing Office. **351:** Figure 12.8 adapted from *Psychology of Work Behavior*, Fourth Edition, by F. J. Landy, p. 638. Copyright © 1989 by Wadsworth, Inc. Reprinted by permission of Brooks/Cole Publishing Company. **352:** Figure 12.9 redrawn from "Job Decision Latitude, Job Demands, and Cardiovascular Disease: A Prospective Study of Swedish Men," by R. A. Karasek, D. Baker, F. Marxer, A. Ahlbom, and T. Theorell, 1981, *American Journal of Public Health, 71*, 694–705. Reprinted by permission. **353:** Figure 12.11 from U.S. Merit Systems Protection Boards, 1981. *Sexual Harassment of Federal Workers: Is It a Problem?* Washington, DC: U.S. Government Printing Office. **354:** Cover image *Sexual Harassment on the Job: What It Is and How to Stop It* by William Petrocelli and Barbara Kate Repa, 1998. Copyright © 1998 Nolo Press, Berkeley, Calif. **359:** Cover image from *The Time Bind: When Work Becomes Home and Home Becomes Work* by Arlie Russell Hochschild, 1997. Copyright © 1997 by Metropolitan Books. **361:** Figure 12.14 adapted from *Job Search: Career Planning Guidebook, Book II*, by R. D. Lock, Brooks/Cole Publishing Company, 1988. **362:** Cover image reprinted with permission from *The 1998 What Color is Your Parachute?* by Richard Nelson Bolles. Copyright © 1998 by Richard Nelson Bolles, Ten Speed Press, P.O. Box 7123 Berkeley, CA, 94707. Available from your local bookseller or call 800-841-2665. Or visit us at www.tenspeed.com.

Chapter 13
369: Figure 13.1 adapted from *The Kinsey Institute New Report on Sex* by J. M. Reinisch, 1990, p. 21. Copyright © 1990 by The Kinsey Institute for Research in Sex, Gender, and Reproduction. Reprinted with permission by St. Martin's Press, Incorporated. **375:** Cover image from *Loving Someone Gay* by Don Clark, 1997. Copyright © 1997 by Celestial Arts. **376:** Figure 13.5 based on *The Kinsey Institute New Report on Sex*, by J. M. Reinisch, 1990, p. 4. Copyright © 1990 by The Kinsey Institute for Research in Sex, Gender, and Reproduction. Reprinted with permission from St. Martin's Press, Incorporated. **377:** Cover image from *The Kinsey Institute New Report on Sex: What You Must Know to Be Sexually Literate*, by J. M. Reinisch with R. Beasley. Copyright © 1990 by The Kinsey Institute for Research in Sex, Gender, and Reproduction. Reprinted with permission by St. Martin's Press, Incorporated. **379:** Figure 13.8 from *The Social Organization of Sexuality: Sexual Practices in the United States*, by E. O. Laumann, J. H. Gagnon, R. T. Michael, and S. Michaels. Copyright © 1994 University of Chicago Press. Reprinted by permission. **380:** Cover image from *Human Sexuality Today* by Bruce M. King, 1999. Copyright © 1999 by Prentice-Hall Inc. **381:** Figure 13.9 from "The Erotic Fantasies of College Students During Coitus," by David Sue, 1979, *Journal of Sex Research, 15*, 303. Reprinted by permission. **383:** Figure 13.11 from "Age, Gender, and Ethnic Differences in Sexual and Contraceptive Knowledge, Attitudes, and Behavior," by D. S. Moore, and P. I. Erickson, *Family and Community Health, 8*(3), November 1985, pp. 38–51. Copyright © 1985, Aspen Publishers, Inc. **384:** Figure 13.12 adapted from *Sex in America: A Definite Survey* by R. T. Michael, J. H. Gagnon, & E. O. Laumann, & G. Kolatta, 1994, Table 8, p. 116. Copyright © 1994 Little, Brown & Company, Inc. **385:** Figure 13.13 from "How We Really Feel About Infidelity," by B. Handy, 1998, *Time Magazine*, August 31, 1998, p. 52–54. Copyright © 1998 Time Inc. **392:** Figure 13.16 adapted from "Frequency of Sexual Dysfunction in 'Normal' Couples," by E. Frank, C. Anderson, and D. Rubenstein, 1978, *New England Journal of Medicine, 299*, 1111–1115. Copyright © 1978 by the New England Journal of Medicine. Reprinted by permission. **393:** Figure 13.17 from *The Social Organization of Sexuality: Sexual Practices in the United States*, by E. O. Laumann, J. H. Gagnon, R. T. Michael, and S. Michaels, p. 369. Copyright © 1994 University of Chicago Press. Reprinted by permission. **395:** Figure 13.18 adapted from *Human Sexuality*, Third Edition by William H. Masters, Virginia E. Johnson, and Robert C. Kolodny, p. 527. Copyright © 1988 by William H. Masters, Virginia E. Johnson, and Robert C. Kolodny. Reprinted by permission of HarperCollins Publishers.

Chapter 14
401: Figure 14.2 art based on *Healthy for Life: Wellness and the Art of Living* by B. K. Williams & S. M. Knight, 1994, figure 30.6. Copyright © 1994 Brooks/Cole Publishing Company, Pacific Grove, Calif. **403:** Cover image from *Is It Worth Dying For?* by Robert S. Eliot and Dennis L.

Breo. Copyright © 1984, 1989 Bantam Books. Reprinted by permission. **406:** Cover image from *Mind Body Medicine: How to Use Your Mind for Better Health*, edited by Daniel Goleman and Joel Gurin. Copyright 1993 Consumers Union of U.S., Inc., Yonkers, NY 10703-1057. Reprinted by permission from Consumer Reports Books, January 1993. To order, call 1-800-500-9760. **408:** Figure 14.7 adapted from *The Health Benefits of Smoking Cessation: A Report of the Surgeon General 1990*, pp. V–XII. U. S. Department of Health and Human Services, U. S. Government Printing Office, Washington, D. C. **410:** Figure 14.9 from *Healthy for Life: Wellness and the Art of Living*, by B. K. Williams and S. M. Knight, p. 11.28, Brooks/Cole Publishing Company, 1994. Based on Wechsler and McFadden for AAA Foundation for Traffic Safety, survey of 1669 college freshmen at 14 Massachusetts institutions. **411:** Figure 14.11 from *Health and Wellness*, Third Edition, by Edlin and Golanty, p. 294. Copyright © 1992, Boston: Jones & Bartlett Publishers, Inc. Reprinted with permission. **416:** Figure 14.13 from *Healthy for Life: Wellness and the Art of Living*, by B. K. Williams and S. M. Knight, p. 6.40, Brooks/Cole Publishing Company, 1994. **418:** Figure 14.15 adapted from "How Different Sports Rate in Promoting Physical Fitness," by C. C. Conrad, *Medical Times*, May 1976, 4–5. Copyright © 1976 by Romaine Pierson Publishers. Reprinted by permission. **419:** Figure 14.16 data from "A Global Report: AIDS in the World," by J. Mann, D. J. M. Tarantola, & T. W. Netter, 1992. Oxford University Press.

Chapter 15
435: Figure 15.3 adapted with permission from the *Diagnostic and Statistical Manual of Mental Disorders*, Fourth Edition, (1994). Copyright © 1994 American Psychiatric Association. **438:** Figure 15.5 from *Fears and Phobias*, by I. M. Marks, 1969, Academic Press. Copyright © 1969 by Isaac Marks. Reprinted by permission. **440:** Cover image from *The Consumers Guide To Psychotherapy* by Jack Engler & Daniel Goleman, 1992. Copyright © 1992 Simon and Schuster. **441:** Figure 15.7 from "Bias in Interpretation of

Ambiguous Sentences Related to Threat in Anxiety," by M. W. Eysenck, K. Mogg, J. May, A. Richards, and A. Mathews, 1991, *Journal of Abnormal Psychology, 100*, pp. 144–150. Copyright © 1991 by the American Psychological Association. Reprinted by permission of the author. **447:** Figure 15.10 from Sarason/Sarason, *Abnormal Psychology: The Problem of Maladaptive Behavior*, Fifth Edition, Copyright © 1987, p. 283. Reprinted by permission of Prentice-Hall, Inc., Englewood Cliffs, NJ. **448:** Figure 15.11 from *Manic-Depressive Illness*, by Frederick K. Goodwin and Kay R. Jamison (p. 132). Copyright © 1990 by Oxford University Press, Inc. Reprinted by permission. **453:** Cover image from *Surviving Schizophrenia: A Family Manual*, by E. Fuller Torrey. Copyright © 1988 Harper & Row. Reprinted by permission of HarperCollins Publishers, Inc. **459:** Figure 15.18 data adapted from "50-year trends in the incidence of anorexia nervosa in Rochester, Minn.: A population-based study'" by A. R. Lucas, C. M. Beard, W. M. O'Fallon, & L. T. Kurland, 1991. *American Journal of Psychiatry, 148*, 917–922. Copyright © 1991 American Psychiatric Group. **460:** Figure 15.19 data from "Cultural expectations of thinness in women," by D. M. Garner, P. E. Garfinkel, D. Schwartz, & M. Thompson, 1980. *Psychological Reports, 47*, 483–491. © 1980 Psychological Reports. Graphic adapted from *Abnormal Psychology: An Investigative Approach* by D. H. Barlow & V. M. Duvand, 1999. Copyright © 1999 Wadsworth Publishing Company, Belmont Calif. **462:** Figure 15.20 data from "Cultural expectations of thinness in women," by D. M. Garner, P. E. Garfinkel, D. Schwartz, & M. Thompson, 1980. *Psychological Reports, 47*, 483–491. Copyright © 1980 Psychological Reports and "Cultural expectations of thinness in women: an update," by C. V. Wiseman, J. J. Gray, J. E. Mosimann & A. H. Ahrens, 1992. *International Journal of Eating Disorders, 11*, 85–89. Copyright © 1992 John Wiley & Sons. Graphic adapted from *Abnormal Psychology: An Investigative Approach* by D. H. Barlow & V. M. Duvand, 1999. Copyright © 1999 Wadsworth Publishing Company, Belmont Calif..

Chapter 16
466: Cover image from *The Psychotherapy Maze*, by O. Ehrenberg and M. Ehrenberg. Copyright © 1986 Aronson. Reprinted by permission. **467:** Figure 16.1 data from "Outpatient Mental Health Care in Nonhospital Settings: Distribution of Patients Across Provider Groups," by M. Oflson and H. A. Pincus, 1996. *American Journal of Psychiatry, 153*, 1353–1356; Figure 16.2 data from "The de Facto US Mental and Addictive Disorders Service System: Epidemiologic Catchment Area Prospective 1-Year Prevalence Rates of Disorders in Services," by D. A. Regier, W. E. Narrow, D. S. Rae, R. W. Manderscheid, B. Z. Locke, & F. K. Goodwin, 1993. *Archives of General Psychiatry, 50*, 85–94. **471:** Figure 16.5 adapted from "Psychoanalysis and Psychoanalytic Therapy," by E. L. Baker. In S. J. Lynn and J. P. Garske (Eds.), *Contemporary Psychotherapies: Models and Methods*, p. 52, 1982. Reprinted by permission of the authors. **473:** Figure 16.6 adapted from *Cognitive Therapy and the Emotional Disorders*, by A. T. Beck, 1976, International Universities Press. Copyright © 1976 by International Universities Press, Inc. Adapted by permission of the publisher. **478:** Figure 16.7 from "Lies of the Mind," by Leon Jaroff, 1993, *Time Magazine*, November 29, 1993, p. 52. Copyright © 1993 Time Inc. Reprinted by permission. **480:** Figure 16.8 from *Methods of Self-Change: An ABC Primer*, by K. E. Rudestam, pp. 42–43, 1980. Copyright © 1980 by Wadsworth, Inc. Reprinted by permission of Brooks/Cole Publishing Company. **483:** Figure 16.12 from data in NIMH-PSC Collaborative Study I and reported in "Drugs in the Treatment of Psychosis," by J. O. Cole, S. C. Goldberg and J. M. Davis, 1966. In P. Solomon (Ed.), *Psychiatric Drugs*, Grune & Stratton. By permission of the author. **487:** Cover image of *Am I Crazy, Or Is My Shrink?* by Larry E. Beutler, Bruce Bongar, & Joel N. Shurkin, 1998. Copyright © 1998 Oxford University Press. **490:** Figure 16.16 adapted from "Meta Analysis of Psychotherapy Outcome Series," by M. L. Smith and G. V. Glass, 1977, *American Psychologist, 32* (September), 752–760. Copyright © 1977 by the American Psychological Association. Adapted by permission.

Name Index

Russell, G. F. M., 458
Russo, N. F., 284, 295, 348, 359
Ruvulo, A., 129
Ryan, C., 374
Ryn, M., 356

S
Saad, L. 373
Sackeim, H. A., 485
Sacks, M. H., 417
Sadd, S., 17
Sadeh, C., 112
Sadker, D., 291
Sadker, M., 291
Sadock, B. J., 474
Saeed, I., 222
Saghir, M. T., 384
Salbolz, E., 269
Sales, E., 321
Salovey, P., 117
Salt, J., 267
Salthouse, T. A., 324
Salvendy, J. T., 474
Samet, J. M., 408
Saminen, G., 165
Samovar, L., 193
Sanders, B., 282
Sanders, G. S., 420
Sanders, M., 235
Sanderson, W. C., 437
Sandler, B. R., 279
Sandler, J., 63, 481
Sanislow, C. A., III, 454
Sansone, C., 237
Santrock, J. W., 7, 9, 333
Saracino, M., 220
Sarason, I. G., 74, 83, 89, 90, 91, 405
Sarason, P. R., 83
Sarrel, P., 239
Savary, L. M., 135
Saxe, G. N., 444
Scanzoni, J., 251
Scarr, S., 54, 330
Schachter, S., 13, 14, 219
Schaef, A. W., 4
Schaefer, E. C., 220
Schaefer, J., 78, 82
Schaeffer, M., 66
Schaffer, D., 340
Schaie, K. W., 323
Schaninger, C. M., 260
Schank, D., 412, 413
Scharfe, E., 233
Schau, C. G., 291
Scheflin, A. W., 478
Scheidlinger, S., 474
Scheier, M. F., 84, 97, 98, 109
Scherg, H., 404
Scheuer, E., 105
Schilit, W. K., 114
Schlaadt, R. G., 408
Schlegel, A., 309
Schlenger, W. E., 80
Schlenker, B. R., 79, 146, 149
Schlessinger, L. C., 6
Schmidlin, A., 194
Schmidt, N., 236
Schmidt, N. B., 439
Schmitt, J. P., 225, 270, 301, 317., 385, 386

Schmitz, J. M., 407, 409
Schneider, N. G., 407, 409
Schnur, D. B., 485
Schober, L. R., 395
Schoen, R., 249, 268, 269
Schofield, J. W., 387
Scholing, A., 480
Schor, J., 1
Schreiber, F. R., 445
Schroeder, A., 65
Schroeder, D. H., 88, 406
Schuldt, W., 199
Schuller, R., 273
Schultis, G. A., 7
Schultz, J., 275
Schultz, J. H., 118
Schulz, R., 321
Schutz, R. W., 311
Schwartz, H. S., 358
Schwartz, J. C., 218
Schwartz, M., 273
Schwartz, P., 230., 252, 256, 270, 284, 294., 371, 379, 382, 384, 385
Schwartzer, R., 46, 403
Scott, K. P., 291
Scratchley, L. S., 140
Scroppo, J. C., 445
Sears, D., 167
Seccombe, K., 20, 248, 254, 319
Seff, M. A., 318
Segal, A., 420
Segal, K. R., 414
Segal, M. W., 219
Segal, N. J., 240
Segerstrom, S. C., 84
Segrin, C., 449
Seibel, M. M., 405
Seidlitz, L., 65
Selff, M. A., 255
Seligman, M. E. P., 9, 84, 85, 98–99, 144–145, 317, 440, 448, 475, 476, 490
Selitzer, J. A., 265
Seltzer, R., 373
Selye, H., 76–77
Semans, J. H., 395
Semin, G. R., 375
Senchak, M., 227
Senecal, C., 112
Sepekoff, B., 372
Serafica, F. C. 344
Sermat, V., 236
Seta, C. E., 64
Seta, J. J., 64
Seymour, R. B., 425
Shaffer, D. R., 232
Shakesby, P. S., 26
Shalenberger, W. R., III, 16
Shannon, P. T., 408
Shapiro, D. A., 476
Shapiro, D. H., Jr., 118
Shapiro, P. A., 404
Sharlin, S., 254
Sharp, L. K., 5, 116
Shavelson, R. J., 139
Shaver, P. R., 199, 200, 218, 231–232, 233, 236, 238
Shaw, D., 235
Shaw, J., 385
Shear, J., 118

Sheedy, C. F., 109–110
Sheehan, P. W., 478
Sheehan, S., 451
Sheehy-Skeffington, A., 183
Sheeran, P., 355
Shehan, C. L., 20, 320
Sheiham, A., 405
Shekelle, R. B., 402
Sheldon, M. B., 345
Shelley, K. J., 340
Shelton, R. L., 281
Shenk, D., 2
Shepperd, J. A., 147
Sher, T. G., 260
Sherer, M., 46
Sherif, M., 168, 172
Sherk, D. L., 149
Sherman, C. B., 408
Sherman, M. F., 64, 301
Sherrod, D., 227
Sherwin, B. B., 368
Sherwood, A., 87
Shiffman, S., 408
Shimizu, H., 218
Shostak, A. B., 265
Shotland, R. L., 240, 241, 242
Shumaker, S., 415
Shurgot, B. A., 220
Shurkin, J. N., 487
Shuval, J. T., 69
Sidden, J., 247
Siebert, A., 22
Siegel, J. M., 83, 90, 405, 417
Siegel, O. 311
Sigler, R. T., 273, 274
Signer, R., 273
Signorelli, N., 292
Silberman, E. K., 471
Silberstein, L. R., 257, 458
Sillars, A., 193
Silver, N., 264
Silver, R., 273
Silverberg, S. B., 255, 318, 331
Silverman, I., 286
Silverman, J. J., 405
Silverman, P. R., 328
Silvern, L., 284
Sime, W., 74
Simeon, D., 438
Simmons, C. H., 218
Simon, G. E., 443
Simon, W., 296, 382, 393
Simoneau, T. L., 456
Simons, A. D., 450
Simonton, D. K., 324, 325
Simpson, C. H. 290
Simpson, J. A., 233, 384
Singelis, T. M., 20
Singer, B., 375
Singer, J., 66
Singer, M. T., 178, 455
Singh, B., 383
Singh, D., 220, 221
Singh, P., 218
Singh, R., 224
Sinnott, J. D., 324
Siscovick, D. S., 417
Skanes, H., 173
Skay, C. L., 112
Skinner, B. F., 43, 45, 55, 224, 479, 486
Skinner, P. H., 281

Skodol, A. E., 436
Slaby, A. E., 484
Slade, P., 458
Slavney, P. R., 443
Smale, B. J. A., 357
Small, I. F., 485, 486
Small, J. G., 485
Small, S. A., 258
Smart, L., 140
Smeaton, G., 224
Smith, A. L., 446
Smith, A. P., 405
Smith, C. A., 73
Smith, D., 487
Smith, D. E., 425
Smith, E. A., 357
Smith, E. R., 162, 172
Smith, G. L., 455
Smith, M., 171
Smith, M., 445
Smith, M. L., 481, 490
Smith, P., 179
Smith, P. A., 280
Smith, R. E., 148
Smith, R. H., 220
Smith, T. W., 87, 381, 402, 403
Smith-Lovin, P., 284
Smock, P. J., 265
Smoll, F. L., 311
Smollar, J., 135
Snodgrass, S. E., 284
Snyder, C. R., 147
Snyder, D., 372
Snyder, K. A., 263
Snyder, M., 151–152, 161, 162, 168 217, 234
Soares, E. J., 370
Soares, J. F., 441
Sobal, J., 458
Sobin, C., 486
Soldow, G. F., 152
Sollie, D. L., 70
Solomon, B., 227
Solomon, J., 329
Solomon, J. C., 274
Solomon, L. J., 374, 432, 433
Solomon, S., 80
Somers, M. D., 254
Sommers-Flanagan, R., 292
Sotiriou, P. E., 25
South, S. J., 250, 265
Sowell, T., 349
Spacapan, S., 71
Spanos, N. P., 477, 444
Spector, I., 379
Spence, J. T., 280, 301
Sperry, R. W., 287
Spiegel, D., 80, 403
Spiegler, M. D., 47, 480
Spiro, A., 319, 344
Spitze, G., 259
Spitzer, M., 451
Sporakowski, M. J., 253
Sprafkin, J. N., 209, 292
Sprecher, S., 223, 234
Springer, S. P., 287
Sriram, T. G., 405
Sroufe, L. A., 233, 329
Stack, S., 267
Stacy, A. W., 87
Stall, R. D., 391
Staneski, R. A., 199, 221

Stanford, M. W., 427
Stanislaw, H., 368
Stankov, L., 323
Stanton, G. C., 139
Stark, E., 275
Starker, S., 7
Starrels, M. E., 255
Statt, D. A., 337
Stattin, H., 311
Stddard, J. J., 408
Steele, J. B., 439
Stein, M. B., 80, 81, 439, 439
Stein, N., 298
Stein, P. J., 247, 249, 250
Stein-Serioussi, A., 145, 196
Steinberg, L., 255, 318
Steiner, H., 104, 460
Steinhausen, H. C., 461
Steinhilber, A., 79
Steinmetz, H., 287
Stejskal, W. J., 59
Stekel, W., 471
Stemberger, R. T., 440
Stephan, W., 164
Stephen, T., 251
Stern, G. S., 71
Sternberg, K. J. 330
Sternberg, R. J., 229, 230–231,
   233, 234
Stets, J., 272
Stevens, G., 220
Stewart, A., 325
Stewart, A. J., 102
Stiles, W. B., 476
Stillion, J. M., 328
Stodghill, R., 369
Stoffer, G. R., 15, 16
Stohs, J. H., 258
Stokes, G., 384
Stokes, J., 200
Stokols, D., 66
Stoll, A. L., 439
Stone, A., 116, 405
Stone, J., 194, 195
Stone, L., 217
Stoney, C. M., 87
Storandt, M., 322
Story, A. L., 145
Strasburger, V. C., 369, 384,
   386
Strassberg, D., 200, 394
Straub, R. O., 100
Strauman, T. J., 132
Straus, M., 272
Strauss, M., 273
Street, S., 66
Strickland, A. L., 326
Strickland, B. R., 284
Striegel-Moore, R. H., 412,
   413, 458, 459
Strober, M., 459
Stroebe, M., 327
Stroh, L. A., 348
Strong, S. R., 490
Strouse, J., 369
Strupp, H. H., 466, 475
Stull, D. E., 319
Stunkard, A. J., 413
Sturgis, E. T., 439
Subrahamanyam, K., 282
Sue, D., 381

Suedfed, P., 82
Sugarman, D., 273
Suh, E., 19
Suinn, R. M., 442
Sullaway, M. E., 224
Sullivan, Q., 223
Sulloway, F. J., 40
Summers, R. J., 349
Super, D. E., 317, 343–344
Surra, C. A., 249, 250
Sussman, N., 190
Swaney, K., 340
Swann, W. B., 141, 145, 163,
   196, 450
Swartz, C. M., 485
Sweeney, P. D., 449
Sweet, J. A., 262, 265, 267
Swim, J., 167
Swisher, S. N., 405
Swoboda, F., 348
Syme, S. L., 83
Szasz, T., 431–432, 433
Szmukler, G. I., 457, 458
Szucko, J., 196
Szymanski, S., 453

T
Tabachnick, B. G., 489
Tajfel, H., 168, 169
Takanishi, R., 314
Tamminga, C. A., 484
Tan, L. S. C., 224
Tanfer, K., 268
Tangri, S. S., 354
Tanke, E., 161
Tannen, D., 208, 302–305
Tanner, J. M., 310
Tarantola, D. J. M., 418
Taris, T. W., 375
Tataryn, D. J., 445
Tatsuoka, M. M., 58
Taub, S., 476
Taubiman, O., 84
Tavris, C., 6, 10, 17, 100, 294,
   299
Tay, K. H., 342
Taylor, C. B., 483
Taylor, D. A., 199, 200
Taylor, D. M., 218
Taylor, R. J., 320
Taylor, S. E., 84, 104, 129, 134,
   141, 144, 145, 162
Tchividjian, L. R., 151
Teachman, J. D., 251
Teasdale, J. D., 99
Tedeschi, R. G., 82
Tellegen, A., 53
Temoshok, L., 404
Tennenbaum, D. L., 318, 331
Terkel, S., 337
Terr, L., 476
Terry, D. J., 97
Tesch, S. A., 316
Test, M., 183
Testa, K., 477
Thalberg, S., 369
Tharp, R., 120, 122
Thayer, J. F., 152
Theorell, T., 350, 351, 352
Thibaut, J. W., 224
Thigpen, C. H., 444
Thomas, K. W., 206

Thomas, M. H., 209
Thomas, V. G., 282, 296
Thomason, B. T., 404, 405
Thompson, A. P., 385, 386
Thompson, E. H., 295
Thompson, S. C., 71
Thomsen, L., 292
Thomson, E., 268
Thornborrow, N. N., 345
Thornduke, P. W., 26
Thornquist, M. H., 87
Thornton, A., 248
Thornton, B., 165
Throckmorton, B., 363
Tibbin, G., 405
Tice, D. M., 112, 140, 147,
   149, 151
Ting-Toomey, S., 218
Toben, M., 439
Tobin-Richards, M. H., 312
Toffler, A., 3
Tohen, M., 447
Tolchinsky, B., 370
Tollefson, G. D., 484
Tolstedt, B., 200
Tondo, L., 484
Tonneson, P., 409
Toohey, M. L., 455
Toomey, R., 453
Torrey, E. F., 40, 453
Touyz, S. W., 460, 461
Town, J., 164
Towne, N., 201
Tracey, Y. J., 343
Trammell, D., 113
Trapnell, R. D., 32
Treas, J., 256
Treasure, J., 458
Treiman, D. J., 345
Triandis, H. C., 135, 218
Trickett, P. K., 274, 275
Tripp, C. A., 271
Trochim, B., 13
Tropp, L. R., 298
Trost, M. R., 286
Truesdale, P., 478
Truxillo, D, M., 297
Tsai, M. 290
Tschann, J. M., 264
Tucker, G. J., 436
Tucker, P., 317, 318
Tucker, V., 386
Tucker-Ladd, C. E., 5, 73
Turner, J. R., 69, 88, 88
Turner, J., 168, 169
Turner, S. M., 438
Twillman, R. K., 224
Tyndall, C. I., 447
Tyrrell, D. A., 405

U
Uchino, B. N., 83
Uhde, T. W., 439
Uhle, S. M., 5
Umberson, D., 83
Umera, A. 290
Ungerleider, J. T., 426
Upshaw, H., 172
Ursano, R. J., 471
Usui, C., 319
Uzzo, R. G., 81

V
Vaillant, G. E., 37, 40, 85, 104
Valene, P., 459
Van Brunt, D., 326
Vance, B. K., 374
Vandeberg, S. G., 282
VanderPlate, C., 404, 405
van der Plight, J., 407
van der Velde, F. W., 407
Van De Vliert, E., 258
Van Houten, R., 333
VanItallie, T. B., 412
Van Putten, T., 454, 483
Van Willigen, M., 18
Van Wormer, K., 6
van Ryn, M., 83
Vaughan, V. C., III, 310
Vaughn, C., 455
Vaux, A., 5, 83, 237
Vavak, C. R., 403
Veccia, E., 194
Veenhoven, R., 17, 18
Veerman, T. J., 351
Ventura, J., 456
Verderber, K., 188, 195, 205,
   207
Verderber, R., 188, 195, 205,
   207
Vernberg, E. M., 80
Verner, E., 265
Vernon, P. A., 54
Veroff, J., 384
Vidmar, N., 273
Vinogradov, S., 474
Vinokur, A. D., 83, 355, 356
Vinsel, A., 200
Viorst, J., 317
Vitaliano, P. P., 102
Vitousek, K. B., 433
Vogt, T., 83
Volk, K., 283, 375
von Baeyer, C. L., 149
Von Glinow, M.A., 348
von Kolke, A., 218
VonKorff, M., 443
Voydanoff, P., 259

W
Wachtel, P. L., 1, 487
Wadden, T. A., 413
Waddil, P. J., 26
Wade, C., 10
Waite, L. J., 267
Wakefield, J. C., 432
Walace-Broscious, A. 344
Waldgeir, D., 181
Walker, I., 6
Walker, L., 273
Walker, L. E., 297
Walker, L. O., 359
Wall, S., 415
Wallace, R. K., 118
Waller, N. G., 32
Wallman, G. U., 488
Walster, E., 164, 220, 223, 228,
   459
Wampler, K. S., 53
Wampold, B. E., 490
Wang, M. A., 64
Wann, D., 168 175
Ward, C. D., 171
Ward, C. M., 342

Subject Index

lie detector and, 196
optimal level of, 74, 75
See also pysiological arousal
Asian Americans, gender roles
and, 290
Asian countries, conformity
and obedience in, 179
*Asserting Yourself: A Practical
Guide for Positive Change*
(Bower & Bower), 211
assertiveness, 210
assertiveness training,
210–213
assumptions, irrational,
107–108
asthma, 405
Athabasca University, 44
atherosclerosis, 400, 401
attachment
day care and, 329–330
infant-mother, 329
attachment process, 231–233
attachment styles, 231, 329
attention
aging and, 324
emotional arousal and, 74
interruption of, 79–80
in observational learning, 46
pressure to perform and, 79
selective, 203
to speaker, 201–202
attitude change, 170–173
attitudes
assertive, 213
defined, 170
similar, 224
toward minority groups, 167
toward sexual aggression,
241
attraction
eye contact and, 192
relationship development
and, 218–223
attractiveness
aging and, 320
confirmation bias and, 161
eating disorders and, 459
happiness and, 18
of information source, 171
readjustment of mental
patients and, 16
relationship formation and,
219–223
stereotypes based on, 164
tactics for, 222
TV emphasis on, 292
attributional style, 144–145
depression and, 448–449
loneliness and, 238
attributions, 161, 448
controllability and, 144
defensive, 165
dimensions of, 161
errors in, 164, 167, 235
in marriages, 261
internal vs. external, 143, 448
self, 143–144
stable vs. unstable, 143–144.
448
audience, imaginary, 312
authenticity, 197
self-presentation and, 152

authoritarian parenting,
330–331, 332
authoritarian personality,
167–168
authoritative parenting, 330,
332
authority, obedience to,
176–178
autoeroticism, 381
autogenic training, 119
autonomic nervous system
(ANS), 75, 77, 87
autonomic reactivity, 87
aversion therapy, 480–481
aversive events, learned helplessness and, 99
avoidance
communication, 202
of conflict, 205, 206
avoidance-avoidance conflict,
67, 242
avoidance behavior, 44, 112
avoidance strategies, 103

B
barbiturates, 422, 423, 424
Barr, Roseanne, 476
basic food groups, 415, 416
basking in reflected glory,
146–147
battering, 272–273
beauty, emphasis on, 220
behavior, defined, 11
behavior modification, 23,
115, 120–125, 490
behavior therapies, 465,
478–481, 486, 487
behavioral approach, to personality, 40–47
behavioral contract, 124, 125
behavioral disengagement, 99
behavioral genetics, 53–54
behavioral rehearsal, 481
behaviorism, 40–41
beliefs, 170
benzodiazepines, 424
bereavement, 327–328
best friends, 228
Big Five personality traits,
31–32, 53, 54, 58
binge eating/purging, 457
biomedical therapies,
465–466, 482–486, 487
biopsychosocial model, 400
bipolar disorders, 445–447,
448
drug treatment for, 484
BIRG (basking in reflected
glory), 146–147
birth control, 386–389
birth order, 39, 53
bisexuality, 229, 367, 371
blaming, 235
blood pressure
aggression and, 100
noise and, 65
Type A personality and, 402
body build, 220–221
body image
disturbed, 457–458
sexual identity and, 367–368
body language, 193–194

body mass index, 412–413
body movement, 193
Boston Couples Study, 234
Boston University, 408
Boston Women's Health Book
Collective, 286
brain
aging and, 321
anxiety disorders and, 439
emotional arousal and, 77,
78
gender differences in,
286–287
mood disorders and, 448
schizophrenic disorders and,
454, 455
brain damage, drug use and,
427
brainstorming, 110
Branch Davidians, 178–179
bulimia nervosa, 458
burnout, 80, 351, 358
Buspar, 483

C
caffeine consumption, 415
CalREN Project, 24
Cambridge diet, 414
cancer, 399
alcohol use and, 411
diet and, 415
exercise and, 416
oral contraceptives and, 387
repression and, 104
stress and, 404
candidiasis, 390
Cannabis, 423, 426
carbohydrates, 416
cardiovascular disease, oral
contraceptives and, 387
cardiovascular reactivity, 87
career advancement, opportunities for, 340, 348
career choice, 337–341
family influences on,
337–338
Holland's model of, 341–343
career counseling, 360
gender bias in, 291
career development, 317
stages of, 343–344
women's, 344–345
career pattern, 318
careers
gender-typed, 340
switching, 341
caregiving styles, 231, 232
Carpenter, Karen, 457
case studies, 16, 51
of midlife crisis, 318–319
catastrophic thinking, 102,
106–108, 473
catatonic schizophrenia, 452
catecholamine, 77
categorizing, of other people,
163, 167
catharsis, 100
causation, 14, 17
central route, to attitude
change, 173

cerebral hemispheres, 287
cervical cap, 388
Challenger disaster, 177
change
cultural, 3
human capacity for, 9
resistance to, 131
stress and, 88–89
as stressor, 68–70
uncertainty and, 3
See also life changes
channels
of communication, 170, 188
of nonverbal communica-
tion, 189
child abuse, 273–274
repressed memories of,
476–478
child care, 317–318
employer-sponsored, 352
child sexual abuse, 274–275
child-rearing, 254–256
dimensions of, 330–331
See also parenting
childlessness, 248, 254
children
access to sexual material by,
370
adult, living at home, 256
aggression in, 208
bereavement in, 328
day care for, 346
development of self-esteem
in, 141–142
of divorced parents, 264
effects of remarriage on, 265,
266
exposure to violence in, 208,
209
of gay parents, 271
gender role socialization of,
288–292
in family life cycle, 254–255
identity development in, 136
launching, 255–256
personality development in,
37–38, 39, 48
psychosexual stages in,
37–38
sex education of, 368–369
sexual abuse of, 274–275
TV viewing by, 291–292
working parents and, 259,
329–330
China, romantic love in, 218
China white, 427
chlamydial infection, 390
chlorpromazine, 482, 483
choking, under pressure, 79
cholesterol, 414–416
Christian men's movement,
3–4
chronic diseases, 399–400,
407
cigarette smoking. *See* smoking
cirrhosis of the liver, 411
clarification, by therapist, 472
clarifying, of speaker's statements, 201–202
class attendance, 25

marriage and, 234
sex and, 384
day care, 329–330, 346
employer-sponsored, 352
deafness, aging and, 324
death, attitudes about, 326
death system, 326
deception
detecting, 195–196
nonverbal communication and, 189, 191
on personality tests, 58
decision making
attitude change and, 173
stress and, 74, 79–80
decoding, of messages, 188
defense mechanisms, 35–37, 102–104, 469
defensive attribution, 165, 167
defensive behavior, 48–49
defensiveness, 203
dejection, as reaction to stress, 74
delusions, 451
delusions of grandeur, 451, 452
dementia, 321
denial, 102, 103, 407
mutual, 204
as stage in dying, 326
dependence, drug, 422, 423, 424, 425
dependent variable, 13, 14
depression, 433, 445–450
cognitive models of, 449
exercise and, 357
gender differences in, 284
learned helplessness and, 99
loneliness and, 236
pessimism and, 145
postpartum, 317
prevalence of, 446
problem solving and, 110
self-attributions and, 143
self-complexity and, 131
self-concept and, 104
smoking and, 404
stress and, 81
treatment of, 486
depressive disorder, 446
causes of, 447–450
cognitive therapy for, 473
drug treatment for, 484
electroshock therapy for, 485–486
heart disease and, 403–404
Derogatis Stress Profile, 109
desensitization, to violence, 209
designer drugs, 427
development
in adulthood, 315–325
in adolescence, 309–314
personality, 313
developmental coordination disorder, 436
developmental tasks, in family life cycle, 252
deviance, 433
diagnosis, 432
Diagnostic and Statistical Manual of Mental Disorders (DSM), 434–436

Diana, Princess, 457
diaphragm, 388
diazepam, 482
Dictionary of Occupational Titles, 338
diet, 322–323
dietary restraint, 413
dieting, 413–414
eating disorders and, 461
diffusion of responsibility, 178
dilemmas, handling, 68
disagreements, 205
disasters
posttraumatic stress disorder and, 80–81
stress and, 63
discipline, 274
disciplining, of children, 45, 209, 330–331, 332–333
disclaimers, 284
disconfirmation bias, 172
discrimination, 166
against gays, 269
gender-based, 296–297
job, 348, 350
modern vs. old-fashioned, 167
diseases
chronic, 2, 399–400, 407
infectious, 2, 399
psychosomatic, 441-442
stress and, 2
dishonesty, 195
disobedience, 177
disorganized schizophrenia, 452
displaced workers, 355
displacement, 36, 100
display rules, 191
dissenters, ethical, 178
dissociative amnesia, 444
dissociative disorders, 443–445
dissociative fugue, 444
dissociative identity disorder, 444
distance zones, 190
distortion, motivational, 203
distraction, as coping method, 116
distributed practice, 26
diversity, in workforce, 348
diversity training, 349
division of labor
gender roles and, 298–299
in marriage, 258
divorce, 248, 251, 252, 262–266
adjusting to, 265
causes of, 261, 262–263
cohabitation and, 268
decision to, 263–264
effects of, 264–265, 345
infidelity and, 386
loneliness and, 236
predicting, 261, 264
remarriage following, 265–266
stress caused by, 263, 264
divorce rates, 218, 262–263
Dole, Bob, 173
domestic chores, 257

domestic violence, 272–275
door-in-the-face technique, 181
dopamine, 454
double bind, in mixed-gender communications, 304–305
double standard, 242, 368
of aging, 320
Dow Jones & Co., 361
downsizing, 346, 355
downtime, 114
Dr. Laura, 4, 9
dream analysis, 469
dreams, archetypes in, 39
drinking, 409–312
See also alcohol
drives, Freud's view of, 34
driving, effect of alcohol on, 410, 411
drug abuse, 100
stress and, 81
drug-centered lifestyle, 424
drug therapy, 482–485, 487
drugs
date rape and, 240
recreational, 422–427
drunk driving, 410, 411
dual-career couples, 259
dual-earner families, 317, 356, 358, 359
dying, process of, 326–327
dyslexia, 282

E
earthquakes, as stressors, 66
eating disorders, 457–461
course and outcome of, 461
culture and, 458, 459
etiology of, 459–461
prevalence of, 458–459
stress and, 81
treatment of, 461
eating patterns, 414–415
eclecticism, in psychotherapy, 487, 490
economic system, American, 1
ecstasy (MDMA), 427
education
career choice and, 338
income and, 347
job opportunities and, 340
effectiveness, vs. efficiency, 114
efficiency, improving, 114
ego, 33, 34
ego integrity, 316
ego threats, 140
egocentrism, in adolescence, 312
ejaculation, premature, 394, 395
elaboration likelihood model, 172–173
Elavil, 484
elderly, 319–320
care of, 255
electroconvulsive therapy (ECT), 485–486
emetic drugs, 480–481
emotion(s), 73
classical conditioning of, 42–43

conveyed by paralanguage, 195
expressed, 455–456
facial expression of, 190–191
heart disease and, 403–404
lie detector and, 196
male gender role and, 294
nonverbal communication of, 189
primary, 191–192
releasing, 115–116
in schizophrenic disorders, 451–452
self-esteem and, 140
stress and, 73–74
suppression of, 115
emotional arousal, interpretation of, 149
Emotional Intelligence: Why It Can Matter More Than IQ (Goleman), 117
emotional release, 100
empathy, 197, 252
in therapy, 472, 491
empiricism, 12
employment
gender discrimination in, 296–297
outlooks for, 338–339
seeking, 360–363
employment agencies, 362
empty nest, 256, 318
encoding, of messages, 188
encounter groups, 48, 474
encounters, initial, 219–220
Encounters with the Self (Hamachek), 131
encouragement, 149
endocrine disorders, 288
endocrine system, 77, 310
aging and, 322
endogamy, 249
enhancement hypothesis, 359
entertainment, 357
environmental stress, 65–66
epidemiology, 436
epididymitis, 390
erectile difficulties, 393–394, 395
erogenous zones, 380
erotic materials, 370
erotic preferences, 368
escape response, 99
est training, 7
estrogens, 368
ethnic groups
premarital intercourse and, 383
stereotypes of, 167
in workforce, 347
ethnic identity, 138
etiology, 432
euphoria, in manic episodes, 447
evolutionary approach, 54
to gender differences, 285–286
to mate selection, 222–223, 250–251
exchange theory, 224–225
executive recruiters, 362
exemplification, 150, 151
exercise, 322, 357, 416–417

heart disease, 322, 399
  alcohol use and, 411
  diet and, 415
  exercise and, 416
  personality and, 400–404
  smoking and, 408
  stress and, 351, 352
heat, as stressor, 65
Heaven's Gate cult, 179
hedge words, 284
helplessness, 73
Hemingway, Ernest, 445
hemispheric specialization, 287
hepatitis, 390
heredity
  in homosexuality, 372–373
  mood disorders and, 448
  obesity and, 412–413
  personality and, 51–54
  psychological disorders and, 439
  schizophrenic disorders and, 454
  See also genetic predisposition/vulnerability
heroin, 422, 423, 424
herpes, 390, 404
heterosexism, 229, 293
heterosexuality, 229, 367, 371
hexagonal model of career choice, 341–343
hidden agenda, 197, 198
Hill, Anita, 353
hiring decisions, 360
Hispanic Americans
  gender roles and, 290
  support networks of, 319
  See also minority groups
histrionic personality, 443
Hitler, Adolf, 176
HIV virus, 418
hobbies, 356
home environment, personality and, 53–54
home office, 346
home team, choking of, 79
homogamy, 249
homophobia, 36, 295, 373
homosexuality, 367, 371–371
  AIDS and, 418
  attitudes toward, 373, 433
  causes of, 372–373
  effects of hiding, 115–116
  genetic basis for, 372–373
homosexuals
  dating criteria of, 220
  loneliness among, 236
  psychological adjustment of, 373–374
  relationships between, 229–230, 268–271
  self-esteem of, 142
  sexual behavior of, 382
honesty, 197
hormones, 77
  aging and, 322
  defined, 287
  gender differences in, 287–288
  at puberty, 310
sex, 368, 372

hostility, 141, 207
  of children toward parents, 333
  heart disease and, 401–403
  rape and, 239
  reducing intergroup, 169
hot reacting, 403
household chores, gender and, 290
housework, in marriage, 257–258
How to Stubbornly Refuse to Make Yourself Miserable About Anything—Yes, Anything! (Ellis), 108
Hughes, Howard, 438–439
Human Sexuality Today (King), 380
human nature, 47, 51
human potential movement, 47
humanism, 47
humanistic theories, 47–51, 55
humor, as stress reducer, 108–109
Hurried Child, The: Growing Up Too Fast, Too Soon (Elkind), 331
hydrophobia, 438
hypnosis, recovery of repressed memories with, 477–478
hypochondriasis, 442–443
hypothalamus, 77
hypotheses, about other people, 161–162

I

I'm Dysfunctional, You're Dysfunctional (Kaminer), 7
id, 33, 34
ideal self, 131
identical twins, 53
  See also twin studies
identification, as defense mechanisms, 36
identity
  congruence and, 152
  defined, 136
  development of, 136–137
  gender differences in, 138
  gender-role, 279, 299–301
  group membership and, 19
  influence of group membership on, 138
  search for, 313
  sexual, 367–368
  sexual orientation and, 373
  social, 168
identity crisis, 137, 313
identity statuses, 137–138, 313, 316
  career maturity and, 344
identity theory, 168, 169
illness
  changing patterns of, 399–400
  life changes and, 68–70
  reactions to, 400, 420–421

stress and, 16, 77, 81–82, 400–406
  See also diseases
illusions, defense mechanisms as, 103–104
imaginary audience, 312
imitation
  in gender-role socialization, 289, 292
  of models, 46, 148–149, 183, 212, 481
imminence, of stressful events, 72
immune functioning
  AIDS and, 418
  social support and, 83
  marijuana and, 427
  stress and 77, 405
impotence, 294, 393, 395
impression formation , 159–166
impression management, 149–150
  facial expression and, 191
  in.job interviews, 363
impressions, first, 165, 199
incest, 274–275
income
  education and, 347
  happiness and, 18
incongruence, 48, 471–472
independent variable, 13, 14
independent vs. interdependent self-systems, 135–136
India, arranged marriages in, 218
individual psychology (Adler), 39–40
individualistic cultures, 19–20
  attributions in, 164
  interpersonal conflict and, 205
  marriage and, 217–218
  self-concept and, 135–136
  self-disclosure and, 200–201
  social influence in, 179
individuality, 135
industrial/organizational psychology, 337
infant attachment, 231 329
infants, inhibited temperament in, 439
infectious diseases, 399
inferiority complex, 39–40, 153
infidelity, 385–386
inflammatory bowel disease, 405
Influence: Science and Practice (Cialdini), 182
information
  accuracy of, 12–13
  retention of, 25–27
information anxiety, 2
information glut, 2
information processing, peripheral vs. central, 172–173
ingratiation, 150, 151
ingroups, 163, 167, 168
inkblot test, 58, 59

insight therapies, 465, 469–478, 487
insincerity, 150
insomnia, stress and, 81
instrumental style, 303
integrity vs. despair, 316
intellectuaization, 103
intelligence
  aging and, 323
  career choice and, 338
  constructive coping and, 104
  emotional, 117
  gender differences in, 281
  happiness and, 18
inter-role conflict, 258
intercourse, sexual, 377–380
  beliefs about, 242
  first experience with, 384
  premarital, 382
interdependence, cooperative, 169
interference, in learning, 26
internal vs. external attributions, 161, 164, 165
internalization, of social norms, 34
Internet, 2
  addiction to, 100–101
  as source of sex information, 369–370
  surfing, 356, 357–358
interpersonal climate, 197
interpersonal communication
  assertive, 210–213
  defined, 187
  See also communication
interpersonal conflict, 204–209
  dealing constructively with, 207
  defined, 204
  managing, 206–207
  nature of, 204–205
  types of, 205–206
  See also conflict
interpersonal distance, 189–190
interpersonal relations, happiness and, 19
interpretation, in psychoanalysis, 470
interrupting, 284
interviews, job, 362–363
intimacy
  as component of love, 230, 233, 234
  confusing sex with, 294–295
  in friendships, 227
  self-disclosure and, 200
  in young adulthood, 315–316
intimacy vs. isolation, 315–316
intimate violence, 272–275, 297
intimidation, 150, 151
intrauterine device (IUD), 388
introverts, 39
inverted-U hypothesis, 74, 75
irrational thinking, 107–108

efficiency in, 165
errors in, 163–165, 167
expectations and, 161–163, 165
key themes in, 165–166
process of, 160
role of attributions in, 161
selectivity of, 165
sources of information for, 159–160
stability of, 165
person-centered theory (Rogers), 48–49
person-centered therapy, 471
personal control, 21
personal fable, 312
personal growth, 47, 49–50
personal orientations, 341–343
personal space, 189–190
personal unconscious, 38
personality
  aging and, 325
  authoritarian, 167–168
  behavioral perspectives on, 40–47
  biological perspectives on, 51–54, 55
  cancer-prone, 404
  career choice and, 341–343
  defined, 31
  evolutionary perspective on, 54
  five-factor model of, 32, 325
  gender differences in, 282–283
  happiness and, 21
  healthy, 49, 50
  heredity and, 51–54
  marital success and, 252
  occupation and, 338
  self-destructive, 407
  as set of response tendencies, 44–45
personality development
  in adolescence, 136–138, 312–314
  in adulthood, 315–316
  Freud's view of, 37–38, 55
  Rogers's view of, 48, 55
  Skinner's view of, 44, 55
personality structure
  Eysenck's model of, 52, 55
  Freud's view of, 33–34, 55
  Rogers's view of, 48, 55
personality tests, 56–59
personality theories
  Adler's individual psychology, 39–40
  diversity of, 54–55
  Freud's psychoanalytic theory, 33–38
  humanistic theories, 47–51
  Jung's analytical theory, 38–39
  psychodynamic theories, 32–40
  trait theories, 31–32
personality traits, 31–32, 52
  anxiety disorders and, 441
  desirable, 224
  eating disorders and, 459

Eysenck's hierarchy of, 52
gender-related, 280
measurement of, 57–58
persuasability and, 172
somatoform disorders and, 443
stability of, 325
personality types, Holland's, 341–343
perspective taking, 252
Perspectives: A Mental Health Magazine, 5
persuasion, 170–173
  in cults, 179
  subliminal, 173–174
persuasion process, 170–172
pessimism, 84, 85, 102
pessimistic explanatory style, 99, 144–145
pet ownership, 83
phallic stage, 38
phobias, 438, 440
  classical conditioning of, 42
phobic disorder, 437–438
  causes of, 440
  treatment for, 480, 490
physical attractiveness. See attractiveness
physical fitness, 416–417
physical health. See health
physical illness. See illness
physiological arousal
  in general adaptation syndrome, 76–77
  lie detector and, 196
  personality and, 52
  stress-induced, 71
physiological reactivity, 403
physiological responses, to stress, 74–77
physique, 220–221
pituitary gland, 77, 310
planning, 113
  of study time, 22
plastic surgery, 368
play
  gender-appropriate, 289–290, 291
  gender differences in, 302
pleasure principle, 33
political attitudes, 32
pollution, 65
polygraph, 196
pornography, 370
  violent, 240–241
positive emotionality, 32
positive feelings, persuasion and, 172
positive reinforcement, 43–44
positive reinterpretation, 109
Positively Gay: New Approaches to Gay and Lesbian Life (Berzon), 375
postpartum distress, 254
postpartum depression, 317
Postponing Sexual Involvement, 369
posttraumatic stress disorder (PTSD), 80–81, 83, 84, 239, 275
posture, 193

poverty, marital satisfaction and, 259
preconscious, 34
predictability, of stressful events, 72
predisposition, to mood disorders, 448
pregnancy, teenage, 312, 382
prejudice, 142, 166–169
  causes of, 167–168
  reducing, 168–169
  in workplace, 349
premarital sex, 382, 383–384
premature ejaculation, 394, 395
prenatal development, sexual, 368, 372
preparedness, 440
pressure, 70–71, 79
  to succeed, 293–294
Pressure Inventory, 71
prevalence, of psychological disorders, 436–437, 446, 450
primacy effect, 165
primary appraisal, of stressful events, 64
primary process thinking, 33
primary sex characteristics, 310, 311
Princeton University, 387
problem solving, 105, 109–110
  aging and, 324–325
  in adolescence, 312
  in interpersonal conflict, 207
procrastination, 112
productivity, 114
  aging and, 324–325
  worker, 346
prognosis, 432
progress, paradox of, 1–3
progressive relaxation, 119
projection, 36
projective tests, 58–59
Promise Keepers, 4
propaganda, 170
protease inhibitors, 418
proxemics, 189–190
proximity, role of, in attraction, 219
Prozac, 484
pseudoconflict, 205
psilocybin, 426
psychiatric nurses, 468
psychiatric social workers, 468
psychiatrists, 467–468, 482, 489
psychic energy, 33
psychoactive drugs, 422–427
psychoanalysis, 33, 453, 469–471, 486
psychoanalytic theory, 33–38
psychobabble, 7
psychodiagnosis, 434–436
psychodynamic approach, to psychotherapy, 471
psychodynamic theories of personality, 32–40
  Adler's theory, 39–40
  criticisms of, 40

Freud's theory, 33–38, 55
Jung's theory, 38–39
psychological dependence, on drugs, 423-424
psychological development. See development
psychological disorders, 55
  classification of, 434–436
  Freud's view of, 38, 55
  gender differences in, 284
  prevalence of, 436–437
  stress and, 81
  treatment for, 465–487
  See also abnormal behavior; specific disorders
psychological tests, 56
psychologists, 11, 466–467, 468, 487
psychology
  careers in, 347
  defined, 11
  as a profession, 11
  as a science, 12
Psychology Today, 226
psychopathology, 431
psychopharmacotherapy, 482–485
psychosexual stages, 37–38
psychosis, amphetamine, 426
psychosocial crises, 313, 315–316
psychosomatic diseases, 73, 81–82, 441–442
psychotherapy
  behavioral approach to, 478–481
  client-centered approach to, 471–472
  cognitive approach to, 473–474
  combining approaches to, 486–487
  costs of, 489–490
  eclectic approach to, 487
  effectiveness of, 475–476, 481, 490
  elements of, 465–468
  false memory controversy in, 476–478
  group approach to, 474–475
  outcomes of, 476, 481, 490
  psychoanalytic approach to, 469–471
  sources of, 488–489
Psychotherapy Maze, The (Ehrenberg & Ehrenberg), 466
puberty, 310, 311, 368
  timing of, 311, 312
pubescence, 310
pubic lice, 389, 390
public self, 149
public speaking, 202
punishment, 45, 123
  in gender-role socialization, 289
  parental, 330, 332–333
Purdue University, 166
Pursuit of Happiness, The Who Is Happy—and Why (Myers), 19

put-downs, assertive
responses to, 213

Q
questionnaires, 16

R
race, eye contact and, 193
racism, 167
radio, advice on, 4
rap music, 370
rape
  alcohol use and, 410
  consequences of, 239–240
  date, 239–243
  drugs and, 240
  incidence of, 239
  prevention of, 242–243
rape victims, 165
rapport talk, 304
rational-emotive therapy, 106, 490
rationality, 47
rationalization, 35
reactance, 182
reaction formation, 36
reaction time, effect of alcohol on, 410
reading
  improving, 23–25
  as leisure activity, 356
Reagan, Ronald, 321
reality principle, 33
reasoning, irrational, 106–108
recall, 25–26
receiver
  of interpersonal messages, 187–188
  of persuasive messages, 172
reciprocity principle, 223
reciprocity norm, 181–182
Recovering from Rape (Ledray), 243
recovery programs, 5
reference groups, 133, 142
reflected glory, 146–147
reflexes, learned, 41
refractory period, 378
regression, 36
rehearsal, 25
  of assertive behavior, 212
  behavioral, 481
reinforcement, 43–44, 121–122
  in gender-role socialization, 289
reinforcement contingencies, 122
reinterpretation, positive, 109
rejection, low self-esteem and, 154, 155
relational aggression, 283
relationships
  abusive, 273, 274
  breakups of, 234, 235
  communal, 226
  conflicts in, 205, 234, 235, 303
  culture and, 217–218
  development of, 218–226
  exchange, 226
  failure of, 234

homosexual, 229–230, 268–271, 371, 385, 386
  ingredients of, 217
  initial attraction in, 218–223
  investments in, 225
  longevity of, 234–235
  priorities in, 270
  rewards and costs in, 225
  romantic, 228–235
  satisfaction in, 224–226
  sexual, 370–371, 375–377, 392–395
  sexual behavior in, 384–386
  in young adulthood, 315–316
  See also friendship(s); marriage
relaxation
  in behavior therapy, 480
  meditation and, 117
relaxation procedures, 119
reliability, of tests, 56–57
religion, happiness and, 19
religious groups, 3
remarriage, 265–266
report talk, 304
repressed memories, 476–478
repression, 35–36, 103, 104
reproductive capacity, 222
research, 12
  correlational, 14–17
  experimental, 13–14
research methods, 13–17
residential density, 65
resistance
  stage of, 76
  to therapist, 470, 491
respondent conditioning. See classical conditioning
response tendencies, 41, 44, 45
responses
  conditioned, 42
  elicited, 42
  emitted, 43
responsibility
  delegating, 112
  diffusion of, 178
résumé, preparing, 360–361
retention, 25–27
retirement, 316, 319, 344
rewards, short-term, 23
rheumatoid arthritis, 404
rhyming, as mnemonic method, 27
rhythm method, 388
Riley Guide, 340
risky behavior, 312
risperidone, 483
road rage, 99, 207, 209
Robbers' Cave State Park, 168, 169
Rockwell International, 177
Rodman, Dennis, 150
rohypnol, 240
role conflict, 358–359
role expectations
  for females, 295, 296
  for males, 293–295
  in marriage, 257–258
role models, development of self-esteem and, 142

role overload, 258
role playing, 212
role-playing exercises, 481
roles, multiple, 296
romance, sex and, 370
romantic relationships, 217, 228–235
  happiness and, 20
  self-disclosure in, 199
  See also relationships
Rorschach test, 58, 59
rumination, 449

S
sadness, as reaction to stress, 74
safe sex, 389, 391
salary, 341
salespeople, techniques of, 180–183
salt intake, 415, 416
samples, free, 181–182
scapegoats, 168
scarcity, feigned, 182
scarcity hypothesis, 359
scare tactics, in drug education, 422
scheduling, of time, 114
schemas, 162
schizophrenic disorders, 450–456
  course and outcome of, 452–453
  etiology of, 454–456
  positive and negative symptoms of, 452–453
  prevalence of, 437, 450
  recovery from, 453–454
  stress and, 81
  subtypes of, 452
  symptoms of, 451–452
  treatment for, 482, 483–484
  vulnerability to, 456
school performance, parenting styles and, 331–332
schools
  as agents of socialization, 291
  children's self-esteem and, 142
  sexual harassment in, 297, 298
  as source of sex information, 369
scientific approach, 12–17
Scientology, 3
search for direction, 3–9
secondary appraisal, of stressful events, 64
secondary process thinking, 33
secondary sex characteristics, 310, 311, 368
secular trend, in timing of puberty, 311
sedatives, 423, 424–425
selective attention, 203
selective serotonin reuptake inhibitors (SSRIs), 484
self
  actual, 131
  authentic, 152

collective, 168
ideal, 131
independent view of, 135–136
interdependent view of, 135–136
ought, 131
public, 149, 152
self-actualization, 50
self-attributions, 143–144, 238
self-blame, 73, 102, 140
self-complexity, 130–131
self-concept
  child's, 135
  defined, 129
  factors shaping, 133–136
  nature of, 129–130
  nonverbal communication and, 196–197
  positive, 138
  realistic, 104
  in Rogers' theory, 48–49, 472
  working, 129
self-concept confusion, 139
self-confidence, gender differences in, 282
self-consciousness, 79
  in adolescence, 312
self-consistency, 145
self-control
  dieting and, 413
  improving, 114–115
  parental acceptance and, 330
  using behavior modification for, 120–125
Self-Creation (Weinberg), 6
self-criticism, 102
self-deception, 40, 102–103, 105
  defense mechanisms and, 36
self-defeating attributions, 238
self-defeating behavior, 112, 147–148, 155
self-destructiveness, 407
Self-Directed Search (SDS), 342
self-discipline, 114–115
self-disclosure, 199–201, 227–228
self-discrepancies, 131–133
self-efficacy, 46–47, 148–149
Self-Efficacy Scale, 46
self-enhancement, 145–148
self-esteem
  aggression and, 140–141
  assertiveness and, 210
  building, 153–155
  career maturity and, 344
  collective, 168
  defined, 138
  determinants of, 141–142, 155
  gender and, 301
  gender bias and, 291, 292
  happiness and, 21
  importance of, 139–141
  loneliness and, 236–237
  male role and, 294
  among minority group members, 142–143

of rape, 239–240, 243
of sexual harassment, 354
video games, 292
Vienna Psychoanalytic
Society, 39
Vietnam veterans, 80, 83, 84
violence
gender differences in,
282–283
intimate, 272–275
self-esteem and, 140–141
television and, 208–209
workplace, 355
violent crimes, 294
alcohol use and, 410
violent pornography, 240–241
viral hepatitis, 390
vision, aging and, 321
visual imagery, to aid retention, 27
Vitamin E, 415
vocalization, 194–195
volunteer activities, 357

W
Waco, Texas, 178–179
wages, gender gap in, 297, 298
warts, genital, 390
wealth, happiness and, 18, 21
Web sites, 2
weight, excess, 412–414
weight gain, with age, 320
weight loss, 413–414
in eating disorders, 457–458
weight loss programs, 123,
124
weight trends, 459, 461

well-being, subjective, 17
wellness programs, 352
Wesleyan University, 163
West Virginia University, 174
What Color Is Your Parachute?
(Bolles), 362
"what-is-good-is-beautiful"
stereotype, 164
*What You Can Change &
What You Can't* (Seligman),
9
whistleblowing, 177–178
Whole Family Center, 256
*Why Marriages Succeed or Fail
. . . and How You Can Make
Them Last* (Gottman), 264
widowhood, 328
withdrawal
communication, 202
social, 99
withdrawal illness, 422, 423,
424, 425
women
attitudes toward sex among,
370–371
in authority position, 305
average weight of, 459, 461
battered, 273
career development for,
344–345
childbirth and, 254
childless, 248
codependency movement
and, 6
diminished aspirations of,
296
double bind for, 304–305

effects of divorce on, 265
identity development in, 138
multiple roles of, 296
occupations for, 340
orgasmic difficulties in, 394,
395
role conflict in, 358–359
role expectations for, 295,
296
sexual harassment of,
353–355
as victims of partner abuse,
272–273
as victims of violence, 297
in workforce, 248, 257, 259,
296, 297, 317, 330,
344–345, 347, 348–349, 359
See also gender
work
balancing with other life
spheres, 356–359
defined, 345
happiness and, 20
marriage and, 258–259
in middle adulthood, 318
retiring from, 316, 319, 344
role of, 337
in young adulthood, 317
work environments, 341
work overload, 350
workaholics, 358, 401
workforce
changing, 347, 352
diversity in, 348
women in, 248, 257, 259,
296, 297, 317, 330,
344–345, 347, 348–349, 359

working self-concept, 129
workplace, 341
innovations in, 352, 353
sexual harassment in,
353–355
trends in, 345–346
violence in, 355
wellness programs in, 352
World Series, 79
World War II, 11

X
Xanax, 482

Y
yeast infection, 390, 404
yoga, 117
*You Just Don't Understand:
Women and Men in
Conversation* (Tannen), 303
*You're Smarter Than You
Think* (Brodsky), 105

Z
Zen, 117
Zoloft, 484

TO THE OWNER OF THIS BOOK:

We hope that you have found *Psychology Applied to Modern Life: Adjustment in the 90s,* Sixth Edition, useful. So that this book can be improved in a future edition, would you take the time to complete this sheet and return it? Thank you.

School and address: _____

Department: _____

Instructor's name: _____

1. What I like most about this book is: _____

_____

2. What I like least about this book is: _____

_____

3. My general reaction to this book is: _____

_____

4. The name of the course in which I used this book is: _____

_____

5. Were all of the chapters of the book assigned for you to read: _____

If not, which ones weren't? _____

6. In the space below, or on a separate sheet of paper, please write specific suggestions for improving this book and anything else you'd care to share about your experience in using the book.

_____

_____

_____

_____

_____

_____

_____

_____

_____

Optional:

Your name: _____ Date: _____

May Brooks/Cole quote you, either in promotion for *Psychology Applied to Modern Life: Adjustment in the 90s*, Sixth Edition, or in the future publishing ventures?

Yes: _____ No: _____

Sincerely,

Wayne Weiten
Margaret A. Lloyd

FOLD HERE

**NO POSTAGE
NECESSARY IF
MAILED IN THE
UNITED STATES**

BUSINESS REPLY MAIL

FIRST CLASS   PERMIT NO. 358   PACIFIC GROVE, CA

POSTAGE WILL BE PAID BY ADDRESSEE

ATT: *Wayne Weiten & Margaret A. Lloyd* _____

**Wadsworth-Brooks/Cole
511 Forest Lodge Road
Pacific Grove, California 93950-9968**

FOLD HERE